Diver! Diver! Diver!

BRIAN CULL

with Bruce Lander

GRUB STREET · LONDON

Published by
Grub Street
4 Rainham Close
London SW11 6SS

British Library Cataloguing in Publication Data
Cull, Brian
  Diver! Diver! Diver!: RAF and American fighter pilots
  battle the V-1 assault over south-east England, 1944
  1. World War, 1939-1945 – Aerial operations, British
  2. World War, 1939-1945 – Aerial operations, American
  3. World War, 1939-1945 – Casualties 4. Fighter pilots -
  Great Britain 5. Fighter pilots - United States
  I. Title II. Lander, Bruce
  940.5'44'941'0922

ISBN-13: 9781904943396

Formatting by Pearl Graphics, Hemel Hempstead

Printed and bound by MPG Ltd, Bodmin, Cornwall

Grub Street only uses FSC
(Forest Stewardship Council) paper for its books.

BRIAN CULL is the author of some of the following Grub Street titles:
AIR WAR FOR YUGOSLAVIA, GREECE and CRETE 1940-41 with
    Christopher Shores and Nicola Malizia
MALTA: THE HURRICANE YEARS 1940-41 with Christopher Shores and
    Nicola Malizia
MALTA: THE SPITFIRE YEAR 1942 with Christopher Shores and Nicola Malizia
BLOODY SHAMBLES Volume 1 with Christopher Shores and Yasuho Izawa
BLOODY SHAMBLES Volume 2 with Christopher Shores and Yasuho Izawa
HURRICANES OVER TOBRUK with Don Minterne
HURRICANES OVER MALTA with Frederick Galea
SPITFIRES OVER SICILY with Nicola Malizia and Frederick Galea
BUFFALOES OVER SINGAPORE with Paul Sortehaug and Mark Haselden
ONE-ARMED MAC with Roland Symons
HURRICANES OVER SINGAPORE with Paul Sortehaug
SPITFIRES OVER MALTA with Frederick Galea
WINGS OVER SUEZ (revised) with David Nicolle and Shlomo Aloni

CONTENTS

ACKNOWLEDGEMENTS

First and foremost, Brian thanks his wife Val for her continued support, encouragement and understanding during the long period of research and writing this tome (some five years), as does Bruce for his wife June's support. Behind every successful man, it is said, is a strong and successful woman – whether he likes it or not! Only joking – where would we be without our ladies?

The authors are deeply indebted to Stephen Henden, compiler of the *Rockets and Flying Bombs* website, for readily agreeing to making his work available to be included in this book. Peter wrote:

> "I have been interested in the V-1 (and V-2) attacks for many years. My family lived in South London during the war, in Beckenham and Dulwich and I was often told stories of the Blitz and the V weapon attacks. My mother, who lived in Beckenham, used to tell a story of how she travelled from Clockhouse Station to Charing Cross on the train to work. One day she looked out of the window and saw a Doodlebug flying along on a parallel course! Everyone just went on reading their newspapers and after what seemed like a long time it veered off and exploded. I recall asking her if she was frightened. She replied, 'Well yes, but you just got used to it!' My Dulwich Grandmother, who lived in Dovercourt Road, used to frequently mention the bombing. I now live a few hundred yards away, in Court Lane, in a house itself damaged by a flying bomb on13 July 1944. Being of an enquiring mind, I wanted to find out exactly what happened in South London during the period. How many bombs, where they fell, what damage was caused and what affect that this had on the post war shape of the area."

Peter's painstaking research over a number of years into the fall of V-1s in South London has provided a valuable background. Both authors, although too young to remember the events, were themselves unwitting witnesses to nearby incidents – Bruce was born and lived in Oldham (as he still does), and was there during the Christmas Eve 1944 assault. "Although I was only three at the time, I seem to remember hearing the air raid sirens." As recorded within, Brian – with his mother, brother and sister – came close to being obliterated by a Diver that fell at Shoot-up-Hill (London) on 15 August 1944, his soldier father having been narrowly missed at Westerham in Kent on 18 June. Is it faith, fate, destiny or luck – call it what you will – that saves one but takes the life of another? Seconds only intervened in the aforementioned incidents, as it did for the author in Rhodesia (now Zimbabwe) many years later. He was not hurt but the unfortunate chap behind him was killed.

We are deeply indebted to the expertise of Chris Goss, author of many fine books dealing with WWII aviation, for providing invaluable material regarding the activities of III/KG3, I, II and III/KG53, II/KG40 and III/KG100 during the period covered. Similarly, eminent German researcher/writer Gerhard Stemmer has supplied much information, while Brian Bines graciously provided copies of loss reports for III/KG3 and KG53. Their expertise and generous contributions have greatly enhanced this study. David Collyer, editor of *Buzz Bomb Diary* compiled by the Kent Aviation Historical Society is thanked for permission to use extracts from their excellent and invaluable publication. Bob Ogley's beautifully produced *Doodlebugs and Rockets* is highly recommended and contains many excellent and evocative photographs of the period. Graham Berry (a cousin) and his son Mark were responsible for providing much assistance with regard to Sqn Ldr Joe Berry DFC. Mainly through their efforts, Joe has not been forgotten.

The authors also acknowledge the assistance of Ruy Horta and Ross McNeill for permitting us to use the medium of their excellent respective websites *12 O'Clockhigh*

(TOCH) and *RAF Commands*, and thus allowing us access to the most generous band of international researcher/writers, who made information available via these websites, including Franek Grabowski (Poland), Daniel J. Cabanilles (France); Chris Charland (Canada); Max Williams; Mark Huxtable; Bob Collis; Tony O'Toole, the latter for inspiration; Mike Howell (USA); Dr Erwin van Loo NIMH (Holland); Michal Havrda (Czech Republic); Michal Plavec (Czech Republic); Robert Schulte (Germany); Many Souffan (France); Erich Brown (USA); Norman Malayney (Canada); Jerry Brewer (Canada); Henk Welting (Holland); Jan Venema, Hans and Elger Abbink (Holland); Steve Brooking (Brenzett Wing researcher); Rick Peck (USA); Del Davis (USA); Randall Bytwerk (USA); Scott Gordon (USA) for information regarding his uncle, former P-61 pilot Al Gordon; Roger Little, son of the late John Little 605 Squadron; Eric Browne, Hon Sec of 616 Squadron Association; Gordon Hobson and Jack Ritch, former 616 Squadron Meteor pilots; Richard Oxby, son of Doug Oxby DSO DFC DFM; Jim Condon, son-in-law of Michael Stanley DFC; Annette and Mike Brampton (Pat Coleman's daughter and son-in-law). Jack 'Paddy' Dalzell, former 74 Squadron pilot; authors Chris Thomas and Andy Thomas; Steve Brew (41 Squadron historian); authors Dr Alfred Price; Bob Cossey; Jan Safarik (Czech Republic); Kent Miller (USA); Paul Sortehaug (New Zealand); Bo Widfeldt (Sweden); Tomas Polak (Czech Republic); Andy Saunders; Chris Shores – for their generous assistance and respective contributions. Good friend, author and researcher *par excellence* Hugh Halliday (Canada) provided much information on RCAF aircrew.

Our gratitude is also extended to Margaret, Aubrey and Steven Sparkes of Tenterden for the loan of a relevant book. The assistance of the staff of the National Archives (formerly PRO) and Bury St Edmunds Public Library is acknowledged. The authors apologise should any contributors have been overlooked; an unintentional oversight. Brian is grateful to computer wizard Kevin Link for saving his work following a disastrous computer crash; and, as always, wishes to acknowledge the importance of the influence that Jack Lee, gentleman and scholar, has had on his life. The authors also thank John Davies for his excellent editing of the manuscript, a tedious but vitally important job, and his staff (Luke and Hannah) at Grub Street Publications.

Please note: There are no prepared lists of V-1 kills from which to extract details apart from entries in squadron ORBs and individual combat reports, not all of which are complete or coherent. Some squadrons completed combat reports in respect of Diver claims, others did not. For example, no combat reports have been found for 486 (RNZAF) Squadron, while 68 Squadron ORB appears to be incomplete. Therefore, the listings contained herein have been compiled from various sources by the authors and may contain errors or omissions. This also applies to serial numbers/individual aircraft letters, some of which may prove to be incorrect. Should errors be found, we apologise profusely, for every effort has been made to ensure accuracy. For the sake of clarity and to reduce repetition, pilots' combat reports have mostly been edited although not altered in content or to mislead. Any additional information or corrections can be sent to briancullauthor@fsmail.net.

There was a popular American song at the time entitled *Lay that Pistol Down Babe* where the words were changed to reflect the topical situation. It went something like this:

> *First you hear the engine,*
> *Then hear it stop!*
> *Then you dive for cover,*
> *Then it goes off pop!*
> *Oh! Shoot that Doodlebug down boys,*
> *Shoot that Doodlebug down!*
> *Hitler's secret weapon,*
> *Shoot that Doodlebug down!*

A typical Londoner was asked how he managed to remain so calm during flying bomb raids: "I see it like this," he said. "It must take the Germans a lot of trouble to make the bloody things, and then they have to get them into those pits and up into the air, and it is quite a long way from France to London, and if they do get to London, they have still got to find Hackney. And even then, it isn't everyone who can find 37, Bulstrode Road, and if they do, its ten-to-one I'm in the pub!"

INTRODUCTION

During the summer months of 1944, the daily onslaught by V-1 jet-propelled pilotless flying bombs – when London and South-Eastern England were targets for the first of Hitler's ominous 'secret weapons' – was countered in the skies of Kent and Sussex by fighter pilots of the newly established Air Defence of Great Britain (ADGB) under the command of Air Marshal Sir Roderic Hill AFC MC. The new weapon soon became feared by those who lived in its path, from Kent and Sussex to South London, and elsewhere that was within range. Many thousands were evacuated from the outer precincts of the capital to safer areas until the threat subsided.

To its designers the flying bomb was known as the Fieseler Fi-103; to the German military machine it was the *FZG76 (Flakzielgerät* – literally anti-aircraft target device, a misleading name to cover its true role); and to the German soldier it was the V-1 (*Vergeltungswaffe 1* – Reprisal Weapon 1), a revenge for the bombing of German cities by the Allies. To the British press, the bewildered public and the fighter pilots flying Tempests and Typhoons, Spitfires and Mustangs, Meteors and Mosquitos, V-1s became known variously as Divers, Buzz Bombs, Flying Bombs, Fly, Doodlebugs, Chuffbombs, Bumblebombs, Dingbats, Robots, Jet-Ships, even Beechcraft (for some unknown reason); by the Poles as *Wariat* (Madman), *Szybotluk* (Window-Buster), or simply *Czarownice* – Witchcraft or Witches; by the Americans as P-planes (Pilotless planes), Robombs or simply Things; and by the indefatigable Eastenders as Farting Furies. One described it thus: "… like an old motorbike, a huge wasp, a tom cat … and then the silence …" Another said: "It sounded like an old Model-T Ford going up a steep hill."

By late 1943, many V-1 'ski' launching sites had being constructed in the Pas-de-Calais by using slave labour in preparation for the bombardment of London, but, thanks to the daring of French agents, the skills of reconnaissance pilots and the diligence of air intelligence units, many of the sites had been located and were soon being targeted by the RAF and USAAF, albeit without great effect. Enough was now known by the Allies to link the flying bomb to a complex of storage depots and concrete structures in Northern France which bombers and fighter-bombers attacked with mixed results. German engineers quickly developed prefabricated launch facilities that mushroomed in France from the Pas-de-Calais to near the mouth of the Seine. RAF and US fighter-bombers, medium bombers and heavy bombers were called upon to take out the sites – codenamed 'Noball' by the RAF – as they were discovered and, while some had been destroyed or otherwise put out of commission, the majority survived. Between 21 December 1943 and 31 May 1944, the RAF's No.2 Group alone flew 4,710 sorties against Noball targets losing 41 aircraft. Another 419 of the attacking bombers were variously damaged by flak. About one-fifth of the attacks were delivered at low level, which called for careful routing. Targets were allocated depending upon the likely anti-aircraft fire. Out of a total of 103 such targets put out of action, No.2 Group was credited with 32 whilst USAAF B-17s and B-24s destroyed 35; American A-20s and B-26s were credited with 28 and fighter-bombers eight[1]. Between 1 January and 12 June 1944 an estimated 2,000 tons of bombs had been dropped on these targets. Nonetheless, up to 140 launching ramps were available along the Pas-de-Calais by mid June 1944 when the assault on the UK commenced[2].

When the launching sites in the Pas-de-Calais were eventually overrun following the Allied landings, other sites were constructed in Holland for use by longer-range missiles (basically the same design but with a 271-gallon fuel tank compared with the 182-gallon tank fitted to the earlier model). Simultaneous to the ground launches, 200 or so redundant He111s were converted to carry a flying bomb slung under one wing, to be operated with little effect in the closing months of 1944, initially by III/KG3 and then KG53. Other forms of flying/guided bombs were also brought into action during this period – Hs293s, Fritz-Xs and *Mistels* by the Germans, BQ-7s and GB-4s by the Americans – none of which had the same impact or success as the V-1.

By the end of the bombardment – 29 March 1945 – approximately 10,500 V-1s had been launched against England, including some 1,500 air-launched from He111s, of which 5,890 crossed the coast. Overland and over the sea, a total of 4,261 were destroyed by the defences. According to official figures, ADGB fighters accounted for 1,902 up to the end of August 1944, but the figure would appear to be nearer 2,250 (see Appendix II). At least a further 80 were destroyed between September 1944 and March 1945. Land-based AA guns shot down a further 1,971, Royal Navy ships' AA 33, while Balloon Command was credited with bringing down 278. Despite these successes, 2,563 bombs penetrated the coastal defences to reach the London area, where 5,582 people were killed as a result, including 207 service personnel, and a further 15,538 were seriously injured of whom 280 were service personnel. Many acts of bravery were performed, not only by members of the emergency services, but also by ordinary members of the public in rescuing trapped victims of the explosions; many of these actions were rewarded, some not. Among those recognized for outstanding performances were three police horses, each awarded the prestigious PDSA Dickin Medal (the animal VC)[3]. Elsewhere in England, mainly in Kent, Sussex and Essex, a further 557 deaths were recorded (including 95 service personnel), with more than 1,700 seriously injured, as a result of 3,327 V-1s crashing to earth.

The V-1 itself proved to be a difficult target to intercept and shoot down, coming in over the Channel by both day and night at heights between 1,000 feet to 2,000 feet (on occasions much higher, the odd one being recorded at eight, nine, even ten thousand feet!) and speeds approaching 400mph. Although the missile could not defend itself, the task for the fighter pilot in shooting it down was not simple or easy, and was fraught with danger for the unwary. The result of an attack from close-range astern was unpredictable, and the bomb would sometimes explode in the air with the pursuer being forced to fly through the debris with not infrequent adverse effect. Some 72 ADGB fighter pilots/crews were killed (see Appendix I) during operations against the new weapon, several of whom died when their target detonated in mid-air, bringing down their own machine, often with fatal consequences; several others were accidentally shot down by British or American AA fire. Air Marshal Hill later commented:

> "During the first six weeks of the attacks, 18 fighters were substantially damaged and five pilots and one navigator killed in this way. Even though the flying bomb could not hit back deliberately, Diver patrols were by no means unattended by risk."

Pilots from almost all Allied countries participated in the destruction of the flying bombs, including British, Canadians, Australians, New Zealanders, South Africans, Dutch, Belgians, Poles, Czechs, Norwegians, Free French, Americans, and even a Swede. Among those who took part were two one-legged pilots (one British, one

French) and another Frenchman who was so shortsighted that he wore spectacles when flying.

During the final V-weapons assault against Antwerp and Liège, where over 4,200 were killed and 10,000 seriously injured in a matter of six months, some 6,000 V-1s were launched.

PREAMBLE

"I ask you: Do you want total war? If necessary, do you want a war more total and radical than anything that we can even imagine today?"
Dr Joseph Goebbels, Propaganda Minister, in his *Sportspalast* speech,
18 February 1943

The use in war of radio-controlled pilotless aeroplanes was under consideration during the early days of World War I, the 'Aerial Target' designed by H.P. Folland being flown at the British Royal Aircraft Establishment at Farnborough sometime in 1916. Two years later the US Army tested the Kettering Aerial Torpedo, known as the 'Bug', at Dayton, Ohio. It was launched off guide rails and upon reaching the vicinity of its intended target the preset timing device would cut the engine, whereupon the bomb-bearing fuselage would plunge to earth, detonating on impact. Although the war ended before any such weapon could be put to operational use, the seed of knowledge had been planted in the minds of many aircraft and weapons designers.

In between wars, the British had become adept in the use of pilotless aerial targets such as the Queen Bee, a radio-controlled Tiger Moth[4], while the Germans were experimenting with rocket-powered piloted and pilotless aircraft as early as 1929. A young aircraft designer, 23-year-old Julius Hatry, had designed and built a rocket-powered sailplane under the sponsorship of Fritz von Opel[5]. In 1940, with RAF Bomber Command unable to inflict much damage to the German war machine, Miles Aircraft Company proposed an unmanned, radio-controlled, Gypsy Major-engined aircraft capable of carrying an underslung 1,000lb bomb an estimated 400 miles. Miles had experimented with a project called Larynx that had been tested in the Iraq desert in 1929. A mock-up of their latest machine, named Hoopla, was built but the Air Ministry showed no interest, which is surprising considering it would have been a low cost machine, easily constructed and could have saved the lives of many airmen at this time. Perhaps it was deemed too simple to be suitable for the job in hand. The Ministry for Aircraft Production reasoned, with typical British sense of fair play: "An unmanned bomb is beneath contempt, because the place of impact could not be controlled accurately and also residential districts and hospitals could be hit." The mock-up, however, was retained until 1948, when it was finally scrapped. Perhaps there had been second thoughts somewhere along the line.

Pulse-jet research was begun in Germany in 1928 by Paul Schmidt. The Fieseler Fi-103/*FZG-76* was designed jointly by Robert Lusser of the Fieseler Aircraft Company and Fritz Gosslau from the Argus engine works. Its maiden flight was carried out on 23 December 1942 from the secret German test site at Peenemünde on the Baltic coast. With a length of 26 feet, wingspan approaching 18 feet, a range of 150 miles, and a maximum speed of 410mph produced by a single Argus AS14 pulse-jet, the flying bomb, with its 1,830lb warhead, was a formidable weapon – and cheap to produce. The 182-gallon fuel tank gave it an endurance of 30 minutes, ample time to reach London from the Pas-de-Calais where the first launching sites were constructed. Although the guidance system was very crude in construction it was sophisticated in conception. Once launched from the specially constructed steam catapult ramp – the so-called 'ski' ramp, since the propulsion unit did not produce sufficient thrust until the flying bomb was up to flight speed, approximately 250mph – or air-launched from specially adapted He111Hs, an autopilot was engaged and this regulated height and speed. However, the aircraft used for the first powered launch was a FW200, this releasing the missile over the Baltic on 10 December 1942. The guidance system consisted of a propeller in the nose. When this had turned a preset number of times (corresponding to the desired range to the target), the counter pushed the missile's rudder hard over, resulting in a dive to the ground, frequently causing many casualties and much damage when the warhead exploded. However, about 20% of all launchings proved defective.

In November 1939, British authorities had secretly acquired from Norway a summary of German technical developments so broad in scope and detailed in nature that the first impression was that it was a hoax. The so-called 'Oslo Report'[6] gained credibility as more weapons appeared, including differing types of radars and a deadly radio-controlled glider-bomb. Top British scientist and defence adviser to the government Dr R.V. Jones commented:

"There are a number of German weapons ... which must be considered seriously. They include: bacterial warfare; new gases; flame weapons; gliding bombs; aerial torpedoes and pilotless aircraft; long-range guns and rockets; new torpedoes, mines and submarines; death rays; engine-stopping rays and magnetic mines."

Among its most intriguing references was mention of a short-range flying bomb (the V-1) and a long-range rocket (the A4 otherwise known as the V-2) carrying high explosives. Exactly what the enemy was creating and what potential it had remained uncertain to the Allies. Intelligence and aerial reconnaissance pointed to a research station at Peenemünde on the Baltic coast. When Prime Minister Churchill was advised of this threat, he informed and warned the House of Commons during one of his periodical reviews of the war situation:

"We must not in any circumstances allow these favourable tendencies [he had been referring to the steadily growing Allied air offensive] to weaken our efforts or lead us to suppose that our dangers are past or that the war is coming to an end. On the contrary, we must expect the terrible foe we are smiting so heavily will make frenzied efforts to retaliate. The speeches of the German leaders, from Herr Hitler downwards, contain mysterious allusions to new methods and new weapons, which will presently be tried against us. It would, of course, be natural for the enemy to spread such rumours in order to encourage his own people, but there is probably more in it than that. For example, we now have experience of a new type of aerial bomb, which the enemy has begun to use in attacks on our shipping, close-quarter attacks on our shipping when at close quarters with the coast. This bomb, which may be described as a sort of rocket-assisted glider, is released from a considerable height, and is then apparently guided towards its target by the parent aircraft.

"It may be that the Germans are developing other weapons on novel lines which they may hope to do us damage and to compensate to some extent for the injury which they are daily receiving from us. I can only assure the House that unceasing vigilance and the best study of which we are capable are given to these possibilities. We have always hitherto found the answer to any of the problems, which have been presented to us. At the same time I do not exclude, and no one must exclude from their minds, that novel forms of attack will be employed, and should they be employed I should be able to show the House in detail the prolonged, careful examination beforehand which brought into force against them."

On the night of 17 August 1943, Bomber Command attacked Peenemünde by moonlight, losing 40 aircraft but causing much damage, consequently delaying the missile campaign by several weeks. It was not long before the muddy waters became clear to British scientists, however, thanks mainly to a daring Danish naval officer, as Dr Jones was later to acknowledge:

"On 22 August [1943] an object had crashed in a turnip field on the island of Bornholm in the Baltic, roughly half-way between Germany and Sweden. It was a small pilotless aircraft bearing the number '*V83*', and it was promptly photographed by the Danish Naval Officer-in-Charge on Bornholm, Lt-Cdr Hasager Christiansen. He also made a sketch, and noted that the warhead was a dummy made of concrete. At first, we were not sure what he had found. From his sketch it was about 14 feet long, and it might have been a rather larger version of the Hs293 glider-bomb that KG100 was now using against our warships in the Mediterranean. Indeed, it turned out that this particular bomb had been released from a Heinkel 111 [possibly CK+UE, operating from the German weapons testing centre at Karlshägen on Peenemünde], but it was in fact a research model ('V' probably stood for *Versuchs* – i.e. research) of the flying bomb about which we were going to hear so much in the next few months."

Some months later, a subsequent report from Stockholm revealed that the skipper of a Danish freighter had witnessed the flight of two missiles that had been fired from a shore installation, which were "… propelled at very high speed by a rocket tube which gave approximately 300 detonations a minute … each detonation appeared to give two flashes in the form of a ring." From Peenemünde the early experimental models of the flying bomb were being tested over the Baltic Sea, but by September 1943 the initial batch of 100 had been fired. The next batch was delayed and by early October only a further 38 had been delivered, this being the total monthly production of the Volkswagen plant at Fallersleben, whereas monthly production of up to 5,000 had been suggested. The scrapping of 2,000 airframes in November because of bad welding further hindered the programme. The weapons programme was set back by many factors, including technical problems with the devices and bureaucratic infighting. Many teething troubles were experienced including premature crashes of the missile following launch. Sometimes a bomb would travel only a few yards from its test catapult before failing. The provisional date for the attack on London (Operation *Kirschkern* – Cherry Stone) was set for 15 December 1943 but had to be postponed. The start of the campaign was then set for May 1944, the flying bomb then being referred to as the *Maikafer* (Maybug), but was again delayed by the lack of missiles. The mass-production timetable was repeatedly compromised but finally, by the end of May some 2,500 operational bombs had been stockpiled with a further 2,500 made available in June. Some 55 launching sites had been constructed in the Pas-de-Calais by slave labour, mainly French, Belgian and Dutch conscripted workers, and these were considered operational for the opening assault. Other sites were still being constructed. Orders were issued. From the Chief of the High Command of the Armed Forces:

The Führer has ordered

1: The long-range bombardment of England will begin in the middle of June. The exact date will be set by the Commander-in-Chief West who will also control the bombardment with the help of LXV Army Corps and 3rd Air Fleet.

2: The following weapons will be employed.
(a) FZG76
(b) FZG76 launched from He111
(c) Long-range artillery
(d) Bomber forces of 3rd Air Fleet

3: Method
(a) Against the main target, London.

The bombardment will open like a thunderclap by night with FZG76 combined with bombs (mostly incendiary) from the bomber forces, and a sudden long-range artillery attack against towns within range. It will continue with persistent harassing fire by night on London. When weather conditions make enemy air activity impossible, firing can also take place by day. This harassing fire, mingled with bombardments of varying length and intensity, will be calculated so that the supply of ammunition is always related to our capacities for production and transport. In addition, six hundred FZG76 will be regarded as a reserve of the High Command of the Armed Forces, to be fired only with the approval of the High Command.

(b) Orders will be given in due course for switching fire to other courses.

4: Bomber planes of the Air Force will co-operate to the exclusion of other tasks, at least at the beginning of the bombardment. Fighter and anti-aircraft defence of firing-points and dumps will be completed and organized at the beginning of the bombardment. All preparations will be made on the assumption that communications with the firing-points will come under heavy attack and may be destroyed.

Keitel
Feldmarschall, Chief of the High Command, 16 May 1944.

There remained some German doubters as to what success the new weapon was likely to achieve, particularly amongst those who realized that British and American technological advances would possibly soon find ways and means of combating the threat. Captain Norman MacMillan[7] later wrote:

"The flying bomb was tested for speed against a captured Spitfire flown by a German pilot. Hitler watched this test. But that Spitfire was a Mark V model, inferior in speed to subsequent Spitfires, Mustangs, Tempests, and Meteors, and so the German premise that their robot's speed could defeat defence by fighters was founded on faulty empirics. German advocates of these new weapons expected much from them. They believed that their very novelty would achieve surprise, and thereby penetrate the orthodox defences, perhaps catastrophically. They obviously did not examine in detail the possibilities of defence against the flying bomb, so overestimated their military worth at their then stage of development."

In addition to ground launching V-1s that came under the control of *Flakregiment 155 (W)* commanded by Oberst Max Watchel, the directive called for air launching from He111s. The responsibility for training selected aircrew fell upon III/KG3 based at Karlshägen (Peenemünde), in particular a specialised unit labelled *Erprobungs-kommando Graudenz*, named after its commander Ltn Karlheinz Graudenz. Training began in May 1944 and was concluded with the test launching of 54 V-1s during the month and the first nine days of June. The first operational flights would be made from Gilze-Rijen on the night of 3-4 July. Of the imminent assault on London, Dr Joseph Goebbels, the Nazi Chief of Propaganda, is recorded as having stated:

"*I suspect that when the first projectiles plunge down onto London, the English public will panic. The Führer and I, bent over a large map of London, have staked off the squares with the most profitable targets. In London twice as many people are crowded into a cramped area as are in Berlin. I know what this means. And London has not had any alarms for the past three-and-a-half years. Imagine the kind of terrible awakening this will be! The offensive means which we deploy are entirely new. There will be no defence and no alarm. There will be no help from Flak and siren. With a bang, our weapons will crash on the unsuspecting city. I can't fully imagine the terrible morale effects of such attacks.*"

Goebbels had earlier indicated that something catastrophic was in store for the people of London when he wrote in *Das Reich*:

"*It will not be long before we are forced to give the enemy far more persuasive proof. The British people above all will be forced to prove whether they in the fifth year of the war possess the same steadfastness as the German people. The worst of this phase of the war is behind us. England is facing it. We did not break. The British must still endure the trial. Whatever happens, we know the horrors of modern war, and we also know that they can be overcome.*"

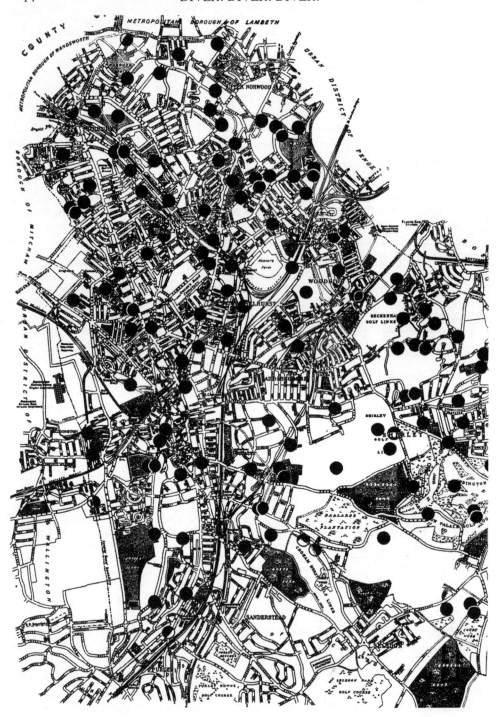

Situation map of V-1s falling on Croydon during this period.

CHAPTER I

A HINT OF THINGS TO COME

*"There are a number of German weapons ... which must be considered seriously. They include
... gliding bombs; aerial torpedoes and pilotless aircraft."*

Dr R.V. Jones

With the certain knowledge that invasion was imminent, the Germans had prepared various means by which they hoped to counter the anticipated armada of ships that would undoubtedly approach the coast of France from British ports. Two of these countermeasures were soon used against Allied shipping building up in various ports. Appreciating that the unguided V-1 would not be sufficiently accurate for this task – indeed, it was designed to be used as a terror weapon against London and other British cities – three other forms of guided weapons were rushed into operation specifically for attacks against ships:

The radio-controlled **Ruhrstahl SD1400X**, known as the 'Fritz-X', was based on a conventional 1,000kg armour-piercing bomb, but fitted with wings and stabilizers. Slung under the wing of its parent aircraft, it was an unpowered free-falling bomb, radio-controlled by an operator aboard the parent aircraft, either a specially adapted Do217 or a four-engined He177. Since the aircraft was required to slow down to enable the bomb aimer to track the missile, it was always vulnerable to anti-aircraft fire or fighter attack.

The **Henschel Hs293** was more advanced and also designed to be carried under the wing of a parent bomber. Work had begun on the project before the outbreak of war. Based on a normal 500kg bomb with wings and fins added, it had a small rocket motor suspended below. Once released it would fall for some 90 metres before the rocket achieved maximum thrust. The first test flight took place on 16 December 1940, the bomb being released from a He111 but it proved a failure when it was realised that the control circuits had been inadvertently reversed during assembly of the guidance system. A second test flight two days later was a complete success. Development continued until by 1943 it was deemed ready for operational use. The main problem was that the parent bomber – again a Do217 or He177 – was required to fly a steady, level path to enable the controller to guide it to its intended target by use of a small control box fitted with a joystick. During this operation, the parent aircraft was potentially an easy target for AA fire or any pursuing fighter. Both the Fritz-X and Hs293 were designed for use against ships not heavily defended by AA fire. Once the Allies had found means of interfering with the control signals, both weapons were rendered practically useless[8]. III/KG100, based at Toulouse under the command of Hptm Wolfgang Vorpahl, had 31 Do217s on its strength, of which fewer than half were serviceable at the beginning of June. I/KG40, less 3 Staffel, was operating He177s[9].

The third secret weapon was the *Mistel* combination comprising an unmanned Ju88 'bomb' launched and guided by a parent Bf109 (and later a FW190), which was less technically sophisticated, but just as potentially lethal, and was based on an idea inspired by the prewar British Short Mayo flying boat combination. For training purposes the Ju88 was fitted with a cockpit section, this being relatively easy to remove to enable the warhead to be fitted in its place. The first live test had taken place in February 1944. While the Fritz-X and Hs293 guided bombs had already been used with limited success in the Mediterranean theatre of operations[10], the *Mistel* was as yet untried in war.

Preliminaries

In the early morning hours of **30 April 1944**, a dozen Do217Ks from III/KG100 attempted to carry out a raid on Plymouth harbour using Fritz-X guided bombs. The main target for the German crews was the battleship *King George V*, but the attack resulted in failure due mainly to the defensive smoke screen over the harbour. Four of the bombs fell on land, two at Laira and two at Stoke, Devon, while two of the Do217s were claimed shot down by Sqn Ldr David Williams DFC RCAF (with Flg Off Clarence Kirkpatrick RCAF) in a Mosquito of 406 (RCAF) Squadron:

> "Closing in at Angels 16, this was identified as a Do217 and attack was made at minimum range while the enemy aircraft was still illuminated. Hits were seen on the starboard engine, causing immediate flames to spread and pieces were seen falling off the wing. The aircraft then spun straight in, landing on the ground. Our aircraft was held illuminated for several minutes and flak was heavy in spite of my every endeavour to call for douse. This was partly due to the subsequent discovery that the Mark II IFF was not working. During this time a second contact had been held at two miles range to starboard at Angels 11, which was then followed out to sea, jinking violently. This was also identified as a Do217 and attack was made at 100 yards with short burst on the starboard side, the enemy aircraft bursting into flame, turning on its back and crashing into the sea. No return fire was experienced in either case."

A third claim was submitted by Wg Cdr Keith Hampshire DSO DFC RAAF, the CO of 456 (RAAF) Squadron (in HK286/RX-A), who was granted a probable:

> "We went down to 500 feet, weaving, to place the target above. The latter was weaving, speed about 200mph. Closing in and obtaining a visual at 2,000 feet, I identified the target as a Do217, confirming this later with the aid of night binoculars. I gave a six-seconds burst and saw a large number of strikes along the port side of the fuselage, mostly at the wing root. The turret gunner of the e/a returned a short burst of fire at the same time, tracer going over the top of our aircraft. The Do217 ceased firing and lost height. I opened fire again a few seconds later, firing a four-seconds burst. Shells could be seen hitting the Dornier's fuselage throughout the burst, and the port wing suddenly went down and the e/a went into a steep spiral from 500 feet. No further fire was experienced from the e/a. A strong blip on the tube disappeared suddenly at a very short range after the e/a went into a steep spiral."

Two Dorniers failed to return from this raid. One – 6N+AD (4701) of StabStaffel carrying Hptm Hermann Pfieffer, Gruppenkommandeur – crashed into the sea just off the harbour, from which only Uffz Friedrich and Uffz Pietzsch survived. A second aircraft – 6N+IT (4716) of 9 Staffel – crashed at Pasture Farm, Blackawton in Devon. Three of Ltn Herbert Palme's crew baled out successfully but Uffz Katzenberger was killed in the crash. Unfortunately, the 'Dornier' claimed by Wg Cdr Hampshire turned out to be Mitchell FR142 of 320 (Dutch) Squadron flown by Lt Cdr Jopie Mulder RNethN on night flying exercise in Herne Bay area. Mulder ordered his crew to bale out, which Flg Off Wjtman did, but the gunner (Sgt Jan de Vos) had left his parachute behind, so the Dutch pilot bravely force-landed his damaged aircraft three miles north-east of Headcorn in Kent.

Slaughter of the Heinkels

Before the V-1 offensive began, however, I and II/KG40 with its He177s capable of carrying both Fritz-X and Hs293 guided bombs, and III/KG100's Do217Ks armed with Hs293s, attempted to interfere with the armada of Allied ships in the Channel and off the French coast. The first RAF claim against one of the missile-carriers was made during the daylight hours of **6 June**, when a Coastal Command Mosquito flown by Flt Sgt L.D. Stoddart of 248 Squadron shot down what was thought to be He177 during a 30-aircraft daylight strike against the St Nazaire submarine base, although it seems that his victim was in fact a reconnaissance Ju88 from 3(F)/123.

He177s and Do217s, together with anti-shipping Ju88s, flew some 150 sorties during the night of **6/7 June**. For scant success, the Heinkels in particular proved easy pickings for the Mosquito night fighter patrols over the beachhead, four aircraft from I/KG40 falling to the guns of 456 (RAAF) Squadron between Le Havre and Cherbourg: Flg Offs Fred Stevens RAAF and Andy Kellett RAAF in HK290/RX-J claimed two:

"Identified target as a He177. At this stage glider-bombs, one under each wing outboard of engine nacelles, and a large four-pronged aerial array in the nose were seen. Dropping back to 100 yards, I opened fire with a two-seconds burst. Port engine of e/a caught fire immediately. Another two two-seconds bursts were given, causing a large white flash in the centre of the fuselage. E/a spun into the sea and exploded. Return fire was experienced from the rear gunner after first burst. *Window* was in profusion but was not seen coming from this aircraft. Continuing the patrol in the same area north of Cherbourg, I was given a vector to another bogey at Angels 4; contact was obtained at three miles dead ahead and below. Speed was increased and height lost and the target was followed through several turns till a visual was obtained at 1,200 feet, slightly to port and at the same level. The target was identified as another He177. I dropped back and made an attack from the dark part of the sky, allowing half-ring deflection at 250 yards. The port engine of the e/a immediately caught fire and another short burst was given but I was dazzled by glare and did not observe any further hits. Breaking away to the dark part of the sky I watched e/a turn to port and lose height in a shallow dive. Fire appeared to be dying out so similar attacks were made again, each being of two-three seconds at a height of 2,000 feet. Strikes all over e/a and bright white flash seen after which the e/a turned vertically to port and dived into the sea, exploding on the water. No glider-bombs or nose-aerial seen. Return fire from rear gunner was experienced on each attack after the initial burst."

Stevens' CO, Wg Cdr Hampshire (in HK286/RX-A) claimed another Heinkel. Having taken off from Ford at 0315, Hampshire and his radar operator Flt Lt Tom Condon RAAF, were given several different vectors before a target appeared:

"A long range visual of over 3,500 feet ensued and I identified the target as a He177 in magnificent full moonlight conditions against a background of white cloud. The glider-bombs were clearly noticeable. I moved 5° to port, range 150 yards, fired a burst and saw large pieces of flaming debris detach from the e/a's port engine, amongst which the port engine appeared to disintegrate. E/a did not burst into flames immediately but five seconds later did so and was seen to burn all the way down to the water. We broke away to give a fix (three miles east of Barfleur: time – 0349)."

Flg Off Ron Pratt RAAF (HK303/RX-H) shot down the fourth:

"I identified the aircraft with the aid of night binoculars as a He177 through thin patches of cloud. The e/a (whose mean speed was 210mph) apparently suspected being stalked and dived to within 200 feet of the sea, climbing then to 400 feet when we closed to 100 yards dead astern. I pressed firing button but nothing happened. E/a opened fire from rear of cockpit, tracer being seen coming straight over and to starboard. I turned hard to port. The He177 again fired, from a parallel course, the fire passing behind our aircraft. E/a then dived down. A firing test was then made, successfully. The situation was reported to control, which wanted to vector us back to base but a six-mile contact was just then obtained to the east on a *Window*-dropper flying south-westerly. At 4,000 feet a visual was obtained on a target taking mild routine evasive action at a height of 500 feet. We moved in and beneath and from side-to-side, easily recognising it as a He177. No bombs were seen to be carried. At 150 yards the e/a, still above, started to turn to port, with the Mosquito coming up to its level (500 feet), where I gave it a short burst. E/a burst into flame immediately at the wing root and in the centre of the fuselage. There was a shower of sparks for about 30 seconds as e/a climbed to 800 feet, then it dived," exploded and disintegrated. Debris began to burn fiercely on the water, near some surface vessels. There was no AA fire, or return fire from the He177."

Five Heinkels in fact failed to return: 1 Staffel lost F8+MH (550206) from which Oblt Siegfried Müller and five of his crew were killed, the other surviving to be taken prisoner. 2 Staffel lost two aircraft and crews, F8+KK (550197) flown by Obfw Hans Timm, and F8+LK (535731) flown by Obfhr Wolfgang Bernrieder. The other two missing aircraft were both from 5 Staffel – F8+IN (550117) commanded by Oblt Jürgen Hanke and the other flown by Obfw Hans Müller. There were no survivors. The body of Uffz Karl Castens, the observer aboard Müller's aircraft, and that of another unidentified German airman, were recovered from the sea by the Royal Navy south-east of the Isle of Wight on 16 June. Both were buried at sea.

The following night (**7/8 June**), a repeat effort was made by the Germans and about a further 150 sorties were flown, the main targets being allied shipping in the Seine bay. 456 (RAAF) Squadron claimed three more Heinkels, two low-flying aircraft by Sqn Ldr Basil Howard RAAF (HK290/RX-J) and one by Plt Off Butch Hodgen RAAF (HK302/RX-Z). Howard reported:

"The aircraft was identified as a He177 with glider-bombs slung outside of engine nacelles. The aircraft continued straight and level as I dropped back to about 100 yards and fired a five-seconds burst from slightly starboard – strikes observed all over starboard side of the aircraft and starboard engine, which burst into flames, with a violent explosion at the starboard wing root. Return fire was observed, apparently from the top dorsal guns and as the aircraft dived steeply to starboard, one of the crew was observed to bale out, passing under starboard wing of Mosquito as chute opened. The enemy aircraft continued diving steeply until it hit the sea in flames, where it exploded with a very violent red explosion and continued to burn on the surface. I immediately called Blackgang for a fix – time about 0105. Patrol was resumed at 5,000 feet and about 15 minutes later another contact was obtained to port and below at 8,000 feet. Followed to investigate through thin stratus cloud. On turning, visual on aircraft was obtained, dropping *Window*. Glider-bombs were again observed outboard of the engines and, as it turned, was definitely identified as a He177. At this stage e/a dived away to port and as he was heading for a layer of thick cloud, a two-seconds burst was given – no strikes were observed but there was very inaccurate return fire from upper dorsal. Another three-seconds burst was fired at about 200 yards range – strikes seen on port engine, which emitted sparks and clouds of white smoke. Another short burst saw a number of strikes on fuselage, but guns ceased firing at this stage. We followed for about one mile when it appeared to catch fire in fuselage, nosed over into vertical position and dived straight into the sea, which it hit with a violent explosion similar to the previous combat. I called for a fix, the time being 0125."

Plt Off Bob Hodgen also witnessed his victim hit the sea:

"Came in behind target to range of 6,000 feet when visual was obtained in bright moonlight. Closed to 1,000 feet range and target positively identified as He177 doing gentle port orbits. I fired a three or four-seconds burst from below and to port at about 800 feet range but as I fired a dark cloud passed between target and the moon and the glare of the gunsight obliterated the target. Return fire was experienced immediately I fired, which passed above our port wing. I tightened my port turn and obtained a visual in bright moonlight again, at about 400 feet and out to starboard. Return fire was now passing over our starboard wing. I closed to a range of between 200 and 300 feet and gave e/a a two-seconds burst, using slight deflection. Starboard motor flashed and burst with a big orange flame. Strikes seen on port wing, which burnt with a very deep red flame. Target lost height in a gentle port spiral turn and hit the sea at 0155. No bombs seen slung under wings."

Flt Lt Jeremy Howard-Williams of the FIU was also up in a Mosquito XIII, departing Manston at 2320 to patrol Orléans/Bricy aerodrome, aided by his radar operator Flg Off Jock MacRae:

"A contact was obtained at two miles and above. This was closed to 3,000 feet on AI and less than 100 yards visually. After some debate as to the identity, black crosses were identified on the wings and the aircraft was identified as a He177. Range was increased to 500-600 feet. Then e/a went into a slow port turn and fire was opened with a two-seconds burst. Immediately a great flash occurred in the port motor and a large piece was seen to fall away. The e/a then peeled off to port and a red glow was seen as it dived under our nose. This was thought to be the e/a on fire but turned out to be [red flare]. I throttled back, put the nose down and gave a one-second burst as I overshot. Strikes were seen. The e/a continued to dive down steeply beneath our aircraft and the visual was lost in the haze. Claim one He177 damaged. Another contact was later closed and recognised as a Liberator."

Two Heinkels were lost, Ltn Kurt Wadle's F8+HK (550211) of 2/KG40, which failed to return, while Oblt Adolf Büsch and his 6 Staffel crew were killed when their aircraft (550083) crashed at Toqueville after they had reported being attacked by a night fighter. A Do217K was shot down by Plt Off Ralph Green RCAF of 406 (RCAF) Squadron (flying HU-D) – possibly 6N+OR (4742) of Stab III/KG100 in which Oblt Oskar Schmidke and his crew were lost. Green reported:

"We [flying with Plt Off A.W. Hillyer RCAF] were on a Night Ranger patrol Lannion to Morlaix area. Near Morlaix a contact was obtained at one mile range, and closing in for a visual identified the target as a Coastal Beaufighter. Patrol was continued on reciprocal and a second contact was made at five miles range – and followed to a visual on a Liberator at Angels 4 off coast. On returning to coast large red flares in shower style were seen appearing from Lannion aerodrome, which was skirted and patrol was resumed over the bay north-east of Morlaix. A head-on contact was then picked up at two miles range on a target at Angels 2. After a hard turn and climb a visual was obtained on a weaving target at 2,000 feet and identified as a Do217, believed to be carrying radio-controlled bombs. Closing in to 75 yards from below and behind, I pulled to left and right to confirm identification, then dropped back to 200 yards and fired two short bursts. Both engines of the enemy aircraft caught fire and the enemy aircraft turned sideways, revealing German markings in the light of the blaze. The enemy aircraft then blew up with its bomb load and plunged into the sea. Patrol was then continued and one more contact was obtained, the target being identified as a Stirling."

Despite the successes by the Mosquito night fighters, inevitably a number of Hs293s were launched and one struck the American destroyer USS (DD726) *Meredith*, which had been towed to the Bay of Seine following damage resulting from striking a mine. Her captain Cdr George Knuepfer USN later wrote:

"On the early morning of the ninth the area was heavily bombed by the enemy and one 2,000-pound bomb landed about 500 yards off the ship's bow and it shook the ship terribly and it had indicated the first evidence of the stern working itself loose. The break of the deck had originally been quite level and now the stern section began rising but still the bulkheads were intact, the bilges were dry and we felt that the ship would eventually be saved and live to fight again. However about ten o'clock on the morning of the 9th, she suddenly gave a terrific crunch and broke in two. There was sufficient time for everybody to jump clear into the water to be picked up by the tugs. The bow slid down aft and the stern slid down forward and just as the bow was about to go underwater, she turned over so that the keel was exposed and she broke in two and rapidly sank out of sight. She sank about thirty-two hours after she was originally struck. As in every serious accident this one had a little bit of its humor. When I was getting ready to leave the ship, one of the chief petty officers said to me, 'I almost forgot *Lurky*.' I said, 'Who is *Lurky*?' He said, 'It's our pet cat that you never knew had been aboard.' I was quite surprised to get the news at such a time, 'cause I had a ship's order that no pets would be allowed on my ship. The destroyer with its steel hot decks is a rather cruel place to keep pets. I've seen so many of them lost overboard, so I didn't want any. This CPO went down into the blacked out chief's quarters and soon came out with this tiny little cat. He tucked her inside his jacket and climbed aboard the tug alongside."

The Australian unit shot down its eighth He177 on the night of **9/10 June** when about 80 sorties were flown by the German crews, Flt Lt Bob Cowper RAAF (HK353/RX-M) being the successful pilot, catching the bomber, which was carrying a pair of Hs293s, off Cap Levy. He also accounted for one of III/KG100's Do217Ks, possibly FhjFw Gerhard Klemp's 6N+JP (336473) of 6 Staffel. Two Heinkels from 2/KG40 were shot down off Cherbourg, with Obfw Josef Henze's F8+SK (535670) crashing at Bonnetable with the loss of the crew; F8+BK (550198) also crashed. From the latter aircraft the crew, apart from the observer, survived. Not all targets were simple to bring down, as Cowper's report revealed:

"I recognised e/a as a He177. E/a carried two large glider-bombs outboard of the engine nacelles. Rear gunner continued to hosepipe fire, not very accurately, throughout the engagement. No engine exhausts were visible, and glider-bombs gave the effect at first of a four-engined aircraft [which, of course, it was]. I fired a one-second burst at 800 feet, obtaining strikes on the port wing. E/a turned steeply starboard and lost height. Another two-seconds burst obtained strikes on starboard wing. E/a was by now close to Cherbourg harbour, and heading for it, still losing height, and was greeted by immediate and heavy flak. He turned 90 degrees starboard, parallel to the coast, and another two-seconds burst at his starboard wing set it ablaze. This wing burned heartily with huge flames and we flew parallel to e/a and slightly above to observe the finish. However, e/a released flaming object and it was seen that the glider-bomb had been ignited and was now flying solo, parallel to, and between, us and the e/a. We immediately closed in to attack again and saw that the starboard wing of the e/a was still burning outward of the engine nacelle. At this juncture e/a dived almost vertically towards the French coast, west of Cherbourg, and following him down we fired a short burst into his rear. No additional effects were noticed. At 300 feet we pulled out of the dive and e/a was still beneath us and just crossing the coastline. Visual was lost owing to me having to give my whole attention to instruments in view of the dangerously low height."

By way of complete contrast, Cowper's second victim was a straightforward interception and was despatched with ruthless efficiency:

"I made a climbing turn to starboard and another contact was immediately obtained at approximately 0405, head-on, slightly starboard, at 4,000 feet and five miles range. This aircraft was dropping *Window*. We continued to climb and, turning to port, came in behind and obtained visual of a Do217 at 2,000 feet. He was carrying one glider-bomb outboard of port nacelle and there was nothing visible under his starboard wing. No exhaust glow was visible and he took no evasive action, although continuing to drop *Window*. One short burst was fired from 450 feet, which set his port engine and inner mainplane ablaze. We took up position above and to port of e/a and watched the fire develop. E/a went into a steep diving turn to port, burning pieces falling off meanwhile. Eventually it hit the beach, a ball of fire, and a brief interval later exploded, lighting up the whole area. No return fire had been experienced."

Plt Off Ivor Sanderson RAAF (HK249/RX-B) continued 456's run when he shot down a Heinkel on the night of **10/11 June**, despite his own aircraft being hit in one wing by return fire. His victim was possibly F8+JH (550175) of 1/KG40 that crashed north of Caen at 0335, in which Obfw Franz Konopek and three of his crew were killed, the other three being captured. Of his victory, Sanderson reported:

"Target was dropping *Window* occasionally but taking no evasive action. A visual was obtained at 2,000 feet range, and we closed to 600 feet to identify it as a He177. When aligning for firing, rear gunner of e/a opened fire at 800 feet with two bursts (containing a lot of tracer). The second burst removed about four feet of the leading edge of the starboard wing outboard on engine. The caused the Mosquito to drop back and swing to one side and it became very difficult to control. I closed again to about 900 feet and slightly below, and fired two long bursts, many strikes being observed round the starboard engine of e/a, which slowly caught fire. E/a began losing height rapidly, fire spreading all over it. E/a finally dropped into sea, burning fiercely, the flaming mass being visible on the sea until we crossed the English coast coming in to base. After being hit, great effort was required to hold the starboard wing of the Mosquito up and to counteract the strong tendency to swing starboard, which made it difficult to bring the sight on to the target. The main spar was bare for six feet outboard of the starboard engine and the Mosquito stalled at 180mph, making it necessary for a very fast approach on landing. It was later found that pieces of shell had pierced the petrol tank, making a two-inch hole which had become re-sealed."

Sqn Ldr Geoff Howitt DFC (HK249/RX-B) claimed a He177 probably destroyed. Two crewmembers aboard a 4 Staffel machine (550221) were wounded as a result of night fighter attack, and this was possibly the aircraft attacked by Howitt, who reported:

"The target was identified by me and navigator [Flt Lt G.N. Irving DFC] using night binoculars as a He177 (no bombs), and it was flying straight and level due east. I gave it two short bursts from 600 feet, dead astern, and strikes were seen on the port wing, fuselage and port engine; the latter streamed smoke immediately and e/a dived steeply and pulled out about 3,000 below. I followed, the target gaining. Closing in to 600 feet, I again opened fire from dead astern with a three-seconds burst, observing a number of strikes concentrated in a bunch on the fuselage and starboard engine nacelle; many sparks and pieces were seen to fly off, and e/a flew steadily for a very short time, and then, turning slightly to starboard, its nose dropped vertically. I followed and pulled out sharply at 2,500 feet when the visual was lost. The heavy trail of smoke from the e/a's engine was seen coming out all the time. Claimed probably destroyed."

Three more He177s were lost on this night, at least two of which were reported to have fallen to AA fire, one crashing into the sea off St Mere Eglise, the other near Lessay. Another Do217K – possibly 6N+KT (4708) of 9/KG100 flown by Ltn Heinz Schul – fell on the night of **11/12 June**, this being claimed by Flg Off Alex Sterrenberg RCAF (MM523) of 409(RCAF) Squadron:

"At 1,200 feet I obtained a visual of the exhausts and at 800 feet both the navigator [Flg Off Clarke RCAF] and myself recognised a Do217 by the position of the exhausts and silhouette. At 200 feet below and to starboard, I fired a two-seconds burst, seeing strikes on fuselage and starboard wing, the starboard engine and wing bursting into flames and burning furiously. Return fire was experienced for about four or five seconds. I closed to 150 yards and delivered a further burst of three-seconds, my navigator observing strikes on top of starboard engine and noticing pieces falling off. The e/a did a slow port spiral, which steepened as it lost height. I followed down to 4,000 feet but was illuminated by three searchlights, almost simultaneously by fairly accurate ack-ack fire, one burst exploding below me and causing the aircraft to drop the port wing violently. I climbed for cloud cover as quickly as I could. Position of combat is estimated to have been in the vicinity of Alençon."

Two more Heinkels were claimed on the night of **12/13 June**, one falling to Flt Lt Reg 'Dusty' Miller DFC (MM526) of 604 Squadron. This was almost certainly F8+FH (550215) of 1/KG40, in which Uffz Rudolf Brühan and his crew was lost. Flying out of Hurn with Wt Off Peter Catchpole as his radar operator, Miller reported:

"We then chased various contacts in cloud at 4,000-5,000 feet. Then, breaking cloud, I observed two clusters of chandelier flares. At the same time my navigator obtained a contact on a target at 3,000 height, two miles range, crossing starboard to port from east to west. I closed in rapidly and obtained a visual at 4,000 feet of the target silhouetted against the flares, I closed in behind and identified it as a He177. The target was turning to port. I then closed to 200 yards and gave him a long burst, observing strikes. The starboard engine of the e/a burst into flames and it peeled off to port and dived into the sea. The wreckage burned for a considerable time, and I went down and took cine camera shots. I returned after about 15 minutes to the area of the combat and the wreckage was still burning."

The other Heinkel fell to Plt Off Len Kearney RCAF of 410 (RCAF) Squadron:

"While we were closing in, the enemy did mild evasive action, dumping out *Window* at the same time. We closed in to about 1,000 feet and obtained a visual. Closed in further to 600 feet and identified it as a He177, carrying an object slung outboard of each engine. We dropped back to 800 feet astern and opened fire, but missed with the first burst. A second burst being fired from approximately 500 feet range, the whole starboard wing root and engine caught fire. A large panel blew off the starboard wing. We pulled off to port and watched the e/a burn. One crewmember was seen to bale out. The e/a started to go down steeply while we did a starboard orbit watching him do so. Flames seemed to be spreading on the e/a. The height was about 6,000 feet and the e/a, going down very steeply, hit the ground with a terrific explosion, which lit us up at 6,000 feet. It then burned fiercely. We pointed our nose down and took a shot with our camera."

The Mosquito (HK459) then suffered an engine fire and Kearney was obliged to carry out an emergency landing on an ALG just beyond the beachhead. The crew survived unhurt but their aircraft was damaged beyond repair. Their victim was an aircraft of 6/KG40, from which Obfw Werner Neuenfeld and his entire crew baled out, two (Uffz Karl Henninger and Fw Alfred Schlegel) sustaining injuries. The Heinkel crashed at Rouville near Bolbec.

The slaughter of the ungainly Heinkels continued the following night (**13/14 June**), one of which fell to 409 (RCAF) Squadron's CO, Wg Cdr Joe Reid RCAF (with Flt Lt Peacock RCAF in MM560):

"I obtained a visual at 1,500 feet but due to the extremely dark background I was unable to identify target definitely until I closed in to 500 feet, when both my navigator, using night binoculars, and myself recognised the target as a He177. I dropped back to 600 feet dead astern, 5° below, and fired a one-and-a-half-seconds burst, hitting the e/a between the two engines and underneath the fuselage. An immediate explosion occurred with great quantities of flaming debris flying off the aircraft, smearing my windscreen and fuselage with oil and matter. The fire extended throughout the length of the plane, which commenced a slow spiral to starboard culminating in a vertical dive and hitting the sea with a still further explosion at 0145. This He177 is claimed destroyed. The position is believed to be 20/25 miles north of Le Havre."

Yet another Heinkel was shot down by Plt Off Stan Williams RAAF flying HK282/RX-L of 456 (RAAF) Squadron, with Flg Off Ken Havord RAAF as his radar operator:

"Turning towards the target, I put nose down and while closing in was told there might be a bogey on my tail. One violent orbit was made but there was no sign of any aircraft. Turning on to the original target, contact was regained at four miles, which was followed through an orbit with constant routine weaving. A little *Window* was dropped early in the chase. Closing to 1,000 feet, a visual was obtained, silhouetted against dark cloud, making identification difficult, so I went below, where aircraft was recognised at 400 feet as a He177. I pulled up the nose and in doing so dropped back a little. I fired from 600 feet range, a two-seconds burst slightly to port. Immediately, a burst of flames came from halfway along the fuselage, and small pieces of debris in profusion came back. The fire ran back slowly along the fuselage and e/a made an easy turn to starboard, losing height slowly, the flames lighting up the sky. Two glider-bombs were clearly seen under the wings. E/a went down vertically, hitting the water with a splash, when many large coloured sparks came up. Orbiting, a fix was obtained just off Fécamp at 0215. Lt Thornley RN was on patrol at the same time and saw an aircraft fall into the sea at the time and place of our combat."

Flt Lt Frank Ellis of 604 Squadron (MM563) also shot down one, with Flt Lt P.C. Williams occupying the radar operator's seat:

"I obtained a visual at 1,500 feet and asked the controller if it was definitely hostile. I then closed in to 350 feet and below and identified the target as a He177 with what I thought were glider-bombs outboard of the engines. Then as I pulled up to dead astern, the e/a peeled off to port. Despite peeling off after him AI and visual contact were lost. I asked the controller for further help and was told that the e/a was five miles away, flying south. My navigator obtained another contact on the e/a at three miles range, flying east. I closed in again as the e/a flew towards a chandelier flare. Another visual was obtained at 1,500 feet on the target flying straight and level. I closed to 400 feet and again identified the target as a He177. I then pulled up dead astern and fired a short burst from 150 yards and observed strikes on the fuselage and port wing root. The e/a exploded in mid air, turned on its back to port and spun down enveloped in flames. I landed at Hurn at 0320 and on examination of my aircraft it was found that pieces of the e/a had caused slight damage to the port mainplane."

A fourth Heinkel was claimed at 0208 by Flt Lt Ian Cosby (HK502) of 264 Squadron:

"The target was continually turning, first port then starboard and throwing out *Window* at 15-seconds intervals. I closed in rapidly and obtained a visual ahead and well above at a range of almost 2,500 feet. Target then dropped three bright yellowish flares. It was an extremely dark moonless night with 10/10th cloud above and identification was very difficult. Target aircraft appeared for a long time as a dark blob. I closed the range and climbed, while target orbited the flares. When almost directly below and at 800 feet range, I with my naked eye and my navigator with night glasses, between us and after some altercation, identified the aircraft as a He177. My navigator, having done all he could to aid me, than sat back, folded his hands on his lap and prepared to enjoy the fun. I then climbed up behind the He177, closed to 200 yards and fired a one-second burst. There was a blinding yellow flash with red sparks round the port wing root and cockpit, debris flew off and I broke away to port. I saw the aircraft well below on my starboard side, crossing to port and losing height rapidly with flames coming from it. I throttled back and the e/a gave a short and very inaccurate burst of tracer roughly in my direction. I throttled right back but even so began passing over it when it blew up with a huge flash."

Five He177s from II/KG40 failed to return from operations this night, including three from 4 Staffel: F8+IM (550146) flown by Oblt Benno Meissner, who was reported missing with his crew, one of whom (Obfw Erwin Scholz) was taken prisoner. There were no survivors from Ltn Jürgen Reichmüller's aircraft (550080), and two members of the crew of 550048 were wounded. 6 Staffel lost Uffz Hermann Klavehn's 550078, together with all the crew, while 550087 was reported shot down by a night fighter with the loss of three of the crew[11].

410 (RCAF) Squadron's Wt Off Wally Price RCAF (HK366) shot down a brace of Hs293-armed Dorniers on the night of **14/15 June**, with Plt Off John Costello RCAF as his radar operator:

"Identified the victim as Do217, using night glasses to do so. Closed in to 400 feet astern and below. Pulled the nose up and fired two short bursts. Target's port engine and wing disintegrated in a flash of orange flame. Mosquito then stalled and went into spin. Pulled out at 2,000 feet and saw a fire burning on the ground directly below us. I claimed this e/a as destroyed. We then continued the patrol and picked up second contact at a range of two miles, height 5,000 feet. Identified as Do217 after closing range to 1,500 feet, again using night glasses. Closed into 400 feet astern and below ... opened fire with a three-five- seconds burst. Strikes were seen on port wing and engine with pieces flying off. Port engine immediately burst into flames and e/a flipped over on its back and went into a spin, burning fiercely. Orbited the burning wreck until it hit the ground and exploded, followed by fire."

Three Dorniers failed to return from operations off Cherbourg – 6N+KR (4748) of KG100's 7 Staffel and 6N+IT (4555) and 6N+HR (4749), both from 9 Staffel. Both the crews commanded by Fw Rudolf Stoll and Obfw Kurt Faust were lost, however from Ltn Dietrich Leydhascher's crew there were two survivors including the pilot, who was wounded. Thus, in just ten nights, the Mosquitos had practically devastated I and II/KG40, shooting down 17 of the four-engined Heinkels. Six Do217Ks of III/KG100 had also been shot down by the Mosquitos during this period. The majority, if not all, of the downed bombers had been carrying either Fritz-X or Hs293 guided bombs. US P-51 pilots claimed two more He177s during daylight patrols over the French coastal region, one of them falling to 1/Lt W.J. McGinty and 2/Lt C.J. Brien Jr of 355thFG, who shared in shooting down F8+IK (550204) of 2/KG40 engaged on a ferry flight on 7 June; Ofhr Hubert Hein and his crew were killed. The next day 1/Lt S.C. Wilkerson of 361stFG claimed another but presumably misidentified his target since there were no He177 losses on this date.

Defence against the V-1 flying bomb fell jointly upon AA Command and the newly established Air Defence of Great Britain (ADGB[12]), which had only recently (November 1943) superseded RAF Fighter Command which had been divided into home defence (ADGB) and 2nd Tactical Air Force (2TAF) for the invasion of Normandy. While the anti-aircraft guns currently formed the first line of defence, ADGB hurriedly reorganised itself to cope with the latest threat from across the Channel. The initial patrols were undertaken by 11 squadrons of fighters, two of them Mosquito-equipped for the period of darkness. Initially, it was not until it was realised that the V-1 could outpace most of the fighters the Allies had available, that the task of shooting them down was bestowed in the main upon the newly introduced Tempest V, with assistance provided by small numbers of Mustang IIIs, also just coming into service, and a few high performance Spitfire XIIs and XIVs. British-based fighters of the USAAF's 8th and 9th Air Forces – P-38s, P-47s and P-51s lacked sufficient low level performance to counter the bombs and were, therefore, not required to contribute to the defence, although, on occasion, eager American pilots did shoot down targets of opportunity. However, following incidents that resulted in the unnecessary death of an RAF pilot and damage to two Tempests and a Spitfire, the Americans were quietly advised to conduct their war against the Germans in France and elsewhere and leave the V-1s to the by-then better-organised British defences. The AOC ADGB, 50-year-old Air Marshal Sir Roderic Hill, was soon to become a favourite of the front-line pilots fighting the new weapon, since he would make flying visits to the various airfields in his personal Tempest V (JN876/RH), undertaking no fewer than 62 anti-V-1 patrols during the course of the campaign while attempting to assess the situation first hand. He was aware of the limitations of some of the units under his command, and later wrote:

> "It was reported that a demonstration by a German pilot with a captured Spitfire had convinced Hitler that our fighters could not catch the flying bomb. This was true of the Spitfire V and almost true of the Spitfire IX, but it was not true of the Spitfire XIV or the Tempest. Even so, these aircraft had no more than a fractional superiority."[13]

The Tempest V was just reaching the squadrons and, in fact, only 3 and 485 (NZ) Squadrons were operational at this time, but soon to be followed by 56 Squadron. These three squadrons would form 150 Wing commanded by Wg Cdr Roland Beamont DSO DFC. Of this period he recalled:

> "I was warned by the AOC that there would be an invasion by V-1s, and told to prepare for it. I started to enquire through intelligence sources about the flying characteristics of these V-1s, but they didn't really know. When we took off to make our first attack on a V-1 I had no definite knowledge of how fast or high it would be travelling, and it wasn't until the second plotting of them on radar that we began to hear information about performance. Then we found out for ourselves when we intercepted them."

Early problems with the Tempest included frequent failures of a seal in the constant-speed propeller hydraulics, which tended to blow under pressure. Plt Off Buck Feldman, an American in the RAF serving with 3 Squadron, wrote:

"I was a personal victim of these faults when I took one of the early Tempests [JN748] up from Bradwell Bay [on 31 May] so that I could test-fire the guns. I was just going out over the Channel when the propeller ran away and went through the stops. I came down towards Romney Marsh and saw it was a choice between landing in a barn or in the canal. I could not see myself landing in a barn, although I remembered having seen it done in the old Hollywood movies, so I chose the canal. The landing bent the wings and knocked me out. When I came to, some British soldiers on manoeuvres nearby were on the scene, and I remember one of them asking me, 'I say, old chap, do you feel like a cup of tea?'"

Another unit operating a mixture of Tempests, Typhoons, Mosquitos and the odd Beaufighter was the Fighter Interception Unit (FIU) based at Wittering. Service pilots and aircrew were attached to the unit, which was involved in testing new equipment in frontline aircraft. Its current programme included the use of the Tempest as a night interceptor and a number of experienced night fighter pilots were seconded to the unit to test the feasibility of using the new, fast fighter in this rôle. Trials proved successful and a small band of pilots were undergoing conversion from twin-engine night fighters to the single-engine Tempest. The unit was under the command of Wg Cdr Chris Hartley and included a bevy of experienced pilots such as Sqn Ldr Tubby Daniel DFC, Flt Lt Alan Wagner DFC and Flt Lt Joe Berry DFC. The advent of the V-1 attacks would prove an ideal opportunity to test their flying skills. The operational detachment would move to Newchurch to be nearer the frontline. Based at Ford NAS was the Royal Navy's equivalent to the FIU, the RN NFIU commanded by Major Skeet Harris DSC of the Royal Marines. Among the aircraft undergoing trials by the Navy was another new type, the Firefly NF1, adapted from the two-seater fleet fighter-reconnaissance version and equipped with the new American ASH radar.

The RAF was also pinning its hopes on Britain's own new secret weapon – the twin-jet Gloster Meteor F.1 fighter[14]. One day in April, Sqn Ldr Les Watts DFC of 616 Squadron, based at West Malling with Spitfires, was called to London, there to learn that his squadron was to move to RAF Culmhead where it was to be the first to equip with the new Meteor jet. Having been advised only to let his flight commanders aware of the conversion, the unit's pilots were kept in the dark until the last moment. Canadian Flg Off Bill McKenzie recalled:

"One day this gorgeous, clapped out Oxford arrived at flight dispersal and the Old Man [Sqn Ldr Watts] announced that this was to be our training aircraft – we were all going to become twin-engine pilots! Then we had a bit of a problem – none of us had ever flown twins, except me. Fortunately, we had a supernumerary flight lieutenant who had ten hours on Oxfords, and he was appointed instructor for the squadron. The next day the CO and myself went out with our instructor – I was in the right-hand seat while the Old Man stood behind me watching (ready to get out fast if he had to!) So he showed me how to taxi, then took off, did a circuit, landed and asked me to taxi back, which I eventually did. I sat at the end of the runway, with sweat running out of the toes of my boots – I figured I had about three minutes to live (I'd a premonition that I was going to die in an Oxford and had nightmares about this. I wasn't afraid of being shot down because I knew I was going to die in an Oxford!) I opened the throttle, got off the ground, did a vicious left turn – almost taking the control tower with me – landed, got out and let the Old Man take over. I felt much better after that. A couple of days later the CO and I flew down to Farnborough where we were to see our new aircraft. We arrived safely and stayed overnight. In the morning we were on our way over to what was known as 'H' hangar, where we discovered what a weird place this experimental station was. One needed nerves of steel! We were walking across the tarmac when, without warning, there was an explosion and 'bang' overhead. An aircraft had just been launched with the help of a rocket!

"We entered the hangar, going through three checkpoints with service police checking our ID cards and demanding signatures. I had my first look at the 'thing' sitting there, looking like a dragon with two big empty eyes. Wg Cdr Willie Wilson was running the show. He had the Meteor pushed out onto the tarmac and handed me two printed sheets, which I looked at:

starting procedure, taxiing procedure, take-off procedure and landing procedure. I jumped in and the Old Man got up the ladder, whilst I sat reading the instructions – finally I pressed Button B, then Button A, and all of a sudden the whining started. One engine was running and I started the other. It was just unreal, too much to accept, and I couldn't believe what was going on. Willie reached down, picked up my helmet and handed it to me. 'OK', he says. 'You're on your own. Go take a trip.' I had to get the instructions again and started with the taxiing procedure. I read it, tried it, and it was very pleasant – the first tricycle gear I had ever operated. You could see out front. There was no 14-feet of Merlin blocking your view. This was super, you could drive right down the runway taxi-strip with lots of visibility and it was very quiet because you were in front of the engines. I got to the end of the runway and had a last look at take-off procedure – full throttle, release brakes – and that was it. I was launched! It was just unreal. I guess I was about 50 miles before I turned around. I was in shock. But it was gorgeous, one of the finest trips I ever made, so simple. I sure enjoyed it. I did about 15 minutes running around, and then, sadly, had to come back and land. Out with the instructions again. I landed and it was the simplest and most pleasant aircraft I'd ever flown. I taxied back and the Old Man went up. We stayed at Farnborough flying Meteors for about a week."

Two of the Wellard-powered Meteors – EE213/G and EE214/G (the G denoted that the aircraft required an armed guard at all times) – were brought up to operational standard and were flown to Culmhead by Sqn Ldr Watts and Flg Off McKenzie (on 20 July) but, before leaving Farnborough, armament tests were carried out by a test pilot on another Meteor. This test resulted in it being written off when ejected shell cases showered the aircraft. McKenzie wrote:

"There wasn't one spent shell case that didn't hit the aircraft, be it wings, fuselage or tailplane. He was lucky to get down alive. When word of this got to London, there was action. I've never seen so much action in my life. Eventually they did get the system modified by putting chutes out of the bottom, which was certainly the obvious place. Fuel consumption on the deck was atrocious, but at high altitude the aircraft came into its own, the speed increased and fuel consumption decreased. But they weren't all that fast. We put 24 pilots through and they never scratched an aircraft. When everybody was through we were transferred to Manston."

One of the first to convert to the Meteor was Flt Lt Dennis Barry:

"We were briefed for our first flights. We clustered around the Meteor, peering into the cockpit while the wing commander [Wilson] went through the cockpit drill, explaining the instruments and the aircraft's flying characteristics. Next we were told we could take off on our first familiarisation flights. This conversion briefing seemed rather sparse, especially as there were very few Meteors available and any written off would have been disastrous – and fatal to the pilot as we did not have any ejection seats. There were no Pilot's Notes available, but we felt confident, if a little over-awed at the prospect of being chosen to fly such a novel aircraft and the honour accorded to 616. As I taxied out to the end of the Farnborough runway in Meteor Mk I EE214/G [later coded YQ-B], I ran through the drill as briefed by the wing commander and then I positioned the aircraft ready for take-off. Throttles forward, maximum power while holding on the brakes, then brakes released and slowly accelerate down the runway. No swing, no drag, and hold the stick level until 80mph indicated, then ease stick back and lift off the runway at 120mph. Wheels up and climb away, retracting the flaps. The rate of climb is originally poor, 500 feet a minute, but as the power builds up the rate increases. Local flying now, the aircraft is quiet with no noise from the engines, only a 'whooshing' sound from the air passing the cockpit, like a glider. The visibility is good with only a shallow nose in front and is similar to being in an airship's observation car. Landing successfully completed, I return to my colleagues satisfied with the aircraft except for the lack of power."

AA defences
The first static AA defences were to be found eight miles off the coast at Herne Bay and Whitstable – seven Maunsell Forts[15] built in 1942, designed to defend the Thames Estuary against attacks by German warships. Four were manned by Royal Navy

personnel, the other three by the Army. The forts were basically anti-aircraft platforms, made up of a central control tower surrounded by six other towers, reached by walkways. The layout reflected a land-based HAA battery. The forts proved effective during the war, accounting for around 22 enemy aircraft, 30 V-1s and an E-boat, and were particularly valuable for extending low height radar coverage over the surface of the estuary, unachievable by shore-based sets at that time, and crucial for plotting enemy mine-laying activities.

Whilst fighter aircraft formed the first line of defence, the next line of defence were almost 200 heavy and a similar number of light AA guns in a belt across central Kent, running from the north bank of the estuary, through Tunbridge Wells, to Leatherhead in the west. On the eastern outskirts of London some 480 balloons provided the final element before the capital city was reached. It soon became apparent that these deployments were inadequate and the guns would be increased to 376 heavy and 540 light weapons, whilst the balloon barrage was subsequently strengthened to some 1,000 balloons. The arrival in England of American AA gun batteries, intended initially for use on the Continent following the invasion, were most welcome and would achieve impressive results in the ensuing weeks. Equipped with SCR584 radar and proximity-fused shells, they would reduce the kill/shell ratio to one bomb destroyed for every 40 shells fired.

First encounters

Although not fully aware of what he had encountered, Flg Off Bob Barckley of 3 Squadron flying Tempest JN755 had already opened the score for the RAF. While flying a night intruder sortie (2305-0100) in the Le Havre area on **8/9 May**, he intercepted and shot down a V-1, obviously part of the test firing preliminaries being conducted by *Flakregiment 155 (W)*:

> "I was on a night intruder operation south of Paris, in the neighbourhood of Evreux. I suddenly saw a bright light in the sky. I thought some idiot had left his navigation light on. So I positioned myself behind it and eventually attacked it west of Le Havre. Now, you never attack anything at night with throttle fully open because it's impossible to judge distance. You gradually open up with more and more speed until you can see outlines of things. I did that, but didn't seem to be making any progress. When I got beyond Le Havre I fired a long burst and it immediately went down. It crashed into the sea in the area of Deauville. At the time I was not aware that it was a V-1, and my logbook refers to it as a 'jet-ship', which showed a degree of prescience on my part."

Apparently, the following night (**9/10 May**) a second Diver was shot down by a Beaufighter crew from 68 Squadron, Flt Lt Len Harvey DSO and Flt Lt Basil St John Wynell-Sutherland (known as Winnie) in WM-C recording the kill[16].

These proved to be the first two of more than 2,000 flying bombs that would fall to the guns of RAF, Commonwealth and Allied fighters in the ensuing months. The scene was thus set for Germany's last throw of the dice. Hitler and his chiefs of staff were confident the forthcoming assault would have such a demoralizing effect on the British people that the government would topple and a call for negotiations to end the war, in favour of the Germans, would surely ensue. That test firings were being undertaken from some of the launch sites appears to have been confirmed by a report in the *Daily Express* of 12 May that stated:

> *"Early yesterday and late last night mysterious orange and red lights appeared in the Straits sky which danced about and dived at tangents before falling suddenly."*

Two weeks later a mystery 'machine' impacted at Sarisbury Green near Fareham in Hampshire, between Portsmouth and Southampton. Witnesses reported hearing:

"... the sound of a strange whining noise in the sky which seemed to be approaching from the direction of the Solent. A few minutes later, a small trail of light was visible and what looked like the outline of a small aircraft became distinguishable against the night sky... an eerie silence fell over the Green. It was followed by a terrific crash ..."

Civil Defence warden Mr B.W. Rands, who lived at Fareham was convinced that it was a flying bomb:

"Official records state that the first V-1 to explode on British soil was at Swanscombe near Gravesend on 13 June 1944, but I suspect the official record is incomplete for an understandable reason. I was on duty in the control room at Fareham on Whit Monday [29 May 1944]. The hour before midnight was still warm after a hot day and there being no 'Red' alert we enjoyed the fresh air outside the doorway. The sound of a plane with an engine making an unusual noise was heard and then something came into view that appeared to have its tail on fire. Moments after it passed over there was an explosion. Wardens Post messages came in of a crashing plane, the crucial one coming from the post at Park Gate, Sarisbury Green, that a plane had crashed on tanks parked at the roadside and there were casualties. Services were despatched and the incident reported to Regional Headquarters. However, almost at once the military took over and supplanted the Civil Defence. And in the early hours of the next morning Region instructed me to delete from copies of all control room messages every reference to 'plane' and substitute 'bomb'. I argued on the evidence of my own eyes but was told that this was an order from Whitehall and was to be obeyed. Later I was convinced I was right and it dawned on me that the secrecy was to deny the Nazis knowledge as to the range and direction of the Doodlebug."

CHAPTER II

OPERATION *KIRSCHKERN* (CHERRY STONE) BEGINS

"The mountain hath groaned and brought forth a mouse."
Comment by Lord Cherwell (Chief Scientific Advisor to the Prime Minister) to
Dr R.V. Jones following the initial salvo of four flying bombs[18].

In the early hours of Monday **12 June**, Oberst Wachtel of *Flakregiment 155 (W)* addressed his commanders in the operation bunker:

"After months of waiting, the hour has come for us to open fire! Today your wait and your work will have their reward. The order to open fire has been issued. Now that our enemy is trying to secure at all costs his foothold on the Continent, we approach our task supremely confident in our weapons; as we launch them, today and in the future, let us always bear in mind the destruction and the suffering wrought by the enemy's terror bombing. Soldiers! *Führer* and Fatherland look to us, they expect our crusade to be an overwhelming success. As our attack begins, our thoughts linger fondly and faithfully upon our native German soil. Long live our Germany! Long live our Fatherland! Long live our *Führer!*"[19]

Many of the launch sites were not ready for the firing of the opening batch of flying bombs planned for the night of **12/13 June**, including the one of which Uffz Otto Neuchel was a member of the crew – in fact, only ten of the 55 firing ramps were ready. The catapult's piston release mechanism had failed on Neuchel's ramp, so he and his colleagues could only watch adjacent sites commence the attack:

"It was not a very graceful sight – like watching an ungainly bird being propelled into flight by a sudden gust of wind. I thought the bombs clumsy and awkward, but was fascinated by the sight just the same."

Between 0330 and 0400 ten flying bombs were launched:

"Six of the ten shots went as planned, but four failed. The flying bombs fell to earth just after firing, sending us diving for cover. One of the crashed bombs failed to explode. The other three burst on impact with an awesome concussion – I didn't remember a bang at all, just a terrible force that rushed right over me and hurt my eardrums."

Local French witnesses to the launching of the flying bombs recalled:

"Suddenly there is a terrific explosion like a hundred bombs going off. Windows in the houses and cottages for miles around rattle; others near by are blown into a thousand fragments by the concussion. The sky and surrounding countryside are lit up with a blinding flash of fiery red light, and an object like a meteor races across the heavens with the roar of an express train." Another said: "When the robot shoots across the sky like a ball of fire, cattle bellow with fear and everyone falls flat to the ground in case it does not work properly."[20]

Of the six bombs winging their way towards London, two disappeared into the depths of the Channel before reaching the English coast. The demise of one of the latter had been witnessed by the crew of Royal Navy motor launch *HDML1383*, which was operating out of Dover, as crewman Louis Gray recalled:

"While heading back to England, we heard an aircraft engine overhead. The craft must have been in trouble, because it carried a long tail of fire and fell into the sea. We headed for the spot but found no survivors. It became clear later we must have seen one of the first of the German V-1s."

A Canadian Mosquito crew returning to base following a night patrol over the beaches saw what they reported as "… a rocket projectile heading northwards and leaving a red trail." People in parts of Kent, Sussex and East London soon heard a strange sound in the sky. The sound was later described as something like a motorbike without a silencer or a badly maintained steam train going up hill. Some also saw what they thought was a burning enemy aircraft crossing the sky with a sword of flame emanating from its tail. The flying bomb had arrived. The first (*sic*) impacted in a potato field at Swanscombe near Gravesend at 0418, without causing any damage. Local man Mr George Darling recalled:

> "There were three air raids in quick succession, with some gunfire in the first two at least. In the second I heard a bomb drop but was puzzled that I could no longer hear the sound of the plane. It turned out to be Hitler's first [*sic*] V-1. It came down in a potato field a few miles from where I was living."[21]

At nearby Gravesend airfield Wg Cdr Peter Wykeham-Barnes DSO DFC, OC 140 Mosquito Wing based at Gravesend, stood talking to his Chief Operations Officer when the flying bomb appeared:

> "It was a quarter past four and the clouded sky was turning from black to grey. We were very weary. All night our aircraft had ranged over Normandy, among the silent villages and above the roads littered with wreckage. As we walked towards our tents we heard an odd noise in the eastern sky, like a motorcycle running under water. Almost before we had picked out the crude cruciform shape and the bright light at its tail we knew what it was, for we had hunted its lairs for months past. We watched it as it flew straight over our heads and bustled on towards London. It had hardly passed when there was a sudden silence, then a pause followed by a reverberating explosion. We stood and looked at the billowing cloud of smoke that showed faintly in the sky towards the river."

At West Malling a Mosquito of 96 Squadron flown by Flt Lt Frank 'Togs' Mellersh DFC was approaching to land when a flying bomb crossed the airfield at 1,500 feet "… going quite slowly and flashing a yellow light from its tail. Another crossed over the drome at about the same height and crashed approximately five miles due south …", wrote the Squadrons' diarist. At Newchurch, current home of 56 Squadron equipped with Spitfires, the unit's diarist commented: "We were all rudely awakened at dawn by a strange noise and to our startled eyes there suddenly appeared the first jet-propelled pilotless aircraft …"

Another flying bomb arrived two minutes later and crashed on Mizbrooks Farm at Cuckfield in Sussex. There were no injuries and very little damage, although the blast blew open the door of a nearby pigsty, allowing the inmates a few hours of freedom. A third V-1 crashed in the back garden of a house in Platt near Borough Green in Kent, demolishing two rows of greenhouses but inflicting no injuries, while a fourth – and the first to reach the capital – dived to the ground and exploded in Grove Road, Bethnal Green at 0425. It hit the railway bridge that carried the Great Eastern Railway across Grove Road, from Liverpool Street Station to Essex and East Anglia. The bridge was badly damaged, as was the railway track. A number of houses were also badly damaged. Six people were killed[22] and a further 30 injured, nine seriously – the first of almost 6,200 fatalities that would be caused in England by the terror weapon over the coming months. There were no more missiles that night.

To make matters worse for the Luftwaffe, a reconnaissance Me410 – 9K+HP (420027) from 6/KG51 flown by Fw Siegfried Schönberger – that had been despatched to report on the success or otherwise of this initial salvo, was shot down by AA fire over London. The Messerschmitt crashed near Choats Manor Way, Barking Marshes and both Schönberger and his observer Uffz Kurt Quatfasel were killed. However, it would seem that a second Me410 did return, its pilot Ltn Fritz Worschek allegedly reporting that he had flown over London during the night and had seen the city ablaze. While Feldmarshall Keitel's rhetoric promised that the "bombardment will open like a thunderclap", the opening salvo was more akin to a 'damp squib'. Although it was an inauspicious debut for Hitler's secret weapon, the age of missile warfare had nevertheless arrived. Based at Lympne airfield on the Kent coast with the Spitfires of 74 Squadron was Flt Lt Don Llewellyn:

> "Some of the boys had been having a night out in Folkestone the night that the first Doodlebugs were launched. We had no idea what they were. I remember hitching a ride back to Lympne on the back of a motorcycle, driving along the coast road with red tracer from Bofors guns streaming out to sea. The tale-tell red glow of the rocket exhaust was not evident that night, perhaps they were in cloud."

3 Squadron's Flt Sgt Ron Pottinger recalled:

> "D-Day had come and gone. We had done our stint of patrols over the beachheads, without incident as far as I was concerned. In addition to the patrols and sweeps we were maintaining a state of readiness from dawn to dusk. Two in the cockpits, engines warmed, two kitted up in dispersal, another pair on five minutes readiness. On 13 June I was among those on the first shift. A truck picked us up from our tents, probably at about 3am and ran us down to dispersal. As we were alighting from the back of the truck there was a strange continuous burping sound and a small dark object flew across, quite low and fast, one tubular shadow on top of another and a long fiery tail behind the upper one. I'm afraid that on that first sighting we all stood and gaped. Then someone shouted, 'Flying Bomb! What are we standing waiting for? Get up and after them!' That ended any chance of 3 Squadron joining the Normandy invasion."

The V-1 was not the only 'flying bomb' threat the Allies had to worry about at this time. Following the Normandy landings, the first of the only five available *Mistels* of II/KG101 was rushed from Nordhausen in Germany to St Dizier airfield in France, for operations against the invasion force. The first to arrive, a *Mistel* complete with a piloted Ju88 (CN+F1) and Bf109 (DM+UC) flown by Fw Bäzner, landed at St Dizier during the morning of **14 June**. At least one more arrived during the day, 5T+CK piloted by Oblt Albert Rheker with Obfw Heinz Lochmüller at the controls of the Messerschmitt (CD+LX). During the late evening, Rheker and Lochmüller were airborne on a training and familiarisation flight when they had the misfortune to be picked up on the radar of marauding Mosquito XIII HK476/RA-O of 410 (RCAF) Squadron, crewed by Flt Lt Wally Dinsdale RCAF and Plt Off J.E. Dunn RCAF, who had been vectored to the area of the Seine. At 2335 a visual was achieved:

> "Several contacts were obtained simultaneously. Pilot obtained a visual immediately at a range of 2,000 feet, height 11,000 feet. Closed to 1,000 feet and identified, with the aid of night glasses, as a Ju88 with a glider-bomb [*sic*] attached to top of the fuselage. Closed in to 750 feet astern and below. Opened fire with a short burst. The cockpit and wing root burst into flames immediately. Enemy aircraft banked slowly to port, then went down in a steep dive burning fiercely leaving a trail of sparks all the way down. It hit the ground with a terrific explosion, lighting up the countryside. Enemy aircraft burnt on the ground. Combat took place at approximately 25 miles south-east of Caen at 2340. The enemy aircraft did no evasive action during the combat."

The *Mistel* crashed about 30 miles south-east of Caen with the loss of Rheker, but the Messerschmitt pilot, Lochmüller, apparently managed to bale out and survived with injuries. The successful Canadian pilot later told newspaper reporters:

> "It was a very awkward thing and lumbered along like an old hippo at about 150mph. I recognised it as a Ju88 but couldn't figure out what the thing on top was. I thought it was one of their glider-bombs mounted in a new way. It was on top, mounted between the rudder and the main wing. My first short burst hit the starboard wing and cockpit of the Junkers. I thought I had killed the pilot but, of course, there was no pilot as the whole thing is controlled from the

fighter on top. Carrying on for a few minutes, circling to port with the fire increasing, he then dropped away and crashed behind the German lines. The explosion lit up the countryside for miles around."

A few minutes later a second *Mistel* Ju88 was almost certainly shot down by Flt Lt John Corre[23] and Flg Off Charles Bines in Mosquito HK502 of 264 Squadron, operating in the same area. Records suggest that four armed *Mistels* led by Oblt Horst Rudat, a former KG55 pilot, attempted to carry out an attack on allied vessels anchored in the bay of the Seine. Rudat later recalled[24]:

"I was able to maintain control of my combination, but my speed was reduced so I ordered the other three aircraft to continue without me. By then darkness had fallen, and as I moved west of Le Havre I saw a British night fighter approaching me. As I had nothing with which to fight back (the armament had been removed from the Messerschmitt to save weight), I aimed the combination in the direction of a collection of landing craft and ships near the shore and released the Ju88. The automatic pilot did not hold the aircraft on one engine, however, and it dived into the sea."

One *Mistel* pilot reported sighting a Mosquito, whereupon he released his Ju88 missile, this probably being Corre's victim:

"At 0008 hours, I was vectored on to a bogey flying at 8,000 feet on a vector of 140 degrees. At 0010 hours, my navigator gave me contact dead ahead two-and-a-half miles. We were then doing 280 IAS. The target was not showing IFF and was doing corkscrew evasive action. We closed quite rapidly and, at 0012, I obtained a visual on a twin-engined mid-wing aircraft – seeing the exhausts – at 1,500 feet. I closed to 200 yards and identified it as a Ju188 [*sic*]. It appeared to have another single-engine aircraft flying immediately above it but upon closer scrutinising, it appeared to be a glider-bomb straddled on the Ju188's back. I dropped back to 200 yards. I gave him a half-second burst and he blew up and disintegrated. The main body of tbe Ju188 went almost vertically into the sea and we saw a large greyish cloud of smoke where it had crashed. I fixed my position 25 miles west of Le Havre."

Another Mosquito crew reported:

"We were on patrol 25 miles west of Le Havre at an altitude of 5,000 to 6,000 feet. Visibility was excellent and a large convoy was observed about four miles to the west. We had a good view, lasting 15 to 20 seconds, of an unusual 'biplane' about a mile away. This had the appearance of a small aircraft attached to the top of a larger twin-engined type. It was possible to see between the two aircraft and they appeared to be connected at the trailing edges of the mainplane. Although we were on a parallel course and must have been seen, no avoiding action was taken by the composite, which proceeded on a dead straight course in the direction of the convoy. Its speed was estimated to be between 200 and 250mph."

Of the initial assault, Prime Minister Churchill wrote in his memoirs:

"*The long-studied assault on England by unmanned missiles now began. The target was Greater London. For more than a year we had argued among ourselves about the character and scale of the attack, and every preparation, which our wits could devise and our resources permit, had been made in good time. In the early hours of June 13, exactly a week after D-Day, four pilotless aircraft crossed our coast. They were the premature result of a German order, sent urgently on D-Day in reaction to our successes in Normandy. One reached Bethnal Green, where it killed six people and injured nine; the others caused no casualties. Nothing further happened until late on June 15, when the Germans started their campaign of 'Vergeltung' (Retaliation) in earnest. More than two hundred of the missiles came against us within twenty-four hours, and over three thousand were to follow in the next five weeks. The flying bomb, as we came to call it, was named V-1 by Hitler, since he hoped – with some reason – that it was only the first of a series of terror weapons which German research would provide.*"

CHAPTER III

THE MOUSE BEGINS TO ROAR[25]

June 1944

"The English showed a courageousness during the buzz bomb season that was unequalled by anyone else so far as my personal knowledge went. They'd go to work in the morning, not knowing if they'd have an office to work in, and in the evening, when they started home, they'd never know whether they had a wife or a home to come back to."

Capt Jack M. Ilfrey USAAF, 20thFG ace

Night 15/16 JUNE

Shortly before midnight a Diver fell at the junction of Gibbon Road and Senate Street (Peckham SE15), killing four. Seven more were killed when another impacted in Raymouth Road, Bermondsey (SE16) at 0017. An ARP report from Ashford noted that a flying bomb had exploded in the air at 0105. Four came down in the Dartford/Medway area in the early hours of the morning, two people being seriously injured by shrapnel in Chatham at 0200, and one being killed and six slightly injured when another impacted in Shepherds Lane/Princes Road, Dartford, at 0353, where eight houses were demolished. Three more fell in the Dartford area at 0340, injuring two people at Stones Wood and another at Eynsford. Two fell in Deptford (SE8), the first in Albyn Road (two killed), and the second, at 0753, impacting in Reginald Square, causing much damage in killing 22 residents. Beckenham received its third bomb of the morning (the first having killed a resident in Eden Way) at 0900, which hit an ARP post in Tootswood Road, killing three wardens. A hour later, as rescue crews were returning from this incident, another Diver impacted opposite Links Road, West Wickham, killing seven rescuers aboard their vehicle.

A fighter brought down one that fell at Lamberhurst at 0750. Croydon received its first Diver – the first of 141 to fall in the borough – one that impacted in Warminster Road, South Norwood. Others fell shortly thereafter in Upper Shirley Road, Selsdon Park Road and Croham Road. Mr Kenneth King, history master at Selhurst Grammar School, wrote in his diary:

"We have passed through the most alarming and hectic night of the war. I went to bed at the usual time and, being very tired, slept so heavily that I was not aware of the P-plane raid that began just before midnight. But about 2.30am I was awakened by the collapse of part of the ceiling of my bedroom – fortunately most of the debris was clear of my bed. The whole atmosphere was filled with what seemed an acrid mist; it proved to be billowing clouds of dust from the wreckage made by the exploding P-plane. In the darkness it was impossible to check the extent of the damage, and, as it seemed quiet again, I went back to bed. But not for many minutes – there was another explosion and again the noise of falling glass and rubble[26]."

Morning revealed that the first Diver had fallen between Northbrook and Pawsons Roads, where a dozen people had been killed. The second had come down in Selhurst New Road, where the casualties were even worse. Another fell in the village of Longford, west of London. Eight of the missiles that penetrated the coastal defences impacted in the Bexley/Sidcup/Crayford areas of South London, causing three deaths in Bexley; nine deaths in Crayford and another in Sidcup, with over 100 more residents suffering injuries, 39 of a serious nature. Bromley and Beckenham received seven bombs, inflicting four fatalities and 60 injuries. A house was damaged in Croydon, as recalled by its owner (Mr John Franklin) to a reporter from the *News Chronicle*:

"When I first caught sight of the plane it appeared to be flying at about 300-400 miles per hour and at a height of 2,000 feet. In size it was rather less than half that of a Spitfire, but it had no propeller or tailplane. It was losing height gradually. Flashes about half the length of the fuselage were coming out behind it; they were reddish-yellow in colour and spat backwards at intervals of about five seconds. Soon after the plane passed over my head its engine cut out and the flashes stopped at the same time. It did a half-turn, then went into a steep dive. It crashed through the top of a roof opposite my own house and then a few seconds later blew up in the road. It seemed to be all surface blast."

A witness to this first serious assault against the capital, Brigadier Norman Elliott Rodger, Chief of Staff 2 Canadian Corps, entered in his diary:

"At midnight the alert blew and I saw red tracer fountaining up in the distance toward Folkestone. Soon it started upward in Dover direction including their rocket battery at a light moving toward us and on which the searchlights were concentrated. As the object approached I realised it was the long-awaited glider-bomb [sic] powered by some sort of a rocket motor. One passed overhead and the tail of flame almost as long as the bomb itself made a wonderful aiming mark and gave out a peculiar noise like a slow running motor. Every gun in the area (and there are many of them) opened up and it was quite a sight – red Bofors tracer and 3.7-inch shell bursts being the main part but I suspect some Brens were also having their fun. Fin [Colonel Findlay Clark, Chief Signals Officer] was sorely tempted to try his revolver at it! Several more bombs passed over or near us during the night and the particles of flak could be heard coming down through the bushes. The bombs continued more infrequently on into the day when Spitfires took up the game and joined in chasing them. Some were shot down by flak and some by aircraft. One pilot didn't swerve quickly enough after squirting at it and was killed in the explosion. The centre of the path of these seemed to be over Folkestone rather than here – and many were finding their way into London – though they were distributed all the way from Colchester to Maidenhead and Surrey and Sussex."

One missile fell on the famous 'Bells of Ouseley' public house, on the banks of the Thames at Old Windsor, where a fire was started. There were two fatalities, four seriously injured and eight less so. Even as far away as rural East Suffolk, the residents of the village of Peasenhall were awakened at 0028 by an explosion in the air over Lodge Farm, which caused blast damage to a number of houses.

The crew of a Naval Swordfish engaged on an anti-shipping patrol off Boulogne – Sub Lt(A) Ron Wadham (pilot) and Sub Lt(A) Tuberville with L/Airman Hunter in NF119/X of 819 Squadron operating from Manston – also witnessed one of the first flying bombs:

"We were in our usual aircraft, and just about to investigate a radar contact off Boulogne, when we saw three orange lights in the sky. We took them to be enemy night fighters, because the German equivalent of our AI radar showed a bright orange light when it was switched on. We took immediate evasive action, and on eventually returning to our contact we found it had reached the safety of Boulogne harbour before our poor old Swordfish managed to get there. We subsequently discovered that what we had seen were actually the exhausts from three Doodlebugs."

Plt Off Buck Feldman of 3 Squadron at Newchurch recalled:

"In the Newchurch Wing we heard the first V-1s come across. The gunners opened up over 180° and the shrapnel was falling all over the airfield and going through our tents. One P-47 Thunderbolt fired at a V-1 over the airfield and the bullet drilled a hole through the hand of one of our airmen lying asleep in his bed."

Another witness was 1/Lt Jack Robinson USAAF of the P-47-equipped 416thFBG based at Great Chart ALG near Ashford:

"Ashford was in a direct line between the launching sites in France and London, in the midst of the ack-ack gun belt set up to defend the city. On the night of 15 June, Ashford saw its first V-1, and the guns opened up like a chapter from 'Buck Rogers' lacing the sky with tracer

bullets. To add to the confusion, a telephone call from HQ had warned of parachute landings on the coast taking place at the same time so our unrehearsed Group Defence Plan went into operation. All personnel were floundering around in the dark, in all sorts of night dress and webbing equipment, but with the essential steel helmets, as shrapnel from ack-ack guns was falling all round. Some dug fox holes and slept in them, and all kept their ears cocked for the ominous sound of motor cut-outs."

American fighter pilot 1/Lt Richard E. Turner USAAF 356thFS/354thFG based at Lashenden ALG near Maidstone, later wrote:

"At 1145pm, most of the group was rudely awakened to the terror of Germany's first secret weapon: the V-1, or flying bomb. We were sleeping peacefully in our bivouac areas when we were literally bounced from our sacks by the muzzle blasts and thunderous reverberations of nearby 90mm gun emplacements. We had seen these emplacements around the area, but had never heard them fire before. It was a bizarre half hour before we found the reason for the excitement. The gunners were shooting at V-1s buzzing overhead toward London. The V-1s had pre-set gyroscopic guidance systems, which kept them on an unwavering course to London, and the fuel was calculated to run out in a pre-set area. The pulsating putter of the V-1's ram jet [sic] engine sounded like a very loud motorcycle going wide out. As long as you could hear them you were safe, but when the engine sound cut off abruptly, they were going into their final destructive dive. Their blast effect was tremendous. These missiles kept us on edge every night until we left for our beachhead."

Based with the 412thFS near Dover was Sgt John R. Kinn USAAF, who recalled:

"I remember the first night the buzz bombs came over in earnest, the AA guns kept shooting but never scored a kill. In fact, they kept firing so long the guns were almost horizontal to the ground and I heard they killed two MPs in their tent. So then they put stops on the guns so they could only be lowered so far. [Later] we used to watch the RAF Typhoons [Tempests?] and Spitfires chasing them and shooting them down. It was like a race to see which could get them first."

A P-47 pilot of the 411thFS, Lt Bill Mather USAAF, remembered the initial onslaught with humour:

"I was with a bunch walking back from Ashford, when old Adolf unleashed a swarm of his nosiest aircraft, which began passing directly overhead, each with a strange glowing light marking its passage. Here they came, buzzing and clattering in from the west and suddenly the peaceful Kentish countryside came alive with a storm of AA weapons, all firing at once. As pilots, we had learned deflection shooting, so we were discussing, with academic vigour, the common tendency of all ground troops to shoot behind the target instead of ahead of it, being altogether too noisy, making loud and derisive comments about the waste of ammunition. We were overheard! Out of the bushes beside the road, came a bullish roar: 'You bloody *****, ***** Yanks, get your ***** arses out of our field of fire!!' and not 50 feet from where we were standing, an entire battery of largish pieces began whanging away over our heads; we lost no time in following orders."[27]

Many who witnessed the initial assault did not necessarily take matters seriously, including 2/Lt John W. McClane USAAF, a B-24 navigator with the 68thBS/44thBG stationed at Shipdham:

"When we first heard that these pilotless flying bombs were being launched, we thought it was an act of desperation on their part, that they had no more pilots or planes to strike back with. In other words, it was very funny to us but later we changed our tune when we went to London on rest leave only to be brought back to reality by five of them exploding close by."

The British could normally be relied upon to produce an essence of humour out of tragedy, as Miss Joyce Brewer of Hastings recalled:

"The first we knew of them was on June 14th when the first one came over Kent and all of the

AA gun sites were given the code name for them, Diver-Diver. The following night my two future brothers-in-law, Jim and Jack, were having supper with us when the sirens sounded and then we heard this awful chugging sound in the skies above. We ran to the front door, the weather was overcast with drizzly rain. The first Doodlebug flew in low over the houses in Mount Pleasant, not that we could see its shape in the dark, just a jet of flame and this horrible unforgettable racket. Jim rushed to the Bofors gun and Jack dived into the bucket seat of the twin Browning machine-guns situated just across the road from our house. He opened up fire immediately and hit an electric pylon in Fir Tree Road and scared the daylights out of a passer-by; the robot machine sailed on unscathed."[28]

To Flt Lt John Musgrave of 605 Squadron fell the distinction of shooting down the first flying bomb of the campaign, when he destroyed his target some 21 miles off Dunkirk. This success was closely followed by another scored by Flt Lt Sailor Parker of 219 Squadron some ten miles north of Gravelines. Two others were shot down by 605 Squadron pilots before dawn.

96 Squadron (Mosquito XIII) West Malling

The CO Wg Cdr Edward Crew DFC took off in HK461 at 0515 in an effort to intercept the flying bombs. The unit's diarist noted:

"The robot bombers started to come in strength tonight and continued in a steady stream into the morning. The ack-ack was terrific and fighters couldn't get anywhere near them, though the CO went up specially to find one and was hit by ack-ack himself."

219 Squadron (Mosquito XVII) Bradwell Bay

Flt Lt G.R.I. Parker	HK248/FK-	V-1	0045	off Gravelines

Flt Lt Sailor Parker[29] reported:

"Patrolling east to west at 3,500 feet south of Dungeness and observed a bright white light at 0040 ... and was able to cut it off and close range to 1,000 yards ... unable to close range further, so gave target a very short burst and no strikes observed, but target blew up about four-five seconds later at 0045. No force of explosion felt. Position ten miles north of Gravelines. No falling debris seen after explosion and everything went black. Informed by control more trade was coming from the south. Almost immediately had visuals on at least six Divers, range about six miles, crossing port to starboard and below. Tried to cut off leading Diver but misjudged range and so intercepted No.2 and No.3, range again about 1,000 yards. Fired several bursts but observed no indications of damage to target. Had to turn away because I was near our coast and AA defences were already engaging leading Divers."

418 (RCAF) Squadron (Mosquito FBVI) Holmsley South

Sqn Ldr Russ Bannock RCAF recalled:

"On the night of 16 June, we were departing on a night intruder sortie and while over Beachy Head at about 2,000 feet we spotted what we thought was a burning aircraft flying at high speed below us and going inland. We called sector ops to alert them of the aircraft in distress but they replied that we were witnessing Hitler's new secret weapon, the V-1 flying bomb. When we returned from our intruder sortie there was great excitement in the ops room as several V-1s had been despatched towards London and 418 were assigned to patrol a sector of the English Channel from dusk until dawn starting the following night."

605 Squadron (Mosquito VI) Manston

Flt Lt J.G. Musgrave	UP-H	V-1	c0040	off Dunkirk
Flg Off P.R. Rudd	UP-	V-1		off Dover
Flg Off J. Reid	UP-	V-1		off Dover

Of his historic first Diver kill of the assault, Flt Lt John Musgrave reported:

"It was like chasing a ball of fire across the sky. It flashed by our starboard side a few thousand feet away at the same height we were flying. I quickly turned to port and gave chase. It was going pretty fast, but I caught up with it and opened fire from astern. At first there was no effect so I closed in another 100 yards and gave it another burst. Then I went closer still and pressed the button again. This time there was a terrific flash and explosion and the thing fell down in a vertical dive into the sea. The whole show was over in about three minutes."

Flt Sgt John Little, navigator to Flt Lt John Rhodes recalled:

"The crisis caused by the advent of the flying bomb hit the Squadron and we had to take on the added task of intercepting these weapons over the Channel with the objective of destroying them. This was not easy with Mosquitos as their top speed was no match for that of the bombs. Tactics were worked out whereby we patrolled over the French coast at about 8,000 feet until we saw the exhaust light of a bomb leaving France. We then turned towards the English coast and went into a steep dive at full throttle, the theory being that the flying bomb would emerge from below our nose and we would be going fast enough to be able to catch it as we levelled out behind it. This worked and the Squadron did well."

London-based *New York Herald Tribune* correspondent Richard L. Tobin's informed copy to his newspaper helped enlighten the American public as well as confused and frightened Londoners and those living in Kent and Sussex:

Robot Planes Hit England's South Coast

The Germans have been using in numbers a formidable new weapon of war, a pilotless plane carrying high explosives, to attack the southern part of England since Tuesday, it was announced officially at London today. This pilotless plane is not, in all probability, radio-controlled, and is essentially only a bomb with wings and an engine to propel it. It is destroyed when it explodes. It is undoubtedly sent into the air by catapult somewhere on the northern coast of France, an area where Allied planes for months have been bombing 'mystery installations', as they did again today. That coast, at the nearest point, is about ninety miles from London. There were dozens of unanswered questions today, such as how the plane works, whether radio really controls it and how expensive it is to manufacture. No one in this country knows the answers, or if anyone does know, he is not saying.

Rate of Output *The rate of manufacture of the new German weapon is important. If it can be made easily and cheaply, it may yet prove important. But since its mechanism must be fairly complex, and since German industry is undoubtedly in disrepair after so much aerial bombing and so many years of war, it does not seem likely that the pilotless plane will turn the tide. The robot bombers were seen by many persons in southern England last night and today. As intense an anti-aircraft barrage as has been put up in some time in that area was augmented by other measures of defense. Eyewitnesses interviewed today by this correspondent said, for example, 'It was a ball of fire as big as a barrage balloon.' 'It looked like a plane on fire.' 'It was going so slow it was like shooting a sitting duck.' 'It scared the hell out of me.'*

Held in Searchlights *Some of the robot bombers were held by searchlights last night for minutes at a time and were seen plainly before they exploded. They looked to some observers like homemade box kites with a fuselage longer than one usually sees on an airplane. They seemed to have a top velocity of 300 miles an hour and a low trajectory. There was a 'phosphorescent' glow about them, which suggested to some eyewitnesses that they might be rocket-propelled after all. Probably a Diesel engine [sic] propels the robot bomber once it is in the air. It has been noted that when the engine stops and a light at the rear end of the device goes out, the explosion of the device follows in five to fifteen seconds. The explosive charge seems, from the effects produced, to be large. The robot bomber amounts to a projectile which is aimed by the Germans in the general direction of a target and may or may not strike it. It looks much like a skyrocket and is launched substantially as skyrockets are.*

Herbert Morrison, *Minister of Home Security, told the House of Commons today, 'It has been known for some time that the enemy was making preparations for the use of pilotless aircraft against this country, and he has now started to use this much-vaunted new weapon. A small number of these missiles were used in the raids of Tuesday morning. A few were scattered over a large area. A larger number were used last night and this morning. On the first occasion, they* caused a few casualties, but the attack was light, and the damage on the whole was inconsiderable. Last night's attack was more serious, and I have not as yet full particulars of the casualties and damage, nor the number of pilotless aircraft destroyed before they could explode. The enemy's preparations have not, of course, passed unnoticed, and counter-measures have already been and will continue to be applied with full vigour. It is, however, probable that the attack will continue and, subject to experience, the usual siren warning will be given for such attacks. Meanwhile, it is important not to give the enemy any information that would help him in directing his shooting by telling him where his missiles have landed. It may be difficult to distinguish these attacks from ordinary air raids, and therefore it has been decided that, for the present, information published about air raids in southern England – that is to say, south of the line from The Wash to the Bristol Channel – will not give any indication where the air raid has taken place, beyond saying that it had occurred in southern England. While I think it right to give the House, at the earliest opportunity, information about the use of this new weapon by the enemy, the available information does not suggest that an exaggerated importance need be attached to this new development. All possible steps are being taken to frustrate the enemy's attempts to supplement his nuisance raiding by means, which do not imperil the lives of his pilots. Meanwhile, the nation should carry on with its normal business. Further, as the raids with pilotless aircraft may occur during the time when the streets are full of people and anti-aircraft guns will be used to shoot down the machines, I must impress on the public the importance of not exposing themselves unnecessarily to danger by remaining in the streets out of curiosity, instead of taking the nearest cover while the guns are firing. For the time being, at any rate, the guns will shoot. But this is liable to review as we go along, in the light of experience, and what is expedient. Members will notice the arrangements we have made with the press with a view to avoiding the enemy knowing where his pilotless aircraft have fallen. I am sure members, in any questions they may put down or supplementary questions or observations, will themselves act up to the practice we have asked the press to observe.'

Statement is Issued The Ministry of Home Security issued tonight a statement about the robot bomber. 'The damage it has caused,' the statement said, 'has been relatively small, and the new weapon will not interfere with our war effort and our sure and steady march to victory. The enemy's aim is clearly, in view of the difficulty of the military situation, to try to upset our morale and interfere with our work. It is essential that there should be the least possible interruption in all work vital to the country's needs at this time, and the government's counsel is that every one should get on with his or her job in the ordinary way, and only take cover when danger is imminent. There is already an efficient system for giving warning of imminent danger in factories. For the general public, the advice is that if they see or hear one of these things or hear gunfire near them, they should keep under cover. When the engine of the pilotless aircraft stops and the light at the end of the machine is seen to go out, it may mean that explosion will soon follow, perhaps in five to fifteen seconds. So take refuge from the blast. Those indoors should keep out of the way of the blast and use the most solid protection immediately available. There is no reason to think that raids by this weapon will be worse than or indeed as heavy as the raids with which the people of this country are already familiar and have borne so bravely.

Nazis Report a Panic The German propaganda machine went into high gear today, talking about panic at London and giving full credit for this alleged development to the secret weapon touted in recent months by Propaganda Minister Paul Joseph Goebbels. Berlin broadcasts declared 'general uprising' of the British people would compel the Allies to stop bombing the German supply system in France beyond the Allies' Normandy beachhead and would force them to attack instead the northern coast of France – where the launching apparatus for the robot bombers is understood to be situated. The Nazis declared, among other things, that the robot bomber is Germany's first secret weapon and that it ushers in a period of reprisals against the British, carries a new type of explosive of especially great force, is a new anti-invasion weapon and has complete novelty and super-effects. One Berlin announcer said: 'One can be happy to be in Berlin tonight instead of in London.' A broadcast by the German Transocean news agency tonight declared: 'Damage of the greatest extent has been caused by new German high explosives in London. Warehouses on the Thames are in flames and rail communications are partly disrupted.' One enemy broadcast described the robot plane as a *'new invasion weapon which works most effectively,' and declared it 'has the importance of a strong air fleet.' The German radio said also: 'There is no German who has not received the announcement with deep satisfaction and a full heart. It will be an eye for an eye and a tooth for a tooth.' Previously, it said, the German air force had been careful to hit only military objectives in Britain, but from now on it will be different, and they (the Allies) will now learn that crimes against the German civilian population and cultural monuments do not remain unpunished.'"*

Friday 16 JUNE

By noon, some 244 V-1s had been launched but 45 had either crashed on take-off or had fallen into the Channel. Seventy-three reached London and about 50 were aimed at Southampton, even East Anglia received four more flying bombs during the day. One of the Divers fell at Baker's Hall Farm at Bures in Essex, damaging farm buildings but causing no casualties. It was initially thought that an aircraft had crashed at high speed. Another fell in a potato field at Weeley in Essex, again thought to be an aircraft. One fell at Chart Sutton at 1013, the victim of a fighter. At 1019 one impacted at Cold Norton near Bradwell Bay, and at 1029 a combination of AA and fighters brought down one that crashed three miles west of Bethersden airfield in Kent, causing minor damage to 15 houses. The gunners at Folkestone brought down their first at 1040. Fighters shot down another that crashed in the Brooklands area at 1220. The fighters also accounted for one that crashed near Frittenden at midday, and two that fell in the Tonbridge/Sevenoaks area at 1155 and 1411. At 1614, Suffolk received its second bomb, which came down at Woolverstone near Ipswich.

Of the total of 26 shot down during the day, a dozen fell to the fighters. The first brought down by day fighters was shot down by 3 Squadron's Flt Sgt Morrie Rose at 0750, the Tempests accounting for the lion's share, 3 Squadron alone being credited with nine destroyed. Wg Cdr Beamont recalled:

"For 150 Wing the week following D-Day was fully occupied with patrols of the invasion front and deeper fighter sweeps beyond the front towards the Paris area, but then a new diversion occurred. In the evening of 15 June the Newchurch Tempest squadrons of 150 Wing were warned to come to 'Readiness' before dawn on the following day, after the arrival of a small number of V-1s during the previous night. Still no detailed intelligence was available as to what to expect beyond the fact that these were small, pilotless aircraft of unspecified shape, travelling it was thought, at about 400mph and at heights up to about 5,000 feet."

3 Squadron (Tempest V) Newchurch

Flt Sgt M.J.A. Rose	JN760/JF-R	V-1	0750	Maidstone
Plt Off S.B. Feldman (US)	JN735/JF-X	V-1	0900-1030	Ashford
Wg Cdr R.P. Beamont ⎤	JN751/RB	V-1	0910-1020	Faversham
Flt Sgt R.W. Cole ⎦	JN761/JF-U			
Flt Lt A.E. Umbers RNZAF	JN745/JF-T	V-1	1900-1040	
Flt Sgt R.W. Pottinger	JN743/JF-P	V-1	1020-1135	Ashford
Flt Lt R. van Lierde (Belg) ⎤	JN862/JF-Z	V-1	1024-1205	Chatham
Flt Sgt D.J. Mackerras RAAF ⎦	JN793/JF-N			
Flt Sgt S. Domanski (Pol)	JN752/JF-S	V-1	1044-1203	Chatham area
Flt Sgt L.G. Everson	JN748/JF-	V-1	1310-1420	Hastings
Flg Off G.A. Whitman ⎤ RCAF (US)	JN743/JF-P	V-1	1320-1430	Lewes area
Flt Sgt J.W. Foster ⎦	JN745/JF-T			

Flt Sgt Morrie Rose opened the scoring when he shot down a flying bomb at 0750. It burst into flames before it crashed on impact south of Maidstone. He was fortunate to return safely after US gunners based on the Romney Marshes blasted a hole through one wing of JF-R, necessitating a wing change. Flt Sgt Ron Pottinger commented:

"We were allowed the space between the guns and the balloons, or the area over the sea. We were more or less obliged to stick to this area, but any gun whether in the area or not had a go. In particular the Americans who were stationed at other airfields on Romney Marshes, and had plenty of ammunition, most of which seemed to be aimed at the following aircraft rather than the Doodlebug. Maurice Rose flying my 'R' for Robert, had half-inch shells through the wing, which meant the wing being changed. Strange to say, it was never so fast after that change. Our own gunners too, were not allowing sufficient deflection and initially their success rate wasn't all that good, which frustrated us, because we also had greater difficulty in shooting them down in the brief time allowed us. However, the gunners had plenty of opportunity for practice and eventually, when provided with proximity fuses, were doing extremely well. Even we were forced to admit it!"

The newspapers were keen to get Flt Sgt Rose's story:

"Today I can tell you that it was my good fortune to be the first pilot to shoot down a Doodlebug in daylight. As a matter of fact, I was very lucky to get into the battle of the Doodlebugs at all. Three days before I shot that first one down, I was on an offensive patrol in France behind the Allied lines in Normandy when I was hit by a German fighter and had to bale out. Luckily I landed safely, but now I had no plane to fly. So I was sent back across the Channel in a supply vessel and returned to my base. As I was going over the Channel I suddenly saw a flying bomb come buzzing towards me. Of course, I had heard about them at briefings but no one had actually seen one in flight before! The Doodlebug was coming straight out of the sun at my aircraft. Even in the glare I could still see the flame from its motor and the noise of the engine sounded like a motorcycle on the blink. I am used to facing Hun fighter pilots who always try to come out of the sun at you – but they twist and turn to make it difficult for you to get a clean shot. But this new Nazi terror weapon didn't deviate an inch as it came straight on towards me. The whole situation seemed crazy, almost unreal. But there was no time to think. I had to set my sights and go into action. I was about to do something no fighter pilot had ever done before – go into battle against a robot enemy. But there was no time for getting a close look at this one. I just fixed it in my sights and gave it a full burst with my guns. Fortunately, the thing blew up in mid-air. The whole incident was all over as quickly as that."

Wg Cdr Roly Beamont shared one with Flt Sgt Bob Cole shortly thereafter, and later wrote:

"Soon after dawn on 16 June, a drizzling wet morning, the expected alert warnings came and with Sergeant Bob Cole as my No.2, we led the Wing into an action which was to continue at maximum intensity for the next six weeks. But now it was all conjecture – what were these pilotless aircraft, and how to destroy them? Immediately after take-off we were given a heading south-east to a point off Folkestone. There was broken cloud at 2,000 feet and rather poor visibility in showers, and when radar control indicated that our target was closing rapidly ahead and then passing down the port side we had still not seen it, so I pulled around in a tight turn to port and at that moment saw a small dark shape go through a break in the clouds. Still at full power we dived to increase to absolute maximum (level) speed, about 410mph indicated at that height, and then suddenly out of the murk to starboard saw what appeared to be a small monoplane with a bulky, glowing jet engine at the back. We crossed in just over Folkestone in heavy rain and rapidly overtook the V-1, which was flying at about 370mph, but it was a very small target and, opening fire from about 400 yards astern, I missed completely with the first burst. Steadying up at about 300 yards, another short burst hit its port outer wing; and then with all the remaining ammunition a long burst hit it first on the fuselage without immediate effect, and finally on the engine which stopped and it began to go down. The V-1 slowed rapidly but remained on an even keel, and as I overtook it on the port side I was able to get a quick look at its slim, pointed fuselage, high mounted ram-jet engine at the back, and short stubby wings. It was painted dull grey overall and the jet pipe at the back was smoke-blackened. I called in Bob Cole to finish it off, which he did with a well-aimed burst and it rolled over on its back and dived into a field south of Maidstone, exploding with a lot of flame and black smoke and a clear goldfish bowl of blossoming shock-wave which was to become a familiar feature of these activities in the weeks ahead."

Plt Off Buck Feldman's first encounter with a flying bomb was nearly his last:

"After we had first been scrambled, we had finished our patrol and were going back to Newchurch when we heard on the radio that there was a V-1 crossing near Ashford. The sky was overcast, but there was a big ray of sunshine coming through a hole in the clouds. The V-1 broke out in front of me. I was right underneath it, and let fly for two or three seconds. When I was only 50 yards away, it blew up into my face. My wingman saw me disappear in a sheet of flame and shouted, 'You are on fire. Bale out.' I thought I had had it, and I found later that the aeroplane in places was burned and blackened."

Of Feldman's lucky escape, Wg Cdr Beamont commented:

"A V-1 was exploded by cannon fire about 400 yards away from the Tempest concerned. The aircraft went straight through the fireball and returned safely but streaked with smoke and evidence of charring, particularly on the fabric-covered elevators and on the rudder, part of which was burnt off. On this occasion the pilot came down with burns on his forearm, and this was traced to ingress of flame from the explosion entering the cockpit through the air ventilator, which was naturally open in the hot summer weather and was positioned immediately above the pilot's throttle hand. The problem was cured simply by keeping the louvre closed. It was certainly impressive to fly straight through the middle of a 2,000lb bomb explosion, but not many pilots were hurt doing it. You couldn't avoid flying through the fireball. As a V-1 exploded it went from 400mph to zero in a fraction of a second. It stopped. You didn't. You were doing 400mph behind it, so in a fraction of a second you went through the fireball. There was no way of avoiding it, and a number of aircraft were damaged and one or two [sic] pilots were brought down and killed. You anticipated every time that it was going to happen. They didn't always blow up. If you knocked a wing off it would just roll down, but once you'd seen an explosion you knew it might happen, so every time you pressed the gun button you were instinctively sucking inside yourself to avoid the explosion. There was a certain amount of adrenalin about the operation."

91 Squadron (Spitfire XIV) Deanland ALG

Flt Lt H.B. Moffett RCAF	RM617/DL-G	V-1	1035-1110	Kenley

Flt Lt Bruce Moffett RCAF opened the scoring for 91 Squadron when he shot a flying bomb that crashed near Kenley: "I sighted it about a mile away, closed in and opened fire. I saw several strikes hit home, then it went into a vertical dive, crashing in an open field and exploding."

486 (RNZAF) Squadron (Tempest V) Newchurch

Wt Off B.J. O'Connor RNZAF	JN809/SA-	V-1	1200	Rye-Dungeness
Plt Off K. McCarthy RNZAF	JN801/SA-L	V-1	1240	Rye

Wt Off Brian O'Connor intercepted 486 Squadron's first flying bomb between Hythe and Dungeness at midday. He delivered three short bursts and it exploded in the air. Within the hour Plt Off Kevin McCarthy got another, which dived into the ground north of Rye. Others were not so lucky, as Plt Off Jack Stafford recalled:

"I caught up to the bomb but when I opened fire my cannon jammed. I was almost shot down by our own flak, which was totally unorganised and fired continually, badly endangering our own fighters. Between the flak barrier and the balloon barrage erected to defend London, we were free to intercept and shoot down the Divers without interference. We patrolled a thousand or two feet higher than the expected altitude of the Divers and were well informed by ground control of their imminent arrival. We would be vectored to the position [at which] the Diver would cross the coast, [and] given a countdown to its arrival. This was absolutely accurate and our indication came with the intense flak barrage that met its arrival. As it passed through the flak we pursued it in a long, gentle diving turn at max revs and boost. They varied in speed and to a lesser extent altitude. We would be doing maybe 450mph at this stage and we had maybe two-and-half minutes to catch it before it entered the balloon barrage."

142 Wing (Spitfire Vb) Horne ALG

Wg Cdr J.M. Checketts RNZAF   AB524/JM-C   V-1   am   Caterham area

New Zealand ace Wg Cdr Johnny Checketts DSO DFC, with a dozen victories to his credit, had just taken command of the newly formed 142 Wing based near Biggin Hill. To counter the threat of low flying Divers he requested that twin machine-guns be set up in front of the IO's hut, so when he was not flying he could take shots at any that came directly over the airfield. When one did, he was not around and the IO duly shot it down, much to his chagrin.

68 Squadron, equipped with Beaufighters but soon to receive Mosquito XVIIs, moved from Fairwood Common to Castle Camps, south of Cambridge and near Saffron Walden. Wg Cdr Dennis Hayley-Bell DFC was in command of the unit that included a number of Czech crews.

Wg Cdr Beamont had more to say following his initial experience:

> "The Tempest proved to have a greater speed margin than all other fighters, and with its excellent gun-aiming stability was immediately successful in destroying ten V-1s over the Channel, Kent and Sussex by midday. On the first day, speed, height, size and best methods of attack were all unknown. In the event, the attack came generally at below 2,000 feet and at speeds between 340 and 370mph IAS; and with a three-foot cross-section fuselage and eight-inch thick wing they proved extremely small targets to hit from the stern quarter which, by virtue of their high speed, was the segment in which the vast majority of fighter attacks ended up. Then there was the question of firing range and how close to go in, relative to the chances of blowing yourself up when the warhead exploded. Starting at 400 yards we experienced much wastage and frequent missing altogether until, when closing to 200 yards before firing, a higher success rate was achieved. I was convinced that the standard Fighter Command 'spread harmonisation' pattern for the guns was unsuitable for this operation and, after failing to obtain official approval, had my own guns point-harmonised at 300 yards. This had an immediate effect for the better on my shooting and I was able to hit the next lot of V-1s with my first burst and with good effect."

Accordingly he ordered all 150 Wing's Tempests' guns be point-harmonised in disregard of Command policy – with two results: the first an immediate and sustained improvement on the Wing's scoring rate, and the second, not unexpectedly, was a different sort of rocket from Headquarters. Interception of these small, fast targets was also a problem. Although the radars could see them they could rarely put a fighter into the 500 yards or nearer position, which was generally necessary for them to be picked up visually in all but perfect light conditions. Beamont continued:

> "The situation became even more difficult by the end of the first week when it became fashionable to do 'training sorties' in the south-east, and the skies of Kent became a sort of free-for-all with fighters of all types and from many Commands joining in. This showed commendable zeal for the fray but it often resulted in confused intercepts, and many V-1s got through when the Tempests were baulked by slower fighters. I reported to 11 Group Headquarters and asked for a special defence zone to be created in which all aircraft would be banned except those few squadrons most suitable for this activity, namely Tempests, Spitfires XII and XIV, and later Mustangs with uprated engines. I also asked for a deployment of the Royal Observer Corps round the coast with signal rockets which they would fire towards any V-1 seen, to give visual clues to the radar-vectored fighters. Within a very few days, thanks to the immediate reaction of Air Vice-Marshal Bouchier of 11 Group, these measures were in operation, and significant improvement in the kill rate was achieved."

Night 16/17 JUNE

One of the flying bombs launched this night malfunctioned and crashed into a nearby French village, killing ten people. Other bombs had apparently suffered damage to their control systems, affecting the compass and causing the missiles to turn around in the opposite direction after launching, there to disappear inland. Known as *Kreisläufer* (circle runners), one crashed near Paris, two near Brussels and one between Soissons and Lâon. Uffz Otto Neuchel of *Flakregiment 155(W)* recalled that on one occasion five flying bombs crashed one after the other just after take-off "the entire world turned red" and he later found out that three launch ramps had been destroyed and about a dozen men killed by the concussion[30]. The site at Avesnes Chaussoy was among the first to have been destroyed when a bomb reared up, stalled and fell back on those who had launched it.

Shortly before midnight, a Diver impacted on tennis courts in South Park, Ilford, the first of 32 flying bombs that were to fall on the borough. Two came down in the Bromley area, at 0100 and 0125, damaging more than 80 houses. Fortunately casualties were relatively light: one killed and 15 injured, four seriously. Two Divers fell on Beckenham in the early hours, the first killing a resident in The Avenue, the second causing damage only. Six houses were damaged at Great Chart near Ashford when a bomb fell at 0345. The worst incident occurred at 0405 when a bomb struck St Mary Abbotts Hospital in Kensington, destroying the children's isolation block, the main nurses' home and four wards. Thirteen patients, mostly children, and five staff were killed. The hospital had to be closed with the loss of 832 beds. Moored in Newhaven harbour with many other vessels was SS *Canterbury*, loaded with troops and awaiting orders to sail for Caen. Suddenly, a flying bomb approached and was promptly shot down by one of the ship's AA guns. Although this spectacle was enjoyed by the troops and crew on board, the gunner's moment of glory was shattered when he was put on a charge as it was against orders to shoot down flying bombs while in the vicinity of Newhaven, as they might fall in the harbour area.[31]

96 Squadron (Mosquito XIII) West Malling

Flt Lt D.L. Ward	HK415/ZJ-R	V-1	2302-0208	over Channel
Sqn Ldr A. Parker-Rees	MM497/ZJ-	V-1	2230	off Dover

Flt Lt Ward opened the scoring for 96 Squadron when he intercepted a Diver between Dungeness and Boulogne. It exploded on the sea following his attack. Shortly thereafter, Sqn Ldr Alistair Parker-Rees shot down a second, which exploded in the air off Dover.

219 Squadron (Mosquito XVII) Bradwell Bay

Wg Cdr A.McN. Boyd	HK348/FK-	V-1	0100-0300	
Sqn Ldr P.L. Burke	HK248/FK-	V-1	0200-0415	off Dungeness

418 (RCAF) Squadron (Mosquito FBVI) Holmsley South

Sqn Ldr E.R. McGill RCAF	TH-	V-1 probable	2330-0210	
Flt Lt D.A. MacFadyen RCAF	HR155/TH-X	V-1	0038-0321	over Channel
	HR155/TH-X	V-1	0038-0321	over Channel
Flt Lt C.J. Evans RCAF	TH-	V-1	0133-0438	Hastings area

Sqn Ldr Russ Bannock RCAF[32] later recalled:

"A barrage of 20 or 30 of these things was launched. We started to patrol, trying to catch them in the usual manner by diving down on them from a couple of thousand feet. We soon found that we couldn't get anywhere near them, and decided to work out a tactic. Two or three of us got together and decided that the only way we could catch these things was to patrol at 10,000 feet in the middle of the Channel. As soon as we saw one launched, we would head out on an intercept course at our height. Instead of heading for it, we turned toward London, and kept looking over our shoulders, dipping the wing until we saw it catching up. When it was directly underneath us, we went into a dive and achieved about 430mph. It [the V-1] would cruise usually at 375mph and we attacked from about a 30-degree angle to avoid any particular debris. We became fairly adept at this. We had some amusing incidents. I had one experience where I fired a burst at one and watched it go into a 180-degree turn after which the auto-pilot straightened it up. It flew back into France and crashed. We did have a few experiences like that. We had another hazard, and that was enemy night fighters. To avoid collision, as soon as we started to dive from 10,000 feet on a V-1 we had to turn our navigation lights on because there might be somebody else diving from the other side. So a few German night fighters would hover around the Channel while we were there, and I'm afraid we lost some of our fellows to them."

Wt Off Guy James' Mosquito NT142, which had taken off at 2233 on anti-Diver patrol over the Channel, may have been a victim of a Luftwaffe night fighter, as suggested, since it FTR, although none of the regular night fighter units made a claim for a Mosquito on this night. James, a RAF pilot, and his Canadian navigator Flg Off Duncan MacFarlane were lost.

605 Squadron (Mosquito VI) Manston

| Sqn Ldr G.J. Wright | UP- | V-1 | 0150-0320 | off Dungeness |

"We set course for the Channel where a large number of Divers were seen heading in a north-westerly direction towards Dungeness. One of these Divers was actually seen to fly on a course of 120 degrees and was heading just south of Calais. Several were seen to be engaged by ground defences and/or night fighters to our port and starboard. We attacked one flying about 300mph at a height of approximately 1,000 feet ten miles south-east of Dungeness, and saw cannon strikes and the Diver immediately exploded. Range very difficult to judge."

405 aircraft from Bomber Command raided many of the V-1 launch sites during the night. Guns opened fire on some of the stragglers, causing AOC Bomber Command Air Marshal Sir Arthur Harris to write to General Sir Frederick Pile, GOC AA Command:

"… the Hun has realised (by his use of Diver) his hope of producing in this country a reaction wholly disproportionate to the threat. I am concerned that this reaction, in so far as AA Command is concerned, is jeopardizing my heavy night-bomber force. If AA gunners are light on the trigger, they will at best hamper my forces and at worst shoot them down. I already have reports that a very large number of my aircraft were engaged on the night June 15-16, 1944, in spite of prior warning of their route. It is entirely deplorable that the Hun should be able to produce a panicky lack of fire discipline among our defences, who have obviously got themselves at times into a state wherein they don't care who or what they hit. With all emphasis, I ask you to ensure that their operations are confined to reasonable measures for the defence of this country without endangering the crews and aircraft of my Command."

General Pile later wrote in his memoirs:

"As a matter of fact, we had a pretty good record, on the whole – as Sir Roderic Hill later pointed out – for not shooting at our own planes, although they very frequently broke all the known rules, came in on routes different from the ones they had notified, failed to show correct recognition signals, flew over gun-defended areas, and generally gave us a very difficult time. Very often we got blamed for the activities of the Americans [when they later arrived] or of the Navy, who were particularly sensitive towards planes approaching their harbours. But, in general, there was very little official quarrelling between the RAF and ourselves."

Saturday 17 JUNE

By 0600, total casualties to date as a result of the flying bomb attack were announced as 18 killed, 166 seriously injured, and 83 slightly injured. This was but a foretaste of what was to come. The *Croydon Advertiser* attempted to make light of the seriousness of the situation:

> *"Dodging the Dingbats is becoming an acquired art in Southern England today. Before people began to know the habits of the brute there was a certain amount of very natural uneasiness. No one quite knew what to expect. But now everyone goes about his or her normal business and when one is heard approaching, most people take appropriate evasive action. In one district they seem to be generally named Dingbats. This word apparently comes from an expressive phrase of RAF men who, when they wish to describe something very fast, say it goes like a dingbat."*

Hitler's 'secret weapon' was now generating fear and terror in Londoners, as well as those in the firing line on the Kent and Sussex coasts. At 1600, a Diver impacted on the 'Surrey Hounds' public house in St John's Hill near Clapham Junction (SW11). The street was crowded with shoppers and 24 persons were killed. Shops and houses were demolished and two passing trolley buses badly damaged. One of the victims of the Battersea bomb was Sylvia White, aged 14. She was shopping with her mother when the air raid siren started:

> "... a man standing in the doorway said: 'There's one of them funny things up there and they're firing at it. It might come down.' He gave me a shove back into the shelter of the shop. The next thing I remember is regaining consciousness in complete blackness, my mother shaking me like a terrier and slapping my face and her voice shouting 'wake up wake up, for God's sake, wake up.' Then I became conscious of other voices calling out saying they knew we were there and they would soon get us out. The bomb had fallen on the baker's and the pub on the other side of the road and the blast had blown in the front door of the butcher's shop and brought down part of the first floor. Thanks to the stranger in the shop doorway I am still alive to tell the tale. When the rescue services had dug us out we were taken to the Granada cinema, which was being used as a casualty clearing station. We were then taken to have our wounds dressed and to be given certificates to say we were official war casualties."

Another Diver came down at Highbury Corner near Arsenal's famous football ground, killing 26 and injuring 150. Surbiton in Surrey received one during the early afternoon, killing a dozen people in Tolworth Park Road, and another hit in Lewisham, killing 13 and seriously injuring a further 17. A flying bomb that fell on New House Farm in Benenden, Kent, killed the farmer, his wife and daughter. Fortunately, there were no casualties when a Diver fell on the village of Nutfield in Surrey. There occurred some superficial damage to property at Staplehurst and Marden caused by cannon fire from a Tempest pursuing a Diver, but no casualties were inflicted.

3 Squadron (Tempest V) Newchurch

Flg Off M.F. Edwards ⎫ Flt Sgt C.W. Orwin ⎭	JN793/JF-N JN761/JF-U	V-1	1520	Folkestone area
Wg Cdr R.P. Beamont ⎫ Flt Lt R. van Lierde (Belg) ⎭	EJ525/RB JN862/JF-Z	V-1 shared	1700	Tenterden area
Plt Off S.B Feldman (US) ⎫ Flt Sgt D.J. Mackerras RAAF ⎭	JN739/JF-W JN735/JF-X	V-1	1950	Dungeness area
Flt Sgt M.J.A. Rose ⎫ Flt Sgt R.W. Cole ⎭	JN769/JF-G JN768/JF-F	V-1	2312	Ham Street area
Wg Cdr R.P. Beamont	EJ525/RB	V-1 damaged	2320	Newchurch area

All four of the squadron's kills were shared, the first exploding on the ground between Folkestone and Hawkinge following an encounter during an afternoon patrol by Flg Off Malcolm Edwards and Flt Sgt Bill Orwin. The Wing Leader and Flt Lt Remi van

Lierde brought down another an hour and a half later, which was seen being chased by two Spitfire XIVs. Both Tempests engaged, as did one of the Spitfires and the Diver crashed north of Tenterden. The third fell to Plt Off Buck Feldman and Flt Sgt Don Mackerras, who reported seeing four Spitfires in the area, but they were unsure if the Spitfires had attacked. The final one fell to Flt Sgts Morrie Rose and Bob Cole without interference, except that of local AA guns, as the latter noted: "Intercept one at Dungeness. Chase it with Flt Sgt Rose. Fire from 600 feet. It crashed and blew up. Our AA continued to fire throughout the chase." Wg Cdr Beamont was up again before midnight but could only claim one damaged:

> "Saw Diver over base at 350mph. Was illuminated and called for douse and opened fire at 700 yards and saw many strikes. S/L did not douse. Diver slowed down and I overshot. Closed again to 200/300 yards. After more strikes Diver turned to port, when intense flak of all varieties came up between Diver and me and I was unable to see target, and had to break."

91 Squadron (Spitfire XIV) Deanland ALG

Flg Off G.C. McKay RCAF	RB174/DL-T	V-1	0520	Redhill area
Flg Off P.A. Schade ⎱	RB180/DL-E	V-1	1550	Hastings
Flg Off A.R. Cruickshank RCAF ⎰	NH654/DL-			

Flg Off Paddy Schade DFM, a Malta ace with 14 victories (one shared) shared this Diver with Flg Off Ray Cruickshank some 20 miles north of Hastings.

229 Squadron (Spitfire IX) Detling

Flt Lt W.D. Idema RCAF (US)	MH852/9R-	V-1	2115 (KiA)	Folkestone

Of the loss of Flt Lt Wally Idema, a 27-year-old American pilot from Michigan, the unit's diarist wrote:

> "Flt Lt Idema returned from providing cover to Mitchells and Bostons bombing Mezidon, overshooting on returning, pulled up and crashed unhurt at 2020. Took off alone at 2055 to search for pilotless aircraft – informed control he was going south-east and not heard from again."

It seems that Idema intercepted a flying bomb but was killed by the explosion. Private R.C. McKenzie of the Canadian Infantry witnessed his loss:

> "My regiment [Calgary Highlanders] was billeted in the empty seafront hotels, in Folkestone. Several of us were standing about the front entrance to our hotel when one of the first Doodlebugs we ever saw came flying towards us across the Channel. The spluttering and popping noise of the damned things drew all our eyes to it. It wasn't very high up when, just as it got almost directly overhead, a Spitfire suddenly dived out from the clouds above the buzz bomb and fired a short burst at it, from very close quarters. As soon as the bullets struck there was a horrendous explosion. The last thing I saw before I was blown backwards into the hotel lobby was the Spitfire being flipped into a backward loop by the terrific blast. Luckily, although we were all shaken up, not one of us witnessing this little drama, was badly hurt, even though there was a lot of glass from the shattered windows flying about. I've often wondered if the Spitfire and the pilot managed to survive. I very much doubt it. Of course, from then on, many buzz bombs came over the Folkestone and Dover areas, but this was my first encounter with one and I strongly believe this was the first Doodlebug to appear over Folkestone, as we were right on the waterfront and would have heard or seen any others[33]."

Shortly thereafter, 229 Squadron despatched two Spitfires to patrol off Hythe. They were subsequently vectored towards a bogey but this turned out to be a friendly aircraft. During the evening a flying bomb crossed Detling airfield. Enthusiasts machine-gunned the pilotless aircraft, causing some consternation to those who found themselves disregarded in the field of fire, surrounded by tracer, while watching outside the mess dispersal.

486 (RNZAF) Squadron (Tempest V) Newchurch

Flg Off T.M. Fenton RNZAF	JN808/SA-	V-1	0630	Sevenoaks
Plt Off R.J. Danzey RNZAF	JN809/SA-M	V-1	1915	Faversham

Flg Off Ike Fenton and Plt Off Ray Danzey doubled the Squadron's score with a brace of flying bombs, both exploding on the ground.

353rdFS/354thFG USAAF (P-51B) Lashenden ALG

1/Lt W.Y. Anderson USAAF	43-12172	V-1	evening	
1/Lt L.H. Powers USAAF	43-	V-1	1845-2330	
	43-	V-1	1845-2330	Lashenden
	43-	V-1 shared	1845-2330	
1/Lt C.G. Bickel USAAF[34]	43-6453	V-1	evening	
	43-6453	V-1	evening	
	43-6453	V-1	evening	

1/Lt William Anderson (a naturalised US citizen born at Kromfors, Sweden) shot down the first flying bomb for the USAAF, apparently followed by five more by two squadron colleagues during the same evening/night. The Group diarist noted:

> "Three of our pilots [Lts Willie Anderson, Lewis Powers and Carl Bickel] went up to chase them. Powers took off first at 1845 and destroyed two buzz bombs before landing at 2330. One of his victories was destroyed over the field (Lashenden) creating quite a thrill for the men, making them dash for their fox holes."

326thFS/362ndFG (P-47) Headcorn ALG

1/Lt E.O. Fisher USAAF[35]	42-26918	V-1	evening
	42-26918	V-1	evening
	42-26918	V-1	evening

Lt Edwin 'Bill' Fisher from Portland Oregon claimed his hat-trick during one sortie. His aircraft carried the name *Shirley Jane III*.

Night 17/18 JUNE

Mosquitos were reported to have shot down six Divers during the night, AA guns getting a magnificent 40 and RAF Regt a further two. One Diver impacted at Ruckinge near Ashford, destroying two houses in which one person was seriously injured and three slightly injured. At 0035, one fell on Lakeside Drive, Bromley, seriously damaging eight houses and injuring nine people, four seriously. Five residents of Streatham (SW2) were killed in Downton Avenue when a Diver exploded at 0107, demolishing ten houses and badly damaging 17 others. A far more serious incident occurred in Deptford (SE16) at 0115 when a Diver came down between Crofton Street and Chilton Street, destroying eight houses and killing 18 residents, while a further 200 houses were damaged by blast. Some 80 houses were damaged in Dartford at 0305 by an impacting Diver, and three people were injured at Sutton-on-Hone shortly thereafter. At 0320, a Diver hit the Crystal Palace end of Penge High Street (SE20), causing extensive damage to property in High Street, Avington Grove and to the local Methodist church. Eleven residents were killed. Four more were killed and six seriously injured when a Diver crashed at West Park/Highcombe Close, Mottingham at 0435, and others were injured at the same time at Bexley. Three more were killed at 0542 when a bomb fell at the junction of High Street/Gwynne Street, Battersea (SW11).

96 Squadron (Mosquito XIII) West Malling

Flt Lt W.J. Gough	MM499/ZJ-V	V-1	2241-0145	off Calais
Flg Off R.F. Ball	HK372/ZJ-	V-1	2350-0235	off Hastings

Flt Lt W.J. Gough   MM499/ZJ-V   V-1 damaged 0050-0320

Flt Lt Bill Gough's first victim exploded in mid-air off Calais following an attack from 300-400 feet. Flg Off Ball engaged his target ten miles off Hastings and opened fire. Strikes were seen and the Diver lost height rapidly and entered cloud but the attack had to be abandoned when ground defences opened up. The Diver was assessed to have been destroyed.

418 (RCAF) Squadron (Mosquito FBVI) Holmsley South

Flt Lt C.J. Evans RCAF	TH-	V-1	0125-0437	overland
Flt Lt R.G. Gray RCAF	TH-	V-1	0238-0507	

Flt Lt Ross Gray, of Edmonton, told an interested Canadian correspondent:

"We had to develop an entirely new technique to fight them. There was certainly nothing in our flying training to give us a hint. For the first couple of nights the most we knew was that Jerry had a new secret weapon, and we had to go get it. We didn't know if the things would blow up in the air and whip us. Some did blow up, of course, and we had to fly through the debris. The flash of the explosion blinded us, and afterward we had to grope our way, guiding the crate by the feel of the controls. As the days went by we began to know what the flying bombs would do, and we began to develop a habit of closing one eye as we shot for a kill, so that when the flash had disappeared – if we were lucky enough to hit the thing – we had one eye serviceable for the darkness. Knocking down the Doodlebugs was harder work than going after enemy aircraft." Gray added that some of the flying bombs showed signs of having been tampered with by French underground agents. One he was attacking suddenly wobbled, veered around, then came flying toward him. He let it go by to crash on the German fortified coast.

456 (RAAF) Squadron (Mosquito XVII) Ford

Lt(A) D.G. Thornley RNVR	HK359/RX-K	V-1 probable 0035		Channel (Q.7745)

A Royal Navy pilot attached to the Australian squadron, Lt(A) Dennis Thornley[36] claimed the unit's first flying bomb kill: "Engaged Diver at 2,000-3,000 feet and saw indistinct flashes. The orange exhaust flame disappeared." However, it was not seen to crash.

605 Squadron (Mosquito VI) Manston

Flt Lt G.C. Wright	UP-	V-1	2400	off Le Touquet
	UP-	V-1	0040	off Le Touquet

Flt Lt George Wright AFC claimed three flying bombs destroyed but was granted only two:

"Airborne Manston 2325 and commenced patrol off French coast near Le Touquet. At 2341 we attacked first Diver from 1,000 yards flying at 320mph. No results seen. The second was attacked from 600 yards with a four-seconds burst. Strikes were very difficult to see owing to cloud and range. The Diver lost height steeply and was lost in thickish cloud. Almost immediately a flash lit up the cloud, caused either by the Diver exploding in the air or crashing in the sea. At 0040 a third was attacked from 800 yards and again from 500 yards. Sparks appeared from the tail end suggesting strikes and the flames seemed to increase in intensity. The Diver dived immediately, almost vertically, and the fire disappeared. No explosion seen but as this attack was carried out about ten miles from the shore and at 2,000 feet, it is claimed as destroyed. A fourth was attacked from 700 yards in part cloud with a long burst, but here we ran out of cannon. The Diver immediately altered course and as flak appeared in the distance in front of us, we broke off to starboard. A searchlight flicked on to the Diver, which seemed to hover in the beam and soon after exploded. At 0047 we attacked a fifth with machine-gun fire only from 250-200 yards and we were subject to a definite slipstream. No results seen, although Diver altered course to starboard, diving into cloud."

Sunday 18 JUNE

Early on Sunday morning, a flying bomb hit one side of Hungerford railway bridge. This was the 500th Diver launched. Later that morning, at 0850, another flying bomb exploded in Rutherford Street, Westminster, killing and injuring scores of people and demolishing two blocks of flats. But even worse was to come. The Guards Chapel in Bird Cage Walk, St James's, was the church used by the Royal Guardsmen based at nearby Wellington barracks. The chapel was packed that morning with Guardsmen, their families and friends. Just past 1100, not long after the service started, the congregation heard a distant buzzing. It gradually grew louder and turned into a roar overhead, which drowned out the singing. The engine cut out and the Diver glided down and hit the roof of the chapel. This was made of concrete, having been rebuilt after damage by incendiary bombs in the blitz. The Diver exploded on impact and the whole roof collapsed on the congregation. Rubble was piled up to ten feet deep in parts. One hundred and twenty-one military and civilians were killed and 141 seriously injured. Among those who perished was Col John Cobbold, OC the Scots Guards, Lt Col The Lord Edward Hay, OC the Grenadier Guards, and the Director of Music Major James Causley-Windram. Only the Bishop of Maidstone, who was conducting the service, escaped totally unhurt. The altar from which he was conducting the service was covered by a portico, which sheltered him from the blast. Legend has it that after the explosion the altar candles were still alight. It took two days to dig the dead and injured out of the devastation. News from this awful tragedy was suppressed at the time although rumours of the disaster soon spread throughout London.

The first of 13 Divers to fall on West Norwood (SE27) arrived at 0438 at the Tivoli Road/Crown Hill junction on the boundary of Lambeth and Croydon. Two houses were demolished and 30 suffered severe damage. There were no reported casualties. Four people were killed in Peckham (SE15) at 0830 following the impact of a Diver at the Redding Road/Unwin Road junction near the depot of the South Metropolitan Gas Company. Streatham (SW2) received its second of the day when a Diver impacted in Lyham Road near Brixton Prison where eight houses were destroyed, 30 damaged and five people killed. Two missiles fell near the docks at Beckton just after 1400, believed to have been victims of Spitfires. It was reported that a Spitfire was seen pursuing a Diver that eventually fell in Annerley Park (Penge SE20) at 1508. Three houses were demolished, 20 severely damaged, with 84 flats and 68 houses suffering blast effect. Surprisingly, only two people were killed.

A Diver, hit by both AA fire and fighters, crashed on Eastbourne at 2025, falling in the vicinity of Charleston Road, Milton Road and Mountney Road, where 41 residents were injured and extensive damage to property inflicted. Kent received a number of unwelcomed visitors, one Diver crashing at Shadoxhurst near Ashford after being shot down by a fighter at 0656. A fighter shot down one at 1146 that fell on Wilmington, seriously injuring six people. A few minutes later another impacted at Meopham, injuring one and damaging three houses. Another that had been hit by both AA and fighters fell at Snargate, slightly injuring three people.

At 1245, a Diver crashed on the slopes of Westerham Hill near Sevenoaks, apparently having been shot down by Flt Sgt Morrie Rose of 3 Squadron. Close to the point of impact was Gunner Harry Cull, formerly of the 9/Middlesex Regiment and now attached to a searchlight unit in support of a nearby heavy Royal Artillery AA gun battery. His unit was housed in tented accommodation but had access to a wooden cookhouse building in which to prepare in-situ meals and for brewing all-important tea. Gunner Cull had just left the immediate vicinity of the site to fetch a pail of water when the flying bomb exploded nearby. The unit's cookhouse was demolished, the searchlight and nearby army lorries damaged and the site officer critically wounded; there was one other less serious injury. Harry escaped with shock, having been knocked over by the blast[37]. He commented wryly: "That was the second time the Germans had tried to kill me, the first being at RAF Honington during the Battle of Britain." His wife and family experienced a similar narrow escape two months later (see 15 August). A witness to the incident, Air Raid Warden Arthur Yeadon, later wrote:

"I was coming back from Sevenoaks on the bus. Just past Brasted I heard the sound of a Doodle on its way, immediately overhead, very low. It was obviously going to have difficulty getting over Westerham Hill. For some reason it went into a vertical dive, there was a flash and a crash and the hillside west of Westerham Hill was enveloped in smoke and dust. I could not see where it had dropped but I knew it was not far from the Hill. The Doodle had hit a tree about 50 yards northwest of Durtnell's house, which was in a pretty bad state and a cottage in the garden was a total wreck. The Durtnells and their two children were in bed and by a miracle none of them was hurt. Mr Durtnell caused some amusement by running around the garden with a bottle of brandy in one hand (for his own fortification) doing his best to catch his tame rabbits whose hutches had been blitzed ... the most pitiful sight was their dog which had caught the full blast of a broken window and was lying there pitted with glass splinters. There was only one thing to do for the poor beast. There were about 40 Army lorries parked along the private road and most of these were damaged. They were supposed to be moving off the following morning but their departure was somewhat delayed. Two soldiers were hurt but these were dealt with by the military authorities. Every house on Pilgrims Way from Betsoms Farm to the Waterworks was damaged in some way."[38]

Fighters and AA brought down another at 1655, which impacted at Smarden, and yet another exploded at Bromley Green at 2025. Another fell on Lullingstone Castle, at 2035, causing damage though no one was hurt. Nearby St Botolphs Church was also damaged. Another victim of fighters crashed into the river at Erith at 2040.

3 Squadron (Tempest V) Newchurch

Flt Lt A.E. Umbers RNZAF	JN768/JF-F	V-1	0442	Grid Q.9191
Flt Lt R. van Lierde (Belg) ⎤	JN862/JF-Z	V-1	0520	Dungeness area
Flt Sgt H.J. Bailey RAAF ⎦	JN759/JF-			
Flt Sgt T.A. McCulloch	JN738/JF-	V-1	0700	Dungeness area
Flt Sgt D.J. Mackerras RAAF	JN752/JF-S	V-1	0815	Biggin Hill
Flt Lt A.E. Umbers RNZAF	JN768/JF-F	V-1	0900	Cranbrook area
Flt Lt A.R. Moore	JN818/JF-	V-1	0955	Rye area
Flg Off G.A. Whitman RCAF (US)	JN735/JF-X	V-1 shared	1145	Bexley area
Flt Lt R. van Lierde (Belg)	JN862/JF-Z	V-1 shared	1155	Ivychurch area
Flt Sgt M.J.A. Rose	JN745/JF-T	V-1	1245	Westerham area
Flt Sgt R.W. Cole	JN759/JF-	V-1	1300	exploded in mid-air
Flg Off M.F. Edwards	JN735/JF-X	V-1	1430	Rye area
Plt Off H.R. Wingate	JN739/JF-W	V-1	1630	Biggin Hill area
Flt Sgt D.J. Mackerras RAAF	JN745/JF-T	V-1	1735	Gatwick area
Flg Off G.E. Kosh	JN735/JF-X	V-1	1800	Rotherfield area
Flt Sgt H.J. Bailey RAAF	JN739/JF-W	V-1	2100	Eastbourne area
Plt Off H.R. Wingate ⎤	JN752/JF-S	V-1	2115	Appledore area
Wt Off R.S. Adcock RAAF ⎦	JN735/JF-X			
Wg Cdr R.P. Beamont	JN862/JF-Z	V-1	2200	exploded in mid-air
	JN862/JF-Z	V-1 shared	2210	Hastings area
Plt Off K.G. Slade-Betts	JN812/JF-M	V-1	2230	Bexhill area
Flt Lt A.E. Umbers RNZAF	JN796/JF-A	V-1	c2300	Dunsford area

| Flg Off R.H. Clapperton | JN765/JF-K | V-1 | 2315 | Hailsham area |
| Flt Sgt M.J.A. Rose | JN735/JF-X | V-1 | 2325 | exploded in mid-air |

The Squadron had a field day, shooting down 22 Divers including three shared, with the majority of the pilots getting on the score sheet. Flt Lt Spike Umbers got the first at 0442:

"Saw Diver south-west of Dungeness at 1,000 feet, speed 390mph. Chased all out and fired from (believed) 400 yards but no results seen. Then realised glare of jet had confused range estimation and that opening range was near 1,000 yards. Closed gradually, firing short bursts until point-blank range. Strikes seen port wing and fuselage. Diver slowed to 250mph. Fired further bursts when told by control of obstructions ahead, so broke away. Diver last seen at 500 feet flying at 200mph. ROC confirmed this Diver crashed at Q.9191."

Flt Lt Remi van Lierde shared the next with Flt Sgt Bert Bailey:

"On take-off saw Diver crossing over Dungeness, speed 360mph at 1,500 feet, but ack-ack from Newchurch caused us to break off. Returned to Dungeness and saw another Diver coming in four miles east of Dungeness, same speed and height. Closed to 500 yards and gave one-second burst, but while no strikes were seen the Diver turned to port. No.2 fired two bursts, again seeing no strikes in glow of jet. Flak again caused us to break, and as I was completing my turn I saw Diver hit the ground and explode."

Flt Sgt McCulloch scored his kill at 0700:

"Saw Diver crossing half-a-mile west of Dungeness. Closed rapidly and gave three bursts from 300 yards to point-blank range. No strikes seen and overshot. Closed again to 150 yards and gave short bursts. Saw strikes on both wings. Diver turned on back and spiralled in."

Australian Flt Sgt Don Mackerras was the next to add to the score sheet:

"Saw Diver at 2,500 feet in breaks in cloud. Chased to Biggin Hill, fired two bursts at 400 yards then two bursts at 250 yards. Starboard wing fell off and Diver exploded on the ground near Biggin Hill Ops Room – confirmed by Duty IO who was blown down while temporarily outside his post of duty."

Flt Lt Umbers was off again at 0850:

"Chased Diver from Dungeness at 2,000 feet, 380mph. Closed to 250 yards, fired several short bursts and saw strikes. Diver went into cloud and was followed. Closed again, fired short bursts and strikes seen on wings and fuselage. Diver staggered, rolled on back and dived in, exploding near a castle, believed in the Cranbrook area."

The next wave of Divers approached shortly before 1000, Flt Lt Bob Moore getting the first:

"Put on Diver west of Dungeness at 2,500 feet. Rapidly overhauled at 450mph and closed to 200 yards. Many strikes seen, particularly on jet. Diver pulled up, turned to port and spiraled into ground, exploding in a field five miles west of Rye."

American Flg Off Lefty Whitman shared his kill with other Tempests:

"Saw Diver off Dungeness at 2,500 feet, speed 400mph+. Fired as it crossed coast, no results. Several other aircraft chasing. Another Tempest pulled ahead then broke away. I closed and saw strikes on jet unit. Another Tempest came from above and fired. Diver went down with jet still operating. Exploded Bexley area on a greenhouse." He commented later: "I dropped one on a greenhouse, and the glass rose up a million feet. What am I going to say to the guy who owns that greenhouse when we go to the pub tonight?"

That made seven Divers down for the morning. The first of the afternoon was shot down by Flt Sgt Morrie Rose:

"Saw Diver coming in south of Rye at 370mph, height 2,000 feet. Chased and closed to 600 yards, firing intermittent bursts causing jet to spit puffs of smoke. Diver slowed. I closed to 400 yards as target dived and crashed into top of hill in Westerham area, exploding."

Flt Sgt Bob Cole had a lucky escape:

"I was closing on it and I didn't hit it the first time, I hit it a bit later on. But when I did it blew up and I went straight through. It burnt the dope off the aircraft. Burnt the rudder. But the aircraft still flew. I went back on patrol and it seemed to be flying all right. But then Bob Moore flew alongside me and told me to return to base. I didn't know what the hell was the matter with the aircraft. All he would say is return to base. He wouldn't say anything else. I didn't know there was a hole in the rudder. I took it up to about 12,000 feet and put the wheels down, flaps down and threw it around. I thought if it breaks up I can get out up here. But not if it breaks up low down. I won't say I was a bit apprehensive coming into land, thinking what the hell is the matter with the damn thing, but it flew just as well on half a rudder as the whole."

Flt Lt Remi van Lierde was obliged to share his kill with Flt Lt Cook of 486 Squadron:

"Saw Diver crossing in north of Dungeness. Fired beam shot at 600 yards and missed. Lined up behind, fired and saw strikes when an aircraft of 486 Sqn came down and skidded right across me. This unseemly performance was repeated. Diver blew up on the ground near Ivychurch, damaging a farm house and a haystack."

Flg Off Edwards got the next, which he saw crossing the coast near Rye at 2,000 feet:

"Dived on it from 700 feet above, fired seven bursts from astern and strikes seen. Blackish smoke came from jet apparatus, which stopped working and Diver crashed and exploded four miles north of Rye."

It was two hours before the next wave of Divers approached, Plt Off Dickie Wingate getting the first at 1630:

"Saw Diver coming in over Hastings at 2,500 feet, speed 410mph. Gave two long bursts at extreme range, no results seen. Chased to Biggin Hill and fired again from 400 yards. Diver shuddered and slowed to 200mph and was losing height when ack-ack opened up and chase had to be given up. Subsequently told by Biggin Hill that this target had crashed."

Number 13 fell to Flt Sgt Don Mackerras, his second of the day:

"Given excellent vectors and got visual two miles south of Eastbourne at 2,500 feet. Closed to 500 yards and fired but strikes seen. Closed to 200 yards and saw strikes on port wing and jet apparatus. Diver lost height and went down steeply, exploding on the ground near Gatwick."

Flg Off George Kosh waded in with another a few minutes later:

"Saw Diver over Hastings at 3,000 feet. Chased to Rotherfield. I opened fire from 600 yards closing to 200 yards and saw strikes, which stopped jet, causing it to emit grey smoke. No.2 [Plt Off Slade-Betts] fired from 300 yards but saw no strikes. Diver lost height, slowed up and glided over a small town, exploding in a small orchard."

The final wave of the day started coming in just before 2100, and again 3 Squadron was ready and waiting with Flt Sgt Bert Bailey knocking down the first:

"Sighted Diver one mile east of Eastbourne at 3,000 feet. Opened fire at 700 yards with three short bursts but no results seen. At 200 yards I fired one long burst and starboard wing came off. Target rolled over and went down, exploding four miles north of Eastbourne."

Plt Off Dickie Wingate and Wt Off Adcock were patrolling when a Diver was spotted over Dungeness at 4,000 feet. Mustangs were observed pursuing it but they failed to score any strikes. Wingate reported:

> "I fired from 200 yards observing strikes, then overshot. No.2 fired from 200 yards with a short burst and Diver went down, exploding on the ground near Appledore."

Wg Cdr Roly Beamont now got in on the action, shooting down two more, one of which he shared:

> "Saw Diver over Beachy Head at 3,400 feet. White 1 fired and missed, a Spit XII fired and no strikes seen, and the target went on unaffected. Closed 300 yards and fired long burst, closing to 150 yards, when the Diver exploded in blue and red flashes, blowing the Tempest on its back and damaging it. Headed for base and saw another Diver pursued by Tempests. Closed and fired three-seconds burst from 300 yards, slowing the Diver to 300mph. Fired again and target slowed to 200mph. Spit XII then fired and Diver crashed north of Hastings."

The next was shot down by Plt Off Slade-Betts:

> "Diver seen crossing in at Rye at 2,000 feet. Opened fire at 500 yards and saw strikes. Closed to 200 yards and tail blown off target with short burst. Diver crashed and exploded in a field north of Bexhill."

This was closely followed by another by Flt Lt Spike Umbers, his third for the day:

> "Target seen over Hastings at 3,000 feet. Dived down and opened fire at 500 yards but could not close. Fired several short bursts and saw strikes on wing and fuselage. Jet became intermittent and port wing root was burning. Target lost height. Chase had to be abandoned owing to proximity of balloons in Dunsford-Biggin area."

Flg Off Ray Clapperton recorded

> "Fired at F/Lt Umbers' target but missed. I went to Beachy Head and saw Diver come in at 2,500 feet. Chased and closed to 400 yards. Fired two bursts. Diver porpoised, went down and exploded in a field west of Hailsham."

The final kill of this very successful day went to Flt Sgt Morrie Rose:

> "Saw Diver over Beachy Head at 2,000 feet with another aircraft on its tail. Dived down and overshot, so throttled back, but on being told by No.1 to go in, closed to 200-300 yards. Fired from slightly below and Diver blew up over Beachy Head."

56 Squadron (Spitfire IX) Newchurch

Flt Lt P.L. Bateman-Jones	MK517/US-P	V-1	1925-2125	Channel

Flt Lt Bateman-Jones was on an evening convoy patrol when he intercepted and shot down a flying bomb, the Squadron's first such kill. Earlier in the day, during a dawn weather recce, Flt Sgts Artie Shaw (ML341/US-G) and Tony Drew (ML351/US-C) intercepted another Diver but although they fired at it, it continued its flight until shot down by a Tempest from 3 Squadron.

91 Squadron (Spitfire XIV) Deanland ALG

Cne J-M. Maridor (FF)	RB161/DL-I	V-1	1200	West Malling area
Sqn Ldr N.A. Kynaston	RB185/DL-	V-1	1420	London outskirts
Sqn Ldr P.McC. Bond	RB161/DL-I	V-1	1510	Croydon/West Malling
Flg Off A.R. Elcock	RB177/DL-J	V-1	1645-1750	West Malling
Flt Lt A. Smith RNZAF ⎫	RB173/DL-	V-1	2015	West Malling area
Flg Off R.A. McPhie RCAF ⎭	RB182/DL-V			
Sqn Ldr P.McC. Bond ⎫	RB161/DL-I			
Flt Lt R.S. Nash ⎪	RB169/DL-Q	V-1	2030	West Malling area
Flt Lt A. Smith RNZAF ⎪	RB173/DL-			
Flg Off R.A. McPhie RCAF ⎭	RB182/DL-V			
Flt Lt R.S. Nash ⎫	RB169/DL-Q	V-1	2040	Gravesend-London
Flt Lt A. Smith RNZAF ⎭	RB173/DL-			

Flg Off R.A. McPhie RCAF	RB182/DL-V	V-1	2210	Croydon area
Flt Lt R.S. Nash	RB169/DL-Q	V-1	2315	Beachy Head
	RB169/DL-Q	V-1 shared	2315-2350	
Sqn Ldr N.A. Kynaston	RB185/DL-	V-1	2320	off Dungeness

Cne Jean-Marie Maridor's kill was five miles north of West Malling. Flt Lt Ray Nash's solo victim exploded in mid-air over Beachy Head, while he shared his second with Tempests. Sqn Ldr Norman Kynaston exploded another in mid-air over Dungeness.

322 (Dutch) Squadron (Spitfire XIV) Hartford Bridge Flats

Flg Off R.F. Burgwal	VL-K	V-1	1530-1700	Hastings area
Flg Off L.M. Meijers	VL-	V-1	1530-1700	Hastings area
Flt Lt L.C.M. van Eendenburg ⎱	RB184/VL-B	V-1 shared	2230	Bexhill area
Flg Off R.F. van Daalen Wetters ⎰	VL-K			

The first anti-Diver patrol was flown at 1310 but without success. The Dutch pilots broke their duck during an afternoon patrol by Flg Off Loekie Meijers and Flg Off Rudi Burgwal:

> "Yellow 2 [Burgwal] saw two Divers travelling inland over Hastings at 1,000 feet. I attacked at 600 yards range. Diver exploded. Yellow 1 [Meijers] also saw Diver crossing the coast at Hastings at 2,000 feet. He attacked from quarter line astern, range 400 yards. Diver turned over and hit the ground at approximately R.2633."

A third Diver was shot down during an evening patrol. Flt Lt Kees van Eendenburg reported:

> "Vectored on Diver, later seen crossing coast one mile west of Bexhill at 1,500 feet travelling north. Attacked from 1,000 feet above, closing in to 400 yards. Broke off and No2 [Flg Off Rudi van Daalen Wetters] attacked from astern, range 600 yards. Both pilots saw big orange flame from Diver and pieces falling off. A Tempest came in and gave several long bursts, causing Diver to explode."

486 (RNZAF) Squadron (Tempest V) Newchurch

Flg Off W.A. Hart RNZAF	JN797/SA-K	V-1	0515	Le Tréport
Flg Off N.J. Powell RNZAF	JN804/SA-R	V-1	0615	off Dungeness
Flt Sgt O.D. Eagleson RNZAF	JN811/SA-Z	V-1	0910	Tonbridge
Plt Off R.J. Danzey RNZAF	JN797/SA-K	V-1	1015	Tonbridge
Flg Off J.G. Wilson RNZAF	JN809/SA-M	V-1 shared	1145	Dartford
Flt Lt V.St.C. Cooke RNZAF	JN801/SA-L	V-1 shared	1155	Ivychurch
Flt Sgt O.D. Eagleson RNZAF	JN804/SA-R	V-1	2040	Newchurch
	JN804/SA-R	V-1	2045	Rye
Flt Sgt B.M. Hall RNZAF	JN809/SA-M	V-1	2100	Sevenoaks
Flt Sgt R.J. Wright RNZAF	JN770/SA-V	V-1	2200	Mayfield
Flg Off J.R. Cullen RNZAF	JN758/SA-Y	V-1	2300	Rye
Flg Off S.S. Williams RNZAF	JN810/SA-P	V-1	2300	off North Foreland

Flg Off Bill Hart was on an early morning Channel patrol when he shot down the flying bomb, which crashed behind Le Tréport – at least one that would not trouble the defences. A second that failed to reach the coast was shot into the sea off Dungeness by Flg Off Pip Powell, while Flt Sgt Ginger Eagleson scored the Squadron's first double, the first falling five miles north of Newchurch airfield. Another to come down near the airfield was shot down by Flt Lt Vaughan Cooke, who was on an air test when the flying bomb suddenly emerged from cloud. He took up the chase and had a crack at it. One burst was sufficient and somewhat to his surprise the bomb turned slowly over in flight and flew along upside down for some distance before diving sharply to explode in a field. Plt Off Ray Danzey had a lucky escape when his target blew up following his attack, his Tempest returning scorched and soot-blackened from the explosion. Flg Off Woe Wilson was obliged to share his kill with a Tempest pilot from 3 Squadron.

142 Wing (Spitfire Vb) Horne ALG

Wg Cdr J.M. Checketts RNZAF	AB524/JM-C	V-1	am	Caterham area

356thFS/354thFG USAAF (P-51D) Lashenden ALG

1/Lt R.E. Turner USAAF	44-13561/AJ-T	V-1	am	Dover area
	44-13561/AJ-T	V-1	am	Calais-Dover

"In the early morning we ran a dive-bombing mission into France which was completed within two hours. On the return trip to base I hovered my flight in a loose orbit at 6,000 feet between Calais and Dover. With plenty of fuel and ammunition left, I was tempted to subtract a few buzz bombs from the many the Germans were sending over to terrorize London. I felt if we could pick them up over the Channel and dive on them, we stood a good chance of knocking them down since they were unable to evade us in any way. I sighted one below and dived on it, pulling out behind it but slightly out of range. I tried to close the distance, but the missile was just a little too fast. I chased the infernal machine for ten minutes alternately diving to gain speed, and pulling up to lob long range bursts at it. Eventually one of my bullets must have scored a chance hit in the engine, for suddenly it emitted a long streamer of yellow flame and lost speed quickly. In a curving dive, it plunged into a vacant field below where it exploded harmlessly. Encouraged by my success I proceeded back to the Channel area to pick up another. I began to wonder how I was going to get the next V-1, because most of my ammo was expended, and my gun barrels had burnt out. Soon I saw another one and made a very steep dive to gain extra overtaking speed. This bomb must have been moving more slowly than the first one, for I almost overran it as I pulled out of my dive. As I flew alongside the little monster I had a new idea. I knew they were controlled by a gyro guidance 'brain', and perhaps this mechanism could be upset without gunfire. I carefully edged close to it and placed my wingtip about a foot under its tiny fin. Rolling my plane suddenly neatly flipped the V-1 upside-down, and it promptly spun into the shallows of the Channel near the English shore where it blew a useless hole in the water. Jubilant with my success I flew back to Maidstone and hastened to tell the other pilots of the new pastime I had discovered."

Later that day the P-51Ds of the 354FG left their base at Lashenden for the Continent, landing at an ALG at Cricqueville (A.2) on the French coast, from where they were to operate henceforth.

365thFS/358thFG (P-47) High Halden

1/Lt L.C. Boze USAAF	CP-	V-1 shared	1650	High Halden area

1/Lt Leslie Boze was on a training flight when he spotted a Diver:

"I was in a good position to attack so with a minor manoeuvre I was dead astern. It was a fast one and I had to use full throttle and water injection (emergency boost) to stay with it. I fired and saw hits. We used armour-piercing incendiary bullets, which give off a brilliant flash upon impact. Meanwhile, a Typhoon [sic] came tearing in from the left in a curve of pursuit on the same V-1 firing 20mm right across my nose. I don't believe he ever saw me as he was in a left bank and I was in his blind spot. I saw that the V-1 was headed straight to the ground. The Typhoon [sic] was getting dangerously close so I dived just in time to witness the explosion of the V-1, not too far off the west end of the east-west runway. I don't know if the Typhoon [sic] hit it or not, but I'm convinced that bird was headed for the ground after my strikes. Anyway, we both claimed it. I never received an official confirmation. I don't know whether he did or not."[39]

It seems probable that the RAF fighter was a Spitfire rather than a Typhoon. 1/Lt Ralph G. Neas – a 367thFS pilot – recalled:

"A Spitfire shot down a V-1 right over High Halden and the bomb landed west of the field a mile or so. The Spitfire was close enough that when the bomb exploded it caused the Spitfire to lose its coolant. It made an emergency landing at our field. We flew the pilot back to his home field in our AT-6."

Fellow pilot 1/Lt Louis L. Wilson Jr added:

"I will always remember the incident of my stand-up bath in the old farm house there at High Halden. Someone had discovered a spigot of water (cold) in the bathroom. As always, we welcomed a bath and were taking turns. The floor was dirty, so we would put a big towel by the washbasin to stand on. When I was just about finished with my bath a loud swooshing noise went just over the roof. I thought it was a buzz bomb that had been shot down, and would explode when it hit the ground. So I hit the deck, naked, right in the middle of all that slimy dirt. No explosion! As I got sheepishly up and looked out the window a Spitfire, engine out, was dead-sticking it onto the runway. Apparently when he shot up the V-1, he flew through the blast, which killed his engine. He made a good landing, I re-bathed."

Another of the American pilots 1/Lt Harry M. Snell took a dislike to the newcomer:

"A British pilot in a Spitfire blew one up close to the field and got damaged from debris. He made a dead-stick landing which impressed me because at the intersection of the two runways, and just before touchdown, he turned that beautiful aircraft so as to land more into wind. I went out to congratulate the pilot as he walked in and found him to be a bit of a snob. A handkerchief protruded from the sleeve of his immaculate, tailored flying suit; his English flying boots beautifully shined. He sniffed as he looked at my muddy combat boots and rumpled GI clothes."[40]

513thFS/406thFG USAAF (P-47) Ashford ALG

1/Lt R.N. Walsh USAAF	L3-	V-1	Channel

Lt Ray 'Nobby' Walsh was credited by some with being the first USAAF fighter pilot to shoot down a Diver, but this was clearly not the case.

512thFS/406thFG USAAF (P-47) Ashford ALG

1/Lt L.E. Hayes USAAF ⎤	4P-	V-1	Ashford area
1/Lt E.F. Mayne USAAF ⎦	4P-		

Lts Lewis Hayes and Ed Mayne shared their target south of Ashford.

Night 18/19 JUNE

A flying bomb hit by AA fire crashed in Eastbourne during the early evening, demolishing many houses in Charleston Road, Milton Road and Mountney Road, and inflicting injuries to 41 residents, though none fatally. Eight Divers fell to night fighters, none to the guns. Young mother Mrs Joan Mansfield, married to an engineer at Hawkers, lived at Walton in Surrey, and recalled:

"It was a Sunday, just another Sunday, with a slight difference. Bren Carriers, manned by Canadians, were patrolling the streets, waiting to have a crack at the bugs as they flew over, hitting targets in Weybridge, sadly with loss of life. We thought we were lucky as the Doodlebugs were now passing over us. We breathed a sigh of relief each time the horrid engine kept going. Some of them were dropping in the river. I can remember my landlady and myself cheering[41]."

But one that fell in Bridge Street, Walton at 0025, killed three, seriously injured four and a further 27 suffered minor injuries.

96 Squadron (Mosquito XIII) West Malling

Flg Off J. Goode	HK406	V-1 damaged c2340	between Hastings
	HK406	V-1 damaged c2340	and Dover

Flt Sgt W.A. McLardy	HK453	V-1	2359	off Beachy Head
	HK453	V-1 damaged c2340		
Sqn Ldr R.N. Chudleigh	HK469	V-1	c0200	off Dungeness
	HK469	V-1 damaged c0200		
Sqn Ldr W.P. Green	MM495	V-1	0320	Hastings area
	MM495	V-1	0410	exploded in mid-air

Flg Off John Goode was credited with two damaged although he had claimed one of these destroyed, having had to break away when AA opened fire. Wt Off Bill McLardy got his first north-east of Beachy Head, but the second was credited even though the Diver was issuing clouds of black smoke when last seen. Sqn Ldr Dick Chudleigh saw his victim explode on impacting the sea off Dungeness, while Sqn Ldr Peter Green shot down his first ten miles north-west of Hastings, where it exploded on the ground, but debris from the second damaged the nose of the Mosquito following his attack from 300 yards range.

219 Squadron (Mosquito XVII) Bradwell Bay

| Sqn Ldr P.L. Burke | HK248 | V-1 | c0330 | Dungeness area |

Three crews from 219 engaged V-1s during their respective patrols, but only Sqn Ldr Pat Burke submitted a claim:

> "Projectile was seen going north-west at 2,000 feet off the French coast. Gave chase and dived from 7,000 feet, speed 330, and opened fire from 400-500 yards. Target continued into cloud. Control informed and minutes later I was informed target had crashed into the ground, Dungeness area at about 0330."

409 (RCAF) Squadron (Mosquito XIII) Hunsdon

| Flg Off C.J. Preece RCAF | MM547 | V-1 | 0050 | West Malling area |

> "As we took off to carry out a defensive patrol over the French beachhead, I noticed a pilotless plane approaching from the south at a height of 1,000 feet, travelling at an estimated speed of 220mph. I positioned myself and was able to get in a two-seconds burst from 150 yards astern as the Diver passed. The navigator saw strikes but as I had to bank to port to avoid the balloon barrage, we were unable to follow the fate of the enemy aircraft. It has been ascertained however the ROC reported a Diver crashed north-east of base at the approximate time of take-off, in the vicinity reported by us, and Balloon Command have confirmed that the crash was not due to balloon action. No anti-aircraft fire was in progress at the time."

605 Squadron (Mosquito VI) Manston

Flt Sgt John Little, Flt Lt John Rhodes' navigator in HJ776/UP-E, noted: "Diver patrol Calais-Boulogne-St Quentin. One pilotless aircraft seen and attacked but owing to our Navy opening fire on us at the same moment we were forced to turn off."

Monday 19 JUNE

It was announced by the British government that 526 people had lost their lives between 16-18 June as a result of the flying bomb assault. By the end of the first week up to 60 V-1s a day were reaching London. In this same period, up to 0600 on Monday morning, RAF day fighters had shot down 63 of the missiles, RAF night fighters a further 25, while USAAF fighters had scored 13 including one shared, AA guns 112, and the RAF Regiment a further two. At this stage, none had fallen to the balloons. A further 16 would fall to RAF fighters during the day, and only two to the guns. Just before 0800, a Diver landed in a cul-de-sac near Vicarage Farm Road, Heston in the Thames Valley. Many houses were damaged in the blast and three people killed, while others were injured. Another fell on Garden House in Benenden, Kent, killing the owner, a 78-year-old widow. One that reached South-East London at 1715 came down at Upper Crane Wharf, Rotherhithe (SE16) killing one person. Another was killed in Brockley (SE4) at 2206 following the explosion of a Diver at the junction of Dalrymple Road and Brockley Road.

Meanwhile, Dr Goebbels' propaganda machine enjoyed a heyday with spurious claims literally to put the fear of death into the British population, and to boost the morale of the German people. A Berlin radio station proclaimed:

"The thick oily clouds of black smoke that have been hanging over London during the past few days are proof of the effectiveness of the new German weapon [which were known to the German public as 'Dynamite Meteors' or 'Hell-Hounds']. There are fires everywhere between Kingston and Bromley and smoke miles high over Southampton and Portsmouth. The British government has given orders for the immediate evacuation of the population, and many trains with thousands of refugees are leaving for the north. The roads leading to London are also chocked with panic-stricken refugees. Seven million Londoners are today forced to resort to camping. Only a few have motors. Most take their pots and pans with them on hand-drawn carts and other improvised vehicles."

Another German radio station broadcasted in English:

"In London life has practically come to a standstill as the rain of secret weapons is continuing almost without interruption. Buckingham Palace has been badly damaged in these raids, but the Royal Family has suffered no injury because they had been evacuated to the safety of a secluded castle in Scotland."

And for the benefit of American listeners, Goebbels' propagandists continued fear mongering:

"The night before last the US Army suffered the heaviest casualties so far. One of the robot machines crashed into a railroad station in London and exploded just when the station was crowded with US soldiers. It has been estimated that between 3,000 and 4,000 US soldiers were killed. American Red Cross nurses have stated that some of the US soldiers were torn to pieces so badly that they could not be identified." The commentator went on to add that a new weapon being developed would eventually be used against New York, while an article in the German press concluded dramatically: *"A fiery circle has been drawn round the town [London] which has been fighting for days for its life against a terrible weapon of attack. In the centre of the town, at the bend of the Thames, fierce fires must be raging. A thin veil of clouds over London is coloured dark red ... in London the fires will never be extinguished."*

3 Squadron (Tempest V) Newchurch

Flg Off M.F. Edwards	JN752/JF-S	V-1	0725	Dungeness area
Flg Off R.E. Barckley	JN759/JF-	V-1	1455	Horley area
Flt Lt A.R. Moore	JN769/JF-G	V-1	1745-1905	exploded in mid-air
	JN769/JF-G	V-1	1745-1905	Tonbridge area
Flg Off G.E. Kosh	JN769/JF-G	V-1	2055	Lewes area
Wg Cdr R.P. Beamont	JN817/JF-H	V-1	2210	Tunbridge Wells area
Flg Off R.E. Barckley	JN768/JF-F	V-1	2145-2245	Biggin Hill area
Flt Lt A.R. Moore	JN755/JF-D	V-1	2310	Rye area
Plt Off S.B. Feldman (US)	JN752/JF-S	V-1	2300	Bexhill area
Plt Off S.B. Feldman (US) ⎫	JN752/JF-S	V-1	2315	Ashford area
Flg Off G.A. Whitman RCAF ⎬ (US) ⎭	JN759/JF-			
Flg Off G.A. Whitman RCAF (US)	JN759/JF-	V-1	2320	Cranbrook area

Flg Off Edwards scored in the morning:

"Put on to Diver above cloud over Dungeness at 2,000 feet. Closed to 150 yards and gave short burst. Strikes on starboard wing. It then dived through cloud, doing slow rolls and exploded on the ground three-four miles north-west of Dungeness."

Flg Off Bob Barckley:

"Saw Diver over Seaford at 1,000 feet. Chased, closed in and fired from 150 yards, having slowed it down with a burst from 600 yards. Saw strikes on jet and fired a further burst from slightly above at 50 yards. Diver went down in a wood west of Horley, where it exploded."

Flt Lt Moore scored a double:

"Vectored on to Diver which had crossed in west of Rye at 2,000 feet. Closed to 250 yards. Give a long burst and it slowed down to 160mph. Lost speed with difficulty and fired again from 100 yards. Diver blew up in the air. Returned to Rye and was put on another Diver, west of Hastings. Chased for ten miles and closed at 400mph. Gave a short burst from 150 yards, setting tail on fire. It lost height and crossed over a small town near Tonbridge, exploding on the ground."

A further seven would fall to the Tempests before midnight, Flg Off George Kosh getting the first of these just before 2100:

"Put on to Diver approaching Beachy Head. Closed to 400 yards, opened fire at 100 yards. Diver turned on its back and went straight down four miles east of Lewes."

Wg Cdr Beamont was up an hour later:

"Warned of a Diver coming in over Pevensey at 3,500 feet, and turned behind it as it was being chased by a Mustang which fired tracer below it. The Diver continued on a steady course and speed. When Mustang broke away, I gave a short burst from 250 yards and it went down over on its back and dived into wood two miles south-west of Tunbridge Wells."

Plt Off Barckley then got his second of the day, and Flt Lt Moore his third, before the two Americans Plt Off Buck Feldman and Flg Off Lefty Whitman provided a grand finale, Feldman reporting:

"I saw a Diver by the flames of its jet at a great distance. And orbited until it was below and then dived and gave short burst at 500 yards, closing to 200 yards with a long burst. Strikes seen and jet stopped. It spiralled gently and exploded in a park at Bexhill. Rejoined [with Whitman] and sighted another Diver ten miles south of Dungeness at 1,500 feet. Dived into line astern and fired two short bursts. Saw pieces fall off and Diver slowed."

Flg Off Whitman takes up the story:

"I then engaged the Diver at 200mph with a short burst from 500 yards. It spiralled down, exploding on the ground eight miles south-west of Ashford."

At this stage Feldman returned to base owing to a faulty radio, while Whitman continued patrolling alone:

"I saw a Diver at 3,000 feet at high speed. Closed and fired from 800 yards, observing strikes. Broke, and closed to line astern and fired another short burst from 300 yards, observing strikes. Red tracer was coming from behind me on starboard quarter and strikes seen (no claim made by other aircraft) and Diver went into a gentle dive and exploded on the ground at Cranbrook."

56 Squadron (Spitfire IX) Newchurch

| Flt Sgt J.E. Hughes | MK715/US-T | V-1 | 0450-0645 | Beachy Head area |

Flt Sgt Hughes' victim exploded in a wood north of Beachy Head.

91 Squadron (Spitfire XIV) Deanland ALG

| Lt H.F. de Bordas (FF) | NH654/DL- | V-1 | 1930 | Beachy Head |

Flt Lt J.W.P Draper RCAF	RM617/DL-G	V-1	1940	Tunbridge Wells
Flt Lt H.B. Moffett RCAF	NH701/DL-A	V-1	2155	Battle
Lt H.F. de Bordas (FF) ⎱	RB181/DL-	V-1	2230	Uckfield
Flg Off J.A. Faulkner RCAF ⎰	RM617/DL-G			
Flt Sgt G. Kay	RB188/DL-K	V-1 shared	2310	off Beachy Head

The flying bomb attacked by Flt Lt Bruce Moffett exploded and knocked off the propeller tip of his aircraft. Lt Henri de Bordas chased his victim inland from Beachy Head before destroying it. Flt Lt Moffett's victim may have been the one that crashed near Vines Cross, Horam, as noted by PC Max Soffner in his diary:

> "Good shot by fighter pilot. Hit in fuel tank, which exploded, and nose fell away. Fuselage jet tube came down undamaged. Warhead at Church Wood, Vines Cross and fuselage and jet propulsion unit at South View Farm."

322 (Dutch) Squadron (Spitfire XIV) Hartford Bridge Flats

Flg Off R.F. Burgwal	VL-D	V-1 shared	0545	Hailsham
Flg Off P.A. Cramerus	VL-	V-1	1830	Beachy Head-Hastings
Flg Off J.W. Dekker	VL-	V-1	2230	Beachy Head-Hastings
Flg Off G.F.J. Jongbloed	RB184/VL-B	V-1 shared	2145	Beachy Head-Hastings

Nine sections patrolled over Hailsham-Hastings-Beachy Head during the day. Flg Off Rudi Burgwal saw a Diver approaching from the south-east at 2,500 feet:

> "I opened fire and hit engine, causing the flying bomb to fall but it was then attacked by three Tempests, following which it exploded."

During the early evening Flg Off Piet Cramerus was vectored onto a flying bomb approaching between Beachy Head and Hastings:

> "Diving from 4,000 feet I caught up with it and gave two short bursts. The starboard wing fell off, causing it to spin to the ground where it exploded."

The missile attacked by Flg Off Jan Dekker exploded in mid-air following a long burst from dead astern, closing to 400 yards. The final kill of the day fell to Flg Off Jan Jongbloed, who sighted his target crossing the coast two miles west of Hastings at 3,000 feet:

> "I chased it for 20 minutes before I was able to close to 500 yards, getting several bursts from dead astern. At the same time another Spitfire attacked from the starboard side and the Diver exploded in mid-air."

Jongbloed was forced to land at Friston with engine trouble believed caused by pieces of debris puncturing the radiator.

332 (Norwegian) Squadron (Spitfire IX) Bognor Regis ALG

Sgt E. Veiersted	MJ253	V-1	c0630	over Channel

Six Spitfires took off at 0550 to carry out patrol over the Channel – four were recalled but the two others were ordered to investigate an incoming Diver, which was engaged by Sgt Elvind Veiersted. Following his attack the Diver exploded and damaged his aircraft, causing the engine to seize. The Norwegian baled out into the Channel, from where he was soon rescued.

486 (RNZAF) Squadron (Tempest V) Newchurch

Flg Off W.L. Miller RNZAF	JN811/SA-L	V-1	0625	Bexhill
Flg Off R.J. Cammock RNZAF[43]	JN810/SA-P	V-1	0630	Beachy Head

Plt Off J.H. Stafford RNZAF	JN803/SA-D	V-1	2037	Wrotham
Flt Lt H.N. Sweetman RNZAF	JN754/SA-A	V-1	2240	Hawkhurst
Flt Lt J.H. McCaw RNZAF	JN770/SA-V	V-1	2316	Dungeness

Not all pilots found the flying bombs easy to shoot down, Wt Off Jim Sheddan being one:

> "Sightings were frequent, interceptions difficult for although our ground speed was over 400mph our target was as fast, some of them faster and it was frustrating to have a flying bomb leave you floundering in its wake as it headed towards London. In warfare, tactics are never static. The bombs flew at 2,000 feet or lower, so the intercepting fighter had to be positioned another 2,000 feet above and directed onto its target by radar. In theory it seemed fool proof. In practice, in hurtling down at near the speed of sound, the bomb because of its dark colouring, was almost invisible against the ground and when seen, the attacker was almost on top of it and the closing speed was frightening. On one occasion, concentrating on the interception and at the same time checking the angle of dive in order to level out directly behind my victim, the bomb did not become visible until less than a hundred yards ahead. It was a case of the hunter becoming the hunted as my plane seemed intent on doing a first-class ramming job. All thought of shooting had vanished. There was only one way to miss that half ton of high explosives and that was to push the control column forward. The motor cut through being starved of fuel and at the same time my head hit the canopy top with a resounding bang. Another lesson learned the hard way, never fly with loose straps. It did not help to hear the plaintive voice of the controller complaining that I must have passed within a few feet of the bomb without seeing it. Somehow it did not appear to be my day."

381stFS/363rdFG USAAF (P-51B) Staplehurst ALG

| Capt J.B. Dalglish USAAF | 42-106769 | V-1 | 2205 | Penshurst area |

Capt James Dalglish and Lt Clifford Davis were scrambled to intercept approaching Divers, one being engaged by Dalglish, a five-victory ace from New York, who reported:

> "I was vectored on to rocket in Hastings area by Snackbar (code name for controller). When I first saw him, I was at 6,000 feet and the rocket at 1,500 feet. I dove past two Spitfires and a Mustang, which were firing at him, and closed on him indicating about 450mph. He was indicating 400 mph. Started firing from about 1,000 yards but did not register hits until at about 400 yards. Scored hits at both wing roots and he toppled to the right and went down in a descending turn, finally crashing in a wooded area near Penshurst. This occurred about 2205. Noticed nothing special about the Diver that I had not read in reports. There was a lot of torque in his slipstream."

514thFS/406thFG USAAF (P-47) Ashford ALG

| 1/Lt J.L. Billington USAAF | 43-25270 | V-1 | | Ashford area |

41 and 610 Squadrons with Spitfire XIIs and XIVs respectively arrived at West Malling to strengthen the anti-V-1 defences.

Night 19/20 JUNE
96 Squadron (Mosquito XIII) Ford

Flt Lt K. Kennedy	HK425/ZJ-	V-1	0012	off Beachy Head
Flt Lt B.A. Primavesi	HK497/ZJ-	V-1	0130	Beachy Head area
Flt Lt D.L. Ward	HK415/ZJ-R	V-1	0400	off Beachy Head

All three Divers fell in the Beachy Head area, the victims of Flt Lts Kennedy and Ward exploding on impact with the sea while Flt Lt Brian Primavesi's target exploded on land.

219 Squadron (Mosquito) Bradwell Bay

Plt Off A. Hollingsworth	HK254	V-1	0305-0525	

418 (RCAF) Squadron (Mosquito FBIV) Holmsley South

Flt Lt C.M. Jasper RCAF (US)[46]	HX811/TH-K	V-1	2230-0040	Channel
Sqn Ldr R. Bannock RCAF	HR147/TH-Z[47]	V-1	0035-0324	Channel

Sqn Ldr Russ Bannock recalled:

> "The first couple of nights, while we were on patrol at around 2,000 feet, we had no success because we were unable to obtain enough speed to close on the V-1. We then worked out a plan whereby we would patrol at 10,000 feet, wait until we saw a V-1 launched on the French coast, and then fly a course to intercept it around mid-Channel. We would then wait for the V-1 to arrive directly underneath. By diving from 10,000 feet, we could attain a speed of 430mph, which gave us about 40 seconds to close. On a clear night the launch from France was visible, producing a large flash, and then the V-1 trailed a long flame from the pulse-jet engine. Bob Bruce [Bannock's navigator] and I vividly recall the occasion when we came up behind the first V-1 that we intercepted from directly behind. Its pulse-jet engine streaming a long flame reminded us of looking straight into a blast furnace. After picking up some small debris from the first V-1, we learned to attack from an angle-off of about 30 degrees. Each one that we destroyed exploded with a vivid white flash, which would temporarily blind us until we pulled away from the explosion. There was always a secondary explosion when the V-1 hit the sea, which led us to conclude that only the fuel tanks exploded when hit with cannon and machine-gun fire and the warhead exploded when it hit the sea."

605 Squadron (Mosquito VI) Manston

Flt Lt A. Michie	UP-	V-1		off Folkestone

> "We were patrolling the Channel between Calais and Folkestone when we spotted the 'fire' from a Diver at about 2,500 feet. Our speed when we attacked was 290mph and after several bursts strikes were observed, followed by a flash and the Diver lost height and crashed into the sea off Folkestone. It continued to burn for a while. A second Diver was attacked later and strikes seen but Diver continued on course and was picked up by searchlights off English coast."

Tuesday 20 JUNE

Biggin Hill Balloon Centre snared its first flying bomb during the day, the missile falling harmlessly into an orchard. Biggin Hill had again become one of the capital's major areas of defence, housing almost 700 balloon personnel including more than 170 WAAFs. That evening, at 1832, a fighter shot down a Diver that crashed at Sutton-on-Hone, damaging 30 houses on Highland Hill and causing 16 casualties, of which four were serious.

3 Squadron (Tempest V) Newchurch

Flt Lt A.E. Umbers RNZAF	JN817/JF-H	V-1	0545	Redhill area
Plt Off S.B. Feldman (US)	JN761/JF-U	V-1	0840	Tonbridge area
Plt Off K.G. Slade-Betts	JN765/JF-K	V-1	0940	Eastbourne area
Plt Off H.R. Wingate	JN735/JF-X	V-1	1335	off Hastings
Wt Off R.S. Adcock RAAF	JN739/JF-W	V-1	1335	Beachy Head area
Plt Off S.B. Feldman (US)	JN735/JF-X	V-1	1905	Eastbourne area
Flg Off G.E. Kosh	JN765/JF-K	V-1	2050	Kenley/Biggin area
Flt Sgt D.M. Smith	JN752/JF-S	V-1	2200	Hastings area
Flg Off R.H. Clapperton	JN738/JF-	V-1	2320	Ashford area

The Tempest pilots added a further nine kills to their tally during the day, Flt Lt Spike Umbers and Plt Offs Buck Feldman and Ken Slade-Betts all scoring during morning patrols. An afternoon section comprising Plt Off Dickie Wingate and Wt Off Adcock also enjoyed success, each shooting down a Diver, the former's crashing into the sea, while the latter's exploded in mid-air:

> "Dived and closed in as it crossed the coast. Fired at 200 yards. Strikes on starboard wing. Closed to 100 yards, fired again and Diver exploded in the air. I flew through the debris."

41 Squadron (Spitfire XII) West Malling

Plt Off N.P. Gibbs	MB875/EB-G	V-1	1900-1940	Eastbourne area
Flg Off K.R. Curtis RCAF	EN229/EB-K	V-1	2050-2150	Battle area

During an evening patrol Plt Off Peter Gibbs saw a V-1 about 12 miles south of Beachy Head, flying at 3,000 feet. He pursued it and closed to 200 yards, whereupon it dived into the ground by the Eastbourne Road at Friston. Later that evening Flg Off Keith Curtis shot off the port wing of another, the bomb exploding near Battle.

91 Squadron (Spitfire XIV) Deanland ALG

Flt Sgt J.A. Brown	NH707/DL-	V-1	2240	Reigate area
Flg Off C.I.M. Ettles RCAF	RB161/DL-I	V-1 shared	2240	Bexhill area

Flg Off Colin Ettles shared his kill with Flt Lt McCaw of 486 Squadron.

322 (Dutch) Squadron (Spitfire XIV) West Malling

Flt Lt L.C.M. van Eendenburg	RB184/VL-B	V-1	1835	Swanley Junction

The Dutch squadron at Hartford Bridge Flats was ordered to take its Spitfire XIVs to West Malling, 18 aircraft departing for its new frontline base. Flt Lt 'Kees' van Eendenburg scored a victory that evening:

> "Patrolling Beachy Head at 5,000 feet when Diver crossed coast at 2,000 feet. Chased Diver and it changed course to go through a gap in the Balloon Barrage. I followed and caught up, giving a long burst at 600 yards. Pieces fell off including half the starboard wing. Diver fell to the ground and exploded three-quarters of a mile north-east of Swanley Junction."

332 (Norwegian) Squadron (Spitfire IX) Bognor Regis ALG

2/Lt H.R. Isachsen ⎫	AH-	V-1	c2100	Redhill
2/Lt O.G. Aanjesen ⎭	MA228/AH-			

The Norwegian squadron was off at 2000 to provide escort for 18 Lancasters tasked to bomb a target in France, but bad weather over the target area caused the operation to be cancelled and the Spitfires returned to base. On the return flight a Diver was observed at 4,500 feet three miles south of Redhill by 2/Lt Hans Isachsen and 2/Lt Ola Aanjesen, who attacked it jointly. It exploded in mid-air and a large piece of debris hit one of the Spitfires although it was able to land safely at base.

486 (RNZAF) Squadron (Tempest V) Newchurch

Plt Off R.J. Danzey RNZAF	JN801/SA-L	V-1	1000	Eastbourne area
Plt Off J.H. Stafford RNZAF	JN808/SA-	V-1	2205	Maidstone area
Flt Lt J.H. McCaw RNZAF	JN758/SA-Y	V-1 shared	2245	Hastings area

610 Squadron (Spitfire XIV) West Malling

Sqn Ldr R.A. Newbery	RB159/DW-D	V-1	1145-1245	Channel
Plt Off R.C. Hussey	DW-	V-1	2050-2155	Channel
Sqn Ldr R.A. Newbery	RB159/DW-D	V-1	2130-2215	Channel
Flt Lt J.B. Shepherd	DW-	V-1	2230-2310	Channel

365thFS/358thFG USAAF (P-47) High Halden

1/Lt D.W. Johnston USAAF	CP-	V-1	c.2300	mid-Channel

Thirty-six P-37s of the 358thFG carried out a late evening fighter-bomber strike against military traffic, road and railways in the Paris-Lâon area. The 365thFS bombed goods wagons in a siding near Beaumont and others at Moisselles. On the return flight a Diver was sighted but Capt Howard L. Gurley USAAF missed his opportunity:

> "I was leading a flight of four when we saw a rocket ahead and below us as we were over the Channel returning to High Halden. Being in the lead I signalled for line astern and down we went. I had the rocket in my gun sight, squeezed the trigger and nothing happened. I had failed to release the gun safety. After I pulled up to go over the rocket, the number 2 man [Lt David Johnston] destroyed it."

The Mosquito XIIIs of **96 Squadron** transferred from West Malling to Ford during the day, the ground crews following.

Night 20/21 JUNE

Two of the Divers that reached South London inflicted at least nine fatalities. One came down at 0103 at the junction of Petworth Street and Bolan Street (SW11), demolishing six houses and damaging a further 20, while the other hit a barrage balloon at 0229 and crashed into flats at the rear of Bradfield House, Wandsworth Road (SW11).

96 Squadron (Mosquito XIII) Ford

Flt Lt F.R.L. Mellersh	MM527/ZJ-	V-1	0035	off Dover
Wg Cdr E.D. Crew	MM449/ZJ-V	V-1	0200	Dungeness area

Flt Lt Togs Mellersh intercepted a Diver east of Dover, closed in to 1,000 feet and shot it down into the sea where it exploded, but Wg Cdr Ed Crew's victim crashed near Dungeness, exploding on impact.

219 Squadron (Mosquito XVII) Bradwell Bay

Flt Lt R. Davey	HK254	V-1 shared	2255-0135	into sea
Sqn Ldr G.M. Merrifield	HK362	V-1	0230	into sea
	HK362	V-1	0245	into sea

Flt Lt Davey had two chases but managed to engage only one at which he opened fire from 200-300 yards. Strikes were seen all over but as he closed in to deliver a final burst, another aircraft nipped in and shot it into the sea. Sqn Ldr Merrifield had a busy 15 minutes during which he had four chases:

> "On first chase nearly collided with another fighter which was chasing same target. Chase abandoned in favour of other fighter – the resins saved a collision. Another chase on Diver, height 4,000 feet. Opened fire at 500-600 feet range; strikes seen and target turned and dived to starboard, exploding on impact. Third chase broken off as another aircraft with nav lights on was dealing with it. Fourth chase: I turned my navigation lights on because of what had happened before. I saw another Diver at 4,000 feet, speed 240mph. Closed, firing range from 1,000-600 feet and opened fire. Port wing must have broken off as target dived quickly to port and exploded on impact."

409 (RCAF) Squadron (Mosquito XIII) Hunsdon

Sqn Ldr R.S. Jephson RCAF	MM510	V-1	0150	Dungeness area

Sqn Ldr Dick Jephson, a Canadian from Victoria, who had shot down a Ju88 ten days earlier, destroyed a Diver over the Channel:

> "At approximately 0147 we obtained a visual at ten miles in mid-Channel. I dived from 9,000 feet and delivered several bursts, seeing pieces fall off. Just as pilotless plane crossed the coast, I delivered a final burst. It seemed to descend on fire and we saw it explode on the ground near Dungeness."

418 (RCAF) Squadron (Mosquito FBVI) Holmsley South

Wt Off J.J.P. McGale RCAF	TH-	V-1 damaged 0027-0202		
Plt Off W.E. Bowhay RCAF	TH-	V-1	0138-0429	

605 Squadron (Mosquito VI) Manston

Flt Off B.F. Miller USAAF	UP-U	V-1	0029	off Eastbourne
Flt Lt G.C. Wright	UP-	V-1		
Flt Lt T.E. Knight	UP-	V-1		

Flt Off Bud Miller, an American junior officer seconded to the RAF for night fighter experience, reported:

> "0023 Diver sighted eight miles south-east of Le Touquet at 1,400 feet. Many short and one long burst from 600 yards. Finally target dived into sea at 0029 ten miles south-east of Eastbourne."

Wednesday 21 JUNE

Erith area received another Diver at 0525, which impacted at Southern Outfall, Cross Ness damaging seven houses in which four were killed and one seriously injured. A total of 48 people were injured, three seriously, when a Diver fell on Nuresey Avenue, Bexley at 0800, and there were further injuries following the explosions of bombs at Sidcup and Erith later in the morning. Addington Road, West Wickham, received a bomb at 0903, damaging 65 houses. One local person died in a public shelter. During the early afternoon an explosion between Queens Road and Clockhouse Road, Beckenham, killed three in addition to inflicting damage to 300 houses. A Croydon schoolmaster, Mr K.M. King, wrote in his journal:

> "During an 'alert' this afternoon, rather than go into the stifling shelter, I went into the school field, whence I could see the massed barrier of barrage balloons which is one of the expedients used to keep the things away from the London district. One of the flying bombs came into sight, streaking across the sky with an RAF plane in hot but ineffectual pursuit, and then I saw the bomb dive with a great explosion and a tall pillar of smoke and dust. It seemed to be in the direction of Grange Wood, and we heard later it fell in Ross Road."

3 Squadron (Tempest V) Newchurch

Flt Sgt R.W. Cole	JN760/JF-R	V-1	0545	Hastings area
	JN760/JF-R	V-1	0600	off Bexhill
Flt Lt A.R. Moore	JN818/JF-	V-1	0810	off Hastings

Flt Sgt Bob Cole added a brace to his tally, the first crashing in open ground ten miles north-west of Hastings. Fifteen minutes later he intercepted another, which exploded in the sea just off Hastings. Two hours later, Flt Lt Moore knocked down another into the sea, some 30 miles south of Hastings, confirmed by his No.2 Flt Sgt Morrie Rose.

41 Squadron (Spitfire XII) West Malling

Plt Off N.P. Gibbs	MB875/EB-G V-1	0745-0845	Hastings-Beachy Head

The Spitfire XIIs flew 19 patrols but only one flying bomb was shot down, Plt Off Peter Gibbs scoring his second kill, which fell between Hastings and Beachy Head.

91 Squadron (Spitfire XIV) Deanland ALG

Flg Off E. Topham	NH707/DL-	V-1	0640	West Malling area
Sqn Ldr P.McC. Bond	RB161/DL-I	V-1	0720	Channel

Flg Off Topham intercepted a Diver flying at 4,000 feet: "Attacked from astern, strikes seen and Diver fell through cloud. It exploded when it hit the ground near West Malling." Just under an hour later Sqn Ldr Peter Bond brought down a second, also engaged at a height of 4,000 feet: "Attacked from astern with two short bursts and Diver seen to fall into sea."

322 (Dutch) Squadron (Spitfire XIV) West Malling

Flt Sgt R.L. van Beers	VL-	V-1	dawn

486 (RNZAF) Squadron (Tempest V) Newchurch

Flg Off S.S. Williams RNZAF	JN866/SA-U	V-1	0645	Dungeness area

Night 21/22 JUNE

A barrage balloon sited at Horton Kirby near Dartford brought down a Diver at 0304, the bomb falling harmlessly in a cornfield. But one that crashed at the junction of Turney Road/Burbage Road in Herne Hill (SE24) destroyed or damaged almost 100 houses and killed four. Another killed six in Tulse Hill (SW2), exploding in Christchurch Road/Lanercos Road area, destroying and damaging 26 houses.

96 Squadron (Mosquito XIII) Ford

Sqn Ldr P.L. Caldwell	MM461	V-1	0340	off Dungeness
	MM461	V-1	0435	off Dungeness

219 Squadron (Mosquito XVII) Bradwell Bay

Flt Lt G.R.I. Parker	HK248	V-1	0001	off Dungeness

"Opened fire at 100 yards. Strikes seen. Pulled above as was overshooting and when in this position target exploded beneath, 10 miles south of Dungeness. It is believed another fighter was in the area."

418 (RCAF) Squadron (Mosquito FBVI) Holmsley South

Flg Off S.P. Seid RCAF	HR149/TH-R	V-1	2230-0146	exploded in mid-air

The Mosquito had its paint burnt off when the Diver exploded. Flg Off Sid Seid, an American Jew from California, was accompanied by Flg Off Dave McIntosh RCAF, who later wrote:

"We had a hell of a time shooting down our first flying bomb. First, we couldn't catch up with one, then we screamed after another before we could get a shot. When we finally hit one, we were much too close and the blast took all the paint off the Mosquito: This is how Sid reported to the Ops Room: 'Jaysyz. There we are going down like a stone in a well and my 'alligator' [navigator] sitting there with his balls in his mouth he's so scared and I'm fingering the tit to get ready for a burst when we go tearing by as if that goddam thing had stopped to let somebody off. Then my alligator lectures me on tactics. Back up we go with my alligator twitching like a dry leaf on the end of a dry twig in a dry wind because he's afraid a Jerry is going to crawl up our ass while we're trying to get up a Doodlebug's ass. Well, we spot another, though my alligator pretends he doesn't see it and says we should go home another way, like the three wise men. Down we go again. I don't know how you're supposed to tell how far away you are. I thought we were about three hundred yards away when I fired. Jaysyz, we weren't three yards away. I'm going to wear dark glasses at night after this.'"

On landing back at base, slightly overdue, they were greeted by a fellow pilot; McIntosh continued:

"A flashlight bobbed around under my wing, the door opened, a ladder came up and with it a blurred face. 'Where in hell have you been?' asked Hal. 'We got a Doodlebug.' 'What did you do, fly right up its ass?' asked Hal. I climbed down the ladder. Sid followed and took Hal's flashlight and played it on the wings and nose. There wasn't an inch of paint anywhere. The Mosquito was black. No roundel, no number, no letters, nothing."

605 Squadron (Mosquito VI) Manston

Flt Off B.F. Miller USAAF	UP-U	V-1

Thursday 22 JUNE

Ham Street was on the receiving end of a Diver shot down by a fighter at 0524, 100 houses sustaining damage while 13 villagers were injured, one seriously. One minute later a second Diver fell at Hall House, Hawkhurst, also the victim of a fighter. Local teenager W. Goodwin recalled:

> "I was still in bed when I heard a flying bomb and then the engine stopped and I heard an explosion. It had landed on the wall surrounding Hall House, demolishing the wall. Our roof tiles were ripped off and we were left looking up at the sky. One of my father's goats was tethered about 30 yards from where the V-1 landed, and when I went to see if she was all right, she was calmly grazing, with only a scratch on her nose. The pulse tube from the Doodlebug had been blown right over her head and had landed in the middle of the field."[50]

Eleven residents of Clapham (SW11) were killed following the explosion of a bomb in Stockwell Park Road at 0658. A second Diver came down in the same general area at 0845, killing one more. Peckham (SE15) was on the receiving end of a Diver that caused 23 deaths at 0850, many of them young female workers at a corset manufacturer in the Nunhead Lane/Peckham Rye area. Three people were killed in Penge (SE20) when a Diver fell on Crampton Road. Two more fell in the Dartford area at 1845, at Southfleet and Lullingstone, one the victim of a fighter. Another came down at the rear of Horton Kirby School. There were no injuries.

3 Squadron (Tempest V) Newchurch

Flt Lt A.E. Umbers RNZAF	JN817/JF-H	V-1	0430-0455
Plt Off H.R. Wingate	JN862/JF-Z	V-1	0450-0600
Flt Lt A.E. Umbers RNZAF	JN862/JF-Z	V-1	0800-0850
Wt Off F.McG. Reid	JN738	V-1	0800-0915
Sqn Ldr A.S. Dredge	JN812	V-1 shared	0855-094
Flg Off G.E. Kosh	JN815	V-1	1605-1740
Flg Off R.H. Clapperton	JN769	V-1	
Plt Off K.G. Slade-Betts	JN755	V-1	1955-2100
Flt Sgt M.J.A. Rose	JN738	V-1	1605-1740

Flt Sgt Pottinger: "W/O Reid shot one down over Romney Marshes near Ham and it landed on a farmhouse, the only building for miles. It killed the old couple in the house. Reid was terribly upset!"

41 Squadron (Spitfire XII) West Malling

Flt Lt C.R. Birbeck ⎱	MB841	V-1	0647	off Pevensey
Flg Off R.E. Anderson RAAF ⎰	MB837/EP-B			
Flt Sgt C.S. Robertson RAAF	MB875/EB-G	V-1 shared	1125-1222	Pevensey area

Flt Lt Clive Birbeck and Flg Off Bob Anderson jointly shot down their victim off Pevensey, Birberk noting: "Opened fire, closing to 150 yards. Hit port wing and Diver spiralled down, emitting flames and black smoke and crashed six miles off Pevensey at 0647." Later, Flt Sgt Colin Robertson also scored his kill off Pevensey, sharing it with a Tempest.

91 Squadron (Spitfire XIV) Deanland ALG

Flg Off K.R. Collier RAAF	RB188/DL-K	V-1	0540	Epsom area
Cne J-M. Maridor (FF)	RB180/DL-E	V-1 shared	0750	Bexhill area
	RB180/DL-E	V-1 shared	0800	Tunbridge Wells area
Flg Off C.I.M. Ettles RCAF	NH698/DL-F	V-1	1900	Gatwick area

Cne Jean-Marie Maridor's second kill probably shared with Wt Off Gus Hooper of 486 Squadron.

137 Squadron (Typhoon 1b) Manston

Although currently engaged on anti-shipping patrols, 137 Squadron was given permission to undertake V-1 interceptions as from this date, when other duties permitted. The Typhoon was a formidable interceptor at low altitude. The pilots soon got into their stride.

Plt Off K.G. Brain	MN191	V-1	0817	off Dungeness
Flt Lt D.G. Brandreth	MN584	V-1	0925	off Dungeness
Wt Off J.A. Horne RAAF	MN627	V-1	1100	off Dungeness
Plt Off K.G. Brain	MN191	V-1	1905	off Dungeness

Flt Lt Matt Wood and Plt Off Ken Brain were on anti-diver patrol off Dungeness when vectored onto an approaching flying bomb. Brain spotted it first at 3,000 feet, opened fire and shot it down into the sea, to open the squadron's account:

"I dived down on Diver, firing a burst from astern from 400 yards. No strikes were observed and the target disappeared under the nose of my aircraft. I pulled away and glimpsed Diver going down and almost immediately a big red flash and clouds of black smoke were seen on the sea by Flt Lt Wood."

He also reported that the Diver was "blackish grey with the top rear structure red." An hour later Flt Lt Brandreth caught another some three miles south-east of Dungeness and also shot this into the sea:

"I attacked from astern firing a long burst from one cannon (the other three would not fire) from 200-300 yards. Strikes were seen on the stern and the usual red glow suddenly developed into a long streak of flame and the Diver dived down, exploding on the sea."

A third flying bomb followed the other two to a watery grave when Wt Off Jack Horne sighted a target 20 miles out to sea, south-west of Dungeness:

"I attacked from astern firing two bursts of cannon from 200-250 yards, seeing flames coming from port wing. The Diver spun in, exploding in the water, blast being felt at 3,000 feet. The Diver was a rusty brown colour and a sheet of flame about 20 feet long was issuing from the stern before the attack."

Shortly before midday, Sqn Ldr Piltingsrud, the Norwegian CO, saw a Diver five miles off Hastings at 2,500 feet, but could not close the range. Pilots were finding the Typhoon wanting in speed at low level. Plt Off Brain was up again during the evening, flying as No.2 to Flt Lt Doug Brandreth. A Diver was sighted 15 miles south-east of Dungeness but they were unable to close on it. Brain then spotted another some four miles south-east of Eastbourne at 5,000 feet. He closed:

"A short burst from 600 yards was followed by a long one from 400 yards from astern. Strikes were seen on both port and starboard wings and the Diver spiralled down, exploding on the sea."

322 (Dutch) Squadron (Spitfire XIV) West Malling

Flt Lt J.L. Plesman	VL-	V-1	0440	exploded in mid-air
Flg Off C.R.R. Manders	VL-	V-1	0555	
Flg Off R.F. van Daalen Wetters	VL-	V-1	1906	

The first kill for the Dutch squadron fell to Flt Lt Jan Plesman[51]:

"Jan could see it moving beneath him on its steady course towards London. He pushed the joystick sharply forward, aligning the Spitfire with the V-1's flight path ahead of him. When he was about a thousand feet behind it he opened fire with his four cannon. He could clearly see the tracer of his ammunition moving over the stubby wings of the flying bomb; adroitly adjusting his own flight path, he saw the tracer enter the V-1. But oddly enough nothing happened and Jan felt utterly disappointed. He persisted, because he was still slightly gaining on the V-1, giving his engine full throttle in order to position himself for further attack. After the distance between the Spit and his quarry had shortened, he fired again. This time the bomb exploded into a big, bubbling ball of orange-red flames straight ahead of him. The resulting debris hurtled through the air, slowly, even majestically, fluttering to earth. His plane shuddered and vibrated madly from the conflagration's after-effects. He barely managed to keep the situation under control. Then he levelled off, and reduced engine power and speed to return to his base in an excellent mood."[52]

486 (RNZAF) Squadron (Tempest V) Newchurch

Flt Lt J.H. McCaw RNZAF	JN758/SA-Y	V-1	0500	Hastings/ Eastbourne
	JN808/SA-N	V-1	0540	Hastings/Rye area
Plt Off K. McCarthy RNZAF	JN801/SA-L	V-1	0555	Cherbourg area
Flg Off W.L. Miller RNZAF	JN794/SA-T	V-1	0600	Hastings area
Plt Off K. McCarthy RNZAF	JN801/SA-L	V-1	0630	Hastings area
Wt Off G.J.M. Hooper RNZAF	JN809/SA-M	V-1	0810 shared	Wrotham area
Flt Lt J.H. McCaw RNZAF	JN821/SA-H	V-1	0930	Newchurch area
Wt Off C.J. Sheddan RNZAF	JN809/SA-M	V-1	1040	in sea
Sqn Ldr J.H. Iremonger RAF	JN808/SA-N	V-1	1120	Crowborough area
Plt Off J.H. Stafford RNZAF	JN803/SA-D	V-1	1910	Battle area

Wt Off Gus Hooper shared his kill with a Spitfire (probably Cne Jean-Marie Maridor of 91 Squadron). Wt Off Jim Sheddan finally opened his account following many frustrating sorties:

"Success when it came was something of an anti-climax. A short chase, then as the dot of the reflector sight settled on the target, a burst of cannon fire and ball of flame. The explosion seemed to blow everything outwards thus forming a tunnel through which the pursuing fighter could safely pass."

610 Squadron (Spitfire XIV) West Malling

Flt Lt J.B. Shepherd ⎫	DW-	V-1	0520-0625	Channel
Flg Off G.M. McKinlay ⎭	RB142/DW-			
Sqn Ldr R.A. Newbery	RB159/DW-D	V-1	0540-0610	Channel
	RB159/DW-D	V-1	0700-0810	Channel
Wt Off R. Roberts	DW-	V-1	1000-1130	Channel

Night 22/23 JUNE

A balloon brought down a Diver at 0156, which caused damage to the RAF camp at Kingsdown. There were no injuries. Among others that reached South-East London, one impacted at 0212 between the junction of Hollydale and Stanbury Road (Peckham SE15), where three residents were killed, and another came down at 0215 in Brockley (SE4), where it killed three residents in the Ewhurst Road/Crofton Park Road area. At 0228, another fell in Carter Street, Walworth (SE17), where it destroyed five houses and killed ten residents. Another was hit by a fighter and crashed near Hope Cottage at Snargate at 0255, one occupant being slightly injured. At 0405, a Diver came down on Rosendale Road, Dulwich (SE22), killing four residents and destroying six houses. Six were killed in Rotherhithe (SE16) at 0413 when a Diver fell at the junction of Moodkee Street and Lower Road, where 23 houses were demolished or badly damaged. At just about the same time another Diver impacted on Greenland Dock (also Rotherhithe), where it struck the steamer SS *Tristram*, the bomb penetrating to the engine room, killing two seamen.

96 Squadron (Mosquito XIII) Ford

Sub Lt(A) W. Lawley-Wakelin RNVR	HK370	V-1	0200	off Beachy Head
Flt Sgt W.A. McLardy	HK433	V-1	c0300	Lympne area
Sqn Ldr R.N. Chudleigh	MM497	V-1	c0300	off Beachy Head
	MM497	V-1	c0300	off Beachy Head
Sqn Ldr W.P. Green	MM495	V-1	0352	off Friston
	MM495	V-1	0359	Worthing area
	MM495	V-1	0415	off Hastings
Flt Lt W.J. Gough	HK499	V-1	0430	Dungeness area

The FAA crew comprising Sub Lt(A) Bill Lawley-Wakelin and Sub Lt(A) Williams shot their victim into the sea some 15 miles off Beachy Head, followed by Flt Sgt McLardy catching a Diver as it approached Lympne. After a burst of fire, the Diver slowed down and lost height. A second burst caused it to dive to ground near Lympne, where it exploded. Sqn Ldr Dick Chudleigh shot both his victims into the sea between Beachy Head and Dungeness, while Sqn Ldr Paddy Green knocked down two into the sea and one on land, the latter impacting near Worthing. The final kill on this successful night fell to Flt Lt Bill Gough, his target gliding down to explode near Dungeness.

418 (RCAF) Squadron (Mosquito FBVI) Holmsley South

Wg Cdr A. Barker RAF	TH-	V-1	0001-0258	
Flg Off S.N. May RCAF	NS837/TH-L	V-1	0228	off Dieppe
	NS837/TH-L	V-1	0353	off Beachy Head
Flt Lt S.H.R. Cotterill RCAF	TH-	V-1	0126-0430	
	TH-	V-1	0126-0430	

Flt Lt Stan Cotterill from Toronto provided copy for a Canadian newspaper correspondent when he described a typical sortie:

"We used to stooge around, just out from the launching area in France. We were the first-line night fighter patrol. Sometimes we could see the actual launchings – a launching looks like a great half-moon of brilliant explosion. Then, when the thing came up, and it could be spotted by the steady glow from the rear end, we dived down vertically on them at full throttle. Several kites would line up on one bomb, and if the first one missed, then the others would go down for a try. After our dive on the thing we would level out and let go with a quick burst, and then if you were too close you'd be thrown all over the sky by the explosion, or flying debris would damage the machine. Sometimes, from a distance, we weren't always sure whether there was a Doodlebug or not, so we used to line up the light with a star, and then, if it moved, in we went."

Flg Off Newton May scored two kills during his patrol off Dieppe:

"At 0228 a Diver was attacked with three two-seconds burst of cannon. It exploded in the air and crashed in to the sea. At 0353 another Diver attacked with four-seconds burst of cannon and machine-gun, two miles south of Beachy Head. Diver exploded on crashing in to the sea."

150 Wing (Tempest V) Newchurch

Wg Cdr R.P. Beamont	EJ525/RB	V-1	night	Hastings area

"I took off for an experimental sortie from Newchurch and succeeded in intercepting and shooting down a V-1 north of Hastings, but it was an imprecise and hazardous occupation at first. The radar interception was made far easier than in daytime of course, by virtue of the fact that the brilliant flame of the pulse-jet could be seen at night for ten or fifteen miles in good weather, and all one had to do was to close at full throttle until at firing range. But here was the problem. With nothing to judge distance by except the light, which got progressively bigger and more dazzling, it was not easy to get into an effective firing range without suddenly over-shooting and possibly even running into the target. There was no way, at night, with eyeballs only, that you could judge your distance from a bright red flame which got brighter and brighter the nearer you got. I found that the best method was to approach the target from astern until we appeared to be within about 1,000 yards and then to descend below it until in a relative position of approximately 100 feet below and 300 yards behind. This could be judged reasonably well by looking up through the transparent canopy and over the top of the windscreen arch. From this situation a gentle climb was made into the dead astern position until preferably the wake of the V-1 was felt in the Tempest and then with the gunsight centred directly on the exhaust flames, a long burst was generally enough to deal with it. That blinding condition would get worse if you exploded the V-1. It was a very exciting experience. Later, the RAE came out with a brilliant stereoscopic device. The pilot would look through his normal gunsight but instead of seeing one bright light he'd see two, and as he drew closer the lights would come together. When they touched he would open fire. That worked."

FIU (Mosquito VIII) Manston

Flt Lt A.D. Wagner	ZQ-	V-1		near Bourges

Friday 23 JUNE

Dr Goebbels (Hitler's Chief of Propaganda) chose this day to make another statement about the V-1 assault to the German press:

"The effect of our bombardment is caused by its uninterrupted duration ... I can imagine that this, apart from all real damage, is slowly getting on everyone's nerves. It is like having a toothache. The pain itself is perhaps not too severe. But when it is gnawing and throbbing in the tooth continuously, day and night, a person thinks he will go mad, he cannot form a clear idea, he does not think of anything but this damned pain."

Eighty houses were damaged in Dartford by a Diver that fell at 0810, inflicting minor injuries to five people. One person was killed near Mill Place, Yalding when a Diver crashed after being shot by a fighter at 1630. A balloon brought down another at 1733, the bomb crashing in Brands Hatch Road, Falkham, where two houses were damaged and three people slightly hurt. A Diver that impacted on Charlton Junction Railway Station killed four civilians including the signalman's wife. The village of Smarden in Kent was hit again at 2103 when a Diver exploded after being shot down by a fighter, injuring two people. A Diver shot down by a fighter at East Peckham near Malling at 2115 slightly injured three, but surprisingly there were no casualties when another victim of the fighters crashed at Laddingford near Yalding at 2255, damaging 22 houses, two seriously. Sidcup received two Divers during the day, at least 30 injuries being reported of which 13 were of a serious nature. A worse incident occurred at 1837, when a Diver fell on Gipsy Road, Welling, killing ten, seriously injuring a dozen, with a further 45 suffering minor injuries. Nine residents were killed in Beechdale Road, Brixton (SW2), where 32 houses were destroyed or damaged, while the bomb that fell on Battersea (SW11) killed six and demolished eight houses in Honeywell Road/Broomwood Road. Four more died in Westfield Road, Beckenham.

3 Squadron (Tempest V) Newchurch

Flt Lt R. van Lierde (Belg)	JN862/JF-Z	V-1 shared	0459	Hastings area
	JN862/JF-Z	V-1	0509	Grid R.1941
	JN862/JF-Z	V-1	0520	off Hastings
Flt Sgt R.W. Pottinger	JN760/JF-R	V-1	0645	Grid Q.9171
Plt Off K.G. Slade-Betts	JN815/JF-	V-1	1630	Appledore area
Flt Sgt M.J.A. Rose	JN865/JF-	V-1	1650	Grid R.1661

Wg Cdr R.P. Beamont	JN751/JF-M	V-1	1709	Grid Q.9369
Flg Off G.A. Whitman RCAF⎱	JN743/JF-P	V-1	1830	Grid Q.99 area
(US) ⎰				
Flt Sgt J.W. Foster	JN760/JF-R			
Sqn Ldr A.S. Dredge	JN812/JF-	V-1	2058	Biddenden Green area
Flt Sgt H.J. Bailey RAAF	JN761/JF-U	V-1	2103	Grid R.1466
Flt Sgt D.J. Mackerras RAAF	JN752/JF-S	V-1	2104	Grid Q.9969
Flt Lt R. van Lierde (Belg)	JN862/JF-Z	V-1 shared	2240	Beachy Head
Flt Sgt R.W. Cole	JN768/JF-F	V-1 shared	2305	Hastings area
Wg Cdr R.P. Beamont ⎱	EJ525/RB	V-1	2315	Hastings area
Flt Lt R. van Lierde (Belg)⎰	JN862/JF-Z			
Flt Sgt R.W. Cole	JN768/JF-F			
Flt Sgt H.J. Bailey RAAF ⎱	JN761/JF-U	V-1	2335	Newchurch area
Plt Off S.B. Feldman (US)⎰	JN793/JF-N			

Flt Lt Remi van Lierde enjoyed an early morning anti-Diver patrol, shooting down three, one of which he shared:

> "Chased Diver over Bexhill area at 2,000 feet. Had to break inland owing to flak. Returned four miles south of Beachy Head and intercepted another Diver approaching Hastings with P/O Danzey of 486 Squadron, firing from long range. As P/O Danzey broke to port, I fired two bursts and saw strikes on the port side of target, which dived steeply and exploded on the ground at 0459. Claimed as shared destroyed with P/O Danzey. Put on to another Diver off Beachy Head at 2,000 feet, speed 340mph. As I was about to open fire, a Spitfire popped up in front and engaged target until all its ammunition was exhausted. No strikes were seen and Diver continued on its course. I closed in and gave several short bursts, which caused Diver to dive in and explode on the ground. Returned to Hastings and saw another Diver approaching off shore. Fired deflection shot but missed, then fired two bursts from astern and saw many strikes. Had to break as a convoy opened fire, then engaged again and Diver crashed, exploding in the sea between the convoy and Hastings."

An hour later, Flt Sgt Ron Pottinger was the next to score:

> "Sighted Diver one mile south of Hastings at 3,500 feet. Closed to 400 yards after several long bursts and shot off port wing. Diver's petrol tank caught fire and Diver turned over and dived in. It was not seen to hit the ground, as evasive action had to be taken from the petrol flames, but the position was fixed by Biggin Hill and this corresponds with an ROC report of a Diver which exploded on the ground at Q.9369 at the relevant time."

There followed a lull before the next wave of Divers came in, two falling in quick time to Plt Off Ken Slade-Betts (at 1639) and Flt Sgt Morrie Rose ten minutes later. Unfortunately, the first of these two crashed onto a small house on the outskirts of a village near Appledore. Both Tempests developed engine problems, which caused them to return early, Slade-Betts belly-landing with a glycol leak at Woodchurch ALG, while Rose force-landed JN865 at Brenzett. Neither was hurt. Wg Cdr Beamont increased his total when he shot down another at 1709:

> "A Diver was sighted one mile off Hastings with two Spitfires in pursuit. First Spitfire opened fire in the Tonbridge area without strikes being seen. I then came in to 400 yards range and fired without result. I closed range to 100 yards and a short burst caused the jet to go out and the Diver to spin in and explode in a wood to the west of Tonbridge."

Sqn Ldr Alan Dredge also shot down one, his victim reported to have crashed into a spinney near Biddenden Green. The next fell to the combined fire of Flg Off Lefty Whitman and Flt Sgt John Foster, their victim crashing two miles north of the balloon barrage inland from Rye. The Australian pairing of Flt Sgts Bert Bailey and Don

Mackerras accounted for two more during their patrol, claiming within minutes of each other.

The Tempests had by now brought down 11 during the day with one shared. More were to follow before midnight, Wg Cdr Beamont sharing another with Flt Lt van Lierde, which crashed just north of Hastings, the Belgian sharing a second with a New Zealand pilot of 486 Squadron (Flg Off Jimmy Cullen), reporting that it crashed on the top of Beachy Head. The final successes fell to Flt Sgt Bob Cole, Flt Sgt Bailey and Plt Off Buck Feldman, who took off as a section from Newchurch just before 2300. Cole reported:

"At 2305, I fired a short burst at a Diver at 3,000 feet as it approached Hastings from out to sea. As soon as it crossed the town I fired again from 150 yards and strikes were seen. Another aircraft attacked from starboard and above, causing me to break. Two other aircraft then fired and Diver crashed and exploded two miles north of Hastings. I saw another Diver at 3,000 feet, speed 400mph-plus, and dived down and fired from 250 yards, causing jet to stop jetting temporarily. Diver slowed down and F/Sgt Bailey and P/O Feldman then attacked. The target went slower still and eventually went in and exploded two miles north of Newchurch. This was confirmed by ground observation from Newchurch airfield."

41 Squadron (Spitfire XII) West Malling

Flt Lt T.A.H. Slack	EB-	V-1 shared	0450	Hastings area
Plt Off J.C.J. Payne	EB-	V-1	0840	Rye area
Flg Off M.A.L. Balaase (Belg)	MB830/EB-	V-1 probable	0830	Hastings area
Flt Lt T. Spencer	MB856/EB-X	V-1	2302	Hastings area

Flt Lt Tom Slack reported that he was first to attack a Diver at 0455 near Hastings, and carried out a second attack but four Tempests intervened, and the bomb was shot down. Plt Off Jimmy Payne and Flg Off Maurice 'Mono' Balaase took off on another patrol at 0800, Payne reporting that his victim exploded following his brief attack, while Balaase's target disappeared into 10/10 cloud with flames coming out of its fuselage, and was awarded a probable since it was not seen to crash. He was then obliged to crash land west of Farley due to fuel shortage; his aircraft was written-off and the Belgian pilot slightly injured. Flt Lt Terry Spencer shot down his victim at dusk north of Hastings:

"At 2302 I fired three bursts of five-seconds each at 350-200 yards. Bomb turned to starboard and blew up on the ground 10-15 miles north-north-east of Hastings. Two Tempests came alongside, overtaking and opening fire."

91 Squadron (Spitfire XIV) Deanland ALG

Flt Lt R.H. Dibnah RCAF	RB173/DL-	V-1	0655	Tonbridge area
Flt Sgt T.B. Burnett	RB174/DL-T	V-1	0655	Sevenoaks area
Flg Off G.H. Huntley	RB181/DL-	V-1 shared	0710	Tunbridge Wells area
Flt Sgt G. Kay	RB165/DL-	V-1	1630	West Malling area
Wg Cdr R.W. Oxspring	NH714/RWO	V-1 shared	1700	Redhill-Edenbridge
Sqn Ldr N.A. Kynaston	RB185/DL-	V-1	1725	Hastings area
	RB185/DL-	V-1	1740	Eastbourne area
Flt Lt H.D. Johnson	RB188/DL-K	V-1 shared	1745	Uckfield area
Flt Sgt G. Kay	RB165/DL-	V-1 shared	1840	Hastings area
Flg Off J.A. Faulkner RCAF	RM617/DL-G	V-1 shared	2125	East Grinstead area
Flg Off K.R. Collier RAAF	NM698/DL-	V-1	2240	East Grinstead area

Several of the squadron's kills were shared with other units, Flg Off Huntley's at 0710 with a Tempest, while Wg Cdr Bobby Oxspring shared with a Tempest and another Spitfire at 1700 between Redhill and Edenbridge. However, Oxspring wrote later that his victim had crashed near Battersea power station:

> "My first encounter occurred at Maidstone, and as I curved after my target I underestimated its speed and found myself in a stern chase. Very slowly I reduced the range until able to fire, and as I did so bits flew off the rear end and the craft plummeted down. Concentrating on the action, I had not kept track of my position until I saw, to my consternation, my target explode on a Nissen hut in the bounds of Battersea power station. The hut disintegrated but I afterwards heard, to my relief, that there were no casualties."

Both Flt Lt Johnny Johnson and Flg Off John Faulkner shared their targets with a Tempest (Flg Off Ray Cammock of 486 Squadron) and a Tempest and a Spitfire respectively, Flt Sgt Geoff Kay also sharing with a Tempest. Flg Off Ken Collier became the first Spitfire pilot to destroy a Diver without firing a shot. He had exhausted his ammunition so placed his wingtip under that of the flying bomb and tipped it over, whereupon it crashed near East Grinstead. The squadron diarist commented:

> "Collier's effort was a clear case of determination crowned at the last moment with success. He came across this particular Diver just after it had crossed over Beachy, and immediately gave chase. Getting within range, he fired, with no apparent effect as it carried straight on. This peeved him somewhat, so he had another go, and in fact several goes, but still nothing happened, and what was worse he ran clean out of ammo. By this time Ken was swearing mad, and was determined to do or die. He therefore formated with it, and with his wing, tipped it over. On his second attempt down it went into a tight spin, but it very nearly landed in the centre of a town. However, it did no damage, and Flg Off Collier thus brought into practice a new method of getting rid of these flying bombs."

The incident was reported in the local newspaper:

> "Quick thinking and cool courage on the part of a fighter pilot probably saved serious casualties from a flying bomb in Southern England on Friday evening. The flying bomb had been attacked and the engine silenced when one of the pursuing pilots, sensing that it was likely to fall and hit some houses, manoeuvred his plane close to it and diverted it from its course by tipping its wing. As a result, the bomb dropped into some gardens at the rear of an old peoples' home. Although the blast smashed all the windows of the place and did structural damage, none of the residents were hurt, apart from some cases of shock."

137 Squadron (Typhoon 1b) Manston

During a morning patrol by Flg Off L. Walker and Flg Off M.J.B. Cole two bombs were seen but the pilots could not close range. Walker gave one a short burst from long range before it entered cloud, but saw no results. In the afternoon Wt Off Horne pursued one at 395mph, but it got away and was last seen flying inland at 3,000 feet. An early evening patrol was similarly frustrated. Wt Off Jimmy Shemeld and Plt Off Gates could only get within 1,000-1,250 yards of the bomb they pursued, firing from long range before it outpaced them. However, they had the satisfaction of seeing it shot down by AA guns north-east of Rye. Flg Off Artie Sames returned from a late patrol without adding to his score. He had chased one Diver towards the balloon barrage, firing at it from 800 yards without result. He broke away to avoid entering the restricted zone but saw a Spitfire continuing the chase. Sames then spotted another and fired at this from 800 yards, again without result, and was forced to break away when shore guns opened up.

The Typhoons also suffered from interference by over-zealous American pilots, as admitted by 1/Lt Frank L. Buckio USAAF, a P-47 pilot with the 367thFS based at High Halden:

"[1/Lt] John Pedigo in CP-J and I in CP-Q had had some major maintenance requiring test hops. We took off together and were lazily flying along when we ran into a couple of Brit Typhoons. We tried to engage for a little fun but they wouldn't play. So we just got in trail with them doing 'lazy-eights' over Dover. All at once the lead Typhoon rolled over on his back and started straight down. We were at 12,000 feet. All at once we realised what was happening. They had been waiting for a V-1 and had obviously been called and vectored onto the incoming missile at 3,000 feet. The altitude difference of course was to allow them to build up enough speed to intercept it. John and I followed them down to join the chase. Soon with our superior downhill speed we had caught up and passed them and the V-1. All we saw was some flak. London came up fast and we had to break off, not only because it was restricted but also encumbered with balloons. When we landed they [the authorities] were waiting for us. They had our letters (CP-Q and CP-J) and said we had interfered with the Brits. I guess we were lucky not to get court-martialled. But our intentions were good. We were only trying to help."[53]

165 Squadron (Spitfire) Detling

Flt Lt A.C.W. Holland	ML204/SK-N	V-1	2045	Rye area
Flg Off T.A. Vance RAAF	MK638/SK-B	V-1	2050	Redhill area
	MK638/SK-B	V-1 shared	2110	Beachy Head
Sqn Ldr M.E. Blackstone	MK425/SK-V	V-1	2220	Wimbledon Common
Lt(A) S.G. Hamblett RNVR[54]	MK426/SK-D	V-1	2220	Hailsham area
Flt Sgt R.J. Hughes RAAF	MK426/SK-D	V-1	2330	Dungeness area

165 Squadron entered the fray during the evening, when Malta veteran Flt Lt Tony Holland shot down a Diver that crashed near a railway line:

"I saw the bomb travelling north-west and picked it up one mile out to sea. IAS of bomb 300mph. Attacked and target fell west of Rye."

This was followed by another falling to the guns of Australian Flg Off Tommy Vance, which came down south of Redhill, before he spotted a second that had been damaged by a Tempest. Opening fire on this, he was rewarded with the satisfaction of witnessing it explode in the air:

"I picked up my [first] target between Redhill and Hastings. Seen to crash south of Redhill. Picked up a second target over Beachy Head. Exploded in the air north of Tonbridge. A piece of cable about five feet in length, similar to an aerial cable, caught round the mirror of my aircraft."

Sqn Ldr Maurice Blackstone[55] possibly got one at 2220:

"I picked up Diver, which was on a north-westerly course, at Beachy Head and gave chase with many other aircraft. After three minutes I was the only fighter left but could not close. IAS of Diver was 375mph at 2,500-3,000 feet. I chased for about ten minutes when light went out. As it slowed up I closed and fired without effect. Pulled away and as it was heading for open ground decided to try and explode it in the air, away from populated areas. Again saw no strikes. Pulled away and on looking again could not see target. Orbited but nothing seen. I only advance this claim subject to confirmation from ground observers that the bomb dived in as I was not in a position to see the final destruction myself. The position was finally in the vicinity of Wimbledon Common."

The CO's claim was later confirmed by the ROC and other ground observers. Another was intercepted at the same time by Lt(A) Selwyn Hamblett RNVR, the Squadron's seconded FAA pilot:

"Saw Diver coming in over Beachy Head. Gave chase, firing several bursts. Had no difficulty in keeping up. Passed over houses and decided to wait until over open country. Once clear of houses gave another burst, seeing several strikes on the tail end. The Diver pulled up steeply and I broke away. On looking again the Diver was seen to dive into the ground and exploded slightly north of Hailsham and 150 yards from a house."

An hour later Flt Sgt Hughes shot down the last one for the day: "Bomb came in slightly to the east of Dungeness. I attacked and it exploded in a wood." It was seen to crash by Flg Off Vance. The successes were marred by the loss of the Squadron's gallant 37-year-old French one-legged pilot Wt Off Albert Zevaco-Lamour[56], whose Spitfire MK738/SK-L crashed two or three miles south-east of Canterbury – believed to have been another victim of AA fire.

322 (Dutch) Squadron (Spitfire XIV) West Malling

Flg Off J. van Arkel ⎱	VL-V	V-1	2145	Tonbridge area
Flg Off M.L. van Bergen ⎰	VL-N			
Maj K.C. Kuhlmann SAAF	NH586/VL-G	V-1	2230	

486 (RNZAF) Squadron (Tempest V) Newchurch

Plt Off R.J. Danzey RNZAF	JN797/SA-K	V-1	0430	exploded on ground
	JN797/SA-K	V-1 shared	0459	Hastings area
Plt Off F.B. Lawless RNZAF	JN859/SA-S	V-1	0513	Hastings area
Flt Sgt B.M. Hall RNZAF	JN809/SA-M	V-1	0600	Battle area
Plt Off K. McCarthy RNZAF	JN754/SA-A	V-1	1515	Willingdon area
	JN754/SA-A	V-1	1610	Newchurch area
Flt Sgt O.D. Eagleson RNZAF	JN794/SA-T	V-1	1705	Uxbridge/East Hoathly
Flg Off W.L. Miller RNZAF	JN808/SA-N	V-1	1735	Hastings area
Flg Off R.J. Cammock RNZAF	JN810/SA-P	V-1 shared	1745	Pevensey Bay area
Flg Off W.L. Miller RNZAF	JN808/SA-N	V-1	1810	Pevensey Bay area
Wt Off C.J. Sheddan RNZAF	JN801/SA-L	V-1	2105	Sevenoaks area
Wt Off S.J. Short RNZAF	JN810/SA-P	V-1	2110	Beachy Head area
Flt Sgt O.D. Eagleson RNZAF	JN794/SA-T	V-1 shared	2120	Beachy Head area
Flg Off J.R. Cullen RNZAF	JN770/SA-V	V-1 shared	2250	Beachy Head area
Wt Off W.A. Kalka RNZAF	JN801/SA-L	V-1	2255	Newchurch area
Flg Off R.J. Cammock RNZAF	JN810/SA-P	V-1	2310	Edenbridge area

Flg Off Ray Cammock shared his kill with a Spitfire of 91 Squadron flown by Flg Off Johnny Johnson. The bomb had already been damaged when Cammock saw that it was probably going to fall on Hastings. He dived after it and succeeded in exploding it just before it made the final plunge earthwards. Flt Sgt Owen Eagleson saw another Diver that had been damaged by a Spitfire glide directly towards a small village north of Eastbourne. He followed it down, fired and exploded it in mid-air before it could do any harm. Plt Off Danzey shared with Flt Lt van Lierde of 3 Squadron.

610 Squadron (Spitfire XIV) West Malling

Sqn Ldr R.A. Newbery	RB159/DW-D	V-1 shared	0440-0520	Channel
Flg Off S.A. Jones ⎱	DW-			
Plt Off B.R. Scamen RCAF ⎰	DW-	V-1	1535-1640	Channel
Wt Off R. Roberts	DW-	V-1 damaged	2005-2110	

Sqn Ldr Bob Newbery shared his victory with a Tempest, as did Flg Off Stan Jones DFM and Plt Off Brian Scamen[57] later in the day. Wt Off Roberts reported damaging a Diver during his 2005-2110 patrol but did not see it crash.

358thFG (P-47) High Halden

A Diver impacted on High Halden ALG at 2105. There were no casualties on the ground although several Americans received a scare, as recalled by Lt Ralph F. Palaia, 367thFS Assistant Intelligence Officer:

"Captain Henry Banke and I were walking across a field near Group HQ when we saw a buzz bomb dive towards the ground. We ran one way and the bomb followed us. We then ran toward a ditch and it too changed course. We finally dove into the nearby ditch just as the bomb struck and exploded a few hundred yards away. It was this bomb that blew out the windows in the headquarters building."

Sgt George C. Long, an armourer, added:

"We had one buzz bomb fall near the base and fairly close to the officers' barracks. You should have seen those officers come out of that barracks. It looked like a bunch of ducks heading for a June-bug convention."

Night 23/24 JUNE

Residents on the Isle of Wight suddenly found themselves in the firing line again, when the first Divers appeared in the night sky. Jock Leal, a local ROC spotter, recalled:

"After a day-long Diver alert, the air raid warning at 10.26 pm was followed by plots of a V-1 which crashed in the Petersfield area, and after further alerts came the sound we were going to hear so often again. This Diver was off the east of the island. We sent the dockyard workers at Cowes to shelter as it roared up Spithead. Fog prevented us from seeing it but we had it placed somewhere near Calshot when the engine started to splutter. For a few seconds silence followed. Then came an explosion. It had crashed at Marchwood, near Southampton."[59]

At 2301, a victim of a night fighter crashed at Rheewall Farm near Brenzett, slightly injuring six persons in a nearby cottage.

219 Squadron (Mosquito XVII) Bradwell Bay

Flt Lt F.E. Clarke	HK260	V-1	2300-0140	Dungeness area

Flt Lt Clarke intercepted a Diver approaching Dungeness and dived down from 8,000 feet. He opened fire from 400 yards, strikes were seen and target crashed inland west of Dungeness.

264 Squadron (Mosquito XIII) Hartford Bridge

Flt Lt J.B. Fox	HK480/PS-	V-1	0052	over sea (also FTR)

Flt Lt John Fox and Plt Off Cliff Pryor's Mosquito FTR; the Mosquito was believed to have been brought down by the explosion of the Diver they were attacking. They were last heard from at 0052.

418 (RCAF) Squadron (Mosquito FBVI) Holmsley South

Flt Lt C.J. Evans RCAF	TH-	V-1	2238-0215	Channel
	TH-	V-1	2238-0215	Channel
	TH-	V-1	2238-0215	Channel
Sqn Ldr E.R.McGill RCAF	TH-	V-1	0129	Channel
Plt Off W.E. Bowhay RCAF[60]	TH-	V-1	2355-0337	Rouen area

After shooting down one Diver, Flt Lt Colin Evans tackled another in mid-Channel. He ran in close and fired and the bomb blew up, blinding him by the blast and debris, knocking out one of his engines. Then, soon after he had regained control of his stricken machine and his sight, he spotted a third bomb and swung in to shoot it down. Of his kill, Plt Off Bill Bowhay reported:

"I went into a shallow dive reaching 360mph. Gave it a short burst from astern and saw strikes. Broke away. Returned, finding it had lost height. Closed to 200 yards, firing two-seconds burst at 50 yards. Diver headed northwards and caused a bright orange flash as it struck the ground three-and-a-half miles north-west of Rouen."

Sqn Ldr Edward McGill reported seeing a large number of amber flares being dropped five miles north of Dieppe during the early stage of his patrol. Then, at 0129, when 20 miles off Le Tréport, he intercepted a Diver: "Fired three one-second bursts of cannon from 300 yards. An aircraft with navigation lights on flew in front, and as we broke away the Diver hit the sea causing a large yellow flash."

605 Squadron (Mosquito VI) Manston

Flg Off B.G. Bensted	HJ799/UP-L	V-1	2356	Channel
	HJ799/UP-L	V-1	2358	Channel
	HJ799/UP-L	V-1 probable	0100	Channel
Flt Lt J.G. Musgrave	UP-H	V-1 damaged	0003	Channel
	UP-H	V-1	0027	Channel
Flg Off J. Reid	HJ776/UP-E	V-1 probable	0250	Channel
Flt Lt J. Singleton	MM415/UP-	V-1		Channel

Flg Off Basil Bensted's report was brief and to the point:

"Off from Manston 2320 [with Sgt C.L. Burrage]. Diver sighted at 2350 at 2,000 feet. Attacked with two bursts but Diver was out of range. At 2356 attacked [second] Diver at 2,000 feet, 350mph. Fired one burst and Diver exploded. At 2358 sighted [third] Diver. Fired two bursts, jet doused and last seen diving into sea. At 0100 saw [fourth] Diver at 2,000 feet, 350mph. Fired three bursts, strikes seen and Diver last seen slowly losing height."

Flt Lt John Musgrave and Flt Sgt Samwell were in action again, having departed Manston at 2310:

"At 2351 Diver sighted at 2,000 feet, climbing, at 370mph. Attacked with four bursts – no result. At 0003 fired two short bursts [at second] and saw strikes. At 0027 carried out one attack [on third], caught fire and crashed in sea. Four more seen coming over from south of Boulogne."

Although they claimed a flying bomb destroyed, Flg Off Reid and Plt Off Phillips were not granted a kill:

"At 0248 a Diver was seen launched a little east of bend in river by Le Touquet. Diver climbed straight up to 4,000 feet at 320mph. At 0250 I attacked and Diver was seen to be in a shallow dive. Diver flew through thin cloud and at 2,500 feet the light disappeared and was not seen again."

While flying one of 605 Squadron's aircraft, Flt Lt Joe Singleton DSO DFC and his navigator Flt Lt W.G. Haslam DFC, from HQ Fighter Command, shot down a Diver.

FIU (Mosquito VIII) Manston

Sqn Ldr W.H. Maguire	ZQ-	V-1		Channel

Shortly after midnight, a reconnaissance Ju188F-1 – F6+JL of 3(F)/122 – was shot down over Suffolk by a Mosquito XVII (HK257) flown by Wg Cdr C.M. Wight-Boycott, CO of 25 Squadron. The aircraft crashed at Padley Water near Chillesford, and four of the crew were killed[62]. Only the gunner Uffz Willi Scheel survived, having been flung out of the doomed machine as it disintegrated. Flt Lt D. Reid, the Mosquito navigator, annotated his combat report: "It was later confirmed that this was a German aircraft carrying boffins, probably in connection with buzz bombs." However, no connection has so far been identified.

Five *Mistels* of II/KG101 from St Dizier airfield led by Oblt Horst Rudat, were tasked to carry out an attack on Allied vessels anchored in the bay of the Seine. Two new combinations (Bf109 NA+YS/Ju88 CN+CK and Bf109 DE+VK/Ju88 G1+QH) had arrived on 18 June to replace earlier losses. Escort was provided by a Staffel of

Bf109Gs from 3/JG301. En route to the target, Rudat's aircraft was hit and damaged by German flak but he carried on until he spotted a British night fighter, when he wisely decided to release the Ju88. In turn, the Mosquito crew had seen the combination, which the navigator initially described as an "unusual biplane." It was at this stage that Rudat separated his Messerschmitt from the missile, and, as the Mosquito closed in for better identification, the Ju88 fell away and was lost against the background of the land. A second Messerschmitt flown by Fw Saalfeld had to release its missile prematurely when the pilot experienced control difficulties. All fighters returned to St Dizier without damage, one pilot reporting some success. However, damage to the proposed targets did not reach the level of destruction hoped for, but at least to the Germans the procedure had proved to be feasible, and to the Allies posed a further new threat. One RN vessel had indeed been damaged in this sortie, as recalled by Lt Peter Meryon RN, First Lieutenant on the destroyer HMS *Nith*:

> "We spent each day directing where the next convoy was to berth for off-loading until the night of 23/24 June when we were attacked by a very secret German air force unit, the Ju88 loaded with explosive. At my action station aft and on the upper deck, I watched with horror – what was to happen? A moonlight night added to the drama. I ordered everyone to tie down and I watched as the Ju88 was released by the mother plane and targeted on us. The wing of the plane cut in half, the sea-boat turned outboard in readiness and crashed alongside with an enormous explosion. Real action then followed onboard, there being quite a few casualties. I think about three dead with one more dying soon afterwards and many injured and, of course, firefighting and damage control. The ship lost power and developed quite a list and both boilers put out of action. Before leaving the beachhead we had to arrange the funerals of the deceased. This entailed wrapping the bodies in canvas, putting heavy weights therein – usually shells and committing the bodies to the deep. Subsequently we were towed back to Cowes [Isle of Wight] for repair."

Saturday 24 JUNE

On the day when announced fatalities from the assault had reached 756 and 2,697 badly injured, the infamous Irish-American William Joyce, aka 'Lord Haw-Haw', made one of his regular 'Germany Calling' broadcasts:

> "*London and southern England have now been under bombardment for more than a week. For nine days, with very little interruption, the V-1 projectiles have been descending on the British capital. May I remind you, the name V-1 has been given to them officially. 'V' is the capital letter of the German word 'Vergeltung', which means 'retaliation', and its use to denote the concept of victory must be familiar to nearly all of my listeners. The very term V-1 implies, of course, that Germany has other new weapons which have not as yet been employed against the enemy. That is a fact, and is a fact which even the British government is beginning to realise. The emergence of V-1 has provided a surprise for Germany's enemies and I believe they will have several other surprises 'before the autumn leaves fall', if I may borrow a phrase which Mr Churchill used on a certain occasion. Germany's military policy in this war is based not on slogging and on squandering but upon a scientific economy and application of energy, but this is the kind of policy the details of which must never be disclosed before the right time. It can reasonably be assumed that the battle in the East against the Bolshevik foes of civilisation will be hard and fierce and there is every reason to believe that the battle in the West against the capitalist agents of Jewish international finance will attain a climax of violence possibly without precedence. But in the closing rounds of this war it will be seen that Germany has conserved her strength to a degree that will confound her enemies.*"[63]

During the early morning, at 0618, a Diver shot down by a fighter hit the Newlands Military Camp at Charing, killing 47 men and seriously injuring a further 28. A few minutes later another was shot down over Smarden and wrecked a bungalow, killing four and fatally wounding two others at Bartley Poultry Farm. At 0700, a Diver impacted in Ellerslie Street, Clapham (SW4), damaging 50 houses and killing five. Twenty minutes later a Diver came down near Endwell Road railway bridge in Brockley (SE4), severely damaging property and killing two residents.

41 Squadron (Spitfire XII) West Malling

Plt Off N.P. Gibbs	MB875/EB-G	V-1	0615	Hastings area
Flt Sgt R.L. Short	EN620/EB-F	V-1 shared	dusk	Channel
Flt Lt T. Spencer	EN224/EB-L	V-1	dusk	Hastings area

Plt Off Peter Gibbs scored his third success when he shot down a V-1 during an early morning patrol south of Hastings. At dusk, Flt Sgt Roger Short was returning from his patrol when he saw the tell-tale flames of a flying bomb behind him. He pulled up, gave a burst and shot it down into the sea. Two other Spitfires were seen firing at it from below and he was obliged to share it.

91 Squadron (Spitfire XIV) Deanland ALG

Flt Lt J.W.P. Draper RCAF	NH654/DL-	V-1	0650	Hastings area
Flt Lt H.D. Johnson	RB188/DL-K	V-1	0650	Hawkhurst area

Flg Off Bill Draper reported: "Diver intercepted over Hastings. Attacked with short bursts and it fell on intersection of railway lines three miles north-east of Hastings." Flt Lt Johnny Johnson scored at the same time: "Diver sighted over Hastings. Attacked with three bursts and Diver turned on its back and exploded on hitting the ground west of Hawkhurst."

137 Squadron (Typhoon 1b) Manston

At 0535 Flt Lt Doug Brandreth (MK134) pursued a flying bomb and fired two short bursts at extreme range but no observed result. He chased it inland for five miles but was unable to close. He estimated its speed in the region of 370mph.

165 Squadron (Spitfire) Detling

Flt Lt I. St.C. Watson	MK811/SK-S	V-1	0625	Biggin Hill area

"Commenced attacks on Diver, closed to 150 yards. Saw many strikes on rear of fuselage. Jet ceased to function, bomb went down into balloon barrage north of Biggin Hill."

350 (Belgian) Squadron (Spitfire Vb) Friston

AB276/MN-U flown by Flg Off Joseph Brosteaux hit by AA over Sussex during his 0435-0630 anti-Diver patrol. However, he was able to return to base and land safely.

486 (RNZAF) Squadron (Tempest V) Newchurch

Flg Off R.J. Cammock RNZAF	JN808/SA-N	V-1	0740	Eastbourne area
	JN808/SA-N	V-1	0810	Eastbourne area
Plt Off K. McCarthy RNZAF	JN803/SA-D	V-1	0810	Eastbourne area

610 Squadron (Spitfire XIV) West Malling

Sqn Ldr R.A. Newbery	RB159/DW-D	V-1	0525-0640	Channel
Sqn Ldr R.A. Newbery ⎫	RB159/DW-D	V-1	0525-0640	Channel
Flg Off P.M. Bangerter ⎭	DW-			

Sqn Ldr Newbery now had five Divers and two shares to his credit, the latest shared with Flg Off Pat Bangerter. Next day the Squadron moved to Westhampnett to counter an apparent V-1 assault in that area.

56 Squadron at Newchurch received its first Tempests during the day, the former Spitfire pilots embarking on an intensive conversion course to bring the Squadron back to operational status. Arriving at the same time to assist with the conversion came Flt Lt Digby Cotes-Preddy GM, a former operational pilot who had in recent times been engaged as a test pilot with Napier Aero Engines. He was now posted back on operations.

Three Tempests from the **FIU** at Wittering were flown to Newchurch to operate at night. Wg Cdr Chris Hartley made two trips and Flt Lt Joe Berry one. The following day Sqn Ldr Daniel arrived with another Tempest (these were probably EJ524/ZQ-Y, EJ530, EJ531 and EJ553/ZQ-L). Flt Lt Jeremy Howard-Williams, also of the FIU, later wrote:

> "It was decided to see whether night fighter pilots could more easily convert to the Tempest than day fighter pilots could convert to all-weather night flying. We at FIU were ordered to convert some of our pilots to the Tempest. Because they had both flown on the abortive Abdullah experiment with Typhoons[64], Teddy Daniel, the flight commander, and Flt Lt Joe Berry, a pilot whom Chris Hartley had managed to grab on his return from the Mediterranean theatre of operations, were the first two. They became the nucleus of a small Tempest detachment, which was to shoot down more than eighty flying bombs in seven weeks. The two pilots arrived at Newchurch in brand-new aircraft. Some dozen airmen were sent by road, to provide the ground party. They set up their tented camp a little apart from the resident day wing, who seemed to regard them with tolerant scorn. The weather immediately showed signs of what it had in store. Low cloud and rain prevented flying on the first three nights. Teddy and Joe suffered some leg pulling in the bar of the officers' mess tent. The other pilots were somewhat relieved that the newcomers were also human. Night fighter pilots, they jeered, could not fly any more than anyone else when the cloud was on the deck."

Night 24/25 JUNE

In the early hours a Diver scored a direct hit on the eastern side of Victoria Station, where 17 people were killed and some 30 injured which included six porters on fire watch duty, although one had a very lucky escape. Just before the flying bomb impacted, he was on the roof of the building watching the searchlights in the night sky. He came back downstairs and opened the door of an empty room. At that moment he heard a Diver's engine cut out overhead and he dived under the cover of a desk. He heard no explosion at all. The only thing that he was conscious of was that he was unable to get his legs under the desk and he could feel rubble falling on them. He was able to get back on his feet and stumble out of the wreckage of the room. The whole of the eastern side station offices were badly damaged. There was also damage to the Grosvenor Hotel and to shops in the Wilton Road area. Deptford (SE8) received another bomb at 0205, which fell between Gosterwood Street and Etta Street, killing eight. A further seven Londoners were killed in Clapham (SW4) at 0356 following a Diver explosion that wrecked a dozen houses in Kepler Road, and a similar number in Solon New Road. Another fell at 0405 in Hillingdon Street between Farmers and Wareham Roads (Camberwell SE5). Fifty houses, four shops and the Freemasons Arms were destroyed, and 23 people killed. All occupants of the public house survived and included Barbara Mcnally, who was just five years old at the time:

> "The bomb blew out the side walls and the building collapsed onto us. Luckily one or some of the girders in the roof of the cellar created a small space above us to stop us all being killed. My dad was the only casualty as the till from the bar above fell on his head and he was very bloody and unconscious. I remember my mum and aunty both crying and praying and shouting for help. I thought I would help by pushing all this debris that was in front of me out of the way. That nearly brought the house down, literally. I don't know how long we were down there but eventually the emergency services heard our shouts and we were pulled out more or less feet first and put in the shelter in the street. I remember looking out of the shelter door as my dad was taken away in an ambulance. The road seemed to be very bright and wet and busy with people running around and hoses and vehicles and dust everywhere. We were very lucky to

have survived, many were killed by that bomb."

Another flying bomb exploded near the end of the runway at Rattlesden airfield in Suffolk, home of the USAAF's 451st Bomb Squadron. One that fell to the combined fire of the guns and a fighter at 0428 crashed in Rochester, where 26 houses were damaged, a further 130 suffering blast effects, with six people injured, two seriously.

96 Squadron (Mosquito XIII) Ford

Wg Cdr E.D. Crew	MM449/ZJ-V	V-1	0110	Worthing area
Flt Lt F.R.L. Mellersh	HK372/ZJ-	V-1	0230	off Dungeness
	HK372/ZJ-	V-1	0305	off Dungeness
Flt Sgt T. Bryan	HK421/ZJ-	V-1	0328	off Eastbourne
	HK421/ZJ-	V-1	0340	Beachy Head area

Wg Cdr Edward Crew and his radar op Wt Off Croydill were lucky to survive when their Mosquito MM449/ZJ-V broke up when chasing a V-1 near Worthing; both baled out safely. Crew later commented: "In the course of shooting down the flying bomb my Mosquito was also destroyed. Bits came off and put both engines out, forcing us to bale out. A very expensive flying bomb!" Flt Lt Mellersh's targets both fell into the sea off Dungeness, the second leaving a trail of sparks about a mile long before bursting into flames. Flt Sgt Tom Bryan's first exploded in the air near Eastbourne, the second on the ground near Beachy Head.

418 (RCAF) Squadron (Mosquito VI) Holmsley South

Flg Off J.H. Phillips RCAF	NT137/TH-T	V-1	0228	Channel
Wt Off J.J.P. McGale RCAF	HJ719/TH-U	V-1		
	HJ719/TH-U	V-1		

Flg Off Jack Phillips reported: "Chased Diver from ten miles off Le Tréport and fired two-seconds burst of cannon from 200 yards astern. Diver glided down to sea and exploded with a bright yellow flash." Wt Off John McGale's Mosquito was damaged by debris following the explosion of his second victim forcing him and his navigator Flg Off E.J. Storey RCAF to bale out over land; both sustained minor injuries. They were picked up safely and taken to Ford.

456 (RAAF) Squadron (Mosquito XVII) Ford

Flt Lt G.R. Houston RAAF	HK264/RX-T	V-1 probable 0405	off Beachy Head

Flt Lt George Houston made several attempts at intercepting Divers and during one, as the Mosquito closed in, another fighter opened fire on it, forcing him away. When finally he managed to engage one, on which he scored several strikes, it continued flying straight and level. However, three minutes later an explosion was seen on the ground, which he thought was possibly his victim, but was credited with a probable only.

605 Squadron (Mosquito VI) Manston

Sqn Ldr I.F. McCall	UP-	V-1	0342	Beachy Head area
Flg Off R.C. Walton RNZAF	UP-	V-1		

Sqn Ldr Ian McCall and Flt Sgt Tom Caulfield scored their first kill:

> "At 0342 Diver seen flying at 3,000 feet. I gave four bursts with cannon and machine-guns and Diver lost height as it approached Beachy Head. I pulled away and saw my target crash and explode behind Beachy Head."

Sunday 25 JUNE

A flying bomb impacted in Locksway Road in Milton, a suburb of Portsmouth. One that fell during the evening, shot down by a fighter, hit Pluckley near Ashford at 2326 without causing damage. Three residents of Beckenham were killed when a bomb hit The Drive, where three houses were destroyed.

3 Squadron (Tempest V) Newchurch

Flt Sgt R.W. Cole	JN768/JF-F	V-1	2100	Hastings area
Flt Sgt M.J.A. Rose	JN817/JF-H	V-1	2136	Goudsbridge area
Sqn Ldr A.S. Dredge	JN812/JF-M	V-1	2150	Hawkhurst area
Flt Lt R. van Lierde (Belg)	JN862/JF-Z	V-1	2310	Ashford area
Flg Off G.A. Whitman RCAF (US)	JN743/JF-P			
Flt Lt R. van Lierde (Belg)	JN862/JF-Z	V-1	2319	Biggin Hill area
Flt Sgt H.J. Bailey RAAF	JN752/JF-S	V-1	2330	Grid R.2650
Flt Sgt D.J. Mackerras RAAF	JN745/JF-T	V-1	2325	Grid R.3565
	JN745/JF-T	V-1 probable	2335	
Plt Off S.B. Feldman (US)	JN761/JF-U	V-1	2335	off Hastings

All eight Divers were brought down in a two-and-half hour spell from 2100 onwards, Flt Sgt Bob Cole getting the first:

> "Sighted Diver four miles south of Rye at 3,000 feet. Closed and attacked from 400 yards, from 300 yards and a third time from 250 yards. The Diver went down and exploded on the ground seven miles north of Hastings."

Flt Sgt Morrie Rose got the next:

> "Sighted Diver between Hastings and Rye. Dived and fired two two-seconds bursts from 100 yards. Both wingtips came off, it flicked over and dived into the outskirts of a small village in the Goudsbridge area."

Sqn Ldr Alan Dredge joined in with one that crashed into a field two miles south-east of Hawkhurst:

> "Fire was opened from 300 yards, closing to 150 yards with three bursts. Strikes were seen on the starboard wing and side of fuselage from second burst, while the third burst caused the starboard wing to crumple. Diver pulled up and the wing came off, and it went into a dive."

Flt Lt Remi van Lierde bagged two, the first of which he shared with Flg Off Lefty Whitman:

> "A Diver was sighted with the aid of ROC rockets. Range was closed to 200 yards and we both fired several bursts. The propulsive unit went out and the Diver glided in, exploding south-west of Ashford. I returned to Dungeness and sighted another Diver four miles inland at 2,000 feet. I closed in and fired a long burst and the Diver exploded on the ground."

The Australian pair Flt Sgts Don Mackerras and Bert Bailey departed Newchurch at 2250, both gaining kills during the patrol, Mackerras reporting:

> "Fired a two-seconds burst from 300 yards, seeing strikes on the jet unit. The Diver lost height by 500 feet and the jet exploded. It then went in and exploded on the ground. I then fired at a second Diver and saw strikes but it was lost in cloud."

Meanwhile, Flt Sgt Bailey was also busy:

> "Sighted Diver coming in over Dungeness with the aid of ROC rockets. I closed to 300 yards but AA fire caused me to break away. I fired two two-seconds bursts and saw strikes but AA again caused me to break away. The Diver went down and crashed, exploding on the ground."

Plt Off Buck Feldman scored the last of the day at 2335:

> "I sighted Diver 20 miles east of Hastings at 2,500 feet. After firing several short bursts from

400 yards the Diver went straight down and exploded in the sea."

41 Squadron (Spitfire XII) West Malling

| Wt Off P.T. Coleman | MB841/EB-C | V-1 | 1850-2000 | Bexhill area |

"I shot down a bomb after Ross Harding had expended his ammunition unsuccessfully on it. Falls and explodes in a field behind Bexhill. This will not count as an enemy aircraft but a special category."

91 Squadron (Spitfire XIV) Deanland ALG

| Flt Lt R.S. Nash | RB169/DL-Q | V-1 | 0425 | Maidstone area |
| Lt H.F. de Bordas (FF) | NH654/DL- | V-1 | 2310 | Tenterden-Ashford |

Flt Lt Nash:

"Diver sighted as taking-off from base and I immediately went into attack, shooting it down near Maidstone, where it exploded on hitting the ground."

The remainder of the day saw no further success, but darkness brought with it a victory and a loss. Lt Henri de Bordas shot down another Diver:

"Vectored on to Diver approaching from Dungeness. Attack made from astern and Diver shot down, exploding on ground between Tenterden and Ashford."

But Wt Off 'Red' Blumer RAAF, who had only recently returned to the Squadron following his escape from France after being shot down the previous year, was killed when RM617/DL-G crashed at 2230 on returning from Staplehurst where he had landed after an anti-Diver patrol.

165 Squadron (Spitfire IX) Detling

| Plt Off R.S.J. Hebron RAAF | MK838/SK-K | V-1 | 2220 | Staplehurst-Marden area |

"Bomb seen three or four miles due south of Dungeness. Closing to 300 yards I made a quarter attack. Nose of bomb dropped and it went down exploding harmlessly in open ground. As I was positioning myself for attack, a Tempest dived down from 9 o'clock and pulled up in front of me. This aircraft carried out a stern attack but no strikes were seen and the bomb continued on its course until I shot it down."

486 (RNZAF) Squadron (Tempest V) Newchurch

Flg Off S.S. Williams RNZAF	JN758/SA-Y	V-1	0500	Newchurch area
Wt Off S.J. Short RNZAF	JN801/SA-P	V-1	2035	Battle area
Flg Off R.J. Cammock RNZAF	JN804/SA-R	V-1	2100	Maidstone area
Flg Off J.R. Cullen RNZAF	JN770/SA-V	V-1	2102	Redhill area
	JN770/SA-V	V-1	2147	Headcorn area
Flg Off W.A. Hart RNZAF	JN809/SA-M	V-1	2205	Newchurch area
Wt Off C.J. Sheddan RNZAF	JN854/SA-G	V-1	2310	Newchurch area
Flg Off R.J. Cammock RNZAF	JN804/SA-R	V-1	2310	Hastings area
Flg Off W.A. Hart RNZAF	JN809/SA-M	V-1	2315	Newchurch area

135 Wing (Spitfire IX) North Weald

| Wg Cdr R.H. Harries | RH-H | V-1 | am | |

381stFS/363rdFG USAAF (P-51B) Staplehurst ALG

| Capt J.B. Dalglish USAAF | 42-106769 | V-1 | 2300 | Thames area |
| | 42-106769 | V-1 | 2320 | Headcorn area |

Capt James Dalglish, who had been ordered to orbit near Staplehurst with his wingman (who subsequently landed), saw an approaching Diver being chased by a Tempest, which overshot, allowing Dalglish to attack but he also overshot. Finally the

Tempest shot down the Diver and Dalglish was vectored on to another:

"No friendly fighters present so I went into attack from 5,000 feet at 400mph, and got several good bursts on the Diver, which made column of flames coming from tail increase. Overshot, but Diver was still on course so I made a second attack, which caused the Diver to spin into the ground and exploded about 15 miles south of the Thames. Headed south west and picked up another Diver over Headcorn and went into attack from 4,000 feet at 350mph. Got several good bursts into Diver, which caused it to loop twice and then hit the ground and explode at about 2320."

85 Squadron at Swannington equipped with Mosquito XVII and XIX night fighters was ordered to help with the night defence against the V-1s, the first sorties being flown that night.

Night 25/26 JUNE
'Doodlebug Night on the Isle of Wight.' The phrase was coined following the intrusion of Divers over the island on this night, as observed by ROC spotter Jock Leal:

"On the night of June 25, no fewer than 16 roared over the island or close to it, three crashing in island waters, and three landing on the island itself – one of them causing bad damage and a death in Newport. It all started at 8.36pm when the siren wailed through misty rain to warn of a V-1 coming west over Selsey Bill. This was quickly followed by a second, both crashing in the Warsash area at 8.45pm. Not long afterwards two more followed the same course, one landing behind Portsmouth and the other in the Southampton area. Now the first Doodlebug to land on the island was on its way. At 9.48pm, the ROC at Bembridge Forelands reported that it had passed overhead, travelling westwards. Two minutes later it had crashed near a searchlight site at North Fairlee. At 9.57pm, another was plotted east of Bembridge on the same course. This, too, landed on the island at Duxmore. The time was 10.05pm. Just over half an hour later another was on its way to crash beyond Portsmouth, and then, at 11.37pm sirens warned of two more coming north-west into Sandown. We saw their flames before we could hear them. The first roared over Newport at 1,000 feet, heading towards Lymington, but the engine of the second began to splutter out over St George's Down and cut out completely somewhere over Whitepit Lane. For a second there was silence. Then, from just off Carisbrooke Road, came the thunder of a great explosion. We felt the blast up on Mount Joy. Below us a lot of damage had been done. It seemed scarcely credible that there was only one fatality.

"At 12.27am, Diver number 10 came up south-east of Sandown to crash in the Netley area, and two more could be seen arriving. One followed its predecessor and landed near Netley, the other passed above Newport. Over the north-west of the island its flame died out. It exploded off Hamstead. We were quiet for a while after that, but the Doodlebug night was not over yet. At 3.30am, Diver number 13 was seen and heard along the south coast of the island. Passing Chale, it crashed into the sea off Brook. The sirens, which had been sounding on and off all night, had hardly given the 'all clear' at 4am, when the ROC gave another alarm, and four minutes later they were wailing again. The 14th V-1of the night was coming up south-east of Sandown. It crossed the east of the island and landed north of Portsmouth. Before the night was over we had one more alert. It was just before 5am, when the sirens went. Two V-1s were on the way. One went over to the east of us, heading for Portsmouth. The other flamed over Newport, where people walked out in the dawn light to look at it. Over Gurnard its motor cut out, and it crashed into the sea near the Egypt Point light-house. The final 'all clear' of a memorable night came at 5.32am."[65]

Half an hour before midnight 11 houses were damaged when a flying bomb impacted at Crow's Green, Great Saling in Essex. One hit by a fighter glided down to land almost intact near Snargate at 2204, and failed to explode. Four minutes after midnight, another victim of fighters crashed near Ivychurch. One of the Divers that evaded the defences fell between Wyndham Road and Elfin Road (Camberwell SE5) at 0130, demolishing 18 houses and killing three residents. Another killed two people at the junction of Creek Side/Bronze Street in Deptford (SE8) at 0350. Another fell at Bethersden near Ashford at 0348, the victim of a night fighter, and at 0440 a balloon cable brought down one at Ash. A vessel of the US Naval Armed Guard Service, the *William A. Jones*, reported shooting down a Diver while on duty off the Normandy beaches. A sister vessel the *James B. Weaver* had claimed two Divers shot down a few days earlier. One US Naval officer commented:

> "We never could get used to those buzz bomb attacks. Kinda like an artillery shell: as long as you can hear them you know you were OK. When that motor on the buzz bomb stopped you had an instant cure for haemorrhoids."

85 Squadron (Mosquito XIX) Swannington

Capt T. Weisteen (Norw)	MM636/VY-A	V-1	0015-0230	

96 Squadron (Mosquito XIII) Ford

Flg Off J. Goode	HK406/ZJ-	V-1	0001	Grid R.4040
	HK406/ZJ-	V-1	0006	Grid R.2141
Flg Off R.F. Ball	HK372/ZJ-G	V-1	0050	Bexhill area
Sqn Ldr P.L. Caldwell	MM461/ZJ-	V-1	0045	Hastings area
Flt Lt N.S. Head	MM492/ZJ-	V-1	0206	off Eastbourne
Sqn Ldr W.P. Green	MM495/ZJ-	V-1	0325	in sea

219 Squadron (Mosquito XVII) Bradwell Bay

Plt Off A. Hollingsworth	HK254/FK-	V-1	2245-0045	Hythe area
	HK254/FK-	V-1	2245-0045	Hythe area
Flt Lt G.R.I. Parker	HK250/FK-	V-1	0300-0500	off Dungeness
	HK250/FK-	V-1	0300-0500	off Dungeness

Plt Off Alec Hollingsworth scored two kills, one crashing seven miles north of Hythe, and the second approximately five miles north of the same town. Flt Lt Sailor Parker also scored two more V-1s to raise his total to five, both shot down into the sea some ten miles south-east of Dungeness.

605 Squadron (Mosquito VI) Manston

Flg Off R.E. Lelong RNZAF	HJ785/UP-T	V-1	0200	Channel
Flg Off A.T. Linn	UP-	V-1	0348	Beachy Head

New Zealander Flg Off Roy Lelong attacked two flying bombs and shot down one:

> "Diver was sighted at 2,000 feet flying at 360mph. After attack it slowed down to 280mph and after three more bursts target exploded. At 0217 sighted another but could not attack owing to range. At 0231 sighted third at 2,000 feet – started to attack but ammo ran out."

Flg Off Arthur Linn also attacked two:

> "Attacked at 0330 off Dungeness at 3,000 feet, without result. At 0348 another Diver sighted 15 miles south of Rye at 3,000 feet, doing 350mph. Three bursts of cannon and machine-gun blew up jet unit and Diver crashed on Beachy Head."

FIU Detachment (Tempest V) Newchurch

Sqn Ldr Daniel and Flt Lt Berry carried out night flying tests during the evening but the weather curtailed night operations.

Monday 26 JUNE

Bad weather prevented much flying. A Diver fell in open country north of Norwich, the first in Norfolk. Another came down close to the billets occupied by the survey section of 4 (Med) Regt of the Canadian Army at Little Selkirk near Caterham in Surrey. Four Canadian soldiers were killed and eight wounded, three seriously. Another fell on a house in Gauden Road, Clapham, the residence of Russian-born Vera Menchik-Stevenson, the reigning Women's World Chess Champion, killing her, her mother and younger sister[66]. Fighters shot down one that fell near Willesborough in Kent. Many people across the south-eastern counties were getting their first close encounters with the missiles, an ARP Warden at Waltham Abbey in Essex, Ted Carter, noting in his journal:

> "For just over two weeks now Jerry has been sending us over a new type of nuisance. Pilotless aircraft, which crash and blow up with the effects of a 1,000kg HE on the surface. Several nights past have witnessed very long alerts and sirens, particularly if overclouded, punctuate the daytime. It seems odd to have daytime alerts again. Last night I stood by and heard about 20 of them drone their way in and explode. During the previous night one fell in Baker Street, Enfield. Today, however, we got one! Dinnertime was just about over and at 1340 a fairly loud bang put everyone on their toes. Not more than a couple of minutes later, possibly not so long, there was a fearful whack, which rattled doors and windows. Running upstairs, we could see smoke rising and guessed it was at Sewardstone. Got car out and went to see. It had fallen in a paddock adjoining the Grange at Sewardstone and had made a mess of the house. Not a door, window, curtain, pane of glass or a ceiling was left intact. A dozen or so fowls dead in the yard. Two casualties were removed. The job was cleared up very quickly."

One Diver reached Walworth (SE17) where it exploded in East Street at 1332, destroying two shops and damaging many houses; five people were killed. Another came down at 1600, exploding in Banstead Road/Nunhead Grove (Peckham SE15), killing two.

3 Squadron (Tempest V) Newchurch

Wt Off J.R.L. Torpey	JN765/JF-K	V-1	1510-1605	

137 Squadron (Typhoon Ib) Manston

Flg Off A.M. Sames RNZAF	MN134/SF-J	V-1	1425-1525	off Bexhill
	MN134/SF-J	V-1	1425-1525	Bexhill area

Flg Off Artie Sames and Flt Sgt Dick Egley (MN191) were off at 1425 to patrol off the coast in the Bexhill area. They sighted a flying bomb at 2,000 feet near Bexhill, which Sames promptly shot down into the sea. A second was sighted at 3,000 feet inland, and this also was downed by the New Zealander. Earlier, at dawn, Flg Off Ralph Johnstone (MN460) and Flt Sgt L.A.V. Burrows (MN429) patrolled the Gravelines-Le Tréport line and, at 0500, had sighted a V-1 at 1,500 feet some two miles north of Le Touquet. Twenty minutes later they saw another ten miles west of Le Touquet, which they chased but just as they started to close on the red glow, it spiralled into the sea and exploded on impact.

486 (RNZAF) Squadron (Tempest V) Newchurch

Flt Lt J.H. McCaw RNZAF	JN758/SA-Y	V-1	1615	Dungeness area

501 Squadron (Spitfire Vb) Westhampnett

Sqn Ldr M.G. Barnett RNZAF	W3702/SD-M	V-1		Bexhill area

While on an air-test Sqn Ldr Gary Barnett[67] engaged and shot down a Diver near Bexhill.

Night 26/27 JUNE

Flakregiment IV/155(W) and part of *II/155(W)* were ordered to target Southampton rather than London, which was regarded by the Germans as one of the most important embarkation ports for invasion troops, the *Flakregiment*'s war diary noting:

> "Contrary to the opinion of the Luftwaffe operations staff, the Supreme Commander West is insisting upon the combating of the southern English ports of Southampton and Portsmouth."

A total of 53 V-1s was launched against the ports with little effect, and the order was rescinded the following day. Three of the four hit by AA near Folkestone exploded in mid-air in fairly quick succession, the other falling near the RASC Barracks at Shorncliffe. Three people were slightly injured when a Diver impacted near Wested Farm at Eynsford at 0546. One that fell at Wormdale Farm near Newington failed to explode, thereby providing further details of its construction. One that reached South London fell in Gauden Road, Clapham (SW4) at 0020, killing 11 residents.

219 Squadron (Mosquito XVII) Bradwell Bay

Flt Lt L. Stephenson	HK248/FK-	V-1	2340-0050	
Flt Lt P.G.K. Williamson	MM690/FK-	V-1	0305	off Dungeness

Of his first kill Flt Lt Peter Williamson reported:

> "Was free-lancing. Combat with target and opened fire at 600 feet down to 200 feet. A second burst from 150-100 feet. Strikes seen on fuselage and on 'fire box'. Formated on target, which was seen to be damaged and with fire coming out of many places. Target then crashed into the sea south of Dungeness."

409 (RCAF) Squadron (Mosquito XIII) Hunsdon

Sqn Ldr R.S. Jephson RCAF	MM510/KP-	V-1	night	Channel

Sqn Ldr Dick Jephson RCAF was attached to 605 Squadron at Manston for the evening and shot down his second Diver.

Tuesday 27 JUNE

An RAF spokesman Sqn Ldr John Strachey broadcast to the nation of the BBC's Home Service in an attempt to reassure the public:

> *"Though the flying bomb has turned out to be militarily negligible that does not mean that its effect may not often be personally tragic. It is almost unbearably sad, at this late stage of the war, to see again the effect of high explosives on an ordinary street of little houses. Apart from the tragedy of those individuals who are killed or badly hurt, there is all the suffering and pain of smashed homes, lost personal possessions, families broken up – and it is being done by the enemy without any real military purpose, at all. As usual there is not the slightest need for anyone to tell the people of southern England to keep steady. They are steadiness itself. In fact, the main thing that needs saying is once again to urge them to take reasonable and sensible precautions. These, remember, are essentially blast bombs. There is no need to describe what the flying bomb looks like and sounds like to listeners who live within range. But you in the rest of the country may not realise just what it is like when these things come over. First you hear a faint humming in the distance, more or less like an ordinary aircraft. Gradually it grows louder, and the note changes till it sounds more like a motorbike with a two-stroke engine being driven through the sky. Soon, if it is a clear day, you see the little aircraft, with the hump on its back, flying along a few thousand feet up.*
>
> *"If it is at night you see a light, which is the exhaust flame, coming out of the back. The noise grows and grows and if the flying bomb goes right over your head it sounds like an express train dashing through the sky. If the noise stops it means that it will drop and explode in anything from five to fifteen seconds or so. That is the time to get away from the windows and take any other reasonable precautions. Our fighters are shooting them down. Our Spitfires and the American Mustangs and Thunderbolts are getting an increasing bag. Our newest fighter, the Tempest, has proved particularly good at this job. And our gunners are also attacking them. We must not expect, I think, that these counter-measures will stop the flying bomb altogether in the immediate future. It always takes a little time completely to overcome a*

new form of attack. But already we have done a good deal to limit the scale of the thing. A lot more is being done. No doubt the best way to ensure that no more flying bombs ever come over is to capture the places from which they are being fired. After all, we have done that already in the case of the Cherbourg launching points."

Damage to the south of the Thames was severe and four main line railway stations had been closed due to direct hits and part of London Underground was out of action. The increased activity called for urgent measures and the Chiefs-of-Staff met to consider options available to them. One idea was to guarantee the immunity of specified German towns from bombing attacks by the RAF and USAAF if the Germans would agree to stop the indiscriminate bombardment. This proposal, together with the suggested use of poison gas and napalm to attack the launching sites, did not find favour with the Allied Supreme Commander, General Eisenhower, nor with the CIGS General Sir Alan Brooke:

"He did not feel that the Germans would abandon a relatively inexpensive campaign that was currently diverting about 50 per cent of the Allied bombing effort from targets in the Reich. A recommendation to use gas on the launching sites was also rejected because the danger to French civilians in surrounding areas was too great."[68]

Two Divers brought down by fighters at 0520 and 0610 crashed near Brooklands and Newchurch respectively, without causing any damage. A Diver shot down by a fighter at 0712 crashed near Ightham near Malling, seriously injuring one person, but the only casualties of an impact in Nash Lane, West Wickham, were two horses in a nearby field, both of whom received slight injuries. A far greater tragedy occurred at midday, when another reached London and impacted at Highbury Corner, killing 26 and injuring more than 150. Many buildings were destroyed in Upper Street, Compton Terrace and St Paul's Road including Highbury and Islington Railway Station and The Cock Tavern. Two more came down in Warden Carter's patch in Waltham Abbey:

"Pilotless aircraft fell in a field at the rear of Lancaster Cottages, Avey Lane. Difficult to locate but a nasty feel when found. Had fallen right on to some cattle sheltering in a corner from the raid. Three cows killed and two so badly injured that they had to be destroyed, and four others slightly injured. Heaps of tangled and twisted metal all over the fields. At about 1215, another blighter came over, getting nearer and nearer. Eventually it became so loud that I thought it must be one of our fighters. Terrific explosion when it did go off. It crashed in Ordnance Road, Enfield, at its junction with Chesterton Road. Four fatal casualties and one or two more injured."

Peckham (SE15) was on the receiving end of three Divers during the day, the first at 1056 (Willow Brook/Summit Road) killing three; the next came down four minutes after midday, killing nine in the Green Hundred/Camelot Road area; and the final one impacted at Rye Hill Park at 2011, killing one. Three people were slightly injured when a Diver exploded near a farmhouse at Marden at 1407, following a meeting with a fighter. All told, during the day, nine Divers crashed in the Malling/Hollingbourne districts of Kent, all victims of fighters bar one, which was shot down by AA fire. Two others shot down by fighters crashed near Ivychurch at 1550, and near Old Romney at 1705. Another shot down by AA at 1735 fell near the church at Hothfield near Ashford, slightly injuring two people. A fighter shot down another at 2032 that crashed at Darland near Gillingham.

1 Squadron (Spitfire LFIXb) Detling

Flg Off R. Bridgeman ⎫	MK997/JX-F			Flimwell/
Flt Sgt K.C. Weller ⎬	ML258/JX-L	V-1	0720-0730	Wadhurst area
Flt Sgt I. Hastings ⎭	MK988/JX-			

Flg Off W.J. Batchelor	ML313/JX-	V-1	1030	Rye area

A patrol led by Flg Off Bob Bridgeman was vectored towards a plot and a Diver was soon sighted near Dungeness at 2,000 feet. The Diver was chased by Bridgeman and his two companions Flt Sgts Ken Weller and Iain Hastings, all three attacking to send it down near Wadhurst, where it exploded on impact:

> "All three made several attacks, which culminated in Diver making violent turn to port and then diving steeply to the ground where it exploded in Flimwell/Wadhurst area, between a farmhouse and outhouses."

Later that morning Flg Off Jack Batchelor intercepted a second Diver one mile out to sea off Hastings:

> "I opened fire at 500 yards from dead astern, closing to 300 yards. After attack jet glow appeared to burn far brighter. Diver then went into cloud. A second attack from close range was then carried out and probably damaged the gyro because Diver turned off course. This attack was carried out in cloud and shortly after Diver disappeared. ROC reported Diver crashing at [Grid] R.3541."

150 Wing (Tempest V) Newchurch

Wg Cdr R.P. Beamont	JK812/JF-M	V-1	am	Ham Street area
	EJ525/RB	V-1	pm	Hastings area
	EJ525/RB	V-1	pm	Hastings area

3 Squadron (Tempest V) Newchurch

Flt Lt R. van Lierde (Belg)	JN862/JF-Z	V-1	0605-0730	
Flt Sgt D.J. Mackerras RAAF	JN760/JF-R	V-1	0750-0855	
Flt Sgt L.G. Everson	JN765/JF-K	V-1	0825-0930	
Flt Sgt J.W. Foster	JN807/JF-Y	V-1 shared	1555	Hastings area
Flt Lt A.E. Umbers RNZAF	JN817/JF-H	V-1	1715-1845	
Flg Off R.H. Clapperton	JN769/JF-G	V-1	1715-1845	
Wt Off J.R.L. Torpey	JN765/JF-K	V-1	1910-2020	
Flt Sgt L.G. Everson	JN769/JF-G	V-1	1945-2110	
Flg Off R. Dryland	JN822/JF-	V-1	2045-2215	
Flt Sgt H.J. Bailey RAAF	JN807/JF-Y	V-1	2205-2305	

The Squadron scored a further ten kills (one shared). Flt Sgt John Foster shared his kill with Wt Off Ginger Eagleson of 486 Squadron.

91 Squadron (Spitfire XIV) Deanland ALG

Sqn Ldr P.McC. Bond	RB161/DL-I	V-1	1100	West Malling
Flg Off R.A. McPhie RCAF	NH698/DL-Y			
Flt Lt R.S. Nash	RB169/DL-Q	V-1	1135	Frittenden area
Flg Off E. Topham	RB183/DL-M	V-1 shared	1215	Detling area
Sqn Ldr P.McC. Bond	RB161/DL-I	V-1	1240	Ashford area
Flg Off J.A. Faulkner RCAF	RM620/DL-E	V-1	2105	exploded in mid-air
Flt Lt H.B. Moffett RCAF	RB161/DL-I	V-1	2125	West Malling area

Six Divers were destroyed including one by Sqn Ldr Peter Bond and Flg Off Ray McPhie who chased it across the airfield at West Malling and brought it down just north of the boundary and close to Offham House, where the Station Commander Wg Cdr J.A. O'Neill DFC lived. Many windows were blown out but no one hurt. No.2 fell to Flt Lt Ray Nash south-west of Frittenden: "Diver sighted approaching Dymchurch. Attacked from astern and it flicked over and exploded in a field." Flg Off Ted Topham was the next to score but had to share his victim: "Diver sighted over Ashford being fired on by a Spit of 322 Sqn. My attack was made from astern and Diver was brought down in a wood south-east of Detling where it exploded."

The CO got another in the Ashford area: "Diver sighted coming in over Dungeness. Attacked from astern at 600 yards range and it flicked over and fell in woods where it exploded." Flt Lt Bruce Moffett and Flg Off John Faulkner took off at 2045 and both scored, the latter reporting: "Vectored on to Diver out in Channel. Attacked from quarter astern and it exploded in the air 15 miles south-east of Dungeness." Flt Lt Moffett observed a wire, some 75 yards long, trailing from the Diver he intercepted: "Vectored on to Diver crossing between Rye and Hastings. Attack made from astern and it made a complete loop, falling after second attack, and exploded in a field five miles south of base."

137 Squadron (Typhoon Ib) Manston

A frustrating day for the Typhoon pilots. The 0730-0830 patrol, flown by Wt Off Jimmy Shemeld and Wt Off Charlie Points sighted a flying bomb but before they could engage, it fell into the sea and exploded, presumably the victim of other fighters. Later in the morning, at 1105, the OC Manston, Wg Cdr Gordon Raphael DFC (a former bomber and night fighter pilot), decided to try his hand and borrowed Typhoon MK586. He soon sighted a Diver but before he was able to manoeuvre behind it, two Spitfires shot it down. He then saw another, closed to short range, only to find that his guns would not fire. To add insult to injury, a Tempest then nipped in and shot it down.

165 Squadron (Spitfire IX) Detling

Flt Sgt R.J. Hughes RAAF	MK426/SK-D	V-1	1600	Maidstone area
Flg Off S.R. Chambers	MJ580/SK-Y	V-1 shared	1820	Tunbridge Wells

Flt Sgt Hughes sighted the flying bomb coming in east of Hastings at 1,000 feet:

> "Picked up ten miles inland. Two Tempests also in pursuit. Then a Spitfire and both Tempests made attacks without result (conditions were very bumpy). I attacked, saw a strike on the left wing. The bomb burst into flame, with much black smoke, and exploded on the ground in a paddock five miles west-south-west of Maidstone."

Two hours later Flg Off Chambers picked up his target south of Pevensey, one mile out to sea at 2,500 feet: "Gave several bursts and saw numerous strikes. Bomb crashed between Tunbridge Wells and Tonbridge, near railway line." The authorities decided that a Tempest from 3 Squadron had fired at the same Diver and the two pilots were each awarded a half kill.

322 (Dutch) Squadron (Spitfire XIV) West Malling

Flt Sgt R.L. van Beers	VL-H	V-1	0920	Beachy Head area
Flt Sgt C. Kooij	VL-Q	V-1 shared	1215	Frittenden area
Flt Sgt J.H. Harms	VL-J	V-1	1353	Grid R.23
	VL-J	V-1	1400	Dungeness area
Flt Lt J.L. Plesman	VL-V	V-1	1443	exploded in mid-air
Flg Off M.L. van Bergen	VL-N	V-1	1825	Malling area
Flg Off J. van Arkel	VL-T	V-1		Edenbridge area

The Squadron flew 60 anti-Diver sorties and shot down seven missiles. Flt Sgt Ronnie van Beers got the first:

> "Patrolling at 6,000 feet five miles north of Beachy Head. Vectored on to Diver. Attacked with three long bursts. Diver fell and exploded, position not known."

It seems that Flt Sgt Cees Kooij shared his kill with Flg Off Topham of 91 Squadron.

Although Flt Sgt Jan Harms claimed two kills, the first one was disallowed:

> "Patrolling over sea four miles south of Hastings when told two Divers were approaching over Bexhill. I saw both, one was zig-zagging. I saw Tempest attack one flying straight and level but missed and broke off. I attacked at 200 yards and Diver blew up in position R.23."

Apparently this was awarded to the Tempest pilot. Harms' second kill was conclusive:

> "Diver approaching Dungeness. I gave two long bursts dead astern. Diver crashed and exploded 50 yards from row of houses in area R.416."

As a result of the next kill, Flt Lt Jan Plesman's Spitfire suffered some damage:

> "Saw Diver approaching west of Hastings. Another pilot of 322 Squadron attacked and I saw strikes. I came in line astern, range 150 yards and gave short bursts. Diver blew up. Small pieces of Diver hit the radiator of my Spitfire."

The Dutch pilots' luck continued when Flg Off van Bergen shot down another:

> "Attacked Diver approaching north of Dungeness at 250 yards range. Diver broke in half and exploded in a field north-west of Malling."

486 (RNZAF) Squadron (Tempest V) Newchurch

Flt Lt N.J. Powell RNZAF	JN866/SA-U	V-1	0617	Hastings area
Flt Lt H.N. Sweetman RNZAF	JN754/SA-A	V-1	1025	Rye area
	JN821/SA-H	V-1	1345	Bexhill area
Wt Off G.J.M. Hooper RNZAF	JN803/SA-D	V-1	1505	Hastings area
	JN803/SA-D	V-1	1522	off Beachy Head
Flg Off W.L. Miller RNZAF	JN811/SA-Z	V-1	1553	off Rye
Wt Off O.D. Eagleson RNZAF	JN794/SA-T	V-1 shared	1555	Hastings area
Flg Off W.L. Miller RNZAF	JN811/SA-Z	V-1	2042	Paddock Wood
Flg Off W.A. Hart RNZAF	JN803/SA-D	V-1	2105	Rye area
Flg Off R.J. Cammock RNZAF	JN794/SA-T	V-1	2140	Rye area

The New Zealanders accounted for another ten Divers, one of which Wt Off Owen Eagleson shared with 3 Squadron's Flt Sgt Foster.

FIU Detachment (Tempest V) Newchurch

Sqn Ldr Daniel and Flt Lt Berry carried out day and night patrols but without success.

381stFS /363rdFG USAAF (P-51) Staplehurst ALG

1/Lt R.B. Freyermuth USAAF[69]	B3-	V-1	2005	Maidstone area

Lt Russel Freyermuth reported:

> "I sighted a P-plane (pilotless) about three miles east of base at about 2005, closed to within 300 yards, chasing it for approximately five minutes, firing intermittent bursts. P-Plane finally swung to right, dove to ground and exploded about five miles west of Maidstone."

68 Squadron Beaufighter KV974/WM-R crewed by Flt Lt Jo Capka DFM (a Czech) and Flt Lt Willie Williams DFM, was ordered by ground control to investigate "a ragged bunch of specks" that had appeared on radar from over the French coast during the late afternoon – it was initially thought possibly another approaching wave of Divers. As the Mosquito neared the formation, the crew was able to identify the bogies as a formation of US B-24s (believed from the 489thBG) returning from a raid on Creil in France, one of which had been badly shot up and was flying on three engines. The Czech pilot later wrote:

> "I had visions of a wounded American pilot struggling with the controls of the bomber and moved quickly in on his tail to fly alongside and see if there was anything that could be done. As I did so I saw the rear-turret traversing to follow us and thought nothing about it. One moment I was studying the Liberator's wounds and the next there was nothing. I heard no

abnormal noise, felt no pain, but just like that I was blind ... I yelled 'What the bloody hell happened?' A hand pulled my helmet from over my right ear and Willie's voice screamed in what sounded like astonished tones: 'The bastard shot us ... that bloody Yank shot us ... the port engine's gone.'"

Despite his injuries, including the loss of his left eye, Capka managed to fly the crippled aircraft back to East Anglia, where it crash-landed on the Suffolk/Essex border after Williams had baled out. Capka, who received burns in the crash, would spend many months recovering[70].

Night 27/28 JUNE

Nine people were killed when a Diver fell on Manor Place, Walworth (SE17) at 2245. Six houses were destroyed in Crampton Street and four in Manor Place. Many others were damaged. A further five Londoners were killed at 0115 when a Diver came down on Barcombe Avenue, Streatham (SW2).

85 Squadron (Mosquito XVII) Swannington

Flg Off P.S. Kendall	MM632/VY-E	V-1	0220-0315

96 Squadron (Mosquito XIII) Ford

Flt Lt F.R.L. Mellersh	HK456/ZJ-K	V-1	0320	off Dungeness
Flt Sgt T. Bryan	HK421/ZJ-	V-1	0340	off Dungeness
Wg Cdr E.D. Crew	HK417/ZJ-	V-1	0340	off Hastings
Flt Lt D.L. Ward	MM524/ZJ-	V-1	0424	off Dungeness

The Divers shot down by Wg Cdr Crew and Flt Lt Togs Mellersh were straight forward and both splashed into the sea following close-range stern attacks, while that shot down by Flt Lt Don Ward lost both its wings before plunging into the sea. Flt Sgt Tom Bryan failed to notice any strikes during his attack but all the same the Diver went into an orbit and then crashed into the sea.

157 Squadron (Mosquito XIX) Swannington

Flt Lt J.G. Benson	MM630/RS-E	V-1		Calais-Le Touquet
Wt Off A.G. McLeod	MM637/RS-P	V-1		

Flt Lt Benson's navigator Flt Lt Lewis Brandon later wrote a graphic account of the difficulties of early night interceptions[71]:

"As Group had called for a maximum effort we made sure 'Eager Beaver' was in fighting trim. She was and at 2255 hours Ben and I found ourselves airborne on an anti-Diver patrol over the Somme Estuary. There was one small change to our usual set-up; the armourers had been instructed to load us with one tracer in every four of our cannon shells. Normally we did not use tracer ammunition in order to maintain the element of surprise. We were soon over the Channel making our way to our patrol point. When we reached it, we informed control. The weather was clear but dark, so we turned on to our north-easterly leg flying at nine thousand feet. 'Well, here we go,' said Ben. 'Some caper this is. I wonder what bright spark at Air Ministry dreamed this one up?' 'Blowed if I know! I'm certainly going to keep my AI switched on. There are dozens of aircraft around.' 'The Jerries are bound to plot a gaggle of aircraft like this. If they put some fighters up there'll be some fun.' I took the visor off the AI indicator. 'Just look at this! There're five aircraft here for a start!' We pressed on regardless for some 40 minutes of our hour's patrol with our remarks getting more caustic all the time. France seemed very dark and peaceful below us. It all seemed such a waste of time.

"Then suddenly it happened. Down there in the blackness we saw a moving light. It was followed in a matter of seconds by another and another, until within a minute there were five little lights below all heading north-east for London. Ben was already turning after the leading light. I switched the navigation lights on and stared out at the moving lights, which were all heading in the same direction but with a considerable space between each of them. They were yellow. I looked at the one we were diving after. It was some way off still but we were fairly whistling down after it. All seemed to be well, then suddenly: 'Christ Almighty!' exploded Ben. 'Just look around us. Let's get the hell out of here!' I looked around. The sky around us was stiff with navigation lights. Almost every fighter on patrol must have seen the lights at the same time and gone screaming down after the leader. We weaved our way through the navigation lights. Ben wasted little time and merely transferred his attention to number three of the lights. This was about a mile behind the first one. Eager Beaver was shuddering a little as we were now diving at well over 320mph, pretty fast for an ordinary night fighter Mozzie.

"Ben had judged the interception beautifully. The Diver was now fairly close below our starboard wing, crossing slightly from starboard to port. All that could be seen was a long yellow flame. What the devil could it be? As Ben made the final turn to bring us behind the Diver, or whatever it might be, we lost sight of it for a second. Then a huge yellow flame swooshed just over our cockpit. We had found it again – the flame looked at least twenty feet long. The Diver was whizzing along very fast indeed at a height of 2,000 feet and flying straight and level. Ben had to keep the throttles full open to keep up with it although we had gathered quite a lot of speed during our dive. We were nicely behind it now. 'Here goes,' said Ben, giving the thing ahead of us a two-seconds burst of cannons. The tracer shells in our ammunition proved their value. But to our dismay we could see them falling well short of the wretched flame thing in front of us. 'It must be a damned sight farther away than it ruddy well looks,' remarked Ben, giving it another short burst. 'It seems to be about two or three hundred yards.' The shells were still dropping short. With each burst of fire our speed had dropped slightly. Even with full throttle Eager Beaver was falling behind. Then a thought struck me. I had been sitting there feeling a bit useless on this job, but as Ben was finding difficulty in judging the range, I could give him the correct range from my AI. Sure enough I could see it clearly, only a small blip but easy to see. I told Ben: 'I've got it on AI. The range is nearly 6,000 feet.' 'Well I'm blowed! I would have thought it was still only about 500 yards off. Well, it's no use chasing this one any more.'

"As we climbed back to patrol height we discussed the strange phenomenon we had seen. It had flown straight and level even though we had been firing tracer at it. It all seemed very queer, but perhaps it might be a pilotless missile after all. I was quite pleased that I could be of some help using my AI as a range finder. We were over the Somme Estuary again, but we could see no more of the yellow lights. The patrol carried on for another ten minutes or so, then we saw another batch of five Divers start off on their journey. This time we had decided to ignore the leading light – which seemed far too popular. We swooped down after number three, with our navigation lights on as before. This time as I looked around I could see only one other pair of lights in pursuit of the Diver. Ben had spotted it too. 'Is he the only one around?' he asked. 'Can't see any more. . . No, nobody else near, anyhow.' 'Right, we're in a better position than he is. Flash the nav lights on and off a couple of times and see if that works.' I did as Ben suggested, but the other aircraft's navigation lights were still there – a little further behind but still there. I reported this to Ben. He was now approaching the tricky part of the whole business, the final swoop. 'Okay. We'll soon fix him.' Although we were still some way from the Diver, far out of firing range, Ben let fly a short burst of cannons. We saw the tracer falling away in front of us. So did the other aircraft. He must have realised that we were better placed for an interception, so he waggled his wings and turned away. Just in time too – Ben did not want anything else to worry him now. The Diver was down on our starboard side, coming in to us at an angle of about fifteen degrees. Ben had kept it below so that he would be able to swoop on it after the final turn that would bring us behind it. He timed it perfectly. As we turned, he put Eager Beaver's nose slightly down and I could see the blip on the AI. The only information he wanted from me was the range.' 'I've got it now. Just under a mile ...we're closing on it nicely ... three thousand. How's it going?' 'Oh, we've still got a bit of height in hand. It looks bloody close now. What range?' "Two thousand ... it's still coming in quite fast ... fifteen hundred now ... twelve hundred.' 'I'll have a go from about two hundred yards. Can't see anything to shoot at but that ruddy great flame. What range? 'Just under a thousand feet. We're still gaining pretty fast.' 'Yes. This isn't going so fast as the first one was.' 'Coming in to eight hundred now ... seven hundred, still gaining ... coming in to six hundred, Okay. Here we go.'

"I looked up as Ben pressed the gun button. We saw the tracer go slap into the flame. Flashes came from it as the shells struck home and sent it spinning into the sea. The strange flame from its tail was still burning until it hit the water. In the meantime, as Ben gave the fairly long burst of cannon fire, Eager Beaver bucked for a moment or two like a Wild West bronco. The cockpit was suddenly filled with cold, rushing air; there was a noise like a heavy sea breaking on a shingle beach and the wind whistled into the cockpit like a hurricane. For the first and only time in all our sorties together Ben said to me: 'You'd better put your parachute on, Brandy.' So I did. After a few moments, however, Eager Beaver seemed to settle herself down to fly fairly smoothly. Ben decided to make for the nearest airfield in case of emergency, as there was obviously something amiss. I gave him a course to steer for Tangmere. I remember hoping that if we did have to jump for it we would at least reach dry land before the worst happened. I am a very keen swimmer, but I prefer to choose the time and place. We reached Tangmere in due course, with Ben flying very gingerly. It was found that Eager Beaver's nose had almost collapsed with the excessive strain caused by our speed coupled with the vibration of the cannons. After this, the noses of Mozzies flying on this job were strengthened."

219 Squadron (Mosquito XVII) Bradwell Bay

| Flt Lt G.R.I. Parker | HK250/FK- | V-1 | 0205 | mid-Channel |

"Sighted target at 3,500 feet, 280 IAS, and chased halfway across the Channel. Opened fire from 1,000 yards down to 300 yards. Strikes on port wing. Broke off and target dived into the sea."

418 (RCAF) Squadron (Mosquito VI) Holmsley South

| Flt Lt S.H.R. Cotterill RCAF | TH- | V-1 | 0051 | Channel |

"Diver seen at 1,600 feet five miles north of Le Touquet. Fired a two-seconds burst from 150 yards, followed by one-and-half-second burst. Strikes seen on starboard wing. Diver spiralled down to sea and blew up on impact."

605 Squadron (Mosquito VI) Manston

Flt Lt J.I. Pengelly	UP-	V-1	0221	over land
Flg Off B.G. Bensted	HJ799/UP-L	V-1	0335	Channel
Sqn Ldr G.J. Wright	UP-	V-1	0427	off Dungeness
Flg Off R.C. Walton RNZAF	UP-	V-1		
	UP-	V-1		
Flt Lt J.R. Rhodes	UP-C	V-1 damaged		off Calais-Le Touquet

Flg Off Jack Pengelly shot down his first flying bomb:

"At 0158 we attacked Diver at 2,000 feet. We chased it across the Channel, closing in, and attacked from astern. The target lost height and crashed one-mile inland at 0204. We saw four or five others at same time but unfortunately had run out of ammo."

An hour later Flg Off Basil Bensted chalked up his third kill:

"Out of six Divers seen we attacked two. First at 0313 at 3,000 feet flying at 400mph, but we could not close range and Diver pulled away. At 0034 we again attacked a Diver travelling at 400mph at 1,000 feet. We saw strikes and Diver caught fire, banked over to port and crashed in the sea at 0335. Range when attacked 600 yards."

Sqn Ldr Wilbur Wright reported:

"Airborne 0216. During the whole patrol ten Divers were seen but only two attacked owing to unfavourable position of Mosquito. At 0245 ten miles south-east of Dungeness we attacked the first Diver at 3,000 feet. No results were seen. At 0427 we attacked a second Diver which was flying at 340mph at 3,000 feet. We were astern and above and as we opened fire we saw strikes and almost instantly saw two other aircraft below us and astern of the Diver. After several strikes from our guns the jet from the target dimmed and flared twice, and it struck the sea. The lower layer of cloud was lit for miles around by the explosion. We fixed the position of the kill two miles east-south-east of Dungeness."

The New Zealand crew of Flg Off Walton and Sgt Pritchard scored a double. Flt Sgt John Little, Flt Lt Rhodes' navigator in UP-C, noted in his logbook: "Patrol Calais-Le Touquet area. Lots [of Divers] seen and four attacked. One definitely hit and slowed down. Closing in for the kill when some one else opened up in front of us."

Wednesday 28 JUNE

A Diver fell on Upton Junior Council School, Iris Avenue, Bexley at 0850, seriously injuring three children and slightly wounding a further one dozen. Another flying bomb fell on Heston in the Thames Valley, this time impacting on the airfield where considerable damage was done, but no one was injured. Twenty-five people were killed at 1249 when a Diver struck a row of houses and shops in Acre Lane by the Town Hall in Brixton (SW2). One of the shops was being used as a rest centre for people previously forced out of their homes by flying bombs. Gauden Road, Clapham SW4, received its second bomb on consecutive days, this one taking a further life. A further severe loss of life occurred at 1734, when a Diver impacted at the corner of Peckham Road and St Giles Road (Camberwell SE5), where it hit a block of flats (Bentley House), killing 19. Shortly thereafter, a Diver exploded in Rectory Road, Beckenham, destroying or damaging 50 properties and taking the life of a resident. A later explosion in Beckenham, at 2005, occurred in Shortlands Road, where a further three people were killed.

Elsewhere, fighters shot down another that fell on Lamb's Farm near Brooklands. And another victim of fighters crashed near Ivychurch at 1300. Americans based at Fowlmere in Cambridgeshire, home of the 339thFG, experienced a near miss when a Diver fell 500 yards from the airfield's control tower at 1410. There was no damage. Another came down south-west of Gravesend airfield, and two more fell at Meopham (1343) and Hartley (2130) after being shot down by fighters, while one brought down by a balloon cable at 2204 fell at New Barn near Southfleet, injuring one person. Five more were brought down by fighters in the Malling/Hollingbourne area during the daylight hours, none causing injuries, but the Diver hit by AA near Staplehurst crashed near a gun site at Great Pagehurst Farm, killing a soldier and seriously injuring another. One Diver was located almost intact, and was found to be carrying a cable-cutting knife installed into the leading edge of the wing, the first such device to be inspected. A subsequent report stated:

"From that date [28 June] until 4 July, out of 68 flying bombs examined, only eight were found to be fitted with the cable-cutting device. These figures however are not necessarily a true guide to the number of flying bombs carrying this device, as much of the wreckage examined has been buried under buildings and the evidence obtained is too scanty to give a definite ruling as to whether or not a cable-cutter had been fitted. The cable-cutter consists of a knife-edged section of hard steel very similar in profile to the device fitted to the leading edge of the wing of the He111. It seems probable that the blade is inserted after the wings are manufactured, and before they are bolted to the main spar. Because the wing leading-edge is of steel, and the clips holding the cable-cutter are not of a very robust construction, it is possible that the knife blade may fold over on impact with a balloon cable and not actually sever it."[72]

1 Squadron (Spitfire LFIXb) Detling

Flg Off D.V. McIntosh	MK901/JX-	V-1 shared	1736	exploded in mid-air
Flg Off E.G. Hutchin	MJ422/JX-	V-1	1830	Minster area
Flt Sgt I. Hastings	MK846/JX-	V-1	2105-2110	Brentwood area
Flt Lt T. Draper Williams	ML118/JX-	V-1	2210-2215	Willards Hill area
Flg Off E.N.W. Marsh	MK988/JX-	V-1	2300	Ashford area

The Squadron accounted for five Divers during the evening, the first falling to Flg Off

McIntosh at 1736, although a Spitfire pilot from 322 Squadron was granted a share in the kill:

> "Yellow Section scrambled – saw Diver approaching on a north-westerly course, at 1,300 feet. I fired a short burst from 200 yards, using full deflection, and Diver exploded in mid-air."

A witness on the ground, LAC Phil Williamson remembers:

> "This chap had just taken off and this V-1 came over. Our pilot got round onto its tail and opened fire and it took a dive right above us. I jumped into a Nissen hut, hit the floor with my hands over my ears, but nothing happened. I came out again and the V-1 had circled round the other side of the airfield and then exploded in a ball of flame. Our pilot pulled round and landed within seconds and we could see all the fabric had gone from the tailplane. A great lump of aluminum from the V-1 suddenly landed near us, clanging along on the concrete."

The second fell to Flg Off Hutchin at 1830:

> "Green Section vectored on to Diver six miles south-east of Canterbury, flying at 2,000 feet. Closed in, firing from 600-350 yards. Jet burned very brightly. Diver slowed up, turned on back and exploded on ground by railway between Halfway House and Minster."

Flt Sgt Iain Hastings reported:

> "Diver sighted east of Folkestone on north-west course, flying at 350mph. Made four attacks, the last one over the Thames Estuary. Strikes seen on port wing. Ammo exhausted so broke away. Diver last seen heading for Brentwood. ROC confirms Diver crashed near Brentwood."

Flt Lt Tom Draper Williams:

> "Vectored onto four Divers coming over in Dungeness area. Saw one at 1,500 feet near Westfield on north-westerly course. Fired short bursts from 300-200 yards from dead astern. Saw strikes and as I pulled away to starboard, Diver dived steeply and crashed near Willards Hill. I was nearly hit by AA from coastal batteries."

The final victory of the day was scored by Flg Off Junior Marsh:

> "Saw Diver near New Romney flying at 1,700-2,000 feet. Closed in from 500-300 yards attacking and observing strikes on rear fuselage and port wing. The Diver went into a gentle dive and flew straight and level for a second or two then made a steep climbing turn to port, finally diving down to explode on the ground four-five miles south of Ashford."

150 Wing (Tempest V) Newchurch

Wg Cdr R.P. Beamont	EJ525/RB	V-1	am	Hastings area

3 Squadron (Tempest V) Newchurch

Flg Off R.H. Clapperton	JN822/JF-	V-1	0625-0745	
	JN822/JF-	V-1	0625-0745	
	JN822/JF-	V-1	0625-0745	
Plt Off G.A. Whitman RCAF (US)	JN807/JF-Y	V-1	0530-0650	
Plt Off K.G. Slade-Betts	JN769/JF-G	V-1	0730-0845	
	JN769/JF-G	V-1	0730-0845	
Plt Off S.B. Feldman (US)	JN743/JF-P	V-1	0730-0805	
Flt Sgt R.W. Cole	JN769/JF-G	V-1 damaged	0925-1105	off Eastbourne
Plt Off H.R. Wingate	JN862/JF-Z	V-1	0930-1050	
Flt Sgt D.M. Smith	JN793/JF-N	V-1	0730-0820	
Flt Lt R. van Lierde (Belg)	JN862/JF-Z	V-1	1220-1305	
Flt Sgt R.W. Pottinger	JN793/JF-N	V-1	1220-1455	

Flg Off Ray Clapperton scored all three in one sortie, thereby bringing up the Squadron's 100th kill in 13 days. Flt Sgt Bob Cole noted in his logbook: "Patrol. Intercept Diver off Eastbourne. Get a piece off. It escaped into cloud." Flt Sgt Ron

Pottinger recalled:

> "On one occasion I was flying No.2 to F/O Kosh, and we and a third pilot were all chasing after the same Doodlebug. I was in the middle and slightly below and behind the other two. As soon as I was within reasonable distance I gave it a good burst and was gratified to see large lumps fly off and the thing go into a nose-dive. I was later complimented on my shooting but told I should have let my No.1 have first whack! I'm afraid my home was in London and I was only interested in stopping the Doodlebugs, never mind the niceties!"

91 Squadron (Spitfire XIV) Deanland ALG

Flt Lt J.W.P. Draper RCAF	RB161/DL-I	V-1	0800	Rye-Hastings
Flt Lt H.D. Johnson	RB183/DL-M	V-1	0800 shared	exploded in mid-air
	RB183/DL-M	V-1	0815	Hastings area

Flt Lt Bill Draper: "Diver seen over the sea and I attacked from astern. Tail unit was knocked off and Diver spun into sea between Rye and Hastings." Flt Lt Johnny Johnson scored a brace:

> "West of Hastings I was vectored on to a Diver. Attacked by one Spit and two Tempests followed by me. It exploded in mid-air. Attacked second Diver south of Hastings and attacked with one-seconds burst and it fell into the sea."

137 Squadron (Typhoon Ib) Manston

Wt Off J.A. Horne RAAF	MN429/SF-	V-1	0440-0540	Dover area

During their early morning patrol of the Cap Gris Nez-Le Tréport line, Wt Off Jack Horne and Flt Sgt L. Burrows sighted five flying bombs, two of which were attacked. The first pulled away before they could open fire, and the second was chased to the Kent coast, hits being observed. However, the bomb maintained its course and the Typhoons had to break away to avoid entering the coastal gun zone. The Typhoons returned to Manston, where Flt Sgt Burrows belly-landed MN351 due to hydraulics failure. Sometime later, Dover ASR telephoned to report that the Diver had in fact crashed seven miles inland and Horne was credited with one confirmed.

> "I saw a flying bomb coming out from France and I turned to chase it. The Doodlebug was doing about 380mph, but I had a slight advantage in height so I put the nose down, opened the throttle, put the pitch in fully fine and got after it. I opened fire at long range but I could see that the cannon-shells were not hitting it and the range was getting greater. In desperation I raised the nose of the Typhoon and fired four pairs of rockets at it (I'd seen no shipping on the reconnaissance). At least one of the rockets hit the bomb, because it started to break up and spun down into a field (I'd gone too far in the chase – we were supposed to break off five miles from the coast to give the flak a chance)."

This was probably the same incident as recorded by 1/Lt Leslie Boze USAAF of the 365thFS. Wt Off Jack Horne continued:

> "The following day, a group captain from an experimental station [probably from the FIU] arrived at Manston in a Mustang, which was equipped with rockets unlike any we'd seen before. They had Bakelite heads with a photo-electric cell, which would trigger the 25lb warhead if the rocket passed close to the Doodlebug. The group captain told me that the rockets had originally been intended as a makeshift anti-aircraft defence earlier in the war [presumably the Z-rocket device]. They loaded my aircraft up with similar rockets which had been sent down by transport and we both stooged up and down the Channel, but no flying bombs appeared that day."

322 (Dutch) Squadron (Spitfire XIV) West Malling

Flg Off L.D. Wolters	VL-N	V-1 shared	1310	Wadhurst area
Wt Off J.A. Maier	VL-Q	V-1	1540	off Hastings

Flg Off G.F.J. Jongbloed	VL-C	V-1	2230	West Malling area
Flt Sgt F. van Valkenburg	NH649/VL-F	V-1	2240	off Beachy Head

Although it would appear that Flg Off Bert Wolters should have been awarded a kill, he was obliged to share it with another pilot:

> "Vectored on Diver crossing coast near Hastings. As I was closing in another Spitfire fired, missed and broke off. I closed to 200 yards, gave short burst, but lost sight of Diver in cloud. Sighted it again, gave long burst and port wing fell off. Diver spun, crashed and exploded near Wadhurst."

Just over two hours later Wt Off Justin Maier shot down another:

> "Whilst patrolling in mid-Channel was vectored on to Diver. Attacked line astern from above, range 150 yards. Further attack from starboard. Diver spun and exploded in sea six miles south of Hastings."

During a late evening patrol Flg Off Jan Jongbloed (in VL-E) had exhausted his ammunition without success so tried to tip the flying bomb with one wingtip, but only succeeded in bending the wingtip. He landed and was off again in VL-C, when he was more successful:

> "Sighted Diver when taking off, chased it and attacked from port, slowing it down. Second attack and Diver crashed and exploded on hilltop north-west of West Malling."

Flt Sgt van Valkenburg got another a few minutes later:

> "Patrolling mid-Channel when vectored on to Diver. Intercepted and attacked dead astern. Diver crashed in sea and exploded six miles south-east of Beachy Head."

486 (RNZAF) Squadron (Tempest V) Newchurch

Flg Off J.G. Wilson RNZAF	JN866/SA-U	V-1	0610	Appledore area
Wt Off O.D. Eagleson RNZAF	JN859/SA-S	V-1	0800	Sevenoaks area
	JN854/SA-G	V-1	1035	Rye area
Flg Off R.J. Cammock RNZAF	JN810/SA-P	V-1	1112	Beachy Head area
Plt Off F.B. Lawless RNZAF	JN859/SA-S	V-1	1405	Hastings area
Flt Sgt B.M. Hall RNZAF	JN809/SA-M	V-1	2245	Rye area
Plt Off R.R. Wright RNZAF	JN804/SA-R	V-1	KiA	Beachy Head area

Plt Off Roland 'Joe' Wright flying SA-R was shot down by AA while on a Diver patrol and crashed into the sea off Beachy Head, losing his life. Wt Off Jim Sheddan wrote:

> "Joe Wright, while on a seaward flight patrol, had pursued a bomb inland and after destroying it was heading back to his offshore patrol line when some American gunners shot his aircraft down and Joe was killed. From the ground at night it should have been a physical impossibility to mistake an aircraft for a flying bomb with that long sheet of flame trailing astern, but the American gunners managed to do it. The last message from Joe was that he was being fired on by our gunners and that his Tempest had been hit and he was going to attempt a forced-landing. In the area he was over a forced-landing in daylight would have been a dicey do, at night he had no show. At the time he was hit he was over land and with enough height to have successfully baled out. Why he did not was difficult to understand. Joe was a popular member of our team and it made us bitter to see him killed in this way. We would have welcomed the opportunity of making a strafing attack on the gunners responsible."

A second Tempest (JN794/SA-T) flown by Plt Off Stamford 'Bill' Williams was also hit by AA fire while on V-1 patrol off Beachy Head but he managed to return safely to Newchurch.

FIU Detachment (Tempest V) Newchurch

Flt Lt J. Berry	EJ524/ZQ-Y[73]	V-1	daytime
	EJ524/ZQ-Y	V-1	daytime
Sqn Ldr E.G. Daniel	EJ531/ZQ-	V-1	daytime
	EJ531/ZQ-	V-1	daytime

Sqn Ldr Daniel and Flt Lt Berry each flew three patrols and both claimed two flying bombs destroyed, all of which were confirmed. Flt Lt Jeremy Howard-Williams recalled:

"On 28 June the clouds lifted a little and the FIU pilots held a conference. The gibes they had suffered were not to be borne another night, so they would go and have a look at the weather. Teddy ordered the covers off the aircraft and they started getting ready to fly. Looking up they could see nothing but an unbroken expanse of low cloud scudding by. The other pilots had not noticed the departure of the pair. In the bar at dusk, the noise of laughter and talk was suddenly shattered by the familiar blast of a Tempest engine. In the silence which followed, the second aircraft added its raucous crackle. Unconscious of the ripple they had caused, Joe followed his flight commander to the end of the line of flares. He saw Teddy's aircraft straighten up, pause and then disappear down the flare path into the murk. He taxied forward, opened the throttle and gathered speed down the runway. Before the last flare had flashed past he was airborne. Wheels up; throttle back; adjust airscrew pitch. The vital drill came automatically as he concentrated on keeping his aircraft climbing on instruments. He changed from aerodrome frequency to sector control. Teddy Daniel's voice crackled through his headphones, acknowledging instructions; there was evidently plenty of trade. In turn he was vectored towards the south. Soon he climbed through the top of the low-cloud layer, with further broken cloud piled up above him. He flew along in a gap between the layers and could now afford to look outside his cockpit. Suddenly he spotted a flickering yellow glow away to the south over the English Channel. Streaking along was his first flying bomb. 'Tally ho!' He took over control of the interception. All too quickly he found that seeing the target was one thing, destroying it another. Control had to be accurate, the engagement swift, otherwise he found himself flying through the lethal AA gun belt."

Following two days of fruitless anti-Diver patrols, **41 Squadron** at West Malling was stood down temporarily due to poor weather conditions in its sector, permitting the pilots to relax and for some to indulge themselves somewhat, as observed by the squadron diarist: "There was a good session in the bar where Flt Lt Burne was undisputed chairman and noggin master." Flt Lt Tommy Burne was one of those gallant airmen who could have sat out the remainder of war considering his disability. In 1942 he had been a Hudson pilot at Singapore, where he was severely wounded, having a leg amputated. Fitted with an artificial leg he volunteered to fly fighters, was posted to 41 Squadron and flew his share of operational sorties including anti-Diver patrols[74].

Night 28/29 JUNE

A Diver exploded in Willow Bank Road (Peckham SE15), close to where one fell the previous day, killing one resident. Two Divers fell on Penge (SE20) during the early morning hours, one impacting in Cottingham Road at 0023, causing much widespread damage and killing three residents. Thirty minutes later a second fell on Laurel Grove, behind Penge High Street, again inflicting severe damage and killing a further three. Four were killed in Upper Norwood (SE19) when a Diver crashed in Gibbs Close at 0423, demolishing eight houses.

85 Squadron (Mosquito XIX) Swannington

Flg Off R.T. Goucher	TA400/VY-J	V-1	2250-0215	Channel

96 Squadron (Mosquito XIII) Ford

Flt Lt I.A. Dobie	HK396/ZJ-	V-1	2240-0050	Channel
	HK396/ZJ-	V-1	2240-0050	Channel
	HK396/ZJ-	V-1	2240-0050	Channel
	HK396/ZJ-	V-1	2240-0050	Channel
Flt Lt F.R.L. Mellersh	HK372/ZJ-G	V-1	2245-0135	Channel
	HK372/ZJ-G	V-1	2245-0135	Channel
	HK372/ZJ-G	V-1	2245-0135	Channel
	HK372/ZJ-G	V-1	2245-0135	Channel
Wg Cdr E.D. Crew	HK456/ZJ-K	V-1	0045-0345	Channel
	HK456/ZJ-K	V-1	0045-0345	Channel

Ten flying bombs brought down by just three crews represented a record and raised the squadron's score to 49 confirmed. Flt Lt Togs Mellersh and Flt Lt Michael Stanley were now the top-scoring crew with nine.

157 Squadron (Mosquito XIX) Swannington

Sqn Ldr J.H.M. Chisholm	MM676/RS-W	V-1 damaged	0106
	MM676/RS-W	V-1	0126

169 Squadron (Mosquito VI) Great Massingham

Wg Cdr N.B.R. Bromley	NT113	V-1 damaged	2245-0315	Channel

Wg Cdr Neil Bromley OBE spotted a Diver taking off from its ramp and pursued it out to sea. Although he reported strikes on both wings it continued on its course and he was unable to confirm its destruction.

605 Squadron (Mosquito VI) Manston

Flt Lt J.R. Rhodes	UP-C	V-1	0005	off Dungeness
Flt Lt A.T. Linn	UP-	V-1	0014	Bexhill area
Flg Off R.C. Walton RNZAF	UP-	V-1		
	UP-	V-1		
Flt Lt G.C. Wright	UP-	V-1	0151	off Rye
	UP-	V-1	0222	off Rye

605's first Diver of the night fell to Flt Lt John Rhodes:

"At 0005 attacked a Diver flying at 2,500 feet. A long burst was fired with no result, so range was closed to about 200 yards and again I opened fire, seeing the target explode, causing slight damage to the Mosquito three miles south of Dungeness. A second Diver was seen flying from Le Touquet area at 2,000 feet. I attacked with three-four-seconds burst, apparently out of range as no result seen. Between Le Touquet and Dungeness five Divers were seen but not in position to attack."

The Mosquito flown by Flg Off Arthur Linn was also damaged by the explosion of their victim:

"At 0001 we gave chase to a Diver inland east of Beachy Head flying at 2,500 feet. I fired several bursts and found I had three cannon stoppages. The ground defences then opened fire at Diver so I immediately broke off attack without seeing results. At 0013, eight to nine miles south-east of Bexhill, I attacked a second Diver at 2,500 feet. I attacked from astern and noticed the target slow down. Opened fire again from dead astern and Diver exploded in mid-air at 0014 some 12 miles north-west of Bexhill. Damage to port engine was caused by explosion."

Flg Off Walton, a New Zealander scored another double, raising his score to five. Flt Lt George Wright scored his third and fourth kills off Rye:

"At 0151 five miles north-east of Rye a Diver was attacked at 3,000 feet and from 4-500 yards. Strikes seen and sparks from jet unit. As we could not close range we broke off attack and watched Diver being picked up by single searchlight – it then exploded in mid-air without further shots being fired. At 0222 at 4,000 feet a second Diver was attacked with two bursts. It was seen to catch fire and appeared to explode on impact with sea. Another was attacked at 0140 five miles south-west of Rye. A second burst was given but no results seen."

Thursday 29 JUNE

Penge (SE20) received its third Diver of the morning at 0615 but this did not cause any casualties, only damage to property, but a fourth fell on an AA site behind Annerley House School (at 1120), killing one soldier and inflicting damage to buildings, Nissen huts and six Z-rocket sites. Z-rocket batteries supplemented the AA guns but were not believed to have been very effective. Bombardier Frank Crown of the Royal Artillery was posted to such a site near New Romney:

"Each launcher fired two rockets, which were about six-feet in length and four inches in diameter, with four tail fins. Most had time fuses. The idea was that the launchers, with some slight variation in elevation and bearing, would form a box-barrage of explosions at a certain height, and that a target would be, hopefully, somewhere in the vicinity! Some shells had proximity fuses, with lenses in their noses, which exploded, or were supposed to, on passing a shadow. Rockets were fired electronically by depressing a lever on the side of the projector and, with 64 (sometimes) rockets fired, the brain suffered some disorientation for a few seconds! The drill after firing was to peer over the side of the launcher to check that both rockets had gone; if not, the launcher was swung on a bearing out to sea and left for a period in case of delayed action."[75]

A fighter shot down a Diver that crashed in West Street, Horsham, at 0500 – no injuries but much damage. Merstham School near Reigate in Surrey was damaged by blast from a flying bomb that exploded in the Corporation Yard in Albury Road, which was just 100 yards from the school. Although damage was extensive there were no serious casualties among the 200 children and staff. One of the Divers shot down by fighters over Kent in the morning crashed at Bromley Green at 1125, four bungalows suffering damage with three persons injured, two seriously. Two more victims of fighters fell at Great Chart (1231) and Shadoxhurst (1315) without causing damage. One that was shot down at 2216 fell at Aldington, injuring two. During the afternoon, islanders on the Isle of Wight had a front seat at a Diver performance which fortunately had a happy ending:

"A V-1 more or less sneaked in – the alert ROC crew at Puckpool just picked the sound up in time, at 5.16pm, workers at Cowes were sent to the shelters as anti-aircraft guns opened fire on the intruder. Shells burst close, it turned on its side two or three times, and then it must have been hit. With engine still full on it spun drunkenly down to explode harmlessly in Osborne Bay."

The cheers of the workers and other witnesses could probably be heard the other side of the Solent. At 1049, a Diver fell in Amesbury Avenue/Hillside Road in Brixton (SW2), killing four. During the evening, at 2020, a flying bomb demolished St Matthew's Church, Cottenham Park in Wimbledon SW20. Two hours later another impacted at the junction of Avignon and Aspinall Roads, Brockley (SE4), killing three more Londoners.

150 Wing (Tempest V) Newchurch

Wg Cdr R.P. Beamont	EJ525/RB	V-1	am	Ashford area
	EJ525/RB	V-1	am	Ashford area

3 Squadron (Tempest V) Newchurch

Flt Lt R. van Lierde (Belg)	JN862/JF-Z	V-1	0430-0555
Flt Sgt S. Domanski PAF	JN752/JF-S	V-1	0430-0550

Flg Off R.E. Barckley	JN755/JF-D	V-1	0530-0645	
Plt Off K.G. Slade-Betts	JN769/JF-G	V-1	0925-1045	
Flt Sgt R.W. Cole	JN759/JF-	V-1	1125-1245	Maidstone area

The Tempests brought down seven more Divers, two of them falling to Wg Cdr Beamont, raising his score to 14 including four shares. Flt Lt Remi van Lierde now had 13 to his credit although 7 were shared with others. Wg Cdr Beamont later recalled:

"The first week of the battle two Tempest pilots were shot down by anti-aircraft guns with the result that deputations were sent to local MPs. The Tempest Wing had their own more immediate satisfaction, however, when by a complete coincidence one of them downed a V-1 into the grounds of a country house used as a mess by the gunners. The resulting explosion blew out all the windows in the mess without hurting anybody, just as the gunner officers were having their breakfast. The Tempest pilots were said to have come back from that particular sortie holding their sides."

Air Vice-Marshal Hill arrived at Newchurch in his Tempest to visit the Squadron and no doubt to congratulate them on their recent successes.

74 Squadron (Spitfire LFIX) Lympne

| Flt Lt D.E. Llewellyn | NH468/4D-N | V-1 | pm | Lympne area |
| Sgt J. Dalzell | RR207/4D-T | V-1 | pm | Lympne area |

Flt Lt Don Llewellyn wrote:

"I was, as B Flight commander, designated to lead the Squadron that day. We were suddenly told we could send up an anti-Diver patrol of two aircraft for the last hour of the daylight readiness. I took Sgt [Paddy] Dalzell as my partner. I had a nasty suspicion that the controllers might favour the more regular patrols, so we ignored their instructions, until they put us on to one which was directed (as we expected) over Lympne. As we approached from the west it was crossing from right to left at our height, just below the cloud level (about 4,000 feet, I think). Because they were supposed to be fast, I pulled up into the cloud, did a 90° turn and came down directly behind it with speed, lined it up and fired. At that moment one of those damned 'free-lance' Tempests came up from below, right in front of me, and I hit him in both wings, directly above Lympne – pieces of aircraft fell on the field and were shown to me afterwards. Since I could do nothing about the Tempest, I went on and shot down the Doodlebug. It turned over to the left and went into a field somewhere to the north of Lympne. When I later phoned to say I had accidentally shot down a Tempest, a bored WAAF said, 'Oh, what, another one?' and rang off. It did not matter anyway. The Tempest was flown by the Newchurch Wing Co [Wg Cdr R.F. Aitken OC 150 Wing], and there were far too many Tempests (and wing commanders!) floating around in everybody's way, in June 1944!"

Sgt Paddy Dalzell remembered:

"I landed at Lympne and a couple of cars (one the CO's) met me on the airfield and enquired if I was all right. It turned out that Llew had been firing at a V-1 and a Tempest appeared between him and the V-1 into the line of fire, hitting and knocking off his wingtip. They thought it was me. I had changed frequency to one used by the ack-ack to hear of any V-1s approaching Kent and therefore did not receive any calls from Llew or base."

24 Wing (Spitfire XIV) Deanland ALG

| Wg Cdr R.W. Oxspring | NH714/RW-O | V-1 | 0955 | Tenterden |

Wg Cdr Bobby Oxspring patrolled with 91 Squadron.

91 Squadron (Spitfire XIV) Deanland ALG

Flt Lt A. Smith RNZAF	RB173/DL-	V-1	0520	Dungeness area
Flg Off E. Topham	NH707/DL-N			
Flt Lt R.S. Nash	RM615/DL-	V-1	0600	Newchurch a/f

	RM615/DL-	V-1	0630	Lydd area
Flg Off E. Topham	RM654/DL-F	V-1	0850	Sittingbourne area
Flg Off G. Balcombe	RB161/DL-I	V-1	1340	West Malling area
Flg Off E. Topham	RB169/DL-Q	V-1	1345	Ashford area
Flt Lt H.D. Johnson	NH701/DL-A	V-1	1645	High Halden area
Flt Lt W.C. Marshall	RB181/DL-W	V-1	1725	exploded in mid-air
Flt Lt H.D. Johnson	RB188/DL-K	V-1	2100	Battle area
Flt Lt H.M. Neil	RB173/DL-	V-1	2220	Newchurch area

91 Squadron flew a record total (for the Squadron) of 66¹/4 hours during the day and accounted for 11 Divers. Three were shot down before breakfast, the first falling to the combined attack of Flt Lt Smith and Flg Off Topham, who brought down their victim into a field near Dungeness. The next two fell to Flt Lt Ray Nash:

"Vectored on to Diver crossing the coast. Shot down, it falling on airfield perimeter track at Newchurch." Thirty minutes later he got his second: "Diver intercepted over Dungeness. Attacked and it fell in a field north-west of Lydd, where it exploded."

Topham was up on his second patrol when he sighted a Diver coming in over Ashford. Following his attack it crashed and exploded in a field near Sittingbourne. Wg Cdr Bobby Oxspring flew a patrol at 0930, catching a Diver 25 minutes later:

"Vectored on Diver four miles east of Dungeness. Shot it down and it exploded when hitting the ground in the Tenterden area."

Flg Off Topham was again successful when flying his third patrol of the day:

"Vectored on a Diver and intercepted east of Dungeness. Shot it down, falling in a field close to an AA gun post six miles south of Ashford."

Next to score was Flg Off George Balcombe:

"Diver sighted 15 miles south of base and attacked. It was set on fire and fell in woods five miles from base, where it exploded."

Flt Lt Johnny Johnson added to his score at 1645:

"Diver sighted over Dymchurch and was set on fire from second burst. It fell in a field near High Halden where it exploded."

Flg Off Bill Marshall reported:

"Sighted Diver over Eastbourne. It was over taken and exploded in mid-air with burst from 150 yards range."

Flt Lt Johnson was up again at 2000, and an hour later scored his second kill of the evening:

"Vectored on Diver west of Bexhill. Shot it down and it exploded in a field east of Battle."

The last kill of the day fell to Flg Off Neil:

"Diver seen three miles south of Dungeness and attacked from dead astern from 100 yards range. Diver spun in and exploded in a field five miles north of Newchurch."

165 Squadron (Spitfire IX) Detling

Flg Off T.D. Tinsey ⎤	ML175/SK-P	V-1	1315	Tenterden area
Flt Sgt I.L. Loch ⎦	ML139/SK-Q			
Flt Sgt V. Porich RAAF	NH401/SK-M	V-1 shared	1640	off Rye
Flt Sgt C.R. Bundara RAAF	MK811/SK-S	V-1	1700	Sevenoaks area
Lt(A) S.G. Hamblett RNVR	MK480/SK-F	V-1	1710	Dungeness

Plt Off J.M. Walton RCAF	MK738/SK-L	V-1	1920	off Hastings
Lt(A) S.G. Hamblett RNVR	MK838/SK-K	V-1	2140	Tonbridge area

165 Squadron had its most rewarding day when accounting for six Divers, the first of which fell to the combined attacks of Flg Off Tommy Tinsey and Flt Sgt Ian Loch at 1315:

> "When just airborne Green Section saw Diver being attacked by Thunderbolts [possibly 22ndFS] without result. Flt Sgt Loch made two attacks the first being a two-seconds burst from 150/200 yards range, the second a two-seconds burst astern at 50/100 yards. I made one attack of two-seconds range from astern and below. The Diver exploded on the ground near Tenterden."

Three hours later Flt Sgt Vic Porich picked up a flying bomb five miles out to sea south of Rye: "Attacked, firing a two-seconds burst at 40-50 yards range. Diver spun into sea two to three miles south of Rye." This was shared with a Tempest from 486(NZ) Squadron flown by Wt Off S.J. Short. Fellow Australian Flt Sgt Colin Bundara made four attacks on the bomb he intercepted north of Sevenoaks: "During last attack there was a large flash and I pulled away. On looking again there was no sign of the Diver." A few minutes later the Navy pilot Lt(A) Selwyn Hamblett scored his second kill ten miles north of Dungeness:

> "Saw Diver three miles south-east of Dungeness. I overshot on my first attack. Made second attack, firing two two-seconds bursts from 200-100 yards astern. Diver exploded in a field."

On a later patrol, at 2140, he caught another:

> "Picked up Diver three miles south of Bexhill. Diver went into cloud and when it emerged I made astern attacks, firing three or four bursts of one-second each from 150-100 yards. During last bursts strikes were seen on the trailing edge of starboard wing. The Diver rolled over and spiralled down to explode in very open country ten miles north-east of Tonbridge."

In between these two kills, Canadian Plt Off John Walton attacked his target over the sea south of Hastings: "Attacked, firing a half-second burst and then a one-second burst from 250 yards range. Large pieces of jet unit fell off and Diver fell into sea five miles south of Hastings."

277 Squadron (ASR Spitfire Vb) Hawkinge

Flt Sgt A.M. Rollo	AD377/BA-	V-1	0904	off Dungeness

Flt Sgt Alex Rollo[76] was flying an ASR search sortie in company with Flt Lt P.D. O'Sullivan as his No.2:

> "Whilst searching for two splashes reported in the sea eight miles south-east of Dungeness, heard on the R/T that a Diver was at 2,500 feet, flying at 300mph. I was then at 3,500 feet, so I dived and engaged it from 500 yards, closing to 150 yards dead astern. First its port wing dropped, then its starboard wing and again the port wing, finally fluttering down to crash and explode in the sea. Confirmed by No.2."

322 (Dutch) Squadron (Spitfire XIV) West Malling

Flg Off F.W.L.S. Speetjens	VL-J	V-1	0635	Luckhurst area
Flg Off G.F.J. Jongbloed	VL-K	V-1	0712	Tenterden area
Flt Sgt M.J. Janssen	VL-D	V-1	0850	Staplehurst area
Flg Off R.F. Burgwal	NH649/VL-F	V-1	1215	Grid R.3951
	NH649/VL-F	V-1	1233	High Halden area
Flg Off M.A. Muller	VL-T	V-1	1710	Salehurst area
Flt Lt J.L. Plesman	VL-W	V-1	1930	off Hastings
Flg Off L.D. Wolters	VL-N	V-1	2047	Battle area
Flg Off F.J.H. van Eijk	NH699//VL-R	V-1	2120	West Malling area

| Flt Sgt W. de Vries | VL-Q | V-1 | 2210 | exploded in mid-air |

The Dutch pilots flew 62 anti-Diver sorties and destroyed ten Divers. Flg Off Frank Speetjens got the first at 0635:

"On the way to patrol Dungeness vectored on Diver crossing coast at Dungeness. Intercepted five miles north of Rye. Made three attacks. Diver broke up and exploded on ground south-east of Luckhurst."

Shortly thereafter, Flg Off Jan Jongbloed got another:

"Vectored on Diver crossing near Dungeness. Attacked from port to line astern. Diver caught fire and exploded on the ground in Tenterden area."

The third of the morning fell to Flt Sgt Janssen:

"Vectored on to Diver crossing north-east of Dungeness. Attacked, pieces fell off, speed reduced to 180mph. Further attack and tail came off. Diver crashed and exploded south of Staplehurst. Yards of wire found on pitot head of my aircraft on landing."

Flg Off Rudi Burgwal bagged a brace:

"Vectored on to Diver crossing the coast. Made quarter attack, range 200 yards. Diver crashed and exploded on the ground." Just over 15 minutes later he got his second: "Vectored on to Diver crossing near Dungeness. Attacked quarter to starboard, range 100 yards. Diver crashed and exploded in open field east of Halden."

There was a lull before the next salvo of V-1s came in, Flg Off Martin Muller shooting down one at 1710:

"Attacked dead line astern, range 200 yards. Diver spun and exploded on the ground just south of Salehurst."

The Diver shot down by Flt Lt Jan Plesman crashed into the sea south of Hastings, where it exploded, but Flg Off Bert Wolters' victim crashed on land near Battle. Flg Off Fraks van Eijk had a tussle with a Tempest to get at another Diver:

"Chased Diver which was being attacked by a Tempest. The Tempest missed and broke away. I then attacked with three long bursts, dead line astern. Diver crashed and exploded west of West Malling."

During his late evening patrol Flt Sgt Bill de Vries was fired upon by light AA and received damage to his starboard aileron, wing, cowling and fuselage, but was able to make a safe landing at the P-47 base at Kingsnorth ALG. He was unhurt:

"Vectored on to Diver crossing one mile south of Folkestone. Attacked line astern, range 200 yards closing to 100 yards. Diver exploded in the air between Ashford and Mersham. During the attack my Spitfire was hit by flak."

486 (RNZAF) Squadron (Tempest V) Newchurch

Plt Off R.J. Danzey RNZAF	JN797/SA-K	V-1	0430	Newchurch area
	JN797/SA-K	V-1	0450	Beachy Head area
Plt Off R.D. Bremner RNZAF	JN821/SA-H	V-1	0620	
Flt Lt H.N. Sweetman RNZAF	JN821/SA-H	V-1	1200	Rye area
Wt Off C.J. Sheddan RNZAF	JN809/SA-M	V-1	1530	Bexhill area
Wt Off S.J. Short RNZAF	EJ527/SA-Q	V-1	1600	Rye area
	EJ527/SA-Q	V-1 shared	1620	Rye area
Flg Off J.R. Cullen RNZAF	JN810/SA-P	V-1	2223	Shoreham area

FIU Detachment (Tempest V) Newchurch

| Flt Lt J. Berry | EJ524/ZQ-Y | V-1 | am | |

Sqn Ldr Daniel and Flt Lt Berry each flew a daytime patrol, and were joined by Flt Lt R.A. Jones who had just been posted to the Detachment. Joe Berry scored the only kill.

22ndFS/36thFG USAAF (P-47) Kingsnorth ALG

Capt C.G. Browne Jr USAAF ⎱	3T-	V-1 shared	1315	Tenterden area
1/Lt C.H. Nott USAAF ⎰	3T-			

Capt Cyril Browne Jr and Lt Hudson Nott possibly attacked the same Diver as that engaged by 165 Squadron, which crashed near Tenterden at 1315. The 22ndFS's diarist noted:

"The bombs didn't worry us very much in themselves because we knew they weren't aimed at us, but the flak from the American anti-aircraft that was thrown up at them from batteries around the field literally covered the sky and eventually the ground. Fortunately, there were no casualties but many were given a quick lesson in religion, particularly when a few bombs were shot down near by. One of these buzz bombs, incidentally, can be claimed by Lt Hudson Nott."

381stFS/363rdFG USAAF (P-51) Staplehurst ALG

1/Lt J. Gervan USAAF[77]	B3-	V-1	2030	off Dungeness

"First seen south-east of Folkestone, about mid-Channel, and shot down about three to five miles from shore, between Folkestone and Dungeness. Altitude 2,000 feet; speed approximately 300mph; time was approximately 2030; range 150 yards. The rocket was below me and I turned into it out of a right turn, closing into range. Fired about four bursts, saw strikes on the machine, bit of the right wing flew off, then the flame stopped and it veered off on its left wing into the Channel."

Night 29/30 JUNE

In the early hours of the morning a Diver impacted on Weald House, on the edge of Crockham Hill Common near Edenbridge in Kent. The house was being used by the London County Council as a home for evacuated children, 22 of whom (all aged under five) were killed or later died from their injuries, together with eight female staff. Fate was extra cruel on this occasion, as, had the bomb not been deflected onto the house when it struck a tree on Mariners Hill, probably all would have survived.

"Rescuers described the carnage and the garden full of twisted metal, cots in which babies had been sleeping, tiny shoes and vests, soft toys, and diminutive pink and blue blankets which were scattered over a wide area, hanging from trees in the garden and far out into the woods and fields."[78]

85 Squadron (Mosquito XVII) Swannington

Flt Lt R.H. Farrell	HK119/VY-S	V-1	2220-0150

96 Squadron (Mosquito XIII) Ford

Sqn Ldr W.P. Green	MM495/ZJ-	V-1	0050	off Beachy Head

Sqn Ldr Peter Green reported that it crashed almost vertically into the sea about ten miles off Beachy Head following a short burst from 250 yards.

409 (RCAF) Squadron (Mosquito XIII) Hunsdon

Mosquito HK460 crewed by Flt Lt Sandy Sanford and Flg Off Allison was recalled from an anti-Diver patrol when the weather closed in. On the way back one engine failed and Sanford headed for Ford to carry out an emergency landing. Here, however, the brakes failed and the Mosquito crashed into some sandbags, wiping off the undercarriage and part of the tail unit. The crew emerged unscathed.

605 Squadron (Mosquito VI) Manston

Wg Cdr G.L. Raphael	UP-	V-1	2358	Channel
Sqn Ldr K.M. Carver	HJ761/UP-P	V-1	0047	Channel
	HJ761/UP-P	V-1	0052	Channel
Wg Cdr N.J. Starr	UP-	V-1	0048	Bexhill area
Flt Lt G.C. Wright	UP-	V-1 damaged	0148	Channel
	UP-	V-1	0221	Channel

Wg Cdr Gordon Raphael DSO DFC, OC RAF Manston, borrowed one of 605 Squadron's Mosquitos and shot down a flying bomb just before midnight:

"A Diver was sighted at 2,000 feet and attacked. A two-seconds burst was fired and Diver crashed and exploded in the sea at 2358. During the patrol very intense, inaccurate light and heavy flak was experienced from Boulogne."

The CO, Wg Cdr Norman Starr DFC at last got in on the act and shot down a flying bomb near Bexhill:

"At 0008, four miles east of Dungeness, Diver was attacked at 2,700 feet. Five bursts but no result seen. At 0035, east of Dungeness, another Diver was attacked. Short bursts were fired but forced to break off attack as a ship opened fire. At 0048 near Bexhill a Diver was attacked at 1,000 feet with two bursts and target exploded in the air. At 0052 west of Dungeness a Diver was seen to crash into cliffs and explode."

Sqn Ldr Kenneth Carver scored his kills in quick succession:

"At 0047 when ten miles south of Dungeness saw Diver at 1,500 feet at 300mph. Attacked with four bursts and target exploded in the air. At 0052 when 15 miles south-west of Dungeness saw Diver at 1,000 feet flying at 300mph. Diver was attacked with four bursts. Target slowed up, lost height to 300 feet and then exploded in the air."

Although he attacked two flying bombs, Flt Lt George Wright was able only to shoot down one:

"At 0148 attacked a Diver with one burst – strikes were seen but target was lost in rain and cloud. At 0151 another Diver was attacked with two or three bursts but no results were seen. At 0221 a third Diver was attacked with two or three bursts. Diver altered course and slowed down to 220mph and was eventually overtaken at 50 feet, still diving but lost when our aircraft went into cloud and experienced St Elmo's fire."

Friday 30 JUNE

Two more residents of Upper Norwood (SE19) were killed at 0840 following the explosion of a Diver at the corner of Hermitage Road and Central Hill. A third fell in the borough shortly thereafter but inflicted damage only. At 0932, a Diver impacted in the Kimberley Avenue/Evelina Road area of Peckham (SE15), killing five. Twenty people were killed, and 29 seriously injured, in Tottenham Court Road W1 (Howland Street) at 1215. But the most devastating incident of the day – indeed, of the whole Diver assault – occurred when a bomb cut out over Waterloo Railway Station and went into a steep dive. It exploded in the street just outside the Air Ministry building in the Aldwych, opposite the BBC at Bush House. The Aldwych was packed with people out on their lunch hours. Others were at their desks and some of the girls from the Air Ministry were sunbathing on the roof. Many people in the street were killed or maimed, more died in the ruins of buses and the girls on the Air Ministry roof also perished. Some workers at the Air Ministry were sucked out of office windows by the blast and vacuum. A BBC employee recalled:

"Through the dust and smoke the casement of the bomb lay burning at the corner of Kingsway:

three victims lay unmoving at the top of the steps only thirty yards from where we had crouched and huddled and figures were scattered all over the road."

In a nearby first aid post she saw the body of a young women with whom she worked:

"She was naked and dead, stripped and killed by the blast. Another I knew came into the building helped by a friend – blood spurting from her wrist and a deep gash in one eye. From approximately 2.15 pm to 5.15 pm we were treating casualties."

At least 48 people lost their lives, 399 more were seriously injured and about 200 less seriously so, although the death toll is believed to have risen as high as 198 following deaths from serious injuries. A reporter, surveying the carnage, eloquently recorded:

"A light mist lifted to unveil the wide pavements littered with the shapes of the dead and wounded. In the canyon of the Aldwych's white masonry they were scattered with the victims of a massacre in some spacious curved arena. And the freshly day-lit terrible scene was further confounded by odd wreckage – the twisted frames of a line of busses parked there, and on the pavement and the road a pathetic snow of currency notes."

Two Divers plunged into the Thames at Rotherhithe, one at Nelson Dock at 0755 and the other at Lawrence Wharf in the afternoon. There were no casualties but some damage was inflicted to nearby property. A Diver fell at Holyoak Road/Brook Drive in Lambeth (SE11) at 0907, destroying and damaging much property and killing nine. Two hours later another came down in East Dulwich (SE22), killing a further three in Henslow and Underhill Roads. Oakland Grove, Penge (SE20) was struck by a Diver at 1118, where four were killed and much damage inflicted. Beckenham received another Diver at 1340 that caused widespread damage to houses and shops but took the life of only one resident. It exploded at the junction of Beckenham Road and Mackenzie Road. Richard Beckett, who was nine years old at the time, later wrote:

"We had an Anderson shelter in the back garden and my father had erected a blast shelter of wooden railway sleepers around the entrance. This I am sure was the only reason that my mother, my two sisters and myself were saved from serious injury. My father was on his way home from work and at the time was only about half a mile away when the bomb came down. Later he told us that from where he was, it looked to him as though it had actually come down on our house. In fact it had come down on the opposite side of the railway track and consequently the railway bank had diverted a lot of the blast. However, our house was severely damaged. What I can distinctly remember is that when the bomb came down I heard no bang, only a loud whooshing noise. When we came out of the shelter, the back of our house, with all the glassless windows looking like hollow eyes, somehow reminded me of a skeleton.

"Also, there was the awful overpowering smell of the stale dust, which probably came out of the house lofts. Suddenly my father came running through the house to make sure that we were all right, which luckily we were. At the same time, the lady from next door appeared in the back garden clutching her baby in her arms and both her face and her baby's were covered in blood. In the weeks that followed we went back to the house several times to collect personal items and two things remain clearly in my mind. At the time of the bomb, my mother had been in the house making jam and when she heard the bomb coming she ran out and just got in the shelter in time. When we went back later, the walls of the kitchen were covered in jam, and the walls of my father's shed were covered in paint where paint pots had exploded and mixed in the paint were hundreds of small ball bearings from a tin which my father had collected over the years."[79]

Two more people were killed when ten houses were destroyed in Howie Street, Battersea (SW11) by a bomb at 1816. A dozen of the fighters' victims over Kent were recorded as impacting near Lydd (0735), Marden (0930), Old Romney, where two bungalows were damaged and two occupants slightly injured (0942), Lydd again (two exploding in the air at 0950), Kingsnorth (1017), Maidstone area (1115), Toll Farm, Newchurch (1630), Manor Farm, New Romney (1634), Monks Horton (1635), Hartsfield Farm (1825), Howletts Farm, Molash (2018, one slightly injured) and Elvey Farm, Egerton (2221), while one brought down by AA crashed near Cheriton Rectory at 2213, slightly injuring five. A flying bomb that fell near Braintree, damaging a cottage in which the three occupants were slightly injured, was found to be carrying radio gear that enabled it to signal its position.

1 Squadron (Spitfire LFIXb) Detling

Flg Off N.E. Brown	MK644/JX-	V-1	1445	off Folkestone
	MK644/JX-	V-1 probable	1450	Dover area
	MK867/JX-	V-1	1600-1710	exploded in mid-air
Flg Off D.R. Wallace	MJ481/JX-	V-1	1600-1710	off Dover
Plt Off K.R. Foskett	MK986/JX-V	V-1 shared	2030	Faversham area
	MK986/JX-V	V-1	2220	Hastings area
Flg Off H.L. Stuart	NH246/JX-	V-1	2220	Bexhill/Pevensey Bay
Wt Off J.W. McKenzie	MK997/JX-F	V-1 shared	c.2220	Hailsham area

Flg Off Neville Brown had a busy afternoon:

"Intercepted Diver five miles south-east of Folkestone, height 4,000 feet. Fired four-seconds burst from starboard quarter, developing into stern attack, 300 yards range closing to 200 yards. Diver heeled over onto starboard wing and then dived into sea just south of Folkestone. Second Diver attacked just north of Dover. Fired a long burst but Diver disappeared into cloud after many strikes seen on starboard side. Ultimate fate of this Diver not known. Claim one destroyed."

Having landed, he was soon off again in another aircraft and accompanied by Flg Off Wallace:

"Vectored on to Diver eight miles south-east of Folkestone. It was just in range over Folkestone but held fire. Gave two short bursts at long range when eight miles inland. Diver exploded in the air after being given half-a-second burst from 200 yards."

Meanwhile, Wallace was vectored onto a Diver coming out of Cap Gris Nez and intercepted out to sea:

"Diver seen at 3,500 feet and I gave one-second burst. Flames from the jet became twice as large, then Diver spun into sea five miles south-west of Dover."

Plt Off Ken Foskett's first victim was attacked three times:

"Overshot twice then made two attacks. Three strikes seen in second attack. Size of flame from jet increased. Diver then rolled on back and went in exploding on some farm buildings. A P-47 was making attacks from port side without any apparent effect."

The P-47 pilot was probably 1/Lt John A. Kelly of the 412thFS based at Woodchurch ALG, who reported sharing a Diver with two Tempests. Foskett landed, refuelled and rearmed and was sent off again:

"Intercepted Diver five miles south of Hastings. Gave three short bursts and Diver went straight in and exploded one-and-a-half miles north-west of Hastings by a wood."

After firing two bursts from 150-200 yards at his selected target, Flg Off Stuart reported:

"Diver started to go down gradually and then went straight down. The fuselage was burning bright red. It turned over and exploded on the ground near houses five miles inland between Bexhill and Pevensey Bay."

Wt Off McKenzie shared his kill with two Spitfires:

> "Intercepted Diver just west of Pevensey Bay. Two Spits had fired previously and I saw strikes, I attacked and saw strikes. Diver went on for 300 yards. Fuselage began to glow and it dived and exploded on ground two-three miles west of Hailsham."

3 Squadron (Tempest V) Newchurch

Flt Sgt J.W. Foster	JN743/JF-P	V-1	0720	Grid R.4838
Plt Off K.G. Slade-Betts	JN755/JF-D	V-1	1117	Maidstone area
Flt Sgt R.W. Cole	JN768/JF-F	V-1	1140	Rye area
Flt Sgt S. Domanski PAF	JN752/JF-S	V-1	1150	off Dungeness
Flg Off R. Dryland	JN822/JF-	V-1	1805	Rye area
Flg Off D.J. Butcher	JN745/JF-T	V-1	2205	Grid R.0055

Flt Sgt John Foster:

> "A Diver was sighted two miles south of Dungeness at 4,500 feet. I attacked and shot its wing off. Diver exploded on the ground."

Plt Off Ken Slade-Betts' victim crashed four miles south of Maidstone after its tail section was shot away. In his logbook Flt Sgt Bob Cole noted:

> "Destroy one Diver one mile west of Rye, plus one in Tonbridge area. Strikes on another. It goes into balloons. Land at Friston for fuel."

The sea claimed Flt Sgt Domanski's target, which was seen to be on fire from its starboard before it went down. Flg Off Dryland's attack caused the jet unit to extinguish and the Diver exploded on the ground four miles south of Rye, while Flg Off Butcher's victim stalled, dived towards the ground and then climbed to 1,000 feet before finally plunging to earth, where it exploded.

91 Squadron (Spitfire XIV) Deanland ALG

Cne J-M. Maridor (FF)	RB188/DL-K	V-1	0720	Biddenden
Flg Off A.R. Elcock	RB182/DL-V	V-1	0945	exploded in mid-air
Flt Lt A. Smith RNZAF	NH703/DL-	V-1	2220	Sandhurst area
Sqn Ldr N.A. Kynaston	RB185/DL-	V-1	2225	Hailsham area

With these four kills the squadron score had increased to 65 Divers destroyed. The first fell to Cne Jean-Marie Maridor at 0720: "Sighted Diver over New Romney. Attacked from astern and shot it down, exploding on hitting the ground near Biddenden." Flg Off Elcock was the next to score: "Sighted Diver over Channel south of Dungeness. Strikes obtained from burst and Diver exploded in the air." New Zealander Flt Lt Smith added another:

> "Vectored on to Diver crossing in over Rye. Other aircraft attacked but no strikes observed. I attacked from dead astern at 300-400 yards and wingtips fell off. Diver spun in, falling in woods near Sandhurst, where it exploded."

Last of the day fell to Sqn Ldr Kynaston:

> "Attacked by Spit of 322 Sqn, who obtained one strike. I attacked from astern from 150 yards range, getting strikes beneath jet mechanism, causing Diver to climb and dive violently, ending finally in dive to port, where it fell in a field near Hailsham."

137 Squadron (Typhoon Ib) Manston

Flg Off R.A. Johnstone RCAF	MN152/SF-	V-1	0700-0800	off Boulogne
Flg Off N.J.M. Manfred RNZAF	MN596/SF-	V-1	0605-0710	off Boulogne
Plt Off K.G. Brain	MN169/SF-Z	V-1	0735-0745	off Boulogne
Plt Off K.G. Brain ⎫	MN169/SF-Z	V-1	0735-0745	off Boulogne
Flt Lt M. Wood RCAF ⎭	MN134/SF-J			

An early morning shipping patrol by two rocket-armed Typhoons in the Cap Gris Nez-Dieppe sector was flown by Canadian Flg Off Ralph Johnstone and Flg Off Noel Manfred, a New Zealander. While passing Boulogne on return, they were vectored on to a bogey, which turned out to be a flying bomb. Manfred attacked with cannons and also fired his rockets, at which the bomb dived into the sea and exploded. Johnstone spotted a second V-1 at 1,500 feet and carried out a beam attack. The bomb immediately crashed into the sea and exploded. The next patrol was just as successful, also destroying two flying bombs off Boulogne. Plt Off Ken Brain sighted the first, firing a long burst from 650 yards. He saw strikes, and then it caught fire, dived into the sea and exploded. Another was seen off Boulogne, which Flt Lt Matt Wood[80] attacked, expending all his ammunition without apparent effect. He contemplated tipping it with his wingtip, but then Brain called up and told his Canadian colleague to stand clear as he fired a short burst from 400 yards. The bomb caught fire and crashed into the sea, where it exploded.

165 Squadron (Spitfire IX) Detling

Flg Off C.M. Lawson RAAF	MK811/SK-S	V-1	1030	Marden area

> "I made a quarter attack from above and to port. I gave one two-seconds burst and saw strikes along the port mainplane. The Diver pulled up and spiralled down through cloud, exploding near a railway line four miles east of Marden."

322 (Dutch) Squadron (Spitfire XIV) West Malling

Flg Off L.M. Meijers	VL-J	V-1	0920	Newchurch area
Flg Off J. van Arkel	VL-D	V-1	1010	Ashford area
Flg Off R.F. Burgwal	VL-E	V-1	1950	Grid R.1837
	VL-E	V-1	2155	Grid R.1930
Flg Off J. Jonker	VL-K	V-1	2200	Grid R.1147

Flg Off Loekie Meijers started the ball rolling with a kill at 0920:

> "Patrolling near Newchurch. Diver crossed in over cloud. Attacked with long burst dead astern, range 200 yards. Diver slowed down to 180mph when it slowly dived through cloud and exploded."

Less than an hour later Flg Off Jan van Arkle got another:

> "Saw Diver coming in to the north-west. Attacked dead astern, range 150 yards, shot wing off. Diver spun and exploded on the ground three miles south-west of Ashford."

Two more fell to Flg Off Rudi Burgwal:

> "Vectored on to Diver. Attacked from starboard, range 300 yards to line astern. Saw hits on wings. Diver crashed and exploded in a small wood." Following his second sortie, he wrote: "Vectored on to Diver crossing east of Hastings. Attacked from port and pieces fell off Diver. Got in line astern and gave short burst, range 150 yards. Diver crashed and exploded."

The last of the day fell to Flg Off Jan Jonker:

> "Vectored on to Diver crossing between Hastings and Bexhill. Attacked from starboard, range 100 yards. Diver exploded in the air and again on the ground."

350 (Belgian) Squadron (Spitfire IX) Friston

Pilots were involved in escorting a convoy off the Sussex coast during the day. One patrol flown by Flg Off Paul Delorme and Sgt Bob Mehuys sighted a V-1 coming in at about 2200, Delorme (EN800) chasing this. He fired all his ammunition but observed no tangible results.

486 (RNZAF) Squadron (Tempest V) Newchurch

Wt Off S.J. Short RNZAF	JN810/SA-P	V-1	0930	off Dungeness
Flt Sgt B.M. Hall RNZAF	N821/SA-H	V-1	1015	Hastings area
Plt Off F.B. Lawless RNZAF	JN811/SA-Z	V-1	1700	Hastings area
Flt Lt E.W. Tanner RNZAF	JN770/SA-V	V-1	1810	Rye area
	JN770/SA-V	V-1	1815	Rye area
	JN770/SA-V	V-1	1835	Cranbrook area
Plt Off J.H. Stafford RNZAF	JN801/SA-L	V-1	2040	Robertsbridge area
Flt Sgt B.M. Hall RNZAF	JN854/SA-G	V-1	2045	Tunbridge Wells area
Flt Lt H.N. Sweetman RNZAF	JN801/SA-L	V-1	2240	Ashford area

Flt Lt Rick Tanner and Wt Off Gus Hooper were on a patrol off Rye but it was Tanner who achieved all the success on this occasion. He sighted a flying bomb at 5,000 feet. Although travelling at 390mph he intercepted and shot it down about six miles from the coast. Five minutes later he shot down a second off Rye, and then attacked a third. This fell near Cranbrook, where it exploded. Wt Off Short's aircraft, SA-P, was hit by AA and crash-landed at Newchurch. The pilot was unhurt.

412thFS/373rdFG USAAF (P-47) Woodchurch ALG

1/Lt H.F. Phelps USAAF	V5-	V-1		Tunbridge Wells
1/Lt J.A. Kelly USAAF	V5-	V-1 shared		Hastings area

Lt Harold Phelps made a solo kill but Lt John Kelly reported sharing his victim with two Tempests but probably attacked the same Diver as that claimed shot down by Plt Off Ken Foskett in a Spitfire LFIXb of 1 Squadron. Sgt John R. Kinn USAAF recalled:

> "Some of them [P-47 pilots] went out over the Channel to wait for the buzz bombs, but the ensuing explosion did damage to one of the planes and that put a stop to their relaxation."

A pilot from 411thFS, Lt Bill Mather USAAF, wrote:

> "When we were flying we were told to keep the hell out of the way of the RAF Spitfires and Tempests, which were much lighter and more manoeuvrable than out lumbering Jugs (P-47s). But the temptation was great, because it seemed that the vast majority of the beastly things came directly over our fragile tents. We did chase a few while airborne, but the RAF fighters let us know they didn't like our intrusion, and we knew for a certainty that the ack-ack boys would gleefully shoot at anything that moved, so we did not press the issue."[81]

5th ERS USAAF (ASR P-47D) Dover ALG

1/Lt J. Tucker USAAF	5F-	V-1		Channel

Lt John Tucker of the 5th Emergency Rescue Squadron was engaged on an ASR patrol over the Channel when he sighted and shot down a Diver. The ASR spotter unit was officially named as Detachment B, part of the 65th Fighter Wing based at Boxted, using cast-off P-47Ds of the 56thFG for air/sea search and rescue duties[82].

Minister of Home Security Herbert Morrison told Parliament:

> *The toll of death, injury and damage to property from these attacks on London is far heavier than is generally appreciated. Though the proportion of persons killed to other casualties is less than in the raids of 1940-41 the total casualties in London for a month of flying bomb attack would, if the present rate of casualties continues, be equal to those of September 1940, the worst month of the Blitz period. In September 1940, 5,546 persons were killed and 7,167 seriously injured in the London Region. In 14 days and nights of attacks by flying bombs up to the morning of the 29 June, 1,679 persons have been killed and about 5,000 seriously injured in the London Region. In this period a total of nearly 270,000 houses in London have been*

damaged, of which over 7,000 have been destroyed ... If damage continues at the present rate for two months, as many London houses will have suffered damage in that period as ... for the nine months of the Blitz. The attacks, though intermittent, go on day and night and the strain upon the people of London is severe. They ... are bearing it admirably, but it would be of the greatest help to the maintenance of their morale ... to give to Londoners what is their due and let them and the country know that we are proud of them."

Night 30 JUNE/1 JULY

Brixton (SW2) was on the receiving end of a Diver at 0349, when it fell between Baytree and Sudbourne Road. At least 60 houses were destroyed or damaged and three people killed. Two Divers fell in the SE19 district, the first impacting between Highland and Lunham Road, Gipsy Hill at 0445, killing five and destroying or damaging some 25 properties. The next followed at 0602, destroying seven houses, damaging 30 more and killing two residents in Gibbs Square, Upper Norwood.

157 Squadron (Mosquito XIX) Swannington

Sqn Ldr J.H.M. Chisholm	TA404/RS-M	V-1	2325
Flt Lt E.J. Stevens	MM674/RS-T	V-1	0141
	MM674/RS-T	V-1	0145

FIU Detachment (Tempest V) Newchurch

Flt Lt J. Berry	EJ524/ZQ-Y	V-1	night
	EJ524/ZQ-Y	V-1	night
	EJ524/ZQ-Y	V-1	night

Flt Lts Berry and Jones each flew three nocturnal sorties, Berry shooting down two in one trip to raise his score to six.

June reminiscences

Of the V-1 offensive, Prime Minister Churchill wrote in his memoirs:

"This new form of attack imposed on the people of London a burden perhaps even heavier than the air raids of 1940 and 1941. Suspense and strain were more prolonged. Dawn brought no relief and cloud no comfort. The man going home in the evening never knew what he would find; his wife, alone all day or with the children, could not be certain of his safe return. The blind, impersonal nature of the missile made the individual on the ground feel helpless. There was little that he could do, no human enemy that he could see shot down."

In her journal (later published[83]) South African authoress Sarah Gertrude Millin wrote:

"Pilotless planes, rocket planes, robot planes, comet planes – people don't yet know what to call them – are attacking England. Here is Hitler's 'Terror'. Here is what he means, would, 'at the decisive moment', bring triumph to Germany. The Things first came on the morning of the 13th. Then again, they came in great numbers on the night of the 15th, and again yesterday morning. They are said to streak across the sky like comets – very straight, at great speed, singly, or in twos or threes, at different heights from roof level upwards. They have a brilliant tail, which darkens before they explode. They give off sparks. Some think they are gyro-controlled, and some that they are radio-controlled. Milton speaks of Satan 'in hollow tube training his devilish enginry.' Men-manned planes have gone up against them. This seems to me the most shocking thing of all – men in machines having to fight machines without men. The idea is to explode them in the air so that they may cause no damage on the earth. The population has been instructed that when the engine of a pilotless aircraft stops and the head of the machine is seen to go out, it may mean that an explosion will soon follow – perhaps in five to fifteen seconds. To take refuge from the blast, even those indoors should use the most solid protection immediately available. Mr Herbert Morrison [Minister of Home Security] says:

'It has been known for some time that the enemy was making preparations for the use of pilotless aircraft against this country. He has now started to use his much-vaunted secret weapon. His aim is clearly, in view of the difficulties of his military situation, to upset our morale and interfere with our work. There is no reason to think that raids of this weapon will be worse than, or, indeed, as heavy as, the raids with which the people of this country are already familiar and have borne so bravely.'

"The moment I heard of 'pilotless aircraft' I thought it was a bad name for them – it gave them too monstrous a significance; it made them, without men, the equals of the aerial machines which need men. More than equals: since they were not tied to the pains, the fears, the weakness, the errors of humanity, their superiors. Mr Morrison makes a mistake, again, when he asks people to bear these rocket raids with those they already know and 'have borne so bravely'. The ghost, even of a loved one, would be frightening. Mr Morrison is now telling the English people not to mind the murderous ghost of a murderer, a murdering robot. How can one meet bravely the animus of something inanimate, something that is itself beyond terror? The rocket bomb seems to me a characteristically German invention: an outcome of the mind that loves musical boxes, musical clocks, clockwork toys, the goose-step, drilling, the crushing of the individual, the subservience of human beings to the State – the whole machinery that is Germany. The Germans call this 'the beginning of the day of vengeance.'"

1/Lt Lloyd Sunderland USAAF 532ndBG Ridgewell:

"One evening we heard the familiar buzz bomb 'phut, phut, phut' and then a big explosion nearby. I learned the next day just how close it came to one of my crew. He had invited a lady friend from London to spend a few days in the country away from the steady V-1 bombardment. There was a vacant cottage near the Ridgewell base and my enterprising crewman exercised squatters' rights in order to provide a comfortable cottage for his friend. In fact, he set her up for light housekeeping with items acquired by moonlight requisition. On the particular evening we heard the V-1, he and his gal decided to walk to the nearby pub to socialise. They had scarcely cleared the premises when the bomb hit their cottage. It totally destroyed the building. All that was left at the scene was a pile of shattered boards, a badly dented GI bunk bed and the pieces of the buzz bomb that looked like a crumpled stovepipe. Fortunately the couple escaped uninjured."

Another American, Capt G. Lee Taylor USAAF, a transport officer based at High Halden ALG, remembered:

"We had nine trucks mounting .50 calibre machine-guns. The V-1s came in fairly slow [sic] at night from across the Channel. They followed a regular route over the wooded area where we camped, then across the truck park and on to London. They seemed to travel at a fairly low altitude. It seemed logical that if we could arrange our trucks in a semi-circle to get a cone of fire as the V-1 came over the woods we just might bring one down. We set up the operation for the following night. It was clear and crisp. Visibility was good. The V-1 came pop-popping into view over the woods, shooting fire from its tail pipe. The .50 calibres opened fire and we shot the stovepipe off a major's tent! We had a staff meeting early the following morning. It was suggested that we leave the V-1s to the anti-aircraft batteries and the fighter planes."[84]

Wg Cdr Beamont recalled:

"After about four weeks of intensive and successful operations I received notification of a VIP visit for a high level investigation of the flying bomb defences; and I was told to provide all facilities and information requested. The visitor turned out to be Mr Duncan Sandys [Chairman of the Government's Anti-Diver Committee] who had been charged by the Prime Minister with reporting on the success or otherwise of the measures being taken against the V-1 attack. Sandys arrived to the accompaniment of the, by then quite normal in the area, sounds of Tempest diving at full power, cannon fire and exploding V-1s. I gave him a general picture of tactics, training standards, details of aircraft performance and aircraft and armament servicing under these intensive operating conditions; and also of the methods employed to coordinate the battle and improve interception and success rates. Mr Sandys listened attentively but without noticeable enthusiasm, and after interruptions on some occasions to watch Tempests intercepting V-1s overhead (and shooting one down just beyond 56 Squadron's dispersal), he said that he had seen all he needed and was ready to leave. After a short silence he suddenly went on to say that we were wasting our time in this flying business – in a few years all this sort of thing would be done by rockets!"

Mr Duncan Sandys later flew a sortie in a Mosquito piloted by 96 Squadron's Wg Cdr Crew, during which a Diver was attacked but missed, before a Tempest attacked and also missed. The Minister's view probably was not altered by his experience.

On the subject of accidental shoot downs of intercepting aircraft by AA gunners, Wg Cdr Beamont commented:

"Sometimes as many as 40 or 50 sorties a day were flown by each of the two Tempest squadrons involved, and pilots' individual scores of two or three V-1s in a day were becoming frequent. Losses were relatively low and although we had a number of Tempests damaged by exploding V-1s and some resulting forced landings, there were few fatalities. The main loss rate during the first three weeks of the campaign was due to over-exuberance on the part of the anti-aircraft gunners who, whenever in range of a V-1, would naturally let go all they had; but without precision radar equipment at that time they invariably tended to under-estimate the lead-angle required, and if their target was being pursued as it so often was by one or two Tempests at approximately two to three hundred yards behind the V-1, the fighters collected the majority of the anti-aircraft bursts. Lives were lost because of this, and there was some considerable tension as a result of it both in the squadrons and among the population of Kent who often saw these unfortunate incidents and eventually caused questions in Parliament on the subject; and there was much comment in the press."

Flt Sgt Morrie Rose of 3 Squadron continued in his piece for the newspapers, giving the readers his first-hand impressions:

"I read recently that tackling the flying bombs is said to be rather like joining in a very fast game of rugger on a very small ground and I can certainly vouch for that. For there is not a lot of space for manoeuvring when you are chasing a Doodlebug and trying to keep clear of the barrage balloons and all the ack-ack fire being put up by the anti-aircraft guns below! Let me tell you what it is like to attack a Doodlebug when you have been scrambled from base or if you should suddenly see one while on patrol. The first thing you hear is the sound like an angry bee and then a tiny speck of light appears over the horizon growing bigger every second. The buzz and the light soon become synchronised into what appears to be a meteor with a flaming orange-red tail. Sometimes near the coast, ack-ack guns will open up below you and you can see red and white tracer shots streaming up towards the robot. Of course, it has become part of our tactics to attack the robots before they reach the coast so we don't run the risk of being hit by the ack-ack fire ourselves!

"As you close up on the robot, it looks rather like a large flame with wings sticking out on either side. Because it is so small, the flying bomb is not easy to hit, but it is still vulnerable. If your bullets strike home on the jet unit, the whole thing catches fire and it goes down with a crash. If you hit the explosives it is carrying, the robot blows up. When we started attacking these machines we trod warily, shooting from long range, but as we have got experienced at this new form of attack, we have found we can close in, sometimes to 100 yards. If you are close when the bomb goes up you sometimes fly through the debris, and some of our Tempests have come back with their paint scorched. Some have even been turned on their backs by the force of the explosion, but the pilot feels no effect except an upward jolt. Often it is not necessary to hit your target cleanly. A few bullets sometimes upset the gyro (automatic pilot) and the robot crashes straight down into the sea. One of our chaps has also discovered that by using his slip-stream it is possible to force the Doodlebugs into a spin. We are now getting expert at intercepting an increasing number of Doodlebugs, and all this practice is helping to make our shooting very accurate."

Having gained some experience flying against the Divers, 3 Squadron's Flt Sgt Bob Cole was able to reflect:

"We thought originally that they would be too fast to catch. But actually they weren't. They cruised at 370mph, while a Tempest would get about 440mph flat out. Of course you couldn't fly flat out all the time – you would use all your fuel up. You would cruise at about 300mph, but you could push it up to 440mph. Tactics were haphazard to start with and then we had standing patrols. You couldn't scramble and catch them. You had to have standing patrols. You would be told where they were crossing and if the weather was good enough you would aim to get a thousand feet and cruise at 300mph and when you saw it you'd shove the nose down and open up. You could overhaul it then. When it went down I used to turn the aircraft on its side as there was quite a kick from the explosion. There was a ton of bomb blowing up and you were only about a thousand yards away. It's a fair way but it's quite a thump. And if it comes up and your aircraft is plan [i.e. full on] to it, it really bangs. Rolling to the side took off some of the shock. We would have a patrol up and then another two in the cockpit, they sat in the cockpit for an hour and if something happened and there was too much activity, they would be sent up. Then two more at fifteen minutes readiness and two at an hour. And as one lot went off you moved up. It was quite a reasonable system. Normally we had patrols from Eastbourne to Hastings, Hastings to Rye and Rye up to Folkestone. Physically it was tiring. At the time we were sleeping on a bag of straw in a tent. And of course these damn things were going over and there was a fair bit of flak. We'd get to bed about midnight and then you were up at half past three and then the first aircraft off before four, just before light. I've been asleep flying actually. I was doing Hastings to Eastbourne. I remember turning over Eastbourne and coming to. I had been out for a couple of minutes. I used to fly on trimming tabs – to give myself something to do, occupy the mind. If you fly up and down the coast on a hot day, and nothing happens, and you have had damn all sleep anyway, I think it's quite easy to drop off. We had one Diver come down near our tent. We wandered out of the tent and walked across to the mess and we heard the engine stop – there was cloud down to about 300 feet and everybody was looking where the hell it was. It came out of the cloud and it was just teetering on the stall. Another 20 yards and it would have hit our tent. Everybody was running like hell across this field to get away from it. It tipped in, just in a stream with a bank, the blast went up and it blew the latrines down but otherwise nobody was hurt.

"I had a couple of close calls. I chased one flying bomb and the damned ack-ack kept firing and that's the only time I broke away. I didn't do it again as it affects your morale actually. I was closing in and had got to about 300 yards. The flak was being pumped up right between me and the thing. So I got out of the way. I could have shot the bloody thing down easily. One night there were two of us up on patrol. It was pitch black. This damned flying bomb, we were on its tail and there was tracer coming up like a wall. We were flying through a V of tracer, with the flying bomb stuck in the middle of it. And you couldn't turn out of it or you would have turned straight into the flak. I kept flying and in the end it went down, so the guns did stop; claimed half of it with whoever I was with. We were both firing at it, though we couldn't see one another of course. And there wasn't just competition from the ground to shoot down the V-1s. In the air too, pilots were keen to get themselves a Diver. There wasn't supposed to be any competition but anybody who was doing an air test would tend to come down, they weren't supposed to, and see what they could see. I know one night – it was a lovely night – I was chasing this damn flying bomb and so were about eight others, including a Meteor. I passed that."

Another 3 Squadron pilot, Flt Sgt Ron Pottinger, recalled:

"One morning I was on readiness and had just left for dispersal, when one came down only about 30 yards from our tent. Fortunately, between it and the tent there was a ditch with raised banks, and this deflected much of the blast upwards. Nevertheless, the tent was split from end to end and the late sleepers shaken out of their beds. Eventually, a three-mile wide band along the coastline was given over to AA guns, and any other device that might prove effective. The main difficulty I found was in seeing the Doodlebug. To gain a speed advantage we usually patrolled above their usual height and with their small size and khaki colour it was not easy to see them against the ground beneath. On one early morning myself and a No.2 were up on patrol and there were huge black cumulus clouds everywhere. We were out over the sea and were continually being guided into the heart of a really fierce thunderstorm. It was black as night, apart from which the rain lashed down so that visibility was nil. I had no alternative but to keep my eyes in the cockpit and fly back the way we had come on instruments. My No.2's eyes would have been glued to me, flying formation, so that the chances of either of us seeing V-1s were zero. But each time we got out of the murk, and were given a fresh course to steer we found ourselves headed straight back into it again. The whole patrol was a complete waste of time. If there were any Doodlebugs around we certainly didn't see them. Another time, I was directed out to sea when there was low cloud down on the deck all along the coast. The only way through was by flying down the valley and out over Hastings. It was like flying down a tunnel, hills on either side and cloud above my head, and not knowing if the tunnel might be blocked. Again we saw no Doodlebugs and then came the difficulty of finding a way back in! One day I was down amongst the tents when one came over quite high and flew in large circles over our part of Kent. Probably it was hit, or possibly there was a fault in its guidance system. Anyway, you can imagine the scramble for cover every time it came overhead, and the almost audible sighs of relief when it passed over. Then it didn't re-appear so presumably it had come down somewhere else."

Of this period 74 Squadron's Flt Lt Don Llewellyn commented:

"It was soon evident that the flight path of the Doodlebugs from one particular launch pad passed directly overhead, but we were incensed that we were not allowed to go up after them. The Spitfire IX was considered too slow and the Tempest and the Spitfire XIV squadrons were the ones used to combat the V-1, although a number of wing commanders and squadron leaders ignored these rules, and went up freelance. Naturally, we and the other squadrons on the Wing complained."

This was confirmed by Wg Cdr Bobby Oxspring DFC, who had just been appointed to command newly formed 24 Fighter Wing (91 and 322 Dutch Squadrons) at West Malling:

"Stationed as we were with our high performance Spit XIVs at West Malling, we were ideally placed to react to the continuous stream of missiles from their launch sites in the Pas-de-Calais. Mounting standing patrols, we and the newly formed high-speed Tempest Wing led by Wg Cdr Roly Beamont were controlled for interceptions by Biggin Hill operations. Unfortunately our initial efforts were often handicapped by an onrush of miscellaneous aircraft from all over the country whose pilots were out to get themselves a Doodlebug. These chaps ranged from elderly staff officers to young pilots who had just joined a squadron. All were strapped to lethal fighters, and none were under operational control of Biggin Hill or anyone else. We dubbed these guys the 'Wolf Pack', and when attacking our targets spent anxious moments dodging streams of lead as they hose-piped at ranges of 2,000 yards or more."

Chasing and shooting down Divers at night proved difficult and often dangerous, as remembered by Flg Off Doug Oxby of 219 Squadron:

"We took off in the early hours (0110) of the 18 June with S/L Merrifield at the helm. I recall we chased and fired on several Divers – but the results were not impressive. No joy that night. A couple of nights later, on 20 June, we took off again for a patrol at precisely the same time, ten past one in the morning and in the same Mosquito, 362. This time, we fixed two of the things. We had learned a few lessons from the previous night's outings. On that occasion, we had trouble just keeping up with them – leave alone shooting one down. Fortunately, despite the Mosquito's apparently flimsy construction, the glued structure usually managed to withstand any damage from chunks of disintegrating pulse-jet. But I wouldn't have wanted to be anywhere nearby if one of those flying bombs exploded mid-air! Just the thought made me feel uneasy. Too much excitement always makes me need the John. Flying through the detonation of a V-1 in a Mosquito though, would have been a different story. Fortunately we were spared that painful experience. I well recall our mechanics having a tough time of it during this period, constantly repairing our blown Merlin engines. Quite often, with the aircraft flying at the limit for extended periods to chase these things, the engine might literally blow a gasket – usually something to do with the supercharger. To keep the aircraft operational for the following night, this meant engine out, fit the new gaskets, re-assemble the engine, and lift back in. Quite a job."

Flt Lt Vic Hester of 138 Mosquito Wing based at Lasham found himself with an unusual task:

"Word came down from Group HQ that the Prime Minister wanted a close-up cine film of a buzz bomb to show on Cinema newsreels, in an endeavour to reassure the public that this new German weapon did not baffle us. The fastest aircraft that could carry a trained cameraman equipped with a 35-mm cine camera was a Mosquito – DZ383, a modified B.IV – which had an all-Perspex nose occupied by a cine cameraman from Pinewood Studios. The modified nose allowed the cameraman to squat and shoot his films at any angle. We also fixed up a 400 feet-reel camera, fixed to shoot straight ahead. We rigged up a simple gun sight for the pilot so that he could operate this particular camera. Our task was to take 35-mm cine footage of selected raids by any squadron in 2 Group. This unusual Mosquito could carry either 4x500lb bombs in the fuselage or extra fuel tanks extending the range by some 300 miles.[85] Between 18 June and 3 July, I piloted Flg Off Oakley on sixteen flights in DZ383 and DZ414, flying mostly out of Biggin Hill, trying to get some good close-ups of these flying bombs. We used two different Mosquitos because our high speed dives were stripping off some of the fabric wing covering and the first aircraft had to go to Lasham for the airframe fitters to get to work with new fabric and the dope brush.

"Buzz bombs, or rather their launching pads were not new to us. We had been bombing them since the previous year. The main building of these launching pads was about the size of a small haystack plus the take-off ramp. Our photographic Mosquito started diving from 10,000 feet and if we spotted a target would pull out of the dive at the last moment in an endeavour to maintain enough speed to keep up with the target for a short while. The 'G' forces experienced whilst pulling out of the dive made it almost impossible for the cameraman to hold and sight the heavy 35-mm camera. We took many pictures of the ground, with the occasional frame or two of a buzz bomb. After about five days Oakley thought he might have got something worth processing, so after landing at Biggin Hill amongst all the balloons that were also trying to catch the buzz bombs, we rushed up to Shepherds Bush Film Studios to get our films processed. Whilst waiting, Oakley took me off to a local pub that he used regularly before the war. The landlord welcomed Oakley with considerable gusto and asked what he was doing in Shepherds Bush. Oakley told him that we had been trying to get a close up of a buzz bomb for some days. The landlord looked at his watch and then said that if we would accompany him to the roof of his five-storey building, in about ten minutes, there would be one passing over. We did in fact accept the offer and sure enough got the best shot so far achieved. We did though, in the end, get a good air-to-air shot of a buzz bomb being shot down."

American fighter ace Capt Jack Ilfrey USAAF of the 20thFG was on short leave in London and experienced what the Londoners had to endure every day:

"The buzz bomb season settled down late that afternoon. I was on the street, walking around aimlessly, when I heard a loud putter like a motorcycle. Suddenly the putter coughed and died. I had heard all about the V-1 buzz bombs from the pilot who had brought me over from France and I knew this buzz bomb was going to hit somewhere pretty close. You could sense that. People stopped walking and stood rooted in their tracks. There came a kind of boom, then an ear-splitting roar. I felt the sidewalk beneath me move. Two blocks away I saw a building, lighted by fire, crumple into the street, and it seemed to me that tons of glass were crashing everywhere. An Englishman, who was standing near me, said it was a good thing that D-Day came when it did or the Germans might have wiped London off the map with their buzz bombs. He said when the buzz bombs first started coming over, all the anti-aircraft guns in London would open upon them but after a week of this, the military decided not to shoot at them and maybe some of the bombs would go on past London, which they did. I was astonished at the casual way the Britisher talked. From his tone of voice, we might have been in the Savoy-Plaza Bar, having a Scotch-and-soda, and I wondered if we Americans would have stood up as well if the tables had been turned. By this time the fire fighters, rescue squads, and the Home Guard were on the scene, and they all swept into action. I tried to do what I could to help but the English moved too swiftly for me. I walked back to my room at the hotel but not to sleep.

"It didn't take London long to set up a good defense against the robot enemy. On later missions I saw great masses of balloons several thousand feet high in the air. These balloon barrages were centered south-east of London – between London and the Channel – and there was also a large concentration of guns placed in this area, which was known as 'Flak Alley.' This strategy greatly eliminated the number of bombs that got over London. The people were taking to the air raid shelters, as they had done during the blitz. In the early part of the afternoon the Londoners would begin making their makeshift beds in the shelters and in the corridors and stations of the subways. By 11pm one could hardly get on and off the subways for all the sleepers around. We Americans tried to be pretty fatalistic about the buzz bombs. We wouldn't go to the air raid shelters. We figured sort of foolishly if our time had come, the bomb with our number on it would find us wherever we were – in the 'American Melody Bar' or in the air raid shelter. The buzz bombs seemed to pursue me. The next morning on my way to headquarters I could tell we were going to have an unwelcomed visitor. The people on the street were freezing up and waiting to see if they were going to have to fall flat on the sidewalk. Sure enough we had to fall flat, and it would have to be raining that morning. The uncertainty was far worse than when the bombers came over. The Britishers had warning then, but the buzz bomb was right there – bringing sudden slaughter, ravaged homes and buildings, and anguish and sorrow."[86]

CHAPTER IV

THE AERIAL ASSAULT INTENSIFIES

July 1944

"The invisible battle has now crashed into the open. We shall now be able to watch its progress at fairly close quarters. Between 100 and 150 flying bombs, each weighing about one ton, are being discharged daily, and have been discharged for the last fortnight or so. A very high proportion of the casualties have fallen upon London, which presents to the enemy a target 18 miles wide by 20 miles deep. The flying bomb is a weapon literally and essentially indiscriminate in its nature, purpose and effect. London will never be conquered and we will never fail."

Prime Minister Winston Churchill in the House of Commons, 6 July 1944

Saturday 1 JULY

A Diver struck the Colindale Hospital in Hendon, killing five airmen, four WAAFs and a nurse. A doctor wrote in his diary:

"The V-1 had fallen in the earth a few feet from the south side of the two-storey block, which had open balconies at the side. The upper housed some 30 men being treated for pulmonary tuberculosis, of whom five on the adjoining open-air balcony lost their lives. In some amazing way nearly all the remainder managed to crawl out of, or were rescued from, the wreckage with comparatively minor injuries. In the ground-floor ward were some five or six WAAFs from Hendon Aerodrome. Of these four were killed, and one nurse – whose bodies were not found until late that day."[87]

Another hit the Corporation Refuse Destructor chimney near Kentons Lane, Old Windsor. A dozen houses were seriously damaged, with another 250 considerably damaged. There were some 60 casualties, 24 of whom were seriously injured, mainly caused by flying glass. Three Divers fell in the Thornton Heath area of Croydon (CR7) during the morning, the first impacting at 0735 in Whitehall Road. Eight houses were destroyed, 30 damaged and five residents killed. Three more died at 0900 when a bomb fell in Hazelmere Road, and a further nine lost their lives in Nursery Road at 0956. Fulham received a bomb at 1535, 15 people being killed in Harwood Terrace/Bagleys Lane (SW6), a further dozen being seriously injured. One person was killed at 1630 in the Coper Cope Road/Lawn Road area of Beckenham (BR3), where much damage was inflicted. At 1827, a Diver fell between Stuart Road and Reynolds Road, Peckham (SE15) destroying or damaging 80 houses, in which 17 people were killed. At 1854, a Diver impacted near The Goat public house between Queen Elizabeth Street and Gainsford Street, Bermondsey (SE1), demolishing the building and others in the vicinity; 18 people died.

3 Squadron (Tempest V) Newchurch

Flt Sgt S. Domanski PAF	EJ582/JF-T	V-1	0515	Channel
	EJ582/JF-T	V-1 damaged c0520		Channel
Flg Off R. Dryland	JN865/JF-	V-1	0520	Rye area

Polish Flt Sgt Domanski reported:

"Good vectors were received on to two Divers in mid-Channel about one mile apart. The first Diver was chased and range closed to 200 yards. Two short bursts from dead astern caused the Diver to crash into the sea and explode. The second Diver was then chased and fired at. Strikes were seen but it was eventually lost in cloud."

This may possibly have been the same Diver engaged by Flg Off Dryland a few minutes later: "I was vectored on to a Diver over Rye and closed. I fired a three-seconds burst from dead astern but Diver was lost in cloud." The IO added: "Biggin Hill have record of a crash at the relevant time (0520) in the same area, and this has been credited to this pilot." Flg Off George Kosh's aircraft JN765/JF-K crashed south-west of Rye while chasing a Diver, and he was killed, believed to have been a victim of the guns. The exact location of the crash was House Field, Winchelsea Marsh, Icklesham, as testified by the subsequent (abbreviated) Police Report submitted by Police Sgt F. Balcombe, who made a gruesome find:

> "At 0545, a Tempest piloted by Flg Off George Kosh, age 22, of 3 Squadron crashed at House Field. The fuselage was shattered to pieces and strewn over a radius of 300 yards, while the engine and cockpit buried itself in the ground. The pilot was buried with the engine, with the exception of one leg which was found near the crater. This leg has been handed over to ... RAF personnel digging for the remains of the dead pilot."

91 Squadron (Spitfire XIV) Deanland ALG

Sqn Ldr N.A. Kynaston	RB185/Dl-	V-1	1520	Maidstone area
Flg Off P.A. Schade	NH701/DL-A	V-1	1820	Horsmonden area
Flt Lt H.M. Neil	RB173/DL-	V-1	1828	Ticehurst area
Flt Lt H.D. Johnson	RB188/DL-K	V-1	1840	off Dungeness
Flt Lt A.R. Cruickshank RCAF	RM615/DL-	V-1	1850	Dymchurch area
Sqn Ldr N.A. Kynaston	RB185/DL-	V-1	2025	Biggin Hill area

Sqn Ldr Norman Kynaston bagged two Divers during the day, the first at 1520: "Diver sighted over Ashford area. Attacked from astern at 150 yards range with short burst and it fell in a field, exploding on hitting the ground." This Diver actually caused much damage in West Beech Drive, Maidstone, where 200 houses were slightly damaged. One person was seriously injured and three slightly hurt. Three hours later Flg Off Paddy Schade got one: "Sighted Diver above cloud and made attack from dead astern at 350/400 yards range. Saw strikes all over Diver, which went into dive, exploding when hitting the ground." The next fell to Flt Lt Neil:

> "Sighted Diver being attacked by another aircraft [probably a Spitfire of 165 Squadron], which fired all its ammunition from a range of 100/200 yards, after which an unsuccessful attempt to tip it over was made. I advised over the R/T that I was about to fire and the other aircraft broke away, whereupon I opened fire from 100 yards range dead astern, obtaining up to ten strikes, causing the Diver to spiral into the ground where it exploded in a hedge."

Flt Lt Johnny Johnson then scored: "Sighted Diver out in the Channel and opened attack from astern at 100 yards range. Strikes were obtained and Diver spun in and exploded in the sea ten miles south-west of Dungeness." No.5 was shot down by Flt Lt Ray Cruickshank: "I was vectored on to Diver south-east of Dungeness and attacked from astern from 100 yards, Diver spinning in and exploding on the ground three miles north-north-east of Dymchurch." Sqn Ldr Kynaston closed a successful day by destroying his second at 2025: "Diver first seen over Bexhill being fired on by Spit IX, who did not hit it. Chased to Biggin where, after obtaining strikes at 600 yards range from dead astern, it was set on fire and dived to earth, where it exploded."

165 Squadron (Spitfire IX) Detling

Plt Off G.P. Bauchman RCAF	MK752/SK-J	V-1	1815	Hastings area
	MK752/SK-J	V-1 shared	1822	Hastings area
Flg Off C.M. Lawson RAAF	MK811/SK-K	V-1	1820	Bexhill area
	MK811/SK-K	V-1	1830	Hastings area
Plt Off R.S.J. Hebron RAAF	MK864/SK-H	V-1	1830	Eastbourne area

Plt Off J.M. Walton RCAF	MK738/SK-L	V-1	1830	Tunbridge Wells area
Flg Off G.P. Armstrong RAAF	MJ221/SK-J	V-1	1900	Hastings area
Flg Off T.D. Tinsey	ML175/SK-P	V-1	2005	Kenley area

Canadian Plt Off George Bauchman was the first to score for 165 Squadron during the evening, catching his victim at 1815:

> "Diver was sighted one mile south of Hastings. Gave chase and waited for Diver to pass over Hastings and then fired a two-seconds burst, observing strikes along port wing and halfway along starboard wing, fuselage and jet unit. The jet burst a bright yellow, port wing dipped and Diver half-rolled, went into a dive and crashed on a house about one mile north of Hastings. Again vectored on to a Diver which was sighted at 1822 about eight miles north of Hastings. On closing saw another Spit engaging it, so held off. The other aircraft fired and many strikes were seen. The Diver pulled up to 5,000 feet, then stall turned on to nearly a reciprocal course and dived to 1,000 feet. It then pulled up to about 3,000 feet. It then went into a 45° glide to 1,000 feet. After this it went into a very shallow dive. Although many Spits were around, neither they nor the one that had fired did anything about it and remained fairly high up. I, with the object of destroying the Diver in the air, engaged, firing a one-second burst. Strikes were seen on the wing and flame from the jet went out. It then went into a steep dive and crashed into a field about six-eight miles north of Hastings."

Flg Off Lawson's first victim exploded in the air eight miles south of Bexhill at 1820. He was then vectored onto a second, which he pursued and shot down in to the sea one mile off Hastings. Plt Off Hebron intercepted south-east of Eastbourne: "Diver exploded in the air 20 miles north-west of Eastbourne on the outskirts of a small village." Canadian Plt Off John Walton sighted a flying bomb over Bexhill but did not attack until it was clear of the town:

> "I gave chase and fired a three-seconds burst from 200 yards, closing down to 100 yards, with no apparent effect. I then closed and fired a one-second burst from 50 yards. Large pieces of the jet unit fell off and the bomb went into a steep dive and exploded in a field 100 yards from a farmhouse. I went down to about 200 feet to ascertain the damage caused. Five or six cows in a nearby field appeared to be unharmed. As far as I could see the only damage to the farmhouse and area was the removal of a few tiles from the roof."

Flg Off Armstrong returned to Detling with his Spitfire covered in soot and with the elevators and rudder partly burned away after his target exploded north of Hastings:

> "I was only 50 yards away at the time and in consequence flew through the wreckage a matter of seconds after it occurred – and as a result my aircraft now bears black camouflage."

The final flying bomb of this successful evening fell south-east of Kenley at 2005, having been shot down by Flg Off Tommy Tinsey who had pursued it from south-east of Eastbourne:

> "Opened fire at 400 yards. Could not close. Saw one strike. Bomb fell near Westerham. No claim [he was then vectored on to another]. Saw Spit open fire from 600 yards. No hits observed. Passed another Spit and opened fire from 100 yards. Gave one one-second burst. Large flash and large piece of jet unit fell away. Diver fell three miles south-east of Kenley."

322 (Dutch) Squadron (Spitfire XIV) West Malling

| Wt Off J.A. Maier | VL-T | V-1 | 1735 | |

486 (RNZAF) Squadron (Tempest V) Newchurch

Plt Off F.B. Lawless RNZAF	JN770/SA-V	V-1	0520	Cranbrook area
Flg Off R.J. Cammock RNZAF	JN866/SA-U	V-1	1900	Bexhill area
Wt Off C.J. Sheddan RNZAF	JN821/SA-H	V-1	1915	Rye area
Flt Lt L.J. Appleton RNZAF	JN873/SA-W	V-1	2106	Pevensey area

Plt Off Kevin McCarthy's aircraft (JN773) suffered engine failure during an anti-Diver patrol and he force-landed, suffering serious injuries, as Wt Off Jim Sheddan remembered: "Kevin was another casualty and although he survived the crash his flying days were over. When next I saw Mac he was in McIndoe's special hospital at East Grinstead having his face straightened out."

316 (Polish) Squadron equipped with Mustang IIIs arrived at West Malling for anti-Diver patrols. The newly appointed CO, Sqn Ldr Bohdan Arct PAF later wrote:

"On 1 July we received posting to West Malling aerodrome in Kent, about half way between London and the south-east coast. This aerodrome was right on the route of the flying bombs and for this reason we anticipated to be in the midst of fighting and chasing the infernal projectiles. I took one flight only to West Malling, as the other had not yet finished modifications. Flying in close formation we beat the drome to show how the Poles fly, then formed an echelon to land with perfect precision. I taxied to dispersal point, switched off the engine, jumped out and reported to the station commander, who was already waiting outside the barrack. 'You certainly know a lot about formation flying,' he said in a friendly manner. 'Well, let's see if your aiming is as good. There is plenty of good shooting around here. Look there, Squadron Leader Arct.' I glanced in the indicated direction and saw the well-known silhouette whizzing past the aerodrome with lightning speed. Guns roared, the bomb cackled overhead and disappeared in the direction of the capital. 'How many of them pass over here, Sir?' I asked. 'Too many! Swarms of them every day. Some blow up around our station, most get to town. Serious damage is being done. Well, Squadron Leader Arct, you'll find yourselves bloody busy, mark my word. The bomb chase has high priority. Good hunting!' The station commander warmly shook my hand and departed. This way I became the leader of the first Polish squadron assigned to combat the flying bomb."

Night 1/2 JULY

One person died when a Diver fell in Salcott Road, Battersea (SW11) at 2326, where ten houses were demolished and 40 more damaged; Bolingbroke Hospital was also damaged. A more serious incident occurred a few minutes later, at 2335, when a Diver impacted in Lambeth (SE11) damaging 20 houses in Saville Place and Sowberry Street, killing 13 residents. Fulham received its second bomb of the day when the Lewis Trust Building in Lisgard Terrace (W14) was hit two minutes before midnight; 14 died and five were seriously injured. Two Divers fell in Beckenham within a few minutes of each other, the first exploding in Albany Street (BR3) at 0310, causing much damage and killing three. Another three died at 0343, when the second impacted in the Kingshall Road/Alders Mead Road area.

605 Squadron (Mosquito VI) Manston

Flg Off P.R. Rudd	UP-	V-1	2314	off Clacton

"At 2300, 20 miles east of base, Diver was sighted at 1,000 feet at 350mph. This was attacked from astern, range 300 yards, with a short burst of cannon. The jet, which had been burning and flickering steadily up to the time of attack, spluttered several times, and then altered course. It was again attacked with machine-guns. Attack broken off 30 miles east of Clacton as range was increasing. Diver was seen to crash by an aircraft from Coltishall (12 Group) presumably 25 Squadron, and time and place confirmed with Sgt Hart at North Weald Control, who had followed the Diver's plot until it disappeared at this particular spot. Patrol was continued but Mosquito was later recalled to base where weather was closing in. Landed at 0015."

Sunday 2 JULY

The Diver that struck Trenholme Road, Penge (SE20) at 0928, killed 11 people and destroyed 21 houses with a further 300 suffering damage. Three Divers came down in the Peckham/Bermondsey area (SE15) within an hour, the first (at 1051) impacting in Hatcham Street/Ilderton Road/Record Street, Bermondsey. A two-storey building was struck and other property badly damaged. Eight people were killed. This area had previously been heavily hit by conventional bombing. The second Diver fell on Radnor Road, Peckham at 1114, destroying ten houses and damaging 50 more, while two residents were killed. A wayward Diver fell in Chestnut Lane, Amersham at about 1052, demolishing one house and severely damaging four more, while a further 135 houses suffered varying degrees of damage. Two residents were killed and 14 others injured. Two more came down in Thornton Heath, Croydon (CR7), the first in Highbury Avenue (three killed) at 1228, the second some 30 minutes later in Chipstead Avenue (one killed). The next, that exploded in Costa Street, Peckham, took six lives. At least 30 houses were damaged. Another fell near the junction of Albemarle Road and Beckenham High Street, and destroyed several shops. Another wayward Diver impacted at Chiltern Street near Stradishall in Suffolk. Another came down on a US Army encampment, as reported in the *Daily Mail*:

> *"An American Army sergeant was entombed for three and a half days beneath the piled wreckage of his billet in southern England, which was shattered by a flying bomb, before he was rescued. Sgt Ed Bearefoot was in a room with two other United States soldiers when the flying bomb dropped and the place fell about them. He was thrown to the floor and the beams collapsed, but somehow stayed fixed above him. Even the great weight of debris crashing down on top of the beams did not dislodge them. Debris was removed piece by piece by rescuers, and when they finally lifted Sgt Bearefoot out unharmed, but dazed, covered in dust, very thirsty and very hungry, he had been in prison for eighty-five and a half hours. He was taken to hospital where he is said to be rapidly recovering. The bodies of his two comrades trapped in the room were brought out later."*

FIU Detachment (Tempest V) Newchurch

Flt Lt J. Berry	EJ524/ZQ-Y	V-1	daytime

Sqn Ldr Daniel and Flt Lt Berry each flew three patrols, only Berry managing to shoot down a flying bomb. Again Flt Lt Jeremy Howard-Williams recalled:

> "The weather remained fickle over the ensuing days and the two pilots were often kept out of the air, but they flew whenever it was at all possible. Joe's favourite technique was to fly some 4,000 feet above the usual target height and, on sighting the now familiar yellow flame, he turned onto the same course and let the missile overtake him underneath. As it passed, he pushed the stick forward and came down on it with the superior speed conferred by his dive. He drew alongside so as to keep out of its slipstream and only at the last moment did he pull into the turbulent wake of the hot air from the tailpipe. The bad weather continued into July. On the second night of the month, Joe got too close to one bomb as it blew up in front of him. Immediately he felt the thud of metal striking his aircraft. The motor faltered, picked up and spluttered along uncertainly. Now was the time when he would have liked a second engine, but that one got him back all right."

Night 2/3 JULY

At 2250, a victim of a night fighter impacted on Brogden Farm near Maidstone. A Diver that fell on Camberwell Station Road (SE5) at 0302 damaged 30 houses and killed five residents. Within the hour another came down between Queens Road and Besson Street in New Cross (SE14), where 32 houses were damaged but only one person killed. However, four were killed in Streatham (SW16) when a bomb exploded in Besley Street at 0457 demolishing four houses.

85 Squadron (Mosquito XIX) Swannington

Capt T. Weisteen (Norw)	MM636/VY-A	V-1	2350-0335

96 Squadron (Mosquito XIII) Ford

Flt Lt F.R.L. Mellersh	MM577/ZJ-N	V-1	0125	off Beachy Head

	MM577/ZJ-N	V-1	0200	off Beachy Head
	MM577/ZJ-N	V-1	0220	off Beachy Head
Flt Sgt T. Bryan	HK421/ZJ-	V-1	0215	Hastings area
Wg Cdr E.D. Crew	NS985/ZJ-	V-1	0220	Beachy Head area
	NS985/ZJ-	V-1	0228	Beachy Head area
	NS985/ZJ-	V-1	0247	Beachy Head area
Flt Lt I.A. Dobie	HK437/ZJ-	V-1	0245	off Dieppe

All three of Flt Lt Togs Mellersh's victims exploded in the sea following his attacks, two about 40 miles south of Beachy Head and the other nearer inshore. He reported that his second target did a steep climb before diving down. By way of contrast, all three of Wg Cdr Crew's victims came down on land north of Beachy Head, on the edge of the gun belt, two gliding down in flames. Flt Sgt Tom Bryan's target also fell on land, exploding approximately ten miles north of Hastings, while Flt Lt Ian Dobie's exploded on the sea 15 miles north of Dieppe.

157 Squadron (Mosquito XIX) Swannington

Flt Sgt S. Astley	MM637/RS-P	V-1	2210-0200	
Flt Lt R.J.V. Smyth	MM646/RS-R	V-1	2215-0220	exploded in mid-air
Sqn Ldr J.G. Benson	MM670/RS-H	V-1	2335-0220	

Sqn Ldr Benson's navigator Flt Lt Brandon wrote:

"We shot down another buzz bomb while we were on a similar type of patrol as before. Again we found that four or five of them were launched together and we made straight for number three. We were the only fighter after it and we had no trouble with it."

Flt Lt Reg Smyth (known as 'Smithie') shot down a flying bomb on his second anti-Diver sortie, the explosion of which blew a hole in the nose of his Mosquito. Neither he nor his navigator Flg Off Laurie Waters was injured.

409 (RCAF) Squadron (Mosquito XIII) Hunsdon

Wt Off R.F. Henke RCAF	MM510/KP-	V-1	0055	off Beachy Head
Flg Off H.F. Pearce RCAF	MM491/KP-	V-1	0125	Beachy Head area

The two Mosquitos departed Hunsdon together for an anti-Diver patrol, both achieving kills: Wt Off Rudi Henke reported:

"Visual was obtained of pilotless aircraft at range of 10-15 miles approaching from the south at a height of 1,500 feet. I turned in behind and, diving from 6,000 feet, opened fire from astern at 2,000 feet, observing strikes. My navigator then advised me that the range was increasing, so I nosed down. Picking up extra speed, I closed to 1,500 feet, firing another burst from dead astern and slightly below, observing no strikes. The navigator again advised that the range was increasing, so I nosed the plane down again. Picking up speed I closed to 700 feet, pulled the nose up and fired from dead astern, observing hits. The Diver burst into flames and expecting it to explode I broke sharply to port, felt the aircraft lurch and observed a red glare illuminating the sky. The claim is confirmed by F/O Pearce who was patrolling in the area at that time."

Thirty minutes later Flg Off Red Pearce got another:

"We observed a visual at range of ten miles, 15 miles off English coast south-east of Beachy Head. I dived from 5,500 feet and attacked from dead astern and opened fire at just over 2,000 feet. No strikes observed. I delivered a second attack at just under 2,000 feet, closing to 1,500 feet, and delivered a third burst, seeing many strikes and pieces falling off. Closed range to 1,000 feet, firing steadily and saw numerous strikes. Three miles inland and at a range of 500 feet, I broke off the engagement as ammunition was exhausted. The Diver was at 300 feet and in a steep dive."

605 Squadron (Mosquito VI) Manston

| Flt Lt J.G. Musgrave | MM429/UP-H | V-1 | 0335 | exploded in mid-air |

"At 0035 we attacked a Diver with two short bursts of cannon from astern at 200-300 yards. Target was about eight miles south of Folkestone at 2,000 feet. Attack continued but broken off on approaching English coast. Strikes had been observed and Diver was seen picked up by searchlight and it exploded in the air (no AA fire) midway between Folkestone and Dungeness."

Monday 3 JULY

The Streatham Hill Theatre, Streatham (SW2) was hit at 0636, one person in the vicinity being killed. Five were killed in Brockley (SE4) following an explosion in Braxfield Road/Commerford Road at 0840. A major incident occurred at 0747 when a bomb came down in Turks Row, Chelsea (SW3), killing 64 US Army servicemen and ten civilians in their living quarters in Sloane Court; a further 54 soldiers were seriously injured. A Diver impacted on the John Sanders store in Uxbridge Road, Ealing, at about 1130. Another Diver, having been shot down, fell in the lines of the Canadian 6 Tank Regiment located at Sandling Park, East Kent. Six soldiers were injured, one seriously. Elsewhere, a Diver crashed into Bridge Street, Folkestone, causing three fatalities and 60 injuries. Nine houses and the Wheatsheaf Inn were destroyed; the licensee of the inn was killed and his wife seriously injured. The devastation in this area was great with almost 1,000 properties being affected. Although it was reported that guns had brought down the bomb, a local witness recalled that he had seen a fighter tip the missile with its wingtip, and that the pilot involved had later visited the area: "What he saw so disturbed him he went insane."[88] Young mother Gwen Chadwick of Newhaven recalled:

"On a beautiful sunny day in July, my friend and I and my baby girl were taking a walk in open farmland near Newhaven when we heard a Doodlebug flying over Mount Pleasant. Having nowhere to shelter we crouched down over the pram and just hoped for the best. At this point a fighter aircraft suddenly appeared out of the blue and fired at the Doodlebug, which exploded in mid-air. The plane then turned in a semi-circle, dipped its wings and appeared to do a victory roll. We could see the pilot waving to us and we were so excited we cheered and waved madly. Then, to our horror, the plane passed over our heads and came down like a stone in the adjoining field and burst into flames, less than 100 yards away. The pilot had not been waving to us. He was trying to warn us to get out of the way. His crash, as we later learned, had been caused by the impact of the Doodlebug exploding. He was a Polish airman and his remains were buried in the local cemetery."[89]

AA gunners at Folkestone hit a Diver at 1530 that subsequently crashed in Denmark Street, Folkestone, causing much destruction. Three persons were killed and 55 injured, eight seriously. Two brought down by fighters in the same general area crashed at Saltwood and Lyminge. That evening, at 2030, a Diver exploded in Woodville Road, Thornton Heath, Croydon (CR7). Eight houses were demolished and many others damaged. Eight residents were killed.

3 Squadron (Tempest V) Newchurch

Flt Lt R. van Lierde (Belg)	EJ525/JF-	V-1	0755	Beachy Head area
Flt Sgt D.J. Mackerras RAAF	JN868/JF-F	V-1	0837	off Dungeness
Plt Off H.R. Wingate	EJ582/JF-T	V-1	1735	exploded in mid-air
	EJ582/JF-T	V-1	1745	exploded in mid-air
	EJ582/JF-T	V-1	1755	exploded in mid-air

Flt Sgt M.J.A. Rose	JN754/JF-	V-1	1830	Ashford area
Plt Off K.G. Slade-Betts	EJ504/JF-	V-1	1900	Hastings area
	EJ504/JF-	V-1	2240	off Hastings

The Squadron scored a further eight kills during the day but suffered the loss of its Polish pilot Flt Sgt Stanislaw Domanski PAF, who was tragically shot down in JN752/JF-S by AA fire and crashed at Playden north of Rye. Flt Lt Remi van Lierde lost his damaged victim in cloud but it was later confirmed to have crashed four miles north of Hailsham. The Diver intercepted by Flt Sgt Don Mackerras disintegrated after its engine had exploded, the warhead and other parts falling into the sea some ten miles off Dungeness. Plt Off Dickie Wingate was the star of the day, scoring a hat trick of kills that all exploded in the air within the space of ten minutes:

"Fired two short bursts from 400 yards dead astern. The Diver exploded in mid-air. Witnessed by No.2. The next Diver was sighted coming in over Hastings. This also exploded in mid-air and was again witnessed by No.2. The third Diver was seen coming in over Hastings gasworks at 2,500 feet. Red 2 fired a short burst without success, and then I closed to 50 yards dead astern and loosed a short burst. The Diver exploded in mid-air."

Plt Off Slade-Betts and Flt Sgt Morrie Rose took off as a section at 1800, the former being vectored on to a Diver north of Hastings: "Attacked with five two-seconds bursts and it exploded in mid-air 15 miles north of Hastings." Rose engaged another over Folkestone:

"Heavy flak was bursting behind the Diver but ceased as I approached. Closed to 300 yards and fired intermittent bursts. Closed to 250 yards and fired a one-second burst with strikes, flame and smoke as a result. The Diver went vertically through cloud and I saw it explode beside a main road believed to be the Ashford-Maidstone. Traffic was seen stopped either side of the crater by the debris which smothered the road."

Slade-Betts was up again at 2145: "I was put on to a Diver 20 miles south of Dungeness. Five short bursts were fired from 300 yards dead astern and the Diver exploded in the sea."

41 Squadron (Spitfire XII) Friston

| Flg Off M.A.L. Balaase (Belg) | EN609/EB- | V-1 | 0634 | Bexhill area |
| Sqn Ldr R.H. Chapman | EN605/EB-R | V-1 | 0715 | off Beachy Head |

Poor weather conditions, with cloud down to almost ground level, made interceptions very difficult although both the CO and Flg Off Mono Balaase gained successes. The Belgian pilot reported that his victim crashed into an open field four miles north of Bexhill. Sqn Ldr Chapman noted:

"I carried out quarter to dead astern attack, closing to 400-300 yards. Diver dived through clouds and into sea at 0715 some 30 miles south-east of Beachy Head."

56 Squadron (Tempest V) Newchurch

| Flt Lt D.V.G. Cotes-Preedy | JN864/US-C | V-1 | 1825 | off Dungeness |

It was appropriate that Flt Lt Digby Cotes-Preedy GM, who had been involved in assisting Squadron pilots to convert to the Tempest, should shoot down the unit's first flying bomb with the new stead:

"Sighted a Diver 30-40 miles south of Dungeness at 2,000 feet. I attacked on the starboard quarter from 50 yards and Diver caught fire, going down at an angle of 45° and exploding in the sea."

Four hours later, Canadian Plt Off David Ness (JN869/US-D) came close to getting a second. Having used up all his ammunition, he unsuccessfully tried three times to flip his target over with his wingtip.

91 Squadron (Spitfire XIV) Deanland ALG

Flt Lt H.B. Moffett RCAF	RB165/DL-L	V-1	1615	Rye area
Flg Off W.C. Marshall	RM615/DL-	V-1	1630	Dymchurch area
Flt Lt H.D. Johnson	RB188/DL-K	V-1	1725	Lympne a/f area
Sqn Ldr N.A. Kynaston	RB185/DL-	V-1 shared	1820	exploded in mid-air
Flt Lt H.D. Johnson	RB165/DL-L	V-1	2059	Ashford area
Sqn Ldr N.A. Kynaston	NH703/DL-	V-1	2140	exploded in mid-air
Flg Off W.C. Marshall	RM654/DL-F	V-1	2145	Hastings area

Canadian Flt Lt Bruce Moffett added to his score at 1615:

> "Vectored on Diver and attacked from astern at 150-200 yards. Diver fell in a field five miles north-west of Rye where it exploded."

Within 15 minutes Flg Off Bill Marshall got a second:

> "Sighted Diver two miles out to sea and made attack from starboard quarter, closing in to dead astern to 75 yards range. Pieces fell of and jet mechanism set on fire. Diver then spun in and exploded in a field three miles north-west of Dymchurch."

Flt Lt Johnny Johnson scored the next:

> "Saw Diver west of Hythe. Attacked from astern from 400 yards range, closing to 150 yards. Strikes seen on port wing, the Diver flicking over and fell in woods east of Lympne aerodrome, where it exploded."

The CO waded in with another but had to share it with the guns:

> "Sighted Diver over Ashford and attacked from dead astern at 200 yards range. Gave first burst with machine-guns only with no appreciable result. A short burst with cannon exploded Diver in the air."

Flt Lt Johnson was off again at 2040 and scored his second of the day:

> "Vectored on Diver three miles out to sea east of Hastings. Attacked with three bursts from dead astern, closing to 200 yards. Strikes were seen and Diver spun in two miles south of Ashford, exploding in a field."

Sqn Ldr Kynaston also scored his second kill of the evening, at 2140:

> "Sighted Diver south of Tonbridge and attacked from astern at 500 yards range. Strikes seen to penetrate wing root and Diver exploded in the air."

Flg Off Bill Marshall concluded a successful day with the final kill some five minutes later:

> "Vectored on to Diver five miles south of Hastings. Attacked from astern from 600 yards, closing in to 150 yards and Diver exploded in the air."

316 (Polish) Squadron (Mustang III) West Malling

Flt Sgt A. Murkowski PAF	FB352/SZ-C	V-1	1910	exploded in mid-air

Of his kill – the first for the PAF – Flt Sgt Toni Murkowski recalled:

> "Because they [the Divers] were such small targets, our guns were harmonised for about 250 yards range. It was a foggy day and most of the pilots had gone to the officers' mess for lunch when the tannoy went and I scrambled to a flying bomb coming over Rye. It took some catching and we were supposed to keep the over-boost revs on for less than ten minutes or it

meant an engine change. I soon saw it and opened fire, but I was too precise and enthusiastic. I never got such a shock in the air as when I hit it – it went up with a terrific explosion. It just blew up in front of me. My God! I never thought the Mustang would stand the shock as I was hit by the pieces and the left wing flew off above me. When I got back my wingtips had to be changed."

Sqn Ldr Arct added:

"Sergeant Pilot Murkowski brought down a flying bomb 20 miles south-east of the station. A large chart was drawn, hung in the dispersal barrack and Murkowski's name with a miniature of the V-1 at the side was written honourably at the top. I wrote 'victory' as I could not find a more suitable word. The word victory is really out of place as regard flying bombs. One did not fight with the 'Witches'. It is obvious that flying bombs did not defend themselves nor would they attack their pursuers, they did not perform aerobatics in fierce dogfighting, did not fire cannons or machine-guns. Nonetheless, strange things happened during these encounters."

322 (Dutch) Squadron (Spitfire XIV) West Malling

Flt Sgt H.C. Cramm	NH699/VL-R	V-1	1700	off Dungeness
Flg Off J. Jonker	RB160/VL-A	V-1	1813	off Dungeness
Flg Off F.J.H. van Eijk ⎫	VL-U	V-1	2300	West Malling area
Plt Off A.A. Homburg ⎭	VL-Y			

The Diver attacked by Flt Sgt Hendrik Cramm exploded and scorched his aircraft though he was able to land safely:

"Patrolling 10-15 miles south of Dungeness when vectored on to Diver. Attacked line astern, range 250 yards, and saw strikes on starboard wing. Diver slowed down and I closed in to 100 yards and attacked again. Diver exploded and my Spitfire was scorched by the explosion."

Flg Off Jan Jonker reported:

"Patrolling 20 miles south of Dungeness and vectored on to Diver but had to break off as Tempest cut in. Saw Tempest fire and miss, then break away. I attacked line astern, slightly below and range 200 yards. Saw strikes on power unit and wings. Diver crashed and exploded in the sea."

An hour before midnight Flg Off Fraks van Eijk, aided by his No2, got another:

"Attacked line astern, range 400 yards. Nothing happened, broke away to let No2 attack. Both pilots saw strikes but still nothing happened. I was unable to fire any more owing to stoppage in cannon, so formated on Diver and tipped it over with my starboard wing. Diver made spiral dive and crashed and exploded in open field ten miles south of West Malling. wingtip of Spitfire slightly damaged."

486 (RNZAF) Squadron (Tempest V) Newchurch

Plt Off R.D. Bremner RNZAF	JN801/SA-L	V-1	0910	Rye area
Flg Off J.R. Cullen RNZAF	JN863/SA-R	V-1	1735	Hastings area
Wt Off O.D. Eagleson RNZAF	JN873/SA-W	V-1	1735	Edenbridge area
Plt Off K.A. Smith RNZAF	JN801/SA-L	V-1	1840	Hastings area
	JN801/SA-L	V-1	1850	Hastings area
Wt Off C.J. Sheddan RNZAF	JN805/SA-E	V-1	2250	Hastings area

Flg Off Dusty Miller was forced to bale out of his Tempest (JN411) after being hit by AA gunfire whilst chasing a flying bomb, but found he was trapped, half in and half out of the cockpit. He finally managed to extricate himself and his parachute opened just in time. Wt Off Jim Sheddan remembered:

"I was on a night patrol with Dusty Miller – he came on the air to say that his motor had packed up. Looking down into the blackness below, with not even a light visible, there was no way that

Dusty was going to survive a forced-landing in those conditions, so my advice to my old mate was to bale out while there was still time. As there was no reply from Dusty it was obvious that he was in no need of my advice, so after making sure that control was aware of the position it was a case of sweating out the remainder of the patrol, then landing and heading for the local pub. Surprise, surprise, who should be standing by the bar, a pint in his hand and his moustache quivering with excitement, but Dusty, surrounded by an admiring crowd as he told of his misadventure. It seemed as though he had landed in or near the pub. It had all the hallmarks of a put up job, but that could not be; Dusty's navigation was not that perfect!"

FIU Detachment (Tempest V) Newchurch

Flt Lt J. Berry	EJ524/ZQ-Y	V-1	daytime

Five patrols were flown by FIU but only Flt Lt Berry succeeded in shooting down a flying bomb.

41 and 610 Squadrons moved to Friston from West Malling to be nearer to their required area of operation.

Night 3/4 JULY

Operation *Rumpelkammer* (Lumber Room) codename for the air-launched V-1 campaign, began when III/KG3 (commanded by Hptm Martin Vetter) launched its first assault against London. Operations had been delayed following a US bomber raid on the airfield at Beauvais-Tillé (on 16 June) to where the Heinkels of III/KG3 had initially flown from their base in Germany; eight aircraft had been destroyed or damaged and the Gruppe had to await fresh supply. Now, 14 V-1-carrying Heinkels commenced take-off from Gilze-Rijen airfield at 2200, following which they headed for a radio or light beacon on the Dutch coast while travelling about 170mph at an altitude of about 1,300 feet. The aircraft then changed to low-level flight over the sea at an altitude of about 160 feet to avoid being detected by British radar. Shortly before release, the Heinkel had to climb to an altitude of 1,650 feet. During that procedure, which took about four minutes, the crews were aware they were being observed by radar located at Foreness, North Foreland and St Margaret's Bay. At this stage the pulse-jet was started, and for about 30 seconds ran on reduced power. Upon release from the mother craft, the bomb's pulse-jet automatically switched to full power. The flying bomb then dropped 980 feet before climbing to the predetermined altitude. Meanwhile, the Heinkel, in a steep turn, again changed to low-level flight and returned home. The first operation was considered a success and none of the launchers was intercepted or otherwise lost.

85 Squadron (Mosquito XIX) Swannington

Capt T. Weisteen (Norw)	MM636/VY-A	V-1	2225-0200

96 Squadron (Mosquito XIII) Ford

Flt Lt N.S. Head	MM461/ZJ-	V-1	2330	Grid R.73
	MM461/ZJ-	V-1	2359	Grid Q.93
Sqn Ldr R.N. Chudleigh	HK376/ZJ-	V-1	2350	Grid W.47
	HK376/ZJ-	V-1	0010	Grid R.34
	HK376/ZJ-	V-1	0050	Grid W.47

Flt Lt Norman Head shot down both his targets in quick succession shortly before midnight, the first emitting a sheet of flame about 50 feet long following his attack and exploded on hitting the sea. The second did a vertical dive from 500 feet before crashing on land. Two of Sqn Ldr Dick Chudleigh's victims were shot down by positioning ahead and above and allowing them to overtake, then shooting them down into the sea. The third caused problems and exploded in mid-air at about 500-600 feet ahead of the Mosquito, which was damaged by the blast.

157 Squadron (Mosquito XIX) Swannington

Flt Lt R.D. Doleman	MM643/RS-F	V-1	2220-0205	
	MM643/RS-F	V-1	2220-0205	

The CO, Wg Cdr Ken Davison, experienced engine problems but was able to safely land MM678/RS-A at Wittering.

418 (RCAF) Squadron (Mosquito VI) Holmsley South

Sqn Ldr R. Bannock RCAF	HR147/TH-Z	V-1	2248-0239	off Abbeville
	HR147/TH-Z	V-1	2248-0239	off Abbeville
	HR147/TH-Z	V-1	2248-0239	off Abbeville

Sqn Ldr Bannock decided the best way to stop the Diver assault was to catch them at their launch pads. He headed for Abbeville and arrived to see a stream of Divers being launched. Despite heavy flak they repeatedly attacked the site and destroyed three over the sea.

605 Squadron (Mosquito VI) Manston

Sqn Ldr K.M. Carver	HJ761/UP-P	V-1	0016	exploded in mid-air
	HJ761/UP-P	V-1 probable	0045	off Beachy Head

"At 2352 saw a Diver destroyed by another aircraft 12 miles south-east of Dungeness. At 0016, south-east of Beachy Head, a Diver was seen at 1,500 feet. This was followed and at Beachy Head target altered course. Its speed was 330mph. Two bursts were fired from 500 yards astern. Strikes were seen and Diver blew up in the air. At 0045, 15 miles north-west of Le Tréport, another Diver was seen at 3,000 feet. It was attacked from 700 yards from astern, strikes were seen and Diver gradually lost height. By this time we had three stoppages out of four cannons. Attack was broken off at 0055 at 1,000 feet at Beachy Head with target still losing height gradually."

Tuesday 4 JULY

Two people were killed and many houses damaged when a Diver fell in Archbishops Park, Lambeth (SE1) at 0855. A flying bomb that impacted in West Norwood (SE27) at 1315 was the first of three that were to decimate the York Hill area. It landed behind the shops in the Norwood Road in the north-west quadrant of the junction with York Hill and totally demolished six houses and severely damaged 20 others in York Hill. In the Norwood Road 30 shops were badly damaged, as were ten houses in Ullswater Road and 11 civilians were killed. Eleven more people were killed at 1800 following the explosion of a bomb on the south side of Trelawn Road, Brixton (SW2), where 50 houses were destroyed or damaged. A Diver impacted in Moffat Road, Thornton Heath (Croydon CR7) at 2112, killing eight and causing much devastation. Another fell at the junction of Gipsy Road and Bentons Road in West Norwood (SE27) at 2137, and was the first of two to fall very close to each other. It demolished ten houses and caused severe damage to 40 others. Six people died in the attack. Another fell on the quarters of US servicemen and WACs in London, inflicting many casualties, and another came down in Norbury SW16, killing six people at 165 Norbury Crescent.

1 Squadron (Spitfire LFIXb) Detling

Flg Off D.H. Davy	MK846/JX-	V-1	0955	Hastings area
Flt Lt T. Draper Williams ⎫	MK726/JX-	V-1	1235	Channel
Flg Off D.R. Wallace ⎭	MK986/JX-V			
Flg Off D.V. McIntosh ⎫	MK644/JX-	V-1	1950	Channel
Flt Sgt K.C. Weller ⎭	ML258/JX-			

Sqn Ldr Lardner-Burke was off at 0930 on an anti-Diver patrol but it was his No.2 Flg Off Dennis Davy who scored:

> "Diver intercepted in the Rye area and attacked above cloud. Strikes observed on jet. Flames died down, engine spluttered and nose of Diver dropped. It turned to port, dived steeply and crashed on a crossroads four miles north-east of Hastings."

Blue Section (Draper Williams and Wallace) was vectored onto a Diver when 20 miles out to sea off Rye. They carried out alternate attacks whereupon the Diver nosed down and crashed into the sea just off the coast. Flt Sgt Ken Weller shared his second kill with Flg Off McIntosh:

> "Yellow 1 and 2 vectored onto Diver 40 miles south of Rye. Owing to low speed of Diver, overshot. Attacked and strikes observed on nose and wings. After attack Diver flew straight and level for a bit then turned on its back, banked to port and rolled out of control into the sea. Diver appeared larger than usual, especially the jet propulsion unit."

Flt Sgt Weller also recalled one of the many hazards of hunting the flying bombs:

> "The closest call I had with one was the day I was vectored towards one in cloud. Control kept saying our two radar plots are together, you must be right on top of it. I just said, well, I'm in cloud and can't see a bloody thing. Suddenly the V-1 came 'whoosh' right by me, within feet of my Spitfire and immediately disappeared again. Scared me fart-less! We patrolled over the Channel, sometimes as far as the French coast trying to pick them up. They would come over at speed, so we were trying to get around 2,000 feet higher than they flew so we could pick up some speed to catch them. Then we got 150-octane petrol, which gave us about another 30mph or so. But this made it necessary for our Spits to have an engine change about every 60 hours."[90]

150 Wing (Tempest V) Newchurch

Wg Cdr R.P. Beamont	JN751/RB	V-1	2305	Edenbridge area

3 Squadron (Tempest V) Newchurch

Plt Off K.G. Slade-Betts ⎱	JN817/JF-H	V-1	1815	Eastbourne area
Wt Off R.S. Adcock RAAF ⎰	JN735/JF-X			
Flg Off R.H. Clapperton	JN755/JF-D	V-1		Hailsham area
Flt Lt R. van Lierde (Belg)	EN525/JF-	V-1	2108	off Beachy Head
	EN525/JF-	V-1	2130	off Hastings
	EN525/JF-	V-1	2145	off Hastings
	EN525/JF-	V-1	2152	Hastings area
Flg Off R.H. Clapperton	JN755/JF-D	V-1	2215	off Hastings
	JN755/JF-D	V-1	2245	off Hastings
	JN755/JF-D	V-1	2300	off Hastings
Flt Lt A.R. Moore	JN818/JF-	V-1	2030	off Pevensey
Plt Off S.B. Feldman (US)	EJ540/JF-P	V-1	2155	Hastings area
Plt Off S.B. Feldman (US) ⎱	EJ540/JF-P	V-1	2157	off Rye
Flt Sgt L.G. Everson ⎰	JN868/JF-F			
Flt Lt A.R. Moore	JN818/JF-	V-1	2300	Rye area
Flt Sgt L.G. Everson	JN868/JF-F	V-1	2315	off Hastings

Plt Off Ken Slade-Betts took off from Newchurch at 1800 and saw a Diver 15 miles south of Bexhill at 3,500 feet. He attacked with five bursts from dead astern and put the jet out. The Diver went on its back and exploded on the sea south of Eastbourne at 1815. Flt Lt Moore's target fell into the sea about 20 yards offshore in Pevensey Bay at 2030. Flt Lt Remi van Lierde and Plt Off Buck Feldman took off together at 2100 and the Belgian was soon vectored onto a flying bomb, the first of four he would shoot down in less than 45 minutes, one of which gave a spectacular display:

> "I closed and attacked from 300 yards with two one-second bursts and the Diver went down

steeply, exploding in a field 12 miles north of Beachy Head at 2108. Saw a second south of Hastings at 2,000 feet and closed to 200 yards. Fired several bursts from dead astern and the Diver went down and exploded in the sea four miles south of Hastings at 2130. Saw a third out to sea at 1,500 feet. Closed to 150 yards and gave a two-seconds burst and the Diver burst into flames, pulled up in front of my Tempest, looped and went into the sea without exploding, skated off, rose to 150 feet then went straight down and exploded about four miles south of Hastings. Saw a fourth on ROC flares between Hastings and Bexhill at 3,000 feet. Closed to 100 yards and gave two-seconds burst and overshot with all ammo exhausted. Called for assistance but as another Tempest was closing, the Diver heeled over and went straight in, exploding on the ground 15 miles north of Hastings at 2152. Just before I overshot, I saw much flame from the jet and the Diver had slowed down with flames from the port side of its fuselage. A Spitfire had come down at high speed and overshot without firing. This was witnessed by my No.2 [Plt Off Feldman]."

Plt Off Feldman shortly afterwards saw another Diver some 20 miles south of Rye at 2,000 feet:

"I closed to about 400 yards and fired two short bursts from dead astern, with strikes. Then closed to 200 yards and gave a further two bursts. The jet flickered and the Diver went down, exploding in the sea ten miles south of Rye at 2155. Another Diver was seen south of Hastings at 2,500 feet. Overtook rapidly and gave short burst from 300 yards, saw strikes and smoke coming from the jet and the Diver slowed perceptibly. Closed to 100 yards and gave three-seconds burst with strikes on the wing and fuselage. The Diver exploded in the air and the warhead exploded on the ground three-five miles north of Hastings at 2157."

One of these he shared with Flt Sgt Everson. The next patrol was just as successful, with Flg Off Clapperton destroying three flying bombs. He reported:

"Took off from Newchurch at 2205 – saw a Diver 15 miles south of Hastings at 2,500 feet. Fired two one-second bursts from dead astern and the Diver crashed and exploded two miles north of Hastings at 2215. Saw second ten miles south of Hastings at 2,500 feet. Closed to 300 yards with a one-second burst. The jet was hit and the Diver exploded on the sea three miles south of Hastings at 2245. Saw a third ten miles south of Hastings at 2,000 feet and closed to 150 yards. Fired a long burst from dead astern. The petrol exploded in the air and the warhead in the sea three miles south of Bexhill/Hastings at 2300."

The night was young and three more flying bombs fell to the Tempests before midnight, one to Flt Lt Moore at 2300, his second of the evening:

"Saw a Diver south of Rye at 3,000 feet. Closed to 250 yards and fired a very long burst from dead astern. The Diver slowed down and went into a steep glide, but I had to break as I was short of petrol and I did not see it hit the ground. It was left 10-15 miles north of Rye."

Wg Cdr Beamont was also airborne and added to his mounting score:

"I took off at 2215 and saw a Diver over Bexhill at 3,500 feet. Closed to 300 yards astern, fired and the Diver went down, exploding near Edenbridge at 2305."

It was left to Flt Sgt Everson to close the show. He sighted his victim 15 miles south of Hastings, closed to 100 yards and fired a one-second burst:

"There was a big flash from the jet and the Diver turned to port and exploded on the sea."

41 Squadron (Spitfire XII) Friston

Flg Off M.A.L. Balaase (Belg)	EN609/EB-	V-1	1645-1810	off Isle of Wight
Flt Sgt F.G. Woollard	MB875/EB-G			

56 Squadron (Tempest V) Newchurch

Flt Sgt H. Shaw	JN875/US-P	V-1	1045	Newchurch area
Flg Off W.R. MacLaren	JN864/US-C	V-1	1718	Redhill area
Sqn Ldr A.R. Hall	JN869/US-D	V-1	1755	off Eastbourne

Sqn Ldr N.E. Hancock	EJ536/US-V	V-1	2010	Tonbridge area
Plt Off J. Harvey	EJ547/US-A	V-1	2125	Sevenoaks area
Flt Sgt D.E. Matthews	JN864/US-C	V-1 shared	2250	off Hastings

Flt Sgt Artie Shaw's victim crashed 10-15 miles west of Newchurch: "Sighted a Diver crossing the coast between Dungeness and Rye at 1,000 feet. Closed, overshot and pulled out to starboard, I then gave a deflection burst and Diver exploded in the air." Flg Off Bill MacLaren, having used all his ammunition, formated with his target and tipped it over with his wing: "After waiting until I had passed several villages, I lifted my port wing and the Diver turned over and went down exploding two miles south-east of Redhill." Sqn Ldr Archie Hall's target crashed into the sea some seven miles east of Eastbourne: "I dived from 5,000 feet and gave a short burst from 300 yards astern and the Diver peeled over and went down."

During the day the Squadron had received a visit from former member and newly decorated and promoted Sqn Ldr Norman Hancock DFC from HQ 85 Group, who managed to wangle a flight in one of the Tempests and succeeded in shooting down another flying bomb that exploded in a field near Tonbridge: "Sighted a Diver two miles west of Hastings at 4,000 feet, speed 385mph. I fired from 600 yards closing to 300 yards astern with a long burst and Diver turned on its back, exploding in a field." Plt Off Harvey's kill fell near Sevenoaks: "I attacked from 100 yards astern and the Diver went in, exploding on the ground." Darkness had descended by the time Flt Sgt Matthews was on patrol, but he succeeded in intercepting a flying bomb south of Hastings, which he and a Spitfire pilot despatched into the sea:

> "Saw a Diver five miles south of Hastings at 3,000 feet. I attacked from the port quarter getting into line astern at 150 yards. The jet caught fire and the Diver lost height to 1,000 feet, when a Spitfire fired a burst from 1,000 yards and the Diver went in the sea one mile south of Hastings."

91 Squadron (Spitfire XIV) Deanland ALG

Flt Lt A.R. Elcock	RB182/DL-V	V-1	1311	Tenterden area
Flt Lt R.S. Nash	RB169/DL-Q	V-1	1615	Uckfield area
Flg Off G.H. Huntley	RB181/DL-W	V-1	1715	Hailsham area
Flt Sgt J.A. Brown	NH697/DL-X	V-1	1835	Epsom area
Flg Off E. Topham	RB181/DL-W	V-1	2155	Sevenoaks area
Flt Lt R.S. Nash	RB169/DL-Q	V-1	2200	Hastings area
Flg Off M.J. Costello RNZAF	NH705/DL-P	V-1 shared	2210	Hastings area

Flg Off Morrie Costello[91] shared his with fellow New Zealander Flg Off Bill Williams of 486 (RNZAF) Squadron.

165 Squadron (Spitfire IX) Detling

Flg Off D.W.J. Southerst RCAF	MK854/SK-H	V-1 shared	2158	Hastings area

> "Saw red flares from Hastings and Bexhill. Gave chase, no vectors. Two aircraft already in pursuit did not seem to be firing. I attacked and Diver went almost vertically down, exploding on the ground between a small lake and the east to west railway ten miles from Hastings."

Much to his chagrin, the Canadian was advised that he would have to share his kill with another.

277 (ASR) Squadron (Spitfire V) Shoreham

Wt Off J.A. Forrest	AD185/BA-	V-1	1725-1805	Channel

316 (Polish) Squadron (Mustang III) West Malling

Wt Off A. Murkowski PAF	FB374/SZ-A	V-1	1115	Lydd-Rye
Flt Sgt A. Pietrzak PAF	FB161/SZ-I	V-1	1145	off Boulogne

Flg Off K. Cynkier PAF	FB384/SZ-Z	V-1	2315	off Bexhill

The Poles of 316 Squadron were soon learning the art of tackling the flying bombs, and also what to avoid, as Sqn Ldr Arct PAF explained:

> "In theory, the engaging of flying bombs by fighters was a simple matter. In practice it was much more complicated. As a rule, one attacked the missile the same way as a normal aircraft: from behind, with a small deflection. Firing straight from the rear was not effective as bullets might slide along the flexible sheet metal of the projectile's fuselage. One had to aim at the framework to hit either the gyroscopes, or the engine and fuel tanks. Owing to the great speed of the missiles, attacks had to be made with height advantage to increase one's speed in diving. Firing from the right distance was of paramount importance. This rule, instructing to open fire at a minimum distance, could in no circumstances be applied against the mischievous 'Witches.' When the pursuing fighter carelessly closed in and pressed the trigger at, say, a hundred yards, and if he accidentally hit the fuses or the front of the fuselage where the high explosives were loaded, the bomb exploded in the air and its splinters and other bits flew towards the pursuer, often causing serious damage."

322 (Dutch) Squadron (Spitfire XIV) West Malling

Flg Off J. Jonker	VL-D	V-1	1857	Grid Q.9328
Flg Off R.F. Burgwal	NH649/VL-F	V-1	2030	Grid Q.9959
Flg Off F.W.L.S. Speetjens	RB160/VL-A	V-1	2248	Redhill area

Flg Off Jan Jonker reported attacking his target from 200 yards: "Saw hits on power unit, which ceased to function but picked up again. Made further attack and Diver crashed and exploded on the ground." Flg Off Rudi Burgwal saw two Tempests attack a Diver as he approached, but saw no strikes from their efforts: "I attacked from astern, range 100 yards. Diver exploded and fell to the ground where it exploded again." Although Flg Off Frank Speetjens reported shooting down his victim, he was not granted a kill: "Saw Diver six miles north-west of Hastings, height 3,000 feet. Attacked line astern, range 200 yards with three short bursts. Diver crashed and exploded seven miles east of Redhill, just north of Redhill-Tonbridge railway line." However, following investigation, a pencilled note by the IO stated: "No record of this." Presumably, Speetjens had mistaken the location of the crash.

486 (RNZAF) Squadron (Tempest V) Newchurch

Flg Off H.M. Mason RNZAF	JN805/SA-E	V-1	1100	Rye area
Flg Off J.R. Cullen RNZAF	JN770/SA-V	V-1	1142	Hastings area
Wt Off O.D. Eagleson RNZAF	EJ537/SA-S	V-1	1226	Dungeness area
Wt Off W.A. Kalka RNZAF	JN809/SA-M	V-1	1523	Beachy Head area
	JN809/SA-M	V-1	1537	Leatherhead
Plt Off F.B. Lawless RNZAF	EJ537/SA-S	V-1	1615	Eastbourne area
Flt Lt H.N. Sweetman RNZAF	JN809/SA-M	V-1	1905	Eastbourne area
Plt Off R.D. Bremner RNZAF	JN854/SA-G	V-1	1935	Hailsham area
Flt Lt N.J. Powell RNZAF	EJ527/SA-Q	V-1	2010	Crowborough area
Plt Off J.H. Stafford RNZAF	JN854/SA-G	V-1	2055	Hailsham area
	JN854/SA-Q	V-1	2135	Tonbridge area
Flg Off S.S. Williams RNZAF	JN820/SA-P	V-1 shared	2210	Ninfield area
Flg Off H.M. Mason RNZAF	JN809/SA-M	V-1 shared	2300	Hastings area
Plt Off R.J. Danzey RNZAF	JN805/SA-E	V-1	2303	Eastbourne area

The New Zealanders accounted for 14 Divers including two shared. Flg Off Bill Williams shared his victim with Flg Off Morrie Costello RNZAF of 91 Squadron. Possibly one of the New Zealanders' victims was the Diver that fell in Astaire Avenue, Eastbourne, where six houses were demolished and others damaged. Fortunately, there were no reported casualties. Another fell on Eastbourne after darkness, impacting in Tutts Barn Lane, doing little damage. Plt Off Duff Bremner's victim fell at Maynards Green, Horam, where it demolished two houses. Local PC Max Soffner was on duty:

> "Thought this one had my name on it. Occupants [of 'Windryidge'] trapped. One killed, four seriously injured, six slightly injured. Shot down by RAF fighter. Bad luck, boy! Still, it could have been worse."

610 Squadron (Spitfire XIV) Friston

Flt Sgt G. Tate	DW-	V-1	1935-2040
Plt Off B.R. Scamen RCAF	DW-	V-1	2130-2235

Both pilots, having exhausted their ammunition, successfully tipped their victims off course with their wingtips, and both were seen to explode on the ground.

FIU Detachment (Tempest V) Newchurch

Sqn Ldr E.G. Daniel	EJ531	V-1

Sqn Ldr Daniel and Flt Lt Jones each flew three patrols. The weather then deteriorated and Tempests diverted to Ford.

A Typhoon from **181 Squadron** based at Coulomb in France dropped in at RAF Oatlands Hill in Wiltshire during the evening, Flg Off Jim 'Slim' Kenny RCAF having been requested to collect some beer for his thirsty comrades, which also meant that he could spend a night in London:

> "Where to store the beer was a problem, though, since the Typhoon was built to fight, not to carry bottles of beer. Finally, a solution was found. Take out two cannons to make room for beer and leave two cannons to defend the valuable freight. After landing at Oatlands Hill, I stored as much beer as I could in my aircraft's wings, behind the cockpit and anywhere else I could find. In all, I managed to hide away eight-dozen pints. Next stop was Redhill but while approaching the airfield in the dusk, I noticed a small aircraft to starboard. It was a buzz bomb, a V-1, and the first I had ever seen. A series of conflicting emotions tore through me. What should I do, attack the V-1 or ignore it and so preserve my precious cargo? I must shoot it down. No, it will break all the bottles. Duty says I must. The Squadron will hate me. Suddenly, the V-1's engine cut out, solving my dilemma. The pilotless bomb fell to earth, letting me and my beer off the hook. After a night in London, I returned to a hero's welcome."[92]

Night 4/5 JULY

A total of 22 Heinkels of III/KG3 departed Gilze-Rijen commencing 2213. All returned safely, the last landing at 0421. A Diver came down in Drakefell Road, Telegraph Hill in Deptford (SE14) at 2347, killing four. Two people were killed in Streatham (SW16) when a bomb fell at 0034 in Leigh Vale South, damaging at least 30 properties. Eight minutes later another exploded in Brixton (SW2), killing six in the Water Lane/Matthews Road area, where much damage was caused to properties. Another flying bomb came down on West Norwood (SE27), impacting close to the local cemetery at 0119. Three shops/houses were demolished in the Norwood Road and 30 others suffered severe damage. The junction of Park Hall Road and Alleyn Road, West Dulwich (SE21), was struck at 0426. Eight houses and the Alleyns Head pub were destroyed, killing three residents.

85 Squadron (Mosquito XVII) Swannington

Flt Lt P.A. Searle	VY-Q	V-1	2220-0135
Flt Lt R.H. Farrell	HK119/VY-S	V-1	0225-0500

96 Squadron (Mosquito XIII) Ford

Flt Lt I.A. Dobie	MM495/ZJ-	V-1	2245-0015	exploded in mid-air
Sub Lt(A) W. Lawley-Wakelin RNVR	HK370/ZJ-L	V-1	0200-0440	Channel

Flt Lt Ian Dobie's victim exploded in the air, and slightly damaged the tail unit of MM495. On this occasion his navigator was Sqn Ldr Jimmy Rawnsley DSO DFC DFM on a visit from 100 Group HQ, who later wrote:

"Dobie was an experienced hand at the game, and he was calm and methodical about the way he went about things. We set off on patrol, but nothing happened for a long time. I pictured to myself the line of fighters strung out all along the south and south-east coasts, beating up and down like yachts waiting for the starting gun. And then the little twinkling flames began to spring up over the French coast. We made a last check around the cockpit, and settled down in our seats. One of the flying bombs was obviously heading our way, and Dobie began to get into position, carefully weighing up the relative courses. He was nicely placed as we ran in for the final turn, but of course I could not keep my mouth shut. 'Don't you think we ought to cut the corner a bit sharper?' I pleaded, afraid of being pushed out of things again by somebody else. 'I don't think so', Dobie said. He knew what he was doing. 'But I will if you like'. He tightened up his turn, and as a result we found ourselves a few seconds later almost vertically above the bomb, swinging from side to side in order to keep it in sight and waiting for it to draw ahead. Our height was 2,500 feet, which gave us an advantage of about a thousand feet over our target. I flattened my face against the side window trying to see the thing. 'Sorry about the turn,' I said. 'He's beginning to draw ahead now!'

"Dobie pushed the nose down and opened up the throttles. I stood up and I could see the bomb as it came into view under our nose, its sleek, shark-like sides gleaming in the light of the wavering plume of flame that trailed behind it. Although the frightful racket of its exhaust was barely audible above the howling of our over-speeding engines, there was something awesome and full of fiendish purpose in the unswerving flight of the bomb, something outrageous in its brazen indifference to close scrutiny. I felt a strong temptation to warn Dobie not to get too close because it might see us. We were rocketing down through the wake of hot exhaust gases, and I had a quick glimpse right into the fiery maw of the beastly thing before I remembered that I had a job to do. I quickly turned my attention to the AI set. 'One thousand feet … nine hundred …' I told Dobie. 'Right,' he said. 'Here goes.' I looked up as the guns crashed briefly; and I immediately ducked down again. The bomb had burst just three hundred yards ahead of us and we were rushing at over one hundred and fifty yards a second straight at the heart of the explosion. For a few seconds the jet of air from the ventilator close to my head blew hot and acrid; but we were still flying. Sitting up and looking back, I saw that the air behind us was full of glowing red fragments still fanning out and floating downwards. Dobie was coolly checking his instruments and pulling up so as to gain precious height. I did a little instrument checking for myself: oil temperatures and pressures normal; fuel all right, even the AI working. But when I looked outside I could see something white sticking up from the elevator balance. 'Don't look now,' I said, 'but we seem to have a foreign body embedded in the tail. I can't see what it is.' 'Have we, though?' Dobie replied. He seemed to be quite unperturbed. 'It feels all right on the controls, but I suppose we'd better go back and have a look at it.' When we landed we found that it was only a piece of fabric that had been torn loose. I realised that Dobie had taken it all in his stride, just as all these crews had been doing for weeks past."[93]

409 (RCAF) Squadron (Mosquito XIII) Hunsdon

Flg Off A.W. Sterrenberg RCAF	MM512/KP-	V-1	0220	Channel

"We were airborne at 0030 to carry out a Diver patrol under Fairchild Control. At approximately 0220 obtained a visual on a pilotless aircraft travelling at 3,000 feet, at speed of 360mph. We dived from 6,000 feet, but were unable to gain. I fired from dead astern at extreme range, the Diver being seen to crash into the sea and explode."

418 (RCAF) Squadron (Mosquito VI) Holmsley South

Flt Lt D.E. Forsyth RCAF	TH-	V-1	0207	over sea

"At 0207 attacked a Diver at 2,000 feet with two two-second bursts from 150 yards. Strikes seen on starboard wing and Diver went down steeply, exploding in an amber flash on hitting the sea."

The squadron was advised – erroneously, as it turned out – that Divers brought down over the sea would count as an enemy aircraft destroyed, and that any brought down over land as half an enemy aircraft destroyed, which brought forth the comment from the squadron diarist:

"This is encouraging for the squadron as these patrols, though recognised as vitally important, had carried previously little incentive."

605 Squadron (Mosquito VI) Manston

Flg Off R.E. Lelong RNZAF	HJ785/UP-T	V-1	0106	Dungeness area
Flg Off A.J. Craven	UP-	V-1	0200	off Hastings
	UP-	V-1 probable	0225	Channel
Flt Lt R.J. Garner	MM414/UP-Y	V-1	0308	off Boulogne

The Squadron's first of the night fell to Flg Off Roy Lelong:

"Attacked Diver at 0106 in mid-Channel at 2,500 feet. Short burst fired from dead astern, strikes seen and flame spluttered but Diver continued on course. I fired a second burst, range about 100 yards and again saw strikes. This time Diver burst into flames, banked over and spiralled down to earth. Crashed in violent explosion ten miles north-west of Dungeness. Another Diver was seen coming from French coast. We positioned for an attack and, as we were above and in front of the Diver, throttled back, but target had vanished."

Flg Off Arnold Craven opened his account with two Divers between Le Touquet and Dungeness:

"Attacked Diver in mid-Channel at 2,500 feet. Two bursts were given from astern, 200 yards – target exploded on hitting the sea off Hastings. At 0225 attacked another target between Le Touquet and Dungeness at 3,000 feet – many strikes seen. All cannon used so gave many bursts with machine-guns. Diver turned and flew steadily on, losing height gradually. This Diver was probably destroyed by crashing into Channel."

The Mosquito piloted by Flt Lt Garner was airborne shortly thereafter:

"At 0252, north of Le Crotoy, Diver sighted at 3,000 feet, travelling at 380mph. Diver was attacked from astern. No results seen. At 0308 another Diver was sighted at 3,000 feet near Boulogne. We fired a one-second burst from 200 yards astern and port wing fell off and target dived into the sea. At 0318 a third Diver was seen coming in from Le Touquet at 3,000 feet. We attacked from astern at 400 yards but no results seen."

That night Mosquitos from **456 (RAAF) Squadron** were again in the right place at the right time, catching Fritz-X-carrying He177s from I/KG40 over the sea north of Cherbourg and shooting down three. One (550210) was from 4 Staffel commanded by Oblt Waldemar Hunold, who was killed with four of his crew; one survivor was taken prisoner. 5 Staffel also lost one (550213), Oblt Jürgen Hauke's aircraft from which there were no survivors, while 6 Staffel lost two aircraft: Heinkel 550203 flown by Fw Johann Dötsch, and 550195 commanded by Oblt Franz Schulte-Vogelheim. There was one survivor only from the two aircraft. One of the Heinkels was shot down over Cognac airfield. Flt Lt Bob Cowper RAAF, with Flg Off Bill Watson RAF in HK356/RX-D, shot down one:

"We were patrolling under Durrington Control. At about 2315 we made contact with an aircraft travelling north and on informing control were advised to investigate with caution. It proved to be a Black Widow [US P-61] complete with TAF and American markings. We continued patrol. At 0030 we were handed over to Blackgang and informed of trade dropping *Window* 40 miles to the west of us, travelling east. We vectored west and were informed that two aircraft were approaching, one at 10,000 feet and the other at 8,000 feet. We flew at 9,000 feet and established contact on one at nine miles, head-on, beneath us, shovelling out *Window* at a great rate. We flew towards it, and eventually turned starboard behind it, and established firm contact ahead and beneath. The target was weaving gently. We closed in, losing height, and obtained a visual beneath and at 2,000 feet range, on a He177. We easily recognised it and with the aid of night glasses established the fact that it was carrying two FX [Fritz-X] bombs outboard of the engine nacelles. We dived well beneath it (because of light conditions and the cloud formation) and followed e/a visually through a hard starboard turn on to a north-westerly course, and then port, during which turn I fired a one-second burst from 500 feet range. The port wing and engine exploded in red flame and burned fiercely at once. I gave it another one-second burst in the fuselage, which again exploded violently, and e/a spun down, blazing furiously, and exploded on striking the water. The wreckage was still burning some minutes later. No return fire was observed. E/a dropped *Window* continuously throughout the engagement. Flg Off Radford of 456 Squadron, on patrol at the time, observed the fire at 0055."

Flg Off Ted Radford RAAF (with Flt Sgt Wally Atkinson RAAF in HK312/RX-G) also accounted for a He177 shortly after Cowper's success:

"We were vectored southerly and south-westerly and at maximum speed climbed to Angels 8. At 0055 while on a southerly vector south of base we saw a burning object falling, which hit the sea to the west of us; this coincides with Flt Lt Cowper's He177. After several vectors a contact was obtained, at about seven miles range, starboard and slightly above. The target was crossing starboard-port at 190-200 IAS. It was taking mild evasive action and using *Window* continuously. We followed it and got a visual at about 2,000 feet range. It was recognised as a He177. Bombs, although not identified as of glider type, were seen outboard of the engine nacelles under each wing. Target turned hard port. I opened fire at 9,000 feet and saw strikes on the fuselage. E/a returned fire fairly accurately from the tail position with red tracer and continued to do so throughout the engagement until just before our last burst. We were not hit. E/a dived through cloud and the visual was lost. Contact was however regained and we closed in again to 900 feet and from dead astern I fired two short bursts, seeing strikes. The height was now down to 1,500 feet. I fired a third time from dead astern and an explosion was seen on the port engine. One of the crew was seen to bale out just before the e/a dived to port into the sea and blew up, burning furiously."

The crew of Plt Off Ivor Sanderson and Charlie Nicholas in HK249/RX-B got the third.[94]

KG100's missile-carrying Do217Ks fared no better, three being reported lost to night fighters – 6N+DT (4718) flown by Ltn Erich Keller of Stab III, shot down at 2238 over Orne; 8 Staffel's Ltn Siegfried Kynast (in 6847), which fell at a minute past midnight off Le Havre; and Fw Simon Obermeier and his crew from 7 Staffel, shot down at 0020 near Isigny. There was one survivor from each crew, including Keller, all of whom were taken prisoner. A fourth Dornier (4710), commanded by Ltn Ludwig Schäfer of 9 Staffel, failed to return from a sortie over the Gironde Estuary. Plt Off Stan Williams/Flg Off Ken Havord of 456(RAAF) Squadron, off from Ford at 2315 in HK282RX-L, reported:

"We were told of bogeys 15 miles north, on a south-easterly course. We obtained a contact at seven miles and commenced a gentle dive at about 300 IAS, maintaining this throughout the interception, the bogey continuing to lose height. At a range of 4,000 feet the target did a slow orbit to starboard and a visual to the north was easily obtained at 2,500-3,000 feet in a clear sky. We closed in to about 1,000 feet in frequent patches of cloud, having throttled back considerably, target speed being about 240-250mph. Target was followed for several minutes at 900 feet range and identified between patches of cloud as a Do217. Navigator, in a dead astern view, saw what he took to be a glider-bomb directly under the fuselage. A four-seconds burst from 600 feet caused strikes, which were seen immediately on the wing just outside the port engine. E/a started to burn straight away, and I directed my fire towards the fuselage, strikes being seen all along the wing as I did so. In about a second the whole aircraft was a ball of fire; it turned slightly starboard and dived straight into the sea, leaving a long trail of small green explosions. Time 0011. No return fire was seen and Mosquito did not seem to be damaged in any way, but about four minutes later the starboard engine started to run very roughly, lost power and caught fire immediately. I quickly feathered the propeller and used the fire extinguisher, successfully, and set course for base and landed without any trouble or further damage. On landing, it was found that a 20mm shell fragment had entered the radiator and also damaged the cabin heating equipment. It was identified as the same type as carried in the Mosquito, so it is assumed that it had come back from the e/a in debris."

Almost simultaneous with the demise of Williams' victim, Sqn Ldr Bill Gill[95] of **125 Squadron** in HK325 shot down another Dornier, some 20 miles south-west of Le Havre:

"My navigator [Flg Off D.C. Hutchins] obtained a contact to starboard, range four and-a-half miles, slightly below our height of 6,000 feet. We closed to 5,000 feet and obtained a visual on a target, which was turning gently to port. From 150 yards my navigator, with the aid of night glasses, identified target as a Do217, with what appeared to be bombs outboard of the engines. The target was then flying straight and level in a northerly direction at 6,000 feet. I fired two short bursts from 150 yards, dead astern, both of which produced strikes on fuselage. E/a burst into flames and, as I broke away, I saw an explosion. E/a then spiralled down with fuselage well on fire. We followed down and I gave a further short burst from 500 yards, but saw no strikes. E/a disappeared into cloud at 3,000 feet in a very steep spiral dive and shortly afterwards there was a glow on the cloud as e/a hit the sea."

It seems likely that one of the Dorniers was the victim of a 21 Squadron Mosquito VI, one of a dozen intruding in the Le Mans-Alençon area, where railway trains and other forms of transport were being targeted. One crew, Flt Off Richard Seage USAAF[96] and Flt Sgt A. Halliday in NS884, reported meeting a Do217 at 0120 flying at 1,000 feet:

"Enemy aircraft, with downward green recognition lights on, sighted [in Grid Q.7388 area]. Closed in to port of e/a and identified as Do217 from 50 yards – then broke away, making attack with cannons (five seconds) from 300-200 yards – strikes seen on port engine. Made second attack from 100 yards with machine-guns. Results unobserved. Claimed damaged."

Wednesday 5 JULY

A Diver landed in the grounds of a chemical factory in Gordon Road, Ilford, seriously injuring a young lady. Heston airfield in the Thames Valley received its second unwelcome visitor, on this occasion resulting in several deaths. Ten more were killed when a Diver came down in Ivy Road, Cricklewoood NW2 at 1313, the explosion seriously injuring a further 25. Another exploded in Streatham High Street (SW16) at 1451, causing much damage and killing one. Trinity Wharf, Rotherhithe (SE16) was struck at 2004, causing severe damage to the motor tug Jean; five barges were also damaged, one worker killed and three injured. Bizarrely, a second Diver crashed in Norbury Crescent (SW16) at 2124, this time hitting No.129 and killing an occupier (the previous day six people had been killed at No.165). Another came down in Croydon (Thornton Heath CR7), killing eight in Curzon Road. Elsewhere, at 1815, a Diver fell in the lines of the Lincoln & Welland Regt of the Canadian Army, located on the southern outskirts of Crowborough in Sussex: "A flying bomb, flying north-west, crashed into a strip of woods immediately adjacent to 2 Coy HQ, resulting in the deaths of seven men and serious injury to 17." Two of the injured later died in hospital.

Detling Wing (Spitfire LFIXb) Detling

Wg Cdr R.P.R. Powell	MK846/JX-	V-1 shared	1225	Laughton area
	MK846/JX-	V-1	2040	off Eastbourne

1 Squadron (Spitfire LFIXb) Detling

Flg Off P.E. Crocker	NH255/JX-	V-1 shared	1225	Laughton area
Flt Lt P.W. Stewart	NH253/JX-	V-1 shared	1248	Laughton area
Flt Sgt I. Hastings	MK997/JX-F	V-1	1255	Gatwick area

Wg Cdr Peter Powell DFC, Wing Commander Flying at Detling, borrowed a 1 Squadron Spitfire and proceeded to help destroy a Diver with Flg Off Crocker:

"Intercepted Diver north of Beachy Head. Strikes seen by No2 during the first two attacks, and on third the jet went out. The Diver went into a glide, turned over and crashed into a field one-and-three-quarter miles north of Laughton, where it exploded."

A few minutes later Flt Lt Stewart got a second in the same area:

"Vectored onto Diver six miles south-east of Beachy Head. Strikes on both wings and smoke from both wings. Diver kept on course. Immediately another Spitfire [apparently Flt Sgt Janssen of 322 Squadron] attacked from astern. Diver dived steeply and exploded on the ground just east of Laughton."

Flt Sgt Iain Hastings chased his target to the fringes of the balloon barrage before he sent it down to crash near Gatwick, but was unable to avoid hitting a balloon cable:

"I broke away to avoid barrage but hit cable, which spun aircraft round. I managed to restore aircraft to an even keel but saw that the outer section starboard wingtip was cut off. I headed for Gatwick, landing safely. Found two opposite blades of propeller damaged."

Obviously keyed up by his earlier kill, Wg Cdr Powell took off for another anti-Diver patrol shortly after 2000, in company with Flg Off Jack Batchelor, and scored again:

"Diver was intercepted 20 miles south of Eastbourne. Strikes were seen all along the fuselage and port wing and wing root. Diver turned over and dived into sea ten miles south of Eastbourne."

3 Squadron (Tempest V) Newchurch

Flt Sgt H.J. Bailey RAAF	EJ582/JF-T	V-1	1715	Beachy Head area
Flg Off M.F. Edwards	EJ525/JF-	V-1	1720	Edenbridge area
Flg Off R. Dryland	JN818/JF-	V-1	1755	Rye area
	JN818/JF-	V-1	1815	Grid 4553
	JN818/JF-	V-1	1835	Falmer area
Flg Off M.F. Edwards	EJ525/JF-	V-1	1845	Tenterden area
	EJ525/JF-	V-1	1930	Tenterden area
Flt Sgt H.J. Bailey RAAF	JN807/JF-Y	V-1	1925	Pevensey area
Plt Off H.R. Wingate	JN793/JF-N	V-1	2145	Edenbridge area
Flt Lt A.E. Umbers RNZAF	JN817/JF-H	V-1 damaged	c2200	Redhill area
Flg Off R. Dryland	JN818/JF-	V-1	2215	off Beachy Head
	JN818/JF-	V-1	2235	off Eastbourne

3 Squadron had another bumper day with 11 Divers destroyed. Flg Off Malcolm Edwards and Flt Sgt Bert Bailey opened the scoring after they had taken off from Newchurch at 1632. Edwards saw a Diver 40 miles south of Dungeness at 3,000 feet:

"I closed to 700 yards dead astern, attacked and obtained strikes. Closed to 300 yards and saw hits on the port wing and the Diver staggered, went down, exploding in the Edenbridge area."

Meanwhile, Flt Sgt Bailey saw a Diver 15 miles south of Beachy Head at 2,500 feet. He closed in to 50 yards range with a half-second burst, following which the 'jet' went out and the Diver went down and exploded on the sea. While these two were still airborne, Flg Off Rod Dryland took off, and soon sighted a flying bomb at 3,000 feet:

"I fired from 150 yards and blew the port wing off and the Diver exploded on the ground one mile north of Rye. Saw second eight miles north of Dungeness at 3,500 feet. Closed to 100 yards and gave a short burst from astern, seeing strikes on the jet and wing. The jet went out and the Diver exploded on the ground. Saw a third five miles south of Beachy Head at 2,000 feet and attacked with a short burst from 150 yards. Strikes were seen and the Diver went down, exploding on the ground east of Falmer."

Flg Off Edwards and Flt Sgt Bailey were off again at 1825, and were soon in action, Edwards sighting a flying bomb about 20 minutes later:

"I saw a Diver 15 miles south of Dungeness at 3,200 feet. Fired from 500 yards closing to 300 yards and Diver rolled over twice and exploded on the ground near Tenterden at 1845. Saw a second Diver over Hastings at 3,000 feet. Several other aircraft were chasing but I overtook them and fired from 200-300 yards and the Diver blew up in the air over Tenterden at 1930."

Five minutes before Edwards' second kill, Flt Sgt Bailey got one:

"I saw a Diver ten miles south of Pevensey at 3,000 feet. Fired two-seconds burst from 150 yards and the Diver rolled over and exploded in the sea about three miles off Pevensey at 1925."

Flt Lt Spike Umbers was unable to confirm his victory:

"Saw a Diver three miles north of Beachy Head at 3,000 feet. Fired a short deflection burst, no strikes, so fired again from 400 yards astern. Again no strikes, so followed through cloud and just before Redhill attacked again from 300 yards. Strikes were seen on fuselage and confirmed by No2. The Diver slowed appreciably and was left in cloud over Redhill."

Plt Off Dickie Wingate took off from Newchurch at 2130 under Beachy Head Control:

"A Diver was seen five miles off Eastbourne. I attacked from 200 yards with a two-seconds burst from astern. Strikes were seen all over the Diver and flames came from the jet. Gave another two-seconds burst and the Diver slowed down and I overshot. The Diver went down, exploding ten miles north-west of Eastbourne at 2145."

Flg Off Rod Dryland, who accompanied Wingate, destroyed two more flying bombs to raise his score to five for the day. He reported:

"Saw a Diver ten miles off the French coast, closed to 150 yards dead astern and gave four short bursts. The jet went out and the Diver went straight down and exploded on the sea six miles south of Beachy Head at 2215. Saw a second Diver ten miles off the French coast at 3,000 feet. Closed from 300 to 100 yards with three medium bursts. The jet was extinguished and the Diver climbed steeply about 2,500 feet and then glided down into the sea four miles south of Eastbourne, exploding at 2235."

41 Squadron (Spitfire XII) Friston

Flg Off R.P. Harding	EN602/EB-	V-1	1440	Rye area

56 Squadron (Tempest V) Newchurch

Flt Lt T.H. Hoare RCAF	EJ547/US-A	V-1	1420	Tonbridge area

"Sighted Diver four miles off Bexhill at 3,500 feet and 390mph. I fired a deflection burst from 500 yards, but saw no strikes. I got into line astern but could not close to less than 1,000 yards. I gave a short burst and Diver slowed down. I gave a long burst from 500 yards and Diver went down."

91 Squadron (Spitfire XIV) Deanland ALG

Flt Lt R.S. Nash	RB169/DL-Q	V-1	1243	Beachy Head area
Cne J-M. Maridor (FF)	NH698/DL-Y	V-1 shared	1450	Cranbrook area
Flt Lt A.R. Cruickshank RCAF	RM615/DL-	V-1	1850	off Dungeness
Flg Off H.M. Neil	RB177/DL-J	V-1	2045	Newchurch area
Cne J-M. Maridor (FF)	RM654/DL-F	V-1	2115	Canterbury area
Wt Off F.A. Lewis	RM620/DL-E	V-1	2250	off French coast

Flt Lt Ray Nash increased his tally shortly after midday:

> "Saw Diver over Eastbourne and attacked from astern at 200 yards range. Strikes seen and Diver fell ten miles north of Beachy Head, exploding in a field."

Cne Jean-Marie Maridor's first was brought down four miles south of Cranbrook, but he had to share it with a Mustang from 316 Squadron flown by Flt Sgt Sztuka:

> "Saw Diver north of Rye being attacked by a Mustang. My attack was made from astern at 100 yards. Saw strikes but one cannon jammed so closed in to 50 yards and gave second burst. Diver went into slow turning dive, so I flew in front of it and with slipstream caused it to spin in four miles south of Cranbrook, exploding in a field."

There followed a four-hour lull before the next wave was intercepted, Flt Lt Ray Cruickshank scoring at 1850:

> "Sighted Diver ten miles south-east of Dungeness. Attacked from astern at 150-70 yards range with several short bursts. Strikes seen every time and Diver climbed steeply and fell into the sea where it exploded."

Flg Off Neil was next to score:

"Saw Diver south of Newchurch and attacked from astern at 75 yards range with short burst. Exploded in the air three miles south-west of Newchurch."

Cne Maridor's second of the day came down five miles south-west of Canterbury:

> "Diver attacked by a Tempest but it overshot. I attacked from astern at 100 yards range. Strikes caused Diver to skid violently and lose speed. A further burst from 50 yards was given and Diver fell five miles south-west of Canterbury, exploding in a field."

Wt Off Lewis rounded off a successful day:

> "Sighted Diver two miles off French coast between Le Touquet and Boulogne. Attack was made from astern and strikes set jet mechanism on fire. Diver fell and exploded in the sea."

165 Squadron (Spitfire IX) Detling

Flg Off T.D. Tinsey	ML175/SK-P	V-1	1945	Wadhurst area

The Diver was sighted six miles south of Bexhill. Flg Off Tommy Tinsey gave chase, as did other aircraft in the vicinity. They attacked without result. Tinsey continued to attack until all ammunition exhausted and managed to slow the flying bomb down from 340mph to 240mph. "I then put my port wing under the Diver's starboard wing and tipped it up. Diver then went down on back, then straight in. Two inches of my port wingtip were bent down about half an inch."

277 (ASR) Squadron (Spitfire Vb) Shoreham

Wg Cdr A.D. Grace	BM122/BA-	V-1	1748	Ashford area
	BM122/BA-	V-1	2250	Dungeness

ASR Spitfire pilot 37-year-old Wg Cdr Alan Grace DFC, CO of 277 Squadron, shot down a brace of Divers during two evening sorties:

> "I found a pilotless aircraft over Folkestone travelling at 300-340mph at height of 2,000 feet. I made a stern attack from slightly below, using machine-guns and cannon. After first attack flame appeared from the pilotless aircraft and it slowed down considerably, and I had to pull away to avoid colliding with it. I then made two more attacks from 400 yards, closing to 200 yards, and then turned away after using all my ammunition. About 30 seconds later I observed the pilotless aircraft to crash and exploded on the ground near Charing. There was definitely no AA fire in the vicinity."

Wg Cdr Grace was off again at 2150, meeting another Diver:

"I found a pilotless aircraft one mile south of Boulogne at 2,000 feet, rising to 3,000 feet. I made a stern attack from slightly below, using machine-guns and cannon at 300-400 yards range. Pilotless aircraft then dived into the sea and exploded five to seven miles south-east of Dungeness."

316 (Polish) Squadron (Mustang III) West Malling

Flg Off T. Karnkowski PAF	FB352/SZ-C	V-1 shared	1328	Ham Street area
Flt Sgt S. Sztuka PAF	FB378/SZ-X	V-1 shared	1445	Rye area
Flt Lt S. Litak PAF	FB376/SZ-Q	V-1	1445	Salehurst area
Wt Off C. Bartłomiejczyk PAF	FB359/SZ-V	V-1	1645	Ashford area
	FB359/SZ-V	V-1	1650	Mereworth area
Flg Off T. Karnkowski PAF	FB384/SZ-Z	V-1	1803	Sutton Valence

Flg Off Tadeusz Karnkowski shared a Diver with Flt Lt van Eendenburg of 332 Squadron one mile west of Ham Street during an afternoon patrol: "Pilotless aircraft sighted below. Dived and range closed to 100 yards when attack opened. Crashed one mile west of Ham Street." Flt Sgt Sztuka's victim fell four miles north-west of Rye, shared with a Spitfire: "Pilotless aircraft seen over Rye Bay. Chased and opened fire at 330 yards from dead astern. Strikes seen and it crashed and exploded." His leader, Flt Lt Litak, also shot one down: "First seen near Hastings crossing the coast. Chased and opened fire at 400 yards closing to 100 yards from dead astern. Crashed three miles north of Salehurst." The star turn however was Wt Off Bartłomiejczyk, who scored a brace in double quick time:

"Diver seen at coast south of Folkestone. Chased and opened fire from 200 yards dead astern. Diver rolled and crashed three miles north-west of Ashford. Ordered to patrol over Ashford. Diver sighted and chased. Opened fire at 400 yards, closing to 250 yards. Last seen beginning to dive inside balloon belt three miles south-west of Mereworth."

Flg Off Karnkowski completed a successful day with his second kill: "Pilotless aircraft sighted by chance south of Pluckley. Chased and attacked from 500 yards dead astern. Strikes observed and pilotless aircraft seen to dive into woods north of Sutton Valence."

322 (Dutch) Squadron (Spitfire XIV) West Malling

Flt Sgt M.J. Janssen	VL-D	V-1 shared	1230	Fairfield area
	VL-D	V-1	1320	Grid R.4377
Flt Lt L.C.M. van Eendenburg	RB184/VL-B	V-1	1229	Grid Q.78
	RB184/VL-B	V-1 shared	1327	Appledore area

Flt Sgt Janssen reported: "Patrolling Dungeness when told Diver was approaching. Attacked line astern, range 200 yards. Shot pieces off tail and Diver went straight down and exploded on the ground in the Fairfield area." Although there is no mention of another Spitfire, apparently Flt Lt Stewart of 1 Squadron attacked the same aircraft. Janssen continued: "Returned to Dungeness and was told Diver coming in four miles west of Dungeness. Intercepted and attacked line astern, range 200 yards. Saw strikes and pieces fall off. Diver crashed and exploded." Once again Janssen was disappointed when his claim was refused, presumably because another pilot also made a claim for the Diver that fell in the specified area. As he was attacking the first flying bomb Flt Lt van Eendenburg noticed tracers coming from behind over his wings:

"Intercepted and attacked seven miles south-east of Maidstone. Line astern, 600 yards range closing to 300 yards. Saw strikes and pieces falling off. Ammo exhausted and noticing balloons below, broke off but saw Diver losing height rapidly and believed to have crashed."

Although claimed destroyed he was not officially awarded a kill. And while shooting at the second missile he saw a Mustang also firing at the same target. This was Flg Off Karnkowski of 316 Squadron who claimed a shared Diver at the same time. Van Eendenburg wrote:

> "Vectored on Diver in mid-Channel, throttled back, fired and missed whilst in steep turn. Got in line astern, range 250 yards, but had stoppage in cannon. Machine-gun fire was non-effective so formated on Diver and tried to tip, but not successful first time so repeated the performance, and whilst doing so noticed tracer coming from behind. I managed to tip Diver which rolled over in a cloud and then crashed and exploded north of Appledore."

A hard-earned kill and a lot of effort for a half share.

150 Wing (Tempest V) Newchurch

Wg Cdr R.P. Beamont	JN751/RB	V-1 shared	1415	Eastbourne area

486 (RNZAF) Squadron (Tempest V) Newchurch

Wt Off C.J. Sheddan RNZAF	JN854/SA-G	V-1 shared	1415	Eastbourne area
Wt Off B.J. O'Connor RNZAF	JN803/SA-D	V-1	1820	off Beachy Head

Wt Off Jim Sheddan unintentionally shared his victim with Wg Cdr Beamont, OC 150 Wing. During the latter's attack on the flying bomb, it transpired that a spent 20mm cartridge from his Tempest entered the radiator of Sheddan's aircraft, obliging him to force-land near Netherfield in Sussex:

> "I had just scored numerous hits on a Diver and was watching as it headed towards the ground, when in front of me there appeared another Tempest and the smoke drifting back from the wings indicated that the pilot was shooting at my wounded bird. As the bomb increased its angle of dive I ranged up alongside and watched as the marksman continued to fire, without any visible strikes. Even if I had not recognised the letters on the aircraft there was no mistaking the fellow in the cockpit – of all people the individual was our Wing Commander Beamont. I was later to discover that when he returned to base he claimed a half share! Concerned with following the bomb down and watching its final destruction there were developments nearer to home that I was unaware of. Bang!
>
> "The engine ground to a stop and with it the propeller. At the speed at which a propeller turns it is invisible to a pilot and it is something of a shock to see it hanging there useless on the front end! Flames were shooting out all over the aircraft and with the associated smoke it was almost like cloud flying. Much too low to attempt to use my parachute, my only hope of survival was to try and find a clear patch and attempt to do a wheels-up landing. The area of Sussex that I was flying over, just inland from Hastings, was heavily wooded and fields scarce and small. In the general panic the one I did pick was just not big enough and by the time I reached its far end, my Tempest was still airborne and travelling much too fast. There was no alternative but to pull up over a high hawthorn hedge and hope that on the other side a suitable area for a crash landing would be available. I went over or through that hedge and on the far side conditions could not have been worse. Directly in front of me was a large plantation of trees with no hope of going over or around them. My last memory was of trees crashing over as the Tempest started a forward somersault."

Sheddan was found barely conscious and rushed to hospital. Fortunately, he was not seriously hurt and was sufficiently recovered to return to flying the following month.

610 Squadron (Spitfire XIV) Friston

Sqn Ldr R.A. Newbery	RB159/DW-D	V-1	2130-2230
Wt Off R.C. White	DW-	V-1	1945-2035
Wt Off J.J. Bonfield	DW-	V-1	1945-2035

Flg Off George McKinlay reported gaining strikes on two flying bombs but made no claims.

FIU Detachment (Tempest V) Newchurch

Flt Lt J. Berry	EJ524/ZQ-Y	V-1	daytime

	EJ524/ZQ-Y	V-1	daytime
Sqn Ldr E.G. Daniel	EJ531/ZQ-	V-1 (killed)	daytime

Flt Lt Berry flew three daylight patrols and shot down two V-1s, but Sqn Ldr Teddy Daniel DFC was killed when his target exploded. His engine stopped due to the blast and the Tempest fell into the sea. Flt Lt Jeremy Howard-Williams noted:

> "In between selecting targets from the salvoes of missiles, Joe Berry listened to the drama on his radio. 'My engine has failed. I am ten miles south of Beachy Head.' Teddy's familiar voice sounded unruffled. The controller asked his height and, when Joe heard that he was at 3,000 feet he knew that he would never reach land. 'Bale out, Teddy,' he chipped in. 'Bale out. 'I'm going to do just that. I'll leave my transmitter on for a fix.' 'Cheerio. We'll have you picked up in a flash.' Joe waited all night by the telephone for word, which never came. At dawn he borrowed a Tiger Moth and scoured the sea for fifteen miles out, but his only reward was the sight of white foam whipped by the wind from the heaving swell. During the next week Teddy's place was taken by Flt Lt Wagner, one of our more experienced pilots."

367thFS/358thFG (P-47) High Halden

1/Lt M.C. Peterson USAAF	CP-	V-1	c2100	Rye area

During the evening the 358thFG provided escort for medium bombers. First to take off at 1859 was the 367thFS, which rendezvoused with their bombers at North Foreland and then escorted them to a target in the Lille section. Taking off about half an hour later were the 365thFS and 366thFS which provided escort for A-20 medium bombers to a target near Beauvais, which was bombed with good results. As the 367thFS made landfall at Rye, on their way back to base, Lt Milford C Peterson spotted a Diver, to which he gave chase at 325mph and successfully destroyed it.

On 5 July **74 Squadron** left Lympne.

Night 5/6 JULY

Divers impacted near Portsmouth and at Lee-on-Solent when, at 0240, came a report of another about 20 miles south-east of Sandown on the Isle of Wight. Within a few minutes it was over the town, and a second later came the flash and thunder of an explosion. It had fallen on the adjoining town of Lake. Much damage was done to property and one person was killed.

85 Squadron (Mosquito XVII/XIX) Swannington

Wt Off W. Alderton	HK299/VY-C	V-1	0025-0340
Flt Sgt L.J. York	MM648/VY-G	V-1	0225-0515

96 Squadron (Mosquito XIII) Ford

Flt Lt F.R.L. Mellersh	MM577/ZJ-N	V-1	2315	Grid W.56
	MM577/ZJ-N	V-1	2359	Grid W.56
Wg Cdr E.D. Crew	MM511/ZJ-	V-1	0210	Grid W.29-W.39
	MM511/ZJ-	V-1	0315	Grid W.29-W.39
	MM511/ZJ-	V-1	0325	Grid W.29-W.39
Sqn Ldr A. Parker-Rees	MM497/ZJ-	V-1	0354	Grid R.40
	MM497/ZJ-	V-1	0415	Grid R.50
Flt Lt D.L. Ward	HK415/ZJ-R	V-1	0425	Grid W.68

137 Squadron (Typhoon Ib) Manston

Flg Off J.C. Holder RCAF	MN584/SF-W	V-1	2155	off Dungeness
Flg Off H.T. Nicholls	MN134/SF-J	V-1	2240	off Boulogne
	MN134/SF-J	V-1	2250	off Boulogne

Two Typhoons of Yellow Section departed Manston at 2145. Flg Off Jim Holder was vectored on to a Diver 15 miles east of Dungeness: "At 2,000 feet at 290mph the target was attacked from dead astern at a range of 250 yards. It dived into sea and exploded." Three quarters of an hour later, Yellow 1 – Flg Off Henry Nicholls – sighted another Diver about eight miles off Boulogne:

"Target was at 2,000 feet. I dived on to it, attacking from above and astern firing a one-second burst from 100 yards. It dived into the sea and exploded. At 2250, I sighted another Diver off Boulogne. I chased and attacked from astern from 500 yards. Target dived into sea and a splash was seen."

While on an earlier patrol Canadian Flt Sgt Bill Flett (EK270) saw a flying bomb crossing the coast near Lympne and closed to 500 yards, but only one gun fired. As he broke away a Tempest nipped in and shot it down. The squadron diarist noted: "One extremely disgruntled pilot landed at 2120."

157 Squadron (Mosquito XIX) Swannington

Sqn Ldr J.G. Benson	MM630/RS-E	V-1	2359-0305
Sqn Ldr J.H.M. Chisholm	MM676/RS-W	V-1	0015
Lt(A) H. Sandiford RNVR	MM674/RS-T	V-1	0234
Sqn Ldr J.H.M. Chisholm	MM676/RS-W	V-1	0330

Sqn Ldr John Chisholm flew two patrols, shooting down a Diver during each. Of Sqn Ldr Benson's success, Flt Lt Brandon wrote:

"On this occasion, however, the brute just would not go down until Ben gave it a really long burst of cannon fire. We were back in 'Eager Beaver' and the vibration from the cannons put some of the instruments on Ben's blind-flying panel out of action. We landed at Ford for repairs at three in the morning and had to wait over two and a half hours before we took off again for Swannington, where we landed at 0615 hours."

409 (RCAF) Squadron (Mosquito XIII) Hunsdon

Flg Off H.S. Ellis RCAF[97]	MM491/KP-	V-1	0203	off Beachy Head
	MM491/KP-	V-1	0230	off Hastings

"At approximately 0200 a visual was obtained on a pilotless aircraft travelling at a height of 3,000 feet at approximately 290mph. We dived from 6,000 feet and, closing in dead astern and at the same height, opened fire at 2,000 feet, but no strikes observed. Closing in to 1,500 feet I gave a long burst, observing strikes, and the propellant seemed to explode. The Diver was seen to dive into the sea and explode, going in about 10 miles south-east of Beachy Head. Visual on second Diver was obtained at a range of 8/10 miles, travelling at a height of 2,000 feet at approximately 360mph. We dived from 10,000 feet and, coming in dead astern at the same height, opened fire at a range of 2,000 feet. Three bursts in all were fired, strikes being observed on the final burst. The speed of the Diver immediately decreased, and we passed it at a speed of 250mph. The pilotless plane was observed to lose height in a gradual dive, hitting the sea and exploding at approximately 0230 in the area 20 miles south of Hastings."

418 (RCAF) Squadron (Mosquito FBIV) Holmsley South

Flt Lt C.M. Jasper RCAF (US)	HR358/TH-K	V-1 damaged 0200		Channel
	HR358/TH-K	V-1	0208	Channel
Plt Off M.H. Sims RCAF	TH-	V-1	0245	Channel
Flt Lt D.E. Forsyth RCAF	TH-	V-1	0317	Channel
	TH-	V-1	0436	Channel

Flt Lt Jasper claimed two but was given credit for only one:

"At 0200 I attacked a Diver about 25 miles south-east of Beachy Head – numerous strikes seen but Diver continued on its course. At 0208 I attacked another Diver – remainder of ammo used and strikes observed. Two minutes later Diver was seen to blow up. Not known if this was caused by our aircraft or by another aircraft in the meantime."

Plt Off Merlin Sims scored some 40 minutes later:

"At 0245 chased Diver at 340mph. Fired two one-second bursts. Diver seen to smoke, catch fire and plunge into the sea 25 miles south of Dungeness. At 0255 chased another Diver and fired one-second burst but no strikes observed. Diver then engaged by coastal gun defences."

Flt Lt Dave Forsyth:

"At 0317 saw a Diver crossing French coast about 20 miles north-east of Dieppe at 2,000 feet. Closed to 150 yards and fired three two-seconds bursts and Diver crashed into sea. At 0436 observed another Diver crossing French coast at same place as previous one. Dived from 7,000 feet on Diver, which was travelling at 380mph at 2,000 feet. Fired two two-seconds bursts and Diver crashed into sea."

605 Squadron (Mosquito VI) Manston

Flt Lt R.J. Garner	MM414/UP-Y	V-1		Channel
Flt Lt J.G. Musgrave	MM429/UP-H	V-1	0211	off Le Touquet
	MM429/UP-H	V-1	0211	off Le Touquet
	MM429/UP-H	V-1 probable	0303	off Dover

Flt Lt John Musgrave enjoyed a busy patrol following his departure from Manston at 0125:

"At 0210 saw eight Divers coming out of Le Touquet area. At 0211 attacked two of them at 3,000 feet, speed 360mph. Attacks were started at 400 yards astern with cannon only; both Divers exploded in the air. At 0225 a bright light was seen at 1,000 feet about five miles west of Boulogne, flying north parallel to the French coast. We attacked it and fired a short burst from extreme range but saw no results. Light then flew into French coast and the light doused. This happened on two other occasions but no other attacks made. On one occasion when the light came out of Boulogne, flak was seen fired behind it. It is considered possible that this was an enemy aircraft acting as a decoy. At 0303 another Diver was seen at 3,000 feet at 320mph, between Dover and Boulogne. This was attacked from astern at about 600 yards range. Attack was continued until about eight miles from Dover. No strikes were seen but the jet then disappeared. It is considered that this Diver was very probably destroyed."

Thursday 6 JULY

With the death toll rising and the damage increasing, many Londoners wrote irate letters to their MPs demanding to have more details of the campaign and asking what the Government intended to do about it. As it was now impossible to apply the censorship policy any longer, Prime Minister Churchill agreed to make a statement in the House on 6 July:

"Up to 6am today, 2,752 people have been killed by flying bombs and about 8,000 have been injured and detained in hospital. The number of flying bombs launched up to 6 am today was 2,754. The firing points in France have been continually attacked for several months and the total weight of bombs so far dropped on these and rocket targets in France and Germany, including Peenemünde, has now reached about 50,000 tons. The invisible battle has now crashed into the open. We shall now be able to watch its progress at fairly close quarters. Between 100 and 150 flying bombs, each weighing about one ton, are being discharged daily, and have been discharged for the last fortnight or so. Considering the modest weight and small penetrative power the damage done by blast effect has been extensive. It cannot be compared with the terrific destruction by fire and high explosive with which we have been assaulting Berlin, Hamburg, Cologne, and scores of other German cities and war manufacturing points ... A very high proportion of the casualties have fallen upon London, which presents to the enemy a target 18 miles wide by 20 miles deep. It offers the unique target of the world for the use of a weapon of such inaccuracy. The flying bomb is a weapon literally and essentially indiscriminate in its nature, purpose and effect. The House will ask: What of the future? Is this attack going to get worse? Will the rocket-bomb come? Will more destructive explosions come? Will there be greater ranges? I can give no guarantee that any of these evils will be finally prevented before the time comes when the soil from which these attacks come has been fully *liberated. I must make it perfectly plain. I don't want any misunderstandings. We shall not allow the battle operations in Normandy, nor the attacks we are making against specific targets in Germany, to suffer. They come first. We must fit in our own domestic arrangements in the general scheme. There is no question of the slightest weakening of the battle. It may be a comfort to some that they are sharing in no small way the burdens of our soldiers overseas."*

Fourteen more lives were lost at 0641 when a Diver came down in Woodvale/Lordship Lane, East Dulwich (SE22), where six houses were demolished and 50 damaged. And a further five were killed at 0925 when a Diver impacted at the junction of Kennington Lane and Vauxhall Street (SE11). A factory and a local school and 30 houses were damaged. Eight more lives were lost at 1434 when a Diver exploded at the junction of Breakspeare Road and Harefield Road, Brockley (SE4).

150 Wing (Tempest V) Newchurch

Wg Cdr R.P. Beamont	JN751/RB	V-1	1415	Pevensey area

3 Squadron (Tempest V) Newchurch

Sqn Ldr A.S. Dredge	JN812/JF-M	V-1	0450	Faversham area
Flt Sgt H.J. Bailey RAAF	JN807/JF-Y	V-1	0450	Grid R.2040
Flg Off R.H. Clapperton	JN818/JF-	V-1	0452	Tonbridge area
Flt Lt A.E. Umbers RNZAF	JN817/JF-H	V-1	0455	Grid R.4570
Flt Lt R. van Lierde	EJ525/JF-	V-1	0455	Tonbridge area
Flg Off M.F. Edwards	EJ582/JF-T	V-1	0510	off Dungeness
Plt Off H.R. Wingate	JN793/JF-N	V-1	0640	Tonbridge area
	JN793/JF-N	V-1 shared	1310	Grid Q.9831

Sqn Ldr Alan Dredge reported:

"I saw a Diver five miles south of Dover at 2,500 feet at 350mph. Intercepted the Diver south of Canterbury and fired a one-and-a-half seconds burst from 100 yards with deflection. Fired again with a one-second burst from 100 yards dead astern. Strikes were seen all over the jet. The Diver slowed to 100mph and turned to the north, losing height and exploded on the ground in the Faversham/Sittingbourne area at 0450."

Flt Lt Spike Umbers and Flg Off Ray Clapperton took off from Newchurch together at 0425, Umbers shooting down his victim from 400 yards range and watched it explode on the ground. His companion caught another at almost the same time, six miles north of Ashford. After scoring strikes on the propulsion unit and port wing, the Diver went down near Tonbridge. The next one fell to Flt Lt Remi van Lierde:

"Saw a Diver six miles off Hastings. Dived from 6,000 feet and gave three two-seconds bursts from 200 yards, observing strikes. The jet went out then came on again with a brighter and longer flame. Overshot as the Diver slowed to 120mph, and went down to 1,500 feet. I orbited and saw flames streaming from the port side of the fuselage. Then another four aircraft attacked and the Diver went down and exploded near Tonbridge at 0455."

The next pair off, Flg Off Malcolm Edwards and Flt Sgt Bert Bailey each scored a kill, Edwards' victim exploding in the air about 15 miles south of Dungeness. Of his kill, Bailey reported:

"I saw a Diver 15 miles south of Bexhill at 3,500 feet, 350mph. A Mosquito fired from 1,000 yards with no result. I then closed to 400 yards and gave a short burst. After crossing the coast I saw another aircraft attack. I then fired a one-and-a-half-seconds burst from astern. Strikes were seen on the jet and the Diver slowed and turned, losing height, exploding on the ground at 0450."

316 (Polish) Squadron (Mustang III) West Malling

Flt Sgt S. Sztuka PAF	FB378/SZ-X	V-1	0640	Wrotham area

"Diver first seen crossing coast at Hastings. Intercepted and opened fire from 60 yards. Throttled back and fired again from dead astern from 400 yards, and closed again to 40 yards. Diver rolled over and crashed two miles south-east of Wrotham inside balloons."

322 (Dutch) Squadron (Spitfire XIV) West Malling
Flt Sgt Hendrik Cramm claimed a flying bomb destroyed but this was disallowed.

486 (RNZAF) Squadron (Tempest V) Newchurch

Wt Off B.J. O'Connor RNZAF	JN803/SA-D	V-1 shared	0450	Marden area
	JN803/SA-D	V-1	0530	Hastings area
Wt Off O.D. Eagleson RNZAF	JN873/SA-W	V-1	0720	Hastings area
Wt Off G.J.M. Hooper RNZAF	JN805/SA-E	V-1	1305	Friston area
	JN805/SA-E	V-1 shared	1310	off Beachy Head
	JN805/SA-E	V-1	1335	off Beachy Head

Wt Off Gus Hooper sighted the first flying bomb 15 miles south of Beachy Head and pursued it towards the coast, where he shot it down in flames. Five minutes later he shared a second with Plt Off Dickie Wingate of 3 Squadron, which exploded in mid-air, and shortly afterwards sent a third into the sea off Beachy Head.

USAAF Squadron (P-47)

1/Lt J.H. Payne USAAF		V-1

On this date Lt John H. 'Jack' Payne USAAF (P-47) reputedly brought down the first of two V-1s. His son wrote:

"The first he knocked down using the method of flying alongside it, getting one wingtip under its wing and tipping it. The gyro got screwed up and the V-1 crashed. When he landed someone yelled at him, saying that the damn thing could have blown up when he tipped it!"

Night 6/7 JULY
III/KG3 mounted another flying bomb assault, eight Heinkels taking off from Rosières (to where one Staffel had been detached for operations) at 0235, all aircraft returning safely shortly after dawn. However, two others had collided on the ground while taxiing for take-off (killing one aircrew member), thus reducing the overall effectiveness of the mission.

85 Squadron (Mosquito XIX) Swannington

Capt T. Weisteen (Norw)	MM636/VY-A	V-1	0025-0250

96 Squadron (Mosquito XIII) Ford

Flt Lt D.L. Ward	HK415/ZJ-R	V-1	2345	into sea
Flt Lt I.A. Dobie	HK438/ZJ-	V-1	0050	over sea
Lt(A) F.W. Richards RNVR	HK433/ZJ-	V-1	0110	exploded in mid-air
Wg Cdr E.D. Crew	MM511/ZJ-	V-1	0100-0355	
Sqn Ldr A. Parker-Rees	MM497/ZJ-	V-1	0213	into sea
Flt Sgt T. Bryan	MM468/ZJ-	V-1	0300-0520	
Flt Lt F.R.L. Mellersh	MM577/ZJ-N	V-1	0300-0520	

Flt Lt Don Ward shot his victim into the sea following attacks from 1,500 feet down to 500 feet, while Flt Lt Ian Dobie last saw his target diving towards the sea from 1,500 feet following two attacks. The chase was abandoned because of a thunderstorm but they were confident that it would crash.

137 Squadron (Typhoon Ib) Manston

Wg Cdr G.L. Raphael (Can)	MN134/SF-J	V-1	2350	off French coast
Flt Lt M. Wood RCAF	MN627/SF-N	V-1	0200	off Dungeness

Flt Sgt L.P. Boucher	MN152/SF-	V-1	0205	Hailsham area
Wg Cdr G.L. Raphael (Can)	MN134/SF-J	V-1	0315	
Flt Lt R.A. Johnstone RCAF	MN134/SF-J	V-1	0445	off Dungeness
Flg Off D.W. Guttridge	MN169/SF-Z	V-1	0600	off Dungeness

Wg Cdr Gordon Raphael, Manston's CO, borrowed a 137 Squadron Typhoon and undertook a patrol off the French coast between Cap Gris Nez and Berck:

"I sighted a Diver flying at 2,000 feet at 340mph. I attacked from astern and opened fire at a range of 300 yards. Diver went into the sea and exploded."

Two more were shot down by a later patrol, Flt Lt Matt Wood getting the first:

"I was patrolling between Dungeness and Le Touquet. At about 0200 I sighted a Diver off the French coast at 6,000 feet. I chased Diver and attacked from astern at 400 yards. I followed up and attacked again from 200-300 yards. Diver's 'light' went out south of Dungeness."

Wood's No.2 Flt Sgt Boucher scored five minutes later:

"At 0205 I sighted a Diver approaching the coast near Pevensey Bay. Target was at 3,500 feet. I chased and attacked from astern. Diver crashed and exploded in the Hailsham area."

Wg Cdr Raphael was up again at 0200 and again reported a success, shooting down his victim at 0315. This was followed by Flg Off Ralph Johnstone's victim, which also fell into the sea:

"At about 0445 I sighted a Diver at Le Touquet. I gave chase and when I had closed to 300 yards I attacked from dead astern. The Diver's 'light' went out and it crashed into the sea near a convoy east of Dungeness."

It was almost daylight by the time Flg Off David Guttridge[98] took off for the last night patrol:

"At about 0600 I was vectored on to a Diver ten miles south of Hastings. Diver was sighted at 2,000-3,000 feet. I dived down to Diver's height and carried out a head-on attack. Strikes seen. Diver went into a steep dive, exploding on hitting the sea."

157 Squadron (Mosquito XIX) Swannington

Flg Off C.N. Woodcock	MM652/RS-S	V-1	0013	off Dieppe
Flt Sgt J.C. Woolley	MM650/RS-J	V-1	0100	
Sqn Ldr J.G. Benson	MM630/RS-E	V-1	0140	
	MM630/RS-E	V-1		
Flt Lt J.O. Mathews	TA392/RS-K	V-1	0205-0540	

Sqn Ldr Benson's navigator Flt Lt Lewis Brandon wrote:

"We were off again just after midnight for another anti-Diver patrol. We were lucky enough to shoot down two of the things on this trip. Again we went after the third of a group of four or five of them. We found nobody else after our first victim and only one other fighter after the second. Ben had the whole business so well taped by now, though, that he easily out-manoeuvred the other chap and we were soon in much the better position to deal with the interception; the other chap saw this and cleared off. The Divers were not always as amenable as we had found them. Flt Lt Mathews and Wt Off Penrose from our squadron had a rather shattering experience one night. They were on patrol and intercepted a Diver. Mathews opened fire a little too soon and had a rather long chase before he shot it down. Not long after, on the same patrol, they had a second chase. This time he was determined to go in close before he opened fire. He did. The thing exploded right in front of him. His Mozzie was thrown about like a feather in a storm for a few seconds. Then he realised that he could see nothing through his windscreen but a warm red glow was coming from behind him somewhere. His fin and rudder were ablaze but a few gentle dives blew that out. With the aid of his navigator he managed to wipe the windscreen clear of some of the soot and muck from the bomb's explosion. Very gingerly he flew the damaged Mosquito back to base, where he landed all right. He informed his ground crew that he thought there was a bit of damage at the back, which they had better look at next morning. The whole station looked at it next morning – it really was a sight to behold. Only the framework of the fin and rudder was left, the rest had burned away. Every scrap of paint on the starboard side of the aircraft had been burnt off. The camouflage paint, the roundels and the squadron markings had completely disappeared; on the port side the paint was still there but it was blistered all over. They had certainly had a narrow escape."

418 (RCAF) Squadron (Mosquito VI) Holmsley South

Flt Lt P.S. Leggat RCAF	TH-	V-1	0000	over Channel
Flt Lt D.A. MacFadyen RCAF	HR155/TH-X	V-1	0011	off Beachy Head
	HR155/TH-X	V-1	0044	off Beachy Head
	HR155/TH-X	V-1 damaged	0053	off Beachy Head
Sqn Ldr R. Bannock RCAF	HR147/TH-Z	V-1	0051	off Beachy Head
	HR147/TH-Z	V-1	0057	off Beachy Head
	HR147/TH-Z	V-1	0132	off Berck-sur-Mer
	HR147/TH-Z	V-1	0210	Hastings area
Flt Lt C.J. Evans RCAF	TH-	V-1	0245	off Dungeness
	TH-	V-1	0305	off Hastings
	TH-	V-1	0315	off Hastings
Flt Lt D.A. MacFadyen RCAF	HR155/TH-X	V-1	0351	off Ault
Flg Off S.P. Seid RCAF (US)	TH-	V-1	0352	Channel

418 had a bumper night, six crews shooting down a dozen Divers. Flt Lt Peter Leggat shot down the first on the stroke of midnight: "Attacked Diver at 450 yards. Four two-second bursts and flames occurred. Diver exploded in the sea." This was followed a few minutes later by Flt Lt Don MacFadyen getting the first of three:

"0011 attacked Diver out of Dieppe, 340 IAS, 2,200 feet – range 300 yards astern, with one two-seconds burst. Strikes seen and Diver exploded in sea 25 miles south-east of Beachy Head. At 0044 attacked second Diver at 2,000 feet, range 500 yards astern with one two-seconds and one four-seconds bursts. Exhaust went out and Diver exploded in the sea 30 miles south-east of Beachy Head. Fired on another Diver at 0053, strikes seen but shot down later by another aircraft."

Sqn Ldr Russ Bannock, who shot down four Divers in one sortie, matter-of-factly reported:

"At 0051 attacked Diver at 3,500 feet, range 400 yards, from astern with one-and-a-half seconds burst. Exploded in sea six miles south of Beachy Head. At 0047 attacked Diver at 2,000 feet, range 350 yards astern with two two-second bursts. Exploded in mid-air and crashed in the sea eight miles off Beachy Head. At 0132 attacked Diver at 1,000 feet, range 600 yards astern with three-and-a-half seconds burst. Exhaust out, and Diver exploded in sea 15 miles due west of Berck-sur-Mer. At 0210 attacked Diver at 3,500 feet, range 400 yards astern with three two-seconds bursts. Diver went into gentle glide, and I followed until it crashed on land three miles north of Hastings."

Of hunting Divers in the dark, Bannock added:

"There were two hazards ... firstly, German coastal radar vectoring night fighters on to our Mosquitos; secondly, there was distinct danger of collision when two aircraft were diving on the same bomb. After some near misses, we all agreed to turn on our navigation lights once we entered the dive. We lost at least two aircraft in our Squadron during these sorties, due in all likelihood to enemy night fighters. On 6 July, at least 40 V-1s were launched during my two-hour patrol but I ran out of ammo after downing the fourth bomb ..."

Flt Lt Colin Evans from Hamilton, Ontario, raised his score to five with this hat-trick, shooting down the third after one of his own engines had stopped:

"At 0245 attacked Diver off Le Touquet from 150 yards astern with two one-second bursts.

Strikes seen and it exploded in the sea ten miles south-east of Dungeness. At 0305 attacked a second Diver from 100 yards astern with four one-second bursts. Exploded violently in the air 15 miles south of Hastings. Debris hit the Mosquito and starboard engine packed up. At 0315 attacked a third Diver (on single engine) with a two-seconds burst. Strikes seen and Diver crashed into sea six miles south-east of Hastings."

Flt Lt MacFadyen was up again on his second sortie of the night, having departed Ford at 0026:

"At 0351 attacked Diver coming out of Ault at 1,500 feet, range 300 yards astern with two three-seconds bursts. Strikes and exhaust out. Exploded in the sea 30 miles north-west of Ault."

Flg Off Sid Seid scored his second kill, but again his Mosquito was damaged, as recalled by his navigator Flg Off Dave McIntosh:

"We got too close again and this time lost an engine. 'Jesus, I guess I'll never learn,' Sid told the mess. 'My alligator [navigator] warned me we were too close, but he always says that anyway. He just sits there and screams pull up or get back or slow down. I've never heard him say full speed ahead or charge.' He was right there. Sid had made another perfect one-engine landing, this time at Ford. We had to wait until the next afternoon before the plane was fixed and that got us out of flying that night."[100]

605 Squadron (Mosquito VI) Manston

Flg Off B.G. Bensted	HJ799/UP-L	V-1 damaged	2348	Channel
	HJ799/UP-L	V-1	2354	Channel
Flt Lt B. Williams	UP-N	V-1	0205	off Dungeness
	UP-N	V-1	0247	off Le Touquet
	UP-N	V-1	0250	off Dungeness
Flg Off P.R. Rudd	UP-	V-1	0253	Channel
	UP-	V-1 shared	0307	Channel

Flg Off Basil Bensted scored his fourth kill:

"Twelve Divers in all were seen and of these three were attacked. At 2348 a Diver was sighted at 1,500 feet at 360mph. This was attacked 20 miles south-east of Dungeness at 600 yards range. All cannon ammo used and many strikes seen but Diver continued on course. At 2354 another Diver seen and attacked at 1,500 feet ten miles south-east of Dungeness with machine-guns only. Attack from astern at 200 yards range – one-and-a-half seconds burst. Target dived into the sea and exploded. At 0134 a third Diver attacked five miles south-west of Dungeness at 1,000 feet. No results were seen."

Flt Lt Brian Williams opened his score with a hat-trick of kills:

"In all we saw eight Divers, attacking three of them. At 0205 Diver was attacked eight miles south of Dungeness at 6,000 feet. Attacked from astern, 500 yards becoming 200 yards, with three bursts of cannon. The jet was doused and about 45 seconds later target exploded in the sea. At 0247 another Diver was attacked from 500 yards astern with one burst, five miles north-west of Le Touquet, at 500 feet. Target exploded in the air. At 0250, 15 miles east of Dungeness at 500 feet, a third Diver was attacked from 880 yards astern with four bursts. This also exploded in the air. All the Divers seemed to be leaving France in the Le Touquet area."

Two more flying bombs fell to 605 before the night was out, Flg Off Peter Rudd having to share his second kill with another aircraft:

"At 0248 saw Diver flying at 1,500 feet at 350mph approximately. Positioned for attack, opening fire at 200-300 yards with cannon and machine-guns. Very many strikes were seen all over the Diver, which started losing height. We had to break off attack at 0253 as another aircraft flew between the Diver and ourselves. Thirty seconds later the Diver was seen to crash into the sea and blow up. A second Diver was tacked from 0304 to 0307, flying at 1,500 feet at 350mph. Several bursts of cannon and machine-guns from 300 yards approximately. Strikes were seen and jet increased considerably in intensity. This attack had to be broken off as another aircraft flew between us and the Diver. This Diver was also seen about 30 seconds later to crash in the sea and explode. We were first to attack both Divers. It was not possible to tell whether the other aircraft attacked either of these Divers as no tracer was used. In view of this, the second Diver is only claimed as shared with another aircraft, but it would be appreciated if this could be stepped up to a destroyed. We saw a further three Divers but did not attack as there were several other aircraft around each."

The unit lost a Mosquito when Flg Off Arnold Craven's aircraft suffered an engine failure on take-off at 0222. Although the aircraft was a write-off, both Craven and his navigator Sgt Len Woodward survived unhurt.

FIU Detachment (Tempest V) Newchurch

Flt Lt J. Berry	EJ524/ZQ-Y	V-1	night
	EJ524/ZQ-Y	V-1	night
	EJ524/ZQ-Y	V-1	night
	EJ524/ZQ-Y	V-1	night
Flt Lt R.A. Jones	ZQ-	V-1	night

Much of Flt Lt Berry's success at night was due to his experimentation – and fearlessness – in the air. Overshooting an unusually slow Diver one night, he noted that the jet flame changed in appearance as he decreased the range. Rapidly closing in on the bomb, he first observed the 'blow-lamp' effect and then a red glow as the jet pipe shone through the flame. He was then able to make out the bomb's silhouette, not more than 100 yards ahead. On opening fire he was temporarily blinded when the bomb exploded. With his aircraft damaged by debris and blast, he was just able to reach base and make a safe landing.

Friday 7 JULY

From a Russian radio broadcast in English on 7 July:

> *"Nobody understands German atrocities better than the Soviet people and they can feel for British women and children who are suffering from Hitler's latest trick. Now the Hitlerites are killing civilians in Britain for the sole purpose of cheering up the downhearted Germans. It is possible that they had the crazy idea that these flying bombs would dampen Britain's fighting spirit, but Churchill's proud words that the operations in Normandy and the bombing of special objectives in Germany would not be affected by Hitler's latest action were greeted with applause, not only in the House of Commons but throughout the freedom-loving world."*

A flying bomb fell in the woods on Church Hill in Merstham (Surrey), causing extensive damage but no casualties. Another came down near the village of Ruckinge in Kent, as recalled by a young teenage girl:

"I lived in a large solidly built bungalow, which stood alone in fields and had been turned into a small holding with various animals. My sister, who was 15$^{1}/_{2}$ years old, my brother who was seven, and I just approaching my 16th birthday were just sitting down to have our tea, when we heard a Doodlebug coming. We heard a Spitfire go up after it, then the machine-gun fire. The Doodlebug's engine stopped so we ducked for cover under the table, but it was too late. We had a direct hit as the Doodlebug landed right in the middle of the bungalow. The blast killed my little brother, knocked out my sister and blew me through a two-foot thick wall and I ended up, suspended by my legs, under the bath. I waited and listened, and then I heard a man's voice so I shouted for help. As soon as he heard me, he called for silence, and then asked me to direct him to us. By this time there were dozens of people there trying to get us out. Suddenly we all heard another Doodlebug, then the Spitfire's guns – again the engine stopped. The man called for everyone to take cover as this second Doodlebug was heading straight for us, but the pilot of the Spitfire kept firing his guns. Luckily for us he shot one wing off the Doodlebug thus tipping it over; it landed on the farm buildings of the next farm, killing the farmer's prize bull, but nobody was hurt as they were all helping rescue us. My brother was killed, my sister had shock and bruises and I had badly crushed legs and bruises. I was buried for two hours before I was finally got out, feeling very dirty, and embarrassed, because the blast had torn all my clothes to shreds."

Two Divers shot down by fighters in the Elham area crashed at Evington Park and Lymbridge Green; there were no casualties. Fighters also brought down Divers that crashed at Birling (1517), and Moores Farm, Yalding (1910).

1 Squadron (Spitfire LFIXb) Detling

Flt Sgt H.J. Vassie	MK987/JX-	V-1	1455	Hailsham area
Flt Lt H.L. Stuart	NH253/JX-	V-1 shared	1630	Hailsham area
Flg Off E.N.W. Marsh	MK986/JX-V	V-1	2135	Hailsham area

The first fell to Flt Sgt Vassie:

"Closed in to attack Diver. In second of attacks Diver nosed down, dropping to 500 feet. I followed in and out of cloud, still firing. Ammo exhausted. I pulled up and away and lost sight of Diver in cloud. Shortly after there was an explosion which lifted my aircraft."

Flt Lt Stuart added a second:

"Vectored onto Diver crossing over at Eastbourne. Attacked in dive from 6,000 feet. Observed strikes on starboard wing and fuselage. Immediately following attack Diver made diving turn to starboard and crashed on a house near a mental hospital five miles north of Hailsham."

The final one fell to Flg Off Junior Marsh:

"After first attack I saw pieces fall off the port wing. Diver dropped wing but regained stability. After second burst rear portion of Diver disintegrated and, smoking badly, dived steeply to earth, exploding one and-a-half miles south of Hailsham."

3 Squadron (Tempest V) Newchurch

Flt Lt A.R. Moore	JN818/JF-	V-1	0510	off Hastings
Flt Lt R. van Lierde (Belg)	JN862/JF-Z	V-1	0546	Cranbrook area
	JN862/JF-Z		0615	off Dungeness
Flg Off R.E. Barckley	JN815/JF-	V-1	1300	East Grinstead area
Flt Sgt H.J. Bailey RAAF	JN807/JF-Y	V-1	1630-1745	
Flt Lt A.E. Umbers RNZAF	JN868/JF-F	V-1	1830-1955	
Plt Off H.R. Wingate	EN521/JF-	V-1	2230	Bexhill area

41 Squadron (Spitfire XII) Friston

Flg Off P.B. Graham	MB856/EB-X	V-1 shared	0540	Hailsham area
Flt Sgt I.T. Stevenson	EB-	V-1 shared	1630	Polegate area

Flg Off Peter Graham sighted a flying bomb approaching Friston and shot it down ten miles west of Hailsham in collaboration with a Tempest. During the afternoon Flt Sgt Jock Stevenson was carrying out an air test when he spotted his victim, which he shared with a Mustang flown by Flt Lt Longin Majewski of 316 Squadron.

56 Squadron (Tempest V) Newchurch

Flt Lt K.A. Wigglesworth ⎱	JN877/US-M	V-1	1215	Hastings area
Sgt G.H. Wylde ⎰	JN857/US-L			

A Diver was sighted five miles south of Hastings at 2,500 feet: Flt Lt Wigglesworth wrote:

"I gave a two-seconds burst from 200 yards astern, breaking away at 50 yards. Sgt Wylde then made a similar attack. I fired again from 150-50 yards and Diver went in, exploding on the ground about four miles north-west of Hastings. Both aircraft returned to patrol. At 1230, Sgt

Wylde had engine trouble and ditched off Beachy Head."

Sgt Geoffrey Wylde managed to scramble into his dinghy and was picked up, none the worse, 20 minutes later by an HSL. The squadron suffered another engine failure at 1700, and Flt Sgt Hughes had to force-land. He was not hurt.

91 Squadron (Spitfire XIV) Deanland ALG

Flt Lt R.S. Nash	RB169/DL-Q	V-1	0540	Dartford area
Flt Lt A.R. Cruickshank RCAF	RB165/DL-L	V-1	1335	Pluckley Station
Flt Lt A.R. Elcock	RM615/DL-	V-1	1515	Rochester area
Flg Off W.C. Marshall	NH720/DL-H	V-1	1523	Tunbridge Wells area
	NH720/DL-H	V-1	1730	Ham Street area
Sqn Ldr N.A. Kynaston	RB185/DL-	V-1	2005	Detling area
Flt Lt A.R. Cruickshank RCAF	RB165/DL-L	V-1	2035	Wormshill area
Flt Lt H.D. Johnson	RB183/DL-M	V-1	2100	Appledore area
Flg Off H.M. Neil	RB174/DL-T	V-1	2100	West Malling area
Sqn Ldr N.A. Kynaston	RB185/DL-	V-1	2135	Ashford area
Flg Off P.A. Schade	RM620/DL-E	V-1	2335	Rye area
Flg Off H.M. Neil	RB174/DL-T	V-1	2336	Dungeness area

91 Squadron scored a round dozen during the day, Flt Lt Ray Nash opening the score during an early morning patrol:

"Saw Diver 15 miles south-east of base and attacked from astern, damaging it and slowing speed. With wing of my aircraft I tipped Diver over. It fell in a wood south of Dartford where it exploded."

Flt Lt Ray Cruickshank got No.2:

"Sighted Diver four miles west of Folkestone fired at by a Mustang from 40 yards, but who did not get strikes. I attacked from astern and 100 yards range and Diver fell, exploding in a field near railway line at Pluckley Station."

Flg Off Arthur Elcock got the next: "Saw Diver south of Rochester and attacked from 90° to astern with one long burst at 400 yards range. Diver fell and exploded in open country." Flg Off Bill Marshall saw a Diver south of Tunbridge Wells at 1523: "Attacked from line astern. Jet unit put out of action and pieces knocked off wing. Diver fell, exploding in a wood south-west of Tunbridge Wells." Marshall was off again an hour later and brought down another: "Sighted Diver over Dymchurch and attacked from above and astern at 300 yards, closing to 200 yards. Big pieces fell off port wing and it spun with jet mechanism still functioning, exploding on the ground." There followed a lull before the next wave of Divers came in, Sqn Ldr Norman Kynaston getting the first of these: "Saw Diver north-west of Ashford and attacked from astern at 150 yards range. Strikes caused Diver to alter course and, after second attack, it fell exploding in a field north of Detling." Flt Lt Cruickshank got his second of the day shortly thereafter: "Sighted Diver north of Ashford and attacked from astern at 100 yards range. Saw strikes and Diver fell west of Wormshill, exploding in a field." The next fell to Flt Lt Johnny Johnson at 2102: "Saw Diver over Ivychurch and attacked from astern at 100 yards range. Diver fell two miles north of Appledore, exploding in a field." This was followed by another success for Flg Off Neil: "Saw Diver south of Ashford and attacked from astern with two bursts from 150 yards and it fell on a large country house two miles west of base, where it exploded." The CO got his second of the evening, this falling eight miles west of Ashford: "Saw Diver over Rye and attacked from astern at 150 yards range. It fell, exploding in a field." Flg Off Paddy Schade shot down a Diver three miles north-west of Rye, this being recorded as 91 Squadron's 100th kill:

> "Warned of approaching Diver. Sighted it five miles out to sea being fired at by another aircraft, who was not getting any strikes. I called over the R/T that I was going to attack and other aircraft broke away. Attack made from 250 yards, closing to 100 yards. Strikes caused Diver to go in dive and I followed it down to 1,500 feet, and when certain that it was crashing, broke away. Diver exploded on hitting ground."

Flg Off Neil scored again to close the innings, his second of the evening: "Saw Diver five miles south of Dungeness. Attacked from astern at 150-100 yards range and it fell, exploding on hitting the ground eight miles north-west of Dungeness."

316 (Polish) Squadron (Mustang III) West Malling

Wt Off F. Marek PAF	FB391/SZ-E	V-1	0510	Battle area
Wt Off W. Grobelny PAF	FB396/SZ-F	V-1	0615	off Beachy Head
Wt Off T. Szymański PAF	FB377/SZ-R	V-1	1519	Appledore area
Sgt J. Mielnicki PAF	FB386/SZ-N	V-1	1540	Bexhill area
Flt Lt L. Majewski PAF	FB351/SZ-B	V-1	1625	Alfriston area
	FB351/SZ-B	V-1 shared	1630	Polegate area
Sgt J. Mielnicki PAF	FB386/SZ-N	V-1	1955	Tonbridge area
Flt Sgt A. Pietrzak PAF	FB161/SZ-I	V-1	1958	off Bexhill

During an early morning patrol, when Wt Off Feliks Marek shot down a flying bomb, his companion Plt Off Konstanty Cynkier[101] was obliged to crash-land on return to West Malling. He was unhurt and his Mustang FB373/SZ-M not seriously damaged. Marek noted: "Diver first seen when on way out five miles south-east of Hastings. Turned and opened fire from dead astern at 200 yards. Strikes all over and it crashed in a field near Battle." An hour later Wt Off Grobelny brought down a second: "Sighted 25 miles south-south-east of Beachy Head. Attacked from port stern from 200 yards. Strikes all over and it crashed in sea." Wt Off Symański was the next to score: "Diver seen crossing the coast near Romney Sands. Intercepted from port astern and opened fire from 300 yards, closing to 200 yards. Saw strikes and it crashed in a field two miles north-west of Appledore." Sgt Mielnicki sighted the first of his two victims over Bexhill: "I formated on it, then throttled back and opened fire at 100 yards from dead astern. Strikes all over. It banked to port and crashed on side of valley near a wood five-eight miles north of Bexhill."

Flt Lt Longin Majewski shot down two in quick succession, sharing the second with Flt Sgt Ian Stevenson of 41 Squadron: "First seen one mile off Selsey Head. Pursued and attacked from dead astern from 400 yards, closing to 150 yards. Strikes on starboard wing and it crashed into hillside near Alfriston." The second was sighted five minutes later between Eastbourne and Beachy Head: "Attacked from dead astern from 200 yards. Strikes all over and seen to crash near Polegate." At 1855, Sgt Mielnicki scored his second of the day:

> "Diver intercepted soon after take-off. Attacked from dead astern from 300 yards, closing to 200 yards. Strikes all over, blue smoke from pilotless aircraft which glided and crashed three miles east of Tonbridge, just north of the railway line."

The successful day for the Poles came to a close at 1958 with the shooting down of another Diver by Flt Sgt Pietrzak: "Intercepted ten miles off French coast. Attacked from starboard rear from 250 yards. Strikes all over and it exploded in the sea ten miles south-south-east of Bexhill."

322 (Dutch) Squadron (Spitfire XIV) West Malling

Flg Off R.F. Burgwal	VL-C	V-1	1230	exploded in mid-air

Flt Sgt C. Kooij	VL-N	V-1	1447	Grid Q.9464
Flt Sgt G.J.H. Dijkman	VL-Y	V-1	1545	Grid R.1753
Flg Off M.A. Muller	VL-W	V-1	1640	Grid R.2568
Wt Off J.A. Maier	NH686/VL-M	V-1	1710	Grid R.4553
Flg Off P.A. Cramerus	VL-V	V-1	1730	Grid R.5561

Flg Off Rudi Burgwal had a narrow escape when his target exploded in mid-air between Ashford and Folkestone: "Vectored onto Diver. Attacked line astern, range 200 yards, closing to 100 yards. Diver exploded and scorched fabric off my Spitfire. I landed at Ashford ALG." Flt Sgt Cees Kooij had two witnesses to his victory:

"Patrolling Beachy, vectored on Diver. Attacked line astern 300 yards, closing to 200 yards. Saw strikes on power unit and flames came out. Diver went down in dive and exploded in a small wood. Two Spitfire XIVs had fired and missed. After I had shot the Diver down they formated on me, pointed at me, and gave me victory signs."

The next to score was Flt Sgt Gerard Dijkman: "Intercepted Diver ten miles north of Bexhill, attacked at 300 yards line astern, closing to 200 yards. Pieces came off after last burst and Diver slowly turned to port and fell in a wood on the edge of a lake." Flg Off Muller saw strikes on the port wing of his target: "Diver did left spiral turn and went straight in." It was then the turn of Wt Off Justin Maier, with a victory shortly after 1700: "Diver intercepted two miles north-west of Dymchurch. Attacked line astern at 250 yards. One short burst. Large pieces came off and Diver crashed into farm buildings." The final score of the day fell to Flg Off Piet Cramerus: "Intercepted Diver one mile south-east of Folkestone. Attacked line astern from 200 yards. One short burst and hit seen on port wing. It crashed half way up a slope of a hill."

486 (RNZAF) Squadron (Tempest V) Newchurch

Flt Lt H.N. Sweetman RNZAF ⎫	JN801/SA-L	V-1 shared	0610	Beachy Head area
Plt Off R.J. Danzey RNZAF ⎭	JN809/SA-M			
Flt Lt H.N. Sweetman RNZAF	JN803/SA-D	V-1	1255	Ashford area
Wt Off O.D. Eagleson RNZAF	EJ527/SA-Q	V-1	1650	Newchurch area
Flg Off R.J. Cammock RNZAF	JN873/SA-W	V-1	1650	Pevensey area
Flg Off J.R. Cullen RNZAF	EJ527/SA-Q	V-1	1930	off Beachy Head
Flg Off H.M. Mason RNZAF	JN732/SA-I	V-1 shared	2315	West Malling area
Wt Off O.D. Eagleson RNZAF	JN873/SA-W	V-1	2340	Dungeness area

610 Squadron (Spitfire XIV) Friston

Flg Off G.M. McKinlay	RB142/DW-	V-1	1525-1625	
	RB142/DW-	V-1	1525-1625	
Flt Lt J.B. Shepherd	DW-	V-1	1615-1730	
Flg Off W.A. Nicholls[102]	DW-	V-1	1915-2030	

610 Squadron's score noted as 21 but in fact it was 19 plus two shares.

USAAF Squadron (P-47)

| 1/Lt J.H. Payne USAAF | | V-1 | | exploded in mid-air |

Lt Jack Payne's son wrote: "He got behind it [the Diver] and shot it down properly with his machine-guns. It blew up, right in front of him! He had to fly through the fireball and debris of a 1,000lb bomb! Damned if you do, damned if you don't!"

Night 7/8 JULY

A minute before midnight, five people were killed when a Diver demolished six houses (and damaged 80) in the Clayton Road/Cicely Road area of Peckham (SE15). At 0321, a Diver impacted in Prince Street Dockyard in Deptford (SE8), which was being used as a US amphibious base. It struck a 1,500-ton tank landing craft on its starboard side, also damaging another LCT moored beside it, causing severe damage and killing 13 USN officers and ratings. Surrounding property on the quayside was also badly damaged.

85 Squadron (Mosquito XVII/XIX) Swannington

Flt Lt R.H. Farrell	VY-O	V-1	2225-0050	
Wg Cdr C.M. Miller	HK349/VY-R	V-1 shared	2225-0125	off Beachy Head
Lt E.P. Fossum (Norw)	MM648/VY-G	V-1	2230-0105	

137 Squadron (Typhoon Ib) Manston

Flg Off J.C. Holder RCAF	MN627/SF-N	V-1	2315	off Hastings
	MN627/SF-N	V-1	2330	off Hastings
Flg Off H.T. Nicholls	MN198/SF-	V-1	2320	off Berck-sur-Mer

Two Typhoons took off from Manston at 2250 on an anti-shipping patrol. They swept Cap Gris Nez without incident before 25-30 Divers were seen and three attacked, Flg Off Jim Holder shooting down two:

"At 2315, 25 miles off Hastings, I attacked from close range a Diver at 2,500 feet, seeing it explode in the air. At 2330 in the same position and similar course, height and speed, I attacked another in a dive from astern and it exploded on the water."

Meanwhile, Flg Off Henry Nicholls got another: "At 2320 off Berck I sighted a Diver at 2,500 feet, which I attacked with cannon from astern. It exploded on the sea."

409 (RCAF) Squadron (Mosquito XIII) Hunsdon

Flt Lt E.G.L. Spiller RCAF	MM512/KP-	V-1 shared	2245-0140	off Beachy Head

"At approximately 0038 we obtained a visual of a flying bomb at 3,000 feet travelling at an estimated speed of 305mph. I dived from 8,000 feet from stern to port quarter and was closing in behind the bomb when I observed tracer bullets passing beneath my wings – from a fighter positioned behind me. I pulled away to port, and climbing, saw the other fighter deliver a second burst, strikes being observed. As the enemy projectile was by this time pulling away from the second fighter and the latter had abandoned the chase, I closed to 1,000 feet from dead astern and opened fire, the Diver bursting into a sheet of rose-coloured flames and hitting the sea ten seconds later. The position is believed to be five miles south-west of Beachy Head." He added: "The kill was confirmed by Wing Commander of 85 Squadron."

It was in fact Wg Cdr Miller of 85 Squadron who was flying the other Mosquito!

418 (RCAF) Squadron (Mosquito VI) Holmsley South

Sqn Ldr R. Bannock RCAF	HR147/TH-Z	V-1	2342	Channel
	HR147/TH-Z	V-1	0001	Channel
Flt Lt S.H.R. Cotterill RCAF	TH-	V-1	0345	Channel
Flg Off J.J. Harvie RCAF	TH-	V-1	0435	Dungeness area

Sqn Ldr Bannock scored again with a brace:

"At 2342, when ten miles south of Hastings, I attacked Diver from 100 yards astern with two-seconds burst. It blew up in mid-air. At 0001, when 20 miles south of Dungeness, I attacked another Diver from 300 yards with five-seconds burst. Diver blew up on hitting the sea."

Flt Lt Stan Cotterill[103]:

"Two Divers seen but unable to engage. At 0345 saw another at 1,500 feet. Fired one-second burst from 100 yards. Diver went down into sea and blew up. Explosion shook Mosquito."

Flg Off Jeff Harvie and his navigator had a close shave when destroying another Diver:

"At 0428 two Divers were seen to come out of Le Touquet area. A burst was fired at first but unable to close. The second Diver passed underneath at 2,500 feet and I dived from 4,500 feet and fired one-and-a-half-seconds burst from 200 yards range. Strikes seen and rear of 'tube' fell off. Diver continued on course, losing height rapidly and crossed the coast at Dungeness at 0432 and crashed eight miles inland at 0435. No AA fire but another aircraft behind us, 600-700 yards range, fired at Diver. The tracer passed us and we saw no strikes [on the Diver] but had to get out of the line of fire to avoid being hit ourselves."

605 Squadron (Mosquito VI) Manston

Flg Off J.C. Worthington RNZAF	UP-	V-1	night	Channel

FIU (Tempest V) Ford

Sqn Ldr A.D. Wagner DFC	EJ581/ZQ-	V-1	night	Channel
Flt Lt R.A. Jones	ZQ-	V-1	night	Channel

Saturday 8 JULY

A Diver fell on Greenwich Police Station. Although several people were trapped in the rubble there were no fatalities. At 2137, another impacted in Oakdale Road, Streatham (SW16), where six people were killed and many houses damaged, some severely.

3 Squadron (Tempest V) Newchurch

Flt Lt A.E. Umbers RNZAF	JN817/JF-H	V-1 shared	1125-1240
Plt Off K.G. Slade-Betts	JN822/JF-	V-1	1900-1945
Flt Lt R. van Lierde (Belg)	JN861/JF-	V-1	1900-1945
Plt Off K.G. Slade-Betts	JN868/JF-F	V-1	2135-2325
Flt Lt A.R. Moore	JN818/JF-	V-1	2255-2350
Flg Off R. Dryland	JN822/JF-	V-1	2255-2330
Plt Off S.B. Feldman (US)	JN862/JF-Z	V-1	2255-2345

At 1230, Sqn Ldr Dredge (JN812/JF-M) took off to fly an anti-Diver patrol accompanied by Grp Capt Legg (JN754) from HQ 11 Group. They returned 35 minutes later having not sighted any targets.

41 Squadron (Spitfire XII) Friston

Flt Sgt P.W. Chattin	MB837/EB-P	V-1	0525	Thames Estuary
Flt Lt P.B. Graham	EB-	V-1		Dungeness area
Flg Off N.P. Gibbs	EN227/EB-	V-1	2151	Eastbourne area

The flying bomb attacked by Flt Sgt Peter Chattin[104] over the Thames Estuary exploded and damaged his aircraft. Despite damage to the mainplanes, radiator, spinner and propeller, he was able to make a safe landing at Friston. Flg Off Peter Gibbs scored his fourth kill whilst engaged on an air test.

56 Squadron (Tempest V) Newchurch

Flt Lt J.G. Mansfield	EJ534/US-O	V-1	2315	Grid Q.8968

"When returning from patrol I sighted a Diver over Beachy Head at 2,500 feet. I gave a short burst from 400 yards closing to 100 yards. The Diver slowed down and I overshot. I came again and fired from 200 yards, the Diver going down and exploding on the ground."

24 Wing (Spitfire XIV) Deanland ALG

Wg Cdr R.W. Oxspring	NH714/RW-O	V-1	2305	Balloon Barrage area
	NH714/RW-O	V-1	2315	West Malling area

Wg Cdr Bobby Oxspring DFC bagged a brace: "Saw Diver south of base and attacked from astern at 300 yards range. Strikes caused it to dive down and explode in balloon area. Seen to hit ground by F/O Costello." Ten minutes later he got his second: "Sighted Diver approaching south of base and attacked from astern at 300 yards. Diver fell, exploding on ground."

91 Squadron (Spitfire XIV) Deanland ALG

Flg Off R.A. McPhie RCAF ⎫	RB182/DL-V	V-1	2300	exploded in mid-air
Flg Off M.J. Costello RNZAF ⎭	NH705/DL-P			

Flg Off Ray McPhie wrote:

"Sighted Diver over Beachy Head at 3,000 feet and attacked from dead astern at 300 yards range. Strikes caused it to lose height rapidly. Followed it down to 1,500 feet. Where another aircraft [apparently that flown by Flg Off Morrie Costello[105]] dived from above and gave a burst which exploded its fuel tank."

165 Squadron (Spitfire IX) Detling

Plt Off J.V. Tynan	MK738/SK-L	V-1	2130	Pevensey/Bexhill
Flt Lt A.C.W. Holland	MJ580/SK-J	V-1	2122	off Beachy Head
	MJ580/SK-J	V-1	2134	exploded in mid-air
Flg Off V. Porich RAAF	MK480/SK-F	V-1	2134	Hailsham/Hellingly
Flt Lt J.K. Porteous RNZAF	ML418/SK-G	V-1	2145	Hailsham area

Plt Off Tynan was forced away from his target at the last moment by AA fire:

"When returning from one chase, was approaching north-west of Hastings when vectored onto Diver four miles out, heading for Pevensey/Bexhill. Obtained visual about one mile inland by Bexhill. Yellow 2 was already astern, so I climbed and flew parallel for about three minutes. Yellow 2 was not closing so I attacked. On second attack saw strikes around jet – streams of smoke and Diver went into gentle dive. A few seconds later light flak opened up and behind Diver and forced me to break sharply upwards, thus losing sight of it. Yellow 2 confirms claim."

Flt Lt Tony Holland scored a brace: "Sighted Diver 15 miles south of Beachy Head. Saw strikes around jet. Toppled over to starboard and dived vertically into sea ten miles offshore. Vectored onto another Diver ten miles south of Eastbourne. Attacked and saw strikes. Instantaneous explosion in mid-air. Slight damage to my aircraft's radiator." Flg Off Vic Porich intercepted his target north of Beachy Head: "Attacked in dive from 5,000 feet. Saw strikes on jet. Flame diminished considerably. Yellow 2 overshot Diver and when he turned he saw it crash."

310 (Czech) Squadron (Spitfire IX) Lympne

Flg Off O. Smik	EN527/NN-	V-1	2128	Ashford area
	EN527/NN-	V-1	2145	Battle area
	EN527/NN-	V-1	2200	Tenterden area

"I was airborne from base at 2125. At approximately 2128, I was at 5,000 feet, speed 300mph. I dived and attacked it from port quarter and below, using cannon only and giving two-seconds burst. I saw red flashes on the fuselage and Diver crashed near Ashford. I resumed patrol and at 2145, again at 5,000 feet, saw a Diver at 2,000 feet, speed 280mph. Dived and made stern attack with machine-guns only, giving finishing burst with cannon. Scored hits on fuselage, and both wings flew off. Diver crashed north-east of Battle. At 2200 I was over the Channel at 4,000 feet. Saw Diver below, speed 300mph. Went down and fired two-seconds burst machine-gun. Saw no strikes owing to heavy rain but Diver exploded and fell near Tenterden. Landed 2235 hours."

312 (Czech) Squadron (Spitfire IX) Lympne

Sqn Ldr M.A. Liškutín	MK670/DU-V	V-1	pm	Ashford/Maidstone

Sqn Ldr Miroslav Liškutín, later wrote:

"Immediately after getting airborne on an air test I saw, by chance, a flying bomb crossing over Dover on its way towards London. My new Spitfire IXA accelerated easily to about 300 knots, and the interception occurred above the main road between Ashford and Maidstone. It was quickly getting dark and becoming difficult to judge the distance behind this glowing jet-pipe. My height over the high ground of the Quarry Hills was under 500 feet. When I thought I was about 250 yards behind the infernal machine, I took careful aim and fired a one-second burst from my cannons. It happened, literally, in a flash. I did not even see the strikes before flying right into the fireball – and out the other side. Fifteen minutes later I landed back at Lympne. My aircraft wasn't seriously damaged, but something had happened to my self-assurance. Between pressing the firing button and entering the fireball, I had a momentary sensation that I was looking at the V-1, and my Spitfire, from some 500 yards away to the left. It was quite clear, despite the darkness, and I must have been a good deal closer than 250 yards from my target."

316 (Polish) Squadron (Mustang III) West Malling

Flt Lt A. Cholajda PAF	FB384/SZ-Z	V-1	2132	Ticehurst area
	FB384/SZ-Z	V-1	2135	Rotherfield
Flg Off T. Karnkowski PAF	FB359/SZ-V	V-1 shared	2150	Beckley area
	FB359/SZ-V	V-1	2155	Robertsbridge
Flt Lt T. Szymankiewicz PAF	FB391/SZ-E	V-1	2200	Beckley area
Flt Sgt A. Murkowski PAF	FB351/SZ-B	V-1	2205	off Dungeness

Flt Lt Antoni Cholajda (known as Ghandi to his friends) shot down two within three minutes:

"First seen ten miles west of Robertsbridge. Opened fire from 200 yards dead astern. Strikes all over and it crashed two miles west of Ticehurst in a wood. Saw second three miles south of Rotherfield. Opened fire from 200 yards dead astern and it exploded two miles north of Rotherfield."

Flg Off Tadeusz Karnkowski scored his first south-east of Beckley, where it crashed into a wood. Five minutes later he attacked another near Sedlescombe: "Opened fire from 200 yards dead astern. Overshot, throttled back and overturned it with port wing – seen to crash two miles east-south-east of Robertsbridge." He then engaged a third Diver and again tried to tip it with his wing, only to damage his own aircraft, which necessitated a belly-landing on his return to West Malling. Of Karnkowski's plight, Sqn Ldr Arct added:

"Karnkowski tried the wing tipping trick. He flew in close formation with a bomb, expertly put his wing under the Witch's wing and jerked the stick. But he did not jerk it violently enough and the evil-minded monster airfly regained its horizontal position. As Karnkowski did not fly away in time, the bomb hit his plane with all its impetus. The effect was more than unpleasant: the Mustang lost the tip of its wing and Karnkowski only with greatest difficulty returned to base."

Two more were shot down by the Poles two hours before midnight, Flt Lt Szymankiewicz getting the first: "Seen crossing the coast near Rye. Attacked frontally. Then attacked from rear. Opened fire at 200 yards dead astern, closing to 50 yards. Strikes all over and it crashed in a wood two miles north of Beckley. Combat photographed by a Spit." Five minutes later Wt Off Murkowski got the other: "Intercepted 15 miles north-west of Le Touquet. Opened fire at 200 yards dead astern. Strikes all over and it crashed into the sea 15 miles south-east of Dungeness."

322 (Dutch) Squadron (Spitfire XIV) West Malling

Flt Sgt H.C. Cramm	VL-T	V-1	0430	Dungeness area
Flg Off R.F. Burgwal	NH586/VL-G	V-1	2127	Grid R.4757

	NH586/VL-G	V-1	2134	
	NH586/VL-G	V-1	2142	
	NH586/VL-G	V-1	2153	
	NH586/VL-G	V-1 shared	2204	
Flg Off J. Jonker	VL-K	V-1	2206	exploded in mid-air
Flt Lt L.C.M. van Eendenburg	RB184/VL-B	V-1	2316	West Malling area

Flt Sgt Hendrik Cramm was up early, taking off at 0321 for a patrol off Dungeness: "Saw Diver approaching Dungeness. Unidentified aircraft opened fire but missed and broke away. I attacked line astern, range 200 yards. Diver crashed and exploded ten miles north of Dungeness." After shooting down four flying bombs in quick succession, Flg Off Rudi Burgwal shared the fifth with two Mustangs. Flg Off Jan Jonker reported: "Vectored on to Diver, attacked line astern, 400 yards. Spitfire IX cut and fired without result. I closed in to 100 yards and gave short burst. Diver exploded in the air over Fairfield." Flt Lt van Eendenburg wrote: "Near Maidstone, coming in to land, saw Dover behind. Opened fire three-quarter starboard attack from 150 yards. Made steep turn and attacked again, line astern, range 200 yards. Diver rolled over and exploded three-quarters of a mile south-west of airfield [West Malling]."

486 (RNZAF) Squadron (Tempest V) Newchurch

Flg Off J.R. Cullen RNZAF	JN770/SA-V	V-1	0535	off Dungeness
Flt Lt J.H. McCaw RNZAF	JN758/SA-Y	V-1	2310	Ashford/Maidstone
	JN758/SA-Y	V-1	2315	West Malling area
	JN758/SA-Y	V-1	2320	West Malling area
Plt Off F.B. Lawless RNZAF	JN770/SA-V	V-1	2320	off Beachy Head
	JN770/SA-Y	V-1	2325	Brewhurst area
Flt Lt J.H. McCaw RNZAF	JN758/SA-Y	V-1	2359	Biggin Hill area

610 Squadron (Spitfire XIV) Friston

Flt Lt H.D. Price	DW-	V-1		exploded in mid-air

Flt Lt Price's aircraft was slightly damaged by debris from the explosion.

Night 8/9 JULY

The gasholder belonging to South Metropolitan Gas Company at Kennington (SE11) took a direct hit from a Diver at 2141, but although eight nearby houses were damaged there were no fatalities. A Diver that fell in Jardine Street/Scarsdale Road area of Camberwell (SE5) shortly before midnight caused much damage and killed one person.

96 Squadron (Mosquito XIII) Ford

Flt Lt W.J. Gough	HK479/ZJ-	V-1	2359	Channel
Sqn Ldr R.N. Chudleigh	HK379/ZJ-F	V-1	2330	Channel
	HK379/ZJ-F	V-1	2350	Channel
	HK379/ZJ-F	V-1	0005	Channel
Flt Lt N.S. Head	HK462/ZJ-	V-1	0030	Channel
Flg Off J. Goode	MM557/ZJ-	V-1	0102-0350	Channel
Sqn Ldr R.N. Chudleigh	HK379/ZJ-F	V-1	0430	Channel
	HK379/ZJ-F	V-1	0435	Channel
	HK379/ZJ-F	V-1	0500	Channel

Sqn Ldr Dick Chudleigh shot down six flying bombs in two sorties, effectively doubling his overall score to a round dozen.

137 Squadron (Typhoon Ib) Manston

| Flt Lt D.G. Brandreth | MN134/SF-J | V-1 | 0210 | off Cap Gris Nez |

Flt Lt Doug Brandreth wrote: "I was orbiting about ten miles north-west of Gris Nez and sighted a Diver. It was flying at 4,500 feet. I followed and carried out an attack from 300 yards range dead astern. I fired a short burst and Diver went down into the sea and exploded." Somewhat earlier, Wt Off A.W. Emslie suffered injury to an eye when his Typhoon MN556 bounced heavily on the runway on landing at 0130, veered off and overturned.

157 Squadron (Mosquito XIX) Swannington

| Wg Cdr W.K. Davison | MM678/RS-A | V-1 | 2308 |

605 Squadron (Mosquito VI) Manston

| Flg Off R.E. Lelong RNZAF | HJ785/UP-T | V-1 | night |

A Mosquito crashed on take-off from Manston although the crew escaped unharmed.

FIU (Tempest V) Ford

Flt Lt J. Berry	EJ524/ZQ-Y	V-1	night
	EJ524/ZQ-Y	V-1	night
	EJ524/ZQ-Y	V-1	night

During a night anti-shipping patrol south-west of Boulogne, a Coastal Command Beaufighter crew from 143 Squadron sighted a Diver at 2355. Attacked with two short bursts but no result seen. Two US vessels *LST312* and *LST384* were reported to have been damaged by a Diver or a glider-bomb off the Normandy coast, probably the latter.

Sunday 9 JULY

Canadian gunners with the 8th Canadian LAA Regiment based at Heathfield in Sussex gained their first kill during the day.

150 Wing (Tempest V) Newchurch

| Wg Cdr R.P. Beamont | JN751/RB | V-1 | | Rye area |

3 Squadron (Tempest V) Newchurch

Flg Off R.E. Barckley	JN817/JF-H	V-1	0425-0545
	JN817/JF-H	V-1	0425-0545
Plt Off K.G. Slade-Betts	JN817/JF-H	V-1	1035-1145
Plt Off H.R. Wingate	EN549/JF-	V-1	2130-2255
Flg Off R.H. Clapperton	JN818/JF-	V-1	2225-2355
	JN818/JF-	V-1	2225-2355

41 Squadron (Spitfire XII) Friston

| Flg Off R.E. Anderson RAAF ⎫ | EN228/EB- | V-1 | 1250 | off Beachy Head |
| Wt Off A.S. Appleton   ⎭ | EN238/EB-Q | | | |

Flg Off Bob Anderson shared the kill with Wt Off Archie Appleton, who wrote: "Opened fire from 600 yards, closing to 50 yards, obtaining strikes. Diver into sea and exploded."

56 Squadron (Tempest V) Newchurch

Flt Lt J.H. Ryan RCAF ⎫	JN864/US-C			
Flg Off L.J. Henderson RAAF ⎭	EJ547/US-A	V-1 shared	2225	off Bexhill
Flt Lt J.H. Ryan RCAF	JN864/US-C	V-1	2230	Old Romney area
Flt Lt K.A. Wigglesworth	JN877/US-M	V-1	2310	East Grinstead area

Flt Lt John Ryan and Flg Off Henderson shared a Diver, which exploded in the sea five miles off Bexhill, with Sqn Ldr Liškutín of 312 (Czech) Squadron and Flg Off Cullen of 486 Squadron, while Ryan's solo victim exploded on the ground near Old Romsey. He reported:

> "Sighted a Diver 30 miles south of Hastings at 3,000 feet. We fired from 500 yards astern, closing to 150 yards, scoring strikes. The Diver slowed down and a Tempest of 486 Squadron then dived down and fired a burst, the Diver going in and exploding in the sea five to ten miles south of Bexhill." He sighted his second target off Dungeness: "I fired from 100 yards astern. The petrol tank exploded and the Diver went down, exploding on the ground at R.4343."

Flt Lt Keith Wigglesworth completed the successful evening with another kill at 2310: "Sighted Diver over Pevensey Bay at 3,000 feet. I dived and fired several bursts from 300 yards astern, closing to 100 yards. The Diver exploded on the ground."

91 Squadron (Spitfire XIV) Deanland ALG

Flt Lt R.S. Nash	RB169/DL-Q	V-1	1205	Paddock Wood
Lt H.F. de Bordas (FF)	NH720/DL-H	V-1	2020	exploded in mid-air
Flg Off K.R. Collier RAAF	RB183/DL-M	V-1	2130	Swanley Junction
Flt Lt J.W.P. Draper RCAF	RM620/DL-E	V-1	2158	Goudhurst area
Flg Off W.C. Marshall	NH701/DL-A	V-1	2206	exploded in mid-air
Flg Off K.R. Collier RAAF	RB183/DL-M	V-1	2220	Chatham area

Flt Lt Ray Nash's victim crashed south of Paddock Wood Station: "Saw Diver cross in over Hastings. Followed it through cloud and attacked from astern at 250 yards range." Lt Henri de Bordas got his in the same general direction: "Saw Diver over Cranbrook and attacked from astern at 400 yards, closing to 200 yards. Diver exploded in the air." Flg Off Ken Collier's first victim fell north-west of Swanley Junction, and his second north-west of Chatham: "Saw Diver south of Maidstone and attacked from astern at 200 yards range. It fell in a field near houses, where it exploded. Saw Diver by marker flares east of Maidstone and attacked from astern at 400 yards range. Shot down in a field." Personnel at West Malling were alarmed to see a low flying Spitfire firing at a Diver from close range as it crossed the airfield, expecting it to explode over their heads at any moment. Fortunately for the riveted audience one of Flg Off Bill Draper's cannons had jammed and he missed shooting it down. A few hours later he was up again and succeeded in bringing down his victim near Goudhurst: "Sighted Diver over Rye and attacked from astern at 600 yards, closing to 400 yards. Diver fell in a field, where it exploded." Flg Off Bill Marshall closed to 75 yards of his target in order to explode it in the air, four miles north-east of Chatham, in a deliberate attempt to save the town of Lydd. Marshall survived the experience[106].

137 Squadron (Typhoon Ib) Manston

New Zealander Flt Sgt Dick Egley (MN134/SF-J) was vectored on to a V-1 during his 2105-2225 patrol, but it was destroyed by another aircraft before he could close in.

310 (Czech) Squadron (Spitfire IX) Lympne

Flt Sgt F. Mareš	EN526/NN-	V-1	2145-2250	exploded in mid-air
Sgt J. Pipa	NH692/NN-	V-1	2257	Folkestone area

Sgt Josef Pipa shot down his target five miles west of Folkestone from about 1,000 feet, while Flt Sgt František Mareš DFM (with five aerial kills under his belt including shares) recalled:

"Having already flown a sortie, an escort to 57 Lancasters bombing the Noball site at Le Hayn, had me landing at dusk after flying through some very dense and lethal flak. Some of our planes had been hit, others were badly damaged and required nursing back in order to force-land at the nearest airfield in England. Although tired from a long day's flying, my loathing for the continued use of the flying bombs spilled over when we were encouraged to volunteer to lay in wait for these devices. After refuelling, I took off with the intention of venting my feelings by shooting down one of these Hitler-inspired monsters. I took off in the dark of night with the full and encouraging co-operation of Flying Control, who I informed over the R/T that I was airborne. I was passed over to the Ops Room from where an angelic voice took over. She gave me a vector to steer and a height to level off at, giving course alterations as necessary. After some 20 minutes of precise guidance, the voice calm and firm announced – 'I have a Witchcraft for you at 11 o'clock below.' No sooner had I received the message than I discerned the flame of the flying bomb racing towards me. While shouting 'Tally-ho', I stood the aircraft on its nose, spiralled through 180 degrees, the throttle opened to its fullest extent, lined the flame in the gunsight and pressed the button. While the cannons loudly responded, the roar of the Spitfire engine began to cough, then gave up in silent protest.

"For a Spitfire to catch up with a Doodlebug, the pilots had to have a good advantage of height, be in the correct position and react speedily. Thanks to the expert guidance given by the Ops Room, such perfect conditions prevailed but by having exploited them a shade too energetically I had disorientated my aircraft's Merlin engine management, thus losing its obedience which meant that I was powerless to blast the thing out of the sky. Just as I began to despair the engine regained its senses, roared into life and I was able to continue with the pursuit of the, by then, more distant witchcraft flame. Both man and machine revitalized, the cannons spitting out their venomous message, I was willing the shells towards the target. Just as I was declaring my mission a failure there was a blinding flash and a terrific explosion, which preceded some very severe turbulence. My feeling was one of gleeful satisfaction as I reported my success to Flying Control. The ever-gentle voice then guided me through the darkness to a safe landing and a night of dreams about the body and soul that was attached to the angelic voice – I slept really well."

312 (Czech) Squadron (Spitfire IX) Lympne

Sqn Ldr M.A. Liškutín   MK670/DU-V   V-1 shared   2225   Rye area

Sqn Ldr Miroslav Liškutín shared his kill with three Tempests, two of 56 Squadron and one from 486 Squadron.

313 (Czech) Squadron (Spitfire IX) Lympne

Sgt K.J. Stojan   ML145/RY-   V-1   0450   Romney Marshes

"I saw Diver approaching the coast at 2,000 feet. I was at 5,000 feet and dived towards it, making a stern attack at 400 yards. I fired one short burst at 200 yards, seeing strikes. I fired another short burst and Diver dived straight down and exploded in an open field in the marshes south of Lympne."

316 (Polish) Squadron (Mustang III) West Malling

Flg Off T. Karnkowski PAF	FB351/SZ-B	V-1	0519	off Dungeness
Flt Lt T. Szymankiewicz PAF	FB391/SZ-E	V-1	0524	off Dungeness
Wt Off J. Feruga PAF	FB378/SZ-X	V-1	2140	off Boulogne
Flt Lt S. Litak PAF	FB351/SZ-B	V-1 shared	2230	Goudhurst area
Flt Lt T. Szymankiewicz PAF	FB396/SZ-F	V-1	2255	off Dungeness

Flg Off Tadeusz Karnkowski got his fifth and final kill (one shared) south-east of Dungeness: "Diver seen over sea 15 miles south-east of Dungeness. Opened fire from 200 yards dead astern. Saw strikes all over and Diver exploded on the sea ten miles south-east of Dungeness." Flt Lt Szymankiewicz got the next five minutes later: "Seen 20 miles south-west of Dungeness. Opened fire from 250 yards dead astern. Diver exploded on the sea." Another crashed into the sea as a result of Wt Off Józef Feruga's attack: "Sighted five miles off Boulogne. Opened fire from 150 yards dead astern.

Strikes all over and it exploded on the sea 15/20 miles north of Boulogne." Of his kill, Flt Lt Litak wrote: "Seen four miles south-east of Hawkhurst. Together with one Tempest, I opened fire from 300 yards dead astern. Strikes all over and it exploded on the ground two miles south of Goudhurst." Flt Lt Szymankiewicz scored his second of the day at 2255: "Seen 15 miles out to sea south-west of Dungeness. Attacked from 180/200 yards dead astern. Flame in tail increased in size and Diver exploded on the sea four miles south-west of Dungeness. Action photographed by a Spitfire."

322 (Dutch) Squadron (Spitfire XIV) West Malling

Flt Sgt H.C. Cramm	NH699/VL-R	V-1	2245	
	NH699/VL-R	V-1	2248	

Flt Sgt Hendrik Cramm scored a double, thereby raising his tally to four destroyed.

486 (RNZAF) Squadron (Tempest V) Newchurch

Flg Off J.R. Cullen RNZAF	JN873/SA-W	V-1	2145	Lydd area
	JN873/SA-W	V-1shared	2220	Bexhill area
Wt Off G.J.M. Hooper RNZAF	JN821/SA-H	V-1	2300	off Beachy Head
	JN821/SA-H	V-1	2310	off Hastings

Flg Off Cullen shared his second kill with two Tempests of 56 Squadron and a Spitfire from 312 Squadron.

610 Squadron (Spitfire XIV) Friston

Flt Sgt I.F. Håkansson (Swed)	RB153/DW-	V-1	0440	off Dungeness
	RB153/DW-	V-1	c0440 (KiA)	off Dungeness
Flt Lt J.B. Shepherd	DW-	V-1	2125-2255	

Flt Sgt Ingvar Fredrik Håkansson, a Swedish volunteer in the RAF, shot down two Divers but then called up to say his engine had cut. The Spitfire crashed into the sea off Dungeness. He baled out over the Channel but was not found by ASR.

FIU (Tempest V) Ford

Flt Lt J. Berry	EJ524/ZQ-Y	V-1	daytime
Flt Lt R.A. Jones	ZQ-	V-1	daytime

The Mustang IIIs of 129 Squadron, under the command of newly appointed Sqn Ldr Peter Thompson DFC, arrived at Brenzett during the day to participate in anti-Diver patrols. One of his pilots, Flg Off Freddie Holmes recalled:

"Our role was to fly two-hour patrols along the French coast between Calais and Le Touquet, an activity a lot less exciting than sitting in one's tent at Brenzett, which was partly within the inland AA zone. It rained shrapnel day and night for several hours at a time, as well as assorted bits of V-1 wreckage. I sometimes took a room at the County Hotel in Ashford to catch up on my sleep. Our duty roster was that each flight would cover from noon to noon, with the other flight resting, but not leaving the area. The Spitfire and Tempest squadrons (from other ALGs) covered the area between the balloons and the coastal gun zone, flying patrols of one hour or, in the case of the Tempest, 45 minutes. The guns were using proximity fuses for the first time and we gave them the credit for being, at last, almost as good as the German flak – but actually they were remarkably accurate, so much so that the Germans began to hold the Doodlebugs back until they could release about 40 at once and hope to saturate our defences. This made things very dull for the fighters most of the time, except that it gave the Mustangs the best of both worlds. We were still mainly flying the French coast patrols, but in addition we had two aircraft per squadron at cockpit readiness, at the end of the runways, to help cope with the new saturation tactic."[107]

Night 9/10 JULY

The first of 30 sorties undertaken by crews of III/KG3 at Rosières commenced at

2310, some crews flying second sorties. One of the Heinkels, 5K+BS of 8 Staffel flown by Uffz Gerhard Alisch, failed to return and was presumed shot down by Naval AA[108]. The final aircraft to return touched down at 0745. One Diver came down in Battersea (SW11) at the junction of Devereaux Road/Thurleigh Road at 0242, killing two residents and destroying eight houses. A further 20 were damaged. A few minutes later another fell in Clapham Road opposite Clapham Road Underground Station (SW9), killing four and destroying/damaging 26 properties. Norfolk received its first Diver, a wayward bomb that impacted at Southborough at 0313. There were no injuries.

25 Squadron (Mosquito XVII) Coltishall

Sqn Ldr W. Hoy	HK244/ZK-	V-1	2220-0135	

68 Squadron (Mosquito XVII) Castle Camps

Flg Off G. Wild	HK241/WM-	V-1	0300	Manston area
Plt Off M.N. Williams	HK242/WM-D	V-1	0445	off Manston

Flg Off Gilbert Wild was advised of an approaching flying bomb. He dived and caught up with it and opened fire just as it was crossing the coast at 2,000 feet. It crashed beside a block of houses near Manston airfield. Plt Off Michael Williams engaged a Diver at which was fired a short burst but no hits were seen. Another flying bomb was sighted about 40 miles east of Manston at 800 feet, its speed estimated at 400mph plus. Williams dived the Mosquito from 6,000 feet and gave two bursts but it drew away. He then dived below to gain speed, climbed up and gave another burst at extreme range. Strikes were seen, followed by a puff of smoke and an explosion. The missile then glided down into the sea.

96 Squadron (Mosquito XIII) Ford

Wt Off W.A. McLardy RAAF	HK396/ZJ-	V-1	0213	off Dungeness
Flt Lt N.S. Head	HK462/ZJ-	V-1	0445	Dungeness area

Wt Off Bill McLardy attacked a Diver from 1,500 feet down to 800 feet from astern. Strikes were seen and Diver exploded in the sea. Flt Lt Norman Head pursued his victim inland and shot it down about three miles from Dungeness, the Diver exploding on the ground.

219 Squadron (Mosquito XVII) Bradwell Bay

Flt Lt P.G.K. Williamson	MM690/FK-	V-1	0310	Manston-Broadstairs
	MM690/FK-	V-1	c0330	off North Foreland

Flt Lt Peter Williamson destroyed 219 Squadron's final two Divers to bring the unit's total to 20:

> "Was free-lancing in the Straits area [Flg Off Fred Forrest[109], navigator] and had two combats with Divers. The first at 2,000 feet. Opened fire from 600 feet, strikes and explosions seen, and target crashed on land. The second was further east at 3,000 feet. Opened fire from 1,000 feet, strikes seen and Diver nose-dived into sea 30 miles east of North Foreland."

409 (RCAF) Squadron (Mosquito XIII) Hunsdon

Wt Off D.J. MacDonald RCAF	MM523/KP-	V-1	0445	Channel

> "We patrolled off Goodwins at 7,000 feet and 20 miles out to sea sighted Diver proceeding from Dunkirk area at 2,000 feet. Dived to attack from dead astern with two short bursts. Flying bomb nosed over and went down vertically to crash into the sea, exploding on impact."

418 (RCAF) Squadron (Mosquito VI) Holmsley South

Sqn Ldr J.B. Kerr RCAF	HR183/TH-	V-1	0010	Channel

Flt Lt C.M. Jasper RCAF (US)	HR358/TH-K	V-1	0015	exploded in mid-air
Flg Off P.R. Brook RCAF	TH-	V-1	0123	Channel

First to score was Sqn Ldr Kerr: "At 0110 attacked Diver from 300 yards dead astern with five two-seconds bursts. Strikes seen and Diver exploded violently in the sea 35 miles north-west of Le Crotoy." The next fell to Flt Lt Jasper:

"At 0015 attacked Diver 15-20 miles south-east of Beachy Head with two-seconds burst from 200 yards, closing to 100 yards dead astern. The Diver exploded in mid-air and although we broke away, slight damage was done to our aircraft. At 0057 port engine failed so returned to Ford."

456 (RAAF) Squadron (Mosquito XVII) Ford

Flt Lt K.A. Roediger RAAF	HK297/RX-V	V-1	0115	Grid W.68

Flt Lt Keith Roediger scored the unit's first confirmed kill when he intercepted a Diver flying at 2,500 feet.

605 Squadron (Mosquito VI) Manston

Flt Lt A. Michie	UP-	V-1	night	Channel
Flt Lt J.G. Musgrave	MM429/UP-H	V-1	night	Channel
Flg Off J.C. Worthington RNZAF	UP-	V-1	night	Channel

854 Squadron FAA (Avenger I) Hawkinge

Sub Lt(A) D.P. Davies RNVR	JZ127/H	V-1	0510	off Dungeness

The Avenger flown by Sub Lt(A) D.P. Davies was operating from Hawkinge on an early morning anti-shipping patrol when a Diver was encountered over the Channel at 2,000 feet – this was shot down by his TAG L/Airman Fred Shirmer who destroyed it at range of 700 yards, firing only 20 rounds. (Shirmer was awarded a Mention in Despatches).

Monday 10 JULY

Two Divers fell on Crawley although one did not explode. The other however impacted on the junction of Oak Road/West Street, killing seven and injuring 44. Fourteen more were killed when a Diver exploded in Palace Square, Penge (SE20) at 1757, many properties also being destroyed or damaged. One person died following the impact of a Diver in Carver Road, Herne Hill (SE24) at 2100. Six houses were destroyed and 50 damaged. A Diver shot down by a fighter at 1445 crashed near Cherry Garden Farm, Harrietsham, slightly injuring one person. Eileen Saunders was a 24-year-old housewife and mother living in the East Sussex market town of Hailsham with a five-month-old daughter. Her husband was away serving in the Army and flying bomb events were a daily occurrence that had to be faced during the high summer of 1944. On one occasion she heard the sound of a V-1 approaching and looked anxiously southwards for its approach but couldn't see it. Suddenly, she realised it was heading from the north and turned to see it heading back to the Channel and towards France from whence it had come – escorted by an RAF fighter at each wingtip! What had caused this directional change, or the eventual outcome, is unknown as is the date upon which it happened, but it is safe to say that it was a welcome and rousing sight leading to a great deal of cheer in the beleagured towns and hamlets as it passed overhead. Less cheering, though, were the sometimes unfortunate results of fighter interceptions of the flying bombs and Eileen was witness to one with a tragic outcome.

"On 10 July I had been shopping in Hailsham, my daughter Pauline with me in her pram. It was a lovely summers day. Suddenly, I heard the horrid roar of engines and on looking towards the outskirts of the town I could see two machines – a fighter and a Doodlebug. I think the fighter was trying to tip the Doodlebug over, or perhaps shoot it down. Thankfully, he succeeded in destroying the horrid creature before it reached Hailsham – otherwise it might easily have hit the town centre. It roared to earth, but with a very sad ending. It fell into a farmyard at Mulbrooks Farm just to the south of Hailsham where it exploded, toppling a haystack under which two farm workers were sheltering. Both were killed – 26-year old Land Army girl Freda Goldsmith and 44-year-old farm labourer Richard Barnes, a member of the Home Guard.

"I shall never forget that day, although it was one of many events that were commonplace in those times."

1 Squadron (Spitfire LFIXb) Detling

Flt Sgt G. Tate	MK744/JX-	V-1	1450	Sevenoaks area
Flg Off T. Wyllie	MK867/JX-	V-1	1722	Crowborough area

Flt Sgt Godfrey Tate: "Intercepted Diver about five miles east of Tunbridge Wells. Attacked from astern at 400 yards, closing to 250 yards. Pieces fell off Diver, then it exploded in the air four miles north-east of Sevenoaks." Flg Off Wyllie reported:

"Intercepted Diver four miles west of Bexhill. After first attack Diver dropped wing and then recovered. After second attack it turned over and spun in. Strikes seen all round jet. Diver in and out of cloud whole time and fell in wood in Crowborough area."

150 Wing (Tempest V) Newchurch

Wg Cdr R.P. Beamont	JN751/RB	V-1		Ashford area

3 Squadron (Tempest V) Newchurch

Flg Off G.A. Whitman RCAF (US)	JN760/JF-R	V-1 shared	1545-1645	
Plt Off S.B. Feldman (US)	EJ582/JF-T			
Flg Off R.E. Barckley	JN817/JF-H	V-1	1630-1740	
	JN817/JF-H	V-1	1630-1740	
Flt Lt R. van Lierde (Belg)	JN862/JF-Z	V-1	2105-2210	

The American pair Flg Off Lefty Whitman and Plt Off Buck Feldman shared their kill with an aircraft from another squadron.

56 Squadron (Tempest V) Newchurch

Flt Sgt H. Shaw	EJ532/US-H	V-1		1105 Pevensey Bay area

"Sighted a Diver ten miles south of Pevensey at 3,000 feet. I closed to 100 yards and fired several bursts, allowing slight deflection from starboard and above. The Diver glided down and exploded on the ground about eight miles north of Pevensey – in a chicken run."

91 Squadron (Spitfire XIV) Deanland ALG

Lt H.F. de Bordas (FF)	RB181/DL-W	V-1	0141	
Flg Off G. Balcombe	NH705/DL-P	V-1	1440	off Beachy Head
Sqn Ldr N.A. Kynaston	NH714/RW-O	V-1	1450	Tunbridge Wells
Flt Sgt T.B. Burnett	RB181/DL-W	V-1	1630	Sevenoaks area
Flg Off E. Topham	NH698/DL-Y	V-1	1920	Wittersham area
Flg Off M.J. Costello RNZAF	RB161/DL-I	V-1	1922	Maidstone area
Sqn Ldr N.A. Kynaston	RB185/DL-	V-1	2049	Hailsham area

129 Squadron (Mustang III) Brenzett

Flt Lt J.P. Bassett	FB222/DV-W	V-1	2015	Hythe area
Flt Lt K.C. Baker RCAF	FB121/DV-V			

Seven anti-Diver patrols were carried out but only one bomb was destroyed, falling to the guns of Flt Lts Bertie Bassett and Kelts Baker, a Canadian[110]. It was intercepted ten miles south-east of Folkestone at 2,000 feet. Baker fired two long bursts, and Bassett several short ones from astern, the Diver eventually impacting close to Hythe, where five people were injured on the ground.

306 (Polish) Squadron (Mustang III) Brenzett

Flt Sgt S. Rudowski PAF	HB871/UZ-E	V-1	1425	Kenley area

Flt Sgt Stanislaw Rudowski opened the scoring for 306 Squadron when his victim crashed south of Kenley.

322 (Dutch) Squadron (Spitfire XIV) West Malling

Flt Lt J.L. Plesman	VL-W	V-1	0020
Flt Lt L.C.M. van Eendenburg	RB184/VL-B	V-1	1440

610 Squadron (Spitfire XIV) Friston

Plt Off B.R. Scamen RCAF	DW-	V-1	1610-1720
Flt Sgt M.P. Harding	DW-	V-1	2140-2255

Plt Off Brian Scamen tipped the Diver with his wingtip after using all his ammunition.

316 Squadron transferred to Friston ALG from West Malling.

Night 10/11 JULY

Acting on false information provided by a double agent, *Flakregiment 155 (W)* was ordered to target Southampton and a total of 22 Divers were plotted approaching the major south coast port, of which ten were brought down by night fighters and AA fire. Impacts were reported at Beaulieu and Brockenhurst in the New Forest while others fell around but not in the city. If ever the folk of the Isle of Wight were fortunate during these nerve-wracking nights, it was on this night, as intimated by observer Jock Leal at Mount Joy:

> "Between the first ROC alarm at 12.24am and the siren's final 'all clear' at 6.07am, no fewer than 22 flying bombs approached or crossed the coast. The first three came in across Sandown, buzzed away over Newport – one of them practically above the Mount Joy post – and crashed respectively off Calshot, in Beaulieu River and near the big Beaulieu airfield. A little more fuel and the two that followed them might have done tremendous damage here – but they just failed to reach the coast. One went down into the sea off Luccombe; the other did the same off Lake. Three more roared in north of the island. The first went into the sea off Bembridge, the others into Spithead off Ryde. Twelve others found mainland targets during that hectic night – at least five hit the Eastleigh district – but the island's luck held even when, just as sirens were sounding a premature 'all clear' at 5.20am, two Divers roared in across Sandown Bay. Over Newport they came, and a moment later one of them started that ominous splutter. Cowes lay beneath – but the deadly craft crashed into the sea just off the town. Its companion, taking a more north-westerly course, actually hit the island. Fortunately its landing place was Newtown Creek."[111]

Meanwhile, II/KG3 launched a further eight from over the North Sea aimed at London, of which four reached their destination.

96 Squadron (Mosquito XIII) Ford

Sqn Ldr A. Parker-Rees	MM562/ZJ-	V-1	2311	off Wrotham
Flt Lt D.L. Ward	MM579/ZJ-	V-1	2346	off Wrotham
	MM579/ZJ-	V-1	2355	off Wrotham
Flt Lt R.V. Bray	MM459/ZJ-	V-1	0025	exploded in mid-air

Wg Cdr E.D. Crew	MM511/ZJ-	V-1	0225	exploded in mid-air

Sqn Ldr Parker-Rees reported intercepting a Diver approaching Wrotham and attacked from dead astern, opening fire at 1,000 feet. The Diver caught fire and dived into the sea. Flt Lt Don Ward scored a double in quick succession, both of his victims falling into the sea off Wrotham. Flg Off James Black reported that his aircraft was shadowed by what appeared to be a FW190 during his 0035-0400 patrol, but he was able to shake off the pursuer after three tight orbits. It seems probable that the shadower was a Tempest rather than a FW190. Wt Off G. Stephens' Mosquito MM495 suffered an engine failure during his patrol but was able to return safely at 0405 on one engine and landed on one wheel. The aircraft was written off in the resultant crash-landing though Stephens and his navigator (Flg Off G. Bradshaw) were unhurt.

264 Squadron (Mosquito XIII) Hartford Bridge

Flt Lt K.G. Rayment	HK514/PS-	V-1	0155-0525	Portsmouth area

On the way to carry out an intruder mission over France, Flt Lt Ken Rayment DFC[112] encountered a Diver ten miles north of Portsmouth: "I closed to 4,000 feet range and opened fire with a half-second burst. The Diver immediately dipped from 7,000 feet and disappeared. There was an explosion in cloud below as it blew up approximately eight miles south of Alton."

409 (RCAF) Squadron (Mosquito XIII) West Malling

Flg Off R. Lee RCAF	MM547/KP-	V-1	2245 (FTR)	off Folkestone

It was believed that Flg Off Bob Lee RCAF (from Quebec) and Flt Sgt Jack Wales RAF were lost when the Diver they were attacking blew up, their aircraft crashing into the sea south of Folkestone.

456 (RAAF) Squadron (Mosquito XVII) Ford

Flt Lt R.G. Houston RAAF	HK264/RX-T	V-1	0110	Grid Q.2575

Flt Lt George Houston scored his first confirmed kill following his interception of a Diver travelling at 300mph over the Channel: "It was flying at 2,000 feet and I approached from dead astern in a dive into a range of 200 feet. I fired 154 rounds and the Diver exploded in the sea."

Tuesday 11 JULY

Deptford Dockyard (SE8) received its second Diver in three days at 1215, workshops and a jetty being demolished, five cranes sustaining severe damage and 11 workers being killed. At 1228, a Diver came down in Hawke Road/Alexandra Drive area of Gipsy Hill (SE19), killing three and causing much damage. West Wickham High Street (BR4) was hit at 1752, the explosion killing one and injuring 20. A bus careered into the pond by the White Hart pub, which was also damaged. Lordship Lane/Court Lane in East Dulwich (SE22) received a second Diver at 1759, this scoring a direct hit on the Fire Station, killing one person. At almost the same time another impacted in Marion Road, Thornton Heath (CR7) killing five and demolishing a dozen houses. Another fell in Annerley Road, Crystal Palace (SE20) at 1809, close to the previous day's explosion when 14 were killed. A further 11 died in this incident that wrecked 18 shops, and severely damaged 15 other properties including the Paxton Arms pub. Four more were killed when a Diver exploded in Sisters Avenue, Clapham (SW11) at 1938; some 20-odd houses were destroyed or damaged. Elsewhere, a second Diver kill was claimed by the gunners of the 8th Canadian LAA Regiment based at Heathfield in Sussex, but this was also to be their last. The victim of a fighter crashed at Plaxtol near Maidstone at 1750, causing damage to the local telephone exchange, but no casualties.

1 Squadron (Spitfire LFIXb) Detling

Flt Sgt I. Hastings	NH466/JX-	V-1 shared	2050	exploded in mid-air
Flt Sgt G. Tate	NH246/JX-	V-1	2050	Hastings area
Flg Off F.W. Town	MK726/JX-	V-1	2105	Rye area

Flt Sgt Iain Hastings: "Chased Diver to Dunsford airfield. Saw strikes and light from jet went out. Diver crashed near Godalming." Of his second kill of the day, he reported: "Fired burst of two seconds. On second burst, while still firing, a [Spitfire] XIV came in front from one o'clock above. Pushed nose down to save hitting XIV. Saw strikes on port wing. While XIV was still firing, the Diver blew up and both of us flew through it." Flt Sgt Godfrey Tate: "Gave burst when four miles north of Hastings. Smoke streamed out of jet and Diver crashed in woods ten miles north of Hastings." Flg Off Freddie Town: "Saw strikes on jet. Diver climbed to cloud about 3,000 feet and rolled over back, then spiralled into the ground seven miles north of Rye."

150 Wing (Tempest V) Newchurch

Wg Cdr R.P. Beamont	JN751/RB	V-1		Hastings area

3 Squadron (Tempest V) Newchurch

Flt Lt R. van Lierde (Belg)	JN862/JF-	V-1	0435-0600
	JN862.JF-	V-1	1230-1325
Flt Lt A.E. Umbers RNZAF	JN817/JF-	V-1	1645-1815
Flt Sgt T.A. McCulloch	JN822/JF-	V-1	1730-1820
Plt Off H.R. Wingate ⎤	EN521/JF-	V-1	1830
Flt Sgt D.J. Mackerras RAAF ⎦	JN868/JF-		

56 Squadron (Tempest V) Newchurch

Flt Lt T.H. Hoare RCAF	JN869/US-D	V-1	1745	Tunbridge Wells area

"Sighted Diver ten miles south of Bexhill at 3,200 feet. I gave several long bursts from 400 yards and another from 700 yards, when the Diver pulled up vertically, stalled and went down, exploding on the ground at R.0555."

91 Squadron (Spitfire XIV) Deanland ALG

Sqn Ldr P.McC. Bond ⎤	RM621/DL-	V-1	0925	Sevenoaks area
Flg Off J. Monihan ⎦	RM620/DL-E			
Sqn Ldr N.A. Kynaston	RB185/DL-	V-1	1547	exploded in mid-air
Lt H.F. de Bordas (FF)	NH720/DL-H	V-1	1748	Ashford area
Sqn Ldr N.A. Kynaston	RB185/DL-	V-1	1940	Ashford area
Flt Lt A.R. Cruickshank RCAF	RB182/DL-V	V-1	2056	exploded in mid-air
	RB182/DL-V	V-1	2058	Tenterden area

Although Sqn Ldr Bond and Flg Off Monihan submitted a claim for one destroyed, their claim was not officially allowed. They reported inflicting damage during their joint attacks from 600 yards to 400 yards, but they were unable to follow up due to the proximity of balloons, though the Diver was seen to explode on the ground. This was possibly the missile that impacted at Borden Farm near Headcorn. Sqn Ldr

Norman Kynaston was more successful: "Saw Diver over Ashford approaching from Folkestone. Attacked from astern at 200 yards range, slowing it down, and after a further burst it exploded in the air." It is believed that the wreckage fell at Thurnham, where a serviceman was slightly injured. Lt Henri de Bordas shot down his target five miles east of Ashford, while Sqn Ldr Kynaston knocked down his second of the day four miles north-west of Ashford. Flt Lt Ray Cruickshank scored his kills in quick succession, the first over Tenterden and the second two minutes later five miles north-west of the town:

> "Saw Diver ten miles south-east of Tenterden and attacked from dead astern at 100 yards range. Short burst exploded Diver in the air, a piece of it doing damage to my aircraft. Saw second Diver three miles south-east of Tenterden being fired at by a Thunderbolt [P-47] with unobserved results. Attacked from above and astern and exploded fuel tank, the warhead exploding on the ground."

129 Squadron (Mustang III) Brenzett

Flg Off F.H. Holmes	FB292/DV-N	V-1	1200	Hastings area
Flg Off J.E. Hartley	FZ130/DV-D	V-1	2115	exploded in mid-air

Flg Off Freddie Holmes caught his victim at midday over Hastings. Closing in from astern, he saw strikes following which the port wing dropped and it crashed to ground. Despite the squadron flying 14 patrols, the next Diver was not engaged until the evening, Flg Off Jim Hartley exploding his target in the air following a short burst from 500 yards.

165 Squadron (Spitfire IX) Detling

Flt Lt J.K. Porteous RNZAF	MK418/SK-G	V-1	1935	Bexhill area
Plt Off A. Scott	MK831/SK-X	V-1	1945	Bexhill area
Flt Sgt G.S. Cameron ⎫	MK854/SK-H	V-1 shared	1945	Rotherfield area
Flt Sgt L. Wright ⎭	MK638/SK-B			

Plt Off Scott scored his second kill in the Bexhill area: "On third attack strikes seen on mainplane. On fourth attack the Diver exploded in the air." Flt Sgts Cameron and Wright shared with two others: "Intercepted five miles north of Bexhill. We both attacked, obtained strikes and saw pieces fall off. After the last attack [by Wright], the Diver spun and exploded on the ground six miles south-east of Rotherfield in a field on the edge of a wood."

306 (Polish) Squadron (Mustang III) Brenzett

Flt Lt J. Siekierski PAF	FB241/UZ-Z	V-1	2000	Grid R.5355

Flt Lt Jan Siekierski intercepted a Diver five miles south-east of Hythe at 1,500 feet. He attacked from astern and fired one long burst, whereupon the Diver spun into the ground five miles south-east of Hythe, where it exploded. Wg Cdr Stanislaw Skalski DFC, OC 133 (Polish) Wing flew his first and only anti-Diver patrol (in FZ315/SS), albeit without any sightings of flying bombs. This was also his last operational flight before handing over command of 133 (Polish) Wing to Wg Cdr Jan Zumbach DFC the following day.

315 (Polish) Squadron (Mustang III) Brenzett

Flt Sgt T. Jankowski PAF	FZ169/PK-R	V-1	1315	Baldslow area
Plt Off G. Świstuń PAF	FX894/PK-Y	V-1	2050	
Flg Off B. Nowosielski PAF	PK-V	V-1	2100	Rye area

Flt Sgt Tadeusz Jankowski opened the scoring for 315 Squadron when he shot down his victim over Hastings at 1315; it crashed and exploded on the ground south of Baldslow.

322 (Dutch) Squadron (Spitfire XIV) West Malling

Flg Off L.M. Meijers	VL-H	V-1	0917	Grid R.2564
Flg Off M.A. Muller	VL-T	V-1	1430	Bexhill area
Flg Off C.R.R. Manders	VL-V	V-1	2055	Grid R.3545
Flg Off F.J.H. van Eijk	VL-U	V-1	2058	exploded in mid-air
Wt Off J.A. Maier	NH686/VL-M	V-1	2103	Grid R.3543

Another successful day for the Dutch pilots saw Flg Off Loekie Meijers open the scoring in the morning: "Patrolling Dymchurch. Vectored on Diver. Intercepted and attacked quarter port to line astern, range 600 yards closing to 300. Saw strikes on starboard wing, which broke off. Diver crashed and exploded." The next fell to Flg Off Martin Muller shortly after lunchtime:

> "Told to go to Bexhill, where Diver was crossing to west. Attacked line astern, 400 yards, and saw strikes on wing roots. Diver crashed and exploded in wood north-west of Bexhill."

486 (RNZAF) Squadron (Tempest V) Newchurch

Plt Off B.M. Hall RNZAF	JN805/SA-E	V-1 shared	1300	Tonbridge area
Wt Off B.J. O'Connor RNZAF	JN767/SA-B	V-1	1740	Ewell area
Plt Off R.J. Danzey RNZAF	JN821/SA-H	V-1 shared	1750	Tonbridge area
Flt Lt J.H. McCaw RNZAF	EN523/SA-X	V-1	1919	Bexhill area
Flg Off R.J. Cammock RNZAF	JN803/SA-D	V-1	1935	Bexhill area

610 Squadron (Spitfire XIV) Friston

Flt Lt B.M. Madden RNZAF ⎫	DW-	V-1	0950-1020	
Flg Off A. Cresswell-Turner ⎭	DW-			
Sqn Ldr R.A. Newbery	RB159/DW-D	V-1	1000-1025	
	RB159/DW-D	V-1	1000-1025	
Flt Sgt J.N. Philpott	DW-	V-1	1400-1445	

New Zealander Flt Lt Brian Madden and Flg Off Tubby Cresswell-Turner jointly attacked the flying bomb and exhausted their ammunition, so Madden flew alongside the bomb and tried to tip it with his wing. Twice the bomb righted itself but his persistence was finally rewarded when it turned over and dived into a wood, where it exploded. Flt Sgt John Philpot opened his account during an afternoon patrol.

41 Squadron moved its Spitfire XIIs to Lympne from Friston. Shortly after its arrival at the new base a Diver appeared over the airfield and was promptly shot down by the airfield defences. The unit's diarist recorded that the score of V-1s destroyed had by now reached 21 but this figure is believed inaccurate, and that the total was actually 17 plus three shared with other squadrons, plus one credited only as a probable. Next day 1 Squadron moved to Lympne from Detling, as did **165 Squadron**.

Night 11/12 JULY

Shortly before midnight 18 Heinkels from III/KG3 set out from Rosières to release their missiles against Southampton. All were back by 0645. Fourteen of the Divers were plotted approaching the city, two falling to coastal guns. Only one caused casualties, nine people being injured at Bitterne in Southampton, the others falling outside the city boundaries. It turned out to be a bad night for the Mosquitos, one failing to return and another suffering damage from the explosion of its target. Isle of Wighters witnessed another night of trauma as more Divers scurried across the island, as recorded by Jock Leal:

> "Eleven more Doodlebugs enlivened the night, but again the island was unscathed. Several came along our coasts on the way to the mainland; one crashed in the sea off Niton and another

west of Calshot, and two came directly over the island. The first crossed Shanklin, and then passed Newport and Parkhurst Forest on its way to land in the Beaulieu area. We spotted the second just east of Ventnor radar pylons as dawn was breaking, and as it came in near the Mount Joy post we had a close-up view of the monster. It roared over Newport like an express train – a train which, luckily for the town, was non-stop. On it went across the Solent. We heard a violent explosion, and through our binoculars saw the trees of the New Forest silhouetted in the glare. It had landed somewhere near Brockenhurst. That night illustrated the value of the spotters' work. Sirens had kept a five-hour public warning but, because we could give a quick alarm when danger really threatened, the men and women on vital war work at Cowes had spent less than two hours in the shelters."[113]

25 Squadron (Mosquito XVII) Coltishall

| Flt Sgt G.T. Glossop | HK305/ZK- | V-1 | 0220-0015 | exploded in mid-air |

Following a one-second burst the Diver exploded in mid-air, damaging the Mosquito, which landed at Manston with starboard engine u/s.

456 (RAAF) Squadron (Mosquito) Ford

Mosquito HK312/RX-G crewed by Flg Off Ted Radford RAAF, a 21-year-old from Western Australia, and Flt Sgt Wally Atkinson RAAF (from NSW) FTR from anti-Diver patrol. The navigator's body was recovered from the sea eight miles south of Littlehampton, and interred in Brookwood Military Cemetery.

Wednesday 12 JULY

At 0857, a Diver scored a direct hit on 'Beechmont', a large rambling house near Sevenoaks, which was in use as a billet for ATS girls maintaining army vehicles stored in nearby Knole Park. Fortunately, most had already left for work when the bomb struck, but nonetheless two girls were killed and 44 injured. A minute later one person was killed in West Wickham (BR4) when a bomb impacted in The Grove, causing much damage. The SS *Tristram* moored in Greenland Dock, Rotherhithe (SE16) was further damaged when a Diver exploded at 1524, having previously suffered a hit on 23 June. The SS *Peebles* nearby was also damaged and six dock workers killed. Beckenham (BR3) received its second fatal bomb of the day, this exploding in Elmers Road at 1914. Considering 24 shops and 230 houses were damaged, some seriously, the fatalities could have been much heavier. Many houses were destroyed or damaged in Grange Road, Thornton Heath (CR7) at 2118, eight residents losing the lives. Elsewhere, Warden Carter on duty in the Waltham Abbey area, part witnessed a fighter kill:

"I could hear all sorts of planes and aero engines, and thought they seemed to be in the vicinity. Then I saw one of our fighters go haring across the sky low down in a south-westerly direction and thought it possible he was after something. However, while I watched him most intently, there came, to my astonishment, the usual 'crump' of an explosion to the north, behind me! Saw the dark column of smoke going up, and located it at Galley Hill. Only damage to nearby nurseries and bungalows, but no casualties."

3 Squadron (Tempest V) Newchurch

Flt Sgt R.W. Pottinger	EJ540/JF-P	V-1 shared	0435-0545
Flg Off M.F. Edwards	EJ582/JF-T	V-1 shared	0630-0745
Flt Sgt D.J. Mackerras RAAF	JN868/JF-F	V-1 shared	1205-1310
Flg Off R.H. Clapperton	JN817/JF-H	V-1	1325-1450
	JN817/JF-H	V-1	1325-1450
Flt Sgt R.W. Cole	JN822/JF-	V-1	1325-1450
Flt Lt R. van Lierde (Belg)	JN862/JF-Z	V-1	1430-1535
Flt Sgt C.W. Orwin	JN735/JF-X	V-1	1430-1545

Flt Sgt J.W. Foster	EJ582/JF-T	V-1	1600-1645	
Sqn Ldr A.S. Dredge	JN812/JF-M	V-1	1720-1800	
Flt Sgt R.W. Cole	JN822/JF-	V-1 shared	1735-1850	
Flt Lt R. van Lierde (Belg)	JN862/JF-Z	V-1	1745-1855	
Flt Sgt J.W. Foster	EJ582/JF-T	V-1	1845-1930	
Flt Sgt D.M. Smith	JN761/JF-U	V-1 shared	1845-1930	
Plt Off K.G. Slade-Betts	JN755/JF-D	V-1	1845-1940	
Flt Lt A.R. Moore	JN818/JF-	V-1	1845-1935	
	JN822/JF-	V-1	1845-1935	
Flt Lt R. van Lierde (Belg)	JN793/JF-N	V-1	2200-2325	
	JN793/JF-N	V-1 shared	2200-2325	
Flt Lt A.R. Moore	JN818/JF-	V-1	2200-2330	

3 Squadron pilots enjoyed another successful day, shooting down 20 Divers of which six were shared with other squadrons. The first fell at dawn and the final shortly before midnight, Flt Lt Moore getting three, Flt Lt Remi van Lierde three and one shared, with doubles being scored by Flg Off Ray Clapperton and Flt Sgt John Foster.

41 Squadron (Spitfire XII) Lympne

| Flt Sgt P.W. Chattin | EN602/EB- | V-1 | 0840 | Ashford area |

Following his earlier experience, Flt Sgt Peter Chattin was understandably a little more cautious when engaging his second flying bomb and succeeded in shooting it down north-west of Ashford.

56 Squadron (Tempest V) Newchurch

Flt Sgt J. Langley ⎫	EJ543/US-U	V-1	0722	East Grinstead
Flt Sgt J.A. Bosley ⎭	JN877/US-M			area
Flt Lt J.H. Ryan RCAF	EJ532/US-H	V-1	1645	exploded in mid-air
Plt Off D.E. Ness RCAF	EJ522/US-F	V-1	1745	Winchelsea area
Sgt G.H. Wylde	EJ526/US-N	V-1	1815	Tonbridge area
Flt Sgt H. Shaw	EJ548/US-G	V-1	1905	Tonbridge area
Flt Lt D.V.G Cotes-Preedy	JN864/US-C	V-1 shared	2117	Staplehurst area

Flt Sgts Langley and Bosley opened the scoring when they sighted a Diver south of East Grinstead at 4,000 feet. They fired deflection bursts from 200-300 yards and the Diver caught fire, gliding down and exploding in the middle of East Grinstead (London Road) where three elderly men were killed and 41 others injured. Up to 400 properties were damaged including a number of shops that were totally destroyed. Within hours of this incident, the King and Queen visited the town and met emergency service workers[114]. The local paper – the *East Grinstead Courier* – reported:

> *"The robot had been shot down and diverted by a fighter who was attempting to bring it down in open country, and he was afterwards so distressed that he drove specially into East Grinstead to apologise for any damage that had been caused."*

Flt Lt John Ryan's victim exploded in mid-air just west of Crowborough: "Sighted Diver north-west of Eastbourne at 3,500 feet. Closed to 75 yards and fired a long burst from dead astern, the Diver exploding." Fellow Canadian Plt Off David Ness got another: "Sighted a Diver south of Winchelsea at 2,700 feet. Fired from 150 yards astern and Diver went down, exploding in a wood."

At 1815, Sgt Geoffrey Wylde shot down the next: "Sighted Diver four miles south of Rye at 3,500 feet. Fired two short bursts from 100 yards astern. The Diver rolled over and went down, exploding on the ground four-five miles west of Rye." Flt Sgt

Artie Shaw increased his score with a kill that fell north-west of Tonbridge: "Sighted a Diver one mile south of Rye at 3,000 feet. Fired short bursts from 100 yards dead astern and the Diver went down, exploding on the ground." Although Flt Lt Digby Cotes-Preedy believed he had shared his kill with a Spitfire, it would seem that it was a Tempest flown by Flt Lt Tanner of 486 (RNZAF) Squadron:

> "Sighted a Diver over Dungeness at 2,600 feet. Fired two-seconds burst from 200 yards dead astern. Strikes were seen and flames from the side of the jet. The Diver slowed to 240mph, losing height, when a Spitfire dived from above and astern, scoring strikes. The Diver crashed, exploding on the ground in the Staplehurst area."

The day's successes were marred, however, by the loss of Flt Lt John Mansfield's aircraft (EJ559/US-L), which was hit by AA while he was chasing a Diver. He force-landed at Ripe near Eastbourne and was seriously injured.

91 Squadron (Spitfire XIV) Deanland ALG

Flg Off J.A. Faulkner RCAF	RB173/DL-	V-1	0715	off Dungeness
Flt Lt J.W.P. Draper RCAF	RM621/DL-	V-1	0830	exploded in mid-air

Canadian Flg Off John Faulkner: "Saw Diver five miles off Dungeness and attacked from quarter astern at 150 yards. Diver exploded on hitting the sea." Fellow Canadian Flt Lt Bill Draper reported "Sighted Diver over the sea south of Dymchurch. Attacked from astern, 100 yards range, and Diver exploded in the air."

129 Squadron (Mustang III) Brenzett

Plt Off E.W. Edwards	FZ143/DV-P	V-1	0849	Dungeness area
Flt Lt R.G. Kleimeyer RNZAF (Aus)	FZ172/DV-A	V-1	0920	Beachy Head area
Flg Off F.H. Holmes	FB222/DV-W	V-1	1510-1725	Folkestone area
Flg Off D.F. Ruchwaldy	FB112/DV-R	V-1	1510-1725	Lydd area
	FB112/DV-R	V-1	1510-1725	Lympne area
Flt Lt K.C. Baker RCAF	FB389/DV-J	V-1	1650-1825	Tunbridge Wells area
Wt Off E. Redhead ⎞ Plt Off J.L.W. Bilodeau RCAF ⎦	FB292/DV-N FB171/DV-S	V-1	1815-2005	off Hastings

For the 26 anti-Diver sorties flown, a return of seven destroyed was rewarding and a great morale-booster for 129. Plt Off Eddie Edwards opened the scoring when he intercepted his target seven-ten miles north of Beachy Head. He fired a long burst from dead astern at 300 yards, at which flame spurted some 40 feet from the jet unit before the Diver crashed and exploded on the ground near Dungeness. The next fell to Australian-born Flt Lt Dutch Kleimeyer[115], who intercepted it one mile north of Beachy Head. He attacked dead astern from 250 yards. A large panel was seen to drop off the Diver, which then entered cloud, but his No.2 (Flt Lt Conroy RAAF) saw it explode on the ground 15 miles north of Beachy Head.

The early afternoon patrol proved to be particularly successful, Flt Lt Des Ruchwaldy DFC[116] destroying two Divers and his No.2 Flg Off Freddie Holmes one, who got the first of the three. Intercepted over Folkestone at 2,000 feet, he attacked from dead astern from 200 down to 100 yards range, his cannon fire cutting off one wingtip. The Diver exploded on the ground five miles north-west of Folkestone. Ruchwaldy engaged his first near Lydd at 3,000 feet, and attacked from dead astern at 250 yards. Diver turned to starboard, dived and exploded on the ground. A few minutes later he sighted another, over Lympne, shooting this down also.

On the next patrol Flt Lt Kelts Baker intercepted his target 15 miles north-west of

Hastings at 2,000 feet, and attacked from dead astern from 600-300 yards. The Diver switch-backed before crashing and exploding one mile north-north-west of Tunbridge Wells. The seventh Diver fell to the combined efforts of Wt Off Eric Redhead and Plt Off John Bilodeau, who intercepted about 15 miles south-east of Hastings. Following their attack the Diver fell away to port and ultimately crashed in the sea about ten miles from the coast.

137 Squadron (Typhoon Ib) Manston

Plt Offs Jack Frost and Ken Brain chased a flying bomb during their 2020-2155 patrol but it was finally shot down by another aircraft some 15 miles inland from Dungeness.

306 (Polish) Squadron (Mustang III) Brenzett

Flt Sgt W. Nowoczyn PAF	FB106/UZ-V	V-1 shared	1740	Ashford area
	FB106/UZ-V	V-1 shared	1815	Tunbridge Wells area
Flg Off A. Beyer PAF	UZ-Y	V-1 shared	1845	Rye area

Flt Sgt Witold Nowoczyn was off at 1655 and intercepted a Diver two miles north of Folkestone at 2,500 feet. He attacked from slightly to starboard from 300 yards and gained strikes, the jet unit giving off clouds of smoke. It rapidly lost speed and when going down a Spitfire (possibly from 322 Squadron) opened fire on it, following which it exploded on the ground near Ashford. Nowoczyn soon came across another Diver six miles north of Hastings, flying at 2,000 feet. He attacked from dead astern at 300/200 yards range. Strikes were seen and the Diver turned to port, losing speed. A Tempest then joined in and opened fire. The Diver exploded on impact north of Tunbridge Wells. The third Diver fell to Flg Off Andrzej Beyer, who intercepted his target west of Rye, flying at 350mph. He attacked from dead astern and the missile went into a flat spin, crashing on the ground. Beyer reported that a Tempest was attacking at the same time but as it was some 300 yards behind him, he considered it unlikely that any hits were achieved. However, the Tempest pilot was credited with a share. Fate dealt a tragic twist for Flt Lt Zygmunt Jelinski, who had flown a couple of anti-Diver patrols during the past two days and was now on a 48-hour pass to see his wife and daughter who lived at Heston in Middlesex. A Diver scored a direct hit on their house, killing Mrs Jelinski and critically injuring his young daughter, who died shortly after. Flt Lt Jelinski was badly injured.

315 (Polish) Squadron (Mustang III) Brenzett

Flt Lt J. Zbrozek PAF	FZ128/PK-X	V-1	1550	Hythe area
Plt Off G. Świstuń PAF	FB174/PK-S	V-1	1700	Hythe area
	FB174/PK-S	V-1	1705	Hythe area

Flt Lt Jerzy Zbrozek reported: "I spotted it three miles south-east of Folkestone and fired on it from a distance of 250 yards. It crashed and exploded three miles north of Hythe." Just over an hour later, Plt Off Gwido Świstuń shot down two flying bombs in quick succession to raise his score to three in two days.

316 (Polish) Squadron (Mustang III) Friston

Flt Sgt A. Pietrzak PAF	FB378/SZ-X	V-1	0705	Appledore area
	FB378/SZ-X	V-1	0742	exploded in mid-air
Wt Off F. Marek PAF	FB383/SZ-J	V-1	0745	Ashford area
Sgt J. Mielnicki PAF	FB391/SZ-E	V-1	1645	Tunbridge Wells area
	FB391/SZ-E	V-1	1650	Reigate area
Wt Off T. Szymański PAF	FB351/SZ-B	V-1	1640	Hastings area
	FB351/SZ-B	V-1	1700	Crowborough area

Sgt Alexandr Pietrzak sighted the first Diver crossing the coast at Dungeness: "Attacked from 200 yards dead astern, closing to 100 yards, Strikes all over and Diver exploded on the ground two miles north-west of Appledore." The blast of his victim exploding severely damaged his aircraft and he was obliged to bale out, landing safely. He reported: "The first burst slowed it down and after the second burst it exploded in the air and damaged the propeller and left side of my aircraft." Sqn Ldr Arct went into greater detail:

"Sgt Pietrzak, in the heat of fighting, closed in to 100 yards and opened accurate fire. He must have hit the fuses, as the bomb exploded in the air. The blast was so powerful that the Mustang lost its propeller and the wings bent to a most peculiar shape. The aircraft went out of control. Fortunately, Pietrzak, a stocky, well-built fellow possessed very quick reflexes. His misfortune happened at 800 metres, he lost quite a lot of precious height and at the last moment got out to save his life. Conclusions were drawn, and we introduced the rule forbidding opening fire from less than 200 yards. This distance could easily be judged both in daytime and at night. When a fighter approached a bomb from behind, which was the usual way of attacking, and when he could see the red-hot ring of the jet engine's exhaust nozzle, it meant the distance was right to open fire. On the other hand, firing from more than 300 metres was rather useless as the V-1 was much smaller than the normal fighter plane and it was easy to miss it from a big distance."

Wt Off Marek's kill was straightforward: "Diver seen crossing coast over Folkestone. Attacked from 200 yards dead astern. Strikes all over and exploded on ground one mile north-west of Ashford." Sgt Mielnicki brought down two within the space of five minutes:

"First seen eight miles north of Hailsham. Attacked from 400 yards dead astern, closing to 300 yards. Strikes all over and Diver exploded on the ground five miles west of Tunbridge Wells. Second seen in same area. Opened fire at 600 yards dead astern in short bursts, closing to 100 yards. Jet unit stopped and Diver exploded on the western outskirts of Reigate."

Wt Off Tadeusz Szymański also brought down two Divers, shooting down the first at 1640: "Attacked east of Beachy Head from 400 yards dead astern. Strikes all over and it exploded in woods approximately 20 miles north." The second caused a few problems:

"I started shooting and saw strikes before my ammunition was finished, but the bomb kept on a dead-level course. Over the town of Hastings I moved into close formation to get a close look at it. The thing was jerking along and the elevator was flapping with each vibration of the crude jet motor. I noticed there were no ailerons and on the front of the bomb was a silly little propeller. It looked ridiculous. We didn't know at the time but this was the aiming device set to dive the bomb into the ground after so many miles. I decided to try and tip the Doodlebug up with my wingtip. As soon as I put my port wing under the Doodlebug's wing, it started lifting and I banked to starboard. I repeated this manoeuvre eleven times but each time it went over so far and then came back. By now the barrage balloons protecting London were in sight and I was becoming rather anxious. I tried a different manoeuvre, hitting it very hard with my wingtip as I went up into a loop. When I recovered my position I found, to my dismay, that the Doodlebug was flying perfectly safe and level – but upside down! Suddenly it dived out of control and crashed in open countryside."

322 (Dutch) Squadron (Spitfire XIV) West Malling

Flg Off C.R.R. Manders	VL-V	V-1	0855	Maidstone area
Flt Sgt M.J. Janssen	VL-E	V-1	1515	Grid R.3968
	VL-E	V-1	1730	River Medway
Flg Off J. Vlug	RB160/VL-A	V-1	1749	Sissinghurst area
Flg Off J. Jongbloed	NH586/VL-G	V-1	2110	Cranbrook area
Wt Off J.A. Maier ⎫ Unknown US P-51 ⎭	RM678/VL-Q	V-1	2110 (killed)	Dungeness area

Flg Off Coen Manders shot down his victim 12 miles east of Maidstone, while Flt Sgt Janssen got his first as it approached Ashford; his second crashed into the River Medway, north of Upchurch. Of his kill, Flg Off Johannes Vlug reported: "Attacked Diver north-west of Rye and it slowed down. Tempest then attacked and broke away. Diver still flying so I attacked from 150 yards. It climbed, rolled over, fell and exploded on the ground near Sissinghurst." The Diver attacked by Flg Off Jongbloed crashed and exploded in a wood south-east of Cranbrook, but the day was marred when Wt Off Justin Maier was killed when the flying bomb he was trying to tip with his wing was shot down by a US P-51. The explosion caught the Spitfire, which fell out of control and crashed.

486 (RNZAF) Squadron (Tempest V) Newchurch

Wt Off O.D. Eagleson RNZAF	EN527/SA-Q	V-1 shared	0505	Dover area
Flt Lt J.H. McCaw RNZAF	JN770/SA-V	V-1	0851	Maidstone area
Flg Off S.S. Williams RNZAF	EN523/SA-X	V-1 shared	1538	Hastings area
Plt Off B.M. Hall RNZAF	JN821/SA-H	V-1	1620	Bexhill area
Wt Off W.A. Kalka RNZAF	JN803/SA-D	V-1	1620	Hastings area
	JN803/SA-D	V-1	1629	Bexhill area
	JN803/SA-D	V-1	1632	Bexhill area
	JN803/SA-D	V-1	1632	Bexhill area
Flt Sgt J.S. Ferguson RNZAF	JN767/SA-B	V-1	1827	Pevensey area
Flt Lt L.J. Appleton RNZAF	JN770/SA-V	V-1 shared	1910	Dungeness area
Flt Lt E.W. Tanner RNZAF	EN528/SA-P	V-1 shared	2115	Rye area

The New Zealanders added a further 11 Divers to their scoreboard, four of which were shared, Wt Off Kalka alone bringing down four.

610 Squadron (Spitfire XIV) Friston

Flt Sgt J.N. Philpott	DW-	V-1	0550-0720	
Flt Lt J.B. Shepherd	DW-	V-1	1540-1655	
Flg Off G.M. McKinlay	RB142/DW-	V-1	1605 (KiA)	Newhaven area
Flt Sgt M.P. Harding	DW-	V-1	1615-1725	
Flt Lt W.M. Lightbourn ⎱	DW-	V-1	1715-1810	
Flg Off G. Watkin RCAF ⎰	DW-			

Flt Sgt John Philpott returned to Friston with his propeller scorched after having flown though the explosion of his victim. Flg Off George McKinlay was ordered up shortly before 1600 to investigate some balloons, when he sighted an approaching Diver, which he attacked over Newhaven. The explosion brought down his aircraft, which crashed at the Brooks, Drove Road, Seaford and the 23-year-old from Gateshead was killed. Eyewitnesses believed the pilot had sacrificed his own life by steering the crippled fighter away from a built-up area. Impressed by his courage, the town clerk wrote to his mother telling her the gallant way in which her son had died. An hour or so later, Flt Lt Warren Lightbourn (from the Bahamas) and Flg Off Gordon Watkin, having exhausted their ammunition, caused their victim to dive into the sea by using their slipstreams. The Squadron diarist commented: "We shoot them down, tip them up, now we blow them over!"

1 Squadron with its Spitfire LFIXbs now left Detling and returned to Lympne, from where it would continue anti-Diver patrols.

Thursday 13 JULY

In the hope of achieving better results and closer co-ordination, General Pile and Air Marshal Hill gave orders moving all guns to the coast and creating two distinct areas for fighters, one over the sea in front of the gun belt and the other inland behind it.

This division of their patrol area made the task of the fighter squadrons more difficult but the new system quickly justified itself. During the second week after the redeployment a record number of bombs was destroyed and the following week the guns exceeded the fighter score for the first time. Moreover, gun batteries and airfields were now more or less in the same areas and, with personal contact between airmen and gunners, harmonious co-operation was soon restored.

A Diver impacted on a works site in York Road, Battersea (SW11) at 1015, killing two workmen. Much widespread damage was caused on the site including the loss of 60 tons of oil and 200 gallons of turpentine, and seven nearby barges loaded with paraffin wax were damaged on the Thames. Forty minutes later another Diver fell on Clapham, killing two and damaging many houses in Lesser Avenue (SW4). Deptford (SE8) received another fatal bomb at 1805, on this occasion two people losing their lives when ten houses were demolished in Hoopwich Street. Two more were killed in Ridgemount Close, Penge (SE20) during the early evening. A flying bomb that impacted outside the Park Hotel in Bromley Road, Farnborough, killed five members of the same family (the Vickers) who were evacuating to a safer part of the country. Another scored a direct hit on the Tiger's Head public house in Lewisham, killing 18 and injuring a further 40. Two more died when a Diver fell in the Bath Terrace/Dickens Square area of the Elephant & Castle (SE1).

3 Squadron (Tempest V) Newchurch

Plt Off K.G. Slade-Betts	JN822/JF-	V-1	0755-0850	
Flt Lt A.R. Moore	JN812/JF-M	V-1	0830-0940	
Flt Lt R. van Lierde (Belg)	JN862/JF-Z	V-1	0930-1040	

41 Squadron (Spitfire XII) Lympne

Plt Off J.C.J. Payne	MB804/EB-T	V-1	1020	Battle area

The Diver crashed east of Battle, Plt Off Jimmy Payne's second kill: "At 1020 Diver seen ten miles south of Hastings. Four two-seconds bursts from 200 yards, dropping back to 250 yards. Diver spun through 5/10 cloud into a wood north of Hastings."

56 Squadron (Tempest V) Newchurch

Flg Off W.R. MacLaren	JN816/US-W	V-1	1000	exploded in mid-air

Flg Off Bill MacLaren intercepted the flying bomb three miles south of Fairlight Cove at 2,000 feet: "I fired a three-seconds burst from 200 yards astern and the Diver slowed to 250mph. I fired another short burst from 80 yards and the Diver exploded in mid-air west of Winchelsea."

91 Squadron (Spitfire XIV) Deanland ALG

Flt Lt R.S. Nash	RB169/DL-Q	V-1	1004	exploded in mid-air
Sqn Ldr N.A. Kynaston ⎫	RB185/DL-	V-1	1500	exploded in mid-air
Lt H. de Bordas (FF) ⎭	NH720/DL-H			

Flt Lt Ray Nash: "Saw Diver over Dungeness being attacked by a Tempest of 486 Squadron without success. Made attack from astern at 250 yards, closing to 100 yards and Diver exploded in the air about 12 miles south of base. Blast and flames did some damage to my aircraft." Sqn Ldr Norman Kynaston and Lt Henri de Bordas shared one: "Diver indicated by 'Snowflake' markers ten miles south of Tunbridge Wells. We both attacked from astern at 150 yards and Diver exploded in the air 15 miles north-west of Penshurst."

129 Squadron (Mustang III) Brenzett

| Flg Off M. Humphries | FB137/DV-C | V-1 | 1615 | off Dungeness |

Flg Off Mike Humphries took off at 1500 accompanied by Wt Off R.L. Thomas RAAF. A Diver was intercepted by Humphries eight miles west of Dungeness at 2,000 feet, flying at 310mph. He attacked from starboard quarter and observed strikes on its fuselage, whereupon it turned over and crashed into the sea where it exploded about 200 yards offshore.

137 Squadron (Typhoon Ib) Manston

| Flg Off A.N. Sames RNZAF | MN169/SF-Z | V-1 | 1410-1530 | exploded in mid-air |

Flg Off Artie Sames sighted Diver three miles off Dungeness, closed from astern to 150 yards, and opened fire. The bomb exploded with the result that the Typhoon was badly blistered and burnt. Despite this, Sames was able to return and land safely.

165 Squadron (Spitfire IX) Lympne

| Flt Sgt A.F.A. McIntosh RCAF | MJ221/SK-T | V-1 | 1730-1745 | Ashford area |

> "Bomb exploded in the Ashford area. I flew through the explosion and my aircraft was slightly damaged. Confirmed by White 1."

316 (Polish) Squadron (Mustang III) Friston

| Sqn Ldr B. Arct PAF | FB374/SZ-A | V-1 | 1005 | Hailsham area |
| Flt Lt L. Majewski PAF | FB383/SZ-J | V-1 | 1453 | Hailsham area |

Despite flying many anti-Diver patrols, Sqn Ldr Arct had not succeeded in opening his score until this morning. Sitting in the cockpit of his Mustang, a flying bomb suddenly spluttered over the airfield. He was scrambled but was too late to catch the missile. However, more trade soon came his way:

> "This time I saw my quarry from a few miles distance. A thin layer of white clouds extended in that direction below me, and the bomb, flying a couple of thousand feet lower, was clearly visible. It was approaching me very quickly, but at a very slight angle. I pushed forward the throttle and control stick. My Mustang roared on full revs, dived slightly, its speed increasing rapidly. The hands of the speed indicator moved: 390 … 400 … then 410, and finally 420 miles per hour. I was now much faster than my target. Closing in and getting ready to open fire, I kept glancing downwards to find a place without any buildings around. My target flew in a straight line and was unable to change course. It also could not increase speed or engage me in dog fighting. It was strange to watch this monstrosity and I could hardly believe that a real, live pilot was not sitting in the fuselage. The dead 'Witch' seemed to be alive, locked like some monstrous freak as it flew on in nervous jerks.
>
> "When deserted hills and woods spread below, I closed in to 200 yards and pressed the trigger, giving a short burst from my four cannons. It was quite an effort to keep the target in my sights. I flew on through the hot whirlpool behind its flaming tail. I was careful not to close in too much. The bomb spat fire like a legendary dragon, slowed down and turning to the left ejected fireworks of sparks. The first burst was accurate, the second deadly. With great satisfaction I watched the 'Witch' diving to end its infamous life. The bomb crashed in an empty field and instantly exploded. The blast jerked my aircraft, a sharp red glow blinded me for a moment and that was all. Another V-1 was rendered harmless, some human lives saved. I returned to West Malling pleased with my first success."

Flt Lt Majewski scored his kill five hours later in the same general area: "Diver seen crossing coast over Pevensey Bay. Opened fire at 300 yards dead astern for three seconds. Diver climbed then crashed and exploded on the ground three miles north of Hailsham."

322 (Dutch) Squadron (Spitfire XIV) West Malling

Flt Sgt M.J. Janssen	RB160/VL-A	V-1	1005
Flt Sgt J.H. Harms	RB141/VL-L	V-1	1030

486 (RNZAF) Squadron (Tempest V) Newchurch

Flg Off H.M. Mason RNZAF	JN732/SA-I	V-1	1004	Tenterden area
	JN732/SA-I	V-1	1032	Bexhill area
Plt Off W.A.L. Trott RNZAF	JN866/SA-U	V-1	1505	Tunbridge Wells area
Wt Off B.J. O'Connor RNZAF	JN866/SA-U	V-1	1715	West Malling area

Night 13/14 JULY

Sixteen Heinkels from III/KG3 operating out of Rosières carried out their latest mission against Southampton, departing just before midnight with the last returning at 0237. Seven Divers passed over the Isle of Wight, as recorded by Jock Leal:

> "Among seven Divers which had us on the alert during the night, one cut out near the mouth of Wootton Creek and crashed into the sea off Osborne. Another also went into the sea, off Sandown Bay. Others landed on the mainland but we were glad to hear that one had been shot down by a night fighter near Basingstoke[117]."

Three fell on the mainland but none within the city precincts of Southampton.

456 (RAAF) Squadron (Mosquito XVII) Ford

Flt Lt K.A. Roediger RAAF	HK297/RX-V	V-1	0148	Grid V.2298

> "The Diver was at 1,500 feet at 320mph when I hit the propulsion unit, causing it to be separated from the main body – exploded in the sea. Another was chased, drawing away at 400mph."

Friday 14 JULY

The British Government announced that up to 0600 on 14 July, the total number of flying bombs plotted as launched was 3,526. The communiqué also stated that since the night of 10/11 July (inclusive) the attack had not been directed against London[118]. However, this did little to allay the fears of the civilian population of the capital, who were leaving in their thousands both through official and unofficial evacuation schemes. By mid-July some 15,000 a day were leaving the terminal stations on packed trains. Some reports describe a situation at the main stations of near panic as people struggled to get tickets and on to the over-flowing trains. It was variously reported that somewhere between 1,500,000 and 2,000,000 people fled the capital during this period. This created an eerie and empty feeling in many parts. Children disappeared from the streets and food, which had been in short supply, became easier to obtain. This mass evacuation would undoubtedly have saved many, many lives.

The V-1s had, as anticipated and not unexpectedly, a very negative effect on morale. There had been a brief period of elation after D-Day, until it was realised that the war was still not going to be over quickly. When death and destruction started to fall from the skies again it was a huge strain on Londoners. They were tired after five years of war and this was the last straw. They became tense and nervous and exhausted through lack of sleep. They were frequently awoken as the sirens kept going off or by the ack-ack guns trying to shoot down the intruders. Many took to sheltering again. The Underground system was hugely popular and also from mid-July a number of the Northern Line stations. The back garden Anderson shelter also became a frequent refuge and bed for many. They were to save countless lives and stood up incredibly well to the V-1 blast. The more recent Morrison shelter, which resembled a large table with a steel top, also gave great protection.

It was a cold dank summer and some of the prevailing impressions of the period are the grey Doodlebugs scuttling along in and out of the heavy clouds. The smell of powdered brick dust and plaster filled the air. Mingling with this was the smell of crushed leaves stripped from trees by the blast waves. In some places spring arrived twice and trees were reported blossoming and leafing again later in the summer due to their confusion at the conditions. Underfoot was the crunch of broken glass and slates from thousands of windows and roofs. The day and night was punctuated with the sight of Doodlebugs coming over, sometimes in flights of ten or more at a time, followed by the ear splitting noise of the engines and then the periodic explosions. Going to work and seeing familiar suburban streets ripped apart, familiar houses, churches, shops and buildings destroyed was an awesome experience but one Londoners soon took in their stride.

1 Squadron (Spitfire LFIXb) Lympne

Flg Off E.N.W. Marsh	MK423/JX-	V-1	1800	off Cap Gris Nez
Flt Lt P.W. Stewart	NH253/JX-	V-1	1835	Tenterden area

Flg Off Junior Marsh: "Saw strikes on port wing and rear of Diver. Left wing dropped but Diver flew straight on. Final burst and jet exploded in ball of flame. Diver winged over and spiralled into sea ten miles off Cap Gris Nez." Thirty-five minutes later Flt Lt Stewart got another: "First burst no strikes observed. Second burst caused belch of flames from rear of Diver, which banked steeply to port and dived into ground. Exploded near farm buildings in the Tenterden area." On the return of 1 Squadron to Lympne airfield, LAC Bill Noakes recalled:

> "We were now right in Doodlebug alley and soon experienced the weight of V-1s coming over. On Romney Marshes, adjacent to the airfield, there appeared to be hundreds of AA guns, which were becoming a bone of contention with the pilots. Picking up a V-1 over the Channel the pilot would chase it across the coast possibly by now in firing range. Suddenly AA guns would open up despite one of our aircraft being near, thus putting him in danger. Pilots were reluctant to back off because they felt they had a better chance of a hit. We were instructed to wear our tin helmets due to the amount of shrapnel that was falling on the airfield, sometimes damaging aircraft on the ground. At night, as we tried to sleep, the AA gunners would be pounding away at a continuous stream of flying bombs. On one occasion one of our aircraft taxied in having just blown up a V-1. When we examined the skin of the machine, the after suction of the explosion had forced outwards some of the moulding that wrapped around the carburettor intake. V-1s flew over the airfield regularly and it was certainly a hectic time dealing with these ghost-like flying machines plus all the ducking and weaving we seemed to do when one was suddenly shot off course and crashed down near the aerodrome."[119]

3 Squadron (Tempest V) Newchurch

Flg Off R.E. Barckley	JN755/JF-D	V-1	0900-1010	Eastbourne area
	JN755/JF-D	V-1	0900-1010	Sevenoaks area
Flg Off R.E. Barckley ⎫ Flt Sgt R.W. Pottinger ⎬	JN755/JF-D JN760/JF-R	V-1	0900-1010	Eastbourne area
Flt Sgt D.J. Mackerras RAAF	JN768/JF-F	V-1	1805-1915	

Flg Off Bob Barckley recalled tipping a Diver:

> "It wasn't impossible to tip them up but quite difficult. I only did it once. On that particular patrol I'd already shot down two, I'd used up all my ammunition when this one came in over Eastbourne ... the thing was flying towards London so I thought I'd better do something, so I decided to tip it over. I had to formate on it in the first place, I found that every time I put my wing under its starboard wing, it just skidded away; I had upset the airflow. On the next try I slipped my wing under it and immediately flipped my stick over to the right, and that tipped its wing right over and it just catapulted into the ground. I saw it hit a wood, well clear of Sevenoaks"[120]

41 Squadron (Spitfire XII) Lympne

Flt Lt K.F. Thiele RNZAF	MB856/EB-X	V-1	1725-1840	Cliff End area

The flying bomb exploded in the air, giving the former bomber ace (recipient of the DSO and DFC) his first aerial kill.

56 Squadron (Tempest V) Newchurch

Wt Off V.L.J. Turner RAAF	EN534/US-O	V-1	1750	Bexhill area

"Took off from Newchurch at 1700 hours. Sighted a Diver ten miles off Bexhill at 2,500 feet. Fired two short bursts from 300 yards closing to 150 yards and Diver went down, exploding in the back garden of a house west of Bexhill." Damage was considerable although there were no fatalities.

91 Squadron (Spitfire XIV) Deanland ALG

Sqn Ldr N.A. Kynaston	RB161/DL-I	V-1	1842	West Malling area

"Saw Diver 15 miles south of base and attacked from astern. First burst set Diver on fire and slowed it down. Second burst and Diver exploded in the air."

137 Squadron (Typhoon) Manston

Flg Off A.N. Sames RNZAF	MN134/SF-J	V-1	0850-0920	off Dungeness

Undeterred by his experience of the previous afternoon, Flg Off Artie Sames pursued another Diver over the sea, this time opening from a more respectable 230 yards, following which it dived into the sea off Dungeness and exploded.

165 Squadron (Spitfire IX) Lympne

Flt Sgt C.R. Bundara RAAF	MJ580/SK-Y	V-1	1435-1535	

315 (Polish) Squadron (Mustang III) Brenzett

Flt Lt J. Zbrozek PAF	FZ155/PK-L	V-1 shared	1835	Grid R.3555

"The Diver was intercepted south of Dungeness at 2,000 feet. Attacked from astern, range 500-200 yards. After I had expended all my ammunition, Diver slowed down to 200mph and made several slight turns. A Spitfire approached and fired and Diver crashed to ground and exploded."

322 (Dutch) Squadron (Spitfire XIV) West Malling

Flt Sgt R. van Beers	VL-H	V-1	1516	Grid R.3967
Flt Sgt M.J. Janssen	VL-C	V-1	1805	Tonbridge area
Flt Lt J.L. Plesman	VL-W	V-1	1826	Robertsbridge area
	VL-W	V-1	1830	exploded in mid-air

Flt Sgt Ronnie van Beers: "Vectored on to Diver over Ashford. Attacked line astern. Saw strikes and flames from propulsion unit. Diver crashed and exploded." Flt Sgt Janssen followed this with one that crashed near Tonbridge: "Vectored on to Diver coming in over Hastings. Attacked line astern, range 200 yards. Petrol tank exploded in the air and Diver crashed and exploded." Flt Lt Jan Plesman scored a double within a few minutes of each other: "Was told Diver crossing in near Hastings. Intercepted and attacked from line astern, range 250 yards. Saw strikes on wings and fuselage. Diver turned over, fell to the ground and exploded. Another reported coming in over Dungeness." This he attacked in similar fashion, the Diver exploding in the air.

486 (RNZAF) Squadron (Tempest V) Newchurch

Flt Lt J.H. McCaw RNZAF	JN758/SA-Y	V-1	0945	Bexhill area
	JN758/SA-Y	V-1	0950	Bexhill area
Wt Off O.D. Eagleson RNZAF	EN523/SA-X	V-1	0955	Eastbourne area
Flg Off S.S. Williams RNZAF	JN860/SA-Z	V-1	1525	Westerham/Sevenoaks

| Flg Off H.M. Mason RNZAF | JN732/SA-I | V-1 shared | 1750 | Bexhill area |
| Flg Off J.R. Cullen RNZAF | JN770/SA-V | V-1 | 1832 | Hastings area |

610 Squadron (Spitfire) Friston

| Flt Sgt J.A. Pope | RB156/DW-O | V-1 damaged 1655-1820 |

Flt Sgt Alan Pope saw strikes on the flying bomb he attacked, but it was not allowed as a kill since it disappeared into cloud. The Squadron reported that a technical party arrived at Friston to modify its Spitfires, to enable them to fly at 21lb boost on 150-octane petrol. After the modifications had been carried out to the CO's RB158/DW-D, a civilian test pilot took it up on a test flight during which he sighted a Diver. It was out of range, however, although he fired at it.

418 (RCAF) Squadron was ordered to transfer from Holmsley South to RAF Hurn, from where it was to continue anti-Diver patrols while also undertaking intruder sorties over the Continent.

Night 14/15 JULY

A total of 23 sorties were flown by the Heinkels of III/KG3, some possibly flying two sorties between 2311, when the first departed Rosières, and 0620, when the last one home landed safely. Again, Southampton was the target. Again, the Isle of Wight was put on alert, as noted by Jock Leal:

> "We had nine Doodlebugs to deal with that night as they passed on their way to the mainland. Some of them came across the island, one so low and close to the Mount Joy post that the girl at regional headquarters, to whom we were transmitting our plots, told us she could hear its roar clearly over the telephone. Another landed on the island, the sixth to hit us – but it dropped on Ventnor golf course. We had sent the Cowes night shifts to shelter twice before the final intruder passed over, intermittently visible in the cloudy dawn. We received the 'all clear' at 5.48am and the Diver alert ended at 7.15am. Those times are worth recording because that was the last night of enemy air attack upon this island. It ended as it began, back in June, 1940, with high explosive on a golf course ..."[121]

Of the 13 that impacted on the mainland, three caused a serious loss of life and many casualties, the most lethal falling at Newcomen Road, Stamshaw in Portsmouth. Here, 15 people were killed and 98 injured. A further six (all evacuees from London) were killed in the village of Goodworth Clatford, 18 miles north of Southampton, while six more were injured, one seriously, at Sholing in Southampton.

25 Squadron (Mosquito XVII) Coltishall

| Plt Off J.E.C. Tait RAAF | HK322/ZK- | V-1 | 0032 | off Dungeness |

> "At 0032 a flying bomb was seen off Dungeness. I dived to 2,200 feet and opened fire at 1,000 feet from dead astern. The light went out after a short burst, but I had to pull up and over the flying bomb to avoid it. I did not actually see the result of my attack but immediately afterwards saw two explosions and I claim the flying bomb as destroyed. I saw another flying bomb but was near the gun belt. Saw two more and attacked one but saw no result."

96 Squadron (Mosquito XIII) Ford

| Flt Sgt T. Bryan | MM468/ZJ- | V-1 | 0130 | Grid Q.773 |

Flt Sgt Tom Bryan intercepted a Diver flying at 1,400 feet, attacking from astern but it had already crossed the coast, whereupon it dived to ground and exploded.

264 Squadron (Mosquito XIII) Hartford Bridge

| Flt Sgt P.N. Lee | HK479/PS-F | V-1 | 2245-0155 | off Cap Gris Nez |

409 (RCAF) Squadron (Mosquito XIII) Hunsdon

| Flg Off W.H. McPhail RCAF[122] | MM555/KP- | V-1 | 0020 | off Bernay |

"Sighted flying bomb at 3,000 feet approaching from the direction of Bernay on a westerly course at 250mph. Dived to intercept at 300mph and attacked from dead astern with two long bursts from 1,000 feet, closing to 250 feet. Diver was burning from end to end as I broke away down to port. Momentarily, the Diver mimicked the manoeuvre as it lost its way and peeled over, then dived vertically into 10/10th cloud."

418 (RCAF) Squadron (Mosquito VI) Hurn
Flg Off S.N. May RCAF   NS837/TH-L   V-1   0213   off Le Touquet

"Attacked Diver at 1,200 feet, five miles off Le Tréport. Much light flak from English coast caused attack to be broken off. Light from Diver disappeared, so claim Diver."

FIU (Tempest V) Ford
Wg Cdr C.H. Hartley   EJ530/ZQ-   V-1   daytime

Flt Lt Jeremy Howard-Williams wrote:

"Chris Hartley decided to spend a few days getting first-hand experience of the problem. He brought five more days of bad weather but managed to destroy a flying bomb. For every bomb destroyed, each pilot probably shot at three or four, but they often had to break off as they approached the gun belt."

422ndNFS USAAF (P-61) Ford
2/Lt Herman E. Ernst USAAF and his radar operator Flt Off Edward H. Kopsel USAAF of the 422ndNFS came close to opening the score for the P-61 night fighters. Having been vectored onto a flying bomb, Ernst descended through the clouds and was approaching his target when the Plexiglas tailcone of his aircraft disintegrated, causing him to abort. The aircraft (42-5547) was landed safely, and it was discovered that the tailcone had exploded under pressure of the dive.

Another Do217 was shot down west of Antwerp, at 0145, by a Mosquito XIII of the FIU flown by Royal Marine pilot Lt John Armour (his second victory) and his Royal Navy navigator Lt(A) P.R.V. Wheeler RNVR:

"Patrolled area east of Brussels for one uneventful hour, and on the point of returning to base, when airfield to westwards was lit and searchlight caused an aircraft to fire four white flares. Turned towards airfield and got a contact at a range of about two miles. Followed contact on steady course for 15 minutes, climbing hard from 1,500 feet to 13,000 feet. Visual obtained at 700 feet and closed to 300 feet. Aircraft identified as Do217 and appeared to be carrying two large objects underslung outboard of the engines. Dropped back a little and opened fire with four-seconds burst. As e/a was turning gently to port, a little deflection was allowed. E/a's port engine burst into flames, which immediately spread to the fuselage. He pulled up and over to port, going into a dive enveloped in flames and exploding on the ground shortly afterwards. No crew seen to bale out."

Although it was assumed that the "two large objects underslung outboard of the engines" were missiles, it seems more likely that they were long-range fuel tanks since no aircraft from KG100 was lost on this occasion.

Saturday 15 JULY
Seven people were killed near London Bridge (SE1) at 1348 following the explosion of a Diver that hit Whiteground Estate, where a block of flats was destroyed. US airman Sgt Donald W. Marner, who had just arrived in the UK, embarked on a train for London there to be greeted by a flying bomb attack:

"At 3.30pm we arrived in London and were welcomed by a robot plane attack. One robot plane exploded one block from the station where I was. A building and four taxicabs were blown to bits. I hit the ground during the attack and was never so scared in all my life. Five robot planes exploded in the hour and a half we were in London. Saw the terrible damage the bombing had done there."

1 Squadron (Spitfire LFIXb) Lympne

Flt Sgt H.J. Vassie	MJ422/JX-	V-1	1733	Detling area

"After last attack Diver spiralled down and exploded some 200 yards from house, which was damaged, five miles east-north-east of Detling."

3 Squadron (Tempest V) Newchurch

Flt Lt A.E. Umbers RNZAF	JN865/JF-	V-1 shared	1720-1805
Flt Sgt T.A. McCulloch	JN868/JF-F	V-1	2015-2120

Flt Lt Spike Umbers shared his kill with Plt Off Bzowski of 306 (Polish) Squadron.

91 Squadron (Spitfire XIV) Deanland ALG

Flt Lt H.B. Moffett RCAF	NH701/DL-A	V-1	1728	Wrotham area

"Saw Diver over Maidstone and attacked from astern from 300 yards. Diver was set well on fire and speed slowed down considerably, the Diver falling in a slow glide and exploded on hitting the ground in the Wrotham area."

306 (Polish) Squadron (Mustang III) Brenzett

Plt Off J. Bzowski PAF	FB358/UZ-C	V-1 shared	1750	Grid R.2744

Plt Off Janusz Bzowski intercepted a Diver south-west of Rye and attacked from dead astern, closing to 150 yards. He fired a three-seconds burst and it lost speed and crashed into the ground. Shared with Flt Lt Umbers of 3 Squadron.

486 (RNZAF) Squadron (Tempest V) Newchurch

Flt Lt J.H. McCaw RNZAF	JN860/SA-Z	V-1	1725	Ashford area
Wt Off G.J.M. Hooper RNZAF	JN803/SA-D	V-1	1740	Rye area

412thFS/373rdFG (P-47)

1/Lt Donald M. Raine USAAF	V5-	V-1		Kingsnorth area

Night 15/16 JULY

An hour after midnight a Diver impacted in Brigstock Road, Thornton Heath (CR7), killing four and causing much damage to property including the local Fire Station. Norbury (SW16) received another Diver at 0432, this exploding in Pollards Hill South and demolishing four houses; one occupier was killed.

25 Squadron (Mosquito XVII) Coltishall

Flt Lt K.V. Panter	HK237/ZK-G	V-1	0040	crashed on land
Plt Off J.E.C. Tait RAAF	HK322/ZK-	V-1	0432	exploded in mid-air
	HK322/ZK-	V-1	0437	exploded in mid-air

Flt Lt Keith Panter's victim crashed and exploded in the gun belt:

"I was airborne from Coltishall at 2225 and handed over to Sandwich Control at 8,500 feet. At the commencement of the patrol I was vectored onto a bogey. Contact was obtained at $5^1/_2$ miles range and after a chase of about eight minutes duration, during which time I closed to 4,000 yards, I was informed that bogey was friendly and was called off. At 0005, when at 3,500 feet, I saw a flying bomb. I dived to 1,700 feet and opened fire from 1,100 feet range. The flying bomb emitted showers of sparks but drew away, so chase was abandoned. I climbed to 3,000 feet and saw another flying bomb. I dived to 1,500 feet to intercept it, but could not get into firing range and abandoned the chase as I saw another fighter to be in a better position. I climbed to 4,000 feet and dived to intercept another flying bomb, but as I commenced to dive

I saw two fighters in a better position, so I broke away and climbed again to 5,000 feet. Almost immediately I saw a flying bomb at 2,000 feet, so I dived to slightly below and opened fire from 800 feet dead astern. Strikes were observed on the propulsion unit and the flying bomb emitted large quantities of sparks. I broke away to port, intending to position myself for a further attack, but I saw the flying bomb dive vertically down and explode on land."

This may have been the Diver that crashed into a field at Withersfield in West Suffolk and caused damage to several houses in Haverhill and Withersfield, slightly injuring one person. It was reported to have been shot down by an RAF fighter.

Plt Off John Tait's aircraft was damaged by blast from his second kill – both radiators were punctured, port wing damaged and the starboard wing caught fire. His navigator Plt Off E.P. Latchford baled out and landed in the sea three miles south-west of Dover, but Tait managed to belly-land safely in a field four miles north of Dover. Tait reported:

"I dived to 5,000 feet and immediately saw a formation of flying bombs at 2-4,000 feet. I dived to 2,000 feet and attacked one, which was straggling. Opened fire at 1,500 feet and flying bomb exploded in the air. I climbed again to 5,000 feet and at 0437 saw a flying bomb approaching head-on. I turned in behind flying bomb and opened fire from 1,000 feet dead astern. The flying bomb immediately exploded and the debris showered over our aircraft without causing any apparent damage. After 15 minutes the port engine caught fire and I ordered the navigator to bale out. I was unable to follow so decided to ditch but when I broke cloud sighted the coast and belly-landed in a cornfield near Whitfield [Withersfield] at 0510 – not hurt."

96 Squadron (Mosquito XIII) Ford

Flt Lt D.L. Ward	MM524/ZJ-	V-1	0104	off Boulogne

The interception by Flt Lt Don Ward was made ten miles north-north-west of Boulogne, and upon being hit the Diver's fuel tank erupted and the missile dived into the sea where it exploded on impact.

264 Squadron (Mosquito XIII) Hartford Bridge

Flt Lt I.H. Cosby	HK481/PS-O	V-1	0015	Hythe area
Flt Sgt P.N. Lee	HK479/PS-F	V-1	0418	Hythe area
Flt Lt R.L. Beverley	HK477/PS-C	V-1	0420	off Dover

Flg Off Cosby: "Shot it down six miles north of Hythe but not seen to crash." Of his kill Flt Lt Beverley reported: "The Diver exploded in the air four miles south of Dover, damaging the Mosquito." The Mosquito sustained a shattered windscreen and other debris damage, but Beverley was able to fly his aircraft safely back to base. The Diver attacked by Flt Sgt Lee also exploded in the air one mile south of Hythe. Flg Off Peter Brooke (HK506/PS-G) had a frustrating evening. On closing in to attack Divers on three occasions his guns failed to fire. It seems that two of the above fell in the Elham district, one impacting at Lympne at 0424, followed by a second four minutes later at Mill Down. There were no casualties.

422nd NFS (P-61) Ford

2/Lt H.E. Ernst USAAF	42-5547	V-1	2248-0105	Beachy Head area

The P-61 crew of 2/Lt Herman Ernst[123] and Flt Off Kopsel soon made up for the disappointment of the previous evening when they scored the first success for the American night fighter. When flying at 3,000 feet off Beachy Head, four Divers were sighted by Ernst, but, as he manoeuvred into position to attack one, a Mosquito nipped in and shot down the bomb. Selecting another target, he dived to attack, closed in and opened fire, whereupon it exploded. Another member of the 422nd recalled:

"They got in behind this buzz bomb off Cherbourg. They were in perfect position. Closing in to 200 feet the pilot opened up. At that time the propulsion unit blew up; boy, smoke and fire and everything else came out! When they got down on the ground, the radar op just looked at the pilot, turned his back on him and walked off."

Sunday 16 JULY
This Sunday morning, at 0747, witnessed a Diver crashing in Rumsey Road, Brixton (SW9), where 50 houses were destroyed or damaged and five people killed. A second fell a short distance away at 1025, killing two people in the Brixton Road/Camberwell New Road area of Kennington (SW9). At almost the same time a Diver came down in Battersea (SW11), exploding in the area of Battersea Street/Lubbock Street, inflicting much damage and killing 16 people. A third fell in Tower Bridge Road, Bermondsey (SE1) at 1027, further damaging St John's Church (a victim of the 1940 bombing) and killing two people. Next hit was Commercial Way, Peckham (SE15), where two people were killed, six houses demolished and 30 damaged at 1110. Later, at 1926, four people were killed when a Diver impacted in Newton Street, Brixton (SW9), damaging the railway line and many houses.

1 Squadron (Spitfire LFIXb) Lympne
Flt Lt T. Draper Williams	ML423/JX-S	V-1	1920	Maidstone area

"Saw strikes on fuselage and wing roots following first attack. Diver dropped starboard wing and made slight diving turn to starboard. Second attack Diver pulled up in climb to port. Went through cloud and saw Diver make turn to starboard and then go down. Crashed in orchard two miles south of Maidstone."

3 Squadron (Tempest V) Newchurch
Flt Lt A.E. Umbers RNZAF	JN822/JF-	V-1	1020-1140	
Flg Off R. Dryland	JN754/JF-	V-1	1320-1425	
	JN754/JF-	V-1	1320-1425	
Flt Sgt H.J. Bailey RAAF	JN807/JF-Y	V-1	1620-1700	

41 Squadron (Spitfire XII) Lympne
Plt Off D.P. Fisher	MB798/EB-U	V-1	1815	Beachy Head area

Flg Off Peter Graham and Plt Off Jackie Fisher (who had just returned to the unit after a six weeks illness) were nearing the end of their patrol when a flying bomb was sighted half a mile away, and below. They dived down from 11,000 feet and Fisher shot it down into the sea 15 miles off Beachy Head, where it exploded on impact.

56 Squadron (Tempest V) Newchurch
Flt Lt T.H. Hoare RCAF	JN867/US-A	V-1	1915	Grid Q.8165

"Sighted a Diver ten miles north of Bexhill at 3,500 feet. Fired a deflection burst from port and above, drew into line astern and fired from 400 yards, scoring strikes. I broke away owing to balloons and left the Diver losing height rapidly. The Diver exploded on the ground."

91 Squadron (Spitfire XIV) Deanland ALG
Flg Off P.A. Schade	RM654/DL-F	V-1	1230	off Dymchurch

"Intercepted Diver four miles south-east of Dymchurch and attacked from astern at 300 yards down to 200 yards range, shooting it down into the sea."

129 Squadron (Mustang III) Brenzett
Flt Lt I.D.S. Strachan RNZAF	FX862/DV-K	V-1	1015	Rye area
Plt Off E.W. Edwards	FB125/DV-F	V-1	1030	Chatham area
Flg Off J.E. Hartley	FZ172/DV-A	V-1	1100	Dungeness area

Fourteen Diver patrols netted three kills, the first falling to Flt Lt Shorty Strachan at 1015, who intercepted it five miles south of Rye.

165 Squadron (Spitfire IX) Lympne

Flt Lt J.K. Porteous RNZAF	ML242/SK-A	V-1	1240	Hythe area
Plt Off A. Scott	ML204/SK-N	V-1	1700	off Dungeness

Flt Lt Porteous' victim crashed at Postling near Elham; there were no casualties. Plt Off Scott: "Intercepted Diver 15 miles south-east of Dungeness. Strikes seen round jet unit. Diver turned over and spiralled in."

306 (Polish) Squadron (Mustang III) Brenzett

Flt Sgt J. Zaleński PAF	FB393/UZ-U	V-1	1650	Rye area
Flt Sgt W. Nowoczyn PAF	FB106/UZ-V	V-1 shared	1640	St Leonards area
Plt Off K. Wacnik PAF	FZ149/UZ-W	V-1	1920	Rye area

Flt Sgt Józef Zaleński saw his victim crash two miles north of Rye following his two attacks, while Flt Sgt Witold Nowoczyn again had to share his victim, this time with a Tempest of 486 Squadron (Flt Sgt Hall). Plt Off Kazimierz Wacnik also brought his target down near Rye, where it exploded about ten miles north-west of the town. Grp Capt Tadeusz Rolski DSO from HQ Polish Air Force flew a sortie in FX987/UZ-R during the afternoon but failed to make any sightings.

322 (Dutch) Squadron (Spitfire XIV) West Malling

Flg Off J. Jongbloed	NH586/VL-G	V-1	1035	Grid R.2472
Flg Off J. van Arkel	VL-V	V-1	1055	Grid R.1565

Flg Off Jan Jongbloed reported: "When proceeding on cannon test saw Diver going into cloud eight to ten miles north-west of Ashford. Intercepted and attacked from starboard, range 300 yards. Noticed wire trailing from Diver. Made further attack, range 150 yards. Diver blew up and exploded on the ground." Flg Off Jan van Arkel was on patrol when he sighted another Diver some three miles north-east of Ashford: "Intercepted and attacked line astern, range 200 yards. Saw strikes on starboard wing, which fell off. Diver crashed and exploded in field."

486 (RNZAF) Squadron (Tempest V) Newchurch

Flt Sgt B.M. Hall RNZAF	JN821/SA-H	V-1 shared	1635	Hastings area
Plt Off R.J. Danzey RNZAF	JN803/SA-D	V-1	1915	Hastings area

FIU (Tempest V) Ford

Sqn Ldr Alan Wagner DFC, CO FIU Tempest detachment at Ford, died when he flew into ground in EJ581 at high speed in fog when pursuing a Diver. Flt Lt Howard-Williams wrote:

> "Then disaster struck the small detachment again. Wagner flew into the ground at high speed in poor visibility and killed himself. It was found later that Tempest altimeters all over-read at high speed near the ground, and the static vent was changed."

Night 16/17 JULY
85 Squadron (Mosquito XIX) Swannington

Lt E.P. Fossum (Norw)	MM648/VY-G	V-1	0200-0520

96 Squadron (Mosquito XIII) Ford

Flg Off J. Goode	MM452/ZJ-	V-1	2240-0015

Flg Off John Goode attacked his target and saw strikes but nothing happened, so he tried to upset it with his slipstream, without apparent success, but was nonetheless credited with its destruction. Presumably the controller confirmed that it disappeared from the radar screen.

264 Squadron (Mosquito XIII) Hartford Bridge

At 0005, Wg Cdr Chris Hartley, CO of the FIU, flying Tempest EJ630, collided with a 264 Squadron Mosquito (HK471/PS-D) while pursuing a flying bomb. Hartley managed to bale out, although he fractured an ankle badly, but the Mosquito crew, 21-year-old Flt Sgt Maurice Hoare from Watford and his 26-year-old navigator Flt Sgt Edward Bishop, were killed when the Mosquito crashed at Borders Farm, Etchingham. Hartley's Tempest crashed at Corner Farm, Broadoak. Jeremy Howard-Williams wrote:

> "Chris Hartley collided with a Mosquito as they both swooped on the same target at night. There were sufficient collisions and near misses, among the night fighters engaged in anti-Diver operations, for pilots to start using navigation lights. This in turn attracted the Luftwaffe, who sent over intruders to profit from some easy pickings. When coupled with accidents caused by exceeding the aircraft flight envelopes, these losses started to assume significant proportions, but still the missiles came over."

422ndNFS (P-61) Ford

Capt R.O. Elmore USAAF	42-5534	V-1	0310-0515	Beachy Head area

Monday 17 JULY

There was a major incident in Walworth (SE17) at 0513, when a Diver exploded in Suffield Road. Seventeen residents were killed, 40 houses demolished and 150 damaged by blast. Brixton (SW9) received another bomb at 0630, when Brassey Square was hit and 60 houses were damaged, many beyond repair; four people were killed. There were four more fatalities at South Wharf, Rotherhithe (SE16) almost three hours later, when a bomb caused severe damage to dockyard buildings.

The new defence system devised by General Pike and Air Marshal Hill came into effect at dawn. The Air Marshal reflected:

> "I felt that one of my main tasks must now be to ensure that the forces directly under my command were made thoroughly familiar with their part in the new plan. I realised that this was a task I must undertake myself. My own staff had their hands full: to devise and apply measures which would ensure that the safety of our own aircraft was not endangered by the Diver defences was only one of many duties that called for much careful staff work and painstaking liaison. The AOC 11 Group and his staff were preoccupied with matters arising out of the operations in Normandy. Realising that this would be so, I had arranged that the Sector Headquarters at Biggin Hill should become a co-ordinating centre for Diver. I found, however, that the practical, hour-to-hour supervision of operations left the Sector Commander and his staff with little time for other work; and it seemed to me that, in any case, the study and dissemination of tactical doctrine and the promotion of disciplined enthusiasm amongst pilots faced with a novel weapon ought to proceed from a rather higher level than that of a Sector Headquarters. I felt that this was a case where I must give a direct lead to the Station and Squadron Commanders concerned with flying bombs."

The AOC's Tempest was soon to be seen scurrying from station to station as he prepared to bolster the morale of the men under his command:

> "Here my practice of sharing actively and frequently in the fighter operations stood me in good stead. Trying to shoot down a missile travelling at six miles a minute while flying at the same speed and a height of perhaps a thousand feet across a narrow belt of undulating country bounded by balloons and guns was a business whose subtleties were not readily appreciable from an office chair. I found that a practical acquaintance with this business had its uses. Not only did it help me to acquire a fund of tactical knowledge that I could hardly have gained in any other way; above all it enabled me to talk on a basis of common understanding and endeavour with the pilots whose devotion it was my task to foster.
> "An incidental advantage of the abolition of the inland gun-belt was that it gave the

searchlights, which remained when the guns had gone, more scope to assist night fighters. Another unlooked-for benefit of the move was that it brought the headquarters of the AA Batteries close to the bases from which our fighters were operating. Immediate and personal contact between Battery Commanders and Station Commanders suddenly became possible and even easy. I found during my first visits to stations after the move that advantage was not always being taken of this proximity. I was shown – as I had been shown for the last five weeks – aircraft whose pilots alleged that the guns had fired at them; I was shown marks of damage said to have been thus infected, and fragments of shell-casing which appeared to have entered aircraft or fallen on airfields. In each case I suggested that the Station Commander concerned should pocket the more portable of these exhibits and, armed with this evidence, go and discuss his grievances, real or imaginary, with the local Battery Commander.

"The hint was taken. The consequences were profound and striking. As a result of these meetings between Station and Battery Commanders, the first requisite of understanding between two parties whose interests must occasionally conflict – the realisation that the other side also has a viewpoint – was attained. The mists of suspicion whose gathering had troubled me so much were dispersed almost overnight. On subsequent visits to the same stations I was again shown aircraft that had suffered minor damage from anti-aircraft fire. But this time, instead of having to listen to grievances against the gunner, I was told of pilots who had flouted discipline and good sense by venturing too near the guns. In short, pilots and gunners were beginning to understand one another's problems and work together. Unity was restored."

41 Squadron (Spitfire XII) Lympne

The Squadron suffered the loss of two of its young pilots when the Spitfire flown by Flt Sgt Roger Short collided in mid-air with a Tiger Moth flown by Flt Sgt Cliff Oddy approximately one mile south of their airfield. Both the 21-year-olds were killed. Investigations undertaken by Wg Cdr Thomas of the Air Ministry's Accidents Branch stated that Oddy, who was flying the unit's Tiger Moth (DV575), turned into the path of Short, who had just taken off in Spitfire MB877. Wg Cdr Thomas found Oddy to blame as he was making an unauthorised low flight over Lympne, when he turned across the path of the Spitfires, which were taking off to participate in an anti-Diver patrol. Oddy, suddenly realising his mistake, turned away sharply, but his reaction was too late and he collided with Short at a height of 200 feet. Little was left of the Spitfire, which crashed straight to the ground, whilst the Tiger Moth spun in and crash-landed in the grounds of Lympne Castle. Oddy was killed immediately, but Short initially survived the accident and died five hours later.

Night 17/18 JULY

Five people were killed when a Diver exploded in Henwood Road, Rotherhithe (SE16) at 0234. Among the 40 properties severely damaged were the buildings of local ship repairers Green & Silley Weir. A wayward Diver crashed in open country having overflown Ipswich in Suffolk. Another came down at Waltham Forest, demolishing the remains of the 600-year-old Low Hall. Warden Carter, whose patch it was, wrote in his diary:

"Local siren went at 0330, and hard on its heels two very loud explosions from pilotless aircraft quite near. A third one came along then, and succeeded in putting the wind up folk. Made a real din and seemed to cut out tight over town. Fortunately it did not dive immediately, but glided on a bit further. Made a strange sound as of corrugated iron being shaken as it continued on its course. Landed not very far away. Counted about twelve near-ones and several more a good way off."

An unfortunate incident occurred during the night when Beaufighter R2080 of 51 OTU from RAF Cranfield in Bedfordshire – presumably on a night exercise – hit an anti-Diver balloon cable. With its port engine on fire, the aircraft crashed at Werke Farm, Kingsdown near Deal. It is believed the crew survived.

25 Squadron (Mosquito XVII) Coltishall

Flt Sgt E.R.C. Lelliott	HK256	V-1	night	
	HK256	V-1	night	over land

Flt Sgt Lelliott shot down one Diver then attacked second – last seen steadily losing height after having to disengage owing to proximity of gun belt; claimed destroyed.

85 Squadron (Mosquito XVII) Swannington

Flt Lt M.H.C. Phillips	VY-B	V-1	0110-0430	off Dungeness

Grp Capt R.G. Slade, Swannington's Station Commander, flew an anti-Diver sortie in one of 85 Squadron's aircraft (VY-D) albeit without success.

96 Squadron (Mosquito XIII) Ford

Sqn Ldr A. Parker-Rees	MM511/ZJ-	V-1	0213	off Cap Gris Nez
	MM511/ZJ-	V-1	0220	off Abbeville
Flt Lt D.L. Ward	MM524/ZJ-	V-1	0400	exploded in mid-air

Sqn Ldr Parker-Rees had an exciting patrol, shooting down two Divers but then being shot down into the sea himself:

> "Diver first seen north of Abbeville, flying due north. I flew parallel with the coast and attacked from astern off Cap Gris Nez. It caught fire in the air and exploded in the sea. At 0220 saw another Diver north of Abbeville on a more westerly course than first Diver. After short burst Diver lost height, then the 'light' went out and explosion seen on the sea."

Parker-Rees then saw tracer passing beneath the nose of his aircraft as the Mosquito came under attack from an Allied night fighter. With the aircraft badly damaged both pilot and observer baled out into the sea, from where they were speedily rescued by HMS *Obedient* and returned safely to land. Flt Lt Don Ward was also patrolling off the French coast when he sighted a Diver some 18 miles north of Boulogne, which exploded in the air following his attack.

157 Squadron (Mosquito XIX) Swannington

Sqn Ldr J.G. Benson	MM630/RS-E	V-1	0127	off Le Touquet
Flt Sgt J.C. Woolley	MM643/RS-F	V-1	0205	off Somme Estuary

264 Squadron (Mosquito XIII) Hartford Bridge

Sqn Ldr F.J.A. Chase	PS-	V-1 probable	2241	Grid R.3755
Flt Lt H.J. Corre	HK516/PS-	V-1	0115	Grid R.3655
Flg Off J. Daber	HK481/PS-O	V-1	0345	West Malling area

All three crews acknowledged the assistance of searchlights when making interceptions.

456 (RAAF) Squadron (Mosquito XVII) Ford

Plt Off I.W. Sanderson RAAF	HK249/RX-B	V-1 damaged		Channel

605 Squadron (Mosquito IV) Manston

Wg Cdr N.J. Starr	UP-	V-1	night	Manston area

The Diver exploded in the air and debris damaged the CO's Mosquito but the crew were unhurt.

FIU (Tempest V) Ford

Flt Lt J. Berry	EJ524/ZQ-Y	V-1	night
	EJ524/ZQ-Y	V-1	night

422ndNFS USAAF (P-61) Ford

Four P-61s up and one crew claimed a Diver shot down, using 513 rounds of 20mm, but not credited.

Tuesday 18 JULY

With operations undertaken on this night by the Heinkels of III/KG3 based at Rosières, 14 sorties were flown without loss. Meanwhile, the Staffeln at Gilze-Rijen were working up to operational level pending joining in the assault on London. At 0619, a third Diver hit the Deptford Dockyard (SE8), inflicting further damage to the US amphibious base and killing two workers. Another fell in Croydon Road, Beckenham (BR3), killing one and causing much damage. At 1634, a Diver fell at the junction of Kennington Lane and Vauxhall Street (SE11), very close to the one that fell 12 days earlier. On this occasion three people were killed. At about 2037, a Diver fell on Elmers End Bus Garage, Beckenham (BR3) and killed 18 including seven employees of London Transport and two members of the Home Guard. A major fire broke out when buses' petrol tanks began to explode. A number of firemen were subsequently badly burned during rescue operations.

1 Squadron (Spitfire LFIXb) Lympne

Flg Off D.H. Davy	ML119/JX-B	V-1 probable		Channel

Flg Off Dennis Davy claimed a Diver shot down into the sea but it was not confirmed and therefore not credited as a kill.

3 Squadron (Tempest V) Newchurch

Flg Off R. Dryland	JN822/JF-	V-1	1521	Grid R.1340
Flt Sgt M.J.A. Rose	JN755/JF-D	V-1	2046	Mayfield area
Flt Lt A.R. Moore	JN815/JF-	V-1	2245	exploded in mid-air
Flt Sgt H.J. Bailey RAAF	JN807/JF-Y			
Flg Off R. Dryland	JN822/JF-	V-1	2345	Hastings area

Flg Off Dryland saw a Diver two miles west of Hastings at 2,000 feet: "A Spitfire dived down and overshot but did not fire. I closed to 100 yards astern and gave a four-seconds burst. Strikes were seen on the wings and the jet. The Diver rolled over with the jet out and went down, exploding on the ground." There was a gap of several hours before the next kill, which fell to Flt Sgt Morrie Rose:

"Saw a Diver west of Hastings at 2,500 feet and closed to attack from 500 yards astern. The Diver climbed to 3,000 feet. I closed to 300 yards and fired intermittently, closing to 200 yards. Numerous strikes were observed and black smoke came out. The Diver went down three or four miles south of Mayfield but was not seen to explode on the ground."

56 Squadron (Tempest V) Newchurch

Flt Sgt H. Shaw	EJ548/US-G	V-1 shared	1815	Maidstone area
Plt Off K. Watts RAAF	EJ522/US-F	V-1 shared	2240	exploded in mid-air

Flt Sgt Artie Shaw shared the kill with a Mustang from 315 Squadron (Plt Off Judek):

"Sighted a Diver north of Tenterden at 1,000 feet. I fired a deflection burst from 100 yards, scoring strikes. Smoke came from the jet, the Diver slowing down to 140mph. A Mustang then fired and the Diver peeled over, exploding on the ground about ten miles south of Maidstone."

This was probably the missile that fell on Harrietsham where a dozen houses were damaged and three residents slightly injured. The Australian Plt Off Watts sighted a Diver near Rye: "I fired a 15° deflection burst from 400 yards, scoring strikes, then fired a second burst. The petrol tank caught fire and the Diver exploded in mid-air about ten miles inland. A Spitfire was firing, causing strikes at the same time."

91 Squadron (Spitfire XIV) Deanland ALG

Flg Off R.A. McPhie RCAF	NH705/DL-P	V-1	1700-1800	Tunbridge Wells area

Canadian Flg Off Ray McPhie reported: "Saw Diver west of Etchingham and attacked from astern at 300 yards. Diver fell near a house and exploded south-east of Tunbridge Wells."

165 Squadron (Spitfire IX) Lympne

Flt Lt I.A.St.C. Watson	MK425/SK-V	V-1	1630	Maidstone area
Flt Lt J.K. Porteous RNZAF	MK738/SK-L	V-1	2245	Tenterden area
Flt Sgt L. Wright	MK401/SK-M	V-1	2248	Staplehurst area

Flt Lt Ivor Watson scored his second kill when he intercepted a Diver over Maidstone: "Piece of jet unit fell off and Diver spiralled in 5 miles west-north-west of Maidstone. Confirmed by Green Section." Both pilots of Red Section scored within minutes of each other, Flt Lt Porteous getting the first. Flt Sgt Wright got the other, his first and only Diver, which he intercepted in the Tenterden area: "Immediately following my final attack, the Diver exploded in the air three miles west of airfield at Staplehurst."

306 (Polish) Squadron (Mustang III) Brenzett

Flt Lt J. Siekierski PAF	FB241/UZ-Z	V-1	1517	Grid R.1148

315 (Polish) Squadron (Mustang III) Brenzett

Flt Sgt J. Bargielowski PAF	FB371/PK-B	V-1	1815	Dymchurch area
Plt Off A. Judek PAF	FB362/PK-A	V-1 shared	1820	Ashford/Redhill

Plt Off Judek shared his kill with Flt Sgt Artie Shaw of 56 Squadron.

322 (Dutch) Squadron (Spitfire XIV) West Malling

Flt Lt L.C.M. van Eendenburg	RB160/VL-A	V-1	1740	Grid R.0761
Flg Off J. Vlug	VL-K	V-1	1937	Grid R.4165
	VL-K	V-1	2206	Grid R.2959

Flt Lt Kees van Eendenburg intercepted a Diver coming in over Hastings:

"Attacked from starboard to astern, range 200 yards closing to 100 yards. In spite of an explosion from the Diver it still went on and another Spitfire fired, but Diver continued on its way. I made another attack from line astern and pieces fell off. Diver caught fire, crashed and exploded."

Flg Off Johannes Vlug brought down two in two separate patrols:

"Off at 1855, patrolling Ashford to Tenterden. Saw Diver over Ashford. Attacked line astern, range 200 yards. Diver crashed and exploded. Off [again] at 2110. Patrolling Ramsgate to Folkestone when told Diver crossing in south of Lympne. Intercepted, closing to 100 yards. Flames came out and Diver crashed and exploded."

486 (RNZAF) Squadron (Tempest V) Newchurch

Sqn Ldr J.H. Iremonger RAF ⎤	JN763/SA-F	V-1	1735	Tenterden area
Flg Off J.R. Cullen RNZAF ⎦	JN770/SA-V			
Flt Lt H.N. Sweetman RNZAF	JN754/SA-A	V-1	2250	Hastings/Bexhill
Flg Off J.R. Cullen RNZAF	JN770/SA-V	V-1 shared	2245	Rye area

501 Squadron at Westhampnett, equipped with a mixture of Spitfire Vs and IXs, received its first two Tempests during the day, as recalled by Flt Sgt 'Ben' Gunn:

"One bright day there was a roar in the sky and a Tempest appeared. After landing, out stepped a little blonde ATA girl who informed us that there were nineteen more Tempests behind her and two Ansons. 'You are being re-equipped,' she said. The CO looked at me and said, 'If she can fly it, so can you – get airborne.'"

Flg Off Jimmy Grottick added:

"The pattern soon became reasonably settled, that is so far as proper patrol lines for the V-1s were concerned, especially at night. At the beginning of June-July 1944, the day approach was very much 'here comes one – let's have a go', and for this purpose the Spitfire Vs and IXs were not much use. It usually meant stooging at about 6,000 feet in order to get a good dive, and only by this means could the Vs and IXs get anywhere near the thing. Only the Spitfire XIIs and the XIVs with their increased power did better in the early stages."[124]

Night 18/19 JULY

A salvo of Divers crossed over Essex on their way to London shortly after midnight, several falling short, as noted by Warden Carter:

"Another 'hot' night. I wonder if I can recall all that took place. Local siren soon after midnight again and one or two explosions sufficiently near to rattle the windows as I hurriedly dressed. First Doodlebug seen came in low down, almost due east to west; the searchlight screen seemed to be on the near side of him and all that could be seen was the glare and glow of the propulsion unit. Darkie Smith's description as a 'bonfire flying through the air' is very apt. It travelled at a good speed and disappeared behind the Town Hall. It cut out soon after and within seconds the church windows rattled to the crash of the explosion. Just missed the sight when a pilotless aircraft hit Tottenham gasworks smack on the largest gas holder; many million cubic feet of gas went up, and I could believe it in the dazzling glare and brilliant light that rose across the sky. Number three of the 'near-ones' came very soon after, this time much higher and seemed almost to be coming up from behind the church. First seen as a bright star, rushing ever nearer with the deep throated pulsing of the jet engine; then the searchlights caught him and he gleamed like a silver fish with a Chinese lantern in its tail as it tore across the sky to the west. By the sound he landed in Enfield somewhere. Heard later that it had landed in Enfield, in Ladysmith Road."

Another wayward Diver impacted at 2227 in a lane beside Gipping Wood at Gipping in Suffolk (14 miles east of Bury St Edmunds). Some damage was done to Wood Farm but there were no casualties. Two residents of Brixton (SW2) were killed at 0406, when a Diver exploded in Effra Parade/Dalberg Road, inflicting damage to 50 properties.

68 Squadron (Mosquito) Castle Camps

Plt Off M.N. Williams	HK242/WM-D	V-1	0330	off Clacton

"I turned on to Diver and gave three short bursts. In the second burst the Diver was seen to be hit, after which the 'light' flared up and went out, and a trail of smoke was seen. The 'light' came on intermittently and after third burst the Diver was seen to strike the sea and explode."

85 Squadron (Mosquito XVII) Swannington

Sqn Ldr B.A. Burbridge	HK349/VY-R	V-1	0010-0420

96 Squadron (Mosquito XIII) Ford

Lt(A) F.W. Richards RNVR	MM492/ZJ-	V-1	2330	exploded in mid-air
Flt Lt F.R.L. Mellersh	MM577/ZJ-N	V-1	0125	off Beachy Head

157 Squadron (Mosquito XIX) Swannington

Wt Off B. Miller	MM643/RS-F	V-1	0130
Wt Off A.G. McLeod	MM649/RS-M	V-1	0422

264 Squadron (Mosquito XIII) Hartford Bridge

Flt Sgt D.R. Callaghan	MM549/PS-	V-1	0017	Grid R.1951

456 (RAAF) Squadron (Mosquito XVII) Ford

Flt Lt K.A. Roediger RAAF	HK297/RX-V	V-1	0135	Grid R.1065

"I fired at 1,200 feet range dead astern. Sparks and bits flew off the propulsion unit and it burst into flames. Crashed and exploded causing a fire on the ground."

422ndNFS (P-61) Ford

1/Lt J.W. Anderson USAAF	42-5543	V-1	2229-0117

1/Lt Willie Anderson attacked a Diver and reported that the 'light' extinguished. It dived steeply to port but P-61 then broke away owing to IAZ.

Wednesday 19 JULY

Elspeth Road in Wandsworth (SW11) was hit at 0758, the explosion destroying six houses and damaging 20 more, killing six people. Two Divers fell in Peckham (SE15) during the early afternoon, the first at 1203 exploding in the Wood Road/Harpers Mews area, where it demolished 13 properties and killed six people. In the second incident, at 1434, 11 people were killed in McKerrell Road. Some 50 properties were damaged in addition to the destruction of six shops. Fighters brought down nine Divers in the Maidstone/Hollingbourne area, two falling near Yalding, two near Marden, two near Staplehurst, with the remaining three impacting at West Farleigh, Lenham and Harrietsham; only one person was slightly injured.

150 Wing (Tempest V) Newchurch

Wg Cdr R.P. Beamont	JN751/RB	V-1		Rye area

3 Squadron (Tempest V) Newchurch

Wt Off R. Hassall RCAF	JN755/JF-D	V-1	0915	Grid R.16??
Plt Off H.R. Wingate	JN760/JF-R	V-1	0958	Tenterden area
Flt Sgt R.W. Cole	JN768/JF-F	V-1	1004	Appledore area
Flt Lt A.R. Moore	JN868/JF-F	V-1	1120	Rye area
	JN868/JF-F	V-1	1155	Dungeness area
Flg Off R. Dryland	JN822/JF-	V-1	1210	Biddenden area
Flg Off R.H. Clapperton	JN815/JF-	V-1	2231	Hastings area

Canadian Wt Off Ralph Hassall opened the scoring at 0915: "Saw a Diver over Rye at 2,000 feet and closed to 300 yards; fired three four-seconds bursts to 100 yards. Strikes were seen on the tail and the rear of the fuselage. The Diver went down and exploded on the ground." Plt Off Dickie Wingate got No.2: "Saw a Diver eight miles north-west of Dungeness at 2,000 feet. Closed to 100 yards astern, fired and saw strikes on the port wing. Fired again and the Diver went down, exploding on the ground." No.3 fell to Flt Sgt Bob Cole: "Saw Diver two miles north of Lydd at 3,000 feet. Closed from 600 yards to 200 yards with short bursts and saw strikes on the starboard wing and tail. The Diver rolled to the right and went down, exploding near Appledore." Two more were shot down by Flt Lt Moore:

"Saw a Diver two miles north of Rye at 3,000 feet. Closed to 250 yards astern and gave two short bursts. The Diver went down and exploded on the ground eight miles north of Rye. Saw second Diver three miles north of Dungeness at 3,000 feet. Close to 200 yards and gave two short bursts. The jet exploded and the Diver went down, exploding on the ground ten miles north of Dungeness."

Flg Off Dryland joined the act and got one shortly after midday: "Saw a Diver two miles from Newchurch at 2,000 feet. Closed to 100 yards and gave a one-second burst, seeing strikes. The Diver rolled over and exploded on the ground near Biddenden." There followed a lull until late evening, when Flg Off Clapperton scored: "Saw a Diver three miles east of Hastings at 2,000 feet. Closed to 50 yards astern and was about to attack when an unidentified aircraft fired from 500 yards astern. I then fired and the petrol blew up. The Diver went down, exploding on the ground ten miles north-east of Hastings."

41 Squadron (Spitfire XII) Lympne

Flg Off M.A.L. Balaase (Belg)	MB880/EB-	V-1 shared	0830	Lamberhurst area

Flg Off Mono Balaase shot down his third flying bomb, shared with a Tempest.

56 Squadron (Tempest V) Newchurch

Plt Off A.S. Miller RAAF	EJ578US-I	V-1	0705	Redhill area
Flt Lt K.A. Wigglesworth	JN877/US-M	V-1	1330	Ashford area
Flt Sgt J. Langley ⎱	EJ522/US-F	V-1	1725	Ashford area
Flt Sgt D.E. Matthews ⎰	JN856/US-S			

Plt Off Miller opened the scoring at 0705: "Sighted a Diver six miles north of Rye at 1,000 feet. Fired a deflection burst from starboard at 150 yards and the Diver went down, exploding on the ground." Flt Lt Keith Wigglesworth got the next: "Sighted Diver three miles east of Ashford. I fired a short burst from 150 yards astern and the Diver's starboard wing came off. It crashed, exploding in open ground, five miles north of Ashford."

24 Wing (Spitfire XIV) Deanland ALG

Wg Cdr R.W. Oxspring	NH714/RWO	V-1	1822	Frant area

"Saw Diver north of Hastings and attacked from astern at 300 yards. Strikes caused Diver to decrease speed to 140mph and drop down to treetop level. After further burst Diver fell in a park near Frant, where it exploded."

91 Squadron (Spitfire XIV) Deanland ALG

Sqn Ldr N.A. Kynaston	RM654/DL-F	V-1	1130	Maidstone area
	RM654/DL-F	V-1	1530	Maidstone area
Lt H.F. de Bordas (FF)	RB165/DL-L	V-1	1827	East Grinstead area

Sqn Ldr Norman Kynaston scored during each of two patrols: "Diver seen west of Ashford and closed in to 300 yards. Attacked from astern and Diver fell two miles south-west of Maidstone, exploding in a field." Four hours later he got his second: "Saw Diver over Ashford and attacked from astern at 150 yards. It fell in a pond three miles west of Maidstone, where it exploded." Lt Henri de Bordas rounded off a successful day with another: "Saw Diver immediately after breaking off chase of another and attacked it from astern at 300 yards range, closing down to 100 yards. Diver fell, exploding alongside a road south-east of East Grinstead."

129 Squadron (Mustang III) Brenzett

Flt Lt D.F. Ruchwaldy	FB395/DV-Y	V-1	0820-1015	Hastings area
Sqn Ldr P.D. Thompson	FB123/DV-H	V-1	1215-1335	Hastings area
Flt Lt I.D.S. Strachan RNZAF ⎱	FX862/DV-K	V-1	1640-1840	Tunbridge Wells area
Wt Off A.J. Foster RAAF ⎰	SR438/DV-L			

Flt Lt Des Ruchwaldy engaged his target two miles west of Ashford at 2,000 feet. Following three short bursts from port quarter, the Diver turned to starboard and spun earthwards. A second was intercepted by Sqn Ldr Peter Thompson shortly after midday, and exploded south-east of Hastings following a long chase, necessary as only one cannon was firing. Later in the day Flt Lt Shorty Strachan and Wt Off Joe Foster, having intercepted their target six miles west of Rye, finally shot it down three miles south-east of Tunbridge Wells, where it exploded on the ground.

306 (Polish) Squadron (Mustang III) Brenzett

Flt Sgt J. Zaworski PAF	FB241/UZ-Z	V-1 shared	1130	off Rye
Flt Sgt S. Rudowski PAF	FB380/UZ-F	V-1	1330	Cranbrook area
	FB380/UZ-F	V-1	1345	Lamberhurst area
	FB380/UZ-F	V-1	1649	Maidstone area

Flt Sgt Zaworski took off at 1105 and a Diver was intercepted two miles south of Rye harbour at 3,000 feet. He fired several short bursts from line astern, 550 yards closing to 200 yards. Bursts seen on engine and right wing. Diver crashed four miles from Rye. Flt Sgt Rudowski shot down his first two during an early afternoon sortie, catching the first near Hastings at 2,000 feet. He fired several short bursts from 400 yards closing to 200 yards, following which the Diver crashed and exploded four miles south-west of Cranbrook. He reported that another aircraft behind him was also seen to fire at the same missile. A second Diver was also intercepted near Hastings, flying at 3,000 feet. He attacked from astern and fired several short bursts down to 100 yards. The Diver slowed down, dived and exploded on the ground in the vicinity of Lamberhurst. Again, other aircraft were seen endeavouring to manoeuvre for position. Flt Sgt Rudowski was up again at 1615 and intercepted another Diver three miles west of Ashford at 2,500 feet. It exploded in mid-air near Maidstone following his attack.

315 (Polish) Squadron (Mustang III) Brenzett

Flt Lt M. Cwynar PAF	FZ157/PK-Z	V-1 shared	1040	Tenterden area
Sqn Ldr E. Horbaczewski PAF	FB382/PK-G	V-1 shared	1148	Appledore area
Flt Sgt K. Kijak PAF	FZ154/PK-N	V-1	1210	Rye area
Flt Sgt T. Jankowski PAF	FZ128/PK-X	V-1 shared	1330	Hastings area
Sqn Ldr E. Horbaczewski PAF ⎤	FB382/PK-G	V-1	1400	Hastings area
Flt Sgt T. Jankowski PAF ⎦	FZ128/PK-X			
Flt Lt H. Pietrzak PAF	FB362/PK-A	V-1	1455	Ashford area
	FB362/PK-A	V-1	1520	Newchurch area
Flt Sgt S. Bedkowski PAF ⎤	FB371/PK-B			
Flt Sgt T. Jankowski PAF ⎬	FZ169/PK-R	V-1	1840	Newchurch area
Flg Off A. Czerwiński PAF ⎦	SR440/PK-J			

The squadron enjoyed a successful 'Witch hunt', shooting down seven flying bombs and sharing one more.

322 (Dutch) Squadron (Spitfire XIV) West Malling

Flt Lt L.C.M. van Eendenburg	RB184/VL-B	V-1	0959	Paddock Wood
Flg Off G.F.J. Jongbloed ⎤	VL-E	V-1	1045	Grid R.3159
Flg Off J. Vlug ⎦	VL-D			
Flg Off R.F. Burgwal	NH649/VL-F	V-1	1133	Wittersham area
Flt Lt J.L. Plesman	VL-W	V-1	1320	Hawkhurst area
Flg Off G.F.J. Jongbloed	VL-E	V-1	1320	Grid R.1535
Flg Off P.A. Cramerus	VL-U	V-1 shared	1825	

The first of the day fell to Flt Lt Kees van Eendenburg:

> "Was told that a Diver was crossing in at Rye. Intercepted and attacked north-west of Tenterden, line astern, range 350 yards. Pieces fell off exhaust and long flame appeared. Diver crashed and exploded."

Flg Offs Jan Jongbloed and Johannes Vlug were patrolling together in the Tenterden-

Ashford area, the former reporting:

> "Vectored on to Diver crossing in at Dungeness. I attacked line astern, range 200 yards, closing to 100 yards. Strikes seen and Diver slowed down and lost height to 1,000 feet. A Mustang then attacked and broke away but Diver went on. F/O Vlug attacked line astern, range 200 yards and Diver crashed and exploded."

Flg Off Rudi Burgwal got another in the same general area just under an hour later: "Intercepted and attacked quarter starboard, range 200 yards. Diver rolled over, crashed and exploded." Two more were shot down at 1320, one falling to Flt Lt Jan Plesman: "Was told Diver was crossing over Hastings. Intercepted and attacked line astern, range 300 yards closing to 200 yards. Saw strikes and Diver crashed and exploded 1,000 yards west of Hawkhurst." The second was shot down by Flg Off Jongbloed: "Vectored on to Diver crossing west of Hastings. Attacked quarter port to astern, range 150 yards. Diver went straight down and exploded in a wood." Flg Off Piet Cramerus shot down the final one but shared it with another pilot.

486 (RNZAF) Squadron (Tempest V) Newchurch

Flg Off S.S. Williams RNZAF	EJ523/SA-X	V-1	1210	Tenterden area

FIU (Tempest V) Ford

Flt Lt J. Berry	EJ524/ZQ-Y	V-1	daytime	
	EJ524/ZQ-Y	V-1	night	
	EJ524/ZQ-Y	V-1	night	
	EJ524/ZQ-Y	V-1	night	
	EJ524/ZQ-Y	V-1	night	
Flt Lt R.L.T. Robb	EJ598/ZQ-U	V-1	night	

Flt Lt Howard-Williams wrote:

> "Joe Berry was now alone; his personal score of bombs destroyed stood at twenty. It was obvious that the detachment's morale was in jeopardy and that something would have to be done; it was equally obvious that Joe would have to do it. He decided to play upon the rivalry shown between the day and night units. He chose a day when low cloud and rain made it hard to see from one side of the aerodrome to the other. As he hurried to his aircraft, head bent against the wind, he shot a quick glance at the day wing's Tempests. Dimly through the veil of rain and vapour could be seen the grey shapes snug behind their chocks; there would be no flying for them today, so he would do the job for them. With a grunt of satisfaction he settled in his seat as the mechanic helped him on with his straps. Soon he had the hood wound forward and his cockpit check complete, then he was taking off in a flurry of spray. Cloud base was only 400 feet, but he broke clear of it again at 3,000 feet. He called control; one bomb in the clear, just one, was all he wanted. And then suddenly there it was; streaking along among the cloud caps he made out the unfamiliar outline of a flying bomb in daylight. A short chase put him in position and he shot it down. On his return to the rain-lashed airfield he could not resist the temptation to fly once, low and fast, across the mess tent. He landed without undue difficulty and taxied in. Grotesque figures in their dripping groundsheet capes – half-a-dozen airmen – came out to greet him. As he approached he could see that they were grinning broadly, despite the rain streaming off their faces. Three new pilots were posted in that day and one of them got his first kill that night; Joe got four. The crisis was over."

Night 19/20 JULY

The Staffeln of III/KG3 at Rosières put up all available aircraft, some of which flew two sorties, prior to handing over to Gilze-Rijen for a week or so. A total of 26 sorties were flown, the first aircraft departing at 2246 and the final one returning at 0610. There were no losses. One of the air-launched flying bombs went astray and fell near Thorpe Abbots in Norfolk, a USAAF supply base, as recorded by the unit's diarist:

> "At 2330, a flying bomb hit near the base. The best of it was they called 'Red Alert' but got no

more than 'Red' called over the tannoy when the explosion came. Salvo sure did get out in a hurry with his equipment on. He was shooting crap and all the boys that were there say it was the fastest they have seen salvo move!"

Three others fell in Essex and ten reached London, two impacting in Edmonton and two in Enfield. He177s were also out and two of these were sighted by the crew of an 850 Squadron Avenger from Perranporth on an anti-shipping patrol off Ushant. The Heinkels were circling a group of destroyers, one being engaged and claimed damaged by the Avenger.

68 Squadron (Mosquito XVII) Castle Camps

Flg Off G.T. Gibson RCAF	HK294/WM-Q	V-1	0016	off Manston

"While off Manston was informed by control that there were Divers approaching in the vicinity. I saw visual due east through haze at 2,000 feet. I dived from 4,000 feet and made head-on attack, opening fire at 1,000 yards and closed to 500 yards. The 'light' went out and explosion occurred. The kill was confirmed by the pilot of an XIX who was in the vicinity and saw the Diver explode."

96 Squadron (Mosquito XIII) Ford

Flg Off J. Goode	MM452/ZJ-	V-1	0115	Channel
Sqn Ldr P.L. Caldwell	HK462/ZJ-	V-1	0115	exploded in mid-air
Sqn Ldr R.N. Chudleigh	MM459/ZJ-	V-1	0405	exploded in mid-air
Sqn Ldr W.P. Green	HK379/ZJ-F	V-1	0415	exploded in mid-air
	HK379/ZJ-F	V-1	0430	Channel
	HK379/ZJ-F	V-1	0505	Channel

Flg Off John Goode opened the scoring when he engaged a Diver at 2,500 feet over the sea (Grid R.4218). Having shot its port wing off, it fell into the sea and exploded. At the same time Sqn Ldr Caldwell got another (Grid R.3006), which exploded in the air. Almost three hours later, Sqn Ldr Dick Chudleigh intercepted a Diver over the sea (Grid W.69), which he attacked from 900-750 feet. Its fuel tank exploded, debris probably causing damage to the Mosquito's starboard engine, obligating a return to base on one engine. Shortly thereafter, Sqn Ldr Peter Green scored another hat-trick, getting his first at 0415 (Grid R.20), which exploded in the air, before shooting the port wing off a second (Grid W.59) and finishing by knocking a third into the sea (Grid W.39) half-an-hour later.

157 Squadron (Mosquito XIX) Swannington

Wt Off A.G. McLeod	MM637/RS-P	V-1	0120	North Sea

264 Squadron (Mosquito XII) Hartford Bridge

Flt Lt I.H. Cosby	MM610/PS-	V-1	0105	Grid R.1465
Flg Off P.deL. Brooke	HK506/PS-G	V-1	2333	Grid R.1064
	HK506/PS-G	V-1	0110	Grid R.2568
	HK506/PS-G	V-1	0123	Grid R.1476
Flt Lt M.M. Davison	HK519/PS-	V-1	0130	Grid R.3961
Flt Lt R.L. Beverley	HK516/PS-	V-1	0320	Grid R.1181

Flg Off Peter de Brooke enjoyed a successful patrol, scoring a hat-trick, the first two exploding on the ground but he was unable to obtain a fix for the third owing to balloons. Both those destroyed by Flt Lt Ian Cosby and Flt Lt Beverley came down over land. Aboard Flt Lt Mike Davison's HK519 as an observer was Lt-Col J.H. Fell RA, Chief Instructor in Searchlights, from AA Command HQ, who later reported:

"I was anxious to get the fighter's viewpoint on S/L-aided interception of flying bombs, and was lucky enough to get a flight. We were airborne at about 2250 and arrived at our orbit at 2320. It was still partially light and it was not too easy to see the orbits. There was some haze and in addition there was broken cloud around 6,000 feet. We were patrolling at 7,000 feet and my only job was to keep a keen lookout for other aircraft. We burned navigation lights the whole time. At about midnight we were warned that trade was approaching. We positioned ourselves as best we could and asked permission to reduce height to just under 6,000 feet because of the cloud. This was granted. Very soon we saw flak – mostly light but with some heavy. SL beams went up and then we saw the flying bomb. We were just getting ready for the chase when we saw it hit. It caught fire and crashed.

"We were told more trade was on the way, so remained in the area. Sure enough, in a couple of minutes we saw the same picture over again, but this time a bomb offered itself as a target. We flew across on a cut-off vector till we were almost over the bomb. This process was enormously assisted by the SL beams, which clearly indicated the course of the target. Once over the little flame we did a tight turn to starboard and simultaneously dived upon it. In a very few seconds (or so it appeared) we were level with the bomb and behind it. The pilot gave it a burst – nothing happened. We closed some more (judging the range is the most difficult part of the job) and gave a second burst. Still nothing happened. Reluctantly the pilot swung away and started to climb. We had dropped to 800 feet and it was not safe to go any further at this height. I feel it is doubtful if this flying bomb reached London at such a low height.

"We went back to patrol. At 0100 we were again warned of trade. Much the same process was repeated except that in doing a cut-off vector we inadvertently went slightly too near the guns and found some tracer around us, though not uncomfortably close. This time there was no mistake. We dived and closed rapidly. The first burst failed to produce results. A second burst produced strikes – then suddenly the flame went out. We saw it dive down – apparently into open country. 'We'd better get out of this' said my pilot, and started to climb and turn. Almost instantaneously we saw a great pink flash and the next moment the Mosquito shuddered violently with the blast. It was not unlike the effect of an air pocket, except that one went up instead of down. We went back to orbit until 0130 and then headed for home as we had not enough fuel left for another chase. We landed at 0200."

418 (RCAF) Squadron (Mosquito VI) Hurn

Sqn Ldr R. Bannock RCAF	HR147/TH-Z	V-1	0114	Channel
	HR147/TH-Z	V-1	0221	Channel

605 Squadron (Mosquito VI) Manston

Flt Lt G.C. Wright	UP-	V-1 probable 0013	off Manston

"At 0012 attacked Diver from 500 yards, height of target 2,500 feet, north-east of Manston. Long burst given from astern and Diver immediately lost height to 1,500 feet. Attack broken off eight miles north of Manston at 0013 with Diver still losing height. The reason for breaking off the attack was that I saw a second Diver and turned to chase, but was unable to position and open fire. At 0245 two Divers flying close together came out from Coxyde area. They appeared to converge and one light extinguished and almost immediately the second one went out. It may be assumed that these Divers collided."

The Squadron IO added, for the attention of Group HQ:

"It would be appreciated if the final assessment of the 'probably destroyed' would be communicated to us for completion of the Squadron total. Sgt Hanson and two corporals of our ground crew definitely state that at about 0015 they were watching a Diver approach Manston airfield from the north-east and they actually saw it lose height rapidly and explode a few miles north of this aerodrome – presumably in the sea. This time coincides with the above claim and we would appreciate your final assessment being forwarded to us."

Thursday 20 JULY

Four people were killed in New Cross (SE14) at 0640, when a Diver exploded between Ommaney Road and Jerningham Road, destroying four houses and damaging others.

3 Squadron (Tempest V) Newchurch

Flg Off R.E. Barckley	JN817/JF-H	V-1	0542	Rye area
Flt Lt B.C. Mackenzie RAAF	JN735/JF-	V-1	0550	Paddock Wood area
Flt Sgt D.J. Mackerras RAAF	JN754/JF-	V-1	0630	Battle area

Flg Off Bob Barckley sighted a Diver over Winchelsea: "Closed to 250 yards and fired with deflection. Closed to 50 yards and gave a two-second burst from astern. The Diver went down, exploding on the ground five miles west of Rye." Australian Flt Lt Mackenzie was off at 0500: "Saw a Diver over New Romney at 2,000 feet and closed to 200 yards. Fired, and many pieces of the wing came off and the Diver went down and exploded north of Paddock Wood." An hour later fellow Australian Flt Sgt Mackerras got another:

"Saw a Diver between Hastings and Bexhill at 2,000 feet. Closed to 300 yards quarter astern and gave one short burst. Closed to 200 yards astern and fired again, observing strikes on the port wing, half of which fell off. The Diver went down and exploded near Battle."

41 Squadron (Spitfire XII) Lympne

Flt Sgt I.T. Stevenson	MB878/EB-	V-1	0644	Channel

"I was on a reciprocal course to Diver until told to turn by control. Closed 150-50 yards and fired a three-seconds burst. Strikes seen and Diver peeled to port and exploded in the sea at 0644."

91 Squadron (Spitfire XIV) Deanland ALG

Flg Off K.R. Collier RAAF	RM685/DL-M	V-1	0620	Lamberhurst area
Flt Lt J.W.P. Draper RCAF	RM686/DL-G	V-1	0823	Tonbridge area
Flg Off K.R. Collier RAAF	RM685/DL-M	V-1	0940	West Malling area
Flt Lt A.R. Cruickshank RCAF	NH703/DL-	V-1	0948	East Grinstead area
Wt Off F.A. Lewis	RM686/DL-G	V-1	1020	Etchingham area

All five Divers were brought down during the morning, the first by Flg Off Ken Collier: "Saw Diver north of Hastings and attacked from 200 yards, closing to 150 yards. Diver fell on farm houses south of Lamberhurst, exploding on impact." The next was shot down by Flt Lt Draper two miles east of Tonbridge: "Sighted Diver crossing in north of Bexhill. Attacked from 150 yards astern and it fell, exploding in a wood." Flg Off Collier was off again at 0820 and at 0940 sighted a Diver over Staplehurst: "Attacked from astern at 350 yards. Diver fell, exploding in a field six miles north of base." Flt Lt Ray Cruickshank saw his target north of Uckfield: "Attacked from astern at 200/150 yards and it fell in field three miles south-east of East Grinstead, where it exploded." Number five for the day went to Wt Off Lewis: "Saw Diver south-west of Etchingham and attacked with short burst from astern at 250 yards. Diver fell on level crossing two miles west of Etchingham, where it exploded."

165 Squadron (Spitfire IX) Lympne

Flt Lt J.K. Porteous RNZAF	MK425/SK-V	V-1	0730	
Flt Sgt C.R. Bundara RAAF	ML139/SK-Q	V-1	0835	Tenterden area

Flt Sgt Colin Bundara[125] reported: "Intercepted ten miles north-west of Tenterden. First burst caused sheet of flame from rear of Diver. Second burst exploded petrol tank. Yellow flash, Diver turned over and went in. Confirmed by No.1."

306 (Polish) Squadron (Mustang III) Brenzett

While chasing a Diver over Kent, Plt Off Zygmunt Kawnik's Mustang (UZ-Y) was hit by AA fire and slightly damaged, though he was able to land safely.

315 (Polish) Squadron (Mustang III) Brenzett

Flt Lt M. Cwynar PAF	FZ157/PK-U	V-1 shared	0640	Newchurch area
Flt Sgt T. Berka PAF	FZ128/PK-X	V-1 shared	0645	Tenterden area
Sqn Ldr E. Horbaczewski PAF	FB382/PK-G	V-1	1050	off Hythe

Flt Lt Michal Cwynar attacked a Diver at 1,500 feet near Newchurch, following which it dived into woods and exploded. He reported that two Tempests had also attacked and fired from long range without result. Flt Sgt Berka had a similar experience: "One Diver destroyed, shared with Tempest. Intercepted near Tenterden at 2,000 feet. Attacked from 500 yards, closing to 200 yards. Diver crashed on the ground at R.1075. Two Tempests fired, but only one hit and slowed down the Diver." Shared with Wt Off Gus Hooper of 486 Squadron. A few hours later, Sqn Ldr Horbaczewski intercepted a Diver three miles south of Hythe: "When flying at 8,000 feet over the gun belt, no gunfire seen, so I dived vertically and, when pulling out, looped in front of Diver. Closed on Diver, which then turned over and crashed into the sea one mile south of Hythe."

322 (Dutch) Squadron (Spitfire XIV) West Malling

Flt Lt J.L. Plesman	VL-W	V-1	0727	Ashford area
Flg Off M.L. van Bergen	VL-U	V-1	0820	Appledore area

The Diver attacked by Flt Lt Jan Plesman fell near Ashford: "While patrolling Margate to Folkestone was told Diver coming in near Dover. Attacked from 150 yards, line astern. Saw strikes and Diver crashed and exploded north-east of Ashford." Shortly after, Flg Off van Bergen got another: "Patrolling north and south of Ashford when told Diver crossing. Attached line astern from 200 yards and Diver crashed and exploded north of Appledore."

486 (RNZAF) Squadron (Tempest V) Newchurch

Plt Off R.D. Bremner RNZAF	JN802/SA-C	V-1 shared	0620	Maidstone area
Wt Off G.J.M. Hooper RNZAF	JN797/SA-K	V-1 shared	0640	West Malling area

Wt Off Gus Hooper shared his victim with Flg Off Michal Cwynar of 315 Squadron.

FIU (Tempest V) Ford

Flt Off B.F. Miller USAAF	ZQ-	V-1

The American NCO pilot seconded from 605 Squadron scored his second kill.

Night 20/21 JULY

In the early hours of the morning, RAF Manston reported an unidentified aircraft in its landing circuit and, at 0240, a Bf109G (White 16/412951[126]) landed safely, its surprised pilot Ltn Horst Prenzel of 1/JG301 having mistaken Manston for a French airfield. He had been patrolling the V-1 launching sites in the Pas-de-Calais from his base at St Dizier when he became lost. Five minutes later a second Bf109G (Yellow 8/163240) on similar duty and from the same Gruppe also attempted to land at Manston, but fearing he was about to overshoot, Fw Manfred Gromill of 3 Staffel raised his undercarriage and carried out a belly landing, causing considerable damage to his aircraft. Both pilots were promptly taken prisoner[127]. Swordfish of 819 Squadron were based at Manston at this time, and N/Air Tom Mogford remembered:

"Almost every type of aircraft landed at Manston, but even we were taken aback at one pair that arrived unexpectedly. One night, two aircraft joined the circuit, and the control tower staff, rather naively, switched on the runway lights. The aircraft promptly landed and, then, silence.

For quite a long time nothing happened, no pilots emerged, no radio contact was made – nothing. The crash crew was sent out to investigate and found two German Messerschmitt fighters, of the very latest type, complete with German pilots! Once he had got his breath back, the duty corporal contacted the tower, and the authorities belatedly swung into action. The pilots were carried off for interrogation and the ME109s were trundled off the runway to a place nearby.

"Came the dawn. A solitary Swordfish rolled slowly round the perimeter track, after returning from a patrol, the weary crew eagerly looking forward to their breakfast bacon and eggs, a war-time treat only available for those who had been on operations. As it approached the tower, the Swordfish came to an abrupt halt. The pilot, well up on aircraft recognition, had spotted the outline of the 109s. A heated discussion took place between pilot and navigator, both by now thoroughly alarmed. They were convinced that they had made a gross error and landed on an airfield on the wrong side of the Channel. Even the TAG had woken up and was wondering what life in a German prison camp was going to be like. Just as the pilot had made up his mind to turn his plane around and leg it for where he hoped home would be, the panic was allayed by the sight of an RAF truck arriving at the tower. A relieved, but shaken, crew then continued on their way. We never learned whether the Germans had made a navigational error, or whether they had simply decided to surrender."

Of the Diver blitz, he added:

"We soon became quite accustomed to this new weapon. No longer did we dash out to gape at them, but, at dusk one evening, the Germans made a determined attempt to swamp our defences and the sky was full of the things. Anti-aircraft guns were blazing away, fighters were swooping to the attack, and in the middle of it all a single Swordfish sailed sedately along without a scratch. Not really as surprising as it sounds, because even the dimmest of gunners could hardly fail to know the difference between an ultra-modern, pilotless aircraft and an escapee from history rumbling along at no more than 80 miles per hour."

Deptford's Dockyard (SE8) was hit by yet another Diver – the fourth in two weeks – where 20 concrete huts used as sleeping quarters by the USN were badly damaged, killing one. Other buildings were also damaged. Another fell at Gibson's Hill, Upper Norwood (SE16) at 0433, destroying four houses and killing an occupant. Two victims of night fighters fell near Malling and Boxley, injuring one person at the former location and damaging 40 houses at the latter.

68 Squadron (Mosquito XVII) Castle Camps
Mosquito (HK242) crewed by Plt Off Michael Williams and his 28-year-old navigator Plt Off Alf Waples FTR. Last fix received at 0510 four miles east of Dover.

96 Squadron (Mosquito XIII) Ford

Flg Off J. Goode ⎫	HK406/ZJ-	V-1	2315	off Hastings
Wt Off W.A. McLardy RAAF ⎰	MM577/ZJ-N			
Sqn Ldr W.P. Green	HK417/ZJ-	V-1	2330-0220	Channel
Wg Cdr E.D. Crew	HK479/ZJ-	V-1	0140	Channel
	HK479/ZJ-	V-1	0207	Channel
Sqn Ldr R.N. Chudleigh[128]	HK379/ZJ-F	V-1	0424	exploded in mid-air
	HK379/ZJ-F	V-1	0506	Channel

Although Flg Off John Goode and Wt Off Bill McLardy each claimed a Diver off Hastings at more or less the same time, the authorities decided that they had attacked the same bomb.

264 Squadron (Mosquito XIII) Hartford Bridge

Flt Lt J.C. Trigg	MM455/PS-Q	V-1	0255	Maidstone area
Flt Lt J.P. Bentley	HK519/PS-	V-1	0420	West Malling area
Flg Off J. Daber	HK472/PS-	V-1	0440	Tunbridge Wells area

456 (RAAF) Squadron (Mosquito XVII) Ford

Flg Off R.G. Pratt RAAF	HK303/RX-	V-1	2320	Grid R.27
Flt Lt C.L. Brooks RAF	HK253/RX-	V-1	2325	Grid R.07
Flg Off F.S. Stevens RAAF	HK290/RX-J	V-1 damaged	2225-0129	over Kent

Flg Off Pratt was off at 2225 and engaged a Diver an hour later: "I attacked it from 600 yards astern and it went into the ground and exploded. Confirmed by searchlight site." A second was brought down at almost the same time by Flt Lt Brooks: "Engaged a Diver at 2325 from 600 yards astern. It exploded on the ground." Flg Off Fred Stevens pursued his target, which was travelling at 400mph at a height of 500 feet, over Kent and observed strikes but had to break away as it entered the balloon barrage.

422ndNFS (P-61) Ford

Capt T. Spelis USAAF	42-5540	V-1	pm	exploded in mid-air

Capt Tadas Spelis and his radar operator Flt Off Eleutherious Eleftherian (known conveniently as 'Lefty'), who were accompanied by the unit's IO Lt Philip M. Guba USAAF, were vectored onto a flying bomb. Spelis closed in to 450 feet before opening fire, following which the bomb exploded. The P-61 was thrown out of control and only with much difficulty was the pilot able to regain control and land safely back at Ford. Examination revealed much blistering of paint and large areas of fabric-covered control surfaces burnt away. Lt Guba recalled:

> "This buzz bomb came flying right by us and it looked like a full moon streaking along like a freight train only it was going several times faster than one. Our pilot was in perfect position to intercept it and we started climbing very fast. I was surprised to witness how close we were before we started firing. The first burst didn't seem to do anything, but the second created a dangerous situation for us. One minute there was almost total darkness and the next we were lit up like the sun had exploded. We had absolutely no time to move right or left so we barrelled right through the centre of the fireball. It blinded everyone in the aircraft and at the time we were diving at a low altitude, so the ground wasn't too far away. We could smell gasoline and feel the intense heat as we went through the explosion. Our R/O yelled over the intercom to see if Capt Spelis was all right, but there was no answer. I began to reach for the escape hatch just as he responded. He had been temporarily blinded by the flash and only a small portion of his vision was usable out of the corner of his eye. He was barely able to see the horizon and began to pull us out. He brought us back to base with some difficulty because of damage to the control surfaces. He learned a lesson the hard way in that you don't fly that close to a V-1 before opening fire."[129]

A second Diver was claimed by another 422ndNFS pilot (possibly 1/Lt Paul A. Smith in 42-5544) but was not awarded.

Friday 21 JULY

Seven people were killed at 0654 when a Diver exploded in Penge High Street/Blenheim Close (SE20), where more than 150 properties were damaged, some severely. A few hours later another fell in the same area, killing another Penge resident. A Diver crashed into Barchester Street in Bow, East London, killing seven and seriously injuring a further 19. Thirty houses were destroyed and a large two-storey building was severely damaged. Deptford (SE8) received its second bomb within four hours, this impacting at the junction of Prince Street/Czar Street – near the Dockyard – killing six and damaging 40 houses. The Diver that fell in Lambeth Road (SE11) at 0815 severely damaged the Eldorado Ice Cream Company's premises and killed one person. Another was killed at 1018 when a Diver came down at the junction of Knights Hill and Furneaux Road, West Norwood (SE27), damaging many houses.

The Diver that exploded in Barry Road/Hindsman Road, East Dulwich (SE21) at 1234 also claimed a life. Fighters brought down six Divers during the day in the Maidstone area, these falling at Nettlestead, Hunton, Staplehurst, Trottiscliffe, Shipbourne and Wrotham. There were no reported casualties.

3 Squadron (Tempest V) Newchurch

Plt Off K.G. Slade-Betts	JN817/JF-H	V-1	c0600	Beachy Head area
	JN817/JF-H	V-1	0630	Beachy Head area
Flt Sgt M.J.A. Rose	EJ504/JF-	V-1	0730	off Hastings
Plt Off K.G. Slade-Betts	JN817/JF-H	V-1	1007	off Hastings

This turned out to be Plt Off Slade-Betts' day, shooting down two during an early morning patrol and another four hours later: "Took off at 0510. Saw a Diver above cloud at 3,000 feet. Closed to 250 yards with several bursts and destroyed it. Saw a second Diver ten miles north of Eastbourne at 3,000 feet. Closed to 200 yards with one burst and saw strikes. The Diver went down and exploded on the ground 14 miles north of Beachy Head." Flt Sgt Morrie Rose added another to his total: "Vectored on to Diver above cloud at 3,500 feet. Closed to 150 yards and gave a one-second burst from astern. The left wing fell off and the Diver spun in, on fire, exploding on the sea 30 miles south of Hastings." Slade-Betts' third of the day was also shot down off Hastings.

41 Squadron (Spitfire XII) Lympne

Wt Off A.S. Appleton	EN602/EB-	V-1	0610	off Hastings

Flg Off Mono Balaase and Wt Off Archie Appleton took off for a dawn patrol, when several flying bombs were seen approaching. They became separated as they each manoeuvred on to a target, Appleton shooting one down some eight miles south of Hastings, while Balaase failed to score.

56 Squadron (Tempest V) Newchurch

Flt Sgt A.C. Drew	EJ522/US-F	V-1	0600	off Hastings
Flg Off W.R. MacLaren	EJ547/US-A	V-1	1800	Grid R.0469

Flt Sgt Tony Drew took off at 0555 and almost immediately sighted a Diver: "I fired from 250 yards astern and the Diver crashed, exploding in the sea off Hastings." It was not until late afternoon that the next successful interception took place, Flg Off Bill MacLaren claiming the kill: "Sighted a Diver over Tenterden at 2,000 feet. I fired a short burst from 200 yards, closing to 50 yards. The port wing came off and the Diver exploded on the ground."

91 Squadron (Spitfire XIV) Deanland ALG

Flt Lt A.R. Cruickshank RCAF	RM649/DL-	V-1	1857	Uckfield area
Flg Off A.R. Elcock	RM685/DL-M	V-1	2004	Tunbridge Wells area

486 (RNZAF) Squadron (Tempest V) Newchurch

Flt Lt J.H. McCaw RNZAF	JN758/SA-Y	V-1	1558	Rye area

Wg Cdr Desmond Scott RNZAF OC 123 Wing later wrote:

"It was from Le Tréport that I flew across to Newchurch in the Romney Marshes to attend my long-delayed Tangmere farewell party. 486 was based there, flying Tempests in pursuit of flying bombs. Before leaving to cross the Channel, my fitter and rigger filled the gun bays of my Typhoon with about four-dozen bottles of champagne. Then I took off and climbed over a high belt of cloud, which covered the Channel. Letting down before coming into land I noticed what I thought were thin streams of petrol leaving the trailing edge of both wings. It had me puzzled, but on landing the mystery was soon solved. The altitude and the vibration had been too much for some of the cargo in the gun bays and the bottles had blown their corks. It proved a happy, if heavy, evening and I was eventually put to bed on the high narrow operating table in station sick quarters. Not that I needed medical attention; they were simply short of what they considered suitable beds for a senior officer. In my condition, I could have slept on my head in a chicken coop. The next morning I had a rude awakening. Someone blew up a flying bomb almost directly over the airfield and a shower of plaster fell from the ceiling. I learnt afterward that it was Jim McCaw – the boy who had been so fond of Tangmere meat pies. He had finished his rest period and was back with his old squadron."

FIU (Tempest V) Ford

Flt Lt J. Berry	EJ524/ZQ-Y	V-1	daytime

Both **85** and **157 Squadron** moved their Mosquitos from Swannington to West Malling during the day.

Six missile-armed Do217s from III/KG100 were tasked to intercept the Royal Navy's 14th Destroyer Escort Group operating off Brest, which was being protected by one Mosquito and three Beaufighters from **406 (RCAF) Squadron** and four Coastal Command Mosquito IVs from **248 Squadron**. The Dorniers were engaged by the fighter escort, Sqn Ldr David Williams RCAF in the 406 Mosquito (MM731) claiming one shot down and sharing a second. Having set an engine of his second victim on fire, he pulled back as the crew were beginning to bale out, only to witness another Mosquito nip in and shoot it down, the Coastal pilot claiming a victory. One of the Beaufighter pilots Flg Off W.H. Meakin RCAF also claimed a Dornier but was hit by return fire and only just managed to regain base. The Coastal pilots reported shooting down two Dorniers, one apiece by Flg Off L.N. Collins (LR346/DM-A) and Flt Lt F.R. Passey AFM (HR127/DM-F), while Flt Lt Stan Nunn (HJ826/DM-R) shared with Flt Sgt W.W. Scott the probable destruction of what was believed to be a He177. However, 30-year-old Walter Scott and his 32-year-old observer Flt Sgt John Blackburn lost their lives when their aircraft HP973/DM-Z crashed into the sea. A brief report of 248's part in the action revealed:

> "At 1320 'F' [Flt Lt Passey] saw enemy aircraft crash into the sea and explode three miles north-west of Escort Group, survivors being picked up. At 1337, sighted Do217, both aircraft ['F' Passey and 'A' Collins] attacked and 'A' claims the e/a as destroyed. At 1348, Do217 sighted, 'F' attacked and saw numerous strikes on fuselage before e/a dived steeply into cloud as if out of control. At 1500, 'F' sighted Do217 and attacked with machine-guns as cannon was exhausted. Strikes were seen on the fuselage as e/a dived steeply into cloud, no return fire being noticed. At 1505, sighted a possible He177 with 'R' [Nunn] and 'Z' [Scott] chasing it and attempted to head off the e/a from the coast. 'Z' was ahead and attacked first from starboard beam, breaking away on fire towards the sea. 'R' then closed to attack from 800-200 yards. Strikes were seen on port wing and fuselage of e/a and this later was seen on fire in a shallow dive before disappearing into cloud. 'R' was hit by return fire and both crew slightly injured."

Meanwhile, two Mosquitos from **235 Squadron** that had been ordered to relieve the escort ran into severe weather, but the crews decided to continue having received a report that the destroyers were being harassed by several Dorniers, carrying glider-bombs. Boring their way through dense clouds and mist down to sea level, through continuous driving rain, the two aircraft deliberately separated to avoid any possible air collision, but as they did so one Mosquito – HR131/LA-Z crewed by Flg Off M.L. Dodd and Flg Off F. McK. Morrison – dipped a wing into the sea and crashed at high speed. The second Mosquito eventually returned to base to report that weather conditions were near impossible to penetrate. The CO, Wg Cdr John Yonge[130], decided to fly the sortie himself (in HR139/LA-D), in company with one volunteer crew (Flg Off D.B. Frost/Flg Off Fuller in HP977/LA-J):

"When Frost and I took off the weather had cleared a little over base, but we had to fly blind, in close formation, to get through the rain and low cloud. We finally broke cloud at 1,400 feet while approaching the patrol area. Then we came into a patch of weather the like of which I had never seen before. We were in a col, with a thunderstorm to the south, sea fog over Brest and Ushant, and continuous rain to the north; it was the most extraordinary combination of weather. Then we reached the patrol area and it was comparatively clear, but we had to vary our height and fly blind from time to time to keep at our task. At 20 minutes past one I had still not found either the destroyers or the reported Dorniers. Then, half an hour later, we sighted two Do217s, with a Mosquito from another Wing opening fire on them at long range. I learned later that the Mosquito [sic] was an ADGB aircraft, and that it was still trying to attack after being hit in its port engine [Meakin of 406]. The pilot had to give it up and fly home as best he could. We jettisoned our wing tanks, opened up to full boost and revs, and attacked the second Dornier at 300 knots. I was just about to open fire when I saw that Frost had already set its port engine on fire. I therefore swung my gunsight on to the leading Dornier and attacked with several bursts of cannon and .303, opening at 800 yards.

"I closed right behind its tail, although he was doing his best to dodge me. Out of the corner of my eye I saw the first German, which Frost had hit, diving in flames and three parachutes floating down to the water. My fire was effective. The Dornier blew up, 100 yards in front of me, so close that streams of his oil blacked me out completely. I had to jerk back the stick to avoid hitting him, and then to fly on instruments until the windscreen wiper had cleaned some of the oil away. Then I could just about peer through the relatively clear spots between the thick German oil and saw the two Dorniers blazing on the sea, and several of the crews in dinghies. It was only then that we saw the destroyers we were defending from the Dorniers for the first time. I spoke to the Navy and told them that both Germans had been shot down in flames, and that the survivors were waiting in the water to be picked up. Frost and I became separated in the thick cloud on the way back, but we landed at base within five minutes of each other. Here I handed the Mosquito over to the ground crew, always there to make us feel that they were part of the effort. They wiped the thick oil from the fuselage; then painted a swastika on it for our victory."

Three Do217Ms were actually shot down; 6N+GC from 7 Staffel flown by Uffz Gustave Schmidt who was rescued together with his crew; one from 8 Staffel 6N+CS flown by Ltn Wolfgang Schirmer, he and his crew perishing; and one from 9 Staffel (6N+GS) flown by Oblt Karl Lamp, who was rescued with one of his crew. A fourth Dornier, although damaged, made it back to base.[131]

Night 21/22 JULY

While fuelling a flying bomb ready for operations at Venlo, two airmen[132] were killed when an explosion occurred; possibly others were injured. Nineteen launches were made, but only two Divers reached London, while seven came down in Essex. Later, a Heinkel from 8/KG3 – 5K+AS flown by Ltn Ludwig Schmalholz – crashed at Jutphas near Utrecht while on an operational flight. There were no survivors[133]. One Diver fell in Calders Place, Streatham (SW2), causing damage to industrial buildings and private dwellings, killing one.

605 Squadron (Mosquito VI) Manston

Flt Lt G.C. Wright	UP-	V-1	0005	Channel
Flt Lt T.E. Knight	UP-	V-1	0333	Channel

Not all flying bombs succumbed to the initial attack. Not only once, but twice did Flt Lt George Wright fly alongside his target before being able to shoot it down:

"At 2359, Diver sighted. I attacked from 300 yards with cannon. Two-to-three seconds bursts. No results seen so I drew up alongside of the Diver to assist in estimating the range. Dropped back to 250 yards and fired another four-seconds burst. Possible strikes were seen so again drew up alongside the Diver and observed that its speed was now 200mph and it was undulating

200 feet in height. A good fire was burning in port of the jet unit and in the body. Drew back and fired off all remaining rounds. Drew to one side and observed large fire in fuselage and target was diving slightly. Another aircraft then attacked and as he broke away Diver blew up and crashed in the sea where the warhead exploded."

Saturday 22 JULY

The British Government announced that the total number of flying bombs plotted as launched up to 0600 on 22 July was 4,056. After a break of five nights (10/11 to 14/15 July), London was again the main target for attacks by night as well as by day. Sixty-three V-1s penetrated the defences and impacted on London during the day, one killing or injuring 175 people in the west of the capital. Three lost their lives in Clive Road/Hamilton Road, West Norwood (SE27) and another was killed at the junction of Bird in Bush Road and Friary Street, Peckham (SE15) at 1025. At least ten houses were damaged in this incident. Two more were killed when a Diver fell in Barnfield Wood Road, Beckenham (BR3) at 1326.

1 Squadron (Spitfire LFIXb) Lympne

Flg Off J.O. Dalley	MJ422/JX-	V-1	2105	Lamberhurst/ Hawkhurst
Flg Off D.H. Davy	ML117/JX-D	V-1 shared	2220	exploded in mid-air

Flg Off Jo Dalley DFM:

"My first V-1 was over farmland on the Weald. On being hit, it reared up vertically and then went straight down into a field full of cows. The cows took off like the start of the Grand National, leapt over a hedge into the next field and then started eating a growing crop within a minute or two. The farmer did not seem very pleased as he ran from his house to recover matters. We always dreaded that a V-1 we might shoot down would fall on a house."

Flg Off Dennis Davy:

"Two Mustangs seen attacking Diver, which slowed down from 350-300mph, but carried on. Mustangs broke away. I attacked and Diver blew up in air – own aircraft damaged by Diver fragments."

150 Wing (Tempest V) Newchurch

Wg Cdr R.P. Beamont	JN751/RB	V-1	pm	Bexhill area
	JN751/RB	V-1	pm	Rye area
	JN751/RB	V-1	pm	Hastings-Eastbourne

3 Squadron (Tempest V) Newchurch

Flt Lt A.R. Moore	JN817/JF-H	V-1	1520	Grid R.0557
	JN817/JF-H	V-1	1535	Biddenden area
Flt Sgt R.W. Cole	JN759/JF-	V-1	1705	Kingsnorth area
Sqn Ldr A.S. Dredge	JN812/JF-M	V-1	1807	Biddenden area
Flt Sgt M.J.A. Rose	EJ504/JF-	V-1	1801	Newenden area
	EJ504/JF-	V-1	1909	Tunbridge Wells area
Flt Lt A.R. Moore	JN817/JF-H	V-1	1917	Hastings area
	JN817/JF-H	V-1	1927	Grid R.1632
Flg Off D.J. Butcher	JN745/JF-T	V-1 shared	2110	Bexhill area
Sqn Ldr A.R. Dredge	JN812/JF-M	V-1	2141	Brookfield area
Flg Off M.F. Edwards	JN862/JF-Z	V-1 shared	2147	Rye area
Flt Sgt R.W. Cole	JN759/JF-	V-1	2147	Pevensey area
	JN769/JF-G	V-1	2209	Grid R.2547
Plt Off H.R. Wingate	EJ521/JF-	V-1 damaged	c.2230	Hastings area
	EJ521/JF-	V-1 damaged	c.2230	Hastings area
	EJ521/JF-	V-1	2250	Tonbridge area

3 Squadron enjoyed another very successful day, accounting for 14 Divers including three shared, of which Flt Lt Moore was credited with four in two patrols, and Flt Sgt Bob Cole getting three, the former bagging his first pair during the early afternoon:

"Saw a Diver north of Rye at 2,500 feet. Closed from 600 yards to 200 yards dead astern with a long and a short burst. It went down, exploding in a wood. Saw the second Diver over Rye at 2,000 feet. Closed to 200 yards dead astern and gave a short burst. The Diver went down and exploded on the ground."

Flt Sgt Bob Cole got his first of the day at 1705: "Saw a Diver six miles north of Dungeness at 3,000 feet. Closed to 200 yards and gave eight short bursts. Saw strikes on starboard wing and the Diver spun in, exploding on the ground south-east of Kingsnorth." The CO got the next, which crashed near Biddenden:

"Saw a Diver over Dungeness at 3,000 feet. Closed to 250 yards below and to starboard and gave a two-seconds burst. Strikes were seen on the jet unit and the Diver climbed slightly into the fringe of the cloud and slowed to 340mph. Closed to 300 yards dead astern and gave two short bursts. The port wing broke off and the Diver spun in, exploding on the edge of a farmyard."

Flt Sgt Morrie Rose's brace were scored an hour apart:

"Saw a Diver four miles east of Hastings at 2,000 feet. Closed to 200 yards astern and gave two long bursts and the Diver went down, exploding on the ground. Saw a second Diver over Bexhill at 2,500 feet. Chased for eight miles when two Spits [probably Wt Off Roberts and Flg Off Watkin of 610 Squadron] turned in front of me from ahead and closed to 400-500 yards, firing long bursts without strikes. The Spits pulled away and I closed to 300 yards and gave two medium bursts, with strikes, and the Diver stalled and dived to 1,500 feet and then carried on in a shallow dive. It was then attacked again by one of the Spits before exploding on the ground five miles south-east of Tunbridge Wells."

Flt Lt Moore got his second brace of the day during an early evening patrol:

"Saw a Diver three miles inland from Hastings at 3,000 feet, with Mustangs firing from 500 yards with one strike but the Diver was still drawing away unaffected. I chased for six miles and then closed to 350 yards. A medium burst from dead astern caused the Diver to go down and explode on the ground eight miles north-west of Hastings. Saw a second Diver three miles north of Bexhill at 2,500 feet. Closed rapidly to 100 yards dead astern and a short burst sent the Diver down. It exploded on the ground."

Flg Off Butcher was obliged to share his kill with two Mustangs (Flg Offs Holmes and Parker of 129 Squadron): "Saw a Diver north of Hastings at 2,000 feet. Closed from 250 yards to 50 yards dead astern, firing short bursts. Strikes were seen all over and the Diver slowed considerably. My engine cut and two Mustangs closed in and finished it off." Sqn Ldr Dredge's report revealed some annoyance when two Mustangs muscled in on his target:

"Saw a Diver over Dungeness at 3,000 feet. Closed to 300 yards and fired. Saw strikes on the starboard wing and fuselage and the Diver half-rolled to starboard and went down, exploding on the ground one mile north-west of Brookfield. Two Mustangs [probably Flt Lt Jan Siekierski and Flg Off Stefan Tronczyński of 306 Squadron] dived in front of my Tempest as the Diver commenced its final plunge and fired just before it hit the ground. This is confirmed by ground witnesses at Brooklands – F/Lt Cotes-Preedy and F/Lt Wigglesworth of 56 Sqdn and F/O Whitman of 3 Sqdn."

Flg Off Edwards and Flt Sgt Bob Cole enjoyed a successful evening patrol, the former reporting: "Saw a Diver over Dungeness at 2,500 feet. Closed to 600 yards and gave two or three long bursts from dead astern and saw strikes. A Tempest then cut in from

above and a Mustang from port. The Diver crashed four miles north-east of Rye."
Meanwhile, Flt Sgt Cole bagged a pair:

> "Saw a Diver over Pevensey at 3,500 feet. Closed to 250 yards dead astern and gave four short bursts. The wings came off and the Diver exploded on the ground seven miles north of Pevensey. Saw second Diver two miles east of Hastings at 3,000 feet and closed to 200 yards. Gave five bursts and the Diver exploded on the ground."

The final success of the day fell to Plt Off Dickie Wingate but not before he frustratingly missed two others:

> "Saw a Diver over Hastings at 2,500 feet. Closed to 500 yards and fired three short bursts and saw strikes on the jet, but had to break owing to balloons. Saw another over Hastings at 2,500 feet and closed to 400 yards. Fired, obtaining a few strikes but another aircraft then passed so broke away. Saw another Diver in searchlight near Tunbridge Wells at 2,500 feet. Closed to 100 yards and fired a long burst. Strikes were seen on the jet and the flame increased. I had to break owing to balloons but saw the Diver explode on the ground three miles west of Tonbridge."

56 Squadron (Tempest V) Newchurch

Flt Lt J.H. Ryan RCAF	EJ578/US-I	V-1	1725	Ashford area
Flt Sgt L. Jackson	JN869/US-D	V-1	1930	Robertsbridge/ Tonbridge
Flg Off W.R. MacLaren	EJ547/US-A	V-1	2105	Grid R.0845
	EJ547/US-A	V-1 shared	2125	Grid R.4147
Flt Lt E.M. Sparrow	EJ536/US-R	V-1	2155	Ashford area

The first of the evening fell to Canadian Flt Lt John Ryan:

> "I sighted a Diver over Folkestone at 2,800 feet, 350mph, and fired a 25-degree deflection burst from port and above. The petrol tank exploded in the air, and the warhead exploded on the ground south-east of Ashford. My aircraft's nose tank was pierced when the petrol tank of the Diver exploded; the oil system was damaged and fabric burned off the rudder, but a successful wheels down force-landing was made at Kingsnorth."

The next fell to Flt Sgt Lawrence Jackson: "Sighted Diver near Robertsbridge at 2,000 feet. Fired all my ammunition from 200 yards astern and the Diver exploded on the ground, near a railway line, between Robertsbridge and Tunbridge Wells." Flg Off Bill MacLaren was off at 2015 and after patrolling for some time was vectored on to a Diver north of Hastings:

> "I fired a long burst from 200 yards, closing to 50 yards, scoring strikes on jet, which went out. The Diver lost considerable height and then the jet came on again, but the shallow dive continued and the Diver exploded on the ground. I sighted a second Diver three miles north of Dungeness at 2,000 feet. I fired, scoring strikes from 250 yards astern, at the same time as a Tempest from another squadron, and the Diver exploded on the ground."

The final kill of the evening was scored by Flt Lt Sparrow: "Sighted a Diver between Rye and Dungeness at 2,000 feet. I fired from 300 yards, closing to 150 yards, scoring strikes and the Diver exploded on the ground south-west of Ashford."

91 Squadron (Spitfire XIV) Deanland ALG

Flg Off E. Topham	NH707/DL-N	V-1	1756	exploded in mid-air
Flt Lt R.S. Nash	RB169/DL-Q	V-1	1930	exploded in mid-air
Flg Off J. Monihan	RB161/DL-I	V-1 shared	2058	Cranbrook area
Flg Off G. Balcombe	RB173/DL-	V-1	2210	exploded in mid-air

Flg Off Monihan shared his kill with a Mustang:

"Saw Diver approach from west of Rye being attacked by Mustang, who broke away apparently having run out of ammunition. No strikes were observed. I then closed in to 150 yards dead astern and Diver fell in field three miles east of Cranbrook where it exploded."

96 Squadron (Mosquito XIII) Ford

Wg Cdr E.D. Crew	NS985/ZJ-	V-1	1430	Newchurch area

While on a daytime cross-country flight with Capt Hughes, an Army liaison officer, Wg Cdr Ed Crew sighted a Diver six-eight miles north of Newchurch. He engaged, shooting off its port wing, whereupon it crashed.

129 Squadron (Mustang III) Brenzett

Sgt R. Sandever	FB171/DV-S	V-1	1505	New Romney
Flg Off D.C. Parker ⎫ Flg Off A.F. Osborne ⎭	FB392/DV-N FX874/DV-G	V-1	1545-1730 1700-1900	Ashford area
Flt Sgt W.A. Jeal	FB121/DV-V	V-1	1700	Ashford area
Wt Off E. Redhead	FB389/DV-J	V-1	1700-1900	Maidstone area
Flg Off A.F. Osborne	FX874/DV-G	V-1 shared	1700-1900	Ashford area
Flg Off F.H. Holmes ⎫ Flg Off D.C. Parker ⎭	FB212/DV-Q FB392/DV-N	V-1 shared	1955-2125	Appledore area
Flg Off F.H. Holmes ⎫ Flg Off D.C. Parker ⎭	FB212/DV-Q FB392/DV-N	V-1 shared	1955-2125	Ashford area
Flt Lt D.F. Ruchwaldy	FZ184/DV-Z	V-1	2015	Dover area
Flg Off A.F. Osborne	FB123/DV-H	V-1 shared	2030-2220	Tonbridge area
Flt Lt J.P. Bassett	FB222/DV-W	V-1 shared	2200	Ashford area

The squadron achieved its best daily score during the afternoon/evening hours, bringing down ten Divers (five shared) during the course of 17 sorties. The first fell to Sgt Sandever, being intercepted near Dungeness at 1505 at 1,500 feet. After two attacks it turned to port and exploded on the ground. The next was shot down by Flt Sgt Jeal west of Folkestone. Dead astern attacks from 150 yards caused the Diver to half-roll and crash north-west of Ashford. Flt Lt Sammy Osborne and Flg Off Denny Parker then brought down one jointly that crashed half-a-mile south of Ashford. Osborne got a second later, but was obliged to share it with a Spitfire, the Diver also impacting close to Ashford. Wt Off Eric Redhead's victim fell ten miles east of Maidstone although was not seen to crash owing to clouds. Two more were shot down by the joint attacks of Flg Offs Holmes and Parker, the first exploding on the ground in the vicinity of Appledore after a Tempest (probably Flg Off Butcher of 3 Squadron) had joined the attack, the second also being shared with another Tempest a few minutes later, this crashing two miles south-east of Tonbridge.

Flt Lt Des Ruchwaldy intercepted his target north of Dover at 2,000 feet. He fired three short bursts from port quarter and dead astern. The Diver exuded smoke, spun and dived to the ground. Flg Off Osborne shared his third of the day with another Mustang (possibly Flt Lt Ruchwaldy) reporting that it crashed two miles south-east of Tonbridge. The last of the day was shot down by Flt Lt Bertie Bassett, aided by a Spitfire. He intercepted the Diver four miles north-west of Dymchurch at 2,000 feet and attacked from starboard quarter and dead astern at 150 yards. Fuel was seen to ignite and the missile commenced its final dive when a Spitfire nipped in front of him, opened fire and caused it to explode in the air four miles south-west of Ashford.

137 Squadron (Typhoon Ib) Manston

Flt Lt Doug Brandreth saw a Diver during his afternoon patrol (1325-1450) but this was shot down by AA fire. He then sighted a second crossing the coast near

Dymchurch. A chase ensued, in which he was joined by a Mosquito, the bomb being shot down before he could get in range.

165 Squadron (Spitfire IX) Lympne

Flg Off T.D. Tinsey	ML175/SK-P	V-1	1705	Sittingbourne area
Flt Sgt R.J. Hughes	MK480/SK-F	V-1	2255	Tonbridge area

Flg Off Tommy Tinsey reported:

"Intercepted north-east outskirts of Ashford. Strikes seen and small fragments flew off. During last attack Diver exploded in the air, with smaller secondary explosion when Diver hit the ground."

306 (Polish) Squadron (Mustang III) Brenzett

Flt Lt J. Siekierski PAF	UZ-S	V-1	1803	Ashford area
	UZ-S	V-1 shared	1810	Tenterden area
Plt Off Z. Kawnik PAF	UZ-Y	V-1 shared	1800	Grid R.3654
Flt Sgt S. Rudowski PAF	FB206/UZ-M	V-1	1940	Grid R.0948
Plt Off Z. Kawnik PAF	UZ-Y	V-1	2112	Rye area
Flg Off C. Gierycz PAF	UZ-N	V-1	2120	Tonbridge area
	UZ-N	V-1	2142	Grid R.3951
Flt Lt J. Siekierski PAF	UZ-S	V-1 shared	2144	Appledore area
Flg Off S. Tronczyński PAF	FZ149/UZ-W	V-1	2157	Brenzett area
Flt Lt J. Siekierski PAF	UZ-S	V-1	2202	Grid R.3342

Flt Lt Jan Siekierski opened the scoring during the early evening, having departed Brenzett at 1710. A Diver was intercepted west of Lympne at 2,500 feet, and a line astern attack was carried out, closing to 300 yards. Diver climbed and then spun to ground, exploding five miles west of Ashford. Second Diver intercepted two miles west of Newchurch at 2,000 feet. Again attacked from astern at 500 yards. Diver was losing height when a Tempest opened fire. The Diver exploded on the ground two miles north of Tenterden. Another section took off at 1730, Plt Off Zygmunt Kawnik intercepting a Diver three miles north of Dymchurch. Following a stern attack it lost speed, but then a Tempest appeared on the scene. The Diver crashed and exploded. A Tempest also interfered as Flt Sgt Stan Rudowski was attacking a Diver he engaged near Hastings, but after his first burst from 200 yards it turned on its back and exploded on the ground. Kawnik was up again and got his second kill near Rye. His companion, Flg Off Czeslaw Gierycz, shot down two more. To end the successful day, Flt Lt Siekierski and Flg Off Stefan Tronczyński destroyed three Divers during their late evening patrol, all exploding on the ground.

315 (Polish) Squadron (Mustang III) Brenzett

Flt Lt H. Pietrzak PAF	FB362/PK-A	V-1 shared	1920	Hastings area
Flt Lt M. Cwynar PAF	FZ154/PK-N	V-1 shared	2110	Rye area
	FZ154/PK-N	V-1 shared	2120	Rye area
Plt Off A. Judek PAF ⎫	FB184/PK-C	V-1	2114	Hastings area
Flt Sgt A. Ciundziewicki PAF ⎬	FB371/PK-B			
Flt Lt K. Stembrowicz PAF	FX903/PK-K	V-1	2118	Lympne area
Flt Sgt A. Ciundziewicki PAF	FB371/PK-B	V-1 shared	2124	Newchurch area
Flt Sgt K. Siwek PAF	FB145/PK-F	V-1	2135	Lympne area
Flg Off A. Czerwiński PAF ⎫	FB161/PK-J	V-1	2140	Brenzett area
Flt Sgt K. Siwek PAF ⎬	FB145/PK-F			

With the onset of darkness, the Poles of 315 came into their own and shot down eight more Divers, of which four were shared with other units.

316 (Polish) Squadron (Mustang III) Friston

Flt Lt S. Marcisz PAF ⎱	FB356/SZ-U	V-1	1610	off Eastbourne
Flg Off W. Wojtyga PAF ⎰	HB839/SZ-V			
Flt Sgt Z. Narloch PAF	HB824/SZ-N	V-1	1921	off Hastings
	HB824/SZ-N	V-1	1930	off Dungeness
Flt Sgt T. Jaskólski PAF	HB845/SZ-Y	V-1	2100	Wadhurst area
Flt Lt A. Cholajda PAF	HB836/SZ-R	V-1	2103	Cranbrook area

The first of the day fell to the joint attack made by Flt Lt Marcisz and Flg Off Wojtyga: "First seen at a point 20 miles south of Eastbourne. We chased and opened fire from 300 yards, closing to 80 yards from dead astern. The Diver rolled and crashed eight miles south of Eastbourne." The next two fell in rapid succession to Flt Sgt Zygfryd Narloch: "First seen about 20 miles south of Hastings. Chased and opened fire from dead astern at 400 yards. Strikes all over. Diver slowed down and crashed ten miles south of Hastings." The second he sighted 30 miles south of Dungeness: "Opened fire from 250 yards. Diver rolled and crashed 20 miles south of Dungeness."

Two more fell in quick succession, the victims of Flt Sgt Jaskólski and Flt Lt Antoni Cholajda. It seems probable that Jaskólski shared his victim: "Chased and opened fire from 500 yards dead astern. After two bursts Diver slowed down. Closed range to 200 yards. Diver rolled and crashed south of Wadhurst. As Diver was going down it was attacked by a Spitfire." Of his kill, Cholajda reported: "Chased and opened fire from 400 yards dead astern. After two bursts Diver slowed down and crashed on the ground two miles west of Cranbrook."

322 (Dutch) Squadron (Spitfire XIV) West Malling

Flg Off G.F.J. Jongbloed	VL-E	V-1	2057	Grid R.0551
Flg Off R.F. Burgwal	VL-C	V-1	2101	Tunbridge Wells
	VL-C	V-1	2112	Grid R.0747

Flg Off Jan Jongbloed reported:

> "Vectored on to Diver crossing in between Hastings and Bexhill. Attacked line astern, 150 yards range. Saw strikes and Diver crashed and exploded. A Mustang tried to cut in from starboard below, endangering my Spitfire."

Flg Off Rudi Burgwal scored a double during his patrol: "Patrolling north of Pevensey Bay and Bexhill when vectored on Diver east of Hastings. A Tempest fired first and then broke away. I attacked line astern, range 150 yards. Diver crashed and exploded in Tunbridge Wells area." His second kill occurred soon after: "Vectored on to Diver over Hastings. Attacked line astern, range 150 yards. Diver engine stopped and picked up again. I attacked again and Diver crashed and exploded."

486 (RNZAF) Squadron (Tempest V) Newchurch

Flg Off R.J. Cammock RNZAF	JN863/SA-R	V-1	1315	Ashford area
Flg Off J.R. Cullen RNZAF	EJ537/SA-S	V-1	1545	Sevenoaks area
Plt Off R.J. Danzey RNZAF	JN801/SA-L	V-1	1637	West Malling area
Flg Off J.R. Cullen RNZAF	EJ523/SA-X	V-1	2115	Rye area

Its probable that the Diver shot down by Plt Off Danzey fell near Borough Green Road, Ightham, where three people were slightly hurt. Damage was caused to Forge House, Ightham Court, the parish church and the local pub.

610 Squadron (Spitfire XIV) Friston

Wt Off R. Roberts ⎱	DW-	V-1 damaged	
Flg Off G. Watkin RCAF ⎰			

Wt Off Roberts and Flg Off Gordon Watkin chased a V-1 during their patrol, registering strikes but were unable to claim a kill.

Night 22/23 JULY
Oakdale Road, Streatham (SW16) received its second Diver at 0119. On this occasion four people were killed, three houses destroyed and a further 30 damaged. During the previous incident (on 8 July) six residents had been killed.

25 Squadron (Mosquito) Coltishall
Flg Off V.H. Linthune	HK300/ZK-	V-1	0240	over sea

Flg Off Vic Linthune wrote:

> "I saw searchlight indicating point of flying bomb and then saw it 6,000 feet away below my port engine. I dived down to 2,000 feet and opened fire with three short bursts. The petrol tank burst and the flying bomb exploded. Almost immediately AA defences opened fire. It is believed warhead fell into the sea. Combat seen by Flt Sgt Glossop, who confirms flying bomb blew up before guns opened fire."

Plt Off John Tait RAAF fired at a V-1 during his 2200-0120 patrol but it was then struck by AA fire from the gun belt and crashed into the sea. He made no claim.

96 Squadron (Mosquito XIII) Ford
Flt Lt F.R.L. Mellersh	MM577/ZJ-N	V-1	2354	Grid R.90
Wg Cdr E.D. Crew	NS985/ZJ-	V-1	0135	Grid W.42
	NS985/ZJ-	V-1	0137	Grid W.80
Flt Sgt T. Bryan	MM468/ZJ-	V-1	0442	Grid R.30

All four Divers were shot down over the Channel and blew up on impact. Flt Lt Togs Mellersh was accompanied by Wg Cdr R.B. Cawood from HQ, and Wg Cdr Edward Crew again had Capt Hughes as observer.

425thNFS USAAF (P-61) Ford
Maj H. Ross USAAF	42-5580	V-1	pm	Channel

Seven P-61s were up in a unified effort during which Major Hardin Ross scored a kill. He reported that he closed from 3,000 feet to 1,200 feet of his target before opening fire, and then shot it down using 160 rounds of 20mm.

Fifteen minutes before midnight, a flight of three RN Avengers from 855 Squadron operating from Hawkinge took off on an anti-E-boat patrol. En route, a Diver was spotted by Sub Lt(A) Roger Johnson RNVR, who allowed his gunner L/Air Stan Norman to fire at it, albeit without result. A few minutes later the Avenger (plus a second) was shot down by return fire from an E-boat flotilla encountered off Dieppe. Johnson was rescued and taken prisoner but his crewman perished.

Sunday 23 JULY
Germany's Propaganda Minster Dr Goebbels again boasted of the effect that the V-1 assault was having on London:

> *"How often over the past months has the English government used its captive press to claim either that there were no German secret weapons, or that if there were, London knew all about them and was prepared for them. If they did not exist, how can they be in use, and if London knew all about them, how is it possible that our V-1s are flying undisturbed toward London, that women and children are being evacuated from the British capital, that the larger part of London's population is sleeping in packed subway stations?"*

1 Squadron (Spitfire LFIXb) Lympne

Flt Sgt H.J. Vassie	MJ481/JX-	V-1	0550	off Dover
Flg Off D.H. Davy	MK986/JX-V	V-1	0824	off Boulogne
	ML423/JX-S	V-1 shared	0830	Kingsnorth ALG

Flt Sgt Vassie reported:

"Intercepted Diver 15 miles south of midway between Folkestone and Dover. Fired one two-seconds burst from 250-300 yards range and saw strikes on jet and wing roots. Diver cartwheeled into sea ten miles south of Dover/Folkestone."

Of his first kill of the day Flg Off Dennis Davy wrote:

"Strikes and pieces fell off. Diver started to climb. Petrol tank hit on second burst. Much flame. Diver turned on reciprocal, turned over and fell into sea eight miles north-east of Boulogne." Having landed, Davy was soon off again in a different aircraft: "Intercepted Diver just south-east of Lympne. Attacked from line astern from 150-200 yards and fired three bursts of three seconds. Strikes on wings and jet and, following final attack, jet belched flames and dived steeply down, exploding on the ground. Whilst it was diving a Mustang came in to attack. Diver crashed three miles south-east of Ashford." A few minutes later he was vectored on to another: "Intercepted two miles inland from Dymchurch-Hythe. Closed in to attack but two Mustangs, one Spitfire and one Tempest attacked first. I saw strikes and Diver started to climb. Other aircraft broke away and it levelled out and continued on course with jet functioning. I went in and attacked from port beam from 150 yards, and after one burst the fuel tanks blew up. Diver turned steeply to port and then dived down, exploding on the perimeter track of Kingsnorth airfield."

The kill was shared with Plt Off Miller of 56, Flg Off Osborne of 129 and Flt Sgt Siwek of 315. Kingsnorth ALG near Ashford, was the home of the 36thFG, and three P-47s were damaged by debris, which also inflicted further damage on a force-landed B-17, causing Flg Off Jo Dalley to recall:

"We gave Davy a mock Iron Cross with Oak Leaves for his destruction of those American aircraft! He also upset the CO by really bending the wingtip of the CO's aircraft [on another occasion] trying to tip over a V-1 after firing all his ammunition. Although perhaps worth a try the V-1 could not be tipped over easily as popular myth has it – the gyro control was too powerful when in full flight. [Sqn Ldr] Lardner-Burke DFC told Davy to 'get with it' in his shooting. Rather rough as the target was very small from the rear but good gunnery should be effective as it was a straight and level target. One must also remember that when the guns fired it immediately knocked 30mph off the speed and was troublesome if the V-1 and Spitfire were both at the same speed – when flat out."

3 Squadron (Tempest V) Newchurch

Flt Lt A.E. Umbers RNZAF ⎫	JN768/JF-F	V-1	0442	Grid Q.9191
Plt Off K.G. Slade-Betts ⎭	JN755/JF-D			
Flt Lt R. van Lierde (Belg) ⎫	JN862/JF-Z	V-1	0520	Dungeness area
Flt Sgt H.G Bailey RAAF ⎭	JN739/JF-W			
Flt Sgt T.A. McCulloch	JN738/JF-	V-1	0700	Dungeness area
Flt Sgt D.J. Mackerras RAAF	JN752/JF-S	V-1	0815	Biggin Hill
Flt Lt A.E. Umbers RNZAF	JN768/JF-F	V-1	0900	Beachy Head
Flg Off G.A. Whitman RCAF (US)	JN735/JF-X	V-1 shared	1145	Bexley area
Flg Off R. van Lierde (Belg)	JN862/JF-Z	V-1 shared	1155	Ivychurch area
Flt Sgt M.J.A. Rose	JN745/JF-T	V-1	1245	Westerham area
Flt Sgt R.W. Cole	JN769/JF-G	V-1	1300	Dymchurch area
Plt Off H.R. Wingate	JN739/JF-W	V-1	1630	Biggin Hill area
Flt Sgt D.J. Mackerras RAAF	JN745/JF-T	V-1	1735	Gatwick area
Flt Sgt H.G. Bailey RAAF	JN739/JF-W	V-1	2100	Eastbourne area
Plt Off H.R. Wingate ⎫	JN752/JF-S	V-1	2115	Appledore area
Wt Off R.S. Adcock RAAF ⎭	JN735/JF-X			

3 Squadron increased its tally by a further 13 kills, including two shares, during the day, no fewer than 11 pilots getting on the scorecard.

41 Squadron (Spitfire XII) Lympne

Flg Off M.A.L. Balaase (Belg)⎱	MB798/EB-U	V-1	1415	off Rye
Plt Off J.C.J. Payne ⎰	MB880/EB-			
Wt Off A.S. Appleton	MB882/EB-B	V-1	1512	Bexhill area

Flg Off Mono Balaase and Plt Off Jimmy Payne engaged a flying bomb over the sea as it approached the Sussex coast, and jointly shot it down into the sea ten miles south of Rye. Payne reported:

"Fired at 300 yards closing to 200, hit port wing causing 45° bank and return to level flight. Strikes on jet causing greyish smoke. Ran out of ammo."

Balaase added:

"[Fired] 200 yards closing to 50 yards, slowing up Diver to 220mph, causing it to glide as though engine u/s, weaving considerably. Both wings holed and rear end of jet came off. Ordered to break owing to gun belt area. Control confirmed from police that Diver was seen to go into sea at 1415."

Wt Off Archie Appleton had a fortunate escape when he flew into the debris from his exploding victim – and suffered no damage; he reported:

"Excellent vectors causing visual. Slowed down and dropped back to 150 yards. One burst of two seconds and Diver blew up with sheet of flame and then burst in air eight miles south of Bexhill."

56 Squadron (Tempest V) Newchurch

Plt Off A.S. Miller RAAF	EJ544/US-J	V-1 shared	0830	Kingsnorth ALG
Flt Sgt L. Jackson	JN869/US-D	V-1 shared	0900	Grid R.4275

Australian Plt Off Miller shared his kill with Flg Off Davy of 1 Squadron, Flg Off Osborne of 129 and Flt Sgt Siwek of 315:

"Sighted Diver five miles south-east of Ashford at 2,000 feet. I fired a 10-degree deflection burst, scoring strikes on the jet at the same time as another Tempest. The Diver exploded on the perimeter track of an American airfield south-west of Ashford."

Thirty minutes later Flt Sgt Lawrence Jackson got another:

"Sighted Diver over Folkestone. I fired from 250 yards astern, scoring strikes on the wing and the Diver slowed down considerably. A Mustang [Plt Off Feliks Migoś of 306 Squadron] then attacked and the Diver exploded on the ground."

91 Squadron (Spitfire XIV) Deanland ALG

Flt Lt R.S. Nash	RM652/DL-	V-1	0601	Deanland area
Sqn Ldr P.McC. Bond	RM624/DL-	V-1	0651	Robertsbridge area
Sqn Ldr N.A. Kynaston	RM654/DL-F	V-1	1520	Gatwick area

Flt Lt Nash saw a Diver approaching south of Deanland: "Attacked from 300 yards astern with short burst. Diver fell on farm buildings one mile south-east of base, where it exploded." Sqn Ldr Bond: "Saw Diver over Rye and attacked from astern at 100 yards and Diver fell, exploding in a field south-east of Robertsbridge."

129 Squadron (Mustang III) Brenzett

Flg Off A.F. Osborne	FB212/DV-Q	V-1 shared	1100-1250	Kingsnorth ALG
Flg Off M. Twomey	FX952-DV-E	V-1	1405	off Dieppe
	FX952-DV-E	V-1 shared	1355-1435	off Hastings

| Flg Off M. Humphries | FB137/DV-C | V-1 shared | 1505-1715 | Hastings area |

The pilots scored one individual and three shared kills during the day, Flg Off Sammy Osborne sharing the first with Flg Off Davy of 1, Plt Off Miller of 56 and Flt Sgt Siwek of 315. The Diver impacted on Kingsnorth ALG near Ashford, causing the squadron diarist to comment:

> "This was of course by no means deliberate, although it did nothing to boost Anglo-American relations."

Flg Off Twomey followed up in the afternoon with two kills, the first intercepted ten miles north of Dieppe at 3,000 feet. He attacked from dead astern and saw hits on starboard wing root. The Diver made a shallow dive to starboard, crashed and exploded in mid-Channel. The second he intercepted 15 miles north of Dieppe and attacked from slightly below and astern. Two pieces fell away and the Diver slowed down to about 350mph. He then formated on the starboard side and tipped Diver's wing up, whereupon it pulled off to port, almost turning on its back. It then righted itself and continued on its course, though 1,000 feet lower. As he was about to repeat his attack, another Mustang came in and fired. The Diver crashed and exploded ten miles west of Hastings. Finally, Flg Off Mike Humphries shared his victory with both a Spitfire and a Tempest. Intercepted three miles north of Hastings, the trio took turns in firing and the Diver crashed eight miles north-west of Hastings.

306 (Polish) Squadron (Mustang III) Brenzett

Flg Off K. Marschall PAF	HB871/UZ-E	V-1	0602	exploded in mid-air
Plt Off F. Migoś PAF	UZ-Q	V-1 shared	0900	Faversham area
Flg Off S. Tronczyński PAF	HB863/UZ-O	V-1	1428	Grid R.2437
	HB863/UZ-O	V-1	1529	Tunbridge Wells area

The Diver attacked by Flg Off Karol Marschall four miles east of Hastings exploded in the air following his close-range attack, though his aircraft was damaged. Plt Off Feliks Migoś reported that his victim went into a double spin before it crashed and exploded on the ground south-west of Faversham (shared with Flt Sgt Jackson of 56 Squadron). During the early afternoon Flg Off Stefan Tronczyński scored a double, both being intercepted east of Hastings. He reported that the second Diver "went into a mad spin" before exploding in a wood five miles south-east of Tunbridge Wells.

315 (Polish) Squadron (Mustang III) Brenzett

Flt Sgt K. Siwek PAF	FX995/PK-E	V-1	0810	Lympne area
	FX995/PK-E	V-1	0817	Mersham area
Flt Lt H. Pietrzak PAF	FB362/PK-A	V-1 shared	0817	Lympne area
Flt Sgt K. Siwek PAF	FX995/PK-E	V-1 shared	0830	Kingsnorth ALG

Flt Sgt Kazimierz Siwek got his first near Smeeth, three miles north-west of Lympne, his second half a mile south of Mersham Railway Station, and then pursued a third. He approached from astern and opened fire at 200 yards range. The flying bomb climbed and another Mustang fired, it went into a dive and crashed on Kingsnorth ALG south-east of Ashford (shared with Flg Off Davy of 1, Plt Off Miller of 56 and Flg Off Osborne of 129).

316 (Polish) Squadron (Mustang III) Friston

| Wt Off P. Syperek PAF | FB353/SZ-H | V-1 | 1420 | off Hastings |

> "Chased and opened fire from 400 yards, closing to 200 yards from dead astern. Diver rolled and crashed in the sea 25 miles south of Hastings."

322 (Dutch) Squadron (Spitfire XIV) West Malling

Flg Off G.F.J. Jongbloed	VL-E	V-1	0937	Grid R.5663
Flg Off C.R.R. Manders	VL-Y	V-1	1520	Grid R.0939

Flg Off Jan Jongbloed scored another kill during his morning patrol between Tenterden and Ashford: "Vectored on to Diver crossing in near Hawkinge. Attacked from port to line astern, range 150 yards. Strikes seen and Diver turned over, crashed and exploded." The Folkestone railway police officer who had previously witnessed the shooting down of a Diver by two Tempests from 3 Squadron, saw the end of another, possibly Jongbloed's victim:

> "I was thinking that it might be a dream after all and there could not be a war waging in such serene surroundings, when I was startled by the approach of another flying bomb, a small black dot coming from Cap Gris Nez. It was in a line, which would pass right over my head. A Spitfire appeared out of the blue and started to chase it. I was fascinated by the sight and speculated whether or not the airman would catch it. Three explosions in a row split the air, seemingly beneath my feet, and I went clean over the back of that seat, finishing up on the turf with my legs in the air. I had forgotten the Bofors gun, in the cliff ledge some 15 feet away. The third round seemed to miss the thing's tail by a hair's breadth. The airman caught it up and fired a short burst. Black smoke appeared from the tail and it subsequently fell in open country at Hawkinge."

It seems that its final destination was Little Pett Bottom Farm; there were no injuries. The only other successful interception was carried out by Flg Off Coen Manders: "Patrolling north of Bexhill and told Diver was crossing in west of Bexhill. Attacked line astern, range 150 yards. Saw strikes on starboard wing and propulsion unit. Diver crashed and exploded."

486 (RNZAF) Squadron (Tempest V) Newchurch

Plt Off W.A.L. Trott RNZAF	JN758/SA-Y	V-1	1515	Hastings area
	JN758/SA-Y	V-1	1530	Etchingham area

610 Squadron (Spitfire XIV) Friston

Plt Off B.R. Scamen RCAF	DW-	V-1	0715-0820
Flt Sgt J.M. Philpott	DW-	V-1	1300-1435

Night 23/24 JULY

The Heinkels of III/KG3 were active again, at least 11 launches being achieved. Five impacted on London, the most serious incident occurring in Canterbury Terrace, Kilburn NW6, where 16 residents were killed at 0440[134]. Another fell in Bailden Street, Deptford (SE8), killing two residents. Four more fell in Essex and two in Hertfordshire.

> "Again the siren sounded soon after midnight," wrote Warden Carter of Waltham Abbey in his diary, "followed by three 'near-ones'. Quite a dark night when I got the car out. A fatal casualty in Honey Lane, when in the light of my headlamp I saw a pussy sitting in the road, too late to take avoiding action. On arrival, found the usual assortment of cars everywhere. The Woodbine public house was a mess, with glass, broken bottles and liquor all over the floor. The remains of the jet propulsion unit lay alongside the road on the grass verge. Two casualties were removed and eight persons evacuated to the rest centre."

25 Squadron (Mosquito XVII) Coltishall

Flt Lt R.J. Lilwall reported that during his 2230-0130 patrol, as he approached a Diver, it dived into the sea on its own accord and therefore he did not make a claim.

68 Squadron (Mosquito XVII) Castle Camps

Flt Lt A.B. Harvey	NT368/WM-L	V-1	night

85 Squadron (Mosquito XVII) West Malling

Flg Off J. Chipperfield	VY-W	V-1	0018	off Thames Estuary
Wg Cdr H deC.A. Woodhouse	VY-F	V-1		

Flg Off Jimmy Chipperfield reported: "Diver first seen at 500 feet in Thames Estuary area, 3,000 feet below. Dived on it and fired a long burst from dead astern at 700 yards. Strikes seen and Diver exploded on impact." Wg Cdr Paddy Woodhouse DFC AFC, currently attending a Mosquito conversion course at 51 OTU, borrowed an 85 Squadron Mosquito and shot down a flying bomb[135].

96 Squadron (Mosquito XIII) Ford

Wt Off W.A. McLardy RAAF	MM577/ZJ-N	V-1	0325	off Beachy Head

"Attacked from 1,000 feet range but no strikes seen, although Diver then crashed into the sea and exploded some 35 miles south-east of Beachy Head."

264 Squadron (Mosquito XIII) Hartford Bridge

Flg Off P.deL. Brooke	HK473/PS-	V-1	0202	Grid Q.9858
	HK473/PS-	V-1	0209	Grid Q.8967

Flg Off Peter Brooke raised his score to five in two sorties with this brace of flying bombs. The first exploded on the ground and the second blew up in the air. The squadron was now taken off anti-Diver patrols and moved to Hunsdon.

418 (RCAF) Squadron (Mosquito VI) Hurn

Sqn Ldr R. Bannock RCAF	HR147/TH-Z	V-1	0001	Channel
	HR147/TH-Z	V-1	0022	Channel

605 Squadron (Mosquito VI) Manston

Flt Lt G.C. Wright	UP-	V-1	0018	Channel

"We patrolled north of Ostende and saw a single Diver which was not in position for an attack. At 0015 we saw a further two Divers. We positioned ourselves behind one of these and fired from astern, range 300 yards. Many strikes were seen – Diver spluttered badly – fire spread over whole body and Diver lost height rapidly and exploded on impact with sea. This claim is substantiated by the crews of two other Mosquitos of this squadron who were in approximate position at the time of the kill."

FIU (Tempest V) Ford

Flt Lt J. Berry	EJ524/ZQ-Y	V-1	night
	EJ524/ZQ-Y	V-1	night
	EJ524/ZQ-Y	V-1	night
	EJ524/ZQ-Y	V-1	night
	EJ524/ZQ-Y	V-1	night
	EJ524/ZQ-Y	V-1	night
	EJ524/ZQ-Y	V-1	night

Possibly two of these fell at 0029 and 0159, when victims of fighters crashed at Offham military camp in Mereworth Woods, and Gravelly Bottom, Kingswood, where two houses were badly damaged. There were no service casualties but one person was seriously injured and another hurt in the second incident. Flt Lt Jeremy Howard-Williams wrote:

"On 23 July he [Flt Lt Berry] shot down seven flying bombs in one night, as many as most people destroyed in the whole campaign. Once again he saw the blinding flash as a bomb blew up in his face at close range. Once again he flew through the violence of the subsiding debris, feeling the full force of the detonation. A fragment of bomb must have hit part of his aircraft, for he felt the shock as something exploded. The Tempest veered sharply. Automatically he

Top: A Diver falling on London somewhere near Piccadilly Station early in the campaign.

Bottom left: Sqn Ldr Joseph Berry DFC, Tempest pilot with 61 kills. *(Mrs J.M. Manser)*

Bottom right: Flt Lt Remi van Lierde DFC, Belgian Tempest pilot with 47 kills.

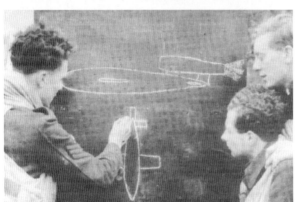

Top left: Flt Lt Francis 'Togs' Mellersh DFC, Mosquito pilot, 44 kills.

Top right: Flt Lt Michael Stanley DFC, Flt Lt Mellersh's R/Op, who shared 37 kills.

Middle left: 3 Squadron's Flt Sgt Bob Cole artistically describing the Diver's profile to Flg Off Bob Barckley (who in fact shot down the very first Diver) and Flg Off Ken Slade-Betts.

Middle right: 501 Squadron Tempests ready for action. (*Andy Saunders*)

Bottom centre: Wt Off Pat Coleman of 41 Squadron.

Bottom right: Canadian Flg Off Jimmy Waslyk scored 504 Squadron's sole Diver victory.

Top: He111 A1+HK (161605) of 2/KG53, with Diver under starboard wing, ready for take-off.

Middle left: Diver over the sea en route for England.

Middle right: Spitfire tipping wing of Diver.

Bottom: Fighter Kill!

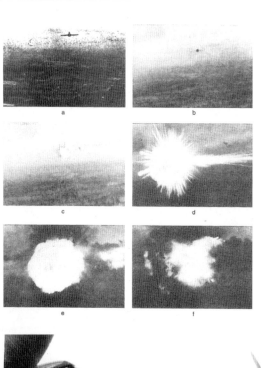

Top left: Flying through the explosion and debris of a kill.

A few of the Mosquito night fighters:

Top right: Flt Lt Sailor Parker (right) and his navigator Wt Off Don Godfrey of 219 Squadron (note 5 Diver kills markings).

Bottom left: Night intruder Flt Lt Eric Smith RCAF scored a kill flying with 107 Squadron.

Below: Sqn Ldr Ross Gray RCAF and his West Indian navigator Flg Off Fred Smith RCAF of 418 (RCAF) Squadron.

BOROUGH OF EASTBOURNE.   AIR RAID INCIDENT July 4th 1944.

CIVILIAN CASUALTIES TREATED AT AVENUE HOUSE FIRST AID POST.

24. PATTENDEN, Fred.W.   44 M.   2 Easton Cottages, Langley Rise.

CIVILIAN CASUALTIES ADMITTED TO ST.MARY'S HOSPITAL.

1.	WHEATLEY, Mrs.Florence.	35 F.	26 Astaire Avenue.	Slight Shock. Confined 2.7.44. (with mother)
2.	WHEATLEY, Barrie F.	2 days.M.	26 " "	(Transferred from Avenue House First Aid Post.
	WILSON, James.	63 M.	58 " "	

RECEIVED
6 JUL 1944

The devastation wrought by a flying bomb on 4 July 1944 at Astaire Avenue, Eastbourne. The bomb had been shot down by gunfire whereupon it dived into the ground and exploded. There were a number of casualties, none fatal, as the casualty report shows.
(Andy Saunders)

S.E.R.C.22.   ARPO.

ARP/6.
To The Controller,
Civil Defence,
Eastbourne.

COUNTY BOROUGH OF EASTBOURNE.

AMENDED 1.

CIVILIAN CASUALTY RETURN.

RECEIVED
6 JUL 1944

5 JUL 1944
RECEIVED

Casualty Bureau,
Torfield Court,
St.Anne's Road,
Eastbourne.

Day 5th July 1944
Month

Date	Incident	DEAD				INJURED AND DETAINED IN HOSPITAL.			INJURED :- OTHER CASES.			MISSING BELIEVED KILLED.		
		M.	W.	C.	Unclassified.	M.	W.	C.	M.	W.	C.	M.	W.	C.
4.7.44.	Flying Bomb brought down Astaire Avenue.													
	Princess Alice Hospital:													
	In-Patients													
	St.Mary's Hospital:					3	5	-						
	In-Patients													
	Avenue House First Aid Post					1	1	1						
									10	11	2			
	TOTALS.					4	6	1	10	11	2			

From Casualty Bureau :- Amendments 6th July 1944.   5

Signed *John Fenton*
Medical Officer of Health.

Top left: Prime Minister Winston Churchill watching AA guns in action against flying bombs, summer 1944. *(Andy Saunders)*

Top right and middle right: German propaganda leaflets aimed at undermining morale of Allied troops serving abroad.

Middle left: One that did not explode – a lucky let-off for the local inhabitants.

Bottom left and bottom right: The British response: a selection of cartoons that appeared in the British press.

"Either STOP the thing or get it UNSTUCK: one or the other… but QUICK !

"GOOD HEAVENS! WE CAN'T WIN A WAR THIS WAY!"

Top left: Flg Off Gordon Hobson.

Top right: Flg Off Bill McKenzie RCAF (left) and Flg Off Jack Ritch RCAF pose with Meteor F.3.

Middle: 616 Squadron pilots pose in front of a Meteor F.1. Flg Off Dixie Dean front row, white scarf; Flg Off Gordon Hobson fifth from right, back row.

Bottom: Flg Off Gordon Hobson with Meteor F.3 named Athena.

Top left: Britain's prewar flying bomb – the Miles Hoopla. It was not put into production.

Top right: Postwar, the V-1 design lived on for a few years, albeit in modified form. The French developed the CT-10 based on the V-1 design. The Royal Navy purchased a number and tested these from Benghaisa Point, Malta. They were not adopted for operational use.

Middle: The author's family circa 1944. Gunner Harry Cull, Royal Artillery, survived a close call on 18 June 1944, when a Diver exploded near his searchlight site at Westerham in Kent and fatally wounded his officer. His wife Lily and their three young children (Joyce, Don and baby Brian) experienced the blast of a Diver that fell near Kilburn Underground Station (London) on 15 August 1944.

Bottom: Look behind you!! Author Brian Cull dwarfed by Duxford's V-1.

corrected the movement, even as he flashed a comprehensive glance at the vital instruments. One of his fuel tanks was reading zero; it must have been holed. Fire in the air, the pilot's nightmare, obviously threatened; to make matters worse, his radio was dead. Carefully descending through cloud over the sea, he flew until he recognised the coastline; from there it was easy. When he filled in his logbook next day, he wrote the following words: '7 destroyed. Petrol tank exploded. R/T u/s.'"

Monday 24 JULY

1 Squadron (Spitfire LFIXb) Lympne

Flg Off F.W. Town	MK926/JX-	V-1	2140	Ashford area
Plt Off K.R. Foskett	MK986/JX-V	V-1 shared	2140	Ashford area

Flg Off Freddie Town reported:

"Control advised Diver approaching Folkestone. Guided by flak I saw Diver and made deflection attack. No strikes seen. Fired further bursts from dead astern. Jet went out and Diver went into gentle dive. Jet started again during dive but it crashed shortly after, exploding in a wood five miles north-east of Ashford."

Plt Off Ken Foskett became a local hero when he shot down a Diver west of Ashford, the bomb falling on a railway line:

"Saw Diver coming through AA and held off while Mustang [Plt Off Kawnik of 306 Squadron] went in to attack. Mustang broke away and Diver still flying straight and level with jet functioning. I then went in at range from 400 to 200 yards and fired two short bursts, seeing numerous strikes. Diver heeled over to port and went in a slow dive to the ground. I broke away and Mustang fired a burst whilst Diver going in, without effect. Diver crashed six miles west of Ashford, 20 yards off rail line near brickworks."

As he pulled away he saw a train approaching. He flew alongside it, dropping and raising his undercarriage in an attempt to warn the driver, who fortunately understood and stopped the train some distance from the damaged track. Later, a letter of appreciation was received by ADGB HQ from grateful passengers[136].

3 Squadron (Tempest V) Newchurch

Flt Lt B.C. Mackenzie RAAF	JN735/JF-X	V-1	0530	Robertsbridge area
Flg Off M.F. Edwards	JN862/JF-Z	V-1 shared	1625	Brenchley area
	JN862/JF-Z	V-1	1635	Tenterden area

Flt Lt Mackenzie was vectored on to a Diver south of Hastings at 2,000 feet: "Closed to 200 yards astern and attacked with a short burst. Hit the jet, which increased the flame. Fired a second burst and hit the starboard wing. The Diver then went down two miles south of Robertsbridge." Flg Off Malcolm Edwards scored a double but had to share one of them with two Spitfires:

"Saw a Diver three miles east of Hastings and, when four miles inland and 800 yards astern, two Spitfires – one DL-J [RB177 from 91 Squadron] – dived in from port and above firing deflection bursts, which caused links and cartridge cases to fall around my aircraft. No strikes were seen and the Spits dropped behind. I closed to 200 yards and fired two long bursts from dead astern. The Diver crashed and exploded in the Brenchley area (R.1560). Saw a second Diver four miles east of Hastings at 2,500 feet. It was being chased by two Mustangs, who were firing. Both Mustangs broke and the Diver continued apparently unaffected. I closed to 50 yards and gave a two-seconds burst from dead astern. Saw strikes all over the Diver. Broke to avoid collision and the Diver went down with the two Mustangs on its tail. It exploded on the ground in the Tenterden area."

91 Squadron (Spitfire XIV) Deanland ALG

Flg Off J.A. Faulkner RCAF	RM654/DL-F	V-1	0529	Hastings area
Flg Off R.A. McPhie RCAF	RM680/DL-	V-1	1505	Eastbourne area

| Flt Lt R.S. Nash | RM624/DL- | V-1 | 1635 | Polegate area |

Flg Off Faulkner was off at 0505 and was soon vectored on to a Diver crossing the coast east of Hastings: "Attacked from 200 yards dead astern and Diver exploded on the ground ten miles north-west of Hastings." Flg Off McPhie intercepted his target ten miles north of Eastbourne: "Attacked from astern at 300 yards. Diver fell, exploding on the ground." Flt Lt Nash took off on the return of McPhie's section: "Saw Diver one mile north of Eastbourne and attacked from astern at 200 yards. Diver fell in wood north of Polegate where it exploded."

306 (Polish) Squadron (Mustang III) Andrews Field

| Flg Off A. Beyer PAF | FB106/UZ-V | V-1 shared | 1623 | Grid R.2049 |
| Plt Off Z. Kawnik PAF | FB393/UZ-U | V-1 shared | 2140 | Ashford area |

Flg Off Andrzej Beyer intercepted north-east of Hastings and saw his victim explode on the ground following a close-range attack during which he registered strikes on both wings. A Tempest of 3 Squadron flown by Flg Off Edwards attacked the same bomb. Plt Off Zygmunt Kawnik shared his kill with a Spitfire flown by Plt Off Ken Foskett of 1 Squadron. Their victim exploded on the ground five miles north-east of Ashford.

315 (Polish) Squadron (Mustang III) Brenzett

| Flt Lt M. Cwynar PAF | FZ157/PK-Z | V-1 | dawn | Folkestone area |

"At dawn we were airborne for an anti-Diver patrol. Before we attained sufficient height, we noticed the mushroom shaped explosions of an AA barrage over the Folkestone area. The guns were firing at the first series of the morning's flying bombs. Not having sufficient height I started to chase one. I was gaining on it but only slowly. When at a proper distance, short bursts of fire were sufficient to damage the V-1's vital component – the gyroscope. Once this part was shot up, the craft veered violently, usually to the left, and dived to the ground. To give the engine a rest, I throttled back, did a leisurely left turn and observed the impact on the ground. It exploded in what looked like, in the morning mist, an orchard of young trees. I turned to a south-east direction and pushed the throttle to increase speed but there was no response! The propeller was idling, driven only by the air speed. At 2,000 feet I had to look for a suitable landing place, a field where, if the worst came to the worst, I could land with the undercarriage in the up position. Luckily, through the morning mist, I spotted a hangar and that could only mean a permanent airfield. In fact there were three hangars to the north-west at West Malling. With the hydraulics working, the undercarriage and flaps down, I landed, stopping in the middle of the airfield. Old memories came flooding back of the days when I was learning to fly and was pleased when I achieved a neat three-point landing on lush, green grass. I telephoned Brenzett from the flying control tower. Sqn Ldr Horbaczewski came over in a jeep, his favourite toy, and brought our chief mechanic. In no time he found that the throttle linkage had jammed somewhere between the pilot's left hand side in the cabin and the engine connection. I was soon on my way back to Brenzett."

Later, he wrote:

"Sqn Ldr Horbaczewski and I decided to try out a night patrol. We chose a clear, moonless night, thinking it would be easier to detect the Doodlebugs' orange-red coloured exhaust flames. We asked our resourceful chief mechanic to prepare the runway's flight path. He had a simple, basic idea of placing a dozen oil-lit lamps in a straight line, along the left side of the Summerfield mesh runway. In the darkness, without the a/c's positional lights, Horbaczewski got airborne for an approximate two-hour long patrol. After his safe landing, I took off to continue the night patrol. We did not intercept any flying bombs that night. Next day, the airfield commander was not pleased. Horbaczewski had not asked permission so that was the end of the night flights."

322 (Dutch) Squadron (Spitfire XIV) West Malling

Flg Off R.F. Burgwal ⎫	VL-K	V-1	1653	Rye area
Flg Off J. Jonker ⎭	VL-D			

Flg Off Rudi Burgwal and Flg Off Jan Jonker jointly shot down a Diver during their patrol:

> "Vectored on to Diver. We both attacked line astern, range 250 yards closing to 100 yards. Strikes were seen. A Mustang and a Tempest also fired but no material damage appeared. We then attacked again and Diver exploded and crashed ten miles north-west of Rye. S/Ldr Kynaston of 91 Squadron confirms that we destroyed the Diver."

486 (RNZAF) Squadron (Tempest V) Newchurch

Flt Lt L.J. Appleton RNZAF	JN863/SA-R	V-1	0526	Canterbury area
Flt Lt E.W. Tanner RNZAF	JN732/SA-I	V-1 shared	1503	Ninfield area

504 Squadron (Spitfire IX) Detling

Flg Off J. Waslyk RCAF	PL263/TM-	V-1	pm	Hailsham area

Canadian Flg Off Jimmy Waslyk[137] from Toronto scored 504's first and only Diver kill:

> "Returning from a test flight down the south coast when I was overtaken by a Diver in the neighbourhood of Hailsham. It was above me so I had to climb quickly. Got on its tail and gave prolonged burst at 200-400 yards range. The jet unit exploded and bomb dived to explode on the ground."

Night 24/25 JULY

III/KG3, operating from Gilze-Rijen, carried out 25 sorties between 2205 and 0524. All the Heinkel crews returned safely. Six Divers hit London, three fell in Hertfordshire and one in Essex.

25 Squadron (Mosquito XVII) Coltishall

Wg Cdr C.M. Wight-Boycott	HK357/ZK-	V-1	2225-0135	Manston area

> "While patrolling off North Foreland at 8,000 feet I was told by control [of approaching flying bomb]. I dived on course 280°, this being the estimated course of the flying bomb. On leaving cloud at 2,000 feet I saw flying bomb slightly below to port. I continued to dive and at 3,000-4,000 feet pulled up slightly at 340mph and fired a very short burst from approximately 1,000 feet. The flying bomb immediately burst and hit the ground about two miles east of Manston aerodrome, setting fire to a haystack or building."

68 Squadron (Mosquito XIX) Castle Camps

Flt Lt F.J. Kemp	MM679/WM-	V-1	night (FTR)	off east coast

68 Squadron lost an aircraft and crew when 30-year-old Londoner Flt Lt Fred Kemp and his navigator Flg Off James Farrar failed to return. They had been despatched to search for a missing bomber when a flying bomb was sighted. Apparently the Mosquito engaged the missile and a message was received from the pilot stating that the bomb had exploded – but then silence. A nearby Mosquito from 219 Squadron was sent to investigate but failed to find any signs of debris or crew[138].

96 Squadron (Mosquito XIII) Ford

Flg Off J. Goode	MM452/ZJ-	V-1	2305	Grid R.3220
	MM452/ZJ-	V-1	2310	exploded in mid-air
Flg Off R.F. Ball	HK372/ZJ-G	V-1	2322	Grid R.0102

Flg Off John Goode noted: "(1) Diver spiralled down and exploded on the sea; (2)

Diver exploded in the air, damaging starboard tailplane." Fifteen minutes later, Flg Off Ball scored a third: "First attack from 400 yards, strikes seen. Diver flew on. Second attack from 250 yards astern. Diver exploded in the sea. About 50 feet of thin wire seen behind, illuminated by flame."

157 Squadron (Mosquito XIX) West Malling

Flt Lt J.O. Mathews	MM671/RS-C	V-1	2305	Tonbridge area
	MM671/RS-C	V-1	2310	Tonbridge area

Flt Lt Mathews scored a brace within five minutes: "Vectored into position above Diver. Dived on it and gave burst from above. Seen to explode on the ground ten miles south-east of Tonbridge." Five minutes later he was vectored on to another: "Vectored to position above Diver. Gave burst from above. Diver exploded on the ground 15 miles south-east of Tonbridge." It seems probable that his second victim fell at Marden Thorn where cottages were damaged and one occupant slightly injured.

605 Squadron (Mosquito VI) Manston

Flt Lt A.J. Craven	UP-	V-1		Channel
Flt Lt R.J. Garner	MM414/UP-Y	V-1	2352	Channel

Flt Lt 'Pete' Garner scored again just before midnight:

"Saw four Divers in all and attacked two. All Divers came from Ostende. Three-four cannon burst from 400-500 yards astern. Attack broken off at 2352 when Diver was seen to explode in the sea. Claim is confirmed by Flg Off Lelong, who saw both the attack and the explosion."

Night 25/26 JULY

Eighteen sorties were flown by III/KG3 from Gilze-Rijen, but possibly only 11 launchings were successful. All aircraft except one had returned safely by 0450. The missing Heinkel, 5K+GT of 9 Staffel flown by Uffz Günter Rohne, had collided with a high mast near Eindhoven at 0010. There were no survivors[139]. London, Essex and Hertfordshire each received three of the unwelcome visitors. Four fighter victims exploded in the Maidstone/Malling/Hollingbourne area in the early hours, damage being inflicted at Goudhurst Road, Marden (one seriously injured), three houses at Aylesford (three slightly hurt), Snoad Farm, Otterden, and Harpole Farm, Detling.

25 Squadron (Mosquito XVII) Coltishall

Wt Off R.G.B. Pickles	HK301/ZK	V-1	0420	Channel

"We were patrolling and at 0420 saw flying bomb at 2,000 feet. I closed the range and opened fire from 400-300 yards with 25° deflection as the flying bomb was crossing from port to starboard. I saw red glow round about petrol tank and the light went out and it commenced to lose height. The flying bomb was not observed to go in but I was informed by Sandwich Control that it was destroyed."

85 Squadron (Mosquito XIX) West Malling

Capt T. Weisteen (Norw)	MM636/VY-A	V-1	0415	West Malling area
	MM636/VY-A	V-1	0455	West Malling area
Flt Lt R.T. Goucher	TA400/VY-J	V-1	0430	Dungeness area

Both of Capt Tarald Weisteen's victims fell near West Malling although 40 minutes apart:

"Dived from 5,000 feet, short burst from astern. Diver exploded on ground five-ten miles east of West Malling. Sighted [second] and dived from 6,000 feet. Fired several bursts from astern. Diver rapidly lost height and exploded on ground five-six miles west of West Malling."

Flt Lt Goucher scored his kill north of Dungeness: "Sighted and granted permission to chase. Dived from 7,000 feet and fired short burst from astern. Diver exploded on the ground."

96 Squadron (Mosquito XIII) Ford

Flt Sgt T. Bryan	MM468/ZJ-	V-1	0045 (FTR)	Channel
Flt Lt F.R.L. Mellersh	MM577/ZJ-N	V-1	0110	Channel
	MM577/ZJ-N	V-1	0117	exploded in mid-air
Flt Lt K. Kennedy	HK425/ZJ-	V-1	0125	Channel (Grid Q.7505)
Flg Off J.D. Black	MM492/ZJ-	V-1	0302	Grid R.1939
Flt Lt D.L. Ward	MM524/ZJ-	V-1	0415	Channel

The night started badly when Flt Sgt Tom Bryan and his navigator Sgt Brian Jaeger were lost when their aircraft failed to return. It is believed they shot down a Diver and then possibly fell victim to friendly fire from the coastal guns. A subsequent search found only an empty Mae West. During the search for the missing crew, the Mosquito (MM494) crewed by Lt(A) Frank Richards RNVR and Lt M.J. Baring RNVR was fired upon by the coastal guns. Despite evasive action the port engine was hit and stopped, Richards carrying out a dead stick landing at Friston, but overshot and collided with stationary Mustang HB882 of 316 (Polish) Squadron. Both aircraft caught fire and were destroyed although Richards and Baring escaped unharmed. Despite these setbacks, five Divers were shot down by daybreak, two falling to Flt Lt Togs Mellersh, the first of which exploded in the sea. Seven minutes later he shot down a second, which exploded in the air and damaged his aircraft. Nonetheless, he was able to return safely to base. His navigator Flt Lt Michael Stanley simply annotated his logbook: "Second blew up and shook us somewhat!" Flt Lt Kennedy's victim also exploded on hitting the sea, while Flg Off Black noted: "Strikes seen and 'aircraft' lost height. It went down steeply and exploded on the ground."

157 Squadron (Mosquito XIX) West Malling

Flt Lt J.W. Caddie	MM681/RS-	V-1	(FTR)	North Foreland

Mosquito MM681/RS-K crewed by Flt Lt John Caddie and Flg Off George Larcey FTR from anti-Diver patrol. Mosquito brought down by explosion.

418 (RCAF) Squadron (Mosquito VI) Hurn

Flg Off J.S. Hill RCAF[140]	TH-	V-1	0405	

605 Squadron (Mosquito VI) Manston

Flt Lt R.J. Garner	MM414/UP-Y	V-1	night	Channel
Flt Lt J.G. Musgrave	MM429/UP-H	V-1	night	Channel

FIU (Tempest V) Ford

Flt Lt J. Berry	EJ524/ZQ-Y	V-1	night	
	EJ524/ZQ-Y	V-1	night	
	EJ524/ZQ-Y	V-1	night	
	EJ524/ZQ-Y	V-1	night	
Flt Lt R.L.T. Robb	ZQ-	V-1	night	

Wednesday 26 JULY

In his speech to Luftwaffe officers at a training camp on this date, Reichführer-SS Heinrich Himmler wildly exaggerated the success of the bombardment:

> *"Regarding the V-1 fire, which is being kept up day and night without interruption – it is never known when it will come. A warning for southern England and London is never possible, which is very nerve-racking and costs a great number of lives. News from London indicates that*

London had 120,000 dead [sic] after four weeks by the beginning of July, which corresponds completely with the numbers of V-1 projectiles that we have sent over [sic] and of which I am well aware. Since we have a rough idea of the effects, we can therefore calculate the number of deaths. Eleven million people are affected by this bombardment from our weapons. That is how many live in both southern England and London. London has eight to nine million inhabitants. That means that 25 per cent of the total English population is affected by this troublesome instrument. This will not cause a sudden change. Here, too, we can expect no miracles. But it is nerve-racking. It is impeding the invasion army's supplies. It is obstructing new assemblies for new landings from the island. It is more than a nuisance. It is something which in a military sense is weakening the power of a nation of a belligerent state."

Before 0800, a further four Divers were shot down by fighters in the Maidstone/Hollingbourne area, one damaging a dozen houses at East Peckham (one slightly injured), Wateringbury (one killed), Ditton, and Mantle Farm, Hollingbourne.

1 Squadron (Spitfire LFIXb) Lympne

Flt Lt I.P. Maskell	NH466/JX-	V-1	0755	Maidstone area
Flg Off D.H. Davy	ML117/JX-D	V-1	1410	off Folkestone
Flg Off D.H. Davy ⎫	ML117/JX-D	V-1	1415	off Lympne
Flt Sgt G. Tate ⎭	MK987/JX-			

Flg Off Dennis Davy reported:

"Control vectored me on to Diver. I closed in and after first attack saw strikes on port wing. Second attack saw many strikes on starboard wing and jet. Diver slowed down. Final burst observed more strikes. Diver turned to port and dived steeply and exploded in sea ten miles south of Folkestone."

He shared a second with Flt Sgt Godfrey Tate (known as Spud and recently posted from 610 Squadron):

"Intercepted Diver ten miles north-west of Boulogne at 2,000 feet. Four divided attacks made from line astern and starboard. Yellow 2 [Tate] attacked first and observed strikes on both wings. I attacked next and scored strikes on port wing, the third attack being made by Yellow 2, who hit the Diver all over, slowing it right down. I then attacked again, seeing strikes on the jet unit. The Diver dropped port wing and began to lose height. Yellow 2 made a final attack and Diver went into sea, exploding about five miles south of Lympne."

Flg Off Jack Batchelor recalled:

"I shared a room with Davy – a great chap. While I was on a 48-hour leave he shot down five V-1s. We were all envious and he was soon known as 'Ace Davy'[141]. At Lympne we had spare time on our hands as normally we only had a few anti-V-1 patrols a day. The mess was at Porte Lympne House. One day we were lying around by the pool and a Halifax bomber with one engine on fire came over at about 12,000 feet and people started to bale out as the pilot turned back towards the sea. However, as we watched, the port undercarriage wheel fell off. It appeared that it was coming straight for us and we all started running. The amusing thing was that a 41 Squadron pilot [Flt Lt Tom Burne], who had lost a leg below the knee was with us, and on these bathing periods would naturally take off his tin leg and hobble about on crutches. What amazed us all as we ran for cover was this guy going past us like a bullet!"[142]

150 Wing (Tempest V) Newchurch

Wg Cdr R.P. Beamont	JN751/RB	V-1 shared		Hailsham area

3 Squadron (Tempest V) Newchurch

Flt Sgt D.J. Mackerras RAAF	JN768/JF-F	V-1	0630	Tunbridge Wells area
Flg Off G.A. Whitman RCAF (US)	EJ504/JF-	V-1 shared	0755	Tunbridge Wells area
Flt Lt A.R. Moore	JN865/JF-	V-1	0803	Beachy Head area

Flt Sgt D.J. Mackerras RAAF	JN768/JF-F	V-1	1425	Ashford area
Flt Lt R. van Lierde (Belg)	JN862/JF-Z	V-1	2208	Bexhill area
Flt Lt R. van Lierde (Belg)	JN862/JF-Z	V-1	2212	Bexhill area
Flg Off M.F. Edwards	JN521/JF-			
Flt Lt R. van Lierde (Belg)	JN862/JF-Z	V-1	2215	Bexhill area
Flg Off R. Dryland	JN865/JF-	V-1	2215	Hastings area

Another successful day for the squadron saw eight more Divers chalked up as destroyed, the first three falling in the morning, two in the Tunbridge Wells area and the other near Beachy Head. Flt Sgt Don Mackerras, who got one of these, added a second in the afternoon:

> "Saw a Diver over Folkestone at 3,000 feet and closed to 400 yards. Saw strikes on jet, then closed to 200 yards and blew wingtip off with short burst. The Diver rolled on its back and went down to 500 feet, leveled out for a moment and then went down, exploding on the ground south of Ashford."

With the onset of darkness, Flt Lt van Lierde took off with Flg Off Malcolm Edwards[143], the Belgian ace shooting down two more and sharing another with Edwards:

> "Saw a Diver south of Bexhill at 3,000 feet. Closed to 400 yards and fired to 200 yards. The Diver went down and exploded on the ground five-six miles north of Bexhill at 2208. Saw a second Diver over Hastings at 2,500/3,000 feet. F/O Edwards attacked from 400 yards closing to 200 yards, obtaining numerous strikes but had to break. I then attacked from 300/400 yards astern and Diver went down at 2212. Saw a third Diver north of Bexhill at 1,500 feet and closed to 300 yards. Gave a short burst and Diver went down, exploding on the ground ten miles north of Bexhill at 2215."

Flg Off Rod Dryland got the last of the day: "Saw Diver over Hastings at 3,000 feet. Attacked from astern, closing from 300 to 100 yards. Strikes were seen and Diver heeled over, having caught fire, and went down, exploding on the ground seven or eight miles north of Hastings."

41 Squadron (Spitfire XII) Lympne

Flg Off M.A.L. Balasse (Belg)	EN609/EB-	V-1	2145	off Beachy Head
Flg Off E.B. Gray	EN605/EB-	V-1	2105-2230	

56 Squadron (Tempest V) Newchurch

Sqn Ldr A.R. Hall	EJ541/US-B	V-1	0750	Maidstone area
Flt Sgt A.C. Drew	JN869/US-D	V-1	1410	Ashford area
	JN869/US-D	V-1	1420	Ashford area

Sqn Ldr Archie Hall sighted his target six miles west of Ashford at 1,000 feet: "I fired from 250 yards astern, scoring strikes on the starboard wing and the Diver exploded on the ground six miles south-west of Maidstone." The CO's No.2 Flg Off R.V. Dennis was flying 700 yards behind him and saw a Mustang also open fire on this Diver but observed no strikes. Flt Sgt Drew enjoyed a successful ten minutes:

> "I sighted Diver off Dymchurch at 2,000 feet. I fired from 150 yards, closing to 100 yards, and the Diver exploded in a field east of Ashford. I sighted a second Diver over Dungeness and fired from 150 yards, using up all my ammunition, without observing any strikes, so I formated on the Diver and tipped it over with my port wing. The Diver went down, exploding in a field south-east of Ashford."

91 Squadron (Spitfire XIV) Deanland ALG

Flt Lt H.D. Johnson	RM624/DL-	V-1	0730	Battle area
Flt Lt A.R. Cruickshank RCAF	RM649/DL-	V-1	0752	Crowborough area
Flt Lt E.G.A. Seghers (Belg)	RM743/DL-	V-1	1420 (KiA)	Hoathly area

| Sqn Ldr N.A. Kynaston | RM654/DL-F | V-1 | 2210 | Bexhill area |
| Flg Off G.H. Huntley | RM653/DL- | V-1 shared | 2245 | Hailsham area |

Flt Lt Johnny Johnson opened the scoring for the day during a morning patrol: "Saw Diver over Pevensey Bay and attacked from astern at 100 yards. Diver fell and exploded in a wood west of Battle." Twenty minutes later, Flt Lt Ray Cruickshank got another: "Saw Diver west of Ninfield and saw strikes on starboard mainplane. Diver spun in, exploding in a wood two miles north-east of Crowborough." Sadly, Flt Lt Gin Seghers misjudged his attack and collided with his target, which exploded and pieces of both machines fell at Ridgewood near Uckfield. Wg Cdr Bobby Oxspring, OC 24 Wing, wrote:

> "Flt Lt Seghers, a Belgian attached to 91 Squadron, lost his life within sight of the airfield when he attacked a target from an awkward angle of fully 90°. Trying to pull enough deflection he lost sight of it under his nose and misjudged his distance. To our horror he struck the warhead which in a deadly flash demolished both target and Spitfire."

Two more were shot down during the evening, Sqn Ldr Norman Kynaston getting the first: "Saw Diver over Bexhill, attacked and it fell, exploding on the ground ten miles north-west of Bexhill."

129 Squadron (Mustang III) Brenzett

Flg Off J.E. Hartley	HB862/DV-G	V-1	0635-0800	Tunbridge Wells area
Flg Off M. Humphries	FB137/DV-C	V-1	0800-0840	Netherfield area
Flt Lt K.C. Baker RCAF[144]	FB395/DV-Y	V-1 shared	1355-1605	Wadhurst area

Flt Lt Kelts Baker reported that he stopped his victim's engine before a Tempest nipped in front of him and caused the Diver to burst into flames and crash to ground.

137 Squadron (Typhoon Ib) Manston

| Flg Off J.C. Holder RCAF[145] | MN134/SF-J | V-1 | 0745 | off Hastings |

Two Typhoons took off from Manston at 0650 to undertake a weather reconnaissance over France. On the return flight Flg Off Jim Holder sighted a Diver 20 miles south-east of Hastings at 2,000 feet: "After a Mustang had broken away after an unsuccessful attack, I fired from astern and the fuel caught fire. The Diver exploded on the sea."

165 Squadron (Spitfire IX) Lympne

Flg Off C.M. Lawson RAAF	ML175/SK-P	V-1	0640	Ashford area
Plt Off A. Scott	MK514/SK-Z	V-1	0800	Maidstone area
Flt Sgt P.T. Humphrey RNZAF	ML175/SK-P	V-1 shared	1420	Ashford area
Flt Sgt G.S. Cameron	NH401/SK-M	V-1 shared	1525-1630	Robertsbridge area

First of the day fell to Flg Off Lawson: "Intercepted near Dymchurch. Strikes seen on fuselage, then petrol exploded – three miles west of Ashford. Confirmed by Black 1." Plt Off Scott got the next: "Intercepted three miles west of Ashford. After fourth attack Diver flicked over on its back and exploded on the ground in a coppice outside Maidstone." New Zealander Flt Sgt Humphrey intercepted five miles north-west of Folkestone: "Tempest attacked and bomb made complete roll but carried on course. I attacked and saw strikes on right wing. Bomb spiralled in near railway line to Canterbury. Confirmed by Blue 1." Flt Sgt Cameron: "Intercepted ten miles north of Hastings. Tempest first seen to go in to attack. Apparently hit Diver. I attacked and flame became very large at rear. Diver went down about three miles south-west of Robertsbridge near a lake."

306 (Polish) Squadron (Mustang III) Brenzett

Flt Lt A. Beyer PAF	FB106/UZ-V	V-1 shared	0610	Grid R.4050
Flt Sgt J. Zaleński PAF	FB241/UZ-Z	V-1 shared	0609	Grid R.3347
	FB241/UZ-Z	V-1	0615	Grid R.1368
Sqn Ldr P. Niemiec PAF	UZ-X	V-1 shared	0741	Grid R.1470
Flt Sgt J. Zaleński PAF	FB241/UZ-Z	V-1	1415	off Hastings
Flt Sgt J. Czeżowski PAF	HB863/UZ-O	V-1 shared	2212	Robertsbridge area

Flt Lt Andrzej Beyer and Flt Sgt Józef Zaleński took off at 0535 and both soon engaged Divers, Beyer intercepting south-east of Lydd. His target slowed down, spewing fuel, before a Spitfire nipped in and finished the job, the Diver exploding in the air. Zaleński engaged his victim seven miles west of Rye, the Diver doing an estimated 410mph. Following his first attack the propulsion unit ceased to function, whereupon another Mustang (probably from 315 Squadron) opened fire when it was about 200 feet above the ground. Zaleński gave another burst and it exploded on the ground. He then engaged another near Ham Street and saw pieces fly off the jet unit. It crashed and exploded near a farm. The next Diver fell to Sqn Ldr Paweł Niemiec near Tenterden, a Tempest finishing it off. Flt Sgt Zaleński scored again during the afternoon, shooting it down into the sea about 15 miles south-south-east of Hastings, while Flt Sgt Jacek Czeżowski shot down another that went in two miles south-east of Robertsbridge, exploding on impact, but was informed that two others had also engaged this bomb.

315 (Polish) Squadron (Mustang III) Brenzett

Wt Off T. Jankowski PAF	FB188/PK-U	3 V-1s	0615, 0625, 0645	
Wt Off T. Słoń PAF	FB174/PK-S			off Hastings
Flg Off T. Haczkiewicz PAF	FZ157/PK-Q	V-1 shared	0743	off Hastings
Flt Sgt S. Bedkowski PAF	FB371/PK-B	V-1	2210	off Hastings

Wt Offs Janowski and Słoń jointly shot down three Divers during their patrol, the first 30 miles south-east of Hastings, the second 40 miles off the coast and the third 15 miles from the French coast.

316 (Polish) Squadron (Mustang) Friston

Wt Off A. Murkowski PAF	FB381/SZ-C	V-1	0615	off Beachy Head
Wt Off W. Grobelny PAF	FB385/SZ-D	V-1	0635	exploded in mid-air
Flt Lt K. Zielonka PAF	FB353/SZ-H	V-1	1446	Tonbridge area
Flt Lt A. Cholajda PAF	FB384/SZ-Z	V-1	2213	off Rye
	FB384/SZ-Z	V-1	2255	off Rye

Wt Off Murkowski scored the first of the day: "Seen 35 miles south of Beachy Head. Chased and opened fire from 150 yards, closing to 100 yards from beam. Diver exploded in the sea." Wt Off Wladyslaw Grobelny: "Opened fire from 400 yards down to 300 yards whereupon the Diver exploded in the air." Flt Lt Zielonka got the next after lunch: "Seen over Sandhurst. Chased and opened fire from 600 yards, closing to 100 yards. Strikes all over. Diver exploded three miles east of Tonbridge in a wood. When Diver was going down a Tempest was firing at it." Flt Lt Antoni Cholajda rapidly shot down two more: "Attacked from dead astern at 300 yards. Diver exploded in the sea 30 miles south of Rye." Three minutes later he got his second: "Seen 35 miles south of Rye. Chased and opened fire from dead astern at 300 yards. Diver crashed into the sea."

322 (Dutch) Squadron (Spitfire XIV) West Malling

Flg Off J. van Arkel	VL-W	V-1	0630	Grid R.0067
Flt Sgt C. Kooij	VL-S	V-1	0632	Grid R.4549
Flg Off R.F. Burgwal	NH649/VL-F	V-1	2205	Hastings area
	NH649/VL-F	V-1 shared	2210	Hastings area
	NH649/VL-F	V-1 shared	2218	Grid Q.8935

Flg Off Jan van Arkel and Flt Sgt Cees Kooij carried out straight forward interceptions and shot down their victims without undue problems, but Flg Off Rudi Burgwal faced stiff competition during his evening patrol:

> "Vectored on to Diver crossing east of Hastings. Attacked starboard to line astern, range 150 yards. Tempest had fired and slowed it up. Diver crashed and exploded 10-15 miles north of Hastings." Five minutes later he was vectored on to another over Hastings: "Mustang and Tempest attacked but Diver went on. I attacked from line astern, range 150 yards, causing Diver to crash and exploded approximately 17 miles north-west of Hastings." Yet another Diver approached Eastbourne a few minutes later, and Burgwal was vectored on to this also: "A Spitfire from 91 Squadron fired and broke away. I attacked line astern, range 100 yards. Petrol exploded and Diver crashed and exploded on the ground."

486 (RNZAF) Squadron (Tempest V) Newchurch

Plt Off R.D. Bremner RNZAF	JN803/SA-D	V-1	0620	Rye area
Flg Off W.A. Hart RNZAF	JN732.SA-I	V-1	0633	Tonbridge area
Flg Off R.J. Cammock RNZAF	EJ523/SA-X	V-1	0745	Bexhill area
Flt Lt J.H. McCaw RNZAF	JN770/SA-V	V-1	0750	Bexhill area
Plt Off K.A. Smith RNZAF	JN803/SA-D	V-1	0810	Pevensey area
Flt Lt V.St.C. Cooke RNZAF	JN763/SA-F	V-1	0820	Battle area
Flg Off R.J. Cammock RNZAF	JN770/SA-V	V-1	1425	Ashford area
Flg Off J.R. Cullen RNZAF	JN770/SA-V	V-1 shared	2210	Pevensey area
Plt Off J.H. Stafford RNZAF	JN803/SA-D	V-1	2230	Hastings area

610 Squadron (Spitfire XIV) Friston

Flt Sgt T.F. Higgs	DW-	V-1	0540-0705

Night 26/27 JULY

III/KG3 operating from the French airfield at Roye/Amy flew a further 19 sorties during the night. All returned safely. A Diver that fell in Streatham (SW2) at 2257 badly damaged a girls' school in Wavette Road. Thirty houses were also damaged and one resident killed. Three more were killed in Clapham (SW4) when a dozen flats and 40 houses in Kings Avenue/Clarence Road were damaged by a Diver at 0144. At almost the same time, another bomb fell in Bramerton Road, Beckenham (BR3), where five people were killed. At 0225, a Diver impacted at Great Warley in Essex. One person was killed, the first fatality in East Anglia, four injured and two houses demolished. Another fell on a street in Barking, where it damaged a number of houses and killed a mother and her 18-year-old daughter. Around this time a flying bomb fell near Barking Creek without causing much damage, but strangely many nearby cyclists found their tyres had deflated, a strange phenomenon apparently caused by the blast of the explosion. A second Diver came down in Beckenham (BR3) at 1744, killing three in St George's Road and causing much damage.

25 Squadron (Mosquito XVII) Coltishall

The crew of Flt Lt Lilwall and Flg Off Norris were again frustrated and denied opening their score when their intended victim again dived into the sea without a shot being fired, causing the pilot to comment: "Apparently it lost its nerve and went into the sea without being molested."

68 Squadron (Mosquito) Castle Camps

Sqn Ldr M.J. Mansfeld	MM683/WM-C	V-1	0135-0145	Castle Camps area

Sqn Ldr Miroslav Mansfeld departed Castle Camps at 0135 and while circling the airfield a Diver was illuminated by a searchlight at 0140. This was immediately engaged and shot down, the explosion seen by many air and groundcrew of A Flight.

85 Squadron (Mosquito XVII) West Malling

Flg Off E.R. Hedgecoe	HK120/VY-P	V-1	0003	Hawkhurst area

Flg Off Edward Hedgecoe engaged a Diver held by searchlights: "Dived from 7,000 feet and fired short burst from astern. Diver exploded on the ground five miles west of Hawkhurst."

96 Squadron (Mosquito XIII) Ford

Flt Lt D.L. Ward	MM524/ZJ-	V-1	2357	exploded in mid-air
Flt Lt F.R.L. Mellersh	MM577/ZJ-N	V-1	0135	Channel
Flt Lt I.A. Dobie	HK437/ZJ-	V-1	0144	Channel
Flt Lt F.R.L. Mellersh	MM577/ZJ-N	V-1	0505	Channel

Flt Lt Don Ward's victim blew up in mid-air following his attack, while those shot down by Flt Lt Togs Mellersh – two in separate patrols – raised his score to 21.

418 (RCAF) Squadron (Mosquito VI) Hurn

Flt Lt C.J. Evans RCAF	TH-	V-1	0142	off Eastbourne
Sqn Ldr R. Bannock RCAF	HR147/TH-Z	V-1	0210	into sea

Flt Lt Colin Evans gained his sixth and final kill:

> "At 0142 a Diver was sighted at 1,500 feet, through a break in the cloud, 20 miles south-west of Beachy Head. Proceeded to dive through cloud, which enabled interception from astern. Dived through cloud on instruments, catching occasional glimpses and finally attacked from astern with three short bursts. Several minor explosions occurred. The Diver went into a steep dive and crashed in the sea ten miles west of Eastbourne."

Sqn Ldr Bannock got another:

> "At 0210 a Diver came out of the Dieppe area at 2,500 feet. We were then at 9,000 feet and the Diver was seen through a hole in the cloud. We flew over to intercept, making S-turns on the Diver's track. When the light appeared just beneath the nose, I dived vertically, pulling out astern at 200-300 yards. The attack was made with three two-seconds bursts of cannon and machine-gun. The Diver went down in a steep glide and exploded on impact with the sea."

But it was not all success, since Sqn Ldr Dick Jephson FTR from a night sortie over France. He reported shooting down a Ju88 but his aircraft was hit by debris from the explosion and his Mosquito (HK462) crashed near Calvados, killing him and his navigator Flg Off John Roberts RCAF.

422NFS USAAF (P-61) Ford

2/Lt L.A. Gordon USAAF	42-5591	V-1 possible	mid-Channel

2/Lt Lewis 'Al' Gordon, flying P-61 'Impatient Widow', recalled:

> "The job was to fly over the English Channel and if possible to shoot them down before they hit London. If we didn't get them before they arrived over the coast, the anti-aircraft ground-based guns tried to do the job. It was important for us to break off the chase before we arrived over the coast or we could be hit by British flak. Since the buzz bombs flew faster than the P-61, we patrolled above their expected altitude and were directed to dive at a point to intersect by GCI (ground radar). I chased several of them and never shot one down, although I almost

got one. The V-1s were so fast that we had to dive on them. I followed it and was coming down on it when, all of a sudden, the damn thing started to gain altitude. And so I chased it up, shot at it, but I don't know for sure if I hit or not. But it splashed into the water. These missions to shoot down buzz bombs were intentionally provided to give the flight crews a taste of combat. Although there was nobody shooting back at you, if you got too close to a V-1, you could shoot yourself down. One of our guys [Capt Spelis] came close to doing just that. He got too close to a buzz bomb and it exploded. His plane came back looking like a cinderblock, completely sooted, from the results of the explosion. But the plane was all right and so was he."

Thursday 27 JULY

Twenty-four people were killed when a flying bomb fell in Church Road, Beckenham. The nearby parish church of St George's was severely damaged by blast and many gravestones were shattered. Two Divers came down in West Norwood (SE27) during the evening. One exploded on the south side of York Hill, killing five and destroying/damaging at least 40 houses. The other fell near Tulse Hill railway bridge, destroying 20 shops and 30 houses, and killing six. The Maidstone area of Kent was again on the receiving end of crippled Divers, victims of fighters. Seven came down between 1525 and 2350. Eastbourne received another at 1925, injuring 34 residents and causing much damage. Across the North Sea, at Mosstofta, north-west of Jämjö in Sweden, a V-1 impacted at 1734, without causing damage or casualties. From where it originated is unclear, but probably it was test firing from Peenemünde.

150 Wing (Tempest V) Newchurch

Wg Cdr R.P. Beamont	JN751/RB	V-1	pm	Bexhill area
	JN751/RB	V-1	pm	Tenterden area

3 Squadron (Tempest V) Newchurch

Flg Off R.H. Clapperton	JN815/JF-	V-1	1515	Maidstone area
Flt Lt R. van Lierde (Belg)	JN862/JF-Z	V-1	1640	Rye area
	JN862/JF-Z	V-1	1645	Tonbridge area
	JN862/JF-Z	V-1	1647	Grid R.1266
	JN862/JF-Z	V-1	2002	Tunbridge Wells area
Flg Off R.H. Clapperton	EJ540/JF-P	V-1	2215	Tunbridge Wells area
Flt Lt R. van Lierde (Belg)	JN862/JF-Z	V-1	2245	Hastings area

Two pilots accounted for seven flying bombs, Flg Off Ray Clapperton getting two, one in the afternoon and the other in the evening: "I saw a Diver over base at 1,500 feet and closed to 200 yards – fired one short burst and saw strikes on the jet and starboard wing. The Diver went down and exploded near Maidstone at 1515." This was probably the Diver that fell between Lancet Lane and Loose Road, Maidstone, causing much damage. At least 300 houses suffered of which six were destroyed. Fourteen people were slightly hurt. He was off again at 2215: "Saw a Diver above cloud at 3,000 feet and closed to 150 yards and gave one short burst. The Diver exploded in mid-air in the Tunbridge Wells area at 2250. My aircraft flew through the debris and was damaged." The star turn was again Flt Lt Remi van Lierde who accounted for five Divers during the course of three busy patrols:

"Saw a Diver over Dungeness at 3,000 feet, closed to 250 yards with a short burst and the Diver went down and crashed near Rye at 1640. Saw a second near base at 2,500 feet. Closed to 400 yards and fired down to 50 yards. Diver went down three miles south of Tonbridge at 1645. Saw a third south of Tonbridge and attacked from astern with two one-second bursts from 100 yards. The jet spluttered and went out. The Diver carried on at reduced speed, losing height but had to be left owing to balloons at R.1266. It is understood that this Diver crashed just outside the IAZ."

The Belgian landed, refuelled and re-armed and was off again at 1925:

> "Saw a Diver east of Eastbourne at 2,500 feet. Closed to 350 yards and attacked with four one-second bursts and tip of Diver's port wing came off. Closed to 200 yards and gave three-seconds burst and Diver burst into flames and the port wing came off. It crashed five miles south-east of Tunbridge Wells." He was off again at 2205: "Saw Diver above cloud in Hastings area at 3,000 feet. Closed to 150 yards and gave one short burst. The petrol exploded and the Diver crashed ten miles north-west of Hastings at 2245."

His score now stood at 39 including eight shared.

41 Squadron (Spitfire XII) Lympne

Flt Sgt C.S. Robertson RAAF	EN602/EB-	V-1	2115	off Dungeness

Flt Sgts Colin Robertson and Jock Stevenson took off at 2030 to carry out an anti-Diver patrol, Robertson catching one some 15 miles south of Dungeness, where he shot it down into the sea:

> "Patrolling mid Channel and warned of approach of Diver ten miles ahead at 3,000 feet. Made three attacks and many strikes observed. Diver altered course to port and lost height rapidly and disappeared through 10/10 cloud at 2,000 feet and into sea."

56 Squadron (Tempest V) Newchurch

Flt Lt R.K. Dean	EJ545/US-Z	V-1	pm	Folkestone area
	EJ545/US-Z	V-1	pm	Lympne area

Flt Lt Dean crash-landed at 2245 and suffered a broken thigh and severe shock.

91 Squadron (Spitfire XIV) Deanland ALG

Sqn Ldr N.A. Kynaston	RM684/DL-	V-1	2115	Staplehurst area
	RM684/DL-	V-1	2130	Tonbridge area

Sqn Ldr Norman Kynaston's first victim fell north of Staplehurst: "Saw Diver four miles south of Tenterden. Attacked from astern at 250 yards range, Diver falling and exploding in a field." No.2 followed 15 minutes later: "Saw Diver west of Rye. Attacked from astern at 300 yards. Both wings shot off and Diver fell, exploding in a wood two miles south of Tunbridge."

129 Squadron (Mustang III) Brenzett

Flt Lt A.C. Leigh	FB364/DV-D	V-1	2035-2255	off Dungeness

Flt Lt Joe Leigh DFM intercepted a Diver 30 miles south of Dungeness and attacked from dead astern with long bursts, closing to 200 yards. The bomb rolled over and exploded in the sea about ten miles offshore.

137 Squadron (Typhoon Ib) Manston

137 Squadron suffered a double tragedy in the morning, when Flg Off Ralph Johnstone RCAF and Flt Sgt Arthur Hack collided in cloud at 0838 during their patrol. Both were killed when their respective aircraft MN830 and MN836 crashed. Flg Off Artie Sames' aircraft (MN198) was armed with air-to-ground rockets, which he fired at a V-1 from a range of 600 yards during a late evening sortie (2230-2330). The salvo was seen to explode about 40 feet above the flying bomb, which then drew slowly out of range apparently undamaged.

165 Squadron (Spitfire IX) Lympne

Flg Off T.D. Tinsey	MK514/SK-Z	V-1	1405	Faversham area
Flt Sgt G.S. Cameron	ML139/SK-Q	V-1 shared	1648	Staplehurst area
Flt Lt B.J. Murch	NH401/SK-M	V-1	1755	
Flg Off G.P. Armstrong RAAF	MJ221/SK-T	V-1 shared	2115	

Flg Off Tinsey: "Intercepted Diver north-east of Ashford. Strikes seen all over and it turned over and went into a cornfield south-west of Faversham. Confirmed by Flt Lt Watson." Flt Sgt Cameron intercepted five miles south of Staplehurst: "Strikes seen and bomb dived in one mile north of Marden." It seems that he was obliged to share his victory with Flt Sgt Rudowski of 306 Squadron.

306 (Polish) Squadron (Mustang III) Brenzett

Flt Sgt J. Pomietlarz PAF	FB358/UZ-C	V-1	1640	Grid R.5862
Plt Off J. Smigielski PAF	UZ-I	V-1	1645	Grid R.3463
Flt Sgt S. Rudowski PAF	FB380/UZ-F	V-1 shared	1652	Staplehurst/ Tonbridge
Plt Off J. Smigielski PAF	UZ-I	V-1 shared	2110	Tunbridge Wells area
Flt Sgt S. Rudowski PAF	FB380/UZ-F	V-1	2140	Grid R.2458

Flt Sgt Jan Pomietlarz shot down another some two miles north-west of Hawkinge, while Plt Off Jan Smigielski got one that impacted near a farmhouse, damaging it and a nearby haystack. Flt Sgt Stan Rudowski fired at his target at the same time that a Spitfire attacked. The starboard wing tore away before the Diver crashed between Staplehurst and Tonbridge. That evening two more were intercepted, Plt Off Smigielski shared his with a Spitfire (probably Flg Off Armstrong of 165 Squadron) and a Mustang (Wt Off Jankowski of 315 Squadron), the Diver exploding on the ground ten miles south-east of Tunbridge Wells, while Flt Sgt Rudowski saw pieces break away from his target before it crashed and exploded on a road.

315 (Polish) Squadron (Mustang III) Brenzett

Flt Lt F. Wiza PAF	FX995/PK-E	V-1	1635	off Dieppe
Wt Off T. Jankowski PAF	FZ143/PK-V	V-1 shared	2110	off Dieppe

486 (RNZAF) Squadron (Tempest V) Newchurch

Flg Off W.A. Hart RNZAF	JN754/SA-A	V-1	1642	Tenterden area
Plt Off R.D. Bremner RNZAF	JN803/SA-D			
Plt Off W.A.L. Trott RNZAF	JN763/SA-F	V-1	1755	West Malling area
Flg Off R.J. Cammock RNZAF	EJ523/SA-X	V-1	1924	Tunbridge Wells area
	EJ523/SA-X	V-1	1930	Hastings area
Flt Lt J.H. McCaw RNZAF	JN770/SA-V	V-1	1927	Hastings/Bexhill
Wt Off O.D. Eagleson RNZAF	EJ586/SA-Z	V-1	2122	Ashford area
Wt Off B.J. O'Connor RNZAF	JN801/SA-L	V-1	2140	Beachy Head area
Flt Lt J.H. McCaw RNZAF	EJ523/SA-X	V-1	2245	Ashford area

616 Squadron (Meteor F.1) Manston

Following its arrival at Manston, Wg Cdr Andrew McDowall DFM was posted in to take command of the Meteor Flight, since it was custom for squadrons equipped with multi-engined aircraft to be commanded by a wing commander. Sqn Ldr Les Watts remained with the unit, however, and continued to command the Spitfire Flight. 616 Squadron received six Welland-powered Meteor F.1s. Also joining the Meteor Flight at Manston was Wg Cdr Hugh 'Willie' Wilson AFC, a very experienced service test pilot from the RAE and one of the pioneers of Meteor flying, who arrived with his personalised aircraft EE224/HJW. The squadron diarist wrote:

"The Meteors go into operation. History is made! The first British jet-propelled aircraft flies in defence of Britain against the flying bomb. At 1430 hours, Flg Off McKenzie [EE219/YQ-D] took off to patrol a line between Ashford and Robertsbridge, this line covering the main 'in-roads' of the flying bomb. Uneventful patrols were made by Wg Cdr McDowall [EE215/YQ-C], Wg Cdr Wilson [HJW], Flg Off Rodger [EE219/YQ-D], Wt Off Wilkes [EE213/YQ-A]."

"Sqn Ldr Watts [EE213/YQ-A] was unfortunate in having trouble with his guns as he was about to open the Squadron's Diver score near Ashford. Flg Off Dean [EE215/YQ-C] sighted one Diver and followed in line astern at 405mph. He closed in to 1,000 yards on the bomb, estimated flying at 390mph when he was turned back by control owing to the proximity of balloons. Pilots are convinced that given favourable weather and good plots nothing can prevent the Meteor knocking down the latest Axis weapon."

Air Marshal Hill, whose decision it was to bring the Meteor into action, later wrote:

"I decided to match jet against jet by trying it out against the flying bomb. At first only a few of these aircraft were available, and various problems including that of limited endurance, had to be overcome before we could get the full benefit out of the Meteor's great speed."

Night 27/28 JULY

III/KG3 suffered three losses – 5K+ER of 7 Staffel (Uffz Karl Schmidt), 5K+LS of 8 Staffel (Uffz Heinz Schmidt), and 5K+HS of 8 Staffel (Uffz Gerd Schwärzel) – during the course of 25 sorties flown from Rosières between 2250 and 0540, some crews having flown twice. In addition, 5K+IR of 7 Staffel force-landed at Amiens with flak damage and a dead gunner (Obgfr Karl-Heinz Temmel). The reasons for the losses remain unknown. There were no night fighter claims so they either fell to gunfire from RN ships at sea or to malfunctions. Three houses were seriously damaged and a further 14 less seriously damaged when a stray flying bomb fell on the village of Benhall in Suffolk at 0632.

25 Squadron (Mosquito XVII) Coltishall

Flt Lt R.J. Lilwall	HK305/ZK-	V-1	2240-0135	
Flg Off K.V. Panter	HK237/ZK-G	V-1	2255-0135	off Manston
	HK237/ZK-G	V-1	2255-0135	off Dungeness

Having been frustrated on two previous occasions when engaging flying bombs, Flt Lt Lilwall finally succeeded in shooting down one: "I patrolled at 7,000 feet and saw flying bomb at 2,000 feet. I dived to 2,000 feet and overshot. I then throttled back, climbed and weaved to get behind flying bomb, which was travelling at 200mph. I opened fire with two short bursts from 800 feet dead astern and scored strikes, causing the flying bomb to break to port and dive into sea." Flg Off Keith Panter shot down two of the four he sighted:

"I was airborne from Coltishall at 2255 hours to carry out an anti-Diver patrol under Sandwich GCI control. We were patrolling south-east of North Foreland at 5,000 feet and at 2253 saw a flying bomb at 2,000 feet travelling at approximately 400mph. I dived to 2,000 feet and fired a short burst from 10 to port from 800 feet with unobserved results. I fired another short burst from 800 feet dead astern and the flying bomb zig-zagged, dived into the sea and exploded about ten miles south-east of Manston. I was then vectored onto another flying bomb, which I saw at 2,000 feet. I dived from 3,500 feet and opened fire from 700 feet dead astern and saw spurts of flame and an orange glow from the flying bomb. The flying bomb blew up in the air off Dungeness as I broke off the attack. The AA guns opened fire just as the flying bomb exploded, but I consider it was destroyed by my attack. I had three more chases but on the first the flying bomb's speed was too great and I could not get into range, and the last one I got to within 3,000 feet, still closing, when AA opened up and I was forced to break away."

85 Squadron (Mosquito XVII) West Malling

Flt Lt R.H. Farrell	HK119/VY-S	V-1	2220-0105

96 Squadron (Mosquito XIII) Ford

Sqn Ldr P.L. Caldwell	MM461/ZJ-	V-1	2244	Channel

137 Squadron (Typhoon Ib) Manston

Flt Lt D.G. Brandreth	MN198/SF-	V-1	0010	off Folkestone

Flt Lt Doug Brandreth achieved an unheralded first in the annals of RAF history when he brought down a Diver using rocket projectiles. He was patrolling off Cap Gris Nez on an anti-shipping sortie when he sighted several V-1s approaching. He picked up one in mid-Channel at 3,000 feet:

"One pair of rockets was fired from 500-600 yards astern, and these appeared to explode above the target and the 'light' on the tail disappeared. The Diver exploded on contact with the water a few seconds later."[147]

418 (RCAF) Squadron (Mosquito VI) Hurn

Sqn Ldr R. Bannock RCAF	HR147/TH-Z	V-1	2356

456 (RAAF) Squadron (Mosquito XVII) Ford

Flt Lt R.B. Cowper RAAF	HK356/RX-D	V-1	2351	Sussex (Grid R.4557)
Flg Off F.S. Stevens RAAF	HK290/RX-J	V-1	2359	Kent (Grid R.2568)
	HK290/RX-J	V-1	0003	Kent (Grid R.2058)

Flt Lt Bob Cowper got his kill over Sussex, opening fire from 800 feet dead astern:

"Many strikes were seen but visual lost shortly afterwards. However, ROC confirmed that a flying bomb exploded on the ground at 2356 at Grid R.4557. A fairly long wire was seen trailing from the bomb."

Both Divers intercepted by Flg Off Fred Stevens fell in Kent: "(1) Attacked at range 1,500 feet, dead astern. This exploded on the ground; (2) Attacked at range 1,200 feet, dead astern. This also exploded on the ground."

150 Wing (Tempest V) Newchurch

Wg Cdr R.P. Beamont	JN751/RB	V-1	night	Pevensey area

Following his two kills during the day, Wg Cdr Beamont flew a night sortie and shot down another Diver. His score now stood at 27 including six shared.

Friday 28 JULY

A Diver came down in Dulwich at 0735, killing four and injuring 40. A worse incident occurred two hours later when a Diver struck the crowded Lewisham town centre at 0941. It exploded in the market area after impacting on the roof of a street level air raid shelter outside Marks and Spencers. Major damage was caused to the shops, which also included Woolworths and Sainsburys and devastation was caused to the market. Fifty-nine people died in this tragedy and a further 124 were very seriously injured. Hundreds of others suffered less serious injury. Casualties occurred in the shops, in the basement café of Woolworths and on passing buses. The Post Office was also badly damaged. This was the worst single V-1 incident in South London. The blast area was particularly large and extended unto 600 yards in each direction. In total about 100 shops were very badly damaged and flats, shops and houses suffered varying degrees of damage across a wide area. At lunchtime another Diver fell in Kensington High Street, killing 45 and injuring a further 170. A very costly day in human lives. Fighters shot down a further five near Maidstone, mainly in the evening. There were no reported casualties.

1 Squadron (Spitfire LFIXb) Lympne

Flg Off J.O. Dalley	MK987/JX-	V-1	2145	off Cap Gris Nez
Flg Off F.W. Town	MK919/JX-	V-1	2145	Staplehurst area
	MK919/JX-	V-1 shared	2215	Lenham area

Flg Off Jo Dalley recalled:

"My second V-1 was perhaps more memorable. It was dusk and over the English Channel beyond the AA belt on the coast. It was a very strange experience. The V-1 had a much longer flame thrust than usual, was flying only at 140mph and at about 2-300 feet. I seem to remember reporting it as being unusual in my combat report. I despatched it promptly; it hit the sea right under me, exploded, and gave me a very sharp kick up the pants. My engine stopped momentarily due to the negative G. The V-1 had been heading directly for Dorchester."[148]

In his combat report he wrote:

"Intercepted it six-eight miles off Cap Gris Nez, flying at 150 feet at 110-130mph. We both agreed [he was flying with Flt Lt Stewart] it is the largest Diver seen with wing span 30-35 feet [normal wingspan 16 feet], with fuselage and jet unit in proportion [!] Diver flying very slowly – skidding with port wing down, and righting itself to straight and level at regular intervals. Two attacks made with flaps down, from astern and 5° above, at range of 300 yards. I saw no strikes after first attack. On second attack saw strikes on jet. Diver nosed down and exploded in sea in mid-Channel. I broke away after final attack and climbed steeply to 500 feet. Fragments from Diver burst around and above me without damage."[149]

Flg Off Freddie Town shot down two Divers, sharing the second with a Mustang pilot:

"Saw Diver coming through AA belt and intercepted it in Tenterden area. One attack made from line astern with three bursts of three-seconds at range of 200 yards. After first attack saw strikes on jet unit. Diver dived down and I followed, firing two more bursts in an endeavour to explode it in mid-air, but Diver crashed in a field one-two miles north-west of Staplehurst. Saw [another] Diver being chased by two Mustangs and two Spitfires, but by using full boost I passed all these aircraft after seeing one Spitfire [apparently a Mustang] fire a short burst without effect. Diver flying at 1,000 feet at 320mph. I intercepted north-east of Ashford. One attack made from line astern from 300 yards range. Closing in I gave another burst of four seconds, seeing strikes on the tail unit. Diver glided steeply and exploded about 30-40 yards from railway track west of Lenham."

3 Squadron (Tempest V) Newchurch

Flt Lt R. van Lierde (Belg)	JN802/JF-	V-1	2230-2330
Flt Sgt D.J. Mackerras RAAF ⎤	JN822/JF-	V-1 shared	2230-2330
Flt Lt R. van Lierde (Belg) ⎦	JN822/JF-		2150-2300
Flt Sgt H.J. Bailey RAAF	JN807/JF-Y	V-1	

56 Squadron (Tempest V) Newchurch

Flt Sgt H. Shaw	JN857/US-P	V-1	1330	Tunbridge Wells area
Plt Off D.E. Ness RCAF	EJ536/US-R	V-1 shared	2135	Robertsbridge area
Flt Lt E.M. Sparrow	JN857/US-P	V-1	2240	Ashford area

Plt Off Ness reported: "I fired from 350 yards astern, scoring strikes on port wing and the Diver exploded on the ground ten miles north of Robertsbridge." Flt Lt Sparrow: "I sighted Diver four miles north of Folkestone at 2,000 feet. I fired from 300 yards astern and Diver exploded on the ground five miles east of Ashford."

91 Squadron (Spitfire XIV) Deanland ALG

Flt Lt H.D. Johnson	RM684/DL-	V-1	0955	Deanland area
Flt Lt R.S. Nash	RM735/DL-	V-1	2143	Pevensey Bay area
Sqn Ldr N.A. Kynaston[150]	RM687/DL-	V-1	2235	Tenterden area
Flg Off J. Monihan	RM651/DL-	V-1	2235	Oxley Green area

During a morning patrol Flt Lt Johnny Johnson saw a Diver four miles north of Pevensey Bay: "I attacked it from astern, range 200 yards. Diver fell and exploded in a wood three miles north of base." Flt Lt Ray Nash increased his tally with another:

"Intercepted Diver crossing coast from Pevensey Bay and attacked it from astern at 150 yards. Diver turned over and exploded in a wood eight miles north of the Bay." Sqn Ldr Norman Kynaston scored his 17th (and final) kill near Tenterden: "Intercepted Diver crossing the coast at Dungeness. Attacked from astern at 330 yards. Diver fell on ground and exploded." The final success of the evening fell to Flg Off Monihan: "Intercepted Diver between Dungeness and Rye. Attacked from astern at 250 yards. Diver spun in and exploded on the ground."

129 Squadron (Mustang III) Brenzett

Flg Off G.R. Dickson RNZAF	FX924/DV-V	V-1 shared	1330-1540	Maidstone area
Flg Off D.C. Parker	FZ178/DV-R	V-1	1520-1605	Ashford area
	FZ178/DV-R	V-1 shared	1520-1605	Tenterden area

Flg Off Reg Dickson[151] intercepted a Diver two miles north-west of Brenzett and scored many strikes during his stern attack. As he overshot, a Spitfire nipped in and shot it down to crash six miles south of Maidstone. Flg Off Denny Parker also had to share one of the two Divers he shot down, the first falling near a lake eight miles south-west of Tenterden. This was shared with the Spitfire pilot. He then engaged second two miles south of Ashford, causing flames to increase from the jet unit. The Diver crashed and exploded five miles north-west of Ashford.

165 Squadron (Spitfire IX) Lympne

Flg Off S.R. Chambers	ML139/SK-Q	V-1	1325	Ashford area

"Strikes seen on rear fuselage and large sheet of flame. Diver stalled in ten miles north-west of Ashford. Confirmed by Flg Off Armstrong."

306 (Polish) Squadron (Mustang III) Brenzett

Plt Off J. Smigielski PAF	UZ-I	V-1	1350	off Rye
Flt Sgt J. Zaleński PAF	FB241/UZ-Z	V-1	2235	off Maidstone

315 (Polish) Squadron (Mustang III) Brenzett

Flt Lt H. Pietrzak PAF	FB188/PK-U	V-1	1335	off Le Touquet

322 (Dutch) Squadron (Spitfire XIV) West Malling

Flt Sgt M.J. Janssen	VL-D	V-1 shared	2220	Grid R.2575
Maj K.C. Kuhlmann SAAF	NH586/VL-G	V-1	2245	Lamberhurst area

Flt Sgt Janssen recorded:

"Attacked line astern, range 200 yards. Another aircraft fired and strikes were seen but Diver went on. I fired again and big explosion was seen from jet unit. Diver crashed and exploded."

Twenty-five minutes later Maj Keith Kuhlmann DFC, the South African CO, shot down another:

"Whilst proceeding on an air test a Diver was seen crossing in over Dungeness. Intercepted and attacked line astern, range 300 yards. Strikes were seen on the propulsion unit and Diver crashed and exploded one mile north-west of Lamberhurst. Another aircraft had fired first but no strikes seen and the aircraft broke away and to port."

349 (Belgian) Squadron (Spitfire IX) Selsey

Flg Off J.F. Moreau	NH464/GE-	V-1	c2145	Tonbridge area

Squadron returning from an escort to bombers attacking No-ball sites west of Lille when Flg Off Jean Moreau sighted a Diver, which he shot down north of Tonbridge.

486 (RNZAF) Squadron (Tempest V) Newchurch

Plt Off F.B. Lawless RNZAF	JN770/SA-V	V-1	1230	Beachy Head area
	JN770/SA-V	V-1	1340	Tunbridge Wells area

610 Squadron (Spitfire XIV) Friston

Plt Off B.R. Scamen RCAF	DW-	V-1	2100-2230

616 Squadron (Meteor F.1) Manston

The Meteors flew a further eight anti-Diver sorties, again without success. In addition to the pilots who operated the previous day, both Flt Lt Mike Graves and Free Frenchman Flg Off Jean Clerc[152] carried out anti-Diver patrols.

FIU (Tempest V) Ford

Flt Lt R.L.T. Robb	EJ598/ZQ-U	V-1	night
	EJ598/ZQ-U	V-1	night

Night 28/29 JULY

At 0015, a Diver exploded in Camberwell Grove (SE5), demolishing a dozen houses and damaging 30 more. Five residents were killed. Five minutes later another person was killed in Paradise Road, Clapham (SW9).

25 Squadron (Mosquito XVII) Coltishall

Flt Lt J. Lomas	HK244/ZK-	V-1	2150-0110	off Dungeness

"At 0005, whilst patrolling at 6,000 feet, I saw a flying bomb 12-15 miles off Dungeness at 2,000 feet. I dived and fired short burst from 2,000 feet dead astern and the flying bomb fuel tank immediately caught fire. The flying bomb then dived into sea and exploded."

A second Mosquito flown by Flt Lt Doug Greaves fired at a flying bomb during his patrol but observed no results.

96 Squadron (Mosquito XIII) Ford

Sqn Ldr W.P. Green	MM495/ZJ-	V-1	0001	Channel
Wg Cdr E.D. Crew	NS985/ZJ-	V-1	0116	Channel
Flg Off R.F. Ball	HK372/ZJ-G	V-1	0507	Grid Q.6941

Sqn Ldr Peter Green reported: "After strikes Diver went into shallow diving turn to port and hit sea with very white explosion."

157 Squadron (Mosquito XIX) West Malling

Flt Lt E.J. Stevens	MM674/RS-T	V-1 shared	0225	West Malling area

Shared with Flt Lt Joe Berry of FIU. 157 Squadron's diarist noted: "This was not the first occasion on which more than one aircraft intercept a Diver. The Beacons were also manned by Tempests and in fact there was often an ugly rush by several aircraft at the same Diver."

605 Squadron (Mosquito VI) Manston

Flg Off B.G. Bensted	HJ799/UP-L	V-1	0010	off Dover
	HJ799/UP-L	V-1	0018	off Deal
	HJ799/UP-L	V-1	0023	off Deal
Flt Lt J.R. Rhodes	HJ809/UP-D	V-1	0011	off Dungeness

Flg Off Basil Bensted raised his score to seven with this hat-trick:

"Between midnight and 0030, 12-15 Divers were seen flying out from between Calais and Cap Gris Nez. Many were seen flying in batches of three with an odd one here and there. We destroyed our first approximately three miles south of Dover at 0010 after diving from 5,000 feet and firing from astern and above. Strikes were seen and Diver lost height and exploded on impact with sea. A few minutes later we destroyed a second Diver at 0018 approximately 20 miles south-east of Deal. Strikes were seen and target hit the sea and exploded. Range about 200 yards. At 0023, a third Diver was destroyed approximately four miles north-east of Deal. After being attacked with several bursts – very stubborn, this one – Diver crashed and exploded on the sea. All three Divers attacked were subject to our guns alone, no other fighters were seen in area at time of destruction. A fourth was later attacked with little success."

Of his second kill, Flt Lt John Rhodes reported:

"Between 0001-0025 some 25-30 Divers were seen to leave the French coast between Cap Gris Nez and Calais. We attacked three and destroyed one ten miles south-east of Dungeness at 0011. We were sitting above and dived down on Diver, firing from astern and above. Strikes were observed and Diver slowed down. We again opened fire, this time from astern and below and strikes were seen. Diver exploded on hitting the sea."

Rhodes' navigator, Flt Sgt John Little added: "The normal tour of ops was 30 trips with 25 on the second. However, with the pressure of the Second Front and the flying bombs, we were asked to carry on at the end of the 30 trips and do a second tour without a break."

FIU (Tempest V) Ford

Flt Lt J. Berry	EJ524/ZQ-Y	V-1 shared	0225	West Malling

Flt Lt Joe Berry during a low-level chase closed to 100 feet before downing the Diver and his aircraft was damaged by the ensuing explosion. To his chagrin he had to share credit with a Mosquito (Flt Lt Stevens of 157 Squadron) who had fired at the same V-1 from 1,000 yards.

"[It] started to dive onto a lighted aerodrome [West Malling]. I closed in and opened fire at about 100 yards giving it a long burst with my cannons, the bomb blew up much to the relief of the flying control officer who was watching it on the aerodrome. Fragments of the bomb were blown into my aircraft and one went into the air intake, jamming the throttle, which was almost wide open. I went home at full speed, whether I liked it or not – fortunately I managed to get down safely."

150 Wing (Tempest V) Newchurch

Wg Cdr R.P. Beamont	JN751/RB	V-1	night	Hastings area
	JN751/RB	V-1	night	Tenterden area

Wg Cdr Beamont scored two more kills, thereby raising his score to 29 including six shared.

207 Squadron (Lancaster)

Sgt J. Marriott (R/G)	PB286/EM-U	V-1	0435	over sea

Flg Off G.H. Montgomery was the pilot of Lancaster EM-U flying at 3,500 feet when a flying bomb was sighted at 1,000 below on the port beam. As it closed in from the port beam, the rear gunner (Sgt Marriott) opened fire at 600/700 yards and continued firing to 300 yards, whereupon it orbited and spiralled down. A flash was seen as it hit the sea. This was witnessed by four members of the crew. Earlier in the flight the gunners aboard this aircraft had claimed two attacking night fighters shot down. One for Bomber Command.

Saturday 29 JULY

A Diver that impacted in Kinsale Road, Peckham (SE15) at 1424 killed four residents and destroyed or badly damaged eight houses. Two surface air raid shelters were partly destroyed, as were 20 houses, when a Diver fell at the junction of Hollyoak Road and Dante Road in the Elephant and Castle (SE11) at 1426. An additional 200 houses were damaged and five people killed. Three more were killed as a result of a Diver exploding at 1432 in Albany Road/Neate Street, Walworth (SE5), where a shop was demolished and several houses damaged. At about 1600, a Diver was heard approaching Lord's cricket ground, where the Army were playing the RAF in front of 3,100 spectators. Jack Robertson, the England and Middlesex opener was facing Bob Wyatt (Warwickshire and England) when the engine cut. It was apparent that it was going to come down very close to, if not on, Lord's. Fortunately for the cricketers and spectators alike, the bomb fell about 200 yards short of the ground and landed in Albert Road, north of Regent's Park. Wyatt, the bowler, had thrown himself to the ground, midway through his run-up, still clutching the ball. With the threat over, he continued his run and bowled to Robertson, who hammered the ball into the grandstand for six, much to the delight of the crowd. It was construed as an act of defiance in the face of the enemy.

Further south, at Sundridge near Sevenoaks, a Diver was brought down by a balloon, as vividly remembered by A.W. Hall, then an eight-year-old schoolboy:

> "A friend and I were in between our house and 'The Warren' when we heard the sound of a V-1. We looked up to see the Doodlebug strike the balloon cable and one wing fell off and fluttered down yards from us; the rest twisted overhead, luckily missing our house, and exploded in a field north of the A25. As was the custom, we grabbed a souvenir; in this case the whole V-1 wing, which we somehow dragged home and hid in the shed. We were subsequently 'arrested' by the police and taken down to another balloon site, east of our house, for a dressing down by an RAF officer."[153]

Fighters shot down two more that fell near Barling Green Farm and Boxley.

3 Squadron (Tempest V) Newchurch

Flt Lt A.R. Moore	JN818/JF-	V-1	1800-1840	
Flt Sgt R.W. Cole	JN768/JF-F	V-1		

41 Squadron (Spitfire XII) Lympne

Flg Off M.A.L. Balaase	EN609/EB-	V-1	1820	Le Touquet
	EN609/EB-	V-1	2125	Romney Marshes

Flg Off Mono Balaase and Plt Off Jimmy Payne were on patrol off Le Touquet when Balaase spotted a flying bomb down below, and dived from 7,000 feet to engage it. He narrowly missed a collision with the bomb and as he pulled round for an attack, saw it dive into the sea and explode. Payne, who witnessed the incident, reported that the bomb had hit Balaase's slipstream as he passed, and rolled over into the sea. Balaase was up again just after 2100 and intercepted another Diver over Romney Marshes. He opened fire and it exploded in the air about one mile south-east of Woodchurch.

56 Squadron (Tempest V) Newchurch

Flt Sgt Tony Drew on anti-Diver patrol entered cloud, following which his Tempest EJ532/US-H emerged in a steep dive to crash at Acrise Place, Kent at 1010. The 20 year-old from Hastings was killed.

91 Squadron (Spitfire XIV) Deanland ALG

Flg Off R.A. McPhie RCAF	RM743/DL-	V-1	1025	Tunbridge Wells area
Flg Off E. Topham	RM743/DL-	V-1	1845	Tunbridge Wells area
Flg Off K.R. Collier RAAF[154]	RM685/DL-M	V-1	2132	Tonbridge area
Flt Lt H.B. Moffett RCAF	RM726/DL-	V-1	2305	Balloon barrage area
Flg Off J.A. Faulkner RCAF	RM688/DL-N	V-1	2310	exploded in mid-air

Flg Off McPhie opened the scoring: "Intercepted Diver west of Etchingham. One burst astern caused it to fall and explode in a wooded area four miles south-east of Tunbridge Wells." Four more fell in the evening, the first being shot down by Flg Off Topham:

"Intercepted Diver over Rye. Came in after two Tempests and two Mustangs all missed it. Saw strikes and Diver dropped in village and exploded eight miles south-east of Tunbridge Wells."

Flg Off Ken Collier scored his seventh (and final) kill five miles east of Tonbridge: "Saw Diver six miles east of Tonbridge. Saw strikes. Diver fell on road and exploded." The Canadian pair Flt Lt Bruce Moffett and Flg Off John Faulkner took off as a patrol at 2225, and each scored. Moffett sighted his target held in searchlights 15 miles south-east of Tunbridge Wells: "Chased it to Tonbridge. Attacked from astern. Diver dropped and exploded on the ground." Five minutes later Faulkner got another: "Saw Diver four miles north-east of Hastings and chased it to Robertsbridge. Gave short burst from astern at 200 yards. Diver exploded in the air."

129 Squadron (Mustang III) Brenzett

Flg Off L.G. Lunn	FX958/DV-E	V-1	2134	Tunbridge Wells area
Wt Off R.L. Thomas RAAF	FB361/DV-B	V-1	2115-2230	Tunbridge Wells area

165 Squadron (Spitfire IX) Lympne

Flt Sgt A.F.A. McIntosh RCAF	ML204/SK-N	V-1 shared	1905	Wadhurst area

"Saw strikes on port wing. Diver slowed up and I was preparing to attack again when a Mustang cut in over the top and nearly collided with Diver. Mustang not seen to fire but Diver lost height and crashed on houses in Wadhurst. Half share claimed."

It would seem that the Mustang pilot was Plt Off Świstuń of 315 Squadron.

306 (Polish) Squadron (Mustang III) Brenzett

Flt Sgt J. Zaleński PAF	FB393/UZ-U	V-1	1020	Grid R.0755

Flt Sgt Józef Zaleński was really getting into his stride, shooting down his sixth Diver (one shared) following two close-range attacks. The engine caught fire and the Diver exploded on the ground in some woods north of Hastings. Tragically, another fighter fell to friendly fire when Flg Off Egon Zygmund (FB241/UZ-Z) on an anti-Diver patrol off Hastings was shot down into the sea by coastal AA at about 1100 while chasing a Diver. He did not survive.

315 (Polish) Squadron (Mustang III) Brenzett

Plt Off G. Świstuń PAF	FZ152/SS	V-1 shared	1844	Wadhurst area
Sqn Ldr E. Horbaczewski PAF	FB382/PK-G	V-1	2130	Dungeness area
	FB382/PK-G	V-1	2148	Hastings area

322 (Dutch) Squadron (Spitfire XIV) West Malling

Flg Off M.L. van Bergen	VL-T	V-1	1935	Tenterden area
Flg Off L.D. Wolters[155]	VL-N	V-1 shared	2147	Tunbridge Wells area

The Diver shot down by Flg Off van Bergen crashed and exploded in a field two miles west of Tenterden. Two hours later Flg Off Bert Wolters reported that several aircraft also attacked the Diver he finally shot down into a field south of Tunbridge Wells.

610 Squadron (Spitfire XIV) Friston

Flt Lt J.B. Shepherd	DW-	V-1	2120-2225

FIU (Tempest V) Ford

Flt Lt J. Berry	EJ524/ZQ-Y	V-1	daytime
	EJ524/ZQ-Y	V-1	daytime

Night 29/30 JULY

III/KG3's run of bad luck continued when one of its aircraft, 5K+FS of 8 Staffel flown by Uffz Alfons Rieger was shot down at 2325 by gunfire from a German convoy in the Scheldt Estuary, which was escorted by six minesweepers from 32.MS-Flotilla. The crippled aircraft crashed near the coastline between Cadzand and Knokke. Rieger and two of his crew were rescued though injured. Two other crewmembers were lost[156]. This was the only loss during the course of 31 sorties from Rosières flown between 2245 and 0653, some crews flying twice.

68 Squadron (Mosquito XVII) Castle Camps

Flg Off J. Adam (Cz)	WM-A	V-1	night	over North Sea

96 Squadron (Mosquito XIII) Ford

Flt Lt I.A. Dobie	HK437/ZJ-	V-1	2257	Channel
Flt Lt F.R.L. Mellersh	MM577/ZJ-N	V-1	0049	Channel

Only two Divers fell to the Mosquitos, either side of midnight, but another crew was lost when MM557 flown by Flg Off James Black and Flt Sgt Leslie Fox FTR from a sortie off the French coast. A call was received at 0457 to say they were baling out off Boulogne. Another Mosquito crew thought they saw a torchlight flashing in the sea in the approximate position, and also saw two stationery vessels (possibly flak ships) some six miles from the spot. On receiving the news of the missing crew, Wg Cdr Crew took off in MM448 to carry out a search and remained over the area until dawn. On breaking through cloud four miles off Boulogne, their Mosquito was hit behind the cockpit by a burst of flak. With the R/T, hydraulics and instruments u/s, Crew returned on the AI beam and crash-landed at Friston on one wheel. The aircraft was written off but Crew and his navigator Flg Off O.D. Morgan survived unhurt.

125 Squadron (Mosquito XVII) Hurn

Flt Sgt A.R. Cooper	HK245/VA-V	V-1	0325	Beachy Head area

> "When at 5,000 feet sighted Diver at 2,000 feet approximately 20 miles south-west of Beachy Head. I tried to intercept from astern, losing visual temporarily but regaining it at 2,000 feet through a break in the cloud. Unable to reduce range and gave short burst with no result. Gave long burst from 500 yards dead astern. Hits and minor explosion were seen. On breaking in cloud another explosion occurred and light disappeared. Lost visual in cloud and on regaining it saw Diver crash and explode on impact. Landed at Ford."

418 (RCAF) Squadron (Mosquito VI) Hurn

Flg Off P.R. Brook RCAF	TH-	V-1	0315	Channel

> "Went into dive and twice overshot. At third attempt throttled back to 300 yards dead astern and closed gradually. Fired three two-seconds bursts and 'light' went out. Diver exploded in the sea."

Sunday 30 JULY

Beckenham (BR3) received another fatal bomb, which killed one person in Oakwood Avenue and caused much damage. The North Kent village of Swanscome was on the receiving end of another lethal bomb at 1130, the Diver exploding in Taunton Road, killing 13, seriously injuring 22 and inflicting various degrees of injury to a further 69. Eight houses were completely demolished and 150 people made homeless. One eyewitness said he saw the Diver being chased by fighters: "The flying bomb began to lose altitude and I thought it would crash in the fields but it hit the village."[157]

1 Squadron (Spitfire LFIXb) Lympne

Flt Sgt Godfrey Tate FTR from an anti-Diver patrol over the Channel following engine trouble while flying MJ422. He baled out into the sea but apparently drowned. Flg Off Dennis Davy, who was leading Yellow Section, reported:

> "While on patrol Yellow 2 (Flt Sgt Tate) called up saying his engine was running rough. Control instructed Section to return to base. Yellow 2 led me by almost a mile and owing to haze was not visible. Shortly after, Yellow 2 called up saying engine was cutting and he was losing height, finally saying he was baling out. Visibility at the time was varying between 500 and 1,000 yards and I was still unable to see him. So I came down until I could see the water and was just in time to see a large splash created by aircraft entering the water. I orbited the spot, searching for pilot/parachute/dinghy but no signs. Only small oil patch. Another section and a Walrus was on its way out, but owing to fuel shortage I had to leave the scene of the crash before they arrived. Position 15 miles south-east of Dungeness."

The subsequent search found nothing. His body was later washed up on the Belgian coast and buried in Leopoldsburg War Cemetery.

3 Squadron (Tempest V) Newchurch

Flg Off R. Dryland	JN815/JF-	V-1	2155-2320
Flt Sgt M.J.A. Rose	JN818/JF-	V-1	
Flt Sgt R.W. Pottinger	JN761/JF-U	V-1 shared	2310-0015

Flt Sgt Ron Pottinger:

> "Then we started doing night patrols, and I didn't like that at all! A fighter is not like a larger plane where things happen comparatively slowly. Without any sort of a reference you can be upside down before you know it, unless you keep your head inside the cockpit, and glue your eyes to the instruments, and then you aren't going to see many Doodlebugs. To assist us, searchlights at intervals along the coast would be arranged in pairs. One with its beam vertical, the other with its beam elevated to about 45 degrees and pointing out to sea. A single plane would patrol between two of the vertical beams, flying figure of eights, turning out towards the sea at either end. The searchlights helped in that you knew where you were, but the light did nothing for your night vision! On the first of these night patrols (30 July) I was directed onto a V-1. I could see the flame from the rear of its engine from some way off, and turned to come up behind it, adjusting the trim of the aeroplane as I did. You can't shoot accurately if the plane is skidding or slipping all over the sky. It's difficult to judge distance at night, but as soon as I thought I was near enough I gave it a long burst of fire. Its fuel caught fire and the whole thing went up in a sheet of flame. I pulled up to avoid flying through the flames, but was pretty well blinded by the explosion. The last thing I saw as I ducked my head into the 'office' to look at my instruments was the grey shape of yet another plane, which pulled up from beneath me passing within 50 feet on my port side and a little ahead, and then vanished into the night. My thought as I went onto instruments was 'How many more moths round this particular flame?' I flew on instruments for a few minutes to let my sight recover a little, and an anxious few minutes it was too! Then I set a course for my friendly searchlight, and resumed patrol. I only had a momentary glimpse of the other aircraft, but I was fairly certain it was a Mosquito. However the next day I was told I had shared the kill with a Spitfire of 91 Squadron. It was amazing how you could shoot one down, with so far as you could see an otherwise empty sky, and yet you would find yourself sharing it with two other pilots who both reckoned they had got it. Mind you, it must have been a terrible job keeping track of it all, with so many coming over at once, but it could also be frustrating for us! The people controlling us would give courses to steer to pick up a Doodlebug, but of course had quite often little idea of the conditions in the air."[158]

56 Squadron (Tempest V) Newchurch

Plt Off D.E. Ness RCAF	EJ534/US-O	V-1	1340	Hastings area

"I fired 10° deflection burst from port and above at 200 yards range, scoring strikes on jet. I made another similar attack from starboard and the Diver exploded on the ground, eight miles north of Hastings."

91 Squadron (Spitfire XIV) Deanland ALG

Sqn Ldr P.McC. Bond	RM652/DL-	V-1 shared	1805	West Malling area
Flt Lt H.B. Moffett RCAF	RM682/DL-	V-1	2345	Sittingbourne area

Sqn Ldr Peter Bond's victim – shared with Flg Off Rudi Burgwal of 322 Squadron – fell close to the airfield, causing the diarist to comment politely: "The CO had the indecency to shoot one down within half-a-mile of the aerodrome – too close, was the general consensus of opinion!" With Flt Lt Bruce Moffett's kill shortly thereafter: "Intercepted Diver east of Hastings, caught in searchlights. Diver fell and exploded in woods after stern attack from 200 yards." Thus, 91 Squadron registered its 104th kill for July, raising its total to 167.

129 Squadron (Mustang III) Brenzett

Flg Off A.F. Osborne	FB212/DV-Q	V-1	1705-1920	off Hastings

When 20 miles south of Hastings at 2,500 feet, the controller warned Flg Off Sammy Osborne that a Diver was behind him and catching him up. He weaved, then saw the Diver approaching rapidly but as it entered his slipstream, it dived into the sea and exploded.

306 (Polish) Squadron (Mustang III) Brenzett

Flt Sgt J. Czeżowski PAF ⎤	FB347/UZ-T	V-1	1338	Appledore area
Flt Sgt J. Zaleński PAF ⎦	FB241/UZ-Z			

316 (Polish) Squadron (Mustang III) Friston

Wt Off W. Grobelny PAF	FB383/SZ-J	V-1	1335	off Hastings

Wt Off Grobelny scored again when he intercepted a Diver in mid-Channel:

"Chased and opened fire from 300 yards astern. Strikes seen all over and pieces of Diver flew off. After a second similar attack, Diver was flying very slowly and starboard wing heavy. Lost in haze."

322 (Dutch) Squadron (Spitfire XIV) West Malling

Flg Off R.F. Burgwal	VL-C	V-1 shared	1802	West Malling area

Flg Off Rudi Burgwal shared his kill with a Spitfire from 91 Squadron flown by Sqn Ldr Peter Bond:

"Patrolling Tenterden when vectored on a Diver crossing Eastbourne. Attacked line astern, range 200 yards. Another Spitfire, from 91 Squadron, also fired and strikes were seen from both Spitfires. Diver crashed and exploded one-and-a-half miles south of base."

486 (RNZAF) Squadron (Tempest V) Newchurch

Flt Lt J.H. McCaw RNZAF	EJ523/SA-X	V-1	1345	Mayfield area

Personnel of **41 Squadron** at Lympne witnessed a flying bomb approaching the airfield at 1345. Local AA opened fire, the bomb was hit, and it carried out a series of perfect slow rolls before falling to earth west of Lympne.

418 (RCAF) Squadron was now instructed to operate from Middle Wallop.

Flg Off Owen Faraday of 219 Squadron flew a Mosquito to Wittering to be interviewed by the **FIU** to see if he was suitable to convert to Tempests. Unfortunately, he collided with an Oxford on landing and both aircraft were written-off. Fortunately, he was not hurt and despite his mishap was accepted by the FIU. Another, most interesting, arrival at Wittering was Tempest EJ535 from TRE Defford flown by Flt Lt Les Leppard. The Tempest was fitted with a compact AN/APS13 radar known as Monica IIIE, and was to be tested for use against Divers at night and/or in bad weather. Flt Lt Leppard carried out the first operational sortie the following night but there proved to be a lack of targets. Although the equipment proved successful, a fault with the lighting system meant that the project did not progress (see Appendix VI).

315 Squadron engaged in bomber escort and took on Bf109s, eight of which were claimed shot down, two by Wt Off Jankowski, and one each by Flt Lt Cwynar, Plt Off Świstuń, Sqn Ldr Horbaczewski, and Wt Off Idrian, with the other two shared by Cwynar, Świstuń, Horbaczewski and Flg Off Nowosielski

Night 30/31 JULY

At least 20 sorties were flown by III/KG3 during the night, nine Heinkels departing at about 2330, followed by a second wave of 11 aircraft at 0255 – probably including crews flying their second sorties. Eight Divers hit the capital and two others fell in Essex. One came down in Greenwich, exploding in Millward Street/Nightingale Vale where it killed two and injured 53.

96 Squadron (Mosquito XIII) Ford

Wg Cdr E.D. Crew	NS985/ZJ-	V-1	2350	Channel
	NS985/ZJ-	V-1	0007	Channel
Flt Lt F.R.L. Mellersh	MM577/ZJ-N	V-1	0047	Channel

137 Squadron (Typhoon Ib) Manston

Flg Off N.J.M. Manfred	MN169/SF-Z	V-1	2305-2355

418 (RCAF) Squadron (Mosquito VI) Middle Wallop

Flt Lt P.S. Leggat RCAF	TH-	V-1	2350	Channel
	TH-	V-1	2357	Channel
Flg Off S.K. Woolley RCAF[159]	PZ342/TH-O	V-1	0250	off Beachy Head

Flt Lt Peter Leggat scored two kills in quick succession:

> "At 2350 a Diver was seen to cross out between Dieppe and Le Tréport at 3,000 feet. I manoeuvred into position above and slightly ahead, then dived down at Diver. At the first attempt I overshot, swung out to the right and came in dead astern at 150 yards. After firing two short bursts of cannon, the Diver became enveloped in a sheet of flame, fell into the sea and blew up. At 2357 a further Diver was sighted on an identical course, height and speed. I repeated the previous tactics but this time did not overshoot, and after a short burst the 'light' on the Diver went out and the Diver spun into the sea, exploding on impact."

These successes were followed by another when Flg Off Stewart Woolley got one off Beachy Head:

> "At 0250 two Divers were seen to cross out at Le Tréport. When seven miles out to sea, the second one was at 3,000 feet. We went into a glide from 8,000 feet, which brought us 150 yards astern of the Diver. A one-second burst was fired, strikes being seen with many sparks flying off. I broke off the attack. The Diver was not seen to explode but I claim one destroyed."

456 (RAAF) Squadron (Mosquito XVII) Ford

Flt Lt W.R.V. Lewis RAAF	HK317/RX-	V-1	2344	Sussex (Grid Q.64)

605 Squadron (Mosquito VI) Manston

Flt Lt J.G. Musgrave	MM429/UP-H	V-1	0327	off Ostende
	MM429/UP-H	V-1	0329	off Ostende
Flt Lt R.C. Walton RNZAF	UP-	V-1		Channel

Two more flying bombs fell to Flt Lt John Musgrave:

"The patrol was carried out between Foreness and north of Ostende and at 0325 we saw approximately eight Divers fly out from the Ostende area at various distances between each other. I dived down from 6,000 feet and positioned myself behind a Diver at 2,500 feet. I opened fire from slightly above and astern with three short bursts and target dived, hit the sea and exploded at 0337. I then immediately turned to port and commenced to orbit and whilst still turning spotted another Diver very close, and attacked this from dead astern at 0329. Diver was at 1,700 feet, speed about 340mph. After firing a burst Diver appeared to stop and crashed into the sea, exploding. A third Diver was immediately attacked but after a very brief burst the cannon shells ran out and no results obtained."

Monday 31 JULY

Thornton Heath (CR7) received another bomb at 1501, this exploding in the Recreation Ground and killing one person, in addition to wrecking many nearby houses. Fighters brought down two Divers in the Elham district during the day, one impacting at Lyminge, the other at Lympne. There were no injuries.

3 Squadron (Tempest V) Newchurch

Flt Lt A.R. Moore	JN865/JF-	V-1	1425-1540

91 Squadron (Spitfire XIV) Deanland ALG

The Squadron lost a veteran pilot when Flg Off Paddy Schade's Spitfire was hit from above by a Tempest flown by Flt Sgt Archie Wilson RNZAF of 486 Squadron as the latter emerged from cloud in pursuit of a Diver. The wingtip of the Tempest tore through the rear of the Spitfire's cockpit and both pilots were killed in the double crash. Following is the police report:

"On 31st July 1944 at 1500hrs a Tempest fighter was in collision with a Spitfire fighter and crashed and burnt out at Sandhurst Lane, Bexhill-on-Sea. Flt Sgt A.A. Wilson 422336 was killed. Serial number of aeroplane EJ586.
    "The Spitfire aeroplane, number RM654, crashed and was totally destroyed at Holmes Farm, Hooe, killing Flt Lt Schade of 91 Squadron RAF. Wreckage guarded by 'G' Troop, 412 Light Anti-Aircraft Bty, RA, Bexhill."

129 Squadron (Mustang III) Brenzett

Flg Off L.G. Lunn	FX958/DV-E	V-1	1400-1505	off Dungeness
Flt Lt R.G. Kleimeyer RNZAF (Aus)	FB361/DV-B	V-1	1720-1925	off Beachy Head

Flg Off Les Lunn intercepted a Diver over the Channel at 2,000 feet. Strikes were seen on fuselage whereupon it slowed down, pulled up, stalled, turned over on its back and exploded in the sea off Dungeness. Flt Lt Dutch Kleimeyer also shot his victim into the sea about 30 miles off Beachy Head.

306 (Polish) Squadron (Mustang III) Brenzett

Flt Sgt S. Rudowski PAF	FB380/UZ-F	V-1	1815	Rye area

Flt Sgt Stan Rudowski was off at 1620 and vectored onto a Diver approaching Rye. Two miles west of the coastal town he intercepted and attacked from slightly below. The Diver lost speed, turned to port and crashed and exploded on the ground.

316 (Polish) Squadron (Mustang III) Friston

Flg Off T. Gora PAF	FB161/SZ-I	V-1	1525	off Hastings
Wt Off P. Syperek PAF	HB821/SZ-L	V-1	1800	off Hastings
Wt Off K. Kobusiński PAF	FB391/SZ-E			

Flg Off Gora intercepted 20 miles south of Hastings: "Attacked from dead astern from

300 yards. Diver exploded in the sea." Two and-a-half hours later, Wt Offs Syperek and Kobusiński jointly shot down a second: "Intercepted 30 miles off the coast. Attacked from 100 yards and opened fire dead astern. Diver exploded in the sea."

610 Squadron (Spitfire XIV) Friston
Flg Off P.M. Bangerter   MN685/DW-L   V-1   1455-1620

Night 31 JULY/1 AUGUST
Gilze-Rijen was responsible for the III/KG3 operations this night, 23 sorties being flown between 2216 and 0415 for no loss. In excess of 350 sorties had been flown since operations began on the night of 3-4 July for the total loss of eight aircraft plus a further two damaged on the ground.

July reminiscences
Newchurch received a visit early in the month from Ernest Hemingway, the distinguished American novelist-cum-correspondent of *Colliers*, and he wrote glowingly of man and machine[160]:

> "All information about tactics employed in the shooting down of pilotless aircraft is out. So there isn't much in this article now, except a guy loving an airplane. Writing under censorship is necessary and proper in time of war, and we all censor out ourselves everything we think might be of any possible interest to the enemy. But in writing about the air on the basis of trying to include colour, detail and emotion, there is a certain analogy to sports writing. The Tempest is a great, gaunt airplane. It is the fastest pursuit job in the world and is as tough as a mule. It has been reported with a speed of 400mph. Its job was to intercept the 'pilotless' planes and shoot them down over the sea or in open country as they came in on their sputtering roar toward London. The squadron flew from four o'clock in the morning until midnight. There were always pilots sitting ready in the cockpits to take off when the Very pistol signalled, and there were always a number of planes on permanent patrol in the air. The fastest I clocked a plane as airborne, from the sound of the pop of the flare pistol that would arc a twin flare over toward the dispersal area from the door of the intelligence hut, was 57 seconds. As the flare popped, you would hear the dry bark of the starting cartridge and the rising scream of the motor, and these hungry, big, long-legged birds would lurch, bounce, and scream off with the noise of two hundred circular saws hitting a mahogany log dead on the nose. They took off downwind, cross-wind, any way the weather lay, and grabbed a piece of the sky and lurched up into it with the long, high legs folding up under them. All day long they shoot down this nameless weapon, day in and day out. The squadron leader is a fine man, tall, small-spoken, with light brown circles under his eyes and the odd purple complexion of a man whose face has been burned away, and he told the story of his exploit to me very quietly and truthfully, standing by the wooden table in the pilots' mess."

Hemingway was obviously referring to Sqn Ldr Alan Dredge DFC, CO of 3 Squadron, who had been shot down and badly burned while flying Hurricanes at Malta in 1941. He enquired about Dredge's most recent flying bomb victim:

> "He was very precise in remembering exactly how it had been, because it was one of the first pilotless aircraft he had shot down, and he was very exact in details. He did not like to say anything personal but it was evidently all right to speak well of the plane. 'You can't just say where you'll shoot them down,' the squadron leader said. Standing there, speaking shyly, patiently and with strange eagerness from behind the purple mask he would always wear now for a face. 'They go very fast, you know.' The wing commander [Beamont] came in. He was short, with a lot of style and a tough, bad tongue. He was twenty-six, I found out later. I had seen him get out of an airplane before I knew he was the wing commander. It did not show then, nor did it show now when he talked. The only way you knew he was the wing commander was the way the other pilots said 'Sir.'"

Flt Sgt Ron Pottinger of 3 Squadron recalled:

"It was on a Doodlebug patrol with F/Sgt Everson as my No.2, when I had yet another undercarriage failure. We were at a height of around 3,000 feet somewhere behind Eastbourne. On this occasion, we had been guided onto an oncoming V-1. Suddenly I saw it way beneath us, travelling in almost the opposite direction. I rolled the plane onto its back and dropped into a half loop, meanwhile trying to keep my eye on the Doodlebug. They were not at all easy to see against the ground. I was near vertical and, travelling at somewhere near 500mph when the plane suddenly and violently dipped downwards and under, trying to do an inverted loop. I throttled back, and heaved back on the control column. It took all my strength with my feet raised onto the upper pedals to pull the plane slowly back into more or less level flight, and a more reasonable speed. By then I had seen that the undercarriage light for the port leg was showing red. My No.2 had stayed with me, he should really have gone after the Doodlebug, but maybe he didn't see it. He confirmed that the port leg was in fact down and swinging loose. Back at base the advice that came over the air was tremendous in quantity, and varied in content. Land with wheels up, land with wheels down. Wg Cdr Beamont settled things by telling me to come in wheels down. I remember circling, uneasily, but too busy to be afraid. On the approach I yanked my safety straps as hard as I could, and made sure the hood was securely locked open. I didn't fancy being trapped in the cockpit again! The landing must have been the best ever. It really greased on, ran for a couple of hundred yards straight and then slowly turned left, despite all my frantic efforts on the right brake, judicious bursts of the throttle etc. It ended up about fifty yards off the runway, and at right angles to it, as if it had turned its back on the whole sorry scene. As I climbed out, everyone came running up, congratulations and smiles everywhere. Beamont congratulated me on the landing."

Fellow 3 Squadron pilot Plt Off Buck Feldman later reflected:

"I shot down 11 V-1s in all, and had eight further interceptions, but the guns got there first each time. Two of my kills were at night. Control had a system of searchlights on the coast between Hastings and Dungeness, with two shining out to sea and two shining upwards. This was the point around which the Tempests were stacked, flying figures of eight, waiting for the V-1s to come over. When the bottom aircraft left the stack, the others would move down. It was an unpopular operation, as it was necessary to fly with navigation lights on to avoid mid-air collisions, and the Germans tried to infiltrate their own aircraft into the pattern. Control would broadcast the code phrase, 'Close your windows' when there was an intruder, as a signal to switch off our navigation lights."

USAAF pilots, often flying independently and unauthorized to engage the flying bombs, tended to cause problems, as Sqn Ldr Arct of 316 Squadron recalled:

"When American pilots happened to join the chase, sometimes complications arose. Flt Sgt Lewicki and Sgt Walasek [these were not the real names of the two pilots involved] of 315 Squadron, while on patrol, were directed inland; which was unusual. That day flying bombs were flying in whole batches. Large groups of them appeared, then a few hours interval followed, and in came the next wave. Ops Room informed the Poles that one of the bombs crossed the coast, evaded the gunners and flew towards London fairly near the pair of Mustangs. A few seconds later the pilots spotted the missile. Walasek closed in first. He got into the line of flight and followed the air-eddies behind the bomb, prepared for a kill. But the situation suddenly changed in a most unexpected way. A Tempest appeared high above, took no notice of the Mustangs and dived towards the bomb at great speed. It got right in front of Walasek, who had to break in a swift evasive turn. Still higher and to the rear, two other Tempests hurried to join this senseless chase, an obvious waste of petrol and of the pilots' energy. A dramatic situation rapidly developed. Hardly had the first Tempest got a chance to fire, when a stately Thunderbolt with American white stars on its wings and fuselage came in sight against the background of blue sky. Obviously its pilot must have noticed the hunt as his soldierly blood boiled, and he dived down at full speed. He was fast enough to join the pursuit and place himself at its tail. Unhappily, the American was full of fighting spirit, but he lacked experience and common sense. Not thinking twice, or perhaps thinking at all, he belched fire from his cannons right through the chain of planes in front of him, aiming at the bomb, but hitting his colleagues. The effect of his intervention was deplorable. Lewicki noticed the

Thunderbolt firing and broke out just in time, but other pilots were less fortunate, as they never expected to be fired at from the back. Walasek hurriedly turned to base with a trail of smoke behind the tail of his Mustang. Two damaged Tempests staggered to their aerodrome, the third escaped in a vertical climb. The bomb, not a bit disturbed by the outstanding show, serenely flew on to London. Only the victorious Thunderbolt remained on the battlefield. It is a debatable point whether its pilot really was proud of himself."

LACW Lorraine Balmforth, the pretty young wife of Wg Cdr Tommy Balmforth DFC, was a volunteer M/T driver at West Malling, to where she had only recently been posted:

"I recall an incredible incident when I was detailed to drive the dental officer to a balloon site for a routine dental inspection. The previous day, my old Standard van had shed its silencer and exhaust system. It was making a shocking noise. On one side of the road was a humped back grass verge, on which two workmen were cutting the grass. They were frantically waving at us to stop. We thought this was a huge joke, relating it to the noise my van was making. However, to our great horror a Doodlebug, which had cut out and was diving down – actually gliding on its back – was in full view. It landed in a field beyond two cottages on the other side of the road. The backs of the houses were blown out and all the windows were smashed. As far as we know, no one was injured; in fact we could not find anyone around. The only real casualty was the dental officer who was shaking like a leaf and deeply shocked. Fortunately I can be very cool in a serious situation and I returned to camp and took him straight to the sick bay."

Derek Reynolds was attached to Tooting Fire Station:

"One bright sunny day in July 1944 I was about to leave the fire station where I had been on shift when looking up saw, to my unbelievable horror, the nose of a dreaded V-1 was very slowly coming into view just above the fire hall. This V-1 was no more than 100 feet up and, what was most unusual about this bomb, it was gliding without engine power. I, of course, expected the bomb to land on the road almost where I stood. I had fallen to the pavement trying to make myself as small as possible and I think I was trying to dig a hole in the concrete, but the bomb made its slow and rocky way, skimming the roofs of houses opposite, finally running out of air and landing with a crash on a small house about 100 yards away. One good thing about this was that as the bomb was so low and had glided some three miles after its engine had cut out, it did not have the force that usually accompanied these bombs, meaning that the area of devastation was greatly reduced and so it destroyed only one house and even left the house opposite the crash with its windows intact."

Maidstone teenager Frank Williams recalled:

"It was interesting to see how the Allied fighters handled this new menace, approaching them rather like a cat stalking a dangerous mouse or rat, or perhaps a mongoose with a snake. A quick dart to the stern of the bomb, a burst of machine-gun or cannon fire, then a very steep bank away from the bomb. On two occasions I saw a very cool approach when a Tempest pilot calmly flew alongside and, with his wingtip tucked under the wing of the V-1, he gently nudged it around. The bomb would head back the way it had come and crash somewhere in the Kent countryside. My brother and his friends who roamed the countryside at that time (it was an ideal time to raid the fruit orchards) were crouching behind a sturdy farm wall, watching a bomb grunt overhead, when suddenly it veered round and came back, necessitating a panicky scaling of the wall to gain the other side for protection."

John Rawlings, the son of the Vicar of Shirley, a once-picturesque village near Croydon, recalled:

"My youth was spent in Shirley village in an area which provided a frontline view. We suffered severe damage from ... flying bombs. Our church [St John's] was damaged by these and the school demolished. On one occasion, whilst helping the verger to dig a grave we counted 17 flying bombs approaching in line abreast, some gliding, some diving and some under power. If hit, we thought at least we could save someone the job of burying us!"[161]

During the summer of 1944, a US Marine Corps carrier group, MAG-51 comprising VMF-511, 512, 513, 514, and VMO-351, was alerted for duty in European waters as part of the proposed Operation 'Danny' project, to undertake strikes against V-1 launching sites using F4U Hellcats armed with the new and yet untried 'Tiny Tim' rocket projectile. This was an unguided 11.75-inch missile with a 590lb warhead considered capable of inflicting much damage to the Noball sites. However, the planners had not taken into account the bitter inter-service rivalry that existed between the US Army and USMC. Cdr Thomas Moorer USMC, who was involved in the project, wrote:

"I was on the NavAirLant staff, and the mission Washington wanted done was to destroy the V-1 launchers which were wreaking havoc in London. Working with the Marine air staff, we developed a plan to use six [*sic*] Marine F4U squadrons, each airplane armed with 'Tiny Tim' rockets. At this time these airborne rockets were the largest anywhere in the world, and carried a heavy punch. Our plan was to put the Marine squadrons on jeep carriers [CVEs], sail to Europe, and launch the F4Us from the North Sea to make a series of massive strikes on the Nazi targets. After all the planning was done, the training was in progress and the logistics in order, I was sent to Washington with a group to brief the highest civilian and military authorities, including General George C. Marshall [the US Army Chief-of-Staff]. The conference room was filled with brass, and only General Marshall was momentarily absent. I was told to go ahead with my briefing. I got well into it, when General Marshall entered the room. I stopped and everybody rose in deference to America's most prestigious military figure. One of his staff generals quickly summarized my briefing to that point. General Marshall listened, but on hearing that US Marine aviators would make the planned attacks, he raised his hand. Rising to his feet, he moved toward the door and said something to the effect, 'That's the end of this briefing. As long as I'm in charge of our armed forces, there will never be a Marine in Europe.' And there never was during WW II."

It was probably just as well that Operation Danny did not come into being, since to effectively launch a 'Tiny Tim' the pilot had to fly low and straight. Some believed the expected pilot casualties would be at least 80%, and most were relieved when this assignment was cancelled. The American aircraft company Fairchild was currently involved in building an unmanned remotely controlled flying bomb known as BQ-3 of which two models were built, but no interest was forthcoming from the USAAF.

But one form of guided bomb that did see limited operational use was the B-17 drone known as the BQ-7, which was literally a flying bomb. The aircraft were stripped of their normal equipment and packed with up to nine tons of explosives, and were fitted with a radio-controlled flight system codenamed 'Double-Azon'. This comprised a television camera placed on the flight deck so that an image of the main instrument panel could be sent back to a controlling aircraft. A second camera was installed inside the Plexiglas nose, which gave a television monitor in the controlling aircraft a view of the ground so that the machine could be directed onto the target. It was planned that a volunteer two-man crew would take the aircraft off the ground and fly it up to an operational altitude of 2,000 feet, point the aircraft in the general direction of the target, arm the explosives for an on-impact detonation, hand over control to the director aircraft that was flying above at 20,000 feet, and then parachute to safety while still over England. The controlling B-17 would then direct the BQ-7 to the target area over the French coast and lock its controls into a crash course into the target before turning to escape. That was the theory. In practice it proved far more difficult. The USAAF had been experimenting for many months with the idea of using war-weary B-17s and a total of 23 redundant bombers were made available to the 562ndBS, part of the 388thBG, based at RAF Honington in Suffolk. The codename given to the operation was 'Aphrodite'[162].

CHAPTER V

THE HEIGHT OF THE ASSAULT

August 1944

"The Angel of Death is abroad in the land, only you can't always hear the flutter of its wings."
Prime Minister Winston Churchill

Tuesday 1 AUGUST
A Diver fell in Border Road/Laurie Park Avenue, Sydenham (SE26) at 0701, killing three. Another caused eight deaths at 1416, when it came down at the junction of New Cross Road/Achilles Street (SE14).

315 (Polish) Squadron (Mustang III) Brenzett
Flt Lt F. Wiza PAF   FX995/PK-E   V-1   1435   Channel

> "A Diver was intercepted over the Channel, at 2,800 feet. After two short bursts from line astern at 300 yards, the Diver dived steeply, crashed and exploded in the sea."

On completing the patrol, Wiza's Yellow Section received a warning from control that they were ten miles from the English coast and gave them a vector to the 'safety lane'. Before crossing the coast all necessary precautions had been made, only to find that the coastal guns opened up with intense fire. Fortunately, no one was hit.

Night 1/2 AUGUST
A dozen sorties were flown by III/KG3's Heinkels during the night, the first departing Gilze-Rijen at 2154 and the final one returning at 0025. There were no losses.

96 Squadron (Mosquito XIII) Ford
Wt Off W.A. McLardy RAAF   HK479/ZJ-   V-1   0345-0600   Channel

Flg Off Ray Ball's Mosquito (MM562) crashed on the edge of the airfield at 0003 while attempting to land on beam in bad weather. Both Ball and his navigator Flg Off Fred Saunders were killed, as was LAC Charlie Allen on the ground.

Wednesday 2 AUGUST
New Cross (SE14) received its second Diver on consecutive days when one crashed in Troutbeck Road at 0631, killing four residents. A Diver impacted 100 yards from the officers' mess at Newchurch ALG at 0815. There was only slight damage and no casualties. One of the most serious incidents of the whole Diver assault occurred at 1302, when a flying bomb hit a restaurant in Beckenham Road, Beckenham (SE), just south of the railway bridge that carries the Beckenham to Crystal Palace railway line. Forty-four people were killed, many instantly and many others were badly injured. As well as the restaurant, huge destruction was caused to the shops and houses. The blast extended many hundreds of yards in each direction and considering the size of the area damaged it is likely that this was one of the heavier and more powerful warheads that were used at this stage of the attacks. One of those killed was the father of one of the young men killed in the Elmers End bus garage incident that occurred on 18 July. The American *Time Magazine* ran an article graphically describing the carnage:

> "The worst that one V-1 flying bomb could do was done in London. It streaked down during the noonday rush on a shop-lined street. Its 2,240 lbs of TNT blew apart a crowded restaurant,

filling the air with knife-edged shards of splintered glass. The blast wrenched off the top deck of a bus, tore apart another bus. Passengers were dazed, their clothing afire. Hours later rescuers still dug for the dead and trapped in the wreckage of the restaurant. The toll was high. But by now most Londoners were convinced that they were in for something infernally worse: a rocket-propelled robomb whose deadly war head might be ten times the size of V-1s, with explosive force far greater than even the RAF's six-ton factory-buster."

3 Squadron (Tempest V) Newchurch

Flt Sgt H.J. Bailey RAAF	JN807/JF-Y	V-1	1250-1405	
	JN807/JF-Y	V-1	1250-1405	

91 Squadron (Spitfire XIV) Deanland ALG

Flt Lt R.S. Nash	RM735/DL-	V-1	1250	exploded in mid-air
	RM735/DL-	V-1 shared	1250	Mayfield area
Sqn Ldr P.McC. Bond	RM687/DL-	V-1	1258	exploded in mid-air

Flt Lt Ray Nash reported: "Saw Diver two miles north of Hastings – gave a short burst at 200 yards, then another at 150 yards. Diver exploded in mid-air." He then immediately engaged a second: "Intercepted Diver ten miles north of Hastings. Short burst at 150 yards. Diver's wing severely damaged. Diver glided down through clouds with excess flame coming from jet unit." This was also fired at by Flt Sgt Ronnie van Beers of 322 Squadron, and Nash withdrew his claim when it was known this would count as the Dutch unit's 100th kill.

129 Squadron (Mustang III) Brenzett

Wt Off E. Redhead	FB364/DV-P	V-1	1204-1407	off Dungeness

Only six Diver patrols flown during the day with just the one success scored by Wt Off Eric Redhead, who intercepted his victim 12-15 miles south of Dungeness at 3,000 feet, flying at 370mph. He attacked it from dead astern at 300-200 yards with short bursts. Strikes were seen and the Diver rolled over to starboard and crashed into the sea, where it exploded.

322 (Dutch) Squadron (Spitfire XIV) West Malling

Flt Sgt R.L. van Beers[163]	VL-C	V-1 shared	1254	Tunbridge Wells area
	VL-C	V-1 shared	1300	Tunbridge Wells area

Flt Sgt Ronnie van Beers shared his first of the day with a pilot of 3 Squadron, and the second with Flt Lt Nash of 91 Squadron, but since the latter would be the Dutch unit's 100th kill, Nash generously withdrew his claim. Van Beers reported:

"Patrolling base when vectored on a Diver crossing over near Bexhill. Attacked line astern, range 150 yards, with long burst. Tail unit blew off and Diver spun through cloud in the Tunbridge Wells area. Returning to patrol area after destroying Diver when second Diver seen below. Attacked with three short bursts, 350 yards line astern. Diver went into shallow dive through cloud and believed to have crashed near balloon barrage in Tunbridge Wells."

616 Squadron (Meteor F.1) Manston

Poor weather had curtailed Meteor operations during the preceding few days, and only four anti-Diver patrols were carried out on this date by Sqn Ldr Les Watts, Flg Off Derek 'Dixie' Dean, Canadian Flg Off Bill McKenzie and Flg Off Jean Clerc (FF) between Ashford and Robertsbridge, albeit without success. The unit's diarist noted: "Meteor aircraft are still the centre of attraction and the Meteor Flight receives many visitors each day. During the evening a visit was made by Grp Capt Fleming, ADGB." The Flight now possessed six operational aircraft, including the two training machines EE213 now YQ-A and EE214/YQ-B. One of the distinguished visitors to manage to take a flight in one of the Meteors was Wg Cdr Roly Beamont, OC 150 Tempest Wing:

"It ought to have been an impressive experience but somehow it was not. The low, thin-fuselaged, blunt-nosed profile was not enhanced by an awkward looking high tail, with two bulges at mid-wing on either side which were distinctly more reminiscent of beer barrels than of aero-dynamically refined engine nacelles. McDowall's briefing was simple and casual. The Meteor, it appeared, was a straightforward aeroplane in most respects but had some limitations as a fighter. It was slow to accelerate and decelerate and it was very fast – but by the time it reached its maximum IAS of about 480mph it was fuel-limited and needed to land! With power set at max continuous, we lumbered quietly round the circuit gaining speed and height slowly. I levelled out to gain speed while checking gunsight and safety catch as this flight over Kent would be well into 'Flying Bomb Alley', which Sector Control advised was currently active. With the nose slightly down, speed increased steadily with no fierce acceleration to about 480mph IAS, faster than I had been in level flight, and still increasing. The fuel gauges were already below half and so it was necessary to haul this projectile round and aim it back to Manston. It had been an interesting experience and I was readily convinced that gas turbines would become the power of the future when more thrust was available. In the meantime it seemed that the Meteor would be regarded as a useful test bed for its jet engines but not by a measure as suitable for fighter operations as they were at this stage of the war. Furthermore, I felt that the cumbersome twin engine, high-tail configuration was unlikely to be capable of development into a truly effective fighter aeroplane, although with greatly increased power/weight ratio it might make a useful interceptor/bomber destroyer."[164]

Night 2/3 AUGUST

7 Staffel of III/KG3, which had transferred to Venlo (Holland) for trial operations, was responsible for the night's raid, but one returning Heinkel (5K+MR) crashed when it attempted to carry out an emergency landing at Kortrijk in Belgium. It smashed into a factory with the loss of Obfhr Friedrich Martin and his crew[165].

One Diver was shot down by AA near Burnham-on-Crouch, Essex. One person was killed at Beulah Hill, Upper Norwood (SE19) at 0044. A serious incident occurred in Pendle Road, Streatham (SW16) at 0308, a dozen people losing their lives. One that fell in Jardin Street/Coburg Road, Camberwell (SE5) at 0340 killed three. Shortly after five in the morning, the second Diver to fall in the Gipsy Road area of West Norwood (SE27) impacted at the junction of Gipsy Road and Auckland Hill. Three residents were killed, including an elderly lady: One young lady wrote:

"My father [a police constable] told me that he tried to console an old man, who was in a state of shock. Apparently he went for a stroll with his dog while his wife cooked the midday dinner [sic]. When he returned, the whole street had been demolished and most of the people were under it, including the old man's wife. My father got the old man a cup of tea and talked to him while they searched for his wife."

Sadly, she was one of the fatalities. Another fell in Norbury Crescent (SW16) at 0625, killing five. David Golfman remembered:

"From the safety of my air raid shelter I was rudely awakened and instinctively knew that the campsite had been hit. I hurriedly arose and ran round to be met with a scene of absolute devastation, death and destruction and found myself in a state of shock. During that fateful forenoon, together with survivors, we wandered around the wreckage, retrieving what we could of the personal belongings of the dead and the living. Those were handed over to wardens and other officials who arrived on the scene, and in a pool of blood and on the spot where I would have been sleeping had I not moved."

96 Squadron (Mosquito XIII) Ford

Lt(A) F.W. Richards RNVR	MM559/ZJ-	V-1	0430	Grid R.4262
	MM559/ZJ-	V-1	0436	Grid R.1276

Lt(A) Frank Richards bagged a brace in double-quick time, both of his victims exploding on the ground. His score now stood at four destroyed. The first fell at Yalding, causing damage to Lees Cottages, and the second on the railway line at Aylesford.

418 (RCAF) Squadron (Mosquito VI) Middle Wallop

A Mosquito flown by Flg Off Stuart May RCAF on anti-Diver patrol was jumped by two unidentified aircraft, the second possibly a Me410, but managed to evade both without damage.

Nine Hs293-armed Do217Ms of III/KG100 set out to attack the road and railway bridges at Pontaubault, south of Avranches, it an attempt to thwart the American breakout from Normandy. The mission was unsuccessful and two of the Dorniers were lost, one of which was 6N+DR (2926) of 8 Staffel. Uffz August Stolzenberg and his crew were killed, while there was one wounded survivor from Obfw Konrad Doser's crew. Both were victims of prowling Mosquitos. Flt Lt Allen Browne RNZAF flying HK532 of 488 (RNZAF) Squadron shot down one:

"I was given a vector at Angels 8. After a matter of minutes my navigator [Wt Off T.F. Taylor RNZAF] reported contact at three miles range. We closed in whilst climbing and a visual was obtained at 2,000 feet range and approximately 1,000 feet above, silhouetted against the moon. The e/a was travelling in a southerly direction, weaving to port and starboard. I closed in to 1,000 feet when e/a crossed the moon and identified it as a Do217, which was confirmed by my navigator using night glasses. I throttled back when reaching same height and closed in to 250 yards and opened fire from dead astern. Strikes were seen on the port engine, which burst into flames. The e/a then pulled up in a stall turn to port. I closed in very rapidly on the turn, so I pulled out to starboard to avoid overshooting. Erratic return fire from dorsal guns was experienced at this time. I then pulled inside his turn to allow for slight deflection, and opened fire with a short burst. The e/a then burst into flames and went down vertically. I did port orbit and saw him burning on the seashore uncovered by the tide – about three or four miles west of Avranches."

The other Dornier fell to 410 (RCAF) Squadron's Sqn Ldr Dean Somerville RCAF, with Flg Off G.D. Robinson RCAF as his navigator in MM477:

"I closed in to 1,000 feet and identified it as a Do217 by pulling off to the starboard and getting a silhouette against the bright northern sky. I pulled back into line astern and opened fire at approximately 800 feet. It appeared that the e/a must have seen me the exact split second I opened fire, for it started a fairly hard starboard turn. On the first burst half of the e/a's port tailplane and port rudder flew off and evidently I must have holed his oil tank, because my windscreen and aircraft became smothered in oil. E/a started doing a steady starboard turn and losing height rapidly as if the pilot had been killed or was having difficulty in controlling his aircraft. After my first burst the combat developed into a dogfight as return fire was experienced from the dorsal and ventral guns of the e/a. No hits appeared to register although the fire appeared uncomfortably close. I re-opened fire every time I got close enough to see the e/a through the oil, which was gradually clearing due to the slipstream, at the same time the e/a kept firing back at me. It appeared that the e/a dived vertically into the ground at the precise moment that I used up all my ammunition. I orbited to port and saw the e/a strike the ground and burn furiously. Position approximately six miles north-west of Ponterosson. Intermittent flak was experienced throughout and on returning to base found that my mainplane had been hit by a 13cm shell inboard of the port engine."

Thursday 3 AUGUST

A Diver fell on Hendon airfield demolishing a barrack block and five accommodation huts, where five airmen were killed and 25 more injured. Soldiers from the nearby Army School of Physical Training billeted at the Hendon Police College assisted RAF personnel in rescuing survivors and clearing debris. A resident of the Druids Way/Kingswood Avenue area of Beckenham (BR3) died at 1055 following an impact, which caused much damage. Two more were killed in Wordsworth Road, Penge (SE20) at 1120.

Three Divers fell in or near Maidstone during the day, two causing casualties: five workmen were killed and a further ten people injured when a bomb exploded at Maidstone West railway station goods yard, and 14 residents of houses near the golf course were injured in the other incident. Fighters and AA accounted for six Divers that fell in Ashford RD (Rural District). The balloon barrage around Dartford was still proving successful, bringing down three Divers during the day. Fighters and balloons brought down nine Divers in the Maidstone RD area. Unfortunately, one Diver fell in Maidstone and caused much damage; five people were killed, seven seriously injured and 40 more suffered minor injuries. Five of the Divers that crashed in Sevenoaks/Tonbridge area were brought down by fighters, AA or balloons. Fighters and AA accounted for all seven Divers that crashed in Tenterden RD. Several properties were damaged in the area and one person reported seriously injured, with a further 22 slightly hurt. Two more fighter victims fell at Harrietsham, injuring two people, and near Ewell Manor, West Farleigh.

1/Lt Jack Robinson USAAF of the P-47-equipped 416thFBG based at Great Chart ALG:

> "On one occasion [believed to have been 3 August] the 514th Fighter Squadron was lined up on the north end of the runway ready for take-off, when the leader saw a V-1 coming directly at him, or so he thought. Fortunately it just missed and came down just across the road at the north end of the runway. We had people injured from Allied ground and aircraft guns and much flak fell around us, but I do not remember anyone being seriously injured. One of our pilots had a .50-calibre machine-gun bullet go through his leg above the knee, but he was lucky as it divided everything and did not cause real extended damage. He soon returned to flying, but was later killed in action."

Another P-47-related incident was recalled by Mr R.R. May, who was an apprentice with Southern Railway works at Ashford:

> "I was working at the Kimberly works and as it was one of the main Southern Railway workshops, we had Air Raid Spotters and warnings were given about planes and V-1s etc. We were told to go to the shelters whenever the warning was given, but as us lads wanted to see all the action going on outside, we would go to the Bofors gun that the work's Home Guard were operating and we saw it firing at a V-1. It was going low over the Torrington Road area – the sky was peppered with black dots and going through all this was a V-1. Then, to our horror, and to the gun crews', we saw a flight of about eight US Thunderbolt fighters. I think that they were returning from a mission in Northern France and were coming in to land at their airfield at Kingsnorth. Anyway, these planes had to take violent evasive action. They managed to avoid being shot down but unfortunately the V-1 escaped in the mêlée and headed on in the direction of Maidstone and disappeared from our sight."

Another eyewitness to this event wrote:

> "The gunfire was accompanied by ... shouts of 'Up a bit', 'Over a bit', etc., but all the bursts of fire missed the flying-bomb. Suddenly about six American Buffalo [*sic*] fighters coming back from a raid over France swooped round to land at Kingsnorth. The American planes were diving in all directions to get out of the way. There was a great shout of 'Trust the Yanks to

make us miss.' The flying-bomb ... got away to London."[166]

Another missile came close to wiping out several distinguished Polish pilots at Brenzett, as recalled by Sqn Ldr Bohdan Arct of 316 Squadron who was visiting his colleagues of 315 Squadron under the command of Sqn Ldr Horbaczewski:

> "The Brenzett Wing, though attached to the Tactical Air Force and initially intended for France, had stayed in England, but retained its field equipment including tents. Horbaczewski rose and went to change his uniform. We intended to go to our Air Headquarters in London, and before leaving Friston I put on my very best uniform. Puffing at a cigarette, I leisurely waited for my friend. I was still smoking when the guns roared and a small, very familiar shape rushed straight towards Brenzett at low altitude, aiming at the centre of the airfield. When it reached the border of the field it wobbled and dived. It must have been damaged by gunfire. There was no time to lose. I looked around, desperately seeking shelter, did not find any and threw myself flat on the ground, shaking from rage and fear, as my best uniform was soiled and I was facing death. But I kept looking up to see what the fiendish projectile intended to do. It flew across the field a few feet over the ground, then surprisingly lifted its cursed nose and climbed westward. I got up and began dusting off my new uniform. Mechanics, who like myself, had lain flat on the ground, returned to their aircraft.
>
> "This persistent specimen of the 'Wunderwaffe' did not leave us in peace. It turned eastward as if intending to go back to its den in France, changed its mind, made a regular orbit over the airfield and again climbed down to land. The whole procedure was repeated. Down I fell, down fell the mechanics and my friend in front of his tent. Our persecutor, proud of its accomplishment, decided not to explode at Brenzett, climbed and set course for its original destination. I cannot possibly repeat here the curses issued then. We all got up, brushed the dust off and ... the third attempt to blow us to bits followed. The evil bomb with diabolical laughter performed the mock landing trick. Scaring us stiff must have satisfied its ego, as it dropped the hide and seek game, flew away, disappeared behind a nearby hill, hit the ground and then the crashing sound of an explosion rang in our ears."

1 Squadron (Spitfire LFIXb) Lympne

Flg Off D.R. Wallace	MK919/JX-	V-1	1153	West Malling area

"Diver in and out of cloud. Strikes seen after fourth attack. Diver climbed slightly. Further burst and Diver spun in to a field four miles south-west of West Malling airfield."

3 Squadron (Tempest V) Newchurch

Flg Off R.H. Clapperton	JN755/JF-D	V-1	0700-0815
	JN755/JF-D	V-1	0700-0815
Flt Sgt R.W. Pottinger	JN760/JF-R	V-1	0800-0905
Flt Lt R. van Lierde (Belg)	JN862/JF-Z	V-1	0800-0920
	JN862/JF-Z	V-1	0800-0920
Flt Lt A.E. Umbers RNZAF	JN817/JF-H	V-1	0900-1030
	JN817/JF-H	V-1	0900-1030
	JN817/JF-H	V-1	0900-1030
	JN817/JF-H	V-1 shared	1026
Plt Off T.A. McCulloch	JN818/JF-	V-1	1000-1120

3 Squadron accounted for another ten Divers, Flt Lt Spike Umbers getting four and Flt Lt Remi van Lierde increasing his tally by two, as did Flg Off Ray Clapperton. Possibly one of the latter's victims fell near Cranbrook, damaging a bus and injuring 20 of its passengers. Sqn Ldr Turner Hughes from HQ 11 Group borrowed a Tempest and flew an anti-Diver sortie during the day but did not sight any Divers.

56 Squadron (Tempest V) Newchurch

Flt Lt J.D. Ross	EJ539/US-K	V-1	1100-1200	Rye area

91 Squadron (Spitfire XIV) Deanland ALG

Flt Lt W.C. Marshall	RM682/DL-	V-1	0914	Robertsbridge area

Lt H.F. de Bordas (FF)	RM685/DL-M	V-1 shared	1105	Mayfield area
Flt Lt H.B. Moffett RCAF	RM726/DL-	V-1	1220	Mayfield area
Cne J-M. Maridor (FF)	RM656/DL-F	V-1	1243 (KiA)	Benenden

Flt Lt Bill Marshall opened the scoring with a Diver that crashed four miles east of Robertsbridge: "Saw Diver coming over Hastings. Gave a short burst at 300 yards, then another at 70 yards. Saw strikes on fuselage and port wing, half of which fell off. Diver went through low cloud." Lt Henri de Bordas attacked his target that had been damaged by Flg Off Tommy Vance of 165 Squadron, in the Mayfield area: "Intercepted Diver four miles north of Bexhill. Gave short burst at 100 yards. Jet unit caught fire and Diver fell and exploded on the ground six miles north of Mayfield." Flt Lt Bruce Moffett shot down his target in the same area: "Diver intercepted coming in east of Hastings. Made two attacks from astern. Diver went down four miles north of Mayfield, exploding in a field."

For Cne Jean-Marie Maridor the day ended in death. He intercepted a Diver over Rolvenden, at which he fired a burst, causing it to go into a glide towards Benenden School, which housed a large military hospital. He dived after it and fired again from close range. The bomb exploded and blew a wing off the Spitfire, which crashed nearby, taking the gallant Frenchman to his death – eight days before he was due to be married. Witnesses were of the opinion that Maridor had deliberately risked his life to prevent the bomb falling on to the school[167]. A schoolmistress at Benenden wrote to the French pilot's fiancée's father:

"I wish I could tell you more about the terrible accident to Captain Maridor. As you can imagine it all happened so quickly we had no time to see much. We were told that in trying to save the hospital and the school where we live, he shot at the flying bomb rather too close. The plane was cut in half and flew over the school. Will you tell your daughter from us all here that his gallant deed saved the lives of soldiers and many small children – I feel this is not much to you but is all I can tell you. I am sending you one of the shells that we picked up in the grounds, it may be a little comfort to your daughter to have one of the shells shot from Captain Maridor's plane."

129 Squadron (Mustang III) Brenzett

Sqn Ldr I.D.S. Strachan RNZAF	FB364/DV-D	V-1	0900+	Lympne area
	FB364/DV-D	V-1	0900+	Leeds Castle area
Flt Lt R.G. Kleimeyer RNZAF (Aus)	FB152/DV-L	V-1	0900-1045	Ham Street area
Flt Lt G.C.D. Green	FX958/DV-E			
Flt Lt G.C.D. Green	FX958/DV-E	V-1 shared	0900-1045	Leeds Castle area
Flt Lt R.G. Kleimeyer RNZAF (Aus)	FB152/DV-L	V-1	0900-1045	Hythe area
	FB152/DV-L	V-1	0900-1045	
Flg Off J.E. Hartley	HB862/DV-G	V-1	1015-1135	
Flg Off L.G. Lunn	FB137/DV-C	V-1	1145-1220	

The first two Divers shot down fell to Sqn Ldr Shorty Strachan, who was carrying out an air test. The first was sighted near Lympne at 3,000 feet and an attack was made at 450 yards with short bursts. Strikes were seen and the Diver lost height with starboard wing down, but was not seen to crash as the CO was warned by Very light to turn away from balloons north-west of Maidstone. A second Diver was then intercepted south-east of Ashford at 1,500 feet. Attacked from port quarter and astern with short bursts. Strikes were seen on fuselage and wings whereupon it turned over to starboard and crashed, exploding on the ground near Leeds Castle.

A third Diver was destroyed jointly by Flt Lts Gerry Green and Dutch Kleimeyer, who intercepted it between Dymchurch and Dungeness at 2,000 feet. They attacked alternately with short bursts down to 50 yards. The Diver slowed down and disappeared into cloud below before emerging to explode in a wood west of Ham Street. Green then engaged another, which he attacked from starboard quarter and line astern, observing strikes. The Diver lost speed and height and as it entered its final dive, a Spitfire nipped in and attacked, causing it to crash and explode in hills one mile north of Leeds Castle. Two more Divers were then destroyed by Kleimeyer, the first intercepted over Hythe at 3,500 feet. Flg Offs Jim Hartley and Les Lunn completed the scoring for the day.

165 Squadron (Spitfire IX) Lympne

Plt Off J.V. Tynan	MK738/SK-L	V-1	1012	Ashford area
Flg Off T.A.Vance RAAF	ML418/SK-G	V-1 shared	1053	Robertsbridge area

Plt Off Tynan's target crashed in what was believed to be Head's Wood, three miles west of Ashford: "Interception made above cloud. Strikes seen all over and jet went out. I went below cloud and saw smoke of explosion. Confirmed by F/O Vance and F/S Porich." Flg Off Tommy Vance shared another: "Intercepted seven miles north of Hastings. Strikes seen, Diver slowed down and engine stopped. It wallooned along and then a Spit XIV [apparently Lt de Bordas of 91 Squadron] attacked, igniting fuel. Confirmed by Red 2."

306 (Polish) Squadron (Mustang III) Brenzett

Wt Off J. Czeżowski PAF	FB393/UZ-U	V-1	1005	Dallington area
Flt Sgt S. Rudowski PAF	FB380/UZ-F	V-1	1016	Hastings area
	FB380/UZ-F	V-1 shared	1026	Grid R.1038

Wt Off Jacek Czeżowski intercepted his target two miles north of Hastings at 2,500 feet and shot it down near Dallington. Flt Sgt Stan Rudowski intercepted his first Diver between Bexhill and Hastings at 3,000 feet. Attacked from slightly below from 300 yards and Diver exploded in the air. He then intercepted a second two miles west of Hastings and attacked from starboard, while a Tempest from 3 Squadron attacked from astern, following which the Diver crashed.

315 (Polish) Squadron (Mustang III) Brenzett

Plt Off G. Świstuń PAF	PK-O	V-1 shared	1015	Hastings area
Flt Lt J. Schmidt PAF	FZ157/PK-Z	V-1 shared	1037	Rye area
	FB367/PK-U	V-1 shared	1215	Hythe area

486 (RNZAF) Squadron (Tempest V) Newchurch

Wt Off O.D. Eagleson RNZAF	JN808/SA-N	V-1	0745	Bexhill area
	JN808/SA-N	V-1	0810	Newchurch area
Flg Off S.S. Williams RNZAF	JN858/SA-Y	V-1	0955	Tonbridge area
	JN858/SA-Y	V-1	1000	Hastings area
Flg Off W.A. Hart RNZAF	JN732/SA-I	V-1	1010	Pevensey area
Plt Off R.D. Bremner RNZAF	JN767/SA-B	V-1	1110	Battle area
Flg Off W.A. Hart RNZAF ⎱	JN732/SA-I	V-1		
Plt Off R.D. Bremner RNZAF ⎰	JN767/SA-B			
Flt Lt N.J. Powell RNZAF	JN808/SA-N	V-1	2334	

610 Squadron (Spitfire XIV) Friston

Wt Off Chalky White and Flt Sgt John Philpott[168] chased and fired at Divers on the first patrol of the day (0915-1020) but both had to break off as they reached the coastal gun belt.

616 Squadron (Meteor F.1) Manston

The Meteor pilots were desperate to break their duck and came close to succeeding during a patrol by Flt Lt Mike Graves. Having sighted a Diver he had no difficulty in overtaking it and was able to fire a two-seconds burst at 400/500 yards range. No results were observed and as he manoeuvred for a second attack a Mustang nipped in front of him and shot it down.

Night 3/4 AUGUST
85 Squadron (Mosquito XVII/XIX) West Malling

Flt Lt R.H. Farrell	HK119/VY-S	V-1	0200	exploded mid-air
Plt Off L.J. York	TA400/VY-J	V-1	0258	off North Foreland
	TA400/VY-J	V-1	0310	off Deal
Flt Lt P.A. Searle	VY-Q	V-1	0332	West Malling area

Flt Lt Ginger Farrell's aircraft was damaged by the explosion of his victim: "Attacked from dead astern from 200 feet. Exploded in mid-air seven miles east of West Malling." He returned to base on one engine, making a safe landing. Plt Off York followed up with two more:

"Attacked from astern from 600-700 yards. Diver exploded in the sea 20 miles east of North Foreland. Attacked [second] from 300 yards increasing to 500 yards. Strikes seen and Diver climbed to 8,000 feet then dived and exploded in the sea five miles east of Deal."

Flt Lt Searle got the last of the night: "Dived from 9,000 feet and attacked from dead astern, range 350 yards. Strikes seen and Diver crashed and exploded seven-eight miles north-east of West Malling."

96 Squadron (Mosquito XIII) Ford

Flt Lt F.R.L. Mellersh	MM577/ZJ-N	V-1	0115	off Dungeness
	MM577/ZJ-N	V-1	0125	off Dungeness
	MM577/ZJ-N	V-1	0150	off Dungeness
	MM577/ZJ-N	V-1	0210	off Dungeness
	MM577/ZJ-N	V-1	0220	off Dungeness
	MM577/ZJ-N	V-1	0245	off Dungeness
	MM577/ZJ-N	V-1	0322	off Dungeness
Wg Cdr E.D. Crew	NS985/ZJ-	V-1	0205	off Dover
	NS985/ZJ-	V-1	0235	off Dover

The unit's diarist commented: "What a night! Nine Divers knocked down by two crews!!" Flt Lt Togs Mellersh and Flt Lt Mike Stanley had a supremely successful sortie, all their victims exploding in the sea between one and 15 miles south-east of Dungeness. Of his final kill Togs saw strikes only and did not witness it crash, but another crew nearby confirmed that it went into the sea just off the coast. Wg Cdr Edward Crew added two more, both going into the sea off Dover. He reported seeing a regular stream of Divers rather than salvos, with a few flying at just 500 feet.

137 Squadron (Typhoon Ib) Manston

| Flt Lt D.G. Brandreth | MN995/SF- | V-1 | 2335 | Channel |

Flt Lt Doug Brandreth was requested by control to use the special rockets he was carrying:

"The first two attacks were carried out on Divers flying at 1,500 feet and 2,500 feet respectively. Attacked from astern, range 600 yards, and rockets exploded 30-40 feet below Diver in each case. After the two unsuccessful attacks with the special RPs, I made contact with a Diver at approximately 2335. I fired a short burst with cannon from astern and saw strikes on the starboard wing and motor. The Diver turned off course and crashed into the sea but did not explode."

157 Squadron (Mosquito XIX) West Malling

Plt Off W.S. Vale RAAF[169]	MM671/RS-C	V-1	0124	West Malling area

Plt Off Bill Vale sighted a Diver over Hawkinge: "Attacked from astern from 600-700 yards. Diver crashed and exploded three miles south-east of base."

418 (RCAF) Squadron (Mosquito VI) Middle Wallop

Flt Lt P.S. Leggat RCAF	TH-	V-1	0257	Channel

"I was flying across the sea from Dieppe to Le Touquet at 9,000 feet and turned to port to track Diver, diving down. Opened fire at 400 yards range with four short bursts. Pulled away as Diver was pulling away at 400mph. One minute afterward the 'light' went out and Diver hit the sea and exploded on impact."

605 Squadron (Mosquito VI) Manston

Sqn Ldr I.F. McCall	UP-	V-1	0305	Manston area

"Saw very many Divers during patrol of which at least eight were destroyed by AA. At 0305 Diver sighted at 1,000 feet. We dived from 4,000 feet, opening fire from astern at about 400 yards as Diver crossed the coast just south of Manston. Three to four bursts. Diver lost height and exploded before reaching the ground."

FIU (Tempest V) Ford

Flt Lt R.L.T. Robb	EJ598/ZQ-U	V-1	night
	EJ598/ZQ-U	V-1	night
Flt Lt C.B. Thornton	ZQ-	V-1	night
	ZQ-	V-1	night
Flg Off R.G. Lucas	ZQ-	V-1	night
	ZQ-	V-1	night
Flt Lt J. Berry	EJ524/ZQ-Y	V-1	night
	EJ524/ZQ-Y	V-1	night
	EJ524/ZQ-Y	V-1	night
	EJ524/ZQ-Y	V-1	night
	EJ524/ZQ-Y	V-1	night

The Tempests brought down a total of 11 Divers during the hours of darkness, five falling to Flt Lt Joe Berry. Unfortunately, detailed records/combat reports have not survived. It seems that two of the FIU's victims crashed at East Sutton and Thurnham shortly before midnight, and possibly at Aylesford, Hushheath Farm, Staplehurst, Hermitage Lane, Maidstone, and Leybourne, where three houses and a church were damaged, and eight people injured, two seriously. These fell between 0127 and 0359.

Six Do217Ms from III/KG100 repeated their attack on the bridges at Pontaubault just before midnight, one crew claiming a hit on the rail bridge with a conventional bomb. One Dornier, 6N+MS of 7 Staffel piloted by Obfw Helmut John, fell to Mosquito MM552 of 604 Squadron flown by Flt Lt Reg Foster DFC (his sixth victory) at 2315 as it manoeuvred to release its Hs293 guided bomb:

"I was told of a bandit flying north at 10,000 feet and given a vector. After climbing to 9,000 feet my observer [Flg Off M.F. Newton] obtained contact at five miles. Visual was obtained at 2,500 feet range. I closed in to 200 yards dead astern and identified target as a Do217. I pulled the nose up and fired a two-seconds burst from 150 yards, as the bandit turned gently starboard. Strikes were seen on the starboard engine. A second burst was fired resulting in a blinding flash from the fuselage and port engine. The bandit then dived, firing from belly position, and we followed. An object thought to be a man baling out, passed under my starboard wing. Bandit continued diving until he was at 5,000 feet and we thought he was finished. At 5,000 feet however he levelled off and I tried another burst but found the gunsight had gone out. Flashes and strikes were seen on the fuselage. As e/a dived to port we were engaged by friendly ack-ack and hit in the port engine, port wing and Perspex roof of cabin. We both received slight cuts to the back of the neck. I fired a fourth burst, hitting e/a's starboard wingtip. E/a continued diving hard to port and at 2,500 feet I pulled out as we were still being heavily engaged by ack-ack. My port engine then became very rough and after making 1,000 feet and getting out of ack-ack, I feathered it and returned to base on one engine, landing at A.8 at 2355."

He added: "Wreckage of a Do217 which crashed between 2325 and 2330 hours, eight miles south of Granville, was found by Major Lewis and Capt Hart of 6th LAA Regiment. I claim one Do217 destroyed."

Friday 4 AUGUST

Waltham Abbey was again in the forefront of Diver activity, one impacting just before 0700 not far from Gilwell Farm, as testified by Warden Carter:

"Located the crater in a cornfield. An assortment of scrap iron again, some quite hot. Jet propulsion unit buried in the crater this time, and round and near the edges some of the chisel edge wire cutter that Jerry is now fixing in the wings to sever balloon barrage cables. While looking round the hole, heard a most awful bang, which echoed and reverberated backwards and forwards between the hills. On getting to a phone I found that a Liberator had crashed and caught fire at Cheshunt. Seems the whole crew were killed."

Beckenham (BR3) received another bomb at 1550, this falling in Cherry Tree Walk, where one person was killed. Dulwich Wood Avenue (SE19) was hit at 1632, one resident being killed. At 1809, a Diver fell on the Bermondsey Wall (SE16), killing three people and injuring nine others. The wharfs were used to store grain and the collapse of the buildings released this. Combined with floods of water from fire brigade hoses, a huge mass resulted which blocked Bermondsey Wall and Loftie Street, where houses and yards were filled to a depth of three-four feet. It was Christmas before demolition and clearance had started. By this time the grain had taken root and started growing.

Elsewhere, the village of Laughton in Sussex was hit by a Diver, inflicting four fatalities. Another, having been tipped by a Tempest, crashed on Funtington ALG (near Chichester) at 1820 where 349 (Belgian) Squadron was based with its Spitfires. One airman was slightly hurt. The bomb impacted about 15 yards from one Spitfire, which was loaded with fuel. Several groundcrew rushed over to the damaged machine and dragged it to safety, although it was later written off. Two others were damaged, one requiring an engine change and the other a replacement wingtip. Fighters brought down five Divers in Ashford RD, including one at 1903 that fell in Victoria Park, Ashford, damaging the Catholic School, the Co-op Bakery, flour mills and a laundry. Three people were seriously injured and 21 others hurt. Two more Divers were brought down by Dartford's balloon defences.

Nine more Divers were accounted for by fighters in the Maidstone RD area, some of the resultant crashes causing casualties on the ground; at least three people were seriously hurt and nine others suffered minor injuries. Fighters were responsible for six of the seven Divers that crashed in the Sevenoaks/Tonbridge area. For people on the ground at Tenterden it was just as terrifying, with fighters shooting down ten Divers and AA one more. Although there was some damage only five people were injured. In the Folkestone area 20 Divers were shot down into the sea by AA and a further eight by fighters. Elsewhere in Kent, Divers shot down by fighters came to earth near the Crown & Horse pub at Langley (two slightly injured), and near Hollidays Farm, while two more exploded in the air over the Fountain Inn (East Peckham) and Redwall Lane, Linton.

1 Squadron (Spitfire LFIXb) Lympne

Flg Off W.J. Batchelor	MJ481/JX-	V-1	1550	Ashford area

"I closed to 250 yards and gave a deflection burst of three seconds, after which the Diver slowed down to 250mph and dropped its starboard wing. I pulled up to avoid overshooting and then came in for another short burst. The Diver then did some aerobatics and crashed in Eastwell Park, five miles north of Ashford."

Wt Off J.W. McKenzie was carrying out an anti-Diver patrol when the engine of his aircraft (NH466) failed, and a belly-landing was made at Thane in Kent, when the pilot was slightly injured and the aircraft written-off.

3 Squadron (Tempest V) Newchurch

Flt Sgt L.G. Everson	JN817/JF-H	V-1	1920-1945
Wt Off J.L.R. Torpey	JN768/JF-F	V-1	1935-2050
Wt Off R. Worley	JN760/JF-R	V-1	2125-2210

41 Squadron (Spitfire XII) Lympne

Flt Lt T.A.H. Slack	EN238/EB-Q	V-1	1610	Isle of Oxley

"I returned from one scramble to report to 'Gizzy' [Lord Gisborough, squadron IO] that I thought I had shot down a Doodlebug in the Ashford area but I had not seen it hit the ground. He made a few phone calls and was told a Doodlebug had exploded half an hour ago in the middle of the Ashford Railway Yards, causing considerable damage to railway property and military equipment destined for the Front in Europe. We both hurriedly agreed not to claim it as shot down by me or anyone else in 41 Squadron. After this unfortunate incident Gizzy said that if Hitler ever heard about all the British equipment I had been responsible for destroying, like the Audax in the desert, the Spitfires in France and in the Channel, and now the marshalling yards at Ashford, he would probably award me the Iron Cross First Class with diamonds and crossed swords. Little did he know that there was soon to be another Spitfire to add to this shameful list."[170]

56 Squadron (Tempest V) Newchurch

Sqn Ldr A.R. Hall	EJ541/US-B	V-1		
Plt Off D.E. Ness RCAF	EJ547/US-A	V-1	1625	Robertsbridge area
	EJ547/US-A	V-1	1635	over land
Sgt A.M.L. Kennaugh	EJ544/US-J	V-1	1825	
Flt Lt J.H. Ryan RCAF	EJ522/US-F	V-1	1900	

91 Squadron (Spitfire XIV) Deanland ALG

Flt Lt A.R. Cruickshank RCAF	RM649/DL-	V-1	1548	Horsham area
Flt Lt H.D. Johnson	RM686/DL-G	V-1	1605	East Grinstead area
Flg Off A.R. Elcock	RM734/DL-	V-1	1905	Tunbridge Wells area
Lt H.F.de Bordas (FF)	RM688/DL-N	V-1	2025	Tunbridge Wells area

Canadian Flt Lt Ray Cruickshank shot down his target five miles south-west of Horsham: "Diver intercepted three miles north of Bexhill and attacked from 300 yards. It fell and exploded on the ground." Flt Lt Johnny Johnson got the next, which crashed one mile south-east of East Grinstead: "Diver intercepted one mile north-west of Crowborough. Attacked from 100 yards. Saw strikes on wings and Diver fell and exploded on the ground." The final two for the day fell near Tunbridge Wells, the first to Flt Lt Elcock: "Intercepted Diver two miles north-east of Etchingham and attacked from 150 yards. It did a slow diving turn to port, fell and exploded in a wood." Lt Henri de Bordas' target was sighted over Hastings: "Attacked from dead astern at 150 yards. Fired short burst and jet unit exploded. Diver fell two miles west of Tunbridge Wells."

129 Squadron (Mustang III) Brenzett

Flt Lt R.J. Conroy RAAF	SR428/DV-L	V-1	pm	
Flt Lt R.G. Kleimeyer RNZAF (Aus)	FB137/DV-C	V-1	evening	
Flg Off P.N. Howard	FB170/DV-U	V-1 shared	pm	
Plt Off E.W. Edwards	FB147/DV-K	V-1	pm	

During an evening patrol Flt Lt Dutch Kleimeyer sighted a flying bomb and overshot on his approach but, turning sharply across the nose of the bomb, the bomb flew into his slipstream, rolled over and crashed.

137 Squadron (Typhoon Ib) Manston

Flg Off A.N. Sames RNZAF	MN134/SF-J	V-1	am	Channel

Flg Off Art Sames gained his fourth and last Diver kill during an early morning sortie, the unit's 30th.

165 Squadron (Spitfire IX) Lympne

Plt Off J.M. Walton RCAF	MK801/SK-E	V-1	1545	Tunbridge Wells area
Flt Lt J.K. Porteous RNZAF	MK854/SK-H	V-1	1815	
Flt Lt B.J. Murch	NH401/SK-M	V-1	1825	Robertsbridge area

Canadian Plt Off John Walton intercepted his target four miles south-east of Tenterden: "Diver commenced to turn westerly after first attack, lost height and finally crashed on a house four miles south-south-west of Tunbridge Wells. Mustang also in vicinity may have fired but not seen to do so, therefore claim is made for one Diver destroyed." Flt Lt Murch reported: "Strikes seen and Diver commenced slow, meandering dive and then spun in to a field two miles west of Robertsbridge."

131 (Polish) Wing (Mustang III) Brenzett

Grp Capt T. Nowierski PAF	HB886/T-N	V-1	2007	New Romsey area

37-year-old Grp Capt Tadeusz Nowierski DFC, former Battle of Britain pilot and currently OC 131 (Polish) Wing, succeeded in shooting down a Diver to add to his tally of combat kills.

306 (Polish) Squadron (Mustang III) Brenzett

Flt Sgt J. Zaworski PAF	UZ-K	V-1	1545	Ashford area
Plt Off J. Bzowski PAF	HB871/UZ-E	V-1	1617	off Hastings
Flt Sgt J. Zaworski PAF	FZ196/UZ-D	V-1	1915	off Bexhill
Flt Lt J. Siekierski PAF	UZ-I	V-1	2017	Tenterden area

Flt Sgt Jan Zaworski intercepted a Diver over Hythe, shooting it down near Ashford. Plt Off Janusz Bzowski got another when he shot a Diver down into the sea 15 miles off Hastings at 1617. Flt Sgt Zaworski was up again during the early evening and engaged another Diver over the Channel about 20 miles off Bexhill. Attacked from astern, the Diver exploded in the air about five miles offshore, damaging his aircraft. Flt Lt Jan Siekierski intercepted two miles north-west of Lydd at 2,000 feet. He attacked from port and astern at 100 yards with three short bursts. Strikes were seen and the Diver climbed before crashing and exploding on the ground one mile north-east of Tenterden.

315 (Polish) Squadron (Mustang III) Brenzett

Flg Off W. Wunsche PAF ⎱	FB123/PK-W	V-1	1550	Rye area
Wt Off T. Słoń PAF ⎰	FZ169/PK-R			

Sqn Ldr Horbaczewski spotted a Diver near Dungeness at which he fired all of his ammunition, but only shot off part of its starboard wing. He reported that Tempest SF-J [*sic*] then engaged and the Diver exploded six miles south-west of Tonbridge and stated that the 'Tempest' pilot was awarded the kill[171].

322 (Dutch) Squadron (Spitfire XIV) West Malling

Flt Lt J. van Arkel	VL-W	V-1	2010	Grid R.9539
Flt Lt J.F. Plesman	VL-Z	V-1	2015-2035	Hailsham area

Flt Lt Jan van Arkel reported: "Vectored on to Diver. Attacked line astern, range 200 yards. Diver exploded in mid-air and again on the ground." Flt Lt Jan Plesman got a second at about the same time: "I saw Diver heading in over Eastbourne. Intercepted and attacked in dive, firing from 200 yards. Diver exploded on the ground two miles north of Hailsham."

486 (RNZAF) Squadron (Tempest V) Newchurch

Wt Off O.D. Eagleson RNZAF	EJ528/SA-P	V-1	1625	Hastings area
Wt Off B.J. O'Connor RNZAF	JN801/SA-L	V-1	1810	Rye area
Plt Off K.A. Smith RNZAF	JN821/SA-H	V-1	1900	Tunbridge Wells area
	JN821/SA-H	V-1	1920	Tunbridge Wells area
	JN821/SA-H	V-1	1935	Maidstone area

610 Squadron (Spitfire XIV) Friston

Flt Lt J.B. Shepherd ⎫	DW-	V-1	1300-1415	
Flg Off J. Doherty ⎬	DW-			

616 Squadron (Meteor F.1) Manston

Flg Off T.D. Dean	EE216/YQ-E	V-1	1616	Tonbridge area
Flg Off J.K. Rodger	EE2??/YQ-	V-1	1640	Tenterden area

Flg Off Dixie Dean reported:

"At 1545 I was scrambled for anti-Diver patrol between Ashford and Robertsbridge. Flying at 4,500 feet, 340mph IAS, I saw one Diver four to five miles south-east of Tenterden flying at 1,000 feet, estimated speed of 365mph (at 1616). From two-and-a-half miles behind the Diver I dived down from 4,500 feet at 470mph. Closing in to attack I found my 4x20mm guns would not fire owing to technical trouble. I then flew my Meteor alongside the Diver for approx 20-30 seconds. Gradually I manoeuvred my wingtip a few inches under the wing of the Diver, then pulling my aircraft upwards sharply, I turned the Diver over on its back and sent it diving to earth approximately four miles south of Tonbridge. On return to Manston I was informed that ROC had confirmed one Diver had crashed at position given by me. This is the first pilotless aircraft to be destroyed by a jet-propelled aircraft."

Shortly afterwards, at 1640, 616 Squadron achieved a second kill when Flg Off Jock Rodger shot down a V-1 that crashed near Tenterden:

"At 1640 I sighted a Diver over Tenterden flying at 3,000 feet and speed of 340mph. I immediately attacked from dead astern and fired a two-seconds burst at range of 350 yards. I saw several hits and saw petrol or oil streaming out of Diver, which continued to fly straight and level. I fired another two-seconds burst from my four cannon, still from 300 yards. Both Meteor and Diver were flying at 340mph. The Diver then went down and exploded on ground about five miles north-west of Tenterden."

616's diarist noted:

"The first flying bomb was destroyed by a jet-propelled aircraft. This note in the squadron history and indeed aviation history can be recorded by Flg Off Dean. The squadron is now thrilled at the first two kills and is ready for more."[172]

A detachment of the USAAF's 562ndBS, operating from the ALG at Woodbridge on the Suffolk coast, carried out the first Operation 'Aphrodite' mission during the day, two BQ-7s and two controlling B-17s being tasked to raid V-weapon sites in France at Siracourt (42-39835) and Watten (42-30342). One BQ-7 ('835) went out of control after the radio operator/engineer – T/Sgt Elemet Most USAAF – had baled out. It crashed, killing 1/Lt John Fisher USAAF when it exploded near Orford, creating a huge crater and destroying two acres of forest. The crew of '342, 1/Lt Fain Pool USAAF and S/Sgt Phillip Enterline USAAF, also suffered slight injuries while evacuating their aircraft, which nonetheless was guided by the mother ship towards the target area where it was believed to have been hit by flak, crashing and exploding north-west of Gravelines. The pilot of an observation aircraft witnessed the death of Lt Fisher:

> "A pilot far below in one of the recon aircraft watched as a pair of legs began to protrude from the navigator's hatch, but suddenly the drone went into another sharp climb, and the legs quickly disappeared back inside the fuselage. Once again the old bomber returned to straight and level flight, and once again a pair of legs came out the bottom. But this time the plane jerked into a sharp climb, stalled quickly, and fell off on the left wing. The recon pilot saw that the B-17 was spinning toward the ground, and he boldly dived his little plane for a closer view. At about 100 feet, he saw a body fall from the open hatch, but body and airplane hit the ground almost at the same time and the same place, and B-17 No.835 blew itself and its pilot to tiny bits in a loud explosion."[173]

Following this inauspicious first attempt, the two controlling aircraft returned to base to carry out the second part of their mission by guiding 41-24639 to Mimoyecques, and 42-3461 to Wizernes. Again one crew found difficulty in abandoning their aircraft. 1/Lt Connie Engel USAAF was seriously injured (necessitating his injured arm having to be amputated), during the bale out from '639, and his radio operator/engineer T/Sgt Cliff Parsons USAAF was slightly injured, with only 1/Lt Frank Houston USAAF and T/Sgt Willard Smith USAAF emerging from '461 without injury. This drone missed its target by 500 yards due to low cloud cover, while '639 crashed before reaching Mimoyecques due to operator error. Of the demise of '461 at Wizernes, a subsequent report by Luftwaffe investigators revealed:

> "Time of attack – 1600 hours, height 300 meters. Aircraft shot down by flak. Attack was directed against construction work. Aircraft exploded upon impact into tiny fragments, which were scattered over a radius of 500-1,500 meters from the point of impact, creating craters of various diameters (one measuring 20 meters). Aircraft maintained course even while attacked by flak and no counter-measures were observed. Whether or not there were accompanying aircraft flying above could not be determined. No traces of a crew or aerial guns were found. A great quantity of explosives must have been used, based on complete destruction of aircraft."

On returning from the Mimoyecques operation, the controlling aircraft flown by 1/Lt Wilf Tooman USAAF found itself caught up in a Diver attack:

> "Desultory flak began blossoming around the B-24, and Tooman dropped a wing in a tight turn and poured on full throttle for the run home, losing altitude and gaining speed with every mile. He passed Dover at some 6,000 feet and he heard a gasp over the intercom and the voice of the tail gunner. 'Hey, we're in the goddamn middle of a goddamn buzz bomb attack!' Tooman looked out and saw the flaming exhaust of a V-1 passing to the right, headed straight for London. Another came by, and a third, and then the B-24 mother ship shuddered in mid-air as a burst of flak went off nearby. 'The Limeys are firing at the V-bombs!' Hargis [Lt Glen Hargis, Bombardier] called out from his vantage point in the nose. Tooman flicked on his radio switch. He was white with rage, compounded of previous encounters with British flak and the disappointment of missing his target at Mimoyecques, and he said evenly and loudly into the microphone: 'Can you please shut off the goddamned artillery? You're down there nice and

safe. We're up here, and there's flak all over the place. This is supposed to be friendly territory.' The flak continued, but no more immediate bursts upset Tooman's equanimity. He flew north-northeast along the coast, out of range of the Dover gunners, until he reached Great Yarmouth, and when he turned inland toward Fersfield at an altitude of 4,000 feet, the British opened up on the B-24 with 40mm automatic weapons. Tooman had been homing on a beacon and had radioed his estimated time of landfall and had turned on his IFF loud and clear, but now once again he had to contend with friendly flak. He put the four-engine bomber into shudderingly violent evasive manoeuvres, dived to gain speed and pull clear of the coastal anti-aircraft stations, and finally burst into peaceful air south of Norwich."[174]

Night 4/5 AUGUST

A Diver fell in Moyser Road, Streatham (SW16) at 0442, killing two residents. Hythe AA began shooting down the incoming Divers as from 0010, and had accounted for 17 splashed in the sea by the end of the day.

85 Squadron (Mosquito XIX) West Malling

Flg Off A.J. Owen	TA400/VY-J	V-1	0430	Tenterden area
Lt E.P. Fossum (Norw)	MM648/VY-G	V-1	0445	Herne Bay area

The Diver shot down by Flg Off Ginger Owen DFM[175] crashed in the vicinity of Tenterden: "Dived from 9,000 feet. Short burst given from dead astern. Diver dived steeply." Norwegian Lt Fossum's target also crashed on land: "Dived from 8,000 feet and opened fire from astern. Diver exploded on the ground in vicinity of Herne Bay."

96 Squadron (Mosquito XIII) Ford

Flg Off J. Goode	MM452/ZJ-	V-1	0445	Channel

418 (RCAF) Squadron (Mosquito VI) Middle Wallop

Sqn Ldr R. Bannock RCAF	HR147/TH-Z	V-1	0430	exploded in mid-air
	HR147/TH-Z	V-1 damaged	0440	Channel
	HR147/TH-Z	V-1	0445	Channel
Flg Off J.J. Harvie RCAF	TH-	V-1	0435	off Le Touquet

Sqn Ldr Russ Bannock scored another double:

"At 0430 a Diver was seen at 3,000 feet. Attacked with three two-seconds bursts of cannon and machine-gun from 250 yards dead astern. Diver blew up in air. Another Diver was seen some miles behind but since there was no time, it was allowed to pass above and slightly to port. As it did so, fired a two-seconds burst from 250 yards. Strikes were seen on port wing so fired another two-seconds burst from astern. No claim. At 0445 attacked further Diver. Diving from 9,000 feet I overshot, but when Diver pulled ahead again, fired three two-seconds bursts from 500 yards dead astern. Diver crashed into the sea and exploded."

Flg Off Jeff Harvie shot down one during the same period:

"After an abortive attack on a Diver which came out from Le Touquet, three Divers were sighted in mid-Channel. The last one was engaged from dead astern at range of 400 yards. Fired a mixed short burst, speed of flying bomb fell off and our aircraft over shot. Turned to starboard and made second attack from dead astern with one three-seconds burst. Diver immediately went down in deep glide and blew up before hitting the sea."

456 (RAAF) Squadron (Mosquito XVII) Ford

Flt Lt K.A. Roediger RAAF	HK297/RX-V	V-1	0451	Sussex (Grid R.0749)

Saturday 5 AUGUST

A flying bomb brought down by a Tempest crashed in Malling Road, Snodland shortly before 1900, demolishing ten houses and damaging many more. Twelve people were killed and 16 seriously injured. Two local doctors displayed great heroism despite being injured themselves. One, a Czech refugee, was holding his surgery when the bomb fell. He was badly cut in the face by glass splinters and bleeding heavily but continued to do what he could for those who had been hurt. The other doctor, who was in the front room of his house, received the full force of the blast and was thrown against the man he was treating. Although his leg was broken he also continued to treat the injured. Among those killed was a nine-year-old girl, who was a patient at the surgery, a police sergeant, his wife and two girls, who were staying with the doctor, and several neighbours. Derek Pantony of Whitstable was crossing an open field at Coxheath, near Maidstone when he saw this flying bomb tipped over by a Tempest. It veered to port before crashing in Snodland. He recalled:

> "The pilot was heavily criticised at the time for employing this well-known tactic but from my position it was clear that if he had opened fire it is highly likely that it would have crashed in the centre of Maidstone, where the casualty rate may have been much higher. I feel the pilot was unjustifiably pilloried."

Another very serious incident occurred at 1645, when a Diver impacted in East Dulwich (SE22) one of the worst in South London. The bomb hit the Co-op store at the corner of Northcross Road in Lordship Lane. The Co-op and six other shops were demolished and 20 houses damaged in Lordship Lane and 40 in Shawbury Road. A Salvation Army hall was also damaged. Twenty-three people died and a further 29 were seriously injured. Three people were killed and four injured in Prestlands Park Road, Sidcup at 1646.

41 Squadron (Spitfire XII) Lympne

Flt Sgt I.T. Stevenson	MB795/EB-	V-1	1900	Maidstone area

Flt Sgt Jock Stevenson[176] saw his victim crash six miles north-west of Maidstone:

> "Saw strikes on each attack, speed reduced to 300mph. Used all ammunition (one cannon jammed). Flew alongside and decided to tip it up with own wing when clear of Maidstone. Diver held same course after tipping but went into a dive and crashed five-six miles north-east of Maidstone near balloons."

56 Squadron (Tempest V) Newchurch

Flt Sgt H. Shaw	JN867/US-H	V-1 shared	1635	Hastings area
	JN867/US-H	V-1 shared	1640	Tunbridge Wells area

91 Squadron (Spitfire XIV) Deanland ALG

Flg Off G.C. McKay	RM653/DL-	V-1	1640	exploded in mid-air
Flg Off J. Monihan	RM651/DL-	V-1	1900	Heathfield area

Flg Off McKay: "Diver intercepted between Crowborough and Tonbridge. Attacked from astern at 400 yards and it blew up in mid-air." Flg Off Monihan: "Sighted Diver five miles west of Heathfield. Attacked from astern at 150 yards and Diver crashed and exploded in a wood." This was probably the bomb that impacted in a cornfield near Horam, where 80 houses were damaged by the blast.

129 Squadron (Mustang III) Brenzett

Flg Off M. Twomey	FX952/DV-E	V-1	pm
Plt Off M. Humphries	FB137/DV-C	V-1	pm
Flg Off F.H. Holmes	FB212/DV-Q	V-1	pm
Plt Off E.W. Edwards	FB389/DV-M	V-1	pm

165 Squadron (Spitfire IX) Lympne

Flg Off C.M. Lawson RAAF	ML175/SK-P	V-1	1625	Robertsbridge area
	ML175/SK-P	V-1	1635	Tunbridge Wells area
Plt Off A. Scott	MK752/SK-W	V-1	1850	off Dungeness
Plt Off T.P.G. Lewin	MJ580/SK-Y	V-1	1855	off Boulogne

Flg Off Lawson survived two lucky escapes:

> "Intercepted Diver south of Hawkhurst. Diver blew up immediately following half-second burst, causing minor damage to my Spitfire and throwing it on its side. Saw second Diver being attacked by Tempest without result [probably Sgt Shaw of 56 Squadron]. Tempest pulled out to one side and I attacked. Second burst caused Diver to explode. Spitfire again clobbered by explosion, causing damage to hood."

Two hours later two more Divers fell to the Squadron, Plt Off Scott getting the first: "During attack Diver commenced to weave and skid, losing height and speed. I broke off as I approached gun area. Controller reported that Diver went into sea and was not claimed by gunners." Five minutes later Plt Off Jock Lewin shot down his first and 165's last V-1: "Intercepted eight-ten miles north-north-west of Boulogne. Saw sheet of flame from Diver and it went straight down, exploding in the sea."

306 (Polish) Squadron (Mustang III) Brenzett

Wt Off W. Nowoczyn PAF	UZ-S	V-1	0715	Bexhill area
Flg Off J. Smigielski PAF	FB358/UZ-C	V-1	1640	off Rye

Wt Off Witold Nowoczyn intercepted Diver east of Bexhill at 2,000 feet and attacked from astern; wing broke off and Diver crashed eight miles north of Bexhill. During the afternoon Flg Off Jan Smigielski engaged another 20 miles south of Rye, and following his attack it glided into the sea and exploded.

316 (Polish) Squadron (Mustang III) Friston

Wt Off T. Szymański PAF	HB835/SZ-P	V-1	0240-0515
	HB835/SZ-P	V-1	0240-0515
Flt Sgt T. Jaskólski PAF	HB839/SZ-V	V-1	0420-0635
Flt Sgt A. Pietrzak PAF	FB383/SZ-J	V-1	0515-0700
	FB383/SZ-J	V-1	0515-0700
Wt Off P. Syperek PAF	FB353/SZ-H	V-1	0515-0750

322 (Dutch) Squadron (Spitfire XIV) West Malling

Flg Off J. Jonker	VL-K	V-1	1635	Grid R.0637
Flg Off R.F Burgwal	RB184/VL-B	V-1	1624	Hastings area
	RB184/VL-B	V-1	1640	Uckfield area

Three Divers fell to the Dutch pilots in quick succession, Flg Off Rudi Burgwal getting the first: "Over R/T told Diver crossing over Hastings. Intercepted and attacked line astern, range 200 yards. Diver crashed and exploded in Hastings area." Eleven minutes later Flg Off Jan Jonker shot down a second: "Vectored on to Diver coming in three miles east of Pevensey Bay. Intercepted and attacked it from slightly below, range 200 yards. Saw strikes on tail unit. Diver crashed and exploded." The third also fell to Burgwal: "After destroying first Diver I was vectored on another crossing in east of Beachy Head. Several other aircraft seen. Gained height and dive attacked to 200 yards. Diver crashed and exploded three-quarters-of-a-mile east of Uckfield."

486 (RNZAF) Squadron (Tempest V) Newchurch

Flg Off H.M. Mason RNZAF	JN801/SA-L	V-1	1852	Newchurch area

501 Squadron (Tempest V) Manston

Flg Off W.F. Polley	EJ598/SD-H	V-1	1825-1910	Ashford area
Flg Off W.F. Polley ⎫	EJ598/SD-H	V-1	1825-1910	Ashford area
Flt Sgt R.W. Ryman ⎭	EJ585/SD-A	V-1		

501 had only just settled in to Manston, having flown over from Westhampnett for operations, Flg Off Bill Polley soon getting into the swing of things, shooting down one and sharing a second with Flt Sgt Roy Ryman.

610 Squadron (Spitfire XIV) Friston

Flt Lt F.A.O. Gaze RAAF	DW-U	V-1	1515-1650

FIU (Tempest V) Ford

Flt Lt J. Berry	EJ524/ZQ-Y	V-1	daytime
	EJ524/ZQ-Y	V-1	daytime
	EJ524/ZQ-Y	V-1	daytime
	EJ524/ZQ-Y	V-1	daytime
	EJ524/ZQ-Y	V-1	daytime

Night 5/6 AUGUST

A total of 22 sorties were flown by III/KG3 operating out of Rosières, one FTR. One of the Divers came down in Brockley (SE14), exploding in Millbank Grove and killing two residents. One Diver brought down by a fighter crashed at Chainhurst near Marden at 0535. Three people were killed and two injured at 0400 when a Diver impacted between Halfway Street and Corbylands Road, Sidcup.

25 Squadron (Mosquito XVII) Coltishall

Flg Off B.G. Nobbs	HK243/ZK-G	V-1	0430	off Dover
	HK243/ZK-G	V-1	0430	off Dover

"I was patrolling at 7,000 feet off Cap Gris Nez and at approximately 0430 saw five flying bombs at 2,000 feet. I dived to attack and opened fire on one flying bomb from a range of 2,000 feet dead astern. I did not observe any results from my attack and had to break away owing to being close to the gun area. I climbed and when at 4,000 feet saw another flying bomb at 2,000 feet. I dived and attacked from dead astern, opening fire from 1,500 feet but did not observe any strikes as the flying bomb drew away out of range. I climbed again to 6,000 feet and saw a flying bomb at 2,000 feet. I dived and opened fire from 900 feet dead astern but had to break away before observing results. All three attacks had to be broken off owing to close proximity of the guns and I was therefore unable to observe results. I was later informed by Sandwich Control that two of the flying bombs which I had attacked were destroyed. I was also informed that I was the only fighter in the area at the time and that the guns were not making any claims. I therefore claim two flying bombs destroyed."

96 Squadron (Mosquito XIII) Ford

Wt Off W.A. McLardy RAAF	HK479/ZJ-	V-1	0509	off Hastings

157 Squadron (Mosquito XIX) West Malling

Flg Off C.N. Woodcock	MM652/RS-S	V-1	0326	Tunbridge Wells area

"First seen crossing Beachy Head engaged by searchlights. Attacked from astern at 600 yards. Diver caught fire and exploded on the ground five miles south-west of Tunbridge Wells."

418 (RCAF) Squadron (Mosquito VI) Middle Wallop

Flg Off P.R. Brook RCAF	TH-	V-1	0348	Channel
Flg Off H. Loriaux RCAF	TH-	V-1	0337	Channel
	TH-	V-1	0340	Channel

French-Canadian Flg Off Hank Loriaux scored a double:

"At about 0330 a number of Divers were seen coming out at Le Tréport. At 0337 dived from 8,000 feet on one travelling at 330 IAS. Made a quarter attack with three one-second bursts. The Diver, which was at 3,500 feet, seemed to slow up. A two-seconds burst at 250 yards caused it to fall to pieces and it dived into the sea, exploding. At 0340 second Diver was attacked. A series of short bursts caused this to blow up in the air. The Mosquito had just broken away in time to avoid the explosion."

Shortly thereafter Flg Off Phil Brook scored his third kill:

"On returning from a Ranger to Munich and when halfway across the Channel, I noticed a Diver behind at 2,000 feet. Circled and gained height and when the Diver was directly underneath the Mosquito, I dived on it and pulled up 500 yards astern. Fired four three-second bursts – 'light' went out and it glided slowly down to the sea, exploding on impact."

456 (RAAF) Squadron (Mosquito XVII) Ford

Wt Off J.E. Semmens RAAF	HK253/RX-	V-1	0330	off Eastbourne
Plt Off S.J. Williams RAAF	HK282/RX-L	V-1	0455	off Dungeness

Both Divers attacked by the Mosquitos fell into the sea. The one engaged by Wt Off John Semmens flew into the gun belt after being hit but then turned south and exploded in the sea. Plt Off Stuart Williams' victim followed soon after and was confirmed by Flg Off Stevens.

425thNFS USAAF (P-61) Ford

1/Lt G.E. Peterson USAAF	42-5581	V-1	2155-0041	off Hastings

Lt Garth Peterson encountered a Diver flying at 180mph. Dived on it and closed to 400 feet astern. Opened fire and saw strikes all over, the propulsion unit stopped and the Diver crashed into the sea 20 miles south of Hastings.

Do217s were again active and Mosquito crews from 488 (RNZAF) Squadron claimed two destroyed, one of which was an Hs293-armed aircraft from III/KG100 flown by Ltn Alfred Schlect that fell near Ponterosson. Flt Lt Peter Hall RAF (with Flg Off R.D. Marriott RNZAF) shot down one at 0052:

"When we reached the Bay of Mont St Michel, we were vectored south-east over land and told that there were some five e/a in the area. We were also warned that there was some *Window* but saw no trace of it throughout the patrol. We were fairly soon vectored on to a bandit on which contact was obtained at four-and-a-half miles and above. After a fairly long chase during which the range steadily increased to six miles on a climbing target, we were called off by control for something nearer. We obtained contact on a second one at two-and-a-half miles at 5,000 feet. After a fairly long chase during which the target climbed from 5,000 feet to 8,000 feet, a visual was obtained at 3,000 feet range. At 1,500 feet range the target went into a slow turn to port during which it was identified as a Do217. In spite of the moon, the lighting conditions were tricky. During the turn we got a side view of the fins and rudders and also saw the black crosses on the wing. Night glasses were used. I opened fire from 100 yards with a short burst but over deflected and saw no strikes. E/a peeled off to port and I gave it a second burst from dead astern as it went down, hitting the fuselage and setting the starboard engine on fire. E/a went into a diving turn, and just before it hit the ground the fire went out, but three seconds later there was an enormous explosion with a great fire and clouds of black smoke."

The second Dornier was claimed by Flt Sgt T.A. MacLean RNZAF at 0217, and another was damaged by the same pilot ten minutes later:

"Almost immediately after obtaining a contact and a visual on a Stirling, I was told to investigate another bogey and given several vectors after which contact was obtained as three miles range on a target taking evasive action. A visual was obtained at a range of 3,000 feet. I closed in and as I did so bogey increased speed to 180 IAS. At a range of 450 feet I identified the bogey as a Do217. This was confirmed by my navigator [Flg Off B.C. Grant RNZAF] assisted by the use of night glasses. I maintained the same position and opened fire with a two-seconds burst. I observed strikes on the port engine, port wing root and fuselage, which set the port engine alight. Debris fell off the engine and from the port wing. The e/a turned over on its back and went down in a vertical dive, hitting the ground with an explosion. The position was ten miles west of Angers. My navigator reported that he had a freelance contact, four miles range. We closed in and visual was obtained at a range of 3,000 feet. I closed in to 100 yards and identified target as a Do217. My navigator confirmed this again using night glasses. I positioned myself to port, slightly below, and opened fire with a short burst. I observed strikes on the port engine and fuselage, from which I could see minor explosions. Simultaneously with my opening fire, the e/a peeled off to port and returned my fire, which did not register any hits on my aircraft. The e/a then commenced violent evasive action and I followed him but did not have an opportunity of positioning myself to open fire again. The e/a continued very violent evasive action down to below 2,000 feet, during which I overshot and visual was lost. Contact was also lost in the ground returns. While the e/a was diving in the evasive action, sparks were seen to issue from its port engine."

Sunday 6 AUGUST

Dartford was on the receiving end of a Diver at 1710, the missile causing massive damage in the Carrington Road area, where 20 homes were wrecked, ten people killed and a further 20 seriously injured. Up to 700 more houses were damaged by the blast. Fighters and guns brought down three Divers that fell in Ashford RD, while balloons accounted for four Divers in the Sevenoaks/Tonbridge area, two others falling to fighters. Two Divers were shot down into the sea off Folkestone by guns, four more being splashed by fighters. A further four were brought down into the sea by Hythe AA.

3 Squadron (Tempest V) Newchurch

Flg Off R. Dryland	JN865/JF-	V-1	1220-1350
	JN865/JF-	V-1	1220-1350
Flt Sgt D.M. Smith	EJ549/JF-	V-1	1320-1410
Flt Sgt L.G. Everson	EJ540/JF-P	V-1	1615-1740

Flt Sgt Don Mackerras RAAF (14 Divers of which three shared) was killed when his Tempest JN759 spun into the ground at Minfield in Sussex during an anti-Diver patrol. He had apparently been attempting to tip a flying bomb with his wingtip. Wg Cdr Beamont flew an anti-Diver patrol between 1900 and 2010 with Mr Bill Humble, Hawker's chief test pilot, as his No.2 in JN817/JF-H. Unfortunately, no Divers were encountered.

56 Squadron (Tempest V) Newchurch

Sgt G.H. Wylde	EJ526/US-N	V-1`	1705	Hastings area
Flt Sgt L. Jackson	EJ544/US-J	V-1	1705	Tunbridge Wells area

91 Squadron (Spitfire XIV) Deanland ALG

Flg Off A.R. Elcock	RM734/DL-	V-1	1725	Burwash area

"Intercepted Diver south of Etchingham. Attacked from astern at 150 yards and strikes seen on wings. Jet unit broke off and fuel tank exploded. Diver fell north-west of Burwash and exploded on the ground."

129 Squadron (Mustang III) Brenzett

Wt Off E. Redhead	FX942//DV-P	V-1	1327	Ham Street area

The Diver was intercepted two miles south-west of Ham Street and attacked from astern down to 200 yards. Its starboard wing dropped and the Diver went vertically down in the middle of a village believed to be Woodchurch.

306 (Polish) Squadron (Mustang III) Brenzett

Flt Lt J. Siekierski PAF	FB393/UZ-U	V-1	1324	Channel
	FB393/UZ-U	V-1	1355	Channel
	FB393/UZ-U	V-1	1709	Ashford area

Flt Lt Jan Siekierski shot down three in two sorties, the first two crashing into the Channel within ten minutes of each other although he lost sight of the second in the haze. During a second sortie he intercepted a Diver north of Brenzett. Following his stern attack he reported that the Diver "started wobbling" before it crashed and exploded three miles south-west of Ashford ALG. Siekierski now had nine Divers to his credit.

315 (Polish) Squadron (Mustang III) Brenzett

Flg Off P. Kliman PAF	FX939/PK-L	V-1	1331	Brenzett area
Flt Sgt J. Donocik PAF	FX945/PK-I	V-1	1332	Dymchurch area

316 (Polish) Squadron (Mustang III) Friston

Flt Lt T. Szymankiewicz PAF	HB824/SZ-N	V-1	0020	off Newhaven
Wt Off W. Grobelny PAF	FB353/SZ-H	V-1	0325	Beachy Head area
Flt Lt L. Majewski PAF	HB821/SZ-L	V-1	0352	off Beachy Head
Wt Off W. Grobelny PAF	FB356/SZ-U	V-1	0430	off Hastings
Flt Lt K. Zielonka PAF	FB353/SZ-H	V-1	0445	Maidstone area
Sqn Ldr B. Arct PAF	HB836/SZ-R	V-1	0445	Tunbridge Wells area
Wt Off T. Szymański PAF	HB824/SZ-N	V-1	1325	off Hastings
	HB824/SZ-N	V-1	1337	off Hastings
Flt Lt L. Majewski PAF	HB821/SZ-L	V-1	1355	off Hastings

The Poles had their best day with nine kills, the first two falling just after midnight. Flt Lt Szymankiewicz getting the first: "Intercepted whilst going out on patrol. Attacked 250-300 yards astern. Jet hit. Diver exploded in the sea about eight miles south-west of Newhaven." Five minutes later his No.2, Wt Off Grobelny, scored in similar circumstances: "Sighted Diver five miles north of Beachy Head. Attacked from 300 yards astern. Diver exploded on the ground about 20 miles north of Beachy Head." Two hours later Flt Lt Majewski got another: "Intercepted Diver when returning from patrol line from gun zone. Attacked from astern from 300 yards. Diver turned swiftly to port. Attacked again and it crashed and exploded in the sea." Wt Off Grobelny was up again soon after, scoring his second kill of the night: "Seen 25 miles south of Hastings. Attacked from quarter astern, then astern. Jet unit hit and Diver crashed in the sea." Flt Lt Zielonka intercepted his target north-west of Dungeness: "Attacked 300 yards astern. Strikes all over port wing and it crashed and exploded on the ground at edge of balloon barrage west of Maidstone." Of his second kill, Sqn Ldr Arct wrote:

> "Owing to various duties I was unable to fly regular night patrols, instead I arranged night aircraft tests. These had really nothing in common with normal tests. I would go up, climb to 10,000 feet and circle, keeping a sharp eye eastward, but was not allowed to fly out over the sea. The glaring spots of incoming bombs were perceptible in darkness from many miles. Furious and very accurate gunfire met them over the coast, but some managed to get through the artillery barrage and that was where I would come in. When bringing down a flying bomb during one of these night aircraft tests I experienced the strange thrill of night aerobatics. My bomb was damaged when passing over the gun belt and as I caught up with it, it whirled in most sophisticated loops, turnovers, rolls and even spins. I followed, firing my guns from all imaginable positions. At last it exploded in the fields, but when I came back to Friston I was absolutely drenched in my own perspiration."

Wt Off Szymański then scored two in double quick time: "Diver seen 15-20 miles south of Hastings. Attacked from astern 350-400 yards. It went into steep dive as I turned away to deal with another Diver in the vicinity. Attacked from astern at 200 yards. Diver exploded in the sea." The last of the day, and his second, fell to Flt Lt Majewski: "Seen and attacked 20 miles south of Hastings. Diver exploded in the sea."

322 (Dutch) Squadron (Spitfire XIV) West Malling

Flt Lt J.F. Plesman	VL-P	V-1	2309	Channel

486 (RNZAF) Squadron (Tempest V) Newchurch

Flg Off J.G. Wilson RNZAF	JN802/SA-C	V-1	0450	West Malling area
Wt Off W.A. Kalka RNZAF	EJ524/SA-M	V-1	1335	Bexhill area
Plt Off W.A.L. Trott RNZAF	EJ528/SA-P	V-1	1347	Newhaven area
Plt Off R.J. Danzey RNZAF ⎫	JN803/SA-D	V-1	1710	Tunbridge Wells
Plt Off R.D. Bremner RNZAF ⎭	EJ524/SA-M			area
Flg Off R.J. Cammock RNZAF	EJ523/SA-Z	V-1	1718	Eastbourne area

Another task force of two BQ-7s (42-30212 with 1/Lt Joe Andrecheck USAAF and T/Sgt Ray Healy USAAF in charge, and 42-31394 with 1/Lt John Sollars USAAF and T/Sgt T.H. Graves USAAF) and four command B-17s was sent out against the V-1 site at Watten, one drone loaded with nine tons of explosives, the other with 160 incendiary bombs and 800 gallons of jellified gasoline (napalm). The crews parachuted clear of the aircraft without incident, but within minutes one of the drones went out of control and crashed into the sea off the French coast. The other drone decided to develop a mind of its own and the explosives-packed aircraft began to circle the industrial area of Ipswich before flying out to sea, where it was harmlessly crashed. Following these failures Operation 'Aphrodite' was put on hold until the guidance system could be rectified[177].

Night 6/7 AUGUST

Twenty-two sorties were flown by crews of III/KG3 from Rosières, the last aircraft back landing safely at 0348. There were no losses.

96 Squadron (Mosquito XIII) Ford

Flt Lt I.A. Dobie	HK437/ZJ-	V-1	0135	off Dungeness

The night's operations were marred by the loss of MM649, flown by RNVR crew Lt(A) Peter Pryor and Sub Lt(A) Doug MacKenzie, which crashed at Finningham Manor near Detling at 0105 on returning from an anti-Diver patrol. Both men died from their injuries. There was only one success. Flt Lt Dobie reported:

> "Strikes seen. Diver lost height. Chase broken off because of proximity to Gun Belt. Operator and W/Cdr Crew saw explosion on sea. Another Diver seen trailing something 2,000 feet behind and below."

418 (RCAF) Squadron (Mosquito VI) Middle Wallop

Flg Off H. Loriaux RCAF	TH-	V-1	0133	

456 (RAAF) Squadron (Mosquito XVII) Ford

Flt Lt K.A. Roediger RAAF	HK297/RX-V	V-1	0135	Grid R.2153

FIU (Tempest V) Ford

Flt Lt C.B. Thornton	ZQ-	V-1	pm	

425thNFS USAAF (P-61) Ford

1/Lt G.E. Peterson USAAF	42-5581	V-1	pm	

The American crew of Lts Garth Peterson and Howe notched their second success on consecutive nights.

Between **2-6 August**, Do217Ms of III/KG100 carrying Hs293s had attacked bridges of the River See and River Selume at the southern end of the Cherbourg peninsular resulting in only slight damage to bridge at Pontaubault for loss of six Do217s. During these attacks Mosquito crews had claimed eight Dorniers destroyed, the last two falling to 488 (RNZAF) and 604 Squadrons during the final night's operations. Flt Lt Allen Browne RNZAF (HK420) had a very successful sortie, shooting down a Ju88 night fighter of III/NJG2 (claimed as a Ju188), before intercepting two Do217s although he was uncertain of their identity at the time, as his combat report reveals:

"Almost immediately [after shooting down the Ju88] control took us over and asked us to investigate another bogey. After several vectors we obtained contact, range three miles, well above and dead ahead. I opened to full throttle and climbed to 10,000 feet, which was approximately bogey's height. I saw a reddish-amber light at a range of 4,000 feet moving from port to starboard. I followed visually and pulled in at full throttle dead behind it. The light then commenced to dive and I followed at 310 ASI but failed to close range. The light was going down very steeply and at a constant angle. AI contact was maintained throughout but I followed without difficulty by sight. I could not identify as I saw no silhouette but was satisfied that it was a very large single circular light. The light hit the ground and exploded and a volume of fire was seen. This explosion occurred roughly west of Rennes. I pulled out of the dive at 500 feet and orbited the burning wreckage."

Although he had not fired a shot, Browne claimed this as a destroyed unidentified enemy aircraft. His report continues:

"A little later [control] asked us to investigate another bogey at about 12,000 feet. Contact was obtained, range three miles at Angels 12. Closed range very slowly though I was at full throttle. Visual 1,500 yards dead ahead on an aircraft taking exceptionally violent evasive action. I could not identify, as I could not close the range and the bogey peeled off to starboard. I followed and experienced a long burst of fire from dorsal turret. I turned to port and lost visual. Contact was picked up again at one-mile range, slightly below to starboard when we were at 3,000 feet. I levelled out and closed in when visual was obtained at 1,000 feet. The aircraft opened fire again with a very erratic burst and missed. The aircraft was still continuing evasive action and half rolled to port, then going down vertically. This caused me to overshoot, as I was not prepared to duplicate the aircraft's manoeuvres at that low altitude. I did a hard turn to port at the same time losing height. At that juncture, while in a hard turn, my navigator and I saw a violent explosion on the ground with large volumes of flame, over to port, which would have been the aircraft's approximate position. By reason of the evasive action and speed of events I was not able at any time throughout the chase to identify the aircraft, which was always below. I endeavoured throughout to position myself but was unsuccessful through the flying skill of the other pilot. I would add that I have never experienced such violent evasive action. The aircraft crashed at 0331 approximately south-west of Rennes."

Flt Lt John Surman (MM448) of 604 Squadron also claimed three victories, a Bf110 and two Dorniers:

"At 0050 when at 4,500 feet we were given a vector towards a bogey, which was 15 miles away. My navigator [Plt Off Clarence Weston] obtained a contact on this target, range three miles, well below and to port. The target did first a port orbit and then a starboard orbit and we gained a visual as the target commenced another port orbit from 2,000 feet, against the moon. We identified it as a Me110. I closed in to 600 feet and gave a two-seconds burst and saw explosion in the port engine, fuselage and starboard engine. E/a dropped out of the sky and exploded on hitting the ground. I was vectored north and resumed patrol and at 0135 we were given easterly vector towards bogey, which we were told was orbiting eight miles away, at 6,000 feet. My navigator obtained a contact at four miles range, slightly above and to the starboard. Target was on a port orbit and climbing. I closed in, gradually climbing and finally obtained a visual when at 11,500 feet. I closed in to 600 feet directly below and identified it as a Do217, the black cross on the wing being clearly visible. I drew up dead astern and gave a short burst from 500 feet. The starboard engine exploded and went on fire, and there was return fire from the e/a. The e/a dived vertically to starboard and exploded as it hit the ground.

"We returned to patrol again and at 0245, when being vectored home, the controller informed me that an aircraft was two miles ahead on my starboard side. I turned starboard and my navigator obtained contact, two miles range, well to starboard. I closed in slowly and from 800 feet obtained a visual and identified from underneath as a Do217. I drew up and gave a short burst from 600 feet. The port engine exploded but did not catch fire, and I overshot. I turned hard port, came in again and saw e/a flying on one engine. I gave another two bursts. Port engine exploded but did not catch fire, and again I overshot. I came round for a third attack. I gave another burst. No strikes were seen and I again overshot and did a tight orbit to come in again. By this time e/a was at 2,000 feet and I gave another burst into the port engine. Engine on fire and e/a then dived hard starboard, hit the ground and exploded."

It would seem that Surman actually accounted for two Bf110 night fighters and one Do217, one of the night fighters flown by Hptm Helmut Bergmann, a 36-victory ace and Staffelkapitän of 8/NJG4. Two Do217Ms were lost – 6N+GR (723054) of 7/KG100, from which Ltn Hans Kieffer and his crew baled out and were taken prisoner – and Ltn Rudolf Engelmann's 6N+AD in the same area, only two of the crew surviving. In addition to the RAF claims, a 422ndNFS P-61 (42-4568) crewed by 2/Lt Eugene D. Axtell USAAF and Flt Off Joseph F. Crew USAAF, operating from Ford, engaged a Do217 at 0310 near Bayeux and exchanged fire; the Dornier dived into clouds near Mont St Michel and was claimed probably destroyed.

Monday 7 AUGUST

Four people were killed in East Dulwich (SE22) when a bomb fell in Underhill/Fiern Road at 0731. Three Divers were brought down by fighters and AA in Ashford RD. Two victims of fighters fell at Monks Horton near Elham at 0725 and 20 minutes later at Little Pett Bottom near Elstead. One victim of a fighter fell on Cliffe Cottages at Boughton Monchelsea and killed one resident, slightly injuring three others.

56 Squadron (Tempest V) Newchurch

Sgt G.H. Wylde	EN526/US-N	V-1	0605	Biddenden area
Flg Off J.J. Payton	JN816/US-V	V-1	0610	Tunbridge Wells area
Flg Off E.C. Goulding	EJ545/US-Z	V-1 shared	0615	Ashford area
Sgt G.H. Wylde	EN526/US-N	V-1	0620	over land

Flg Off Goulding shared a Diver with Flg Off Czerwiński of 315 Squadron.

91 Squadron (Spitfire XIV) Deanland ALG

Flg Off A.R. Elcock	RM694/DL-	V-1	0601	Etchingham area
Flt Lt H.D. Johnson	RM684/DL-	V-1	0722	Hastings area
Lt H.F. de Bordas (FF)[178]	RM686/DL-G	V-1	0804	Appledore area

Flg Off Arthur Elcock reported: "Owing to half light I was uncertain of my position when first sighted Diver. Attack was made from 150 yards astern and Diver fell in open countryside ten miles north-north-east of Etchingham with jet unit still functioning." Another fell to Flt Lt Johnny Johnson seven miles north-west of Hastings: "Diver sighted over Bexhill and attacked from 250 yards astern, knocking off wings. Diver spun in, exploding on the ground." Frenchman Lt Henri de Bordas got the final one of the morning: "Diver crossed over Dungeness. Attack was made from astern, wing was hit and it fell in a field one mile north of Appledore."

129 Squadron (Mustang III) Brenzett

Flg Off D.C. Parker	HB862/DV-G	V-1	0603	Canterbury area
	HB862/DV-G	V-1	0610	Faversham area
Plt Off E.W. Edwards	FB389/DV-M	V-1	0725-0915	Dymchurch area

306 (Polish) Squadron (Mustang III) Brenzett

Plt Off K. Wacnik PAF	FB347/UZ-T	V-1	0558	Brenzett area
Flt Sgt J. Zaleński PAF	FB393/UZ-U	V-1	0722	Dallington area

315 (Polish) Squadron (Mustang III) Brenzett

Flg Off A. Czerwiński PAF	FX878/PK-F	V-1 shared	0615	exploded in mid-air
Plt Off G. Świstuń PAF	FZ157/PK-Q	V-1 shared	1055	Brenzett area

Flg Off Andrzej Czerwiński lost contact with ground control but sighted a Diver near Rye. He joined a Tempest (Flg Off Goulding of 56 Squadron) in attacking this bomb, which exploded in the air four miles south-east of Tonbridge.

316 (Polish) Squadron (Mustang III) Friston

Wt Off C. Bartłomiejczyk PAF	HB849/SZ-W	V-1	0140	mid-Channel
	HB849/SZ-W	V-1	0142	mid-Channel
	HB849/SZ-W	V-1	0143	mid-Channel
	HB849/SZ-W	V-1	0145	mid-Channel
Flt Lt Z. Przygodski PAF[179]	HB839/SZ-V	V-1	0140	mid-Channel
Flt Sgt S. Sztuka PAF	HB835/SZ-P	V-1	0605	Tenterden area
	HB835/SZ-P	V-1	0609	Hastings area
Flt Lt L. Majewski PAF	FB396/SZ-F	V-1	1100	off Hastings

Following on from their success of the previous day/night operations, the Poles brought down a further eight Divers including four by Wt Off Czeslaw Bartłomiejczyk in the space of five minutes:

> "Diver sighted 15 miles off coast. Attacked astern from 150 yards and Diver exploded in the sea. Second Diver seen at 100 feet. Attacked from astern at 200 yards and it exploded in the sea."

The third followed a minute later having been attacked in the same manner, as did the fourth: "Attacked from astern and Diver exploded in the sea." These kills raised his score to six. Flt Lt Przygodski also scored at this time: "Seen in mid-Channel and attacked from 400 yards astern. Exploded in the sea about eight miles from the coast." Flt Sgt Sztuka followed with a brace: "Intercepted over Dungeness. Attacked from astern from 250 yards. Strikes seen and it crashed north-west of Tenterden." Number two followed four minutes later: "Seen over the coast near Hastings. Attacked from beam 600 yards closing to 100 yards. Crashed on the ground near large house." Flt Lt Majewski closed the day's scoring with another at 1100: "Intercepted 40 miles south of Hastings. Attacked from astern 200 yards and it crashed in the sea."

322 (Dutch) Squadron (Spitfire XIV) West Malling

Flg Off R.F. Burgwal[180]	VL-L	V-1	2306	

486 (RNZAF) Squadron (Tempest V) Newchurch

Flg Off R.J. Cammock RNZAF	JN863/SA-R	V-1	0603	Dungeness area

501 Squadron (Tempest V) Manston

Flg Off R-C. Deleuze (FF)	EJ599/SD-W	V-1	0520-0620	Tenterden area

616 Squadron (Meteor F.1) Manston

Flg Off T.D. Dean	EE2??/YQ-	V-1	0620	Robertsbridge area

The unit's diarist wrote: "Another success today to Flg Off Dean, who shot down a Diver east of Robertsbridge at 0620. Congratulations to Dixie on his second success." Dean's combat report reveals:

"At approximately 0620, I intercepted a Diver four miles east of Robertsbridge. The Diver was flying at 1,000 feet and estimated speed of 390mph. I came into attack line astern at 400mph and opened fire with all four cannon at 700 yards. I continued firing in short bursts, closing into 500 yards. Strikes seen and pieces fell off from the Diver's starboard wing. Finally I broke away, having expended my ammunition, and saw Diver go down in shallow dive. It was not possible to see the Diver crash owing to prevailing ground mist. It was later confirmed by ROC that Diver had crashed at 0625."

The diarist continued: "The Rt.Hon. Sir Archibald Sinclair, Secretary of State for Air, arrived on Station. He was greeted by Wg Cdr McDowall at dispersal, where all the pilots were introduced. Sir Archibald was keen and interested to hear first hand news from the pilots. During the visit Flg Off Rodger and Flg Off McKenzie were scrambled and thus afforded a fine opportunity to show off the Meteor." The Squadron now had 33 pilots who had converted to flying the Meteor and had progressed to A and B Flights from the original one Flight, although only a dozen aircraft were currently on strength.

FIU (Tempest V) Ford

Flt Lt J. Berry	EJ524/ZQ-Y	V-1	daytime
	EJ524/ZQ-Y	V-1	daytime
	EJ524/ZQ-Y	V-1	daytime
	EJ524/ZQ-Y	V-1	daytime
Flg Off E.L. Williams (Rhod)	EJ524/ZQ-Y	V-1	
Flg Off R.G. Lucas	EJ553/ZQ-L	V-1	
Flt Lt R.L.T. Robb	EJ598/ZQ-U	V-1	
	EJ598/ZQ-U	V-1	

Possibly at least two of the FIU's victims fell during the hours of darkness, Diver crashes occurring at East Peckham at 0150 (four slightly injured) and at the entrance to Cobtree Zoo, Boxley (one slightly injured).

Night 7/8 AUGUST

The Heinkels of III/KG3 were out again from Rosières, 23 sorties being flown without loss. One Diver came down in Baldwin Avenue, Eastbourne, shortly before midnight. Many houses were damaged but no fatalities were reported. One of those shot down by a fighter fell near an agricultural hostel between Hawkhurst and Benenden, killing four and injuring 33.

96 Squadron (Mosquito XIII) Ford

Flt Lt F.R.L. Mellersh	Spitfire IX MH473	V-1	2210-0030	
	Spitfire IX MH473	V-1	2210-0030	
	MM577/ZJ-N	V-1	0455	Channel
	MM577/ZJ-N	V-1	0503	Channel

Flt Lt Togs Mellersh borrowed Spitfire IX MH473 from the Night Fighter Development Wing at Ford to try his luck – and shot down two Divers. He then shot down two more while flying his usual Mosquito: "Intercepted at 2,000 feet. Glided down some distance before hitting the sea. Grid W.6397. Intercepted at 2,000 feet. Opened fire at 800 feet. Dived straight in and exploded in the sea Grid W.5092."

157 Squadron (Mosquito XIX) West Malling

Flt Lt J.O. Mathews	TA401/RS-D	V-1	0507	West Malling area
	TA401/RS-D	V-1	0513	exploded in mid-air
Sqn Ldr J.H.M. Chisholm	MM676/RS-W	V-1	0555	over land

Flt Lt Mathews shot down two in quick succession: "Both Divers attacked from astern. First dived and exploded on the ground. Second exploded in the air, damaging my aircraft. Both combats took place south-east of base." Sqn Ldr Chisholm reported: "Attacked from astern 500 yards range. Diver exploded on the ground."

418 (RCAF) Squadron (Mosquito VI) Middle Wallop

Flg Off S.N. May RCAF	NS837/TH-L	V-1	2316	Brighton area
Flt Lt P.S. Leggat RCAF	TH-	V-1	0136	Channel
Flg Off H.E. Miller RAF	TH-	V-1	0141	off Le Tréport

Flg Off Stuart May intercepted eleven miles off the Brighton coast and chased it across the coast, firing as he did so: "Strikes were seen and flames were seen from the tail. The Diver crossed the coast near Brighton, when it was held by searchlights and crashed on land. No AA fire was observed." Flt Lt Peter Leggat experienced a more exciting chase: "At 0132 when patrolling off the coast of Dieppe at 9,000 feet, a salvo of four Divers was seen to cross out. One was selected and I dived down, but just before coming within range, the starboard cabin window blew out, so broke away and regained height. No.2 in the salvo was then picked out. Two attacks made from 350 yards dead astern. Diver commenced to glow brightly, turned over and went into the sea, exploding on impact at 0136." Of his kill Flg Off Bert Miller[181] reported: "When patrolling off the French coast ten miles south of Le Tréport, two Divers came out at 4,000 feet, IAS 350mph. The first was selected for attack. I dived down and fired three one-second bursts of cannon and machine-gun from dead astern. The Diver was seen to hit the sea and explode."

456 (RAAF) Squadron (Mosquito XVII) Ford

Sqn Ldr B. Howard RAAF	HK323/RX-R	V-1	2304	Grid Q.8779
	HK323/RX-R	V-1	2314	Grid Q.7947

425thNFS USAAF (P-61) Ford

Capt F.V. Sartanowicz USAAF	42-5582	V-1	night	Channel

Capt Francis Sartanowicz sighted an approaching flying bomb and dived to attack. Closing to 600 feet, he saw strikes on the propulsion unit, whereupon the bomb dived into the Channel.

Another Do217M failed to return, an aircraft of 8/KG100 reportedly shot down by AA, but Flg Off John Smith[182] (with Flg Off Les Roberts) of 604 Squadron in MM465 claimed two Do217s, one of which was obviously Ltn Hans-Joachim Schildknecht's aircraft. The other may have been an aircraft from III/KG2 that crash-landed at Achmer. Smith's report revealed:

"I was told that an e/a was coming from port to starboard flying in a westerly direction. My navigator obtained a contact, range two-and-a-half miles. I lost height and turned towards the target, closing the range and obtained a visual at 4,000 feet. I closed in on the port side and slightly below the target, identifying it from 100 yards as a Do217. The e/a turned starboard and opened fire from the top turret, narrowly missing me. I fired a short burst and saw strikes on the fuselage. The e/a started to go down and I followed, firing another burst and seeing more strikes. The e/a continued to go down and eventually burst into flames. I saw it crash and explode in the Rennes area. Another contact was almost immediately made, crossing from port to starboard. A visual was obtained. I closed to 600 feet, identified the e/a as a Do217, my navigator confirming this with the aid of night glasses, fired two bursts from 600 feet dead astern, and saw strikes on the fuselage. I crossed to starboard side of e/a as it went down in a shallow dive, closed in and fired another burst from 100 yards. The e/a had smoke coming out of it and went down in a steep dive. I orbited, saw it crash and explode about ten miles east of the first target."

Tuesday 8 AUGUST

Dartford's balloons accounted for two more Divers. A Diver that was shot down at 0857 and crashed at Bidborough, near Tonbridge, was reported as carrying 24 1kg incendiary bombs.

316 (Polish) Squadron (Mustang III) Friston

Flt Lt T. Szymankiewicz PAF	FB396/SZ-F	V-1	0200	off Beachy Head

"Intercepted about 20 miles south-west of Beachy Head. Attacked from astern from 300 yards. Diver crashed in the sea."

616 Squadron (Meteor F.1) Manston

Difficulties with the 20mm Hispano cannon installation in the Meteor had been overcome, but in helping to eradicate the faults, pilots encountered further difficulties in attaining accurate speed control as Flg Off Mike Cooper recalled:

"The problem with the guns was caused by up draught in the under-fuselage ejector slots preventing the empty shell cases from being ejected. Modifications were made and the guns fired perfectly. However, during the gun failure investigations pilots were called upon to carry out many airborne gun-firing tests. A favourite area in which to test the guns were the mud flats in the Thames Estuary. We found that if we dived down to fire the guns at the same steep angle that we were used to with the Spitfire, the Meteor's speed became too great for comfort near the ground. The Meteor Is were not fitted with airbrakes thus we had to fly in at a much more shallow angle, almost parallel with the ground. Now unfortunately, the projectiles flung a shower of mud upwards and our speed took us right through it. Several Meteors returned with the metal of the engine nacelle, wings and fuselage dented or torn."

Night 8/9 AUGUST

A further 13 sorties were flown by III/KG3 crews. All returned safely to Rosières, the last landing shortly before midnight.

96 Squadron (Mosquito XIII) Ford

Sqn Ldr W.P. Green	MM568/ZJ-	V-1	2255	off Beachy Head

456 (RAAF) Squadron (Mosquito XVII) Ford

Sqn Ldr G.L. Howitt RAF	HK249/RX-B	V-1	2307	over land

"I attacked from dead astern, range 800-1,000 feet. In turning away after the attack, the target was lost but almost immediately there was an explosion on the ground. No other aircraft were in the vicinity."

FIU (Tempest V) Ford

Flg Off E.L. Williams (Rhod)	EJ630/ZQ-Y	V-1	night

425thNFS USAAF (P-61) Ford

1/Lt J.L. Thompson USAAF	42-5582	V-1	night

Flg Off Terry Wood/Flg Off R. Leafe from 604 Squadron in MM528 claimed another Do217 at 0010:

"The controller gave me westerly vectors and informed me that the target was crossing from starboard to port, range one mile. My navigator obtained a contact. I turned after the target, closed in quickly and obtained a visual at 2,000 feet above and slightly to port. The target was at 6,000 feet, weaving slightly at an estimated speed of 180 IAS. I closed to 500 feet and identified it as a Do217, my navigator confirming this with the aid of night glasses. I fired a short burst from 500 feet dead astern and saw strikes and a large explosion in the starboard engine. The e/a dived almost vertically to starboard and exploded on hitting the ground. S/Ldr Furse of 604 Squadron was also on patrol and saw the e/a go down and explode. It is known to be in the Brest Peninsula area."

Tragically, it seems that their victim was Albemarle P1501 of 296 Squadron rather than a Dornier. The Albemarle flown by Wt Off Bruce Stenning RAAF was engaged on a supply dropping SOE mission, having departed Brize Norton at 2205. The 27-year-old Australian from NSW and his RAF crew[183] were lost.

Wednesday, 9 AUGUST

A second Diver was reported to have been carrying 1kg incendiary bombs when it exploded over Lamberhurst following fighter attack. The American *Time* magazine continued its account of the impact of the Divers on Londoners in general, written mainly for the consumption of its readers back home:

> *"The 'Things' came over in increasing salvos. The number of robombs destroyed in southern England's elaborate and still-growing system of defense rose; but more and more got through. Londoners learned a few items of their defense-in-depth, heard that RAF fighter pilots, as they had in the bomb blitzes, were again doing a legendary job. London's defense is triple-decked, but most of its details are under strong censorship lock. The system goes to work almost at the instant of the robot bomb's launching. The course of each missile is plotted, its flight checked to the end. If the bomb reaches the English coast (many are reported crashing a few hundred yards from their take-off platforms), they are first attacked by a record concentration of ack-ack guns. If the robomb gets through, it runs into a wide belt of fighter planes – Spitfires, Mustangs, Mosquitoes, Tempests. Pilots of the day force are in readiness from an hour before dawn to an hour after dark. It is a dangerous business: the RAF rewards it by giving Distinguished Flying Crosses for every ten robombs downed [sic]. The highest individual score last week was 27 shot down, credited to Rene [sic] van Lierde, a Belgian. Fighters chase the 'Things' to the edges of a balloon barrage that would scare off a bomber pilot. But many a pilotless bomber gets through. They got through last week upon a hospital, upon a family of six in a backyard shelter, upon apartment houses, upon more shops and buses. Londoners, shaken but still full of understatement, talked mostly about the lucky misses. One bomb sailed close over a crowd at a band concert in Hyde Park, landed a scant 500 yards away, killed only two. The band went on playing 'On Steps of Glory.'"*

1 Squadron (Spitfire LFIXb) Lympne

Flt Lt J.J. Jarman	MK659/JX-	V-1 shared	0716	Hailsham area

"Attacked from astern and above from 400-100 yards and fired one burst of one-second. Diver went steeply down after attack and, as I broke away, I saw a Tempest go in to attack, but not seen to fire. Red 1 saw Diver explode on ground just south-west of Hailsham."

The Tempest was probably that flown by Flt Lt Appleton of 486(RNZAF) Squadron, who also claimed a Diver at 0716.

41 Squadron (Spitfire XII) Lympne

Flt Lt T. Spencer	MN875/EB-	V-1	0640	Wadham area
Flg Off H. Cook[184]	MB878/EB-	V-1	0645	Channel

315 (Polish) Squadron (Mustang III) Brenzett

Flt Lt K. Stembrowicz PAF	FB362/PK-A	V-1	0642	Staplehurst area

"Intercepted one mile east of Brenzett at 3,000 feet. First burst from 30° starboard, range 200 yards, then from line astern. Several short bursts from 400 yards. Diver slowed down – last burst fired from 200 yards. Diver banked to port and crashed north of Ashford-Tonbridge railway line, north of Staplehurst."

316 (Polish) Squadron (Mustang III) Friston

Wt Off T. Szymański PAF	HB835/SZ-P	V-1	2315	mid-Channel
	HB835/SZ-P	V-1	2317	mid-Channel
Flt Lt T. Szymankiewicz PAF	FB396/SZ-F	V-1	0845	off Hastings

322 (Dutch) Squadron (Spitfire XIV) West Malling

Flt Lt L.C.M. van Eendenburg	VL-I	V-1	2310

486 (RNZAF) Squadron (Tempest V) Newchurch

Flt Lt H.N. Sweetman RNZAF	EJ577/SA-F	V-1	0645	Hastings area
Flt Lt L.J. Appleton RNZAF	JN808/SA-N	V-1	0716 shared	Beachy Head area

Flt Lt Appleton probably shared Diver with Flt Lt Jarman of 1 Squadron.

91 Squadron was officially taken off anti-Diver operations and moved to Hawkinge to re-equip with Spitfire LFIXs under the command of Sqn Ldr Peter Bond. Squadron's score of V-1s now stood at 184, although two more would be shot down on 23 and 26 August. The Squadron's XIVs were handed over to **402 (RCAF) Squadron** in exchange for the latter's LFIXs, the Canadian unit commencing anti-Diver operations three days later.

Night 9/10 AUGUST
96 Squadron (Mosquito XIII) Ford

Sqn Ldr P.L. Caldwell	MM461/ZJ-	V-1	0417	Channel
				Grid.R5215

157 Squadron (Mosquito XIX) West Malling

Flt Lt E.J. Stevens	MM674/RS-T	V-1	0424	West Malling area

"Picked up near Dover. Dived from 8,000 feet. Short burst given from above, 300 yards range. Diver lost height to 1,000 feet before exploding on the ground five miles north-east of base."

418 (RCAF) Squadron (Mosquito VI) Middle Wallop

Flt Lt D.E. Forsyth RCAF	TH-	V-1	0444	off Dover

"Between 0401 and 0445, approximately 16 Divers were seen to leave the French coast. At 0444 a Diver crossed north of Bivalle at 9,000 feet. As the Mosquito was at 8,000 feet we climbed to 9,000 feet and orbited to await the Diver, which appeared to be travelling at slower speed and a much higher altitude than usual [an extraordinary height for a V-1]. Attacked from quarter astern with three two-seconds bursts. Strikes seen and Diver commenced to lose height rapidly. I then turned to chase second Diver and saw first explode on impact with the sea ten miles south of Dover."

456 (RAAF) Squadron (Mosquito XVII) Ford

Flt Lt K.A. Roediger RAAF	HK297/RX-V	V-1	0400	Grid R.1440

FIU (Tempest V) Ford

Flt Lt R.L.T. Robb	EJ598/ZQ- U	V-1	night	
	EJ598/ZQ-U	V-1	night	
Flt Lt C.B. Thornton	EJ555/ZQ-	V-1	night	

Thursday 10 AUGUST
A Diver fell in Patmos Road/Lothian Street, Kennington (SW9) at 2109, killing five people. Two Divers crashed in Ashford RD, the victims of fighters. Two more were victims of Dartford's balloons.

150 Wing (Tempest V) Newchurch

Wg Cdr R.P. Beamont	JN751/RB	V-1	pm	Tenterden area

3 Squadron (Tempest V) Newchurch

Flg Off R.H. Clapperton	EJ504/JF-	V-1	1410-1535
	EJ504/JF-	V-1	1410-1535
Flt Lt A.R. Moore	JN818/JF-	V-1	1615-1735
	JN818/JF-	V-1	1615-1735

129 Squadron (Mustang III) Brenzett

Flg Off L.G. Lunn	FB389/DV-M	V-1	2101	Appledore area
Flg Off J.E. Hartley	FB147/DV-K	V-1	c2110	Newchurch area
Plt Off E.W. Edwards	HB862/DV-G	V-1	c2130	Lympne area

Three Divers were destroyed, the first by Flg Off Les Lunn who intercepted over Lydd. Following his stern attack it rolled to starboard and crashed two miles north of Appledore. The second was intercepted by Flg Off Jim Hartley over Dymchurch at 3,000 feet. When hit, the Diver dropped to starboard and then pulled up, whereupon Hartley fired again and it crashed to ground two miles north-west of Newchurch. The third Diver spun down one mile east of Lympne aerodrome following Plt Off Eddie Edwards' close stern attack. This is believed to have been the missile that came down to earth more or less intact on The Firs Farm, Hawkinge.

322 (Dutch) Squadron (Spitfire XIV) West Malling

Flt Lt J.L. Plesman	VL-W	V-1	0438

501 Squadron (Tempest V) Manston

Sqn Ldr Gary Barnett RNZAF and 20 pilots from 501 were posted to 274 Squadron, also at Manston, which was re-equipping with Tempests, Barnett designated to take command when the incumbent CO, Sqn Ldr James 'Stocky' Edwards RCAF DFC DFM, completed his tour. To replace Barnett as CO of 501, newly promoted Sqn Ldr Joe Berry DFC arrived and was accompanied by five other experienced Tempest pilots from FIU, Flt Lts Jackson Robb and Cyril Thornton, Flg Offs R.G. 'Lucky' Lucas[185] and Ernie Williams, and the American Flt Off Bud Miller USAAF. 501 Squadron now became a night fighter unit operating solely against the flying bomb assault. Sqn Ldr Berry commented:

> "I was called away yesterday and received instruction about the role of 501 against the night intruders. It was said to me that these instructions came from the Prime Minister himself, to the effect that the Squadron must consider itself expendable and thus will take off to try to effect interception in any weather conditions, even though all other squadrons are grounded, this, because it was felt that the threat of the V-1 is so great that people on the ground must at least 'hear' fighters airborne whenever there is a V-1 warning. So the Squadron will get airborne even if it is quite impossible to make an interception."

The decision to use the Tempest in this role was thrust upon Air Marshal Hill due to the fact that most of the Diver activity now occurred at night. He later wrote:

> "For the fighters the chief problem arose out of the fact that all activity was now at night. There was a natural tendency to suppose that interception at night would be easier than in daylight simply because the tongue of flame emitted by the bomb was so conspicuous in the dark. Unfortunately, seeing the bomb was not enough: pilots had also to estimate its range, and this proved extremely difficult, as anyone who has tried to judge his distance from a light on a dark night will understand. Sir Thomas Merton, the distinguished spectro-scopist, designed a simple range-finder which eventually proved of great value to pilots; but individual skill and experience remained the biggest factor in overcoming this difficulty. Some pilots showed remarkable aptitude for this work, so baffling to many."

616 Squadron (Meteor F.1) Manston

| Flg Off T.D. Dean | EE2??/YQ- | V-1 | 2105 | Ashford area |

Flg Off Dixie Dean bagged his third V-1:

"While under Kingsley Control I saw a Diver coming west of Folkestone. The Diver was flying at 5,000 feet at an estimated speed of 200mph. Diving down from 6,000 feet, I intercepted the Diver as it came out of the gun belt north-west of Folkestone at 2105. I made two orbits of the Diver, then came in to attack. No other aircraft were seen in the vicinity at the time. Two bursts of cannon were fired, one one-second burst at 10° deflection, range 200 yards, and one two-seconds burst from line astern at 100 yards. Pieces were seen to fall off the wings and the Diver turned on its back and commenced to spin to ground. While the Diver was spinning down, two other aircraft believed to be Tempests, were seen to cannon the Diver, which was seen to crash and explode five miles north-west of Ashford."

Flg Off H.J. Moon was flying close by in another Meteor, some 2,000 yards behind, and confirmed that no other aircraft was in the vicinity when Dean attacked, but that two Tempests were seen to fire at the Diver as it spun to earth.

During the day Wg Cdr S.D. Felkin, on behalf of ADI (K), issued a revealing Air Ministry Intelligence Summary (No.554) to those in High Command who needed to know:

"A P/W [Prisoner of War] of 4/KG66 who paid a visit to Roye/Amy airfield on July 26, stumbled across the fact that a unit based at that airfield was equipped with He111s equipped for the launching of Flying Bombs against England. This P/W and his crew flew to Roye/Amy to have the aircraft compass swung. They arrived during the afternoon and immediately took their aircraft to the compass-swinging base. After a few minutes the Station Commander himself arrived on the scene and told the crew in no uncertain terms to take the aircraft out of sight into a blast shelter, so that no activity on the airfield should be disclosed to Allied aircraft. They were ordered to stay overnight and to have the compass swung at first light on the following morning. Later that same evening, P/W was at the flying control when a number of lorries arrived bringing 15 or 16 crews in flying kit. He spoke to some of those crews, most of whom were young and inexperienced, and was told that they were flying He111s against England. P/W and his crew ridiculed the idea, but the crews insisted that it was true but would give no further information.
    "On the following day P/W and his crew made enquiries of some of the ground staff, who told them that the He111 crews were in fact taking off from Roye/Amy with one Flying Bomb attached to each aircraft, and that sorties usually lasted about one hour. They learned that the Flying Bomb was attached in some way to the starboard side of the fuselage of the He111; the automatic pilot of the Flying Bomb, they were told, was started by the crew of the He111 whilst airborne. An air of secrecy pervaded the airfield and guards were posted at regular intervals; no activity, which could be seen from the air, took place during daylight. The P/W was able to look into some of the hangars on the east side of the airfield, and saw some large hand-drawn trucks with a low wheel-base, which he assumed were for transporting the Flying Bombs from storage to the aircraft."

Night 10/11 AUGUST

There was again a reduced effort by III/KG3, just 13 sorties being flown from Rosières without loss. A *Mistel* pilotless Ju88 bomb (5T+CK of 2/KG101) came down at Slade Bottom Farm, Bonley near Andover in Hampshire at 2335 after being launched against shipping in the Channel. The aircraft disintegrated when the warhead exploded, although the wrecked airframe allowed British technical experts to examine the construction of the missile. It transpired that one of the *Mistel* Messerschmitt pilots had become disorientated and, when he found that he was approaching the south coast of England, released his missile and made home for France.

96 Squadron (Mosquito XIII) Ford

Flt Lt F.R.L. Mellersh	MM577/ZJ-N	V-1	0055	off Beachy Head

Flt Lt Togs Mellersh's latest victim crashed into the sea 20 miles south-east of Beachy Head. Wg Cdr Crew's Mosquito NS985 suffered starboard engine failure while pursuing a flying bomb and he was obliged to return to Ford on one engine.

125 Squadron (Mosquito XVII) Middle Wallop

Sqn Ldr E.G. Barwell	HK355/VA-T	V-1	0050	off Beachy Head

Sqn Ldr Eric Barwell's combat report revealed:

"Left Middle Wallop at 2225 on anti-Diver patrol. At 0050 whilst patrolling ten miles south of Beachy Head, approximately ten Divers were seen. I attacked one at 1,000 feet, speed 330mph. A four-seconds burst, closing from 800 to 500 feet. The Diver caught fire, debris fell off and whilst I was still firing, the Diver exploded and fell into the sea."

Barwell later expanded on this report, when he recalled:

"Sometimes you could see the V-1s quite a long way away at night from the flames coming from their funny engines. I saw one or two but couldn't get near them; I then suddenly got an idea of how to do it. When the next one came along I had the advantage of height and turned at the right sort of time. These things were going faster than the Mosquito could fly straight and level, so one had to have height advantage to get near to them. I told my chaps that if you were going to attack a V-1 you had to close one eye on firing, and that if you saw any bits flying off the thing you had to break away immediately. Then if it blew up, it wouldn't bring you down with it. Having told my chaps all this, I saw this V-1 and got too excited. I didn't close one eye, started firing at it and was determined to get it down, which I did. It then blew up in front of me with a great 'Whoosh' and I was temporarily blinded, but managed to climb. I couldn't see any instruments, but was able to get control and landed with two pieces of shrapnel in the aircraft."

157 Squadron (Mosquito XIX) West Malling

Sqn Ldr J.H.M. Chisholm	MM674/RS-T	V-1	0047	over land

"Dived from 8,000 feet to Diver's height, then found Diver's speed was 240mph. Throttled back hard and allowed Diver to get to 300 yards. Short burst given. Jet motor and petrol tank exploded. Large burning mass explosion seen below cloud shortly after."

Friday 11 AUGUST

One person died in Stradella Road, Herne Hill (SE24) when a Diver fell at 0729. Three Divers crashed in Ashford RD following engagement by fighters and AA. A Diver that fell at 0705 in Cleveland Road, Welling, damaged 18 houses and injured 37 people including 13 seriously.

41 Squadron (Spitfire XII) Lympne

Flg Off J.F. Wilkinson	EN609/EB-	V-1 shared	1418	Brabourne area

Flg Off John Wilkinson shared his victim with a Mustang of 315 Squadron flown by Flt Sgt Bargielowski:

"At 10,000 feet informed by control of Diver approaching from sea. Dived to 3,000 feet and flew beside it to lose speed, positioned in behind, firing cannons and machine-guns. Saw strikes. Diver nosed down and exploded in a field near Brabourne at 1418. Mustang in vicinity. Half share."

129 Squadron (Mustang III) Brenzett

Flg Off G.R. Dickson RNZAF	FX924/DV-V	V-1	1300-1440	Ashford area
Flt Lt J.P. Bassett	FB130/DV-W	V-1 shared	1400-1545	Ashford area

The Diver intercepted by Flg Off Reg Dickson two miles east of Brenzett crashed 800 yards south of Ashford ALG. Flt Lt Bertie Bassett's target had apparently been damaged by AA fire and was trundling along at 250mph when he opened fire from astern. It rolled over and crashed five miles south-east of Ashford.

315 (Polish) Squadron (Mustang III) Brenzett

Flt Sgt J. Bargielowski PAF	FX878/PK-F	V-1 shared	1415	Folkestone area

Shared with Flg Off John Wilkinson of 41 Squadron.

130 Squadron with Spitfire XIVs moved from Tangmere to Lympne to take part in anti-V-1 patrols.

Night 11/12 AUGUST

A renewal of effort saw 25 sorties flown by III/KG3 Heinkels from Rosières between 2204 and 0213. There were no losses. But on the ground, two people were killed when a Diver impacted in Nunhead (SE15), causing much damage in the Ivydale Road/Inverton Road area. Dartford's balloons accounted for four Divers during the hours of darkness, two of which exploded in the air. Some damage was caused to properties but no casualties resulted. The guns at Folkestone and Hythe brought down 11 more before they reached the coast.

25 Squadron (Mosquito XVII) Coltishall

Flt Sgt G.T. Glossop	HK301/ZK-	V-1	0050-0350	Dover area
	HK301/ZK-	V-1	0050-0350	off Dover

Flt Sgt Glossop was on patrol south of Manston to Cap Gris Nez when a Diver was sighted:

> "I saw flying bomb at 1,500 feet travelling at approximately 150mph. Owing to slow speed of flying bomb I had to weave and do a couple of orbits to keep behind it. I opened fire from 1,000 feet, giving three short bursts and saw strikes. I then had to break away as I was near the gun area. At 0240 I saw two flying bombs at 1,000 feet, about two miles apart. I dived and opened fire from 1,200 feet on leading flying bomb but broke away on being informed by control that I was approaching gun area. I then attacked the second flying bomb but again had to break off before observing results. At 0305, when south of Dover, I saw a flying bomb at 1,000 feet, tracking at 240/300mph. I dived from 6,000 feet and opened fire from 1,000 feet. After the third burst flame went out and flying bomb dived into the sea and exploded. ROC confirms the first and fourth flying bombs which I attacked as destroyed."

85 Squadron (Mosquito XVII) West Malling

Wt Off W. Alderton	HK299/VY-C	V-1	0301	Maidstone area

> "Diver seen between Maidstone and Dungeness. Opened fire from above and astern. Petrol tank exploded and Diver crashed and exploded on the ground south of Maidstone."

This Diver was probably the one that crashed at Boughton Monchelsea at 0307, damaging two houses and slightly injuring one occupant.

96 Squadron (Mosquito XIII) Ford

Flt Lt F.R.L. Mellersh	MM577/ZJ-N	V-1	2255	off Beachy Head
Flt Lt I.A. Dobie	HK437/ZJ-	V-1	0115	Channel

Flt Lt Togs Mellersh reported: "Attacked Diver at 1,500 feet. Strikes seen. Light went out. Dived into sea 20 miles south-east of Beachy Head." This was followed by a second shot down by Flt Lt Ian Dobie: "Intercepted at 1,000 feet. Sparks seen after each of three bursts. Turned east, dived into the sea and exploded."

125 Squadron (Mosquito) Middle Wallop

Flt Lt G.E. Dunfee	HK291/VA-	V-1	2306	off Beachy Head
Flt Sgt K.W. Ramsay	HK240/VA-	V-1	0120	mid-Channel

Flt Lt Geoffrey Dunfee reported:

> "We were airborne from Middle Wallop at 2200 to patrol between Beachy Head and Dieppe. At approximately 2306 two Divers were seen to come from the Dieppe area. Intercepted one and orbited until Diver was in favourable position to attack. Dived from 9,000 feet and slightly astern. Diver at 2-3,000 feet at 300mph. Fired one two-seconds burst from dead astern at 600 yards. Strikes seen, engine flared up and pieces seen to fall off. Diver exploded on sea approximately 30 miles south-east of Beachy Head."

Flt Sgt Ramsay recorded:

> "At approximately 0115 a salvo of six Divers was picked up in mid-Channel at 2,000 feet. I came in dead astern and fired five two-seconds bursts at 300-400 yards range. Strikes seen and Diver turned to port. It glided down to the sea and exploded on impact 10 miles south of Beachy Head at 0120."

157 Squadron (Mosquito XIX) West Malling

Wt Off B. Miller	TA400/VY-J	V-1	0030-0330	
Wt Off S. Astley	MM674/RS-T	V-1	0125	off Maidstone

Wt Off Miller was using an 85 Squadron aircraft. Of his kill Wt Off Astley reported:

> "Dived from 8,000 feet. Two bursts given from 2,500 feet, closing in. Diver lost height and disappeared beneath cloud. Broke away and explosion seen beneath cloud. Confirmed by GCI."

418 (RCAF) Squadron (Mosquito VI) Middle Wallop

Flg Off S.P. Seid RCAF	TH-	V-1	0105	Channel
Flt Lt F.M. Sawyer RCAF	TH-	V-1	0112	Channel

Flg Off Dave McIntosh had this to say about the third Diver shot down by his pilot, Flg Off Sid Seid:

> "We got a V-1 so fast I didn't have time to be scared. We were just leaving the English coast for our patrol station over France and the Channel when Sid spotted a Doodlebug coming at us. We were on a collision course. Sid pressed the firing button and yanked the stick to starboard at the same time. The V-1 exploded and none of the debris hit us. 'They'll never believe it,' I said. 'Sure they will. I'll tell 'em you plotted it all the way across on your magic box and gave me the angle and time to shoot.' 'But the Gee box can't do that.' 'Hell, the other pilots will never know that.'"[186]

456 (RAAF) Squadron (Mosquito XVII) Ford

Flt Lt G.R. Houston RAAF	HK264/RX-T	V-1	2301	Channel (Grid R.31)
Sqn Ldr B. Howard RAAF	HK282/RX-L	V-1	0308	Channel

501 Squadron (Tempest V) Manston

Flt Lt E.L. Williams (Rhod)	EJ555/SD-Y	V-1	2210-0005
Flt Lt C.B. Thornton	EJ558/SD-U	V-1	2315-2330
	EJ558/SD-U	V-1	2315-2330
	EJ558/SD-U	V-1	2315-2330
Flg Off R.G. Lucas	EJ553/ZQ-L	V-1	2335-0135
Flt Off B.F. Miller USAAF	EJ584/SD-Q	V-1	2350-0140
	EJ584/SD-Q	V-1	2350-0140
	EJ584/SD-Q	V-1	2350-0140

The FIU detachment soon got into its stride and brought down eight flying bombs in a short space of time. Flt Lt Cyril Thornton's score now stood at seven Divers. The

American Flt Off Bud Miller raised his score to six.

Saturday 12 AUGUST

274 Squadron at Detling, newly equipped with Tempest Vs, flew its first anti-V-1 patrols during the day, albeit without success. The pilots had approached the introduction of the Tempest with some trepidation, as recalled by the CO Sqn Ldr 'Stocky' Edwards DFC DFM RCAF :

> "My pilots were a little anxious about flying the new Tempest. However, the first aircraft was delivered by the Air Transport Auxiliary, and the pretty young lady who piloted it powdered her nose and put lipstick on before she got out of the cockpit, so they decided that the Tempest was not that difficult to fly."

A similar experience to that had heartened the pilots of 501 Squadron when they had received their first Tempest. Sqn Ldr Edwards flew only eight anti-Diver patrols, without success, before his tour expired, and Sqn Ldr Gary Barnett RNZAF took command.

From **96 Squadron** Sqn Ldr Peter Green DFC moved to **219 Squadron** to take command.

Following the failure of the USAAF's Operation 'Aphrodite', the USN attempted to step in with its own version of a flying bomb – the similarly guided US Navy PB4Y-1 Liberator – which was to be despatched to strike at Mimoyecques. Having successfully taken off with Lt Joseph Kennedy USN[187] and Lt Wilford Willy USN on board, the drone (T-11/32271) suddenly disintegrated while flying at 2,000 feet over the Blythe estuary close to Southwold, apparently due to an electrical fault causing premature detonation. Both pilots were killed and damage caused to more than 150 houses. The crew aboard the accompanying controlling aircraft witnessed the awful scene:

> "[Lt] Harry Wherry's mother ship was about 400 yards behind the drone and several hundred feet above it, and since [Lt John] Anderson was still controlling from the other plane, several members of Wherry's crew were watching through the pilot's windshield. They saw the drone begin a slow turn to the left, but just as the left wing dipped a few degrees below the horizontal, there was a blinding flash of light, and the bright afternoon sky became incandescent. Where the drone had been there was now a yellow nucleus edged in smoke, with fire and flame going straight up and down from it, like a pair of giant Roman candles. In a split second the nucleus had turned into a greenish-white cylinder of fire, slightly compressed in the middle like an hourglass and flattened out on top. The column burned brightly, almost as vividly as a welder's torch seen at close range, and just as suddenly it was gone, leaving black smoke streaming away in the wind and a few small fires in the wood below."[188]

Night 12/13 AUGUST

An all-out effort was made by III/KG3, it crews flying 36 sorties from Rosières, some probably flying two missions. All returned safely. A serious incident occurred at 0130 with the explosion of a bomb in Knights Hill Square, West Norwood (SE27), which killed eight residents. Peckham (SE15) received a bomb at 0210 that killed two people in Scilla Road/Claude Road. Elsewhere, in rural Suffolk, twenty-five houses received severe blast damage in the pretty village of Cockfield near Bury St Edmunds following the impact of a flying bomb at 0620. The Diver hit the top of a tree, breaking off the warhead, which exploded but did not destroy the rest of the missile. Surprisingly there were no casualties.

85 Squadron (Mosquito XVII) West Malling
Wg Cdr H.deC.A. Woodhouse   MM632/VY-E   V-1   0440 (FTR)   Channel

Sqn Ldr B.A. Burbridge	HK349/VY-R	V-1	0610	off Maidstone
Flt Lt P.A. Searle	HK120/VY-P	V-1	0631	Channel

Wg Cdr Paddy Woodhouse DFC AFC again borrowed an 85 Squadron Mosquito (MM632/VY-E) to carry out an anti-Diver patrol during which he shot down a Diver but FTR. He and his navigator Flt Lt Walter Weir, a 29-year-old from Glasgow, were both killed. Sqn Ldr Branse Burbridge shot his victim into the sea: "Dived from 7,000 feet. Short burst given from 1,000 feet. Diver caught fire and dived towards ground. Did not see explosion but confirmed by ROC as ten miles south of Maidstone." Twenty minutes later, Flt Lt Searle got another: "Dived from 6,000 feet. Short burst from 1,200 feet. Diver caught fire and dived into sea eight miles from coast."

96 Squadron (Mosquito XIII) Ford

Flt Lt W.J. Gough	HK479/ZJ-	V-1	2255	Channel
	HK479/ZJ-	V-1 damaged	c2300	Channel
Flt Sgt J. Gallivan	HK433/ZJ-	V-1 damaged	0025-0310	Channel
Flt Lt N.S. Head	MM460/ZJ-	V-1	0345	Channel

418 (RCAF) Squadron (Mosquito VI) Middle Wallop

Sqn Ldr R. Bannock RCAF	HR147/TH-Z	V-1	2300	near Boulogne
Sqn Ldr R.G. Gray RCAF	HR148/TH-B	V-1	0120	off Hastings
Flg Off H.E. Miller RAF	TH-	V-1	0243	off Le Tréport
	TH-	V-1	0407	off Le Tréport

Sqn Ldr Russ Bannock opened the scoring for the night with an unusual kill:

"Five Divers were seen coming out of the Dieppe area. Fired all cannon from approximately 500 yards astern. Strikes seen and Diver slowed up, dropping right wing several times then righting itself. Just before reaching the Gun Belt, the Diver turned on to 120°, flew back to France and crashed on land near Boulogne, after I had followed and fired two bursts of machine-gun."

Sqn Ldr Ross Gray got the second, shooting it into the sea ten miles south-east of Hastings. The final two fell to Flt Lt Bert Miller:

"At 0243 attacked Diver which left Le Tréport at 4,000 feet. Fired half-second burst from 100 yards, Fuel tank exploded and Diver went into the sea exploding on impact 22 miles north-west of Le Tréport. At 0407 chased a Diver from Dieppe on similar course. Fired remaining ammunition. Reduced speed to 180 IAS and climbed to 6,000 feet. Diver climbed past Mosquito to 7,500 feet, speed about 160mph. The jet spluttered, stopped and Diver went down into the sea, exploding 40 miles north-west of Le Tréport."

456 (RAAF) Squadron (Mosquito XVII) Ford

Flt Lt R.G. Pratt RAAF	HK303/RX-	V-1	0145	Channel
Sqn Ldr G.L. Howitt RAF	HK249/RX-B	V-1	0352	exploded in mid-air

Flt Lt Pratt reported: "At 0145 attacked from dead astern, range 1,000 feet, a flying bomb at 1,000 feet, speed 350mph. It exploded on the sea at R.1805." Two hours later, Sqn Ldr Geoff Howitt got another: "Attacked from dead astern a flying bomb, height 1,500 feet, speed 250mph. It exploded in the air in Grid Q.94."

501 Squadron (Tempest V) Manston

Sqn Ldr J. Berry	EJ590/SD-L	V-1	0123	Sandhurst area
	EJ590/SD-L	V-1	0613	West Malling area

During the hours of darkness patrols were kept up. Sqn Ldr Berry shot down two Divers, one on each patrol:

"I was on patrol under Watling Control when I saw Diver coming in direction of Rye at 2,000 feet at 400mph. I immediately closed in and from 150 yards astern I opened fire. I saw strikes on the motor and the Diver crashed four miles north of Sandhurst at 0123."

This was probably the bomb that came down in the churchyard of the medieval St Laurence Church at Hawkhurst, causing considerable damage to the church and its windows. Some 25 houses and shops were damaged and three residents slightly injured, as recalled by Mr W. Goodwin[189]: "A Diver shot down by a fighter landed in the churchyard – the church, the vicarage, and the graveyard were badly damaged. As well, three shops in the village and some 25 houses were also damaged." Berry was up again at 0410:

> "On my second patrol under Watling Control the weather at base was reported as raw. I flew over, headed to avert to Ford and on the way there trade was reported coming over Dungeness. I saw one Diver and turned in behind it. Height was 1,600 feet, speed 190mph. I fired two bursts from dead astern, range 150-300 yards. No results. Third burst from 250 yards and Diver exploded in the air. Position approximately six miles south-west of West Malling at 0613 (claim is in daylight)."

Sunday 13 AUGUST
274 Squadron lost its first Tempest during the day when EJ637 flew into a hillside north-west of Elham near Canterbury early in the morning in poor visibility. 21-year-old Flt Sgt Royston Ryman from Cardiff was killed.

The Americans were planning to introduce their own guided bomb at this time, known as the GB-4. In theory two of these radio-controlled 2,000lb bombs, each fitted with a small television receiver in the nose, were to be carried on racks beneath a specially modified B-17G, but low-resolution pictures and inferior radio equipment caused much disappointment and poor results. Nonetheless, the B-17 (42-40043) with a crew from the 388thBG, set out to attack Le Havre, accompanied by another B-17 carrying five American engineers and technicians to observe the results, and also a P-38 and a Mosquito PRXVI (MM370) to photograph the results. Unfortunately, the latter approached too close to the GB-4 after it had been released, and was brought down by shrapnel and blast from the explosion. Both GB-4s missed the target by almost a mile. Another attempt would be made a week later using the same aircraft to attack the U-boat base at La Pallice, again without success, while a third attempt was abandoned due to cloud cover, after which the project was called off due to unreliable equipment.[190]

Night 13/14 AUGUST
III/KG3 crews flew only 19 sorties this night, almost half the number of the previous night. All returned safely but Rosières was about to be evacuated in the face of the Allied advance. The aircraft were ferried to Venlo (Holland) and the ground personnel followed. It would be a week before operations resumed. Victims of fighters fell at Mereworth, Ulcombe and Staplehurst.

96 Squadron (Mosquito XIII) Ford

Flt Lt F.R.L. Mellersh	Spitfire IX MH473	V-1	pm	
	Spitfire IX MH473	V-1	pm	
Wt Off W.A. McLardy RAAF	MM495/ZJ-	V-1	0048	Channel
Flt Lt W.J. Gough	HK438/ZJ-	V-1	0425	Channel

Flt Lt Togs Mellersh again borrowed Spitfire IX MH473 from NFDW and repeated his performance of the previous week, shooting down two more Divers. Two more fell to Mosquito crews, Wt Off Bill McLardy getting the first: "Numerous strikes seen. Petrol blew up and Diver exploded on the sea. Seen by F/O Williams of 456 Squadron." Flt Lt Bill Gough got the second: "After one burst Diver lost height gradually. Further burst given and Diver exploded on sea." The Squadron lost another crew, however, when MM452 veered across the runway on take-off, went through a blister hangar and crashed into a brick wall, where it caught fire outside the Station HQ. Both Flt Sgt Leslie Read and his navigator Wt Off Bill Gerrett were killed. The cause of the accident was not determined.

418 (RCAF) Squadron (Mosquito VI) Middle Wallop

Flg Off S.P. Seid RCAF	TH-	V-1	2257	Channel
Flt Lt L.E. Evans RCAF	TH-	V-1	2310	Channel

Flt Lt Evans: "At 2310, when ten miles south of Beachy Head, I made diving stern attack from 300 yards on Diver, with one one-second burst. Diver went straight into the sea and exploded."

456 (RAAF) Squadron (Mosquito XVII) Ford

Flg Off S.J. Williams RAAF	HK282/RX-L	V-1	0047	Channel

Crews reported sighting one flying bomb at 400 feet and two at 8,000 feet, one of which was shot down by AA fire. Flg Off Stuart Williams made his interception at 1,000 feet: "It glided down and exploded on the sea just off the coast in Grid R.2520. No AA fire seen at the time."

501 Squadron (Tempest V) Manston

Sqn Ldr J. Berry }	EJ590/SD-L	V-1	2255	Sevenoaks area
Flg Off R.L.T. Robb }	EJ598/SD-H			
Flg Off R.L.T. Robb	EJ558/SD-U	V-1	0300-0435	

Sqn Ldr Joe Berry scored another, shared with Flg Off Jackson Robb:

> "While on patrol north of Hastings under Watling Control, a Diver was seen approaching at 1,800 feet at 330mph. I closed in and fired from 250-50 yards astern. Twice I saw strikes on the Diver. I had to break away because of balloons when the Diver was at 1,200 feet travelling at 280mph. The Diver crashed and exploded at 2255 near Sevenoaks."

On a second patrol Robb shot down another, his tenth.

Monday 14 AUGUST

AA guns based on the Kent coast shot down a Diver at 1410 but, tragically, it fell on Twiss Road, Hythe, killing five and injuring a further 17 of whom five suffered serious injuries. By now, batteries of the newly arrived US 127thAAA Regiment were operational, one battalion located at Dover accounting for 56 definite kills in the coming weeks.

41 Squadron (Spitfire XII) Lympne

Flg Off Peter Graham (MB831) had a nerve-wracking experience when he intercepted a flying bomb early in the morning. Having dived almost vertically from 12,000 feet to get onto its tail, he came in behind it at 250 yards and the Spitfire was promptly thrown onto its back by the force of the flying bomb's slipstream. After recovery, he attempted to get astern by diving and then climbing up. Following a short burst, the Spitfire was again troubled by the slipstream. On closing in for the kill for a third time, the bomb serenely entered the balloon barrage and escaped.

In a break from anti-Diver patrols, the Mustangs of **316 (Polish) Squadron** carried out a Ranger operation during which Sqn Ldr Bohdan Arct shot down a Bf109, Flg Off Antoni Cholajda claimed a Fw190 and a Bf109, and Wt Off Józef Feruga a Bf109.

25 Squadron was instructed to transfer Flt Lts Keith Panter and R.J. Lilwall to **501 Squadron** to convert to Tempests for night flying operations, while Flg Off Gilbert Wild and Flt Lt Horry Hansen transferred from **68 Squadron**. **274 Squadron** moved over from Detling to West Malling to continue anti-Diver patrols.

Night 14/15 AUGUST
The AA guns at Folkestone and Hythe were very busy during the night, sharing the destruction of 16 Divers, all of which fell into the sea before reaching the coast.

25 Squadron (Mosquito XVII) Coltishall
Flt Lt J.S. Limbert	HK357/ZK-	V-1	2335-0300	off Dover
Flg Off J.F.R. Jones	HK243/ZK-G	V-1	0325-0610	off Dover

The Mosquitos scored two kills during the night, the first by Flt Lt Limbert who departed Coltishall at 2335:

> "I was patrolling at 9,000 feet south of Dover and saw a salvo of eight flying bombs leaving the enemy coast. I dived and attacked flying bomb, which was at 1,000 feet and tracked at 360mph. I attacked from dead astern, closing from 1,100 feet to 600 feet and fired bursts of two-seconds. I saw strikes and flying bomb dived into sea and exploded. I attacked another at 2,000 feet, tracking at approximately 400mph, but could not get into effective range."

Flg Off Jones shot down the second at 0440:

> "I was patrolling at 9,000 feet off Dover and saw flying bomb at 2,500 feet, speed 370mph. I turned to starboard, dived and attacked flying bomb from 20° port, opening fire with two-seconds burst from 3,000 feet. The light went out immediately and the flying bomb dived into the sea and exploded."

85 Squadron (Mosquito XIX) West Malling
Plt Off L.J. York	MM648/VY-G	V-1	0030-0320	Channel
Flt Lt T.W. Redfern	TA400/VY-J	V-1	0400-0610	Channel

96 Squadron (Mosquito XIII) Ford
Sqn Ldr A. Parker-Rees	HK525/ZJ-	V-1	0238	Channel
Flt Lt F.R.L. Mellersh	MM577ZJ-/N	V-1	0417	Channel (Grid R.8022)
	MM577/ZJ-N	V-1	0430	Channel (Grid R.6342)

Sqn Ldr Parker-Rees engaged a Diver at 1,000 feet over the Channel and shot it down into the sea, whereupon it exploded (Grid R.3722). Flt Lt Togs Mellersh was up again in the NFDW's Spitfire IX but had no luck on this occasion. Later he flew a second sortie, this time in his Mosquito, again with Wg Cdr R.B. Cawood from Group HQ, trying out a new range-finder. He shot down two Divers, both of which exploded on hitting the sea.

157 Squadron (Mosquito XIX) West Malling
Flt Lt R.D. Doleman	MM678/RS-A	V-1	0230	West Malling area

> "Dived on it near coast. Two short bursts given 400 yards range. Diver caught fire near base, crashing someway inside balloons."

456 (RAAF) Squadron (Mosquito XVII) Ford
Plt Off R.D. Hodgen RAAF	HK302/RX-	V-1	0207	Channel

Plt Off Butch Hodgen reported: "Climbed sharply to 4,000 feet then vertically dived to 1,500 feet. Fired but broke away without seeing it crash. One seen by Plt Off York of 85 Squadron to explode at same time and place."

605 Squadron (Mosquito) Manston

Flg Off B.G. Bensted	HJ799/UP-L	V-1	0235	off Calais

"Off at 0200. During patrol off Dutch islands no Divers seen, but when we returned to base Diver activity was observed from Calais area. We made an attack on one Diver flying at 1,500 feet from astern at 200 yards. Many strikes were seen and bits flew off. The flying bomb then dived and exploded on impact with the sea at 0235."

854 Squadron FAA (Avenger I) Hawkinge

Lt(A) A.F. Voak RNVR	FN854/G	V-1	0210	off Dunkirk

The crew of the FAA Avenger, on an anti-shipping patrol, sighted a Diver at approximately 2,000 feet, speed 300 knots. Lt(A) Allan Voak fired several long bursts with front guns and flying bomb exploded in the air.

He177s of 2/KG40 were operating from Schwäbisch Hall. North of Barfleur Hptm Stolle's F8+AN (550077) was attacked by a 422ndNFS P-61, at which the tail gunner Uffz Fabinger got in a telling burst. With one engine on fire, the P-61, 42-4591 flown by 2/Lt Al Gordon and 2/Lt Creel H. Morrison, regained its French base but nosed over on landing and was written-off. The crew survived unhurt, as Al Gordon recalled:

"On my eleventh mission we were doing a night patrol over the English Channel, and we got a bogey. So they put us on a heading to intercept, and pretty soon my RO says, 'I got him.' And we called GCI, and said, 'We have him.' We closed in, and my RO would tell me, gentle port, gentle starboard, increase your speed, decrease your speed. And he brought me in. It was a Heinkel 177 bomber. Unfortunately he saw me before I saw him, and his tail gunner cut loose, knocking out my starboard engine, which immediately caught fire. Some of the enemy fire entered the top of my canopy, and lodged in and exploded the hydraulic reservoir just above and behind my head. That knocked out part of the hydraulic system. Fortunately the P-61 controls didn't operate hydraulically; they were operated by cables. So the hydraulic failure didn't affect the flyability of the plane. My first reaction was complete shock – they didn't tell us about this! Then all the training kicked in and I proceeded to function. I was scared, of course. I'd have to be a liar to say I wasn't. But I was so damn busy, trying to fly the aircraft at that point that I really didn't have much time to think about it.

"But I knew that I was in trouble, and I was trying to work my way out of it. I could communicate with my RO over the radio, but in hindsight I should have talked more, because he didn't know what the hell I was doing, and he was scared to death. So here I am, a flamer, 50 miles out over the English Channel. I feathered the starboard engine right away – I did the right thing there. And I dove it a little bit to gain speed, and put the fire out. My radio was still somewhat operational, so GCI vectored me back. My guess is that it might have been fifteen minutes before we reached the airfield, but it seemed like a long, long time. I came in on one engine, and I lowered my landing gear, not realizing that my nose wheel had been shot out from under me. Considering everything, it was a good landing, except that when it came time for the nose wheel to drop, there was no nose wheel. So I skidded on the front of the plane to a stop. Nobody was hurt, but I learned a valuable lesson on that mission. Never come in for an attack from the rear, shallow – so the tail gunner can see you. Rather you synchronize speed and heading well below the bogey, then identify, drop back, and shoot. The important thing is to live beyond an experience like this and of course learn from it. One tends to be a little more cautious, increasing one's chances of lasting through the war."

Tuesday 15 AUGUST

The guns at Folkestone shot down 15 Divers and Hythe accounted for seven more, all falling harmlessly into the sea. Fighters brought down four Divers in Ashford RD, two of these having exploded in mid-air. Fighters shot down one Diver at about 0900 that crashed near Eastwood House, Ulcombe, injuring two. At 1835, a Diver exploded in the grounds of Pinhoe Hall near RAF Stradishall, a moated house standing on high ground to the south of Hundon. The house and outbuildings were extensively damaged but no one was injured. During the evening a Diver fell on a big house in Shoot-up-Hill (NW2) near to Kilburn Underground Station. One witness recalled:

> "The flying bomb made a direct hit on the house. This building entirely disappeared. Houses very close were so badly damaged as to be uninhabitable, and the wing of one had to be demolished. Other houses within a very considerable circle were damaged to the extent of broken windows, stripped of tiles, and other minor damage. Windows were broken in buildings more than half a mile away."

There were many casualties and dead (13) and injured people were dug out of the wreckage; three of those recovered later died from their injuries[191].

41 Squadron (Spitfire XII) Lympne

Flg Off C.J. Malone RCAF	EN622/EB-	V-1 shared	0920	Ashford area
Wt Off P.T. Coleman	MB875/EB-G	V-1	0920	Ashford area
Flt Lt R.P. Harding	MB795/EB-	V-1	1845	Ivychurch area

Flg Off Jack Malone intercepted a Diver as it left the gun belt and with the aid of a Mustang, (Flt Lt Kleimeyer of 129 Squadron) it was shot down and crashed two miles north-west of Ashford. Wt Off Pat Coleman shot down another, as noted in his diary: "I shot one down near Ashford. It explodes in the air and I easily pull clear of the explosion – fired from 250 yards." He was up again at 1720 as No.2 to Flt Lt Ross Harding. No sightings were made during their patrol but on returning to base, Harding spotted a bomb, which he attacked with a two-seconds burst, following which it dived to ground just north of Ivychurch, where it exploded in a field.

56 Squadron (Tempest V) Newchurch

Flt Sgt J.S. Ferguson	EJ536/US-R	V-1	evening	

129 Squadron (Mustang III) Brenzett

Flt Lt R.G. Kleimeyer RNZAF (Aus)	FB137/DV-C	V-1 shared	0920	Ashford area

Intercepted near Hythe at 3,000 feet, the Diver caught fire when attacked from astern and crashed two miles north-west of Ashford. Apparently shared with Flg Off Malone of 41 Squadron.

274 Squadron (Tempest V) West Malling

Flt Lt O.E. Willis	EJ628/JJ-	V-1	1845	Sittingbourne area

Flt Lt Willis opened the Squadron's score when he shot down a flying bomb during the early evening: "Diver was picked up over Dover and attacked from 300 yards range from astern, after which it was seen to be on fire. Shortly afterwards it dived into sandy soil beside a narrow creek two miles north of Sittingbourne."

306 (Polish) Squadron (Mustang III) Brenzett

Wt Off W. Nowoczyn PAF	UZ-V	V-1	0925	Ashford area

Wt Off Witold Nowoczyn scored his fifth and final kill following the interception of a Diver north-west of Brenzett airfield. He attacked from 300/250 yards whereupon the jet unit caught fire and the Diver crashed four miles west of Ashford.

315 (Polish) Squadron (Mustang III) Brenzett

Flt Sgt J. Donocik PAF	FB162/PK-D	V-1	1424	Sandgate area

Flt Sgt J. Bargielowski PAF	FZ143/PK-V	V-1	1558	Hawkinge area

350 (Belgian) Squadron (Spitfire XIV) Friston

Sgt H.A. Boels (Belg)	RM748/MN-	V-1	0904	Ashford area
Flg Off R. Vanderveken (Belg)	RM655/MN-			

486 (RNZAF) Squadron (Tempest V) Newchurch

Wt Off O.D. Eagleson RNZAF	EJ635/SA-T	V-1 shared	0900	Newchurch area
Flg Off R.J. Cammock RNZAF	EJ528/SA-P	V-1	1409	Rye area
Flt Lt K.G. Taylor-Cannon RNZAF	JN808/SA-N	V-1	1548	

Flt Lt Taylor-Cannon's victim possibly crashed near White Lodge, Boughton Monchelsea, slightly injuring one person.

616 Squadron (Meteor F.1) Manston

Flt Sgt Donald Gregg, a 21-year-old recent addition to the Squadron, was killed attempting to land EE226[192] at Great Chard ALG after abortive attempt to fly to High Halden, from where he was to join the Readiness Section. He was the RAF's first jet fatality.

Night 15/16 AUGUST

25 Squadron (Mosquito) Coltishall

Flt Lt A.E. Marshall DFM	HK243/ZK-G	V-1	0530	off South Foreland

"I was patrolling south of South Foreland at 8,000 feet and saw three flying bombs, two at 800 feet, the other at 2/3,000 feet, at approximately five-minute intervals. At 0530 I saw another at 2/3,000 feet. I dived and attacked this, opening fire from approximately 300 yards range. After first burst weapon [radar] went u/s and it was difficult to judge range effectively. As I turned away from the attack, I saw the flying bomb explode in the air."

68 Squadron (Mosquito XVII) Castle Camps

Flt Lt A.B. Harvey	WM-Y	V-1		
	WM-Y	V-1		

This brace raised Flt Lt Len Harvey's score to four, with his fifth following three weeks later.

85 Squadron (Mosquito XIX) West Malling

Capt T. Weisteen (Norw)	VY-B	V-1	0716	off Folkestone

The Norwegian pilot intercepted a Diver about 14 miles south-east of Folkestone:

"Dived from 5,000 feet and attacked from above and astern from 1,800 feet down to 1,400 feet. Diver burst into flames and crashed into the sea three to four miles south-east of Folkestone."

501 Squadron (Tempest V) Manston

Sqn Ldr J. Berry	EJ590/SD-L	V-1	0400-0600	West Malling
	EJ590/SD-L	V-1	0400-0600	
Flt Lt C.B. Thornton	EJ558/SD-U	V-1 damaged		near Hastings

Sqn Ldr Berry used only 60 rounds of 20mm to destroy both flying bombs. One of his victims crashed on West Malling airfield, the explosion breaking many windows but did not cause any casualties. Except for short intervals when roaming balloons made flying dangerous, patrols were kept up during the hours of darkness. Flt Lt Cyril Thornton chased a Diver from Hastings to the balloon barrage. He fired at it and saw strikes but the Diver was apparently unharmed and went on its way.

605 Squadron (Mosquito VI) Manston

Flt Lt J.G. Musgrave	MM429/UP-H	V-1	2332	off Coxyde

MM429/UP-H	V-1	2332	off Coxyde

The second of Flt Lt John Musgrave's two kills was claimed destroyed in unusual circumstances, a total of only 12 cannon shells being fired during the action:

> "Patrolled uneventfully off Dutch and Belgian coasts until 2328, when we spotted two Divers travelling very close together at 500 feet a few miles north of Coxyde. We were flying a north-east course at this time and immediately turned to port and dived down from 6,000 feet to 500 feet and opened fire from slightly above and astern. During this time the navigator had noticed the two Divers were flying exceptionally close together – a matter of a few yards apart – on the same course and were travelling about 380-400mph. I fired from 200 yards range and selected the starboard one as my target – strikes were seen after about a-third-of-a-second burst and Diver lost height and dived into the sea, exploding on impact. The navigator had been watching the port Diver and immediately the cannon shells struck the other Diver, the one under observation wobbled and definitely tilted over to port – then disappeared completely."

Following the Allied landings in Southern France, Do217s of III/KG100 approached the beaches and released the Hs293s at the massed transport vessels offshore, one striking *LST282* off St Raphael. The craft caught fire with the loss of some 40 US personnel. Three of the attacking Dorniers were shot down. Two nights later, five Do217s attempted to carry out a repeat attack, but two aircraft aborted the mission and one jettisoned its Hs293. The remaining two released their missiles and two near misses were claimed including one by the crew of 6N+DR equipped with a Fritz-X.

Wednesday 16 AUGUST

A serious incident occurred in Deptford (SE8) at 0718, when a Diver fell in Grove Street/Dockyard – the seventh Diver to fall in this area – killing seven people. Another came down at the junction of High Street and Hoe Street, Walthamstow (E17), killing 17 and seriously injuring 62. Nine more were killed in Brockley (SE4) as a result of an explosion in Endwell Road at 1832. Fighters and AA brought down seven Divers in Ashford RD during the day. A Diver shot down by a fighter at 0800 crashed on the parish church at Little Chart, two miles south of Charing, Kent. Another, hit by a fighter, crashed at Detling aerodrome, causing damage to the control tower and slightly injuring three airmen. Six of the fighters' victims crashed in the Maidstone/Malling/Hollingbourne area in a four-hour period, injuring four at Plaxtol, two at Aylesford, and one at Harrietsham. Kent coastal gunners had another bumper day, Hythe reporting 30 Divers shot down into the sea with fighters getting another six just offshore, while Folkestone gunners scored a dozen kills. But not all gunsites were chalking up kills. The experiences of a Bofors unit at Tenterden was nothing short of discouraging but, as one gunner, recalled:

> "Before many hours passed the flying-bombs were coming over in bulk – three, four, five or six in the sky at one time. We never scored a hit. When the bomb went out of range and we disengaged, one gunner would point his clenched fist in the air and shout 'Bastard!' at the bomb and immediately every man on the site, including the officer, would follow suit. Then we would all look at each other and laugh like hell … our way of letting off steam."[193]

150 Wing (Tempest V) Newchurch

Wg Cdr R.P. Beamont	JN751/RB	V-1	pm	Ashford area

3 Squadron (Tempest V) Newchurch

Plt Off H.R. Wingate	EJ549/JF-	V-1	1740-1855	
Flt Lt R. van Lierde (Belg)	EJ557/JF-	V-1	1915-2045	
Flt Sgt R.W. Cole	JN768/JF-F	V-1	1945-2010	West Malling airfield

Flt Sgt Bob Cole:

> "I chased this one and I couldn't hit the blasted thing for some reason. I got up to West Malling aerodrome. Then I fired and hit it and I saw it go down, and it was spinning right over the aerodrome. I thought bloody hell what a place to shoot it down. It went in between the sergeants' and officers' mess. It didn't kill anybody."

Wg Cdr John Wray DFC from HQ flew an anti-Diver patrol in JN815 during the morning, accompanied by Wt Off Ralph Hassell as his No.2, but no Divers were sighted.

41 Squadron (Spitfire XII) Lympne

Flt Sgt V.J. Rossow RAAF	MB857/EB-	V-1	1650	Ashford area
Flg Off P.B. Graham	MB831/EB-	V-1	1820	Wrotham area

Flt Sgt Bill Rossow reported strikes and starboard wing broke off, following which the Diver spun in five miles north-west of Ashford. During his patrol Flg Off Peter Graham saw flares ten miles north-west of Tenterden from 12,000 feet and dived down to investigate. He saw a flying bomb being attacked by a Meteor and two Tempests but considered they were out of range, so he dived down beneath them as they broke away and pulled up behind the bomb. He fired two short bursts, which caused its starboard wing to fall off and the bomb was last seen spinning down near Wrotham. He did not see it crash as he had to pull up to avoid balloons.

56 Squadron (Tempest V) Newchurch

Flt Sgt L. Jackson	EJ547/US-A	V-1	0645-0755	Headcorn area
Plt Off I.N. MacLaren	EJ536/US-R	V-1	1645-1800	
Flt Lt D.V.G. Cotes-Preddy	EJ721/US-C	V-1	1845-2015	

129 Squadron (Mustang III) Brenzett

Wt Off R.L. Thomas RAAF	FB138/DV-X	V-1 shared	1955	Marden area

130 Squadron (Spitfire XIV) Lympne

Flg Off G. Jones	RM750/AP-	V-1	0730	Rochester area
Sgt P.E.H. Standish	RM744/AP-	V-1 shared	1950	Tonbridge area
Plt Off W.W. Brown	RM741/AP-	V-1	2000	Rochester area

Of the Squadron's first kill, Flg Off Jones stated that he fired two short bursts following which the flying bomb burst into flames. The next was not destroyed until the evening, by Sgt Peter Standish: "Intercepted north-east of Tenterden. Dived on Diver, saw strikes. Three Tempests and one Mustang broke in on attack, then further attack by me. Diver went down six miles east of Tonbridge." Although he claimed it as a solo kill, it seems that it was shared by Flg Off Lyne of 274 and Wt Off Thomas of 129. Plt Off Brown scored his one and only kill at 2000:

> "Saw strikes on Diver after which an excessive burst of flame came out of the tail and starboard wing dropped considerably. The Diver dived towards the ground at a shallow angle and I broke near balloons. Judge Diver to hit ground two miles north-west of Rochester."

274 Squadron (Tempest V) West Malling

Flt Lt O.E. Willis	EJ640/JJ-	V-1	0705	Sittingbourne area
Flt Lt J.A. Malloy RCAF	EJ640/JJ-	V-1	1615	
Flt Lt L.P. Griffiths RNZAF	EJ647/JJ-	V-1	1905	Faversham/ Sittingbourne
Flg Off J.W. Lyne	EJ634/JJ-	V-1 shared	1950	Hastings
	EJ634/JJ-	V-1 shared	1955	Hastings
	EJ634/JJ-	V-1	2005	Ashford area
Flt Lt J.A. Malloy RCAF	EJ633/JJ-	V-1	2050	Grid R.3488

Flt Lt Willis scored his second kill during the early morning:

> "Saw Diver coming in over Hythe and told control. Dived to obtain speed and, climbing up to
> intercept, saw Mustang firing at it from 200 yards, but no strikes scored. The Mustang pulled
> away and Diver was still flying straight and level. Halfway between Ashford and Maidstone I
> opened fire at 300 yards range. It lost height and crashed near a chalk quarry two-three miles
> north of Maidstone."

During the afternoon, Flt Lt John Malloy destroyed one by tipping with his wingtip:
"I sighted a Diver just inland of Dover at 2,000 feet. I chased it to Rainham, opening
fire from 800 yards but saw no strikes. I closed in and tipped it over with my wingtip.
It crashed on the railway line near Rainham." This was possibly the incident
witnessed by AFS Fireman Harold Collyer: "I was on duty in Deal when I saw a
Mustang just off the coastline pull in and dive behind a V-1 and tip it with its wing.
That one crashed at Woodenesborough, demolishing a row of cottages." Flt Lt
Griffiths got his between Faversham and Sittingbourne: "I sighted a Diver ten miles
north-west of Lympne at 2,000 feet. I chased it to Faversham, firing from 200 yards
range. I saw strikes on it before it crashed and exploded."

It fell to Flg Off John Lyne to enjoy the greater success by shooting down one and
sharing two others with Mustangs:

> "I saw a Diver between Hythe and Ashford at 2,000 feet. I shot it down from 200 yards about
> five miles north-west of Ashford. It exploded on the ground. I saw another 10-15 miles north
> of Hastings at 2,000 feet, and scored strikes on it from 250 yards range. A Mustang then
> appeared and we both continued firing at it. The Diver crashed, exploding on the ground about
> 15 miles north of Hastings. Almost immediately I saw another at 2,000 feet. A Mustang pilot
> and I fired and I scored strikes from 200 yards. It crashed and exploded on the ground north of
> Hastings."

Flt Lt Malloy got his second of the day, again by tipping it:

> "I picked up a Diver near Dover, flying at 2,000 feet, at 350mph. I chased it to the Isle of
> Sheppey area but failed to score strikes, so I closed in and tipped it over with my wingtip. It
> exploded on the ground. A Meteor [pilot] confirmed my claim."

306 (Polish) Squadron (Mustang III) Brenzett

Flt Sgt S. Rudowski PAF	FB380/UZ-F	V-1 shared	0940	Maidstone area
Flg Off K. Marschall PAF	HB871/UZ-E	V-1		Tonbridge area
Flt Lt J. Wisiorek PAF	FB350/UZ-P	V-1	1658	Grid R.2964
	FB350/UZ-P	V-1 shared	1731	Ham Street area
Wt Off J. Rogowski PAF	FB358/UZ-C	V-1	1750	Appledore area
	FB358/UZ-C	V-1 shared	1900	Tunbridge Wells area

When attacking his target near Hythe, Flt Sgt Stan Rudowski's aircraft was hit in the
wing by gunfire from a Meteor that also attacked the same Diver, that flown by Flg
Off Bill McKenzie. Rudowski wrote:

> "I fired short bursts from 300 yards down to 200 yards. It started to dive but at the same time
> a pilot of a Meteor fired on this V-1 and also damaged the wing of my Mustang."

The Diver exploded on the ground four miles north-east of Maidstone. Flt Lt Karol
Marschall intercepted a Diver west of Brenzett at 3,000 feet. He attacked from astern
down to 300 yards, whereupon the Diver lost speed and the jet caught fire. As he
overshot, a Tempest nipped in and shot it down near Tonbridge, where it exploded. Flt
Lt Jan Wisiorek reversed the roles when he engaged a Diver being attacked by a
Tempest. He fired short bursts from astern and the Diver exploded on the ground. Wt
Off Jan Rogowski's first Diver was intercepted over Rye at 2,000 feet. He attacked

from port and then astern, closing to 350 yards. The Diver slowed down and went into a steep dive before crashing and exploding in a field near Appledore. He then intercepted a second east of Rye, slowing it down considerably. As he broke away a Tempest appeared. The Diver rolled over, crashed and exploded near a farm about seven miles from Tunbridge.

315 (Polish) Squadron (Mustang III) Brenzett

Flg Off B. Nowosielski PAF	HB849/PK-M	V-1	0711	Ashford area
Plt Off G. Świstuń PAF	FX865/PK-X	V-1	0710	Dymchurch area
Flt Sgt K. Siwek PAF	FX878/PK-F	V-1	1835	Hythe area
	FX878/PK-F	V-1	1950	New Romney area
	FX878/PK-F	V-1	1955	Dymchurch area

350 (Belgian) Squadron (Spitfire XIV) Friston

Flt Sgt L. Verbeeck	RM655/MN-	V-1	1015-1155	over land
Plt Off J. Lavigne ⎫	RM701/MN-O	V-1	1835-2000	exploded in mid-
Sgt P. Leva ⎭	RM693/MN-S			air

402 (RCAF) Squadron (Spitfire XIV) Hawkinge

Flg Off E.A.H. Vickers RCAF	RM731/AE-	V-1	0710	Hawkinge airfield
Flg Off H. Cowan RCAF	RM737/AE-	V-1	0838	Channel (Grid R.7142)
Flt Lt D. Sherk RCAF	RM680/AE-	V-1	0833	Channel (Grid R.8030)

Flg Off Ed Vickers opened the scoring for the Canadian unit when he sighted a Diver at 2,000 feet four miles west of Cap Gris Nez:

> "Closed to ack-ack zone off Folkestone using all ammo. Saw strikes and Diver lost 1,000 feet. Broke off attack at ack-ack zone. Diver crashed south of Hawkinge drome."

In fact, it impacted very close to 402's dispersal, causing slight damage but no casualties. During a later patrol, both Flt Lt Don Sherk and Flg Off Henry Cowan shot their victims into the sea, the former reporting:

> "I sighted the Diver about ten miles north-west of Boulogne. I was travelling toward Boulogne so I turned to the right to attack. The robot was climbing and I got a short burst immediately after turning into it. It continued to climb and I pursued it. I closed to 200 yards and gave two four-seconds bursts and then overshot. I made an orbit and then attacked again, this time observing strikes on the starboard wing root. The Diver started to spiral down and exploded in the sea."

Flg Off Cowan[194] enjoyed similar success:

> "A Diver was reported crossing out at Cap Gris Nez at 3,000 feet. My height at that time was 10,000 feet. Sighted Diver's 'flash' and went in pursuit. Opened fire at 300 yards and kept firing until about 50 yards, then pulled up to slow down and get another shot at it. Criss-crossed over the top of it but it had slowed down too much and I didn't manage to get into firing position again. Twenty seconds later it dived into the sea and exploded."

486 (RNZAF) Squadron (Tempest V) Newchurch

Flt Sgt J. Steedman RNZAF	EJ528/SA-P	V-1	1655	Tenterden area
	EJ528/SA-P	V-1	1737	West Malling area
Flt Lt H.N. Sweetman RNZAF	JN732/SA-I	V-1	1815	Dungeness area
Wt Off O.D. Eagleson RNZAF	EJ635/SA-T	V-1	1815	Rye area
	EJ635/SA-T	V-1	1825	Maidstone area
	EJ635/SA-T	V-1	1835	Ashford area
Plt Off K.A. Smith RNZAF	JN808/SA-N	V-1	1905	Tenterden area

Flt Lt W.L. Miller RNZAF   JN803/SA-D   V-1   1907   Tonbridge area

610 Squadron (Spitfire XIV) Friston
Four pilots found themselves diverted from Diver patrols when they were requested
to shoot down a barrage balloon that had broken away from its moorings. This was
duly despatched into the Channel by Plt Offs Bangerter, Nicholls, Doherty and
Finbow.

616 Squadron (Meteor F.1) Manston
Flg Off W.H. McKenzie RCAF	EE225/YQ-	V-1 shared	0940	Maidstone area
Flg Off M.M. Mullenders (Belg)	EE2??/YQ-	V-1	1833	Ashford area
Wg Cdr A. McDowall	EE2??/YQ-	V-1 damaged evening		Tenterden area
	EE2??/YQ-	V-1 damaged evening		Tenterden area

Following an uneventful scramble and patrol, Flg Off Bill McKenzie was about to
land at Manston when control advised that Divers were coming in, and he was sent
back to orbit five miles south-east of Ashford at 3,000 feet, where a Diver was soon
sighted:

> "I positioned to 700 yards behind and 500 feet below Diver. A Mustang (Flt Sgt Stan
> Rudkowski of 306 Squadron) attacked from line astern and fired from 250 yards. No strikes
> were observed and the Diver continued on a straight and level course. The Mustang then pulled
> upwards and broke away. I immediately attacked from astern from 400 yards and fired a four-
> seconds burst. Strikes were seen all over the Diver and the starboard wing fell off. Diver then
> rolled over on its back and went down to explode on ground approximately eight miles east of
> Maidstone." He later recalled: "It went into a farmer's field, all stoked with grain for
> harvesting. After that thing hit, it was laid bare. I thought, 'My God, they talk about the poor
> people in London, and here's this poor guy who has just had his whole year's work wiped out.'
> But I got a buzz bomb!"

The Mustang pilot involved, Flt Sgt Stanislaw Rudowski of 306 Squadron, apparently
complained that the Meteor had bounced him and damaged his aircraft. Belgian Flg
Off Prule Mullenders was on a routine anti-Diver patrol in the vicinity of Ashford
when a Diver was seen about five miles south of Ashford at 2,000 feet:

> "Three Typhoons [sic] were seen to attack and break away. It is not certain whether Typhoons
> actually fired at Diver. I immediately dived from 3,000 feet, overtook and closed in to 100
> yards, firing short bursts from line astern. Strikes were seen on fuselage and jet. As I broke
> away the Diver was seen to go down and explode on the ground."

Wg Cdr Andy McDowall DFM attacked two Divers during an evening patrol north-
west of Tenterden but each time had to break off due to proximity of the balloon
barrage. Strikes were seen on both Divers but their fates were not observed.
Unfortunately, the Diver shot down by Flg Off Mullenders impacted on the goods
storage area of Ashford railway station, as recalled by Mr R.R. May, an apprentice
with Southern Railway at Ashford:

> "There were a lot of workers at the rail works who came from Folkestone, Dover, Deal and
> Canterbury so the evening trains were always full. On that evening I was standing in the train
> corridor, on the side facing the railway works, when I saw a V-1 coming in quite low in line
> with the main railway line. It was about over Willesborough, and we all thought that it was
> going to pass over, but as it got closer a Meteor suddenly came out of the sky and slowed down
> in front of the V-1. It seemed to nudge the V-1's short wingtip, which caused the V-1 to go
> haywire; it coughed and spluttered then silence – then it just dropped like a stone; but the jet
> just carried on its way over the Great Chart area. There was a loud bang, an explosion, and it
> rained boxes as the V-1 had hit the goods storage area by the station. The signalman in his box
> had a lucky escape and a few steam engines were damaged, but that V-1 didn't reach London.
> Empty ammunition boxes and other debris were soon cleared up and our train left for home –
> a little late!"

An eyewitness commented on the Oak Lane incident:

> "Next day the pilot of the Meteor jet fighter came down to the scene of the tragedy and was overcome by what he saw, learning of the deaths he had inadvertently caused. It was stressed that he could not possibly have known the Doodlebug would swoop down and dive under the railway bridge as the train came along the line. There were open fields and orchards all round the scene and it could have fallen harmlessly in any of these without killing anyone. It was also pointed out to him that if he had not brought it down, it might well have carried on to fall in Gillingham, Chatham or Rochester, causing a larger number of deaths. It was just pure bad luck."

Four people were reported seriously injured and five others hurt. One or two may have succumbed to their injuries.

Thursday 17 AUGUST

Fighters brought down three Divers in Ashford RD, one of which caused serious injury to a person on the ground when it crashed in Ruckinge. AA gunners at Folkestone increased their tally by 27 Divers shot down into the sea, Hythe gunners claiming 16 more. ARP Warden Ted Carter at Waltham Abbey was still logging events in his diary:

> "Today, at long last, I have seen a Doodlebug in daylight. Coming in straight and high from the south-east. Looked just like a Spitfire in the distance, but as he drew nearer and passed over, all the details could be seen – wings, tail jet propulsion unit and all. Flames were stabbing out from the tail, against the dullish sky, and with his engine still booming he went into a gracefully sweeping curved dive to land behind the trees towards Goffs Oak. A few seconds after came the crump and billowing mushroom of dark brown smoke. Six persons were killed and a number injured."

Several that reached London in the morning caused fatalities: one at Ivydale Road, Nunhead (SE15), close to where a bomb fell the previous week, killed two more residents. Just under three hours later, at 0923, another fell at Lawrence Wharf, Rotherhithe (SE16), killing three, followed a minute later by another in Rotherhithe Street, Bermondsey that killed 17 and injured 62. Another very serious incident occurred when Battersea (SW11) was hit in the afternoon, a dozen people losing their lives in Lavender Hill, in the area of Beauchamp Road/Mossbury Road, at 1530; a further 25 sustained serious injuries, of whom 16 later died. Two more were killed in Honor Oak (SE22) at 1700.

3 Squadron (Tempest V) Newchurch

Plt Off H.R. Wingate	EJ549/JF-	V-1	0645-0725
	EJ549/JF-	V-1	0645-0725
Flt Sgt R.W. Cole	JN768/JF-F	V-1	0640-0800

41 Squadron (Spitfire XII) Lympne

Flt Lt R.P. Harding	MB854/EB-Z	V-1	0745	Brenzett area
Flg Off P.B. Graham	MB831/EB-	V-1	2035	Ashford area

Flt Lt Ross Harding intercepted his target over Old Romney. Three short bursts followed by numerous strikes and the flying bomb crashed one-and-a-half miles north-east of Brenzett. His aircraft was then hit by AA fire though he was able to land safely. The next pair off was not so fortunate. Flg Offs Peter Graham and 'Charlie' van Goens (Dutch) departed Lympne at 0905 but the weather was so bad that Graham decided to abort the mission and return to Lympne. Contact was lost with van Goens who was last heard calling out in Dutch and it was presumed that his Spitfire MB880 had been shot down by AA near Folkestone. Despite a search he was not found. Flg

Off Graham was up again on an evening sortie and succeeded in shooting down his second flying bomb on consecutive days, his victim crashing in Denge Wood between Ashford and Canterbury.

56 Squadron (Tempest V) Newchurch

Sqn Ldr A.R. Hall	EJ541/US-B	V-1	0645-0745	
	EJ541/US-B	V-1	0645-0745	

130 Squadron (Spitfire XIV) Lympne

Sgt P.E.H. Standish	RM744/AP-	V-1	0615	Tenterden area
	RM744/AP-	V-1	0626	Dover area
Flg Off K.M. Lowe RAAF	RM757/AP-	V-1	0745	Wye area
Plt Off F.C. Riley RAAF	RM760/AP-	V-1	0912	Brook area

Sgt Peter Standish reported:

> "(1) Intercepted west of Dungeness, over Rye. Saw strikes and after second attack light went out and Diver went in one mile south-east of Tenterden (2) Intercepted one mile west of Dover. After firing, light went out and it turned in four miles north-west of Dover. Confirmed by White 1, P/O Riley."

Flg Off Lowe got the next south-west of Rye: "Saw Diver above cloud. Gave burst, Diver turned port, jet stopped and Diver spun in. Confirmed by F/Lt Scott. Tempest in vicinity not in position to fire." No.4 fell to Plt Off Riley: "Intercepted south-east of Ashford. Attacked from below with two short bursts, seeing Diver burst into flames and crash through cloud, one mile west of Brook." During a late evening patrol, Plt Off E.C.W. Matthew's aircraft NH701 suffered a fractured crankshaft and the pilot glided toward High Halden ALG, but overshot and the Spitfire was considerably damaged although Matthew was only slightly injured.

274 Squadron (Tempest V) West Malling

Wg Cdr J.F. Fraser	EJ628/JJ-G	V-1	morning	West Malling area

Wg Cdr Joe Fraser DFC[195] from Group HQ borrowed a 274 Squadron Tempest and scored a kill east of West Malling. The Squadron was then ordered to move again, this time to Manston.

306 (Polish) Squadron (Mustang III) Brenzett

Flt Lt M. Wedzik PAF	UZ-V	V-1	0630	West Malling area
Flt Lt W. Klawe PAF	UZ-V	V-1 shared	0845	Ashford area
Flt Sgt J. Zaleński PAF	UZ-T	V-1	0914	Rye-Dymchurch
Flt Lt J. Siekierski PAF	UZ-	V-1	2038	exploded in mid-air

Flt Lt Marion Wedzik intercepted a Diver over New Romney and attacked from astern from 400 down to 250 yards. The jet unit stopped and the Diver disappeared into cloud two miles south of West Malling. The Diver attacked by Flt Lt Włodzimierz Klawe crashed and exploded seven miles west of Ashford following three short bursts. Wt Off Józef Zaleński's target went down vertically near Rye, while that shot down by Flt Lt Jan Siekierski exploded in the air over Kingsnorth.

315 (Polish) Squadron (Mustang III) Brenzett

Flt Sgt J. Donocik PAF	FZ169/PK-R	V-1	0915	Dymchurch area
Flg Off P. Kliman PAF	FX939/PK-L	V-1	1910	Hawkinge area

402 (RCAF) Squadron (Spitfire XIV) Hawkinge

During a patrol of the Folkestone-Lympne area, Flg Off D.W. Hastings RCAF chased a Diver near Dymchurch but entered the gun belt and had to break away when his aircraft (RM743) was hit and he was slightly injured. However, he managed to land safely at Newchurch.

616 Squadron (Meteor F.1) Manston

Flg Off J.R. Ritch RCAF	EE217/YQ-J	V-1	0657	Chart Sutton area
Wt Off T.S. Woodacre	EE218/YQ-F	V-1	0700	Faversham area
Flt Sgt R. Easy	EE2??/YQ-	V-1	1355	Canterbury/ Maidstone

This proved to be the Meteors' big day with three Divers falling to the jets, the first shot down by Canadian Flg Off Jack Ritch:

"A Diver was seen flying at 2,000 feet from direction of Hastings to Maidstone. I intercepted in vicinity of Tenterden at 0654. Two Tempests were seen flying approximately behind the Diver. One Tempest was seen to fire but no strikes were observed. I was then flying alongside the leading Tempest. The Tempests then broke away and the Diver continued on its course straight and level. I went in to attack and fired one long burst from line astern at 150 to 100 yards. Strikes were seen and the Diver rolled over and fell to explode on the ground four miles south of Maidstone."

Ritch's companion, Wt Off Sid Woodacre, got a second a few minutes later:

"While on anti-Diver patrol under Biggin Hill control, I saw a Diver coming in south of Dover and intercepted it three miles south of Canterbury. A Mustang was seen 700-1,000 yards astern of the Diver but this did not fire. I had no difficulty in overtaking both Mustang and Diver and then attacked and fired three short bursts at 200 yards. Strikes were seen on starboard wing of Diver, which rolled over and went down and was seen to explode on ground ten miles south of Faversham."

Flt Sgt 'Sam' Easy was orbiting High Haldon after being scrambled by Biggin Hill Control, when he was advised of three Divers approaching Ashford at 1,000-3,000 feet, and was ordered to intercept one north-west of Ashford:

"I opened my attack from line astern with one burst of one second at 400 yards. Observing a few strikes on starboard wing root, I closed in and fired from slightly below and astern at 250-200 yards. Three more two-seconds bursts were fired and strikes were observed all over the Diver, which then appeared to waggle its wings and climb slightly to port. More strikes were seen when I fired another burst of two seconds. Diver then fell away to starboard and was seen to explode in a field close to Canterbury/Maidstone railway line."

At Manston there occurred a near-fatal incident involving Wg Cdr Wilson's personal aircraft EE224/HJW, which was accidentally damaged by cannon fire. The aircraft was standing at dispersal when, at 1750, the pilot of Meteor EE225, Flg Off Bill McKenzie, inadvertently fired the cannon. Four ground crew including LACs John Keal and Leonard Wibrew were injured, as was Rolls-Royce representative Mr N. Glover. The Canadian was found to be negligent and was disciplined, although Wg Cdr McDowall insisted this was an aircraft malfunction and not pilot error.

Night 17/18 AUGUST

Folkestone and Hythe guns shot down 11 Divers between them up to 0725.

605 Squadron (Mosquito VI) Manston

Flt Lt B. Williams	UP-	V-1	pm	Channel
	UP-	V-1	pm	Channel

Friday 18 AUGUST

Many train passengers had a miraculous escape when a Diver impacted beside the Oak Lane, Newington (Kent), railway bridge, effectively demolishing it, right in the path of the approaching London to Margate express. The engine and tender jumped the gap but the first two carriages crashed onto the road. Of the 600 people on board, eight were killed and 33 seriously injured. Apparently the Diver had been engaged by a fighter. Local teenager Don Deacon recalled:

> "My friend and I were sitting on our bikes outside the house when we heard a V-1 approaching. And also cannon fire. To the east, probably over Faversham, we saw a Spitfire catch up with the flying bomb and flip it over with its wingtip. It was very exciting. We decided to go and see the wreckage, indicated by a column of smoke. When we got there the carnage was terrible. The V-1 had hit and destroyed the railway bridge on the main line near Upchurch. It had hit a few seconds before the Margate express had reached the same spot. The engine had jumped the gap but the rest of the train had rolled down the embankment."[196]

41 Squadron (Spitfire XII) Lympne

Plt Off E. Gray RAAF ⎱	EN228/EB-	V-1	0700	Hollingbourne
Wt Off J.P.N. Ware RAAF ⎰				area

The Australian pair Plt Off Ricky Gray and Wt Off Jimmy Ware attacked their target north-west of Ashford, as the latter reported: "I fired a two-second burst from dead astern. Diver burst into flames and went down in a field north of Hollingbourne, where it exploded on impact. Confirmed by two pilots of 130 Squadron." The crippled Diver crashed at Court Farm, Hucking, where cottages and the church were damaged. Fortunately, only one person was slightly injured.

129 Squadron (Mustang III) Brenzett

Flt Lt D.F. Ruchwaldy	FB178/DV-R	V-1	0610-0810	off Boulogne

130 Squadron (Spitfire XIV) Lympne

During an evening patrol, Flg Off R. Keating's Spitfire was struck by a Mustang of 306 Squadron that had been climbing beneath him – although damaged, Keating managed to control his aircraft to a successful emergency landing at Woodchurch. He was unhurt. The other pilot was not so fortunate, Plt Off Feliks Migoś losing his life when his aircraft crashed (see below).

316 (Polish) Squadron (Mustang III) Friston

Flt Lt A. Cholajda PAF	HB835/SZ-P	V-1	0715	Channel

> "Diver seen mid-Channel. Attacked dead astern from 600 yards. Explosion seen on left wing. Smoke poured from jet. Diver climbed at 180°, turned, looped and crashed into the sea."

350 (Belgian) Squadron (Spitfire XIV) Friston

Flt Sgt L. Verbeeck	RM760/MN-	V-1	0825-0945	off Dungeness
Plt Off J. Wustefeld	RM748/MN-	V-1	1600-1715	off Dungeness

486 (RNZAF) Squadron (Tempest V) Newchurch

Flt Lt N.J. Campbell RNZAF	EJ523/SA-Z	V-1	0705	Haywards Heath
				area

With a reduction in trade for many of the ADGB squadrons, one or two were permitted to undertake Rodeos over France, including **315 (Polish) Squadron**. Sqn Ldr Horbaczewski led his dozen Spitfires in a sweep in the Beauvais area, meeting 20 FW190s circling Beauvais airfield, a further two-dozen heading eastwards and about a dozen more preparing to take off. The German fighters from I/JG2, II and III/JG26, appeared to have been taken by complete surprise and 13 were promptly shot down, two of which crash-landed. Ten of the Luftwaffe pilots were killed and two wounded. The only Polish loss was that of Sqn Ldr Horbaczewski himself, who was seen to shoot down three of the German fighters before his own demise[197]. Thirteen

Mustangs from **306 (Polish) Squadron** also participated in the sweep, the formation led by Wg Cdr Jan Zumbach DFC. No enemy aircraft or flak was encountered but on the return flight Plt Off Feliks Migoś' aircraft (FB206/UZ-M) collided with a Spitfire of 130 Squadron and the Polish pilot was killed.

Night 18/19 AUGUST
157 Squadron (Mosquito XIX) West Malling
Sqn Ldr Benson and Flt Lt Brandon departed West Malling on an anti-Heinkel patrol, as the latter recalled:

> "We were sent on a low-level patrol just off the Dutch islands. The idea was to try to intercept the launching aircraft, which were mostly [*sic*] Heinkels. If we could shoot the Heinkel down before it launched its toy, so much the better. Almost from the moment we arrived on patrol we began a series of chases that got us nowhere. We spotted some lights on one of the islands, but they went out as we approached and we could see nothing when we got there. Then we had two long and difficult chases on aircraft, both of which turned out to be Mosquitos. We then saw what we thought must be a launching some way off. No AI contact appeared however. Again we saw a launching some distance from us but had no joy when we investigated it. Finally we returned to West Malling tired and rather dejected."

456 (RAAF) Squadron (Mosquito XVII) Ford

Flt Lt K.A. Roediger RAAF	HK297/RX-V	V-1	2324	over land (Grid R.2262)

> "Attacked a flying bomb from astern, height 1,200 feet, speed 360mph, from a range of 1,200 feet. The target dived straight in and exploded on the ground."

501 Squadron (Tempest V) Manston

Flg Off R.G. Lucas	EJ584/SD-Q	V-1 probable	0120-0330	West Malling area
Plt Off R.H. Bennett	EJ553/ZQ-L	V-1	0325	West Malling area
Flg Off W.F. Polley	EJ591/SD-Z	V-1	0305-0340	

Flg Off Lucas attacked Diver and saw parts of the engine fall away but then it entered balloon barrage and was not seen to crash. Plt Off Bennett reported:

> "I saw a Diver cross at Dungeness at 4,000 feet, speed 410mph. It was illuminated by searchlights. I closed in astern to 350 yards and fired four bursts. I saw a number of strikes. The Diver swerved, went into a dive towards the ground and exploded north of West Malling."

A Diver crossing at Dungeness was engaged by Plt Off Ron Bennett:

> "I saw a Diver at 4,000 feet, speed 410mph, intercepted by searchlight. I closed in astern to 350 yards and fired four bursts. I saw a number of strikes. The Diver swerved, went into a dive and crashed and exploded north of West Malling at 0325."

605 Squadron (Mosquito VI) Manston

Flt Lt B. Williams	UP-	V-1	0315	off Dungeness
	UP-	V-1	0327	off Le Touquet

Flt Lt Brian Williams shot down two Divers in fairly quick succession to raise his score to five in two sorties, having achieved a hat-trick a few weeks earlier:

> "During the patrol, at 0310, a group of eight Divers were sighted crossing the French coast between Le Touquet and Boulogne. Height varied but averaged about 2,000 feet and speed around 320mph. At 0315 I gave one Diver a short burst from dead astern at 400 yards range. Strikes were seen and Diver exploded in the air about three-quarters of a mile off Dungeness. At 0324 we spotted another Diver, speed, course and height approximately the same as No.1. Attacked again from astern, and slightly above, and after two bursts Diver blew up at 0327 about eight-ten miles north-west of Le Touquet."

Saturday 19 AUGUST

Six Divers crashed in Tenterden RD as a result of fighter action, but only minor damage resulted, and no casualties. At least one flying bomb crossed the Norfolk coast during the day, causing the diarist at the USAAF's supply base at Thorpe Abbotts to comment: "They called a 'red alert' over the tannoy at 1500 today, but the buzz bomb had crashed before we heard the alert."

3 Squadron (Tempest V) Newchurch

Plt Off H.R. Wingate	EJ549/JF-	V-1	0600-0710	
	EJ549/JF-	V-1	0600-0710	
Flt Sgt R.W. Cole	JN768/JF-F	V-1	1355-1525	

41 Squadron (Spitfire XII) Lympne

Flt Lt T. Spencer	MB875/EB-G	V-1	0645	Appledore area

Flt Lt Terry Spencer brought down his fourth Diver shortly before 0700, firing only a half-second burst. It crashed in a field two miles north-west of Appledore.

56 Squadron (Tempest V) Newchurch

Flt Sgt L. Jackson	EJ548/US-G	V-1	0630-0710	Folkestone area

Flt Sgt Artie Shaw force-landed EJ578/US-I due to glycol leak while on an anti-Diver patrol but was unhurt.

129 Squadron (Mustang III) Brenzett

Flg Off J.E. Hartley	FB125/DV-F	V-1	0600-0740	off Dymchurch
Wt Off T. Hetherington	SR436/DV-T	V-1	1930-2135	off Boulogne
Wt Off E. Redhead	FB125/DV-F	V-1	1930-2135	off Dungeness

Flg Off Jim Hartley intercepted a Diver south-west of Boulogne and finally shot off its starboard wing, causing it to crash in the sea seven miles south of Dymchurch. Wt Off Tommy Hetherington caused his victim to crash into the sea north-west of Boulogne when he crossed in front of the Diver at 250 yards, whereupon it was caught by his slipstream and exploded on impact with the sea. The third Diver, intercepted by Wt Off Eric Redhead 15 miles north of Boulogne, also crashed into the sea.

130 Squadron (Spitfire XIV) Lympne

Flt Lt K.J. Matheson ⎫	RM760/AP-	V-1	0630	off Boulogne
Plt Off R.J. Martin RCAF ⎭	RM744/AP-			
Flt Sgt G.W. Hudson	RM760/AP-	V-1 damaged	1435	Channel
Flt Sgt G.W. Hudson ⎫	RM760/AP-	V-1 probable	2111	Ashford area
Wt Off D.H. White ⎭	RM744/AP-			

Flt Lt Matheson wrote:

> "Saw Diver to starboard at two miles, eight miles north-west of Boulogne. Closed on port beam to dead astern. Fired two-seconds burst. After first strikes Diver nosed upwards. I broke away. Diver had slowed down to 200mph. P/O Martin attacked. It caught fire, dived in, exploding in sea."

Flt Sgt Hudson did not enjoy successful encounters, his first at 1435 resulted in a 'damaged' only. Later that evening he was up with Wt Off David White when another Diver was encountered, which both attacked and saw strikes, but since they did not see it crash, they were not credited with a kill. The latter reported:

> "Opened fire at 450 yards from port quarter, closing to 250 yards astern. Saw strikes but had to break as overshooting. Tried to come in again and renew attack but unable to overtake. Found guns considerable handicap."

306 (Polish) Squadron (Mustang III) Brenzett

Flt Lt W. Klawe PAF	HB863/UZ-O	V-1	0643	Grid R.2760
	HB863/UZ-O	V-1	0649	Grid R.4255
Flt Sgt E. Dowgalski PAF	UZ-S	V-1	0605-0745	Grid R.3353
Flt Lt W. Klawe PAF ⎱	HB863/UZ-O	V-1 shared	0647	Grid R.4051
Flt Sgt E. Dowgalski PAF ⎰	UZ-S			
Flt Sgt J. Zaleński PAF	FB350/UZ-P	V-1	2106	Tonbridge area
Flt Lt A. Beyer PAF	UZ-Y	V-1	2115	Grid R.3043

Flt Lt Włodzimierz Klawe intercepted the first Diver west of Appledore and attacked from dead astern. Strikes were seen and it went into a steep dive, crashed and exploded. The second was engaged west of Brenzett at 2,000 feet. Again he carried out a stern attack and Diver poured black smoke and slowed down. As he pulled away, a Tempest moved in and opened fire, the Diver exploding on the ground. Klawe then intercepted a third two miles south-east of Ham Street and shot this down, his claim being verified by a pilot of 315 Squadron. Meanwhile, Flt Sgt Eugeniusz Dowgalski shot down one that he intercepted three miles north-east of Rye, and then got a second, which he reported went into a steep dive before hitting the ground. It transpired this was the same missile engaged by Klawe and the Tempest. Later, both Flt Sgt Józef Zaleński and Flt Lt Andrzej Beyer shot down Divers, the former seeing his explode on the ground seven miles west of Tonbridge in the balloon barrage area, while Beyer's went into a loop before it spun down and crashed.

315 (Polish) Squadron (Mustang III) Brenzett

Flt Sgt K. Siwek PAF	FB371/PK-B	V-1	1445	Appledore area

Crashed at Yalding, damaging buildings but only one person was slightly injured.

316 (Polish) Squadron (Mustang III) Friston

Flt Lt T. Kwiatkowski PAF	HB831/SZ-T	V-1	0645	off Dungeness
Flt Sgt Z. Narloch PAF	HB824/SZ-N	V-1	1515	off Dungeness
Wt Off J. Feruga PAF	HB848/SZ-W	V-1	1517	off Dungeness
Flt Sgt Z. Narloch PAF ⎱	HB824/SZ-N	V-1	1520	off Dungeness
Wt Off J. Feruga PAF ⎰	HB848/SZ-W			
Wt Off J. Feruga PAF	HB848/SZ-W	V-1	2130	off Dungeness

Flt Lt Kwiatkowski had a choice of targets when he intercepted five Divers about six miles off Cap Gris Nez:

"The first got through. Pursued second and attacked ten miles south of Dungeness. It exploded in the sea. I observed three of the other Divers – apparently unattacked – explode in the sea about ten miles north of Boulogne."

Off Józef Feruga and Flt Sgt Zygfryd Narloch departed Friston at 1320 to carry out an anti-Diver patrol and succeeded in shooting down three. Narloch got the first:

"Diver sighted ten miles north of Boulogne. Pursued and attacked from 200 yards astern to 15 miles south of Dungeness. Diver seen by [Feruga] to disintegrate and explode in the sea." Feruga got one two minutes later: "Diver sighted about ten miles north of Boulogne. Pursued and attacked 20 miles south-east of Dungeness. Port wing blown off. Exploded in sea."

Three minutes later they jointly pursued a third, which Narloch attacked from astern while Feruga attacked from port. It crashed into the sea about three miles south of Dungeness. Feruga flew another patrol later in the evening and scored his third kill of the day:

"Diver intercepted 15 miles south of Dungeness. Attacked from line astern, firing two short bursts from 300 yards. Diver pulled steeply up, turned on its back, went into a steep dive and crashed in the sea."

486 (RNZAF) Squadron (Tempest V) Newchurch

Flt Sgt R.J. Campbell RNZAF	JN802/SA-C	V-1	2120	Rye area

616 Squadron (Meteor F.1) Manston

Flg Off G.N. Hobson	EE217/YQ-J	V-1	0646	Ashford area
	EE217/YQ-J	V-1 shared	0700	Ashford area
Flt Sgt P.G. Watts	EE2??/YQ-	V-1	2110	West Malling area
Flt Sgt B. Cartmel	EE2??/YQ-	V-1 damaged		Chilham area

Flg Off Gordon Hobson came close to scoring a double having been vectored to the Ashford area:

> "One Diver was seen and intercepted a few miles west of Ashford. I attacked from line astern and closed in from 800 to 500 yards then fired one two-seconds burst. Strikes were seen all over. Continuing to fire I finally closed to 100 yards when, after a final burst, the Diver rolled over and exploded on the ground a few miles west of Ashford. A second Diver was seen just south of Tenterden, flying at 3,000 feet at 300mph. I made attack from starboard and saw strikes following five-seconds burst of fire. As I turned to attack again, a Tempest attacked from line astern and fired from 300 yards. The Diver tipped over and exploded on the ground a few miles south-west of Ashford."

Flt Sgt Watts was scrambled at 2050:

> "While patrolling south-west of Tenterden a Diver was sighted at 2,000 feet, with two Mustangs pursuing in line astern. I turned towards the Diver and to starboard of the Mustangs. The leading Mustang fired, no results observed. Closing in from astern I opened fire from 400 yards but did not see any strikes. Continuing to close in I fired again from 200 yards. Immediately the Diver turned on its back and went down in a spin."

The Diver was confirmed to have crashed at Teston, six miles south-east of West Malling at 2110. Flt Sgt Brian Cartmel[198] narrowly missed opening his account when his gunsight bulb failed while firing at a Diver, on which he saw several strikes. He could only claim a damaged.

Night 19/20 AUGUST

AA gunners at Hythe brought down a dozen Divers during the hours of darkness, their colleagues at Folkestone accounting for 18 more in a twelve-hour period up to 0600.

85 Squadron (Mosquito XIX) West Malling

Sqn Ldr B.A. Burbridge	VY-B	V-1	2150-0035	off Dungeness

501 Squadron (Tempest V) Manston

Flt Lt H. Burton	EJ603/SD-M	V-1	2205-2340	

The squadron ORB stated:

> "Patrols were flown during the hours of darkness. Activity was reported early and Flt Lt Burton destroyed a flying bomb. There was again activity at dawn and a section was scrambled. Sqn Ldr Berry made two patrols in a Mosquito (UP-U) to see the effect of searchlight dousing and Diver interception from the point of view of the Mosquito. On the first patrol he was accompanied by Flg Off East, the Intelligence Officer, and on the second by Captain Payne, the squadron searchlight officer. A Diver was sighted and attacked at about 0100 but without result."

Sunday 20 AUGUST

Midday witnessed the arrival of a Diver in Twickenham Road, Feltham, where 11 people died and 13 were seriously injured. Three died in Studley Road, Stockwell (SW4) at 1418, and two more were killed in the afternoon in Walworth (SE17) following the explosion of a bomb in the Westmorland Street area.

3 Squadron (Tempest V) Newchurch

Flg Off R.H. Clapperton	JN865/JF-	V-1	1940-2110	

This turned out to be Flg Off Clapperton's final flying bomb kill, raising his tally to 22.

41 Squadron (Spitfire XII) Lympne

Plt Off E. Gray RAAF	EN228/EB-	V-1	1625	off Folkestone

The Diver that Plt Off Ricky Gray sighted off Cap Gris Nez was pursued towards the Kent coast and was finally shot down with two bursts of cannon fire, the burning bomb falling into the sea seven miles offshore from Folkestone.

56 Squadron (Tempest V) Newchurch

Sqn Ldr A.R. Hall	EJ541/US-B	V-1	1540-1610	

Sqn Ldr Hall reported that a Tempest from 3 Squadron was also involved in this kill, but apparently no claim was submitted by the latter.

129 Squadron (Mustang III) Brenzett

Flg Off I.G. Wood	FB392/DV-N	V-1	0903	Meopham Green area
Flg Off M. Twomey	FB125/DV-F	V-1	1315-1525	off Cap Gris Nez

Two Divers were destroyed during the day, the first by Flg Off Chippy Wood, who intercepted west of Romney just before 0900. He attacked from slightly below whereupon it entered cloud. Biggin Hill checked and confirmed that a Diver had crashed at 0903 south-east of Meopham Green. During the early afternoon Flg Off Twomey shot down a Diver into the sea some 20 miles north-west of Cap Gris Nez. The successes were marred by the loss of Plt Off John Bilodeau RCAF, who took off at 1150 on an anti-Diver patrol in company with Flg Off Denny Parker, and was killed when his Mustang FB395/DV-Y spun in through cloud and crashed shortly after midday.

130 Squadron (Spitfire XIV) Lympne

Wt Off J. Edwards ⎤	AP-	V-1	1445	off Dover
Plt Off J.P. Meadows ⎦	RM693/AP-			

Wt Off Edwards reported: "Intercepted Diver ten miles south-west of Dover. Attacked. Saw increase of flame from exhaust but no effect on flight. Unable to close range." Plt Off Jack Meadows added: "Followed Edwards and after four-seconds burst Diver began to go down in long glide towards east of Folkestone. Disappeared in cloud. Claim probable." The ROC reported to Biggin Hill that a Diver had crashed into the sea at the right time and place and the kill was subsequently awarded.

315 (Polish) Squadron (Mustang III) Brenzett

Flt Lt J. Schmidt PAF	HB849/PK-M	V-1	0750	New Romney area
	HB849/PK-M	V-1	0800	New Romney area

350 (Belgian) Squadron (Spitfire XIV) Friston

Flt Sgt P. Leva	RM701/MN-O	V-1	1450-1605	

After using all his ammunition and observing many strikes, Flt Sgt Pino Leva tipped the Diver with his starboard wingtip, causing it to crash and explode. The Spitfire returned safely albeit with a bent wingtip.

501 Squadron (Tempest V) Manston

Sqn Ldr J. Berry	EJ584/SD-Q	V-1	0635	West Malling area

Sqn Ldr Berry was up again at 0615, on this occasion in his Tempest:

> "I was scrambled for Divers reported coming in and was controlled by Biggin Hill. Two were
> reported coming in over Dungeness. I was six miles north of Rye when I saw a Diver coming
> in over cloud at 2,400 feet at 380mph. I attacked from astern, firing from 200 yards with two
> bursts. The Diver exploded in the air at 0635 and crashed south of West Malling."

610 Squadron (Spitfire XIV) Friston

Flg Off J. Lee ⎫	DW-	V-1	1550-1710
Flg Off N. McFarlane RCAF ⎰	DW-		

Flg Offs Lee and McFarlane fired at the V-1 and slowed it down before being forced
to break away on reaching the gun zone. They were granted a kill since the plot was
seen to fade from the radar screens.

Night 20/21 AUGUST
96 Squadron (Mosquito XIII) Ford

Flt Lt W.J. Gough	HK479/ZJ-	V-1	0430	Grid R.3722

Diver intercepted over the sea at 2,000 feet: "Bits flew off; flame turned yellow. Diver
flew on, losing height. Explosion felt (in cloud), and I had to turn hard away, also to
avoid gun belt when AA opened up half-a-mile ahead. Confirmed by F/O Goode."

125 Squadron (Mosquito XVII) Bradwell Bay
Mosquito HK291, being homed through the gun belt when in distress, was shot down
by AA fire off Hastings as it was assumed by the gunners to be a flying bomb.
Navigator Flg Off B.A. Williams baled out but the pilot 31-year-old Flt Lt Geoffrey
Dunfee was killed.

418 (RCAF) Squadron (Mosquito VI) Middle Wallop

Plt Off R.H. Thomas RCAF	MM426/TH	V-1	0217	over sea

> "A salvo of Divers seen to cross north of Berck-sur-Mer. Dived from 6,000 feet and fired three
> one-second bursts from 600 yards dead astern. Strikes seen and Diver went down in a slow
> glide and exploded in the sea approximately ten miles south of Dungeness."

Monday 21 AUGUST
Willesden (NW10) received another bomb at 1247, this impacting in College Road
and killing 20, seriously injuring a further 29. That evening, at 2017, another fell in
Wharncliffe Gardens, St Marylebone (SE25), where another 29 lives were lost and 58
seriously injured. AA gunners in the Dover area had a field day, shooting down at least
36 Divers into the sea.

150 Wing (Tempest V) Newchurch

Wg Cdr R.P. Beamont	JN751/RB	V-1	Sevenoaks area

This was Wg Cdr Roland Beamont's final flying bomb kill, raising his total to 32
including 6 shares.

501 Squadron (Tempest V) Manston
Flt Lt Cyril Thornton was killed in a flying accident when his Tempest EJ602/SD-P
crashed at Woodnesborough, Kent.

Night 21/22 AUGUST
Following a week's break from operations due to its transfer from Rosières to Venlo,
III/KG3 launched 21 sorties from its new base between 2150 and 0200. One Heinkel
crashed on take-off. All others returned safely. There followed another break in

operations and it would be a further week before the next III/KG3 mission. A Diver fell at Hartlip, in a straight line south of the Oak Lane disaster (that occurred on 16 August) and within sight of each other. This flying bomb had been released over the Thames Estuary – Sheppey area. It had crossed Sheppey, the North Kent marshes and Upchurch, but by the time it had reached Hartlip it was very low. It struck the top of some elm trees near the detached farm cottages known as 'Roman Villas' and fell onto them. One woman was killed but her husband, son and daughter survived. Another person was killed in Lordship Lane, East Dulwich (SE22) at 0500, and two more in West Norwood (SE27) at 0729, when a Diver exploded in the York Hill area.

No successful engagements were reported by fighters on Tuesday 22 August, nor during the night of 22/23 August. But the Kent AA defences scored heavily, eight falling to Folkestone gunners and 18 to Hythe – all falling into the sea. However, Wg Cdr Hampshire, CO of 456 (RAAF) Squadron was scrambled at 2350 on report of approaching aircraft. The intruder turned out to be a Do217, which was subsequently shot down by the Dover guns.

Wednesday 23 AUGUST
On the wider front, Paris was liberated on this date and by the end of the month British and Canadian troops were sweeping on towards the Pas-de-Calais, causing units of *Flakregiment 155(W)* to withdraw to prepared ski sites in Holland. But until these were fully operational and longer-range missiles available, London was effectively out of range – or so it was believed.

At 0801, another Diver fell onto buildings in Oakleigh Road, Brunswick Park, East Barnet (N11), killing 33 and injuring 212. Next day another bomb fell nearby, but fortunately it exploded on the North Sports Field in the same general area without inflicting much damage and no injuries. A Diver impacted just east of RAF Stradishall in Suffolk, coming down 100 yards north-east of the village church, its register recording:

> "0915. Church blasted by flying bomb. All the windows blown out and roofs damaged. Walls cracked, mullions broken, tool shed damaged."

The following Sunday the church was packed for a thanksgiving but only three villagers had sustained minor injuries in an explosion that could have taken many lives.

Further south, Folkestone guns brought down a dozen Divers and a fighter was seen to shoot down another just off the coast.

41 Squadron (Spitfire XII) Lympne

Flt Lt T. Spencer	MB882/EB-B	V-1	0820	Ashford area
	MB882/EB-B	V-1	0907	Harrietsham area
Flt Lt D.J. Reid RAAF	MB853/EB-	V-1 shared	2045	Ashford area
Flt Sgt V.J. Rossow RAAF	EB-	V-1 damaged		off Cap Gris Nez

The first of Flt Lt Terry Spencer's two kills was assessed to be the squadron's 50th:

> "Sighted flying bomb east of Folkestone as it left the gun belt. Two-seconds burst and it crashed by the railway line four miles south-east of Ashford. Informed of another Diver and that it would pass four miles due west of Ashford. Saw flares and dived down from 10,000 feet. Saw Diver at 4,000 feet. Closed in and fired, no strikes seen until second bursts, when strikes on port side and wing. Petrol tank exploded and Diver flicked over and went in west of railway line near Harrietsham."

Some 20 houses and farm buildings were damaged and the railway line was blocked.

Flt Lt Dennis Reid reported that he dived from 4,000 feet to position himself behind his target. He saw strikes and flame but then a Tempest cut in and Diver crashed ten miles north-west of Ashford.

56 Squadron (Tempest V) Newchurch

Wt Off V.L.J. Turner RAAF[199]	EJ526/US-N	V-1	0845-0920	

91 Squadron (Spitfire LFIX) Deanland ALG

Flg Off E. Topham	MK998/DL-	V-1	1925-2105	West Malling area

Flg Off Ted Topham was engaged in an uneventful fighter sweep with the rest of the squadron in the Amiens-Abbeville area. On returning to base he intercepted and shot down a flying bomb south-west of West Malling airfield.

129 Squadron (Mustang III) Brenzett

Wt Off A.J. Foster RAAF	FX983/DV-E	V-1	0755-0930	Headcorn area

Wt Off Joe Foster intercepted a Diver over New Romney and shot it down near Headcorn, where it was last seen diving through cloud.

130 Squadron (Spitfire XIV) Lympne

Sgt P.E.H. Standish	RM744/AP-	V-1	0903	off Dover
Flt Lt K.J. Matheson	RM760/AP-	V-1	0920	exploded mid-air
Plt Off W. Dobbs RCAF⎤	RM756/AP-	V-1	2055	Channel
Flt Sgt G. Lord ⎦	RM749/AP-B			

Sgt Peter Standish took his score to four when he shot down one into the sea off Dover: "After second burst starboard wing fell off. Diver did two rolls and then went down." Flt Lt Matheson's target exploded near Ashford:

> "Intercepted four miles west of Ashford. Saw at least four friendly aircraft including Tempests and Mustangs chasing Diver. Closed in from astern and slightly below, firing from 300-200 yards. Long burst – about four seconds. Diver exploded in mid-air and I passed through debris. Two feet of film taken during firing and explosion."

Canadian Plt Off Bill Dobbs shared another with Flt Sgt Geoff Lord[200]:

> "Intercepted five miles north-west of Gris Nez. On first attack saw strikes and Diver slowed down to 200mph and I overshot. Attacked again from astern and saw further strikes. No.2 [F/Sgt Lord] then attacked and hit Diver in port wing – Diver crashed into the sea ten miles south-west of Folkestone."

274 Squadron (Tempest V) Manston

Flt Lt L.A. Wood	EJ646/JJ-	V-1	2030	Ashford area
	EJ646/JJ-	V-1 shared	2035	Detling

Flt Lt Wood's first victim crashed five miles north of Ashford, and the second (shared with a Mustang) exploded in the air south of Detling aerodrome:

> "I sighted a Diver flying through the gun belt at 2,500 feet. It came through unharmed and I fired a burst from astern at a range of 250 yards. A Spit had been firing before with no apparent success, and this aircraft pulled away. After my attack the Diver went straight down into a wood five or six miles north of Ashford. I observed another Diver on my port side and I pulled round and chased it. When I was about 400 yards away, a Mustang pulled up in front of me and fired, scoring hits. The Diver went into a vertical dive over Detling aerodrome but recovered and started to fly south at 1,000 feet. The Mustang did not attack again so, as the Diver was heading for Bearsted, I fired a short burst from starboard and the Diver exploded in the air about 100 yards in front of me. After the explosion I found my oil pressure was falling so headed for Detling, where I landed. A piece of the Diver had pierced the oil cooler. The destruction of this Diver was witnessed by several officers at Detling."

277 (ASR) Squadron (Spitfire Vb) Shoreham

Flt Lt T.G.V. Roden	BA-	V-1	2055	Deal area

ASR Spit pilot Flt Lt Roden shot down 277 Squadron's fifth and last flying bomb:

> "At 2055, while returning from an ASR patrol off Deal, sighted white warning flares on my port. I dived down from 4,000 feet to 1,500 feet. Diver approached dead ahead and after two fighters pulled away, I gave one two-seconds burst at 400 yards, while Bofors gun also fired. Diver crashed on the ground."

306 (Polish) Squadron (Mustang III) Brenzett

Flt Lt W. Klawe PAF	FB393/UZ-U	V-1 shared	0919	Ashford area
	UZ-V	V-1 shared	2054	Grid R.3068

Flt Lt Włodzimierz Klawe intercepted the first Diver over Dymchurch at 2,500 feet. After two short bursts it slowed down and as he broke away another aircraft finished it off. It blew up in the air three miles north-west of Ashford. Klawe was successful again in the evening, intercepting over Rye. He closed in to 300 yards and saw pieces fly off the propulsion unit and the tail break off. The bomb went into a gentle climb before it crashed. Although he did not mention seeing other aircraft, apparently the Diver was also attacked by a Tempest or a Mustang.

315 (Polish) Squadron (Mustang III) Brenzett

Flt Sgt T. Berka PAF ⎫	FB367/PK-V	V-1	2045	Folkestone area
Wt Off R. Idrian PAF ⎭	HB849/PK-M			
Flt Sgt T. Berka PAF	FB367/PK-V	V-1	2054	Elham area

402 (RCAF) Squadron (Spitfire XIV) Hawkinge

Flt Sgt W.G. Austin RCAF	RM686/AE-	V-1	2040	Ashford area

> "I turned and dived from 6,000 feet, getting on to it about two miles south-east of Maidstone. I closed to 200 yards, firing a five-seconds burst. Strikes on starboard wing and the Diver began losing altitude. At this time red rockets were fired in front of me. I broke to starboard and saw a column of black smoke rising from a point about two miles on what was then my starboard side. Cine gun used. Bromley Observer's Post confirms this claim."

486 (RNZAF) Squadron (Tempest V) Newchurch

Wt Off C.J. Sheddan RNZAF	EJ577/SA-F	V-1	2041	Rye area

610 Squadron (Spitfire XIV) Friston

Wt Off Roberts chased a Diver south of Dungeness during a late evening patrol (2010-2115) but was unable to close. The Diver's speed was estimated as 420mph.

Night 23/24 AUGUST

Folkestone guns brought down 14 Divers and another was shot down into the sea just offshore. Hythe AA accounted for 20 more, with fighters shooting down four just off the coast. All of these successes were achieved during a twelve-hour period ending 0600.

96 Squadron (Mosquito XIII) Ford

Flt Lt D.L. Ward	MM524/ZJ-	V-1	0243	Channel
Flt Lt B.A. Primavesi	HK469/ZJ-	V-1	0245	Channel
Flt Lt F.R.L. Mellersh	MM577/ZJ-N	V-1	0605	Channel
	MM577/ZJ-N	V-1	0617	Channel

Flt Lts Don Ward and Brian Primavesi scored within two minutes of each other, both victims exploding on impacting the sea. Flt Lt Togs Mellersh continued his run with another brace: "(1) Pulled up, stalled and dived and exploded in the sea (2) Glided gently and exploded on sea."

157 Squadron (Mosquito XIX) West Malling

Flt Sgt P. Merrall	MM652/RS-S	V-1	0135-0410	Channel
Sqn Ldr J.H.M. Chisholm	MM674/RS-T	V-1	0345-0650	Channel

456 (RAAF) Squadron (Mosquito XVII) Ford

Flt Lt K.A. Roediger RAAF	HK297/RX-V	V-1	0245	Channel
	HK297/RX-V	V-1	0250	Channel

Flt Lt Keith Roediger raised his score to nine with two Divers over the Channel: "(1) Saw strikes and motor stopped; flying bomb dived in and exploded (2) Strikes seen. Diver climbed and then burst into flames and dived in." Two other Divers were unsuccessfully engaged by Wg Cdr Hampshire and Plt Off Butch Hodgen.

501 Squadron (Tempest V) Manston

Flg Off R-C. Deleuze (FF)⎱	EJ607/SD-N	V-1	0545-0710
Flg Off R.C. Stockburn ⎰	EJ599/SD-W		

Thursday 24 AUGUST

Seven people were killed – believed to have been all Home Guard soldiers – when a Diver fell on a gun site in Annerley Road, Penge (SE20) at 1952, very close to the impact that occurred on 29 June. The guns at Folkestone and Hythe had a highly successful day and accounted for some 65 Divers that crashed into the sea.

3 Squadron (Tempest V) Newchurch

Flt Lt A.E. Umbers RNZAF⎱	JN817/JF-H	V-1 shared	0620-0750
Wt Off F.McG. Reid[201] ⎰	JN755/JF-D		
Wt Off J.I.T. Adams RAAF	EJ549/JF-	V-1	0715-0845

91 Squadron (Spitfire LFIX) Deanland ALG

Although not on an anti-Diver patrol, Diver ace Flt Lt Ken Collier baled out over the sea due to engine trouble. Flt Sgt Ernest Cartwright, 277 Squadron Walrus Wop/AG:

> "My log book notes that we picked up a Flt Lt Collier of 91 Squadron. We were later informed that he was the first pilot to bring down a Doodlebug by tipping it with his wing, after running out of ammunition. During this period, aircraft flying below a certain height were only allowed to fly out to sea in certain places, namely Dungeness and North Foreland, but the ack-ack gunners were inclined to be a little trigger-happy. As I remember, one day we crossed the coast at Dungeness and then proceeded to fly up the coast at, what we had thought, was a safe distance from the shore. There was also quite a heavy mist hanging over the sea, and then suddenly we saw these little explosions around us, much too close for comfort. The sound of the Walrus engine was quite distinctive and not unlike a V-1. This episode taught us a valuable lesson! One night, when sleeping in the crew room at dispersal, I recall hearing an almighty bang and the next morning, when we went outside, finding the tail section of a V-1 lying at the dispersal between two of our aircraft. I also remember standing outside our crew room one day, and watching a V-1 approaching over Folkestone with a Tempest diving after it. The Tempest opened fire, hitting the V-1, and then it flew straight through the explosion. We fully expected to see the Tempest in trouble, but she flew serenely on; all in a day's work for those boys!"[202]

130 Squadron (Spitfire XIV) Lympne

Plt Off J.P. Meadows	RM693/AP-	V-1 shared	0740	off Dungeness

Plt Off Jack Meadows shared his kill with Tempests from 3 Squadron:

> "Intercepted 12 miles south-east of Dungeness. Saw strikes on Diver immediately after opening fire and Diver began to lose speed and height. After a further attack by a Tempest, the Diver went into a steep dive and plunged into the sea."

This was 130 Squadron's 12th and last Diver, of which three were shared.

274 Squadron (Tempest V) Manston

Flt Lt L.P. Griffiths RNZAF	EJ647/JJ-	V-1 shared	0705	Channel

"I saw a Diver at 3,000 feet. I attacked from 400 yards astern and saw no strikes. A Spit XVI next attacked but no strikes seen and he pulled away. Diver continued on same course and speed. I then made another attack from 250 yards astern and saw strikes. The Diver went down and exploded in the sea."

316 (Polish) Squadron (Mustang III) Friston

Sgt J. Mielnicki PAF	HB845/SZ-Y	V-1	2040	Dymchurch area
	HB845/SZ-Y	V-1	2050	off Dungeness

402 (RCAF) Squadron (Spitfire XIV) Hawkinge

Flg Off W.S. Harvey RCAF	RM734/AE-	V-1 shared	0705	
Flt Lt J.A.H.G. de Niverville RCAF	RM727/AE-	V-1	1810	Ashford area

Flg Off Bill Harvey shared his victory with a Tempest (Flt Lt Griffiths of 274 Squadron), while Flt Lt Joe de Niverville[203] scored the Canadian unit's last kill when his victim crashed east of Ashford:

"I first saw Diver about one mile east of Folkestone. I dived down on it but was forced to pull up again because of flak. I waited until the Diver was clear of the flak and came down again, firing from 400 yards to 200 yards. I saw strikes on the starboard side of the jet unit. Another burst and two large pieces flew off the wing. It wobbled from side to side and began to loose altitude quickly. My last glimpse of it was seeing it diving through cloud at about 1,000 feet. I looked back and saw a pillar of brown smoke rising into the cloud. Green 2, who was slightly above, saw the right wing fall off and a few seconds later saw a large chunk of the left wing fly off. The Diver then went straight down."

The Diver impacted in the village of Bodsham near Elmsted where 20 houses were damaged. There were no reported casualties.

Friday 25 AUGUST
274 Squadron (Tempest V) Manston

Flt Lt O.E. Willis	EJ634/JJ-	V-1	0705	Ashford area

"I attacked from astern, 200 yards range, firing short bursts and saw strikes."

The Diver came down in the Ashford area.

Night 25/26 AUGUST
A Diver killed a dozen people when it fell in Carrington Road, Dartford.

605 Squadron (Mosquito VI) Manston

Flt Lt J.G. Musgrave	MM429/UP-H	V-1	pm	Channel

Saturday 26 AUGUST
Air Marshal Sir Roderic Hill flew into Friston in his personal Tempest.

91 Squadron (Spitfire LFIX) Deanland ALG

Flg Off E. Topham	MK293/DL-	V-1	1125-1325

Whilst engaged on escort to RAF Marauders raiding St Justen (Ramrod 1231), Flg Off Ted Topham again sighted a flying bomb, which he shot down as his tenth kill (one shared), and the Squadron's 186th and final victory.

Night 26/27 AUGUST
A total of 18 Divers were shot down by Folkestone and Hythe guns in less than an hour.

96 Squadron (Mosquito XIII) Ford

Flt Lt F.R.L. Mellersh	MM577/ZJ-N	V-1	0636	off Dungeness

This was Flt Lt Togs Mellersh's 43nd Diver kill, raising the squadrons' tally to 176 destroyed. He reported: "Attacked Diver at 1,500 feet. Engine stopped, climbed hard to port and dived in 15 miles off Dungeness."

125 Squadron (Mosquito XVII) Middle Wallop

Flt Lt A.D.Boyle	HK316/VA-	V-1	0150	over land

"At 0150 Diver was seen 15-20 miles inland from Cap Gris Nez, height 4,000 feet, speed 360mph. I dived on it from 8,000 feet and closing to 2,500 feet fired three one-second bursts from astern and below. Strikes were seen. I had to break away as approaching gun belt. Soon after, controller confirmed that the Diver had considerably slowed up and a few minutes later that it had come down inland."

501 Squadron (Tempest V) Manston

Flg Off R.G. Lucas	EJ590/SD-L	V-1	0120-0330	
Flt Lt G.L. Bonham RNZAF	EJ597/SD-D	V-1	0535-0735	
	EJ597/SD-D	V-1	0535-0735	
	EJ597/SD-D	V-1	0535-0735	
	EJ597/SD-D	V-1	0535-0735	
Plt Off R.H. Bennett	EJ593/SD-B	V-1	0605-0720	West Malling area
Flg Off W.F. Polley	EJ598/SD-H	V-1	0610-0735	exploded in mid-air

After bringing down four Divers, Flt Lt Gordon Bonham found he was short of fuel and put down on farmland, as recalled by local teenager Alan Palmer:

"On a very foggy Sunday morning, a Hawker Tempest landed near Kingsden Farm and so I made it my business to inspect the plane. I met the pilot, a New Zealander wearing an RAF uniform, coming out of the fog. He told me he had run short of fuel and was unable to reach his base at Manston. He had shot down a V-1, which exploded in front of him and resulted in the plane being scratched from front to back as he flew through the debris. Out of ammunition he encountered a second V-1 that he destroyed by flying alongside and tipping its wing with his wingtip. The V-1 became unstable and crashed to the ground. He encountered two more V-1s, which he disposed of in the same manner! Now short of fuel as well as being out of ammunition explained why he landed near Kingsden. The pilot telephoned Manston from the farmhouse to notify them of the situation and joined us for breakfast and lunch! The laborious task of refuelling his plane was done using 4-gallon cans carried from a lorry to the plane. Once refuelled he departed, but not before giving us an air display!"[204]

Of his second kill Plt Off Ron Bennett reported:

"I was on patrol near Ashford when I saw a Diver approach north of Dungeness at 4,000 feet, speed 410mph. I closed to 500 yards and fired several short bursts and saw hits. The light went out and the Diver lost speed and height, crashing and exploding on the ground north of West Malling."

Flg Off Bill Polley had a lucky escape when the Diver he attacked blew up:

"The area of chase was very limited as we patrolled between the coastal batteries which fired at everything that moved (including ourselves) and the armoured balloons which were also very lethal. We had minutes at the most to find our target, get into position and fire before breaking off very rapidly! Very often we were too close to our targets before we got the opportunity to fire and the big danger was getting an airburst. On one occasion I was chasing a V-1 too quickly and I knew that I was overhauling the bomb too quickly and also that I was very close to the armoured balloons. I fired a long burst and pulled up steeply to starboard, almost above the V-1, just as it exploded. The blast caught my left wing and tumbled the aircraft in a series of snap rolls. After what seemed an eternity the aircraft regained its stability. The only problem was that I saw the searchlights (marking the line of the armoured balloons) apparently starting somewhere above my head and going down to the ground. As my gyros had tumbled it took me many ageing moments to realise that I was upside down. We were always very wary of the Tempest and avoided spinning the aircraft as it had a reputation of being anything but stable, but after that flight I had a lot more affection for the Tempest and confidence in it."[205]

605 Squadron (Mosquito VI) Manston

Flt Lt J.G. Musgrave	MM429/UP-H	V-1	0153	Channel

"Before patrol line was reached, two Divers were seen out from south of Boulogne too far distant to attack. During patrol at 0150 Diver seen to fly out from between Boulogne and Hardelot at 4,000 feet, speed 340mph. We were flying at 7,000 feet and when Diver was well clear of French coast, dived to attack and gave in all six bursts of cannon and machine-gun fire. Many strikes were seen and jet spluttered. As I approached the English coast I pulled away to port and instantaneously the Diver blew up with a terrific flash. The guns did not open fire and no other fighters were seen to engage or to be in the area."

Sunday 27 AUGUST

At 0718, a Diver fell in the Manor House Road/Sidney Road area of Brixton (SW9), killing four. Four Divers crashed in Tenterden RD, having been shot down by fighters, but only three people were slightly injured.

3 Squadron (Tempest V) Newchurch

Plt Off H.R. Wingate	EJ577/JF-	V-1	0640-0750

Plt Off Dickie Wingate's score of flying bombs tallied 19 (one shared) following this latest kill.

41 Squadron (Spitfire XII) Lympne

Flt Lt T. Spencer	MB850/EB-F	V-1	0720	Rye area

Flt Lt Terry Spencer was conducting an air test in MB850 when he saw a Diver over Romney Marsh. Opened fire from 100 yards 15 miles north of Rye, following which the bomb exploded – the squadron diarist noted that he returned somewhat shaken by the experience.

56 Squadron (Tempest V) Newchurch

Flg Off W.R. MacLaren	JN816/US-W	V-1	0635-0725	
Flt Sgt H. Shaw	EJ548/US-G	V-1	0720-0820	Ham Street area

274 Squadron (Tempest V) Manston

Flg Off J.W. Woolfries	EJ628/JJ-	V-1	0645	Hollingbourne area

The Diver was shot down between Hollingbourne and Doddington. Flg Off Woolfries' combat report reveals:

"Sighted a Diver coming in over Dymchurch at 0645. After it had passed through the gun belt I got into position but saw a Tempest below close astern. I kept slightly above until the other aircraft had expended all its ammunition and had broken away. I saw no strikes scored and Diver continued on course with 'flame' still burning. I then attacked from astern, opening fire from 250 yards. On the third short burst the Diver crashed and exploded in a wood east of Maidstone."

315 (Polish) Squadron (Mustang III) Brenzett

Flt Sgt J. Donocik PAF	FX945/PK-I	V-1 shared	0752	Ashford area

"Intercepted Diver near Dymchurch at 2,500 feet. A Tempest fired from 700 yards as I closed. I fired from 300 yards, line astern. Jet unit blew up and flying bomb crashed in woods three and-a-half miles south-west of Ashford."

486 (RNZAF) Squadron (Tempest V) Newchurch

Flt Lt J.R. Cullen RNZAF	JN770/SA-V	V-1	0709	Tenterden area

610 Squadron (Spitfire XIV) Friston

Flt Sgt T.F. Higgs	DW-	V-1	0630-0700	Tunbridge Wells

This was Flt Sgt Tom Higgs'[206] second kill.

Night 27/28 AUGUST

25 Squadron (Mosquito XVII) Coltishall

Plt Off B. Travers	HK304/ZK-	V-1	2345-0235	Pas-de-Calais area
	+ Bf109			

The Mosquito flown by Plt Off Barney Travers was vectored after a bogey, which turned out to be a flying bomb. This was attacked and shot down in flames. It exploded on hitting the ground a few miles inland from the French coast. Travers also shot down a Bf109 over the Pas-de-Calais, an aircraft of 1/JG301 that was part of the force defending the launch sites. Fw Martin Schulze was wounded but managed to bale out before his aircraft crashed. Travers reported:

> "We were told by control of a bogey and given several vectors. Eventually a workable contact was obtained at 10,000 feet to port. The bogey was orbiting and changing height between 4,500 and 7,500 feet at a speed of 260mph. I closed the range to approximately 300 feet and obtained a visual on the exhausts but could not see the aircraft. The bogey continued to orbit and I followed but was unable to close the range. The bogey then crossed the French coast. I followed and was able to close the range and at 100 feet identified the aircraft as a Me109. The identification was confirmed by my navigator [Plt Off Alex Patterson]. I dropped back to 200 feet range and opened fire from dead astern, firing at position indicated by e/a's exhausts, and continued firing until the e/a burst into flames. I then saw the e/a turn over onto its back, dive vertically down and hit the ground [at 0125] where it continued to burn. My navigator also saw the flash as the e/a hit the ground. I then continued anti-Diver patrol for 45 minutes before returning to base."

501 Squadron (Tempest V) Manston

Flt Lt G.L. Bonham RNZAF	EJ607/SD-N	V-1	0525-0700	Rye area

Flt Lt Gordon Bonham was engaged in a night flying test when he was vectored onto a flying bomb near Rye.

Monday 28 AUGUST

The AOC was up in his Tempest during the height of the day's Diver assault and was well satisfied with what he saw:

> "Flying towards the south coast, I could see over Romney Marsh a wall of black smoke marking the position of the Diver barrage. From time to time a fresh salvo would be added to repair the slow erosion of the wind. On the far side of the barrage fighters were shooting down flying bombs into the Channel; on the nearer side more fighters waited on its fringe to pounce on the occasional bomb that got so far. The whole was as fine a spectacle of co-operation as any commander could wish to see."

Of the 97 bombs that approached the shores on this date, only four reached London, the fighters accounting for 23, the AA guns 65 (58 falling to Folkestone and Hythe gunners) and the balloons a further two. Fifty-nine of the 90 fell into the sea. A Diver shot down by a fighter crashed near Headcorn at 1410, causing damage to buildings but no casualties. One that exploded in a chalk pit at Stone, near Dartford, was found to be carrying propaganda leaflets as part of the psychological warfare now being waged by the Germans. Another canister of leaflets was found following the crash of a Diver at Madam Court Farm, Frinstead. Fighters were responsible for all seven Divers that crashed in Tenterden RD, two people being seriously injured when one exploded at Merrington.

3 Squadron (Tempest V) Newchurch

Flt Sgt R.W. Cole	JN768/JF-F	V-1	1755-1915	
	JN768/JF-F	V-1	1755-1915	
Wt Off J.I.T. Adams RAAF	EJ525/JF-	V-1	2100-2140	

Flt Sgt Bob Cole's score reached 21 (one shared) with this brace.

41 Squadron (Spitfire XII) Lympne

Flt Lt T. Spencer	EN229/EB-K	V-1		Rye area

Although 41 Squadron had officially been taken off anti-Diver patrols, Flt Lt Terry Spencer shot down one near Rye for the unit's 53rd and last victory.

56 Squadron (Tempest V) Newchurch

Flt Sgt H. Shaw	EJ548/US-G	V-1	1400-1505

129 Squadron (Mustang III) Brenzett

Flg Off J.E. Hartley	HB860/DV-J	V-1	1315-1520	off Dymchurch
Flt Lt G.C.D. Green	FZ128/DV-A	V-1	1325-1520	off Hastings
Flt Lt A.C. Leigh	SR428/DV-L	V-1	1510-1645	off Dungeness
Flt Lt R.G. Kleimeyer RNZAF (Aus)	FZ128/DV-A	V-1	1640-1820	exploded in mid-air
Flg Off J.E. Hartley	FX924/DV-V	V-1	1755-1905	off Dungeness
Flt Lt R.C. Conroy RAAF	SR428/DV-L	V-1	1755-1950	off Dungeness
	SR428/DV-L	V-1	1755-1950	off Dungeness
Flt Lt P.N. Howard	FB170/DV-U	V-1	2055-2130	over land

Between 0610 and 2130, 24 aircraft carried out a dozen Diver patrols and shot down eight of the missiles. Flg Off Jim Hartley destroyed the first of the day, which he stated appeared to be twice the normal size (!) Intercepted over Boulogne at 7,500 feet and flying at 200mph, he fired from 400 yards down to 100 yards astern and below, but saw no results. He then flew in front of it, hoping to upset the gyro with his slipstream but again no success, so he lowered his flaps and came up 300 yards astern. Having fired a short burst the propulsion unit was set alight at 10,000 feet (an extraordinary height for a V-1; possibly misprint for 1,000 feet). The Diver crashed into the sea two miles south of Dymchurch. The second Diver was destroyed by Flt Lt Gerry Green, who intercepted his victim ten miles north-west of Boulogne. He carried out an attack from astern and the Diver splashed into the sea two miles east of Hastings. Flt Lt Joe Leigh intercepted a Diver ten miles south of Dungeness. It fell into the sea eight miles offshore following an attack from 200 yards astern.

The Diver attacked by Flt Lt Dutch Kleimeyer exploded in the air, slightly damaging his aircraft, while the starboard wing was shot off Flg Off Jim Hartley's victim, which then spun down into the sea 20 miles south-east of Dungeness. Flt Lt Guns Conroy shot down the first of his brace with cannons, the Diver spinning into the sea 25 miles south-east of Dungeness, but the second was caught in his slipstream and exploded in the sea in the same general area. To round off this successful day, Flt Lt Phil Howard intercepted a Diver 15 miles west of Boulogne and pursued it to the Kent coast, scoring strikes on wing roots and fuselage. Pieces were seen breaking away before it entered the gun belt and crashed.

306 (Polish) Squadron (Mustang III) Brenzett

Flt Lt J. Wisiorek PAF	FB347/UZ-T	V-1	1405	Grid R.3564

Wt Off J. Rogowski PAF	FX979/UZ-A	V-1	1425	Canterbury area
	FX979/UZ-A	V-1	1440	Canterbury area
Wt Off J. Pomietlarz PAF	FX979/UZ-A	V-1	1618	Grid R.4344

Flt Lt Jan Wisiorek intercepted a Diver at 2,500 feet near Hythe. He attacked from astern, following which it slowed up, then went into the ground vertically and exploded. A few minutes later Wt Off Jan Rogowski intercepted a Diver off Folkestone at 9,000 feet. Its jet unit extinguished and it went into a vertical dive, crashing and exploding north-west of Canterbury. Fifteen minutes later he shot down a second, which also crashed and exploded near Canterbury. Wt Off Jan Pomietlarz shot down one more at 1618, having intercepted it over Lydd at 3,000 feet. He reported that the Diver went into a steep dive and exploded on the ground.

315 (Polish) Squadron (Mustang III) Brenzett

Flt Lt J. Polak PAF	HB849/PK-M	V-1 shared	1443	Dungeness area
Wt Off R. Idrian PAF	FX995/PK-E	V-1	1538	off Boulogne
Wt Off T. Jankowski PAF	FB367/PK-V	V-1	1615	off Boulogne
	FB367/PK-V	V-1	1645	off Dungeness

486 (RNZAF) Squadron (Tempest V) Newchurch

Plt Off W.A.L. Trott RNZAF	JN863/SA-R	V-1	1625	Tenterden area

610 Squadron (Spitfire XIV) Friston

Flg Off P.M. Bangerter	RM739/DW-O	V-1	1355-1530	off Dungeness
	RM739/DW-O	V-1	1355-1530	off Dungeness

While Flg Off Pat Bangerter scored two kills, his New Zealand colleague Flt Sgt Bill Shaw attacked a third without success.

616 Squadron (Meteor F.1) Manston

Flg Off G.N. Hobson	EE217/YQ-J	V-1	1658	Tenterden area
Flt Sgt E. Epps	EE2??/YQ-			

At 1625, Flg Off Gordon Hobson and Flt Sgt Eddie Epps were scrambled at 1625 and ordered to orbit Tenterden. A Diver was seen coming in at 2,000 feet, flying at 380mph. Hobson reported:

> "I intercepted the Diver about two miles north of Tenterden at 1657. Three Tempests were seen 2,000 yards behind and on the same course as Diver. The Tempests appeared to be losing ground and gradually fell behind. Diving down in a shallow dive from 4,000 feet, I passed over the Tempests and fired two three-seconds bursts at 300 yards from behind and slightly above Diver. Strikes were seen on the Diver, which dipped on its starboard wing and continued on its course. Continuing to close in I fired one three-seconds burst from 100 yards. The Diver immediately spun to earth and exploded. No other aircraft was seen at the time of the attack but as I broke away to starboard after seeing the Diver spin down, I saw another Meteor breaking away to port."

This was Flt Sgt Epps, who added:

> "I attacked level behind and opened fire at 300 yards with one short burst. Strikes were seen as the Diver dipped on its starboard wing. I continued to fire a few more short bursts and saw the Diver spin and explode on the ground. As I broke away to port I saw another Meteor break away to my right."

The Mosquito XIXs of **157 Squadron** moved back to Swannington to resume intruder sorties over the Continent. The Squadron had claimed 41 V-1s including one shared.

Tuesday 29 AUGUST

Kent coastal gunners had another field day, Folkestone batteries shooting down 32

Divers, while Hythe gunners got a further 26. One of the last Divers to fall on south-east London glided down at 1404, its wing colliding with the steeple of Eltham's parish church (SE9). The subsequent explosion killed two and injured 50 more. A Diver shot down by a fighter near Leigh in Kent also contained propaganda leaflets. Four others, all victims of fighters, fell at Offham, Chart Sutton (three slightly injured), Stockbury and Hucking, between 1210-1405. Eleven people were injured, two seriously, when a Diver fell at Lydd, damaging some 200 houses.

3 Squadron (Tempest V) Newchurch

Flt Sgt J.W. Foster	EJ582/JF-T	V-1	1730-1845
Flg Off R.E. Barckley	JN755/JF-D	V-1	1930-2020

Having scored the RAF's first Diver kill way back on 8 May, Flg Off Bob Barckley shot down his 13th and appropriately 3 Squadron's last and 303rd.

56 Squadron (Tempest V) Newchurch

Flt Sgt H. Shaw	EJ548/US-G	V-1	1115-1225	Cranbrook area
Flg Off R.V. Dennis	JN816/US-W	V-1	1325-1450	Maidstone area

129 Squadron (Mustang III) Brenzett

Flg Off J.E. Hartley	SR436/DV-T	V-1	1130-1340	Folkestone area
Flg Off I.G. Wood	FX924/DV-V	V-1	1315-1440	
Flt Lt D.F. Ruchwaldy	FB178/DV-R	V-1	1530-1745	off Dungeness
	FB178/DV-R	V-1 shared	1530-1745	Brenzett area
	FB178/DV-R	V-1	1530-1745	off Boulogne
	FB178/DV-R	V-1	1530-1745	
Flt Lt J.P. Bassett	FB130/DV-W	V-1 shared	1700-1855	Lydd area
Flg Off A.F. Osborne	FB392/DV-N	V-1	1830-2020	off Le Touquet

The first Diver of the day was destroyed by Flg Off Hartley, who intercepted five miles west of Ambleteuse. He fired four short bursts and the propulsion unit caught fire and the Diver exploded in the air approximately ten miles south of Folkestone. Flg Off Chippy Wood shot down his victim into the sea off Dungeness after observing strikes on both wings. Flt Lt Des Ruchwaldy was the star turn with four Divers shot down during his patrol, one of which he shared with AA defences. The first was shot down in mid-Channel. Almost immediately he tagged onto a second, which he attacked with short bursts. The Diver turned over, righted itself and flew into the gun belt at Dungeness, where it was hit by AA fire and crashed near Brenzett. The third was intercepted over Boulogne at 2,000 feet, where Ruchwaldy's Mustang came under fire from a ship in the harbour. He reported that the Diver was caught in his slipstream and crashed into the sea a mile off the coast, but admitted that it might have been shot down by the ship's flak. Either way he was credited with its destruction.

No.4 was engaged 15 miles west of Boulogne at 1,500 feet. Following a short burst his guns jammed, so he tipped it with his wing and it crashed into the sea five miles east of Dungeness. Flt Lt Bertie Bassett also intercepted a Diver west of Boulogne, which he attacked from dead astern. Strikes were observed and pieces flew off. Excess flame issued from the jet unit and it crashed and exploded near Lydd. The final Diver fell to Flg Off Sammy Osborne, who intercepted ten miles north-west of Le Touquet. He closed in to 300 yards and strikes were seen, the bomb turning to port and entering a dive. The final crash was not witnessed due to 10/10th cloud.

274 Squadron (Tempest V) Manston

Flt Lt L.A. Wood	EJ686/JJ-	V-1 shared	1356	Maidstone area
Flt Sgt N.G. Carn[207]	EJ620/JJ-	V-1	1405	Maidstone area
Flt Lt D.C. Fairbanks RCAF (US)	EJ647/JJ-	V-1	1733	exploded in mid-air

Sqn Ldr M.G. Barnett RNZAF	EJ645/JJ-	V-1	1923	West Malling area

Flt Lt Wood and his No.2 (Flt Sgt Carn) scored kills within a few minutes of each other, Wood sharing his with another aircraft five miles north of Ashford:

> "At 1348 I sighted a Diver about five miles north-west of Dymchurch at 2,500 feet. I attacked from 300 yards astern, closing rapidly to 150 yards and saw strikes on starboard side of target. I positioned myself for further attack and found Mustang flying alongside. We both fired from 200 yards astern and Diver glided down, exploding about 30 yards from railway track five miles north of Maidstone."

Flt Sgt Norman Carn's victim fell near Maidstone: "I was vectored at 1400 on a Diver coming in over Folkestone at 2,000 feet. With a Meteor and two Tempests I chased it and attacked from 200 yards astern, closing in to 50 yards for my second burst. The Diver went in and exploded in a field near Maidstone." American Flt Lt David Fairbanks' target blew up in mid-air:

> "At 1730 I sighted a Diver coming in over Lympne at 2,500 feet, travelling at 390-400mph. I opened fire from 200 yards astern and it exploded in mid-air over Puckley. A Spit XIV and a Tempest also fired at it but they were out of range and there was no result from their attacks."

Sqn Ldr Gary Barnett's report revealed the near chaos that reigned in the sky when more than one fighter attempted to shoot down the same Diver:

> "I sighted Diver crossing in three miles east of Rye at 3,000 feet. It was chased by a Tempest, which closed in to 100 yards but I saw no strikes as it broke away. Earlier in the attack, when the Tempest was firing from 200 yards, a Mustang dived steeply and opened fire from 400 yards with no possibility of hitting the target, firing directly through the line of flight of the Tempest. The Mustang was unable to close and eventually broke away. Seeing the Diver still flying straight and level, I opened fire from 200 yards and scored strikes on the starboard wing. The Diver went in and exploded two miles south of West Malling."

306 (Polish) Squadron (Mustang III) Brenzett
Flt Lt A. Beyer PAF	HB863/UZ-O	V-1	1207	Dungeness area

The squadron scored what it believed was its final kill when Flt Lt Andrzej Beyer shot down a Diver that was last seen entering 10/10th cloud after its jet unit had stopped, following his attack north of Dungeness (the squadron's final kill was actually achieved six months later over Holland).

315 (Polish) Squadron (Mustang III) Brenzett
Wt Off K. Kijak PAF	PK-O	V-1	1200	off Boulogne
Flt Lt F. Wiza PAF	FX878/PK-F	V-1 shared	1349	Newchurch area

Flt Lt Wiza shared his kill with Plt Off Hall of 486 Squadron. Sqn Ldr J. Zulikowski (PK-B) from ADGB HQ flew a sortie with 315 Squadron (1300-1450):

> "Prior to my official posting to 306 Squadron, I visited 133 Wing twice in my new capacity of a Staff Officer at HQFC. On both occasions I took the opportunity to get familiar with Mustang aircraft and did some local flying. During my second visit, I even had the opportunity to give chase to a V-1, which just happened to have crossed the coastline on its way to London. However, as I was inching my approach to his tail, a Tempest dived in front of me and got the bug first, which exploded instantly. As one of the main routes of the flying bombs was passing over Brenzett, it was a great show to watch our fighters pursuing these intruders without regard to the anti-aircraft guns' shells, which competed successfully with our fighters by using proximity fuses, thus creating a high rate of scoring. During the night, the artillery, being left in the field on their own, was doubling the effort to get the bombs. It was unnerving to find, the following morning, our canvas tents torn by the fragments of artillery shrapnel. No wonder that some wore helmets during their sleep, for protection!"

486 (RNZAF) Squadron (Tempest V) Newchurch

Wt Off B.J. O'Connor RNZAF	EJ577/SA-F	V-1	1208	West Malling area
Plt Off K.A. Smith RNZAF	JN770/SA-V	V-1	1320	Ashford area
Plt Off B.M. Hall RNZAF	JN803/SA-D	V-1 shared	1358	Rye area
Flg Off R.J. Cammock RNZAF	JN863/SA-R	V-1	1848	Tonbridge area
Plt Off J.H. Stafford RNZAF	JN803/SA-D	V-1	1915	Tonbridge area

610 Squadron (Spitfire XIV) Friston

Flg Off P.M. Bangerter ⎫	DW-	V-1	1215-1320	off Dungeness
Plt Off H.C. Finbow ⎭	DW-			

616 Squadron (Meteor F.1) Manston

Flg Off H. Miller	EE2??/YQ-	V-1	1415	Sittingbourne area

Flg Off Hugh Miller shot down his first and 616's last V-1, raising its score to 14 including one shared. He reported:

> "I intercepted a Diver just north of Ashford. Two Tempests were seen 600 yards behind the Diver. Both fired but no strikes were observed. Owing to the Tempests flying line astern of the Diver I was forced to make a beam attack from port and fired three two-seconds bursts at 100 yards. Strikes were seen on port wing. I again attacked, this time from above and slightly behind at 400 yards. By this time the two Tempests, still line astern, appeared to close in on the Diver. I observed strikes from my fire and the Diver rolled over and exploded on the ground four miles south-west of Sittingbourne."

Wg Cdr Andy McDowall DFM flying EE222/YQ-G on an anti-Diver patrol during the afternoon ran out of fuel and crash-landed south of Manston. Flg Off Mike Cooper recalled:

> "Wg Cdr McDowall was the first victim of engine failure. Running short of fuel and unable to reach base he force-landed in a field. Following normal Spitfire forced-landing procedure, he came in with wheels up but because of the smooth, clean lines of the Meteor's belly, the plane careered across the field and through hedges before coming to a rest. It was a complete write-off, though the Wing Commander himself was uninjured. This incident was the reason for an order that all future forced landings in Meteors were to be carried out with wheels down."

In fact, Wg Cdr McDowall suffered a few cuts but nothing serious[208]. Another anti-Diver patrol was flown by Flt Lt Dennis Barry in EE227/YQ-Y[209], albeit without success.

Night 29/30 AUGUST

Heinkels launched seven flying bombs during the night, two of which fell in Essex and one west of Aylesbury, Bucks. Two reached London.

Wednesday 30 AUGUST

With the onslaught trailing off, Folkestone gunners had to be satisfied with just ten Divers destroyed during the day. Dartford's balloon barrage accounted for its 50th Diver at 0749, this slightly injuring seven people at the Darenth Training Colony when it crashed and exploded.

274 Squadron (Tempest V) Manston

Cne J. Vassier (FF)	EJ628/JJ-	V-1	0943	Ashford area
Flg Off J.W. Woolfries	EJ646/JJ-	V-1	1203	

Cne Jean Vassier, a 36-year-old short-sighted Frenchman who wore spectacles when flying, scored his first and only kill five miles north of Ashford:

> "I sighted Diver crossing in between Folkestone and Hythe at 5,000 feet and still climbing. I

engaged it above 10/10th cloud about five miles north-east of Ashford. I fired from astern and below from 150 yards and Diver exploded in mid-air."

610 Squadron (Spitfire XIV) Friston

Wt Off Jack Bonfield took off on a late evening patrol (2030-2130) with Flt Lt Pat Bangerter. About 15 miles off Boulogne when thick cloud was encountered, Bangerter turned to skirt round it but Bonfield disappeared. Presumably his aircraft (RB150) crashed into the sea. His body was later washed up on the Dutch coast. 610 Squadron recorded that it had flown 2,055 hours on anti-V-1 patrols and had shot down 50 missiles for the loss of three pilots killed.

Night 30/31 AUGUST

In the morning hours, between 0312 and 0640, some 20 Divers were launched by Heinkels of III/KG3, apparently with Gloucester as their target, but only eight crossed the coast and of these six fell in Suffolk and two in Essex. Of the Suffolk impacts, one injured seven people at Harleston at 0445, and three fell near Ipswich, at Raydon, Great Wenham and Chapel St Mary but caused no injuries. Another, that fell to a fighter at 0553, crashed near Whitstable in Kent, injuring four people, one seriously.

One of the Heinkels FTR, Uffz Lorenz Gruber's 8 Staffel machine (5K+BS) crashed at Vossenberg at 0500 during the return flight. There were no survivors[210]. This was the final operation for the month, bringing the total sorties flown for August to 228 for the loss of three aircraft, one of which crashed within the vicinity of the airfield from which it was operating, a much better return than for the previous month.

25 Squadron (Mosquito XVII) Coltishall

Flg Off B.G. Nobbs in HK243/ZK-G sighted two V-1s during his 0330-0630 patrol. The first dived into the sea before he could open fire. He then attacked the second but it continued on its course, apparently undamaged.

96 Squadron (Mosquito XIII) Ford

Flt Lt I.A. Dobie	HK437/ZJ-	V-1	0600	off Cap Gris Nez

Flt Lt Ian Dobie reported seeing a wave of a dozen Divers leaving Cap Gris Nez at 0550. He engaged one that drew away, but broke away when it was illuminated by a searchlight near the gun belt. He then searched for another target and saw one at 6,000 feet. He closed to 1,000 feet and fired three bursts. Strikes were observed all over and the Diver crashed into the sea.

456 (RAAF) Squadron (Mosquito XVII) Ford

Sqn Ldr B. Howard RAAF	HK323/RX-R	V-1	0551	exploded in mid-air
	HK323/RX-R	V-1	0556	Channel (Grid R.7046)

Sqn Ldr Bas Howard scored his fourth and fifth kills in rapid succession:

"Diver seen crossing coast at Gris Nez at 2,000 feet, speed 380mph. Too fast to intercept, though I fired from 2,000 feet. No results. Second Diver seen just south of Gris Nez. Fired from 1,500 feet dead astern and Diver exploded in the air, debris hitting the aircraft. Saw third Diver south of Gris Nez above cloud at 6,000 feet, climbing slightly. I penetrated tops of clouds to find flying bomb just on tail, so dropped back to 1,200 feet and, from dead astern, fired three bursts. Strikes seen each time and flames changed colour. Shower of sparks. Light went out and it glided down very slowly and exploded in sea."

Wt Off G.B. Gould (HK248) saw a Diver coming in over the Thames Estuary at 0500, but when closing in from 4,000 feet saw another aircraft intervene so abandoned the chase. At 0515, south-east of Dover, he was vectored onto a second Diver but was again forestalled by another aircraft opening fire from behind and had to break away.

501 Squadron (Tempest V) Manston
Flg Off E.L. Williams (Rhod)   EJ585/SD-A   V-1   0330-0525   Herne Bay area

Thursday 31 AUGUST
As if to make one final impression, several waves of Divers were launched across the Channel. Most failed to reach their targets, allowing the coastal gunners to blaze away and increase their impressive tallies. Folkestone guns brought down 19, and witnessed fighters shoot down three more; Hythe guns got nine, while Dover AA also had a successful day, shooting down a further six into the sea. The guns located in the New Romney area brought down a further five that fell into the sea, taking their tally for the month to at least 160. However, one that evaded the defences exploded near Lydden Spout Coastal battery, injuring four soldiers. A Diver that fell at Aldingham in Ashford RD spewed out many German propaganda leaflets, as did one that was shot down by a fighter and crashed near Park Wood Cottages, Hollingbourne.

56 Squadron (Tempest V) Newchurch
Flt Sgt H. Shaw   EJ548/US-G   V-1   1145-1300   Rye area

This proved to be Flt Sgt Artie Shaw's tenth (four shared) and final kill.

274 Squadron (Tempest V) Manston
Flg Off J.M. Mears   EJ611/JJ-   V-1   1120-1200   Gravesend area

Flg Off John Mears was responsible for 274 Squadron's 20th (including four shares) and last flying bomb kill:

> "Sighted Diver coming in north of Dover at 5/6,000 feet. The Diver was climbing through cloud and reached 8,500 feet before I attacked over Sittingbourne from 350 yards astern. The 'light' went out and it glided to Gravesend where it exploded in the river."

486 (RNZAF) Squadron (Tempest V) Newchurch
Wt Off B.J. O'Connor RNZAF   JN802/SA-C   V-1   1918   Maidstone area

This turned out to be 486's last and 241st Diver kill. These victories had been marred by the loss of three pilots killed and ten injured, with 17 aircraft destroyed or damaged beyond repair. Most of the casualties resulted from aircraft being caught in the flames or struck by debris from bursting bombs.

501 Squadron (Tempest V) Manston
Sqn Ldr J. Berry   EJ596/SD-C   V-1   0550   Faversham area

This proved to be Sqn Ldr Joe Berry's final Diver kill, taking his score to 59 and two shared:

> "I was patrolling under Watling Control over Ashford and to the west when I saw a Diver in the Sandwich area at 3,000 feet at 250mph, at 0545. I closed in to 300 yards dead astern and fired a short burst, which knocked pieces off the propulsion unit. I fired again from 150 yards and saw more strikes. The Diver exploded on the ground in the Faversham area at 0550."

Unknown date in August
1/Lt Noble Wright USAAF of the 4thBS was returning from a raid in his B-24 named 'Dynamite 'N Dodo' when a Diver was sighted and was shot down by one of the gunners, Sgt George W. Baldwin. This was apparently the only flying bomb shot down by a US bomber.

4thBS/34thBG (B-24) USAAF
Sgt G.W. Baldwin USAAF   42-52755   V-1   daytime   over sea

August reminiscences
Sqn Ldr Joe Berry DFC of 501 Squadron was invited by the BBC to broadcast to the nation in an effort to reassure the population that the defences were getting on top of the flying bomb situation:

"There are probably those of you among my listeners tonight who imagine that tackling a robot which cannot shoot back or take evasive action is – to use a popular service term – 'a piece of cake'. Nothing could be further from the truth, I assure you. As many of you will probably know the first of these flying bombs – or Doodlebugs as they are popularly called – were fired at us by the Germans during the daytime. Our fighter pilots could see them coming and were able to pick a lot of them off in the air. Soon the Germans started to send them over at night when the only thing that was visible were the flames coming from their jet engines. To start with, some of our day fighter pilots were sent to try to intercept the robots. Normally these pilots in their Tempests and Spitfires are crack shots, but it soon became apparent that they were not sufficiently at home in the dark clouds of night. Because of the urgency of the situation, it was decided by the RAF top brass to see if some of the night pilots could convert to flying the Tempest more easily than the day fighter pilots could convert to all weather night flying. There were those who were sceptical about the plan, I know, because I was one of the night fighter pilots involved right from the very start. And because I already had some experience of attacking the Doodlebugs in daylight, I can tell you that flying against them by night proved even more dangerous. Fortunately, we became very successful and are now in a position to tackle the robots at whatever time they appear in our skies. Of course, when the first flying bombs came over the Channel from France in the middle of June, very little was known about their habits and construction, and all fighter pilots had to experiment and swap experiences to work out the best method of destroying them or shooting them down. We had to find out how near we could get to the flying bomb and shoot without the risk of being blown up by it, and I have to tell you that some brave men died before the answer was obtained.

"We patrol at between 5,000 and 6,000 feet, that's about 3,000 feet higher than the path of the average flying bomb. The first thing we usually see is a small light rather hard to distinguish from a star coming in from the sea, then the searchlights light up and point out the direction from which the bomb is coming. The guns go into action and we wait for the bombs that get through the gun belt, as soon as we spot a bomb that's run the gauntlet successfully we make a diving turn and go down after it, finishing our dive just behind the bomb and opening fire at a range of about 250 yards. The Doodlebug doesn't go down easily it will take a lot of punishment and you have to aim at the propulsion unit, that's the long stove pipe, as we call it on the tail, if your range and aim are dead on you can see pieces flying of the stove pipe the big white flame at the end goes out and down goes the bomb. Sometimes it dives straight to earth, but other times it goes crazy and gives a wizard display of aerobatics before finally crashing, Sometimes the bomb explodes in mid-air and the flash is so blinding that you can't see a thing for about ten seconds, you hope to be the right way up when you are able to see again, because the explosion often throws the fighter about, and some times turns it upside down.

"It was on the lawn of a cottage in southern England close to an airfield that, every evening, one of the joint important little councils of war took place during the first stages of the battle, with the flying bombs. The cottage was a wing intelligence office, and on its lawn the pilots of a Tempest squadron, led by Wing Commander Roland Beamont, gathered to compare notes and discuss their experiences. Methods of approaching and attacking the robots would be discussed one evening, tried out the next day during ops, and then reported on that evening. During this experimental period nobody worked harder than the Wingco who flew day after day from light till dusk, and finally the perfect method of attack was evolved, the approach from astern at an acute angle. Results were immediate; the 'bag' went up hand over fist and casualties dropped equally sharply. They were long summer days for the pilots, some of them frequently spending 20 of the 24 hours within sight of their machines. They had to grab some

*shut-eye whenever they could. But they soon had the satisfaction of using only 150 rounds for
each 'Doodle' destroyed compared with more than 500 at first.*

*"It was in July that I was posted as a Squadron Leader to organise night flying against the
Doodlebugs. Although my squadron had to put up with a lot of leg pulling in the officers' mess
whenever low cloud prevented us from flying, once we were airborne there were usually rich
pickings to be had. On the 23rd of July I had the chance to demonstrate how good our
technique had become when I shot down seven of these robots in one night!"*

Sqn Ldr Berry's sister Ivy remembered:

"He became much older in two years. He looked like a 30-year-old, while in fact he was only
24. There were times when he flew for 48 hours chasing the flying bombs. One day he fell
asleep and woke up just in time to miss the cable of a barrage balloon. I met him in August
1944 in Nottingham, he looked very bad and I asked him whether he was hunting the V-1s.
Surprised, he answered and admitted it but told me to keep quiet as the aeroplane [the Tempest]
was still on the secret list. I said to Joe that this was impossible, as the name of the aeroplane
had already been mentioned in the newspapers. He then answered that this type of aeroplane
was known to the Germans as a day fighter and not a night fighter. After this Joe asked me how
I had found out that he was chasing the Doodlebugs. I told him that he never spoke about a co-
pilot, as he usually did, and his letters contained no news. So I suspected a single-seater fighter.
After I had heard that questions were being asked in Parliament about the identity of the pilot
who had shot so many V-1s, mixed with his tired face, I concluded that it must be my brother
Joe."

A Meteor pilot recalled:

"It [the Meteor] was very fast, of course. Faster than the Tempest or the Spitfire, and well
armed with cannon. One problem was acceleration. The first jet engines were not very quick to
gain speed, not nearly as quick as the piston-engine fighters being used to hunt the V-1. The
Meteor took a long runway. But that was to be our job, hunting the Doodlebugs. The Meteor
was considered too precious to be used in combat. Didn't want the Germans to have a copy,
since they were very quick to find and exploit any weakness. And the toll on our civilians in
London was terrible from the buzz bombs. We were needed up there to bring them down. We
had learned a lot about destroying those flying bombs. Not all was good news. Pilots were
blown from the sky by pieces and bits after they had hit a V-1. It was a very dangerous business.
I have to add there was some danger from our own anti-aircraft guns. The lads were shooting
at anything in the air. They didn't always distinguish between the V-1 and the aircraft chasing
it. There were also P-51s, Spitfires, Mosquitos and Tempests besides the Meteor hunting the V-
1. It made for a lot of bullets in the air. Meteor pilots took off at the first news from the radar
stations that V-1s were crossing the Channel. They climbed to altitudes well above that of the
bombs. Once the buzzers passed through the hail of flak, it was the Meteor's turn. The radar
officer would tell us where they were and when they were coming. We would set up, prepare
ourselves by getting to the right position and the right altitude. When we saw them, we began
diving. By diving down on the bombs, we had plenty of speed to hand. Some people called us
'Divers' for just that reason, but in the RAF the real 'Divers' were the V-1s diving down when
their engine cut. So many pilots were lost, we came up with a new technique for dealing with
the Doodlebugs. With our speed, we could formate right next to them. Very, very gently we slid
over until our Meteor's wingtip was underneath the wingtip of the V-1. There is a layer of high-
speed air coming over and under and around the wingtip of an aircraft. By slowly lifting up our
wingtip, the wing of the V-1 was lifted. We didn't have to touch her if we were careful. Over
she went. Down she went. Ka-boom! Our territory was generally over farming country, with a
few villages. Of course if we were approaching a village, we didn't tip the V-1. We waited. Very
little real damage was done."

Flt Sgt Bob Cole of 3 Squadron:

"One V-1 was shot down by one of our people and hit Shorecliffe barracks. And another one
that I could have shot down was hit by someone else and went down in the main street in
Bexhill, right in the middle of the street. But one I shot down one morning, went down about

30 yards from a house. I went down and had a look. It had blown all the tiles off. I didn't see any movement."

Flt Lt Bob Bruce RCAF of 418 Squadron, Sqn Ldr Russ Bannock's navigator:

"By 28 August we had destroyed 18 over the sea, and one whose speed was much reduced by our fire before we ran out of ammo. We were frustrated to watch it limp over the English coast before it exploded on the ground. As navigator, I had little to do but record the time and position of the kills, and recover those parts of my body, which had dropped into my boots as we pulled out of the dive. I was a victim of airsickness."

The sky at night over the Channel could be quite dangerous for others preoccupied with their own duties, as recalled by L/Air Tom Mogford, TAG aboard a Swordfish of 819 Squadron operating out of Manston:

"At dusk one evening, passing near Dover at about 800 feet on our way out, the sky was suddenly full of buzz bombs. Some dozen or so of the things passed above and either side of us in the space of two minutes. It was an attempt to flood the defences and every gun for miles around was letting rip. The old Swordfish sailed blithely through it all without a scratch, not surprisingly really, as it would take a very thick ack-ack gunner to mistake a Stringbag – bogging along fully loaded at some 75 knots – for a Doodlebug."[211]

HMML445 of the 21st Motor Launch Flotilla operated out of Dover during the August/September period, as recalled by crewmember Maurice Gilbraith:

"While at Dover we were fitted with a small rocket gun that fired parachute flares and sometimes we used to patrol the French coast off Boulogne, with the other seven vessels in the Flotilla. When we saw a V-1 fired from the shore, we would launch a flare [known as 'Snowflakes' by the RAF] to help the fighters patrolling over the Channel to locate them. We saw many shot down and many that were toppled over by the fighters going alongside them and tipping their wings. During one of our escort jobs, a British Ack-Ack shell fired at a V-1 near Rye Bay, exploded underneath our ship and it split one of our petrol tanks, so we had to put into Rye to have a new one fitted. The good part for us was the extra leave we had while the repairs were being carried out, and it was smashing going home to the quiet North East after all the shelling and V-1s we'd had in Dover."

As a young lad Cecil Smith lived in Carshalton, Surrey when a flying bomb struck a house two doors away:

"I was in the shelter when I heard the sound of a Doodlebug going overhead and I just couldn't resist the temptation to stick my head out of the door to have a look. You see, there were no grown-ups to stop me and the flying bombs were a bit of a game to all of us youngsters, anyhow. Well, I looked out and saw this huge black shape with flames pouring out of the end right overhead. The engine stopped and even as I jumped back into the shelter and slammed shut the door, I could hear it hitting a house a couple of doors away from ours. There was an enormous explosion and then all hell let loose. We felt a terrific tremor and when we opened the shelter door we could see that the whole of the back of our house had been blown away and the wall had fallen onto where we were hiding. But for the strength of that shelter we would all have been crushed flat. I remember that my brother Leslie ran straight out of the shelter and stepped onto a red-hot piece of metal that badly burnt his foot. And then I saw my mother who was carrying my baby sister Margaret emerging from the ruins of the kitchen. Behind her there was one of our neighbours all covered in glass. I later found out that this woman had panicked and tried to get out of the house as the bomb fell. She had pushed past my mother just as the back door had been blown in, showering her with hundreds of glass splinters. If she had stayed where she was the blast would have hit my mother and her baby. That night all we children were sent away to another shelter while the rescue workers did what they could. At least half a dozen of the houses had been destroyed and a couple of people killed. But perhaps the biggest surprises of all came when I went back to the house the next day. The explosion had caused a wardrobe belonging to my father to be literally blown out of his bedroom down the garden and it had ended up in the branches of an apple tree! And when we began to root around in the house to salvage some of our possessions, my mother was horrified to find that the place had been looted during the night. Someone had actually ransacked our home and stolen some money from a desk drawer."[212]

Another incident which left behind a vivid description of what it was like to be caught up in the drama of being on the receiving end of a flying bomb attack, was graphically recalled by Mr W.A.E. Jones, who told the *Daily Herald*:

"Splintered bark whipped clean from the beech trees by the blast sears past my head. A cold, swishing wind like a miniature tornado carries my hat away. The ground quakes. Great spouts of mud splatter down. Through the choking, oily smoke, I can see the tall trees bowing, cracking, falling. The leaves fall. They fall languidly. My car is buried under a mantle of green until it looks like a curved mound of camouflage. A woman lies near me. She is dead. One of her shoes has been ripped from her foot. Her stocking is torn open. Her little brown dog is there too. His country walk ended in death for him. Now the leaves are mercifully covering him. An old man – his tweeds are plastered with soil – peers from a bush, says shakily, 'Where did it go?' So I point to a tangle of green metal that has dug itself into the grass a few yards from us. It is all that is left of the flying bomb that roared down on us a minute ago. I had a ringside seat for this robot, and I am able to write about it because a tree saved my life. It took the blast. There's no symmetry about that tree now. It has been stripped of its branches. It looks now like a decrepit, bare old skeleton creaking dolefully as it droops over the scene. Down one side of the tree the bark has been sheered off. The sharpest knife couldn't have done a cleaner job. The robot bomb raced towards us in a downward glide. We dived for cover. We huddled in the grass waiting. Then the explosion. When I could hear again I listened to a woman's voice crying shakily, 'Look, look. I'm alive!' The woman was leaning from a wrecked window. Her home was a ruin. But she was still alive and she wanted us to know all about it. Then there were more voices. On all sides there were more voices of people who had survived their nearest brush with death. We began to realise at that moment that we had all escaped – save the old woman and her dog. A butcher's boy cycling by jumped from his machine. He tore his apron from him, offered it for bandages for the wounded. Nurses from a hospital in their impeccable white uniforms dashed into the debris as it still creaked and heaved. They brought comfort with them. They brought soothing words with them and cool fingers to tend the injured. A barmaid – she was a big woman – loomed up. She had a tray of drinks with her. She was mighty popular."

Sqn Ldr Barwell of 125 Squadron remembered:

"We had a squadron of Americans attached to us with the P-61 Black Widow night fighter aircraft, which was a very fine aeroplane. The Americans had very good pilots, but the only thing was they hadn't crewed up with navigators for any length of time, and they were not very efficient at finding enemy aircraft. We became very frustrated because they kept missing the enemy aircraft they were chasing; we had to give them priority and they just didn't find them. This culminated really in one of the Americans chasing a German, losing him and the German sinking the ship, which was our control centre. After that episode, we did not give the Americans priority in the air."

Flt Lt Dick Leggett, also of 125 Squadron, added:

"We had so many night fighters messing about we often spent the night chasing our chums, especially if the IFF was not turned on. As there were normally about 100 Mosquitos and 20 Germans, the 'bogey' nearly always turned out to be a Mosquito. Black Widow crews were keen to fire. They were so trigger-happy that it became embarrassing. Much later, I heard one 'kill' on my R/T one night. He fired, then I heard him claiming a Me410. 'I've hit it! It's on fire! It's going down in flames!' Then I heard the RAF pilot's voice say, 'He missed by at least six feet! I'm not hit. I'm not going down in flames!' It was a Mosquito!"

CHAPTER VI

THE HEINKEL HUNTERS

September 1944 – March 1945

"I could even see the thing hanging under the wing. But before I could fire, somebody went and lit the blue touch paper. There was a dirty great flash as the bomb went whooshing off on its way, and for the next five minutes I could see sweet Fanny. I had to pull up in case I hit the deck, and that was that!"

Mosquito pilot

With the overrun of most of the ski launch sites in the Pas-de-Calais, the V-1 assault diminished – for a while. Most people in London and southern England hoped and prayed that this heralded the end of the fearful attacks but, in the event, had to endure several more weeks of living on their nerves. On the Continent, fighter-bombers of the RAF and USAAF continued to hunt down launch sites and depots.

Only three flying bombs were brought down by fighters on **1 September**, one by Flt Sgt Ben Gunn of 274 Squadron at 1153:

"I was patrolling east to west of Folkestone when, at 1150, I sighted a Diver at 1,500 feet three miles north-west of Dover. I turned on to it and closed from 800-350 yards astern and saw strikes on target. The Diver turned over on its back and crashed ten miles south-west of Canterbury."

It crashed between Waltham and Petham. The second fell to 129 Squadron's CO Sqn Ldr Peter Thompson (FB123/DV-H) and the final one was shot down in the early afternoon by Wt Off Tommy Hetherington (HB860/DV-J) also of 129 Squadron, the Mustang unit's 66th and final kill. Having used all his ammunition, he succeeded in causing the Diver to crash into the sea five miles off Dover by use of his aircraft's slipstream. Flying with him on this occasion was Flg Off Freddie Holmes:

"Tommy and I spotted one east of Calais, lost it in cloud for a moment, and then found ourselves ahead of it, and so well placed that it was rolled over by Hetherington's slipstream and forced to dive in the sea."

Another Diver fell on Hawkinge airfield and damaged Spitfire XIV RM695 of 350 Squadron, and there were casualties when Ipswich received an unwelcomed visitor that impacted in Meryon Road, killing one and injuring 31 others. Four bungalows were demolished. Another exploded just outside the perimeter of Ipswich Airport, demolishing a requisitioned house and killing an RAF NCO. But, all in all, the end of the campaign seemed in sight. Records show that by this date, the effective end of the assault from France, 8,617 V-1s had been ground-launched against the UK. III/KG3 had air-launched about 410, of which some 300 had been intended for London, 90 aimed at Portsmouth and 20 directed at Gloucester. Of those targeted at London, only 160 reached the coast and only 50 or so penetrated the defences to reach the capital.

However, the Germans still had plenty of aces to play, and that night an attack was carried out by the four remaining *Mistels* on charge with II/KG101, when shipping in the Channel was again the target[213]. The attack was to be co-ordinated with that of bomb-carrying FW190s from 2/KG200, but was not successful. Two of the Ju88 'flying bombs' crossed the English coast, one of which eventually crashed at Warsop, north of Mansfield in Nottinghamshire at 2330, where it exploded and flung pieces of wreckage over a quarter of a mile. The other Ju88 went in the other direction and crashed at Hothfield, near Ashford at 2345, where the explosion created a crater 12 feet deep and 40 feet across. Following this unsuccessful operation, II/KG101 was now disbanded and in its place a new *Mistel* unit, III/KG66 commanded by Hptm Kurt Capesius, came into being at Burg near Magdeburg. The same night saw 23 sorties by Heinkels of III/KG3 operating from Venlo – repeated on the night of **4/5 September** (18 sorties) – with batches of V-1s being air-launched towards London, Portsmouth, Southampton and Gloucester. Three of these actually came down in East Anglia – at Hill Farm, Felixstowe, at Langham and at Dedham – and one reached Eyeworth in Bedfordshire. Three more came down in Hertfordshire (at Kings Walden, Stagenhoe and Ware).

Veteran Luftwaffe bomber pilot Horst Juventus, who had been posted to III/KG3 for training in flying bomb launching techniques, recalled of this period:

> "We assumed it meant the end of the Luftwaffe's bomber force, and we were not far wrong. But after a while we were shown how the new flying bombs could be launched from our bombers and a few crews including our own were moved to another base in Holland where we were instructed how to fly a set course over the sea in order to launch the V-1, which was attached to the underside of a Heinkel 111. It was obviously a very indiscriminate weapon and to no good purpose. But we had our orders. With the V-1 attached the Heinkel's performance was of course weakened. We flew off from Gilze-Rijen over the North Sea for some distance before igniting the V-1's motor and releasing it. The things could be a positive menace as they did not always fly true, and we felt in great danger with the contraption beneath us. I was sure some crews released them as soon as they were out of sight of land in order to be free of them."

Mosquito MM680 from 68 Squadron crewed by Flt Sgts James Brill and John Walter was vectored towards an incoming flying bomb, which was sighted and attacked. Although strikes were observed on the missile, they were unable to shoot it down. Their target was seen to fly past their base at Castle Camps before diving to earth near Roydon. Two more were destroyed during a 0515-0640 patrol by two Tempests from 501 Squadron, Flg Off Lulu Deleuze (EJ591/SD-Z) and Flg Off Keith Panter (EJ551/SD-S) both engaging their targets over the Thames Estuary. Panter's kill fell at Aldham, seven miles west of Colchester; and Deleuze's victim crashed at Dedham, seven miles north-east of Colchester.

The end of the V-1 blitz – or not!

> *"As a result of our advances on the Continent, the enemy has been driven out of all areas where he was able to launch flying bombs against London from the normal static launching sites. No such launchings have taken place since 6 September. However, airborne launchings from specially adapted He111s based on airfields in North-West Germany have taken place on a small scale."*

So stated a General Note on Operations, ACIGS meeting, which also revealed that from the start of the attack up to 6 September, casualties for the country as a whole had been 5,817 killed, 17,086 seriously injured and 22,870 slightly injured. The vast majority of the casualties were suffered in London, where the figures were 5,381 killed, 15,777 seriously injured and 18,256 slightly injured. The same summary recorded that during this same period 8,095 flying bombs had been launched, of which 2,337 had reached London and 3,823 were destroyed by the combined defences. Of the latter, fighter aircraft had 'officially' destroyed 1,902, AA Command had accounted for 1,657 and Balloon Command 264. The next day Duncan Sandys, the Chairman of the War Cabinet Committee told the press:

> "Except possibly for a few last shots, the Battle of London is over – we have beaten Hitler's secret weapon, the V-1, which was to have terrorised Britain into making a negotiated peace."

On 8 September, at 1848, the first V-2 exploded on London[214]. Prime Minister

Churchill called a meeting shortly thereafter, Minister of Home Security Herbert Morrison one of those attending; he later wrote:

"I attended a very small meeting of ministers, with the Prime Minister in the chair. I was pressing, not for the first time, for more effort by the Air Staff against the flying bomb sites in Northern France. This was at a time when much of our air offensive was against German industry and communications as part of the strategic action in preparation for D-Day. As Minister of Home Security I was, of course, correct in putting forward my views on minimizing the menace of the V-1 and V-2 to the civil population. [Professor] Lindemann set out to prove that the flying bombs were not so serious as I made out. He produced some figures, which indicated that each Doodlebug launched by the enemy was responsible for killing one person. He added that, while this was unfortunate, the V-1 was obviously not really a menace. As everyone was only too well aware that the noisy transit of these flying bombs, the awe of a pilotless aeroplane, and the quantity of them had all contributed to a fear among the people possibly, if temporarily, greater than in the conventional raids of a couple of years before, I was angry at this remote and impersonal view of the situation.

'Prime Minister,' I said, 'the Professor is good at statistics and I am not in a position to dispute his figures; they may be right. But what is disputed is that the Prof does not understand the human aspects and he does not trouble to find out or imagine what actually happens when one of these flying bombs explodes. First of all he assumes that they drop over a wide area. But you may get as many as ten within one borough, for example in Hackney. When they drop they not only kill the Professor's one person – one bomb may kill several – but they wound a considerable number. They destroy or damage the homes, furniture and possessions of humble people. The hospital services do not merely put the ten corpses from the ten V-1s of the Professor's statistics into the mortuary; they have the injured from the ten incidents. Civil Defence has a big job, and the local authority has to find accommodation for the bombed-out families. If a factory is hit, there may be only one person killed, but production will be interrupted and people thrown out of work. Finally, while there will be no real panic, the people, knowing that they are within range of V-1s, will be in a state of anxiety. My submission is that the sooner we destroy these flying bomb sites and stores the better, and it is my duty to say so.'"

Meanwhile, III/KG3 was now effectively disbanded and renamed I/KG53 although it temporarily retained its former identity (and code markings, 5K+) with regard to its Staffeln, with newly promoted Maj Vetter in command. 7/KG3 (1/KG53) was commanded by Oblt Erhard Banneick and based at Varrelbusch, with 8/KG3 (2/KG53) under Hptm Horst Zander at Ahlhorn, while 9/KG3 (3/KG53) was at Vechta under Hptm Werner Brandt's control. Maj Herbert Wittman was given command of the reformed II/KG53[215], with its Staffeln at Bad Zwischenahn (4 Staffel, Hptm Heinz Zöllner), Jever (5 Staffel, Hptm Erhard Schier) and Wittmund (6 Staffel, Hptm Wilhelm Bautz), while III Gruppe was reformed under the command of Maj Emil Allmendinger, with Staffeln based at airfields on the German/Danish border – Leck (7 Staffel, Hptm Heinz Grünswald), Schleswig (8 Staffel, Oblt Günther Böhnet) and Eggebek (9 Staffel, Hptm Alfred Bischowski). III/KG3 continued to spearhead the launching operations, drawing crews from the other Gruppen as and when required.

Thirteen He111s of I/KG53 from Varrelbusch (one other had crashed on take-off with Fw Heinrich Güls and his crew of 5K+IS losing their lives) launched their weapons just before dawn on **16 September**. Three of these were shot down into the sea, two by RN gunners and one by a Mosquito of 96 Squadron flown by Flt Lt Ian Dobie:

"One batch of two Divers seen at 0535, too far to engage. Second batch of two Divers seen at 0600. Crossed in front of one Diver from starboard to port at approximately 150 feet and roughly same height. Diver immediately started to go down with engine running and exploded in the sea."

Two more were shot down by a Tempest flown by Flt Off Bud Miller USAAF (EJ603/SD-M) of 501 Squadron, who reported:

"I was scrambled under Trimley Control from Bradwell Bay for Diver reported coming in on a course of 285 degrees at 2,500 feet and 340mph. I dived down on it and closed in from 500 yards astern and opened fire. I saw strikes on the tail unit. Control told me to break off the engagement and I did so. I saw the Diver losing height and crash and exploded on the ground near RAF Castle Camps 30 seconds after my attack at 0606 hours. I saw a second one at 0608 hours heading over Bradwell Bay at 340mph. I closed in astern and opened fire from 500 yards, closing in to 50 yards. Diver blew up in mid-air."

Most of those that crossed the coast crashed in Essex, one impacting in St Awdry's Road/Ripple Road, Barking (13 fatalities and 17 seriously injured); others fell at Langham, Aldham, and Wakes Colne. One hit the water tower at Saffron Walden at 0610 and shook men of 4thFG based at nearby Debden airfield. Another came down at Woolwich. Of the renewed assault, General Sir Frederick Pile, in charge of Britain's AA defences, noted at this time:

"After an interval of 11 days, the air-launched attacks were renewed, and we found that the enemy was extending his lines of attack over East Anglia to the north of the Diver Box. Moreover, Intelligence reports indicated that further elements of the Luftwaffe were being converted to the rôle of flying-bomb carriers. Now, early in September, with the lessons of the South Coast fresh in our minds, we had made a plan to have 96 static guns ready for an immediate move to the East Coast. The work of building portable platforms was begun, and gun-towing vehicles and transporters were made ready in the appropriate places. Between September 16 and 18, six light anti-aircraft batteries were redeployed in the Diver Box to cover the withdrawal of the RAF Regiment, which began on the 18th. In the next three days orders went out for the move of sixteen more heavy and nine more light batteries to redeploy in the Harwich area, and some additional equipment was sent to provide three new sites round Yarmouth and Lowestoft. But, just as these forces were starting their move, there came the disturbing news that the enemy was launching attacks well to the north of the Harwich area. It looked at that moment as if the Luftwaffe had got us properly on the run. As fast as we moved northward, so might the Hun each time anticipate us. And, from our point of view, there was a limit to this northward trend. The manpower cuts had left us the merest shadow of our former selves. No longer were we able to deploy in the grand manner. The only thing we could do was to extend our attenuated forces as far as we could and live in the pious hope that there was either some kind of limit to the area over which the enemy could deliver his attack, or that he would prefer to batter away at London in preference to Northern England."

Another Heinkel (14 had departed Varrelbusch) was lost the following night (**16-17 September**) when Uffz Hans Jördens ditched 5K+ET in Lake Braassemermeer; he and his crew survived but the aircraft was totally destroyed. Apparently the Heinkel was a victim of 'friendly fire', returning crews complaining of coming under fire from light flak on no fewer than nine occasions in just two nights. An Ultra intercept noted: "An aircraft of 9/KG3 shot up and ditched at 0900 in Lake Brassemer [*sic*] near Leyden. Varrelbusch informed." During the night of **17/18 September**, a Mosquito from 96 Squadron was successful in bringing down a flying bomb, Flt Lt Charles Bailey in HK526 catching his victim over land at 0246.

On **18 September**, while on an early afternoon (1244-1445) reconnaissance sortie over Zoutkamp in Holland, TacR Spitfire pilot Flt Lt D.A.J. Draper of 4 Squadron in PA852 reported sighting what he believed was a Do217 five miles from Ijmuiden at 22,000 feet – with a V-1 mounted above the fuselage. He carried out a dummy attack – the Spitfire XI was unarmed – whereupon he reported that the V-1 was released and the Dornier evaded and escaped. He may have in fact misidentified the aircraft – only Heinkels were able to carry a V-1, and this suspended from the wing. This sighting was possibly the cause for the British authorities to initially believe that the Heinkels also carried the V-1 mounted above the fuselage. However, there were other weird and wonderful contraptions flying in hostile skies at this time[216].

Heinkels roamed over the North Sea again on the night of **18/19 September**, 14 aircraft having departed Varrelbusch shortly after midnight. One aircraft from 8 Staffel, 5K+HS, crashed at Scharl in Friesland with the loss of Obfw Karl-Heinz Holze and his crew[217]. An eyewitness to the crash, eight-year-old Jan Venema, recalled many years later:

> "It was early in the morning and my mother was waking me up because I had to go to school. Suddenly she saw a burning aeroplane coming straight for our farm. Fortunately for us, the aeroplane crashed about 50 metres away from our farm. Another farmer, who was milking his cows in that very field with his back turned to the scene, got the fright of his life! My oldest brother immediately went over to the wreckage. Soon after the crash German soldiers on motorbikes sealed off and secured the area. A civilian county employee and German soldiers recovered the remains of the crew on the same day. When the mortal remains had been removed, the local population was allowed to go to the wreck. Some parts of the aeroplane were taken as souvenirs. A youth took some unexploded ammunition and during his attempts to defuse it was seriously injured. The incident cost him an eye." [218]

Essex received more uninvited visitors, one of which impacted at Maldon, and another at Manningtree. Two fell on Hornchurch within a few minutes of each other, killing four and injuring 29 at 0433, the second bomb killing ten and injuring 38 some seven minutes later. Dozen of houses were destroyed or damaged, and 20 more were demolished at Mitcham in Surrey. One person was killed in Norbury (SW16). On the nights of 19/20 September (21 sorties), and 22/23 September (13 sorties), Heinkels of III/KG3 were very active, all aircraft returning safely to Varrelbusch. A flying bomb that penetrated the defences fell at Little Baddow in Essex at 0145, killing one, injuring two and badly damaging seven houses. To counter this latest threat, Mosquito squadrons moved into Castle Camps (25 and 68 Squadrons), Coltishall (125 Squadron) and Manston.

On **20 September**, HK345 of 68 Squadron crewed by Flt Sgt Tom Wilson, a 20-year-old from Sussex, and his Welsh navigator Flt Sgt John Jenkins failed to return from an evening anti-Diver patrol off the Dutch islands. They had been vectored on to a flying bomb (21 sorties were flown by III/KG3) by control at 2043, but then silence. It is assumed that their aircraft was brought down by the explosion of their target. Wg Cdr Howden carried out two search sorties but failed to sight any signs of crew or wreckage. Diary entries made by Sgt Donald W. Marner USAAF of the 357thFG at Leiston confirmed the route taken by many of the flying bombs as they crossed the East Anglian coastline:

> "About 7pm a buzz bomb roared directly across our hut, not more than 75 to 100 feet above us. Terrifying roar and yellow flames had me plenty scared. Saw two others go over, one exploding a few miles from our base. At 5am the morning of 21st another roared across the field and exploded six miles from here. I have a piece of that one. 23rd: Saw three buzz bombs over air base very low. One exploded nearby. About 1,500 anti-aircraft guns were moved in this area – this is now called Buzz Bomb Alley. All Doodlebugs that are hitting England are crossing the coast in line with our base."

One of these impacted on the beach close to the experimental radar facility at Bawdsey Manor near Felixstowe, without causing damage or casualties. One that fell in a field at Chediston in Suffolk, some nine miles west of Southwold, was found to have the serial number 701422 stencilled on a fragment. Another, that damaged three houses at Hacheston near Ipswich, was found to be numbered 701427[219].

Despite the counter-offensive measures, V-1s continued to dodge the defences. Damage was done to property at Bethnal Green on the night of 19/20 September, at Wandsworth on 20/21, Hatfield (Herts) on 22/23 September. A V-1 that overflew Newmarket on 24 September crashed near Burwell in Cambridgeshire. 501 Squadron's Flg Off Wild had a lucky escape on the night of **23 September**:

"At around midnight, Gilbert Wild was chasing a V-1; he was just giving his Tempest (EJ603/SD-M) full throttle so that he could reach overtaking speed, when the engine seized up. He had seconds in which to gain height, head westwards to avoid the Essex marshes and bale out. He saw the Tempest explode and set fire to a barn as he landed in the top of a cherry tree, close to the Leather Bottle pub at Shrub End. He was eventually rescued by Sgt Sydney Hunt of the Royal Engineers before spending the next two hours in the police station, 'helping with enquiries'. The fault with the Tempest was eventually traced to an air lock occurring when the fuel tanks were switched over."[220]

The next success came on the night of 23/24 September when Flg Off R.A. Henley in HK362 of 25 Squadron claimed a Heinkel probably destroyed:

"I was airborne at 2130 under Coltishall Control and handed over to Neatishead GCI and then Greyfriars, to patrol. A bogey at 3,000 feet was given immediately by Greyfriars when I was 5,000 feet and gave chase, but no contact presented itself for some minutes owing to an error in elevation given to me by control. This was probably due to the distance of the target. My navigator advised me to lose height and contact was made at half-a-mile range. Closing in to 100 yards at height of 400 feet, a visual was obtained on target above at 800 feet. I pulled up and together with my navigator identified aircraft as a He111. Dropping back to 200 yards I opened fire from dead astern with a one-second burst on e/a flying straight and level, causing glowing fragments to fly off e/a. A further two-seconds burst produced the same results and I last saw the e/a losing height, turning to port, flying into cloud. Contact was then lost and I returned to base."

It seems likely that this was 5K+IR (168334) of 7/KG3, which crashed at Hankenberge returning from its mission, none of Uffz Herbert Böhling's crew surviving[221]. A second mission was flown later that morning by III/KG3, and 25 Squadron's CO, Wg Cdr Leicester Mitchell (HK357) claimed another Heinkel as probably destroyed:

"I took off from Coltishall at 0305 and was vectored onto a bogey about 60 miles east of base. I saw a flying bomb leaving the bogey and this was also observed on the AI, control immediately afterwards giving the bogey as a bandit. I followed for about 15 minutes in thick cumulus cloud without obtaining a visual, although on three occasions the range was closed on AI to about 400 feet. The e/a then dived away to port and contact was lost. I was then vectored on to a second bogey, given almost immediately as a bandit as again a flying bomb was seen launched in a westerly direction. AI contact was obtained at four miles range on a jinking target. Range was closed on AI to 850 feet in thick cloud, and at 400-500 feet a visual was obtained in a break in the clouds. As the e/a turned to starboard both my navigator and myself recognised it as a He111. A long burst from 800 feet range produced strikes on the starboard wing root and, as it disappeared into cloud, was seen by Flt Lt Cox, with the aid of night glasses, to turn hard starboard and go down. The combat took place at 1,000 feet and it is considered unlikely that the e/a could have pulled out from the dive before hitting the water. Greyfriars Control states that only one aircraft emerged from the combat. No return fire was experienced."

It would seem that his target was 5K+ES of 7/KG53, which failed to return from its mission. Oblt Günther Böhnet (the Staffelkapitän) and his crew were reported missing[222]. Following the loss of Oblt Böhnet, Hptm Josef Dengg took command of 7 Staffel.

On this same night Flg Off Ted Ledwidge chased two Heinkels but both were lost in clouds. He then made a further contact but as he closed in on his target visually recognised it as a wayward Lancaster, and pulled away. Flt Sgt Glossop (HK280) had a close shave when he was pursuing another contact when his aircraft came under attack from astern, tracers seen whipping over his wings. The aircraft was not hit. His assailant was presumably another Mosquito. Joy of success was twinged with sadness for the Squadron when 23-year-old Flt Lt John Limbert from Finchley and his navigator Flg Off Henry Cook were lost when attacking a Diver. Presumably their aircraft (HK300) had been badly damaged by the explosion of the missile. Flying from Odiham, Flt Lt Togs Mellersh of 96 Squadron (in MM577/ZJ-N) intercepted a flying bomb out to sea. When hit, it climbed to 8,000 feet in cloud before falling into the sea, the crash witnessed by another Mosquito flown by Flt Lt Kennedy. This was Mellersh's 44th and final kill, 37 of which had been assisted by his navigator Flt Lt Michael Stanley. Sqn Ldr Jimmy Rawnsley from 100 Group recalled a conversation he had with a Mosquito crew who had been hunting Heinkels:

"I talked with one of the crews right after they had landed from a long, tiring patrol off the Dutch coast. They had had a frustrating experience, and they were understandably indignant. 'We were close behind him for miles,' the navigator wailed, 'but he was so close to the water we just couldn't get at him without swimming. I had to watch the radar altimeter as well as the AI while the skipper tried to spot him.' 'Didn't he pull up at all to launch the bomb?' I asked. 'I'll say he did', the pilot broke in bitterly. 'I closed in and spotted him … I could even see the thing hanging under the wing. But before I could fire somebody went and lit the blue paper. There was a dirty great flash as the bomb went whooshing off on its way, and for the next five minutes I could see sweet Fanny. I had to pull up in case I hit the deck, and that was that!'"[223]

The early morning hours of **25 September** saw a second confirmed success for the Heinkel-hunters, Wt Off Len Fitchett RCAF[224] (MM589/KP-U) of 409 (RCAF) Squadron shooting down 20-year-old Ltn Helmut Denig's He111 5K+AR of 7/KG3, one of ten Heinkels operating from Handorf between 2144 and 0207. The aircraft exploded and damaged the Mosquito, which was written off following a forced-landing at Lille. Wt Off Fitchett's subsequent report revealed:

"We [Fitchett's navigator was Sgt Alec Hardy] were airborne from base at 0300 to carry out a defensive patrol. At approximately 0500 we were vectored after a bandit travelling east at a height of 10,000 feet, the range given by control being eight miles. As we were at 16,000 feet I dove down to 10,000 feet and my navigator picked up an AI contact to starboard and slightly below, at a range of two miles, the target carrying out mild evasive action by weaving gently from side to side and reducing height gradually. I closed to 1,000 feet, slightly below, where I obtained a visual and at 500 feet both my navigator and I recognised the bandit as a He111, which by this time was flying at 8,000 feet. The e/a must have seen us for he peeled off to port, attempting to gain cloud cover, the tops of which were at 7,500 feet. I followed and opened fire at 100 feet; a terrific explosion occurring with pieces flying off and the e/a plummeted to earth [near Maastricht] in flames. In view of the short distance it was impossible to avoid flying through some of the debris and our aircraft was damaged. As it was vibrating a great deal I requested an emergency homing and landed at B.51 [Lille] at 0610."

As was the case all too often when the Heinkels were shot down, there were no survivors[225].

501 Squadron's Tempests continued to fly all-weather patrols. The American Flt Off Bud Miller (EJ538/SD-R) shot down his ninth and final flying bomb but Flt Lt Gordon 'Snowy' Bonham DFC was killed when his Tempest EJ590/SD-L crashed in bad weather at Spitfield Farm in Essex. The New Zealander, who had flown against the Japanese at Singapore in 1942, had five V-1s to his credit. Of the four Divers that penetrated the defences, one fell at Chertsey in Surrey, one in Essex and one at Hessett, five miles east of Bury St Edmunds; the latter exploded in the middle of

Mellfield Woods, damaging Hill Farm, Freewood Farm and Mellfield Cottage; there were no casualties.

Wt Off Mervin Woodthorpe and Flt Sgt D.J. Long of 96 Squadron in HK526, scored their only success on the night of **26/27 September**, when one flying bomb fell at Edmonton (25 injured, 11 seriously), three came down in Essex, one in Cambridgeshire, one in Hertfordshire, and three more in Suffolk. Sqn Ldr Miroslav Liškutín, CO of 312 (Czech) Squadron that had recently moved to North Weald, wrote:

> "Due to the new developments in enemy activity, it became rather 'hot' even at North Weald, where the flying bombs arrived in increasing numbers. One of these V-1s was accidentally caught in the huge radio mast complex near our airfield and exploded uncomfortably close to the officers' mess accommodation. Surprisingly, that particular one-ton of TNT did not cause casualties or serious damage."

The next success against the V-1 launchers came on the night of 28/29 September. Wg Cdr Leicester Mitchell of 25 Squadron in HK357 had better luck on this occasion and succeeded in shooting down two Heinkels in quick succession:

> "I was scrambled from base at 0500 and vectored towards anticipated trade. On reaching patrol position I immediately saw flying bomb being launched. My height at this time was 3,500 feet. I carried out a diving turn towards the flying bomb, at the same time informing Greyfriars Control, who in turn informed me of bandit in same position, turning to port. Losing height to 600 feet in a turn, contact was obtained at two-and-a-half miles range, 45° to port, which I followed in a turn, closing range at 200 feet height, and obtained visual at 1,300 feet, to starboard – identified by my navigator with the aid of night glasses as a He111, and confirmed by myself as the range was closed. A short burst from 400 feet dead astern on e/a caused a violent explosion and I was forced to make a hard climbing starboard turn to avoid debris, which flew from the e/a. Turning back over position of e/a's crash, saw flames on the sea which continued to burn for two to three minutes. Returning to our patrol line at 0540, I saw another flying bomb launched. I turned towards flying bomb, losing height and informing Greyfriars Control of my bearing, who gave me a vector towards e/a's turn to port and eventually obtained contact on a converging course. Waiting until the range closed to approximately one mile, I carried out a hard turn to port in order to close in behind e/a, losing height to 150 feet and closed range rapidly. My speed at this time was 220mph, e/a's 180 to 190mph. A visual was then obtained at 1,500 feet range and identified with aid of night glasses as He111. A short burst from 600 feet caused pieces to fly off starboard wing. Allowing slightly more deflection, my second burst from 400 feet caused port engine of e/a to burst into flames. It lost height rapidly and crashed in flames in the sea at 0545. A return was made to the patrol line and a search for survivors until 0615 but without result."

One of his victims was 5K+AT flown by 9 Staffelkapitän Oblt Erhard Banneick, who was posted missing with his crew. The other was 5K+CT, also from 9 Staffel, in which Uffz Willi Döhring and his crew was similarly posted as missing[226]. III/KG3 had flown 20 sorties between 1935 and 0758, suffering just the two losses. The only other contacts made by the patrolling Mosquitos of 25 Squadron turned out to be a Royal Navy Avenger intercepted by Flg Off Henley, and a Warwick recognised in good time by Sqn Ldr Arnsby. 68 Squadron's Flt Lt Humphrey Humphreys (MM680) claimed his first flying bomb during a patrol off The Hague:

> "We saw two flying bombs 30 miles west of The Hague and turned to chase them, but when in position the flying bomb dived into the sea. On returning to the patrol line contact was made with another at 4,000 feet, three-and-a-half miles. Lost height in cloud to 1,500 feet and closed to one-and-a-half miles. Flying bomb dived to port and we followed. It crashed into the sea at 2140."

Another fell to Flt Lt Lilwall (EJ600/SD-F) of 501 Squadron during a 0435-0630 patrol, although he had to share it with the Mosquito (MM446) flown by Flt Lt Kennedy of 96 Squadron. Another Tempest pilot was lost this same night when Flg Off Owen Faraday, who had been flying anti-Diver sorties with 219 (Mosquito) Squadron before being posted to fly Tempests on similar duties, crashed in EJ626/SD-E near St Osyth in Essex following engine failure and was killed. Flt Lt Arthur Woods DFC in UP-D of 605 Squadron, returning to Manston following a sortie to Norway, shot down a flying bomb that had been launched by one of the Heinkels, his only success against these missiles although he had an impressive score against enemy aircraft:

> "At 2038 sighted Diver at 500 feet ten miles east-south-east of Wattisham airfield. Attacked at 2041 from dead astern and saw strikes, sparks and bits shoot off. The Diver must have lost height slightly as on second attack it exploded in the air at 250 feet. Range down to 100 yards from dead astern. Position of explosion five miles west of Stradishall airfield. No other fighters in the area."

All seven Divers that crossed the coast fell in East Anglia (two in Essex, one of which was Flt Lt Lilwall's victim), one in Hertfordshire, one in Cambridgeshire and three in Suffolk – at Chelmondiston, near Lynes Hall, Edwardstone and Burthorpe Farm, Barrow, just five miles west of Bury St Edmunds. Fortunately, there were no injuries.

Next morning (**29 September**), two Mosquito XIXs from 157 Squadron were out searching the North Sea off Cromer for signs of missing colleagues who had failed to return from a night sortie in MM646[227]. Whilst flying at low level, one of these encountered a Me410 from SeenotGr.80, presumably searching for signs of the missing Heinkels. The Messerschmitt promptly shot down Mosquito MM643/RS-F crewed by Flt Lt Sidney Waddington and Flg Off Edward Lomas, but was then attacked by the other, flown by Flt Lt P.W. Vincent (TA391/RS-N), who claimed it probably destroyed some 12 miles east-south-east of Great Yarmouth. However, the Me410 (believed to have been F4+3C) returned safely to its base at Jever, Oblt Langer reporting that he had destroyed a 'Halifax ' that he had encountered at a height of 50 metres.

That night (**29/30 September**), 25 Squadron's Plt Off Barney Travers in HK298 sighted a flying bomb, but, as he closed range, "… it went haywire and started orbiting and climbing ..." The squadron diarist added a note in the ORB: "A doubtful friend appeared behind his aircraft and rather upset his enjoyment of a mad buzz bomb!" The only other contact made by 25 Squadron on this night was made by Flg Off J.F.R. Jones who intercepted two bogies, only to find they were both Mosquitos. However, 96 Squadron's Flt Lt Charles Bailey shot one down while flying HK526 with Flg Off Weston at 0425. More fell in East Anglia, mainly in rural areas and thereby caused little damage, but one demolished a row of cottages at Ardleigh in Essex, where four were killed and five others injured. Two others also fell in Essex, one in Cambridgeshire, one in Hertfordshire, one in Kent and one in Sussex. On the last night of the month, one impacted near the Suffolk market town of Sudbury. This may have been the incident noted by Cpl Ray Ingham USAAF of the 535thBS (381stBG) based at Ridgewell, who wrote in the unit's war diary:

> "One of our fighters shot down a buzz bomb west of the base last night and a few minutes later a second pilotless plane crashed, the latter near Birdbrook. All this action took place at 2000 hours."

The diarist at the USAAF supply base at Thorpe Abbots in Norfolk, from where a number of flying bombs had been witnessed during September, wrote: "Last night we had some buzz bombs over the base and land near here. Makes a guy sit up and take notice." A few days later, he commented:

> "Four buzz bombs went over early this morning and one was only about 150 feet in the air. It even shook the huts a little when it went over. The new name for this place is now 'Buzz Bomb Alley'. Had two more during the day and one after chow tonight."

A US 8th Air Force raid by 750 heavy bombers against airfields at Bielfeld, Hamm, Munster and Handorf that night included amongst the casualties at the latter airfield 7/KG3's Staffelkapitän and Training Officer, Hptm Heinz Grünswald, who was killed. His replacement as commander of 7 Staffel was Hptm August Lauerer. Records show that a total of 177 V-1s was launched by the Heinkels on 13 nights in September.

At the beginning of October, III/KG66 at Burg reported 15 *Mistels* on strength of which ten were serviceable. Its first operation, planned for the night of 3 October, proved disastrous. Five aircraft from 8/KG66 took off at dusk from Burg to attack the bridge at Nijmegen. Weather conditions were poor and on the way to the target, three of the *Mistels* crashed into the Teutoburger Wald, the heavily forested area between Rheine and Bielefeld. Oblt Horst Polster, the Staffelkapitän, was killed, as were Uffz Fritz Scheffler and Uffz Paul Baranski. The remaining two Messerschmitt pilots were unable to find their target and jettisoned their missiles, but this did not help one of them, Fw Franz Heckmann, who was then shot down by fighters over southern Holland. Later in the month, two Ju88s from I/KG66 arrived at Handorf to co-operate with KG53 in an endeavour to increase the accuracy of their launching. The two aircraft were equipped with the most up-to-date navigational aids. However, the experiment was deemed unsuccessful and the crews soon returned to their own unit.

The Royal Navy's NFIU now received permission to participate occasionally in anti-Diver operations, using Coltishall in Norfolk for evaluation trials of the Firefly NF1 against the V-1-carrying Heinkels. In charge of a detachment of two aircraft (DT933 and MB419) was Lt(A) J.H. Kneale RNVR, who recalled:

> "Because the Heinkels came over in very small numbers, and rather more night fighters were scrambled to meet them, it was often a matter of chance which of the defending aircraft were best placed to be directed on to targets identified by the coastal radar. This fact, together with the few occasions when NFIU Fireflies were scrambled to join the RAF night fighters, meant that the opportunities for actual combat were very limited."[228]

The CO of 96 Squadron, Wg Cdr Edward Crew, decided to try out a Mustang III in an attempt to catch a flying bomb on 1 October, but failed to intercept any during his 1855-2130 patrol in FB379. 29 Squadron equipped with Mosquito XVIIs at Hunsdon now received instructions to carry out 'Heinkel hunting' sorties over the North Sea and to intrude the launch sites in Holland, although with a marked reduction in Diver activity, some of the Mosquito VI units were released from anti-Diver patrols including 605 Squadron based at Coltishall. On one of the first of the intruder sorties, on the night **2/3 October**, HJ799/UP-L crewed by stalwarts Flt Lt Basil Bensted and Plt Off Cyril Burrage failed to return from a sortie to the Baltic.This successful crew had eight Divers to their credit.

Between **5** and **11 October**, another mini V-1 blitz was instigated and a total of 62 V-1s were launched from the 75 He111s that operated out of Varrelbusch. Nine of the flying bombs fell on London. During this period 16 people were killed at Hornsey, eight at Wanstead, six at Chertsey, four at Harrow and two at Surbiton. The explosion in Blake Hall Crescent, Wanstead was attended by Divisional Fire Officer Cyril Demarne, who recalled:

> "As we toiled, several V-1s roared across the sky and there came a chorus of 'Seig Heil! Seig Heil!' from hundreds of German throats in the PoW camp, a few hundred yards along the road.

How I prayed for one of them to come down smack in the centre of that compound but my prayer went unanswered and the bombs flew on, to crash in Poplar or Stepney or points west. Casualties were relatively light and we were able to clear up rather more quickly than usual and make our way home. There was no knowing where or when the next buzz bomb would dive. The PoW camp came near to disaster about a week later, when a flying bomb crashed on the anti-aircraft rocket installation on the opposite side of Woodford Road, killing a number of gunners and ATS girls. The blast set fire to dry grass on the site and it was by a narrow margin only that the NFS stopped the fire before it reached the magazines – crude corrugated-iron sheds with openings screened with hessian curtains protecting the rockets laid out in racks. It was a close shave."[229]

One of the Divers fell to Tempest pilot Flg Off Johnny Johnson of 501 Squadron (EJ605/SD-K) during his 1915-2130 patrol. The Mosquito crews of 25 Squadron found themselves in the forefront this time, Flt Lt Jones (HK239) catching a Heinkel off the Norfolk coast on the night of 5/6 October, one of 11 that had taken off at 1814. Jones reported:

"I was airborne from Coltishall at 1900. We were patrolling at 3,000 feet under Greyfriars Control and obtained several contacts, but were called off by control and informed that targets were friendly. We were then informed that there was a bandit and were vectored onto it. Almost immediately my navigator obtained contact at four-and-a-half miles range, 70° to starboard, slightly below with target crossing to starboard. I turned hard starboard and brought the target dead ahead. I closed in a stern chase, at 260 ASI with target losing height and when at 2,500 feet range saw flying bomb released. Target then turned to port, dived and leveled out at 1,200 feet. I followed closing the range and obtained a visual at 1,500 feet and identified target as He111, silhouetted against the dark sky. The target began to weave gently and continued to lose height and, as I closed to 800 feet, I fired a short burst from astern with unobserved results. I closed to 600 feet, fired again from dead astern and scored strikes on the fuselage. The e/a continued to lose height and speed and I closed to 300 feet and fired again, scoring many strikes on the fuselage and about the starboard wing root. A fire, which started in the starboard wing root, went out shortly afterwards, but the e/a continued to lose height. I followed, but had to pull out at 200 feet and in so doing overshot the e/a at 160mph. I turned hard to starboard to try to regain contact and as I turned on an easterly course, I saw a large fire burning on the water in approximately the same position as I overshot the e/a."

This was apparently Uffz Klaus Schulte's 5K+FS of 8/KG3, which ditched 50 miles off Great Yarmouth; the observer Uffz Anton Schlick was lost but the remainder of the crew took to their dinghies. Spitfires from 278 (ASR) Squadron were off at first light to protect a Warwick searching for the downed crew. A dinghy with three airmen – Schulte and two of his crew, Uffz Heinz Weber and Obgfr Heinz Müller – in it was spotted initially and, later, a second dinghy with one person (Uffz Walter Kirchvogel, the W/Op) aboard. A rescue launch was requested and *RML550* was soon on its way together with two relief Spitfires. Meanwhile, the Warwick dropped a life raft to the airmen but this collapsed in the rough seas. The Spitfires then attempted to release their dinghies but both refused to be jettisoned. When *RML550* skippered by Lt S.G. Sheppard RNVR arrived on the scene, only one dinghy could be located, that which contained the three airmen, causing 277 Squadron's diarist to comment: "The three bods were survivors from a Doodle Heinkel – anti-climax!" The difficulties involved in rescuing airmen from the sea is highlighted by fellow RNVR launch commander Lt Alan Rowe's account of this incident[230]:

"It was of course extremely important to get hold of any survivors, so that they could be interrogated to find out more about this new method of launching the V-1 missiles. An intensive search at first light was soon successful, a Warwick aircraft reporting that it was circling a dinghy containing three of the German crew. The duty boat replacing us was *RML550* so, at

0715 on the 6th, [Lt] Sheppard was on his way. The weather, which had been gradually worsening the day before, had now started to reach gale force, which meant that it was too rough to send a faster HSL. In fact, Shep was given the option of returning if conditions were too rough. But he was told how important it was to get these men before their own ASR service could rescue them, so that they could be interrogated by our intelligence men. He was determined, therefore, to go ahead. '550 corkscrewed and plunged into the heavy seas whipped up by the north-easterly gale. As the morning went on, the weather grew steadily worse. The waves were crashing over the bow, hitting the wheelhouse and flooding over the open bridge. Speed had to be reduced and the boat began to suffer storm damage. Several fittings on the decks were smashed and six feet of the rubbing strake were carried away by the force of the waves hitting the port bow. To add to the danger, a drifting mine loomed up dead ahead. Fortunately it was spotted in time for Shep to take avoiding action. For some reason, Shep was unable to make contact with the Warwick, which was orbiting the dinghy but, at about 1050, another Warwick flew past on its way to relieve the first one and they were able to get in touch on VHF.

"An hour later this pilot called Shep up to say that he was orbiting a man in the water. This put Shep in a dilemma: should he go first to the rescue of this man, who had no dinghy to support him? He reasoned, however, that as it would take over two hours to reach him, and his survival seemed extremely unlikely in those weather conditions, it was more practical to go on to the first and nearer target. Soon, a group of Spitfires got in touch with '550 and one of them came to check the course and distance to the dinghy, which was about ten miles away. Ploughing on through the heavy seas, Shep at last sighted red Very lights being fired from the surface dead ahead. He briefed his crew on the need to keep a constant watch on the Germans and not to speak to them.

"Shortly afterwards, Spike Gill, hoisting himself on to the flag locker, just caught sight of a Warwick circling ahead and glimpsed what appeared to be a yellow sail. Spike, going to the port boom, wondered how, in those seas, they were going to be able to put out the scrambling nets without their being torn away. Then he saw the grey, boat-shaped German dinghy, with a small sail and two one-man dinghies trailing behind. In the larger dinghy were three men who attempted to ignore the lines thrown to them and refused to lower their sail. Shep manoeuvred as close to them as possible, turning beam-on to the sea in order to get them under his lee. The ship was rolling so heavily that the guardrails were going under the water. But this proved to be an advantage because, as the ship drifted down on to the dinghy and she rolled to port once again, the dinghy came rising up on the wave-crest close enough to be grabbed by Spike and his mates. As they rolled back to starboard, the German airmen came tumbling out on to the deck and were seized, searched and taken to the sick bay by Spike and the other guards. The dinghy itself had been grasped and made fast by a line to the guardrail.

"When the rescued men had been stripped and bedded down in the sick bay, guarded by Spike and his mates, with loaded Smith and Wesson revolvers, Shep, who could speak a certain amount of German, came aft to tell them, 'You are on a ship of the Royal Navy, and prisoners of war. If you attempt to escape, the guard has orders to shoot you.' They did not in fact display any further reluctance to co-operate. Indeed they were anxious to volunteer information about their two other comrades, one of whom appeared to be the airman spotted by the Warwick. They accepted meekly Shep's instructions not to speak to one another and remained quietly in their bunks, although they were quite fit and unhurt. Their names were: Klaus Schulte, pilot, Heinz Muller and Heinz Weber, air gunners. Shep then carried on to take up the search, with the Warwick, for their comrade. They spent four hours, in worsening weather conditions, searching the area without success. The sea was so rough, in fact, that the aircraft had difficulty in even seeing the RML, according to Shep, who had to fire flares to show where he was! At last they were recalled and ordered to take their prisoners to Parkeston Quay at Harwich and hand them over to the Intelligence Officer, before they could take their well-earned rest, around midnight, back in Felixstowe."

Upon interrogation by the RAF, an account was obtained from the survivors and made available in ADI(K) Report No.579:

"These three P/W, the pilot, the B/M and the gunner, had come to grief on a flying bomb launching sortie. They proved to be the toughest P/W seen for a long time, and the information contained in the present report was only obtained after prolonged interrogation. At 1700 hours on 5 October, three crews of 8/KG3 were collected from their billets in Grossenkneten and taken by lorry to the airfield at Ahlhorn. After briefing they were taken to their aircraft, which were standing at the end of the runway, each loaded with a flying bomb. The aircraft took off at one-minute intervals, +FS manned by this crew starting third. Full runway lighting was turned on, with the addition of a single static searchlight at the end of the runway. +FS flew over land at a height of 300 metres. According to the pilot, the observer had been given a course over land in three legs, each turning point being marked by a low-powered visual beacon with a two-letter Morse characteristic. The aircraft flew to the north of Arnhem and crossed the Zuidersee; after leaving the Dutch coast three more legs were to be flown, each at a deviation of 30° from the preceding leg. The pilot maintained a height of 100 metres over the sea and only used his FuGe101 altimeter sparingly as an occasional check to the barometric temperature. After flying for over an hour and when on the second leg over the sea, the pilot found that the oil pressure of the starboard engine had dropped to zero. The flying bomb was jettisoned but the aircraft could not maintain height and the pilot ditched. The W/T operator was lost with the aircraft and the remainder of the crew took to their dinghies; the observer drifted away from his companions and was lost."

The pilot had earlier stated that their aircraft had not been attacked. He also confirmed that this was his third operational flight with 8/KG3 and advised that on his first sortie his bomb had simply fallen into the sea. A Diver damaged by AA fire over Colchester during the night turned over on its back and crashed near Reed Hall. Soldiers who were in a hut in its direct line had a remarkable escape when the falling bomb was diverted by a tree. Three reached London, exploding in Surbiton (two killed), Heston (15 injured), and Edgware, where five were killed and 40 injured, one of whom suddenly arrived at the local WVS incident office:

"The phenomenon of 'bomb happiness' appeared in the form of a man with blood stains down his shirt and joy all over his face. He could not stop talking. He said, 'I have lost everything. Suddenly – Bang! – Just like that. I cannot even find my wife. Nobody seems to know, would you believe it? Rations books, marriage certificates, my father's letters to my mother, kids' birth certificates – the whole lot. Well. I mean, what can I do? We were asleep. I have come to ask you if you know where Christine is …' and so on, waving his arms about and appealing to the audience between laughs. Told his wife and little girl were in hospital, neither of them seriously injured, he went off to see them, just as he was, before anyone could stop him."[231]

On the evening of **6/7 October**, at 1832, a further 11 Heinkels set out from Varrelbusch to release their missiles over the North Sea, again meeting Mosquitos from 25 Squadron. The night brought forth losses for both sides. HK256 crewed by Flg Off Jack Henderson and Flg Off Roland Nicholls crashed into the sea while attacking a Heinkel. Henderson survived and was taken prisoner but his navigator was killed. However, a Heinkel was shot down by Flt Lt Alf Marshall DFM in HK257, 40 miles east of Southwold, who reported:

"I was airborne from Coltishall at 1850 and patrolled at 2,500 feet under Hopton GCI control. Shortly after commencing patrol I saw a flying bomb released and informed control, who gave me vectors and then informed me that the target was dead ahead. Almost immediately afterwards my navigator obtained contact at one-and-a-half miles range, dead ahead at a height of 600 feet. I closed the range to 1,800 feet at approximately 280mph and had to throttle back to avoid overshooting the target. I closed again and at 800 feet obtained visual on four exhaust glows and my navigator then identified the target as a He111. The target was then above at 800-900 feet, so I pulled up and closing to 150 yards range opened fire with a two-seconds burst. An explosion occurred at the port wing root and the e/a disintegrated. I broke starboard and climbed to avoid flying debris and saw a large piece of the burning e/a going down in a slow dive. Shortly afterwards my navigator obtained a further contact at three-and-a-half miles range, but contact was lost as I turned starboard on to it."

This was almost certainly 5K+KS of 8/KG3 flown by Ltn Hans Böhne[232] and was Alf Marshall's 20th air victory including two probables, but his first at night. He had formerly been a Hurricane day fighter pilot[233]. Another patrolling Mosquito, HK241 from 68 Squadron piloted by Flg Off John Haskell shot down a Diver at 1954:

"Approximately 20 miles off Southwold we dived from 5,000 feet and fired one burst but flying bomb was out of range. Second attacked 30 miles off Southwold. The flying bomb was seen at 900 feet, speed about 340mph. Dropped down from 2,500 feet to 900 feet and opened fire at 1,000 feet range. Fired two bursts from dead astern. Flying bomb crashed into the sea and was seen to explode."

Flg Off Jan Adam pursued a second Diver at 2005, but was unable to close the range. However, he was satisfied to observe it dive into the sea before reaching the coast. Tempests from 501 Squadron were airborne and Flg Off Lulu Deleuze (EJ584/SD-Q) shot down one for his fourth kill between 1855 and 2105.

On the following night (**7/8 October**), 25 Squadron's Plt Off Barney Travers and Plt Off Alex Patterson in HK285 encountered a Heinkel off the Norfolk coast, and claimed it damaged:

"I was airborne from base at 1850. We were patrolling at 3,000 feet and I saw a flying bomb released and travel very low. I informed control and turned in direction of where the flying bomb was released and my navigator reported three successive contacts to port, dead ahead and to starboard respectively, all at approximately nine miles range. We singled out the starboard contact and were following it when I saw, at 6,000 feet range, another flying bomb released to port. The flames from the flying bomb illuminated momentarily the e/a, which I identified as a He111. I turned to port in the direction of the e/a and my navigator picked up contact at 5,000 feet range. The target was turning slowly to port and losing height. I closed to 3,000 feet range but as I thought I might overshoot, I throttled back. The target started to draw away and lose height so I increased speed up to 220 ASI and closed again to 700 feet. The height of the target by this time was 400 feet and I obtained a visual. I closed to 450 feet range as target lost height to 200 feet. I opened fire with approximately six-seconds burst from dead astern and saw strikes on fuselage of e/a. I pulled out to starboard to observe results and e/a was still losing height and, when at 75 feet, I had to pull up to avoid going in and lost sight of e/a and also lost contact. Contact was not regained."

This was possibly another aircraft from 7/KG3, Uffz Winfried Brender's 5K+KR being reported missing[234]. One Diver impacted at Little Yeldham in Essex, where two cottages and the church were seriously damaged. A few minutes later a second bomb fell on Greenstead Green, also in Essex, seriously damaging three cottages while blast damaged sixty houses and the village school. The occasional flying bomb was still being intercepted by Tempests of 501 Squadron, Flt Lt Ernie Williams DFC (in EJ590/SD-L) shooting down one to raise his personal score to five. Flt Lt Humphrey Humphreys of 68 Squadron (in HK344) scored a double including one by unconventional means:

"We closed to 500 yards and gave flying bomb three bursts – unable to close further. No immediate results seen but controller states flying bomb [blip] immediately disappeared from screen. Saw another approaching head-on – overshot but weaved and got in front of it when slipstream hit the flying bomb, which was then seen to crash into the sea."

It was not all success, however, and one V-1 that escaped the fighters and guns hit a balloon cable in the village of Fawkham near Gravesend and demolished several houses. There were many casualties including 17 killed and 54 injured (20 seriously) at Hornsey (N8) in London, when a Diver impacted in Park Road/Barrington Road at 0052. One of the many Heinkels lost to causes other than the British defences crashed this night. Crews were required to gain their bearings on the way out with the southern mast of the German navigation beacon *Sonne Elektra* on the Dutch coast at Groet-Petten. At 1929, Fw Lothar Gall's aircraft, 5K+DS of 8/KG3 collided with the mast and crashed onto a house in the coastal village of Groet. The crew was killed[235]. It was rumoured that some local people tried to break up the remains of the flying bomb, that had separated from the wreckage of the aircraft and was laying on the beach, because they thought it was a petrol tank with some valuable petrol still in it. When the Germans arrived on the scene they set about blowing up the remains of the weapon in situ.

Sgt Donald W. Marner USAAF at Leiston had cause to make another 'buzz bomb' entry in his diary for the night of **9/10 October**:

"Was awakened at 1am by red air alert. Saw a buzz bomb come over at treetop level and explode less than a mile from our base. In the morning I went to see it and brought several pieces back. [One fragment bore the serial number 254805[236]]. Two farm houses destroyed and many windows broken in Saxmundham."

At least two Heinkels were lost during the night, 5K+ER of 7/KG3 (Fhj Volker Happel) and 5K+CR (Fw Anton Schmid) of 8 Staffel colliding in mid-air at 0115 and crashing near Leeuwarden with the loss of both crews[237]. One of these came down at Nijemirdum, the explosion damaging many houses but inflicting no casualties on the ground. Most of the damage comprised broken windows and damaged roof tiles, the local church alone losing 50 windows, as revealed in the subsequent Dutch police report, although one crafty local resident submitted a recompense claim for a 'missing' wristwatch! Due to the extensive damage in the area, it was supposed that at least one aircraft was carrying its V-1. On the other side of the water, one Diver that evaded the defences fell on Hatfield (Herts) at 0500, killing eight and seriously injuring 30.

Flt Lt Ernie Williams (in Tempest EJ590/SD-L) of 501 Squadron got another flying bomb on the night of **11/12 October**, which crashed near Great Dunmow in Essex, followed by one more the following night (**12/13 October**) when flying EJ605/SD-K, while others were destroyed by Flt Lt A.T. Langdon-Down (EJ593/SD-B), Flt Lt Clive Birbeck (EJ598/SD-H), and Flt Lt Richard Bradwell DFC (EJ589/SD-J), the latter's victim falling harmlessly in a field near Coggeshall. Flt Lt Charles Bailey of 96 Squadron in Mosquito HK526 shot down another: "Attacked Diver and saw strikes and pieces fall off. It lost height to 800 feet but had to withdraw to allow Tempest [Flt Lt Langdon-Down of 501 Squadron in EJ593/SD-B] a shot. It crashed west of Chelmsford." Three civilians died when a Diver impacted on their house, possibly the one that fell on Russell Gardens N20. An even greater tragedy occurred on the night of **13/14 October**, a flying bomb claiming the lives of ten civilians. A missile that fell on the Suffolk coastal town of Southwold caused much damage but surprisingly no casualties: blast damage to 357 houses, 68 shops, three churches, the cottage hospital and fire station was reported. Another blew up over Raydon airfield near Hadleigh, the engine narrowly missing the bomb dump concealed in Raydon Great Wood. Wt Off Edward Wojczynski PAF, a Polish pilot who had recently been posted to 501 from 307 (Polish) Mosquito Squadron, shot down his first Diver (Tempest EJ763/SD-X), which crashed four miles east of Billericay, but, by a strange quirk of coincidence, this night also saw the loss of a Mosquito crew from 307 Squadron, who were hunting down a Heinkel over the North Sea. Flt Sgt Franciszek Kot PAF, the Polish pilot and his Czech navigator Wt Off Vladimir Kepák in DZ302/EW-V engaged the flying bomb. This apparently exploded in mid-air and took the Mosquito down with it. The authorities credited the crew with bringing down the

Heinkel launcher also, and this may have been Uffz Werner Weiffen's 5K+FR that crashed on return, in which the crew perished[238].

On the night of **14/15 October**, the diarist of US 100thBG based at Eye in Suffolk wrote:

"Tonight, around 2000 hours, when Sgt Pirtle and I were coming from the Sergeants club we saw quite a bit of ack-ack going up in the air over near Great Yarmouth, at least in that general direction, and watched until we saw a big explosion. They must have hit a buzz bomb because there was a big explosion in the air. Really was a sight to see."

Another wayward Diver crashed at Nayland but landed harmlessly in a meadow. Another, that came down more or less intact at Hopton in Suffolk, exploded as a bomb disposal officer (Lt C.H. Bassett) attempted to remove the fuse. Meanwhile, Flg Off John Haskell of 68 Squadron (in HK344) bagged a brace of flying bombs over the North Sea, one at 0139 and the second a few minutes later:

"Closed to 1,000 feet and fired three bursts. The light [exhaust flame] went out and flying bomb exploded and dived into the sea. Saw another flying bomb coming up behind, so turned towards it – flying at 900 feet at 280mph. Fired head-on at 2,000 feet, no result. Fired again at 300 feet and it exploded and crashed into the sea."

Flg Off Lulu Deleuze of 501 Squadron (Tempest EJ589/SD-J) also scored a double, taking his score to six, one of his kills coming down at Steeple in Essex at 0150. The local newspaper, the *Essex County Standard*, reported:

"In the early hours of Sunday morning a flying bomb fell in a meadow and caused damage to some houses in a village, four being rendered uninhabitable. Those damaged included a public house. A number of people suffered minor injuries, the most serious being a young girl, Jane Collins, who received cuts to her arms and head from flying glass. The robot is believed to have been hit by a plane and pieces of it were found half-a-mile away."

The following night (**15/16 October**), Sqn Ldr Norman Head, flying MM460 of 96 Squadron, scored his seventh kill, at 0451, shooting a Diver down into the sea, one of 19 that had been air-launched. Nine fell to the guns. One that escaped the defences reached London at 0150 and fell at the junction of Athenlay Road/Fernholm Road, Nunhead (SE15), where eight residents were killed. More Divers fell to 501 Squadron's Tempests on the following two nights, Flg Off Ron Bennett (EJ580/SD-G) shooting one down which crashed north-west of North Weald on **16/17 October**:

"I was under Trimley Control and saw a Diver crossing at Clacton, coned in searchlight at 1,500 feet. I dived down and from 1,000 yards astern opened fire and continued firing. Flg Off Polley flew up alongside the Diver, giving me the range. The Diver was hit and began to climb, while I followed, firing at it. At 4,000 feet the Diver exploded in the air north-west of North Weald at 2030."

68 Squadron's CO, Wg Cdr George Howden DFC[239] (with Flt Lt D.M. Norris-Smith in HK349) came close to getting a V-1-carrying Heinkel shortly after 2000:

"Having received information and several vectors, AI contact made with bandit about 1955, approximately 50 miles east of Lowestoft. Target head-on, about 3,000 feet. Turned and chased at 1,100 feet and gained height, dead astern. Closed to 300 yards before visual obtained under dark cloud. Target still unidentified so closed in to 150 yards, speed 180mph, when huge flash and flame dazzled me. Flying bomb seen falling beneath an He111, with large flame gradually becoming less and in five to ten seconds the flying bomb had dropped or dived several hundred feet and proceeded normally. Heinkel broke upwards to port at moment of release. To avoid collision with flying bomb I turned violently to starboard and dived. Flash and glow caused trouble in sighting. Visual and contact lost and not regained."

Wt Off Edward Wojczynski PAF (EJ763/SD-X) got his second Diver the following night (**17/18 October**). Some 70 houses were damaged in Kirby-le-Soken in Essex when a Diver impacted amongst them. During the period from **18/19 October** until the end of the month, there was a further increase in activity. Despite the successes achieved by the defences, not all of the bombs could be stopped and one that reached London fell at the junction of Lower Fore Street and Fairfield Road, Edmonton, killed 12 people and seriously injured 29. Several came down in East Anglia, killing five in Halton Crescent, Ipswich, where a further 28 were injured. This was the worst Diver incident to occur in East Anglia. One bomb came down near the USAAF base at Lavenham in Suffolk although it caused no damage or casualties. A Heinkel of 9/KG3 failed to return, Obfw Werner Schmidt-Reich and his crew[240] of 5K+LT being reported missing. Two of the flying bombs were shot down by Mosquitos, Flt Sgt Alf Bullus of 68 Squadron getting one at 2032 while flying HK237/WM-S: "We turned into an attack from starboard and closed to 500 yards. Flying bomb was travelling at 340mph at 400 feet. Gave three short bursts, the light went out and the bomb exploded and crashed into the sea." Flt Lt Dick Leggett (HK247) of 125 Squadron shot down the second.

Flg Off George Gibson RCAF of 68 Squadron (HK294/WM-Q) got one on the following night (**19/20 October**): "Saw several flying bombs – short bursts at four but no hits seen. At 0458 a further bomb seen at 1,500 feet flying at 200mph. Closed to within 700 yards and short burst given. Light of flying bomb went out, which was then seen to explode and crash into the sea." A brace of Divers fell to Wt Off D. Lauchan, also of 68 Squadron, in HK294/WM-Q: "We closed to 300 yards and gave short burst – flying bomb exploded and crashed into sea (0450). Saw another flying bomb approaching dead ahead. Dived and closed to 400 yards and fired three short bursts. Strikes were seen, the light went out and then immediately exploded." Flg Off Keith Panter (EJ599/SD-W) of 501 Squadron brought down another Diver shortly after 0500.

Another Heinkel was lost on the night of **20/21 October**, 5K+BT flown by Uffz Albert Fleischmann, failing to return to base. It transpired that it had crashed at Cloppenburg near Oldenburg with the loss of all aboard[241]. A flying bomb was shot down by Flg Off Lulu Deleuze of 501 Squadron (EJ584/SD-Q) on the night of **22/23 October**, crashing north of Woodford. Two more fell to Flg Off Johnny Johnson (EJ538/SD-R) shortly before midnight. Another Heinkel from 1/KG53 (5K+ER) crashed in the North Sea off Zandvoort, in which one member of the crew (Obgfr Walter Hasler) was drowned; the survivors were rescued. The following night (**23/24 October**) saw 501 Squadron add to its laurels when both Flg Off Don Porter (EJ589/SD-J) and Flg Off Ron Bennett (SD-P) shot down Divers. The latter reported: "Patrolling under Trimley Control when I saw a Diver crossing in over the coast near Harwich, speed 280mph, at 500 feet. I chased it and closing in fired three long bursts, observed strikes and the Diver crashed west of North Weald at 0115." Two people were killed and 69 injured when a Diver impacted at the junction of Orsett Road and Derby Road in Grays, Essex, at 1940. An hour into the new day, a second came down near the town.

III/KG3 (I/KG53) having borne the brunt of these early operations, the other two Staffeln were now introduced – but two of the Heinkel launchers were claimed during the night of **24/25 October**, one by Flt Lt Desmond Tull DFC flying a Beaufighter of the FIU, who shot down his victim some 60 miles east of Great Yarmouth. This was probably 5K+ES of 2/KG53 flown by Obfw Othmar Hämmerle[242] and was Tull's ninth victory, including one probable:

"We proceeded to position approximately 30 miles east-south-east of Coltishall. At 1930 we were told of trade 12 miles ahead and saw three Divers passing on the starboard side. No joy however as bombers were already heading for home. Then, after patrolling north and south, we were given trade five miles ahead. Throttled back to 180mph. Target dead ahead, crossing to starboard. Almost immediately we established contact. Turned starboard after target, closing to two miles, and saw flying bomb released. Target then turned to port, losing height. We followed and closed to 2,500 feet where a visual was established. Continued closing to 1,000 feet and identified target as He111. I pulled up dead astern at a range of 250 yards, height 700 feet, ASI 200mph and fired a three-seconds burst. Strikes were seen and a shower of debris came back, followed by an opening parachute. The target was clearly illuminated by a concentration of red sparks, apparently caused by an explosion in the aircraft. I fired another burst of four seconds. Strikes were seen and the target fell away to port in a violent spin. It was seen to hit the sea at 1945. This was later confirmed by control."

The other Heinkel was claimed by Flg Off Bill Beadle (HK310/VA-J) of 125 Squadron and would appear to have been A1+BL of 3/KG53, which returned to base 45% damaged and with a dead crewman (Fw Karl Proksch) aboard, having been attacked by a night fighter. Of his third victory Beadle reported:

"We were airborne from Coltishall at 1815. At 1905 we were told of trade and reduced height to 1,500 feet. Shortly afterwards contact was obtained at four-and-a-half miles range, dead ahead and at 1,500 feet. By giving port and starboard turns the navigator [Flg Off R.A. Pargeter] brought us 3,000 feet dead astern of the target. I then throttled back, put down 20° flap and reduced speed to 150 IAS. I obtained visual on target straight ahead and slightly above. Looking through night glasses I saw the flash of a bomb being released and identified it as He111. No exhausts visible. On releasing the bomb, e/a started a slow turn to port; ending in a dive to sea level in an easterly direction, and visual was lost momentarily. I did a steep port turn down to 100 feet, still retaining contact and regained visual from 1,500 feet astern on target, which was climbing to 300 feet. I reduced speed to 120-150mph and closing in slowly, gave a short burst from 900 feet range, observing strikes on the port engine. Rear gunner of e/a immediately opened fire, but without result, green tracers going over our starboard wing. Target reduced to 150 feet [above the sea] and following behind I gave another burst from 700 feet, obtaining strikes on fuselage but this time there was no return fire. Target started gentle weaving, and from 400 feet I gave another two-seconds burst, hitting port engine, which caught fire. Target went down still further to 100 feet, and coming into 30 yards, I gave a final one-second burst, hitting the fuselage. E/a immediately went into a steep vertical peel off to starboard, as I did a steep turn to port, going up to 300 feet. Looking back, the navigator saw a large flash at zero feet. Turning round quickly, I went down to 100 feet over the area, but no further contact was obtained."

One of the flying bombs that evaded the fighter patrols crossed the coast and killed eight civilians. Two of the flying bombs launched by Heinkels were shot down by a 68 Squadron Mosquito (HK347) piloted by Sqn Ldr John Wright, the first at 1934 and the second a few minutes later:

"Flying bomb seen below – chased and fire opened at 1,500 feet, but it disappeared into cloud after first burst. Vectored onto it and visual obtained. Three further bursts and it dived into cloud again but shortly afterwards there was a huge flash and flying bomb crashed into the sea. Regained height and another flying bomb seen on port side and slightly below. Chase was given and I gave short burst, range approximately 1,000 feet. Could not close range so gave two more bursts. Light went out and the flying bomb exploded."

501 Squadron's Flt Lt Clive Birbeck (EJ598/SD-H) scored a Diver kill just before midnight, while on the following night (**25/26 October**), Flt Lt Bob Stockburn (EJ558/SD-U) brought down two, and Flt Lt Jackson Robb (EJ555/SD-Y) another; this was Robb's 13th and final kill. 68 Squadron continued its run of successes when Sqn Ldr Miroslav Mansfeld DFC (in MM683/WM-C with Plt Off Slavomil Janáček) shot down another over the North Sea at 1925: "One seen coming in with another

behind it at 500 feet. I failed to overtake the first one, which got away. Second also got away by superior speed. Dived on third from 6,000 feet, firing short bursts from 1,000 feet. The light went out and a big flash was seen in the water." A second V-1 was shot down 20 minutes later by one of the American pilots, 1/Lt Sam Peebles USN, attached to 68 Squadron for night fighter experience, aided by Ens Dock Grinndal USN in HK344: "The first three flying bombs were lost in cloud, but next one was attacked from 200 yards range at approximately 400 feet above the sea, travelling at 350mph. Short burst, the light went and the flying bomb exploded." One of the Navy's Firefly NF1s was scrambled from Coltishall, MB419 flown by the detachment commander Lt Jimmy Kneale, with Lt Harrison operating the radar, but R/T failure obliged them to return to base. The same crew scrambled again two nights later but no trade came their way.

One of the flying bombs to evade the defences came down on the railway line at Palmers Green station in Enfield. Three nights later (**28/29 October**), 501's Flt Lt Ernie Williams (EJ590/SD-L) shot down his tenth flying bomb. One that evaded the defences came down in Deptford (SE14), killing one person in Milton Court Road. Flg Off Jimmy Grottick (EJ555/SD-Y) got his first two nights later (**30/31 October**), a night that saw another Heinkel fall to the guns of a Mosquito, on this occasion HK325 flown by Sqn Ldr Bill Gill of 125 Squadron. He shot down A1+BM of 4/KG53 in which Fw Theodor Warwas and his crew[243] were lost, and claimed a second as probably destroyed; the latter was later reduced to a 'damaged' only status. Gill reported:

"We turned hard starboard on navigator's instructions, and obtained a contact at 6,000 feet range, target above. I had previously obtained a fleeting visual on a Heinkel 111 as it passed above us on the opposite vector. We closed range rapidly to 4,000 feet when I started to get fleeting visuals on the target flying through broken cloud. Target, having released its bomb, was turning port and started to go down slightly. I closed range rapidly to 1,000 feet and opened fire, giving a long burst, obtaining many strikes on starboard engine and fuselage. Many pieces flew off and it started to go down steeply. I gave a further burst and obtained more strikes on the tail but was now overshooting, so had to break away. Enemy aircraft went down to sea level, straightened out and started to climb again for cover. As it was now climbing very slowly, I did a complete orbit and commenced AI search again, regained contact at 4,000 feet range and closed in rapidly to find target again taking violent evasive action and climbing slightly with engine smoking. Gave it another long burst from 1,000 feet range and obtained many strikes all on the starboard side of the fuselage. This set e/a alight and it went straight down into the sea. From a quick glance there appeared to be no survivors. Reported kill to Hopton.

"We immediately obtained further contacts towards north-east of us and after a little while obtained contact on another target, first appearing out of heavy rainstorms about two miles dead ahead – target 1,200-1,500 feet. On navigator's instructions turned hard starboard and whilst doing so obtained visual on He111 about 4,000 feet away, just dropping its chuff [bomb]. Closed range rapidly and at 2,000 feet e/a turned hard to port across our bows. Turned after it, with range closing rapidly to about 1,000 feet, opened fire at it, obtaining a few strikes. The curve of the pursuit brought me round behind the e/a and with a further burst I obtained many strikes on the tail of the e/a. My ammunition had now run out and I had at the same time overshot e/a, which was now climbing steeply and very slowly for thicker cloud cover. We did a complete orbit to try and regain contact but were unable to do so. Flt Lt Haigh confirms that port engine was u/s and a considerable amount of smoke was coming from e/a when last seen."

Fifteen people were killed in the south-eastern counties during the night by Divers and a further three were killed in West Ham just after dawn. Whilst all incidents when death and injury occurred were tragic, the Diver that struck the Marie Hotel at Coulsdon in London at 0650 was particularly appalling. The hotel was being used as an old people's private hotel. Seventeen of the residents were killed and ten more seriously injured. There was a friendly fire incident that same evening when a B-17 from the 379thBG at Kimbolton, on a night training flight, erroneously entered a restricted area and was fired on by HAA guns engaging Divers coming in over the Suffolk/Essex coast. With one wing on fire, 1/Lt Charles W. Goodier USAAF ordered his crew to bale out. All landed safely, the B-17 falling in a field at Manor Farm, Knodishall in Suffolk. Coastal watchers located within Pakefield Lighthouse at Lowestoft had a nasty shock when a Diver was spotted 100 feet above the waves heading straight for them. With no time to call HQ, the lighthouse was speedily evacuated – just in time to see the bomb plunge harmlessly into the sea in front of them. During another attack, the tower of the 15th century St Andrew's Church at Chelmondiston in Suffolk was hit and damaged by a Diver. Known as the 'Cursed Tower', it was said to have been cursed by a local witch and was subsequently burned down. In later years it was rebuilt, only to be struck by lightning and burned down again. Then along came the Diver. The church was finally rebuilt in 1957.

Towards the end of the month, two Beaufighters (including V8385/ZQ-F) from the Fighter Interception Development Squadron (formerly the FIU) were flown to Coltishall, current home of 125 Squadron's Mosquitos. One of the Beaufighter pilots, Sqn Ldr Jeremy Howard-Williams DFC explained:

> "The Heinkels which were launching the V-1s over the North Sea gave the Mosquitos charged with the task of intercepting them a certain amount of trouble, funnily enough because the Mosquitos were too fast. So somebody at Fighter Command suggested bringing Beaufighters out of retirement for the job, since they had a much lower stalling speed than the Mosquito. We already had several Beaufighters with Mk.VIII AI in an operational condition, so we were naturals for the trials."

Royal Navy frigate HMS *Caicos*, fitted out as a floating radar station and fighter control centre, was now employed for duties in the North Sea to help detect the launchers. A total of 282 V-1s had been launched by KG53 on 20 nights during the month.

November 1944 started relatively quietly for the defences, Flt Lt Ernie Williams of 501 Squadron in Tempest EJ590/SD-L shooting down another V-1 on the night of **3/4 November**, his 11th and final kill, while Flg Off Don Porter (EJ605/SD-K) got another. The following night (**4/5 November**) saw the commencement of another mini-Diver blitz, with 17 Heinkels of III/KG53 (which had been strengthened by the addition of two extra Staffeln) heading the assault once again. During this seven-night blitz, a dozen Heinkels failed to return, more than half falling to the night fighters. It did not take long for the Beaufighters of the FIDS at Coltishall to prove their worth, since one of the Heinkels was shot down by Sqn Ldr Howard-Williams:

> "Mac [Flg Off F.J. MacRae] and I take a Beau (V8385/ZQ-F) with AI Mk VIII to Coltishall again. This time Hopton gives us trade at 1,500 feet, crossing port to starboard but say they can give no more help. I point the Beau to port a bit and Mac soon gets a contact at one-and-a-half miles. We let it cross us and I lower 30° of flap for the approach. We close to a visual quickly and it is a Heinkel going west at 140mph, looking for all the world like a sinister black crow as it prepares to release its flying bomb from underneath the right wing. I am fed up with firing one-second bursts at port or starboard engines and then waiting for the immediate explosion, which only seems to occur in other people's combat reports. Nobody's going to survive a ditching in the North Sea for long tonight anyway, so I take aim on the centre of the Hun's fuselage and hold my thumb on the gun button. Things start happening immediately, a nice big fire breaks out and he nose-dives straight into the drink, complete with flying bomb, where a pool of burning fuel spreads briefly on the surface sending flames dancing on the water."

Howard-Williams had just received a course to return to base when another Heinkel was sighted:

"At that moment there is a flame in the sky about two miles away to our left, as a Heinkel ignites a flying bomb. The enemy aircraft is clearly illuminated as it banks away to port and Mac gets a contact as soon as I head towards it. By this time we are down to 500 feet and, scared of overshooting, I have the throttles three-quarters open nevertheless. The sky is completely black ahead and there is no horizon; how I wish for a radio altimeter such as we have on one or two of our Mosquitos. I go on losing height until 250 feet is showing on the altimeter, then 200 feet and finally 150. I have to hope that the barometric pressure hasn't changed in favour of Sir Isaac, and force myself to go lower; I still can't see the sea, nor will I until we hit it at this rate. The AI can give some sort of indication of height. I open the throttles wide but the echo finally disappears in the ground returns, which tend to be obstructive at such low altitudes. We lose that one."

The night turned out to be disastrous for the crews of II/KG53. Of the 14 aircraft that took off from Varrelbusch commencing 1715, five failed to return. The crew commanded by Hptm Heinz Zöllner, 4 Staffelkapitän in A1+AM, was posted missing[244] – believed to have been Howard-Williams' victim – as were the crews of Ltn Heinz Redde of 6 Staffel in A1+EP[245], Obfw Fritz Jost, also of 4 Staffel, in A1+KM, Ltn Willi Hansen in A1+CM (4 Staffel), Uffz Walter Weider in A1+BM (4 Staffel). It is believed that the other two aircraft were lost due to premature detonation of the flying bomb each was carrying, caused by a fault in the electrical system. In addition to these losses, Obfhr Karl-Heinz Mallach and two[246] of his crew from 2 Staffel were killed when their aircraft (A1+GK) crash-landed at Kotwijk in Holland; only Obgfr Anton Kartak survived, albeit injured. Six aircraft totally lost along with 23 aircrew for very little return.

The following night (**5-6 November**) was equally as disastrous, with a further five Heinkels being lost: A1+CN (Fw Karl Wiaweg/5 Staffel), A1+LN (Obfw Ernst Lösche/5 Staffel), A1+BN (Ltn Alfred Schacht/5 Staffel), A1+AC (Uffz Walter Schulz[247]) of 4 Staffel, and A1+FN (Obfw Paul Flir[248]) of 5 Staffel. It would seem that either AC or FN was the victim of night fighter attacks, since both crews reported such before their demise. Indeed, 68 Squadron Mosquito (TA389) crew Flt Sgt Les Neal and Flt Sgt E. Eastwood claimed a Heinkel over the North Sea. Neal recorded:

"We were under Dunwich Control and informed that trade was approaching and at once given various vectors until we obtained a contact at one-and-a-half miles range at 1,000 feet with target below, going west. We dropped 100 feet, closing to 2,500 feet. Target was then above. Closed in at 160 IAS, target travelling at 150mph. We overshot. We then returned to patrol. At 2040, we were vectored and obtained contact at two miles range, at Angels 500 feet, with target at same height and crossing port to starboard. We closed in to 1,000 feet and target weaved slightly. Increased speed and` climbed. We then closed to 500 feet range and saw e/a release flying bomb. Visual lost due to glare. Contact, however, retained. E/a followed in path of flying bomb for 20/30 seconds, losing height gradually, and then made hard turn to starboard. We followed on AI and obtained visual at 150/200 yards at 900 feet height and identified target as He111. At 2045 we gave a two-seconds burst. Strikes were seen on fuselage and e/a dived steeply to starboard and crashed into the sea."

The other Heinkel was almost certainly shot down by Sqn Ldr Bill Maguire DFC (with Flg Off W.D. Jones DFC) of the FIDS in a Beaufighter, as noted by Sqn Ldr Howard-Williams:

"The unit had one more success with the Beaufighter when Bill Maguire shot down another V-1-carrying Heinkel. After that, Fighter Command decided to call off the experiment on the grounds that the Beaufighter would not be resurrected anyway, so there was no point in getting the resident Mosquito crews' backs up."

At least one of the 17 crews from II/KG53 airborne that night was instructed to carry out an attack on Portsmouth and, at about 1900, sirens were sounded on the Isle of

Wight as the Heinkel flew down the Channel towards East Sussex. It released the missile in the direction of Portsmouth but in fact it impacted near Littlehampton. One of the flying bombs launched by the Heinkels was shot down at 2020 by AA guns near Aldeburgh, its warhead falling near a gun site at Gorse Hill where three soldiers were injured.

Hptm Heinz Rehfeld now took command of the heavily depleted 4/KG53 following the loss of Hptm Zöllner, and Hptm Siegfried Jessen, who had commanded 7 Staffel earlier in the year, took over the reins of 9 Staffel from Hptm Bischowski. Since RAF night fighters claimed only three of the missing ten aircraft, it seems probable that some of the losses were due to premature detonation of the bombs. The following night Ltn Karl Glauner of 1 Staffel carried out his first operational sortie, A1+DP departing Hesepe at 1835, and returning safely just over three hours later.

During the evening of **8/9 November**, a Diver reached London and hit the 'Gaumont State' in Holloway, England's second largest cinema. The massive street frontage boasted a 200-seat restaurant with outdoor terrace seating and a broadcasting studio. The cinema, foyer and auditorium were in French Renaissance style. Following the explosion only the main walls and the foyer survived, the auditorium having been completely destroyed. Nine Divers came down in Kent, two in Essex and one in Sussex. The most serious incident occurred at Rochester at 2045, when a Diver impacted at the junction of Grafton Avenue and Gerrards Avenue, killing eight and seriously injuring 17. The two that came down in Essex were the victims of Tempests, Flt Lt Richard Bradwell (EJ589/SD-J) catching one north-west of Chelmsford that eventually crashed at Leadon Roding at 2049, while Flg Off Don Porter (EJ605/SD-K) shot down a second that sadly crashed in Palmerston Road, South Stifford. One person was killed and 23 seriously injured. One of the Heinkels (A1+KK) involved FTR with the loss of Obfw Clemens Bergmann and his 2 Staffel crew, while an aircraft from 6 Staffel crash-landed during which the gunner Obfw Herbert Tauchmann was injured. Flg Off Ted Ledwidge, with Wt Off C.A. Bonner in 25 Squadron's MT474, managed to shoot down two flying bombs over the North Sea during his 2010-2200 patrol.

"We were airborne from Castle Camps at 2012 to carry out anti-Diver patrols over the North Sea. We were told to patrol at 7,000 feet. Before we crossed the coast we saw a Diver being fired at by AA and control informed us that there was trade developing. On crossing the coast we saw two Divers about two miles apart and well below us; these were seen to explode after being hit by AA fire. We then saw several Divers to the north and south of us. Control gave us trade south-east and we saw a Diver at 1,000/1,500 feet. We turned onto it and dived down to 1,500 feet and fired two long bursts from 500 yards dead astern. Diver was travelling at 280mph in and out of cloud. Results of the first attack were unobserved so a further two short bursts were fired from 500 yards dead astern. The flame went out and the flying bomb was not seen again. We broke away, climbed and went east as control informed us that there was more trade to the east and south-east. When at 3,000 feet we saw another Diver approaching head-on, well below and travelling in and out of cloud. We turned in front of Diver and dived down to obtain speed but then had to weave to let Diver overtake. We closed to 400 yards and fired two short bursts from astern and slightly above as Diver passed into cloud. We pulled out to starboard to observe results and saw Diver explode in the air."

More success was to come for 25 Squadron on the following night (**9/10 November**). Out over the North Sea, Mosquito MV521 crewed by Flt Lts Jim Lomas[249] and Norman Fleet shot down one more of the V-1 launchers, the Heinkel being observed to crash into the sea 35 miles east of Clacton.

"We were scrambled from Castle Camps at 1840 to carry out anti-Diver-carrier patrol over the North Sea. Many Divers were seen but these were ignored. Control then vectored us south and after a few minutes we saw a Diver launched approximately ten miles away from us. We were given two more vectors and informed that there were two enemy aircraft in the area. We turned to port, losing height, and contact was obtained at four-and-a-half miles range. Our height was then 400 feet. We did a hard starboard turn and then a gentle turn, bringing the target 10,000 feet dead ahead. We climbed to approximately the same height as the target, which was at 800 feet, closed in and obtained visual of exhausts at 1,800 feet range. We closed in at 190 IAS and when at 800 feet range identified the target as a He111. The e/a did not take any evasive action and we closed to 175-150 yards and opened fire with two short bursts from dead astern. After the first burst the port wing root burst into flames, and the second burst set fire to the port fuselage. The e/a went down in a controlled glide and after ditching broke into several pieces, which burned on the sea."

This was probably A1+LK of 2 Staffel flown by Fw Rupert Dorn, which FTR. A second Heinkel, apparently bearing the markings VL+YR (sic[250]) but from 1 Staffel, crashed with the death of the pilot (Uffz Hermann Hurrle) and two of his crew. This may have been the victim of Wt Off K.R. Cookson of 68 Squadron in HK251, who claimed a probable: "We obtained contact at 1,000 feet at three-and-a-half miles range. Turned on to target and went down to 200 feet to get below it. Visual at 900 feet range on Heinkel flying at 150mph. Opened fire but saw no strikes." Flt Lt Richard Bradwell (EJ589/SD-J) of 501 Squadron shot down his third flying bomb during the night, this also causing casualties on the ground when it crashed in Mount Crescent, Brentwood at 2205. Three people were killed and eight seriously injured. Another fell to a 25 Squadron Mosquito crew, Plt Offs D.J. Carter and W.J. Hutchinson in MT474, during their 1720-2015 patrol, as reported:

"At approximately 1900, control reported Diver activity and told us to keep a sharp lookout to starboard. We saw four Divers well below. We singled out one and dived to 600 feet, closed and opened fire at 400 yards, but unable to observe results as Diver and Mosquito illuminated by searchlight. Climbed to 2,500 feet and almost immediately saw another Diver approaching head-on. Turned hard to port, dived to 500 feet and opened fire from 350 yards dead astern. Flame [from engine] extinguished and Diver exploded on hitting the sea."

The same crew (Plt Offs Carter and Hutchinson) shot down another Diver (again in MT474) the following night (**10/11 November**): "Airborne at 1815 and patrolled at 1,500 feet under Dulwich GCI. At 1955 saw Diver to starboard approaching almost head-on. Turned hard to port and dived from 1,500 feet to 500 feet. Opened fire with two short bursts from dead astern. Diver lost height and dived into the sea where it exploded." Three flying bombs fell to the Tempests of 501 Squadron, two being shot down by Flt Lt Monty Burton during two separate patrols while flying EJ591/SD-Z, with a third falling to Flg Off John Maday in EJ672/SD-V. Another 25 Squadron victory against the launchers was notched up the same night, when Flt Lt Doug Greaves DFC (with Flg Off Milton Robbins DFC in MT492) shot down the Heinkel over the sea about 70 miles east of Lowestoft. This was the tenth and final victory for the successful pairing who had flown together in North Africa the previous year:

"We were scrambled from Castle Camps at 0030 on indications of Diver-carrier activity over the North Sea. After about an hour we were informed that there might be some activity in the area. Shortly afterwards several Divers were seen at about 600 feet. We went down to 200 feet, weaved about and obtained a contact at two-and-a-half miles range. We closed at 190 IAS to 150 feet astern and slightly to port and obtained a visual on e/a, identified as He111, at height of 200 feet. We opened fire with a long burst from dead astern. Strikes, followed by a sheet of flame, were seen on the starboard engine and wing root. Difficulty was experienced in firing at this height owing to the necessity for keeping an eye on the altimeter. We climbed to 4,000 feet and saw the Heinkel, on fire, slide slowly to starboard into the sea. The wreckage was still burning three minutes later when we left the area."

Wt Off Arthur Brooking and Plt Off Bob Finn (HK348) of 68 Squadron claimed a second Heinkel:

> "We were under Happisburgh Control and informed that trade was approaching. We saw four flying bombs released and we reduced to 700 feet. We then got a freelance contact at 700 feet at two-and-a-half miles range on target slightly above. We closed to 2,000 feet, losing height to 300 feet to keep target above, speed of which was 180 IAS. We closed to 1,200 feet, when we got a visual, and then gradually reduced range while flying through patchy cloud. We opened fire from 600 feet and saw strikes on starboard wing root and fuselage. Pieces flew off and a glow of burning was visible inside fuselage. We broke starboard to avoid flying debris and a few seconds later saw burning wreckage on the sea. No return fire was experienced and no evasive action was taken by the target."

125 Squadron's Flt Lt Gilbert Simcock failed to see his victim crash and was therefore credited with only a probable. Flying with Flg Off N.E. Heijne as his navigator in HK263, he reported:

> "I saw what proved to be a flying bomb being released and asked control if any information was available. Control had no information so we turned in direction of flying bombs. We obtained a contact on target crossing from starboard to port, going east, but control turned us away from this and then turned us back. As we were turning back I saw, slightly behind us, a He111 by the light of its flying bomb. Turned towards it and obtained contact at three miles, our height being 1,000 feet and target's about 1,500 feet. Target did a wide turn to port and slowly lost height to 200 feet, approximate IAS 200mph. Followed on AI through heavy shower and closed in, getting visual at 800 feet. Target was then down to 150 feet, IAS 150mph. I originally intended to shadow e/a on AI hoping that he would gain height on approaching coast, but as there was more very dirty weather ahead, decided to open fire at once rather than risk losing contact. Opened fire with long burst at 600 feet, closing to 400 feet. Target then at 100 feet height. Many strikes were seen on port engine and port wing root and on port side of fuselage. There was a large whitish-yellow flash from the port engine and large piece flew back from it. My observer reported seeing another flash from the port side of the fuselage, but I did not see this. E/a immediately slowed down and went into steep port bank. I had to break away to avoid collision. Broke starboard and then turned back to port again and attempted to regain contact. We searched the area thoroughly at about 75 feet, scanning up, but no contact obtained. The sea was very rough with white horses, and it was extremely dark, so consider it unlikely, as it was not on fire, that I would be able to see it hit the sea. I claim one He111 probably destroyed."

A total of 29 sorties were flown by the Heinkel crews, some flying twice during the night. First off was airborne from Varrelbusch at 1758, and last to return landed at 0510. It was another bad night for KG53, two aircraft from 4 Staffel failing to return from operations: A1+NM flown by Obfhr Walter Strump and A1+HM by Ltn Günther Scholz, plus one from 3 Staffel, Obfhr Wilhelm Janssen's A1+AB. There were no survivors from any of the crews. 1 Staffel's Ltn Glauner was one of the lucky pilots, having carried out his fourth successful sortie (in A1+GP) in as many nights, and would be followed by another the following night.

Tragically, another so-called 'friendly fire' incident occurred on the evening of **14 November**. Mosquito HK289/WM-K of 68 Squadron took off from Coltishall at 1805 in the hands of one of the unit's attached American crews[251], Lts Joe Black from Virginia and Tom Aitken from Pennsylvania, both USN Reserve officers. At 1849, the crew advised their controller that they had a contact on their radar and were hot in pursuit. At 1909 hours, a Diver passed over the gun batteries at Hopton flying south-west. Right behind it as it roared in towards the coastal gun batteries was Black's Mosquito. The night fighter crews had been thoroughly briefed on the procedures for crossing the coast in fighter-free zones such as this. These involved losing speed and height, and circling at a set distance from the coast showing their navigation lights or using coloured Very lights to show the 'colours of the day'. Presumably, Lts Black and Aitken were so focused on overhauling and shooting down the Diver[252] that they failed to notice their proximity to the gun belt. A searchlight illuminated the Mosquito (which bore a striking resemblance to the Me410), and the 3.7 inch heavy gun batteries, under orders to engage any aircraft not following the laid-down procedure outlined above, opened fire. Dozens of proximity-fused shells exploded around the Mosquito, which fell in flames in a field on Decoy Farm, Blundeston, disintegrating and killing both crewmen. The subsequent Court of Enquiry placed the blame on the shoulders of Lt Aitken who, it concluded, should have warned his pilot of their proximity to the guns. A second Mosquito was also crippled by HAA gunfire whilst crossing the coast at Southwold, but this time Wg Cdr Leicester Mitchell and Flt Lt Dennis Cox were able to bale out. Their aircraft, MV526 from 25 Squadron, was being guided by Trimley GCI through the defences owing to fuel shortage, but the guns at Southwold opened fire and damaged the Mosquito, which crashed near Garboldisham in Suffolk. The wing commander sprained an ankle on landing. The Navy's Lt(A) Jimmy Kneale was up again in Firefly MB419 but severe weather conditions hampered any chance of a contact.

II/KG53 lost another Heinkel this night, 4 Staffel machine A1+KP crashing on return from a sortie, in which the pilot Fw Karl Oehl was seriously injured and his observer Fw Georg Fiebig was killed; two others were slightly injured. However, eight of the 37 Divers launched reached London where two serious incidents were recorded. One bomb fell at St Pancras (NW1) at 0030, killing 18 people and injuring a further 20, and causing much damage. Within 30 minutes another came down at Sutton, 11 residents of Frogmore Gardens, Henley Avenue and Windsor Avenue losing their lives; 18 others were injured. Many properties were destroyed or damaged.

Two Divers that fell in East Anglia at this time caused widespread damage. One impacted on the night of **17/18 November** in the small market town of Hadleigh on the Essex/Suffolk border (inflicting 11 serious and five slight casualties); one man later died, a former soldier who had just been discharged from the army due to shell shock. The other fell two nights later (**19/20 November**) at Carlton Colville near Lowestoft on the Norfolk coast (two killed, 17 injured), but a total of 21 flying bombs were shot down by the guns off Harwich and Felixstowe. On this same night Flg Off Doug Arnold RAAF of 456 (RAAF) Squadron (with Flg Off J.B. Stickley RAAF in HK246/RX-U) intercepted a Heinkel some 75 miles east of Lowestoft, and shot it down into the Ijsselmeer near Molkwerum. There were no survivors from Fw Rudolf Ripper's crew aboard A1+NN of 5/KG53. Arnold's report revealed:

"We were airborne from Ford at 1855 ... and while flying south, I saw flying bombs to the south. A flying bomb was seen to start up dead astern. Control, on being informed of this, confirmed the presence of trade about eight miles away. I turned port on reciprocal, height 3,000 feet, and a contact was obtained at 12,000 feet range to starboard and below, at about 2015. I turned to starboard to place target dead ahead. The contact established, the target proceeded to fly a complete orbit. I went down to get below. The target dived and I followed it down in steps until it settled at 500 feet in a continuous weave. Holding the target dead ahead and level, I obtained the first visual at 700 feet and identified it as a He111. There was no Window or other special features seen. Closing in, a first burst of two-three seconds was fired from 400 feet. No strikes were seen but e/a returned fire from the ventral position with a medium burst of green tracer, and we got the impression that the Mosquito was hit (on landing damage was found in the trailing edge of one of the blades of the starboard propeller and also in the leading edge of the starboard wing; the latter believed to be from debris from the propeller blade). After this, e/a turned to port and I fired another burst, seeing strikes on the e/a's starboard engine, fire breaking out there and extending inboard. A third burst was fired with no observed results, and e/a climbed suddenly to 1,200 feet, still burning, where it partially broke up, a burning section falling away to starboard. E/a turned over starboard in a stall turn, to port of the Mosquito, and dropped, burning, into the sea, where a shower of sparks was seen just before the flames doused. There was no explosion on impact."

The threat posed by the V-1-carrying Heinkels was beginning to cause ADGB a headache, since standing patrols did not seem to be the answer. In an effort to overcome the problem of detection, it was proposed that an ASV-equipped Wellington be borrowed from Coastal Command for the purpose of patrolling the suspected launching area, at which point an accompanying Mosquito or Beaufighter would then be called in to shoot down the Heinkel and V-1. Thus, on **21 November**, a Wellington from 407(RCAF) Squadron flown by Flt Lt M.S. McLean RCAF was detailed to join the FIDS at Ford from where the crew was to practise for its new rôle. Among the crew was Plt Off Ross Hamilton RCAF, the Wop/air gunner:

> "After a short period of intense training, mainly homing in on fast-flying Beaufighters at very low altitude, at night and in daylight over the Channel, we began operations from Manston to Coltishall as quickly as possible. Two boffins from RAE flew every trip with us, training and ops. As the Heinkels would normally pick only the foulest nights to go out, it was necessary for the Wimpy and its escort to follow suit. It was very dicey trying to maintain 100 feet altitude in a Wellington over water at night without special instrumentation (the regular altimeter was useless in this situation.). However, one of the trusty boffins soon came up with a solution – a 'radio altimeter.' This consisted of a white light bulb on the pilot's instrument panel, which would illuminate – at a height of 100 feet. Unfortunately the aircraft could be lower than this, and a lot of attention was needed on the controls to keep the little light blinking on and off – but never on fully for any length of time. Very rudimentary, but it worked. We also had a quick flight to the maintenance unit at St David's to have dual controls installed on the Wimpy. Flying at 100 feet for sustained periods, particularly at night and in awful weather conditions, placed a severe strain on the skipper, so the flying chore was shared. There was also the factor that if an engine even hiccupped we could be in the drink and one pilot alone would be hard pressed to cope with the immediate response requirements. This was particularly so with an aircraft which hadn't exactly been designed for this specialised work and was still some 2,000 pounds overweight – even without the depth charges on board."[253]

The Wellington crew would be ready for operations at the beginning of January, under the codename Operation 'Vapour'. In the meantime, from Coltishall on the night of **21/22 November**, Lt(A) Mike Howell RNVR (with Lt(A) Lester as his radar operator) was scrambled in Firefly MB419 and vectored on to an approaching Diver. It was picked up on the radar but disappeared almost immediately, as though it dived into the sea: "With the Firefly we hadn't the turn of speed to actually catch a flying bomb, but if we could have got close enough for a few seconds to have a crack at it with the cannon we might have been lucky. The alternative was to catch the parent aircraft, the Heinkel, which would have made the Luftwaffe a little more cautious."[254] The same crew had another scramble in the early hours of the following morning, albeit without success. Flt Lt Monty Burton (SD-Z) of 501 Squadron chalked up another flying bomb kill shortly after midnight on **22/23 November**. The night witnessed another Heinkel loss when A1+KH of 1 Staffel crashed at Osterode near Bramsche at 2330. Flhj Wilhelm Wolfshol, the pilot, and his observer Uffz Georg Grill were killed; the other three, Ltn Alfred Rauh, Uffz Johann Nissters and Obfw Hans Bernhart were seriously injured. The Suffolk and Essex coastal guns scored a very satisfactory 25 kills on the night of **23/24 November**, when Flt Lt Burton (again in EJ591/SD-Z) claimed his fifth. He recalled:

> "That particular afternoon the boffins appeared with their latest invention consisting of a piece

of corrugated glass, about seven inches long by about four inches wide, which was stuck to the windscreen with the corrugations vertical. The idea being that once behind a V-1, its jet flame would be reflected in each corrugation and on closing in, the side reflections would move towards the centre and when only one light showed in the centre you were at the correct firing range (250/300 yards) – all very simple. That night it was very dark with thick low cloud; I tracked a V-1 at seven hundred feet and eagerly watched the light centring on the glass gadget; when the light became a central unit, I fired. Of course, I was far too close and the bomb exploded in my face with pieces hitting my aircraft in various places. Worst of all, I was completely blinded by the explosion and couldn't see my instruments – so at two hundred feet I was flying at great speed, not knowing if I was going upwards, sideways – or downwards! Eventually my sight returned and I went back to base where I was interrogated by a strange Army officer – probably another boffin. Needless to say I promptly ejected the glass sight. Some time later I received a letter from the North Avenue Wardens Post at Chelmsford who confirmed the destruction of the flying bomb close to the Boarded Barns Estate, and expressed his gratitude for the probable saving of lives and property. I was most gratified to them to go to such trouble as they had plenty of problems of their own."

The guns brought down a further 11 Divers the following night (**24/25 November**), which also saw the destruction of a He111 by a Mosquito of 456 (RAAF) Squadron, Flg Off Fred Stevens RAAF and Flg Off Andy Kellett RAAF being the successful crew in HK290/RX-J. They caught A1+BH ten miles off Texel at 0510 after they had chased it for 25 minutes. The doomed 1/KG53 Heinkel, with V-1 still attached, crashed into the sea a few miles west of Egmond with the loss of its crew[255]. The body of the pilot, Fw Kurt Hillmann, was washed ashore two days later near the coastal village of Callantsoog, some ten miles south of Den Helder. The Australian pilot from Victoria reported:

"We were airborne from Ford at 0300. We were patrolling under Bawdsey at 2,500 feet and, seeing flying bombs on a westerly course, reported these. We had just turned when three or four bright flashes were seen off the starboard wing, about 1,000 feet below, corresponding with control reporting a bogey to the east. We turned to starboard and dived to 1,500 feet and observed two contacts to port, both about two miles range. The nearest of these was chosen and it appeared to be flying in an easterly direction and taking evasive action. We went down to 500 feet in pursuit. Control was told that this was being investigated but the message was apparently not heard owing to the aircraft being so low. Target settled down on a mean track at 500 feet. Closing very slowly (due to the fact that the C-scope was u/s), a visual was obtained at 800 feet range but shortly afterwards lost before recognition could be effected owing to the target making a violent starboard turn. I made a half-orbit and contact was immediately regained, and after ten minutes the target was seen again. There was no cloud but it was very dark. At 800 feet range the target opened fire twice but did not hit us, and at 600 feet range, at a height of 900 feet, it was identified as a He111. At 600 feet range I opened fire with a two-seconds burst. The e/a's port engine immediately caught fire, and closing to 150 feet, another two-seconds burst was fired, this appearing to go right through the fuselage. In the light of the flames the fin and rudder were noticed as being of a peculiar dull light grey camouflage. We broke away to starboard, very close to the e/a, which could be seen to be going into a gentle dive, flames from the port engine spreading. E/a hit the water and wreckage bounced over the surface, leaving a sea of flame."

However, another Mosquito (HK317) from the Australian unit failed to return from an anti-Diver patrol and 21-year-old Australian Wt Off John Mulhall RAAF from Victoria and his Welsh navigator Flg Off Jimmy Jones from Glamorgan, also 21, were posted missing. It is not known if their aircraft was brought down by the explosion of a flying bomb or was lost to other causes. One of the Navy's Fireflies (DT933) was up from Coltishall, flown by Lt(A) Jimmy Kneale, but was not vectored on to any of the incoming missiles. One of the sorties was flown by Ltn Glauner of 1/KG53 (in A1+GP) now operating from Wittmundhafen. A Diver that escaped the attention of the defences crashed in Hampstead (NW9), where it badly damaged 44 houses in Kingsbury Road, killed 12 and seriously injured 29 others. It was the turn of one of the US P-61s to shoot down a flying bomb on the night of **26/27 November**, 1/Lt Paul A. Smith USAAF[256] of the 422ndNFS (flying 42-5544 'Lady Gen'), operating from Belgian base A.78 (Florennes), being the successful pilot. It was the ninth (or possibly tenth) and final success for the P-61s. The same crew reported that they had also shot down a Heinkel at 0325 over Holland near Hillegom. Indeed, they had. It was not however a KG53 machine but a converted transport of 1/TG30, possibly that flown by Obfw Ernst Fiala who was killed with his crew while on a mission to supply the besieged Dunkirk garrison. Records pertaining to KG53's activities reveal that 316 V-1s had been launched on just 13 nights during November.

December 1944 brought with it a continued assault by the Heinkels, with London remaining the focus of their attention. On the night of **4/5 December**, III/KG53 launched 20 Heinkels from Schleswig, Leck and Eggebek between 1650 and 1710. Two of these crash-landed shortly thereafter, one coming down in Husum, the other at Laland/Schleswig. It seems that both crews survived. At 2052 the first of the returning Heinkels landed, the last to return touching down at 2320. Four had suffered emergencies and had released their bombs prematurely, one falling in the Zuidersee, one in the Gotteskogsee, a third at Grid reference W.1 (the predetermined point for launching), and the other over the North Sea, the latter presumably the 'red flash' reported by the 68 Squadron crew. Two others had failed to launch. The 'red flash' was observed by Wt Off James Brill and Flt Sgt John Walter, the crew of HK348, who radioed they were going down to investigate, but FTR. The cause of their loss remains unknown, but possibly the Mosquito flew into the sea. It seems likely that they had attacked a Heinkel of 7 Staffel flown by Uffz Claus Jahvos before their demise. KG53 was quite satisfied with this operation:

"Take-off was excellent. *Sonne Husum* and *Merkur* (radio beam stations) good signals. Radio failure [affecting four aircraft] originated by heavy rain. The landing operation was good but suffered communication due to FuG16 radio failure. Emergency landings and emergency drops resulted from radio failure. This result is acceptable for the first mission."

On the following night (**5/6 December**), of 15 launches by the Heinkels, only seven Divers approached the coast. Three of these fell to the guns of 501 Squadron's Flt Lt Burton (EJ697/SD-N), Flg Off Johnny Johnson (EJ585/SD-A) and Sqn Ldr Parker-Rees (SD-P), while Flt Sgt D.J. James (HK417) of 96 Squadron brought down the unit's 180th and final kill at 2010. Burton's victim crashed in rural Essex, and that shot down by Parker-Rees fell at Chignall St James near Chelmsford, where some damage was done to Chignall Hall. Another was shot down by the Tempests on the night of **7/8 December**, Flt Lt Don Porter (EJ605/SD-K) and Flt Lt Langdon-Down (EJ593/SD-B) sharing the kill, which came down near East Hornan Hall near Brentwood. One that eluded the defences crashed in a garden in West Mersea but inflicted no injuries. One of the Heinkel launchers FTR with the loss of Obfw Nikolaus Mertes and his crew of A1+AM; none of the crew survived. Two nights later (**9/10 December**) a stray Diver impacted at Chelmindiston in Suffolk, killing one and injuring 20. Once again, a Heinkel FTR, Uffz Günter Lis and his 1 Staffel crew of A1+FH being posted as missing; the body of the observer Obfhr Kurt Tornier was washed up on the coast of Sweden three months later. On this night Ltn Glauner of 1 Staffel clocked up his seventh sortie. The following night (**10/11 December**) witnessed 15 launches by the Heinkels, but only eight Divers approached the coast, two of which were shot down by Naval AA over the sea and the remaining six fell to inland AA. One reached London before it was hit, falling in Fairfax Road, Tottenham at 1903. Thirteen people died and 88 were injured, 30 seriously. Many properties were destroyed and damaged.

On the evening of **12 December**, III/KG53 launched 17 Heinkels between 2022 and 2108 from Schleswig, Leck and Eggebek. Of these, two crews were obliged to carry out emergency releases – one due to engine failure and the other owing to failure of blind flying instruments, whereupon the weapon was released over the city of Schleswig. The official report stated: "Barriers installed and recovery actions already started", suggesting the V-1 fell into the river or a canal. Two crews reported that the engines of their bombs failed to start and another failed following release. Heinkels from I/KG53 were still operating from Bad Zwischenahn, Ltn Glauner now flying A1+CP logging his eighth sortie, but 1 Staffel, at least, returned to operate from Wittmundhafen the next day. A radar-equipped Firefly NF1 (MB419) from the NFIU detachment at Coltishall was scrambled to investigate three of four contacts that appeared to be He111s, but without success although after chasing one ASH contact across the North Sea in very bad weather, Lt(A) Jimmy Kneale RNVR fired one long-range burst at the Heinkel without observable effect: "In the absence of a blind-flying facility this was no more than an opportunist attempt, and no results were claimed." Engine problems when off the Dutch coast then forced the Firefly to return to Coltishall. Five further anti-Diver patrols were carried out by the Firefly detachment, all without success. The conclusions drawn of the Firefly's capability as a night fighter were generally satisfactory. Official records for KG53 show that between 1 and 13 December, on six nights, some 90 V-1s were launched.

Round about this time, US fighter pilots Lts Bud Fortier and James Duffy, P-51 pilots with the 355thFG stationed in Essex, were on a two-day leave in London, as Fortier recalled:

"We got to London before noon and after checking in at the officers' hotel on Jermyn Street, we headed for the 'Rainbow Club' for lunch. As we walked along Regent Street, crowded with shoppers, we suddenly heard the unmistakable sound of a V-1's pulse-jet engine. We looked up and saw it clearly, less than a thousand feet high, nearly overhead. Everyone on the crowded sidewalk stopped and stared up at it. The rasping, buzzing sound of the engine stopped. The V-1 slanted down towards the ground. It seemed to be headed right for us. We flattened ourselves against the wall of a large building, and we had a lot of company. We looked as if we were all plastered against the walls. The V-1 passed overhead, about 200 feet up, and crashed with an ear-splitting roar about three blocks away. Almost instantly, the traffic – pedestrian and vehicular – that had come to a standstill, was back to normal. As Duff and I stepped away from the wall, a scrawny little woman – she looked to be in her late sixties – passed us, muttering to herself, 'Bloody nuisance, these buzz bombs!'"

The early morning hours of **18 December** witnessed the next operation by III/KG53, the first of 28 Heinkels taking off at 0302. Seven crews reported unsuccessful launches – two with engines failed to start, two with engines that did not reach full power while three fell directly into the sea due to technical failure. Three crews reported being fired on by their own ships shortly after take-off, but no damage resulted. One crew reported sighting a twin-engined night fighter, which did not attack, although Plt Off K.D. Goodyear/Plt Off J. Burrows of 125 Squadron claimed a He111 damaged:

"We saw two flying bombs being released and went in that direction. Three contacts were obtained at the same time at three-and-a-half miles range, at 800 feet height. Contacts turned port in a westerly direction and we put down 10° of flap and followed for about eight minutes, gradually reducing the range. All three were taking evasive action by diving and climbing and changing course. Eventually one broke off to starboard, so decided to follow it, and chased it for some minutes, with target taking hard evasive action. Saw reddish orange glow of exhausts at 1,500 feet and obtained visual on He111 at 1,000 feet. E/a then at 500 feet height, speed 170 IAS. We put down another 5° of flap, dropped below and astern and opened fire from 1,000 feet, observing strikes on starboard engine. E/a immediately dived down to 400 feet, then climbed to starboard at 140 IAS. Following it up we closed to 600 feet and saw small bright light of starboard engine on fire. Opened fire again but struck the slipstream, which turned us practically over on our back. Visual lost."

Of the operation, III/KG53 reported:

"Take-off and landing as planned without event. The weather and wind complied with the forecast, only cloud over the sea was more than expected. Good usage of navigational aids except *Merkur* and *Auster* [beacons]. Proposed for next mission to use only *Sonne Husum*. Alternatively, *Auster* must be replaced by a more powerful unit. No plane could read *Auster*. The flying success was mainly eliminated by the failure of the bombs."

Had III/KG53 but known the fate of those Divers that had been successfully launched, the crews would have been totally dispirited. Four fell to the Tempests of 501 Squadron with Flg Off Lulu Deleuze (EJ762/SD-V) destroying his eighth and final flying bomb during the night. Wt Off Edward Wojczynski PAF (EJ580/SD-G) and Flt Lt Lilwall (SD-P) each got one, as did Wt Off S.H. Balam (EJ607/SD-N): "Sighted Diver held by searchlight. I climbed to position myself behind and fired three medium bursts from extreme range. After my third burst it dived steeply and light became brighter. I was unable to follow it down but about one minute later I saw a fire appear on the ground some ten miles north-west of Chelmsford at 0410." Coastal guns accounted for 17 more, with three that evaded the defences falling at Skeffington in Leicestershire, Radlett in Hertfordshire and Stanmore, Middlesex, causing little damage and inflicting only one casualty.

Early on the morning of **23 December**, the first of 23 Heinkels from III/KG53 began taking off from Schleswig and Eggebek. Two aborted due to radio failure and failure of FuG101 respectively. Another crashed on take-off and was badly damaged, while a fourth (A1+LR) crashed offshore from Den Helder shortly after take-off, killing Uffz Robert Rösch and two of his crew. III/KG53's subsequent report was far from encouraging:

"Taxi and take-off operation at Schleswig was terrible. Due to carelessness of the marshaller and due to the stupid parking of lorries, three planes damaged during taxi. One plane crashed due to pilot error after take-off and was completely destroyed. One plane crashed during take-off due to engine trouble. This resulted in a blockage of the runway for 20 minutes. Two planes could not start because of radio or electrical failures. One plane could not start because engine starter failed. Two planes had to return because of radio and direction finder failure. The offences – and behaviour of those responsible – will be checked immediately and, if required, punished. Out of 20 [missiles] released, nine failed because of engine failure. Research results for the reason will follow via the Gruppe engineer. The result of the mission was poor."

One of the Heinkels was claimed by Mosquito XVII HK247 of 125 Squadron, the crew of Flt Lt Dick Leggett and Flg Off Egbert Midlane having stalked their victim for almost an hour:

"Took-off from Coltishall at 0550 … the first indication of activity was a flying bomb crossing starboard to port about two miles away and at same level. I turned starboard in assumed direction of launching aircraft. Shortly afterwards saw a flare being dropped dead ahead, obviously from target. Went round to starboard after contact, eventually finishing dead behind, target still at 1,000 feet. Followed for three minutes when target turned. Followed on this vector for about 30 minutes at speed 145 IAS. Closed range into 500/600 feet on several occasions but no visual because of cloud. Target turned and started to take some evasive action by weaving port and starboard, and reduced height to 300 feet, in cloud all the time. At this time what was thought to be one contact split into two and we followed nearer target for some time with other target about one mile ahead. Nearer target started to take hard evasive action and after a chase of about 55 minutes from initial contact, we closed into 700 feet as light improved. Got visual on He111 at 300 yards range, 300 feet height, fighter slightly below. Exhaust of e/a visible. Gave two-seconds burst from astern and below from 200 yards and saw strikes below fuselage and inboard of port engine. As we broke to starboard saw e/a alight from stem to stern and large explosion in fore part. Saw it hit and glow for some minutes at 0745."

It would seem that their victim was A1+HT of 9/KG53, Obfw Kramer's Heinkel being attacked at 0750 by a Mosquito at sea level, and suffering some damage and it crash-landed at Leck. The observer (Uffz Hans Gunz) was killed and Uffz Hans Höhler, the radio operator, who had been wounded in the neck, suffered concussion in the crash. The survivors reported that the Heinkel had just launched its bomb when the night fighter attacked. Two Heinkels were also fired at by German craft when off the Dutch coast although neither was hit.

On **Christmas Eve**, in one final all-out effort by the Luftwaffe to show that the threat was not over, an estimated 50 Heinkels from Stab, I and III/KG53 (including Ltn Glauner of 1 Staffel flying his tenth sortie) set out from the various bases for a surprise V-1 attack aimed at Manchester, 17 aircraft from III Gruppe departing Schleswig and Eggebek between 0258 and 0345. Three aircraft were unable to take off due to electrical problems and another burst a tyre, causing a 15-minute delay. Three crews from III Gruppe reported malfunction of their missiles, while another saw their bomb fall into the sea, where it exploded. The raid was witnessed by British fishermen in the North Sea who reported that some of the "rockets" had failed to ignite and had just fallen harmlessly into the sea. The RAF coastal radar station at Lowestoft picked the raid up in its infancy and alerted the defences along the coast. The Humber AA defences opened up as the Divers approached but failed to destroy any.

In total, 31 of the bombs reached the target area with 15 falling in the Manchester vicinity. The first impacted at Chorley at 0530, killing 30 chickens in a hen coup, but one that fell on a row of cottages in Abbey Hills Road in Oldham killed 32 people and seriously injured 49. A further six people died when another landed on Chapel Street in Tottington, near Bury, Greater Manchester, where it destroyed a row of cottages. One of eight injured died later in hospital. The remaining bombs fell over a wide area of north-west and north England; seven came down in Yorkshire and another in the Humber Estuary, three in Derbyshire, two in Lincolnshire, one each in Nottinghamshire, Northamptonshire and Co. Durham. The latter landed on a cricket ground at Tudloe at 0605, the blast damaging 22 houses and injuring 11 of the occupants. In total, 42 people were killed and over one hundred seriously injured. Many homes suffered damage but no military and industrial areas were affected. Unfortunately for the local population, 103 Home Guard AA Battery, located in Manchester's Alexandra Park, had recently been stood down, since any aerial threat to the area had been assumed to have ended. A member[257] of the Battery wrote in his diary:

"The attack of V weapons on the North has caused rather a stir among the Northerners, who in my opinion, had thought themselves free from any further enemy action. It was to me very galling not to be manning our guns. Not an AA gun was going off. It was as at the beginning of the war, when the enemy had the sky to himself. During two-and-a-half-years on the guns we saw no action, and now we are stood down, the enemy planes come back."

Although night fighters were directed to the area, only the Mosquito flown by Flt Sgt Alf Bullus/Flg Off L.W. Edwards of 68 Squadron enjoyed any success, having departed Coltishall at 0520:

"Vectors given by control were followed and contact was made to port, four miles range and well below. Target travelling west. We turned to port and behind. At the end of our turn we were behind at 4,000 feet range, target then at 500 feet height, reduced to 300 feet as we closed in. Visual of He111 obtained at 1,200 feet range. No exhaust visible. We then fired three two-seconds bursts, the first from 200 feet obtained strikes on starboard wing root, a second burst at 100 feet, which was below centre of fuselage, and the third burst at 50 feet which resulted in strikes on port engine and port wing root. Target then burst into flames and did an uncontrolled climbing turn to port and peeled off into the sea. It was observed to be on fire at least five minutes."

Their victim was A1+AR of 7/KG53 flown by Uffz Herbert Neuber, who was reported missing together with his crew[258]. Another crew reported sighting a single-engined fighter, which was possibly one of the Naval Fireflies from the NFIU Detachment based at Coltishall.

This unexpected and undefended assault aimed at Manchester caused repercussions, and led to the Minister for Home Security issuing a warning to all Civil Defence regions:

"The recent flying bomb attack on the North, which may well be repeated and may be extended to other areas, has emphasised the importance of ensuring that the Civil Defence services are kept up on a state of operational efficiency. Many wardens' posts have been shut, and in some areas, wardens' posts are only open for a short period in the early evening. Many depots are now only manned on the siren sounding or enemy action occurring. Telephones should be tested frequently at these posts to be used for operations. All personnel must be definitely informed of their obligations to turn out on an alert, or on enemy action occurring ... and of the consequences which may follow a failure to report for duty."

General Sir Frederick Pile, GOC AA defences, could not be held to blame, and he later wrote:

"We had everything prepared. Suitable accommodation had been earmarked and all the administrative details lined up. It was unfortunate, therefore, that more than a month went by and in spite of our repeated requests, no permission to deploy was forthcoming from the War Office. Then, suddenly, in the early hours of December 24, enemy aircraft launched approximately 40 flying bombs across the coast, most of them between Spurn Head and Mablethorpe, in an attack upon Manchester. Though many of the bombs fell in widely scattered areas throughout the Midlands, the attack achieved some measure of success. Too late the War Office reacted. The same day an immediate, though limited, deployment was sanctioned. Sixty heavy anti-aircraft guns with the normal anti-Diver equipment moved up, followed, two days later, by four Light AA troops. Search-light detachments for providing orbit beacons and navigational warning lights were also moved forward. The whole deployment took place, over Christmas, in terrible weather.

"On Christmas Day and Boxing Day progress was held up by a thick fog, which was followed by a hard frost, during which the task of emplacing the gun platforms was a difficult one. To add to everything else, there were heavy falls of snow along the Yorkshire coast which made roads impassable and which actually isolated two of the sites for three days. Even in perfect weather the deployment would have been an arduous one for at all times movement was difficult over the low-lying and marshy ground south of the Humber. The roads were few and poor. Bridges had to be strengthened. In the weather that we had that Christmas, the move was more of a nightmare than most such moves. But by December 29 it was almost completed, and the guns were in position to engage the flying bombs that never came that way again."

There did occur another scare three days later when the air raid sirens sounded at Rochdale in Lancashire, causing the local people to fear another V-1 assault, but it transpired that the subject of the scare was a bomb-laden US B-24 that had developed problems when flying over the area. Although it did not crash, the danger of an explosion was considered sufficient to justify a public warning. Although the attack on Manchester had caused little material damage, Hitler apparently convinced himself of its value when he wrote (on 28 December):

"We are causing continual disturbances to the English industrial regions through these flying bombs."

Despite being overwhelmed on the continent, Luftwaffe commanders continued with their plans to carry the war to Britain. On **28 December**, Ju188D A6+FH (230443) of 1(F)/120 flown by Uffz Werner Grundmann was despatched from Sola, Norway to carry out a recce of Scapa Flow to evaluate the numbers and types of warships, to prepare for the long-intended *Mistel* raid on the mighty naval base. However, the Ju188 developed engine trouble and Oblt Werner Neugebauer, the observer captain of the aircraft, ordered the crew to bale out. Only Uffz Heinz Josef survived and was taken prisoner after he had surrendered himself to civilians at a house he had approached. He was surprised to learn that he was not in the Orkneys but on the west coast of Scotland. The aircraft had ditched in Loch Broom near the picturesque fishing village of Ullapool at 1800. The body of Neugebauer was later washed ashore but Uffz Grundmann and Uffz Heinrich Kostner were both reported missing. The lack of intelligence due to the loss delayed a possible strike on the naval base, and in January two Ar234Bs[259] were sent to Baumbacha airfield, a *Mistel* base, to continue reconnaissance of Scapa Flow[260]. In the event, the attack never materialized. But some were still defiant. On the last day of the year, Oberstlt Wolf, commander of *Flakregiment 155 (W)*, issued the following Order of the Day:

"For the second time in the history of our Regiment and the use of our weapons, we are standing on the threshold of a New Year. We learn with intense inner pleasure how despite the bitter defensive fighting on all fronts here, in our area a German counter-attack has started up which has already substantial successes to its credit and which hopefully will later expand into a major blow against our enemies in the West. After two years of reverses, Germany is once more attacking: That is the reply that the German soldier and the German people are offering to our enemies and to their plans to annihilate us. It shows the strength that lies in us when we keep this in our thoughts and, with iron will, stand closely together. We can therefore enter the New Year full of happy hopes. We know what is awaiting us, and are aware of the difficulties of the fighting we still have to face. We are equally convinced that under Adolf Hitler's leadership we shall achieve victory for our just cause. Our sacred task in the New Year will therefore be to play our part with all our strength.

Long live the Führer!
Long live our people and our Fatherland!"

The New Year brought with it renewed hope for a speedy end to the war – optimism for the British and their Allies, desperation for the Germans. To help counter the Heinkel threat, Operation 'Vapour' (Wellington ASV-assisted detection of Heinkels) began, Plt Off Ross Hamilton RCAF recalling:

"Our nocturnal patrols in the 'control' aircraft were usually carried out along a given line up and down the Dutch coast from whence the Heinkels came up. We were normally accompanied by a Mosquito or a Beaufighter, or a combination of both – one to get the Heinkel and the other the V-1 if it had already been launched. Three deadly escorts tailed along a mile or so behind the Wimpy and away from the slipstream, the Mossie with its undercart down, plus a bit of flap, so as not to overtake the plodding Wimpy and still stay above stalling speed, including an orbit or two from time to time. The Beaufighter had a much lower stalling speed than the Mossie but his problems of staying airborne were much the same. Both remained very alert waiting for the radio call from the Wimpy when a contact turned up on our long-range ASV radar. At this point there was an immediate transmission to escort one and he was given course to steer that would put him on the tail of the bogey. Now with blips of both the hunted and the hunter on the screen it was a matter of providing continuous and accurate vectors to the fighter as he closed on the target. As soon as he was in the range scope of his AI night fighting radar (about three miles) and now at 1,500 feet, he would announce, 'Tally-Ho' and begin stalking for the kill and positive ID. The system worked well, and plans were soon in the works to form a full squadron of ASV-equipped Wellingtons with 407 (RCAF) Squadron crews as the nucleus. The boffins were also hoping to supersede the Wellingtons with Liberators eventually, the idea being that, with almost double the endurance, continuous patrols could be enacted round the clock, with the escort fighters replacing each other on the patrol line from various bases on the east coast of the UK."[261]

Sqn Ldr Jeremy Howard-Williams was one of the FIDS pilots selected to try out the new system in earnest, flying his first such sortie on 2 January:

"Mac and I fly one of the new Mosquito NF30s on Operation Vapour. Intelligence had told us that the Hun was coming but they had forgotten to tell the Hun. The Mk30 is a heavy aircraft, even when fuel tanks are nearly empty; approach speed is 150 and you come over the hedge at 130mph." Three days later the same pair flew another sortie: "Operation Vapour again. We take a Beau this time and are scrambled from Coltishall. We are too late and, anyway, the Wimpy's ASV is u/s. Thank God we have a radio altimeter this time and have done some practice in daylight to convince us of its reliability. We fly in the dark at 50 feet (fairly) happily."

The Heinkels of KG53 were now operating from Schleswig-Holstein airfield, close to the Danish border. But bad weather conditions on the night of **3/4 January** caused yet further despair for the desperate crews of III/KG53. At 2130, A1+GK (110264) of 9 Staffel crashed at Bjerndrup Ostermark near Kliplev in southern Denmark, with the loss of Uffz Herbert Jürgens and his entire crew[262]. Local eyewitnesses to the crash suggested that Jürgens had attempted to carry out an emergency landing but hit a small dyke. A second Heinkel from 2/KG53 – A1+DK (162378) – came down at Leck, killing Flgfr Herbert Rose and his crew[263], while an aircraft (700128) from 7 Staffel crashed at Gammellund killing Ltn Siegesmund Kasberg, Uffz Gerhard Tanner and Obgfr Hubert Turks. Fortune again smiled on 1 Staffel's Ltn Glauner and his crew of A1+GP who safely returned from their three-hour sortie.

A dozen Divers were brought down by the coastal guns during a night that was to witness the last major air-launched raid – a good start to the New Year. Forty-five launches were made over the North Sea. Of the missiles that crossed the coast, four fell in Suffolk as victims of the guns, coming down at Aldeburgh, Ellough, Bredfield and Hopton; three in Norfolk (Deopham Green, Sutton, Hempnall); five in Essex, at Goose Green, High Ongar, Langham, North Weald, and Shelley; one each at Heydon, (Cambs), Godmanchester (Hunts) and Moulsoe (Bucks); and one reached London, coming down in Lewisham but causing no injuries.

The defenders suffered another loss when Mosquito XVII HK296 from 68 Squadron flown by Wt Off Arthur Brooking and Plt Off Bob Finn FTR from an anti-Diver patrol over the North Sea during the evening. They reported shooting down a Heinkel – but then silence. Their victim was almost certainly another aircraft of 9/KG53 (700520) which FTR from its mission over the North Sea. The Heinkel eventually crashed at Björköby in Sweden after Uffz Heinz Krause and crew had baled out; all were posted missing although it is believed that Fw Erich Schulz survived, injured[264]. Whether the Mosquito was hit by debris or by return fire is not known. The following night (**5/6 January**), a single raid was made between 2210-2225, ten missiles being launched of which five aborted. Two of the five were subsequently shot down by the guns, but two others caused serious incidents when they fell in London. Eleven people were killed in Beckenham (Burnhill Road/Fairfield Road), with 22 injured; and a further 14 died in Lambeth a few minutes later following an explosion at the junction of Fentiman Road and Carroun Road, some 36 more suffering injuries.

Another Heinkel fell to Wg Cdr Russ Bannock, now CO of 406 (RCAF) Squadron, on the night of **6/7 January**, Hptm Siegfried Jessen and his 9/KG53 crew being killed in A1+HT (162181). Of his seventh victory, Bannock reported:

"I spent many hours trying to catch some of these fellows but they were really far too smart. Many times my radar operator would say, 'We've got a fix at 400 yards. He's dead ahead, and 20 degrees below.' I would look down and see the wave tops right below me and not dare go any lower. [On this night] we made landfall at Pellworm at 2010 and proceeded towards Husum aerodrome, which was lit with outer perimeter lights and double flare path. We immediately commenced to do a right-hand circuit at about 400 feet and obtained a head-on contact on an aircraft. We turned hard about and picked up the contact again at 4,000 feet, almost dead ahead, and followed it across the aerodrome, obtaining a visual at 1,000 feet. As I closed in to identify, I interrogated with a 'waggle your wings, bogey', with no response. From dead below and slightly behind we identified the aircraft as a He111. The aircraft was burning a blue resin light inboard of the starboard engine. I dropped back to 600 feet and fired a one-second burst. The e/a immediately burst into flames and spun down into a wooded dispersal area at the south-west corner of the aerodrome. The airfield immediately doused so we flew towards Schleswig, which had a searchlight navigational marker over it. At approximately 2035, I heard a 'waggle your wings, bogey', which seemed very close, causing me to waggle violently. However, I soon found I wasn't the intended victim for an aircraft immediately went down in flames, crashing approximately four miles north-west of Schleswig."

Bannock also witnessed another Heinkel crash following engine failure – Ltn Kurt Neubert and his crew from 7/KG53, flying A1+CR were reported missing from an operational sortie.

But still the Divers came over, the occasional one slipping the defences. At 0615 on **12 January**, one landed near the front door of Capel Green Farm, Capel St Andrews near Woodbridge in Suffolk. It had been winged by AA fire from the guns of 7th City of London Regt stationed locally. The warhead did not explode and it was the most perfect example of the seven that landed in England undetonated. Having been defused by Capt H.J. Hunt and his bomb disposal team, the casing was eventually sent to the USA. Another fell on Manor Farm, Great Holland in Essex. The following night (**13/14 January**), the Heinkels were back including Ltn Glauner of 1 Staffel in A1+GP (0010-0300). Flt Lt Langdon-Down (in Tempest EJ605/SD-K) shot down a V-1 in the Sidcup area during his 2155-2320 patrol. Seven Divers got through, one killing ten and injuring 17 at Southwark (SE5) at 0155. Many houses were damaged in Horsman Street and Bethwin Road, from where most of the casualties came. And on the morning of **14 January**, a Diver landed near Bury Green Cemetery at Cheshunt, killing a mother and her daughter. Sqn Ldr Jeremy Howard-Williams was up in a FIDS Beaufighter again to co-operate with Flt Lt Mac McLean's ASV Wellington:

"Operation Vapour. A Beaufighter and AI Mk VIII again, but this time using Manston as our advanced base. We take off and latch on behind the Wimpy, then stooge out towards the Dutch coast together. Our tame boffin, E.J. Smith, has worked out a patrol so that the Wimpy can guarantee to cover a Heinkel flying at 150mph if it crosses out of Holland between certain points. If the Wimpy has started its northward leg and just misses the Heinkel as it enters the area, we shall be back again on the southward leg before the Hun has flown out of the vital zone. We patrol for a short while and are then ordered off the 'tow line' and given an interception. 'We have several customers', says the controller happily. All seems to be working and the weather is playing its part. Calm enough to let us fly at under 100 feet, with a nice trace of horizon – not that I look out of the cockpit at that height, having my eyes glued to my instruments to make sure that I don't stray too low, or slip height a little on the turn. 'All targets are flying west and we have chosen one for you. He is crossing to port, range one mile.' Never have I felt the clinical nature of an interception more keenly than tonight: we know for certain that our target is hostile and he has been selected for execution. 'Contact,' calls Mac. 'Turn port gently. Range 4,000 feet. Target slightly above.'

"As soon as he has stabilised the situation and is prepared to continue the interception without further help, I call the airborne controller and pass him the appropriate code word. 'Judy' [code word signifying satisfactory AI contact. We will continue the interception ourselves]. I switch on the amplified intercom, which shuts out all R/T so that Mac can continue his patter uninterrupted. The target turns north for some strange reason, but we close happily. Eventually I can see it and we close to 150 yards and about 60° up. It's a bloody Wellington. I look again and make Mac get the Ross night glasses on it, willing it to be a Heinkel. But it's a Wimpy all right so we don't waste any more time on it. On calling our own Wellington, we are told that all other trade has gone westwards and that we are to return to patrol position. And that is the nearest we get to the Luftwaffe that night. The Heinkels are certainly over, and it's just bad luck that the controller chose the one and only friendly aircraft from all the blips he had on his tube. Our jinx is operating again."[265]

A Mosquito NF30 (NT245/A) from 125 Squadron was also up and under the control of the Wellington, Flt Lt Dick Leggett having a similar experience to that of Howard-Williams:

"Midi [Flg Off Midlane] and I were delighted to be given our first patrol time, which was re-affirmed by our intelligence as the likely period when the Heinkels were outbound from the Dutch coast. Hence, shortly after joining up with the Wellington, we were not surprised to hear, on our VHF control channel, from Mr Smith that he had trade for us. Under his excellent close control we reduced height to 100 feet. Within a few minutes Midi obtained a form contact and took over from Mr Smith. Although it was a dark night and we were flying through broken low stratus cloud this was to be a sure kill for us. Speed was synchronized with the target at 120mph on a course towards Norfolk at a height of 270 feet. With my gun button on 'fire' we struggled through the severe downwash of slipstream from the target and quickly achieved a visual sighting to about 100 yards. To our utter disappointment the aircraft was not a Heinkel but a Warwick – a derivative of the Wellington! In strong language I announced my frustration to Mr Smith, who replied, 'Shoot it down as it must be hostile.' A fierce argument followed as he explained the target was not responding to IFF interrogation, so get on with it! Naturally, Midi and I would have been delighted to add a 'sitting duck' to our score so we stupidly nudged closer and closer in an attempt to convince ourselves it was an enemy aircraft. We virtually flew in formation with it, re-affirmed there was no V-1 missile underslung and that it was a Warwick. There was no way I was going to destroy the aircraft with 'friendly fire' – despite the protestations of Mr Smith. Although our Wellington, with its brood of night fighters, patrolled throughout the long night, the Heinkel raid remained unscathed."

This was to be KG53's swansong – with fuel no longer available, the unit effectively disbanded even though the Luftwaffe's Order of Battle dated 20 January showed an establishment of 101 He111s of which 79 were serviceable: StabKG53, one aircraft (u/s); I/KG53, 37 aircraft (25 u/s); II/G53, 33 aircraft (29 u/s) and III/KG53, 30 aircraft (24 u/s). Some of these were later strafed by Allied fighters but most were later destroyed by placing explosives in vital parts. At the war's end, the main airfields used by KG53 were in British hands and a count of airframes revealed 86 abandoned/demolished machines at Eggebek (32), Husum (17), Leck (21) and Schleswig (16). Presumably, the majority of these were former KG53 machines. During the month, Major Herbert Wittmann, Gruppenkommandeur of II/KG53 was advised of the award of the Knight's Cross with Oak Leaves, while Oblt Otto Engel of 5 Staffel received the Knight's Cross on completion of 400 operational sorties including a number of V-1 launchings; the Knight's Cross was also awarded to Hptm Ernst Ebeling of the Geschwader Stab, Ltn Georg Ackermann of II Gruppe Stab, and Oblt Rudolf Küster (6 Staffel). Several crewmembers were also recognised in this manner, Oblt Alois Huhla (6 Staffel), Obfw Franz Mund (6 Staffel), Obfw Walter

Richter (5 Staffel), and Obfw Fritz Steudel (II Gr.Stab).

Following a relatively quiet February, a Diver mini-blitz from the long-range launch sites in northern Holland erupted in early March. Air Marshal Hill wrote:

> "The attack began in the early hours of the 3rd March. The first bomb to reach this country got through the defences and fell at Bermondsey at 0301 hours. The next six bombs were all destroyed by anti-aircraft fire: five of them exploded in the air and the sixth fell into the sea. After a lull of nine hours the attack was resumed in the afternoon of the same day and continued intermittently until noon on the 4th, when there was another lull. Ten bombs came over during this second burst of fire: four of them were destroyed by the guns and only two reached London."

One of these released unfused incendiaries as it exploded in the air over Walton Cliffs near Frinton in Essex. One reached its destination and hit Bermondsey.

The constant barrage of V-1s combined with heavy intruder activity the previous night made gunners jumpy and when an unannounced aircraft crossed the Clacton area in overcast on the night of **4/5 March**, HAA opened fire. Their victim was a B-17G (43-37516 Tondalayo) of the 406thBS(P), returning from a leaflet-dropping sortie over Holland at 2110. It is believed that the pilot, Lt Col Earl J. Aber Jr USAAF was killed in the air and that 2/Lt Maurice Harper USAAF held the doomed aircraft steady to allow the crew to bale out, which all nine safely did, but Harper left it too late to save himself and was killed when the B-17 crashed into the River Stour. Slightly more lucky were the crew of a 68 Squadron Mosquito (NT365) that was operating under Greyfriars GCI. Given a vector by the ground controller, the Mosquito came under fire from ground defences. With port engine hit and the aircraft falling out of control, Wt Off Lauchlan and his observer Plt Off Bailey baled out safely. Air Marshal Hill continued:

> "The second lull came to an end late in the morning of the 5th March. Thereafter, until activity finally ceased on the 29th March, there was spasmodic activity punctuated by intervals of quiet. The performance of the guns during this phase was outstanding. Indeed, it was so good that, in view of the unexpected lightness of the attack, I was able to dispense with the Meteors and five of the six Mustang squadrons, which returned to their former duties."

306 Squadron's Sqn Ldr Jozef Jeka (UZ-B) shot down a Diver on the evening of **6 March**, after he intercepted it between Malden and West Harmingfield during his 1255-1445 patrol. He attacked from astern from 300/200 yards and after his third burst the Diver turned over to port and dived to ground near to a farm (Grid M.1818). Not to be outdone, Flg Off Johnny Johnson (EJ580/SD-G) of 501 Squadron shot down another next day (**7 March**). He saw the Diver at 4,000 feet heading due west just east of Chelmsford, and opened fire from 400-300 yards. The Diver fell almost immediately and crashed near North Weald. One Diver that evaded the defences on 14 March came down at 0923 in Bellevue Road, Ealing, killing a dozen residents and seriously injuring 22. Flt Lt Stanislaw Blok PAF of 315 Squadron shot down a Diver on **24 March**, and the next day Flt Lt Janusz Bibrowicz PAF gained 315 Squadron's 53rd and the PAF's final kill. Bibrowicz took off from Andrews Field at 0745 and three miles south of Saffron Walden attacked the Diver. Opening fire from 800 yards, he closed in and fired three more short bursts, whereupon it exploded in mid-air at 0752. The final one to fall to the ADGB was shot down by Flt Lt Jimmy Grottick of 501 Squadron on the night of **26/27 March**:

> "That evening I had been assigned to cockpit readiness, which meant that one took to one's cockpit, strapped in, and was 'listening out' on the radio. At 0235, I was given scramble, and soon after take-off, (I was flying EJ599 SD-W), I was vectored roughly south-west, and began to climb. It was a clear night, but without a moon. It wasn't long before I could see the jet light

of a V-1 at about 1,000 feet and travelling very, very fast. It was some distance ahead and about two miles off to the port side. I turned towards it and eventually came in through a 180° approach – I recollect that at the bottom of my dive and on the final approach I was clocking 580mph! Allowing the distance to decrease, throttling back as I came into range, and then at about 300 yards down to about 200 yards, I opened fire with a three-to-four-seconds burst. There were immediate strikes and then the flame feathered, the gyro obviously toppled and the intruder veered off course and dived into the ground near North Weald."

ARP Warden Ted Carter at Waltham Abbey was on duty when one of the last Divers to fall in England impacted at Caverhambury:

"Siren this morning about 0745, followed shortly by the sound of a Doodle. By the noise of the engine it was not far away, but before we could get outside to see him, there was a bump not nearly so loud as expected. Found it in one of the paddocks attached to Caverhambury Kennels. Very slight damage round about. Apparently it had hit a tree and exploded almost before it reached the ground. The usual smell of burnt earth and hot metal. [Fitted] with the new plywood wings. The first Doodle in the area since last September, and in daylight too!"

Of the final batch of Divers to cross the coast on **29 March**, four came down in East Anglia. At 0004, one impacted at Great Holland in Essex, followed at 0856 by one that damaged six houses in the village of Datchworth in Hertfordshire. Just under an hour later, at 0940, another fell at Little Oakley (Essex), damaging 31 houses, two farms and the church; and at 0958 one impacted on a farm at Great Wigborough, also in Essex. The fifth travelled all the way to Kent and crashed at Iwade near Sittingbourne at 1000, causing slight damage and no casualties. Royal Marine AA gunners on the gun platform erected some 12 miles off Felixstowe on Roughs Tower (nicknamed Churchill Fort) shot down the final Diver off Orfordness at 1243.

A total of 2,419 Divers had fallen on the London boroughs, killing 5,582 people including 207 service personnel. Croydon was the worst hit with no fewer that 142 incidents being recorded, while 19 more fell on the periphery of the town. 211 residents were killed, 697 seriously injured and 1,277 slightly injured. Wandsworth was a close second with 126 strikes, followed by Lewisham with 117. Kent received 1,444 (killing 152 and injuring 1,716), Sussex 886 (approximately 40 deaths), Essex 412 (in excess of 60 killed), and 295 came down in Surrey (at least 20 killed). Many others fell harmlessly in the sea or in rural areas including 93 in Suffolk (at least 17 of these falling in West Suffolk) and 13 in Norfolk, although casualties and damage did occur in these areas. The final death toll from these missiles was estimated to be 6,184 killed and 17,981 persons seriously injured. In his subsequent *Despatch*, Air Marshal Hill stated that a total of 3,957 flying bombs – out of the 9,251 plotted and reported (although 10,500 were launched against England) – were shot down by the defences: 1,846 plus two shared by the fighters; 1,878 plus one shared by the guns; and 231 plus two shared by the balloons. As with most statistics, the AOC's are at variance with those calculated by other official sources, which state that the RAF destroyed 1,979, although Appendix II would suggest an even higher figure. AA Command was credited with 1,971, Balloon Command with 278, and Royal Navy AA with 33 – a grand total of 4,261. There is also the question of those V-1s shot down by USAAF fighters (approximately 40), which do not appear to have been included in official figures.

In his *Despatch*, published in 1948, Air Marshal Sir Roderic Hill reflected on the success of his Command and the final days of the war in general:

"On the broader issue of the extent to which the Germans were right, in the military, sense, to develop their two long-range weapons and put them into operation, a number of questions naturally arise. Would several thousand fighters have been worth more to the enemy than the 20,000 flying bombs and 3,000 rockets [V-2s], or thereabouts, which he aimed at England and Continental cities? Put thus, the issue is misleadingly simple; the fighters would have been no use without pilots, ground crews, bases, and supplies of aviation spirit greater than the Germans could command. If this effort had been put into the production of bombers instead, the Germans would still have been no better off: the crews and the aviation spirit would not have been forthcoming. And indeed, since by the time the most important decisions were taken the Luftwaffe had lost much of its striking power, the devotion of so much skill and manpower to the flying bomb and the A-4 [V-2] is at least understandable. The former was an ingenious weapon, which we might not have overcome if we had been less well prepared; the latter a notable advance on anything that had gone before, and a source of problems with which the nations are still grappling. The sponsors of these engines of destruction may be pardoned for a certain lack of judgment if they fancied themselves on the brink of changes comparable to those which followed the rifled barrel and the machine-gun.

"Whatever the pros and cons of the German policy which lay behind the operation of the flying bomb and the A-4 rocket, it is probable that, as the end approached, the German measures to stave off general defeat became less well co-ordinated and more involuntary. I have tried to show why I think it more than doubtful whether Hitler could have developed a decisive attack with the flying bomb and the rocket in 1944, whatever targets had been chosen. I have suggested that in fact he was confronted with the peremptory need of a sign, which would show his followers that England was being attacked, and so mitigate to some degree the terror that was coming upon them. Where action is taken under forces of overwhelming compulsion there can hardly be a question of fastidious strategic judgement. Nonetheless, in the complex and often tangled web of German strategy one important thread was missing. Though hidden at first by reason of the great number of aircraft deployed to lead off the German land campaigns, its absence became more obvious as operations went on. I refer to the German failure to think consistently in terms of air power. The Luftwaffe was allowed to run down, and no big enough measures were set in train for its continuous replenishment, especially in respect of competent bomber crews. The result of this neglect was a progressive loss of air superiority, at first over the occupied territories and finally over the living space of Germany. If, as Koller [General Karl Koller, Chief of Luftwaffe Operations Staff] had said, the flying bomb and the A-4 rocket were to be regarded as a substitute for the strategic bomber force, the cardinal mistake was to suppose that these novel weapons could be used effectively in the absence of air superiority, which alone could have provided reasonable immunity from air attack. Only air superiority could ensure that the places where the missiles were stored, serviced and fired, the crews who fired them, and the vehicles, which carried them by road and rail, would not be subject to systematic interference.

"By the time the flying bomb and rocket campaigns were got under way, the Allies had gained a high degree of air superiority over all the areas from which the weapons could be fired. Hence we were in a position to conduct a counter-offensive at will, and without serious hindrance from enemy aircraft, wherever targets might present themselves and whenever the scale of attack by the Germans was sufficient to warrant the diversion of Allied bombers from their main task. Sometimes – as with the rail interdiction programme of the tactical air forces – operations conceived with the main task in view served a dual purpose, and no diversion was involved. Moreover, this vital condition of air superiority, for which we had fought without respite since the Battle of Britain, enabled us constantly to improve the system of air defence whose application to new threats I have endeavoured to describe. Because we had air superiority we found ourselves free to adapt the system to novel circumstances and keep it in action day and night, with scarcely a rap from the German bombers not an hour's flying away. The problems of air defence, which have been described, will not remain static. They may recur in new forms in the future. The scientific advances, which the Germans used so spectacularly, if unsuccessfully, gave us a foretaste of hazards against which it is our business to provide. As science goes forward, and fresh discoveries lead to changes in the apparatus and methods of air defence, fertility in research and skill in engineering will provide better tools and weapons; but these are only raw materials of progress. What we need to do, above all, is to give rein to the qualities of mind and imagination which can take the growing mass of technical knowledge and mould what it brings forth to fit the shape of things to come." (see Appendix VIII)

CHAPTER VII

THE ASSAULT ON ANTWERP AND LIÈGE

October 1944 – March 1945

"In the two robomb sieges of Liège more than a thousand V-bombs fell and detonated in the city. Nothing was untouched – every aspect of life suffered. With great loss of life and untold human misery, civilian men, women and children and Allied military personnel were caught in the city of terror."

Major Gregory, US Army

On 1 September 1944, as the Germans retreated towards the Reich, Supreme Allied Commander General Eisenhower ordered a broad front advance to hold the Germans at bay and not overstretch the Allied supply lines. North of the line, General Montgomery's forces were given priority until the Belgian port of Antwerp could be secured. Capture of the vast port facilities would obviously greatly improve the supply situation for the advancing Allied armies. The British 11th Armoured Division duly captured the city and port intact on 4 September, but failed to seize the bridges over the Albert Canal, and when the British troops tried to cross a few days later the bridges were blown by the retreating Germans, who still had control of South Beveland and Walcheren.

In early October, Hitler ordered that all V-weapons should now target London and Antwerp exclusively. It seems that there were no plans to use either weapon against the advancing Russians on the Eastern Front[266]. SS General Hans Kammler received the orders for the bombardment of Antwerp under the codename 'Anton'. On 7 October, a V-2 range-finding shot impacted near Antwerp. It fell in the community of Brasschaat, without causing any casualties, but six days later a V-2 destroyed several buildings on the corner of Schildersstraat and Karel Rogierstraat. There were reports of many citizens being crushed under the tons of rubble. Later that same day, another rocket exploded in the city. Early morning of 21 October witnessed *Flakregiment 155(W)'s 23 Batterie* at Büchel (12 miles south of Mayen in the Eifel Mountains) launch the opening salvo of V-1s aimed at Antwerp and by the afternoon nine had reached the city, while a further four had crashed prematurely. *22 Batterie* at Laufeld followed suit on 24 October, but by the end of the month only 27 of the 337 flying bombs launched had reached greater Antwerp; 47 had crashed prematurely[267].

American Brig-Gen C.H. Armstrong arrived in Antwerp on 10 November, briefed to form 'Anti-Flying Bomb Commando Antwerp X' (Command Antwerp X). This would comprise American, British and Polish anti-aircraft units (22,000 men) to be stationed in an arc outside the city to form a protective barrier against the flying bombs, and would be deployed to counter any change in direction of the main attack. But of course the guns could not prevent Divers penetrating the defences, sometimes with catastrophic results. On 16 November, a Diver hit a boys' orphanage on Durlestraat, killing 36 and injuring 125 including many boys. During the month, 2TAF and ADGB began operating squadrons of Spitfire fighter-bombers to seek out and destroy the launch sites. By 6 December, some 2,738 V-1s had been launched against continental targets, of which 818 (almost 30%) had crashed prematurely or off target. During December, 52% of V-1s launched at the city were brought down by the guns. On 12 December, a V-2 hit the 'Rex' cinema in Antwerp killing 492 people, mostly British troops. Another 500 were injured. By the end of the year, a further 174

V-1s had fallen in greater Antwerp (64 in November, 110 in December), plus a staggering 314 V-2s. More than a thousand homes had been destroyed and 13,000 heavily damaged in Diver attacks alone in Antwerp, with 1,500 civilians killed and hundreds injured.

The New Year started no better than the previous one had ended. Shortly after midnight on New Year's Eve the city was struck by another flying bomb. Then, on 2 January, the city registered no less than 20 V-1 strikes. The heavy snow made rescue work almost impossible. The very centre of Antwerp was now desolate. By the end of January, a further 117 V-1s and 155 V-2s had impacted, although the guns had brought down 64% of incoming missiles (V-1s). February saw an increase of the total number of V-1s evading the defences, 224 registering hits, as did 59 V-2s, even though the guns had scored a resounding 72% of the Divers approaching the city. By the end of the month the guns were deployed in a double belt stretching from due north to due east. Although the equipment in use by Antwerp X included the SCR584 radar, the conditions in Belgium and Holland were far from ideal for full effectiveness. The V-1 presented a smaller 'pip' than did fighter aircraft. To the experienced radar operator a V-1 could be further distinguished by its straight and level flight path, but occasionally RAF fighters were mistaken for V-1s because they used a straight and level approach to land at the numerous airfields surrounding Antwerp, and were fired upon[268]. The assault gradually declined in March (86 V-1s, 42 V-2s) as the launch sites were overrun by the advancing allied armies. During March a V-1 impacted between the 5th and 6th floors of the 24-story Boerentoren tower block in Antwerp, but failed to demolish the building. The last flying bomb to fall on Antwerp impacted on 30 March. During the V-weapon onslaught, over a period of 175 days and nights, no fewer than 4,000 V-1s and more than 1,700 V-2s were launched at greater Antwerp. Of those, 628 V-1s came down on the city; in addition, 570 V-2s fell within its periphery. Fortunately for the population, only 30% of V-1s aimed at the city reached their target. Even so, 3,700 civilians were killed and some 6,000 injured. 150 Divers had fallen in the dock area, killing 53 military and 131 civilians, severely injuring over 500 more. Reportedly 150 ships were damaged by V-weapons. Command Antwerp X suffered 32 soldiers killed and 298 wounded. The guns were credited with destroying 2,183 V-1s. A resident of Antwerp, who lived through the terrifying ordeal, Charles Ostyn, recalled:

> "Although the V-2 was terrible, the most scary for us in Antwerp was the 'little dingbat' or the V-1. We could hear them come from a long distance when they crossed the Allied anti-aircraft gun belt around the city but too many got through. They had a characteristic rattle or buzz and flew overhead at high speed clearly visible. When the motor stopped it came down in a long curve and delivered its one ton of explosives on our citizens. We had about fifteen or twenty seconds to dive for cover when the engine cut out, which saved many lives. In January and February the V-1s were a real scourge on the city. Later, in March, the Allied gunners got the upper hand and managed to bring down most of the incoming V-1s. I have to admit though things would have been very different if General Kammler had thrown double the amount of rockets onto our heads, it was more like a steady drizzle not a full-scale bombardment. I suppose the fear factor had a lot to do with this, with V-2 it lasted only a few seconds and it was all over, no time to think or do anything."[269]

Liège was also targeted by the Germans (since it was a major US depot), as was Ghent, although the latter escaped serious damage, while Brussels received 55 V-1s in four days. Liège received its first V-1 on 20 November, quickly followed by two more. On 22 November, a Diver ricocheted off the top of a trolley bus and hit the upper floors of a girls' school, killing 36 and injuring many more. Two days later, one hit the 15th General Hospital, killing a dozen and injuring 15. On 17 December, following a lull, a V-1 hit the fuel depot in Liège and blew up 400,00 gallons of petrol. A freight train was hit in Guillemins station on 21 December, which destroyed or damaged some 20 wagons. This was followed by one that fell on the 28th General Hospital on Boxing Day, but only one patient was killed – a wounded German POW. US Army Major Gregory wrote:

> "Mere words are highly inadequate to portray the terror and noise and death which all occur at the height of battle or bombing. In the two robomb sieges of Liège more than a thousand V-bombs fell and detonated in the city. Nothing was untouched – every aspect of life suffered. With great loss of life and untold human misery, civilian men, women and children and Allied military personnel were caught in the city of terror. Civilian and army hospitals, stores, dwellings, telephone offices, theatres and railroad yards all suffered direct hits. The V-1s, travelling at high speed and with terrifying noise, would suddenly, from a great height, cut off and dive into the city."

By the end of the assault on Liège, 92 soldiers had been killed and 336 wounded. There were 1,158 civilian casualties. An estimated 97% of all buildings were destroyed or damaged in the city.

Between 1-12 January 1945, due to malfunctions, 124 Divers fell on German troops, killing four and wounding 60 others. The Luftwaffe's 5th Flak Division acting commander Oberst Eugen Walter, in a lecture at a conference in Berlin, pointed at the inadequacies that plagued the operations of the *Flakregiment 155(W)*. He admitted technical faults of the Fi-103 were responsible for the premature crashes. As a result of these failures a total of 22 German civilians had been killed and 228 had been wounded, 24 houses had been destroyed and 101 damaged on German soil. In addition to this, there were reports about damage to woods, crops and the traffic network.

With the end of the V-weapons assault on Antwerp and Liège came the statistics – it was recorded that a total of 6,087 Divers had been aimed at the two cities, in addition to 153 V-2s, total casualties being estimated as at least 4,500 killed and 10,000 seriously injured.

For those on the ground, their first experiences of meeting the flying bomb at close quarters could be terrifying, as testified by these two stories, which must have been typical. Polish war correspondent Wladyslaw Kisielewski, visiting Polish forces in the Flanders, found himself so terrorized:

> "It looked as though the night would be quiet, but just after midnight I was awakened by a rumble: 'Flying bombs', I thought. 'Why the hell are they sending them now?' I sat up and listened attentively. 'No danger', I muttered. They are going on full revs, they don't cut off. It means that they are going further on, so I can sleep in peace. I must have said it at the wrong moment. Almost at the same instant the engine of an incoming bomb went dead. Hurriedly I put on my trousers and ran to the staircase where I collided with an artilleryman running from another room. We rolled downstairs and in our predicament did not hear the crack of branches broken by a flying bomb landing in the vicinity. We only heard the dull thud on the ground. Embracing one another we waited for the explosion, which should blow us to pieces together with the whole building. It was now so quiet, that I distinctly heard my heart thumping and my wristwatch ticking. It lasted eternal seconds. 'Will that bloody bastard never explode?' hysterically yelled somebody from the corner. This screaming question changed our quiet, nervous and dying gasps into an infernal cacophony of shrieks. 'Every man for himself!' roared a deep voice.
>
> "We rushed to the entrance door, stamping on each other's feet in pitch darkness. The major pushed everybody aside and reached the door first. His silhouette loomed in the opening, then he jumped up and disappeared in darkness issuing a strident cry. The same repeated with the second, third and fourth escaper. It turned out that the bomb had got entangled in branches,

its wings broke off and the fuselage glided down to rest motionless by the doorstep of our quarters. Every escaper stepped on it in the darkness and on realising what he was doing, jumped up in panic, shrieking with fright. When I grasped the situation, I broke the window and escaped that way."

This may have been the bomb that was noticed to be different from others examined. The nose cone was made of wood instead of metal and it was quickly realized that the reduction in weight would help to allow longer range, meaning that London could again be targeted from launch sites in Holland. Meanwhile, US soldier Orv Iverson, serving with 926th Signal Battalion, was one of those to arrive at Liège at the height of the Diver bombardment. His harrowing account of what it was like to survive a close call follows herewith:

"The road to Liège was congested so we did not arrive until late at night. The weather was near freezing. Rain was changing to snow. Just as we arrived in Liège a buzz bomb cut out above us. We were on top of the load on the six by six truck. We jumped off the truck and crawled under it in the slushy snow just as the buzz bomb exploded.

"On the night of 28 December, I finished my duty at midnight. Even though the bombs were falling very close, I crawled into my cot, pulled the blankets over me, and placed my jacket over my feet to help keep them warm. Immediately, I fell asleep. The next thing I found myself buried under the wooden chalkboard that had been hanging on the wall above my head. A buzz bomb had exploded just outside of our window. It was difficult to breathe. There was a strong smell of gunpowder. My cot had broken from the weight of the debris resting on the wooden chalkboard. I was able to extricate myself from the debris. As I emerged I could see just less than twenty feet from me, a blue flame. I believe it was a magnesium part from the buzz bomb. I hurried as fast as I could in the opposite direction over piles of debris. As I was passing through what was left of the doorway, I could see one of the GIs. He was face up, buried under large beams. His face was pure white in the moonlight. He did not make any moves so I assumed he was dead. Later I found out he had survived.

"I tried to go to the building across the street where the others were housed. I staggered almost all the way, but I collapsed by a wall. The next thing I knew I was being carried by a very large GI into the building, where I was put on a cot. I began regaining my senses on the cot when a lieutenant was brought in. He was bleeding badly from a large flap of skin hanging from his cheek. I got up to give him my cot and as I got out the door two medics grabbed me and attempted to put me in their ambulance. However, just as I was getting into the ambulance, Jim came along and told me there was a need to help dig out the GIs who were still buried. The sky had cleared so the moonlight cast an eerie effect over the demolished building which only minutes before had been our dormitory where most of the GIs were sleeping soundly. Broken glass and snow was all around us. The blood from my leg injuries had caused my pants to stick to my feet. I was coughing up blood and had blood trailing from my nostrils. My chest was giving me some pain. It seemed like some kind of a dream I was locked into. I didn't seem to feel the cold. It was as if the pain and cold were irrelevant.

"At first I came upon Sergeant H. Some of the other GIs were feverishly pulling away with their bare hands the bricks that covered him. Apparently he died instantly while he slept on his cot. We carried his body out of the debris and the medics took him away. In the meantime we could hear the muted voices of the kitchen crew from far under the debris. There were some timbers, which left an opening, so with flashlights we could see someone's hand. By now more help was arriving so we took turns pulling off the debris at a feverish rate. After a while we did not hear any sounds coming from under the debris. It was too late. No one was alive. We found Fritz in his bunk. There was blood oozing from his ears, but seemingly no apparent injuries that caused his death. I must have passed out again, at least I cannot remember much until I woke when daylight arrived and found myself on a pile of debris in what was left of the basement of the building across the street."

RAF 2TAF/US 9thAF claims against V-1s

An American P-47 pilot succeeded in bringing down a V-1 round about this time. 1/Lt

Melvyn Paisley USAAF[270] of the 390thFS/366thFG later wrote:

"Our field at Asch had a temporary air, sitting on a nondescript piece of unwooded land off to the side of a scrub pine forest. The landing strip was a transportable steel mat, plopped onto the barren earth and mashed down by the weight of the bulky P-47s. Our briefing room was now housed in a musty tent and took on an eerie look irrespective of the time of day. One single light glowed overhead casting dancing shadows in the cavernous darkness. It wasn't long, before we were back in the air and back in the thick of the war. The first mission out, I heard a frantic call over the radio from the last man off the target, as I broke away from the target. Tail-end Charlie screamed to his element leader, 'Break hard, left. Bogey coming in on your left. Nine o'clock. High!' I passed into some low clouds and before I knew it, I was in the muck all on my own. Climbing above the overcast I took a look, then started an immediate let down. Our field was not far away. At eight thousand feet I broke out of the clouds, and as I emerged, an object caught my eye at eight o'clock. It was low, maybe two thousand feet below me, steady on course and black as night. With a brisk 'phut … phut … phut,' the Jerry V-1 buzz bomb sped on its course to England or maybe Antwerp. I recalled something one of my squadron mates had told me over a gin fizz. He talked about a gyro, which guided the V-1s straight ahead until they ran out of fuel; 'I bet if you garbled up the gyro somehow, maybe by tipping the damned thing over, it would fall to the ground.' I shoved the throttle to the wall and went into a shallow dive, following close behind the V-1 for 50 miles, plotting its course on my kneepad map. It was on a line to Brussels and in just a matter of time it would be there.

"If the Jerries had everything set just right, it would run out of fuel just as it got to the city. Now was the time to try what we had talked about as we sat under our squadron slogan, drinking gin fizzes. Surveying the area, I noticed there was mostly farmland ahead of the V-1 path. The land was ploughed, but the tiny houses were far apart from one another. It looked good enough to me, so I switched on the water injection and moved up on the V-1, carefully placing my wing under its wingtip. The Doodlebug was much steadier than my Jug, probably owing to the absence of a nervous pilot flying it. 'Steady, now old Jug! This is for Mom's relatives down there.' With a prodding right roll of my aileron, my Jug friend tipped the V-1's right wing to the sky. Within seconds, the V-1 lost its brains and tumbled downward. Rolling back, I took a short blast at the black body as it fell, hoping to get a little camera coverage. What a stupid move that was. My plane lurched upwards as the V-1 burst into the open field below, barely escaping the explosion which sent hordes of mud spurting into the air."

Since it was not practical for fighters to intercept Divers approaching Antwerp and Liège due to the short flight times and low altitude of attack, combined with the obvious dangers from the massed anti-aircraft guns ranged for this purpose, there were no plans for fighter defence although most units within the area permitted its pilots to engage them if conditions prevailed. During December 1944, Grp Capt Desmond Scott RNZAF DSO DFC, OC 123 Typhoon Wing based at Gilze-Rijen, shot down 'several' Divers while flying Typhoon MN941/DJS, including one that exploded in the air:

"Flying bombs and V-2 rockets were an ever-present threat at Gilze-Rijen. We were in the mouth of what was known as 'Antwerp Alley'. Flying bombs from Germany and across the River Maas would converge above our airfield on their way to Antwerp, and the sky would often snarl to the sound of their ram-jet engines [sic]. In one 24-hour period, 148 flying bombs passed over our aerodrome. In the evening and at night their approach could be seen from a great distance. Sometimes, after the day's work was over, I would leave my caravan office, take to the skies, and try to shoot some of them down. I would fly to meet them, and as they passed under me three or four thousand feet below I would roll over, gain speed, and dive after them. They were normally too fast for a Typhoon in level flight and I had to let them get a good 200 yards ahead before opening fire, or their explosion could blow me up too. So once they overtook me, I had little time to work in. It was not polite of me to shoot them down over our own airfield, nor could I follow them far into 'Antwerp Alley', which was heavily defended by our own flak and out of bounds. My only chance was on the far side of the Maas, which was in enemy territory, or in the few miles between our airfield and 'Antwerp Alley'. I succeeded in blowing up only one in the air, but I sent several to earth where they exploded. One, unfortunately, landed close to a Dutch village, where the explosion injured several inhabitants. My only consolation was that it might otherwise have reached Antwerp and killed several hundreds. But the incident flattened my enthusiasm and henceforth I left the flying bombs to our AA gunners.

"Flying bombs would often behave strangely. After lunch one day we were sitting outside the officers' mess enjoying some winter sunshine when a bomb appeared directly overhead. It circled the mess twice just above the treetops, then made off back towards Germany! Another time I was motoring from the airfield to the mess, accompanied by Squadron Leader Hines, my loyal senior administration officer and ever-present shadow. Suddenly he saw the bright flame of a bomb approaching on our right. Normally we took no notice of them, unless their engine stopped. When this happened they immediately keeled over, dived to the ground and exploded. This bomb passed above the station wagon at about 2,000 feet, and then its motor suddenly cut out. I slammed on the brakes and we both dived into the roadside ditch. There was dead silence. Not even a thud. It must have glided on and made a belly landing in a distant field without exploding."

On **16 December**, a Diver crashed on Eindhoven, killing and injuring many. Two days later, on **18 December**, Flt Lt Dennis Sweeting DFC of 198 Squadron was leading a section of Typhoons in formation flying practice when a Diver was sighted. He gave chase but it proved too fast for his Typhoon (MN951/A) although he fired a burst at long range, without seeing any results. On the night of **22-23 December**, among the many intruder and night fighter Mosquitos operating over the Continent was an XIX (TA404) from 157 Squadron flown by Sqn Ldr Dolly Doleman DFC, who had just shot down a Ju88 west of Limburg when he spotted a Diver: "Saw a buzz bomb in Malmédy area on way back. Just getting nicely in position when some brown job opened up with one solitary gun, missed the buzz bomb and frightened us away. I hope it landed on their headquarters!"

The next success came on Christmas Eve (**24/25 December**), a Diver falling to a Mosquito VI fighter-bomber (HR254/L) of 107 Squadron flown by Flt Lt Eric Smith RCAF and Flg Off R.A. Pratt RCAF during an intruder sortie (1833-2035) to attack and harass all movement in Wittlich-Vianden area. He was on patrol with another Mosquito, piloted by F/L John Conlin RCAF. Conlin was the first to notice four or five Divers headed for Antwerp. Smith made a near-effortless one-quarter attack on one and lost sight of it going down. He made no claim at the time, but it was confirmed as destroyed by Intelligence including army reports. His logbook entry noted:

"Ops Patrol – same area as above [Weiswambach – Call – Arhweiler – Mayen]; 3 x 500-lb on road junction in Tonsdorf. Petrol tank exploded and burned from cannon. Other transport cannoned. Buzz bomb attack. Bomb destroyed. Confirmed as destroyed by 2 Group."

Four nights later (**29 December**) a Mosquito from 29 Squadron flown by Flt Lt R.A. Wigglesworth/Flg Off Bloomfield shot down a Diver over Brussels. Wt Off Max Thomas of 401 (RCAF) Squadron ended the year on a high note, shooting down a Diver on **31 December**. The Canadian Spitfire IXs were returning to base at B.80 (Vokel) with aircraft in the circuit when a Diver flew over the strip. Ground personnel and fellow pilots were able to witness the action, when Thomas (in NH240) gave chase and promptly shot it down from 500 yards, the bomb falling harmlessly into a field a few miles south-west of the airstrip.

Round about this time Canadian Typhoon pilot Flg Off Bill Baggs of 164 Squadron realised that a Diver may well have saved his life. Following a rocket attack on targets in Reichwald forest, he had become disorientated: "The weather was poor, with cloud base of 1,500 feet. The light and medium flak was murderous. My instruments toppled and the compass was spinning. Suddenly a V-1 bomb filled my windscreen, coming at me head-on. I pushed the stick forward, diving, and missed the missile by a few feet." When he recovered his senses, he thought it strange that the Diver should be flying in the wrong direction, before it dawned on him that it was he who was in fact flying towards the German lines. Making a smart turn-a-round he reached base safely.

Mosquito VI fighter-bombers of 21 Squadron operating from Thorney Island carried out intruder patrols over railways leading up to the Bulge on New Year's Day (**1 January 1945**). Weather closed in at Thorney Island and the Mosquitos diverted to Epinoy. During their patrol (1915-2310) Sqn Ldr Albert Henderson DFC and Flt Lt Bill Moore RAAF in NT200 shot down a Diver, as did Flt Lt Eric Swaine DFC and Plt Off Albert Holt in PZ397 during their patrol (1940-2300). On the night of **3/4 January**, RCAF crew Flg Off Charles Redecker and Flg Off M.E. Zimmer in a 418 (RCAF) Squadron Mosquito attacked a Diver near St Vith; they saw it crash but were not sure if they had hit it. The following night (**4/5 January**) between 0245 and 0615, 14 Mosquito VIs of 487 (RNZAF) Squadron intruded the St Vith-Houffalize area when three Divers were sighted. Flg Off A.N.Wilson (PZ195/L) attacked two but results were observed on one only, when a large flash was seen and "the light went out." Flt Lt D.V. Patterson (NT184/P) also attacked one and saw fragments fly off. Flg Off A.J. McMahon and Flt Sgt K.Gowlett in Mosquito VI MM398 of 464 (RAAF) Squadron attacked a flying bomb but there was no confirmation that they had shot it down. Spitfire IXs of 127 Squadron were currently based at Woensdrecht (B.79) in Holland. A Diver fell close to the base on **14 January**, as humorously recorded by Plt Off Ted Smith:

"A V-I flying bomb 'shook us rigid' as the airmen are wont to say. We were in our big room in the hut where we sleep. We had just been released. In addition to people and beds, we had three canvas toilet bowls on wooden stands – each with dirty shaving water. Suddenly we heard a shocking roar of engine blast, and Larry standing next to the door, jumped. 'Get out!' he yelled. 'Fuckin' one-nineties!' Everybody charged the door, and jammed in a mass of flesh, as an enormous explosion seemed to lift the entire hut from its base. We fell through the door, and the big space in the outer blast wall. Smoke was rising between the pines, way beyond the officers' quarters, and the air was full of debris. It took us many minutes to deduce the cause. It was a flying bomb that had the misfortune to run into icing clouds. It had been gradually forced down by the weight of ice until it struck the trees straight and level at over 350 miles an hour. After all the excitement died, everyone went away. Everyone that is, but Gordie and Dave. They were both in bathtubs, next door to each other, in the bathhouse. Both dived head down into the water as the wire reinforced windows shattered. Both of them received minor cuts and abrasions on the cheeks of their arses. They spent the next hour or more in surgery, with Doc picking out shafts of glass and glass splinters from their arses."

A claim was made on **22 January**, when TacR pilot Flt Lt Geoffrey Collinson AFC[273] of 4 Squadron recorded shooting down a Diver near Antwerp. Plt Off Paddy Dalzell of 74 Squadron (who had shot down a Diver way back in June) shot down three more while based at Deurne (B.70):[272]

"I remember one day we were returning from an op over northern Holland at 2,000 feet to land at Deurne, and a V-1 overtook me about 30 yards on my starboard and on the same heading. As I had very little ammunition left, I tipped its wing and it went down into a field."

Of another occasion (**11 February**) he recalled:

"I was returning to land and on my downward leg at 1,000 feet a V-2 landed below me and pushed me up a few feet. I remember seeing a flash in the corner of my eye just before, so I guess I had the luck of the Irish (which I am!)."

Deurne was also the base for 413 RSU, and one of its repair jobs, Typhoon PD616 of 197 Squadron, was severely damaged and written off by the explosion. On 25 February, Lt Jean Carre of 340 Squadron (Spitfire IX TB338/GW-D) on a morning patrol sighted a Diver south of Arnhem at 1025, which he attacked from astern but no result observed. 605 Squadron's Flt Lt Brian Williams (UP-S) got his sixth and final kill on the night of **27 February**, shortly before midnight, one of two he attacked. Flt Lt Lionel Frost[274] of 74 Squadron was more successful and shot one down three days later (**28 February**), which was en route to Antwerp. He was returning from a weather recon in PT399 when he encountered the Diver at about 1025. 74 Squadron was part of 145 Wing commanded by Wg Cdr Bill Crawford-Compton DSO DFC:

> "Bill Crawford-Compton was as averse to Doodlebugs as everyone else, as several surviving stories testify. On one occasion he was walking across the aerodrome in a brand new barathea uniform. Halfway across, a V-1 approached and then cut out immediately overhead. With an anguished cry of 'Oh my God, my new uniform!' Crawford-Compton got down on to his hands and toes on the wet, muddy tarmac in the 'push up' position, assiduously trying to keep his uniform out of contact with the ground. He stayed that way until the V-1 exploded some distance off!"[275]

On the same date, Flg Off Jan Jongbloed, 222 Squadron's Dutch pilot who had accounted for nine V-1s while flying with 322 Squadron, also shot down a V-1 approaching Antwerp. A Mosquito crew from 488 Squadron narrowly missed an opportunity to shoot down a flying bomb, as recalled by Flg Off Norman Crookes, the navigator aboard Flt Lt Ray Jeff's aircraft:

> "We were not assigned to any V-1 patrols but we did see the V-1s. In fact one almost took our tail off one day when we were flying from Amiens to Gilze-Rijen in Holland where we used to do a detachment until we were eventually (the squadron) posted to Gilze-Rijen. We were to do a night fighter patrol because most of the action was in that area and we were skimming across the cloud top at about 5,000 feet when this V-1 appeared going at 90 degrees to us and it kept very close to our tail."

A Diver was shot down by a Mosquito from 418 (RCAF) Squadron flown by Flt Lt Guy Hackett RCAF on the night of **2 March**, during a close-support sortie to the Hengelo district of Holland. It was seen to crash near Zutphen. One of the last Divers to be shot down by an aircraft fell to Lancaster gunners on the night of **3/4 March**, when 212 Lancasters and ten Mosquitos attacked Ladbergen aqueduct on the Dortmund-Ems Canal, which was breached in two places. Seven Lancasters failed to return. Near the target area, Sgts J.D. Longworth and E.M. Marton, the gunners aboard Wg Cdr S.G. Birch's 619 Squadron Lancaster PD414/B shot down a V-1, one that was probably heading for Antwerp. This was the second known flying bomb kill for a Lancaster crew. Another unlikely claimant was a Spitfire reconnaissance pilot from 2 Squadron, Flg Off J.A. Henderson:

> "I was flying No.2 to Flt Lt Thornton [on **10 March**] on a weather recce in westerly direction [at 0930]. My No.1 sighted a V-1 heading approximately south-west of Arnhem, about 500 feet below us. Turning port I closed in and gave it a short burst from 200 yards. Strikes were seen on the starboard wing and the V-1 spiralled towards the ground, bursting on impact six miles south-west of Arnhem."

A Diver probably fell to the guns of a Mosquito VI, NT202/A of 305 Squadron, on the night of **16/17 March**, during an intruder search in the Osnabrück-Hanover-Rheine-Bremen area, when Flt Sgt A. Mierzwa PAF spotted a flying bomb near Hollen following his attack on a railway crossing. Strikes were seen on its tail unit before it was lost from sight.

Sqn Ldr N.R. Wynn in Mosquito MM577 of 604 Squadron reported chasing a Diver in Nijmegen area on **20 March**, but was unable to catch it due to its estimated speed of 450mph. During a sweep by US P-47s of the 368thFG on **21 March**, pilots of the 397thFS carried out a strafe of an airfield, which may have been Alt-Lönnewitz in northern Germany, although it was reported to be a Czech airfield. 1/Lt Clifford J. Price USAAF claimed the destruction of "four Do217s loaded with V-1s under their wings". If the airfield attacked was indeed Alt-Lönnewitz, these would have been He111s of KG53, four of which were destroyed in a strafing attack by Allied fighters on this date. The next success occurred on **25 March**, Sgt-Chef Pierre Girardeau-Montaut (flying Spitfire IX TB394/GW-S of 340 Squadron) and Sgt-Chef Jean Guichard (TB335/GW-L) shot down a Diver en route to Antwerp at 0615. It was observed by the two Frenchmen to crash on the ground. This may have been the incident witnessed by a gunner aboard Lt Bill Rutherford's B-24J of the 733rdBS, 453rdBG, returning from a raid on Arnsburg, Germany. Sgt William E. Brown Jr recalled:

"We were coming back from a mission and they just blew it up in the sky – two Spitfires. Pretty damn close, maybe a mile. I just happened to spin my turret when I saw them. I yelled at the pilot, 'Bill, look up ahead.' And there, out of the blue were two Spitfires coming out of the clouds. They had enough speed to pick the baby up and Bam! They got it. The V-1 was a little bit higher than us, the sun reflected on it."

Another fell that evening to New Zealand Mosquito intruder pilot Flt Lt John Worthington flying UP-S of 605 Squadron, his third Diver kill. 409 (RCAF) Squadron's Flg Off Martin Kent RCAF (MM554) scored the last flying bomb kills for fighters on the night of **27/28 March** during his 2355-0255 patrol. He reported:

"Just at the end of our patrol, we observed three salvos of four or five Divers each [salvo], launched from the vicinity immediately north-east of Arnhem. We immediately dived to attack and closing slowly opened fire from 1,000 feet dead astern, the bomb flying at a height of 2,000 feet, at approximately 250mph. Strikes were observed and the engine apparently damaged, for the flame went out. The Diver went in and exploded on the ground at approximately 0115 in the vicinity of Rheden. Shortly after, we attacked another Diver travelling at Angels 2 with an IAS of 250mph. Strikes were again observed, some of which apparently hit the elevator, for the flying bomb immediately began to fly erratically, climbing and diving violently, before going on and exploding in the vicinity of Rade. An attack on a third Diver proved abortive."

The V-weapon campaign was over. The war was over. The civilian population, in London and elsewhere in Britain, could now rest easy with the knowledge that death could no longer strike silently from the sky at any moment of the day or night. Prime Minister Churchill, in his victory broadcast to the nation on 13 May 1945, summed the matter up:

There was one final danger from which the collapse of Germany has saved us. In London and the south eastern counties we have suffered for a year from various forms of flying-bombs - perhaps you have heard about this – and rockets, and our Air Force and our ack-ack batteries have done wonders against them. In particular the Air Force turned in good time on what then seemed very slight and doubtful evidence, hampered and vastly delayed all German preparations. But it was only when our Armies cleaned up the coast and overran all the points of discharge, and when the Americans captured vast stores of rockets of all kinds near Leipzig, which only the other day added to the information we had, and when all the preparations being made on the coasts of France and Holland could be examined in detail, in scientific detail, that we knew how grave had been the peril, not only from rockets and flying-bombs but from multiple long-range artillery which was being prepared against London. Only just in time did the Allied armies blast the viper in his nest. Otherwise the autumn of 1944, to say nothing of 1945, might well have seen London as shattered as Berlin.

EPILOGUE

On 29 July **2007**, some 62 years after the last Diver fell on England, the following report appeared in British newspapers:

"Police closed streets near London's Canary Wharf financial district on Saturday [28 July 2007] after an unexploded flying bomb from World War II was found on a construction site. Bomb disposal experts were called in to make the V-1 missile safe after it had been unearthed close to the East London complex that houses 80,000 office workers during the working week, police said. At weekends the area is busy with shoppers and visitors. Police closed several roads around the site in Millharbour, a road in the former docklands. Ambulance, fire and police are there and the building site has been evacuated, a London police spokesman said. The area was cordoned off. Thousands of V-1s, nicknamed Doodlebugs, were fired at the capital during the war, with the docks as the prime target. Hundreds of unexploded bombs from the war are buried across the country, according to government figures. They are unearthed from time to time, often during building excavations. Canary Wharf's tenants include Bank of America, Barclays, Citigroup, HSBC, the Independent newspaper group, and Reuters."

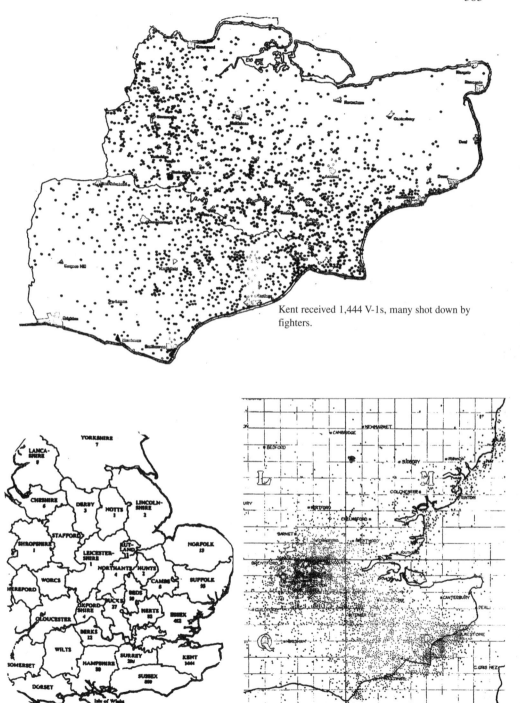

Kent received 1,444 V-1s, many shot down by fighters.

Snap-shot of where the V-1s fell.

Where the Divers fell in South-East England, including London.

APPENDIX I
ROLL OF HONOUR
ADGB Pilots & Navigators who lost their lives during
anti-Diver operations 1944-45

"So much for Darwin's theory of the survival of the fittest, because it was usually the bravest and fittest who were first to die."

Flt Lt Tom Slack 41 Squadron

Night 16-17/6/44
Wt Off Guy B. JAMES
Flg Off Duncan W. MacFARLANE RCAF (Nav)
418 (RCAF) Sqn
Mosquito VI NT142
FTR anti-Diver patrol

17/6/44
Flt Lt Walter D. IDEMA RCAF (US)
229 Sqn Spitfire IX MH852
Killed by explosion of V-1

23/6/44
Wt Off Albert ZEVACO-LAMOUR (FF)
165 Sqn Spitfire IX MK738
Believed shot down by own AA

Night 24-25/6/44
Flt Lt John D. FOX
Plt Off Clifford A. PRYOR (Nav)
264 Sqn Mosquito XIII HK480
Believed killed by explosion of V-1

25/6/44
Wt Off Richard.A.B. BLUMER RAAF
91 Sqn Spitfire XIV RM617
Crashed on return from anti-Diver patrol

28/6/44
Plt Off Roland J. WRIGHT RNZAF
486 (RNZAF) Sqn Tempest V JN804
Shot down by own AA

1/7/44
Flg Off E. KOSH
3 Sqn Tempest V JK765
Believed shot down by own AA

3/7/44
Flt Sgt Stanislaw DOMANSKI PAF
3 Sqn Tempest V JN752
Shot down by own AA

5/7/44
Sqn Ldr Edward G. DANIEL DFC
FIU Tempest V EJ531
Killed by explosion of V-1

9/7/44
Flt Sgt Ingvar F. HÅKANSSON (Sw)
610 Sqn Spitfire XVI RB153
Believed killed by explosion of V-1

Night 10-11/7/44
Flg Off Robert E. LEE RCAF
Flt Sgt Jack W. WALES RAF (Nav)
409 (RCAF) Sqn Mosquito XIII MM547
Believed killed by explosion of V-1

Night 11-12/7/44
Flg Off Edward G. RADFORD RAAF
Flt Sgt Walter E. ATKINSON RAAF (Nav)
456 (RAAF) Sqn Mosq XVII HK312
FTR anti-Diver patrol

12/7/44
Wt Off Justin A. MAIER (Dutch)
Flg Off George M. McKINLAY
322 (Dutch) Sqn Spitfire XIV RM67
610 Sqn Spitfire XIV RB142
Killed by explosion of V-1
Killed by explosion of V-1

16/7/44
Sqn Ldr Alan D. WAGNER DFC
FIU Tempest V EJ581
Flew into ground in fog while pursuing V-1

18/7/44
Flt Sgt Maurice F. HOARE
Flt Sgt Edward L. BISHOP (Nav)
264 Sqn Mosquito XIII HK471
Air collision with Tempest of FIU

Night 20-21/7/44
Flg Off Michael N. WILLIAMS
Flg Off Arthur G. WAPLES (Nav)
68 Sqn Mosquito XVII HK242
FTR anti-Diver patrol

Night 24-25/7/44
Flt Lt Fred J. KEMP
Flg Off James FARRAR (Nav)
68 Sqn Mosquito XIX MM679
Believed killed by explosion of V-1

Night 25-26/7/44
Flt Lt John W. CADDIE
Flg Off George LARCEY (Nav)
157 Sqn Mosquito XIX TA392
FTR anti-Diver patrol

26/7/44
Flt Lt Eugene G.A. SEGHERS (Belg)
91 Sqn Spitfire XIV RM743
Collision with V-1

27/7/44
Flg Off Ralph A. JOHNSTONE RCAF
Flt Sgt Arthur HACK
137 Sqn Typhoon 1b MN830
137 Sqn Typhoon 1b MN836
Air collision while on anti-Diver patrol

29/7/44
Flt Sgt Anthony C. DREW | 56 Sqn Tempest V EJ532 | Crashed during anti-Diver patrol

29/7/44
Flg Off Egon ZYGMUND PAF | 306 (Pol) Sqn Mustang III FB241 | Shot down by own AA

30/7/44
Flt Sgt Godfrey TATE | 1 Sqn Spitfire IX MJ422 | Engine failure, baled out into Channel

Night 30/7/44
Flg Off James D. BLACK
Flt Sgt Leslie W. FOX (Nav) | 96 Sqn Mosquito XIII MM557 | FTR off Boulogne

31/7/44
Flg Off Paudrick A. SCHADE DFM | 91 Sqn Spitfire XIV RM654 | Air collision with below
Flt Sgt Archibald A. WILSON RNZAF | 486 (RNZAF) Sqn Tempest V EJ586 | Air collision with above

Night 1-2/8/44
Flg Off Raymond F. BALL
Flg Off Frederick G. SAUNDERS (Nav) | 96 Sqn Mosquito XIII MM562 | Crashed on airfield when landing, killing member of
LAC Charles L. ALLEN | 96 Sqn groundcrew | groundcrew

3/8/44
Cne Jean-Marie MARIDOR DFC (FF) | 91 Sqn Spitfire XIV RM656 | Killed by explosion of V-1

6/8/44
Flt Sgt Donald J. MACKERRAS RAAF | 3 Sqn Tempest V JN759 | Spun in and crashed while attempting to tip V-1

Night 7/8/44
Lt(A) Peter F. PRYOR RNVR
Sub-Lt(A) Douglas MacKENZIE RNVR (Nav) | 157 Sqn Mosquito XIX MM649 | Crashed on return from anti-Diver patrol

Night 12-13/8/44
Wg Cdr Henry deC.A. WOODHOUSE DFC AFC | 85 Sqn Mosquito XIX | Believed killed by explosion of V-1
Flt Lt Walter WEIR (Nav) | MM632 |

13/8/44
Flt Sgt Royston W. RYMAN | 274 Sqn Tempest V EJ637 | Crashed in poor visibility

Night 14/8/44
Flt Sgt Leslie R. READ
Wt Off William C.A. GERRETT (Nav) | 96 Sqn Mosquito XIII MM452 | Crashed on take-off

15/8/44
Flt Sgt Donald A. GREGG | 616 Sqn Meteor F.1 EE226 | Killed in crash-landing

17/8/44
Flg Off Rijklof VAN GOENS (Dutch) | 41 Sqn Spitfire XII MB880 | Shot down by own AA

18/8/44
Pilot Off Feliks MIGOŚ PAF | 306 (Pol) Sqn Mustang III FB206 | Collision with Spitfire

20/8/44
Plt Off John L.W. BILODEAU RCAF | 129 Sqn Mustang III FB395 | Spun in while on anti-Diver patrol

Night 20-21/8/44
Flt Lt Geoffrey E. DUNFEE | 125 Sqn Mosquito XVII HK291 | Shot down by own AA; navigator baled out and rescued.

21/8/44
Flt Lt Cyril B. THORNTON | 501 Sqn Tempest V EJ602 | Killed in flying accident

30/8/44
Wt Off Jack J. BONFIELD | 610 Sqn Spitfire XIV RB150 | Crashed into sea while on anti-Diver patrol

Night 20/9/44
Flt Sgt Thomas WILSON
Flt Sgt John F. JENKINS (Nav) | 68 Sqn Mosquito XVII HK345 | Believed killed by explosion of V-1

25/9/44
Flt Lt Gordon L. BONHAM DFC RNZAF | 501 Sqn Tempest V EJ590 | Crashed in bad weather during anti-Diver patrol

Night 24-25/9/44
Flt Lt John F. LIMBERT
Flg Off Henry S. COOK (Nav) | 25 Sqn Mosquito XVII HK300 | Believed killed by explosion of V-1

Night 6-7/10/44
Flg Off Owen P. FARADAY | 501 Sqn Tempest V EJ626 | Crashed, engine failure

Night 6-7/10/44

Flg Off Roland A. NICHOLLS (Nav)	25 Sqn Mosquito XVII HK256	Believed shot down by return fire from He111 (pilot rescued)

Night 13-14/10/44

Flt Sgt Franciszek KOT PAF Wt Off Vladimir KEPÁK (Cz) (Nav)	307 Sqn Mosquito VI DZ302	Believed killed by explosion of V-1

Night 14/11/44

1/Lt Joseph BLACK USN 1/Lt Thomas AITKEN USN (Nav)	68 Sqn Mosquito XVII HK289	Shot down by own AA

Night 24/11/44

Wt Off John L. MULHALL RAAF Fg Off James D. Jones (Nav)	456 (RAAF) Sqn Mosquito XVII HK317	FTR anti-Diver sortie

Night 4/12/44

Wt Off James B. BRILL Flt Sgt John H. WALTER (Nav)	68 Sqn Mosquito XVII HK348	FTR anti-Diver patrol

Night 5/1/45

Wt Off Arthur R. BROOKING Plt Off Robert B. FINN (Nav)	68 Sqn Mosquito XVII HK296	Possibly shot down by return fire from He111

Additionally: Lt Col Earl J. Aber Jr USAAF and 2/Lt Maurice Harper USAAF of the 40thBS(P) lost their lives when their B-17 was accidentally shot down by HAA guns engaging V-1s.

APPENDIX II

V-1 KILLS BY RAF/RNZAF/RCAF/RAAF/PAF/USAAF FIGHTER ACTION

NB: The figures in parenthesis indicating the daily number of V-1s destroyed by fighters have been compiled from the following lists and are not necessarily 'official' credits. Identity of navigator, if applicable, follows pilot's name

Night 8-9/5/44 (1 V-1 destroyed by fighters)

Flg Off R.E. Barckley	Tempest V JN755	3 Sqn	V-1

Night 9-10/5/44 (1 V-1 destroyed by fighters)

Flt Lt A.B. Harvey/ Flt Lt B.StJ. Wynell-Sutherland (Nav)	Mosquito MM683	68 Sqn	V-1

Night 15-16/6/44 (4 V-1s destroyed by fighters)

Flt Lt J.G. Musgrave/ Flt Sgt F.W. Samwell (Nav)	Mosquito VI MM429	605 Sqn	V-1
Flt Lt G.R.I. Parker/ Flt Sgt D.L. Godfrey (Nav)	Mosquito XVII HK248	219 Sqn	V-1
Flt Lt P.R. Rudd/ Flg Off D. Messingham (Nav)	Mosquito VI UP-	605 Sqn	V-1
Flg Off J. Reid/ Flt Sgt R.E. Phillips (Nav)	Mosquito VI UP-	605 Sqn	V-1

16/6/44 (13 V-1s destroyed by fighters)

Wg Cdr R.P. Beamont	Tempest V RB751	150 Wing	1/2 V-1
Flt Sgt M.J.A. Rose	Tempest V JN760	3 Sqn	V-1
Plt Off S.B. Feldman (US)	Tempest V JN735	3 Sqn	V-1
Flt Sgt R.W. Cole	Tempest V JN761	3 Sqn	1/2 V-1
Flt Lt A.E. Umbers RNZAF	Tempest V JN745	3 Sqn	V-1
Flt Sgt R.W. Pottinger	Tempest V JN743	3 Sqn	V-1
Flt Lt R. van Lierde (Belg)	Tempest V JN862	3 Sqn	1/2 V-1
Flt Sgt D.J. Mackerras RAAF	Tempest V JN793	3 Sqn	1/2 V-1
Flt Sgt S. Domanski PAF	Tempest V JN752	3 Sqn	V-1
Flt Sgt L.G. Everson	Tempest V JN748	3 Sqn	V-1
Flg Off G.A. Whitman RCAF (US)	Tempest V JN743	3 Sqn	1/2 V-1
Flt Sgt J.W. Foster	Tempest V JN745	3 Sqn	1/2 V-1
Flt Lt H.B. Moffett RCAF	Spitfire XIV RM617	91 Sqn	V-1
Wt Off B.J. O'Connor RNZAF	Tempest V JN809	486 (RNZAF) Sqn	V-1
Plt Off K. McCarthy RNZAF	Tempest V JN801	486 (RNZAF) Sqn	V-1
Wg Cdr J.M. Checketts RNZAF	Spitfire Vb AB524	142 Wg	V-1

Night 16-17/6/44 (9 V-1s destroyed by fighters)

Flt Lt D.L. Ward/ Flg Off E.D. Eyles (Nav)	Mosquito XIII HK415	96 Sqn	V-1
Sqn Ldr A. Parker-Rees/ Flt Lt G.E. Bennett (Nav)	Mosquito XIII MM497	96 Sqn	V-1

Flt Lt F.R.L. Mellersh/	Mosquito XIII HK370	96 Sqn	V-1
Flt Lt M.J. Stanley (Nav)			
Wg Cdr A.McN. Boyd/	Mosquito XVII HK348	219 Sqn	V-1
Flt Lt C. Bailey (Nav)			
Sqn Ldr P.L. Burke/	Mosquito XVII HK248	219 Sqn	V-1
Flg Off L.E.S. Whalley (Nav)			
Sqn Ldr E.R. McGill RCAF/	Mosquito VI TH-	418 (RCAF) Sqn	V-1 probable
Flg Off F.D. Hendershot RCAF (Nav)			
Flt Lt D.A. MacFadyen RCAF/	Mosquito VI HR155	418 (RCAF) Sqn	2 V-1
Flg Off J.D. Wright RCAF (Nav)			
Flt Lt C.J. Evans RCAF/	Mosquito VI TH-	418 (RCAF) Sqn	V-1
Flg Off S. Humblestone RAF (Nav)			
Sqn Ldr G.J. Wright/	Mosquito VI UP-	605 Sqn	V-1
Flg Off R.P. Bourne (Nav)			

17/6/44 (18 V-1s destroyed by fighters including 9^1/$_2$ by USAAF)

Wg Cdr R.P. Beamont	Tempest V EJ525	150 Wg	^{1}/$_2$ V-1
Flg Off M.F. Edwards	Tempest V JN793	3 Sqn	^{1}/$_2$ V-1
Flt Sgt C.W. Orwin	Tempest V JN761	3 Sqn	^{1}/$_2$ V-1
Flt Lt R. van Lierde (Belg)	Tempest V JN862	3 Sqn	^{1}/$_2$ V-1
Plt Off S.B. Feldman (US)	Tempest V JN739	3 Sqn	^{1}/$_2$ V-1
Flt Sgt D.J. Mackerras RAAF	Tempest V JN735	3 Sqn	^{1}/$_2$ V-1
Flt Sgt M.J.A. Rose	Tempest V JN769	3 Sqn	^{1}/$_2$ V-1
Flt Sgt R.W. Cole	Tempest V JN768	3 Sqn	^{1}/$_2$ V-1
Flg Off G.C. McKay RCAF	Spitfire XIV RB174	91 Sqn	V-1
Flg Off P.A. Schade	Spitfire XIV RB180	91 Sqn	^{1}/$_2$ V-1
Flg Off A.R. Cruickshank RCAF	Spitfire XIV RM654	91 Sqn	^{1}/$_2$ V-1
Flt Lt W.D. Idema RCAF (US)	Spitfire IX MH852	229 Sqn	V-1 (also KiA)
Flg Off T.M. Fenton RNZAF	Tempest V JN808	486 (RNZAF) Sqn	V-1
Plt Off R.J. Danzey RNZAF	Tempest V JN809	486 (RNZAF) Sqn	V-1
1/Lt W.Y. Anderson USAAF	P-51D	354thFS USAAF	V-1
1/Lt L.H. Powers USAAF	P-51D	354thFS USAAF	2^1/$_2$ V-1
1/Lt C.G. Bickel USAAF	P-51D	354thFS USAAF	3 V-1
1/Lt E.O. Fisher USAAF	P-47	377thFS USAAF	3 V-1

Night 17-18/6/44 (6 V-1s destroyed by fighters)

Flt Lt W.J. Gough/	Mosquito XIII MM499	96 Sqn	V-1
Flt Lt C. Matson (Nav)			
Flg Off R.F. Ball/	Mosquito XIII HK372	96 Sqn	V-1
Flg Off F.G. Saunders (Nav)			
Flt Lt C.J. Evans RCAF/	Mosquito VI TH-	418 (RCAF) Sqn	V-1
Flg Off S. Humblestone RAF (Nav)			
Flt Lt R.G. Gray RCAF/	Mosquito VI HK148	418 (RCAF) Sqn	V-1
Flg Off F.D. Smith (Nav)			
Lt(A) D.G. Thornley RNVR/	Mosquito XVII HK359	456 (RAAF) Sqn	V-1 probable
Sub-Lt(A) D.R.H. Phillips RNVR (Nav)			
Flt Lt G.C. Wright/	Mosquito VI UP-	605 Sqn	2 V-1
Flg Off J.G. Insall (Nav)			+ V-1 probable

18/6/44 (51 V-1s destroyed by fighters including 4^1/$_2$ by USAAF)

Wg Cdr R.P. Beamont	Tempest V JN862	150 Wg	1^1/$_2$ V-1
Flt Sgt T.A. McCulloch	Tempest V JN738	3 Sqn	V-1
Flt Sgt D.J. Mackerras RAAF	Tempest V JN752/JN745	3 Sqn	2 V-1
Flt Lt A.E. Umbers RNZAF	Tempest V JN768/JN796	3 Sqn	3 V-1
Flt Lt A.R. Moore	Tempest V JN818	3 Sqn	V-1
Flg Off G.A. Whitman RCAF (US)	Tempest V JN735	3 Sqn	^{1}/$_2$ V-1
Flg Off R. van Lierde (Belg)	Tempest V JN862	3 Sqn	^{1}/$_2$+^{1}/$_2$ V-1
Flt Sgt M.J.A. Rose	Tempest V JN745	3 Sqn	2 V-1
Flt Sgt R.W. Cole	Tempest V JN769	3 Sqn	V-1
Flg Off M.F. Edwards	Tempest V JN735	3 Sqn	V-1
Plt Off H.R. Wingate	Tempest V JN739	3 Sqn	1^1/$_2$ V-1
Flg Off G.E. Kosh	Temperst V JN735	3 Sqn	V-1
Flt Sgt H.J. Bailey RAAF	Temperst V JN739	3 Sqn	1^1/$_2$ V-1
Wt Off R.S. Adcock RAAF	Tempest V JN735	3 Sqn	^{1}/$_2$ V-1
Plt Off K.G. Slade-Betts	Tempest V JN755/JN812	3 Sqn	V-1
Flg Off R.H. Clapperton	Tempest V JN765	3 Sqn	V-1
Flt Lt P.L. Bateman-Jones	Spitfire IX MK517	56 Sqn	V-1
Cne J-M. Maridor (FF)	Spitfire XIV RB161	91 Sqn	V-1
Sqn Ldr N.A. Kynaston	Spitfire XIV RB185	91 Sqn	2 V-1
Sqn Ldr P.McC. Bond	Spitfire XIV RB161	91 Sqn	1^1/$_4$ V-1
Flg Off A.R. Elcock	Spitfire XIV RB177	91 Sqn	V-1
Flt Lt A. Smith RNZAF	Spitfire XIV RB173	91 Sqn	^{1}/$_2$+ ^{1}/$_2$+^{1}/$_4$ V-1

Flg Off R.A. McPhie RCAF	Spitfire XIV RB182	91 Sqn	$1^{1}/_{2}+^{1}/_{4}$ V-1
Flt Lt R.S. Nash	Spitfire XIV RB169	91 Sqn	$1^{1}/_{2}+^{1}/_{2}+^{1}/_{4}$ V-1
Flg Off R.F. Burgwal Dutch)	Spitfire XIV VL-K	322 (Dutch) Sqn	V-1
Flg Off L.M. Meijers (Dutch)	Spitfire XIV VL-	322 (Dutch) Sqn	V-1
Flt Lt L.C.M. van Eendenburg (Dutch)	Spitfire XIV RB184	322 (Dutch) Sqn	$^{1}/_{3}$ V-1
Flg Off R.F. van Daalen Wetters (Dutch)	Spitfire XIV VL-K	322 (Dutch) Sqn	$^{1}/_{3}$ V-1
Flg Off W.A. Hart RNZAF	Tempest V JN797	486 (RNZAF) Sqn	V-1
Flg Off N.J. Powell RNZAF	Tempest V JN804	486 (RNZAF) Sqn	V-1
Flt Sgt O.D. Eagleson RNZAF	Tempest V JN811/JN804	486 (RNZAF) Sqn	3 V-1
Plt Off R.J. Danzey RNZAF	Tempest V JN797	486 (RNZAF) Sqn	V-1
Flg Off J.G. Wilson RNZAF	Tempest V JN809	486 (RNZAF) Sqn	$^{1}/_{2}$ V-1
Flt Lt V.St.C. Cooke RNZAF	Tempest V JN801	486 (RNZAF) Sqn	$^{1}/_{2}$ V-1
Flt Sgt B.M. Hall RNZAF	Tempest V JN809	486 (RNZAF) Sqn	V-1
Flt Sgt R.J. Wright RNZAF	Tempest V JN770	486 (RNZAF) Sqn	V-1
Flg Off J.R. Cullen RNZAF	Tempest V JN758	486 (RNZAF) Sqn	V-1
Flg Off S.S. Williams RNZAF	Tempest V JN810	486 (RNZAF) Sqn	V-1
Wg Cdr J.M. Checketts RNZAF	Spitfire Vb AB524	142 Wg	V-1
1/Lt R.E. Turner USAAF	P-51D 44-13561	356thFS USAAF	2 V-1
1/Lt L.C. Boze USAAF	P-47 CP-	365thFS USAAF	$^{1}/_{2}$ V-1
1/Lt L.E. Hayes USAAF	P-47 4P-	512thFS USAAF	$^{1}/_{2}$ V-1
1/Lt E.F. Mayne USAAF	P-47 4P-	512thFS USAAF	$^{1}/_{2}$ V-1
1/Lt R.N. Walsh USAAF	P-47 L3-	513thFS USAAF	V-1

Night 18-19/6/44 (6 V-1s destroyed by fighters)

Flt Sgt W.A. McLardy RAAF/ Flt Sgt Devine (Nav)	Mosquito XIII HK453	96 Sqn	V-1
Sqn Ldr R.N. Chudleigh/ Flg Off H.D. Ayliffe (Nav)	Mosquito XIII HK469	96 Sqn	V-1
Sqn Ldr W.P. Green/ Flt Sgt A.R. Grimstone (Nav)	Mosquito XIII MM495	96 Sqn	2 V-1
Sqn Ldr P.L. Burke/ Flg Off L.E.S. Whalley (Nav)	Mosquito XVII HK248	219 Sqn	V-1
Flg Off C.J. Preece RCAF/ Flg Off W.H. Beaumont RCAF (Nav)	Mosquito XIII MM547	409 (RCAF) Sqn	V-1

19/6/44 (27 V-1s destroyed by fighters including 2 by USAAF)

Wg Cdr R.P. Beamont	Tempest V JN817	150 Wg	V-1
Flg Off M.F. Edwards	Tempest V JN752	3 Sqn	V-1
Flg Off R.E. Barckley	Tempest V JN759/JN768	3 Sqn	2 V-1
Flt Lt A.R. Moore	Tempest V JN769/JN755	3 Sqn	3 V-1
Flg Off G.E. Kosh	Tempest V JN769	3 Sqn	V-1
Plt Off S.B. Feldman (US)	Tempest V JN752	3 Sqn	$1^{1}/_{2}$ V-1
Flg Off G.A. Whitman RCAF (US)	Tempest V JN759	3 Sqn	$1^{1}/_{2}$ V-1
Flt Sgt J.E. Hughes	Spitfire MK715	56 Sqn	V-1
Flt Lt J.W.P Draper RCAF	Spitfire XIV RM617	91 Sqn	V-1
Flt Lt H.B. Moffett RCAF	Spitfire XIV NH701	91 Sqn	V-1
Lt H.F. de Bordas (FF)	Spitfire XIV RB181	91 Sqn	$1^{1}/_{2}$ V-1
Flg Off J.A. Faulkner RCAF	Spitfire XIV RM617	91 Sqn	$^{1}/_{2}$ V-1
Flt Sgt G. Kay	Spitfire XIV RB188	91 Sqn	$^{1}/_{2}$ V-1
Flg Off R.F. Burgwal (Dutch)	Spitfire XIV VL-D	322 (Dutch) Sqn	$^{1}/_{2}$ V-1
Flg Off P.A. Cramerus (Dutch)	Spitfire XIV VL-	322 (Dutch) Sqn	V-1
Flg Off J.W. Dekker (Dutch)	Spitfire XIV VL-	322 (Dutch) Sqn	V-1
Flg Off G.F.J. Jongbloed (Dutch)	Spitfire XIV RB184	322 (Dutch) Sqn	$^{1}/_{2}$ V-1
Sgt E. Veiersted (Norw)	Spitfire IX MJ253	332 (Norw) Sqn	V-1
Flg Off W.L. Miller RNZAF	Tempest V JN811	486 (RNZAF) Sqn	V-1
Flg Off R.J. Cammock RNZAF	Tempest V JN810	486 (RNZAF) Sqn	V-1
Plt Off J.H. Stafford RNZAF	Tempest V JN803	486 (RNZAF) Sqn	V-1
Flt Lt H.N. Sweetman RNZAF	Tempest V JN754	486 (RNZAF) Sqn	V-1
Flt Lt J.H. McCaw RNZAF	Tempest V JN770	486 (RNZAF) Sqn	V-1
Capt J.B. Dalglish USAAF	P-51B 42-106769	381stFS USAAF	V-1
1/Lt J.L. Billington USAAF	P-47 43-25270	514thFS USAAF	V-1

Night 19-20/6/44 (7 V-1s destroyed by fighters)

Flt Lt K. Kennedy/ Flg Off O.D. Morgan (Nav)	Mosquito XIII HK425	96 Sqn	V-1
Flt Lt B.A. Primavesi/ Flg Off R.L. Wilson (Nav)	Mosquito XIII HK497	96 Sqn	V-1
Flt Lt D.L. Ward/ Flg Off E.D. Eyles (Nav)	Mosquito XIII HK415	96 Sqn	V-1
Plt Off A. Hollingsworth/ Plt Off E.G. Alcock (Nav)	Mosquito XVII HK254	219 Sqn	V-1
Flt Lt C.M. Jasper RCAF (US)/	Mosquito VI HR358	418 (RCAF) Sqn	V-1

Flt Lt O.A.J. Martin RCAF (Nav)			
Sqn Ldr R. Bannock RCAF/	Mosquito VI HK147	418 (RCAF) Sqn	V-1
Flg Off R.R.F. Bruce RCAF (Nav)			
Flt Lt A. Michie/	Mosquito VI UP-	605 Sqn	V-1
Wt Off J. Tredwen (Nav)			

20/6/44 (22 V-1s destroyed by fighters including 1 by USAAF)

Flt Lt A.E. Umbers RNZAF	Tempest V JN817	3 Sqn	V-1
Plt Off S.B. Feldman (US)	Tempest V JN761/JN735	3 Sqn	2 V-1
Plt Off K.G. Slade-Betts	Tempest V JN765	3 Sqn	V-1
Plt Off H.R. Wingate	Tempest V JN735	3 Sqn	V-1
Wt Off R.S. Adcock RAAF	Tempest V JN739	3 Sqn	V-1
Flg Off G.E. Kosh	Tempest V JN765	3 Sqn	V-1
Flt Sgt D.M. Smith	Tempest V JN752	3 Sqn	V-1
Flg Off R.H. Clapperton	Tempest V JN738	3 Sqn	V-1
Plt Off N.P. Gibbs	Spitfire XII MB875	41 Sqn	V-1
Flg Off K.R. Curtis RCAF	Spitfire XII EN229	41 Sqn	V-1
Sgt J.A. Brown	Spitfire VIV NH707	91 Sqn	V-1
Flg Off C.I.M. Ettles RCAF	Spitfire XIV RB161	91 Sqn	$1/_2$ V-1
Flt Lt L.C.M. van Eendenburg (Dutch)	Spitfire XIV RB184	322 (Dutch) Sqn	V-1
2/Lt H.R. Isachsen (Norw)	Spitfire IX AH-	332 (Norw) Sqn	$1/_2$ V-1
2/Lt O.G. Aanjesen (Norw)	Spitfire IX MA228	332 (Norw) Sqn	$1/_2$ V-1
Plt Off R.J. Danzey RNZAF	Tempest V JN801	486 (RNZAF) Sqn	V-1
Plt Off J.H. Stafford RNZAF	Tempest V JN808	486 (RNZAF) Sqn	V-1
Flt Lt J.H. McCaw RNZAF	Tempest V JN758	486 (RNZAF) Sqn	$1/_2$ V-1
Sqn Ldr R.A. Newbery	Spitfire XIV RB159	610 Sqn	2 V-1
Plt Off R.C. Hussey	Spitfire XIV DW-	610 Sqn	V-1
Flt Lt J.B. Shepherd	Spitfire XIV DW-	610 Sqn	V-1
1/Lt D.W. Johnston USAAF	P-47 CP-	365thFS USAAF	V-1

Night 20-21/6/44 (9 V-1s destroyed by fighters)

Flt Lt F.R.L. Mellersh/	Mosquito XIII MM527	96 Sqn	V-1
Flt Lt M.J. Stanley (Nav)			
Wg Cdr E.D. Crew/	Mosquito XIII MM499	96 Sqn	V-1
Wt Off J.R. Croysdill (Nav)			
Flt Lt R. Davey/	Mosquito HK254	219 Sqn	$1/_2$ V-1
Wt Off A. Whitby (Nav)			
Sqn Ldr G.M. Merrifield/	Mosquito XVII HK362	219 Sqn	2 V-1
Flg Off D.A. Oxby (Nav)			
Sqn Ldr R.S. Jephson RCAF/	Mosquito XIII MM510	409 (RCAF) Sqn	V-1
Flg Off J. Roberts RCAF (Nav)			
Plt Off W.E. Bowhay RCAF/	Mosquito VI TH-	418 (RCAF) Sqn	V-1
Flt Sgt H.K. Naylor RAF (Nav)			
Flt Off B.F. Miller USAAF/	Mosquito VI UP-U	605 Sqn	V-1
Flg Off J.C. Winlaw (Nav)			
Flt Lt G.C. Wright/	Mosquito VI UP-	605 Sqn	V-1
Flg Off J.G. Insall (Nav)			
Flt Lt T.E. Knight/	Mosquito VI UP-	605 Sqn	V-1
Flg Off A.J. Davey (Nav)			

21/6/44 (8 V-1s destroyed by fighters)

Flt Sgt R.W. Cole	Tempest V JN760	3 Sqn	2 V-1
Flt Lt A.R. Moore	Tempest V JN818	3 Sqn	V-1
Plt Off N.P. Gibbs	Spitfire XII MB875	41 Sqn	V-1
Flg Off E. Topham	Spitfire XIV NH707	91 Sqn	V-1
Sqn Ldr P.McC. Bond	Spitfire XIV RB161	91 Sqn	V-1
Flt Sgt R.L. van Beers (Dutch)	Spitfire XIV VL-	322 (Dutch) Sqn	V-1
Flg Off S.S. Williams RNZAF	Tempest V JN866	486 (RNZAF) Sqn	V-1

Night 21-22/6/44 (5 V-1s destroyed by fighters)

Sqn Ldr P.L. Caldwell/	Mosquito XIII MM461	96 Sqn	2 V-1
Flg Off K.P. Rawlins (Nav)			
Flt Lt G.R.I. Parker/	Mosquito XVII HK248	219 Sqn	V-1
Flt Sgt D.L. Godfrey (Nav)			
Flg Off S.P. Seid RCAF/	Mosquito VI HR149	418 (RCAF) Sqn	V-1
Flg Off D.N. McIntosh RCAF (Nav)			
Flt Off B.F. Miller USAAF/	Mosquito VI HJ775	605 Sqn	V-1
Flg Off J.C. Winlaw RCAF (Nav)			

22/6/44 (34 V-1s destroyed by fighters)

Flt Lt A.E. Umbers RNZAF	Tempest V JN817/JN862	3 Sqn	2 V-1
Plt Off H.R. Wingate	Tempest V JN862	3 Sqn	V-1
Wt Off F.McG. Reid	Tempest V JN738	3 Sqn	V-1
Sqn Ldr A.S. Dredge	Tempest V JN812	3 Sqn	$1/_2$ V-1

Flg Off G.E. Kosh	Tempest V JN815	3 Sqn	V-1
Flt Sgt M.J.A. Rose	Tempest V JN738	3 Sqn	V-1
Flg Off R.H. Clapperton	Tempest V JN769	3 Sqn	V-1
Plt Off K.G. Slade-Betts	Tempest V JN755	3 Sqn	V-1
Flt Lt C.R. Birbeck	Spitfire XII MB841	41 Sqn	$1/2$ V-1
Flg Off R.E. Anderson RAAF	Spitfire XII MB837	41 Sqn	$1/2$ V-1
Flt Sgt C.S. Robertson RAAF	Spitfire XII MB875	41 Sqn	$1/2$ V-1
Flg Off K.R. Collier RAAF	Spitfire XIV RB188	91 Sqn	V-1
Cne J-M. Maridor (FF)	Spitfire XIVRB180	91 Sqn	$1 1/2$ V-1
Flg Off C.I.M. Ettles RCAF	Spitfire XIV NH698	91 Sqn	V-1
Plt Off K.G. Brain	Typhoon Ib MN191	137 Sqn	2 V-1
Flt Lt D.G. Brandreth	Typhoon Ib MN584	137 Sqn	V-1
Wt Off J.A. Horne RAAF	Typhoon Ib MN627	137 Sqn	V-1
Flt Lt J.L. Plesman (Durch)	Spitfire XIV VL-	322 (Dutch) Sqn	V-1
Flg Off C.R.R. Manders (Dutch)	Spitfire XIV VL-	322 (Dutch) Sqn	V-1
Flg Off R.F. van Daalen Wetters (Dutch)	Spitfire XIV VL-	322 (Dutch) Sqn	V-1
Flt Lt J.H. McCaw RNZAF	Tempest V JN758/808/821	486 (RNZAF) Sqn	3 V-1
Plt Off K. McCarthy RNZAF	Tempest V JN801	486 (RNZAF) Sqn	2 V-1
Flg Off W.L. Miller RNZAF	Tempest V JN794	486 (RNZAF) Sqn	V-1
Wt Off G.J.M. Hooper RNZAF	Tempest V JN809	486 (RNZAF) Sqn	$1/2$ V-1
Wt Off C.J. Sheddan RNZAF	Tempest V JN809	486 (RNZAF) Sqn	V-1
Sqn Ldr J.H. Iremonger RAF	Tempest V JN808	486 (RNZAF) Sqn	V-1
Plt Off J.H. Stafford RNZAF	Tempest V JN803	486 (RNZAF) Sqn	V-1
Flt Lt J.B. Shepherd	Spitfire XIV DW-	610 Sqn	$1/2$ V-1
Flg Off G.M. McKinlay	Spitfire XIV RB142	610 Sqn	$1/2$ V-1
Sqn Ldr R.A. Newbery	Spitfire XIV RB159	610 Sqn	2 V-1
Wt Off R. Roberts	Spitfire XIV DW-	610 Sqn	V-1

Night 22-23/6/44 (15 V-1s destroyed by fighters)

Sub-Lt(A) W. Lawley-Wakelin RNVR/ Sub-Lt(A) Williams RNVR (Nav)	Mosquito XIII HK370	96 Sqn	V-1
Flt Sgt W.A. McLardy RAAF/ Sgt Devine (Nav)	Mosquito XIII HK433	96 Sqn	V-1
Sqn Ldr R.N. Chudleigh/ Flg Off H.D. Ayliffe (Nav)	Mosquito XIII MM497	96 Sqn	2 V-1
Sqn Ldr W.P. Green/ Wt Off A.R. Grimstone (Nav)	Mosquito XIII MM495	96 Sqn	3 V-1
Flt Lt W.J. Gough/ Flg Off C. Matson (Nav)	Mosquito XIII MM499	96 Sqn	V-1
Wg Cdr A. Barker RAF/ Plt Off W.A.R. Stewart RCAF (Nav)	Mosquito VI TH-	418 (RCAF) Sqn	V-1
Flg Off S.N. May RCAF/ Plt Off J.D. Ritch RCAF (Nav)	Mosquito VI NS837	418 (RCAF) Sqn	2 V-1
Flt Lt S.H.R. Cotterill RCAF/ Flt Sgt E.H. McKenna RAF (Nav)	Mosquito VI TH-	418 (RCAF) Sqn	2 V-1
Flt Lt A.D. Wagner/ Flg Off E.T. Orringe (Nav)	Mosquito VIII ZQ-	FIU	V-1
Wg Cdr R.P. Beamont	Tempest V EJ525	150 Wg	V-1

23/6/44 (46 V-1s destroyed by fighters)

Wg Cdr R.P. Beamont	Tempest V JN751/EJ525	150 Wg	$1 1/2$ V-1
Flt Lt R. van Lierde (Belg)	Tempest V JN862	3 Sqn	$2+1/2+1/2+1/2$ V-1
Flt Sgt R.W. Pottinger	Tempest V JN760	3 Sqn	V-1
Plt Off K.G. Slade-Betts	Tempest V JN815	3 Sqn	V-1
Flt Sgt M.J.A. Rose	Tempest V JN865	3 Sqn	$1/2$ V-1
Flg Off G.A. Whitman RCAF (US)	Tempest V JN743	3 Sqn	$1/2$ V-1
Flt Sgt J.W. Foster	Tempest V JN760	3 Sqn	$1/2$ V-1
Sqn Ldr A.S. Dredge	Tempest V JN812	3 Sqn	V-1
Flt Sgt H.J. Bailey RAAF	Tempest V JN761	3 Sqn	$1+1/3$ V-1
Flt Sgt D.J. Mackerras RAAF	Tempest V JN752	3 Sqn	V-1
Flt Sgt R.W. Cole	Tempest V JN768	3 Sqn	$1/2+1/3$ V-1
Plt Off S.B. Feldman (US)	Tempest V JN793	3 Sqn	$1/3$ V-1
Flt Lt T.A.H. Slack	Spitfire XII EN238	41 Sqn	$1/2$ V-1
Plt Off J.C.J. Payne	Spitfire XII EB-	41 Sqn	V-1
Flg Off M.A.L. Balaase (Belg)	Spitfire XII MB830	41 Sqn	V-1 probable
Flt Lt T. Spencer	Spitfire XII MB856	41 Sqn	V-1
Wg Cdr R.W. Oxspring	Spitfire XIV NH714	24 Wg	$1/2$ V-1
Flt Lt R.H. Dibnah RCAF	Spitfire XIV RB173	91 Sqn	V-1
Flt Sgt T.B. Burnett	Spitfire XIV RB174	91 Sqn	V-1
Flg Off G.H. Huntley	Spitfire XIV RB181-	91 Sqn	$1/2$ V-1
Flt Sgt G. Kay	Spitfire XIV RB165	91 Sqn	$1 1/2$ V-1
Sqn Ldr N.A. Kynaston	Spitfire XIV RB185	91 Sqn	2 V-1

Flt Lt H.D. Johnson	Spitfire XIV RB188	91 Sqn	$^1/_2$ V-1
Flg Off J.A. Faulkner RCAF	Spitfire XIV RM617	91 Sqn	$^1/_2$ V-1
Flg Off K.R. Collier RAAF	Spitfire XIV NM698	91 Sqn	V-1
Flt Lt A.C.W. Holland	Spitfire IX ML204	165 Sqn	V-1
Flg Off T.A. Vance RAAF	Spitfire IX MK638	165 Sqn	$1^1/_2$ V-1
Sqn Ldr M.E. Blackstone	Spitfire IX MK425	165 Sqn	V-1
Lt(A) S.G. Hamblett RNVR	Spitfire IX MK426	165 Sqn	V-1
Flt Sgt R.J. Hughes RAAF	Spitfire IX MK426	165 Sqn	V-1
Flg Off J. van Arkel (Dutch)	Spitfire XIV VL-V	322 (Dutch) Sqn	$^1/_2$ V-1
Flg Off M.L. van Bergen (Dutch)	Spitfire XIV VL-N	322 (Dutch) Sqn	$^1/_2$ V-1
Maj K.C. Kuhlmann SAAF	Spitfire XIV NH586	322 (Dutch) Sqn	V-1
Plt Off R.J. Danzey RNZAF	Tempest V JN797	486 (RNZAF) Sqn	$1^1/_2$ V-1
Plt Off F.B. Lawless RNZAF	Tempest V JN859	486 (RNZAF) Sqn	V-1
Flt Sgt B.M. Hall RNZAF	Tempest V JN809	486 (RNZAF) Sqn	V-1
Plt Off K. McCarthy RNZAF	Tempest V JN754	486 (RNZAF) Sqn	2 V-1
Flt Sgt O.D. Eagleson RNZAF	Tempest V JN794	486 (RNZAF) Sqn	$1^1/_2$ V-1
Flg Off W.L. Miller RNZAF	Tempest V JN808	486 (RNZAF) Sqn	2 V-1
Flg Off R.J. Cammock RNZAF	Tempest V JN810	486 (RNZAF) Sqn	$1^1/_2$ V-1
Wt Off C.J. Sheddan RNZAF	Tempest V JN801	486 (RNZAF) Sqn	V-1
Wt Off S.J. Short RNZAF	Tempest V JN810	486 (RNZAF) Sqn	V-1
Flg Off J.R. Cullen RNZAF	Tempest V JN770	486 (RNZAF) Sqn	$^1/_2$ V-1
Wt Off W.A. Kalka RNZAF	Tempest V JN801	486 (RNZAF) Sqn	V-1
Sqn Ldr R.A. Newbery	Spitfire XIV RB159	610 Sqn	$^1/_2$ V-1
Flg Off S.A. Jones	Spitfire XIV DW-	610 Sqn	$^1/_2$ V-1
Plt Off B.R. Scamen RCAF	Spitfire XIV DW-	610 Sqn	$^1/_2$ V-1

Night 23-24/6/44 (12 V-1s destroyed by fighters)

Flt Lt F.E. Clarke/	Mosquito XVII HK260	219 Sqn	V-1
Flt Lt H.M. Friend (Nav)			
Flt Lt J.B. Fox/	Mosquito XIII HK480	264 Sqn	V-1 (also FTR)
Plt Off C. Pryor (Nav)			
Flt Lt C.J. Evans RCAF/	Mosquito VI TH-	418 (RCAF) Sqn	3 V-1
Flg Off S. Humblestone RAF (Nav)			
Sqn Ldr E.R.McGill RCAF/	Mosquito VI TH-	418 (RCAF) Sqn	V-1
Flg Off F.D. Hendershot RCAF (Nav)			
Plt Off W.E. Bowhay RCAF/	Mosquito VI TH-	418 (RCAF) Sqn	V-1
Flt Sgt H.K. Naylor RAF (Nav)			
Flg Off B.G. Bensted/	Mosquito VI HJ799	605 Sqn	2 V-1+ probable
Sgt C.L. Burrage (Nav)			
Flt Lt J.G. Musgrave/	Mosquito VI MM429	605 Sqn	V-1
Flt Sgt F.W. Samwell (Nav)			
Flg Off J. Reid/	Mosquito VI HJ776	605 Sqn	V-1 probable
Flt Sgt R.E. Phillips (Nav)			
Flt Lt J. Singleton/	Mosquito VI MM415	605 Sqn	V-1
Flt Lt W.G. Haslam (Nav)			
Sqn Ldr W.H. Maguire/	Mosquito VIII ZQ-	FIU	V-1
Flt Lt W.D. Jones (Nav)			

24/6/44 (10 V-1s destroyed by fighters)

Plt Off N.P. Gibbs	Spitfire XII MB875	41 Sqn	V-1
Flt Sgt R.L. Short	Spitfire XII EN620	41 Sqn	$^1/_2$ V-1
Flt Lt T. Spencer	Spitfire XII EN224	41 Sqn	V-1
Flt Lt J.W.P. Draper RCAF	Spitfire XIV RM654	91 Sqn	V-1
Flt Lt H.D. Johnson	Spitfire XIV RB188	91 Sqn	V-1
Flt Lt I. St.C. Watson	Spitfire IX MK811	165 Sqn	V-1
Flg Off R.J. Cammock RNZAF	Tempest V JN808	486 (RNZAF) Sqn	2 V-1
Plt Off K. McCarthy RNZAF	Tempest V JN803	486 (RNZAF) Sqn	V-1
Sqn Ldr R.A. Newbery	Spitfire XIV RB159	610 Sqn	$1^1/_2$ V-1
Flg Off P.M. Bangerter	Spitfire XIV DW-	610 Sqn	$^1/_2$ V-1

Night 24-25/6/44 (10 V-1s destroyed by fighters)

Wg Cdr E.D. Crew/	Mosquito XIII MM499	96 Sqn	V-1
Wt Off J.R. Croysdill (Nav)			
Flt Lt F.R.L. Mellersh/	Mosquito XIII HK372	96 Sqn	2 V-1
Flt Lt M.J. Stanley (Nav)			
Flt Sgt T. Bryan/	Mosquito XIII HK421	96 Sqn	2 V-1
Flg Off B.J. Friis (Nav)			
Flg Off J.H. Phillips RCAF/	Mosquito VI NT137	418 (RCAF) Sqn	V-1
Plt Off B. Job RAF (Nav)			
Wt Off J.J.P. McGale RCAF/	Mosquito VI HJ719	418 (RCAF) Sqn	2 V-1
Flg Off E.J. Storey RCAF (Nav)			
Flt Lt G.R. Houston RAAF/	Mosquito XVII HK264	456 (RAAF) Sqn	V-1 probable

Flg Off L.C. Engberg RAAF (Nav)
Sqn Ldr I.F. McCall/	Mosquito VI UP-	605 Sqn	V-1
Flt Sgt T. Caulfield (Nav)			
Flg Off R.C. Walton RNZAF/	Mosquito VI UP-	605 Sqn	V-1
Sgt F. Pritchard RNZAF (Nav)			

25/6/44 (23 V-1s destroyed by fighters including 2 by USAAF)
Flt Sgt R.W. Cole	Tempest V JN768	3 Sqn	V-1
Flt Sgt M.J.A. Rose	Tempest V JN817	3 Sqn	V-1
Sqn Ldr A.S. Dredge	Tempest V JN812	3 Sqn	V-1
Flt Lt R. van Lierde (Belg)	Tempest V JN862	3 Sqn	1 1/2 V-1
Flg Off G.A. Whitman RCAF (US	Tempest V JN743	3 Sqn	1/2 V-1
Flt Sgt H.J. Bailey RAAF	Tempest V JN752	3 Sqn	V-1
Flt Sgt D.J. Mackerras RAAF	Tempest V JN745	3 Sqn	V-1+ probable
Plt Off S.B. Feldman (US)	Tempest V JN761	3 Sqn	V-1
Wt Off P.T. Coleman	Spitfire XII MB841	41 Sqn	V-1
Flt Lt R.S. Nash	Spitfire XIV RB169	91 Sqn	V-1
Lt H.F. de Bordas (FF)	Spitfire XIV RM654	91 Sqn	V-1
Plt Off R.S.J. Hebron RAAF	Spitfire IX MK838	165 Sqn	V-1
Flg Off S.S. Williams RNZAF	Tempest V JN758	486 (RNZAF) Sqn	V-1
Wt Off S.J. Short RNZAF	Tempest V JN801	486 (RNZAF) Sqn	V-1
Flg Off R.J. Cammock RNZAF	Tempest V JN804	486 (RNZAF) Sqn	2 V-1
Flg Off J.R. Cullen RNZAF	Tempest V JN770	486 (RNZAF) Sqn	2 V-1
Flg Off W.A. Hart RNZAF	Tempest V JN809	486 (RNZAF) Sqn	2 V-1
Wt Off C.J. Sheddan RNZAF	Tempest V JN854	486 (RNZAF) Sqn	V-1
Wg Cdr R.H. Harries	Spitfire IX RHH	135 Wg	V-1
Capt J.B. Dalglish USAAF	P-51 42-106769	381stFS USAAF	2 V-1

Night 25-26/6/44 (13 V-1s destroyed by fighters)
Capt T. Weisteen (Norw)/	Mosquito XIX MM636	85 Sqn	V-1
Flg Off F.G. French (Nav)			
Flg Off J. Goode/	Mosquito XIII HK406	96 Sqn	2 V-1
Flg Off V.A. Robinson (Nav)			
Flg Off R.F. Ball/	Mosquito XIII HK372	96 Sqn	V-1
Flg Off F.G. Saunders (Nav)			
Sqn Ldr P.L. Caldwell/	Mosquito XIII MM461	96 Sqn	V-1
Flg Off K.P. Rawlins (Nav)			
Flt Lt N.S. Head/	Mosquito XIII MM492	96 Sqn	V-1
Sgt Foskett (Nav)			
Sqn Ldr W.P. Green/	Mosquito XIII MM495	96 Sqn	V-1
Wt Off A.R. Grimstone (Nav)			
Plt Off A. Hollingsworth	Mosquito XVII HK254	219 Sqn	2 V-1
Plt Off E.G. Alcock (Nav)			
Flt Lt G.R.I. Parker/	Mosquito XVII HK250	219 Sqn	2 V-1
Flt Sgt D.L. Godfrey (Nav)			
Flg Off R.E. Lelong RNZAF/	Mosquito VI HJ785	605 Sqn	V-1
Flt Sgt J.A. McLaren (Nav)			
Flg Off A.T. Linn/	Mosquito VI UP-	605 Sqn	V-1
Wt Off W. Harrison (Nav)			

26/6/44 (5 V-1s destroyed by fighters)
Wt Off J.R.L. Torpey	Tempest V JN765	3 Sqn	V-1
Flg Off A.M. Sames RNZAF	Typhoon Ib MN134	137 Sqn	2 V-1
Flt Lt J.H. McCaw RNZAF	Tempest V JN758	486 (RNZAF) Sqn	V-1
Sqn Ldr M.G. Barnett RNZAF	Spitfire Vb W3702	501 Sqn	V-1

Night 26-27/6/44 (3 V-1s destroyed by fighters)
Flt Lt L. Stephenson/	Mosquito XVII HK248	219 Sqn	V-1
Plt Off G.A. Hall (Nav)			
Flt Lt P.G.K. Williamson/	Mosquito XVII MM690	219 Sqn	V-1
Flg Off F.E. Forrest (Nav)			
Sqn Ldr R.S. Jephson RCAF/	Mosquito XIII MM510	409 (RCAF) Sqn	V-1
Flg Off J. Roberts RCAF (Nav)			

27/6/44 (37 V-1s destroyed by fighters including 1 by USAAF)
Flg Off R. Bridgeman	Spitfire IX MK997	1 Sqn	1/3 V-1
Flt Sgt K.C. Weller	Spitfire IX ML258	1 Sqn	1/3 V-1
Flt Sgt I. Hastings	Spitfire IX MK988	1 Sqn	1/3 V-1
Flg Off W.J. Batchelor	Spitfire Vb ML313	1 Sqn	V-1
Wg Cdr R.P. Beamont	Tempest V JK812/EJ525	150 Wg	2 V-1
Flt Lt R. van Lierde (Belg)	Tempest V JN862	3 Sqn	V-1
Flt Sgt D.J. Mackerras RAAF	Tempest V JN760	3 Sqn	V-1
Flt Sgt L.G. Everson	Tempest V JN765/JN769	3 Sqn	2 V-1
Flt Sgt J.W. Foster	Tempest V JN807	3 Sqn	1/2 V-1

Flt Lt A.E. Umbers RNZAF	Tempest V JN817	3 Sqn	V-1
Flg Off R.H. Clapperton	Tempest V JN769	3 Sqn	V-1
Wt Off J.R.L. Torpey	Tempest V JN765	3 Sqn	V-1
Flg Off R. Dryland	Tempest V JN822	3 Sqn	V-1
Flt Sgt H.J. Bailey RAAF	Tempest V JN807	3 Sqn	V-1
Sqn Ldr P.McC. Bond	Spitfire XIV RB161	91 Sqn	$1^1/_2$ V-1
Flg Off R.A. McPhie RCAF	Spitfire XIV NH698	91 Sqn	$^1/_2$ V-1
Flt Lt R.S. Nash	Spitfire XIV RB169	91 Sqn	V-1
Flg Off E. Topham	Spitfire XIV RB183	91 Sqn	$^1/_2$ V-1
Flt Lt H.B. Moffett RCAF	Spitfire XIV RB161	91 Sqn	V-1
Flg Off J.A. Faulkner RCAF	Spitfire XIV RM620	91 Sqn	V-1
Flt Sgt R.J. Hughes RAAF	Spitfire IX MK426	165 Sqn	V-1
Flg Off S.R. Chambers	Spitfire IX MJ580	165 Sqn	$^1/_2$ V-1
Flt Sgt R.L. van Beers (Dutch)	Spitfire XIV VL-H	322 (Dutch) Sqn	V-1
Flt Sgt J.H. Harms (Dutch)	Spitfire XIV VL-J	322 (Dutch) Sqn	2 V-1
Flt Lt J.L. Plesman (Dutch)	Spitfire XIV VL-V	322 (Dutch) Sqn	V-1
Flg Off M.L. van Bergen (Dutch)	Spitfire XIV VL-N	322 (Dutch) Sqn	V-1
Flt Sgt C. Kooij (Dutch)	Spitfire XIV VL-Q	322 (Dutch) Sqn	$^1/_2$ V-1
Flg Off J. van Arkel (Dutch)	Spitfire XIV VL-T	322 (Dutch) Sqn	V-1
Flt Lt N.J. Powell RNZAF	Tempest V JN866	486 (RNZAF) Sqn	V-1
Flt Lt H.N. Sweetman RNZAF	Tempest V JN754	486 (RNZAF) Sqn	2 V-1
Wt Off G.J.M. Hooper RNZAF	Tempest V JN803	486 (RNZAF) Sqn	2 V-1
Flg Off W.L. Miller RNZAF	Tempest V JN811	486 (RNZAF) Sqn	2 V-1
Wt Off O.D. Eagleson RNZAF	Tempest V JN794	486 (RNZAF) Sqn	$^1/_2$ V-1
Flg Off W.A. Hart RNZAF	Tempest V JN803	486 (RNZAF) Sqn	V-1
Flg Off R.J. Cammock RNZAF	Tempest V JN794	486 (RNZAF) Sqn	V-1
1/Lt R.B. Freyermuth USAAF	P-51 B3-	381stFS USAAF	V-1

Night 27-28/6/44 (14 V-1s destroyed by fighters)

Flg Off P.S. Kendall/ Flt Lt C.R. Hill (Nav)	Mosquito XVII MM632	85 Sqn	V-1
Flt Lt F.R.L. Mellersh/ Flt Lt M.J. Stanley (Nav)	Mosquito XIII HK456	96 Sqn	V-1
Flt Sgt T. Bryan/ Plt Off B.J. Friis (Nav)	Mosquito XIII HK421	96 Sqn	V-1
Wg Cdr E.D. Crew/ Sgt B. Jaeger (Nav)	Mosquito XIII HK417	96 Sqn	V-1
Flt Lt D.L. Ward/ Flg Off E.D. Eyles (Nav)	Mosquito XIII MM524	96 Sqn	V-1
Flt Lt J.G. Benson/ Flt Lt L. Brandon (Nav)	Mosquito XIX MM630	157 Sqn	V-1
Wt Off A.G. McLeod/ Flg Off L. Mulroy (Nav)	Mosquito XIX MM637	157 Sqn	V-1
Flt Lt G.R.I. Parker/ Flt Sgt D.L. Godfrey (Nav)	Mosquito XVII HK250	219 Sqn	V-1
Flt Lt S.H.R.Cotterill RCAF/ Flt Sgt E.H. McKenna RAF (Nav)	Mosquito VI TH-	418(RCAF) Sqn	V-1
Flt Lt J.I. Pengelly/ Flg Off L.R. Page (Nav)	Mosquito VI UP-	605 Sqn	V-1
Flg Off B.G. Bensted/ Sgt C.L. Burrage (Nav)	Mosquito VI HJ799	605 Sqn	V-1
Sqn Ldr G.J. Wright/ Flg Off R.P. Bourne (Nav)	Mosquito VI UP-	605 Sqn	V-1
Flg Off R.C. Walton RNZAF/ Flg Off Strickland (Nav)	Mosquito VI UP-	605 Sqn	2 V-1

28/6/44 (34 V-1s destroyed by fighters)

Flg Off D.V. McIntosh	Spitfire IX MK901	1 Sqn	$^1/_2$ V-1
Flg Off E.G. Hutchin	Spitfire IX MJ422	1 Sqn	V-1
Flt Sgt I. Hastings	Spitfire IX MK846	1 Sqn	V-1
Flt Lt T. Draper Williams	Spitfire IX ML118	1 Sqn	V-1
Flg Off E.N.W. Marsh	Spitfire IX MK988	1 Sqn	V-1
Wg Cdr R.P. Beamont	Tempest V EJ525	150 Wg	V-1
Flg Off R.H. Clapperton	Tempest V JN822	3 Sqn	3 V-1
Plt Off G.A. Whitman RCAF (US)	Tempest V JN807	3 Sqn	V-1
Plt Off K.G. Slade-Betts	Tempest V JN769	3 Sqn	2 V-1
Plt Off S.B. Feldman (US)	Tempest V JN743	3 Sqn	V-1
Plt Off H.R. Wingate	Tempest V JN862	3 Sqn	V-1
Flt Sgt D.M. Smith	Tempest V JN793	3 Sqn	V-1
Flt Lt R. van Lierde (Belg)	Tempest V JN862	3 Sqn	V-1
Flt Sgt R.W. Pottinger	Tempest V JN793	3 Sqn	V-1
Flt Lt J.W.P. Draper RCAF	Spitfire XVI RB161	91 Sqn	V-1

Flt Lt H.D. Johnson	Spitfire XVI RB183	91 Sqn	1^1/$_2$ V-1
Wt Off J.A. Horne RAAF	Typhoon Ib MN429	137 Sqn	V-1
Flg Off L.D. Wolters (Dutch)	Spitfire XIV VL-N	322 (Dutch) Sqn	^{1}/$_2$ V-1
Wt Off J.A. Maier (Dutch)	Spitfire XIV VL-Q	322 (Dutch) Sqn	V-1
Flg Off G.F.J. Jongbloed (Dutch)	Spitfire XIV VL-C	322 (Dutch) Sqn	V-1
Flt Sgt F. van Valkenburg (Dutch)	Spitfire XIV NH649	322 (Dutch) Sqn	V-1
Flg Off J.G. Wilson RNZAF	Tempest V JN866	486 (RNZAF) Sqn	V-1
Wt Off O.D. Eagleson RNZAF	Tempest V JN859/JN854	486 (RNZAF) Sqn	2 V-1
Flg Off R.J. Cammock RNZAF	Tempest V JN810	486 (RNZAF) Sqn	V-1
Plt Off F.B. Lawless RNZAF	Tempest V JN859	486 (RNZAF) Sqn	V-1
Flt Sgt B.M. Hall RNZAF	Tempest V JN809	486 (RNZAF) Sqn	V-1
Plt Off R.R. Wright RNZAF	Tempest V JN804	486 (RNZAF) Sqn	V-1 (also KiA)
Flt Lt J. Berry	Tempest V EJ524	FIU	2 V-1
Sqn Ldr E.G. Daniel	Tempest V EJ531	FIU	2 V-1

Night 28-29/6/44 (18 V-1s destroyed by fighters)

Flg Off R.T. Goucher/	Mosquito XIX TA400	85 Sqn	V-1
Flt Lt C.H. Bulloch (Nav)			
Flt Lt I.A. Dobie/	Mosquito XIII HK396	96 Sqn	4 V-1
Flg Off E.A. Johnson (Nav)			
Flt Lt F.R.L. Mellersh/	Mosquito XIII HK372	96 Sqn	4 V-1
Flt Lt M.J. Stanley (Nav)			
Wg Cdr E.D. Crew/	Mosquito XIII HK456	96 Sqn	2 V-1
Sgt B. Jaeger (Nav)			
Sqn Ldr J.H.M. Chisholm/	Mosquito XIX MM676	157 Sqn	V-1
Flt Lt E. Wylde (Nav)			
Flt Lt J.R. Rhodes/	Mosquito VI UP-C	605 Sqn	V-1
Flt Sgt J.H. Little (Nav)			
Flt Lt A.T. Linn/	Mosquito VI UP-	605 Sqn	V-1
Wt Off W. Harrison (Nav)			
Flg Off R.C. Walton RNZAF/	Mosquito VI UP-	605 Sqn	2 V-1
Sgt F. Pritchard RNZAF (Nav)			
Flt Lt G.C. Wright/	Mosquito VI UP-	605 Sqn	2 V-1
Flg Off J.G. Insall (Nav)			

29/6/44 (48 V-1s destroyed by fighters including 2 by USAAF)

Wg Cdr R.P. Beamont	Tempest V EJ525	150 Wg	2 V-1
Flt Lt R. van Lierde (Belg)	Tempest V JN862	3 Sqn	V-1
Flt Sgt S. Domanski PAF	Tempest V JN752	3 Sqn	V-1
Flg Off R.E. Barckley	Tempest V JN755	3 Sqn	V-1
Plt Off K.G. Slade-Betts	Tempest V JN769	3 Sqn	V-1
Flt Sgt R.W. Cole	Tempest V JN759	3 Sqn	V-1
Wg Cdr R.W. Oxspring	Spitfire XIV NH714	24 Wg	V-1
Flt Lt D.E. Llewellyn	Spitfire IX NH468	74 Sqn	V-1
Sgt J. Dalzell	Spitfire IX RR207	74 Sqn	V-1
Flt Lt A. Smith RNZAF	Spitfire XIV RB173	91 Sqn	^{1}/$_2$ V-1
Flt Lt R.S. Nash	Spitfire XIV RM615	91 Sqn	2 V-1
Flg Off E. Topham	Spitfire XIV RM654/707/RB169	91 Sqn	2^1/$_2$ V-1
Flg Off G. Balcombe	Spitfire XIV RB161	91 Sqn	V-1
Flt Lt H.D. Johnson	Spitfire XIV NH701/RB188	91 Sqn	2 V-1
Flt Lt W.C. Marshall	Spitfire XIV RB181	91 Sqn	V-1
Flt Lt H.M. Neil	Spitfire XIV RB173	91 Sqn	V-1
Flg Off T.D. Tinsey	Spitfire IX ML175	165 Sqn	^{1}/$_2$ V-1
Flt Sgt I.L. Loch	Spitfire IX ML139	165 Sqn	^{1}/$_2$ V-1
Flt Sgt V. Porich RAAF	Spitfire IX NH401	165 Sqn	^{1}/$_2$ V-1
Flt Sgt C.R. Bundara RAAF	Spitfire IX MK811	165 Sqn	V-1
Lt(A) S.G. Hamblett RNVR	Spitfire IX MK480/MK838	165 Sqn	2 V-1
Plt Off J.M. Walton RCAF	Spitfire IX MK738	165 Sqn	V-1
Flt Sgt A.M. Rollo	Spitfire Vb AD377	277 Sqn (ASR)	V-1
Flg Off F.W.L.S. Speetjens (Dutch)	Spitfire XIV VL-J	322 (Dutch) Sqn	V-1
Flg Off G.F.J. Jongbloed (Dutch)	Spitfire XIV VL-K	322 (Dutch) Sqn	V-1
Flt Sgt M.J. Janssen (Dutch)	Spitfire XIV VL-D	322 (Dutch) Sqn	V-1
Flg Off R.F. Burgwal (Dutch)	Spitfire XIV NH649	322 (Dutch) Sqn	2 V-1
Flg Off M.A. Muller (Dutch)	Spitfire XIV VL-T	322 (Dutch) Sqn	V-1
Flt Lt J.L. Plesman (Dutch)	Spitfire XIV VL-W	322 (Dutch) Sqn	V-1
Flg Off L.D. Wolters (Dutch)	Spitfire XIV VL-N	322 (Dutch) Sqn	V-1
Flg Off F.J.H. van Eijk (Dutch)	Spitfire XIV NH699	322 (Dutch) Sqn	V-1
Flt Sgt W. de Vries (Dutch)	Spitfire XIV VL-Q	322 (Dutch) Sqn	V-1
Plt Off R.J. Danzey RNZAF	Tempest V JN797	486 (RNZAF) Sqn	2 V-1
Plt Off R.D. Bremner RNZAF	Tempest V JN821	486 (RNZAF) Sqn	V-1
Flt Lt H.N. Sweetman RNZAF	Tempest V JN821	486 (RNZAF) Sqn	V-1
Wt Off C.J. Sheddan RNZAF	Tempest V JN809	486 (RNZAF) Sqn	V-1

Wt Off S.J. Short RNZAF	Tempest V EJ527	486 (RNZAF) Sqn	1^1/$_2$ V-1
Flg Off J.R. Cullen RNZAF	Tempest V JN810	486 (RNZAF) Sqn	V-1
Flt Lt J. Berry	Tempest V EJ524	FIU	V-1
Capt C.G. Browne USAAF	P-47 3T-	22ndFS USAAF	^{1}/$_2$ V-1
1/Lt C.H. Nott USAAF	P-47 3T-	22ndFS USAAF	^{1}/$_2$ V-1
1/Lt J. Gervan USAAF	P-51 B3-	381stFS USAAF	V-1

Night 29-30/6/44 (7 V-1s destroyed by fighters)

Flt Lt R.H. Farrell/	Mosquito XVII HK119	85 Sqn	V-1
Flt Sgt R. Chappell (Nav)			
Sqn Ldr W.P. Green/	Mosquito XIII MM495	96 Sqn	V-1
Wt Off A.R. Grimstone (Nav)			
Wg Cdr G.L. Raphael/	Mosquito VI UP-	605 Sqn	V-1
Flg Off L.R. Page (Nav)			
Sqn Ldr K.M. Carver/	Mosquito VI HJ761	605 Sqn	2 V-1
Flg Off R. Birrell (Nav)			
Wg Cdr N.J. Starr/	Mosquito VI UP-	605 Sqn	V-1
Plt Off J. Irvine (Nav)			
Flt Lt G.C. Wright/	Mosquito VI UP-	605 Sqn	V-1
Flg Off J.G. Insall (Nav)			

30/6/44 (37 V-1s destroyed by fighters including 2^1/$_2$ by USAAF)

Flg Off N.E. Brown	Spitfire LFIXb MK644/867	1 Sqn	2 V-1+ probable
Flg Off D.R. Wallace	Spitfire LFIXb MJ481	1 Sqn	V-1
Plt Off K.R. Foskett	Spitfire LFIXb MK986	1 Sqn	1^1/$_2$ V-1
Flg Off H.L. Stuart	Spitfire LFIXb NH246	1 Sqn	V-1
Wt Off J.W. McKenzie	Spitfire LFIXb MK997	1 Sqn	^{1}/$_2$ V-1
Flt Sgt J.W. Foster	Tempest V JN743	3 Sqn	V-1
Plt Off K.G. Slade-Betts	Tempest V JN755	3 Sqn	V-1
Flt Sgt R.W. Cole	Tempest V JN768	3 Sqn	V-1
Flt Sgt S. Domanski PAF	Tempest V JN752	3 Sqn	V-1
Flg Off R. Dryland	Tempest V JN822	3 Sqn	V-1
Flg Off D.J. Butcher	Tempest V JN745	3 Sqn	V-1
Flt Lt A.R. Elcock	Spitfire XIV RB182	91 Sqn	V-1
Cne J-M. Maridor (FF)	Spitfire XIV RB188	91 Sqn	V-1
Flt Lt A. Smith RNZAF	Spitfire XIV NH703	91 Sqn	V-1
Sqn Ldr N.A. Kynaston	Spitfire XIV RB185	91 Sqn	V-1
Flg Off R.A. Johnstone RCAF	Typhoon Ib MN152	137 Sqn	V-1
Flg Off N.J.M. Manfred RNZAF	Typhoon Ib MN596	137 Sqn	V-1
Plt Off K.G. Brain	Typhoon Ib MN169	137 Sqn	1^1/$_2$ V-1
Flt Lt M. Wood RCAF	Typhoon Ib MN134	137 Sqn	^{1}/$_2$ V-1
Flg Off C.M. Lawson RAAF	Spitfire IX MK811	165 Sqn	V-1
Flg Off L.M. Meijers (Dutch)	Spitfire XIV VL-J	322 (Dutch) Sqn	V-1
Flg Off J. van Arkel (Dutch)	Spitfire XIV VL-D	322 (Dutch) Sqn	V-1
Flg Off R.F. Burgwal (Dutch)	Spitfire XIV VL-E	322 (Dutch) Sqn	2 V-1
Flg Off J. Jonker (Dutch)	Spitfire XIV VL-K	322 (Dutch) Sqn	V-1
Wt Off S.J. Short RNZAF	Tempest V JN810	486 (RNZAF) Sqn	V-1
Flt Sgt B.M. Hall RNZAF	Tempest V JN770	486 (RNZAF) Sqn	V-1
Plt Off F.B. Lawless RNZAF	Tempest V JN811	486 (RNZAF) Sqn	V-1
Flt Lt E.W. Tanner RNZAF	Tempest V JN770	486 (RNZAF) Sqn	3 V-1
Plt Off J.H. Stafford RNZAF	Tempest V JN801	486 (RNZAF) Sqn	V-1
Flt Sgt B.M. Hall RNZAF	Tempest V JN854	486 (RNZAF) Sqn	V-1
Flt Lt H.N. Sweetman RNZAF	Tempest V JN801	486 (RNZAF) Sqn	V-1
1/Lt H.F. Phelps USAAF	P-47 V5-	412thFS USAAF	V-1
1/Lt J.A. Kelly USAAF	P-47 V5-	412thFS USAAF	^{1}/$_2$ V-1
1/Lt J. Tucker USAAF	P-47 5F-	5thERS (ASR)	V-1

Night 30/6-1/7/44 (6 V-1s destroyed by fighters)

Sqn Ldr J.H.M. Chisholm/	Mosquito XIX TA404	157 Sqn	V-1
Flt Lt E. Wylde (Nav)			
Flt Lt E.J. Stevens/	Mosquito XIX MM674	157 Sqn	2 V-1
Flg Off L. Butt (Nav)			
Flt Lt J. Berry	Tempest V EJ524	FIU	3 V-1

1/7/44 (20 V-1s destroyed by fighters)

Flt Sgt S. Domanski PAF	Tempest V EJ582	3 Sqn	V-1
Flg Off R. Dryland	Tempest V JN865	3 Sqn	V-1
Sqn Ldr N.A. Kynaston	Spitfire XIV RB185	91 Sqn	2 V-1
Flg Off P.A. Schade	Spitfire XIV NH701	91 Sqn	V-1
Flt Lt H.M. Neil	Spitfire XIV RB173	91 Sqn	V-1
Flt Lt H.D. Johnson	Spitfire XIV RB188	91 Sqn	V-1
Flt Lt J.A. Cruickshank RCAF	Spitfire XIV RM615	91 Sqn	V-1
Plt Off G.P. Bauchman RCAF	Spitfire IX MK752	165 Sqn	1^1/$_2$ V-1

Flg Off C.M. Lawson RAAF	Spitfire IX MK811	165 Sqn	2 V-1
Plt Off R.S.J. Hebron RAAF	Spitfire IX MK864	165 Sqn	V-1
Plt Off J.M. Walton RCAF	Spitfire IX MK738	165 Sqn	V-1
Flg Off G.P. Armstrong RAAF	Spitfire IX MJ221	165 Sqn	V-1
Flg Off T.D. Tinsey	Spitfire IX ML175	165 Sqn	V-1
Wt Off J.A. Maier (Dutch)	Spitfire XIV VL-T	322 (Dutch) Sqn	V-1
Plt Off F.B. Lawless RNZAF	Tempest V JN770	486 (RNZAF) Sqn	V-1
Flg Off R.J. Cammock RNZAF	Tempest V JN866	486 (RNZAF) Sqn	V-1
Wt Off C.J. Sheddan RNZAF	Tempest V JN821	486 (RNZAF) Sqn	V-1
Flt Lt L.J. Appleton RNZAF	Tempest V JN873	486 (RNZAF) Sqn	V-1

Night 1-2/7/44 (1 V-1 destroyed by fighters)

Flg Off P.R. Rudd/	Mosquito VI UP-	605 Sqn	V-1
Flg Off D. Messingham (Nav)			

2/7/44 (1 V-1 destroyed by fighters)

Flt Lt J. Berry	Tempest V EJ524	FIU	V-1

Night 2-3/7/44 (15 V-1s destroyed by fighters)

Capt T. Weisteen (Norw)/	Mosquito XIX MM636	85 Sqn	V-1
Flg Off F.G. French (Nav)			
Flt Lt F.R.L. Mellersh/	Mosquito XIII MM577	96 Sqn	3 V-1
Flt Lt M.J. Stanley (Nav)			
Flt Sgt T. Bryan/	Mosquito XIII HK421	96 Sqn	V-1
Plt Off B.J. Friis (Nav)			
Wg Cdr E.D. Crew/	Mosquito XIII NS985	96 Sqn	3 V-1
Sgt B. Jaeger (Nav)			
Flt Lt I.A. Dobie/	Mosquito XIII HK437	96 Sqn	V-1
Flg Off E.A. Johnson (Nav)			
Flt Sgt S. Astley/	Mosquito XIX MM637	157 Sqn	V-1
Plt Off G.T. Lang (Nav)			
Flt Lt R.J.V. Smyth/	Mosquito XIX MM646	157 Sqn	V-1
Flg Off L. Waters (Nav)			
Sqn Ldr J.G. Benson/	Mosquito XIX MM670	157 Sqn	V-1
Flt Lt L. Brandon (Nav)			
Wt Off R.F. Henke RCAF/	Mosquito XIII MM510	409 (RCAF) Sqn	V-1
Sgt L.A. Emmerson RCAF (Nav)			
Flg Off H.F. Pearce RCAF/	Mosquito XIII MM491	409 (RCAF) Sqn	V-1
Plt Off P.J. Smith RCAF (Nav)			
Flt Lt J.G. Musgrave/	Mosquito VI MM429	605 Sqn	V-1
Flt Sgt F.W. Samwell (Nav)			

3/7/44 (28 V-1s destroyed by fighters)

Flt Lt R. van Lierde (Belg)	Tempest V EJ525	3 Sqn	V-1
Flt Sgt D.J. Mackerras RAAF	Tempest V JN868	3 Sqn	V-1
Plt Off H.R. Wingate	Tempest V EJ582	3 Sqn	3 V-1
Flt Sgt M.J.A. Rose	Tempest V JN754	3 Sqn	V-1
Plt Off K.G. Slade-Betts	Tempest V EJ504	3 Sqn	2 V-1
Flg Off M.A.L. Balaase (Belg)	Spitfire XII EN609	41 Sqn	V-1
Sqn Ldr R.H. Chapman	Spitfire XII EN605	41 Sqn	V-1
Flt Lt D.V.G. Cotes-Preedy	Tempest V JN864	56 Sqn	V-1
Flt Lt H.B. Moffett RCAF	Spitfire XIV RB165	91 Sqn	V-1
Flt Lt W.C. Marshall	Spitfire XIV RM615/RM654	91 Sqn	2 V-1
Flt Lt H.D. Johnson	Spitfire XIV RB188/RB165	91 Sqn	2 V-1
Sqn Ldr N.A. Kynaston	Spitfire XIV RB185/NH703	91 Sqn	1¹/2 V-1
Flt Sgt A. Murkowski PAF	Mustang III FB352	316 (Pol) Sqn	V-1
Flt Sgt H.C. Cramm (Dutch)	Spitfire XIV NH699	322 (Dutch) Sqn	V-1
Flg Off J. Jonker (Dutch)	Spitfire XIV RB160	322 (Dutch) Sqn	V-1
Flg Off F.J.H. van Eijk (Dutch)	Spitfire XIV VL-U	322 (Dutch) Sqn	¹/2 V-1
Plt Off A.A. Homburg (Dutch)	Spitfire XIV VL-Y	322 (Dutch) Sqn	¹/2 V-1
Plt Off R.D. Bremner RNZAF	Tempest V JN801	486 (RNZAF) Sqn	V-1
Flg Off J.R. Cullen RNZAF	Tempest V JN863	486 (RNZAF) Sqn	V-1
Wt Off O.D. Eagleson RNZAF	Tempest V JN873	486 (RNZAF) Sqn	V-1
Plt Off K.A. Smith RNZAF	Tempest V JN801	486 (RNZAF) Sqn	2 V-1
Wt Off C.J. Sheddan RNZAF	Tempest V JN805	486 (RNZAF) Sqn	V-1
Flt Lt J. Berry	Tempest V EJ524	FIU	V-1

Night 3-4/7/44 (11 V-1s destroyed by fighters)

Capt T. Weisteen (Norw)/	Mosquito XIX MM636	85 Sqn	V-1
Flg Off F.G. French (Nav)			
Flt Lt N.S. Head/	Mosquito XIII MM461	96 Sqn	2 V-1
Flg Off A.C. Andrews (Nav)			
Sqn Ldr R.N. Chudleigh/	Mosquito XIII HK376	96 Sqn	3 V-1

Flg Off H.D. Ayliffe (Nav)			
Flt Lt R.D. Doleman/	Mosquito XIX MM643	157 Sqn	2 V-1
Flg Off G. Brooks (Nav)			
Sqn Ldr R. Bannock RCAF/	Mosquito VI HR147	418 (RCAF) Sqn	3 V-1
Flg Off R.R.F. Bruce RCAF (Nav)			
Sqn Ldr K.M. Carver/	Mosquito VI HJ761	605 Sqn	V-1+ probable
Flg Off R. Birrell (Nav)			

4/7/44 (53 V-1s destroyed by fighters)

Flg Off D.H. Davy	Spitfire LFIXb MK846	1 Sqn	V-1
Flt Lt T. Draper Williams	Spitfire LFIXb MK726	1 Sqn	$^1/_2$ V-1
Flg Off D.R. Wallace	Spitfire LFIXb MK986	1 Sqn	$^1/_2$ V-1
Flg Off D.V. McIntosh	Spitfire LFIXb MK644	1 Sqn	$^1/_2$ V-1
Flt Sgt K.C. Weller	Spitfire LFIXb ML258	1 Sqn	$^1/_2$ V-1
Plt Off K.G. Slade-Betts	Tempest V JN817	3 Sqn	$^1/_2$ V-1
Wt Off R.S. Adcock RAAF	Tempest V JN735	3 Sqn	$^1/_2$ V-1
Flt Lt R. van Lierde (Belg)	Tempest V EN525	3 Sqn	4 V-1
Flg Off R.H. Clapperton	Tempest V JN755	3 Sqn	4 V-1
Flt Lt A.R. Moore	Tempest V JN818	3 Sqn	2 V-1
Plt Off S.B. Feldman (US)	Tempest V EJ540	3 Sqn	$1^1/_2$ V-1
Flt Sgt L.G. Everson	Tempest V JN868	3 Sqn	$1^1/_2$ V-1
Wg Cdr R.P. Beamont	Tempest V JN751	150 Wg	V-1
Flg Off M.A.L. Balaase (Belg)	Spitfire XII EN609	41 Sqn	$^1/_2$ V-1
Flt Sgt F.G. Woollard	Spitfire XII MB875	41 Sqn	$^1/_2$ V-1
Flt Sgt H. Shaw	Tempest V JN875	56 Sqn	V-1
Flg Off W.R. MacLaren	Tempest V JN864	56 Sqn	V-1
Sqn Ldr A.R. Hall	Tempest V JN869	56 Sqn	V-1
Sqn Ldr N.E. Hancock	Tempest V EJ536	56 Sqn	V-1
Plt Off J. Harvey	Tempest V EJ547	56 Sqn	V-1
Flt Sgt D.E. Matthews	Tempest V JN864	56 Sqn	$^1/_2$ V-1
Flt Lt A.R. Elcock	Spitfire XIV RB182	91 Sqn	V-1
Flt Lt R.S. Nash	Spitfire XIV RB169	91 Sqn	2 V-1
Flg Off G.H. Huntley	Spitfire XIV RB181	91 Sqn	V-1
Flt Sgt J.A. Brown	Spitfire XIV NH697	91 Sqn	V-1
Flg Off E. Topham	Spitfire XIV RB181	91 Sqn	V-1
Flg Off M.J. Costello RNZAF	Spitfire XIV NH705	91 Sqn	$^1/_2$ V-1
Flg Off D.W.J. Southerst RCAF	Spitfire IX MK854	165 Sqn	$^1/_2$ V-1
Wt Off J.A. Forrest	Spitfire Vb AD185	277 (ASR) Sqn	V-1
Wt Off A. Murkowski PAF	Mustang III FB374	316 (Pol) Sqn	V-1
Flt Sgt A. Pietrzak PAF	Mustang III FB161	316 (Pol) Sqn	V-1
Flg Off K. Cynkier PAF	Mustang III FB384	316 (Pol) Sqn	V-1
Flg Off J. Jonker (Dutch)	Spitfire XIV VL-D	322 (Dutch) Sqn	V-1
Flg Off R.F. Burgwal (Dutch)	Spitfire XIV NH649	322 (Dutch) Sqn	V-1
Flg Off F.W.L.S. Speetjens (Dutch)	Spitfire XIV RB160	322 (Dutch) Sqn	V-1
Flg Off M.H. Mason RNZAF	Tempest V JN805/JN809	486 (RNZAF) Sqn	$1^1/_2$ V-1
Flg Off J.R. Cullen RNZAF	Tempest V JN770	486 (RNZAF) Sqn	V-1
Wt Off O.D. Eagleson RNZAF	Tempest V EJ537	486 (RNZAF) Sqn	V-1
Wt Off W.A. Kalka RNZAF	Tempest V JN809	486 (RNZAF) Sqn	2 V-1
Plt Off F.B. Lawless RNZAF	Tempest V EJ537	486 (RNZAF) Sqn	V-1
Flt Lt H.N. Sweetman RNZAF	Tempest V JN809	486 (RNZAF) Sqn	V-1
Plt Off R.D. Bremner RNZAF	Tempest V JN854	486 (RNZAF) Sqn	V-1
Flt Lt N.J. Powell RNZAF	Tempest V EJ527	486 (RNZAF) Sqn	V-1
Plt Off J.H. Stafford RNZAF	Tempest V JN854	486 (RNZAF) Sqn	2 V-1
Flg Off S.S. Williams RNZAF	Tempest V JN820	486 (RNZAF) Sqn	$^1/_2$ V-1
Plt Off R.J. Danzey RNZAF	Tempest V JN805	486 (RNZAF) Sqn	V-1
Flt Sgt G. Tate	Spitfire XIV DW-	610 Sqn	V-1
Plt Off B.R. Scamen RCAF	Spitfire XIV DW-	610 Sqn	V-1
Sqn Ldr E.G. Daniel	Tempest V EJ531	FIU	V-1

Night 4-5/7/44 (8 V-1s destroyed by fighters)

Flt Lt P.A. Searle/	Mosquito XVII VY-Q	85 Sqn	V-1
Flg Off B.J.P. Simpkins (Nav)			
Flt Lt R.H. Farrell/	Mosquito XVII HK119	85 Sqn	V-1
Flt Sgt R. Chappell (Nav)			
Flt Lt I.A. Dobie/	Mosquito XIII MM495	96 Sqn	V-1
Flt Lt Rawnsley (Nav)			
Sub-Lt(A) W. Lawley-Wakelin RNVR/	Mosquito XIII HK370	96 Sqn	V-1
Sub-Lt(A) Williams RNVR (Nav)			
Flg Off A.W. Sterrenberg RCAF/	Mosquito XIII MM512	409 (RCAF) Sqn	V-1
Flg Off J.P. Clarke RCAF (Nav)			
Flt Lt D.E. Forsyth RCAF (US)/	Mosquito VI TH-	418 (RCAF) Sqn	V-1
Flg Off R.T. Esam RAF (Nav)			

Flg Off R.E. Lelong RNZAF/ Flt Sgt J.A. McLaren (Nav)	Mosquito VI HJ785	605 Sqn	V-1
Flg Off A.J. Craven/ Sgt L.W. Woodward (Nav)	Mosquito VI UP-	605 Sqn	V-1+ probable
Flt Lt R.J. Garner/ Flg Off B.J. Duncan (Nav)	Mosquito VI MM414	605 Sqn	V-1

5/7/44 (42 V-1s destroyed by fighters including 1 by USAAF)

Wg Cdr R.P.R. Powell	Spitfire LFIXb MK846	1 Sqn	1¹/₂ V-1
Flg Off P.E. Crocker	Spitfire LFIXb NH255	1 Sqn	¹/₂ V-1
Flt Lt P.W. Stewart	Spitfire LFIXb NH253	1 Sqn	¹/₂ V-1
Flt Sgt I. Hastings	Spitfire LFIXb MK997	1 Sqn	V-1
Flt Sgt H.J. Bailey RAAF	Tempest V EJ582/JN807	3 Sqn	2 V-1
Flg Off M.F. Edwards	Tempest V EJ525	3 Sqn	3 V-1
Flg Off R. Dryland	Tempest V JN818	3 Sqn	5 V-1
Plt Off H.R. Wingate	Tempest V JN793	3 Sqn	V-1
Flg Off R.P. Harding	Spitfire XII EN602	41 Sqn	V-1
Flt Lt T.H. Hoare RCAF	Tempest V EJ547	56 Sqn	V-1
Flt Lt R.S. Nash	Spitfire XIV RB169	91 Sqn	V-1
Cne J-M. Maridor (FF)	Spitfire XIV NH698/654	91 Sqn	1¹/₂ V-1
Flt Lt A.R. Cruickshank RCAF	Spitfire XIV RM615	91 Sqn	V-1
Flt Lt H.M. Neil	Spitfire XIV RB177	91 Sqn	V-1
Wt Off F.A. Lewis	Spitfire XIV RM620	91 Sqn	V-1
Flg Off T.D. Tinsey	Spitfire IX ML175	165 Sqn	V-1
Wg Cdr A.D. Grace	Spitfire Vb BM122	277 (ASR) Sqn	2 V-1
Flg Off T. Karnkowski PAF	Mustang III FB352/FB384	316 (Pol) Sqn	1¹/₂ V-1
Flt Sgt S. Sztuka PAF	Mustang III FB378	316 (Pol) Sqn	¹/₂ V-1
Flt Lt S. Litak PAF	Mustang III FB376	316 (Pol) Sqn	V-1
Wt Off C. Bartłomiejczyk PAF	Mustang III FB359	316 (Pol) Sqn	2 V-1
Flt Sgt M.J. Janssen (Dutch)	Spitfire XIV VL-D	322 (Dutch) Sqn	1¹/₂ V-1
Flt Lt L.C.M. van Eendenburg (Dutch)	Spitfire XIV RB184	322 (Dutch) Sqn	1¹/₂ V-1
Wg Cdr R.P. Beamont	Tempest V JN751	150 Wg	¹/₂ V-1
Wt Off C.J. Sheddan RNZAF	Tempest V JN854	486 (RNZAF) Sqn	¹/₂ V-1
Wt Off B.J. O'Connor RNZAF	Tempest V JN803	486 (RNZAF) Sqn	V-1
Sqn Ldr R.A. Newbery	Spitfire XIV RB159	610 Sqn	V-1
Wt Off R.C. White	Spitfire XIV DW-	610 Sqn	V-1
Wt Off J.J. Bonfield	Spitfire XIV DW-	610 Sqn	V-1
Flt Lt J. Berry	Tempest V EJ524	FIU	2 V-1
Sqn Ldr E.G. Daniel	Tempest V EJ531	FIU	V-1 (also killed)
1/Lt M.C. Peterson USAAF	P-47 CP-	367thFS USAAF	V-1

Night 5-6/7/44 (26 V-1s destroyed by fighters)

Wt Off W. Alderton/ Flg Off R. Caistor (Nav)	Mosquito XVII HK299	85 Sqn	V-1
Flt Sgt L.J. York/ Flt Sgt T.F. Fry (Nav)	Mosquito XVII MM648	85 Sqn	V-1
Flt Lt F.R.L. Mellersh/ Flt Lt M.J. Stanley (Nav)	Mosquito XIII MM577	96 Sqn	2 V-1
Wg Cdr E.D. Crew/ Sgt B. Jaeger (Nav)	Mosquito XIII MM511	96 Sqn	3 V-1
Sqn Ldr A. Parker-Rees/ Flt Lt G.E. Bennett (Nav)	Mosquito XIII MM497	96 Sqn	2 V-1
Flt Lt D.L. Ward/ Flg Off E.D. Eyles (Nav)	Mosquito XIII HK415	96 Sqn	V-1
Sqn Ldr J.G. Benson/ Flt Lt L. Brandon (Nav)	Mosquito XIX MM630	157 Sqn	V-1
Sqn Ldr J.H.M. Chisholm/ Flt Lt E. Wylde (Nav)	Mosquito XIX MM676	157 Sqn	2 V-1
Lt(A) H. Sandiford RNVR/ Lt(A) H. Thompson RNVR (Nav)	Mosquito XIX MM674	157 Sqn	V-1
Flg Off H.S.Ellis RCAF/ Wt Off W.N. MacNaughton RCAF (Nav)	Mosquito XIII MM491	409 (RCAF) Sqn	2 V-1
Flt Lt C.M. Jasper RCAF (US)/ Flt Lt O.A.J. Martin RCAF (Nav)	Mosquito VI HR358	418 (RCAF) Sqn	V-1
Plt Off M.H. Sims RCAF/ Plt Off J.D. Sharples RCAF (Nav)	Mosquito VI TH-	418 (RCAF) Sqn	V-1
Flt Lt D.E. Forsyth RCAF (US)/ Flg Off R.T. Esam RAF (Nav)	Mosquito TH-	418 (RCAF) Sqn	2 V-1
Flt Lt R.J. Garner/ Flg Off B.J. Duncan (Nav)	Mosquito VI MM414	605 Sqn	V-1
Flt Lt J.G. Musgrave/ Flt Sgt F.W. Samwell (Nav)	Mosquito VI MM429	605 Sqn	2 V-1+ probable

Flg Off J.C. Holder RCAF	Typhoon Ib MN584	137 Sqn	V-1
Flg Off H.T. Nicholls	Typhoon Ib MN134	137 Sqn	2 V-1

6/7/44 (15 V-1s destroyed by fighters including 1 by USAAF)

Sqn Ldr A.S. Dredge	Tempest V JN812	3 Sqn	V-1
Flt Sgt H.J. Bailey RAAF	Tempest V JN807	3 Sqn	V-1
Flg Off R.H. Clapperton	Tempest V JN818	3 Sqn	V-1
Flt Lt A.E. Umbers RNZAF	Tempest V JN817	3 Sqn	V-1
Flt Lt R. van Lierde (Belg)	Tempest V EJ525	3 Sqn	V-1
Flg Off M.F. Edwards	Tempest V EJ582	3 Sqn	V-1
Plt Off H.R. Wingate	Tempest V JN793	3 Sqn	$1^1/_2$V-1
Wg Cdr R.P. Beamont	Tempest V JN751	150 Wg	V-1
Flt Sgt S. Sztuka PAF	Mustang III FB378	316 (Pol) Sqn	V-1
Wt Off B.J. O'Connor RNZAF	Tempest V JN803	486 (RNZAF) Sqn	$1^1/_2$ V-1
Wt Off O.D. Eagleson RNZAF	Tempest V JN873	486 (RNZAF) Sqn	V-1
Wt Off G.J.M. Hooper RNZAF	Tempest V JN805	486 (RNZAF) Sqn	$2^1/_2$ V-1
1/Lt J.H. Payne USAAF	P-47	Unknown unit USAAF	V-1

Night 6-7/7/44 (41 V-1s destroyed by fighters)

Capt T. Weisteen (Norw)/ Flg Off F.G. French (Nav)	Mosquito XIX MM636	85 Sqn	V-1
Flt Lt D.L. Ward/ Flg Off E.D. Eyles (Nav)	Mosquito XIII HK415	96 Sqn	V-1
Flt Lt I.A. Dobie/ Flg Off E.A. Johnson	Mosquito XIII HK438	96 Sqn	V-1
Lt(A) F.W. Richards RNVR/ Lt(A) M.J. Baring RNVR (Nav)	Mosquito XIII HK433	96 Sqn	V-1
Wg Cdr E.D. Crew/ Sgt B. Jaeger (Nav)	Mosquito XIII MM511	96 Sqn	V-1
Sqn Ldr A. Parker-Rees/ Flt Lt G.E. Bennett (Nav)	Mosquito XIII MM497	96 Sqn	V-1
Flt Sgt T. Bryan/ Plt Off B.J. Friis (Nav)	Mosquito XIII MM468	96 Sqn	V-1
Flt Lt F.R.L. Mellersh/ Flt Lt M.J. Stanley (Nav)	Mosquito XIII MM577	96 Sqn	V-1
Flg Off C.N. Woodcock/ Flg Off L. Butt (Nav)	Mosquito XIX MM652	157 Sqn	V-1
Flt Sgt J.C. Woolley/ Flt Sgt E. Barrie (Nav)	Mosquito XIX MM650	157 Sqn	V-1
Sqn Ldr J.G. Benson/ Flt Lt L. Brandon (Nav)	Mosquito XIX MM630	157 Sqn	2 V-1
Flt Lt J.O. Mathews/ Wt Off A. Penrose (Nav)	Mosquito XIX TA392	157 Sqn	V-1
Flt Lt P.S. Leggat RCAF/ Flt Lt F.L. Cochrane RCAF (Nav)	Mosquito VI TH-	418 (RCAF) Sqn	V-1
Flt Lt D.A. MacFadyen RCAF/ Flg Off J.D. Wright RCAF (Nav)	Mosquito VI HR155	418 (RCAF) Sqn	3 V-1
Sqn Ldr R. Bannock RCAF/ Flg Off R.R.F. Bruce (Nav)	Mosquito VI HR147	418 (RCAF) Sqn	4 V-1
Flt Lt C.J. Evans RCAF/ Flg Off S. Humblestone RAF (Nav)	Mosquito VI TH-	418 (RCAF) Sqn	3 V-1
Flg Off S.P. Seid RCAF (US)/ Flg Off D.N. McIntosh RCAF (Nav)	Mosquito VI TH-	418 (RCAF) Sqn	V-1
Flg Off B.G. Bensted/ Sgt C.L. Burrage (Nav)	Mosquito VI HJ799	605 Sqn	V-1
Flt Lt B. Williams/ Wt Off S. Hardy (Nav)	Mosquito VI UP-N	605 Sqn	3 V-1
Flg Off P.R. Rudd/ Flg Off D. Messingham (Nav)	Mosquito VI UP-	605 Sqn	$1^1/_2$ V-1
Wg Cdr G.L. Raphael (Can)	Typhoon Ib MN134	137 Sqn	2 V-1
Flt Lt M. Wood RCAF	Typhoon Ib MN627	137 Sqn	V-1
Flt Sgt L.P. Boucher	Typhoon Ib MN152	137 Sqn	V-1
Flt Lt R.A. Johnstone RCAF	Typhoon Ib MN134	137 Sqn	V-1
Flg Off D.W. Guttridge	Typhoon Ib MN169	137 Sqn	V-1
Flt Lt J. Berry	Tempest V EJ524	FIU	4 V-1
Flt Lt R.A. Jones	Tempest V ZQ-	FIU	V-1

7/7/44 (48 V-1s destroyed by fighters including 1 by USAAF)

Flt Sgt H.J. Vassie	Spitfire LFIXb MK987	1 Sqn	V-1
Flt Lt H.L. Stuart	Spitfire LFIXb NH253	1 Sqn	$^1/_2$ V-1
Flg Off E.N.W. Marsh	Spitfire LFIXb MK986	1 Sqn	V-1
Flt Lt A.R. Moore	Tempest V JN818	3 Sqn	V-1

Flt Lt R. van Lierde (Belg)	Tempest V JN862	3 Sqn	2 V-1
Flg Off R.E. Barckley	Tempest V JN815	3 Sqn	V-1
Flt Sgt H.J. Bailey RAAF	Tempest V JN807	3 Sqn	V-1
Flt Lt A.E. Umbers RNZAF	Tempest V JN868	3 Sqn	V-1
Plt Off H.R. Wingate	Tempest V EN521	3 Sqn	V-1
Flg Off P.B. Graham	Spitfire XII MB856	41 Sqn	$^1/_2$ V-1
Flt Sgt I.T. Stevenson	Spitfire XII EB-	41 Sqn	$^1/_2$ V-1
Flt Lt K.A. Wigglesworth	Tempest V JN877	56 Sqn	$^1/_2$ V-1
Sgt G.H. Wylde	Tempest V JN857	56 Sqn	$^1/_2$ V-1
Flt Lt R.S. Nash	Spitfire XIV RB169	91 Sqn	V-1
Flt Lt A.R. Cruickshank RCAF	Spitfire XIV RB165	91 Sqn	2 V-1
Flt Lt A.R. Elcock	Spitfire XIV RM615	91 Sqn	V-1
Flt Lt W.C. Marshall	Spitfire XIV NH720	91 Sqn	2 V-1
Sqn Ldr N.A. Kynaston	Spitfire XIV RB185	91 Sqn	2 V-1
Flt Lt H.D. Johnson	Spitfire XIV RB183	91 Sqn	V-1
Flt Lt H.M. Neil	Spitfire XIV RB174	91 Sqn	2 V-1
Flg Off P.A. Schade	Spitfire XIV RM620	91 Sqn	V-1
Wt Off F. Marek PAF	Mustang III FB391	316 (Pol) Sqn	V-1
Wt Off W. Grobelny PAF	Mustang III FB396	316 (Pol) Sqn	V-1
Wt Off T. Szymański PAF	Mustang III FB377	316 (Pol) Sqn	V-1
Sgt J. Mielnicki PAF	Mustang III FB386	316 (Pol) Sqn	2 V-1
Flt Lt L. Majewski PAF	Mustang III FB351	316 (Pol) Sqn	$1^1/_2$ V-1
Flt Sgt A. Pietrzak PAF	Mustang III FB161	316 (Pol) Sqn	V-1
Flg Off R.F. Burgwal (Dutch)	Spitfire XIV VL-C	322 (Dutch) Sqn	V-1
Flt Sgt C. Kooij (Dutch)	Spitfire XIV VL-N	322 (Dutch) Sqn	V-1
Flt Sgt G.J.H. Dijkman (Dutch)	Spitfire XIV VL-Y	322 (Dutch) Sqn	V-1
Flg Off M.A. Muller (Dutch)	Spitfire XIV VL-W	322 (Dutch) Sqn	V-1
Wt Off J.A. Maier (Dutch)	Spitfire XIV NH686	322 (Dutch) Sqn	V-1
Flg Off P.A. Cramerus (Dutch)	Spitfire XIV VL-V	322 (Dutch) Sqn	V-1
Flt Lt H.N. Sweetman RNZAF	Tempest V JN801/JN803	486 (RNZAF) Sqn	$1^1/_2$ V-1
Plt Off R.J. Danzey RNZAF	Tempest V JN809	486 (RNZAF) Sqn	$^1/_2$ V-1
Wt Off O.D. Eagleson RNZAF	Tempest V EJ527/JN873	486 (RNZAF) Sqn	2 V-1
Flg Off R.J. Cammock RNZAF	Tempest V JN873	486 (RNZAF) Sqn	V-1
Flg Off J.R. Cullen RNZAF	Tempest V EJ527	486 (RNZAF) Sqn	V-1
Flg Off H.M. Mason RNZAF	Tempest V JN732	486 (RNZAF) Sqn	$^1/_2$ V-1
Flg Off G.M. McKinlay	Spitfire XIV RB142	610 Sqn	2 V-1
Flt Lt J.B. Shepherd	Spitfire XIV DW-	610 Sqn	V-1
Flg Off W.A. Nicholls	Spitfire XIV DW-	610 Sqn	V-1
1/Lt J.H. Payne USAAF	P-47	Unknown unit USAAF	V-1

Night 7-8/7/44 (13 V-1s destroyed by fighters)

Flt Lt R.H. Farrell/	Mosquito XVII VY-O	85 Sqn	V-1
Flt Sgt R. Chappell (Nav)			
Wg Cdr C.M. Miller/	Mosquito XVII HK349	85 Sqn	$^1/_2$ V-1
Flg Off R.O. Symon (Nav)			
Lt E.P. Fossum (Norw)/	Mosquito XVII MM648	85 Sqn	V-1
Capt C. Bjørn (Norw) (Nav)			
Flt Lt E.G.L. Spiller RCAF/	Mosquito XIII MM512	409 (RCAF) Sqn	$^1/_2$ V-1
Flg Off J.E. Donaghue RCAF (Nav)			
Sqn Ldr R. Bannock RCAF/	Mosquito VI HR147	418 (RCAF) Sqn	2 V-1
Flg Off R.R.F. Bruce RCAF (Nav)			
Flt Lt S.H.R. Cotterill RCAF/	Mosquito VI TH-	418 (RCAF) Sqn	V-1
Flt Sgt E.H. McKenna RAF (Nav)			
Flg Off J.J. Harvie RCAF/	Mosquito VI TH-	418 (RCAF) Sqn	V-1
Flg Off P.A. Alexander RAF (Nav)			
Flg Off J.C. Worthington RNZAF/	Mosquito VI UP-	605 Sqn	V-1
Plt Off F.A. Friar RNZAF (Nav)			
Flg Off J.C. Holder RCAF	Typhoon Ib MN627	137 Sqn	2 V-1
Flg Off H.T. Nicholls	Typhoon Ib MN198	137 Sqn	V-1
Sqn Ldr A.D. Wagner	Tempest V EJ581	FIU	V-1
Flt Lt R.A. Jones	Tempest V ZQ-	FIU	V-1

8/7/44 (43 V-1s destroyed by fighters)

Flt Lt A.E. Umbers RNZAF	Tempest V JN817	3 Sqn	$^1/_2$ V-1
Plt Off K.G. Slade-Betts	Tempest V JN822/JN868	3 Sqn	2 V-1
Flt Lt R. van Lierde (Belg)	Tempest V JN861	3 Sqn	V-1
Flt Lt A.R. Moore	Tempest V JN818	3 Sqn	V-1
Flg Off R. Dryland	Tempest V JN822	3 Sqn	V-1
Plt Off S.B. Feldman (US)	Tempest V JN862	3 Sqn	V-1
Flt Sgt P.W. Chattin	Spitfire XII MB837	41 Sqn	V-1
Flt Lt P.B. Graham	Spitfire XII B-	41 Sqn	V-1
Flg Off N.P. Gibbs	Spitfire XII EN227	41 Sqn	V-1

Flt Lt J.G. Mansfield	Tempest V EJ534	56 Sqn	V-1
Flg Off R.A. McPhie RCAF	Spitfire XIV RB182	91 Sqn	$^1/_2$ V-1
Flg Off M.J. Costello RNZAF	Spitfire XIV NH705	91 Sqn	$^1/_2$ V-1
Wg Cdr R.W. Oxspring	Spitfire XIV NH714	91 Sqn	2 V-1
Plt Off J.V. Tynan	Spitfire IX MK738	165 Sqn	V-1
Flt Lt A.C.W. Holland	Spitfire IX MJ580	165 Sqn	2 V-1
Flg Off V. Porich RAAF	Spitfire IX MK480	165 Sqn	V-1
Flt Lt J.K. Porteous RNZAF	Spitfire IX ML418	165 Sqn	V-1
Flg Off O. Smik (Cz)	Spitfire IX EN527	310 (Czech) Sqn	3 V-1
Sqn Ldr M.A. Liškutín (Cz)	Spitfire IX MK670	312 (Czech) Sqn	V-1
Flt Lt A. Cholajda PAF	Mustang III FB384	316 (Pol) Sqn	2 V-1
Flg Off T. Karnkowski PAF	Mustang III FB359	316 (Pol) Sqn	$1^1/_2$ V-1
Flt Lt T. Szymankiewicz PAF	Mustang III FB391	316 (Pol) Sqn	V-1
Flt Sgt A. Murkowski PAF	Mustang III FB351	316 (Pol) Sqn	V-1
Flt Sgt H.C. Cramm (Dutch)	Spitfire XIV VL-T	322 (Dutch) Sqn	V-1
Flg Off R.F. Burgwal (Dutch)	Spitfire XIV NH586	322 (Dutch) Sqn	$4^1/_2$ V-1
Flg Off J. Jonker (Dutch)	Spitfire XIV VL-K	322 (Dutch) Sqn	V-1
Flt Lt L.C.M. van Eendenburg (Dutch)	Spitfire XIV RB184	322 (Dutch) Sqn	V-1
Flg Off J.R. Cullen RNZAF	Tempest V JN770	486 (RNZAF) Sqn	V-1
Flt Lt J.H. McCaw RNZAF	Tempest V JN758	486 (RNZAF) Sqn	4 V-1
Plt Off F.B. Lawless RNZAF	Tempest V JN770	486 (RNZAF) Sqn	2 V-1
Flt Lt H.D. Price	Spitfire XIV DW-	610 Sqn	V-1

Night 8-9/7/44 (15 V-1s destroyed by fighters)

Flt Lt W.J. Gough/	Mosquito XIII HK479	96 Sqn	V-1
Flt Lt C. Matson (Nav)			
Flt Lt N.S. Head/	Mosquito XIII HK462	96 Sqn	V-1
Flg Off A.C. Andrews (Nav)			
Flg Off J. Goode/	Mosquito XIII MM557	96 Sqn	V-1
Flg Off V.A. Robinson (Nav)			
Sqn Ldr R.N. Chudleigh/	Mosquito XIII HK379	96 Sqn	6 V-1
Flg Off H.D. Ayliffe (Nav)			
Wg Cdr W.K. Davison/	Mosquito XIX MM678	157 Sqn	V-1
Flt Lt Austin (Nav)			
Flg Off R.E. Lelong RNZAF/	Mosquito VI HJ785	605 Sqn	V-1
Flt Sgt J.A. McLaren (Nav)			
Flt Lt D.G. Brandreth	Typhoon Ib MN134	137 Sqn	V-1
Flt Lt J. Berry	Tempest V EJ524	FIU	3 V-1

9/7/44 (35 V-1s destroyed by fighters)

Flg Off R.E. Barckley	Tempest V JN817	3 Sqn	2 V-1
Plt Off K.G. Slade-Betts	Tempest V JN817	3 Sqn	V-1
Plt Off H.R. Wingate	Tempest V EJ549	3 Sqn	V-1
Flg Off R.H. Clapperton	Tempest V JN818	3 Sqn	2 V-1
Wg Cdr R.P. Beamont	Tempest V JN751	150 Wg	V-1
Flg Off R.E. Anderson RAAF	Spitfire XII EN228	41 Sqn	$^1/_2$V-1
Wt Off A.S. Appleton	Spitfire XII EN238	41 Sqn	$^1/_2$ V-1
Flt Lt J.H. Ryan RCAF	Tempest V JN864	56 Sqn	$1^1/_2$ V-1
Flg Off L.J. Henderson RAAF	Tempest V EJ547	56 Sqn	$^1/_2$ V-1
Flt Lt K.A. Wigglesworth	Tempest V JN877	56 Sqn	V-1
Flt Lt R.S. Nash	Spitfire XIV RB169	91 Sqn	V-1
Lt H.F. de Bordas (FF)	Spitfire XIV NH720	91 Sqn	V-1
Flg Off K.R. Collier RAAF	Spitfire XIV RB183	91 Sqn	2 V-1
Flt Lt J.W.P. Draper RCAF	Spitfire XIV RM620	91 Sqn	V-1
Flt Lt W.C. Marshall	Spitfire XIV NH701	91 Sqn	V-1
Flt Sgt F. Mares (Cz)	Spitfire IX EN526	310 (Czech) Sqn	V-1
Sgt J. Pipa (Cz)	Spitfire IX NH692	310 (Czech) Sqn	V-1
Sqn Ldr M.A. Liškutín (Cz)	Spitfire IX MK670	312 (Czech) Sqn	$^1/_2$ V-1
Sgt K.J. Stojan (Cz)	Spitfire IX ML145	313 (Czech) Sqn	V-1
Flg Off T. Karnkowski PAF	Mustang III FB351	316 (Pol) Sqn	V-1
Flt Lt T. Szymankiewicz PAF	Mustang III FB391/FB396	316 (Pol) Sqn	2 V-1
Wt Off J. Feruga PAF	Mustang III FB378	316 (Pol) Sqn	V-1
Flt Lt S. Litak PAF	Mustang III FB351	316 (Pol) Sqn	$^1/_2$ V-1
Flt Sgt H.C. Cramm	Spitfire XIV NH699	322 (Dutch) Sqn	2 V-1
Flg Off J.R. Cullen RNZAF	Tempest V JN873	486 (RNZAF) Sqn	$1^1/_4$ V-1
Wt Off G.J.M. Hooper RNZAF	Tempest V JN821	486 (RNZAF) Sqn	2 V-1
Flt Sgt I.F. Håkansson (Swed)	Spitfire XIV RB153	610 Sqn	2 V-1 (also KiA)
Flt Lt J.B. Shepherd	Spitfire XIV DW-	610 Sqn	V-1
Flt Lt J. Berry	Tempest V EJ524	FIU	V-1
Flt Lt R.A. Jones	Tempest V ZQ-	FIU	V-1

Night 9-10/7/44 (15 V-1s destroyed by fighters plus 1 by FAA)

Sqn Ldr W. Hoy/	Mosquito XVII HK244	25 Sqn	V-1

Flt Lt R.W. Dalton (Nav)			
Flg Off G. Wild/	Mosquito XVII HK241	68 Sqn	V-1
Flg Off F.F. Baker (Nav)			
Plt Off M.N. Williams/	Mosquito XVII HK24	68 Sqn	V-1
Flg Off A.G. Waples (Nav)			
Wt Off W.A. McLardy RAAF/	Mosquito XIII HK396	96 Sqn	V-1
Sgt Devine (Nav)			
Flt Lt N.S. Head/	Mosquito XIII HK462	96 Sqn	V-1
Flg Off A.C. Andrews (Nav)			
Flt Lt P.G.K. Williamson/	Mosquito XVII MM690	219 Sqn	2 V-1
Flg Off R.E. Forrest (Nav)			
Wt Off D.J. MacDonald RCAF/	Mosquito XIII MM523	409 (RCAF) Sqn	V-1
Flt Sgt W.D. King (Nav)			
Sqn Ldr J.B. Kerr RCAF/	Mosquito VI HR183	418 (RCAF) Sqn	V-1
Flg Off P. Clarke RCAF (Nav)			
Flt Lt C.M. Jasper RCAF (US)/	Mosquito VI HR358	418 (RCAF) Sqn	V-1
Flt Lt O.A.J. Martin RCAF (Nav)			
Flg Off P.R. Brook RCAF/	Mosquito VI TH-	418 (RCAF) Sqn	V-1
Flg Off A.D. McLaren RCAF (Nav)			
Flt Lt K.A. Roediger RAAF/	Mosquito XVII HK297	456 (RAAF) Sqn	V-1
Flt Lt R.J.H. Dobson RAAF (Nav)			
Flt Lt A. Michie/	Mosquito VI UP-	605 Sqn	V-1
Wt Off J. Tredwen (Nav)			
Flt Lt J.G. Musgrave/	Mosquito VI MM429	605 Sqn	V-1
Flt Sgt F.W. Samwell (Nav)			
Flg Off J.C. Worthington RNZAF/	Mosquito VI UP-	605 Sqn	V-1
Plt Off F.A. Friar RNZAF (Nav)			
Sub-Lt(A) D.P. Davies RNVR/	Avenger I JZ127/Z	854 FAA Sqn	V-1
L/A F. Shirmer RNVR (TAG)			

10/7/44 (21 V-1s destroyed by fighters)

Flt Sgt G. Tate	Spitfire LFIXb MK744	1 Sqn	V-1
Flg Off T. Wyllie	Spitfire LFIXb MK867	1 Sqn	V-1
Flg Off R.E. Barckley	Tempest V JN817	3 Sqn	2 V-1
Flt Lt R. van Lierde (Belg)	Tempest V JN862	3 Sqn	V-1
Flg Off G.A. Whitman RCAF (US)	Tempest V JN760	3 Sqn	$1/2$ V-1
Plt Off S.B. Feldman (US)	Tempest V EJ582	3 Sqn	$1/2$ V-1
Wg Cdr R.P. Beamont	Tempest V JN751	150 Wg	V-1
Flt Sgt H. Shaw	Tempest V EJ532	56 Sqn	V-1
Lt H.F. de Bordas (FF)	Spitfire XIV RB181	91 Sqn	V-1
Flg Off G. Balcombe	Spitfire XIV NH705	91 Sqn	V-1
Sqn Ldr N.A. Kynaston	Spitfire XIV NH714/RB185	91 Sqn	2 V-1
Flt Sgt T.B. Burnett	Spitfire XIV RB181	91 Sqn	V-1
Flg Off E. Topham	Spitfire XIV NH698	91 Sqn	V-1
Flg Off M.J. Costello RNZAF	Spitfire XIV RB161	91 Sqn	V-1
Flt Lt J.P. Bassett	Mustang III FB222	129 Sqn	$1/2$ V-1
Flt Lt K.C. Baker RCAF	Mustang III FB121	129 Sqn	$1/2$ V-1
Flt Sgt S. Rudowski PAF	Mustang III HB871	306 (Pol) Sqn	V-1
Flt Lt J.L. Plesman (Dutch)	Spitfire XIV VL-W	322 (Dutch) Sqn	V-1
Flt Lt L.C.M. van Eendenburg (Dutch)	Spitfire XIV RB184	322 (Dutch) Sqn	V-1
Plt Off B.R. Scamen RCAF	Spitfire XIV DW-	610 Sqn	V-1
Flt Sgt M.P. Harding	Spitfire XIV DW-	610 Sqn	V-1

Night 10-11/7/44 (8 V-1s destroyed by fighters)

Sqn Ldr A. Parker-Rees/	Mosquito XIII MM562	96 Sqn	V-1
Flt Lt G.E. Bennett (Nav)			
Flt Lt D.L. Ward/	Mosquito XIII MM579	96 Sqn	2 V-1
Flg Off E.D. Eyles (Nav)			
Flt Lt R.V. Bray/	Mosquito XIII MM459	96 Sqn	V-1
Flg Off O.D. Morgan (Nav)			
Wg Cdr E.D. Crew/	Mosquito XIII MM511	96 Sqn	V-1
Sgt B. Jaeger (Nav)			
Flt Lt K.G. Rayment/	Mosquito XIII HK514	264 Sqn	V-1
Flg Off H.J. Bone (Nav)			
Flg Off R.E. Lee RCAF/	Mosquito XIII MM547	409 (RCAF) Sqn	V-1 (also FTR)
Flt Sgt J.W. Wales RAF (Nav)			
Flt Lt R.G. Houston RAAF/	Mosquito XVII HK264	456 (RAAF) Sqn	V-1
Flg Off L.C. Engberg RAAF (Nav)			

11/7/44 (36 V-1s destroyed by fighters)

Flt Sgt I. Hastings	Spitfire LFIXb NH466	1 Sqn	$1/2$ V-1
Flt Sgt G. Tate	Spitfire LFIXb NH246	1 Sqn	V-1

Flg Off F.W. Town	Spitfire LFIXb MK726	1 Sqn	V-1
Flt Lt R. van Lierde (Belg)	Tempest V JN862	3 Sqn	2 V-1
Flt Lt A.E. Umbers RNZAF	Tempest V JN817	3 Sqn	V-1
Flt Sgt T.A. McCulloch	Tempest V JN822	3 Sqn	V-1
Plt Off H.R. Wingate	Tempest V EN521	3 Sqn	$^1/_2$ V-1
Flt Sgt D.J. Mackerras RAAF	Tempest V JN868	3 Sqn	$^1/_2$ V-1
Wg Cdr R.P. Beamont	Tempest V JN751	150 Wg	V-1
Flt Lt T.H. Hoare RCAF	Tempest V JN869	56 Sqn	V-1
Sqn Ldr P.McC. Bond	Spitfire XIV RM621	91 Sqn	$^1/_2$ V-1
Flg Off J. Monihan	Spitfire XIV RM620	91 Sqn	$^1/_2$ V-1
Sqn Ldr N.A. Kynaston	Spitfire XIV B185	91 Sqn	2 V-1
Lt H.F. de Bordas (FF)	Spitfire XIV NH720	91 Sqn	V-1
Flt Lt A.R. Cruickshank RCAF	Spitfire XIV RB182	91 Sqn	2 V-1
Flg Off F.H. Holmes	Mustang III FB292	129 Sqn	V-1
Flg Off J.E. Hartley	Mustang III FZ130	129 Sqn	V-1
Flt Lt J.K. Porteous RNZAF	Spitfire IX MK418/SK-G	165 Sqn	V-1
Plt Off A. Scott	Spitfire IX MK831/SK-X	165 Sqn	V-1
Flt Sgt G.S. Cameron	Spitfire IX MK854/SK-H	165 Sqn	$^1/_2$ V-1
Flt Sgt L. Wright	Spitfire IX MK638/SK-B	165 Sqn	$^1/_2$ V-1
Flt Lt J. Siekierski PAF	Mustang III FB241	306 (Pol) Sqn	V-1
Flt Sgt T. Jankowski PAF	Mustang III FZ169	315 (Pol) Sqn	V-1
Plt Off G. Świstuń PAF	Mustang III FX894	315 (Pol) Sqn	V-1
Flg Off B. Nowosielski PAF	Mustang III PK-V	315 (Pol) Sqn	V-1
Flg Off L.M. Meijers (Dutch)	Spitfire XIV VL-H	322 (Dutch) Sqn	V-1
Flg Off M.A. Muller (Dutch)	Spitfire XIV VL-T	322 (Dutch) Sqn	V-1
Flg Off C.R.R. Manders (Dutch)	Spitfire XIV VL-V	322 (Dutch) Sqn	V-1
Flg Off F.J.H. van Eijk (Dutch)	Spitfire XIV VL-U	322 (Dutch) Sqn	V-1
Wt Off J.A. Maier (Dutch)	Spitfire XIV NH686	322 (Dutch) Sqn	V-1
Plt Off B.M. Hall RNZAF	Tempest V JN805	486 (RNZAF) Sqn	$^1/_2$ V-1
Wt Off B.J. O'Connor RNZAF	Tempest V JN767	486 (RNZAF) Sqn	V-1
Plt Off R.J. Danzey RNZAF	Tempest V JN821	486 (RNZAF) Sqn	$^1/_2$ V-1
Flt Lt J.H. McCaw RNZAF	Tempest V EN523	486 (RNZAF) Sqn	V-1
Flg Off R.J. Cammock RNZAF	Tempest V JN803	486 (RNZAF) Sqn	V-1
Flt Lt B.M. Madden RNZAF	Spitfire XIV DW-	610 Sqn	$^1/_2$ V-1
Flg Off A. Cresswell-Turner	Spitfire XIV DW-	610 Sqn	$^1/_2$ V-1
Sqn Ldr R.A. Newbery	Spitfire XIV RB159	610 Sqn	2 V-1
Flt Sgt J.N. Philpott	Spitfire XIV DW-	610 Sqn	V-1

Night 11-12/7/44 (1 V-1 destroyed by fighters)

Flt Sgt G.T. Glossop/	Mosquito XVII HK305	25 Sqn	V-1
Flt Sgt B.W. Christian (Nav)			

12/7/44 (62 V-1s destroyed by fighters including $^1/_2$ by USAAF)

Flt Sgt R.W. Pottinger	Tempest V EJ540	3 Sqn	$^1/_2$ V-1
Flg Off M.F. Edwards	Tempest V EJ582	3 Sqn	$^1/_2$ V-1
Flt Sgt D.J. Mackerras RAAF	Tempest V JN868	3 Sqn	$^1/_2$ V-1
Flg Off R.H. Clapperton	Tempest V JN817	3 Sqn	2 V-1
Flt Sgt R.W. Cole	Tempest V JN822	3 Sqn	$1^1/_2$ V-1
Flt Lt R. van Lierde (Belg)	Tempest V JN862	3 Sqn	$3^1/_2$ V-1
Flt Sgt C.W. Orwin	Tempest V JN735	3 Sqn	V-1
Flt Sgt J.W. Foster	Tempest V EJ582	3 Sqn	2 V-1
Sqn Ldr A.S. Dredge	Tempest V JN812	3 Sqn	V-1
Flt Sgt D.M. Smith	Tempest V JN761	3 Sqn	$^1/_2$ V-1
Plt Off K.G. Slade-Betts	Tempest V JN755	3 Sqn	V-1
Flt Lt A.R. Moore	Tempest V JN818/JN822	3 Sqn	3 V-1
Flt Sgt P.W. Chattin	Spitfire XII EN602	41 Sqn	V-1
Flt Sgt J. Langley	Tempest V EJ543	56 Sqn	$^1/_2$ V-1
Flt Sgt J.A. Bosley	Tempest V JN877	56 Sqn	$^1/_2$ V-1
Flt Lt J.H. Ryan RCAF	Tempest V EJ532	56 Sqn	V-1
Plt Off D.E. Ness RCAF	Tempest V EJ522	56 Sqn	V-1
Sgt G.H. Wylde	Tempest V EJ526	56 Sqn	V-1
Flt Sgt H. Shaw	Tempest V EJ548	56 Sqn	V-1
Flt Lt D.V.G Cotes-Preedy	Tempest V JN864	56 Sqn	$^1/_2$ V-1
Flg Off J.A.Faulkner RCAF	Spitfire XIV RB173	91 Sqn	V-1
Flt Lt J.W.P. Draper RCAF	Spitfire XIV RM621	91 Sqn	V-1
Plt Off E.W. Edwards	Mustang III FZ143	129 Sqn	V-1
Flt Lt R.G. Kleimeyer RNZAF (Aus)	Mustang III FZ172	129 Sqn	V-1
Flg Off F.H. Holmes	Mustang III FB222	129 Sqn	V-1
Flg Off D.F. Ruchwaldy	Mustang III FB112	129 Sqn	2 V-1
Flt Lt K.C. Baker RCAF	Mustang III FB389	129 Sqn	V-1
Wt Off E. Redhead	Mustang III FB292	129 Sqn	$^1/_2$ V-1
Plt Off J.L.W. Bilodeau RCAF	Mustang III FB171	129 Sqn	$^1/_2$ V-1

Flt Sgt W. Nowoczyn PAF	Mustang III FB106	306 (Pol) Sqn	$1/2+1/2$ V-1
Flg Off A. Beyer PAF	Mustang III UZ-Y	306 (Pol) Sqn	$1/2$ V-1
Flt Lt J. Zbrozek PAF	Mustang III FZ128	315 (Pol) Sqn	V-1
Plt Off G. Świstuń PAF	Mustang III FB174	315 (Pol) Sqn	2 V-1
Flt Sgt A. Pietrzak PAF	Mustang III FB378	316 (Pol) Sqn	2 V-1
Wt Off F. Marek PAF	Mustang III FB383	316 (Pol) Sqn	V-1
Sgt J. Mielnicki PAF	Mustang III FB391	316 (Pol) Sqn	2 V-1
Wt Off T. Szymański PAF	Mustang III FB351	316 (Pol) Sqn	2 V-1
Flg Off C.R.R. Manders (Dutch)	Spitfire XIV VL-V	322 (Dutch) Sqn	V-1
Flt Sgt M.J. Janssen (Dutch)	Spitfire XIV VL-E	322 (Dutch) Sqn	2 V-1
Flg Off J. Vlug (Dutch)	Spitfire XIV RB160	322 (Dutch) Sqn	V-1
Flg Off J. Jongbloed (Dutch)	Spitfire XIV NH586	322 (Dutch) Sqn	V-1
Wt Off J.A. Maier (Dutch)	Spitfire XIV RM678	322 (Dutch) Sqn	$1/2$ V-1 (also KiA)
Wt Off O.D. Eagleson RNZAF	Tempest V EN527	486 (RNZAF) Sqn	$1/2$ V-1
Flt Lt J.H. McCaw RNZAF	Tempest V JN770	486 (RNZAF) Sqn	V-1
Flg Off S.S. Williams RNZAF	Tempest V JN821	486 (RNZAF) Sqn	V-1
Wt Off W.A. Kalka RNZAF	Tempest V JN803	486 (RNZAF) Sqn	4 V-1
Flt Sgt J.S. Ferguson RNZAF	Tempest V JN770	486 (RNZAF) Sqn	$1/2$ V-1
Flt Lt E.W. Tanner RNZAF	Tempest V EN528	486 (RNZAF) Sqn	$1/2$ V-1
Flt Sgt J.N. Philpott	Spitfire XIV DW-	610 Sqn	V-1
Flt Lt J.B. Shepherd	Spitfire XIV DW-	610 Sqn	V-1
Flg Off G.M. McKinlay	Spitfire XIV RB142	610 Sqn	V-1 (also KiA)
Flt Sgt M.P. Harding	Spitfire XIV DW-	610 Sqn	V-1
Flt Lt W.M. Lightbourn	Spitfire XIV DW-	610 Sqn	$1/2$ V-1
Flg Off G. Watkin RCAF	Spitfire XIV DW-	610 Sqn	$1/2$ V-1
Unknown US P-51 USAAF	P-51	Unknown unit USAAF	$1/2$ V-1

Night 12-13/7/44
No claims

13/7/44 (18 V-1s destroyed by fighters)

Plt Off K.G. Slade-Betts	Tempest V JN822	3 Sqn	V-1
Flt Lt A.R. Moore	Tempest V JN812	3 Sqn	V-1
Flt Lt R. van Lierde (Belg)	Tempest V JN862	3 Sqn	V-1
Plt Off J.C.J. Payne	Spitfire XII MB804	41 Sqn	V-1
Flg Off W.R. MacLaren	Tempest V JN816	56 Sqn	V-1
Flt Lt R.S. Nash	Spitfire XIV RB169	91 Sqn	V-1
Sqn Ldr N.A. Kynaston	Spitfire XIV RB185	91 Sqn	$1/2$ V-1
Lt H. de Bordas (FF)	Spitfire XIV NH720	91 Sqn	$1/2$ V-1
Flg Off M. Humphries	Mustang III FB137	129 Sqn	V-1
Flg Off A.N. Sames RNZAF	Typhoon Ib MN169	137 Sqn	V-1
Flt Sgt A.F.A. McIntosh RCAF	Spitfire IX MJ221	165 Sqn	V-1
Sqn Ldr B. Arct PAF	Mustang III FB374	316 (Pol) Sqn	V-1
Flt Lt L. Majewski PAF	Mustang III FB383	316 (Pol) Sqn	V-1
Flt Sgt M.J. Janssen (Dutch)	Spitfire XIV RB160	322 (Dutch) Sqn	V-1
Flt Sgt J.H. Harms (Dutch)	Spitfire XIV RB141	322 (Dutch) Sqn	V-1
Flg Off H.M. Mason RNZAF	Tempest V JN732	486 (RNZAF) Sqn	2 V-1
Plt Off W.A.L. Trott RNZAF	Tempest V JN866	486 (RNZAF) Sqn	V-1
Wt Off B.J. O'Connor RNZAF	Tempest V JN866	486 (RNZAF) Sqn	V-1

Night 13-14/7/44 (1 V-1 destroyed by fighters)

Flt Lt K.A. Roediger RAAF/	Mosquito XVII HK297	456 (RAAF) Sqn	V-1
Flt Lt R.J.H. Dobson RAAF (Nav)			

14/7/44 (22 V-1s destroyed by fighters)

Flg Off E.N.W. Marsh	Spitfire LFIXb MK423	1 Sqn	V-1
Flt Lt P.W. Stewart	Spitfire LFIXb NH253	1 Sqn	V-1
Flg Off R.E. Barckley	Tempest V JN755	3 Sqn	$21/2$ V-1
Flt Sgt R.W. Pottinger	Tempest V JN760	3 Sqn	$1/2$ V-1
Flt Sgt D.J. Mackerras RAAF	Tempest V JN768	3 Sqn	V-1
Flt Lt K.F. Thiele RNZAF	Spitfire XII MB856	41 Sqn	V-1
Wt Off V.L.J. Turner RAAF	Tempest V EN534	56 Sqn	V-1
Sqn Ldr N.A. Kynaston	Spitfire XIV RB161	91 Sqn	V-1
Flg Off A.N. Sames RNZAF	Typhoon Ib MN134	137 Sqn	V-1
Flt Sgt C.R. Bundara RAAF	Spitfire IX MJ580	165 Sqn	V-1
Flt Lt J. Zbrozek PAF	Mustang III FZ155	315 (Pol) Sqn	$1/2$ V-1
Flt Sgt R. van Beers (Dutch)	Spitfire XIV VL-H	322 (Dutch) Sqn	V-1
Flt Sgt M.J. Janssen (Dutch)	Spitfire XIV VL-C	322 (Dutch) Sqn	V-1
Flt Lt J.L. Plesman (Dutch)	Spitfire XIV VL-W	322 (Dutch) Sqn	2 V-1
Flt Lt J.H. McCaw RNZAF	Tempest V JN758	486 (RNZAF) Sqn	2 V-1
Wt Off O.D. Eagleson RNZAF	Tempest V EN523	486 (RNZAF) Sqn	V-1
Flg Off S.S. Williams RNZAF	Tempest V JN860	486 (RNZAF) Sqn	V-1
Flg Off H.M. Mason RNZAF	Tempest V JN732	486 (RNZAF) Sqn	$1/2$ V-1

Flg Off J.R. Cullen RNZAF	Tempest V JN770	486 (RNZAF) Sqn	V-1
Wg Cdr C.H. Hartley	Tempest V EJ530	FIU	V-1

Night 14-15/7/44 (5 V-1s destroyed by fighters)

Plt Off J.E.C. Tait RAAF/	Mosquito XVII HK322	25 Sqn	V-1
Plt Off E.P. Latchford (Nav)			
Flt Sgt T. Bryan/	Mosquito XIII MM468	96 Sqn	V-1
Plt Off B.J. Friis (Nav)			
Flt Sgt P.N. Lee/	Mosquito XIII HK479	264 Sqn	V-1
Plt Off R. Thomas (Nav)			
Flg Off W.H. McPhail RCAF/	Mosquito XIII MM555	409 (RCAF) Sqn	V-1
Plt Off P.J. Smith RCAF (Nav)			
Flg Off S.N. May RCAF/	Mosquito VI NS837	418 (RCAF) Sqn	V-1
Plt Off J.D. Ritch RCAF (Nav)			

15/7/44 (7 V-1s destroyed by fighters including 1 by USAAF)

Flt Sgt H.J. Vassie	Spitfire LFIXb MJ422	1 Sqn	V-1
Flt Lt A.E. Umbers RNZAF	Tempest V JN865	3 Sqn	$^1/_2$ V-1
Flt Sgt T.A. McCulloch	Tempest V JN868	3 Sqn	V-1
Flt Lt H.B. Moffett RCAF	Spitfire XIV NH701	91 Sqn	V-1
Plt Off J. Bzowski PAF	Mustang III FB358	306 (Pol) Sqn	$^1/_2$ V-1
Flt Lt J.H. McCaw RNZAF	Tempest V JN860	486 (RNZAF) Sqn	V-1
Wt Off G.J.M. Hooper RNZAF	Tempest V JN803	486 (RNZAF) Sqn	V-1
1/Lt D. M. Raine USAAF	P-47 V5-	412thFS USAAF	V-1

Night 15-16/7/44 (8 V-1s destroyed by fighters including 1 by USAAF)

Flt Lt K.V. Panter/	Mosquito XVII HK237	25 Sqn	V-1
Plt Off A.W. Mogg (Nav)			
Plt Off J.E.C. Tait RAAF/	Mosquito XVII HK322	25 Sqn	2 V-1
Plt Off E.P. Latchford (Nav)			
Flt Lt D.L. Ward/	Mosquito XIII MM524	96 Sqn	V-1
Flg Off E.D. Eyles (Nav)			
Flt Lt I.H. Cosby/	Mosquito XIII HK481	264 Sqn	V-1
Flt Lt E.R. Murphy (Nav)			
Flt Lt R.L. Beverley/	Mosquito XIII HK477	264 Sqn	V-1
Flg Off P.G. Sturley (Nav)			
Flt Sgt P.N. Lee/	Mosquito XIII HK479	264 Sqn	V-1
Plt Off R. Thomas (Nav)			
2/Lt H.E. Ernst USAAF/	P-61 42-5547	422ndNFS USAAF	V-1
Flt Off E.H. Kopsel USAAF (R/O)			

16/7/44 (19 V-1s destroyed by fighters)

Flt Lt T. Draper Williams	Spitfire LFIXb ML423	1 Sqn	V-1
Flt Lt A.E. Umbers RNZAF	Tempest V JN822	3 Sqn	V-1
Flg Off R. Dryland	Tempest V JN·54	3 Sqn	2 V-1
Flt Sgt H.J. Bailey RAAF	Tempest V JN807	3 Sqn	V-1
Plt Off D.P. Fisher	Spitfire XII MB798	41 Sqn	V-1
Flt Lt T.H. Hoare RCAF	Tempest V JN867	56 Sqn	V-1
Flg Off P.A. Schade	Spitfire XIV RM656	91 Sqn	V-1
Flt Lt I.D.S. Strachan RNZAF	Mustang III FX862	129 Sqn	V-1
Plt Off E.W. Edwards	Mustang III FB125	129 Sqn	V-1
Flg Off J.E. Hartley	Mustang III FZ172	129 Sqn	V-1
Flt Lt J.K. Porteous RNZAF	Spitfire IX ML242	165 Sqn	V-1
Plt Off A. Scott	Spitfire IX ML204	165 Sqn	V-1
Flt Sgt J. Zaleński PAF	Mustang III FB393	306 (Pol) Sqn	V-1
Flt Sgt W. Nowoczyn PAF	Mustang III FB106	306 (Pol) Sqn	$^1/_2$ V-1
Plt Off K. Wacnik PAF	Mustang III FZ149	306 (Pol) Sqn	V-1
Flg Off J. Jongbloed (Dutch)	Spitfire XIV NH586	322 (Dutch) Sqn	V-1
Flg Off J. van Arkel (Dutch)	Spitfire XIV VL-V	322 (Dutch) Sqn	V-1
Flt Sgt B.M. Hall RNZAF	Tempest V JN821	486 (RNZAF) Sqn	$^1/_2$ V-1
Plt Off R.J. Danzey RNZAF	Tempest V JN803	486 (RNZAF) Sqn	V-1

Night 16-17/7/44 (3 V-1s destroyed by fighters including 1 by USAAF)

Lt E.P. Fossum (Norw)/	Mosquito XIX MM648	85 Sqn	V-1
Capt C. Bjørn (Norw) (Nav)			
Flg Off J. Goode/	Mosquito XIII MM452	96 Sqn	V-1
Flg Off V.A. Robinson (Nav)			
Capt R. O. Elmore USAAF/	P-61 42-5534	422ndNFS USAAF	V-1
Flt Off L.F. Mapes USAAF (R/O)			

17/7/44
No claims

Night 17-18/7/44 (13 V-1s destroyed by fighters)

Flt Sgt E.R.C. Lelliott/	Mosquito XVII HK256	25 Sqn	2 V-1

Flt Sgt B.R. Netherwood (Nav)			
Flt Lt M.H.C. Phillips/	Mosquito XVII VY-B	85 Sqn	V-1
Flt Lt D.V. Smith (Nav)			
Sqn Ldr A. Parker-Rees/	Mosquito XIII MM511	96 Sqn	2 V-1
Flt Lt G.E. Bennett (Nav)			
Flt Lt D.L. Ward/	Mosquito XIII MM524	96 Sqn	V-1
Flg Off E.D. Eyles (Nav)			
Sqn Ldr J.G. Benson/	Mosquito XIX MM630	157 Sqn	V-1
Flt Lt L. Brandon (Nav)			
Flt Sgt J.C. Woolley	Mosquito XIX MM643	157 Sqn	V-1
Flt Sgt E. Barrie (Nav)			
Sqn Ldr F.J.A. Chase/	Mosquito XIII PS-	264 Sqn	V-1 probable
Flg Off A.F. Watson (Nav)			
Flt Lt H.J. Corre/	Mosquito XIII HK516	264 Sqn	V-1
Flg Off C.A. Bines (Nav)			
Flg Off J. Daber/	Mosquito XIII HK481	264 Sqn	V-1
Flt Sgt J.A. Heathcote (Nav)			
Wg Cdr N.J. Starr/	Mosquito VI UP-	605 Sqn	V-1
Plt Off J. Irvine (Nav)			
Flt Lt J. Berry	Tempest V EJ524	FIU	2 V-1

18/7/44 (17 V-1s destroyed by fighters)

Flg Off D.H. Davy	Spitfire LFIXb ML119	1 Sqn	V-1 probable
Flg Off R. Dryland	Tempest V JN822	3 Sqn	2 V-1
Flt Sgt M.J.A. Rose	Tempest V JN755	3 Sqn	V-1
Flt Lt A.R. Moore	Tempest V JN815	3 Sqn	$^1/_2$ V-1
Flt Sgt H.J. Bailey RAAF	Tempest V JN807	3 Sqn	$^1/_2$ V-1
Flt Sgt H. Shaw	Tempest V EJ548	56 Sqn	$^1/_2$ V-1
Plt Off K. Watts RAAF	Tempest V EJ522	56 Sqn	$^1/_2$ V-1
Flg Off R.A. McPhie RCAF	Spitfire XIV NH705	91 Sqn	V-1
Flt Lt I.A.St.C. Watson	Spitfire IX MK425	165 Sqn	V-1
Flt Lt J.K. Porteous RNZAF	Spitfire IX MK738	165 Sqn	V-1
Flt Sgt L. Wright	Spitfire IX MK401	165 Sqn	V-1
Flt Lt J. Siekierski PAF	Mustang III FB241	306 (Pol) Sqn	V-1
Flt Sgt J. Bargielowski PAF	Mustang III FB371	315 (Pol) Sqn	V-1
Plt Off A. Judek PAF	Mustang III FB362	315 (Pol) Sqn	$^1/_2$ V-1
Flt Lt L.C.M. van Eendenburg (Dutch)	Spitfire XIV RB160	322 (Dutch) Sqn	V-1
Flg Off J. Vlug (Dutch)	Spitfire XIV VL-K	322 (Dutch) Sqn	2 V-1
Sqn Ldr J.H. Iremonger RAF	Tempest V JN763	486 (RNZAF) Sqn	$^1/_2$ V-1
Flg Off J.R. Cullen RNZAF	Tempest V JN770	486 (RNZAF) Sqn	$^1/_2$+$^1/_2$ V-1
Flt Lt H.N. Sweetman RNZAF	Tempest V JN754	486 (RNZAF) Sqn	V-1

Night 18-19/7/44 (9 V-1s destroyed by fighters including 1 by USAAF)

Plt Off M.N. Williams/	Mosquito XVII HK242	68 Sqn	V-1
Flg Off A.G. Waples (Nav)			
Sqn Ldr B.A. Burbridge/	Mosquito XVII HK349	85 Sqn	V-1
Flt Lt F.S. Skelton (Nav)			
Lt(A) F.W. Richards RNVR/	Mosquito XIII MM492	96 Sqn	V-1
Lt(A) M.J. Baring RNVR (Nav)			
Flt Lt F.R.L. Mellersh/	Mosquito XIII MM577	96 Sqn	V-1
Flt Lt M.J. Stanley (Nav)			
Wt Off B. Miller/	Mosquito XIX MM643	157 Sqn	V-1
Flt Sgt R. Crisford (Nav)			
Wt Off A.G. McLeod/	Mosquito XIX MM649	157 Sqn	V-1
Flg Off L. Mulroy (Nav)			
Flt Sgt D.R. Callaghan/	Mosquito XIII MM549	264 Sqn	V-1
Plt Off R. Dauncey (Nav)			
Flt Lt K.A. Roediger RAAF/	Mosquito XVII HK297	456 (RAAF) Sqn	V-1
Flt Lt R.J.H. Dobson RAAF (Nav)			
1/Lt J.W. Anderson USAAF/	P-61 42-5543	422ndNFS USAAF	V-1
Flt Off J.W. Morgan USAAF (R/O)			

19/7/44 (35 V-1s destroyed by fighters)

Wt Off R. Hassall RCAF	Tempest V JN755	3 Sqn	V-1
Plt Off H.R. Wingate	Tempest V JN760	3 Sqn	V-1
Flt Sgt R.W. Cole	Tempest V JN768	3 Sqn	V-1
Flt Lt A.R. Moore	Tempest V JN868	3 Sqn	2 V-1
Flg Off R. Dryland	Tempest V JN822	3 Sqn	V-1
Flg Off R.H. Clapperton	Tempest V JN815	3 Sqn	V-1
Wg Cdr R.P. Beamont	Tempest V JN751	150 Wg	V-1
Flg Off M.A.L. Balaase (Belg)	Spitfire XII MB880	41 Sqn	$^1/_2$ V-1
Plt Off A.S. Miller RAAF	Tempest V EJ578	56 Sqn	V-1

Flt Lt K.A. Wigglesworth	Tempest V JN877	56 Sqn	V-1
Flt Sgt J. Langley	Tempest V EJ522	56 Sqn	$1/2$ V-1
Flt Sgt D.E. Matthews	Tempest V JN856	56 Sqn	$1/2$ V-1
Sqn Ldr N.A. Kynaston	Spitfire XIV RM656	91 Sqn	2 V-1
Wg Cdr R.W. Oxspring	Spitfire XIV NH714	91 Sqn	V-1
Lt H.F. de Bordas (FF)	Spitfire XIV RB165	91 Sqn	V-1
Flt Lt D.F. Ruchwaldy	Mustang III FB395	129 Sqn	V-1
Sqn Ldr P.D. Thompson	Mustang III FB123	129 Sqn	V-1
Flt Lt I.D.S. Strachan RNZAF	Mustang III FX862	129 Sqn	$1/2$ V-1
Wt Off A.J. Foster RAAF	Mustang III SR438	129 Sqn	$1/2$ V-1
Flt Sgt J. Zaworski PAF	Mustang III FB241	306 (Pol) Sqn	$1/2$ V-1
Flt Sgt S. Rudowski PAF	Mustang III FB380	306 (Pol) Sqn	3 V-1
Flt Lt M. Cwynar PAF	Mustang III FZ157	315 (Pol) Sqn	$1/2$ V-1
Sqn Ldr E. Horbaczewski PAF	Mustang III FB382	315 (Pol) Sqn	$1/2+1/2$ V-1
Flt Sgt K. Kijak PAF	Mustang III FZ154	315 (Pol) Sqn	V-1
Flt Sgt T. Jankowski PAF	Mustang III FZ128	315 (Pol) Sqn	$1/2+1/2+1/3$ V-1
Flt Lt H. Pietrzak PAF	Mustang III FB362	315 (Pol) Sqn	$2 1/3$ V-1
Flg Off A. Czerwinski PAF	Mustang III SR440	315 (Pol) Sqn	$1/3$ V-1
Flt Lt L.C.M. van Eendenburg (Dutch)	Spitfire XIV RB184	322 (Dutch) Sqn	V-1
Flg Off G.F.J. Jongbloed (Dutch)	Spitfire XIV VL-E	322 (Dutch) Sqn	$1 1/2$ V-1
Flg Off J. Vlug (Dutch)	Spitfire XIV VL-D	322 (Dutch) Sqn	$1/2$ V-1
Flg Off R.F. Burgwal (Dutch)	Spitfire XIV NH649	322 (Dutch) Sqn	V-1
Flt Lt J.L. Plesman (Dutch)	Spitfire XIV VL-W	322 (Dutch) Sqn	V-1
Flg Off P.A. Cramerus (Dutch)	Spitfire XIV VL-U	322 (Dutch) Sqn	$1/2$ V-1
Flg Off S.S. Williams RNZAF	Tempest V EJ523	486 (RNZAF) Sqn	V-1
Flt Lt J. Berry	Tempest V EJ524	FIU	V-1 (day)

Night 19-20/7/44 (21 V-1s destroyed by fighters)

Flg Off G.T. Gibson RCAF/	Mosquito XVII HK294	68 Sqn	V-1
Sgt B.M. Lack (Nav)			
Flg Off J. Goode/	Mosquito XIII MM452	96 Sqn	V-1
Flg Off V.A. Robinson			
Sqn Ldr P.L. Caldwell/	Mosquito XIII HK462	96 Sqn	V-1
Flg off K.P. Rawlins (Nav)			
Sqn Ldr R.N. Chudleigh/	Mosquito XIII MM459	96 Sqn	V-1
Flg Off H.D. Ayliffe (Nav)			
Sqn Ldr W.P. Green/	Mosquito XIII HK379	96 Sqn	3 V-1
Sqn Ldr Cook (Nav)			
Wt Off A.G. McLeod/	Mosquito XIX MM637	157 Sqn	V-1
Flg Off L. Mulroy (Nav)			
Flt Lt I.H. Cosby/	Mosquito XIII MM610	264 Sqn	V-1
Flt Lt E.R. Murphy (Nav)			
Flg Off P.deL. Brooke/	Mosquito XIII HK506	264 Sqn	3 V-1
Plt Off J. Hutchinson (Nav)			
Flt Lt M.M. Davison/	Mosquito XIII HK519	264 Sqn	V-1
LtCol J.H. Fell RA (Ob)			
Flt Lt R.L. Beverley/	Mosquito XIII HK516	264 Sqn	V-1
Flg Off P.G. Sturley			
Sqn Ldr R. Bannock RCAF/	Mosquito VI HR147	418 (RCAF) Sqn	2 V-1
Flg Off R.R.F. Bruce RCAF (Nav)			
Flt Lt G.C. Wright/	Mosquito VI UP-	605 Sqn	V-1 probable
Flg Off J.G. Insall (Nav)			
Flt Lt J. Berry	Tempest V EJ524	FIU	4 V-1 (night)
Flt Lt R.L.T. Robb	Tempest V EJ598	FIU	V-1

20/7/44 (17 V-1s destroyed by fighters)

Flg Off R.E. Barckley	Tempest V JN817	3 Sqn	V-1
Flt Lt B.C. Mackenzie RAAF	Tempest V JN735	3 Sqn	V-1
Flt Sgt D.J. Mackerras RAAF	Tempest V JN754	3 Sqn	V-1
Flt Sgt I.T. Stevenson	Spitfire XII MB878	41 Sqn	V-1
Flg Off K.R. Collier RAAF	Spitfire XIV RM685	91 Sqn	V-1
Flt Lt J.W.P. Draper RCAF	Spitfire XIV RM686	91 Sqn	V-1
Flt Lt A.R. Cruickshank RCAF	Spitfire XIV NH703	91 Sqn	V-1
Wt Off F.A. Lewis	Spitfire XIV RM686	91 Sqn	V-1
Flt Lt J.K. Porteous RNZAF	Spitfire IX MK425	165 Sqn	V-1
Flt Sgt C.R. Bundara RAAF	Spitfire IX ML139	165 Sqn	V-1
Flt Lt M. Cwynar PAF	Mustang III FZ157	315 (Pol) Sqn	$1/2$ V-1
Flt Sgt T. Berka PAF	Mustang III FZ128	315 (Pol) Sqn	$1/2$ V-1
Sqn Ldr E. Horbaczewski PAF	Mustang III FB382	315 (Pol) Sqn	V-1
Flt Lt J.L. Plesman (Dutch)	Spitfire XIV VL-W	322 (Dutch) Sqn	V-1
Flg Off M.L. van Bergen (Dutch)	Spitfire XIV VL-U	322 (Dutch) Sqn	V-1

Plt Off R.D. Bremner RNZAF	Tempest V JN802	486 (RNZAF) Sqn	$^1/_2$ V-1
Wt Off G.J.M. Hooper RNZAF	Tempest V JN797	486 (RNZAF) Sqn	$^1/_2$ V-1
Flt Off B.F. Miller USAAF	Tempest V ZQ-	FIU	V-1

Night 20-21/7/44 (12 V-1s destroyed by fighters including 1 by USAAF)

Flg Off J. Goode/	Mosquito XIII HK406	96 Sqn	$^1/_2$ V-1
Flg Off V.A. Robinson (Nav)			
Wt Off W.A. McLardy RAAF/	Mosquito XIII MM577	96 Sqn	$^1/_2$ V-1
Sgt Devine (Nav)			
Sqn Ldr W.P. Green/	Mosquito XIII HK417	96 Sqn	V-1
Wt Off A.R. Grimstone (Nav)			
Wg Cdr E.D. Crew/	Mosquito XIII HK479	96 Sqn	2 V-1
Wt Off J.R. Croysdill (Nav)			
Sqn Ldr R.N. Chudleigh/	Mosquito XIII HK379	96 Sqn	2 V-1
Flg Off H.D. Ayliffe (Nav)			
Flt Lt J.C. Trigg/	Mosquito XIII MM455	264 Sqn	V-1
Flt Lt G.E. Smith (Nav)			
Flt Lt J.P. Bentley/	Mosquito XIII HK519	264 Sqn	V-1
Plt Off C.W. Auld (Nav)			
Flg Off J. Daber/	Mosquito XIII HK472	264 Sqn	V-1
Flt Sgt J.A. Heathcote (Nav)			
Flg Off R.G. Pratt RAAF/	Mosquito XVII HK303	456 (RAAF) Sqn	V-1
Flg Off S.D.P. Smith RAAF (Nav)			
Flt Lt C.L. Brooks RAF/	Mosquito XVII HK253	456 (RAAF) Sqn	V-1
Wt Off R.J. Forbes RAF (Nav)			
Capt T. Spelis USAAF/	P-61 42-5540	422ndNFS USAAF	V-1
Flt Off E. Eleftherian USAAF (R/O)			

21/7/44 (11 V-1s destroyed by fighters)

Plt Off K.G. Slade-Betts	Tempest V JN817	3 Sqn	3 V-1
Flt Sgt M.J.A. Rose	Tempest V EJ504	3 Sqn	V-1
Wt Off A.S. Appleton	Spitfire XII EN602	41 Sqn	V-1
Flt Sgt A.C. Drew	Tempest V EJ522	56 Sqn	V-1
Flg Off W.R. MacLaren	Tempest V EJ54	56 Sqn	V-1
Flt Lt A.R. Cruickshank RCAF	Spitfire XIV RM649	91 Sqn	V-1
Flg Off A.R. Elcock	Spitfire XIV RM685	91 Sqn	V-1
Flt Lt J.H. McCaw RNZAF	Tempest V JN758	486 (RNZAF) Sqn	V-1
Flt Lt J. Berry	Tempest V EJ524	FIU	V-1 (day)

Night 21-22/7/44 (2 V-1s destroyed by fighters)

Flt Lt G.C. Wright/	Mosquito VI UP-	605 Sqn	V-1
Flg Off J.G. Insall (Nav)			
Flt Lt T.E. Knight/	Mosquito VI UP-	605 Sqn	V-1
Flg Off A.J. Davey (Nav)			

22/7/44 (60 V-1s destroyed by fighters)

Flg Off J.O. Dalley	Spitfire LFIXb MJ422	1 Sqn	V-1
Flg Off D.H. Davy	Spitfire LFIXb ML117	1 Sqn	$^1/_2$ V-1
Flt Lt A.R. Moore	Tempest V JN817	3 Sqn	4 V-1
Flt Sgt R.W. Cole	Tempest V JN759	3 Sqn	3 V-1
Sqn Ldr A.S. Dredge	Tempest V JN812	3 Sqn	2 V-1
Flt Sgt M.J.A. Rose	Tempest V EJ504	3 Sqn	2 V-1
Flg Off D.J. Butcher	Tempest V JN745	3 Sqn	$^1/_2$ V-1
Flg Off M.F. Edwards	Tempest V JN862	3 Sqn	$^1/_2$ V-1
Plt Off H.R. Wingate	Tempest V EJ521	3 Sqn	V-1
Wg Cdr R.P. Beamont	Tempest V JN751	150 Wg	3 V-1
Flt Lt J.H. Ryan RCAF	Tempest V EJ578	56 Sqn	V-1
Flt Sgt L. Jackson	Tempest V JN869	56 Sqn	V-1
Flg Off W.R. MacLaren	Tempest V EJ547	56 Sqn	$1^1/_2$ V-1
Flt Lt E.M. Sparrow	Tempest V EJ536	56 Sqn	V-1
Flg Off E. Topham	Spitfire XIV NH707	91 Sqn	V-1
Flt Lt R.S. Nash	Spitfire XIV RB169	91 Sqn	V-1
Flg Off J. Monihan	Spitfire XIV RB161	91 Sqn	$^1/_2$ V-1
Flg Off G. Balcombe	Spitfire XIV RB173	91 Sqn	V-1
Wg Cdr E.D. Crew/	Mosquito XIII NS985	96 Sqn	V-1 (day)
Capt Hughes RA (Ob)			
Sgt R. Sandever	Mustang III FB171	129 Sqn	V-1
Flg Off D.C. Parker	Mustang III FB392	129 Sqn	$^1/_2+^1/_2+^1/_2$ V-1
Flg Off A.F. Osborne	Mustang III FX874/FB123	129 Sqn	$^1/_2+^1/_2+^1/_2$ V-1
Flt Sgt W.A. Jeal	Mustang III FB121	129 Sqn	V-1
Wt Off E. Redhead	Mustang III FB389	129 Sqn	V-1
Flg Off F.H. Holmes	Mustang III FB212	129 Sqn	$^1/_2+^1/_2$ V-1
Flt Lt D.F. Ruchwaldy	Mustang III FZ184	129 Sqn	V-1

Flt Lt J.P. Bassett	Mustang III FB222	129 Sqn	$^1/_2$ V-1
Flg Off T.D. Tinsey	Spitfire IX ML175	165 Sqn	V-1
Flt Sgt R.J. Hughes	Spitfire IX MK480	165 Sqn	V-1
Flt Lt J. Siekierski PAF	Mustang III UZ-S	306 (Pol) Sqn	$2+^1/_2+^1/_2$ V-1
Plt Off Z. Kawnik PAF	Mustang III UZ-Y	306 (Pol) Sqn	$^1/_2$ V-1
Flt Sgt S. Rudowski PAF	Mustang III FB206	306 (Pol) Sqn	V-1
Plt Off Z. Kawnik PAF	Mustang III UZ-Y	306 (Pol) Sqn	V-1
Flg Off C. Gierycz PAF	Mustang III UZ-N	306 (Pol) Sqn	2 V-1
Flg Off S. Tronczyński PAF	Mustang III FZ149	306 (Pol) Sqn	V-1
Flt Lt H. Pietrzak PAF	Mustang III FB362	315 (Pol) Sqn	$^1/_2$ V-1
Flt Lt M. Cwynar PAF	Mustang III FZ154	315 (Pol) Sqn	$^1/_2+^1/_2$ V-1
Plt Off A. Judek PAF	Mustang III FB184	315 (Pol) Sqn	$^1/_2$ V-1
Flt Sgt A. Ciundziewicki PAF	Mustang III FB371	315 (Pol) Sqn	$^1/_2+^1/_2$ V-1
Flt Lt K. Stembrowicz PAF	Mustang III FX903	315 (Pol) Sqn	V-1
Flt Sgt K. Siwek PAF	Mustang III FB145	315 (Pol) Sqn	$1^1/_2$ V-1
Flg Off A. Czerwiński PAF	Mustang III FB161	315 (Pol) Sqn	$^1/_2$ V-1
Flt Lt S. Marcisz PAF	Mustang III FB356	316 (Pol) Sqn	$^1/_2$ V-1
Flg Off W. Wojtyga PAF	Mustang III HB839	316 (Pol) Sqn	$^1/_2$ V-1
Flt Sgt Z. Narloch PAF	Mustang III HB824	316 (Pol) Sqn	2 V-1
Flt Sgt T. Jaskólski PAF	Mustang III HB845	316 (Pol) Sqn	V-1
Flt Lt A. Cholajda PAF	Mustang III HB836	316 (Pol) Sqn	V-1
Flg Off G.F.J. Jongbloed (Dutch)	Spitfire XIV VL-E	322 (Dutch) Sqn	V-1
Flg Off R.F. Burgwal (Dutch)	Spitfire XIV VL-C	322 (Dutch) Sqn	2 V-1
Flg Off R.J. Cammock RNZAF	Tempest V JN863	486 (RNZAF) Sqn	V-1
Flg Off J.R. Cullen RNZAF	Tempest V EJ537	486 (RNZAF) Sqn	V-1
Plt Off R.J. Danzey RNZAF	Tempest V JN801	486 (RNZAF) Sqn	V-1
Flg Off J.R. Cullen RNZAF	Tempest V EJ523	486 (RNZAF) Sqn	V-1

Night 22-23/7/44 (6 V-1s destroyed by fighters including 1 by USAAF)

Flg Off V.H. Linthune/	Mosquito XVII HK300	25 Sqn	V-1
Flg Off A.B. Cumbers RNZAF (Nav)			
Flt Lt F.R.L. Mellersh/	Mosquito XIII MM577	96 Sqn	V-1
Wg Cdr R.B. Cawood (Ob)			
Wg Cdr E.D. Crew/	Mosquito XIII NS985	96 Sqn	2 V-1
Capt Hughes RA (Ob)			
Flt Sgt T. Bryan/	Mosquito XIII MM468	96 Sqn	V-1
Sgt B. Jaeger (Nav)			
Maj H. Ross USAAF/	P-61 42-5580	425thNFS USAAF	V-1

23/7/44 (36 V-1s destroyed by fighters)

Flt Sgt H.J. Vassie	Spitfire LFIXb MJ481	1 Sqn	V-1
Flg Off D.H. Davy	Spitfire LFIXb MK986/ML423	1 Sqn	$1^1/_2$ V-1
Flt Lt A.E. Umbers RNZAF	Tempest V JN768	3 Sqn	$1^1/_2$ V-1
Plt Off K.G. Slade-Betts	Tempest V JN755	3 Sqn	$^1/_2$ V-1
Flt Lt R. van Lierde (Belg)	Tempest V JN862	3 Sqn	$^1/_2+^1/_2$ V-1
Flt Sgt H.G Bailey RAAF	Tempest V JN739	3 Sqn	$1^1/_2$ V-1
Flt Sgt T.A. McCulloch	Tempest V JN738	3 Sqn	V-1
Flt Sgt D.J. Mackerras RAAF	Tempest V JN752/JN745	3 Sqn	2 V-1
Flg Off G.A. Whitman RCAF (US)	Tempest V JN735	3 Sqn	$^1/_2$ V-1
Flt Sgt M.J.A. Rose	Tempest V JN745	3 Sqn	V-1
Flt Sgt R.W. Cole	Tempest V JN769	3 Sqn	V-1
Plt Off H.R. Wingate	Tempest V JN739	3 Sqn	$1^1/_2$ V-1
Wt Off R.S. Adcock RAAF	Tempest V JN735	3 Sqn	$^1/_2$ V-1
Flg Off M.A.L. Balaase (Belg)	Spitfire XII MB798	41 Sqn	$^1/_2$ V-1
Plt Off J.C.J. Payne	Spitfire XII MB880	41 Sqn	$^1/_2$ V-1
Wt Off A.S. Appleton	Spitfire XII MB882	41 Sqn	V-1
Plt Off A.S. Miller RAAF	Tempest V EJ544	56 Sqn	$^1/_2$ V-1
Flt Sgt L. Jackson	Tempest V JN869	56 Sqn	$^1/_2$ V-1
Flt Lt R.S. Nash	Spitfire XIV RM652	91 Sqn	V-1
Sqn Ldr P.McC. Bond	Spitfire XIV RRM624	91 Sqn	V-1
Sqn Ldr N.A. Kynaston	Spitfire XIV RRM656	91 Sqn	V-1
Flg Off A.F. Osborne	Mustang III FB212	129 Sqn	V-1
Flg Off M. Twomey	Mustang III FX952	129 Sqn	$1^1/_2$ V-1
Flg Off M. Humphries	Mustang III FB137	129 Sqn	$^1/_2$ V-1
Flg Off K. Marschall PAF	Mustang III HB871	306 (Pol) Sqn	V-1
Plt Off F. Migoś PAF	Mustang III UZ-Q	306 (Pol) Sqn	$^1/_2$ V-1
Flg Off S. Tronczyński PAF	Mustang III HB863	306 (Pol) Sqn	2 V-1
Flt Sgt K. Siwek PAF	Mustang III FX995	315 (Pol) Sqn	$2^1/_2$ V-1
Flt Lt H. Pietrzak PAF	Mustang III FB362	315 (Pol) Sqn	$^1/_2$ V-1
Wt Off P. Syperek PAF	Mustang III FB353/SZ-H	316 (Pol) Sqn	V-1
Flg Off G.F.J. Jongbloed (Dutch)	Spitfire XIV VL-E	322 (Dutch) Sqn	V-1

Flg Off C.R.R. Manders (Dutch)	Spitfire XIV VL-Y	322 (Dutch) Sqn	V-1
Plt Off W.A.L. Trott RNZAF	Tempest V JN758	486 (RNZAF) Sqn	2 V-1
Plt Off B.R. Scamen RCAF	Spitfire XIV DW-	610 Sqn	V-1
Flt Sgt J.M. Philpott	Spitfire XIV DW-	610 Sqn	V-1

Night 23-24/7/44 (16 V-1s destroyed by fighters)

Flt Lt A.B. Harvey/	Mosquito XVII/NT368	68 Sqn	V-1
Flt Lt B.StJ. Wynell-Sutherland (Nav)			
Flg Off J. Chipperfield/	Mosquito XVII VY-W	85 Sqn	V-1
Flt Sgt J. Stockley (Nav)			
Wg Cdr H deC.A. Woodhouse/	Mosquito XVII VY-F	85 Sqn	V-1
Flt Lt W. Weir (Nav)			
Wt Off W.A. McLardy RAAF/	Mosquito XIII MM577	96 Sqn	V-1
Flt Sgt Devine (Nav)			
Flg Off P.deL. Brooke/	Mosquito XIII HK473	264 Sqn	2 V-1
Plt Off J. Hutchinson (Nav)			
Sqn Ldr R. Bannock RCAF/	Mosquito VI HR147	418 (RCAF) Sqn	2 V-1
Flg Off R.R.F. Bruce RCAF (Nav)			
Flt Lt G.C. Wright/	Mosquito VI UP-	605 Sqn	V-1
Flg Off J.G. Insall (Nav)			
Flt Lt J. Berry	Tempest V EJ524	FIU	7 V-1

24/7/44 (12 V-1s destroyed by fighters)

Flg Off F.W. Town	Spitfire LFIXb MK926	1 Sqn	V-1
Plt Off K.R. Foskett	Spitfire LFIXb MK986	1 Sqn	$1/2$ V-1
Flt Lt B.C. Mackenzie RAAF	Tempest V JN735	3 Sqn	V-1
Flg Off M.F. Edwards	Tempest V JN862	3 Sqn	$1 1/2$ V-1
Flg Off J.A. Faulkner RCAF	Spitfire XIV RM654	91 Sqn	V-1
Flg Off R.A. McPhie RCAF	Spitfire XIV RM680	91 Sqn	V-1
Flt Lt R.S. Nash	Spitfire XIV RM624	91 Sqn	V-1
Flg Off A. Beyer PAF	Mustang III FB106	306 (Pol) Sqn	$1/2$ V-1
Plt Off Z. Kawnik PAF	Mustang III FB393	306 (Pol) Sqn	$1/2$ V-1
Flt Lt M. Cwynar PAF	Mustang III FZ157	315 (Pol) Sqn	V-1
Flg Off R.F. Burgwal (Dutch)	Spitfire XIV VL-K	322 (Dutch) Sqn	$1/2$ V-1
Flg Off J. Jonker (Dutch)	Spitfire XIV VL-D	322 (Dutch) Sqn	$1/2$ V-1
Flt Lt L.J. Appleton RNZAF	Tempest V JN863	486 (RNZAF) Sqn	V-1
Flt Lt E.W. Tanner RNZAF	Tempest V JN732	486 (RNZAF) Sqn	$1/2$ V-1
Flg Off J. Waslyk RCAF	Spitfire IX PL263	504 Sqn	V-1

Night 24-25/7/44 (9 V-1s destroyed by fighters)

Wg Cdr C.M. Wight-Boycott/	Mosquito XVII HK357	25 Sqn	V-1
Flt Lt D.M. Reid (Nav)			
Flt Lt F.J. Kemp/	Mosquito XIX MM679	68 Sqn	V-1 (also FTR)
Flg Off J. Farrar (Nav)			
Flg Off J. Goode/	Mosquito XIII MM452	96 Sqn	2 V-1
Flg Off V.A. Robinson (Nav)			
Flg Off R.F. Ball/	Mosquito XIII HK372	96 Sqn	V-1
Flg Off F.G. Saunders (Nav)			
Flt Lt J.O. Mathews/	Mosquito XIX MM671	157 Sqn	2 V-1
Wt Off A. Penrose (Nav)			
Flt Lt A.J. Craven/	Mosquito VI UP-	605 Sqn	V-1
Sgt L.W. Woodward (Nav)			
Flt Lt R.J. Garner/	Mosquito VI MM414	605 Sqn	V-1
Flg Off B.J. Duncan (Nav)			

25/7/44
No claims

Night 25-26/7/44 (19 V-1s destroyed by fighters)

Wt Off R.G.B. Pickles/	Mosquito XVII HK301	25 Sqn	V-1
Wt Off L.E. Ashton (Nav)			
Capt T. Weisteen (Norw)/	Mosquito XIX MM636	85 Sqn	2 V-1
Flg Off F.G. French (Nav)			
Flt Lt R.T. Goucher/	Mosquito XIX TA400	85 Sqn	V-1
Flt Lt C.H. Bulloch (Nav)			
Flt Sgt T. Bryan/	Mosquito XIII MM468	96 Sqn	V-1 (also FTR)
Sgt B. Jaeger (Nav)			
Flt Lt F.R.L. Mellersh/	Mosquito XIII MM577	96 Sqn	2 V-1
Flt Lt M.J. Stanley (Nav)			
Flt Lt K. Kennedy/	Mosquito XIII HK425	96 Sqn	V-1
Flg Off O.D. Morgan (Nav)			
Flg Off J.D. Black/	Mosquito XIII MM492	96 Sqn	V-1
Flt Sgt L.W. Fox (Nav)			
Flt Lt D.L. Ward/	Mosquito XIII MM524	96 Sqn	V-1

Flg Off E.D. Eyles (Nav)			
Flt Lt J.W. Caddie/	Mosquito XIX MM681	157 Sqn	V-1 (also FTR)
Flg Off G. Larcey (Nav)			
Flg Off J.S. Hill RCAF/	Mosquito VI TH-	418 (RCAF) Sqn	V-1
Flt Sgt G.W. Roach RCAF (Nav)			
Flt Lt R.J. Garner/	Mosquito VI MM414	605 Sqn	V-1
Flg Off B.J. Duncan (Nav)			
Flt Lt J.G. Musgrave/	Mosquito VI MM429	605 Sqn	V-1
Flt Sgt F.W. Samwell (Nav)			
Flt Lt J. Berry	Tempest V EJ524	FIU	4 V-1
Flt Lt R.L.T. Robb	Tempest V ZQ-Y	FIU	V-1

26/7/44 (53 V-1s destroyed by fighters)

Flt Lt I.P. Maskell	Spitfire LFIXb NH466	1 Sqn	V-1
Flg Off D.H. Davy	Spitfire LFIXb ML117	1 Sqn	1^1/$_2$ V-1
Flt Sgt G. Tate	Spitfire LFIXb MK987	1 Sqn	^{1}/$_2$ V-1
Flt Sgt D.J. Mackerras RAAF	Tempest V JN768	3 Sqn	2 V-1
Flg Off G.A. Whitman RCAF (US)	Tempest V EJ504	3 Sqn	^{1}/$_2$ V-1
Flt Lt A.R. Moore	Tempest V JN865	3 Sqn	V-1
Flt Lt R. van Lierde (Belg)	Tempest V JN862	3 Sqn	2^1/$_2$ V-1
Flg Off M.F. Edwards	Tempest V JN521	3 Sqn	^{1}/$_2$ V-1
Flg Off R. Dryland	Tempest V JN865	3 Sqn	^{1}/$_2$ V-1
Wg Cdr R.P. Beamont	Tempest V JF-M	150 Wg	^{1}/$_2$ V-1
Flg Off M.A.L. Balasse (Belg)	Spitfire XII EN609	41 Sqn	V-1
Flg Off E.B. Gray	Spitfire XII EN605	41 Sqn	V-1
Sqn Ldr A.R. Hall	Tempest V EJ541	56 Sqn	V-1
Flt Sgt A.C. Drew	Tempest V JN869	56 Sqn	2 V-1
Flt Lt H.D. Johnson	Spitfire XIV RM624	91 Sqn	V-1
Flt Lt A.R. Cruickshank RCAF	Spitfire XIV RM649	91 Sqn	V-1
Flt Lt E.G.A. Seghers (Belg)	Spitfire XIV RM743	91 Sqn	V-1 (also KiA)
Sqn Ldr N.A. Kynaston	Spitfire XIV RM656	91 Sqn	V-1
Flg Off G.H. Huntley	Spitfire XIV RM653	91 Sqn	^{1}/$_2$ V-1
Flg Off J.E. Hartley	Mustang III HB862	129 Sqn	V-1
Flg Off M. Humphries	Mustang III FB137	129 Sqn	V-1
Flt Lt K.C. Baker RCAF	Mustang III FB395	129 Sqn	^{1}/$_2$ V-1
Flg Off J.C. Holder RCAF	Typhoon Ib MN134	137 Sqn	V-1
Flg Off C.M. Lawson RAAF	Spitfire IX ML175	165 Sqn	V-1
Plt Off A. Scott	Spitfire IX MK514	165 Sqn	V-1
Flt Sgt P.T. Humphrey RNZAF	Spitfire IX	165 Sqn	^{1}/$_2$ V-1
Flt Sgt G.S. Cameron	Spitfire IX NH401	165 Sqn	^{1}/$_2$ V-1
Flt Lt A. Beyer PAF	Mustang III FB106	306 (Pol) Sqn	^{1}/$_2$ V-1
Flt Sgt J. Zaleński PAF	Mustang III FB241	306 (Pol) Sqn	2_ V-1
Sqn Ldr P. Niemiec PAF	Mustang III UZ-X	306 (Pol) Sqn	^{1}/$_2$ V-1
Flt Sgt J. Czeżowski PAF	Mustang III HB863	306 (Pol) Sqn	^{1}/$_2$ V-1
Wt Off T. Jankowski PAF	Mustang III FB188	315 (Pol) Sqn	1^1/$_2$ V-1
Wt Off T. Słoń PAF	Mustang III FB174	315 (Pol) Sqn	1^1/$_2$ V-1
Flg Off T. Haczkiewicz PAF	Mustang III FZ157	315 (Pol) Sqn	^{1}/$_2$ V-1
Flt Sgt S. Bedkowski PAF	Mustang III FB371	315 (Pol) Sqn	V-1
Wt Off A. Murkowski PAF	Mustang III FB381	316 (Pol) Sqn	V-1
Wt Off W. Grobelny PAF	Mustang III FB385	316 (Pol) Sqn	V-1
Flt Lt K. Zielonka PAF	Mustang III FB353	316 (Pol) Sqn	V-1
Flt Lt A. Cholajda PAF	Mustang III FB384	316 (Pol) Sqn	2 V-1
Flg Off J. van Arkel (Dutch)	Spitfire XIV VL-W	322 (Dutch) Sqn	V-1
Flt Sgt C. Kooij (Dutch)	Spitfire XIV VL-S	322 (Dutch) Sqn	V-1
Flg Off R.F. Burgwal (Dutch)	Spitfire XIV NH649	322 (Dutch) Sqn	1^1/$_2$+^{1}/$_2$ V-1
Plt Off R.D. Bremner RNZAF	Tempest V JN803	486 (RNZAF) Sqn	V-1
Flg Off W.A. Hart RNZAF	Tempest V JN732	486 (RNZAF) Sqn	V-1
Flt Lt J.H. McCaw RNZAF	Tempest V JN770	486 (RNZAF) Sqn	V-1
Flg Off R.J. Cammock RNZAF	Tempest V EJ523/JN770	486 (RNZAF) Sqn	2 V-1
Plt Off K.A. Smith RNZAF	Tempest V JN803	486 (RNZAF) Sqn	V-1
Flt Lt V.St.C. Cooke RNZAF	Tempest V JN763	486 (RNZAF) Sqn	V-1
Flg Off J.R. Cullen RNZAF	Tempest V JN770	486 (RNZAF) Sqn	^{1}/$_2$ V-1
Plt Off J.H. Stafford RNZAF	Tempest V JN803	486 (RNZAF) Sqn	V-1
Flt Sgt T.F. Higgs	Spitfire XIV DW-	610 Sqn	V-1

Night 26-27/7/44 (8 V-1s destroyed by fighters)

Sqn Ldr M.J. Mansfeld (Cz)/	Mosquito XVII MM683	68 Sqn	V-1
Flt Lt S.A. Janáček (Cz) (Nav)			
Flg Off E.R. Hedgecoe/	Mosquito XVII HK120	85 Sqn	V-1
Flg Off N.L. Bamford (Nav)			
Flt Lt D.L. Ward/	Mosquito XIII MM524	96 Sqn	V-1
Flg Off E.D. Eyles (Nav)			

Flt Lt F.R.L. Mellersh/ Flt Lt M.J. Stanley (Nav)	Mosquito XIII MM577	96 Sqn	2 V-1
Flt Lt I.A. Dobie/ Flg Off E.A. Johnson (Nav)	Mosquito XIII HK437	96 Sqn	V-1
Flt Lt C.J. Evans RCAF Flg Off S. Humblestone RAF (Nav)	Mosquito VI TH-	418 (RCAF) Sqn	V-1
Sqn Ldr R. Bannock RCAF Flg Off R.R.F. Bruce RCAF (Nav)	Mosquito VI HR147	418 (RCAF) Sqn	V-1
2/Lt L.A. Gordon USAAF/ 2/Lt C.H. Morrison USAAF (R/O)	P-61 42-5591	422ndNFS USAAF	V-1 possible

27/7/44 (29 V-1s destroyed by fighters)

Flg Off R.H. Clapperton	Tempest V JN815/EJ540	3 Sqn	2 V-1
Flt Lt R. van Lierde (Belg)	Tempest V JN862	3 Sqn	5 V-1
Wg Cdr R.P. Beamont	Tempest V JN751	150 Wg	2 V-1
Flt Sgt C.S. Robertson RAAF	Spitfire XII EN602	41 Sqn	V-1
Flt Lt R.K. Dean	Tempest V EJ545	56 Sqn	2 V-1
Sqn Ldr N.A. Kynaston	Spitfire XIV RM684	91 Sqn	2 V-1
Flt Lt A.C. Leigh	Mustang III FB364	129 Sqn	V-1
Flg Off T.D. Tinsey	Spitfire IX MK514	165 Sqn	V-1
Flt Sgt G.S. Cameron	Spitfire IX ML139	165 Sqn	1/2 V-1
Flt Lt B.J. Murch	Spitfire IX NH401	165 Sqn	1/2 V-1
Flg Off G.P. Armstrong RAAF	Spitfire IX MJ221	165 Sqn	1/2 V-1
Flt Sgt J. Pomietlarz PAF	Mustang III FB358	306 (Pol) Sqn	V-1
Plt Off J. Smigielski PAF	Mustang III UZ-I	306 (Pol) Sqn	1 1/2 V-1
Flt Sgt S. Rudowski PAF	Mustang III FB380	306 (Pol) Sqn	1 1/2 V-1
Flt Lt F. Wiza PAF	Mustang III FX995	315 (Pol) Sqn	V-1
Wt Off T. Jankowski PAF	Mustang III FZ143	315 (Pol) Sqn	1/2 V-1
Flg Off W.A. Hart RNZAF	Tempest V JN754	486 (RNZAF) Sqn	1/2 V-1
Plt Off R.D. Bremner RNZAF	Tempest V JN803	486 (RNZAF) Sqn	1/2 V-1
Plt Off W.A.L. Trott RNZAF	Tempest V JN763	486 (RNZAF) Sqn	V-1
Flg Off R.J. Cammock RNZAF	Tempest V EJ523	486 (RNZAF) Sqn	2 V-1
Flt Lt J.H. McCaw RNZAF	Tempest V JN770/EJ523	486 (RNZAF) Sqn	2 V-1
Wt Off O.D. Eagleson RNZAF	Tempest V EJ586	486 (RNZAF) Sqn	V-1
Wt Off B.J. O'Connor RNZAF	Tempest V JN801	486 (RNZAF) Sqn	V-1

Night 27-28/7/44 (10 V-1s destroyed by fighters)

Flt Lt R.J. Lilwall/ Flg Off D.A. Norris (Nav)	Mosquito XVII HK305	25 Sqn	V-1
Flg Off K.V. Panter/ Plt Off A.W. Mogg (Nav)	Mosquito XVII HK237	25 Sqn	2 V-1
Flt Lt R.H. Farrell/ Flt Sgt Checkley (Nav)	Mosquito XVII HK119	85 Sqn	V-1
Sqn Ldr P.L. Caldwell/ Flg Off K.P. Rawlins (Nav)	Mosquito XIII MM461	96 Sqn	V-1
Sqn Ldr R. Bannock RCAF/ Flg Off R.R.F. Bruce RCAF (Nav)	Mosquito VI HR147	418 (RCAF) Sqn	V-1
Flt Lt R.B. Cowper RAAF/ Flt Lt W. Watson RAAF (Nav)	Mosquito XVII HK356	456 (RAAF) Sqn	V-1
Flg Off F.S. Stevens RAAF/ Wt Off W.A.H. Kellett RAAF (Nav)	Mosquito XVII HK290	456 (RAAF) Sqn	2 V-1
Flt Lt D.G. Brandreth	Typhoon Ib MN198	137 Sqn	V-1
Wg Cdr R.P. Beamont	Tempest V JN751	150 Wg	V-1

28/7/44 (25 V-1s destroyed by fighters)

Flg Off J.O. Dalley	Spitfire LFIXb MK987	1 Sqn	V-1
Flg Off F.W. Town	Spitfire LFIXb MK919	1 Sqn	1 1/2 V-1
Flt Lt R. van Lierde (Belg)	Tempest V JN802/JN822	3 Sqn	1 1/2 V-1
Flt Sgt D.J. Mackerras RAAF	Tempest V JN822	3 Sqn	1/2 V-1
Flt Sgt H.J. Bailey RAAF	Tempest V JN807	3 Sqn	V-1
Flt Sgt H. Shaw	Tempest V JN857	56 Sqn	V-1
Plt Off D.E. Ness RCAF	Tempest V EJ536	56 Sqn	1/2 V-1
Flt Lt E.M. Sparrow	Tempest V JN857	56 Sqn	V-1
Flt Lt H.D. Johnson	Spitfire XIV RM684	91 Sqn	V-1
Flt Lt R.S. Nash	Spitfire XIV RM735	91 Sqn	V-1
Sqn Ldr N.A. Kynaston	Spitfire XIV RM687	91 Sqn	V-1
Flg Off J. Monihan	Spitfire XIV RM651	91 Sqn	V-1
Flg Off G.R. Dickson RNZAF	Mustang III FX924	129 Sqn	1/2 V-1
Flg Off D.C. Parker	Mustang III FZ178	129 Sqn	1 1/2 V-1
Flg Off S.R. Chambers	Spitfire IX ML139	165 Sqn	V-1
Plt Off J. Smigielski PAF	Mustang III UZ-I	306 (Pol) Sqn	V-1
Flt Sgt J. Zaleński PAF	Mustang III FB241	306 (Pol) Sqn	V-1

Flt Lt H. Pietrzak PAF	Mustang III FB188	315 (Pol) Sqn	V-1
Flt Sgt M.J. Janssen (Dutch)	Spitfire XIV VL-D	322 (Dutch) Sqn	¹/₂ V-1
Maj K.C. Kuhlmann SAAF	Spitfire XIV NH586	322 (Dutch) Sqn	V-1
Flg Off J.F. Moreau (Belg)	Spitfire IX NH464	349 (Belgian) Sqn	V-1
Plt Off F.B. Lawless RNZAF	Tempest V JN770	486 (RNZAF) Sqn	2 V-1
Plt Off B.R. Scamen RCAF	Spitfire XIV DW-	610 Sqn	V-1
Flt Lt R.L.T. Robb	Tempest V EJ598	FIU	2 V-1

Night 28-29/7/44 (9 V-1s destroyed by fighters plus 1 by RAF bomber)

Flt Lt J. Lomas/	Mosquito XVII HK244	25 Sqn	V-1
Flt Lt N.B. Fleet (Nav)			
Sqn Ldr W.P. Green/	Mosquito XIII MM495	96 Sqn	V-1
Wt Off A.R. Grimstone (Nav)			
Wg Cdr E.D. Crew/	Mosquito XIII NS985	96 Sqn	V-1
Sqn Ldr Smith (Nav)			
Flg Off R.F. Ball/	Mosquito XIII HK372	96 Sqn	V-1
Flg Off F.G. Saunders (Nav)			
Flt Lt E.J. Stevens/	Mosquito XIX MM674	157 Sqn	¹/₂ V-1
Flg Off L. Butt (Nav)			
Flg Off B.G. Bensted/	Mosquito VI HJ799	605 Sqn	3 V-1
Flt Sgt C.R. Couchman (Nav)			
Flt Lt J.R. Rhodes/	Mosquito VIHJ809	605 Sqn	V-1
Flt Sgt J.H. Little (Nav)			
Wg Cdr R.P. Beamont	Tempest V JN751	150 Wg	2 V-1
Flt Lt J. Berry	Tempest V EJ524	FIU	¹/₂ V-1
Sgt J. Marriott (R/G)	Lancaster PB286	207 Sqn	V-1

29/7/44 (19 V-1s destroyed by fighters)

Flt Lt A.R. Moore	Tempest V JN818	3 Sqn	V-1
Flt Sgt R.W. Cole	Tempest V JN768	3 Sqn	V-1
Flg Off M.A.L. Balaase (Belg)	Spitfire XII EN609	41 Sqn	2 V-1
Flg Off R.A. McPhie RCAF	Spitfire XIV RM743	91 Sqn	V-1
Flg Off E. Topham	Spitfire XIV RM743	91 Sqn	V-1
Flg Off K.R. Collier RAAF	Spitfire XIV RM685	91 Sqn	V-1
Flt Lt H.B. Moffett RCAF	Spitfire XIV RM726	91 Sqn	V-1
Flg Off J.A. Faulkner RCAF	Spitfire XIV RM688	91 Sqn	V-1
Flg Off L.G. Lunn	Mustang III FX958	129 Sqn	V-1
Wt Off R.L. Thomas RAAF	Mustang III FB361	129 Sqn	V-1
Flt Sgt A.F.A. McIntosh RCAF	Spitfire IX ML204	165 Sqn	¹/₂ V-1
Flt Sgt J. Zaleński PAF	Mustang III FB393	306 (Pol) Sqn	V-1
Plt Off G. Świstuń PAF	Mustang III FZ152	315 (Pol) Sqn	¹/₂ V-1
Sqn Ldr E. Horbaczewski PAF	Mustang III FB382	315 (Pol) Sqn	2 V-1
Flg Off M.L. van Bergen (Dutch)	Spitfire XIV VL-T	322 (Dutch) Sqn	V-1
Flg Off L.D. Wolters (Dutch)	Spitfire XIV VL-N	322 (Dutch) Sqn	¹/₂ V-1
Flt Lt J.B. Shepherd	Spitfire XIV DW-	610 Sqn	V-1
Flt Lt J. Berry	Tempest V EJ524	FIU	2 V-1 (day)

Night 29-30/7/44 (5 V-1s destroyed by fighters)

Flg Off J. Adam (Cz)/	Mosquito XVII WM-A	68 Sqn	V-1
Sgt F. Gemrod (Cz) (Nav)			
Flt Lt I.A. Dobie/	Mosquito XIII HK437	96 Sqn	V-1
Flg Off E.A. Johnson (Nav)			
Flt Lt F.R.L. Mellersh/	Mosquito XIII MM577	96 Sqn	V-1
Flt Lt M.J. Stanley (Nav)			
Flt Sgt A.R. Cooper/	Mosquito XVII HK245	125 Sqn	V-1
Flt Sgt P.J. O'Malley (Nav)			
Flg Off P.R. Brook RCAF/	Mosquito VI TH-	418 (RCAF) Sqn	V-1
Flg Off A.D. McLaren RCAF (Nav)			

30/7/44 (9 V-1s destroyed by fighters)

Flg Off R. Dryland	Tempest V JN815	3 Sqn	V-1
Flt Sgt M.J.A. Rose	Tempest V JN818	3 Sqn	V-1
Flt Sgt R.W. Pottinger	Tempest V JN761	3 Sqn	¹/₂ V-1
Plt Off D.E. Ness RCAF	Tempest V EJ534	56 Sqn	V-1
Sqn Ldr P.McC. Bond	Spitfire XIV RM652	91 Sqn	¹/₂ V-1
Flt Lt H.B. Moffett RCAF	Spitfire XIV RM682	91 Sqn	V-1
Flg Off A.F. Osborne	Mustang III FB212	129 Sqn	V-1
Flt Sgt J. Czeżowski PAF	Mustang III FB347	306 (Pol) Sqn	¹/₂ V-1
Flt Sgt J. Zaleński PAF	Mustang III FB241	306 (Pol) Sqn	¹/₂ V-1
Wt Off W. Grobelny PAF	Mustang III FB383	316 (Pol) Sqn	V-1
Flg Off R.F. Burgwal (Dutch)	Spitfire XIV VL-C	322 (Dutch) Sqn	¹/₂ V-1
Flt Lt J.H. McCaw RNZAF	Tempest V EJ523	486 (RNZAF) Sqn	V-1

Night 30-31/7/44 (11 V-1s destroyed by fighters)

Wg Cdr E.D. Crew/	Mosquito XIII NS985	96 Sqn	2 V-1
Wt Off J.R. Croysdill (Nav)			
Flt Lt F.R.L. Mellersh/	Mosquito XIII MM577	96 Sqn	V-1
Flt Lt M.J. Stanley (Nav)			
Flt Lt P.S. Leggat RCAF/	Mosquito VI TH-	418 (RCAF) Sqn	2 V-1
Flt Lt F.L. Cochrane RCAF (Nav)			
Flg Off S.K. Woolley RCAF/	Mosquito VI PZ342	418 (RCAF) Sqn	V-1
Flg Off W.A. Hastie RCAF (Nav)			
Flt Lt W.R.V. Lewis RAAF/	Mosquito XVII HK317	456 (RAAF) Sqn	V-1
Flg Off R.S. Wilmott RAAF (Nav)			
Flt Lt J.G. Musgrave/	Mosquito VI MM429	605 Sqn	2 V-1
Flt Sgt F.W. Samwell (Nav)			
Flt Lt R.C. Walton RNZAF/	Mosquito VI UP-	605 Sqn	V-1
Sgt F. Pritchard RNZAF (Nav)			
Flg Off N.J.M. Manfred RNZAF	Typhoon Ib MN169	137 Sqn	V-1

31/7/44 (7 V-1s destroyed by fighters)

Flt Lt A.R. Moore	Tempest V JN865	3 Sqn	V-1
Flg Off L.G. Lunn	Mustang III FX958	129 Sqn	V-1
Flt Lt R.G. Kleimeyer RNZAF (Aus)	Mustang III FB361	129 Sqn	V-1
Flt Sgt S. Rudowski PAF	Mustang III FB380	306 (Pol) Sqn	V-1
Flg Off T. Gora PAF	Mustang III FB161	316 (Pol) Sqn	V-1
Wt Off P. Syperek PAF	Mustang III HB821	316 (Pol) Sqn	$^1/_2$ V-1
Wt Off K. Kobusiński PAF	Mustang III FB391	316 (Pol) Sqn	$^1/_2$ V-1
Flg Off P.M. Bangerter	Spitfire XIV MN685	610 Sqn	V-1

1/8/44 (1 V-1 destroyed by fighters)

Flt Lt F. Wiza PAF	Mustang III FX995	315 (Pol) Sqn	V-1

Night 1-2/8/44 (1 V-1 destroyed by fighters)

Wt Off W.A. McLardy RAAF/	Mosquito XIII HK479	96 Sqn	V-1
Flt Sgt Devine (Nav)			

2/8/44 (6 V-1s destroyed by fighters)

Flt Sgt H.J. Bailey RAAF	Tempest V JN807	3 Sqn	2 V-1
Flt Lt R.S. Nash	Spitfire XIV RM735	91 Sqn	$1^1/_2$ V-1
Sqn Ldr P.McC. Bond	Spitfire XIV RM687	91 Sqn	V-1
Wt Off E. Redhead	Mustang III FB364	129 Sqn	V-1
Flt Sgt R.L. van Beers	Spitfire XIV VL-C	322 (Dutch) Sqn	$^1/_2$+$^1/_2$ V-1

Night 2-3/8/44 (2 V-1s destroyed by fighters)

Lt(A) F.W. Richards RNVR/	Mosquito XIII MM559	96 Sqn	2 V-1
Lt (A) M.J. Baring RNVR (Nav)			

3/8/44 (36 V-1s destroyed by fighters)

Flg Off D.R. Wallace	Spitfire LFIXb MK919	1 Sqn	V-1
Flg Off R.H. Clapperton	Tempest V JN755	3 Sqn	2 V-1
Flt Sgt R.W. Pottinger	Tempest V JN760	3 Sqn	V-1
Flt Lt R. van Lierde (Belg)	Tempest V JN862	3 Sqn	2 V-1
Flt Lt A.E. Umbers RNZAF	Tempest V JN817	3 Sqn	$3^1/_2$ V-1
Plt Off T.A. McCulloch	Tempest V JN818	3 Sqn	V-1
Flt Lt J.D. Ross	Tempest V EJ539	56 Sqn	V-1
Flt Lt W.C. Marshall	Spitfire XIV RM682	91 Sqn	V-1
Lt H.F. de Bordas (FF)	Spitfire XIV DL-M	91 Sqn	$^1/_2$ V-1
Flt Lt H.B. Moffett RCAF	Spitfire XIV RM726	91 Sqn	V-1
Cne J-M. Maridor (FF)	Spitfire XIV RM656	91 Sqn	V-1 (also KiA)
Sqn Ldr I.D.S. Strachan RNZAF	Mustang III FB364	129 Sqn	2 V-1
Flt Lt R.G. Kleimeyer RNZAF (Aus)	Mustang III FB152	129 Sqn	$2^1/_2$ V-1
Flt Lt G.C.D. Green	Mustang III FX958	129 Sqn	$^1/_2$+$^1/_2$ V-1
Flg Off J.E. Hartley	Mustang III HB862	129 Sqn	V-1
Flg Off L.G. Lunn	Mustang III FB137	129 Sqn	V-1
Plt Off J.V. Tynan	Spitfire IX MK738	165 Sqn	V-1
Flg Off T.A.Vance RAAF	Spitfire IX ML418	165 Sqn	$^1/_2$ V-1
Wt Off J. Czeżowski PAF	Mustang III FB393	306 (Pol) Sqn	V-1
Flt Sgt S. Rudowski PAF	Mustang III FB380	306 (Pol) Sqn	$1^1/_2$ V-1
Plt Off G. Świstuń PAF	Mustang III PK-O	315 (Pol) Sqn	$^1/_2$ V-1
Flt Lt J. Schmidt PAF	Mustang III FZ157/FB367	315 (Pol) Sqn	$^1/_2$+$^1/_2$ V-1
Wt Off O.D. Eagleson RNZAF	Tempest V JN808	486 (RNZAF) Sqn	2 V-1
Flg Off S.S. Williams RNZAF	Tempest V JN858	486 (RNZAF) Sqn	2 V-1
Flg Off W.A. Hart RNZAF	Tempest V JN732	486 (RNZAF) Sqn	$1^1/_2$ V-1
Plt Off R.D. Bremner RNZAF	Tempest V JN767	486 (RNZAF) Sqn	$1^1/_2$ V-1
Flt Lt N.J. Powell RNZAF	Tempest V JN808	486 (RNZAF) Sqn	V-1

Night 3-4/8/44 (28 V-1s destroyed by fighters)

Flt Lt R.H. Farrell/	Mosquito XVII HK119	85 Sqn	V-1
Flt Sgt Checkley (Nav)			
Plt Off L.J. York/	Mosquito XVII TA400	85 Sqn	2 V-1
Flt Sgt T.F. Fry (Nav)			
Flt Lt P.A. Searle/	Mosquito XVII VY-Q	85 Sqn	V-1
Flg Off B.J.P. Simpkins (Nav)			
Flt Lt F.R.L. Mellersh/	Mosquito XIII MM577	96 Sqn	7 V-1
Flt Lt M.J. Stanley (Nav)			
Wg Cdr E.D. Crew/	Mosquito XIII NS985	96 Sqn	2 V-1
Wt Off J.R. Croysdill (Nav)			
Plt Off W.S. Vale RAAF/	Mosquito XIX MM671	157 Sqn	V-1
Flt Lt A.E. Ashcroft (Nav)			
Flt Lt P.S. Leggat RCAF/	Mosquito VI TH-	418 (RCAF) Sqn	V-1
Flt Lt F.L. Cochrane RCAF (Nav)			
Sqn Ldr I.F. McCall/	Mosquito VI UP-	605 Sqn	V-1
Sgt T. Caulfield (Nav)			
Flt Lt D.G. Brandreth	Typhoon Ib MN995	137 Sqn	V-1
Flt Lt R.L.T. Robb	Tempest V EJ598	FIU	2 V-1 (night)
Flt Lt C.B. Thornton	Tempest V ZQ-	FIU	2 V-1 (night)
Flg Off R.G. Lucas	Tempest V ZQ-	FIU	2 V-1 (night)
Flt Lt J. Berry	Tempest V ZQ-	FIU	5 V-1 (night)

4/8/44 (37 V-1s destroyed by fighters)

Flg Off W.J. Batchelor	Spitfire LFIXb MJ481	1 Sqn	V-1
Flt Sgt L.G. Everson	Tempest V JN817	3 Sqn	V-1
Wt Off J.L.R. Torpey	Tempest V JN768	3 Sqn	V-1
Wt Off R. Worley	Tempest V JN760	3 Sqn	V-1
Flt Lt T.A.H. Slack	Spitfire XII EN238	41 Sqn	V-1
Sqn Ldr A.R. Hall	Tempest V EJ541	56 Sqn	V-1
Plt Off D.E. Ness RCAF	Tempest V EJ547	56 Sqn	2 V-1
Sgt A.M.L. Kennaugh	Tempest V EJ544	56 Sqn	V-1
Flt Lt J.H. Ryan RCAF	Tempest V EJ522	56 Sqn	V-1
Flt Lt A.R. Cruickshank RCAF	Spitfire XIV RM649	91 Sqn	V-1
Flt Lt H.D. Johnson	Spitfire XIV RM686	91 Sqn	V-1
Flg Off A.R. Elcock	Spitfire XIV RM734	91 Sqn	V-1
Lt H.F.de Bordas (FF)	Spitfire XIV RM688	91 Sqn	V-1
Flt Lt R.J. Conroy RAAF	Mustang III SR428	129 Sqn	V-1
Flt Lt R.G. Kleimeyer RNZAF (Aus)	Mustang III FB137	129 Sqn	V-1
Flg Off P.N. Howard	Mustang III FB170	129 Sqn	1/2 V-1
Plt Off E.W. Edwards	Mustang III FB147	129 Sqn	V-1
Flg Off A.N. Sames RNZAF	Typhoon Ib MN134	137 Sqn	V-1
Plt Off J.M. Walton RCAF	Spitfire IX MK801	165 Sqn	V-1
Flt Lt J.K. Porteous RNZAF	Spitfire IX MK854	165 Sqn	V-1
Flt Lt B.J. Murch	Spitfire IX NH401	165 Sqn	V-1
Grp Capt T. Nowierski PAF	Mustang III HB886	131 (Pol) Wg	V-1
Flt Sgt J. Zaworski PAF	Mustang III UZ-K	306 (Pol) Sqn	V-1
Plt Off J. Bzowski PAF	Mustang III HB871	306 (Pol) Sqn	V-1
Flt Sgt J. Zaworski PAF	Mustang III FZ196	306 (Pol) Sqn	V-1
Flt Lt J. Siekierski PAF	Mustang III UZ-I	306 (Pol) Sqn	V-1
Flg Off W. Wunsche PAF	Mustang III FB123	315 (Pol) Sqn	1/2 V-1
Wt Off T. Słoń PAF	Mustang III FZ169	315 (Pol) Sqn	1/2 V-1
Flt Lt J. van Arkel (Dutch)	Spitfire XIV VL-W	322 (Dutch) Sqn	V-1
Flt Lt J.F. Plesman (Dutch)	Spitfire XIV VL-Z	322 (Dutch) Sqn	V-1
Wt Off O.D. Eagleson RNZAF	Tempest V EJ528	486 (RNZAF) Sqn	V-1
Wt Off B.J. O'Connor RNZAF	Tempest V JN801	486 (RNZAF) Sqn	V-1
Plt Off K.A. Smith RNZAF	Tempest V JN821	486 (RNZAF) Sqn	3 V-1
Flt Lt J.B. Shepherd	Spitfire XIV DW-	610 Sqn	1/2 V-1
Flg Off J. Doherty	Spitfire XIV DW-	610 Sqn	1/2 V-1
Flg Off T.D. Dean	Meteor F1 EE216	616 Sqn	V-1
Flg Off J.K. Rodger	Meteor F1 YQ-	616 Sqn	V-1

Night 4-5/8/44 (7 V-1s destroyed by fighters)

Flg Off A.J. Owen/	Mosquito XIX TA400	85 Sqn	V-1
Flg Off J.S.V. McAllister (Nav)			
Lt E.P. Fossum (Norw)/	Mosquito XIX MM648	85 Sqn	V-1
Capt C. Bjørn (Norw) (Nav)			
Flg Off J. Goode/	Mosquito XIII MM452	96 Sqn	V-1
Flg Off V.A. Robinson (Nav)			
Sqn Ldr R. Bannock RCAF/	Mosquito VI HR147	418 (RCAF) Sqn	2 V-1
Flg Off R.R.F. Bruce RCAF (Nav)			
Flg Off J.J. Harvie RCAF	Mosquito VI TH-	418 (RCAF) Sqn	V-1

Flg Off P.A. Alexander RAF (Nav)
Flt Lt K.A. Roediger RAAF/   Mosquito XVII HK297   456 (RAAF) Sqn   V-1
Flt Lt R.J.H. Dobson RAAF (Nav)

5/8/44 (32 V-1s destroyed by fighters)

Flt Sgt I.T. Stevenson	Spitfire XII MB795	41 Sqn	V-1
Flt Sgt H. Shaw	Tempest V JN867	56 Sqn	$^1/_2+^1/_2$ V-1
Flg Off G.C. McKay	Spitfire XIV RM653	91 Sqn	V-1
Flg Off J. Monihan	Spitfire XIV RM651	91 Sqn	V-1
Flg Off M. Twomey	Mustang III FX952	129 Sqn	V-1
Plt Off M. Humphries	Mustang III FB137	129 Sqn	V-1
Flg Off F.H. Holmes	Mustang III FB212	129 Sqn	V-1
Plt Off E.W. Edwards	Mustang III FB389	129 Sqn	V-1
Flg Off C.M. Lawson RAAF	Spitfire IX ML175	165 Sqn	2 V-1
Plt Off A. Scott	Spitfire IX MK752	165 Sqn	V-1
Plt Off T.P.G. Lewin	Spitfire IX MJ580	165 Sqn	V-1
Wt Off W. Nowoczyn PAF	Mustang III UZ-S	306 (Pol) Sqn	V-1
Flg Off J. Smigielski PAF	Mustang III FB358	306 (Pol) Sqn	V-1
Wt Off T. Szymański PAF	Mustang III HB835	316 (Pol) Sqn	2 V-1
Flt Sgt T. Jaskólski PAF	Mustang III HB839	316 (Pol) Sqn	V-1
Flt Sgt A. Pietrzak PAF	Mustang III FB383	316 (Pol) Sqn	2 V-1
Wt Off P. Syperek PAF	Mustang III FB353	316 (Pol) Sqn	V-1
Flg Off J. Jonker (Dutch)	Spitfire XIV VL-K	322 (Dutch) Sqn	V-1
Flg Off R.F Burgwal (Dutch)	Spitfire XIV RB184	322 (Dutch) Sqn	2 V-1
Flg Off H.M. Mason RNZAF	Tempest V JN801	486 (RNZAF) Sqn	V-1
Flg Off W.F. Polley	Tempest V EJ598	501 Sqn	$1^1/_2$ V-1
Flt Sgt R.W. Ryman	Tempest V EJ585	501 Sqn	$^1/_2$ V-1
Flt Lt F.A.O. Gaze RAAF	Spitfire XIV DW-U	610 Sqn	V-1
Flt Lt J. Berry	Tempest V EJ524	FIU	5 V-1 (day)

Night 5-6/8/44 (10 V-1s destroyed by fighters)

Flg Off B.G. Nobbs/   Mosquito XVII HK243   25 Sqn   2 V-1
Plt Off Bernard (Nav)
Wt Off W.A. McLardy RAAF/   Mosquito XIII HK479   96 Sqn   V-1
Flt Sgt Devine (Nav)
Flg Off C.N. Woodcock/   Mosquito XIX MM652   157 Sqn   V-1
Flt Lt L. Scholefield (Nav)
Flg Off H. Loriaux RCAF/   Mosquito VI TH-   418 (RCAF) Sqn   2 V-1
Flt Lt W. Sewell RCAF (Nav)
Flg Off P.R. Brook RCAF/   Mosquito VI TH-   418 (RCAF) Sqn   V-1
Flg Off A.D. McLaren RCAF (Nav)
Wt Off J.E. Semmens RAAF/   Mosquito XVII HK253   456 (RAAF) Sqn   V-1
Wt Off H.A. Nitschke RAAF (Nav)
Plt Off S.J. Williams RAAF   Mosquito XVII HK282   456 (RAAF) Sqn   V-1
Flg Off K.W. Havord RAAF (Nav)
1/Lt G.E. Peterson USAAF/   P-61 42-5581   425thNFS USAAF   V-1
2/Lt J.A. Howe USAAF (R/O)

6/8/44 (29 V-1s destroyed by fighters)

Flg Off R. Dryland	Tempest V JN865	3 Sqn	2 V-1
Flt Sgt D.M. Smith	Tempest V EJ549	3 Sqn	V-1
Flt Sgt L.G. Everson	Tempest V JN817	3 Sqn	V-1
Flt Lt R. van Lierde (Belg)	Tempest V EJ540	3 Sqn	V-1
Sgt G.H. Wylde	Tempest V EJ526	56 Sqn	V-1
Flt Sgt L. Jackson	Tempest V EJ544	56 Sqn	V-1
Flg Off A.R. Elcock	Spitfire XIV RM734	91 Sqn	V-1
Wt Off E. Redhead	Mustang III FX942	129 Sqn	V-1
Flt Lt J. Siekierski PAF	Mustang III FB393	306 (Pol) Sqn	3 V-1
Flg Off P. Kliman PAF	Mustang III FX939	315 (Pol) Sqn	V-1
Flt Sgt J. Donocik PAF	Mustang III FX945	315 (Pol) Sqn	V-1
Flt Lt T. Szymankiewicz PAF	Mustang III HB824	316 (Pol) Sqn	V-1
Wt Off W. Grobelny PAF	Mustang III FB353/FB356	316 (Pol) Sqn	2 V-1
Flt Lt L. Majewski PAF	Mustang III HB821	316 (Pol) Sqn	2 V-1
Flt Lt K. Zielonka PAF	Mustang III FB353	316 (Pol) Sqn	V-1
Sqn Ldr B. Arct PAF	Mustang III HB836	316 (Pol) Sqn	V-1
Wt Off T. Szymański PAF	Mustang III HB824	316 (Pol) Sqn	2 V-1
Flt Lt J.F. Plesman (Dutch)	Spitfire XIV VL-P	322 (Dutch) Sqn	V-1
Flg Off J.G. Wilson RNZAF	Tempest V JN802	486 (RNZAF) Sqn	V-1
Wt Off W.A. Kalka RNZAF	Tempest V EJ524	486 (RNZAF) Sqn	V-1
Plt Off W.A.L. Trott RNZAF	Tempest V EJ528	486 (RNZAF) Sqn	V-1
Plt Off R.J. Danzey RNZAF	Tempest V JN803	486 (RNZAF) Sqn	$^1/_2$ V-1
Plt Off R.D. Bremner RNZAF	Tempest V EJ524	486 (RNZAF) Sqn	$^1/_2$ V-1

Flg Off R.J. Cammock RNZAF	Tempest V EJ523	486 (RNZAF) Sqn	V-1

Night 6-7/8/44 (8 V-1s destroyed by fighters including 1 by USAAF)

Flt Lt I.A. Dobie/	Mosquito XIII MM487	96 Sqn	V-1
Flg Off E.A. Johnson (Nav)			
Flg Off H. Loriaux RCAF/	Mosquito VI TH-	418 (RCAF) Sqn	V-1
Flt Lt W. Sewell RCAF (Nav)			
Flt Lt K.A. Roediger RAAF/	Mosquito XVII HK297	456 (RAAF) Sqn	V-1
Flt Lt R.J.H. Dobson RAAF (Nav)			
1/Lt G.E. Peterson USAAF	P-61 42-5581	425thNFS USAAF	V-1
2/Lt J.A. Howe USAAF (R/O)			
Flt Lt C.B. Thornton	Tempest V ZQ-	FIU	V-1

7/8/44 (32 V-1s destroyed by fighters)

Sgt G.H. Wylde	Tempest V EN526	56 Sqn	V-1
Flg Off J.J. Payton	Tempest V JN816	56 Sqn	V-1
Flg Off E.C. Goulding	Tempest V EJ545	56 Sqn	1/2 V-1
Sgt G.H. Wylde	Tempest V EN526	56 Sqn	V-1
Flg Off A.R. Elcock	Spitfire XIV RM694	91 Sqn	V-1
Flt Lt H.D. Johnson	Spitfire XIV RM684	91 Sqn	V-1
Lt H.F. de Bordas (FF)	Spitfire XIV RM686	91 Sqn	V-1
Flg Off D.C. Parker	Mustang III HB862	129 Sqn	2 V-1
Plt Off E.W. Edwards	Mustang III FB389	129 Sqn	V-1
Plt Off K. Wacnik PAF	Mustang III FB347	306 (Pol) Sqn	V-1
Flt Sgt J. Zaleński PAF	Mustang III FB393	306 (Pol) Sqn	V-1
Flg Off A. Czerwiński PAF	Mustang III FX878	315 (Pol) Sqn	1/2V-1
Plt Off G. Świstuń PAF	Mustang III FZ157	315 (Pol) Sqn	1/2 V-1
Wt Off C. Bartłomiejczyk PAF	Mustang III HB849	316 (Pol) Sqn	4 V-1
Flt Lt Z. Przygodski PAF	Mustang III HB839	316 (Pol) Sqn	V-1
Flt Sgt S. Sztuka PAF	Mustang III HB835	316 (Pol) Sqn	2 V-1
Flt Lt L. Majewski PAF	Mustang III FB396	316 (Pol) Sqn	V-1
Flg Off R.F.Burgwal (Dutch)	Spitfire XIV VL-L	322 (Dutch) Sqn	V-1
Flg Off R.J. Cammock RNZAF	Tempest V JN863	486 (RNZAF) Sqn	V-1
Flg Off R-C. Deleuze (FF)	Tempest V EJ599	501 Sqn	V-1
Flg Off T.D. Dean	Meteor F.1 YQ-	616 Sqn	V-1
Flt Lt J. Berry	Tempest V EJ524	FIU	4 V-1 (day)
Flg Off E.L. Williams	Tempest V EJ524	FIU	V-1
Flg Off R.G. Lucas	Tempest V EJ553	FIU	V-1
Flt Lt R.L.T. Robb	Tempest V EJ598	FIU	2 V-1

Night 7-8/8/44 (13 V-1s destroyed by fighters including 1 by USAAF)

Flt Lt F.R.L. Mellersh	Spitfire XI MH473	96 Sqn	2 V-1
Flt Lt F.R.L. Mellersh/	Mosquito XIII MM577	96 Sqn	2 V-1
Flt Lt M.J. Stanley (Nav)			
Flt Lt J.O. Mathews/	Mosquito XIX TA401	157 Sqn	2 V-1
Wt Off A. Penrose (Nav)			
Sqn Ldr J.H.M. Chisholm/	Mosquito XIX MM676	157 Sqn	V-1
Flt Lt E. Wylde (Nav)			
Flg Off S.N. May RCAF/	Mosquito VI NS837	418 (RCAF) Sqn	V-1
Plt Off J.D. Ritch RCAF (Nav)			
Flt Lt P.S. Leggat RCAF/	Mosquito VI TH-	418 (RCAF) Sqn	V-1
Flt Lt F.L. Cochrane RCAF (Nav)			
Flg Off H.E. Miller RAF/	Mosquito VI TH-	418 (RCAF) Sqn	V-1
Sgt W. Hooper RCAF (Nav)			
Sqn Ldr B. Howard RAAF/	Mosquito XVII HK323	456 (RAAF) Sqn	2 V-1
Flg Off J.R. Ross RAAF (Nav)			
Capt F.V. Sartanowicz USAAF/	P-61 42-5582	425thNFS USAAF	V-1
1/Lt E.M. Van Sickles USAAF (R/O)			

8/8/44 (1 V-1 destroyed by fighters)

Flt Lt T. Szymankiewicz PAF	Mustang III FB396	316 (Pol) Sqn	V-1

Night 8-9/8/44 (4 V-1s destroyed by fighters including 1 by USAAF)

Sqn Ldr W.P. Green/	Mosquito XIII MM568	96 Sqn	V-1
Wt Off A.R. Grimstone (Nav)			
Sqn Ldr G.L. Howitt RAF/	Mosquito XVII HK249	456 (RAAF) Sqn	V-1
Flg Off G.N. Irving RAF (Nav)			
1/Lt J.L. Thompson USAAF/	P-61 42-5582	425thNFS USAAF	V-1
Flt Off J.E. Downey USAAF (R/O)			
Flg Off E.L. Williams	Tempest V EJ630	FIU	V-1

9/8/44 (9 V-1s destroyed by fighters)

Flt Lt J.J. Jarman	Spitfire LFIXb MK659	1 Sqn	1/2 V-1
Flt Lt T. Spencer	Spitfire XII MN875	41 Sqn	V-1

Flg Off H. Cook	Spitfire XII MB878	41 Sqn	V-1
Flt Lt K. Stembrowicz PAF	Mustang III FB362	315 (Pol) Sqn	V-1
Wt Off T. Szymański PAF	Mustang III HB835	316 (Pol) Sqn	2 V-1
Flt Lt T. Szymankiewicz PAF	Mustang III FB396	316 (Pol) Sqn	V-1
Flt Lt L.C.M. van Eendenburg (Dutch)	Spitfire XIV VL-I	322 (Dutch) Sqn	V-1
Flt Lt H.N. Sweetman RNZAF	Tempest V EJ577	486 (RNZAF) Sqn	V-1
Flt Lt L.J. Appleton RNZAF	Tempest V JN808	486 (RNZAF) Sqn	$1/_2$ V-1

Night 9-10/8/44 (7 V-1s destroyed by fighters)

Sqn Ldr P.L. Caldwell/	Mosquito XIII MM461	96 Sqn	V-1
Flg Off K.P. Rawlins (Nav)			
Flt Lt E.J. Stevens/	Mosquito XIX MM674	157 Sqn	V-1
Flg Off L. Butt (Nav)			
Flt Lt D.E. Forsyth RCAF (US)/	Mosquito VI TH-	418 (RCAF) Sqn	V-1
Flg Off R.T. Esam RAF (Nav)			
Flt Lt K.A. Roediger RAAF/	Mosquito XVII HK297	456 (RAAF) Sqn	V-1
Flt Lt R.J.H. Dobson RAAF (Nav)			
Flt Lt R.L.T. Robb	Tempest V EJ598	FIU	2 V-1
Flt Lt C.B. Thornton	Tempest V EJ555	FIU	V-1

10/8/44 (10 V-1s destroyed by fighters)

Wg Cdr R.P. Beamont	Tempest V JN751	150 Wg	V-1
Flg Off R.H. Clapperton	Tempest V EJ504	3 Sqn	2 V-1
Flt Lt A.R. Moore	Tempest V JN818	3 Sqn	2 V-1
Flg Off L.G. Lunn	Mustang III FB389	129 Sqn	V-1
Flg Off J.E. Hartley	Mustang III FB147	129 Sqn	V-1
Plt Off E.W. Edwards	Mustang III HB862	129 Sqn	V-1
Flt Lt J.L. Plesman (Dutch)	Spitfire XIV VL-W	322 (Dutch) Sqn	V-1
Flg Off T.D. Dean	Meteor F.1 YQ-	616 Sqn	V-1

Night 10-11/8/44 (3 V-1s destroyed by fighters)

Flt Lt F.R.L. Mellersh/	Mosquito XIII MM577	96 Sqn	V-1
Flt Lt M.J. Stanley (Nav)			
Sqn Ldr E.G. Barwell/	Mosquito XVII HK355	125 Sqn	V-1
Flt Lt D.A. Haigh (Nav)			
Sqn Ldr J.H.M. Chisholm/	Mosquito XIX MM674	157 Sqn	V-1
Flt Lt E. Wylde (Nav)			

11/8/44 ($2^1/_2$ V-1s destroyed by fighters)

Flg Off J.F. Wilkinson	Spitfire XII EN609	41 Sqn	$1/_2$ V-1
Flg Off G.R. Dickson RNZAF	Mustang III FX924	129 Sqn	V-1
Flt Lt J.P. Bassett	Mustang III FB130	129 Sqn	$1/_2$ V-1
Flt Sgt J. Bargielowski PAF	Mustang III FX878	315 (Pol) Sqn	$1/_2$ V-1

Night 11-12/8/44 (21 V-1s destroyed by fighters)

Flt Sgt G.T. Glossop/	Mosquito XVII HK301	25 Sqn	2 V-1
Flt Sgt B.W. Christian (Nav)			
Wt Off W. Alderton/	Mosquito XVII HK299	85 Sqn	V-1
Flg Off J.S.V. McAllister (Nav)			
Flt Lt F.R.L. Mellersh/	Mosquito XIII MM577	96 Sqn	V-1
Flt Lt M.J. Stanley (Nav)			
Flt Lt I.A. Dobie/	Mosquito XIII HK437	96 Sqn	V-1
Flg Off E.A. Johnson (Nav)			
Flt Lt G.E. Dunfee/	Mosquito XVII HK291	125 Sqn	V-1
Plt Off B.A. Williams (Nav)			
Flt Sgt K.W. Ramsay/	Mosquito XVII HK240	125 Sqn	V-1
Flt Sgt T.K. Foote (Nav)			
Wt Off B. Miller/	Mosquito XIX TA400	157 Sqn	V-1
Flt Sgt Crawford RAAF (Nav)			
Wt Off S. Astley/	Mosquito XIX MM674	157 Sqn	V-1
Plt Off G.T. Lang (Nav)			
Flg Off S.P. Seid RCAF/	Mosquito VI TH-	418 (RCAF) Sqn	V-1
Flg Off D.N. McIntosh RCAF (Nav)			
Flt Lt F.M. Sawyer RCAF/	Mosquito VI TH-	418 (RCAF) Sqn	V-1
Flg Off J.E. Howell RCAF (Nav)			
Flt Lt G.R. Houston RAAF/	Mosquito XVII HK264	456 (RAAF) Sqn	V-1
Flg Off L.C. Engberg RAAF (Nav)			
Sqn Ldr B. Howard RAAF/	Mosquito XVII HK282	456 (RAAF) Sqn	V-1
Flg Off J.R. Ross RAAF (Nav)			
Flt Lt E.L. Williams	Tempest V EJ555	501 Sqn	V-1
Flt Lt C.B. Thornton	Tempest V EJ558	501 Sqn	3 V-1
Flg Off R.G. Lucas	Tempest V EJ553	501 Sqn	V-1
Flt Off B.F. Miller USAAF	Tempest V EJ584	501 Sqn	3 V-1

12/8/44
No claims

Night 12-13/8/44 (13 V-1s destroyed by fighters)

Wg Cdr H.deC.A. Woodhouse/	Mosquito XVII MM632	85 Sqn	V-1 (also FTR)
Flt Lt W. Weir (Nav)			
Sqn Ldr B.A. Burbridge/	Mosquito XVII HK349	85 Sqn	V-1
Flt Lt F.S. Skelton (Nav)			
Flt Lt P.A. Searle/	Mosquito XVII HK120	85 Sqn	V-1
Flg Off B.J.P. Simpkins (Nav)			
Flt Lt W.J. Gough/	Mosquito XIII HK479	96 Sqn	V-1
Flt Lt C. Matson (Nav)			
Flt Lt N.S. Head/	Mosquito XIII MM460	96 Sqn	V-1
Flg Off A.C. Andrews (Nav)			
Sqn Ldr R. Bannock RCAF/	Mosquito VI HR147	418 (RCAF) Sqn	V-1
Flg Off R.R.F. Bruce RCAF (Nav)			
Sqn Ldr R.G. Gray RCAF	Mosquito VI HK148	418 (RCAF) Sqn	V-1
Flg Off F.D. Smith RCAF (Nav)			
Flg Off H.E. Miller RAF/	Mosquito VI TH-	418 (RCAF) Sqn	2 V-1
Sgt W. Hooper RCAF (Nav)			
Flt Lt R.G. Pratt RAAF/	Mosquito XVII HK303	456 (RAAF) Sqn	V-1
Flg Off S.D.P.Smith RAAF (Nav)			
Sqn Ldr G.L. Howitt RAF/	Mosquito XVII HK249	456 (RAAF) Sqn	V-1
Flg Off G.N. Irving RAF (Nav)			
Sqn Ldr J. Berry	Tempest V EJ590	501 Sqn	2 V-1

13/8/44
No claims

Night 13-14/8/44 (10 V-1s destroyed by fighters)

Flt Lt F.R.L. Mellersh	Spitfire IX MH473	96 Sqn	2 V-1
Wt Off W.A. McLardy RAAF/	Mosquito XIII MM495	96 Sqn	V-1
Flt Sgt Devine (Nav)			
Flt Lt W.J. Gough/	Mosquito XIII HK438	96 Sqn	V-1
Flt Lt C. Matson (Nav)			
Flg Off S.P. Seid RCAF/	Mosquito VI TH-	418 (RCAF) Sqn	V-1
Flg Off D.N. McIntosh RCAF (Nav)			
Flt Lt L.E. Evans RCAF/	Mosquito VI TH-	418 (RCAF) Sqn	V-1
Flg Off S. Humblestone RAF (Nav)			
Plt Off S.J. Williams RAAF/	Mosquito XVII HK282	456 (RAAF) Sqn	V-1
Flg Off K.W. Havord RAAF (Nav)			
Sqn Ldr J. Berry	Tempest V EJ590	501 Sqn	1/2 V-1
Flg Off R.L.T. Robb	Tempest V EJ598	501 Sqn	1 1/2 V-1

14//8/44
No claims

Night 14-15/8/44 (10 V-1s destroyed by fighters plus 1 by FAA)

Flt Lt J.S. Limbert/	Mosquito XVII HK357	25 Sqn	V-1
Flg Off H.S. Cook (Nav)			
Flg Off J.F.R. Jones/	Mosquito XVII HK243	25 Sqn	V-1
Flg Off Skinner (Nav)			
Plt Off L.J. York/	Mosquito XIX MM648	85 Sqn	V-1
Flt Sgt T.F. Fry (Nav)			
Flt Lt T.W. Redfern/	Mosquito XIX TA400	85 Sqn	V-1
Sgt J.F. Lewis (Nav)			
Sqn Ldr A. Parker-Rees/	Mosquito XIII HK525	96 Sqn	V-1
Flt Lt G.E. Bennett (Nav)			
Flt Lt F.R.L. Mellersh/	Mosquito XIII MM577	96 Sqn	2 V-1
Wg Cdr R.B. Cawood (Ob)			
Flt Lt R.D. Doleman/	Mosquito XIX MM678	157 Sqn	V-1
Flt Lt D.C. Bunch (Nav)			
Plt Off R.D. Hodgen RAAF/	Mosquito XVII HK302	456 (RAAF) Sqn	V-1
Flt Sgt A. McCormick RAF (Nav)			
Flg Off B.G. Bensted/	Mosquito VI HJ799	605 Sqn	V-1
Sgt C.L. Burrage (Nav)			
Lt(A) A.F. Voak RNVR	Avenger I FN854	854 (FAA) Sqn	V-1

15/8/44 (11 V-1s destroyed by fighters)

Flg Off C.J. Malone RCAF	Spitfire XII EN622	41 Sqn	1/2 V-1
Wt Off P.T. Coleman	Spitfire XII MB875	41 Sqn	V-1
Flt Lt R.P. Harding	Spitfire XII MB795	41 Sqn	V-1
Flt Sgt J.S. Ferguson	Tempest V EJ536	56 Sqn	V-1
Flt Lt R.G. Kleimeyer RNZAF (Aus)	Mustang III FB137	129 Sqn	1/2 V-1

Flt Lt O.E. Willis	Tempest V EJ628	274 Sqn	V-1
Wt Off W. Nowoczyn PAF	Mustang III UZ-V	306 (Pol) Sqn	V-1
Flt Sgt J. Donoclik PAF	Mustang III FB162	315 (Pol) Sqn	V-1
Flt Sgt J. Bargielowski PAF	Mustang III FZ143	315 (Pol) Sqn	V-1
Sgt H.A. Boels (Belg)	Spitfire XIV RM748	350 (Belg) Sqn	1/2 V-1
Flg Off R. Vanderveken (Belg)	Spitfire XIV RM655	350 (Belg) Sqn	1/2 V-1
Wt Off O.D. Eagleson RNZAF	Tempest V EJ635	486 (RNZAF) Sqn	1/2 V-1
Flg Off R.J. Cammock RNZAF	Tempest V EJ528	486 (RNZAF) Sqn	V-1
Flt Lt K.G.Taylor-Cannon RNZAF	Tempest V JN808	486 (RNZAF) Sqn	V-1

Night 15-16/8/44 (8 V-1s destroyed by fighters)

Flt Lt A.E. Marshall/	Mosquito XVII HK243	25 Sqn	V-1
Flg Off C.A. Allen (Nav)			
Flt Lt A.B. Harvey/	Mosquito XVII WM-Y	68 Sqn	2 V-1
Flt Lt B.StJ. Wynell-Sutherland (Nav)			
Capt T. Weisteen (Norw)/	Mosquito XIX VY-B	85 Sqn	V-1
Flg Off F.G. French (Nav)			
Flt Lt J.G. Musgrave/	Mosquito VI MM429	605 Sqn	2 V-1
Flt Sgt F.W. Samwell (Nav)			
Sqn Ldr J. Berry	Tempest V EJ590	501 Sqn	2 V-1

16/8/44 (41 V-1s destroyed by fighters)

Wg Cdr R.P. Beamont	Tempest V JN751	150 Wg	V-1
Plt Off H.R. Wingate	Tempest V EJ549	3 Sqn	V-1
Flt Lt R. van Lierde (Belg)	Tempest V EJ557	3 Sqn	V-1
Flt Sgt R.W. Cole	Tempest V JN768	3 Sqn	V-1
Flt Sgt V.J. Rossow RAAF	Spitfire XII MB857	41 Sqn	V-1
Flg Off P.B. Graham	Spitfire XII MB831	41 Sqn	V-1
Flt Sgt L. Jackson	Tempest V EJ547	56 Sqn	V-1
Plt Off I.N. MacLaren	Tempest V EJ536	56 Sqn	V-1
Flt Lt D.V.G. Cotes-Preddy	Tempest V EJ721	56 Sqn	V-1
Wt Off R.L. Thomas RAAF	Mustang III FB138	129 Sqn	1/2 V-1
Flg Off G. Jones	Spitfire XIV RM750	130 Sqn	V-1
Sgt P.E.H. Standish	Spitfire XIV RM744	130 Sqn	1/2 V-1
Plt Off W.W. Brown	Spitfire XIV RM741	130 Sqn	V-1
Flt Lt O.E. Willis	Tempest V EJ640	274 Sqn	V-1
Flt Lt J.A. Malloy RCAF	Tempest V EJ640/EJ633	274 Sqn	V-1
Flt Lt L.P. Griffiths RNZAF	Tempest V EJ647	274 Sqn	V-1
Flg Off J.W. Lyne	Tempest V EJ634	274 Sqn	1 1/2+1/2 V-1
Flt Sgt S. Rudowski PAF	Mustang III FB380	306 (Pol) Sqn	1/2 V-1
Flg Off K. Marschall PAF	Mustang III HB871	306 (Pol) Sqn	V-1
Flt Lt J. Wisiorek PAF	Mustang III FB350	306 (Pol) Sqn	1 1/2 V-1
Wt Off J. Rogowski PAF	Mustang III FB358	306 (Pol) Sqn	1 1/2 V-1
Flg Off B. Nowosielski PAF	Mustang III HB849	315 (Pol) Sqn	V-1
Plt Off G. Świstuń PAF	Mustang III FX865	315 (Pol) Sqn	V-1
Flt Sgt K. Siwek PAF	Mustang III FX878	315 (Pol) Sqn	3 V-1
Flt Sgt L. Verbeeck (Belg)	Spitfire XIV RM655	350 (Belg) Sqn	V-1
Plt Off J. Lavigne (Belg)	Spitfire XIV RM701	350 (Belg) Sqn	1/2 V-1
Sgt P. Leva (Belg)	Spitfire XIV RM693	350 (Belg) Sqn	1/2 V-1
Flg Off E.A.H. Vickers RCAF	Spitfire XIV RM731	402 (RCAF) Sqn	V-1
Flg Off H. Cowan RCAF	Spitfire XIV RM737	402 (RCAF) Sqn	V-1
Flt Lt D. Sherk RCAF	Spitfire XIV RM680	402 (RCAF) Sqn	V-1
Flt Sgt J. Steedman RNZAF	Tempest V EJ528	486 (RNZAF) Sqn	2 V-1
Flt Lt H.N. Sweetman RNZAF	Tempest V JN732	486 (RNZAF) Sqn	V-1
Wt Off O.D. Eagleson RNZAF	Tempest V EJ635	486 (RNZAF) Sqn	3 V-1
Plt Off K.A. Smith RNZAF	Tempest V JN808	486 (RNZAF) Sqn	V-1
Flt Lt W.L. Miller RNZAF	Tempest V JN803	486 (RNZAF) Sqn	V-1
Flg Off W.H. McKenzie RCAF	Meteor F.1 EE225	616 Sqn	1/2 V-1
Flg Off M.M. Mullenders (Belg)	Meteor F.1 YQ-	616 Sqn	V-1

17/8/44 (20 V-1s destroyed by fighters)

Plt Off H.R. Wingate	Tempest V EJ549	3 Sqn	2 V-1
Flt Sgt R.W. Cole	Tempest V JN768	3 Sqn	V-1
Flt Lt R.P. Harding	Spitfire XII MB854	41 Sqn	V-1
Flg Off P.B. Graham	Spitfire XII MB831	41 Sqn	V-1
Sqn Ldr A.R. Hall	Tempest V EJ541	56 Sqn	2 V-1
Sgt P.E.H. Standish	Spitfire XIV RM744	130 Sqn	2 V-1
Flg Off K.M. Lowe RAAF	Spitfire XIV RM757	130 Sqn	V-1
Plt Off F.C. Riley RAAF	Spitfire XIV RM760	130 Sqn	V-1
Wg Cdr J.F. Fraser	Tempest V EJ628	274 Sqn	V-1
Flt Lt M. Wedzik PAF	Mustang III UZ-V	306 (Pol) Sqn	V-1
Flt Lt W. Klawe PAF	Mustang III UZ-V	306 (Pol) Sqn	1/2 V-1

Flt Sgt J. Zaleński PAF	Mustang III UZ-T	306 (Pol) Sqn	V-1
Flt Lt J. Siekierski PAF	Mustang III UZ-	306 (Pol) Sqn	V-1
Flt Sgt J. Donocik PAF	Mustang III FZ169	315 (Pol) Sqn	V-1
Flg Off P. Kliman PAF	Mustang III FX939	315 (Pol) Sqn	V-1
Flg Off J.R. Ritch RCAF	Meteor F.1 EE217/YQ-J	616 Sqn	V-1
Wt Off T.S. Woodacre	Meteor F.1 EE218/YQ-F	616 Sqn	V-1
Flt Sgt R. Easy	Meteor F.1 YQ-	616 Sqn	V-1

Night 17-18/8/44 (2 V-1s destroyed by fighters)

Flt Lt B. Williams/	Mosquito VI UP-	605 Sqn	2 V-1
Wt Off S. Hardy (Nav)			

18/8/44 (6 V-1s destroyed by fighters)

Plt Off E. Gray RAAF	Spitfire XII EN228	41 Sqn	¹/₂ V-1
Wt Off J.P.N. Ware RAAF	Spitfire XII EB-	41 Sqn	¹/₂ V-1
Flt Lt D.F. Ruchwaldy	Mustang III FB178	129 Sqn	V-1
Flt Lt A. Cholajda PAF	Mustang III HB835	316 (Pol) Sqn	V-1
Flt Sgt L. Verbeeck (Belg)	Spitfire XIV RM760	350 (Belg) Sqn	V-1
Plt Off J. Wustefeld (Belg)	Spitfire XIV RM748	350 (Belg) Sqn	V-1
Flt Lt N.J. Campbell RNZAF	Tempest V EJ523	486 (RNZAF) Sqn	V-1

Night 18-19/8/44 (5 V-1s destroyed by fighters)

Flt Lt K.A. Roediger RAAF/	Mosquito XVII HK297	456 (RAAF) Sqn	V-1
Flt Lt R.J.H. Dobson RAAF (Nav)			
Flt Lt B. Williams/	Mosquito VI UP-	605 Sqn	2 V-1
Wt Off S. Hardy (Nav)			
Flg Off R.G. Lucas	Tempest V EJ584	501 Sqn	V-1 probable
Plt Off R.H. Bennett	Tempest V EJ553	501 Sqn	V-1
Flg Off W.F. Polley	Tempest V EJ591	501 Sqn	V-1

19/8/44 (25 V-1s destroyed by fighters)

Plt Off H.R. Wingate	Tempest V EJ549	3 Sqn	2 V-1
Flt Sgt R.W. Cole	Tempest V JN768	3 Sqn	V-1
Flt Lt T. Spencer	Spitfire XII MB875	41 Sqn	V-1
Flt Sgt L. Jackson	Tempest V EJ548	56 Sqn	V-1
Flg Off J.E. Hartley	Mustang III FB125	129 Sqn	V-1
Wt Off T. Hetherington	Mustang III SR436	129 Sqn	V-1
Wt Off E. Redhead	Mustang III FB125	129 Sqn	V-1
Flt Lt K.J. Matheson	Spitfire XIV RM760	130 Sqn	¹/₂ V-1
Plt Off R.J. Martin RCAF	Spitfire XIV RM744	130 Sqn	¹/₂ V-1
Flt Sgt G.W. Hudson	Spitfire XIV RM760	130 Sqn	¹/₂ V-1 probable
Wt Off D.H. White	Spitfire XIV RM744	130 Sqn	¹/₂ V-1 probable
Flt Lt W. Klawe PAF	Mustang III HB863	306 (Pol) Sqn	2¹/₂ V-1
Flt Sgt E. Dowgalski PAF	Mustang III UZ-S	306 (Pol) Sqn	1¹/₂ V-1
Flt Sgt J. Zaleński PAF	Mustang III FB350	306 (Pol) Sqn	V-1
Flt Lt A. Beyer PAF	Mustang III UZ-Y	306 (Pol) Sqn	V-1
Flt Sgt K. Siwek PAF	Mustang III FB371	315 (Pol) Sqn	V-1
Flt Lt T. Kwiatkowski PAF	Mustang III HB831	316 (Pol) Sqn	V-1
Flt Sgt Z. Narloch PAF	Mustang III HB824	316 (Pol) Sqn	1¹/₂ V-1
Wt Off J. Feruga PAF	Mustang III HB848	316 (Pol) Sqn	2¹/₂ V-1
Flt Sgt R.J. Campbell RNZAF	Tempest V JN802	486 (RNZAF) Sqn	V-1
Flg Off G.N. Hobson	Meteor F.1 EE217	616 Sqn	1¹/₂ V-1
Flt Sgt P.G. Watts	Meteor F.1 YQ-	616 Sqn	V-1

Night 19-20/8/44 (2 V-1s destroyed by fighters)

Sqn Ldr B.A. Burbridge/	Mosquito XIX VY-B	85 Sqn	V-1
Flt Lt F.S. Skelton (Nav)			
Flt Lt H. Burton	Tempest V EJ603	501 Sqn	V-1

20/8/44 (11 V-1s destroyed by fighters)

Flg Off R.H. Clapperton	Tempest V JN865	3 Sqn	V-1
Plt Off E. Gray RAAF	Spitfire XII EN228	41 Sqn	V-1
Sqn Ldr A.R. Hall	Tempest V EJ541	56 Sqn	V-1
Flg Off I.G. Wood	Mustang III FB392	129 Sqn	V-1
Flg Off M. Twomey	Mustang III FB125	129 Sqn	V-1
Wt Off J. Edwards	Spitfire XIV AP-	130 Sqn	¹/₂ V-1
Plt Off J.P. Meadows	Spitfire XIV RM693	130 Sqn	¹/₂ V-1
Flt Lt J. Schmidt PAF	Mustang III HB849	315 (Pol) Sqn	2 V-1
Flt Sgt P. Leva (Belg)	Spitfire XIV RM701	350 (Belg) Sqn	V-1
Sqn Ldr J. Berry	Tempest V EJ584	501 Sqn	V-1
Flg Off J. Lee	Spitfire XIV DW-	610 Sqn	¹/₂ V-1
Flg Off N. McFarlane RCAF	Spitfire XIV DW-	610 Sqn	¹/₂ V-1

Night 20-21/8/44 (2 V-1s destroyed by fighters)

Flt Lt W.J. Gough/	Mosquito XIII HK479	96 Sqn	V-1

Flt Lt C. Matson (Nav)
Flg Off R.H. Thomas RAF/   Mosquito VI MM426   418 (RCAF) Sqn   V-1
Flg Off G.J. Allin RAF (Nav)

21/8/44 (1 V-1 destroyed by fighters)
Wg Cdr R.P. Beamont   Tempest V JN751   150 Wg   V-1

22/8/44
No claims

23/8/44 (16 V-1s destroyed by fighters)
Flt Lt T. Spencer   Spitfire XII MB882   41 Sqn   2 V-1
Flt Lt D.J. Reid RAAF   Spitfire XII MB853   41 Sqn ^{1}/$_2$ V-1
Wt Off V.L.J. Turner RAAF   Tempest V EJ526   56 Sqn   V-1
Flg Off E. Topham   Spitfire LFIX MK998   91 Sqn   V-1
Wt Off A.J. Foster RAAF   Mustang III FX983   129 Sqn   V-1
Sgt P.E.H. Standish   Spitfire XIV RM744   130 Sqn   V-1
Flt Lt K.J. Matheson   Spitfire XIV RM760   130 Sqn   V-1
Plt Off W. Dobbs RCAF   Spitfire XIV RM756   130 Sqn ^{1}/$_2$ V-1
Flt Sgt G. Lord   Spitfire XIV RM749   130 Sqn ^{1}/$_2$ V-1
Flt Lt L.A. Wood   Tempest V EJ646   274 Sqn   1^1/$_2$ V-1
Flt Lt T.G.V. Roden   Spitfire Vb BA-   277 (ASR) Sqn   V-1
Flt Lt W. Klawe PAF   Mustang III FB393   306 (Pol) Sqn ^{1}/$_2$+^{1}/$_2$ V-1
Flt Sgt T. Berka PAF   Mustang III FB367   315 (Pol) Sqn   1^1/$_2$ V-1
Wt Off R. Idrian PAF   Mustang III HB849   315 (Pol) Sqn ^{1}/$_2$ V-1
Flt Sgt W.G. Austin RCAF   Spitfire XIV RM686   402 (RCAF) Sqn   V-1
Wt Off C.J. Sheddan RNZAF   Tempest V EJ577   486 (RNZAF) Sqn   V-1

Night 23-24/8/44 (9 V-1s destroyed by fighters)
Flt Lt D.L. Ward/   Mosquito XIII MM524   96 Sqn   V-1
Flg Off E.D. Eyles (Nav)
Flt Lt B.A. Primavesi/   Mosquito XIII HK469   96 Sqn   V-1
Flt Lt P. Houghton (Nav)
Flt Lt F.R.L. Mellersh/   Mosquito XIII MM577   96 Sqn   2 V-1
Flt Lt M.J. Stanley (Nav)
Flt Sgt P. Merrall/   Mosquito XIX MM652   157 Sqn   V-1
Sgt F. Fraser (Nav)
Sqn Ldr J.H.M. Chisholm/   Mosquito XIX MM674   157 Sqn   V-1
Flt Lt E. Wylde (Nav)
Flt Lt K.A. Roediger RAAF/   Mosquito XIVII HK297   456 (RAAF) Sqn   2 V-1
Flt Lt R.J.H. Dobson RAAF (Nav)
Flg Off R-C. Deleuze (FF)   Tempest V EJ607   501 Sqn ^{1}/$_2$ V-1
Flg Off R.C. Stockburn   Tempest V EJ599   501 Sqn ^{1}/$_2$ V-1

24/8/44 (6 V-1s destroyed by fighters)
Flt Lt A.E. Umbers RNZAF   Tempest V JN817   3 Sqn ^{1}/$_2$ V-1
Wt Off F.McG. Reid   Tempest V JN755   3 Sqn ^{1}/$_2$ V-1
Wt Off J.I.T. Adams RAAF   Tempest V EJ549   3 Sqn   V-1
Plt Off J.P. Meadows   Spitfire XIV RM693   130 Sqn ^{1}/$_2$ V-1
Flt Lt L.P. Griffiths RNZAF   Tempest V EJ647   274 Sqn ^{1}/$_2$ V-1
Sgt J. Mielnicki PAF   Mustang III HB845   316 (Pol) Sqn   2 V-1
Flg Off W.S. Harvey RCAF   Spitfire XIV RM734   402 (RCAF) Sqn ^{1}/$_2$ V-1
Flt Lt J.A.H.G. de Niverville RCAF   Spitfire XIV RM727   402 (RCAF) Sqn   V-1

25/8/44 (1 V-1 destroyed by fighters)
Flt Lt O.E. Willis   Tempest V EJ634   274 Sqn   V-1

Night 25-26/8/44 (1 V-1 destroyed by fighters)
Flt Lt J.G. Musgrave/   Mosquito VI MM429   605 Sqn   V-1
Flt Sgt F.W. Samwell (Nav)

26/8/44 (1 V-1 destroyed by fighters)
Flg Off E. Topham   Spitfire LFIX MK293   91 Sqn   V-1

Night 26-27/8/44 (10 V-1s destroyed by fighters)
Flt Lt F.R.L. Mellersh/   Mosquito XIII MM577   96 Sqn   V-1
Flt Lt M.J. Stanley (Nav)
Flt Lt A.D.Boyle/   Mosquito XVII HK316   125 Sqn   V-1
Flg Off H.M. Friesher RAAF (Nav)
Flt Lt J.G. Musgrave/   Mosquito VI MM429   605 Sqn   V-1
Flt Sgt F.W. Samwell (Nav)
Flg Off R.G. Lucas   Tempest V EJ590   501 Sqn   V-1
Flt Lt G.L. Bonham RNZAF   Tempest V EJ597   501 Sqn   4 V-1
Plt Off R.H. Bennett   Tempest V EJ593   501 Sqn   V-1
Flg Off W.F. Polley   Tempest V EJ598   501 Sqn   V-1

27/8/44 (7 V-1s destroyed by fighters)

Plt Off H.R. Wingate	Tempest V EJ577	3 Sqn	V-1
Flt Lt T. Spencer	Spitfire XII MB850	41 Sqn	V-1
Flg Off W.R. MacLaren	Tempest V JN816	56 Sqn	V-1
Flt Sgt H. Shaw	Tempest V EJ548	56 Sqn	V-1
Flg Off J.W. Woolfries	Tempest V EJ628	274 Sqn	V-1
Flt Sgt J. Donocik PAF	Mustang III FX945	315 (Pol) Sqn	1/2 V-1
Flt Lt J.R. Cullen RNZAF	Tempest V JN770	486 (RNZAF) Sqn	V-1
Flt Sgt T.F. Higgs	Spitfire XIV DW-	610 Sqn	V-1

Night 27-28/8/44 (2 V-1s destroyed by fighters)

Plt Off B. Travers/	Mosquito XVII HK304	25 Sqn	V-1 + Bf109
Plt Off A. Patterson (Nav)			
Flt Lt G.L. Bonham RNZAF	Tempest V EJ607	501 Sqn	V-1

28/8/44 (24 V-1s destroyed by fighters)

Flt Sgt R.W. Cole	Tempest V JN768	3 Sqn	2 V-1
Wt Off J.I.T. Adams RAAF	Tempest V EJ525	3 Sqn	V-1
Flt Lt T. Spencer	Spitfire XII EN229	41 Sqn	V-1
Flt Sgt H. Shaw	Tempest V EJ548	56 Sqn	V-1
Flg Off J.E. Hartley	Mustang III HB860	129 Sqn	2 V-1
Flt Lt G.C.D. Green	Mustang III FZ128	129 Sqn	V-1
Flt Lt A.C. Leigh	Mustang III SR428	129 Sqn	V-1
Flt Lt R.G. Kleimeyer RNZAF (Aus)	Mustang III FZ128	129 Sqn	V-1
Flt Lt R.C. Conroy RAAF	Mustang III SR428	129 Sqn	2 V-1
Flt Lt P.N. Howard	Mustang III FB170	129 Sqn	V-1
Flt Lt J. Wisiorek PAF	Mustang III FB347	306 (Pol) Sqn	V-1
Wt Off J. Rogowski PAF	Mustang III FX979	306 (Pol) Sqn	2 V-1
Wt Off J. Pomietlarz PAF	Mustang III FX979	306 (Pol) Sqn	V-1
Flt Lt J. Polak PAF	Mustang III HB849	315 (Pol) Sqn	1/2 V-1
Wt Off R. Idrian PAF	Mustang III FX995	315 (Pol) Sqn	V-1
Wt Off T. Jankowski PAF	Mustang III FB367	315 (Pol) Sqn	2 V-1
Plt Off W.A.L. Trott RNZAF	Tempest V JN863	486 (RNZAF) Sqn	V-1
Flg Off P.M. Bangerter	Spitfire XIV RM739	610 Sqn	2 V-1
Flg Off G.N. Hobson	Meteor F.1 EE217	616 Sqn	1/2 V-1
Flt Sgt E. Epps	Meteor F.1 YQ-	616 Sqn	1/2 V-1

29/8/44 (23 V-1s destroyed by fighters)

Flt Sgt J.W. Foster	Tempest V EJ582	3 Sqn	V-1
Flg Off R.E. Barckley	Tempest V JN755	3 Sqn	V-1
Flt Sgt H. Shaw	Tempest V EJ548	56 Sqn	V-1
Flg Off R.V. Dennis	Tempest V JN816	56 Sqn	V-1
Flg Off J.E. Hartley	Mustang III SR436	129 Sqn	V-1
Flg Off I.G. Wood	Mustang III FX924	129 Sqn	V-1
Flt Lt D.F. Ruchwaldy	Mustang III FB178	129 Sqn	3 1/2 V-1
Flt Lt J.P. Bassett	Mustang III FB130	129 Sqn	1/2 V-1
Flg Off A.F. Osborne	Mustang III FB392	129 Sqn	V-1
Flt Lt L.A. Wood	Tempest V EJ686	274 Sqn	1/2 V-1
Flt Sgt N.G. Carn	Tempest V EJ620	274 Sqn	V-1
Flt Lt D.C. Fairbanks RCAF (US)	Tempest V EJ647	274 Sqn	V-1
Sqn Ldr M.G. Barnett RNZAF	Tempest V EJ645	274 Sqn	V-1
Flt Lt A. Beyer PAF	Mustang III HB863	306 (Pol) Sqn	V-1
Wt Off K. Kijak PAF	Mustang III PK-O	315 (Pol) Sqn	V-1
Flt Lt F. Wiza PAF	Mustang III FX87	315 (Pol) Sqn	1/2 V-1
Wt Off B.J. O'Connor RNZAF	Tempest V EJ577	486 (RNZAF) Sqn	V-1
Plt Off K.A. Smith RNZAF	Tempest V JN770	486 (RNZAF) Sqn	V-1
Plt Off B.M. Hall RNZAF	Tempest V JN803	486 (RNZAF) Sqn	1/2 V-1
Flg Off R.J. Cammock RNZAF	Tempest V JN863	486 (RNZAF) Sqn	V-1
Plt Off J.H. Stafford RNZAF	Tempest V JN803	486 (RNZAF) Sqn	V-1
Flg Off P.M. Bangerter	Spitfire XIV DW-	610 Sqn	1/2 V-1
Plt Off H.C. Finbow	Spitfire XIV DW-	610 Sqn	1/2 V-1
Flg Off H. Miller	Meteor F.1 YQ-	616 Sqn	V-1

Night 29-30/8/44
No claims

30/8/44 (2 V-1s destroyed by fighters)

Cne J. Vassier (FF)	Tempest V EJ628	274 Sqn	V-1
Flg Off J.W. Woolfries	Tempest V EJ646	274 Sqn	V-1

Night 30-31/8/44 (4 V-1s destroyed by fighters)

Flt Lt I.A. Dobie/	Mosquito XIII HK437	96 Sqn	V-1
Flt Lt E.A. Johnson (Nav)			
Sqn Ldr B. Howard RAAF/	Mosquito XVII HK323	456 (RAAF) Sqn	2 V-1

Flt Lt T. Condon RAAF (Nav)

Flg Off E.L. Williams	Tempest V EJ585	501 Sqn	V-1

31/8/44 (4 V-1s destroyed by fighters)

Flt Sgt H. Shaw	Tempest V EJ548	56 Sqn	V-1
Flg Off J.M. Mears	Tempest V EJ611	274 Sqn	V-1
Wt Off B.J. O'Connor RNZAF	Tempest V JN802	486 (RNZAF) Sqn	V-1
Sqn Ldr J. Berry	Tempest V EJ596	501 Sqn	V-1

??/8/44 (1 V-1 destroyed by USAAF bomber)

Sgt G.W. Baldwin USAAF (AG)	B-24 42-52755	4thBS/34thBG	V-1

1/9/44 (3 V-1s destroyed by fighters)

Flt Sgt A.E. Gunn	Mustang III JJ-	274 Sqn	V-1
Sqn Ldr P.D. Thompson	Mustang III FB123	129 Sqn	V-1
Wt Off T. Hetherington	Mustang III HB860	129 Sqn	V-1

Night 4-5/9/44 (2 V-1s destroyed by fighters)

Flg Off R-C. Deleuze (FF)	Tempest V EJ591	501 Sqn	V-1
Flg Off K.V. Panter	Tempest V EJ551/SD-S	501 Sqn	V-1

Night 8-9/9/44 (1 V-1 destroyed by fighters)

Flt Lt A.B. Harvey/	Mosquito XVII WM-N	68 Sqn	V-1
Flt Lt B.StJ. Wynell-Sutherland (Nav)			

Night 15-16/9/44 (3 V-1s destroyed by fighters)

Flt Lt I.A. Dobie/	Mosquito XIII HK437	96 Sqn	V-1
Flt Lt E.A. Johnson (Nav)			
Flt Off B.F. Miller USAAF	Tempest V EJ603	501 Sqn	2 V-1

18/9/44 (1 V-1 destroyed by fighters)

Flt Lt D.A.J. Draper	Spitfire XI PA852	4 Sqn	V-1 (?)

Night 18-19/9/44 (1 V-1 destroyed by fighters)

Flt Lt C.A. Bailey/	Mosquito XIII HK526	96 Sqn	V-1
Flg Off G.E. Weston (Nav)			

Night 20-21/9/44 (1 V-1 destroyed by fighters)

Flt Sgt T. Wilson/	Mosquito XVII HK345	68 Sqn	V-1
Flt Sgt J.F. Jenkins (Nav)			

Night 24-25/9/44 (4 V-1s destroyed by fighters)

Flt Lt J.F. Limbert	Mosquito XVII HK300	25 Sqn	V-1
Flt Lt F.R.L. Mellersh/	Mosquito XIII MM577	96 Sqn	V-1
Flt Lt M.J. Stanley (Nav)			
Flt Off B.F. Miller USAAF	Tempest V EJ558	501 Sqn	V-1

Night 27-28/9/44 (1 V-1 destroyed by fighters)

Wt Off M. Woodthorpe/	Mosquito XIII MM492	96 Sqn	V-1
Flt Sgt D.J. Long (Nav)			

Night 28-29/9/44 (3 V-1s destroyed by fighters)

Flt Lt H. Humphreys/	Mosquito XVII	68 Sqn	V-1
Flg Off P.A. Robertson (Nav)			
Flt Lt K. Kennedy/	Mosquito XIII MM446	96 Sqn	1/2 V-1
Flg Off O.D. Morgan (Nav)			
Flt Lt A.G. Woods/	Mosquito VI UP-D	605 Sqn	V-1
Plt Off W.H. Johnson (Nav)			
Flt Lt R.J. Lilwall	Tempest V EJ600	501 Sqn	1/2 V-1

Night 30/9-1/10/44 (1 V-1 destroyed by fighters)

Flt Lt C.A. Bailey/	Mosquito XIII HK526	96 Sqn	V-1
Flg Off G.E. Weston (Nav)			

Night 5-6/10/44 (1 V-1 destroyed by fighters)

Flg Off J.A.L. Johnson	Tempest V EJ605	501 Sqn	V-1

Night 6-7/10/44 (2 V-1s destroyed by fighters)

Flg Off J.H. Haskell/	Mosquito XVII HK241	68 Sqn	V-1
Flg Off J. Bentley (Nav)			
Flg Off R-C. Deleuze (FF)	Tempest V EJ584	501 Sqn	V-1

Night 7-8/10/44 (3 V-1s destroyed by fighters)

Flt Lt H. Humphreys/	Mosquito HK344	68 Sqn	2 V-1
Flg Off P.A. Robertson (Nav)			
Flt Lt E.L. Williams	Tempest V EJ590	501 Sqn	V-1

Night 11-12/10/44 (1 V-1 destroyed by fighters)

Flt Lt E.L. Williams	Tempest V EJ590	501 Sqn	V-1

Night 12-13/10/44 (4 V-1s destroyed by fighters)

Flt Lt C.A. Bailey/	Mosquito XIII HK526	96 Sqn	¹/₂ V-1
Flg Off G.E. Weston (Nav)			
Flt Lt A.T. Langdon-Down	Tempest V EJ593	501 Sqn	¹/₂ V-1
Flt Lt C.R. Birbeck	Tempest V EJ598	501 Sqn	V-1
Flt Lt E.L. Williams	Tempest V EJ605	501 Sqn	V-1
Flt Lt R. Bradwell	Tempest V EJ589	501 Sqn	V-1

Night 13-14/10/44 (2 V-1s destroyed by fighters)

Flt Sgt F. Kot PAF/	Mosquito VI DZ302	307 (Pol) Sqn	V-1 (also KiA)
Wt Off V. Kepák (Cz) (Nav)			
Wt Off E. Wojczynski PAF	Tempest V EJ763	501 Sqn	V-1

Night 14-15/10/44 (4 V-1s destroyed by fighters)

Flg Off J.H. Haskell/	Mosquito XVII HK344	68 Sqn	2 V-1
Flg Off J. Bentley (Nav)			
Flg Off R-C. Deleuze (FF)	Tempest V EJ589	501 Sqn	2 V-1

Night 15-16/10/44 (1 V-1 destroyed by fighters)

Sqn Ldr N.S. Head/	Mosquito XIII MM460	96 Sqn	V-1
Flg Off A.C. Andrews (Nav)			

Night 16-17/10/44 (1 V-1 destroyed by fighters)

Flg Off R.J. Bennett	Tempest V EJ580	501 Sqn	V-1

Night 17-18/10/44 (1 V-1 destroyed by fighters)

Wt Off E. Wojczynski PAF	Tempest V EJ763	501 Sqn	V-1

Night 18-19/10/44 (2 V-1s destroyed by fighters)

Flt Sgt A. Bullus/	Mosquito XVII HK237	68 Sqn	V-1
Flg Off L.W. Edwards (Nav)			
Flt Lt R.W. Leggett/	Mosquito XVII HK247	125 Sqn	V-1
Flg Off E. Midlane (Nav)			

Night 19-20/10/44 (4 V-1s destroyed by fighters)

Flg Off G.T. Gibson RCAF/	Mosquito XVII HK294	68 Sqn	V-1
Sgt B.M. Lack (Nav)			
Wt Off D. Lauchan/	Mosquito XVII HK294	68 Sqn	2 V-1
Flt Sgt H. Bailey (Nav)			
Flg Off K.V. Panter	Tempest V EJ599	501 Sqn	V-1

Night 22-23/10/44 (3 V-1s destroyed by fighters)

Flg Off R-C. Deleuze (FF)	Tempest V EJ584	501 Sqn	V-1
Flg Off J.A.L. Johnson	Tempest V EJ538	501 Sqn	2 V-1

Night 23-24/10/44 (2 V-1s destroyed by fighters)

Flg Off D.A. Porter	Tempest V EJ589	501 Sqn	V-1
Flg Off R.H. Bennett	Tempest V SD-P	501 Sqn	V-1

Night 24-25/10/44 (3 V-1s destroyed by fighters)

Sqn Ldr J.D. Wright/	Mosquito XVII HK347	68 Sqn	2 V-1
Flg Off W.H. McCulloch (Nav)			
Flt Lt C.R. Birbeck	Tempest V EJ598	501 Sqn	V-1

Night 25-26/10/44 (5 V-1s destroyed by fighters)

Sqn Ldr M. Mansfeld (Cz)/	Mosquito XVII MM683	68 Sqn	V-1
Flt Lt S.A. Janáček (Cz) (Nav)			
Lt F.W. Peebles USN/	Mosquito XVII HK344	68 Sqn	V-1
Ens D. Grinndal USN (Nav)			
Flt Lt R.C. Stockburn	Tempest V SD-U	501 Sqn	2 V-1
Flt Lt R.L.T. Robb	Tempest V SD-Y	501 Sqn	V-1

Night 28-29/10/44 (1 V-1 destroyed by fighters)

Flt Lt E.L. Williams	Tempest V EJ590	501 Sqn	V-1

Night 30-31/10/44 (1 V-1 destroyed by fighters)

Flg Off A.J. Grottick	Tempest V SD-Y	501 Sqn	V-1

Night 3-4/11/44 (2 V-1s destroyed by fighters)

Flt Lt E.L. Williams	Tempest V EJ590	501 Sqn	V-1
Flg Off D.A. Porter	Tempest V EJ605	501 Sqn	V-1

Night 8-9/11/44 (3 V-1s destroyed by fighters)

Flg Off E.J. Ledwidge/	Mosquito XVII MT474	25 Sqn	V-1
Flg Off C.A. Bonner (Nav)			
Flt Lt R. Bradwell	Tempest V EJ589	501 Sqn	V-1
Flg Off D.A. Porter	Tempest V EJ605	501 Sqn	V-1

Night 9-10/11/44 (2 V-1s destroyed by fighters)

Plt Off D.J. Carter/	Mosquito XVII MT474	25 Sqn	V-1

Plt Off W.J. Hutchinson (Nav)
Flt Lt R. Bradwell   Tempest V EJ589   501 Sqn   V-1

Night 10-11/11/44 (4 V-1s destroyed by fighters)
Plt Off D.J. Carter/   Mosquito XVII MT474   25 Sqn   V-1
Plt Off W.J. Hutchinson (Nav)
Flt Lt H. Burton   Tempest V EJ591   501 Sqn   2 V-1
Flg Off J.M. Maday   Tempest V EJ672   501 Sqn   V-1

Night 22-23/11/44 (1 V-1 destroyed by fighters)
Flt Lt H. Burton   Tempest V SD-Z   501 Sqn   V-1

Night 23-24/11/44 (1 V-1 destroyed by fighters)
Flt Lt H. Burton   Tempest V EJ591   501 Sqn   V-1

Night 26-27/11/44 (1 V-1 destroyed by USAAF)
1/Lt P.A. Smith USAAF   P-61 42-5544   422ndNFS USAAF   V-1
2/Lt R.E. Tierney USAAF (R/O)

Night 24-25/11/44 (1 V-1 destroyed by fighters)
Flg Off F.S. Stevens RAAF/   Mosquito XVII HK290   456 Sqn   V-1 + He111
Flg Off W.A.H. Kellet RAAF (Nav)

Night 5-6/12/44 (4 V-1s destroyed by fighters)
Flt Sgt D.J. James/   Mosquito XIII HK417   96 Sqn   V-1
Flt Lt G.M. Ross (Nav)
Flt Lt H. Burton   Tempest V EJ697   501 Sqn   V-1
Flg Off J.A.L. Johnson   Tempest V EJ585   501 Sqn   V-1
Sqn Ldr A. Parker-Rees   Tempest V SD-P   501 Sqn   V-1

Night 7-8/12/44 (1 V-1 destroyed by fighters)
Flg Off D.A. Porter   Tempest V EJ605   501 Sqn $^{1}/_{2}$ V-1
Flt Lt A.T. Langdon-Down   Tempest V EJ593   501 Sqn $^{1}/_{2}$ V-1

Night 17-18/12/44 (4 V-1s destroyed by fighters)
Flg Off R-C. Deleuze (FF)   Tempest V EJ762   501 Sqn   V-1
Wt Off E. Wojczynski PAF   Tempest V EJ580   501 Sqn   V-1
Flt Lt R.J. Lilwall   Tempest V SD-P   501 Sqn   V-1
Wt Off S.H. Balam   Tempest V EJ607   501 Sqn   V-1

??/12/44 (1 V-1 destroyed by fighters)
Grp Capt D.J. Scott RNZAF   Typhoon Ib MN941   123 Wg   V-1

??/12/44 (1 V-1 destroyed by fighters)
Grp Capt D.J. Scott RNZAF   Typhoon Ib MN941   123 Wg   V-1

??/12/44 (1 V-1 destroyed by fighters)
Grp Capt D.J. Scott RNZAF   Typhoon Ib MN941   123 Wg   V-1

Night 24-25/12/44 (1 V-1 destroyed by fighters)
Flt Lt E.G. Smith RCAF/   Mosquito VI HR254   107 Sqn   V-1
Flg Off R.A. Pratt RCAF (Nav)

29/12/44 (1 V-1 destroyed by fighters)
Flt Lt R.A. Wigglesworth/   Mosquito XVII   29 Sqn   V-1
Flg Off Bloomfield (Nav)

1/1/45 (2 V-1s destroyed by fighters)
Sqn Ldr A.C. Henderson/   Mosquito VI NT200   21 Sqn   V-1
Flt Lt W.A. Moore RAAF (Nav)
Flt Lt E. Swaine/   Mosquito VI PZ397   21 Sqn   V-1
Plt Off A. Holt (Nav)

Night 3-4/1/45 (1 V-1 destroyed by fighters)
Flg Off C.R. Redecker RCAF/   Mosquito VI TH-   418 (RCAF) Sqn   V-1
Flg Off M.E. Zimmer RCAF (Nav)

Night 4-5/1/45 (1 V-1 destroyed by fighters)
Flg Off A.N. Wilson/   Mosquito VI PZ195   487 Sqn   V-1
Flg Off E.O. Davies (Nav)
Flt Lt D.V. Patterson/   Mosquito VI NT184   487 Sqn   V-1 probable
Flg Off J.S. Spearing (Nav)

Night 13-14/1/45 (1 V-1 destroyed by fighters)
Flt Lt A.T. Langdon-Down   Tempest V EJ605   501 Sqn   V-1

22/1/45 (1 V-1 destroyed by fighters)
Flt Lt G. Collinson   Spitfire XI   4 Sqn   V-1

?? /2/45 (1 V-1 destroyed by fighters)
Plt Off J. Dalzell   Spitfire LFIXE NH367   74 Sqn   V-1

??/2/45 (1 V-1 destroyed by fighters)
Plt Off J. Dalzell	Spitfire LFIXE NH367	74 Sqn	V-1

??/2/45 (1 V-1 destroyed by fighters)
Plt Off J. Dalzell	Spitfire LFIXE NH367	74 Sqn	V-1

27/2/45 (1 V-1 destroyed by fighters)
Flt Lt B. Williams/	Mosquito VI UP-S	605 Sqn	V-1
Wt Off S. Hardy (Nav)			

28/2/45 (2 V-1s destroyed by fighters)
Flt Lt L.S .Frost	Spitfire LFIXE PT399	74 Sqn	V-1
Flg Off G.F.J. Jongbloed (Dutch)	Tempest V ZD-	222 Sqn	V-1

Night 2-3/3/45 (1 V-1 destroyed by fighters)
Flt Lt G. Hackett RCAF/	Mosquito VI TH-	418 (RCAF) Sqn	V-1
Flg Off W.S. Brittain RCAF (Nav)			

Night 3-4/3/45 (1 V-1 destroyed by bomber)
Sgt J.D. Longworth (AG	Lancaster PD414	619 Sqn	1/2 V-1
Sgt E.M. Marton (AG)	Lancaster PD414	619 Sqn	1/2 V-1

6/3/45 (1 V-1 destroyed by fighters)
Flt Lt J. Jeka PAF	Mustang III UZ-B	306 (Pol) Sqn	V-1

Night 16-17/3/45
Flt Sgt A. Mierzwa PAF/	Mosquito VI NT202	305 (Pol) Sqn	V-1 probable
Flg Off B.F. Panek PAF (Nav)			

24/3/45 (1 V-1 destroyed by fighters)
Flt Lt S. Blok PAF	Mustang III KH492	315 (Pol) Sqn	V-1

25/3/45 (2 V-1s destroyed by fighters)
Flt Lt H. Bibrowicz PAF	Mustang III FB155	315 (Pol) Sqn	V-1
Sgt-Chef P. Girardeau-Montaut (FF)	Spitfire XVI TB394	340 (FF) Sqn	1/2 V-1
Sgt-Chef J. Guichard (FF)	Spitfire XVI TB335	340 (FF) Sqn	1/2 V-1

Night 25-26/3/45 (2 V-1s destroyed by fighters)
Flt Lt A.J. Grottick	Tempest V EJ599	501 Sqn	V-1
Flt Lt J.C. Worthington RNZAF/	Mosquito VI UP-	605 Sqn	V-1
Plt Off F.A. Friar RNZAF (Nav)			

Night 26-27/3/45 (2 V-1s destroyed by fighters)
Flg Off M.G. Kent RCAF/	Mosquito VI MM554	409 (RCAF) Sqn	2 V-1
Plt Off J. Simpson RCAF (Nav)			

Credits awarded to RAF, Commonwealth and PAF squadrons reveal many discrepancies when compared to squadron claims, usually since the powers-that-be subsequently decided that two or more pilots were responsible for the actual shooting down of a Diver. The following compilation is based on information contained in this study gleaned from ORBs, combat reports, logbooks and diaries (NB: totals include shares added together):

	Recorded	Squadron claim	Other sources*
3 Squadron (Tempest V)	317 1/2 (Wg Cdr R.P. Beamont + 32)	303	288-305 1/2
486 (RNZAF) Squadron (Tempest V)	246 3/4	241	223
91 Squadron (Spitfire XIV)	181 1/2 (Wg Cdr R.W. Oxspring + 4 1/2)		185-189
96 Squadron (Mosquito XIII)	189	180	165-174
322 (Dutch) Squadron (Spitfire XIV)	119+2/3		108 1/2
129 Squadron (Mustang III)	88	66	66-86
418 (RCAF) Squadron (Mosquito VI)	86	83	79 1/2
FIU (Tempest V)	84 1/2 (including 2 by Mosquito VIIIs)		86 1/2
316 (Pol) Squadron (Mustang III)	84 1/2	74+5/12 (PAF credit)	74
501 Squadron (Tempest V)	83 (including 1 by Spitfire Vb)		72-95
605 Squadron (Mosquito VI)	82 1/2	75	71
56 Squadron (Tempest V)	72 1/2 (including 2 by Spitfire IXs)		70-77
306 (Pol) Squadron (Mustang III)	72 1/2	57+7/12 (PAF credit)	60
315 (Pol) Squadron (Mustang III)	65 1/2	53+1/12 (PAF credit)	53
165 Squadron (Spitfire IX)	59 1/2		50 3/4
41 Squadron (Spitfire XII)	51 1/2		44+1/3-81
610 Squadron (Spitfire XIV)	48 1/2	50	46 1/2
1 Squadron (Spitfire IX)	41 1/2		47+1/6
157 Squadron (Mosquito XIX)	41 1/2		36 1/2
85 Squadron (Mosquito XVII)	37 1/2 (Wg Cdr H.deC.A. Woodhouse + 2)		18
137 Squadron (Typhoon Ib)	31		29
456 (RAAF) Squadron (Mosquito XIX)	29	29	29
25 Squadron (Mosquito XVII)	26		27
68 Squadron (Mosquito XVII)	27		24
264 Squadron (Mosquito XIII)	20		18

274 Squadron (Tempest V)	18½	20	19
219 Squadron (Mosquito XVII)	18½		12
409 (RCAF) Squadron (Mosquito XIII)	13½		–
616 Squadron (Meteor F.1)	13		12½
130 Squadron (Spitfire XIV)	12		11½
74 Squadron (Spitfire IX)	6		–
125 Squadron (Mosquito XIV)	6		5½
350 (Belg) Squadron (Spitfire XIV)	6		–
277 Squadron (Spitfire Vb)	5		–
402 (RCAF) Squadron (Spitfire XIV)	5½		–
310 (Czech) Squadron (Spitfire IX)	3		3
312 (Czech) Squadron (Spitfire IX)	1¼		–
313 (Czech) Squadron (Spitfire IX)	1		–
504 Squadron (Spitfire IX)	1		–
229 Squadron (Spitfire IX)	1		–
222 Squadron (Tempest V)	1		1
349 (Belg) Squadron (Spitfire IX)	1		–
307 (Pol) Squadron (Mosquito VI)	1		–
340 (FF) Squadron (Spitfire XVI)	1		–
29 Squadron (Mosquito XIII)	1		

150 Wing (Tempest V)	32	Wg Cdr R.P. Beamont (noted above with 3 Squadron)
24 Wing (Spitfire XIV)	4½	Wg Cdr R.W. Oxspring (noted above with 91 Squadron)
123 Wing (Typhoon Ib)	3+	Grp Capt D.J. Scott RNZAF
142 Wing (Spitfire Vb)	2	Wg Cdr J.M. Checketts
135 Wing (Spitfire IX)	1	Wg Cdr R.H. Harries
131 (Pol) Wing (Mustang III)	1	Grp Capt T. Nowierski PAF

Miscellaneous units

4 Squadron (Spitfire XI)	2	–
21 Squadron (Mosquito VI)	2	–
107 Squadron (Mosquito VI)	1	–
487 Squadron (Mosquito VI)	1	–
854 Squadron FAA (Avenger I)	2	–
207 Squadron (Lancaster I)	1	–
619 Squadron (Lancaster I)	1	–

USAAF Credits

354thFS (P-51)	6½	365thFS (P-47)	1½	–
381stFS (P-51)	5	22ndFS (P-47)	1	–
422ndNFS (P-61)	5	512thFS (P-47)	1	–
425thNFS (P-61)	5	513thFS (P-47)	1	–
377thFS (P-47)	3	514thFS (P-47)	1	–
412thFS (P-47)	2½	367thFS (P-47)	1	–
356thFS (P-51)	2	5ERS (P-47)	1	–
Unknown P-47 unit	2	4thBS (B-26)	1	–
Unknown P-51 unit	½			

Tempest V = 851¾ V-1 kills

3 Squadron	317½
486 (RNZAF)	246¾
FIU	82½
501 Squadron	83
56 Squadron	70½
274 Squadron	18½
222 Squadron	1
150 Wing	32

Spitfire XIV = 377⅔ V-1 kills

91 Squadron	181½
322 (Dutch) Squadron	119+⅔
610 Squadron	48½
130 Squadron	12
350 (Belg) Squadron	6
402 (RCAF) Squadron	5½
24 Wing	4½

Mustang III = 246½ V-1 kills

129 Squadron	88
316 (Pol) Squadron	84½
306 (Pol) Squadron	72½
315 (Pol) Squadron	65½
131 (Pol) Wing	1

Spitfire IX = 116¼ V-1 Kills

165 Squadron	59½
1 Squadron	41½
74 Squadron	6
310 (Czech) Squadron	3
312 (Czech) Squadron	1¼
313 (Czech) Squadron	1
504 Squadron	1
229 Squadron	1
349 (Belg) Squadron	1
135 Wing	1

Spitfire XII = 41½ V-1 Kills

41 Squadron	51½

Spitfire Vb = 7 V-1 Kill

277 Squadron	5
142 Wing	2

Spitfire XVII = 1 V-1 Kill

340 (FF) Squadron	1

Typhoon Ib = 34 V-1 Kills

137 Squadron	31
123 Wing	3

Meteor F.1 = 12 V-1 Kills

616 Squadron	12

Mosquito XIII = 223½ V-1 Kills

96 Squadron	189
264 Squadron	20
409 (RCAF) Squadron	13½

Mosquito VI = 173½ V-1 Kills

418 (RCAF) Squadron	86
605 Squadron	82½
21 Squadron	2

Mosquito XVII = 140 V-1 Kills

85 Squadron	39½
456 (RAAF) Squadron	29
68 Squadron	27

29 Squadron	1	107 Squadron	1	25 Squadron	26
		309 (Pol) Squadron	1	219 Squadron	$18^{1}/_{2}$
		487 Squadron	1		

| **Mosquito XIX = $41^{1}/_{2}$ V-1 Kills** | | **Mosquito XIV = 6 V-1 Kills** | | **Mosquito VIII = 2 V-1 Kills** | |
| 157 Squadron | 41 | 125 Squadron | 6 | FIU | 2 |

* See *Aces High* Volume 2 by Christopher Shores.

APPENDIX III

THE TOP SCORERS

Sqn Ldr Joseph Berry DFC**   **61 V-1s destroyed including 2 shared**
Joe Berry was born on 28 February, 1920, in Tursdale, Co. Durham. He joined the Civil Service on leaving school and was working in Nottingham when he volunteered to join the RAFVR in August 1940. On completion of training he was posted to 256 Squadron to fly Defiant night fighters. The following year he was transferred to 255 Squadron on Beaufighter VIFs, and with this unit was posted to the Mediterranean theatre of ops, shooting down three German aircraft in late 1943 (Me210 on 8-9/9/43; Me210 on 9-10/9/43; Ju88 on 23-24/10/43). On completion of his tour, he was awarded a DFC and returned to England, where he was posted to the FIU. In the summer of 1944 he shot down 61 Divers including two shared, while flying Tempest Vs with the FIU and later as CO of 501 Squadron, receiving a Bar to his DFC.
Early in the morning of 2 October 1944, at 0535, he led three Tempests of 501 Squadron from Bradwell Bay to fly a Ranger sortie to Bad Zwischenahn, about 40 kilometres inside Germany. This area was known to be well defended. At a height of 45 feet the Tempests crossed the Dutch coastline and flew inland via the German radar station near Veendam, in the northern part of Holland. There, about 0615, a light anti-aircraft gun opened fire on the low flying fighters and Sqn Ldr Berry's aircraft (EJ600/SD-F) was hit and dived to earth. Over the radio his voice was heard to declare calmly: "Carry on chaps, I've had it." According to Dutch eyewitnesses on the ground, he managed to climb his crippled aircraft to 450 feet but had not sufficient height to bale out and the Tempest crashed at Kibblegaarn, where it burned out. Two local inhabitants, Mr. A. Jager and Mr. S.de Lange, arrived at the scene of the crash. They pulled Berry, who was already dead, out of the burning machine and tried to extinguish the flames on his uniform. His identity tags could not be found. Only a small cigarette box with the initials J.B. and a small medicine box was found on the body. Two hours later the Germans arrived and took the body away. A second Bar to his DFC was announced in February 1946.

Flt Lt Remi van Lierde DFC**   **47 V-1s destroyed including 13 shared**
Born in Belgium on 14 August 1915, Remi van Lierde joined the Belgian Air Force and was briefly involved in the May 1940 battles until shot down and wounded. He escaped to England via Spain after the fall of his country and attended 57 OTU. Commissioned, he was posted to 609 Squadron in 1942, flying Spitfires and Typhoons. He was successful during Ranger operations in 1943, shooting down six German aircraft, and destroying one on the ground (FW190 on 20/1/43; Ju52/3m on 26/3/43; He111 at night on 14-15/5/43; Bf109 on 30/7/43; Ju88, plus one on the ground, on 5/10/43; Bf110 on 30/11/43). Converting to the Tempest in 1944 he joined 3 Squadron and accounted for 47 V-1s including 13 shared and by the end of the war had received two Bars to his DFC. Postwar he commanded 350 (Belgian) Squadron until October 1946. He rejoined the Belgian Air Force and retired as a Colonel in 1968. He died in 1990.

Flt Lt Francis Richard Lee 'Togs' Mellersh DFC*   **44 V-1s destroyed**
Togs Mellersh was born on 30 July 1922 in Edwalton, Notts, the son of Air Vice-Marshal Sir Francis Mellersh KBE AFC, a WWI fighter ace. He joined the RAFVR in 1940 (51 OTU) and on completion of training was posted to 29 Squadron flying Beaufighter night fighters. In late 1942 he was posted to 600 Squadron in North Africa and during the next eight months claimed eight victories including one probable (two Ju88s on 18-19/4/43; Ju52/3m on 8-9/5/43; Z1007bis and Ju88 on 12-13/7/43; He111 on 29-30/7/43; SM84 probable on 3-4/8/43; Ju88 on 9/10/43), for which he was awarded a DFC. On returning to England he was posted to the FIU before joining 96 Squadron on Mosquito XIIIs, and in the summer of 1944 accounted for 43 Divers destroyed by the end of September, assisted in the destruction of 36 of these by his navigator Flt Lt Michael Stanley DFC (see below). He then rejoined the FIU, which had become FIDS (Fighter Interception Development Squadron), and with this unit shot down a Ju88 on 11-12/4/45 while flying a Mosquito XXX. He was awarded a Bar to his DFC. Postwar he remained in the RAF until retirement in 1977 as an Air Vice-Marshal. He died in 1997.

Flt Lt Michael John Stanley DFC (Navigator)   **37 V-1s destroyed (with Flt Lt Mellersh)**
Born in Birkenhead on 8 March 1915, Michael Stanley became a student priest in 1932, but abandoned his religious vocation in 1937. When he volunteered for the RAF in 1940 he was a student teacher. He qualified as a sergeant observer the following year and was posted to 29 Squadron flying Beaufighters, where he teamed up with Plt Off Togs Mellersh. Without having gained any successes, they were posted to North Africa in 1943 and joined 600 Squadron, still flying Beaufighters. Over the next few months Mellersh shot down eight German and Italian aircraft but only two of these were claimed while flying with Michael – two Ju88s on the night of 18-19/4/43. On returning to the UK, still teamed up with Togs Mellersh, Michael was firstly posted to the FIU before joining 96 Squadron on Mosquito XIIIs, and assisted Togs in shooting down 37 Divers. He received an immediate award of the DFC in July 1945, the citation noting the participation in the destruction of three Ju88s and 36 [*sic*] flying bombs. He remained in the RAF postwar and retired as a Squadron Leader. He died in 1981.

Wg Cdr Roland Prosper Beamont DSO* DFC*   **32 V-1s destroyed including six shared**
Born in Chichester, Sussex on 10 August 1920, he joined the RAF in January 1939. By November of that year he was in France with 87 Squadron and was in action during the May 1940 fighting, scoring four victories (Do17 on 13/5/40; Bf110 on 14/5/40; Do17 on 15/5/40; Ju88 on 17/5/40). He then flew during the Battle of Britain, claiming three and one shared, plus two probables (shared Ju88 on 24/7/40; Bf110 and a probable on 15/8/40; Do17 and Bf109 on 25/8/40; Bf109 probable on

12/10/40) and awarded a DFC. In December 1941 he was posted to Hawkers as a production test pilot and flew early Typhoons. Posted initially to 56 Squadron when the Typhoon became operational, he then joined 609 Squadron and became CO. He flew many train-busting ops on the Typhoon, for which he was awarded a DSO and Bar to DFC. Promoted to Acting Wg Cdr, he was given command of 150 Wing flying Tempests and destroyed a Ju88 on the ground on 28/5/44. He shot down a Bf109 on 8/6/44 before becoming involved in the flying bomb campaign, often flying with 3 Squadron, and was credited with 32 V-1s (six shared) destroyed. He shot down a FW190 on 2/10/44 but was then shot down by flak on 12/10/44 and became a POW until the end of the war. A Bar to his DSO had been awarded in July. Postwar he joined Glosters as a test pilot before joining English Electric as chief test pilot, flying the prototype Canberra, the P-1 (later to be known as the Lightning in RAF service), and the ill-fated TSR2. He received a CBE in 1969 and eventually retired in 1979. He died in 2001.

Other pilots who destroyed 20 or more V-1s were:

Flg Off **Raymond Hedley CLAPPERTON** DFC 3 Squadron Tempest V = 24 (POW 29/9/44)

Flg Off **Robert Walton COLE** DFC 3 Squadron Tempest V = 24 including four shared (POW 26/11/44)

Flt Lt **Arthur Robert MOORE** DFC 3 & 56 Squadrons Tempest V = 24 including one shared

Flg Off **Rudolf Frans BURGWAL** (Dutch) 322 Squadron Spitfire XIV = 23 including three shared (KiA 12/8/44)

Flg Off **Owen David EAGLESON** DFC RNZAF 486 (RNZAF) Squadron Tempest V = 23 including three shared (POW 2/5/45)

Flg Off **Raymond John CAMMOCK** RNZAF 486 (RNZAF) Squadron Tempest V = 21 including one shared (KiA 6/10/44)

Sqn Ldr **Norman Arthur KYNASTON** DFC* 91 Squadron Spitfire XIV = 21 (KiA 15/8/44)

Wg Cdr **Edward Dixon CREW** DSO DFC* 96 Squadron Mosquito XIII = 21 (Died 2002)

Plt Off **H. Richard WINGATE** 3 Squadron Tempest V = 21 including two shared

Flt Lt **James Hugh McCAW** DFC RNZAF 486 (RNZAF) Squadron Tempest V = 20 including one shared

Flt Lt **Raymond Stanley NASH** DFC 91 Squadron Spitfire XIV = 20 including three shared

Plt Off **Kenneth Gordon SLADE-BETTS** DFC 3 Squadron Tempest V = 20 including one shared (KiA 29/12/44)

APPENDIX IV

MOSQUITO CLAIMS AGAINST MISSILE-CARRYING HE177s/DO217s

April – August 1944

29-30/4/44

Sqn Ldr D.J. Williams RCAF	406 (RCAF) Sqn HU-O	2 Do217s	6N+AD/4701(StabIII/KG100) FTR
			6N+IT/4716 (9/KG100) FTR
Wg Cdr K.M. Hampshire RAAF	456 (RAAF) Sqn HK286	Do217 probable	Mitchell FR142 320 Sqn shot down in error

6-7/6/44

Flg Off F.S. Stevens RAAF	456 (RAAF) Sqn HK290	2 He177s	Five He177s FTR:
Wg Cdr K.M. Hampshire RAAF	456 (RAAF) Sqn HK286	He177	F8+MH/550206 (1/KG40)
Flg Off R.G. Pratt RAAF	456 (RAAF) Sqn HK303	He177	F8+KK/550197(2/KG40)
			F8+LK/535731 (2/KG40)
			F8+IN/550117 (5/KG40)
			F8+?? (5/KG40)

7-8/6/44

Sqn Ldr B. Howard RAAF	456 (RAAF) Sqn HK290	2 He177s	Two He177s FTR:
Plt Off R.D. Hodgen RAAF	456 (RAAF) Sqn HK302	He177	F8+HK/550211 (2/KG40);
			F8+??/550083 (6/KG40)
Flt Lt J. Howard-Williams	FIU	He177 damaged	
Plt Off R. Green RCAF	406 (RCAF) Sqn HU-D	Do217	6N+OR/4742(StabIII/KG100) FTR

9-10/6/44

Flt Lt R.B. Cowper RAAF	456 (RAAF) Sqn HK353	He177	Two He177s of 2/KG40 FTR:
			F8+BK/550198
			F8+SK/535670.

10-11/6/44

Sqn Ldr G.L. Howitt RAF	456 (RAAF) Sqn HK249	He177 probable	F8+??/550221 (4/KG40) damaged
Plt Off I.W. Sanderson RAAF	456 (RAAF) Sqn HK249	He177	F8+JH/550175 (1/KG40) FTR

11-12/6/44

Flg Off A.W. Sterrenberg RCAF	410 (RCAF) Sqn MM523	Do217	6N+KT/4708 (9/KG100) FTR

12-13/6/44

Flt Lt R.A. Miller	604 Sqn HK526	He177	F8+FH/550215 (1/KG40) FTR
Plt Off L.J. Kearney RCAF	410 (RCAF) Sqn HK459	He177	F8+?? (4/KG40) FTR

13-14/6/44

Wg Cdr J.W. Reid RCAF	409 (RCAF) Sqn MM560	He177	Five He177s FTR:
Plt Off S.J. Williams RAAF	456 (RAAF) Sqn HK282	He177	F8+IM/550146 (4/KG40)
Flt Lt F.C. Ellis	604 Sqn MM563	He177	F8+??/550098 (4/KG40)
Flt Lt I.H. Cosby	264 Sqn HK502	He177	F8+??/550080 (4/KG40)
			F8+??/550078 (6/KG40)
			F8+??/550089 (6/KG40)

14-15/6/44

Wt Off W.F. Price RCAF	410 (RCAF) Sqn HK366	2 Do217s	Three Do217s FTR:
			6N+KR/4748 (7/KG100)
			6N+IT/4555 (9/KG100)
			6N+HR/4749(9/KG100)

4-5/7/44

Flt Lt R.B. Cowper RAAF	456 (RAAF) Sqn HK356	He177	Four He177s FTR:
Plt Off I.W. Sanderson RAAF	456 (RAAF) Sqn HK249	He177	F8+??/550210 (4/KG40)
Flg Off E.C. Radford RAAF	456 (RAAF) Sqn HK312	He177	F8+??/550213 (5/KG40)
			F8+??/550203 (6/KG40)
			F8+??/550195 (6/KG40)
Plt Off S.J. Williams RAAF	456 (RAAF) Sqn HK282	Do217	Six Do217s III/KG100 FTR:
Sqn Ldr L.W.G. Gill	125 Sqn HK325	Do217	6N+DT/4718 (Stab)
Flt Lt J.B. Kerr RCAF	418 (RCAF) Sqn	Do217	6N+??/6847 (8/KG100)
			6N+??/3037 (7/KG100)
			6N+??/3060 (7/KG100)
			6N+??/ 3061 (7/KG100)
			6N+??/4710 (9/KG100)

14-15/7/44

Lt J.O. Armour RM	NFIS Mosq	Do217	Not KG40 or KG100

21/7/44

Wg Cdr J.V. Yonge	235 Sqn	Do217	Three Do217s KG100 FTR
Fg Off D.B. Frost	235 Sqn	Do217	
Flg Off L.N. Collins	248 Sqn	Do217	
Flt Lt F.R. Passey	248 Sqn	Do217	
Flt Lt S.G. Nunn	248 Sqn	Do217 probable	
Flt Lt S.G. Nunn ⎫ Flt Sgt W.W. Scott ⎭	248 Sqn	He177 probable	
Sqn Ldr D.J. Williams RCAF	406 (RCAF) Sqn	Do217 + Do217 shared	
Flg Off W.H. Meakin RCAF	406 (RCAF) Sqn	Do217	

2-3/8/44

Sqn Ldr D.M. Somerville RCAF	410 (RCAF) Sqn MM477	Do217	6N+DR/2926 & 6N+??
Flt Lt A.E. Browne RNZAF	488 (RNZAF) Sqn HK532	Do217	(both 8/KG100) FTR

3-4/8/44

Flg Off R.J. Foster	604 Sqn MM552	Do217	6N+MS/3057 (7/KG100) FTR

5-6/8/44

Flt Lt P.F.L. Hall	488 (RNZAF) Sqn MM513	Do217	6N+?? (Stab III/KG100) FTR
Flt Sgt T.A. MacLean RNZAF	488 (RNZAF) Sqn MM502	Do217, Do217 damaged	
2/Lt E.D. Axtell USAAF	422ndNFS USAAF	Do217 probable	

6-7/8/44

Flt Lt A.E. Browne RNZAF	488 (RNZAF) Sqn HK420	2 Do217	6N+GR & 6N+AD
Flt Lt J.C. Surman	604 Sqn MM448	Do217	(both 7/KG100 FTR)

7-8/8/44

Flg Off J.S. Smith	604 Sqn MM465	2 Do217	6N+?? (8/KG100) FTR

8-9/8/44

Flg Off T.R. Wood	604 Sqn MM528	Do217 probable	Not Do217 (Albemarle P1501 of 296 Sqn shot down in error)

APPENDIX V

MOSQUITO/BEAUFIGHTER CLAIMS AGAINST HE111 V-1 LAUNCHERS III/KG3, I, II & III/KG53

23-24/9/44

Flg Off R.A. Henley	25 Sqn HK362	He111 probable	5K+IR/168334 (7/KG3) FTR
Wg Cdr L.J. Mitchell	25 Sqn HK357	He111 probable	5K+ES/8222 (7/KG3) FTR

24-25/9/44

Wt Off L.E. Fitchett RCAF	409 (RCAF) Sqn MM589	He111	5K+AR/8474 (7//KG3)

28-29/9/44

Wg Cdr L.J. Mitchell	25 Sqn HK357	2 He111s	5K+AT/161726 (9/KG3)
			5K+CT/8428 (9/KG3)

5-6/10/44

Flt Lt J.F.R. Jones	25 Sqn HK239	He111	5K+LS/700272 (8/KG3)

6-7/10/44

Flt Lt A.E. Marshall	25 Sqn HK257	He111	5K+KS/161225 (8/KG3)

7-8/10/44

Plt Off B. Travers	25 Sqn HK285	He111 damaged	5K+KR/161898 (7/KG3) FTR

13-14/10/44

Flt Sgt K. Kot PAF (FTR)	307 (Pol) Sqn DZ302	He111	5K+FR/700639 (7/KG3) crashed

24-25/10/44

Flt Lt D.T. Tull	FIDS Beaufighter	He111	5K+ES/161530 (2/KG53)
Flg Off W.A. Beadle	125 Sqn HK310	He111	A1+BL/8504 (3/KG53) 45% damaged

30-31/10/44

Sqn Ldr L.W.G. Gill	125 Sqn HK325	He111	A1+BM/700253 (4/KG53)
		He111 damaged	

4-5/11/44

Sqn Ldr J. Howard-Williams	FIDS Bftr V8385	He111	See losses listed below*

5-6/11/44

Flt Sgt L.W. Neal	68 Sqn TA389	He111	Prob A1+FN/700666 (5/KG53)
Sqn Ldr W.H. Maguire	FIDS Beaufighter	He111	and A1+AC/700878 (4/KG53)

9-10/11/44

Flt Lt J. Lomas	25 Sqn MV521	He111	A1+LK/8134 (2/KG53)
Wt Off K.R. Cookson	68 Sqn HK251	He111 probable	

10-11/11/44

Flt Lt D.H. Greaves	25 Sqn MT492	He111	Three He111s FTR:
Wt Off A.R. Brooking	68 Sqn HK348	He111	A1+AB/162080 (3/KG53)
Flt Lt G.E. Simcock	125 Sqn HK263	He111 probable	A1+NM/161924 (4/KG53)
			A1+HM/700862 (4/KG53)

19-20/11/44

Flt Lt D.A. Arnold RAAF	456 (RAAF) Sqn HK246	He111	A1+NN/162377 (5/KG53)

24-25/11/44

Flg Off F.S. Stevens RAAF	456 (RAAF) Sqn HK290	He111	A1+BH/110304 (3/KG53)

26-27/11/44

1/Lt Paul A. Smith USAAF	422ndNFS USAAF P-61 42-5544	He111	Not KG53 but 1/TG30

17-18/12/44

Plt Off K.D. Goodyear	125 Sqn	He111 damaged	

22-23/12/44

Flt Lt R.W. Leggett	125 Sqn HK247	He111	A1+HT/8156 (9/KG53) crash-landed

23-24/12/44

Flt Sgt A. Bullus	68 Sqn	He111	A1+AR/700733 (7/KG53)

3-4/1/45

Wt Off A.R. Brooking	68 Sqn HK296	He111	A1+BM/700520 (2/KG53)

5-6/1/45

Wg Cdr R. Bannock RCAF	406 (RCAF) Sqn	He111	A1+HT/162181 (9/KG53)

Other known III/KG3/KG53 operational losses:

July 1944

6-7/7/44	Two He111 (III/KG3) collided on the ground at Rosières (one crewman killed)
10-11/7/44	He111 5K+BS/161306 (8/KG3) FTR (Uffz Gerhard Alisch and crew killed)
21-22/7/44	He111 5K+AS/160257 (8/KG3) FTR (Ltn Ludwig Schmalholz and crew killed)
26-27/7/44	He111 5K+GT/161230 (9/KG3) hit mast near Eindhoven (Uffz Günter Rohne and crew killed)
28-29/7/44	He111 5K+ER/160923 (7/KG3) FTR (Uffz Karl Schmidt and crew)
	He111 5K+LS/160972 (8/KG3) FTR (Uffz Heinz Schmidt and crew)
	He111 5K+HS/160980 (8/KG3) FTR (Uffz Gerd Schwärzel and crew)
	He111 5K+IR/161363 (7/KG3) crash-landed Amiens, flak-damaged (one crewman killed)
29-30/7/44	He111 5K+FS/8269 (8/KG3) shot down by own AA (Uffz Alfons Rieger; two crew killed)

August 1944

2-3/8/44	He111 5K+MR/8268 (7/KG3) emergency landing in Belgium – crashed (Obfhr Friedrich Martin and crew killed)
21-22/8/44	He111 5K+?? (III/KG3) crashed on take-off Venlo
30-31/8/44	He111 5K+BS/16771 (8/KG3) crashed Vossenberg (Uffz Lorenz Gruber and crew killed)

September 1944

15-16/9/44	He111 5K+IS/161439 (7/KG3) crashed on take-off (Fw Heinrich Güls and crew killed)
16-17/9/44	He111 5K+ET (9/KG3) shot down by own flak (Uffz Hans Jördens and crew survived)
18-19/9/44	He111 5K+HS/160571 (8/KG3) crashed at Scharl, Friesland (Obfw Karl-Heinz Holze and crew killed)
25-26/9/44	He111 5K+IR/168334 (7/KG3) crashed 15km south-east Osnabrück (Fw Herbert Böhling and crew killed)
29-30/9/44	US bombing raid on Handorf airfield killed amongst others Hptm Heinz Grünswald, Staffelkapitän 7/KG3

October 1944

7-8/10/44	He111 5K+DS/160969 (8/KG3) collided with beacon and crashed on Dutch coast (Fw Lothar Gall and crew killed)
9-10/10/44	He111 5K+ER/700245 (7/KG3) and 5K+CR/161920 (8/KG3) collided in mid air and crashed near Leeuwarden, killing Fhj Volker Happel and Fw Anton Schmid and their respective crews
18-19/10/44	He111 5K+LT/8339 (9/KG3) FTR (Obfw Werner Schmidt-Reich and crew killed)
20-21/10/44	He111 5K+BT/7000040 (3/KG53) FTR (Uffz Albert Fleischmann and crew killed)
22-23/10/44	He111 5K+ER/161619 (1/KG3) crashed in sea off Zandvoort (Obgfr Walter Hasler drowned)

November 1944

4-5/11/44*	He111 A1+AM/701235 (4/KG53) FTR (Hptm Heinz Zöllner and crew killed)
	He111 A1+KM/161412 (4/KG53) FTR (Ofw Fritz Jost and crew killed)
	He111 A1+EP/700863 (6/KG53) FTR (Ltn Heinz Redde and crew killed)
	He111 A1+BM/701403 (4/KG53) FTR (Uffz Walter Weider and crew killed)
	He111 A1+CM/701113 (4/KG53) FTR (Ltn Willi Hansen and crew killed)
	(NB one of the above claimed by Beaufighter from FIDS)
	He111 A1+GK/8540 (2/KG53) crashed near Katwijk (Ofhr Karl-Heinz Mallach and two crewmembers killed, one survived injured)
5-6/11/44	He111 A1+CN/161002 (5/KG53) FTR (Fw Karl Wiaweg and crew killed)
	He111 A1+BN/160146 (5/KG53) FTR (Ltn Alfred Schacht and crew lost)
	He111 A1+LN/8553 (5/KG53) FTR (Obfw Ernst Lösche and crew killed)
8-9/11/44	He111 A1+?P (6/KG53) belly-landed (w/o); one crewman slightly injured
9-10/11/44	He111 V4+YR/162436 (1/KG53) crashed (Uffz Hermann Hurrle and two crew killed)
13-14/11/44	He111 A1+KP/161756 (4/KG53) crashed (Fw Karl Oehl seriously injured and one killed)
22-23/11/44	He111 A1+KH/700638 (1/KG53) crashed Osterode near Bramsche (Fhj Wilhelm Wolfshol and Uffz Georg Grill killed; three seriously injured)
23/11/44	He111 A1+IL 3/KG53 crashed (Uffz Hans Jördans & crew)

December 1944

4/12/44	He111 crash-landed Husum
	He111 8226 (7/KG53) crash-landed Laland (Uffz Claus Jahvos and crew)
6-7/12/44	He111 A1+AM/700036 (4/KG53) FTR (Obfw Nikolaus Mertes and crew killed)
9-10/12/44	He111 A1+FH/161442 (1/KG53) FTR (Uffz Günter Lis and crew killed)
22-23/12/44	He111 A1+LR/700647 crashed Busdorf (Uffz Robert Rösch and crew killed)

January 1945

3-4/1/45	He111 A1+BK/8067 (2/KG53) FTR (Obfw Christian Dreyer and crew killed)
	He111 A1+DK/162378 (2/KG53) FTR (Fw Heinz Kowalski and crew killed)
	He111 A1+HL/162376 (3/KG53) crashed Flensburg (Obfw Georg Murr and one killed, two seriously injured)
	He111 A1+LM/162105 (4/KG53) crashed Ansetzen (Gfr Fritz Fischer and three killed, one seriously injured)
	He111 A1+FR/160591 (7/KG53) crashed near Copenhagen (Oblt Fritz Jensen and crew baled out, one killed)
	He111 A1+KR/161540 (7/KG53) FTR (Oblt Hans-Harro Werner and crew killed)
	He111 A1+NR/700128 (7/KG53) crashed Gammellund (Ltn Siegesmund Kasberg and crew killed)

He111 A1+AT/8188 (9/KG53) FTR (Fw Rudolf Wimplinger and crew killed)

He111 A1+GK/110264 (9/KG53) crashed Klipplev (Uffz Herbert Jurgens and crew killed)

6-7/1/45   He111 A1+CR/ 70195 (7/KG53) FTR (Ltn Kurt Neubert and crew missing)

February/March 1945

26/2/45   Three He111s of II/KG53 (7973, 8444 and 700731) were strafed and destroyed by Allied fighters at Wittmund

10/3/45   He111 (700133 of III/KG53) crash-landed and was 85% destroyed. Ltn Wietfeld, the pilot, was killed

21/3/45   Four He111s of III/KG53 (including 700115, 700129 and 700254) were strafed and destroyed by Allied fighters at Alt-Lönnewitz*.

It is recorded that 77 He111s of III/KG3 and KG53 were lost to all causes while on operations, of which a dozen or so from II/KG53 were allegedly lost in two operations in early/mid-December due to premature detonation of the V-1 shortly after take-off[276]. This would appear to be incorrect and probably referred to emergency launchings caused by technical problems. However, it seems likely that several Heinkels from II Gruppe did suffer premature detonations in early November. As recorded above, Mosquito and Beaufighter crews were credited with 23 and three probables, two of the latter almost certainly being destroyed. Royal Navy ships patrolling the North Sea were credited with shooting down ten more.

*American P-47 pilot Lt Clifford J. Price USAAF of 397thFS/368thFG reported the result of an attack on a Czech airfield shortly before the end of the war: "I came on four Do217 bombers, which were loaded with V-1 rockets under their wings. I was in perfect position so my single strafing run destroyed all four bombers, plus a Bf109. I was awarded the DFC [US] for that mission."

APPENDIX VI

THE ELECTRONIC WAR AND THE TEMPEST

Although unlike many other types of aircraft in the RAF's arsenal throughout the Second World War, the Hawker Tempest had nothing much to do with 'Electronic Warfare'. With this technology in its infancy the pilot's eyes, in a fast and manoeuvrable single-seater fighter aircraft were deemed to be at the time sufficient for the work these types of aircraft undertook. This kind of 'Electronic Wizardry' was the realm of bombers and fighter-bombers, with numerous 'Measure and Counter Measure' devices being developed and up-dated for navigation, search and protection. One such radar device was the AN/APS 13, codenamed Monica IIIE, developed in this form by the boffins of the Bomber Support Development Unit (BSDU) at Defford in Worcestershire; this unit was also home to the Telecommunications Research Establishment (TRE) and the Telecommunications Flying Unit (TFU).

The AN/APS 13 tail-warning device was designed to alert the aircraft's crew in the event of an enemy fighter attack from the rear. It was first deployed by the RAF in June 1943 but unfortunately it was quickly countered by the Luftwaffe's electronics experts when this system was recovered from a downed bomber and reverse engineered. It then materialized in Luftwaffe aircraft as the *Flensburg*, which was used with great effect to home-in on any Monica emissions. Even though Monica was easy to operate and worked satisfactorily, when it was discovered that this system hade been compromised, the device was taken out of use. It was not until 7 July 1944, with the battle against the V-1 in full swing that the Air Ministry decided to give Monica another try. It had become immediately obvious after the first few encounters with V-1s that detecting a means of this menace quickly enough to do anything about it in the clouded skies and poor visibility over the English Channel and mainland would be very useful. The first trials of the Monica IIIE as a range indicator against the flying bomb were carried out by the FIU at Wittering in a Mosquito VI borrowed from the BSDU, but instead of this device being a backward-looking system, it was reversed and became a forward-looking system. These trials again were successful, and after much re-engineering and size-reducing, the system was fitted into the cockpit of a Tempest V (EJ535) belonging to the TFU. This Tempest was flown from Defford by Flt Lt L.J. Leppard, in late July, to Newchurch to be evaluated by the pilots of the FIU detachment that were already fully engaged in night operations against the flying bombs. The CO of the detachment was Flt Lt Joe Berry DFC, who had previously served with the TFU at Defford, from the end of December 1943 to mid-February 1944, after his tour of duty had expired flying Beaufighters in the Mediterranean.

Selected pilots (Flt Lt Leppard, Flt Lt Joe Berry, Flg Off Cyril Thornton and Flight Officer Bud Miller USAAF) flew evaluation tests by night and day on a dozen occasions against the flying bombs or their own aircraft as targets when no flying bombs were available. One of the main physical differences between the Monica IIIE devise fitted in the Tempest V from that of all the other systems fitted in the other aircraft, was the replacement of the Mark V (PI) display tube with a simple, small orange warning light fitted to the right of the Tempest's gun-sight. Once a flying bomb had broken the beam and activated the warning light, the pilot knew he was within range of his target.

Secret Trials of the AN/APS 13 as a Range Indicator (FIU Report No.254 10 August 1944)

Introduction

Verbal instructions were received by Fighter Interception Unit from Air Defence Great Britain to carry out trials of AN/APS 13 as a method of range finding in Tempest aircraft, operating against Flying Bombs at night. A Tempest V aircraft, fitted with the equipment, was delivered from Defford to the FIU Tempest Detachment at RAF Newchurch, for trials, at the end of July.

Description of Equipment

The AN/APS 13 consists of a Unit of approximately 15" by 8" by 10" overall dimensions, mounted on the port side of the aircraft behind the pilot. The pilot's control box is mounted on the starboard knock out panel and carries an on/off switch and a test switch for the indicator lamp, which is mounted near the gun sight. The indicator lamp will light up at a range, which is pre-set on the ground. A single dipole aerial is carried on the port wing near the wingtip. The overall weight of the equipment is approximately 25lbs.

Nature of Trials

Since returning from Newchurch to Wittering for adjustment, the equipment has been flown six times by day and six times by night by the FIU Tempest detachment. The day trials have been carried out on target aircraft, owing to the shortage of Divers when required; but all the night trials have been done with Divers as targets.

Results of Trials

When the aircraft was delivered from Defford the range was pre-set at 800 yards and the light was permanently on at low levels. The aircraft was returned to Wittering where the range was set at 300 yards and the aircraft returned to Newchurch. During each of the twelve test flights the warning lamp came on at ranges of 300 to 350 yards, or when flying at less than 1,500 feet above the ground. The light remains on to zero range. The dimming of the bulb is considered adequate.

Conclusion

As the equipment is small, and extremely easy to operate, it is ideal for Tempest aircraft. The present range setting is just within the firing range and should remain as it is. It gives no indication of closing speed, but this is not important, as the pilot can tell whether he is closing by the increase of the intensity of the flame from the propulsion unit of the bomb.

Recommendation

The pilot's control panel and cabling is at present installed on the emergency jettison panel and in this position might cause difficulty in abandoning the aircraft. It is suggested that this unit be moved to a position on the same side of the fuselage above the petrol cocks.

The simplicity of this device though had unfortunate side effects – any flying below 1,500 feet would cause the warning light to illuminate. This was found to be ground echoes from the system giving a false reading, which was never a problem in high-flying bombers. Once again, despite its potential, since a large number of flying bombs came over the coast at 1,500 feet or less, the constant illumination of the warning light made this system non-practical and it was again taken out of use. However, by then, the majority of Divers were falling to the new proximity fused shells being used by the AA guns and the greater use of Tempests, Mustangs and Meteors. Tempest EJ535, *sans* Monica equipment, was later issued to 486 (RNZAF) Squadron and was lost shortly thereafter.

Graham Berry

APPENDIX VII

SCIENCE FACT OR SCIENCE FICTION?

One of the many ideas proposed to find a way of defeating the V-1 assault on London could have emanated from the pen of H.G. Wells – but it was the brainchild of eminent US scientist Dr Don Hare and his team at Airborne Instruments Laboratory:

"One very interesting proposal to emerge from the Airborne Instruments Laboratory was a jammer to counter the V-1 flying bomb. This weapon was invulnerable to radio countermeasures in the normal sense of the word: it employed no radar or radio guidance whose signals could be jammed. Azimuth guidance was by means of a magnetic compass controlling a gyro, which operated the rudder via a servo system. Nevertheless even this weapon could have been jammed. The problem was passed to Dr Don Hare and his team at AIL and they figured out a way that was absolutely fantastic. Their idea was to form a magnetic loop employing existing railway lines, suitably interconnected, all the way around London – a circumference of about 60 miles. This loop would be energized with a hefty current to make it into a giant magnetic deflector. They worked on a system, which would have required something like 1,000 amps DC, to provide the necessary magnetic field to deflect the compass of a flying bomb at 1,000 feet. The power requirement for the system would have been of the order of 20 to 30 megawatts, which would have meant dedicating quite a large [commercial] power station for this purpose. The system was very seriously considered and design work began on some of the necessary equipment. While the device was still in the conceptual stage, however, Allied ground troops overran the area in Northern France from which most of the flying bombs were being launched against England. So the idea came to nothing. The jammer to counter the V-1 must hold the record, easily, for the most powerful electronic countermeasures equipment ever considered."

Extracted from *The History of US Electronic Warfare* by Dr Alfred Price (with permission).

APPENDIX VIII

PILOTED FLYING BOMBS

The Luftwaffe's *Leonidas* Staffel
The Imperial Japanese Navy's *Jinrai* Buntai

Fieseler R-1V Reichenberg – Germany's piloted flying bomb

With the continuing and ever-intensifying USAAF daylight bombing raids over occupied Northern Europe and Germany causing grave concern for Hitler and his commanders, many ideas were considered to counter the threat. Although the Americans were taking heavy punishment and grievous losses in machines and men, the USA's ability to make available speedy replacements in both aircraft and aircrew would mean desperate measures would be required to stem the tide. In May 1944, Hauptsturmführer Otto Skorzeny and the celebrated female test pilot Flugkapitän Hanna Reitsch proposed using a manned V-1 as a suicide weapon, which, with its 1,874lb warhead, would cause havoc amongst the tightly packed US bomber formations. The idea gained credence amongst some of the Luftwaffe and a number of V-1s were modified to accommodate a pilot and tested at the Luftwaffe's Rechlin/Lärz Test Centre, home of KG200. The first of the training models was a single-seater V-1 with cushioned skids and landing flaps; the second model was a two-seater fitted with dual controls but no power unit. The operational model of course had no landing gear but was fitted with a jettisonable canopy to allow the pilot a slim chance of baling out before contact was made with the intended target. Once the programme had gained momentum, there was no shortage of volunteer pilots, who were labelled *Selbstopfermänner* (self-sacrifice men), and their unit the *Leonidas* Staffel[277].

Meanwhile, a testing programme was under way at Rechlin/Lärz, as recalled by one of KG200's most experienced test pilots Hptm Hans-Werner Lerche, who piloted the He111:

"The reason for these flights, the actual object of these tests was probably the intended use of such manned V-1 missiles for the so-called 'self-sacrifice' attacks. It was said that some well-known pilots had volunteered for these operations, which did not offer any chance of survival, and certainly did not correspond to our mentality. Our test programme envisaged a series of test launches with the manned V-1 to prove the feasibility or otherwise of this concept. To start with, these launches were to be carried out at an altitude of about 3,000 m (10,000 feet) without power. In the beginning everything went off quite well with three pilots whom I had known since my gliding days. However, when on subsequent flights the V-1 pulse-jet engine had to be started, some critical incidents occurred. The first pilot had to bale out and was lucky to pass clear of the V-1 tail assembly. The second pilot managed all right until just before landing, when the V-1 pulse-jet engine suddenly started again during levelling-off, probably due to the inclined position of the fuel tank. The thrust of the pulse-jet above the centre of gravity generated a moment of nose-heaviness, which the pilot counteracted by vigorous pulling of the elevator control. Then the pulse-jet stopped again, the V-1 stalled, and the pilot wrenched his spine. The third pilot had no luck either: he was hit on the head by the cockpit hood, which had come off in flight, probably because it was not completely locked. He suffered severe injuries but managed to land the V-1 with a fractured skull. The first loss of a pilot's life came during subsequent flights. As far as I know further test flights with the manned V-1 were then continued by Flugkapitän Hanna Reitsch."[278]

Indeed, Hanna Reitsch did carry out a number of test flights, about which she wrote in her memoirs:

"I volunteered to test the prototype, but the experimental station at Rechlin insisted on using their own pilots. On a warm summer's day, Otto Skorzeny and I attended the first test at Lärz. On arriving, we found the plane ready to start. The V-1 was hanging under the right wing of the Heinkel 111 bomber. Fascinated, we followed the Heinkel as it took off with its burden and climbed higher and higher. Then the moment came when we saw the test pilot detach his plane from the bomber and drop away in the V-1 like some small, swift bird. The pilot flew in tight turns until, on a dead-straight course, he began to lose height, gliding at an ever-steeper angle towards the earth. It did not take us long to realise that this behaviour of the machine was in no way intended by the pilot. The machine disappeared from sight and shortly after we heard an explosion in the distance and saw a column of black smoke rising in the summer air. For half an hour we waited, fearing to hear the news, until at last the report came through that the pilot was severely injured but still alive. It transpired that the crash had been caused, not by some structural defect in the aircraft, but through the pilot's own inadvertence. He had unintentionally pressed the catch to the sliding hood of the cockpit and, half stunned by the force of the air-current, had lost control over the plane.

"The day after, a second pilot took off in the V-1. He, too, came to grief, though escaping with his life. From then on, Heinz Kensche[279] and I were allowed to take over the prototype tests of the piloted V-1. My first flight passed without incident and the next eight or ten flights were also successful, though not without their awkward moments. On one occasion, for example, the pilot of the He111 had just released me from beneath the bomber's wing, when his plane grazed the rear of the V-1. There was a loud rending noise, as if the tail of my plane had been broken right off. Though only just able to continue to control the plane, I managed to make a smooth landing, finding, when I inspected it, that the tail had been crumpled and twisted to the right through an angle of almost thirty degrees. It seemed a miracle that it had not come right off. On another occasion, I was testing the behaviour of the two-seater model of the V-1 at a wide range of speed along an inclined flight-path, flying at speeds up to 530mph. During the test, a sack of sand, which had been wedged in the front seat on my instructions to supply extra weight, somehow broke loose and shifted position. In blissful ignorance, I tried to flatten out at speed and suddenly found that I could not move the elevator. I had not enough height, or time, to be able to bale out by parachute and had to risk all on a last, faint chance of saving myself and the plane. Just before the machine reached the ground, I pushed her nose down and then, with all the response I could get from the elevator, quickly pulled out again. This manoeuvre checked the plane just enough for me to be able to make a landing, though an extremely hard one which splintered the skids and the hull. I emerged without a scratch. On yet another test-flight, I was trying out the V-1 fully loaded at high speeds. For this test we had built a water-tank into the hull. As the landing skids were too fragile to stand up to the shock of landing when heavily loaded (for the operational machine would be crashed straight into its target) we had fitted a draining plug in the tank, operated by moving a lever, so that the water could be let out before landing. Otherwise, the pilot would most certainly receive an unpleasant surprise. I started to test the V-1 at about 18,000 feet with the consequence that the draining hole froze up. When I tried to move the lever to open the drain-plug at 4,500 feet, I found that it would not budge. The plane was now gliding rapidly downwards and as no engine was fitted to this model, time was all-important. In a frenzy of desperation, I gripped and clawed at the lever till my fingers were bleeding. The earth was stretching up nearer and nearer towards me. At last, with only a few hundred feet to go, the lever suddenly moved and there was just time to drain out most of the water. Lucky! When the tests had been satisfactorily completed, we began to train the men we had chosen to be instructors of the other volunteers, using the two-seater model of the V-1. Though any average pilot could fly the V-1 without difficulty once it was in the air, to land it called for exceptional skill, in that it had a very high landing speed and, moreover, in training it was the glider model, without engine, that was usually employed. The training period, therefore, made heavy demands on all concerned."

Despite the apparent success of the testing programme – although test pilot Heinz Kensche was killed on 5 March 1945 – and the enthusiasm of Hanna Reitsch and others, the new commanding officer of KG200, the distinguished bomber pilot Oberst Werner Baumbach, was horrified to learn that pilots were volunteering to became suicide pilots and immediately called a halt to further training, a courageous act as he later recalled: "My refusal to collaborate in such idiocy, and even command it, was within an inch of costing me and my officers our heads." Naturally, Hanna Reitsch[280] was unhappy with the decision:

"A formidable difficulty was the total failure on the part of higher authority to appreciate that the Suicide Group was no stunt, but a collection of brave, clear-headed and intelligent Germans who seriously believed, after careful thought and calculation, that by sacrificing their own lives they might save many times that number of their fellow countrymen and ensure some kind of future for their children. But this conception was too cold to kindle the imaginations of Himmler and Goebbels. Himmler suggested that the suicide-pilots should be recruited among the incurably diseased, the neurotics and the criminals so that through a voluntary death they might redeem their 'honour'. Goebbels hasted to exploit the Group for propaganda purposes by summoning its members to his Ministry and reciting to them a premature panegyric on the theme of heroism."

When Hitler agreed that German soldiers should not be expected to sacrifice their lives without a chance of survival, the programme was officially terminated by Oberst Baumbach and the volunteer pilots dispersed accordingly.

MXY-7 *Ohka* – Japan's piloted flying bomb

In a desperate measure to counter the US Navy's command of the seas around the Japanese homeland and islands, the Imperial Japanese Navy called for volunteer pilots to fly the revolutionary *Ohka* (Cherry Blossom) flying bomb on its one-way trip to destruction – and glory for its doomed pilot. The flying bomb was the brainchild of Ensign Mitsuo Ota, who presented his idea to the Imperial Japanese Navy in the summer of 1944. It called for a small wooden aircraft propelled by three solid-fuel rockets and a 1,200kg explosive warhead. The flying bomb was to be carried in the bomb bay of a converted G4M Betty bomber and then flown towards the target, when the bomb would be guided by its entombed pilot to crash onto the selected ship. The initial powered flight took place in October 1944 and production was immediately put in hand. By March 1945, when production ceased, some 750 had been manufactured.

The *Jinrai Buntai* of the 721st Naval Air Group was established on 1 October at Kōnoike to train the volunteers, using the MXY-7K1 trainer fitted with retractable landing skids. The suicide volunteers were known as Thunder Gods, a name given also to other suicide pilots/crews who flew conventional aircraft on such missions. The first operation was planned for 21 March 1945, the unit having moved to Kanoya Naval Base in southern Kyūshū under the command of Cdr Kunihiro Iwaki. The first mission turned out to be a disaster when the 15 G4M carriers were intercepted by USN F6F Hellcats before they were in range. Nine were shot down within ten minutes while the remaining six jettisoned their pilotless *Ohkas* but to no avail – all were shot down with the loss of all bomber crews and the Thunder God pilots. These included Lt Kentaro Mitsuhashi (the commander), Sub-Lt Yuzura Ogata, and Petty Officers Ataru Shimamura, Tomio Matsuo and Naokichi Kameda. The next operation took place on 1 April, six G4Ms being involved. Although all were shot down, some managed to release their *Ohkas* before their own demise, the US battleship *West Virginia* being struck (four killed, seven wounded), as were three transports, the *Alpine*, *Achernar* and *Tyrrell*. One of the bombers had on board PO1c Keisuke Yamamura as the *Ohka* pilot, and he survived the crash, being rescued from the sea.

Nine G4Ms carried out the next attack, on 12 April, an *Ohka* piloted by Reserve Lt Saburō Doi sinking the destroyer USS *Mannert L. Abele* (according to the returning G4M pilot) in which 73 of her crew were killed, while the USS *Stanley* was also hit. One *Ohka* was actually shot down by AA fire from the destroyer USS *Jeffers*, just 50 yards from possible impact. Only one G4M returned. The next three missions were equally as disastrous for the Japanese, all seven *Ohka*-carrying G4Ms being shot down on 14 April, four out of six two days later, and three of four on 28 April. None of the *Ohkas* scored hits on the ships. However, the destroyer USS *Shea* and *Gayety* were both damaged by *Ohkas* on 4 May, although six of the seven G4Ms were shot down. Another success followed on 11 May when the destroyer USS *Hugh W. Hadley* was hit. The penultimate assault planned using 11 G4Ms on 25 May failed due to bad weather and the carriers returned with their charges, including PO1c Yamamura (survivor of the earlier crash), who had been strapped into the *Ohka*. The final attack on 22 June witnessed the loss of four of the six G4Ms for no success. Again, the fortunate PO1c Yamamura was a survivor, his *Ohka* failing to release from the mother aircraft and he was returned to base. Surely the gods had decided that he was not to sacrifice his life for his country. Japanese historian Hatsuho Naito wrote: "Of the total of 185 planes used in *Ohka* attacks, 118 were destroyed, taking the lives of 438 persons including 56 Thunder God pilots and 372 mother-plane crew members."[281]

The Japanese also had plans to build a piloted version of the Fi-103, based on the German Fieseler R-1V *Reichenberg*, with one model intended to take off from simple landing strips around the Japanese mainland coastline, jettisoning its undercarriage while doing so, while another was to be air-launched with a pulse-jet fitted beneath the fuselage rather than on top. The dramatic ending of the Japanese war prevented either version progressing beyond the drawing board. Following the surrender of the Japanese armed forces, General Kawabe, commander of kamikaze operations to the Imperial General Staff, addressed an American commission thus:

"We do not wish the kamikaze tactics to be described by the term 'suicide-attacks'. Right up until the end, we believed we could outweigh your material and scientific superiority by the force of our moral and spiritual convictions."

APPENDIX IX

OPERATIONS APHRODITE, ANVIL & CASTOR

Operation Aphrodite

4/8/44

B-17F 42-30342 (Watten)	1/Lt Fain H. Pool USAAF	injured on baling out
Shot down by flak Gravelines	S/Sgt Phillip Enterline USAAF	injured on baling out
B-17G 42-39835 (Siracourt)	1/Lt John W. Fisher USAAF	killed in crash
Crashed near Orford	T/Sgt Elmer Most USAAF	baled out safely
B-17F 42-3461 (Wizernes)	1/Lt Frank L. Houston USAAF	baled out safely
Crashed 500 yards short of target	T/Sgt Willard D. Smith USAAF	baled out safely
B-17F 41-24639 (Mimoyecques)	1/Lt Cornelius A. Engel USAAF	seriously injured on b/out
Crashed prematurely (error)	T/Sgt Cliff A. Parsons USAAF	injured on baling out

6/8/44

B-17F 42-30212 (Watten)	1/Lt Joe P. Andrecheck USAAF	baled out safely
Crashed in sea off Ipswich	T/Sgt Ray Healy USAAF	baled out safely
B-17G 42-31394 (Watten)	1/Lt John Sollars USAAF	baled out safely
Crashed in sea off French coast	T/Sgt H. Graves USAAF	baled out safely

Operation Anvil

12/8/44

PB4Y 32271 (Mimoyecques)	Lt Joseph P. Kennedy USN	both killed due to
Exploded in air over Blythe	Lt Wilford J. Willy USN	premature detonation

3/9/44

B-24D 42-63954 (Heligoland)	Lt Ralph Spalding USN*	baled out safely
		Crashed on island of Düne (error)

Operation Castor

11/9/44

B-17F 42-30180 (Heligoland)	1/Lt Richard W. Lindahl USAAF	killed when chute FTO
Shot down by flak short of the target	1/Lt Donald E. Salles USAAF	baled out safely

14/9/44

B-17F 42-30363 (Hemmingstedt)	1/Lt M.P. Hardy USAAF	baled out safely
Crashed short of target	1/Lt E. Hadley USAAF	baled out safely
B-17G 42-39827 (Hemmingstedt)	1/Lt W.G. Haller USAAF	baled out safely
Crashed into sea (error)	2/Lt C.L. Shinault USAAF	baled out safely

15/10/44

B-17F 42-30039 (Heligoland)	1/Lt R. Betts USAAF	baled out safely
Shot down by flak short of target	2/Lt M. Garvin USAAF	baled out safely
B-17G 42-37743 (Heligoland)	1/Lt W. Patton USAAF	baled out safely
Narrowly missed target	1/Lt J.W. Hinner USAAF	baled out safely

30/10/44

B-17F 42-30066 (Heligoland)	1/Lt Glen A. Barnes USAAF	baled out safely
Crashed nr Trollhattan, Sweden (error)	1/Lt R. McCauley USAAF	baled out safely
B-17F 42-3438 (Heligoland)	1/Lt W.C. Gaither USAAF	baled out safely
Crashed in North Sea out of fuel	1/Lt W.M. Dunnuck USAAF	baled out safely

5/12/44

B-17G 42-39824 (Hanover)	1/Lt T.H. Barton USAAF	baled out safely
Shot down by flak near Haldorf	1/Lt F.E. Bruno USAAF	baled out safely
B-17F 42-30353 (Hanover)	1/Lt R.F. Butle USAAF	baled out safely
Landed without exploding**	1/Lt K.T. Walters USAAF	baled out safely

1/1/45

B-17F 42-30178 (Oldenburg)	2/Lt J. Stein USAAF	baled out safely
Shot down by flak, crashed without exploding	1/Lt E. Morris USAAF	baled out safely
B-17F 42-30237 (Oldenburg)	Capt J. Hodson USAAF	baled out safely
Shot down by flak, exploded	1/Lt L. Lawing USAAF	baled out safely

* Lt Ralph Spalding USN was killed when his aircraft crashed into a mountain on returning to the United States on completion of his tour.

** Apparently a contingent of German troops approached this aircraft and ordered out the non-existent crew. When there was no response, they battered in the door and entered with drawn pistols. A few seconds later the aircraft exploded.

APPENDIX X

DR GOEBBELS' PROPHETICAL PREDICTIONS

Dr Paul Joseph Goebbels, fanatical to the end although correct in some of his predictions, made one of his last announcements in February 1945 to the people of what remained of near-defeated Germany:

"What will the world look like in the year 2000? Stalin, Churchill and Roosevelt have determined it, at least insofar as the German people are concerned. One may however doubt if they and we will act in the predicted manner. No one can predict the distant future, but there are some facts and possibilities that are clear over the coming fifty years. For example, none of the three enemy statesmen who developed this brilliant plan will still be alive, England will have at most 20 million [*sic*] inhabitants, our children's children will have had children, and the events of this war will have sunk into myth [*not so*]. One can also predict with a high degree of certainty that Europe will be a united continent in the year 2000. One will fly from Berlin to Paris for breakfast in fifteen minutes, and our most modern weapons will be seen as antiques [*correct, but the V-1 was ultimately developed into today's cruise missile, while the V-2 was the forerunner of US and former-USSR space rockets*], and much more. Germany, however, will still be under military occupation according to the plans of the Yalta Conference, and the English and Americans will be training its people in democracy. How empty the brains of these three charlatans must be – at least in the case of two of them!

"The third, Stalin, follows much more far-reaching goals than his two comrades. He certainly does not plan to announce them publicly, but he and his 200 million slaves will fight bitterly and toughly for them. He sees the world differently than do those plutocratic brains. He sees a future in which the entire world is subjected to the dictatorship of the Moscow Internationale, which means the Kremlin. His dream may seem fantastic and absurd, but if we Germans do not stop him, it will undoubtedly become reality. That will happen as follows: If the German people lay down their weapons, the Soviets, according to the agreement between Roosevelt, Churchill and Stalin, would occupy all of East and south-east Europe along with the greater part of the Reich [*true until the late 1980s/early 1990s*]. An iron curtain [*Churchill was credited with coining this term, but clearly not so*] would fall over this enormous territory controlled by the Soviet Union, behind which nations would be slaughtered.

"It is more than naive for the British prime minister to plan for the political and social status of the Reich in the year 2000. In the coming years and decades, England will probably have other concerns. It will have to fight desperately to maintain a small portion of its former power in the world [*true*]. It received the first blows in the First World War, and now during the Second World War faces the final *coup-de-grâce*. One can imagine things turning out differently, but it is now too late. The Führer made numerous proposals to London, the last time four weeks before the war began. He proposed that German and British foreign policy work together, that the Reich would respect England's sea power as England would respect the Reich's land power, and that parity would exist in the air. Both powers would join in guaranteeing world peace, and the British Empire would be a critical component of that peace. Germany would even be ready to defend that Empire with military means if it were necessary. Under such conditions, Bolshevism would have been confined to its original breeding grounds.

"Germany will not be occupied by its enemies in the year 2000 [*true*]. The German nation will be the intellectual leader of civilized humanity [*one of them, anyway*]. We are earning that right in this war [*incorrect*]. This world struggle with our enemies will live on only as a bad dream in people's memories. Our children and their children will erect monuments to their fathers and mothers for the pain they suffered, for the stoic steadfastness with which they bore all, for the bravery they showed, for the heroism with which they fought, for the loyalty with which they held to their Führer and his ideals in difficult times [*incorrect*]. Our hopes will come true in their world and our ideals will be reality. We must never forget that when we see the storms of this wild age reflected in the eyes of our children. Let us act so that we will earn their eternal blessings not their curses."

Goebbels became Reich Chancellor for one day only, following Hitler's death. On 1 May 1945 he allowed his wife Magda to kill their six young children before they both committed suicide. Goebbels was a Roman Catholic, and aged 47 when he died.

APPENDIX XI

POSTWAR DEVELOPMENT OF THE V-1 BY THE ALLIES

By July 1944, the Americans had produced and launched at Eglin AFB the first reverse-engineered V-1 (the Republic AAF MX-544/JB-2 – Jet Bomber 2 Thunderbug). A ton of salvaged V-1 parts had been flown to Wright-Patterson Field on 12 July, from which 13 copies were built in short time. In late July the USAAF ordered 1,000 copies, but when General Spaatz, commanding US strategic bomber forces in Europe, decided against using them against the Germans on the grounds that they were not sufficiently accurate to warrant the trouble, the plan was dropped in September, by which time 1,391 JB-2s had been built, two of which had been air launched from B-17G test beds. By January 1946, the USN had become involved in missile development for its ships, and the USN Loon copy of the V-1 was launched, the forerunner of the Regulus ship-launched cruise missile. The USAAF also modified a P-51D (44-63528) by fitting a Marquardt ramjet under each wing to increase its performance, rather than utilize it as a flying bomb; these looked remarkably like a pair of propulsion units as used on V-1s or the Me328. Apparently with the latter the Germans were unable to keep the pulsing of the jets in sync and, as a result, the mismatched pulses of the jets just about tore the aircraft apart. The P-51 was used to carry out extensive testing until August 1948 when it was lost in an accident. One of the ramjets flamed out and as the test pilot tried to get a relight, the ramjet exploded in a massive fireball. Fortunately, he was able to roll the aircraft over and successfully bale out. The burning aircraft plummeted to the ground and was totally destroyed.

Meanwhile in Britain, Fairey Aviation was approached by the Air Ministry to design and build a ship-to-air flying bomb for use against the Japanese kamikaze attacks now threatening the British and American fleets approaching the Japanese mainland. Named Stooge, it was seven-and-a-half feet long and weighed about 740lbs, of which 220lbs was made up of an explosive warhead. It was to be fired by Royal Navy ships from a ramp launcher by four solid-fuelled Swallow booster rockets, which provided a combined 5,600lb thrust for just less than two seconds. A liquid-fuelled sustainer engine with a 760lb thrust then carried the Stooge to a maximum estimated speed of 500mph and radio-guided to a maximum range of eight miles. It was tested at Aberporth in Cardigan Bay (Wales) but due to the abrupt ending of the Japanese war there was no longer a use for such a weapon, and the project was cancelled. However, the experience and expertise gained did allow Fairey Aviation the opportunity to develop the Fireflash air-to-air guided missile for the postwar RAF.

In late July 1944, British scientists were requested by the government to share their knowledge of the V-1 with their Soviet counterparts, and even despatched wreckage for them to analyse. It has been suggested that the missile involved had been salvaged from the North Sea by Royal Navy divers. In return, a British and American technical team travelled to the recently captured Blizna Test Centre to study V-2 parts, fuels and launchers. A few days later the first V-2 was launched against the United Kingdom. By October 1944, Russian engineer Vladimir Chelomei had been appointed to produce a reverse-engineered V-1 for the Soviets, using machine tools purchased from the British, and by December flight-testing had begun. On 18 January 1945, full production was ordered for the Chelomei design but the decision was later rescinded due to the inaccuracy of the missiles. Nonetheless, test firings continued and by August 1945 some 63 missiles had been launched in Uzbeckistan. Testing and development dragged on for a further five years after which it was decided that accuracy could still not be achieved, and the programme was terminated. One development was the Type 16X, a twin-engined missile that could be launched from a TU-2 carrier. Another development that had progressed in the Soviet Union was the piloted version of the V-1 into a ground attack aircraft, called the EF-126. Five Jumo 226-engined copies were built but on the second test flight the unfortunate coerced German pilot was killed.

The only other countries to copy the V-1 were France and Sweden. The French NORD Company began work in 1947 on the CT-10, a drone that commenced test flying in 1949. It was smaller that the original V-1 and had twin rudders; it was designed to be ground launched or air launched from a LeO451 medium bomber. About 400 were built and some were sold to the USA and United Kingdom. The Royal Navy carried out trials at Malta but missiles being developed by both the USA and USSR rapidly superseded the design. SAAB of Sweden however continued to develop the basic design into the ultimate RB08A, which had an integral engine and butterfly tail, for use on ships.

ENDNOTES

1 As stated by Michael Bowyer in *2 Group RAF.*

2 The authors' recommend Steve Darlow's *Sledgehammers for Tintacks* (published by Grub Street) for further reading on Bomber Command attacks on V-1 sites.

3 Instituted in 1943 by Maria Dickin CBE OBE (1870-1951), founder of the People's Dispensary for Sick Animals (PDSA), the three police horses to receive the Dickin Medal were Olga, Upstart and Regal. The first two awards were in connection with Diver incidents and Olga's citation read: *"On duty when a flying bomb demolished four houses in Tooting and a plate-glass window crashed immediately in front of her. Olga, after bolting for 100 yards, returned to the scene of the incident and remained on duty with her rider, controlling traffic and assisting rescue organisations."* Upstart's citation stated: *"While on patrol duty in Bethnal Green a flying bomb exploded within 75 yards, showering both horse and rider with broken glass and debris. Upstart was completely unperturbed and remained quietly on duty with his rider controlling traffic etc until the incident had been dealt with."* Regal's award was in connection with incendiary bombs: *"Was twice in burning stables caused by explosive incendiaries at Muswell Hill. Although receiving minor injuries, being covered by debris and close to the flames, this horse showed no signs of panic."* As a matter of interest, 18 dogs also received the award, mainly for rescue work, but not only for the actions of 1944.

4 In 1937 the RAF had established a Pilotless Aircraft Section at RAF Henlow using Queen Bees for co-operation with Army Anti-Aircraft units. At the end of 1940 the name was changed to Pilotless Aircraft Unit and later operated from RAF Manorbier with up to 35 Queen Bees. And that is probably about as far as the British pilotless aircraft programme progressed. For his work with the unit Flt Lt The Hon. Michael Adderley received an AFC (he later flew as an exchange pilot in Korea with the USAF). The Queen Bee was a radio-controlled pilotless target derivative of the Tiger Moth, and was first flown on 5 January 1935. A total of 380 were built for the RAF, mainly for live-target gunnery practise on various AA ranges. These had wooden, plywood-covered fuselages, in contrast to the Tiger Moth's metal fabric-covered structure.

5 The aircraft, named RAK-1, had a typical sailplane wing, under which a pod was suspended to accommodate the pilot and sixteen solid rocket engines. The tailplane was mounted on booms behind the wing and high out of the way of the rocket exhaust. Opel successfully piloted it over 10 miles in 75 seconds of flight on 30 September 1929 but landed heavily, damaging the aircraft beyond repair. Opel planned to build a second rocket plane, but apparently lost interest before the project was completed.

6 In November 1939, a package was discovered in the office of the British Naval Attaché in Oslo, deposited – it is believed – by a high-ranking Luftwaffe officer, whose identity has never been discovered. The package contained highly secret information on the latest weapons being developed by Germany, and mention was made of a secret testing site located at Peenemünde on the Baltic coast, where such weapons as the embryonic V-1 and V-2, the Fritz-X guided bomb, and jet and rocket engines were being tested. The documents were passed to MI6 and were deemed to be authentic, which is when Dr R.V. Jones became involved.

7 Military historian and author of *The Royal Air Force in the Second World War.*

8 By the end of hostilities KG100 had flown a total of 65 operations involving 487 aircraft armed with either Hs293s or Fritz-Xs. It was estimated that 319 missiles had been operationally launched of which 215 correctly functioned. During these

operations, in both the Mediterranean and European theatres, a total of 40 warships and 39 merchant vessels were claimed destroyed or damaged, for the loss of 48 aircraft.

9 Wellingtons from 205 Group based in Sardinia would bomb the factory at Portres Des Valence and, under cover of this diversionary attack, Webster's men of the Marquis were to go into the plant and attempt to snatch a Hs293. The operation was laid on for the night of 10/11 May 1944. The first wave of 12 Wellingtons were to bomb both a wall surrounding the plant, and nearby the factory. En route the Wellingtons encountered a freak storm with strong winds. One bomber was shot down and two others forced down by terrible weather while the rest returned to base. One Wellington did reach the area and dropped a flare path to make the target visible from the air. The freak storm cleared in time allowing a second diversionary force of 12 Wellingtons to attack 15 minutes later. Meanwhile, the Maquis approached the factory on time, but found the surrounding wall and structure intact. About a mile away the diversionary attack by the Wellingtons was carried out on schedule, but without a breach in the walls, the Maquis could not enter the compound, so they returned to the hills. Another attempt was scheduled for the second week in June. But the invasion on 6 June forced transfer of all missiles to northern France in an attempt to sink the Allied ships in the channel (courtesy Norman Malayney).

10 The 41,650-ton Italian flagship *Roma* was sunk by a Fritz-X in September 1943, when it and other warships of the Italian Navy were en route to Malta following the surrender of Italian forces. The Royal Navy battleship HMS *Warspite* had been put out of commission for six months by this weapon, while the American cruisers USS *Philadelphia* and *Savannah* had been heavily damaged, and the light cruiser HMS *Spartan* sunk during attacks by Fritz-X bombs. A Henschel Hs293 was credited with the first successful guided missile attack when it sank the sloop HMS *Egret* on 27 August 1943. Several Hs293-armed Do217s had fallen to Spitfires from GCII/7 on 30/9/43 including one shared by Lt Henri Jeandet. A photograph of his aircraft depicts his score painted below the cockpit including one symbol beneath which is written 'Fi-103'. It is believed this referred to an Hs293 he apparently shot down during the attack against KG100's Dorniers, and not a V-1 as suggested.

11 The casualties aboard the five Heinkels were: 550146: Oblt Benno Meissner, Obfw Karl Schöllmann, Fw Hans Kuhm, Uffz Heinz Krüger, Uffz Heinrich Krapt; 550080: Lt Jürgen Reichmüller, Gfr Günter Stetka, Obfw Fritz Fünfotück, Uffz Josef Kistenfeger, Gfr Helmut Strasser, Uff Wilhelm Mohr; 550078: Uffz Hermann Klavehn, Uffz Ernst Koch, Uffz Gerhard Sonnenwald, Obgfr Helmut Sietl, Uffz Max Stolzenberg, Obfw Walter Wiermann; 550048: Uffz Alois Willfahrt, Uffz Franz Schmidt; 550087: Fw Heinrich Lyding, Uffz Bruno Zwahl, Uffz Georg Scharff.

12 In June 1926, the original Air Defence Great Britain had been formed and so-named, and remained as such until July 1936 when it was renamed Fighter Command.

13 Supplement to the *London Gazette*, 20 October 1948.

14 Air Commodore Sir Frank Whittle, the jet pioneer, was somewhat rueful about the events that surrounded the development of his jet engine design, one of the main reasons being lack of official support despite AVM Tedder (later Lord Tedder) stating in 1940 that the project was *"a potential war winner."* He reflected: *"Neither BTH [British Thompson-Houston] nor Rover had personnel competent for the design work involved. Of the firms mentioned, only the team led by Frank Halford of de Havilland had any impact on jet-engine development. Both BTH and Rover attempted to improve on Power Jets designs, and failed miserably. I and my Power Jets colleagues protested vigorously, only to make ourselves very unpopular with the officials responsible for these inept policies. This very sorry state of affairs dragged on until early 1943 when, at last, Rolls-Royce took over from Rover (long after I had wanted to involve them). The scene changed overnight. Rolls-Royce got the W.2B through the prescribed 125-hour type test, giving its full designed performance, within three months. It went into action as the Welland in the Meteor F.1 in August 1944, though by this time the Germans had the Me262 (powered by Junkers 004 engines) in production in much greater numbers.*

"We suffered from other delays due to bombing. The foundry of High Duty Alloys, on whom we depended for compressor casings and other castings, was severely damaged by a direct hit. What would have been our only spare compressor impeller was dropped and scrapped during a daylight raid by a single hit-and-run bomber. These things cost us three to six months. Another factor which allowed the Germans to gain on us was the Ministry's insistence on a 125-hour type test. The Germans argued, with rather brutal logic, that fighters did not last for more than 25 hours in combat operations, so engines were allowed to go into production on that premise. In short, the succession of avoidable delays may have totalled about seven and-a-half years. The RAF could have been equipped with Meteors and Vampires, or the like, by about 1937, and bombers with turbofan engines, based on our LR.1 turbofan, by about 1939. The LR.1, which would have been the world's first turbofan, was never completed, again because of Ministry policy."

15 See *The Maunsell Sea Forts* by F.R. Turner.

16 Although this does not appear in 68 Squadron's ORB, which is clearly incomplete, it is recorded in Flt Lt Albert 'Len' Harvey's logbook (Len Harvey was a famous British boxer of the time, hence the nickname). During his first tour with 600 Squadron, Len Harvey shot down a German bomber on his first op (claimed as a He111 but actually a Ju88, on 7/6/42) but his Beaufighter was hit by return fire and ditched; he was awarded an immediate DSO for helping to save the life of his navigator. Before completing his tour he claimed a Heinkel as probably destroyed. In 1943 he joined 68 Squadron and claimed a He111 on 6/7/43, a Ju88 on 13/7/43, a Bf110 possible on 13/9/43, another Ju88 on 3/2/44 and a Heinkel probable on 7/2/44, raising his score to four and three probables. Sadly, his final claim on 28/5/44 for a Ju88 turned out to be a Mosquito of 604 Squadron.

17 See Peter Haining's *The Flying Bomb War*.

18 See Dr R.V. Jones' *The Secret War*.

19 See *The Flying Bomb* by Richard Anthony Young.

20 Quotes extracted from *The Flying Bomb War* by Peter Haining.

21 Extracted from *Doodlebugs and Rockets* by Bob Ogley.

22 The first fatalities were: Mrs Ellen Woodcraft aged 19 and her eight-month-old baby, Tom; Lennie Sherman aged 12; Dora Cohen (55), Willie Rogers (50) and Connie Day (32).

23 Flt Lt Howard Corre DFC was killed on 19/5/51 when the Tiger Moth (DF211) he was flying crashed.

24 In an interview with Dr Alfred Price, author of *The Last Days of the Luftwaffe*.

25 Phrase coined by Bob Ogley, author of *Doodlebugs and Rockets*.

26 Extracted from *Croydon in the 1940s and 1950s*.

27 See *Buzz Bomb Diary* by David Collyer.

28 See *www.battle-abbey.co.uk/joycesdbug*.

29 Flt Lt Gartrell Parker trained as a Wop/AG in the RAF and was attached to the Fleet Air Arm at Malta in 1940/41 and flew sorties in Swordfish and Fulmars, work for which he received a DSM (hence the nickname Sailor). Later remustered as a pilot and was posted to 219 Squadron in 1944 as a flight lieutenant. By the time the war ended he had been credited with ten victories (one probable) and six V-1s, and awarded the DFC and Bar. Postwar he became a test pilot and was awarded the AFC but was killed in 1963 testing a Buccaneer.

30 See *V for Vengeance* by David Johnson.

31 When *Canterbury* finally sailed, on 22 June, many flying bombs were seen heading for England and several of these were shot down by the ship's gunners.

32 Sqn Ldr Russ Bannock – later Wg Cdr DSO DFC+ who ended the war with 9 kills and $18^1/2$ V-1s to his credit – was born in Canada of an Austrian father by the name of Bahnuk (changed to Bannock on the eve of WWII). Two of Russ Bannock's cousins served with the Luftwaffe in WWII.

33 The loss of Flt Lt Wally Idema RCAF: Excerpt from letter Major N.F. Harrison (the SAAF CO of 229 Squadron, Detling) wrote to Mrs W. Idema (mother), 19 June 1944: "Ki (as we called him) took off with the squadron on the evening of the 17th June to escort some bombers to France, but had to turn back almost at once on account of oil leak in his machine. On landing here, his aircraft was damaged, though he himself was not hurt. He was very disappointed at having missed the 'show', for Ki is always exceedingly keen for flying and fighting, and also chagrined at having made a bad landing. He took the first opportunity of going up again, about three-quarters of an hour later, when he went to test a Spitfire. He could have completed the task in twenty minutes, but while he was up the Germans began sending off some of their robot-planes towards London, and Ki called up on his radio-telephone, saying that he was going south-east to meet the robots and try to shoot them down. That was about 9.30pm. After that he was not heard calling again, nor did anyone report seeing his plane.

"Sometimes when pilots are missing we can make a shrewd guess at what has become of them. In Ki's case we know nothing at all and can say nothing either to soften or shorten the period of uncertainty and anxiety, which, I assure you, we share. We can only speculate. The course he was steering would ultimately have brought him to the French coast between Boulogne and Calais, where he may have been shot down and made prisoner; or his engine may have failed over the Channel, in which case he may have found safety in his rubber dinghy. In either case he may also have been killed. There is nothing to indicate what actually happened. His absence is a great loss to the squadron, where his courage and pugnacity in the air, and his good nature and generosity on the ground made him popular with pilots and ground crew alike. Only a couple of weeks ago he stirred us all by entering Boulogne harbour, flying very low amongst intense gun fire, and damaging enemy shipping there." The American pilot's body was washed up on the French coast and buried at St Croix.

A Court of Inquiry was held on 22 August 1944 with one member (Wg Cdr C.H. Schofield) and one witness (Major N.F Harrison SAAF). It indicated that Idema had flown 500 hours overseas, 350 hours on Spitfires. Air Defence Great Britain felt that the case had been mishandled by Harrison, hence the time lapse between loss and inquiry. Circumstances of the loss were described by Wg Cdr Schofield as follows: (a) On June 17th, F/Lt Idema took off as one of a squadron formation on an operational flight. He left the formation with an oiled up windscreen and on landing at base overshot and damaged his aircraft. On his own authorisation he took another aircraft off and said he was looking for Divers. Aircraft and pilot were not seen again. (b) F/Lt Idema was not empowered to authorise this flight. He described it as an air test but told Flying Control he was looking for Divers. It appears most likely he indulged in a private operation on his own over the Channel. The reason for his non-return cannot be ascertained but may have been enemy action, or engine failure. (c) I have no recommendations to make. The report noted, *"S/Ldr [sic] Harrison has been severely warned about the bad flying discipline of his pilots."*

34 1/Lt Carl Bickel from Nebraska had one air victory at this time, but would be credited with a further four and one shared to become an ace.

35 Following these successes against Divers, 1/Lt Edwin Fisher from Oregon went on to shoot down seven enemy aircraft during July and August. He was killed in a flying accident postwar.

36 Lt Thornley RN earlier in his career had been a Walrus pilot aboard the cruiser HMS *Gambia*.

37 Although not outwardly injured in this incident, Gunner Harry Cull (the author's late father) in later life suffered from severe intermittent back problems that may have been as a result of the blast.

38 See *Westerham & Crockham Hill in the War* by Helen Long. Arthur Yeadon was the London manager for the Leeds Permanent Building Society, who lived in rented accommodation in Westerham.

39 See *Thunderbolts over High Halden* by Graham J. Hukins.

40 *Ibid.*

41 See *Raiders Overhead* by Stephen Flower.

42 What the Germans were completely unaware of was that agents sent to England to report on the fall and accuracy of the V-1s had been captured. Some had been eliminated while others became double agents including Juan Pujol – a Spaniard known as 'Garbo' to the British and 'Rufus' to the Germans – who reported, via his network, that the bulk of the missiles were overshooting the aiming point, Tower Bridge, by up to seven miles. On receiving this information, Oberst Watchel was persuaded to make adjustments of range and bearing, whereupon the majority of the missiles would impact in Kent. Pujol received both the MBE and the Iron Cross from his grateful 'employers' in recognition of his valuable service.

43 Flg Off Ray Cammock had served as an NCO pilot with 253 Squadron in North Africa in 1943, being credited with the destruction of an SM79 and a share of a second on 5/4/43. After shooting down $20^1/2$ V-1s he was killed in action on 6/10/44.

44 Capt James Dalglish had joined the RCAF in late 1941 and received his wings in October 1942. Posted to 613 Squadron, a tactical reconnaissance unit flying Mustang Is, he was credited with damaging a Bf109 on 18/7/43. He transferred to the USAAF later in the year and claimed five victories while flying P-51Bs with the 344thFS. He then served briefly with the 381stFS before joining 353rdFS, with which he scored four more victories.

45 Lt James Billington FTR from a sortie over France on 24/6/44.

46 Flt Lt Clarence Jasper, an American in the RCAF, had scored an unusual victory two months earlier while on an intruder sortie over France. Believing he had shot down a FW190 – quite an unusual victory for a Mosquito – records show that he had in fact destroyed a NA57 (Harvard in the RAF), a machine that had been captured from the French and put into service with the Luftwaffe as a trainer, operating with JG107 at Nancy.

47 Sqn Ldr Bannock's Mosquito HK147/TH-Z carried the name 'Hairless Joe'.

48 See *Croydon in the 1940s and 1950s.*

49 Extracted from *Thanks for the Memory* by Laddie Lucas, and from Dave McIntosh's highly entertaining *Terror in the*

Starboard Seat. Both Sid Seid and Dave McIntosh survived the war, but the American lost his life on 6/12/65 when searching in his private aircraft for three men missing in a boat off the Palau islands.

50 See *Buzz Bomb Diary*.

51 Jan Plesman's father had founded KLM Royal Dutch Airlines in 1919. During the German invasion of Holland in May 1940, Jan had flown antiquated Fokker D-17 biplanes. His older brother Hans had been credited with three kills while flying Fokker D-21s. Jan escaped to England via Spain in May 1941 and joined the RAF. He was shot down and killed while attacking a flak train on 1/9/44.

52 As recorded (slightly edited) by Albert Plesman in *Jan Plesman: A Flying Dutchman*.

53 See *Thunderbolts over High Halden*.

54 While serving with 893 Squadron aboard HMS *Formidable* in late 1942, Lt Hamblett was one of four pilots who shot down an RAF Hudson in error for an Italian SM79.

55 Sqn Ldr Maurice Blackstone later received a DFC and AFC before losing his life on 19/3/51 when the Hastings (WD478) in which he was flying crashed.

56 37-year-old Wt Off Albert Zavaco-Lamour lost his leg following an incident at Gazala landing ground in Libya on 19/12/41. Flying a Hurribomber of 80 Squadron, his aircraft crashed on take-off and the bomb exploded. Fitted with an artificial leg he pleaded to return to operations despite his disability and age.

57 Plt Off Brian Scamen had earlier flown with 165 Squadron and had shared in the destruction of a Ju88 on 9/5/43.

58 See *Thunderbolts over High Halden*.

59 See *Isle of Wight at War* by H.J.T. Leal.

60 Plt Off Bill Bowhay from Alberta was killed in a flying accident in HR149/TH-R on 23/7/44.

61 Flt Lts Singleton and Haslam had destroyed seven and damaged three German aircraft during night operations with 25 Squadron in 1942/43.

62 Oblt H-G. Kasper (pilot), Oblt G. Hupka (observer), Uffz B. Morweiser and Uffz P. Werkhausen.

63 William Joyce, born in New York of an Irish Republican father, was hanged on 3 January 1946 at Wandsworth Prison. His farewell note ended defiantly: "In death, as in this life, I defy the Jews who caused this last war: and I defy the power of Darkness which they represent. I warn the British people against the aggressive Imperialism of the Soviet Union. May Britain be great once again; and, in the hour of greatest danger to the West, may the standard of the *Hakenkreuz* (swastika) be raised from the dust. I am proud to die for my ideals; and I am sorry for the sons of Britain who have died without knowing why."

64 'Abdullah' was a homing device that received signals from German *Würzburg* radar sites that would enable, it was hoped, Typhoons fitted with this to home in on the sites and destroy them. A special flight of Typhoons from the FIU was thus equipped but the operation failed when the Germans switched off the radar when the plot got within ten miles. The idea then fizzled out.

65 See *Isle of Wight at War*.

66 38-year-old Vera Menchik-Stevenson, daughter of a Czech father and British mother, and widow of Rufus Stevenson, had won the 1st Women's World Chess Championship in 1927, and had successfully defended it in 1930, 1931, 1933, 1935, 1937 and 1939.

67 Early in 1942, when serving with 485 (RNZAF) Squadron, Barnett's Spitfire was shot down over France. He evaded capture, and with the help of French Resistance people eventually reached Gibraltar from where he was flown back to the UK.

68 Extracted from *Impact* by Benjamin King & Timothy Kutta.

69 Lt Freyermuth from Muscatine, Iowa, had joined the RCAF and had received his initial fighter training in Canada before transferring to the USAAF.

70 See *Red Sky at Night* by Jo Capka. He had earlier flown Wellingtons with 311 Squadron, the unit with which he won his DFM.

71 See *Night Flyer* by Sqn Ldr Lewis Brandon DSO DFC.

72 From a report published in *AA Command Intelligence Review* No.194 dated 15 July 1944.

73 ZQ-Y is believed to have been the Tempest flown regularly by Flt Lt Joe Berry while with the FIU, and is shown as his mount in the claims lists; however, he may have flown other aircraft on occasions.

74 Flt Lt Tommy Burne continued to fly with 41 Squadron and was promoted CO. On 24/2/45 he was again severely wounded, this time in the chest, but succeeded in flying his Spitfire back to base, a feat for which he was awarded a DSO.

75 See *Buzz Bomb Diary*.

76 Flt Sgt Alex Rollo (277 Squadron) later flew Tempests with 80 Squadron and was shot down on 15/4/45, being taken prisoner. Postwar he remained in the RAF and flew Tempests with 249 Squadron in the Middle East, but died on 11/9/48 following a severe bout of bronchitis.

77 Lt Gervan was one of six 363rdFG pilots shot down by flak on 4/7/44, three of whom were killed including Gervan, who was last seen near St Lô.

78 See *Westerham & Crockham Hill in the War*.

79 See Peter Henden's website *Flying Bombs and Rockets.com*. Interestingly, Richard Beckett recalled that the carcass of the Diver remained on the nearby railway bank well into the 1960s.

80 Flt Lt Matt Wood was shot down by flak and killed near Vimoutiers (France) on 18/8/44.

81 See *Buzz Bomb Diary*.

82 The 5thERS was established in May 1944, using war-weary P-47Ds discarded by the 56thFG; in fact, the P-47s carried the letters 'WW' (for war-weary) on the fin just below the serial number. The first to arrive was 42-75855. Its task was to carry out ASR spotting patrols over the North Sea and almost 250 sorties were flown during the first month alone.

83 See *Fire out of Heaven* by Sarah Gertrude Millin, a Lithuanian-born South African novelist, one of the most popular of the day.

84 See *Thunderbolts over High Halden*.

85 Flt Lt Hester added: "In fact these extra fuel tanks, when new, carried 80-gallons of Courage's Best Bitter to our colleagues stationed on B.5 landing strip near Bayeux in August 1944. I've continued to be amazed how short a time it took for the British Army and Air Force to consume over 600 pints of beer! We were not on the strength of any of the three squadrons that made up 138 Wing, so we could not use any known squadron letters on our aircraft, so a question mark was painted in place

of a letter. The first attempt, by a Polish airman went wrong, as he got the question mark the wrong way round on one side!" (See *Mosquitopanik!* by Martin Bowman.)

86 Extracted from *Happy Jack's Go Buggy*.

87 See *Front Line Folkestone* Folkestone Hythe and District Herald July 1945.

88 This incident allegedly occurred on July 6 at 1304, but in fact would have been 3 July.

89 Extracted from *Number One in War and Peace* by Norman Franks.

90 See *The Doodlebugs*.

91 Flg Off Morrie Costello had served with 249 Squadron at Malta towards the end of 1942 and into early 1943, and had been credited with three destroyed and two damaged.

92 On 1 August 1944, Flg Off Slim Kenny was shot down by flak and became a POW.

93 See *Night Fighter* by C.F. Rawnsley & Robert Wright. Sqn Ldr 'Jimmy' Rawnsley had been Wg Cdr John Cunningham's navigator and had assisted in 17 of Cunningham's 20 night fighter kills.

94 Plt Off Ivor Sanderson's combat report for this action has not been located.

95 Sqn Ldr Bill Gill had flown Tiger Moths and suchlike with the Burma Volunteer Air Force during the Japanese invasion of Burma in late1941/early 42. He later took command of 125 Squadron.

96 Flight Officer Richard M. Seage USAAF received the British DFC in November 1944.

97 Flt Lt Ellis and Plt Off MacNaughton were killed together in a flying accident on 12/12/44.

98 Flg Off David Guttridge was killed in action on 28/9/44 when his Typhoon was shot down by flak near Kassel.

99 Flt Lt C.N. Woodcock and his navigator Flg Off L. Butt were both killed on 1/9/44 when their Mosquito MM652/RS-S was involved in a mid-air collision with another (flown by Flt Lt R.J. Smyth) during an AI practice. Smyth was able to land his damaged aircraft but MM652 crashed seven miles north-east of Swannington.

100 See *Terror in the Starboard Seat*.

101 Flg Off Cynkier was killed in action 3/9/44.

102 Plt Off Nicholls was shot down and made POW on 10/12/44.

103 Flt Lt Stan Cotterill DFC and his navigator Sgt E.H. McKenna had shot down three Ju52/3m transports and a Ju188 on the night of 6/7 July 1944, to which they added a Bf109 damaged on 3 September. Flying a day intruder to the Vienna area on 17 October, when he was seen to shoot down another Ju52/3m by his colleague Flg Off Stuart May (who was shot down on this mission). Cotterill's aircraft FTR to the UK following take-off from an Italian airfield. Lost with him was his navigator Flt Lt Colin Finlayson RCAF DFC. Their bodies were later recovered and buried in the Belgrade British Military Cemetery.

104 Although Flt Sgt Peter Chattin survived this incident, he was shot down and killed in combat with a FW190 on 3 September 1944.

105 Not shown in ORB but apparently recorded in Flg Off Morrie Costello's logbook.

106 Bill Marshall died at the age of 87 in 2005. The following year a plaque was unveiled at The Royal Mail public house in Lydd (presented by Kent brewery Shepherd Neame) to pay tribute to Bill's action, which undoubtedly saved lives and prevented much damage and destruction.

107 See *Mustang Wing* by John Anthony Moor.

108 Uffz Alisch and his crew – Obgfr Karl-Heinz Witzel, Obgfr Engelbert Haarem, Obgfr Josef Bohlscheid and Obgfr Werner Heimann – were reported missing presumed killed.

109 38-year-old Flg Off Fred Forrest, a former transport officer, had dropped rank to fly as aircrew. He assisted his pilot in the destruction of four aircraft and three V-1s and was awarded a DFC.

110 Kelts Baker was born in Singapore of Canadian parents.

111 See *Isle of Wight at War*.

112 Captain Ken Rayment was co-pilot of the Ambassador carrying the Manchester United football team that crashed at Munich Airport on 6/2/58, in which several players were killed. He died from his injuries.

113 See *Isle of Wight at War*.

114 A year earlier, almost to the day, a Do217 had unleashed its load of bombs on East Grinstead, killing 108 residents and injuring a further 235, some seriously. The V-1 fell close to the same spot.

115 Flt Lt Bob Kleimeyer, an Australian of Dutch ancestry (hence his nickname) had joined the RNZAF and had flown Spitfires at Malta in late 1942/early 1943.

116 Malayan-born Flt Lt Des Ruchwaldy had been awarded the DFC for ten aerial victories (including three probables) while flying Spitfires in 1941 (with 603 Squadron) and 1943 (with 129 Squadron).

117 See *Isle of Wight at War*.

118 As reported in *AA Command Intelligence Review* No.194 dated 15 July 1944.

119 See *Number One at War and Peace*.

120 See *There Shall Be Wings* by Max Arthur.

121 See *Isle of Wight at War*.

122 Flg Off McPhail was killed attempting a single-engine landing on 12/1/45; also killed was his navigator Flg Off J.E. Donaghue.

123 Lt Herman Ernst – of obvious German ancestry – from Philadelphia, was later credited with five air kills while flying the P-61.

124 Extracted from *Fear Nothing* by David Watkins.

125 Flt Sgt Colin Bundara, known as Bunny, was later posted to 127 Squadron flying Spitfires in Holland. An amusing incident occurred one day in January 1945, as related by his friend Plt Off Ted Smith (see *Spitfire Diary*): "It seems that he went down to the bogs this for his morning constitutional and took the first cubicle, by the main door. The Germans built the cubicles without doors. Bunny was sitting on the first throne when in came an officer from 66 Squadron. Bunny looked up from the Australian newspaper he was reading, and welcomed the flight lieutenant with his usual, 'Good'ay, mate.' Apparently the officer was not amused. 'Who in hell do you think you are, sergeant. Don't you know that I'm an officer?' Bunny held the intruder's gaze, and replied, 'First of all, cobber, I'm a flight sergeant, not sergeant. Second, you can throw every page of the King's Rules and Regulations at me, and I'll never give you a salute when I'm taking a shit! You got that, cobber?' We all laughed over that one." Sadly, Bunny was dead a few days later, having activated a booby-trap while inspecting an abandoned Bf109. He died from shock following the amputation of his foot.

126 'White 16' was flown to RAE Farnborough and allotted serial TP814. It became part of No.1426 Enemy Aircraft Flight and toured British and American airfields in company with other captured aircraft. However, it crashed on take-off on 23/11/44 and was destroyed.

127 Both pilots had two victories to their credit; Prenzel having claimed two Lancasters destroyed on the night of 5-6/7/44 and Gromill two Lancasters on the night of 7-8/7/44.

128 Sqn Ldr Richard Chudleigh departed 96 Squadron shortly thereafter to take command of a flight in 151 Squadron. His aircraft was damaged by an exploding train during one of his first sorties, necessitating a crash-landing during which his navigator Flg Off Jack Ayliffe was killed.

129 Quote extracted from the article *Chasing V-1s* by noted American author Warren E. Thompson in *FlyPast* March 2005.

130 Wg Cdr Yonge, aged 38, one of the oldest COs flying on operations, had been commissioned in the RAF in December 1925.

131 Uffz Schmidt's crew, who were all rescued and taken prisoner, comprised Uffz August Reidenbach, Uffz Hans Hofgartner and Uffz Georg Dabitz. Ltn Schirmer's missing crew were Uffz Eugen Joos, Uffz Gotthard Siewert and Uffz Karl Pohl, while Oblt Lamp and Uffz Artur Stotter were rescued and made prisoner but Fw Wilhelm Fabry and Uffz Hans Schott were reported missing.

132 Uffz Gerhard Pabel and Obgfr Mathias Wilde.

133 Apart from the pilot those killed were Gfr Wilhelm Dietz, Obgfr Karl-Heinz Hilleker, Obgfr Karl-Heinz Burghardt and Gfr Ernst Schiemann.

134 This impacted very close to where the author's grand parents lived.

135 Wg Cdr Paddy Woodhouse DFC had previously served as a day fighter pilot with 610 and 71 Squadron (CO of the latter) before being promoted to lead the Tangmere Wing, and was credited with five victories (two shared).

136 See *Number One at War and Peace*.

137 Having also shared in shooting down a Ju88 while with 504 Squadron, James Waslyk was posted to Italy where he joined 417(RCAF) Squadron and was soon killed in action, on 20/1/45.

138 Flt Lt Fred Kemp's wife Ellen and their children had recently been killed when a Diver fell on their house in Charlton, London. His 20-year-old navigator James Farrar was a promising novelist and poet; some of his work was published postwar.

139 Those killed with Uffz Rohne were Fw Günther Albrecht, Uffz Walter Langer, Uffz Erich Unterdörfel and Uffz Willy Wetzel.

140 Flg Off Hill RCAF and his navigator Flg Off Roach RCAF FTR from an intruder sortie on 1/11/44.

141 Dennis Davy remained in the RAF postwar but was killed in a flying accident on 18/2/51, when the Valetta transport in which he was acting as navigator carried out a wheels-up emergency landing at Bromma in Sweden. The pilot, Wg Cdr R.I.K. Edwards, and all passengers survived, albeit some with injuries; Davy was the only fatality.

142 Extracted from *Number One in War and Peace*.

143 Flt Lt Malcolm Edwards from Bath was killed in action on 29/12/44.

144 Flt Lt Kelts Colfax Baker, a 27-year-old married Canadian, died by his own hand on 18/10/44.

145 Plt Off Jim Holder, a 22-year-old from Ontario, was shot down off Colynsplaat (Friesland) by flak and killed on 4/8/44.

146 The missing crews were: 5K+ER Uffz Karl Schmidt, Fw Adam Märs, Gfr Hans Behrendt, Uffz Franz Haas and Uffz Ernst Bondarenko; 5K+LS Uffz Heinz Schmidt, Uffz Adolf Schneider, Uffz Alban Schorer, Obgfr Otto Hemmer and Uffz Hans Seufert; 5K+HS Uffz Gerd Schwarzel, Obgfr Wille Bauer, Uffz Alfred Schneider, Obgfr Karl-Heinz Benua and Obgfr Waldemar Naujoks.

147 On 10 August 1939 during a clash between Soviet I-16s and Japanese fighters over Mongolian/Manchurian border, two Japanese aircraft were claimed shot down by air-to-air rockets fired by the I-16s. Developed during the 1930s for aerial use, four RS-82 3.23-inch solid fuel rockets were carried under each wing of the I-16s. This was the first recorded use of air-to-air rocket projectiles.

148 Extracted from *Number One in War and Peace*.

149 It is difficult to know what to make of the claim of a double-size V-1 – there are no records to substantiate this.

150 Sqn Ldr Norman Kynaston DFC, CO of 91 Squadron, was lost on 15/8/44.

151 As an NCO pilot Reg Dickson had flown Spitfires at Malta with 601 Squadron in 1942, and had survived being blown out of his aircraft by a direct hit from Malta's fiercesome AA barrage. Although wounded he was rescued from the sea.

152 Flg Off Jean Clerc had previously flown Spitfires with 602 Squadron and claimed one aerial victory and four probables/damaged. One source suggests that he also claimed three V-1s, but this cannot be substantiated. He was awarded the Croix de Guerre. Postwar changed his name to Clerc-Scott.

153 See *Buzz Bomb Diary*.

154 Flg Off Ken Collier RAAF (91 Squadron) was killed in action on 5/12/44.

155 Flg Off Lambertus Wolters (322 Squadron) shot down three V-1s including one shared. On 16/9/44 he and Flg Off C.R.R. Manders collided in the air, resulting in the death of Wolters. Manders baled out safely.

156 Rescued with Uffz Rieger were Uffz Rudolf Noreike and Gfr Egid Pollinger; Gfr Hans Gründler and Obgfr Waldemar Lahn were lost.

157 See *Doodlebugs and Rockets*.

158 See *A View from The Office*.

159 Flg Off Stewart Woolley's Mosquito was shot down by flak on 2/10/44, he and his navigator Flg Off Hastie becoming POWs. Just prior to being hit, Woolley had shot down an Arado 96 trainer possibly an aircraft from *Flugzeugführerschule 43*.

160 Ernest Hemingway's account has been edited by the author to fit the required criteria.

161 See *Doodlebugs and Rockets*.

162 The first use in war of a radio-controlled flying bomb was achieved by the Italians during the Royal Navy's Operation Pedestal to get supplies and reinforcements through to Malta in August 1942. Using a standard SM79 tri-motor bomber filled with 1,000kg of explosives and fitted with remote control, an attack was launched on 12 August against the British convoy. The SM79 was taken up by M.llo Mario Badij, who baled out as arranged, and control of the flying bomb was assumed by Generale BA Ferdinando Raffaelli, the inventor of the device, flying aboard an accompanying Z1007bis bomber, with an escort of five G50bis fighters from 24°Gruppo CT. Unfortunately for the Italians, the radio-controlled device malfunctioned and the flying bomb droned on until its fuel was exhausted, finally crashing into the slope of Mount Khenchela, to the south

of Constantine in Vichy French Algeria, leaving a large crater and a bemused military.

163 Flt Sgt Ronnie van Beers had served with the NEIAF in Java in 1941/42 and had been evacuated to Australia in March 1942.

164 Later in the year (1944) a detachment of Meteors was sent to the USAAF base at Debden for fighter affiliation duties with the US 8th Air Force, as recalled by Flt Lt Dennis Barry: "The Americans wanted to practise anti-jet combat tactics, having met Me262s over Germany. In the time we were there our small formation had to contend with virtual armadas of up to 140 B-17s or B-24s plus escorts. Wg Cdr Wilson commented in his report on these trials, that the results must have proved very depressing to the Americans as it would appear that the Meteors could sail in as and when they pleased, each 'destroying' two or three Fortresses or Liberators, and pull away with the escort fighters (even Mustangs) not being able to do much about it." It would seem that Wg Cdr Beamont's early assessment that the Meteor could have been an effective bomber destroyer might have been correct. Capt Fred McIntosh USAAF, one of those who flew a P-47 against the Meteor, recalled: "After our encounter with the German jet on 1 November, we occasionally practiced against the British jet – ' Teapot', the Brits called it (?) We tried to devise manoeuvres and tactics for the P-47 against jet fighters. Even though the British jet was not as good as the Me262, it became obvious to us that if the German pilot knew what he was doing, you were dead meat." (see *American Raiders* by Wolfgang Samuel).

165 Killed along with Martin were Gfr Georg Gattnar, Gfr Edmund Weigelt, Obgfr Rudi Fiedler and Uffz Arthur Mohr.

166 See *The Doodlebugs*.

167 General Valin, C-in-C Free French Air Force attended the funeral and there followed a posthumous presentation of the *Legion d'Honneur* to the fallen pilot.

168 Flt Sgt John Philpott volunteered for a posting to a Typhoon squadron and left 610 Squadron on 15 August. He was killed in action fourteen days later.

169 Plt Off William Vale RAAF and his navigator Flt Lt Alf Ashcroft DFC FTR from a sortie on the night of 6/7 October 1944.

170 See *Happy is the Day*, Tom Slack's humorous memoirs. His 'debt' to the RAF comprised one Audax (force-landed with engine failure during an attempted raid on Baghdad by aircraft from 4 FTS in April 1941) and three Spitfires (shot down over France 18/7/43 by Bf109, baled out, evaded and returned to England; shot down by flak 18/6/44, baled out into Channel and rescued; crash-landed France 23/8/44 following engine failure, POW).

171 SF-J was a Typhoon of 137 Squadron (not a Tempest) so presumably was the aircraft flown by Flg Off Sames when he shot down a Diver during a morning sortie.

172 Both Flg Offs Dixie Dean and Jock Rodger (who had flown Blenheims with 21 Squadron in 1940) received a Mention in Despatches for their achievements.

173 Extracted from *Aphrodite: Desperate Mission* by Jack Olsen.

174 *Ibid.*

175 Flg Off Alan Owen had been awarded the DFM while serving with 600 Squadron in the Middle East, where he had shot down six enemy aircraft. He ended the war with 16 including one probable, and a DFC.

176 Flt Sgt Ian Stevenson was later commissioned and awarded a DFC. In the closing months of the war he was credited with two FW190s shot down, one probable and one damaged, to add to his three V-1s (one shared).

177 The USAAF BQ-7 flying bomb programme suffered another setback on 11 September, 1/Lt Richard W. Lindahl USAAF losing his life when his parachute failed to open after he had baled out from 42-30180, which was destined for Heligoland. A loop of the static line had caught around his shoulder and he died of a broken back. Death would have been instantaneous. His co-pilot 1/Lt Donald E. Salles USAAF landed safely. Fortunately, this proved to be the final fatality although ten more missions would be flown before a halt was called to the ill-fated scheme (see Appendix VII). The US Navy in the Pacific had similarly been operating an unmanned assault drone (BQ-4) without much success. However, by the end of the Japanese war, the US Navy had developed a fully guided bomb similar in concept to the German Hs293, and this was used with great success, USN Squadron VPB-123 being credited with sinking 67 Japanese ships between May and August 1945. The Japanese considered the activities of the squadrons based at Yontan Field to be important enough to merit the expenditure of a specialised suicide attack force. On 24 May 1945, the commandos were flown in under cover of darkness aboard three Ki-21s. Two were shot down in flames, along with five of their fighter escorts. The remaining Sally landed wheels up on the airstrip. The attackers quickly dispersed throughout the area, throwing satchel charges and grenades into parked aircraft and engaging the Marine perimeter defence forces in firefights. One VPB-109 aircraft was destroyed and another damaged beyond repair before the commandos were eliminated.

A 1946 USN report revealed: "Navy planes launched the first fully automatic guided missiles used in combat by any nation. Using Navy-developed self-controlled, air-borne homing missiles, land-based patrol squadrons of Fleet Air Wing One took a heavy toll of Jap shipping during the final months of the war. A closely guarded war secret until long after V-J Day. The flying bomb was known only by its code name Bat. The Navy's flying bomb had its beginning in the early days of the war long before Japan had used Baka bombs or launched its Kamikaze attacks. Designed and developed at the request of Bureau of Ordnance, the Bat bears the official designation of SWOD Mk 9. While it was primarily used with Privateers, the Bat has also been successfully carried and released by Catalinas, Mariners, Mitchells, Venturas, Corsairs, Tigercats, Avengers, and Helldivers in actual operations or in tests. The Bat actually is a 1,000 lb bomb mounted in a glider-type airframe equipped with radar transmitter and receiver. Power for the Bat's glide is derived from speed of the parent plane and the force of gravity. The flying bomb's low angle of flight makes it possible for the plane to release its missile well out of range of the target's anti-aircraft fire. While designed primarily for use against sea targets, Bats under proper conditions may be effectively used against land targets. They are carried either as weapons of opportunity or for specific missions against special targets. In making a Bat attack, the pilot of the parent plane locates and selects a target, keeping well outside the enemy's AA range. Through an electronic indicator that displays target data from the radar in the Bat, the operator in the parent plane is able to set the flying bomb's direction equipment for homing on the selected target. The closest type of cooperation is necessary between pilot and the Bat operator. When radar equipment in the Bat is finally set for its homing run, the flying bomb is released. From that time on the Bat homes automatically on its selected target independent of the mother plane. Guided by the radar echoes its receiver picks up, the Bat homes accurately on its target despite visibility or violent evasive manoeuvres. The Bat does not restrict flight operations of the parent plane nor does it appreciably affect flight characteristics. The launching plane's effectiveness with rockets, cannon or machine guns is not altered by having Bats attached. Though the Bat is already considered obsolescent, some of the principles used in it may be applicable in the future."

178 Lt Henri de Bordas received a DFC, gazetted in October 1949. Prior to his service with 91 Squadron he had flown with 131 Squadron and had claimed a FW190 destroyed on 6/12/42.

179 Flt Lt Przygodski (316 Squadron) was killed in action 8/9/44.

180 Flg Off Rudi Burgwal was shot down by flak and killed on 12/8/44.

181 Later in the year Flt Lt Herbert 'Bert' Miller shot down a Bf109 and a Ju88, but FTR from a daylight sortie on 22/2/45.

182 Flg Off John Smith was killed in a flying accident on 2/1/45.

183 Flt Sgts E. Abell, A.F. Elwood, C.A. Hammond and F.N. Manton.

184 Flg Off Harry Cook had flown during the Battle of Britain and had six victories (including three probables) to his credit.

185 Shortly following his arrival at Manston, Flg Off Lucas contracted TB and was hospitalised.

186 See *Terror in the Starboard Seat*.

187 Lt Joe Kennedy USN was the son of the US Ambassador to London and older brother of the future US President John F. Kennedy.

188 Extracted from *Aphrodite: Desperate Mission*.

189 See *Buzz Bomb Diary*.

190 While the Americans were thus experimenting with several forms of flying bomb in Europe, their enemy in the Pacific was doing the same in Japan, albeit by paper balloon! North America's experience of 'flying bomb' warfare occurred during late 1944/early 1945, when bomb-carrying balloons – known to the Japanese as *Fugos*, meaning windship weapon – launched by the Japanese from sites on Honshu made the crossing of the Pacific using the jet stream. With components manufactured by Seiko, Toshiba and Hitachi (all well-known postwar Japanese electronics companies), each paper balloon carried four 12kg incendiary bombs and one 15kg high-explosive anti-personnel bomb. At least 300 of the estimated 9,000 launched crossed the Canadian and American coasts and caused a small number of forest fires, but the only casualties occurred as a result of a tragic accident near Bly in Oregon on 5 May 1945, when picnicking young teenagers found an unexploded bomb still tethered to its balloon. It exploded killing six including the wife of the Rev. Archie Mitchell, who was in charge of the church party. A few of the balloons were intercepted and shot down by USN F6Fs and USAAF P-38s stationed in the Aleutians and California, the first by a P-38 near Navy Alturas on 10/1/45, and another on 25/1/45 south-west of Shemya Island; five were shot down during February (one in Washington State on 21st, one over North Bend, Oregon next day, one by a P-38 over Calistoga, California on 23rd, the fourth over Attu Island on 24th, and one on 27th over Bethal, Alaska). A further four were shot down during March – one on 10th over Ephrata, Washington and another over the same state (over Chimicum) on 13th, a third over Reno, Nevada by a P-63 on 22nd, and the final one for March over Baja, California on 28th. No fewer than 14 were shot down during April, nine by P-38s of the 54th FS on 11th two by USN F6Fs on 12th and 13th, and three over Alaska on 13th, 14th and 16th. The final balloon shot down by US fighters fell on 19/7/45, some 420 miles east of Tokyo, which was thought to be a biological weapon. Meanwhile, the Canadian forces were doing their best to assist, Kittyhawks (P-40s) of 133 Squadron RCAF based at Sea Island, British Columbia accounted for one on 21/2/45 (by Plt Off Edward E. Maxwell RCAF in 866/R ex-42-105865), and another on 10/3/45 (Plt Off John O. Patten RCAF in 858/F ex-42-105192); a Canso (Catalina) of 6(BR) Squadron flown by Sqn Ldr Russell L. Moodie RCAF forced another into the sea on 12/3/45.

191 This was undoubtedly the occasion when the author's mother Lily and her three young children (Donald aged eight, Joyce aged six and baby Brian) were visiting her brother Tony in nearby Palmerston Road, where he kept a tobacconist-cum-grocery shop. The blast blew out the shop windows and frightened all inside. Subsequently, little Joyce suffered from a head twitch all of her life until her untimely death. Their father, Gunner Harry Cull, had earlier experienced his own brush with a Diver (see 17 June).

192 616 Squadron received EE229 to replace EE226.

193 See *The Doodlebugs*.

194 Flg Off Henry Cowan was born in 1920 at Dinslaken, Germany, to Jewish parents as Heinz Cowan. The family fled to Belgium and then to Canada in 1939. He was killed in action on 19/4/45, with a FW190 destroyed to his credit.

195 Wg Cdr Joe Fraser DFC had flown Gladiators with 112 Squadron in Greece in early 1941 and was credited with 10 victories (one shared) for which he received the DFC. On his return to the UK he was posted to Training Command and was CGI at 71 OTU in 1942. He was killed in a car crash in Ankara, Turkey in August 1946.

196 Account by Don Deacon, extracted from *Doodlebugs and Rockets*.

197 In addition to the three FW190s credited to Sqn Ldr Horbaczewski (which raised his score to 16½), others were claimed by Flt Sgt K. Siwek (three), Flt Lt H. Pietrzak (three), Flt Sgt J. Bargielowski (two), and one apiece by Plt Off G. Świstuń, Flg Off E. Nowosielski, Flt Sgt K. Kijak and Flt Lt J. Schmidt.

198 Flt Sgt Brian Cartmel, a 24-year-old from Preston was killed on 29/4/45 when his Meteor III (EE273/YP-K) collided in cloud with EE252/YP-G flown by Sqn Ldr Les Watts DFC, who was also killed.

199 Wt Off Valton Turner went on to shoot down four enemy aircraft and was awarded a DFC. He remained in the RAAF postwar and served with 77 (RAAF) Squadron on Meteors in Korea 1951-52, receiving a bar to the DFC.

200 Geoff Lord went on to claim six enemy aircraft including one shared and was awarded a DFC.

201 Wt Off Frank Reid, who had been awarded an AFM before joining 3 Squadron, was killed in action on 1/10/44.

202 The sight of the ungainly Walrus often brought hoots of derision from American aircrew, but many changed their tune when it came to plucking them out of the sea.

203 Flt Lt Joe de Niverville, the son of an air vice-marshal, remained in the RCAF postwar and was killed in a flying accident on 19/7/54.

204 See *Fear Nothing* by David Watkins.

205 Flt Sgt Tom Higgs from Hampshire was KiA on 18/12/44.

206 Flt Sgt Norman Carn was KiA 30/9/44.

207 In May 1945 Wg Cdr McDowall became a test pilot with Rolls-Royce. Later, in November 1945, he flew one of the two Lockheed YP-80 jets that had been sent to the UK for testing, force-landing this aircraft (44-83027) due to a fractured fuel pipe.

208 EE227 was later transferred to the RAE and was fitted with Rolls-Royce RB50 Trent turboprops. Following the initial delivery of eight Meteors including two for training purposes, a further six arrived during August. The original batch was believed to have been EE213/G (later coded YQ-A), EE214/G (coded YQ-B), EE215/YQ-C, EE216/YQ-E, EE217/YQ-J,

EE218/YQ-F, EE219/YQ-D and EE224/HJW. The subsequent batch of six were EE220, EE221, EE222/YQ-G, EE225, EE226, EE227/YQ-Y. Following the loss of EE224 and EE226, EE228 and EE229/YQ-W arrived as replacements. Later in the year the first batch of Meteor F.3s arrived, when the F.1s were despatched to either 1335 CU at Colerne for conversion training purposes (where EE228 was coded XL-P) or back to the RAE/AAEE/Rolls-Royce or Power Jets for experimental work.

209 The crew of 5K+BS were Fw Karl Koch, Uffz Norbert Wiemers, Gfr Eugen Kauffeldt and Gfr Egon Bahr.

210 See *Swordfish* by Ray Sturtivant.

211 Extracted from *The Flying Bomb War*.

212 II/KG101 had been withdrawn from St Didier to Rheine-Main airfield in Germany on 19 August. It is believed that one further operation had been undertaken against Allied shipping in July, albeit without success.

213 The V-2 assault would see a total of 1,115 rockets arrive over England. 517 fell on London, killing 2,754 people, 6,523 were injured. The assault lasted seven months; the last missile to crash on London (27 March 1945) killed 127 people and wounded 423.

214 II/KG53 was in need of replenishment following a disastrous August for the Gruppe. It had lost five aircraft during operations to air drop supplies to German troops, and then, on 28 August, while transferring its aircraft from Rouvres to Babenhausen (when the route was reportedly clear of Allied air activity) lost A1+AM (five aircrew and five ground crew killed), A1+MP (four killed, two wounded), A1+NP (one killed, four wounded), A1+KP (six wounded), A1+LP (two killed, six wounded), A1+IP (eight believed killed), A1+CP (9 believed killed) shot down by US fighters from the 56th and 353rd FGs.

215 Could what Flt Lt Draper observed have been a test flight of one of the Germans' latest designs? There are several candidates (see photos section): a Do17Z fitted with a Lorin ramjet mounted on the fuselage; a Do217 fitted similarly with a Sänger ramjet; or a Do217K which carried a DFS228 rocket-powered research aircraft on its back; there may have been other designs, such was the brilliance of German technology. However, German air historian/author Gerhard Stemmer doubts this: "All test flights of experimental aircraft took place over Bavaria. No crew would have been so stupid to fly such an immobile aircraft to Holland in September 1944, which was under the direct control of Allied fighters. Maybe what the pilot saw was a *Mistel* from *Einsatzgruppe KG101*, which was active during some days in September over Dutch territory from bases near Frankfurt. On the other hand, all these missions were flown shortly before nightfall."

216 Towards the end of the war a V-1 airframe fitted with an undercarriage was adapted to carry fuel for the Ar234 jet bomber to increase its range. The development was named *Deichselschlepp* (air trailer) and the idea was for the winged fuel tank to be towed behind the bomber, the linkage containing the fuel pipe. Once the fuel had been transferred, the towed tank would be jettisoned. Although tested, the plan did not come to fruition. There was also a plan to launch an armed V-1 by such means, and alternatively from a cradle mounted above the Ar234's fuselage.

217 Uffz Herbert Schwitalla, Uffz Erich Kästner, Fw Herbert Just and Uffz Gerhard Sauermann were all killed with their pilot.

218 Information provided by Jan Venema via Hans and Elger Abbink.

219 See *Air-Launched Doodlebugs* by Peter J.C. Smith.

220 See *Fear Nothing*.

221 Killed with Fw Böhling were Uffz Paul Janetzki, Fw Heinrich Hollmann, Uffz Erich Cieszka and Uffz Leo Kajewicz (the third member of the crew with a Polish-sounding name).

222 Missing with Oblt Bohnet were Obfhr Helmut Trommer, Obfw Karl Flickenschild, Fw Peter Mechtel and Fw Franz Kern.

223 See *Night Fighter*.

224 Len Fitchett volunteered to fly for the embryonic Israeli air force in 1948 and was killed when his Mosquito was shot down by ground fire.

225 Lost with Ltn Denig were Uffz Hans-Heinrich Hollemann, Uffz Karl Geibel, Obfw Max Schütze and Uffz Albert Reinhardt.

226 The missing crews were: 5K+AT Oblt Erhard Banneick, Fw Fritz Menzel, Fw Arthur Sieber, Stabfw Ernst Hampel, and Fw Kurt Hallmann; 5K+CT Uffz Willi Döhring, Gfr Harry Held, Gfr Karl-Heinz Regnet, Gfr Erhart Meyer, and Gfr Karl Rupp.

227 It has been suggested that MM646 crewed by Flt Lt Peter Fry and Flg Off Henry Smith may have been accidentally shot down by a US P-61.

228 Extracted from *Fairey Firefly* by William Harrison.

229 Extracted from *The Blitz – Then and Now*.

230 See *Air-Sea Rescue in World War Two* by Alan Rowe.

231 See *Air-Launched Doodlebugs*.

232 Lost with Ltn Bohne were Fw Willi Romey, Uffz Heinz Wagner, Uffz Walter Ahnert, and Uffz Gerhard Adrian.

233 Flt Lt Alf Marshall and his navigator were killed on 27/11/44 during an air test; a witness (LAC West) to the accident recalled: "The aircraft had been up for about ten minutes when we saw it approaching the drome in a slight dive. As it was almost overhead the pilot pulled it up into a fast steep climb and we distinctly saw something fly off the wing, after which the wings began to disintegrate. It had gained quite a lot of height when we saw that there was hardly any wing left outboard of the engines. The aircraft then seemed to just fall out of the sky as it continued to break up. It fell in a field nearby and later on that evening we went over to see it, but found only an engine and a wheel and a large amount of splintered wood. After an inspection of the wreckage by the plane's makers it was decided that a tear in the wing skin might have caused the air stream to get inside the wing causing the rest of the skin to come adrift and then cause the aircraft to break up. After that, we always had to wear canvas shoes when climbing on to the Mossies."

234 The crew of 5K+KR comprised Uffz Winfried Brender, Uffz Heinrich Kachold, Uffz Hans-Joachim Kuhlmann, Uffz Günter Kalff, and Uffz Ewald Weber.

235 In addition to Fw Gall, Fw Mathias Obermayer, Fw Heinz Dahms, Uffz Peter Damtraut and Obgfr Kurt Busch were killed in the crash.

236 According to *Air-Launched Doodlebugs*.

237 Those lost in the collision in addition to the pilots were: 5K+ER Uffz Werner Friedmann, Obgfr Manfred Thöle, Uffz Alfred Rutscho, Gfr Waldemar Winkel; 5K+CR Uffz Hans Schiessl, Obgfr Gerhard Lessing, Gfr Rudolf Vogel, Gfr Gerhard Pfau.

238 With Uffz Weiffen were Uffz Friedrich Wahl, Uffz Erich Stengel, Uffz Horst Schulze, and Obgfr Heinrich Authorsen.

239 Wg Cdr George Howden was an Australian in the RAF and had been awarded a DFC for two confirmed aerial victories and three damaged in night actions.

240 Obfw Schmidt-Reich's crew were Oblt Konrad Engel (the Gruppe senior observer), Uffz Richard Tietze, Uffz Günther Beyer, and Uffz Max Ordnung.

241 Those killed with Uffz Fleischmann were Uffz Richard Rothe-Oswald, Fw Alfred Orban, Obgfr Hermann Wenck, and Uffz Bruno Weber.

242 Obfw Hämmale's crew comprised Obfw Georg Stolp, Fw Werner Jacobs, Uffz Kurt Gütlein, and Obgfr Werner Oberbeck.

243 Lost with Fw Warwas were Uffz Julius Magin, Uffz Wilhelm Simon, Uffz Kurt Brendler, and Obgfr Wolfgang Müller.

244 Included in Hptm Zöllner's crew was observer Obfw Karl Christmann, who had received the RK in April, as had Zöllner. The other three crewmembers were Fw Erich Schneider, Obfw Fritz Marhoun and Fw Leonhard Dollmeer.

245 Ltn Redde's crew comprised Obgfr Herbert Jüng, Fw Peter Weinnan, Uffz Erich Bögan, and Obgfr Richard Parzinski.

246 The two crewmembers killed in the crash were Obgfr Paul Rohl and Uffz Karl Welzel.

247 Uffz Schulz' crew comprised Obgfr Günter Kudszus, Obgfr Werner Gasner, Uffz Helmut Reichmann, and Uffz Karl Küchler.

248 Obfw Flir's crew comprised Obgfr Fritz Plöger, Uffz Hermann Andergassen, Obgfr Willi Marr and Uffz Herbert Hübsch.

249 Sqn Ldr Jim Lomas DFC was killed on 13/6/53 when Meteor NF11 (WM258) of 264 Squadron crashed.

250 Although the records state VL this should probably be V4, the markings for KG1, from which Geschwader the Heinkel was possibly transferred for duty with I/KG53.

251 Lts Black and Aitken (68 Squadron) were part of the ten-man team of USN flyers undergoing operational training in Britain to gain experience in night-fighting techniques, which the Americans hoped to make good use of against the Japanese in the Pacific. It is sad to relate that only four survived the experience to return to the USA.

252 The Diver Lts Black and Aitken had been pursuing fell harmlessly at Berkhamsted a few minutes later.

253 See www.airmuseum.ca.

254 Extracted from *Fairey Firefly*.

255 In addition to Fw Hillmann, Uffz Rudolf Martin, Fw Ludwig Klalber, Uffz Jürgen Hauser and Uffz Josef Faürnig were also lost.

256 1/Lt Paul Smith from Montana ended the war with six aerial kills, including one probable.

257 T.C. Baskerville, as quoted in Peter J.C. Smith's *Flying Bombs over the Pennines*.

258 Uffz Neuber's crew included Obfw Heinrich Kock, Uffz Fritz Reinhard, and Fw Otto Wieland.

259 One such jet reconnaissance aircraft (from 1(F)/123) was shot down by a Tempest flown by Sqn Ldr David Fairbanks (who had shot down a Diver on 29/8/44) as it approached its home base at Rheine following a sortie to Hull to 11/2/45.

260 2/KG200's *Mistel* operations had just about run the course. A Ju88/FW190 *Mistel* destroyed on ground, plus second damaged, by Flt Lt Roy Lelong (Fighter Experimental Flight Mosquito VI) on 14 February, during an attack on Tirstup airfield that saw the destruction of two combinations comprising Ju88G (714623)/FW190 (380328) and Ju88S (330565)/FW190 (733683). A third combination (Ju88G 714150/FW190 737388) was damaged, and a further Ju88G (714659) destroyed. On 3 March, three Ju88A-4/Bf109F-4 combinations from *Mistelstaffel* 2/KG200 were shot down by P-51Ds 355thFG near Boizenburg at 1230 hours, although the fighter carriers were thought to be FW190s. Lt Col Elwyn Righetti claimed Ju88 shot down and FW190 probable, then Ju88/FW190, Lt Patrick D. Moore claimed a Ju88, and Lt Richard G. Gibbs a Ju88/FW190 combination. In fact, Ju88 (888590) piloted by Ofhr Franz Pietschmann was totally destroyed with the deaths of all three crewmen on board; a second Ju88 (883652) was also shot down, with the loss of Fw Willi Kallhaff and his two crew members, while the third flown by Fw Fritz Lorbach force-landed although one of the crew was killed. All three Bf109s were shot down – 10053 flown by Obgfr Joachim Uhlig, 737989 (Oblt Otto Barkhardt) and 13149 (Obfw Arnold Kiskin) and all three pilots were killed. On 18 March, P-51s of the 364thFG while providing escort to heavy bombers returning from a raid on Berlin, spotted a *Mistel* was taking off from an airfield near Parchim and attacked. Lt John C. Hunter claimed the FW190 destroyed while Lt Edward Chlevin accounted for the lower component, which he thought was a He111. The aircraft was probably from KG(J)30.

261 See www.airmuseum.ca.

262 Fhr Franz Wiethaupt, Uffz Heinz Wagner, Obgfr Erich Kesmitski and Obfw Herbert Lange.

263 Flgr Rose's crew comprised Fw Heinz Kowalski, Gfr Gerhard Täschner and Obgfr Hans Olm.

264 Uffz Obenauer and Obgfr Terbach were also posted missing.

265 See Jeremy Howard-Williams' *Night Intruder*.

266 On 8 February 1945, Russian fighter pilot PoW Mikhail Devyatayev, a 10-victory ace of 104 GIAP, who had been shot down on 13/7/44, escaped from Peenemünde airfield on Usedom Island, to where he had been sent to help repair the airfield. While working on the runway Devyatayev, who had disguised his identity as a pilot, espied a He111 that had been refuelled ready for take-off, complete with a V-1 slung underwing. He and nine other POWs made a swift decision to escape, climbed aboard while Devyatayev started the engines and took off before the Germans could react. The aircraft was flown to a Russian-occupied airfield. Apparently the He111 belonged to Erprobungsstelle Karlshägen, a unit commanded by Oblt Carl-Heinz Graudenz, its task to train new crews of KG53.

267 By the end of the war *Flakregiment 155 (West)* had lost 189 dead, 71 missing and 321 wounded – more than 10% of its strength – due mainly to launching accidents.

268 See *Impact*.

269 Extracted from *Antwerp: City of Sudden Death* (website).

270 1/Lt Mel Paisley from Oregon ended the war with five aerial victories.

271 Flt Lt Eric Smith later flew F-86s in the Korean War.

272 See *Spitfire Diary* by E.A.W. Smith.

273 Flt Lt Geoffrey Collinson had served the war in Training Command (being awarded the AFC in June 1944) until posted to 4 Squadron in late 1944; he also claimed two Bf109s destroyed (according to his logbook) while with this unit, which was primarily a PR squadron.

274 Flt Lt Lionel Frost had been attached to the 358thFS, 355thFG, with which he had claimed one victory and another

damaged, plus two damaged on the ground. He was awarded a DFC.
275 See Bob Cossey's *Tigers*.
276 According to Richard Young in *The Flying Bomb*.
277 King Leonidas and his Spartan warriors sacrificed themselves in 480BC in a successful attempt to buy time for Athens by defending the pass at Thermopylae against superior numbers of Persian troops, thus allowing Athens to be evacuated. Their sacrifice became symbolic with disciplined resistance, hence the name chosen for the Luftwaffe's proposed suicide Staffel.
278 Extracted from *Luftwaffe Test Pilot* by Hans-Werner Lerche.
279 Heinz Kensche was forced to bale out during a test flight, but survived.
280 Hanna Reitsch was 32-years-old at the time of the V-1 testing programme. She died in 1979 aged 67.
281 See *Thunder Gods* by Hatsuho Naito.

SELECT BIBLIOGRAPHY

Aces High Volume 2: Christopher Shores
AckAck: General Sir Frederick Pile
Air-Launched Doodlebugs: Peter J.C. Smith
Air-Sea Rescue in World War Two: Alan Rowe
Aphrodite: Desperate Mission: Jack Olsen
A View from the Office: R.W. Pottinger
Bombers over Sussex 1943-45: Pat Burgess & Andy Saunders
Buzz Bomb Diary: David G. Collyer
Croydon in the 1940s and 1950s: Croydon History Society
Doodlebugs and Rockets: Bob Ogley
Fairey Firefly: William Harrison
Fear Nothing: David Watkins
Fighter Nights: John Bennett
Fire out of Heaven: Sarah Gertrude Millin
Flying Bombs over the Pennines: Peter J.C. Smith
Happy is the Day: Tom Slack
Impact: Benjamin King & Timothy Kutta
Isle of Wight at War: H.J.T. Leal
Jan Plesman: A Flying Dutchman: Albert Plesman
Mistel: Robert Forsyth
Mosquitopanik!: Martin Bowman
Mustang Wing: Anthony John Moor
Night Fighter: C.F. Rawnsey & Robert Wright
Nightfighter Navigator: Richard and Doug Oxby (forthcoming)
Night Flyer: Lewis Brandon DSO DFC
Night Intruder: Jeremy Howard-Williams
Number One in War and Peace: Norman Franks and Mike O'Connor
Red Sky at Night: Jo Capka
Sledgehammers for Tintacks: Steve Darlow
Spitfire Command: Grp Capt Bobby Oxspring
Spitfire Diary: E.A.W. Smith
Swordfish: Ray Sturtivant
Terror in the Starboard Seat: Dave McIntosh
The Blitz – Then and Now: Winston Ramsey (Ed)
The Doodlebugs: Norman Longmate
The Flying Bomb: Richard Anthony Young
The Flying Bomb War: Peter Haining
The History of US Electronic Warfare: Dr Alfred Price

The Royal Air Force in the World War: Capt Norman MacMillan MC AFC
The Wild Winds: Paul Sortehaug
There Shall Be Wings: Max Arthur
Thunderbolts over High Halden: Graham J. Hukins
Tigers: Bob Cossey
V for Vengeance: David Johnson
V-1 Flying Bomb 1942-52: Steven J. Zaloga
Westerham & Crockham Hill in the War: Helen Long
2 Group RAF: Michael Bowyer
315 Squadron: Wojtek Matusiak, Robert Gretzyngier & Piotr Wiśniewski
Supplement to the London Gazette, 20 October 1948

Internet Websites
Flying Bombs and Rockets: Peter Henden
Twelve O'Clock High: Ruy Horta
RAF Commands: Ross McNeill
The Diary of an ARP Warden – Edward Carter, Waltham Abbey (unidentified website)

INDEX OF PERSONNEL
(EXCLUDING ENDNOTES)

PAF Personnel

USN Personnel (Aircrew)

Other British/American/Allied Military Personnel

German – Others

NOTES

NOTES

NOTES

NOTES

NOTES

NOTES

NOTES